Collins *gem*

Collins

BESTSELLING BILINGUAL DICTIONARIES

Spanish

Dictionary

HarperCollins Publishers
Westerhill Road
Bishopbriggs
Glasgow
G64 2QT
Great Britain

Eighth Edition/Octava Edición 2009

Reprint 10 9 8 7 6 5 4 3 2 1

© William Collins Sons & Co. Ltd
1982, 1989
© HarperCollins Publishers 1993,
1998, 2001, 2004, 2006, 2009

ISBN 978-0-00-728449-8

Collins Gem® is a registered trademark
of HarperCollins Publishers Limited

www.collinslanguage.com

A catalogue record for this book is
available from the British Library

Random House Mondadori, S.A.
Travessera de Gràcia 47–49, 08021
Barcelona

www.diccionarioscollins.com

ISBN 978-84-253-4313-1

Typeset by/Fotocomposición por
Wordcraft, Glasgow

Supplement typeset by/
Fotocomposición de la Guía del viajero
por Davidson Pre-Press, Glasgow

Printed in Italy by/Impreso en Italia
por LEGO Spa, Lavis (Trento)

When you buy a Collins dictionary
or thesaurus and register on
www.collinslanguage.com for the
free online and digital services, you
will not be charged by HarperCollins
for access to Collins free Online
Dictionary content or Collins free
Online Thesaurus content on that
website. However, your operator's
charges for using the internet on
your computer will apply. Costs
vary from operator to operator.
HarperCollins is not responsible for
any charges levied by online service
providers for accessing Collins free
Online Dictionary or Collins free
Online Thesaurus on
www.collinslanguage.com using
these services.

HarperCollins does not warrant
that the functions contained in
www.collinslanguage.com content
will be uninterrupted or error free,
that defects will be corrected, or that
www.collinslanguage.com or the
server that makes it available are
free of viruses or bugs. HarperCollins
is not responsible for any access
difficulties that may be experienced
due to problems with network, web,
online or mobile phone connection.

Acknowledgements
We would like to thank those
authors and publishers who kindly
gave permission for copyright
material to be used in the Collins
Word Web. We would also like to
thank Times Newspapers Ltd for
providing valuable data.

PUBLISHING DIRECTOR/DIRECTORA DE PUBLICACIONES
Catherine Love

MANAGING EDITOR/DIRECCIÓN EDITORIAL
Gaëlle Amiot-Cadey

EDITOR/REDACCIÓN
Genevieve Gerrard

CONTRIBUTORS/COLABORADORES
José Martín Galera
Wendy Lee
Cordelia Lilly
José María Ruiz Vaca
Malihé Sanatian

SERIES EDITOR/COLECCIÓN DIRIGIDA POR
Rob Scriven

ÍNDICE

CONTENTS

Estamos muy satisfechos de que hayas decidido comprar este diccionario y esperamos que lo disfrutes y que te sirva de gran ayuda ya sea en el colegio, en el trabajo, en tus vacaciones o en casa.

Esta introducción pretende darte algunas indicaciones para ayudarte a sacar el mayor provecho de este diccionario; no sólo de su extenso vocabulario, sino de toda la información que te proporciona cada entrada. Esta te ayudará a leer y comprender – y también a comunicarte y a expresarte – en inglés moderno. Este diccionario comienza con una lista de abreviaturas utilizadas en el texto y con una ilustración de los sonidos representados por los símbolos fonéticos.

EL MANEJO DE TU DICCIONARIO

La amplia información que te ofrece este diccionario aparece presentada en distintas tipografías, con caracteres de diversos tamaños y con distintos símbolos, abreviaturas y paréntesis. Los apartados siguientes explican las reglas y símbolos utilizados.

ENTRADAS

Las palabras que consultas en el diccionario – las entradas – aparecen ordenades alfabéticamente y en color para una identificación más rápida. La palabra que aparece en la parte superior de cada página es la primera entrada (si aparece en la página izquierda) y la última entrada (si aparece en la página derecha) de la página en cuestión. La información sobre el uso o la forma de determinadas entradas aparece entre paréntesis, detrás de la transcripción fonética, y generalmente en forma abreviada y en cursiva

(p. ej.: (*fam*), (*Com*)). En algunos casos se ha considerado
oportuno agrupar palabras de una misma familia (**nación,
nacionalismo**; **accept, acceptance**) bajo una misma entrada
que aparece en color.

Las expresiones de uso corriente en las que aparece una
entrada se dan en negrita (p. ej.: **hurry**: [...] **to be in a ~**).

SÍMBOLOS FONÉTICOS

La transcripción fonética de cada entrada inglesa
(que indica su pronunciación) aparece entre corchetes,
inmediatamente después de la entrada (p. ej. **knife** [naif]).
En las páginas xv-xviii encontrarás una lista de los
símbolos fonéticos utilizados en este diccionario.

TRADUCCIONES

Las traducciones de las entradas aparecen en caracteres
normales, y en los casos en los que existen significados
o usos diferentes, éstos aparecen separados mediante
un punto y coma. A menudo encontrarás también otras
palabras en cursiva y entre paréntesis antes de las
traducciones. Estas sugieren contextos en los que la
entrada podría aparecer (p. ej.: **alto** (*persona*) o (*sonido*))
o proporcionan sinónimos (p. ej.: **mismo** (*semejante*)).

PALABRAS CLAVE

Particular relevancia reciben ciertas palabras inglesas y
españolas que han sido consideradas palabras 'clave' en
cada lengua. Estas pueden, por ejemplo, ser de utilización
muy corriente o tener distintos usos (**de, haber; get, that**).
La combinación de triángulos y números te permitirá

distinguir las diferentes categorías gramaticales y los
diferentes significados. Las indicaciones en cursiva y entre
paréntesis proporcionan además importante información
adicional.

FALSOS AMIGOS

Las palabras que se prestan a confusión al traducir han
sido identificadas. En tales entradas existen unas notas
que te ayudaran a evitar errores.

INFORMACIÓN GRAMATICAL

Las categorías gramaticales aparecen en forma abreviada
y en cursiva después de la transcripción fonética de cada
entrada (vt, adv, conj). También se indican la forma
femenina y los plurales irregulares de los sustantivos
del inglés (child, -ren).

We are delighted that you have decided to buy this Spanish dictionary and hope you will enjoy and benefit from using it at school, at home, on holiday or at work.

This introduction gives you a few tips on how to get the most out of your dictionary – not simply from its comprehensive wordlist but also from the information provided in each entry. This will help you to read and understand modern Spanish, as well as communicate and express yourself in the language. This dictionary begins by listing the abbreviations used in the text and illustrating the sounds shown by the phonetic symbols.

USING YOUR DICTIONARY

A wealth of information is presented in the dictionary, using various typefaces, sizes of type, symbols, abbreviations and brackets. The various conventions and symbols used are explained in the following sections.

HEADWORDS

The words you look up in a dictionary – 'headwords' – are listed alphabetically. They are printed in colour for rapid identification. The headwords appearing at the top of each page indicate the first (if it appears on a left-hand page) and last word (if it appears on a right-hand page) dealt with on the page in question.

Information about the usage or form of certain headwords is given in brackets after the phonetic spelling. This usually appears in abbreviated form and in italics (e.g. (*fam*), (*Com*)).

Where appropriate, words related to headwords are grouped in the same entry (**nación, nacionalismo; accept, acceptance**) and are also in colour. Common expressions in which the headword appears are shown in a different bold roman type (e.g. **cola:** [...] **hacer ~**).

PHONETIC SPELLINGS
The phonetic spelling of each headword (indicating its pronunciation) is given in square brackets immediately after the headword (e.g. **cohete** [ko'ete]). A list of these symbols is given on pages xv-xviii.

TRANSLATIONS
Headword translations are given in ordinary type and, where more than one meaning or usage exists, these are separated by a semi-colon. You will often find other words in italics in brackets before the translations. These offer suggested contexts in which the headword might appear (e.g. **fare** *(on trains, buses)* or provide synonyms (e.g. **litter** *(rubbish)* o *(young animals)*). The gender of the Spanish translation also appears in italics immediately following the key element of the translation, except where this is a regular masculine singular noun ending in 'o', or a regular feminine noun ending in 'a'.

KEY WORDS
Special status is given to certain Spanish and English words which are considered as 'key' words in each language. They may, for example, occur very frequently or have several types of usage (e.g. **de, haber; get, that**). A combination of triangles and numbers helps you to distinguish different

parts of speech and different meanings. Further helpful information is provided in brackets and italics.

FALSE FRIENDS

Words which can be easily confused have been identified in the dictionary. Notes at such entries will help you to avoid these common translation pitfalls.

GRAMMATICAL INFORMATION

Parts of speech are given in abbreviated form in italics after the phonetic spellings of headwords (e.g. *vt*, *adv*, *conj*). Genders of Spanish nouns are indicated as follows: *nm* for a masculine and *nf* for a feminine noun. Feminine and irregular plural forms of nouns are also shown (**irlandés, esa**; **luz** (*pl* **luces**)).

ABREVIATURAS

ABBREVIATIONS

abreviatura	ab(b)r	abbreviation
adjetivo, locución adjetiva	adj	adjective, adjectival phrase
administración	Admin	administration
adverbio, locución adverbial	adv	adverb, adverbial phrase
agricultura	Agr	agriculture
anatomía	Anat	anatomy
Argentina	Arg	Argentina
arquitectura	Arq, Arch	architecture
el automóvil	Aut(o)	the motor car and motoring
aviación, viajes aéreos	Aviac, Aviat	flying, air travel
biología	Bio(l)	biology
botánica, flores	Bot	botany
inglés británico	BRIT	British English
Centroamérica	CAM	Central America
química	Chem	chemistry
comercio, finanzas, banca	Com(m)	commerce, finance, banking
informática	Comput	computing
conjunción	conj	conjunction
construcción	Constr	building
compuesto	cpd	compound element
Cono Sur	CS	Southern Cone
cocina	Culin	cookery
economía	Econ	economics
eletricidad, electrónica	Elec	electricity, electronics
enseñanza, sistema escolar y universitario	Escol	schooling, schools and universities
España	ESP	Spain
especialmente	esp	especially
exclamación, interjección	excl	exclamation, interjection
femenino	f	feminine
lengua familiar (! vulgar)	fam(!)	colloquial usage (! particularly offensive)
ferrocarril	Ferro	railways
uso figurado	fig	figurative use
fotografía	Foto	photography
(verbo inglés) del cual la partícula es inseparable	fus	(phrasal verb) where the particle is inseparable
generalmente	gen	generally
geografía, geología	Geo	geography, geology
geometría	Geom	geometry

ABREVIATURAS		ABBREVIATIONS
historia	Hist	history
uso familiar	inf(!)	colloquial usage
(! vulgar)		(! particularly offensive)
infinitivo	infin	infinitive
informática	Inform	computing
invariable	inv	invariable
irregular	irreg	irregular
lo jurídico	Jur	law
América Latina	LAM	Latin America
gramática, lingüística	Ling	grammar, linguistics
masculino	m	masculine
matemáticas	Mat(h)	mathematics
masculino/femenino	m/f	masculine/feminine
medicina	Med	medicine
México	MÉX, MEX	Mexico
lo militar, ejército	Mil	military matters
música	Mús, Mus	music
substantivo, nombre	n	noun
navegación, náutica	Náut, Naut	sailing, navigation
sustantivo numérico	num	numeral noun
complemento	obj	(grammatical) object
	o.s.	oneself
peyorativo	pey, pej	derogatory, pejorative
fotografía	Phot	photography
fisiología	Physiol	physiology
plural	pl	plural
política	Pol	politics
participio de pasado	pp	past participle
preposición	prep	preposition
pronombre	pron	pronoun
psicología, psiquiatría	Psico, Psych	psychology, psychiatry
tiempo pasado	pt	past tense
química	Quím	chemistry
ferrocarril	Rail	railways
religión	Rel	religion
Río de la Plata	RPL	River Plate
	sb	somebody
Cono Sur	SC	Southern Cone
enseñanza, sistema escolar y universitario	Scol	schooling, schools and universities
singular	sg	singular
España	SP	Spain
	sth	something

sujeto	*su(b)j*	(grammatical) subject
subjuntivo	*subjun*	subjunctive
tauromaquia	*Taur*	bullfighting
también	*tb*	also
técnica, tecnología	*Tec(h)*	technical term, technology
telecomunicaciones	*Telec, Tel*	telecommunications
imprenta, tipografía	*Tip, Typ*	typography, printing
televisión	*TV*	television
universidad	*Univ*	university
inglés norteamericano	*US*	American English
verbo	*vb*	verb
verbo intransitivo	*vi*	intransitive verb
verbo pronominal	*vr*	reflexive verb
verbo transitivo	*vt*	transitive verb
zoología	*Zool*	zoology
marca registrada	®	registered trademark
indica un equivalente cultural	≈	introduces a cultural equivalent

SPANISH PRONUNCIATION

VOWELS

a	[a]	pata	not as long as *a* in *far*. When followed by a consonant in the same syllable (i.e. in a closed syllable), as in a*mante*, the *a* is short, as in *bat*
e	[e]	me	like *e* in they. In a closed syllable, as in *gente*, the *e* is short as in *pet*
i	[i]	pino	as in *mean* or *machine*
o	[o]	lo	as in *local*. In a closed syllable, as in *control*, the *o* is short as in *cot*
u	[u]	lunes	as in *rule*. It is silent after q, and in *gue*, *gui*, unless marked *güe*, *güi* e.g. *antigüedad*, when it is pronounced like *w* in *wolf*

SEMIVOWELS

i, y	[j]	bien hielo yunta	pronounced like *y* in *yes*
u	[w]	huevo fuento antigüedad	unstressed *u* between consonant and vowel is pronounced like *w* in *well*. See notes on *u* above.

DIPHTHONGS

ai, ay	[ai]	baile	as *i* in *ride*
au	[au]	auto	as *ou* in *shout*
ei, ey	[ei]	buey	as *ey* in *grey*
eu	[eu]	deuda	both elements pronounced independently [e] + [u]
oi, oy	[oi]	hoy	as *oy* in *toy*

CONSONANTS

b	[b,β]	boda bomba labor	see notes on *v* below
c	[k]	caja	*c* before *a*, *o*, *u* is pronounced as in *cat*
ce, ci	[θe,θi]	cero cielo	*c* before *e* or *i* is pronounced as in *thin*
ch	[tʃ]	chiste	*ch* is pronounced as *ch* in *chair*
d	[d,ð]	danés ciudad	at the beginning of a phrase or after l or n, *d* is pronounced as in English. In any other position it is pronounced like *th* in *the*

xv

g	[g,ɣ]	gafas paga	g before a, o or u is pronounced as in gap, if at the beginning of a phrase or after n. In other positions the sound is softened
ge, gi	[xe,xi]	gente girar	g before e or i is pronounced similar to ch in Scottish loch
h		haber	h is always silent in Spanish
j	[x]	jugar	j is pronounced similar to ch in Scottish loch
ll	[ʎ]	talle	ll is pronounced like the y in yet or the lli in million
ñ	[ʃ]	niño	ñ is pronounced like the ni in onion
q	[k]	que	q is pronounced as k in king
r, rr	[r,rr]	quitar garra	r is always pronounced in Spanish, unlike the silent r in dancer. rr is trilled, like a Scottish r
s	[s]	quizás isla	s is usually pronounced as in pass, but before b, d, g, l, m or n it is pronounced as in rose
v	[b,β]	vía	v is pronounced something like b. At the beginning of a phrase or after m or n it is pronounced as b in boy. In any other position the sound is softened
z	[θ]	tenaz	z is pronounced as th in thin

f, k, l, m, n, p, t and x are pronounced as in English.

STRESS
The rules of stress in Spanish are as follows:

(a) when a word ends in a vowel or in n or s, the second last syllable is stressed:
    patata, patatas; come, comen
(b) when a word ends in a consonant other than n or s, the stress falls on the last syllable:
    pared, hablar
(c) when the rules set out in (a) and (b) are not applied, an acute accent appears over the stressed vowel:
    común, geografía, inglés

In the phonetic transcription, the symbol ['] precedes the syllable on which the stress falls.

LA PRONUNCIACIÓN INGLESA

VOCALES

	Ejemplo inglés	Explicación
[ɑ:]	father	Entre *a* de padre y *o* de noche
[ʌ]	but, come	*a* muy breve
[æ]	man, cat	Con los labios en la posición de *e* en pena y luego se pronuncia el sonido *a* parecido a la *a* de carro
[ə]	father, ago	Vocal neutra parecida a una *e* u *o* casi muda
[ə:]	bird, heard	Entre *e* abierta y *o* cerrada, sonido alargado
[ɛ]	get, bed	Como en perro
[ɪ]	it, big	Más breve que en *si*
[i:]	tea, see	Como en *fino*
[ɔ]	hot, wash	Como en torre
[ɔ:]	saw, all	Como en *por*
[u]	put, book	Sonido breve, más cerrado que *burro*
[u:]	too, you	Sonido largo, como en *uno*

DIPTONGOS

	Ejemplo inglés	Explicación
[aɪ]	fly, high	Como en *fraile*
[au]	how, house	Como en *pausa*
[ɛə]	there, bear	Casi como en *vea*, pero el sonido *a* se mezcla con el indistinto [ə]
[eɪ]	day, obey	*e* cerrada seguida por una *i* débil
[ɪə]	here, hear	Como en *manía*, mezclándose el sonido *a* con el indistinto [ə]
[əu]	go, note	[ə] seguido por una breve *u*
[ɔɪ]	boy, oil	Como en *voy*
[uə]	poor, sure	*u* bastante larga más el sonido indistinto [ə]

CONSONANTES

	Ejemplo inglés	Explicación
[b]	big, lobby	Como en tumban
[d]	mended	Como en conde, andar
[g]	go, get, big	Como en grande, gol
[dʒ]	gin, judge	Como en la *ll* andaluza y en Generalitat (*catalán*)
[ŋ]	sing	Como en vínculo
[h]	house, he	Como la jota hispanoamericana
[j]	young, yes	Como en ya
[k]	come, mock	Como en caña, Escocia
[r]	red, tread	Se pronuncia con la punta de la lengua hacia atrás y sin hacerla vibrar
[s]	sand, yes	Como en casa, sesión
[z]	rose, zebra	Como en desde, mismo
[ʃ]	she, machine	Como en chambre (*francés*), roxo (*portugués*)
[tʃ]	chin, rich	Como en chocolate
[v]	valley	Como f, pero se retiran los dientes superiores vibrándolos contra el labio inferior
[w]	water, which	Como la u de huevo, puede
[ʒ]	vision	Como en journal (*francés*)
[θ]	think, myth	Como en receta, zapato
[ð]	this, the	Como en hablado, verdad

f, l, m, n, p, t y x iguales que en español.

El signo [*] indica que la r final escrita apenas se pronuncia en inglés británico cuando la palabra siguiente empieza con vocal. El signo ['] indica la sílaba acentuada.

SPANISH VERB TABLES

1 Gerund 2 Imperative 3 Present 4 Preterite 5 Future 6 Present subjunctive 7 Imperfect subjunctive 8 Past participle 9 Imperfect

Etc indicates that the irregular root is used for all persons of the tense, e.g. oír: 6 oiga, oigas, oigamos, oigáis, oigan

agradecer 3 agradezco 6 agradazca *etc*

aprobar 2 aprueba 3 apruebo, apruebas, aprueba, aprueban 6 apruebe, apruebes, apruebe, aprueben

atravesar 2 atraviesa 3 atravieso, atraviesas, atraviesa, atraviesan 6 atraviese, atravieses, atraviese, atraviesen

caber 3 quepo 4 cupe, cupiste, cupo, cupimos, cupisteis, cupieron 5 cabré *etc* 6 quepa *etc* 7 cupiera *etc*

caer 1 cayendo 3 caigo 4 cayó, cayeron 6 caiga *etc* 7 cayera *etc*

cerrar 2 cierra 3 cierro, cierras, cierra, cierran 6 cierre, cierres, cierre, cierren

COMER 1 comiendo 2 come, comed 3 como, comes, come, comemos, coméis, comen 4 comí, comiste, comió, comimos, comisteis, comieron 5 comeré, comerás, comerá, comeremos, comeréis, comerán 6 coma, comas, coma, comamos, comáis, coman 7 comiera, comieras, comiera, comiéramos, comierais, comieran 8 comido 9 comía, comías, comía, comíamos, comíais, comían

conocer 3 conozco 6 conozca *etc*

contar 2 cuenta 3 cuento, cuentas, cuenta, cuentan 6 cuente, cuentes, cuente, cuenten

dar 3 doy 4 di, diste, dio, dimos, disteis, dieron 7 diera *etc*

decir 2 di 3 digo 4 dije, dijiste, dijo, dijimos, dijisteis, dijeron 5 diré *etc* 6 diga *etc* 7 dijera *etc* 8 dicho

despertar 2 despierta 3 despierto, despiertas, despierta, despiertan 6 despierte, despiertes, despierte, despierten

divertir 1 divirtiendo 2 divierte 3 divierto, diviertes, divierte, divierten 4 divirtió, divirtieron 6 divierta, diviertas, divierta, divirtamos, divirtáis, diviertan 7 divirtiera *etc*

dormir 1 durmiendo 2 duerme 3 duermo, duermes, duerme, duermen 4 durmió, durmieron 6 duerma, duermas, duerma, durmamos, durmáis, duerman 7 durmiera *etc*

empezar 2 empieza 3 empiezo, empiezas, empieza, empiezan 4 empecé 6 empiece, empieces, empiece, empecemos, empecéis, empiecen

entender 2 entiende 3 entiendo, entiendes, entiende, entienden 6 entienda, entiendas, entienda, entiendan

ESTAR 2 está 3 estoy, estás, está, están 4 estuve, estuviste, estuvo, estuvimos, estuvisteis, estuvieron 6 esté, estés, esté, estén 7 estuviera etc

HABER 3 he, has, ha, hemos, han 4 hube, hubiste, hubo, hubimos, hubisteis, hubieron 5 habré etc 6 haya etc 7 hubiera etc

HABLAR 1 hablando 2 habla, hablad 3 hablo, hablas, habla, hablamos, habláis, hablan 4 hablé, hablaste, habló, hablamos, hablasteis, hablaron 5 hablaré, hablarás, hablará, hablaremos, hablaréis, hablarán 6 hable, hables, hable, hablemos, habléis, hablen 7 hablara, hablaras, hablara, habláramos, hablarais, hablaran 8 hablado 9 hablaba, hablabas, hablaba, hablábamos, hablabais, hablaban

hacer 2 haz 3 hago 4 hice, hiciste, hizo, hicimos, hicisteis, hicieron 5 haré etc 6 haga etc 7 hiciera etc 8 hecho

instruir 1 instruyendo 2 instruye 3 instruyes, instruye, instruyen 4 instruyó, instruyeron 6 instruya etc 7 instruyera etc

ir 1 yendo 2 ve 3 voy, vas, va, vamos, vais, van 4 fui, fuiste, fue, fuimos, fuisteis, fueron 6 vaya, vayas, vaya, vayamos, vayáis, vayan 7 fuera etc 9 iba, ibas, iba, íbamos, ibais, iban

jugar 2 juega 3 juego, juegas, juega, juegan 4 jugué 6 juegue etc

leer 1 leyendo 4 leyó, leyeron 7 leyera etc

morir 1 muriendo 2 muere 3 muero, mueres, muere, mueren 4 murió, murieron

6 muera, mueras, muera, muramos, muráis, mueran 7 muriera etc 8 muerto

mover 2 mueve 3 muevo, mueves, mueve, mueven 6 mueva, muevas, mueva, muevan

negar 2 niega 3 niego, niegas, niega, niegan 4 negué 6 niegue, niegues, niegue, neguemos, neguéis, nieguen

ofrecer 3 ofrezco 6 ofrezca etc

oír 1 oyendo 2 oye 3 oigo, oyes, oye, oyen 4 oyó, oyeron 6 oiga etc 7 oyera etc

oler 2 huele 3 huelo, hueles, huele, huelen 6 huela, huelas, huela, huelan

parecer 3 parezco 6 parezca etc

pedir 1 pidiendo 2 pide 3 pido, pides, pide, piden 4 pidió, pidieron 6 pida etc 7 pidiera etc

pensar 2 piensa 3 pienso, piensas, piensa, piensan 6 piense, pienses, piense, piensen

perder 2 pierde 3 pierdo, pierdes, pierde, pierden 6 pierda, pierdas, pierda, pierdan

poder 1 pudiendo 2 puede 3 puedo, puedes, puede, pueden 4 pude, pudiste, pudo, pudimos, pudisteis, pudieron 5 podré etc 6 pueda, puedas, pueda, puedan 7 pudiera etc

poner 2 pon 3 pongo 4 puse, pusiste, puso, pusimos, pusisteis, pusieron 5 pondré etc 6 ponga etc 7 pusiera etc 8 puesto

preferir 1 prefiriendo 2 prefiere 3 prefiero, prefieres, prefiere, prefieren 4 prefirió, prefirieron 6 prefiera, prefieras, prefiera, prefiramos, prefiráis, prefieran 7 prefiriera etc querer 2 quiere 3 quiero, quieres, quiere, quieren 4 quise, quisiste, quiso, quisimos, quisisteis, quisieron 5 querré etc 6 quiera, quieras, quiera, quieran 7 quisiera etc

reír 2 ríe 3 río, ríes, ríe, ríen 4 reí, rieron 6 ría, rías, ría, riamos, riáis, rían 7 riera etc

repetir 1 repitiendo 2 repite 3 repito, repites, repite, repiten 4 repitió, repitieron 6 repita etc 7 repitiera etc

rogar 2 ruega 3 ruego, ruegas, ruega, ruegan 4 rogué 6 ruegue, ruegues, ruegue, roguemos, roguéis, rueguen

saber 3 sé 4 supe, supiste, supo, supimos, supisteis, supieron 5 sabré etc 6 sepa etc 7 supiera etc

salir 2 sal 3 salgo 5 saldré etc 6 salga etc

seguir 1 siguiendo 2 sigue 3 sigo, sigues, sigue, siguen 4 siguió, siguieron 6 siga etc 7 siguiera etc

sentar 2 sienta 3 siento, sientas, sienta, sientan 6 siente, sientes, siente, sienten

sentir 1 sintiendo 2 siente 3 siento, sientes, siente, sienten 4 sintió, sintieron 6 sienta, sientas, sienta, sintamos, sintáis, sientan 7 sintiera etc

SER 2 sé 3 soy, eres, es, somos, sois, son 4 fui, fuiste, fue, fuimos, fuisteis, fueron 6 sea etc 7 fuera etc 9 era, eras, era, éramos, erais, eran

servir 1 sirviendo 2 sirve 3 sirvo, sirves, sirve, sirven 4 sirvió, sirvieron 6 sirva etc 7 sirviera etc

soñar 2 sueña 3 sueño, sueñas, sueña, sueñan 6 sueñe, sueñes, sueñe, sueñen

tener 2 ten 3 tengo, tienes, tiene, tienen 4 tuve, tuviste, tuvo, tuvimos, tuvisteis, tuvieron 5 tendré etc 6 tenga etc 7 tuviera etc

traer 1 trayendo 3 traigo 4 traje, trajiste, trajo, trajimos, trajisteis, trajeron 6 traiga etc 7 trajera etc

valer 2 vale 3 valgo 5 valdré etc 6 valga etc

venir 2 ven 3 vengo, vienes, viene, vienen 4 vine, viniste, vino, vinimos, vinisteis, vinieron 5 vendré etc 6 venga etc 7 viniera etc

ver 3 veo 6 vea etc 8 visto 9 veía etc

vestir 1 vistiendo 2 viste 3 visto, vistes, viste, visten 4 vistió, vistieron 6 vista etc 7 vistiera etc

VIVIR 1 viviendo 2 vive, vivid 3 vivo, vives, vive, vivimos, vivís, viven 4 viví, viviste, vivió, vivimos, vivisteis, vivieron 5 viviré, vivirás, vivirá, viviremos, viviréis, vivirán 6 viva, vivas, viva, vivamos, viváis, vivan 7 viviera, vivieras, viviéramos, vivierais, vivieran 8 vivido 9 vivía, vivías, vivía, vivíamos, vivíais, vivían

volver 2 vuelve 3 vuelvo, vuelves, vuelve, vuelven 6 vuelva, vuelvas, vuelva, vuelvan 8 vuelto

VERBOS IRREGULARES EN INGLÉS

PRESENTE	PASADO	PARTICIPIO	PRESENTE	PASADO	PARTICIPIO
arise	arose	arisen	dream	dreamed,	dreamed,
awake	awoke	awoken		dreamt	dreamt
be (am, is, are; being)	was, were	been	drink	drank	drunk
			drive	drove	driven
bear	bore	born(e)	dwell	dwelt	dwelt
beat	beat	beaten	eat	ate	eaten
become	became	become	fall	fell	fallen
begin	began	begun	feed	fed	fed
bend	bent	bent	feel	felt	felt
bet	bet,	bet,	fight	fought	fought
	betted	betted	find	found	found
bid (at auction, cards)	bid	bid	flee	fled	fled
			fling	flung	flung
bid (say)	bade	bidden	fly	flew	flown
bind	bound	bound	forbid	forbad(e)	forbidden
bite	bit	bitten	forecast	forecast	forecast
bleed	bled	bled	forget	forgot	forgotten
blow	blew	blown	forgive	forgave	forgiven
break	broke	broken	forsake	forsook	forsaken
breed	bred	bred	freeze	froze	frozen
bring	brought	brought	get	got	got,
build	built	built			(US) gotten
burn	burnt,	burnt,	give	gave	given
	burned	burned	go (goes)	went	gone
burst	burst	burst	grind	ground	ground
buy	bought	bought	grow	grew	grown
can	could	(been able)	hang	hung	hung
cast	cast	cast	hang (suspend)		
catch	caught	caught	hang (execute)	hanged	hanged
choose	chose	chosen	have	had	had
cling	clung	clung	hear	heard	heard
come	came	come	hide	hid	hidden
cost (be valued at)	cost	cost	hit	hit	hit
			hold	held	held
cost (work out price of)	costed	costed	hurt	hurt	hurt
			keep	kept	kept
creep	crept	crept	kneel	knelt,	knelt,
cut	cut	cut		kneeled	kneeled
deal	dealt	dealt	know	knew	known
dig	dug	dug	lay	laid	laid
do (does)	did	done	lead	led	led
draw	drew	drawn	lean	leant,	leant,

PRESENTE	PASADO	PARTICIPIO	PRESENTE	PASADO	PARTICIPIO
	leaned	leaned	shine	shone	shone
leap	leapt,	leapt,	shoot	shot	shot
	leaped	leaped	show	showed	shown
learn	learnt,	learnt,	shrink	shrank	shrunk
	learned	learned	shut	shut	shut
leave	left	left	sing	sang	sung
lend	lent	lent	sink	sank	sunk
let	let	let	sit	sat	sat
lie (lying)	lay	lain	slay	slew	slain
light	lit,	lit,	sleep	slept	slept
	lighted	lighted	slide	slid	slid
lose	lost	lost	sling	slung	slung
make	made	made	slit	slit	slit
may	might	–	smell	smelt,	smelt,
mean	meant	meant		smelled	smelled
meet	met	met	sow	sowed	sown,
mistake	mistook	mistaken			sowed
mow	mowed	mown,	speak	spoke	spoken
		mowed	speed	sped,	sped,
must	(had to)	(had to)		speeded	speeded
pay	paid	paid	spell	spelt,	spelt,
put	put	put		spelled	spelled
quit	quit,	quit,	spend	spent	spent
	quitted	quitted	spill	spilt,	spilt,
read	read	read		spilled	spilled
rid	rid	rid	spin	spun	spun
ride	rode	ridden	spit	spat	spat
ring	rang	rung	spoil	spoiled,	spoiled,
rise	rose	risen		spoilt	spoilt
run	ran	run	spread	spread	spread
saw	sawed	sawed,	spring	sprang	sprung
		sawn	stand	stood	stood
say	said	said	steal	stole	stolen
see	saw	seen	stick	stuck	stuck
seek	sought	sought	sting	stung	stung
sell	sold	sold	stink	stank	stunk
send	sent	sent	stride	strode	stridden
set	set	set	strike	struck	struck
sew	sewed	sewn	strive	strove	striven
shake	shook	shaken	swear	swore	sworn
shear	sheared	shorn,	sweep	swept	swept
		sheared	swell	swelled	swollen,
shed	shed	shed			swelled

PRESENTE	PASADO	PARTICIPIO	PRESENTE	PASADO	PARTICIPIO
swim	swam	swum	wear	wore	worn
swing	swung	swung	weave(on loom)	wove	woven
take	took	taken			
teach	taught	taught	weave(wind)	weaved	weaved
tear	tore	torn	wed	wedded, wed	wedded, wed
tell	told	told			
think	thought	thought	weep	wept	wept
throw	threw	thrown	win	won	won
thrust	thrust	thrust	wind	wound	wound
tread	trod	trodden	wring	wrung	wrung
wake	woke, waked	woken, waked	write	wrote	written

a

7 (*razón*): **a 30 céntimos el kilo** at 30 cents a kilo; **a más de 50 km/h** at more than 50 kms per hour

8 (*dativo*): **se lo di a él** I gave it to him; **vi al policía** I saw the policeman; **se lo compré a él** I bought it from him

9 (*tras ciertos verbos*): **voy a verle** I'm going to see him; **empezó a trabajar** he started working o to work

10 (+ *infin*): **al verlo, lo reconocí inmediatamente** when I saw him I recognized him at once; **el camino a recorrer** the distance we *etc* have to travel; **¡a callar!** keep quiet!; **¡a comer!** let's eat!

abad, esa [a'βað, 'ðesa] *nm/f* abbot/ abbess; **abadía** *nf* abbey

abajo [a'βaxo] *adv* (*situación*) (down) below, underneath; (*en edificio*) downstairs; (*dirección*) down, downwards; **el piso de ~** the downstairs flat; **la parte de ~** the lower part; **¡~ el gobierno!** down with the government!; **cuesta/río ~** downhill/downstream; **de arriba ~** from top to bottom; **el ~ firmante** the undersigned; **más ~** lower o further down

abalanzarse [aβalan'θarse] *vr*: **~ sobre** o **contra** to throw o.s. at

abanderado, -a [aβande'raðo] *nm/f* (*portaestandarte*) standard bearer; (*de un movimiento*) champion, leader; (*MÉX: linier*) linesman, assistant referee

abandonado, -a [aβando'naðo, a] *adj* derelict; (*desatendido*) abandoned; (*desierto*) deserted; (*descuidado*) neglected

abandonar [aβando'nar] *vt* to leave; (*persona*) to abandon, desert; (*cosa*) to abandon, leave behind; (*descuidar*) to neglect; (*renunciar a*) to give up; (*Inform*) to quit; **abandonarse** *vr*: **~se a** to abandon o.s. to; **abandono** *nm* (*acto*) desertion, abandonment; (*estado*) abandon, neglect; (*renuncia*) withdrawal, retirement; **ganar por**

PALABRA CLAVE

[a] (*a* + *el* = *al*) *prep* **1** (*dirección*) to; **fueron a Madrid/Grecia** they went to Madrid/Greece; **me voy a casa** I'm going home

2 (*distancia*): **está a 15 km de aquí** it's 15 kms from here

3 (*posición*): **estar a la mesa** to be at table; **al lado de** next to, beside; **a la puerta**

4 (*tiempo*): **a las 10/a medianoche** at 10/midnight; **a la mañana siguiente** the following morning; **a los pocos días** after a few days; **estamos a 9 de julio** it's the ninth of July; **a los 24 años** at the age of 24; **al año/a la semana** a year/week later

5 (*manera*): **a la francesa** the French way; **a caballo** on horseback; **a oscuras** in the dark

6 (*medio, instrumento*): **a lápiz** in pencil; **a mano** by hand; **cocina a gas** gas stove

abandono to win by default

abanico [aβa'niko] nm fan; (Náut) derrick

abarcar [aβar'kar] vt to include, embrace; (LAM: acaparar) to monopolize

abarrotado, -a [aβarro'taðo, a] adj packed

abarrotar [aβarro'tar] vt (local, estadio, teatro) to fill, pack

abarrotero, -a [aβarro'tero, a] (MÉX) nm/f grocer; **abarrotes** (MÉX) nmpl groceries; **tienda de abarrotes** (MÉX, CAM) grocery store

abastecer [aβaste'θer] vt: ~ (de) to supply (with); **abastecimiento** nm supply

abasto [a'βasto] nm supply; **no dar ~ a** to be unable to cope with

abatible [aβa'tiβle] adj: **asiento ~** tip-up seat; (Auto) reclining seat

abatido, -a [aβa'tiðo, a] adj dejected, downcast

abatir [aβa'tir] vt (muro) to demolish; (pájaro) to shoot o bring down; (fig) to depress

abdicar [aβði'kar] vi to abdicate

abdomen [aβ'ðomen] nm abdomen; **abdominales** nmpl (tb: **ejercicios abdominales**) sit-ups

abecedario [aβeθe'ðarjo] nm alphabet

abedul [aβe'ðul] nm birch

abeja [a'βexa] nf bee

abejorro [aβe'xorro] nm bumblebee

abertura [aβer'tura] nf = apertura

abeto [a'βeto] nm fir

abierto, -a [a'βjerto, a] pp de **abrir** ▷ adj open

abismal [aβis'mal] adj (fig) vast, enormous

abismo [a'βismo] nm abyss

ablandar [aβlan'dar] vt to soften; **ablandarse** vr to get softer

abocado, -a [aβo'kaðo, a] adj (vino) smooth, pleasant

abochornar [aβotʃor'nar] vt to embarrass

abofetear [aβofete'ar] vt to slap

(in the face)

abogado, -a [aβo'ɣaðo, a] nm/f lawyer; (notario) solicitor; (en tribunal) barrister (BRIT), attorney (US); **abogado defensor** defence lawyer o (US) attorney

abogar [aβo'ɣar] vi: ~ **por** to plead for; (fig) to advocate

abolir [aβo'lir] vt to abolish; (cancelar) to cancel

abolladura [aβoʎa'ðura] nf dent

abollar [aβo'ʎar] vt to dent

abombarse [aβom'barse] (LAM) vr to go bad

abominable [aβomi'naβle] adj abominable

abonado, -a [aβo'naðo, a] adj (deuda) paid(-up) ▷ nm/f subscriber

abonar [aβo'nar] vt (deuda) to settle; (terreno) to fertilize; (idea) to endorse; **abonarse** vr to subscribe; **abono** nm payment; fertilizer; subscription

abordar [aβor'ðar] vt (barco) to board; (asunto) to broach

aborigen [aβo'rixen] nmf aborigine

aborrecer [aβorre'θer] vt to hate, loathe

abortar [aβor'tar] vi (malparir) to have a miscarriage; (deliberadamente) to have an abortion; **aborto** nm miscarriage; abortion

abovedado, -a [aβoβe'ðaðo, a] adj vaulted, domed

abrasar [aβra'sar] vt to burn (up); (Agr) to dry up, parch

abrazar [aβra'θar] vt to embrace, hug

abrazo [a'βraðo] nm embrace, hug; **un ~** (en carta) with best wishes

abrebotellas [aβreβo'teʎas] nm inv bottle opener

abrecartas [aβre'kartas] nm inv letter opener

abrelatas [aβre'latas] nm inv tin (BRIT) o can opener

abreviatura [aβreβja'tura] nf abbreviation

abridor [aβri'ðor] nm bottle opener;

teatro) to put on; (*film*) to show; (*fiesta*) to hold; **dar algo a algn** to give sb sth *o* sth to sb; **dar de beber a algn** to give sb a drink; **dar de comer** to feed

2 (*producir: intereses*) to yield; (*fruta*) to produce

3 (*locuciones + n*): **da gusto escucharle** it's a pleasure to listen to him; *V tb* **paseo**

4 (*+ n: = perífrasis de verbo*): **me da asco** it sickens me

5 (*considerar*): **dar algo por descontado/entendido** to take sth for granted/as read; **dar algo por concluido** to consider sth finished

6 (*hora*): **el reloj dio las 6** the clock struck 6 (o'clock)

7: **me da lo mismo** it's all the same to me; *V tb* **igual, más**

▷ *vi* **1 dar con**: **dimos con él dos horas más tarde** we came across him two hours later; **al final di con la solución** I eventually came up with the answer

2: **dar en** (*blanco, suelo*) to hit; **el sol me da en la cara** the sun is shining (right) on my face

3: **dar de sí** (*zapatos etc*) to stretch, give

darse *vr* **1**: **darse por vencido** to give up

2 (*ocurrir*): **se han dado muchos casos** there have been a lot of cases

3: **darse a**: **se ha dado a la bebida** he's taken to drinking

4: **se me dan bien/mal las ciencias** I'm good/bad at science

5: **dárselas de**: **se las da de experto** he fancies himself *o* poses as an expert

dardo ['darðo] *nm* dart

dátil ['datil] *nm* date

dato ['dato] *nm* fact, piece of information; **datos personales** personal details

dcha. *abr* (= *derecha*) r.h.

d. de C. *abr* (= *después de Cristo*) A.D.

○ **PALABRA CLAVE**

de [de] (*de + el = del*) *prep* **1** (*posesión*) of; **la casa de Isabel/mis padres** Isabel's/my parents' house; **es de ellos** it's theirs

2 (*origen, distancia, con números*) from; **soy de Gijón** I'm from Gijón; **de 8 a 20** from 8 to 20; **salir del cine** to go out of o leave the cinema; **de 2 en 2** 2 by 2, 2 at a time

3 (*valor descriptivo*): **una copa de vino** a glass of wine; **la mesa de la cocina** the kitchen table; **un billete de 10 euros** a 10 euro note; **un niño de tres años** a three-year-old (child); **una máquina de coser** a sewing machine; **ir vestido de gris** to be dressed in grey; **la niña del vestido azul** the girl in the blue dress; **trabaja de profesora** she works as a teacher; **de lado** sideways; **de atrás/delante** rear/front

4 (*hora, tiempo*): **a las 8 de la mañana** at 8 o'clock in the morning; **de día/noche** by day/night; **de hoy en ocho días** a week from now; **de niño era gordo** as a child he was fat

5 (*comparaciones*): **más/menos de cien personas** more/less than a hundred people; **el más caro de la tienda** the most expensive in the shop; **menos/más de lo pensado** less/more than expected

6 (*causa*): **del calor** from the heat

7 (*tema*) about; **clases de inglés** English classes; **¿sabes algo de él?** do you know anything about him?; **un libro de física** a physics book

8 (*adj + de + infin*): **fácil de entender** easy to understand

9 (*oraciones pasivas*): **fue respetado de todos** he was loved by all

10 (*condicional + infin*) if; **de ser posible** if possible; **de no terminarlo hoy** if I etc don't finish it today

dé [de] *vb* V **dar**

debajo [de'βaxo] *adv* underneath; **~ de** below, under; **por ~ de** beneath

debate [de'βate] *nm* debate; **debatir** *vt* to debate

deber [de'βer] *nm* duty ▷ *vt* to owe ▷ *vi*: **debe (de)** it must, it should; **deberes** *nmpl* (Escol) homework; **deberse** *vr*: **~se a** to be owing o due to; **debo hacerlo** I must do it; **debe de ir** he should go

debido, -a [de'βiðo, a] *adj* proper, just; **~ a** due to, because of

débil ['deβil] *adj* (persona, carácter) weak; (luz) dim; **debilidad** *nf* weakness; dimness

debilitar [deβili'tar] *vt* to weaken; **debilitarse** *vr* to grow weak

débito ['deβito] *nm* debit; **débito bancario** (LAM) direct debit; (BRIT) o billing (us)

debutar [deβu'tar] *vi* to make one's debut

década ['dekaða] *nf* decade

decadencia [deka'ðenθja] *nf* (estado) decadence; (proceso) decline, decay

decaído, -a [deka'iðo, a] *adj*: **estar ~** (abatido) to be down

decano, -a [de'kano, a] *nm/f* (de universidad etc) dean

decena [de'θena] *nf*: **una ~** ten (or so)

decente [de'θente] *adj* decent

decepción [deθep'θjon] *nf* disappointment

> No confundir **decepción** con la palabra inglesa *deception*.

decepcionar [deθepθjo'nar] *vt* to disappoint

decidir [deθi'ðir] *vt*, *vi* to decide; **decidirse** *vr*: **~se a** to make up one's mind to

décimo, -a ['deθimo, a] *adj* tenth ▷ *nm* tenth

decir [de'θir] *vt* to say; (contar) to tell; (hablar) to speak ▷ *nm* saying; **decirse** *vr*: **se dice que** it is said that; **es ~** that is (to say); **~ para sí** to say to o.s.;

querer ~ to mean; **¡dígame!** (Tel) hello!; (en tienda) can I help you?

decisión [deθi'sjon] *nf* (resolución) decision; (firmeza) decisiveness

decisivo, -a [deθi'siβo, a] *adj* decisive

declaración [deklara'θjon] *nf* (manifestación) statement; (de cargo) declaration; **declaración fiscal o de la renta** income-tax return

declarar [dekla'rar] *vt* to declare ▷ *vi* to declare; (Jur) to testify; **declararse** *vr* to propose

decoración [dekora'θjon] *nf* decoration

decorado [deko'raðo] *nm* (Cine, Teatro) scenery, set

decorar [deko'rar] *vt* to decorate; **decorativo, -a** *adj* ornamental, decorative

decreto [de'kreto] *nm* decree

dedal [de'ðal] *nm* thimble

dedicación [deðika'θjon] *nf* dedication

dedicar [deði'kar] *vt* (libro) to dedicate; (tiempo, dinero) to devote; (palabras: decir, consagrar) to dedicate, devote; **dedicatoria** *nf* (de libro) dedication

dedo ['deðo] *nm* finger; **hacer ~** (fam) to hitch (a lift); **dedo anular** ring finger; **dedo corazón** middle finger; **dedo (del pie)** toe; **dedo gordo** (de la mano) thumb; (del pie) big toe; **dedo índice** index finger; **dedo meñique** little finger; **dedo pulgar** thumb

deducción [deðuk'θjon] *nf* deduction

deducir [deðu'θir] *vt* (concluir) to deduce, infer; (Com) to deduct

defecto [de'fekto] *nm* defect, flaw; **defectuoso, -a** *adj* defective, faulty

defender [defen'der] *vt* to defend; **defenderse** *vr* (desenvolverse) to get by

defensa [de'fensa] *nf* defence ▷ *nm* (Deporte) defender, back; **defensivo, -a** *adj* defensive; **a la defensiva** on the defensive

defensor, a [defen'sor, a] *adj*
defending ▷ *nm/f* (*abogado defensor*)
defending counsel; (*protector*)
protector

deficiencia [defi'θjenθja] *nf*
deficiency

deficiente [defi'θjente] *adj*
(*defectuoso*) defective; **~ en** lacking o
deficient in; **ser un ~ mental** to be
mentally handicapped

déficit ['defiθit] (*pl* **~s**) *nm* deficit

definición [defini'θjon] *nf* definition

definir [defi'nir] *vt* (*determinar*) to
determine, establish; (*decidir*) to
define; (*aclarar*) to clarify; (*Inform*) to
define

definitivo, -a [defini'tiβo, a] *adj*
definitive; **en definitiva** definitively;
(*en resumen*) in short

deformación [deforma'θjon] *nf*
(*alteración*) deformation; (*Radio etc*)
distortion

deformar [defor'mar] *vt* (*gen*) to
deform; **deformarse** *vr* to become
deformed; **deforme** *adj* (*informe*)
deformed; (*feo*) ugly; (*malhecho*)
misshapen

defraudar [defrau'ðar] *vt*
(*decepcionar*) to disappoint; (*estafar*)
to defraud

defunción [defun'θjon] *nf* death,
demise

degenerar [dexene'rar] *vi* to
degenerate

degradar [deɣra'ðar] *vt* to debase,
degrade; **degradarse** *vr* to demean
o.s.

degustación [deɣusta'θjon] *nf*
sampling, tasting

dejar [de'xar] *vt* to leave; (*permitir*)
to allow, let; (*abandonar*) to abandon,
forsake; (*beneficios*) to produce, yield
▷ *vi*: **~ de** (*parar*) to stop; (*no hacer*) to
fail to; **~ a un lado** to leave o set aside;
~ entrar/salir to let in/out; **~ pasar** to
let through

del [del] (= **de** + **el**) V **de**

delantal [delan'tal] *nm* apron

delante [de'lante] *adv* in front;
(*enfrente*) opposite; (*adelante*) ahead; **~**
de in front of, before

delantera [delan'tera] *nf* (*de vestido,
casa etc*) front part; (*Deporte*) forward
line; **llevar la ~ (a algn)** to be ahead
(of sb)

delantero, -a [delan'tero, a] *adj*
front ▷ *nm* (*Deporte*) forward,
striker

delatar [dela'tar] *vt* to inform on
o against, betray; **delator, a** *nm/f*
informer

delegación [deleɣa'θjon] *nf* (*acción,
delegados*) delegation; (*Com: oficina*)
office, branch; **delegación de policía**
(*Méx*) police station

delegado, -a [dele'ɣaðo, a] *nm/f*
delegate; (*Com*) agent

delegar [dele'ɣar] *vt* to delegate

deletrear [deletre'ar] *vt* to spell (out)

delfín [del'fin] *nm* dolphin

delgado, -a [del'ɣaðo, a] *adj* thin;
(*persona*) slim, thin; (*tela etc*) light,
delicate

deliberar [deliβe'rar] *vt* to debate,
discuss

delicadeza [delika'ðeθa] *nf* (*gen*)
delicacy; (*refinamiento, sutileza*)
refinement

delicado, -a [deli'kaðo, a] *adj*
(*gen*) delicate; (*sensible*) sensitive;
(*quisquilloso*) touchy

delicia [de'liθja] *nf* delight

delicioso, -a [deli'θjoso, a] *adj*
(*gracioso*) delightful; (*exquisito*)
delicious

delimitar [delimi'tar] *vt* (*función,
responsabilidades*) to define

delincuencia [delin'kwenθja]
nf delinquency; **delincuente** *nmf*
delinquent; (*criminal*) criminal

delineante [deline'ante] *nmf*
draughtsman/woman

delirante [deli'rante] *adj* delirious

delirar [deli'rar] *vi* to be delirious,
rave

delirio [de'lirjo] *nm* (*Med*)
delirium; (*palabras insensatas*)
ravings *pl*

delito | 84

delito [de'lito] nm (gen) crime; (infracción) offence

delta ['delta] nm delta

demacrado, -a [dema'kraðo, a] adj: **estar ~** to look pale and drawn, be wasted away

demanda [de'manda] nf (pedido, Com) demand; (petición) request; (Jur) action, lawsuit; **demandar** [deman'dar] vt (gen) to demand; (Jur) to sue, file a lawsuit against

demás [de'mas] adj: **los ~ niños** the other o remaining children ▷ pron: **los/ las ~** the others, the rest (of them); **lo ~** the rest (of it)

demasía [dema'sia] nf (exceso) excess, surplus; **comer en ~** to eat to excess

demasiado, -a [dema'sjaðo, a] adj: **~ vino** too much wine ▷ adv (antes de adj, adv) too; **~ libros** too many books; **¡esto es ~!** that's the limit!; **hace ~ calor** it's too hot; **~ despacio** too slowly; **~s** too many

demencia [de'menθja] nf (locura) madness

democracia [demo'kraθja] nf democracy

demócrata [de'mokrata] nmf democrat; **democrático, -a** adj democratic

demoler [demo'ler] vt to demolish; **demolición** nf demolition

demonio [de'monjo] nm devil, demon; **¡~s!** hell, damn!; **¿cómo ~s?** how the hell?

demora [de'mora] nf delay

demos ['demos] vb V **dar**

demostración [demostra'θjon] nf (Mat) proof; (de afecto) show, display

demostrar [demos'trar] vt (probar) to prove; (mostrar) to show; (manifestar) to demonstrate

den [den] vb V **dar**

denegar [dene'ɣar] vt (rechazar) to refuse; (Jur) to reject

denominación [denomina'θjon]

nf (acto) naming; **Denominación de Origen** see note

● **DENOMINACIÓN DE ORIGEN**
●
● The **Denominación de Origen**,
● abbreviated to **D.O.**, is a
● prestigious classification awarded
● to food products such as wines,
● cheeses, sausages and hams
● which meet the stringent quality
● and production standards of the
● designated region. **D.O.** labels
● serve as a guarantee of quality.

densidad [densi'ðað] nf density; (fig) thickness

denso, -a ['denso, a] adj dense; (espeso, pastoso) thick; (fig) heavy

dentadura [denta'ðura] nf (set of) teeth pl; **dentadura postiza** false teeth pl

dentera [den'tera] nf (grima): **dar ~ a algn** to set sb's teeth on edge

dentífrico, -a [den'tifriko, a] adj dental ▷ nm toothpaste

dentista [den'tista] nmf dentist

dentro ['dentro] adv inside ▷ prep: **~ de** in, inside, within; **por ~** (on the) inside; **mirar por ~** to look inside; **~ de tres meses** within three months

denuncia [de'nunθja] nf (delación) denunciation; (acusación) accusation; (de accidente) report; **denunciar** vt to report; (delatar) to inform on o against

departamento [departa'mento] nm sección administrativa, department, section; (LAM: apartamento) flat (BRIT), apartment

depender [depen'der] vi: **~ de** to depend on; **depende** it (all) depends

dependienta [depen'djenta] nf saleswoman, shop assistant

dependiente [depen'djente] adj dependent ▷ nm salesman, shop assistant

depilar [depi'lar] vt (con cera) to wax; (cejas) to pluck

deportar [depor'tar] vt to deport
deporte [de'porte] nm sport; **hacer
~** to play sports; **deportista** adj
sports cpd ▷ nmf sportsman/woman;
deportivo, -a adj (club, periódico)
sports cpd ▷ nm sports car
depositar [deposi'tar] vt (dinero) to
deposit; (mercancías) to put away, store;
depositarse vr to settle
depósito [de'posito] nm (gen)
deposit; (almacén) warehouse, store;
(de agua, gasolina etc) tank; **depósito de
cadáveres** mortuary
depredador, a [depreða'ðor, a] adj
predatory ▷ nm predator
depresión [depre'sjon] nf
depression; **depresión nerviosa**
nervous breakdown
deprimido, -a [depri'miðo, a] adj
depressed
deprimir [depri'mir] vt to depress;
deprimirse vr (persona) to become
depressed
deprisa [de'prisa] adv quickly,
hurriedly
derecha [de're(t)ʃa] nf right(-hand)
side; (Pol) right; **a la ~** (estar) on the
right; (torcer etc) (to) the right
derecho, -a [de'retʃo, a] adj right,
right-hand ▷ nm (privilegio) right;
(lado) right(-hand) side; (leyes) law
▷ adv straight, directly; **siga todo ~**
carry o (BRIT) go straight on; **derechos**
nmpl (de aduana) duty sg; (de autor)
royalties; **tener ~ a** to have a right to;
derechos de autor royalties
deriva [de'riβa] nf: **ir o estar a la ~** to
drift, be adrift
derivado [deri'βaðo] nm (Com)
by-product
derivar [deri'βar] vt to derive;
(desviar) to direct ▷ vi to derive, be
derived; (Náut) to drift; **derivarse** vr to
derive, be derived; to drift
derramamiento [derrama'mjento]
nm (dispersión) spilling;

derramamiento de sangre bloodshed
derramar [derra'mar] vt to spill;
(verter) to pour out; (esparcir) to scatter;
derramarse vr to pour out
derrame [de'rrame] nm (de líquido)
spilling; (de sangre) shedding; (de
tubo etc) overflow; (pérdida) leakage;
derrame cerebral brain haemorrhage
derredor [derre'ðor] adv: **al o en ~ de**
around, about
derretir [derre'tir] vt (gen) to melt;
(nieve) to thaw; **derretirse** vr to melt
derribar [derri'βar] vt to knock
down; (construcción) to demolish;
(persona, gobierno, político) to bring
down
derrocar [derro'kar] vt (gobierno) to
bring down, overthrow
derrochar [derro'tʃar] vt to
squander; **derroche** nm (despilfarro)
waste, squandering
derrota [de'rrota] nf (Náut) course;
(Mil, Deporte etc) defeat, rout; **derrotar**
vt (gen) to defeat; **derrotero** nm
(rumbo) course
derrumbar [derrum'bar] vt (edificio)
to knock down; **derrumbarse** vr to
collapse
des etc vb V **dar**
desabrochar [desaβro'tʃar] vt
(botones, broches) to undo, unfasten;
desabrocharse vr (ropa etc) to come
undone
desacato [desa'kato] nm (falta de
respeto) disrespect; (Jur) contempt
desacertado, -a [desaθer'taðo, a]
adj (equivocado) mistaken; (inoportuno)
unwise
desacierto [desa'θjerto] nm
mistake, error
desaconsejar [desakonse'xar] vt to
advise against
desacreditar [desakreði'tar] vt
(desprestigiar) to discredit, bring into
disrepute; (denigrar) to run down
desacuerdo [desa'kwerðo] nm
disagreement, discord
desafiar [desa'fjar] vt (retar) to

challenge; (*enfrentarse a*) to defy

desafilado, -a [desafi'laðo, a]
adj blunt

desafinado, -a [desafi'naðo, a]
adj: **estar ~** to be out of tune

desafinar [desafi'nar] vi (*al cantar*) to
be o go out of tune

desafío etc [desa'fio] vb V **desafiar**
▷ nm (*reto*) challenge; (*combate*) duel;
(*resistencia*) defiance

desafortunado, -a
[desafortu'naðo, a] adj (*desgraciado*)
unfortunate, unlucky

desagradable [desaɣra'ðaβle]
adj (*fastidioso, enojoso*) unpleasant;
(*irritante*) disagreeable

desagradar [desaɣra'ðar] vt
(*disgustar*) to displease; (*molestar*) to
bother

desagradecido, -a [desaɣraðe'θiðo,
a] adj ungrateful

desagrado [desa'ɣraðo] nm
(*disgusto*) displeasure; (*contrariedad*)
dissatisfaction

desagüe [des'aɣwe] nm (*de un líquido*)
drainage; (*cañería*) drainpipe; (*salida*)
outlet, drain

desahogar [desao'ɣar] vt (*aliviar*) to
ease, relieve; (*ira*) to vent;
desahogarse vr (*relajarse*) to relax;
(*desfogarse*) to let off steam

desahogo [desa'oɣo] nm (*alivio*)
relief; (*comodidad*) comfort, ease

desahuciar [desau'θjar] vt (*enfermo*)
to give up hope for; (*inquilino*) to evict

desairar [desai'rar] vt (*menospreciar*)
to slight, snub

desalentador, a [desalenta'ðor, a]
adj discouraging

desaliño [desa'liɲo] nm slovenliness

desalmado, -a [desal'maðo, a] adj
(*cruel*) cruel, heartless

desalojar [desalo'xar] vt (*expulsar,
echar*) to eject; (*abandonar*) to move out
of ▷ vi to move out

desamor [desa'mor] nm (*frialdad*)
indifference; (*odio*) dislike

desamparado, -a [desampa'raðo,

a] adj (*persona*) helpless;
(*lugar: expuesto*) exposed; (*desierto*)
deserted

desangrar [desan'grar] vt to bleed;
(*fig: persona*) to bleed dry; **desangrarse**
vr to lose a lot of blood

desanimado, -a [desani'maðo,
a] adj (*persona*) downhearted;
(*espectáculo, fiesta*) dull

desanimar [desani'mar] vt
(*desalentar*) to discourage; (*deprimir*)
to depress; **desanimarse** vr to lose heart

desapacible [desapa'θiβle] adj (*gen*)
unpleasant

desaparecer [desapare'θer] vi (*gen*)
to disappear; (*el sol, la luz*) to vanish;
desaparecido, -a adj missing;
desaparición nf disappearance

desapercibido, -a [desaperθi'βiðo,
a] adj (*desprevenido*) unprepared; **pasar
~** to go unnoticed

desaprensivo, -a [desapren'siβo, a]
adj unscrupulous

desaprobar [desapro'βar] vt
(*reprobar*) to disapprove of; (*condenar*) to
condemn; (*no consentir*) to reject

desaprovechado, -a
[desaproβe'tʃaðo, a] adj (*oportunidad,
tiempo*) wasted; (*estudiante*) slack

desaprovechar [desaproβe'tʃar]
vt to waste

desarmador [desarma'ðor] (*MÉX*)
nm screwdriver

desarmar [desar'mar] vt (*Mil, fig*) to
disarm; (*Tec*) to take apart, dismantle;
desarme nm disarmament

desarraigar [desarrai'ɣar] vt to
uproot; **desarraigo** nm uprooting

desarreglar [desarre'ɣlar] vt
(*desordenar*) to disarrange; (*trastocar*) to
upset, disturb

desarrollar [desarro'ʎar] vt (*gen*) to
develop; **desarrollarse** vr to develop;
(*ocurrir*) to take place; (*Foto*) to develop;
desarrollo nm development

desarticular [desartiku'lar] vt
(*hueso*) to dislocate; (*objeto*) to take
apart; (*fig*) to break up

desasosegar [desasose'ɣar] vt
(inquietar) to disturb, make uneasy

desasosiego etc [desaso'sjeɣo] vb
V **desasosegar** ▷ nm (intranquilidad)
uneasiness, restlessness; (ansiedad)
anxiety

desastre [de'sastre] nm disaster;
desastroso, -a adj disastrous

desatar [desa'tar] vt (nudo) to untie;
(paquete) to undo; (separar) to detach;
desatarse vr (zapatos) to come
untied; (tormenta) to break

desatascar [desatas'kar] vt (cañería)
to unblock, clear

desatender [desaten'der] vt no
prestar atención a, to disregard;
(abandonar) to neglect

desatino [desa'tino] nm (idiotez)
foolishness, folly; (error) blunder

desatornillar [desatorni'ʎar] vt to
unscrew

desatrancar [desatran'kar] vt
(puerta) to unbolt; (cañería) to clear,
unblock

desautorizado, -a [desautori'θaðo,
a] adj unauthorized

desautorizar [desautori'θar]
vt (oficial) to deprive of authority;
(informe) to deny

desayunar [desaju'nar] vi to have
breakfast ▷ vt to have for breakfast;
desayuno nm breakfast

desazón [desa'θon] nf anxiety

desbarajuste [desβara'xuste] nm
confusion, disorder

desbaratar [desβara'tar] vt
(deshacer, destruir) to ruin

desbloquear [desβloke'ar] vt
(negociaciones, tráfico) to get going
again; (Com: cuenta) to unfreeze

desbordar [desβor'ðar] vt
(sobrepasar) to go beyond; (exceder)
to exceed; **desbordarse** vr (río) to
overflow; (entusiasmo) to erupt

descabellado, -a [deskaβe'ʎaðo, a]
adj (disparatado) wild, crazy

descafeinado, -a [deskafei'naðo, a]
adj decaffeinated ▷ nm decaffeinated
coffee

descalabro [deska'laβro] nm blow;
(desgracia) misfortune

descalificar [deskalifi'kar] vt to
disqualify; (desacreditar) to discredit

descalzar [deskal'θar] vt (zapato) to
take off; **descalzo, -a** adj barefoot(ed)

descambiar [deskam'bjar] vt to
exchange

descaminado, -a [deskami'naðo,
a] adj (equivocado) on the wrong road;
(fig) misguided

descampado [deskam'paðo] nm
open space

descansado, -a [deskan'saðo, a] adj
(gen) rested; (que tranquiliza) restful

descansar [deskan'sar] vt (gen) to
rest ▷ vi to rest, have a rest; (echarse)
to lie down

descansillo [deskan'siʎo] nm (de
escalera) landing

descanso [des'kanso] nm (reposo)
rest; (alivio) relief; (pausa) break;
(Deporte) interval, half time

descapotable [deskapo'taβle] nm
(tb: **coche ~**) convertible

descarado, -a [deska'raðo, a] adj
shameless; (insolente) cheeky

descarga [des'karɣa] nf (Arq, Elec,
Mil) discharge; (Náut) unloading;
descargable [deskar'ɣaβle]
adj downloadable; **descargar**
[deskar'ɣar] vt to unload; (golpe) to
let fly; **descargarse** vr to unburden
o.s.; **descargarse algo de Internet** to
download sth from the internet

descaro [des'karo] nm nerve

descarriar [deska'rrjar] vt
(descaminar) to misdirect; (fig) to lead
astray; **descarriarse** vr (perderse) to
lose one's way; (separarse) to stray;
(pervertirse) to err, go astray

descarrilamiento
[deskarrila'mjento] nm (de tren)
derailment

descarrilar [deskarri'lar] vi to be
derailed

descartar [deskar'tar] vt (rechazar)

to reject; (*eliminar*) to rule out;
descartarse vr (*Naipes*) to discard;
~se de to shirk

descendencia [desθen'denθ ja] nf
(*origen*) origin, descent; (*hijos*) offspring

descender [desθen'der] vt
(*bajar: escalera*) to go down ▷ vi to
descend; (*temperatura, nivel*) to fall,
drop; **~ de** to be descended from

descendiente [desθen'djente] nmf
descendant

descenso [des'θenso] nm descent;
(*de temperatura*) drop

descifrar [desθi'frar] vt to decipher;
(*mensaje*) to decode

descolgar [deskol'ɣar] vt (*bajar*)
to take down; (*teléfono*) to pick up;
descolgarse vr to let o.s. down

descolorido, -a [deskolo'riðo, a] adj =
descolorido, -a [deskolo'riðo, a] adj
faded; (*pálido*) pale

descompasado, -a
[deskompa'saðo, a] adj (*sin
proporción*) out of all proportion;
(*excesivo*) excessive

descomponer [deskompo'ner] vt
(*desordenar*) to disarrange, disturb; (*Tec*)
to put out of order; (*dividir*) to break
down (into parts); (*fig*) to provoke;
descomponerse vr (*corromperse*) to
rot, decompose; (*LAM Tec*) to break
down

descomposición [deskomposi'θjon]
nf (*de un objeto*) breakdown; (*de fruta
etc*) decomposition; **descomposición
de vientre** (*ESP*) stomach upset,
diarrhoea

descompostura [deskompos'tura]
nf (*MÉX: avería*) breakdown, fault;
(*LAM: diarrea*) diarrhoea

descomprimir [deskompri'mir]
(*Internet*) to unzip

descompuesto, -a
[deskom'pwesto, a] adj (*corrompido*)
decomposed; (*roto*) broken

desconcertado, -a
[deskonθer'taðo, a] adj disconcerted,
bewildered

desconcertar [deskonθer'tar] vt

(*confundir*) to baffle; (*incomodar*) to
upset, put out; **desconcertarse** vr
(*turbarse*) to be upset

desconchado, -a [deskon'tʃaðo, a]
adj (*pintura*) peeling

desconcierto etc [deskon'θjerto] vb
V **desconcertar** ▷ nm (*gen*) disorder;
(*desorientación*) uncertainty; (*inquietud*)
uneasiness

desconectar [deskonek'tar] vt to
disconnect

desconfianza [deskon'fjanθa] nf
distrust

desconfiar [deskon'fjar] vi to be
distrustful; **~ de** to distrust, suspect

descongelar [deskonxe'lar] vt to
defrost; (*Com, Pol*) to unfreeze

descongestionar
[deskonxestjo'nar] vt (*cabeza, tráfico*)
to clear

desconocer [deskono'θer] vt
(*ignorar*) not to know, be ignorant of

desconocido, -a [deskono'θiðo, a]
adj unknown ▷ nm/f stranger

desconocimiento
[deskonoθi'mjento] nm falta de
conocimientos, ignorance

desconsiderado, -a
[deskonsiðe'raðo, a] adj
inconsiderate; (*insensible*) thoughtless

desconsuelo etc [deskon'swelo] vb
V **desconsolar** ▷ nm (*tristeza*) distress;
(*desesperación*) despair

descontado, -a [deskon'taðo, a]
adj: **dar por ~ (que)** to take (it) for
granted (that)

descontar [deskon'tar] vt (*deducir*)
to take away, deduct; (*rebajar*) to
discount

descontento, -a [deskon'tento, a]
adj dissatisfied ▷ nm dissatisfaction,
discontent

descorchar [deskor'tʃar] vt to
uncork

descorrer [desko'rrer] vt (*cortinas,
cerrojo*) to draw back

descortés [deskor'tes] adj (*mal
educado*) discourteous; (*grosero*) rude

descoser [desko'ser] vt to unstitch;
  descoserse vr to come apart (at the
  seams)

descosido, -a [desko'siðo, a] adj
  (Costura) unstitched

descreído, -a [deskre'iðo, a] adj
  (incrédulo) incredulous; (falto de fe)
  unbelieving

descremado, -a [deskre'maðo, a]
  adj skimmed

describir [deskri'βir] vt to describe;
  descripción [deskrip'θjon] nf
  description

descrito [des'krito] pp de **describir**

descuartizar [deskwarti'θar] vt
  (animal) to cut up

descubierto, -a [desku'βjerto, a] pp
  de **descubrir** ▷ adj uncovered, bare;
  (persona) bareheaded ▷ nm (bancario)
  overdraft; **al** ~ in the open

descubrimiento [deskuβri'mjento]
  nm (hallazgo) discovery; (revelación)
  revelation

descubrir [desku'βrir] vt to discover,
  find; (inaugurar) to unveil; (vislumbrar)
  to detect; (revelar) to reveal, show;
  (destapar) to uncover; **descubrirse** vr
  to reveal o.s.; (quitarse sombrero) to take
  off one's hat; (confesar) to confess

descuento etc [des'kwento] vb V
  descontar ▷ nm discount

descuidado, -a [deskwi'ðaðo, a]
  adj (sin cuidado) careless; (desordenado)
  untidy; (olvidadizo) forgetful;
  (dejado) neglected; (desprevenido)
  unprepared

descuidar [deskwi'ðar] vt (dejar)
  to neglect; (olvidar) to overlook;
  descuidarse vr (distraerse) to be
  careless; (abandonarse) to let o.s. go;
  (desprevenirse) to drop one's guard;
  ¡descuida! don't worry!; **descuido**
  nm (dejadez) carelessness; (olvido)
  negligence

○ **PALABRA CLAVE**

desde ['desðe] prep **1** (lugar) from;

desde Burgos hasta mi casa hay 30
km it's 30 km from Burgos to my house
2 (posición): **hablaba desde el balcón**
she was speaking from the balcony
3 (tiempo: + adv, n): **desde ahora** from
now on; **desde la boda** since the
wedding; **desde niño** since I etc was
a child; **desde 3 años atrás** since 3
years ago
4 (tiempo: + vb, fecha) since; for; **nos
conocemos desde 1992/desde hace
20 años** we've known each other since
1992/for 20 years; **no le veo desde
1997/desde hace 5 años** I haven't seen
him since 1997/for 5 years
5 (gama): **desde los más lujosos hasta
los más económicos** from the most
luxurious to the most reasonably
priced
6: **desde luego (que no)** of course
(not)
▷ conj: **desde que**: **desde que
recuerdo** for as long as I can
remember; **desde que llegó no ha
salido** he hasn't been out since he
arrived

desdén [des'ðen] nm scorn

desdeñar [desðe'nar] vt (despreciar)
  to scorn

desdicha [des'ðitʃa] nf (desgracia)
  misfortune; (infelicidad) unhappiness;
  desdichado, -a adj (sin suerte)
  unlucky; (infeliz) unhappy

desear [dese'ar] vt to want, desire,
  wish for

desechar [dese'tʃar] vt (basura) to
  throw out o away; (ideas) to reject,
  discard; **desechos** nmpl rubbish sg,
  waste sg

desembalar [desemba'lar] vt to
  unpack

desembarazar [desembara'θar] vt
  (desocupar) to clear; (desenredar) to free;
  desembarazarse vr: **~se de** to free o.s.
  of, get rid of

desembarcar [desembar'kar] vt
  (mercancías etc) to unload ▷ vi to

disembark

desembocadura [desemboka'ðura]
nf (de río) mouth; (de calle) opening

desembocar [desembo'kar] vi (río)
to flow into; (fig) to result in

desembolso [desem'bolso] nm
payment

desembrollar [desembro'ʎar]
vt (madeja) to unravel; (asunto,
malentendido) to sort out

desemejanza [deseme'xanθa] nf
dissimilarity

desempaquetar [desempake'tar]
vt (regalo) to unwrap; (mercancía) to
unpack

desempate [desem'pate] nm (Fútbol)
replay, play-off; (Tenis) tie-break(er)

desempeñar [desempe'ɲar] vt
(cargo) to hold; (papel) to perform; (lo
empeñado) to redeem; **~ un papel** (fig)
to play (a role)

desempleado, -a [desemple'aðo, a]
nm/f unemployed person; **desempleo**
nm unemployment

desencadenar [desenkaðe'nar]
vt to unchain; (ira) to unleash;
desencadenarse vr to break loose;
(tormenta) to burst; (guerra) to break out

desencajar [desenka'xar] vt (hueso)
to dislocate; (mecanismo, pieza) to
disconnect, disengage

desencanto [desen'kanto] nm
disillusionment

desenchufar [desentʃu'far] vt to
unplug

desenfadado, -a [desenfa'ðaðo,
a] adj (desenvuelto) uninhibited;
(descarado) forward; **desenfado** nm
(libertad) freedom; (comportamiento)
free and easy manner; (descaro)
forwardness

desenfocado, -a [desenfo'kaðo, a]
adj (Foto) out of focus

desenfreno [desen'freno] nm
wildness; (de las pasiones) lack of
self-control

desenganchar [desengan'tʃar] vt
(gen) to unhook; (Ferro) to uncouple

desengañar [desenga'ɲar] vt to
disillusion; **desengañarse** vr to
become disillusioned; **desengaño**
nm disillusionment; (decepción)
disappointment

desenlace [desen'laθe] nm outcome

desenmascarar [desenmaska'rar]
vt to unmask

desenredar [desenre'ðar] vt (pelo) to
untangle; (problema) to sort out

desenroscar [desenros'kar] vt to
unscrew

desentenderse [desenten'derse]
vr: **~ de** to pretend not to know about;
(apartarse) to have nothing to do with

desenterrar [desente'rrar] vt (to)
exhume; (tesoro, fig) to unearth, dig up

desentonar [desento'nar] vi (Mús)
to sing (o play) out of tune; (color)
to clash

desentrañar [desentra'ɲar] vt
(misterio) to unravel

desenvoltura [desenβol'tura]
nf ease

desenvolver [desenβol'βer] vt
(paquete) to unwrap; (fig) to develop;
desenvolverse vr (desarrollarse) to
unfold, develop; (arreglárselas) to cope

deseo [de'seo] nm desire, wish;
deseoso, -a adj: **estar deseoso de** to
be anxious to

desequilibrado, -a [desekili'βraðo,
a] adj unbalanced

desertar [deser'tar] vi to desert

desértico, -a [de'sertiko, a] adj
desert cpd

desesperación [desespera'θjon]
nf (impaciencia) desperation, despair;
(irritación) fury

desesperar [desespe'rar] vt to
drive to despair; (exasperar) to drive
to distraction ▷ vi: **~ de** to despair of;
desesperarse vr to despair, lose hope

desestabilizar [desestaβili'θar] vt
to destabilize

desestimar [desesti'mar] vt
(menospreciar) to have a low opinion of;
(rechazar) to reject

desfachatez [desfatʃa'teθ] nf (*insolencia*) impudence; (*descaro*) rudeness

desfalco [des'falko] nm embezzlement

desfallecer [desfaʎe'θer] vi (*perder las fuerzas*) to become weak; (*desvanecerse*) to faint

desfasado, -a [desfa'saðo, a] adj (*anticuado*) old-fashioned; **desfase** nm (*diferencia*) gap

desfavorable [desfaβo'raβle] adj unfavourable

desfigurar [desfixu'rar] vt (*cara*) to disfigure; (*cuerpo*) to deform

desfiladero [desfila'ðero] nm gorge

desfilar [desfi'lar] vi to parade; **desfile** nm procession; **desfile de modelos** fashion show

desgana [des'ɣana] nf (*falta de apetito*) loss of appetite; (*apatía*) unwillingness; **desganado, -a** adj: **estar desganado** (*sin apetito*) to have no appetite; (*sin entusiasmo*) to have lost interest

desgarrar [desɣa'rrar] vt to tear (up); (*fig*) to shatter; **desgarro** nm (*en tela*) tear; (*aflicción*) grief

desgastar [desɣas'tar] vt (*deteriorar*) to wear away o down; (*estropear*) to spoil; **desgastarse** vr to get worn out; **desgaste** nm wear (and tear)

desglosar [desɣlo'sar] vt (*factura*) to break down

desgracia [des'ɣraθja] nf misfortune; (*accidente*) accident; (*vergüenza*) disgrace; (*contratiempo*) setback; **por ~** unfortunately; **desgraciado, -a** [desɣra'θjaðo, a] adj (*sin suerte*) unlucky, unfortunate; (*miserable*) wretched; (*infeliz*) miserable

desgravar [desɣra'βar] vt (*impuestos*) to reduce the tax o duty on

desguace [des'ɣwaθe] (ESP) nm junkyard

deshabitado, -a [desaβi'taðo, a] adj uninhabited

deshacer [desa'θer] vt (*casa*) to break up; (*Tec*) to take apart; (*enemigo*) to defeat; (*diluir*) to melt; (*contrato*) to break; (*intriga*) to solve; **deshacerse** vr (*disolverse*) to melt; (*despedazarse*) to come apart o undone; **~se de** to get rid of; **~se en lágrimas** to burst into tears

deshecho, -a [des'etʃo, a] adj undone; (*roto*) smashed; (*persona*): **estar ~** to be shattered

desheredar [desere'ðar] vt to disinherit

deshidratar [desiðra'tar] vt to dehydrate

deshielo [des'jelo] nm thaw

deshonesto, -a [deso'nesto, a] adj indecent

deshonra [des'onra] nf (*deshonor*) dishonour; (*vergüenza*) shame

deshora [des'ora]: **a ~** adv at the wrong time

deshuesadero [deswesa'ðero] (MÉX) nm junkyard

deshuesar [deswe'sar] vt (*carne*) to bone; (*fruta*) to stone

desierto, -a [de'sjerto, a] adj (*casa, calle, negocio*) deserted ⊳ nm desert

designar [desix'nar] vt (*nombrar*) to designate; (*indicar*) to fix

desigual [desi'ɣwal] adj (*terreno*) uneven; (*lucha etc*) unequal

desilusión [desilu'sjon] nf disillusionment; (*decepción*) disappointment; **desilusionar** vt to disillusion; to disappoint; **desilusionarse** vr to become disillusioned

desinfectar [desinfek'tar] vt to disinfect

desinflar [desin'flar] vt to deflate

desintegración [desinteɣra'θjon] nf disintegration

desinterés [desinte'res] nm (*desgana*) lack of interest; (*altruismo*) unselfishness

desintoxicarse [desintoksi'karse] vr (*drogadicto*) to undergo detoxification

desistir [desis'tir] vi (*renunciar*) to

desleal | 92

stop, desist

desleal [desle'al] adj (infiel) disloyal; (Com: competencia) unfair; **deslealtad** nf disloyalty

desligar [desli'γar] vt (desatar) to untie, undo; (separar) to separate; **desligarse** vr (de un compromiso) to extricate o.s.

desliz [des'liθ] nm (fig) lapse; **deslizar** vt to slip, slide

deslumbrar [deslum'brar] vt to dazzle

desmadrarse [desma'ðrarse] (fam) vr (descontrolarse) to run wild; (divertirse) to let one's hair down; **desmadre** (fam) nm (desorganización) chaos; (jaleo) commotion

desmán [des'man] nm (exceso) outrage; (abuso de poder) abuse

desmantelar [desmante'lar] vt (deshacer) to dismantle; (casa) to strip

desmaquillador [desmakiʎa'ðor] nm make-up remover

desmayar [desma'jar] vi to lose heart; **desmayarse** vr (Med) to faint; **desmayo** nm (Med: acto) faint; (: estado) unconsciousness

desmemoriado, -a [desmemo'rjaðo, a] adj forgetful

desmentir [desmen'tir] vt (contradecir) to contradict; (refutar) to deny

desmenuzar [desmenu'θar] vt (deshacer) to crumble; (carne) to chop; (examinar) to examine closely

desmesurado, -a [desmesu'raðo, a] adj disproportionate

desmontable [desmon'taβle] adj (que se quita: pieza) detachable; (plegable) collapsible, folding

desmontar [desmon'tar] vt (deshacer) to dismantle; (tierra) to level ▷ vi to dismount

desmoralizar [desmorali'θar] vt to demoralize

desmoronar [desmoro'nar] vt to wear away, erode; **desmoronarse** vr (edificio, dique) to collapse; (economía)

to decline

desnatado, -a [desna'taðo, a] adj skimmed

desnivel [desni'βel] nm (de terreno) unevenness

desnudar [desnu'ðar] vt (desvestir) to undress; (despojar) to strip; **desnudarse** vr (desvestirse) to get undressed; **desnudo, -a** adj naked ▷ nm/f nude; **desnudo de** devoid o bereft of

desnutrición [desnutri'θjon] nf malnutrition; **desnutrido, -a** adj undernourished

desobedecer [desoβeðe'θer] vt, vi to disobey; **desobediencia** nf disobedience

desocupado, -a [desoku'paðo, a] adj at leisure; (desempleado) unemployed; (deshabitado) empty, vacant

desodorante [desoðo'rante] nm deodorant

desolación [desola'θjon] nf (de lugar) desolation; (fig) grief

desolar [deso'lar] vt to ruin, lay waste

desorbitado, -a [desorβi'taðo, a] adj (excesivo: ambición) boundless; (deseos) excessive; (: precio) exorbitant

desorden [de'sorðen] nm confusion; (político) disorder, unrest

desorganización [desorγaniθa'θjon] nf (de persona) disorganization; (en empresa, oficina) disorder, chaos

desorientar [desorjen'tar] vt (extraviar) to mislead; (confundir, desconcertar) to confuse; **desorientarse** vr (perderse) to lose one's way

despabilado, -a [despaβi'laðo, a] adj (despierto) wide-awake; (fig) alert, sharp

despachar [despa'tʃar] vt (negocio) to do, complete; (enviar) to send, dispatch; (vender) to sell, deal in; (billete) to issue; (mandar ir) to send away

despacho [des'patʃo] nm (oficina) office; (de paquetes) dispatch; (venta) sale; (comunicación) message; **~ de billetes o boletos** (LAM) booking office

espacio [des'paθjo] adv slowly

esparpajo [despar'paxo] nm self-confidence; (pey) nerve

esparramar [desparra'mar] vt (esparcir) to scatter; (líquido) to spill

especho [des'petʃo] nm spite

espectivo, -a [despek'tiβo, a] adj (despreciativo) derogatory; (Ling) pejorative

espedida [despe'ðiða] nf (adiós) farewell; (de obrero) sacking

espedir [despe'ðir] vt (visita) to see off, show out; (empleado) to dismiss; (inquilino) to evict; (objeto) to hurl; (olor etc) to give out o off; **despedirse** vr: **~se de** to say goodbye to

espegar [despe'xar] vt (gen) to unstick ▷ vi (avión) to take off; **despegarse** vr to come loose, come unstuck; **despego** nm detachment

espegue etc [des'pexe] vb V **despegar** ▷ nm takeoff

espeinado, -a [despei'naðo, a] adj dishevelled, unkempt

espejado, -a [despe'xaðo, a] adj (lugar) clear, free; (cielo) clear; (persona) wide-awake, bright

espejar [despe'xar] vt (gen) to clear up ▷ vi (el tiempo) to clear; **despejarse** vr (tiempo, cielo) to clear (up); (misterio) to become clearer; (cabeza) to clear

espensa [des'pensa] nf larder

espeñarse [despe'ɲarse] vr to hurl o.s. down; (coche) to tumble over

esperdicio [desper'ðiθjo] nm (despilfarro) squandering; **desperdicios** nmpl (basura) rubbish sg (BRIT), garbage sg (US); (residuos) waste sg

esperezarse [despere'θarse] vr to stretch

esperfecto [desper'fekto] nm (deterioro) slight damage; (defecto) flaw, imperfection

espertador [desperta'ðor] nm alarm clock

despertar [desper'tar] nm awakening ▷ vt (persona) to wake up; (recuerdos) to revive; (sentimiento) to arouse ▷ vi to awaken, wake up; **despertarse** vr to awaken, wake up

despido etc [des'piðo] vb V **despedir** ▷ nm dismissal, sacking

despierto, -a etc [des'pjerto, a] vb V **despertar** ▷ adj awake; (fig) sharp, alert

despilfarro [despil'farro] nm (derroche) squandering; (lujo desmedido) extravagance

despistar [despis'tar] vt to throw off the track o scent; (confundir) to mislead, confuse; **despistarse** vr to take the wrong road; (confundirse) to become confused

despiste [des'piste] nm absent-mindedness; **un ~** a mistake o slip

desplazamiento [desplaθa'mjento] nm displacement

desplazar [despla'θar] vt to move; (Náut) to displace; (Inform) to scroll; (fig) to oust; **desplazarse** vr (persona) to travel

desplegar [desple'xar] vt (tela, papel) to unfold, open out; (bandera) to unfurl; **despliegue** etc [des'plexe] vb V **desplegar** ▷ nm display

desplomarse [desplo'marse] vr (edificio, gobierno, persona) to collapse

desplumar [desplu'mar] vt (ave) to pluck; (fam: estafar) to fleece

despoblado, -a [despo'βlaðo, a] adj (sin habitantes) uninhabited

despojar [despo'xar] vt (alguien: de sus bienes) to divest of, deprive of; (casa) to strip, leave bare; (alguien: de su cargo) to strip of

despojo [des'poxo] nm (acto) plundering; (objetos) plunder, loot; **despojos** nmpl (de ave, res) offal sg

desposado, -a [despo'saðo, a] adj, nm/f newly-wed

despreciar [despre'θjar] vt (desdeñar) to despise, scorn; (afrentar) to slight; **desprecio** nm scorn, contempt; slight

desprender [despren'der] vt (broche) to unfasten; (olor) to give off; **desprenderse** vr (botón: caerse) to fall off; (broche) to come unfastened; (olor, perfume) to be given off; **~se de algo que ...** to draw from sth that ...

desprendimiento [desprendi'mjento] nm (gen) loosening; (generosidad) disinterestedness; (de tierra, rocas) landslide; **desprendimiento de retina** detachment of the retina

despreocupado, -a [despreoku'paðo, a] adj (sin preocupación) unworried, nonchalant; (negligente) careless

despreocuparse [despreoku'parse] vr not to worry; **~ de** to have no interest in

desprestigiar [despresti'xjar] vt (criticar) to run down; (desacreditar) to discredit

desprevenido, -a [despreβe'niðo, a] adj (no preparado) unprepared, unready

desproporcionado, -a [desproporθjo'naðo, a] adj disproportionate, out of proportion

desprovisto, -a [despro'βisto, a] adj: **~ de** devoid of

después [des'pwes] adv afterwards, later; (próximo paso) next; **~ de comer** after lunch; **un año ~** a year later; **~ se debatió el tema** next the matter was discussed; **~ de corregido el texto** after the text had been corrected; **~ de todo** after all

desquiciado, -a [deski'θjaðo, a] adj deranged

destacar [desta'kar] vt to emphasize, point up; (Mil) to detach, detail ▷ vi (resaltarse) to stand out; (persona) to be outstanding o exceptional; **destacarse** vr to stand out; to be outstanding o exceptional

destajo [des'taxo] nm: **trabajar a ~** to do piecework

destapar [desta'par] vt (botella) to open; (cacerola) to take the lid off; (descubrir) to uncover; **destaparse** vr (revelarse) to reveal one's true character

destartalado, -a [destarta'laðo, a] adj (desordenado) untidy; (ruinoso) tumbledown

destello [des'teʎo] nm (de estrella) twinkle; (de faro) signal light

destemplado, -a [destem'plaðo, a] adj (Mús) out of tune; (voz) harsh; (Med) out of sorts; (tiempo) unpleasant, nasty

desteñir [deste'nir] vt to fade ▷ vi to fade; **desteñirse** vr to fade; **esta tela no destiñe** this fabric will not run

desternillarse [desterni'ʎarse] vr: **~ de risa** to split one's sides laughing

desterrar [deste'rrar] vt (exiliar) to exile; (fig) to banish, dismiss

destiempo [des'tjempo]: **a ~** adv out of turn

destierro etc [des'tjerro] vb V **desterrar** ▷ nm exile

destilar [desti'lar] vt to distil; **destilería** nf distillery

destinar [desti'nar] vt (funcionario) to appoint, assign; (fondos): **~ (a)** to set aside (for)

destinatario, -a [destina'tarjo, a] nm/f addressee

destino [des'tino] nm (suerte) destiny; (de avión, viajero) destination; **con ~ a Londres** (barco) (bound) for London; (avión, carta) to London

destituir [destitu'ir] vt to dismiss

destornillador [destorniʎa'ðor] nm screwdriver

destornillar [destorni'ʎar] vt (tornillo) to unscrew; **destornillarse** vr to unscrew

destreza [des'treθa] nf (habilidad) skill; (maña) dexterity

destrozar [destro'θar] vt (romper) to smash, break (up); (estropear) to ruin; (nervios) to shatter

destrozo [des'troθo] nm (acción) destruction; (desastre) smashing; **destrozos** nmpl (pedazos) pieces; (daños) havoc sg

destrucción [destruk'θjon] nf destruction

destruir [destru'ir] vt to destroy

Jesuso [des'uso] nm disuse; **caer en ~** to become obsolete

desvalijar [desbali'xar] vt (persona) to rob; (casa, tienda) to burgle; (coche) to break into

desván [des'βan] nm attic

desvanecer [desβane'θer] vt (disipar) to dispel; (borrar) to blur; **desvanecerse** vr (humo etc) to vanish, disappear; (color) to fade; (recuerdo, sonido) to fade away; (Med) to pass out; (duda) to be dispelled

desvariar [desβa'rjar] vi (enfermo) to be delirious

desvelar [desβe'lar] vt to keep awake; **desvelarse** vr (no poder dormir) to stay awake; (preocuparse) to be vigilant o watchful

desventaja [desβen'taxa] nf disadvantage

desvergonzado, -a [desβerɣon'θaðo, a] adj shameless

desvestir [desβes'tir] vt to undress; **desvestirse** vr to undress

desviación [desβja'θjon] nf deviation; (Auto) diversion, detour

desviar [des'βjar] vt to turn aside; (río) to alter the course of; (navío) to divert, re-route; (conversación) to sidetrack; **desviarse** vr (apartarse del camino) to turn aside; (: barco) to go off course

desvío etc [des'βio] vb V **desviar** ⊳ nm (desviación) detour, diversion; (fig) indifference

desvivirse [desβi'βirse] vr: **~ por** (anhelar) to long for, crave for; (hacer lo posible por) to do one's utmost to

detallar [deta'ʎar] vt to detail

detalle [de'taʎe] nm detail; (gesto) gesture, token; **al ~** in detail; (Com) retail

detallista [deta'ʎista] nmf (Com) retailer

detective [detek'tiβe] nmf detective;

detective privado private detective

detención [deten'θjon] nf (arresto) arrest; (prisión) detention

detener [dete'ner] vt (gen) to stop; (Jur) to arrest; (objeto) to keep; **detenerse** vr to stop; (demorarse): **~se en** to delay over, linger over

detenidamente [deteniða'mente] adv (minuciosamente) carefully; (extensamente) at great length

detenido, -a [dete'niðo, a] adj (arrestado) under arrest ⊳ nm/f person under arrest, prisoner

detenimiento [deteni'mjento] nm: **con ~** thoroughly; (observar, considerar) carefully

detergente [deter'xente] nm detergent

deteriorar [deterjo'rar] vt to spoil, damage; **deteriorarse** vr to deteriorate; **deterioro** nm deterioration

determinación [determina'θjon] nf (empeño) determination; (decisión) decision; **determinado, -a** adj specific

determinar [determi'nar] vt (plazo) to fix; (precio) to settle; **determinarse** vr to decide

detestar [detes'tar] vt to detest

detractor, a [detrak'tor, a] nm/f slanderer, libeller

detrás [de'tras] adv (tb: **por ~**) behind; (atrás) at the back; **~ de** behind

detrimento [detri'mento] nm: **en ~ de** to the detriment of

deuda ['deuða] nf debt; **deuda exterior/pública** foreign/national debt

devaluación [deβalwa'θjon] nf devaluation

devastar [deβas'tar] vt (destruir) to devastate

deveras [de'βeras] (MÉX) nf inv: **un amigo de (a) ~** a true o real friend

devoción [deβo'θjon] nf devotion

devolución [deβolu'θjon] nf (reenvío) return, sending back; (reembolso)

repayment; (Jur) devolution
devolver [deβol'βer] vt to return;
(lo extraviado, lo prestado) to give back;
(carta al correo) to send back; (Com)
to repay, refund ▷ vi (vomitar) to be sick
devorar [deβo'rar] vt to devour
devoto, -a [de'βoto, a] adj devout
▷ nm/f admirer
devuelto pp de **devolver**
devuelva etc vb V **devolver**
di etc vb V **dar; decir**
día ['dia] nm day; ¿qué ~ es? what's
the date?; **estar/poner al ~** to be/keep
up to date; **el ~ de hoy/de mañana**
today/tomorrow; **al ~ siguiente** (on)
the following day; **vivir al ~** to live from
hand to mouth; **en pleno ~** by day, in daylight;
en pleno ~ in full daylight; **Día de la
Independencia** Independence Day;
Día de los Muertos (MÉX) All Souls'
Day; **Día de Reyes** Epiphany; **día
feriado** (LAM) holiday; **día festivo** (ESP)
holiday; **día lectivo** teaching day; **día
libre** day off
diabetes [dja'βetes] nf diabetes
diablo ['djaβlo] nm devil; **diablura**
nf prank
diadema [dja'ðema] nf tiara
diafragma [dja'fraɣma] nm
diaphragm
diagnóstico [diaɣ'nostiko] nm =
diagnosis
diagonal [djaɣo'nal] adj diagonal
diagrama [dja'ɣrama] nm diagram
dial [djal] nm dial
dialecto [dja'lekto] nm dialect
dialogar [djalo'xar] vi: **~ con** (Pol) to
hold talks with
diálogo ['djaloɣo] nm dialogue
diamante [dja'mante] nm diamond
diana ['djana] nf (Mil) reveille; (de
blanco) centre, bull's-eye
diapositiva [djaposi'tiβa] nf (Foto)
slide, transparency
diario, -a ['djarjo, a] adj daily ▷ nm
newspaper; **a ~** daily; **de ~** everyday
diarrea [dja'rrea] nf diarrhoea
dibujar [diβu'xar] vt to draw,

sketch; **dibujo** nm drawing; **dibujos
animados** cartoons
diccionario [dikθjo'narjo] nm
dictionary
dice etc vb V **decir**
dicho, -a [di'tʃo, a] pp de
decir ▷ adj: **en ~ países** in the
aforementioned countries ▷ nm
saying
dichoso, -a [di'tʃoso, a] adj happy
diciembre [di'θjembre] nm
December
dictado [dik'taðo] nm dictation
dictador [dikta'ðor] nm dictator;
dictadura nf dictatorship
dictar [dik'tar] vt (carta) to dictate;
(Jur: sentencia) to pronounce; (decreto) to
issue; (LAM: clase) to give
didáctico, -a [di'ðaktiko, a] adj
educational
diecinueve [djeθi'nweβe] num
nineteen
dieciocho [djeθi'otʃo] num eighteen
dieciséis [djeθi'seis] num sixteen
diecisiete [djeθi'sjete] num
seventeen
diente ['djente] nm (Anat, Tec) tooth;
(Zool) fang; (: de elefante) tusk; (de
ajo) clove
diera etc vb V **dar**
diesel ['disel] adj: **motor ~** diesel
engine
diestro, -a ['djestro, a] adj (derecho)
right; (hábil) skilful
dieta ['djeta] nf diet; **estar a ~** to be
on a diet
diez [djeθ] num ten
diferencia [dife'renθja] nf
difference; **a ~ de** unlike; **diferenciar**
vt to differentiate between ▷ vi to
differ; **diferenciarse** vr to differ, be
different; (distinguirse) to distinguish
o.s.
diferente [dife'rente] adj different
diferido [dife'riðo] nm: **en ~** (TV etc)
recorded
difícil [di'fiθil] adj difficult
dificultad [difikul'taðh] nf difficulty;

(problema) trouble

dificultar [difikul'tar] *vt (complicar)* to complicate, make difficult; *(estorbar)* to obstruct

difundir [difun'dir] *vt (calor, luz)* to diffuse; *(Radio, TV)* to broadcast; **~ una noticia** to spread a piece of news; **difundirse** *vr* to spread (out)

difunto, -a [di'funto, a] *adj* dead, deceased ▷ *nm/f* deceased (person)

difusión [difu'sjon] *nf (Radio, TV)* broadcasting

diga *etc vb* V **decir**

digerir [dixe'rir] *vt* to digest; *(fig)* to absorb; **digestión** *nf* digestion; **digestivo, -a** *adj* digestive

digital [dixi'tal] *adj* digital

dignarse [diɣ'narse] *vr* to deign to

dignidad [diɣni'ðað] *nf* dignity

digno, -a [ˈdiɣno, a] *adj* worthy

digo *etc vb* V **decir**

dije *etc vb* V **decir**

dilatar [dila'tar] *vt (cuerpo)* to dilate; *(prolongar)* to prolong

dilema [di'lema] *nm* dilemma

diluir [dilu'ir] *vt* to dilute

diluvio [di'luβjo] *nm* deluge, flood

dimensión [dimen'sjon] *nf* dimension

diminuto, -a [dimi'nuto, a] *adj* tiny, diminutive

dimitir [dimi'tir] *vi* to resign

dimos *vb* V **dar**

Dinamarca [dina'marka] *nf* Denmark

dinámico, -a [di'namiko, a] *adj* dynamic

dinamita [dina'mita] *nf* dynamite

dínamo [ˈdinamo] *nf* dynamo

dineral [dine'ral] *nm* large sum of money, fortune

dinero [di'nero] *nm* money; **dinero en efectivo o metálico** cash; **dinero suelto** (loose) change

dio *vb* V **dar**

dios [djos] *nm* god; **¡D~ mío!** (oh,) my God!; **¡por D~!** for heaven's sake!; **diosa** [ˈdjosa] *nf* goddess

diploma [di'ploma] *nm* diploma

diplomacia [diplo'maθja] *nf* diplomacy; *(fig)* tact

diplomado, -a [diplo'maðo, a] *adj* qualified

diplomático, -a [diplo'matiko, a] *adj* diplomatic ▷ *nm/f* diplomat

diputación [diputa'θjon] *nf (tb: ~ provincial)* ≈ county council

diputado, -a [dipu'taðo, a] *nm/f* delegate; *(Pol)* ≈ member of parliament *(BRIT)* ≈ representative *(US)*

dique [ˈdike] *nm* dyke

diré *etc vb* V **decir**

dirección [direk'θjon] *nf* direction; *(señas)* address; *(Auto)* steering; *(gerencia)* management; *(Pol)* leadership; **dirección única o prohibida** one-way street/no entry

direccional [direkθjo'nal] *(MÉX) nf (Auto)* indicator

directa [di'rekta] *nf (Auto)* top gear

directiva [direk'tiβa] *nf (tb: junta ~)* board of directors

directo, -a [di'rekto, a] *adj* direct; *(Radio, TV)* live; **transmitir en ~** to broadcast live

director, a [direk'tor, a] *adj* leading ▷ *nm/f* director; *(Escol)* head (teacher) *(BRIT)*, principal *(US)*; *(gerente)* manager/ess; *(Prensa)* editor; **director de cine** film director; **director general** managing director

directorio [direk'torjo] *(MÉX) nm (telefónico)* phone book

dirigente [diri'xente] *nmf (Pol)* leader

dirigir [diri'xir] *vt* to direct; *(carta)* to address; *(obra de teatro, film)* to direct; *(Mús)* to conduct; *(negocio)* to manage; **dirigirse** *vr*: **~se a** to go towards, make one's way towards; *(hablar con)* to speak to

dirija *etc vb* V **dirigir**

disciplina [disθi'plina] *nf* discipline

discípulo, -a [dis'θipulo, a] *nm/f* disciple

Discman® [ˈdiskman] *nm*

Discman®

disco ['disko] nm disc; (Deporte) discus; (Tel) dial; (Auto: semáforo) light; (Mús) record; **disco compacto/de larga duración** compact disc/long-playing record; **disco de freno** brake disc; **disco flexible/duro o rígido** (Inform) floppy/hard disk

disconforme [diskon'forme] adj differing; **estar ~ (con)** to be in disagreement (with)

discordia [dis'korðja] nf discord

discoteca [disko'teka] nf disco(theque)

discreción [diskre'θjon] nf discretion; (reserva) prudence; **comer a ~** to eat as much as one wishes

discreto, -a [dis'kreto, a] adj discreet

discriminación [diskrimina'θjon] nf discrimination

disculpa [dis'kulpa] nf excuse; (pedir perdón) apology; **pedir ~s a/por** to apologize to/for; **disculpar** vt to excuse, pardon; **disculparse** vr to excuse o.s.; to apologize

discurso [dis'kurso] nm speech

discusión [disku'sjon] nf (diálogo) discussion; (riña) argument

discutir [disku'tir] vt (debatir) to discuss; (pelear) to argue about; (contradecir) to argue against ▷ vi (debatir) to discuss; (pelearse) to argue

disecar [dise'kar] vt (conservar: animal) to stuff; (: planta) to dry

diseñar [dise'ɲar] vt, vi to design

diseño [di'seɲo] nm design

disfraz [dis'fraθ] nm (máscara) disguise; (excusa) pretext; **disfrazar** vt to disguise; **disfrazarse** vr: **disfrazarse de** to disguise o.s. as

disfrutar [disfru'tar] vt to enjoy ▷ vi to enjoy o.s.; **~ de** to enjoy, possess

disgustar [disɣus'tar] vt (no gustar) to displease; (contrariar, enojar) to annoy, upset; **disgustarse** vr (enfadarse) to get upset; (dos personas)

to fall out

⚠ No confundir **disgustar** con la palabra inglesa **disgust**.

disgusto [dis'ɣusto] nm (contrariedad) annoyance; (tristeza) grief; (riña) quarrel

disimular [disimu'lar] vt (ocultar) to hide, conceal ▷ vi to dissemble

diskette [dis'ket] nm (Inform) diskette, floppy disk

dislocarse [dislo'karse] vr (articulación) to sprain, dislocate

disminución [disminu'θjon] nf decrease, reduction

disminuido, -a [disminu'iðo, a] nm/f: **~ mental/físico** mentally/physically handicapped person

disminuir [disminu'ir] vt to decrease, diminish

disolver [disol'βer] vt (gen) to dissolve; **disolverse** vr to dissolve; (Com) to go into liquidation

dispar [dis'par] adj different

disparar [dispa'rar] vt, vi to shoot, fire

disparate [dispa'rate] nm (tontería) foolish remark; (error) blunder; **decir ~s** to talk nonsense

disparo [dis'paro] nm shot

dispersar [disper'sar] vt to disperse; **dispersarse** vr to scatter

disponer [dispo'ner] vt (arreglar) to arrange; (ordenar) to put in order; (preparar) to prepare, get ready ▷ vi: **~ de** to have, own; **disponerse** vr: **~se a o para hacer** to prepare to do

disponible [dispo'niβle] adj available

disposición [disposi'θjon] nf arrangement, disposition; (voluntad) willingness; (Inform) layout; **a su ~** at your service

dispositivo [disposi'tiβo] nm device, mechanism

dispuesto, -a [dis'pwesto, a] pp de **disponer** ▷ adj (arreglado) arranged; (preparado) disposed

disputar [dispu'tar] vt (carrera) to compete in

disquete [disˈkete] nm floppy disk, diskette

distancia [disˈtanθja] nf distance; **distanciar** [distanˈθjar] vt to space out; **distanciarse** vr to become estranged; **distante** [disˈtante] adj distant

diste vb V **dar**

disteis vb V **dar**

distinción [distinˈθjon] nf distinction; (elegancia) elegance; (honor) honour

distinguido, -a [distinˈɣiðo, a] adj distinguished

distinguir [distinˈɣir] vt to distinguish; (escoger) to single out; **distinguirse** vr to be distinguished

distintivo [distinˈtiβo] nm badge; (fig) characteristic

distinto, -a [disˈtinto, a] adj different; (claro) clear

distracción [distrakˈθjon] nf distraction; (pasatiempo) hobby, pastime; (olvido) absent-mindedness, distraction

distraer [distraˈer] vt (atención) to distract; (divertir) to amuse; (fondos) to embezzle; **distraerse** vr (entretenerse) to amuse o.s.; (perder la concentración) to allow one's attention to wander

distraído, -a [distraˈiðo, a] adj absent-minded; (entretenido) amusing

distribuidor, a [distriβwiˈðor, a] nm/f distributor; **distribuidora** nf (Com) dealer, agent; (Cine) distributor

distribuir [distriβuˈir] vt to distribute

distrito [disˈtrito] nm (sector, territorio) region; (barrio) district; **Distrito Federal** (MÉX) Federal District; **distrito postal** postal district

disturbio [disˈturβjo] nm disturbance; (desorden) riot

disuadir [diswaˈðir] vt to dissuade

disuelto [diˈswelto] pp de **disolver**

DIU nm abr (= dispositivo intrauterino) IUD

diurno, -a [ˈdjurno, a] adj day cpd

divagar [diβaˈɣar] vi (desviarse) to

digress

diván [diˈβan] nm divan

diversidad [diβersiˈðað] nf diversity, variety

diversión [diβerˈsjon] nf (gen) entertainment; (actividad) hobby, pastime

diverso, -a [diˈβerso, a] adj diverse; **~s libros** several books; **diversos** nmpl sundries

divertido, -a [diβerˈtiðo, a] adj (chiste) amusing; (fiesta etc) enjoyable

divertir [diβerˈtir] vt (entretener, recrear) to amuse; **divertirse** vr (pasarlo bien) to have a good time; (distraerse) to amuse o.s.

dividendos [diβiˈðendos] nmpl (Com) dividends

dividir [diβiˈðir] vt (gen) to divide; (distribuir) to distribute, share out

divierta etc vb V **divertir**

divino, -a [diˈβino, a] adj divine

divirtiendo etc vb V **divertir**

divisa [diˈβisa] nf (emblema) emblem, badge; **divisas** nfpl foreign exchange sg

divisar [diβiˈsar] vt to make out, distinguish

división [diβiˈsjon] nf (gen) division; (de partido) split; (de país) partition

divorciar [diβorˈθjar] vt to divorce; **divorciarse** vr to get divorced; **divorcio** nm divorce

divulgar [diβulˈɣar] vt (ideas) to spread; (secreto) to divulge

DNI (ESP) nm abr (= Documento Nacional de Identidad) national identity card

Dña. *abr* (= doña) Mrs

do [do] *nm* (Mús) do, C

dobladillo [doβla'ðiʎo] *nm* (de vestido) hem; (de pantalón: vuelta) turn-up (BRIT), cuff (US)

doblar [do'βlar] *vt* (número: papel) to fold; (caño) to bend; (la esquina) to turn, go round; (film) to dub ▷ *vi* to turn; (campana) to toll; **doblarse** *vr* (plegarse) to fold (up), crease; (encorvarse) to bend; **~ a la derecha/izquierda** to turn right/left

doble ['doβle] *adj* double; (de dos aspectos) dual; (fig) two-faced ▷ *nm* double ▷ *nmf* (Teatro) double, stand-in; **dobles** *nmpl* (Deporte) doubles *sg*; **con ~ sentido** with a double meaning

doce ['doθe] *num* twelve; **docena** *nf* dozen

docente [do'θente] *adj*: **centro/personal ~** teaching establishment/staff

dócil ['doθil] *adj* (pasivo) docile; (obediente) obedient

doctor, a [dok'tor, a] *nm/f* doctor

doctorado [dokto'raðo] *nm* doctorate

doctrina [dok'trina] *nf* doctrine, teaching

documentación [dokumenta'θjon] *nf* documentation, papers *pl*

documental [dokumen'tal] *adj*, *nm* documentary

documento [doku'mento] *nm* (certificado) document; **documento adjunto** (Inform) attachment; **documento nacional de identidad** identity card

dólar ['dolar] *nm* dollar

doler [do'ler] *vt*, *vi* to hurt; (fig) to grieve; **dolerse** *vr* (de su situación) to grieve, feel sorry; (de las desgracias ajenas) to sympathize; **me duele el brazo** my arm hurts

dolor [do'lor] *nm* pain; (fig) grief, sorrow; **dolor de cabeza/estómago/muelas** headache/stomachache/toothache

domar [do'mar] *vt* to tame

domesticar [domesti'kar] *vt* = **domar**

doméstico, -a [do'mestiko, a] *adj* (vida, servicio) home; (tareas) household; (animal) tame, pet

domicilio [domi'θiljo] *nm* home; **servicio a ~** home delivery service; **sin ~ fijo** of no fixed abode; **domicilio particular** private residence

dominante [domi'nante] *adj* dominant; (persona) domineering

dominar [domi'nar] *vt* (gen) to dominate; (idiomas) to be fluent in ▷ *vi* to dominate, prevail

domingo [do'mingo] *nm* Sunday; **Domingo de Ramos/Resurrección** Palm/Easter Sunday

dominio [do'minjo] *nm* (tierras) domain; (autoridad) power, authority; (de las pasiones) grip, hold; (de idiomas) command

don [don] *nm* (talento) gift; **~ Juan Gómez** Mr Juan Gómez, Juan Gómez Esq (BRIT)

- **DON/DOÑA**
-
- The term **don/doña** often
- abbreviated to **D./Dña** is placed
- before the first name as a mark
- of respect to an older or more
- senior person – eg Don Diego,
- Doña Inés. Although becoming
- rarer in Spain it is still used
- with names and surnames on
- official documents and formal
- correspondence – eg "Sr. D. Pedro
- Rodríguez Hernández", "Sra. Dña.
- Inés Rodríguez Hernández".

dona ['dona] (MÉX) *nf* doughnut, donut (US)

donar [do'nar] *vt* to donate

donativo [dona'tiβo] *nm* donation

donde ['donde] *adv* where ▷ *prep*: **el coche está allí ~ el farol** the car is over there by the lamppost o where the lamppost is; **en ~** where, in which

dónde ['donde] adv where?; **¿a ~ vas?** where are you going (to)?; **¿de ~ vienes?** where have you been?; **¿por ~?** where?, whereabouts?

dondequiera [donde'kjera] adv anywhere; **por ~** everywhere, all over the place ▷ conj: **~ que** wherever

donut® [do'nut] (ESP) nm doughnut, donut (US)

doña ['dona] nf: **~ Alicia** Alicia; **~ Victoria Benito** Mrs Victoria Benito

dorado, -a [do'raðo, a] adj (color) golden; (Tec) gilt

dormir [dor'mir] vt: **~ la siesta** to have an afternoon nap ▷ vi to sleep; **dormirse** vr to fall asleep

dormitorio [dormi'torjo] nm bedroom

dorsal [dor'sal] nm (Deporte) number

dorso ['dorso] nm (de mano) back; (de hoja) other side

dos [dos] num two

dosis ['dosis] nf inv dose, dosage

dotado, -a [do'taðo, a] adj gifted; **~ de** endowed with

dotar [do'tar] vt to endow; **dote** nf dowry; **dotes** nfpl (talentos) gifts

doy [doj] vb V **dar**

drama ['drama] nm drama; **dramaturgo** [drama'turɣo] nm, f dramatist, playwright

drástico, -a ['drastiko, a] adj drastic

drenaje [dre'naxe] nm drainage

droga ['droɣa] nf drug; **drogadicto, -a** [droɣa'ðikto, a] nm/f drug addict

drogarse [dro'ɣarse] vr to take drugs

droguería [droɣe'ria] nf hardware shop (BRIT) o store (US)

ducha ['dutʃa] nf (baño) shower; (Med) douche; **ducharse** vr to take a shower

duda ['duða] nf doubt; **no cabe ~** there is no doubt about it; **dudar** vt, vi to doubt; **dudoso, -a** [du'ðoso, a] adj (incierto) hesitant; (sospechoso) doubtful

duela etc vb V **doler**

duelo ['dwelo] vb V **doler** ▷ nm (combate) duel; (luto) mourning

duende ['dwende] nm imp, goblin

dueño, -a [ˈdweɲo, a] nm/f (propietario) owner; (de pensión, taberna) landlord/lady; (empresario) employer

duermo etc vb V **dormir**

dulce ['dulθe] adj sweet ▷ adv gently, softly ▷ nm sweet

dulcería [dulθe'ria] (LAM) nf confectioner's (shop)

dulzura [dul'θura] nf sweetness; (ternura) gentleness

dúo ['duo] nm duet

duplicar [dupli'kar] vt (hacer el doble de) to duplicate

duque ['duke] nm duke; **duquesa** nf duchess

durable [du'raβle] adj durable

duración [dura'θjon] nf (de película, disco etc) length; (de pila etc) life; (curso: de acontecimientos etc) duration

duradero, -a [dura'ðero, a] adj (tela etc) hard-wearing; (fe, paz) lasting

durante [du'rante] prep during

durar [du'rar] vi to last; (recuerdo) to remain

durazno [du'raθno] (LAM) nm (fruta) peach; (árbol) peach tree

durex ['dureks] (MÉX, ARG) nm (tira adhesiva) Sellotape® (BRIT), Scotch tape® (US)

dureza [du'reθa] nf (calidad) hardness

duro, -a ['duro, a] adj hard; (carácter) tough ▷ adv hard ▷ nm (moneda) five-peseta coin o piece

DVD nm abr (= disco de vídeo digital) DVD

e

E abr (= este) E

e [e] conj and

ébano ['eβano] nm ebony

ebrio, -a ['eβrjo, a] adj drunk

ebullición [eβuʎi'θjon] nf boiling

echar [e'tʃar] vt to throw; (agua, vino) to pour (out); (empleado: despedir) to fire, sack; (hojas) to sprout; (cartas) to post; (humo) to emit, give out ▷ vi: **~ a correr** to run off; **~ una mirada** to give a look; **~ sangre** to bleed; **echarse** vr to lie down; **~ llave a** to lock (up); **~ abajo** (gobierno) to overthrow; (edificio) to demolish; **~ mano a** to lay hands on; **~ una mano a algn** (ayudar) to give sb a hand; **~ de menos** to miss; **~se atrás** (fig) to back out

eclesiástico, -a [ekle'sjastiko, a] adj ecclesiastical

eco ['eko] nm echo; **tener ~** to catch on

ecología [ekolo'xia] nf ecology; **ecológico, -a** adj (producto, método) environmentally-friendly; (agricultura) organic; **ecologista** adj

ecological, environmental ▷ nmf environmentalist

economía [ekono'mia] nf (sistema) economy; (carrera) economics

económico, -a [eko'nomiko, a] adj (barato) cheap, economical; (ahorrativo) thrifty; (Com: año etc) financial; (: situación) economic

economista [ekono'mista] nmf economist

Ecuador [ekwa'ðor] nm Ecuador; **ecuador** nm (Geo) equator

ecuatoriano, -a [ekwato'rjano, a] adj, nm/f Ecuadorian

ecuestre [e'kwestre] adj equestrian

edad [e'ðað] nf age; **¿qué ~ tienes?** how old are you?; **tiene ocho años de ~** he's eight (years old); **de ~ mediana/avanzada** middle-aged/advanced in years; **la E~ Media** the Middle Ages

edición [eði'θjon] nf (acto) publication; (ejemplar) edition

edificar [eðifi'kar] vt, vi to build

edificio [eði'fiθjo] nm building; (fig) edifice, structure

Edimburgo [eðim'burxo] nm Edinburgh

editar [eði'tar] vt (publicar) to publish; (preparar textos) to edit

editor, a [eði'tor, a] nm/f (que publica) publisher; (redactor) editor ▷ adj publishing cpd; **editorial** adj editorial ▷ nm leading article, editorial; **casa editorial** publisher

edredón [eðre'ðon] nm duvet

educación [eðuka'θjon] nf education; (crianza) upbringing; (modales) (good) manners pl

educado, -a [eðu'kaðo, a] adj: **bien/mal ~** well/badly behaved

educar [eðu'kar] vt to educate; (criar) to bring up; (voz) to train

EE. UU. nmpl abr (= Estados Unidos) US(A)

efectivamente [efectiβa'mente] adv (como respuesta) really, precisely; (verdaderamente) really; (de hecho) in fact

efectivo, -a [efek'tiβo, a] adj

effective; (real) actual, real ▷ nm: **pagar en ~** to pay (in) cash; **hacer ~ un cheque** to cash a cheque

efecto [e'fekto] nm effect, result; **efectos** nmpl (efectos personales) effects; (bienes) goods; (Com) assets; **en ~** in fact; (respuesta) exactly, indeed; **efecto invernadero**greenhouse effect; **efectos especiales/ secundarios/sonoros**special/side/ sound effects

efectuar [efek'twar] vt to carry out; (viaje) to make

eficacia [efi'kaθja] nf (de persona) efficiency; (de medicamento etc) effectiveness

eficaz [efi'kaθ] adj (persona) efficient; (acción) effective

eficiente [efi'θjente] adj efficient

egipcio, -a [e'xipθjo, a] adj, nm/f Egyptian

Egipto [e'xipto] nm Egypt

egoísmo [eɣo'ismo] nm egoism

egoísta [eɣo'ista] adj egoistical, selfish ▷ nmf egoist

Eire ['eire] nm Eire

ej. abr (= ejemplo) eg

eje ['exe] nm (Geo, Mat) axis; (de rueda) axle; (de máquina) shaft, spindle

ejecución [exeku'θjon] nf execution; (cumplimiento) fulfilment; (Mús) performance; (Jur: embargo de deudor) attachment

ejecutar [exeku'tar] vt to execute, carry out; (matar) to execute; (cumplir) to fulfil; (Mús) to perform; (Jur: embargar) to attach, distrain (on)

ejecutivo, -a [exeku'tiβo, a] adj executive; **el (poder) ~** the executive (power)

ejemplar [exem'plar] adj exemplary ▷ nm example; (Zool) specimen; (de libro) copy; (de periódico) number, issue

ejemplo [e'xemplo] nm example; **por ~** for example

ejercer [exer'θer] vt to exercise; (influencia) to exert; (un oficio) to practise ▷ vi (practicar): **~ (de)** to

practise (as)

ejercicio [exer'θiθjo] nm exercise; (período) tenure; **hacer ~** to take exercise; **ejercicio comercial**financial year

ejército [e'xerθito] nm army; **entrar en el ~** to join the army, join up; **ejército del aire/de tierra**Air Force/Army

ejote [e'xote] (MÉX) nm green bean

○ PALABRA CLAVE

el [el] (f la, pl los, las, neutro lo) art def 1the; **el libro/la mesa/los estudiantes** the book/table/students

2(con n abstracto: no se traduce): **el amor/la juventud** love/youth

3(posesión: se traduce a menudo por adj posesivo): **romperse el brazo** to break one's arm; **levantó la mano** he put his hand up; **se puso el sombrero** she put her hat on

4(valor descriptivo): **tener la boca grande/los ojos azules** to have a big mouth/blue eyes

5(con días) on; **me iré el viernes** I'll leave on Friday; **los domingos suelo ir a nadar** on Sundays I generally go swimming

6(lo +adj): **lo difícil/caro** what is difficult/expensive; (cuán): **no se da cuenta de lo pesado que es** he doesn't realise how boring he is

▷ pron demos ʈ **mi libro y el de usted** my book and yours; **las de Pepe son mejores** Pepe's are better; **no la(s) blanca(s) sino la(s) gris(es)** not the white one(s) but the grey one(s)

ʈ **lo de: lo de ayer** what happened yesterday; **lo de las facturas** that business about the invoices

▷ pron relativo 1(indef): **el que: el (los) que quiera(n) que se vaya(n)** anyone who wants to can leave; **llévese el que más le guste** take the one you like best

2(def): **el que: el que compré ayer** the one I bought yesterday; **los que se van** those who leave

3: **lo que: lo que pienso yo/más me gusta** what I think/like most
▷ *conj*: **el que: el que lo diga** the fact that he says so; **el que sea tan vago me molesta** his being so lazy bothers me
▷ *excl*: **¡el susto que me diste!** what a fright you gave me!
▷ *pron personal* **1** (*persona: m*) him; (*: f*) her; (*: pl*) them; **lo/las veo** I can see him/them
2 (*animal, cosa: sg*) it; (*: pl*) them; **lo** (*o* **la**) **veo** I can see it; **los** (*o* **las**) **veo** I can see them
3 (*como sustituto de frase*): **lo: no lo sabía** I didn't know; **ya lo entiendo** I understand now

él [el] *pron* (*persona*) he; (*cosa*) it; (*después de prep: persona*) him; (*: cosa*) it; **de ~** his

elaborar [elaβo'rar] *vt* (*producto*) to make, manufacture; (*preparar*) to prepare; (*madera, metal etc*) to work; (*proyecto etc*) to work on o out

elástico, -a [e'lastiko, a] *adj* elastic; (*flexible*) flexible ▷ *nm* elastic; (*un elástico*) elastic band

elección [elek'θjon] *nf* election; (*selección*) choice, selection; **elecciones generales** general election *sg*

electorado [elekto'raðo] *nm* electorate, voters *pl*

electricidad [elektriθi'ðað] *nf* electricity

electricista [elektri'θista] *nmf* electrician

eléctrico, -a [e'lektriko, a] *adj* electric

electro... [elektro] *prefijo*
electro...; **electrocardiograma** *nm* electrocardiogram; **electrocutar** *vt* to electrocute; **electrodo** *nm* electrode; **electrodomésticos** *nmpl* (electrical) household appliances

electrónica [elek'tronika] *nf* electronics *sg*

electrónico, -a [elek'troniko, a] *adj* electronic

electrotren [elektro'tren] *nm* express electric train

elefante [ele'fante] *nm* elephant

elegancia [ele'ɣanθja] *nf* elegance, grace; (*estilo*) stylishness

elegante [ele'ɣante] *adj* elegant, graceful; (*estiloso*) stylish, fashionable

elegir [ele'xir] *vt* (*escoger*) to choose, select; (*optar*) to opt for; (*presidente*) to elect

elemental [elemen'tal] *adj* (*claro, obvio*) elementary; (*fundamental*) elemental, fundamental

elemento [ele'mento] *nm* element; (*fig*) ingredient; **elementos** *nmpl* elements, rudiments

elevación [eleβa'θjon] *nf* elevation; (*acto*) raising, lifting; (*de precios*) rise; (*Geo etc*) height, altitude

elevado [ele'βaðo] *adj* high

elevar [ele'βar] *vt* to raise, lift (up); (*precio*) to put up; **elevarse** *vr* (*edificio*) to rise; (*precios*) to go up

eligiendo *etc vb* V **elegir**

elija *etc vb* V **elegir**

eliminar [elimi'nar] *vt* to eliminate, remove

eliminatoria [elimina'torja] *nf* heat, preliminary (round)

élite ['elite] *nf* elite

ella ['eʎa] *pron* (*persona*) she; (*cosa*) it; (*después de prep: persona*) her; (*: cosa*) it; **de ~** hers

ellas ['eʎas] *pron* (*personas y cosas*) they; (*después de prep*) them; **de ~** theirs

ello ['eʎo] *pron* it

ellos ['eʎos] *pron* they; (*después de prep*) them; **de ~** theirs

elogiar [elo'xjar] *vt* to praise; **elogio** *nm* praise

elote [e'lote] (*MÉX*) *nm* corn on the cob

eludir [elu'ðir] *vt* to avoid

email [i'mel] *nm* email; (*dirección*) email address; **mandar un ~ a algn** to email sb, send sb an email

embajada [emba'xaða] *nf* embassy

embajador, a [embaxa'ðor, a] nm/f ambassador/ambassadress

embalar [emba'lar] vt to parcel, wrap (up); **embalarse** vr to go too fast

embalse [em'balse] nm (presa) dam; (lago) reservoir

embarazada [embara'θaða] adj pregnant ▷ nf pregnant woman
  No confundir **embarazada** con la palabra inglesa embarrassed.

embarazo [emba'raθo] nm (de mujer) pregnancy; (impedimento) obstacle, obstruction; (timidez) embarrassment; **embarazoso, -a** adj awkward, embarrassing

embarcación [embarka'θjon] nf (barco) boat, craft; (acto) embarkation, boarding

embarcadero [embarka'ðero] nm pier, landing stage

embarcar [embar'kar] vt (cargamento) to ship, stow; (persona) to embark, put on board; **embarcarse** vr to embark, go on board

embargar [embar'ɣar] vt (Jur) to seize, impound

embargo [em'barɣo] nm (Jur) seizure; (Com, Pol) embargo

embargue etc V **embargar**

embarque etc [em'barke] vb V **embarcar** ▷ nm shipment, loading

embellecer [embeʎe'θer] vt to embellish, beautify

embestida [embes'tiða] nf attack, onslaught; (carga) charge

embestir [embes'tir] vt to attack, assault; to charge, attack ▷ vi to attack

emblema [em'blema] nm emblem

embobado, -a [embo'βaðo, a] adj (atontado) stunned, bewildered

embolia [em'bolja] nf (Med) clot

émbolo ['embolo] nm (Auto) piston

emborrachar [emborra'tʃar] vt to make drunk, intoxicate; **emborracharse** vr to get drunk

emboscada [embos'kaða] nf ambush

embotar [embo'tar] vt to blunt, dull

embotellamiento [emboteʎa'mjento] nm (Auto) traffic jam

embotellar [embote'ʎar] vt to bottle

embrague [em'braxe] nm (tb: **pedal de –**) clutch

embrión [em'brjon] nm embryo

embrollo [em'broʎo] nm (enredo) muddle, confusion; (aprieto) fix, jam

embrujado, -a [embru'xaðo, a] adj bewitched; **casa embrujada** haunted house

embrutecer [embrute'θer] vt (atontar) to stupefy

embudo [em'buðo] nm funnel

embuste [em'buste] nm (mentira) lie; **embustero, -a** adj lying, deceitful ▷ nm/f (mentiroso) liar

embutido [embu'tiðo] nm (Culin) sausage; (Tec) inlay

emergencia [emer'xenθja] nf emergency; (surgimiento) emergence

emerger [emer'xer] vi to emerge, appear

emigración [emixra'θjon] nf emigration; (de pájaros) migration

emigrar [emi'xrar] vi (personas) to emigrate; (pájaros) to migrate

eminente [emi'nente] adj eminent, distinguished; (elevado) high

emisión [emi'sjon] nf (acto) emission; (Com etc) issue; (Radio, TV: acto) broadcasting; (: programa) broadcast, programme (BRIT), program (US)

emisora [emi'sora] nf radio o broadcasting station

emitir [emi'tir] vt (olor etc) to emit, give off; (moneda etc) to issue; (opinión) to express; (Radio) to broadcast

emoción [emo'θjon] nf emotion; (excitación) excitement; (sentimiento) feeling

emocionante [emoθjo'nante] adj (excitante) exciting, thrilling

emocionar [emoθjo'nar] vt (excitar) to excite, thrill; (conmover) to move, touch; (impresionar) to impress

emoticón [emoti'kon], **emoticono** [emoti'kono] nm smiley

emotivo, -a [emo'tiβo, a] adj emotional

empacho [em'patʃo] nm (Med) indigestion; (fig) embarrassment

empalagoso, -a [empala'ɣoso, a] adj cloying; (fig) tiresome

empalmar [empal'mar] vt to join, connect ▷ vi (dos caminos) to meet, join; **empalme** nm joint, connection; junction; (de trenes) connection

empanada [empa'naða] nf pie, pasty

empañarse [empa'narse] vr (cristales etc) to steam up

empapar [empa'par] vt (mojar) to soak, saturate; (absorber) to soak up, absorb; **empaparse** vr: ~se de to soak up

empapelar [empape'lar] vt (paredes) to paper

empaquetar [empake'tar] vt to pack, parcel up

empastar [empas'tar] vt (embadurnar) to paste; (diente) to fill; **empaste** nm (de diente) filling

empatar [empa'tar] vi to draw, tie; **~on a dos** they drew two-all; **empate** nm draw, tie

empecé etc vb V **empezar**

empedernido, -a [empeðer'niðo, a] adj hard, heartless; (fumador) inveterate

empeine [em'peine] nm (de pie, zapato) instep

empeñado, -a [empe'naðo, a] adj (persona) determined; (objeto) pawned

empeñar [empe'nar] vt (objeto) to pawn, pledge; (persona) to compel; **empeñarse** vr (endeudarse) to get into debt; **~se en** to be set on, be determined to

empeño [em'peno] nm (determinación, insistencia) determination, insistence; **casa de ~s** pawnshop

empeorar [empeo'rar] vt to make worse, worsen ▷ vi to get worse, deteriorate

empezar [empe'θar] vt, vi to begin, start

empiece etc vb V **empezar**

empiezo etc vb V **empezar**

emplasto [em'plasto] nm (Med) plaster

emplazar [empla'θar] vt (ubicar) to site, place, locate; (Jur) to summons; (convocar) to summons

empleado, -a [emple'aðo, a] nm/f (gen) employee; (de banco etc) clerk

emplear [emple'ar] vt (usar) to use, employ; (dar trabajo a) to employ; **emplearse** vr (conseguir trabajo) to be employed; (ocuparse) to occupy o.s.

empleo [em'pleo] nm (puesto) job; (puestos: colectivamente) employment; (uso) use, employment

empollar [empo'ʎar] (ESP: fam) vt, vi to swot (up); **empollón, -ona** (ESP: fam) nm/f swot

emporio [em'porjo] (LAM) nm (gran almacén) department store

empotrado, -a [empo'traðo, a] adj (armario etc) built-in

emprendedor, a [emprende'ðor, a] adj enterprising

emprender [empren'der] vt (empezar) to begin, embark on; (acometer) to tackle, take on

empresa [em'presa] nf (de espíritu etc) enterprise; (Com) company, firm; **empresariales** nfpl business studies; **empresario, -a** nm/f (Com) businessman(-woman)

empujar [empu'xar] vt to push, shove

empujón [empu'xon] nm push, shove

empuñar [empu'nar] vt (asir) to grasp, take (firm) hold of

○ **PALABRA CLAVE**

en [en] prep 1 (posición) in; (: sobre) on;

está en el cajón it's in the drawer; **en Argentina/La Paz** in Argentina/La Paz; **en la oficina/el colegio** at the office/school; **está en el suelo/quinto piso** it's on the floor/the fifth floor

2 (*dirección*) into; **entró en el aula** she went into the classroom; **meter algo en el bolso** to put sth into one's bag

3 (*tiempo*) in; on; **en 1605/3 semanas/invierno** in 1605/3 weeks/winter; **(el mes de) enero** in the month of January; **en aquella ocasión/época** on that occasion/at that time

4 (*precio*) for; **lo vendió en 20 dólares** he sold it for 20 dollars

5 (*diferencia*) by; **reducir/aumentar en una tercera parte/un 20 por ciento** to reduce/increase by a third/20 per cent

6 (*manera*): **en avión/autobús** by plane/bus; **escrito en inglés** written in English

7 (*después de vb que indica gastar etc*) on; **han cobrado demasiado en dietas** they've charged too much to expenses; **se le va la mitad del sueldo en comida** he spends half his salary on food

8 (*tema, ocupación*): **experto en la materia** expert on the subject; **trabaja en la construcción** he works in the building industry

9 (*adj* + *en* + *infin*): **lento en reaccionar** slow to react

enaguas [e'naɣwas] *nfpl* petticoat *sg*, underskirt *sg*

enajenación [enaxena'θjon] *nf* (*Psico: tb*: **~ mental**) mental derangement

enamorado, -a [enamo'raðo, a] *adj* in love ▷ *nm/f* lover; **estar ~ (de)** to be in love (with)

enamorar [enamo'rar] *vt* to win the love of; **enamorarse** *vr*: **~se de algn** to fall in love with sb

nano, -a ['nano, a] *adj* tiny ▷ *nm/f* dwarf

encabezamiento [enkaβeθa'mjento] *nm* (*de carta*) heading; (*de periódico*) headline

encabezar [enkaβe'θar] *vt* (*movimiento, revolución*) to lead, head; (*lista*) to head, be at the top of; (*carta*) to put a heading to

encadenar [enkaðe'nar] *vt* to chain (*together*); (*poner grilletes a*) to shackle

encajar [enka'xar] *vt* (*ajustar*): **~ (en)** to fit (into); (*fam: golpe*) to give ▷ *vi* to fit (well); (*fig: corresponder a*) to match

encaje [en'kaxe] *nm* (*labor*) lace

encallar [enka'ʎar] *vi* (*Náut*) to run aground

encaminar [enkami'nar] *vt* to direct, send

encantado, -a [enkan'taðo, a] *adj* (*hechizado*) bewitched; (*muy contento*) delighted; **¡~!** how do you do, pleased to meet you

encantador, a [enkanta'ðor, a] *adj* charming, lovely ▷ *nm/f* magician, enchanter/enchantress

encantar [enkan'tar] *vt* (*agradar*) to charm, delight; (*hechizar*) to bewitch, cast a spell on; **me encanta eso** I love that; **encanto** *nm* (*hechizo*) spell, charm; (*fig*) charm, delight

encarcelar [enkarθe'lar] *vt* to imprison, jail

encarecer [enkare'θer] *vt* to put up the price of; **encarecerse** *vr* to get dearer

encargado, -a [enkar'xaðo, a] *adj* in charge ▷ *nm/f* agent, representative; (*responsable*) person in charge

encargar [enkar'xar] *vt* to entrust; (*recomendar*) to urge, recommend; **encargarse** *vr*: **~se de** to look after, take charge of; **~ algo a algn** to put sb in charge of sth; **~ a algn que haga algo** to ask sb to do sth

encargo [en'karxo] *nm* (*tarea*) assignment, job; (*responsabilidad*) responsibility; (*Com*) order

encariñarse [enkari'narse] *vr*: **~ con**

to grow fond of, get attached to
encarnación [enkarna'θjon] nf
incarnation, embodiment
encarrilar [enkarri'lar] vt (tren) to
put back on the rails; (fig) to correct,
put on the right track
encasillar [enkasi'ʎar] vt (fig) to
pigeonhole; (actor) to typecast
encendedor [enθende'ðor] nm
lighter
encender [enθen'der] vt (con
fuego) to light; (luz, radio) to put on,
switch on; (avisar: pasión) to inflame;
encenderse vr to catch fire; (excitarse)
to get excited; (de cólera) to flare up; (el
rostro) to blush
encendido [enθen'diðo] nm (Auto)
ignition
encerado [enθe'raðo] nm (Escol)
blackboard
encerrar [enθe'rrar] vt (confinar) to
shut in, shut up; (comprender, incluir) to
include, contain
encharcado, -a [entʃar'kaðo, a] adj
(terreno) flooded
encharcarse [entʃar'karse] vr to
get flooded
enchufado, -a [entʃu'faðo, a] (fam)
nm/f well-connected person
enchufar [entʃu'far] vt (Elec) to
plug in; (Tec) to connect, fit together;
enchufe nm (Elec: clavija) plug; (: toma)
socket; (de dos tubos) joint, connection;
(fam: influencia) contact, connection;
(: puesto) cushy job
encía [en'θia] nf gum
encienda etc vb V **encender**
encierro etc [en'θjerro] vb V **encerrar**
▷ nm shutting in, shutting up;
(calabozo) prison
encima [en'θima] adv (sobre) above,
over; (además) besides; **~ de** (en) on,
on top of; (sobre) above, over; (además
de) besides, on top of; **por ~ de** over;
¿llevas dinero **~**? have you (got) any
money on you?; **se me vino ~** it took
me by surprise
encina [en'θina] nf holm oak

encinta [en'θinta] adj pregnant
enclenque [en'klenke] adj weak,
sickly
encoger [enko'xer] vt to shrink,
contract; **encogerse** vr to shrink,
contract; (fig) to cringe; **~se de
hombros** to shrug one's shoulders
encomendar [enkomen'dar] vt to
entrust, commend; **encomendarse**
vr: **~se a** to put one's trust in
encomienda etc [enko'mjenda]
vb V **encomendar** ▷ nf (encargo)
charge, commission; (elogio) tribute;
encomienda postal (LAM) package
encontrar [enkon'trar] vt (hallar)
to find; (inesperadamente) to meet, run
into; **encontrarse** vr to meet (each
other); (situarse) to be (situated); **~se
con** to meet; **~se bien (de salud)** to
feel well
encrucijada [enkruθi'xaða] nf
crossroads sg
encuadernación
[enkwaðerna'θjon] nf binding
encuadrar [enkwa'ðrar] vt (retrato)
to frame; (ajustar) to fit, insert;
(contener) to contain
encubrir [enku'βrir] vt (ocultar) to
hide, conceal; (criminal) to harbour,
shelter
encuentro etc [en'kwentro] vb V
encontrar ▷ nm (de personas) meeting;
(Auto etc) collision, crash; (Deporte)
match, game; (Mil) encounter
encuerado, -a (MÉX) [enkwe'raðo,
a] adj nude, naked
encuesta [en'kwesta] nf inquiry,
investigation; (sondeo) (public)
opinion poll
encumbrar [enkum'brar] vt
(persona) to exalt
endeble [en'deβle] adj (persona)
weak; (argumento, excusa, persona) weak
endemoniado, -a [endemo'njaðo,
a] adj possessed (of the devil);
(travieso) devilish
enderezar [endere'θar] vt (poner
derecho) to straighten (out);

(: *verticalmente*) to set upright; (*situación*) to straighten o sort out; (*dirigir*) to direct; **enderezarse** *vr* (*persona sentada*) to straighten up

endeudarse [endeu'ðarse] *vr* to get into debt

endiablado, -a [endja'βlaðo, a] *adj* devilish, diabolical; (*travieso*) mischievous

endilgar [endil'xar] (*fam*) *vt*: **~le algo a algn** to lumber sb with sth

endiñar [endi'ɲar] (ESP: *fam*) *vt* (*bofetón*) to land, belt

endosar [endo'sar] *vt* (*cheque etc*) to endorse

endulzar [endul'θar] *vt* to sweeten; (*suavizar*) to soften

endurecer [endure'θer] *vt* to harden; **endurecerse** *vr* to harden, grow hard

enema [e'nema] *nm* (Med) enema

enemigo, -a [ene'miɣo, a] *adj* enemy, hostile ▷ *nm/f* enemy

enemistad [enemis'tað] *nf* enmity

enemistar [enemis'tar] *vt* to make enemies of, cause a rift between; **enemistarse** *vr* to become enemies; (*amigos*) to fall out

energía [ener'xia] *nf* (*vigor*) energy, drive; (*empuje*) push; (Tec, Elec) energy, power; **energía eólica** wind power; **energía solar** solar energy o power

enérgico, -a [e'nerxiko, a] *adj* (*gen*) energetic; (*voz, modales*) forceful

energúmeno, -a [ener'xumeno, a] (*fam*) *nm/f* (*fig*) madman(-woman)

enero [e'nero] *nm* January

enfadado, -a [enfa'ðaðo, a] *adj* angry, annoyed

enfadar [enfa'ðar] *vt* to anger, annoy; **enfadarse** *vr* to get angry o annoyed

enfado [en'faðo] *nm* (*enojo*) anger, annoyance; (*disgusto*) trouble, bother

énfasis ['enfasis] *nm* emphasis, stress

enfático, -a [en'fatiko, a] *adj* emphatic

enfermar [enfer'mar] *vt* to make ill ▷ *vi* to fall ill, be taken ill

enfermedad [enferme'ðað] *nf* illness; **enfermedad venérea** venereal disease

enfermera [enfer'mera] *nf* nurse

enfermería [enferme'ria] *nf* infirmary; (*de colegio etc*) sick bay

enfermero [enfer'mero] *nm* (male) nurse

enfermizo, -a [enfer'miθo, a] *adj* (*persona*) sickly, unhealthy; (*fig*) unhealthy

enfermo, -a [en'fermo, a] *adj* ill, sick ▷ *nm/f* invalid, sick person; (*en hospital*) patient; **caer o ponerse ~** to fall ill

enfocar [enfo'kar] *vt* (*foto etc*) to focus; (*problema etc*) to approach

enfoque *etc* [en'foke] *vb* V **enfocar** ▷ *nm* focus

enfrentar [enfren'tar] *vt* (*peligro*) to face (up to), confront; (*oponer*) to bring face to face; **enfrentarse** *vr* (*dos personas*) to face o confront each other; (Deporte: *dos equipos*) to meet; **~se o con** to face up to, confront

enfrente [en'frente] *adv* opposite; **la casa de ~** the house opposite, the house across the street; **~ de** opposite, facing

enfriamiento [enfria'mjento] *nm* chilling, refrigeration; (Med) cold, chill

enfriar [enfri'ar] *vt* (*alimentos*) to cool, chill; (*algo caliente*) to cool down; **enfriarse** *vr* to cool down; (Med) to catch a chill; (*amistad*) to cool

enfurecer [enfure'θer] *vt* to enrage, madden; **enfurecerse** *vr* to become furious, fly into a rage; (*mar*) to get rough

enganchar [engan'tʃar] *vt* to hook; (*dos vagones*) to hitch up; (Tec) to couple, connect; (Mil) to recruit; **engancharse** *vr* (Mil) to enlist, join up

enganche [en'gantʃe] *nm* hook; (ESP Tec) coupling, connection; (*acto*) hooking (up); (Mil) recruitment, enlistment; (MÉX: depósito) deposit

engañar [enga'ɲar] vt to deceive; (estafar) to cheat, swindle; **engañarse** vr (equivocarse) to be wrong; (disimular la verdad) to deceive o.s.

engaño [en'gaɲo] nm deceit; (estafa) trick, swindle; (error) mistake, misunderstanding; (ilusión) delusion; **engañoso, -a** adj (tramposo) crooked; (mentiroso) dishonest, deceitful; (aspecto) deceptive; (consejo) misleading

engatusar [engatu'sar] (fam) vt to coax

engendro [en'xendro] nm (Bio) foetus; (fig) monstrosity

englobar [englo'βar] vt to include, comprise

engordar [engor'ðar] vt to fatten ⊳ vi to get fat, put on weight

engorroso, -a [engo'rroso, a] adj bothersome, trying

engranaje [engra'naxe] nm (Auto) gear

engrasar [engra'sar] vt (Tec: poner grasa) to grease; (: lubricar) to lubricate, oil; (manchar) to make greasy

engreído, -a [engre'iðo, a] adj vain, conceited

enhebrar [ene'βrar] vt to thread

enhorabuena [enora'βwena] excl: ¡~! congratulations! ⊳ nf: dar la ~ a to congratulate

enigma [e'niɣma] nm enigma; (problema) puzzle; (misterio) mystery

enjambre [en'xambre] nm swarm

enjaular [enxau'lar] vt to (put in a) cage; (fam) to jail, lock up

enjuagar [enxwa'xar] vt (ropa) to rinse (out)

enjuague etc [en'xwaxe] vb V **enjuagar** ⊳ nm (Med) mouthwash; (de ropa) rinse, rinsing

enjugar [enxu'xar] vt to wipe (off); (lágrimas) to dry; (déficit) to wipe out

enlace [en'laθe] nm link, connection; (relación) relationship; (tb: ~ matrimonial) marriage; (de carretera,

trenes) connection; **enlace sindical** shop steward

enlatado, -a [enla'taðo, a] adj (alimentos, productos) tinned, canned

enlazar [enla'θar] vt (unir con lazos) to bind together; (atar) to tie; (conectar) to link, connect; (LAM: caballo) to lasso

enloquecer [enloke'θer] vt to drive mad ⊳ vi to go mad

enmarañar [enmara'ɲar] vt (enredar) to tangle (up), entangle; (complicar) to complicate; (confundir) to confuse

enmarcar [enmar'kar] vt (cuadro) to frame

enmascarar [enmaska'rar] vt to mask; **enmascararse** vr to put on a mask

enmendar [enmen'dar] vt to emend, correct; (constitución etc) to amend; (comportamiento) to reform; **enmendarse** vr to reform, mend one's ways; **enmienda** nf correction; amendment; reform

enmudecer [enmuðe'θer] vi (perder el habla) to fall silent; (guardar silencio) to remain silent

ennoblecer [ennoβle'θer] vt to ennoble

enojado, -a [eno'xaðo, a] (LAM) adj angry

enojar [eno'xar] vt (encolerizar) to anger; (disgustar) to annoy, upset; **enojarse** vr to get angry; to get annoyed

enojo [e'noxo] nm (cólera) anger; (irritación) annoyance

enorme [e'norme] adj enormous, huge; (fig) monstrous

enredadera [enreða'ðera] nf (Bot) creeper, climbing plant

enredar [enre'ðar] vt (cables, hilos etc) to tangle (up), entangle; (situación) to complicate, confuse; (meter cizaña) to sow discord among o between; (implicar) to embroil, implicate; **enredarse** vr to get entangled, get tangled up; (situación to get complicated; (*persona*) to get embroiled; (LAM: *fam*) to meddle

enredo [en'reðo] *nm* (*maraña*) tangle; (*confusión*) mix-up, confusion; (*intriga*) intrigue

enriquecer [enrike'θer] *vt* to make rich, enrich; **enriquecerse** *vr* to get rich

enrojecer [enroxe'θer] *vt* to redden ▷ *vi* (*persona*) to blush; **enrojecerse** *vr* to blush

enrollar [enro'ʎar] *vt* to roll (up), wind (up)

ensalada [ensa'laða] *nf* salad; **ensaladilla (rusa)** *nf* Russian salad

ensanchar [ensan'tʃar] *vt* (*hacer más ancho*) to widen; (*agrandar*) to enlarge, expand; (*Costura*) to let out; **ensancharse** *vr* to get wider, expand

ensayar [ensa'jar] *vt* to test, try (out); (*Teatro*) to rehearse

ensayo [en'sajo] *nm* test, trial; (*Quím*) experiment; (*Teatro*) rehearsal; (*Deporte*) try; (*Escol, Literatura*) essay

enseguida [ense'ɣiða] *adv* at once, right away

ensenada [ense'naða] *nf* inlet, cove

enseñanza [ense'naɲθa] *nf* (*educación*) education; (*acción*) teaching; (*doctrina*) teaching, doctrine; **enseñanza (de) primaria/secundaria** elementary/secondary education

enseñar [ense'ɲar] *vt* (*educar*) to teach; (*mostrar, señalar*) to show

enseres [en'seres] *nmpl* belongings

ensuciar [ensu'θjar] *vt* (*manchar*) to dirty, soil; (*fig*) to defile; **ensuciarse** *vr* to get dirty; (*bebé*) to dirty one's nappy

entablar [enta'βlar] *vt* (*recubrir*) to board (up); (*Ajedrez, Damas*) to set up; (*conversación*) to strike up; (*Jur*) to file ▷ *vi* to draw

ente ['ente] *nm* (*organización*) body, organization; (*fam: persona*) odd character

entender [enten'der] *vt* (*comprender*) to understand; (*darse cuenta*) to realize ▷ *vi* to understand; (*creer*) to think,

believe; **entenderse** *vr* (*comprenderse*) to be understood; (*ponerse de acuerdo*) to agree, reach an agreement; **~ de** to know all about; **~ algo de** to know a little about; **~ en** to deal with, have to do with; **~ mal** to misunderstand; **~se con algn** (*llevarse bien*) to get on o along with sb; **~se mal** (*dos personas*) to get on badly

entendido, -a [enten'diðo, a] *adj* (*comprendido*) understood; (*hábil*) skilled; (*inteligente*) knowledgeable ▷ *nm/f* (*experto*) expert ▷ *excl* agreed!; **entendimiento** *nm* (*comprensión*) understanding; (*inteligencia*) mind, intellect; (*juicio*) judgement

enterado, -a [ente'raðo, a] *adj* well-informed; **estar ~ de** to know about, be aware of

enteramente [entera'mente] *adv* entirely, completely

enterar [ente'rar] *vt* (*informar*) to inform, tell; **enterarse** *vr* to find out, get to know

enterito [ente'rito] (RPL) *nm* boiler suit (BRIT), overalls (US)

entero, -a [en'tero, a] *adj* (*total*) whole, entire; (*fig: honesto*) honest; (*: firme*) firm, resolute ▷ *nm* (*Com: punto*) point

enterrar [ente'rrar] *vt* to bury

entidad [enti'ðað] *nf* (*empresa*) firm, company; (*organismo*) body; (*sociedad*) society; (*Filosofía*) entity

entiendo *etc vb* V **entender**

entierro [en'tjerro] *nm* (*acción*) burial; (*funeral*) funeral

entonación [entona'θjon] *nf* (*Ling*) intonation

entonar [ento'nar] *vt* (*canción*) to intone; (*colores*) to tone; (*Med*) to tone up ▷ *vi* to be in tune

entonces [en'tonθes] *adv* then, at that time; **desde ~** since then; **en aquel ~** at that time; (*pues*) **~** and so

entornar [entor'nar] *vt* (*puerta, ventana*) to half-close, leave ajar; (*los ojos*) to screw up

entorno [en'torno] nm setting, environment; **~ de redes** (Inform) network environment

entorpecer [entorpe'θer] vt (entendimiento) to dull; (impedir) to obstruct, hinder; (: tránsito) to slow down, delay

entrada [en'traða] nf (acción) entry, access; (sitio) entrance, way in; (Inform) input; (Com) receipts pl, takings pl; (Culin) starter; (Deporte) innings sg; (Teatro) house, audience; (billete) ticket; **~s y salidas** (Com) income and expenditure; **de ~** from the outset; **entrada de aire** (Tec) air intake o inlet

entrado, -a [en'traðo, a] adj: **~ en años** elderly; **una vez ~ el verano** in the summer(time), when summer comes

entramparse [entram'parse] vr to get into debt

entrante [en'trante] adj next, coming; **mes/año ~** next month/year; **entrantes** nmpl starters

entraña [en'traɲa] nf (fig: centro) heart, core; (raíz) root; **entrañas** nfpl (Anat) entrails; (fig) heart sg; **entrañable** adj close, intimate; **entrañar** vt to entail

entrar [en'trar] vt (introducir) to bring in; (Inform) to input ▷ vi (meterse) to go in, come in, enter; (comenzar): **~ diciendo** to begin by saying; **hacer ~** to show in; **me entró sed/sueño** I started to feel thirsty/sleepy; **no me entra** I can't get the hang of it

entre [entre] prep (dos) between; (más de dos) among(st)

entreabrir [entrea'βrir] vt to half-open, open halfway

entrecejo [entre'θexo] nm: **fruncir el ~** to frown

entredicho [entre'ðitʃo] nm (Jur) injunction; **poner en ~** to cast doubt on; **estar en ~** to be in doubt

entrega [en'treγa] nf (de mercancías) delivery; (de novela etc) instalment; **entregar** vt (dar) to hand over, deliver; **entregarse** vr (rendirse) to surrender, give in, submit; (dedicarse) to devote o.s.

entremeses [entre'meses] nmpl hors d'œuvres

entremeter [entreme'ter] vt to insert, put in; **entremeterse** vr to meddle, interfere; **entremetido, -a** adj meddling, interfering

entremezclar [entremeθ'klar] vt to intermingle; **entremezclarse** vr to intermingle

entrenador, a [entrena'ðor, a] nm/f trainer, coach

entrenarse [entre'narse] vr to train

entrepierna [entre'pjerna] nf crotch

entresuelo [entre'swelo] nm mezzanine

entretanto [entre'tanto] adv meanwhile, meantime

entretecho [entre'tetʃo] (cs) nm attic

entretejer [entrete'xer] vt to interweave

entretener [entrete'ner] vt (divertir) to entertain, amuse; (detener) to hold up, delay; **entretenerse** vr (divertirse) to amuse o.s.; (retrasarse) to delay, linger; **entretenido, -a** adj entertaining, amusing; **entretenimiento** nm entertainment, amusement

entrever [entre'βer] vt to glimpse, catch a glimpse of

entrevista [entre'βista] nf interview; **entrevistar** vt to interview; **entrevistarse** vr to have an interview

entristecer [entriste'θer] vt to sadden, grieve; **entristecerse** vr to grow sad

entrometerse [entrome'terse] vr: **~ (en)** to interfere (in o with)

entumecer [entume'θer] vt to numb, benumb; **entumecerse** vr (por el frío) to go o become numb

enturbiar [entur'βjar] vt (el agua)

to make cloudy; (fig) to confuse;
enturbiarse vr (oscurecerse) to become
cloudy; (fig) to get confused, become
obscure

entusiasmar [entusjas'mar] vt to
excite, fill with enthusiasm; (gustar
mucho) to delight; **entusiasmarse**
vr: **~se con o por** to get enthusiastic o
excited about

entusiasmo [entu'sjasmo] nm
enthusiasm; (excitación) excitement

entusiasta [entu'sjasta] adj
enthusiastic ▷ nmf enthusiast

enumerar [enume'rar] vt to
enumerate

envainar [embai'nar] vt to sheathe

envalentonar [embalento'nar] vt
to give courage to; **envalentonarse** vr
(pey: jactarse) to boast, brag

envasar [emba'sar] vt (empaquetar)
to pack, wrap; (enfrascar) to bottle;
(enlatar) to can; (embolsar) to pocket

envase [em'base] nm (en paquete)
packing, wrapping; (en botella)
bottling; (en lata) canning; (recipiente)
container; (paquete) package; (botella)
bottle; (lata) tin (BRIT), can

envejecer [embexe'θer] vt to make
old, age ▷ vi (volverse viejo) to grow old;
(parecer viejo) to age

envenenar [embene'nar] vt to
poison; (fig) to embitter

envergadura [emberɣa'ðura] nf
(fig) scope, compass

enviar [em'bjar] vt to send; **~ un
mensaje a algn** (por movil) to text sb, to
send sb a text message

enviciarse [embi'θjarse] vr: **~ (con)**
to get addicted to

envidia [em'biðja] nf envy; **tener
~ a** to envy, be jealous of; **envidiar**
vt to envy

envío [em'bio] nm (acción) sending;
(de mercancías) consignment; (de dinero)
remittance

enviudar [embju'ðar] vi to be
widowed

envoltura [embol'tura] nf (cobertura)

cover; (embalaje) wrapper, wrapping;
envoltorio nm package

envolver [embol'βer] vt to wrap (up);
(cubrir) to cover; (enemigo) to surround;
(implicar) to involve, implicate

envuelto [em'bwelto] pp de
envolver

enyesar [enje'sar] vt (pared) to
plaster; (Med) to put in plaster

enzarzarse [enθar'θarse] vr: **~ en**
(pelea) to get mixed up in; (disputa) to
get involved in

épica ['epika] nf epic

epidemia [epi'ðemja] nf epidemic

epilepsia [epi'lepsja] nf epilepsy

episodio [epi'soðjo] nm episode

época ['epoka] nf period, time; (Hist)
age, epoch; **hacer ~** to be epoch-
making

equilibrar [ekili'βrar] vt to balance;
equilibrio nm balance, equilibrium;
mantener/perder el equilibrio to
keep/lose one's balance; **equilibrista**
nmf (funámbulo) tightrope walker;
(acróbata) acrobat

equipaje [eki'paxe] nm luggage;
(avíos): **hacer el ~** to pack; **equipaje de
mano** hand luggage

equipar [eki'par] vt (proveer) to equip

equipararse [ekipa'rarse] vr: **~ con**
to be on a level with

equipo [e'kipo] nm (conjunto de
cosas) equipment; (Deporte) team; (de
obreros) shift; **~ de música/de hi-fi**
music centre

equis ['ekis] nf inv (the letter) X

equitación [ekita'θjon] nf horse
riding

equivalente [ekiβa'lente] adj, nm
equivalent

equivaler [ekiβa'ler] vi to be
equivalent o equal

equivocación [ekiβoka'θjon] nf
mistake, error

equivocado, -a [ekiβo'kaðo, a] adj
wrong, mistaken

equivocarse [ekiβo'karse] vr to be
wrong, make a mistake; **~ de camino**

to take the wrong road

era ['era] vb V **ser** ▷ nf era, age

erais vb V **ser**

éramos vb V **ser**

eran vb V **ser**

eras vb V **ser**

erección [erek'θjon] nf erection

eres vb V **ser**

erigir [eri'xir] vt to erect, build;
erigirse vr: **~se en** to set o.s. up as

erizo [e'riθo] nm (Zool) hedgehog;
erizo de mar sea-urchin

ermita [er'mita] nf hermitage;
ermitaño, -a [ermi'taɲo, a] nm/f
hermit

erosión [ero'sjon] nf erosion

erosionar [erosjo'nar] vt to erode

erótico, -a [e'rotiko, a] adj erotic;
erotismo nm eroticism

errante [e'rrante] adj wandering,
errant

erróneo, -a [e'rroneo, a] adj
(equivocado) wrong, mistaken

error [e'rror] nm error, mistake;
(Inform) bug; **error de imprenta**
misprint

eructar [eruk'tar] vt to belch, burp

erudito, -a [eru'ðito, a] adj erudite,
learned

erupción [erup'θjon] nf eruption;
(Med) rash

es vb V **ser**

esa ['esa] (pl **~s**) adj demos V **ese**

ésa ['esa] (pl **~s**) pron V **ése**

esbelto, -a [es'βelto, a] adj slim,
slender

esbozo [es'βoθo] nm sketch, outline

escabeche [eska'βetʃe] nm brine; (de
aceitunas etc) pickle; **en ~** pickled

escabullirse [eskaβu'ʎirse] vr to slip
away, to clear out

escafandra [eska'fandra] nf (buzo)
diving suit; (escafandra espacial)
space suit

escala [es'kala] nf (proporción, Mús)
scale; (de mano) ladder; (Aviac) stopover;
hacer ~ en to stop o call in at

escalafón [eskala'fon] nm (escala de

salarios) salary scale, wage scale

escalar [eska'lar] vt to climb, scale

escalera [eska'lera] nf stairs pl,
staircase; (escala) ladder; (Naipes) run;
escalera de caracol spiral staircase;
escalera de incendios fire escape;
escalera mecánica escalator

escalfar [eskal'far] vt (huevos) to
poach

escalinata [eskali'nata] nf staircase

escalofriante [eskalo'frjante] adj
chilling

escalofrío [eskalo'frio] nm (Med)
chill; **escalofríos** nmpl (fig) shivers

escalón [eska'lon] nm step, stair; (de
escalera) rung

escalope [eska'lope] nm (Culin)
escalope

escama [es'kama] nf (de pez,
serpiente) scale; (de jabón) flake; (fig)
resentment

escampar [eskam'par] vb impers to
stop raining

escandalizar [eskandali'θar] vt to
scandalize, shock; **escandalizarse**
vr to be shocked; (ofenderse) to be
offended

escándalo [es'kandalo] nm scandal;
(alboroto, tumulto) row, uproar;
escandaloso, -a adj scandalous,
shocking

escandinavo, -a [eskandi'naβo, a]
adj, nm/f Scandinavian

escanear [eskane'ar] vt to scan

escaño [es'kaɲo] nm bench; (Pol) seat

escapar [eska'par] vi (gen) to escape,
run away; (Deporte) to break away;
escaparse vr to escape, get away;
(agua, gas) to leak (out)

escaparate [eskapa'rate] nm shop
window; **ir de ~** to go window-
shopping

escape [es'kape] nm (de agua, gas)
leak; (de motor) exhaust

escarabajo [eskara'βaxo] nm beetle

escaramuza [eskara'muθa] nf
skirmish

escarbar [eskar'βar] vt (tierra) to

scratch

escarceos [eskar'θeos] nmpl: **en mis ~ con la política ...** in my dealings with politics ...; **escarceos amorosos** love affairs

escarcha [es'kartʃa] nf frost;
escarchado, -a [eskar'tʃaðo, a] adj (Culin: fruta) crystallized

escarlatina [eskarla'tina] nf scarlet fever

escarmentar [eskarmen'tar] vt to punish severely ▷ vi to learn one's lesson

escarmiento etc [eskar'mjento] vb
V **escarmentar** ▷ nm (ejemplo) lesson; (castigo) punishment

escarola [eska'rola] nf endive

escarpado, -a [eskar'paðo, a] adj (pendiente) sheer, steep; (rocas) craggy

escasear [eskase'ar] vi to be scarce

escasez [eska'seθ] nf (falta) shortage, scarcity; (pobreza) poverty

escaso, -a [es'kaso, a] adj (poco) scarce; (raro) rare; (ralo) thin, sparse; (limitado) limited

escatimar [eskati'mar] vt to skimp (on), be sparing with

escayola [eska'jola] nf plaster

escena [es'θena] nf scene; **escenario** [esθe'narjo] nm (Teatro) stage; (Cine) set; (fig) scene

No confundir **escenario** con la palabra inglesa scenery.

escenografía nf set design

escéptico, -a [es'θeptiko, a] adj sceptical ▷ nm/f sceptic

esclarecer [esklare'θer] vt (misterio, problema) to shed light on

esclavitud [esklaβi'tuð] nf slavery

esclavizar [esklaβi'θar] vt to enslave

esclavo, -a [es'klaβo, a] nm/f slave

escoba [es'koβa] nf broom; **escobilla** nf brush

escocer [esko'θer] vi to burn, sting;
escocerse vr to chafe, get chafed

escocés, -esa [esko'θes, esa] adj Scottish ▷ nm/f Scotsman(-woman), Scot

Escocia [es'koθja] nf Scotland

escoger [esko'xer] vt to choose, pick, select; **escogido, -a** adj chosen, selected

escolar [esko'lar] adj school cpd
▷ nmf schoolboy(-girl), pupil

escollo [es'koʎo] nm (obstáculo) pitfall

escolta [es'kolta] nf escort; **escoltar** vt to escort

escombros [es'kombros] nmpl (basura) rubbish sg; (restos) debris sg

esconder [eskon'der] vt to hide, conceal; **esconderse** vr to hide;
escondidas (LAM) nfpl: **a escondidas** secretly; **escondite** nm hiding place; (ESP: juego) hide-and-seek; **escondrijo** nm hiding place, hideout

escopeta [esko'peta] nf shotgun

escoria [es'korja] nf (de alto horno) slag; (fig) scum, dregs pl

Escorpio [es'korpjo] nm Scorpio

escorpión [eskor'pjon] nm scorpion

escotado, -a [esko'taðo, a] adj low-cut

escote [es'kote] nm (de vestido) low neck; **pagar a ~** to share the expenses

escotilla [esko'tiʎa] nf (Náut) hatch(way)

escozor [esko'θor] nm (dolor) sting(ing)

escribible [eskri'βiβle] adj writable

escribir [eskri'βir] vt, vi to write; **~ a máquina** to type; **¿cómo se escribe?** how do you spell it?

escrito, -a [es'krito, a] pp de **escribir** ▷ nm (documento) document; (manuscrito) text, manuscript; **por ~** in writing

escritor, a [eskri'tor, a] nm/f writer

escritorio [eskri'torjo] nm desk

escritura [eskri'tura] nf (acción) writing; (caligrafía) (hand)writing; (Jur: documento) deed

escrúpulo [es'krupulo] nm scruple; (minuciosidad) scrupulousness; **escrupuloso, -a** adj scrupulous

escrutinio [eskru'tinjo] nm (examen atento) scrutiny; (Pol: recuento de votos) count(ing)

escuadra [es'kwaðra] *nf* (Mil etc) squad; (Náut) squadron; (flota: de coches etc) fleet; **escuadrilla** *nf* (de aviones) squadron; (LAM: de obreros) gang

escuadrón [eskwa'ðron] *nm* squadron

escuálido, -a [es'kwaliðo, a] *adj* skinny, scraggy; (sucio) squalid

escuchar [esku'tʃar] *vt* to listen to ▷ *vi* to listen

escudo [es'kuðo] *nm* shield

escuela [es'kwela] *nf* school; **escuela de artes y oficios**(ESP) ≈ technical college; **escuela de choferes**(LAM) driving school; **escuela de manejo** (MÉX) driving school

escueto, -a [es'kweto, a] *adj* plain; (estilo) simple

escuincle, -a [es'kwinkle, a] *nm* (MÉX: fam) *nm/f* kid

esculpir [eskul'pir] *vt* to sculpt; (grabar) to engrave; (tallar) to carve; **escultor, a** *nm/f* sculptor(-tress); **escultura** *nf* sculpture

escupidera [eskupi'ðera] *nf* spittoon

escupir [esku'pir] *vt*, *vi* to spit (out)

escurreplatos [eskurre'platos] (ESP) *nm inv* draining board; drainboard (US)

escurridero [eskurri'ðero] (LAM) *nm* draining board (BRIT), drainboard (US)

escurridizo, -a [eskurri'ðiθo, a] *adj* slippery

escurridor [eskurri'ðor] *nm* colander

escurrir [esku'rrir] *vt* (ropa) to wring out; (verduras, platos) to drain ▷ *vi* (líquidos) to drip; **escurrirse** *vr* (secarse) to drain; (resbalarse) to slip, slide; (escaparse) to slip away

ese [ˈese] (f **esa**, pl **esos, esas**) *adj demos* V **ese**

ése [ˈese] (f **ésa**, pl **ésos, ésas**) *pron* (sg) that (one); (pl) those (ones); **...** **éste ...** the former ... the latter ...; **no me vengas con ésas** don't give me any

more of that nonsense

esencia [e'senθja] *nf* essence; **esencial** *adj* essential

esfera [es'fera] *nf* sphere; (de reloj) face; **esférico, -a** *adj* spherical

esforzarse [esfor'θarse] *vr* to exert o.s., make an effort

esfuerzo *etc* [es'fwerθo] *vb* V **esforzarse** ▷ *nm* effort

esfumarse [esfu'marse] *vr* (apoyo, esperanzas) to fade away

esgrima [es'rrima] *nf* fencing

esguince [es'rinθe] *nm* (Med) sprain

eslabón [esla'ßon] *nm* link

eslip [ez'lip] *nm* pants pl (BRIT), briefs pl

eslovaco, -a [eslo'ßako, a] *adj, nm/f* Slovak, Slovakian ▷ *nm* (Ling) Slovak, Slovakian

Eslovaquia [eslo'ßakja] *nf* Slovakia

esmalte [es'malte] *nm* enamel; **esmalte de uñas**nail varnish o polish

esmeralda [esme'ralda] *nf* emerald

esmerarse [esme'rarse] *vr* (aplicarse) to take great pains, exercise great care; (afanarse) to work hard

esmero [es'mero] *nm* (great) care

esnob [es'nob] (pl **~s**) *adj* (persona) snobbish ▷ *nmf* snob

eso [ˈeso] *pron* that, that thing o matter; **~ de su coche** that business about his car; **~ de ir al cine** all that about going to the cinema; **a ~ de las cinco** at about five o'clock; **en ~** thereupon, at that point; **~ es** that's it; **¡~ sí que es vida!** now that's really living!; **por ~ te lo dije** that's why I told you; **y ~ que llovía** in spite of the fact it was raining

esos *adj demos* V **ese**

ésos *pron* V **ese**

espabilar *etc* [espaßi'lar] = **despabilar** *etc*

espacial [espa'θjal] *adj* (del espacio) space *cpd*

espaciar [espa'θjar] *vt* to space (out)

espacio [es'paθjo] *nm* space; (Mús) interval; (Radio, TV) programme (BRIT),

program (us); **el ~** space: **espacio aéreo/exterior** air/outer space; **espacioso, -a** adj spacious, roomy
espada [es'paða] nf sword; **espadas** nfpl (Naipes) spades
spaguetis [espa'ɣetis] nmpl spaghetti sg
espalda [es'palda] nf (gen) back; **espaldas** nfpl (hombros) shoulders; **a ~s de algn** behind sb's back; **estar de ~s** to have one's back turned; **tenderse de ~s** to lie (down) on one's back; **volver la ~ a algn** to cold-shoulder sb
espantajo [espan'taxo] nm = **espantapájaros**
espantapájaros [espanta'paxaros] nm inv scarecrow
espantar [espan'tar] vt (asustar) to frighten, scare; (ahuyentar) to frighten off; (asombrar) to horrify, appal; **espantarse** vr to get frightened o scared; to be appalled
espanto [es'panto] nm (susto) fright; (terror) terror; (asombro) astonishment; **espantoso, -a** adj frightening, terrifying; astonishing
España [es'paɲa] nf Spain; **español, -a** adj Spanish ▷ nm/f Spaniard ▷ nm (Ling) Spanish
sparadrapo [espara'ðrapo] nm (sticking) plaster (BRIT), adhesive tape (US)
esparcir [espar'θir] vt to spread; (diseminar) to scatter; **esparcirse** vr to spread (out), to scatter; (divertirse) to enjoy o.s.
espárrago [es'parraɣo] nm asparagus
esparto [es'parto] nm esparto (grass)
espasmo [es'pasmo] nm spasm
espátula [es'patula] nf spatula
special [es'peθjal] adj special; **especialidad** [espeθjali'ðað] nf speciality (BRIT), specialty (US)
specie [es'peθje] nf (Bio) species; (clase) kind, sort; **en ~** in kind
specificar [espeθifi'kar] vt to

specify; **específico, -a** adj specific
espécimen [es'peθimen] (pl **especímenes**) nm specimen
espectáculo [espek'takulo] nm (gen) spectacle; (Teatro etc) show
espectador, a [espekta'ðor, a] nm/f spectator
especular [espeku'lar] vt, vi to speculate
espejismo [espe'xismo] nm mirage
espejo [es'pexo] nm mirror; **(espejo) retrovisor** rear-view mirror
espeluznante [espeluθ'nante] adj horrifying, hair-raising
espera [es'pera] nf (pausa, intervalo) wait; (Jur: plazo) respite; **en ~ de** waiting for; **(con expectativa)** expecting
esperanza [espe'ranθa] nf (confianza) hope; (expectativa) expectation; **hay pocas ~s de que venga** there is little prospect of his coming; **esperanza de vida** life expectancy
esperar [espe'rar] vt (aguardar) to wait for; (tener expectativa de) to expect; (desear) to hope for ▷ vi to wait; to expect; to hope; **hacer ~ a algn** to keep sb waiting; **~ un bebé** to be expecting (a baby)
esperma [es'perma] nf sperm
espeso, -a [es'peso, a] adj thick; **espesor** nm thickness
espía [es'pia] nmf spy; **espiar** vt (observar) to spy on
espiga [es'piɣa] nf (Bot: de trigo etc) ear
espigón [espi'ɣon] nm (Bot) ear; (Náut) breakwater
espina [es'pina] nf thorn; (de pez) bone; **espina dorsal** (Anat) spine
espinaca [espi'naka] nf spinach
espinazo [espi'naθo] nm spine, backbone
espinilla [espi'niʎa] nf (Anat: tibia) shin (bone); (grano) blackhead
espino, -a [es'pinoso, a] adj (planta) thorny, prickly; (asunto) difficult

espionaje [espjo'naxe] nm spying, espionage

espiral [espi'ral] adj, nf spiral

espirar [espi'rar] vt to breathe out, exhale

espiritista [espiri'tista] adj, nmf spiritualist

espíritu [es'piritu] nm spirit; **Espíritu Santo** Holy Ghost o Spirit; **espiritual** adj spiritual

espléndido, -a [es'plendiðo, a] adj (magnífico) magnificent, splendid; (generoso) generous

esplendor [esplen'dor] nm splendour

espolvorear [espolβore'ar] vt to dust, sprinkle

esponja [es'ponxa] nf sponge; (fig) sponger; **esponjoso, -a** adj spongy

espontaneidad [espontanei'ðað] nf spontaneity; **espontáneo, -a** adj spontaneous

esposa [es'posa] nf wife; **esposas** nfpl handcuffs; **esposar** vt to handcuff

esposo [es'poso] nm husband

espray [es'prai] nm spray

espuela [es'pwela] nf spur

espuma [es'puma] nf foam; (de cerveza) froth, head; (de jabón) lather; **espuma de afeitar** shaving foam; **espumadera** nf (utensilio) skimmer; **espumoso, -a** adj frothy, foamy; (vino) sparkling

esqueleto [eske'leto] nm skeleton

esquema [es'kema] nm (diagrama) diagram; (dibujo) plan; (Filosofía) schema

esquí [es'ki] (pl ~s) nm (objeto) ski; (Deporte) skiing; **esquí acuático** water-skiing; **esquiar** vi to ski

esquilar [eski'lar] vt to shear

esquimal [eski'mal] adj, nmf Eskimo

esquina [es'kina] nf corner; **esquinazo** [eski'naθo] nm: **dar esquinazo a algn** to give sb the slip

esquirol [eski'rol] (ESP) nm strikebreaker, scab

esquivar [eski'βar] vt to avoid

esta ['esta] adj demos V **este²**

está vb V **estar**

ésta pron V **éste**

estabilidad [estaβili'ðað] nf stability; **estable** adj stable

establecer [estaβle'θer] vt to establish; **establecerse** vr to establish o.s.; (echar raíces) to settle (down); **establecimiento** nm establishment

establo [es'taβlo] nm (Agr) stable

estaca [es'taka] nf stake, post; (de tienda de campaña) peg

estacada [esta'kaða] nf (cerca) fence, fencing; (palenque) stockade

estación [esta'θjon] nf station; (del año) season; **estación balnearia** seaside resort; **estación de autobuses** bus station; **estación de servicio** service station

estacionamiento [estaθjona'mjento] nm (Auto) parking; (Mil) stationing

estacionar [estaθjo'nar] vt (Auto) to park; (Mil) to station

estadía [esta'ðia] (LAM) nf stay

estadio [es'taðjo] nm (fase) stage, phase; (Deporte) stadium

estadista [esta'ðista] nm (Pol) statesman; (Mat) statistician

estadística [esta'ðistika] nf figure, statistic; (ciencia) statistics sg

estado [es'taðo] nm (Pol: condición) state; **estar en ~** to be pregnant; **estado civil** marital status; **estado de ánimo** state of mind; **estado de cuenta** bank statement; **estado de sitio** state of siege; **estado mayor** staff; **Estados Unidos** United States (of America)

estadounidense [estaðouni'ðense] adj United States cpd, American ▷ nmf American

estafa [es'tafa] nf swindle, trick; **estafar** vt to swindle, defraud

estáis vb V **estar**

estallar [esta'ʎar] vi to burst; (bomba)

to explode, go off; (*epidemia, guerra, rebelión*) to break out; **~ en llanto** to burst into tears; **estallido** *nm* explosion; (*fig*) outbreak

estampa [es'tampa] *nf* print, engraving; **estampado, -a** [estam'paðo, a] *adj* printed ▷ *nm* (*impresión: acción*) printing; (*: efecto*) print; (*marca*) stamping

estampar [estam'par] *vt* (*imprimir*) to print; (*marcar*) to stamp; (*metal*) to engrave; (*poner sello en*) to stamp; (*fig*) to stamp, imprint

estampida [estam'piða] *nf* stampede

estampido [estam'piðo] *nm* bang, report

estampilla [estam'piʎa] (LAM) *nf* (*postage*) stamp

están *vb* V **estar**

estancado, -a [estan'kaðo, a] *adj* stagnant

estancar [estan'kar] *vt* (*aguas*) to hold up, hold back; (*Com*) to monopolize; (*fig*) to block, hold up; **estancarse** *vr* to stagnate

estancia [es'tanθja] *nf* (ESP, MÉX: *permanencia*) stay; (*sala*) room; (RPL: *de ganado*) farm, ranch; **estanciero** (RPL) *nm* farmer, rancher

estanco, -a [es'tanko, a] *adj* watertight ▷ *nm* tobacconist's (shop), cigar store (US)

● **ESTANCO**
●
● Cigarettes, tobacco, postage
● stamps and official forms are all
● sold under state monopoly in
● shops called **estancos**. Although
● tobacco products can also be
● bought in bars and quioscos they
● are generally more expensive.

estándar [es'tandar] *adj, nm* standard

estandarte [estan'darte] *nm* banner, standard

estanque [es'tanke] *nm* (*lago*) pool, pond; (Agr) reservoir

estanquero, -a [estan'kero, a] *nm/f* tobacconist

estante [es'tante] *nm* (*armario*) rack, stand; (*biblioteca*) bookcase; (*anaquel*) shelf; **estantería** *nf* shelving, shelves *pl*

○ **PALABRA CLAVE**

estar [es'tar] *vi* **1** (*posición*) to be; **está en la plaza** it's in the square; **¿está Juan?** is Juan in?; **estamos a 30 km de Junín** we're 30 kms from Junín

2 (+ *adj: estado*) to be; **estar enfermo** to be ill; **está muy elegante** he's looking very smart; **¿cómo estás?** how are you keeping?

3 (+ *gerundio*) to be; **estoy leyendo** I'm reading

4 (*uso pasivo*): **está condenado a muerte** he's been condemned to death; **está envasado en ...** it's packed in ...

5 (*con fechas*): **¿a cuántos estamos?** what's the date today?; **estamos a 5 de mayo** it's the 5th of May

6 (*locuciones*): **¿estamos?** (*¿de acuerdo?*) okay?; **¿listo?** ready?

7. **estar de: estar de vacaciones/ viaje** to be on holiday/away o on a trip; **está de camarero** he's working as a waiter

8: **estar para: está para salir** he's about to leave; **no estoy para bromas** I'm not in the mood for jokes

9: **estar por** (*propuesta etc*) to be in favour of; (*persona etc*) to support, side with; **está por limpiar** it still has to be cleaned

10: **estar sin: estar sin dinero** to have no money; **está sin terminar** it isn't finished yet

estarse *vr*: **se estuvo en la cama toda la tarde** he stayed in bed all afternoon

estas ['estas] adj demos V **este²**

éstas pron V **éste**

estatal [esta'tal] adj state cpd

estático, -a [es'tatiko, a] adj static

estatua [es'tatwa] nf statue

estatura [esta'tura] nf stature, height

este¹ ['este] nm east

este² ['este] (f **esta**, pl **estos, estas**) adj demos ⊳ pron (sg) this; (pl) these

esté etc vb V **estar**

éste ['este] (f **ésta**, pl **éstos, éstas**) pron (sg) this (one); (pl) these (ones); **ése ... ~ ...** the former ... the latter ...

estén etc vb V **estar**

estepa [es'tepa] nf (Geo) steppe

estera [es'tera] nf mat(ting)

estéreo [es'tereo] adj inv, nm stereo; **estereotipo** nm stereotype

estéril [es'teril] adj sterile, barren; (fig) vain, futile; **esterilizar** vt to sterilize

esterlina [ester'lina] adj: **libra ~** pound sterling

estés etc vb V **estar**

estética [es'tetika] nf aesthetics sg

estético, -a [es'tetiko, a] adj aesthetic

estiércol [es'tjerkol] nm dung, manure

estigma [es'tixma] nm stigma

estilo [es'tilo] nm style; (Tec) stylus; (Natación) stroke; **algo por el ~** something along those lines

estima [es'tima] nf esteem, respect; **estimación** [estima'θjon] nf (evaluación) estimation; (aprecio, afecto) esteem, regard; **estimado, a** adj esteemed; **E~ señor** Dear Sir

estimar [esti'mar] vt (evaluar) to estimate; (valorar) to value; (apreciar) to esteem, respect; (pensar, considerar) to think, reckon

estimulante [estimu'lante] adj stimulating ⊳ nm stimulant

estimular [estimu'lar] vt to stimulate; (excitar) to excite

estímulo [es'timulo] nm stimulus; (ánimo) encouragement

estirar [esti'rar] vt to stretch; (dinero, suma etc) to stretch out; **estirarse** vr to stretch

estirón [esti'ron] nm pull, tug; (crecimiento) spurt, sudden growth; **dar o pegar un ~** (fam: niño) to shoot up (inf)

estirpe [es'tirpe] nf stock, lineage

estival [esti'βal] adj summer cpd

esto ['esto] pron this, this thing o matter; **~ de la boda** this business about the wedding

Estocolmo [esto'kolmo] nm Stockholm

estofado [esto'faðo] nm stew

estómago [es'tomaxo] nm stomach; **tener ~** to be thick-skinned

estorbar [estor'βar] vt to hinder, obstruct; (molestar) to bother, disturb ⊳ vi to be in the way; **estorbo** nm (molestia) bother, nuisance; (obstáculo) hindrance, obstacle

estornudar [estornu'ðar] vi to sneeze

estos ['estos] adj demos V **este²**

éstos pron V **éste**

estoy vb V **estar**

estrado [es'traðo] nm platform

estrafalario, -a [estrafa'larjo, a] adj odd, eccentric

estrago [es'traxo] nm ruin, destruction; **hacer ~s en** to wreak havoc among

estragón [estra'xon] nm tarragon

estrambótico, -a [estram'botiko, a] adj (persona) eccentric; (peinado, ropa) outlandish

estrangular [estrangu'lar] vt (persona) to strangle; (Med) to strangulate

estratagema [estrata'xema] nf (Mil) stratagem; (astucia) cunning

estrategia [estra'texja] nf strategy; **estratégico, -a** adj strategic

estrato [es'trato] nm stratum, layer

estrechar [estre'tʃar] vt (reducir) to narrow; (Costura) to take in; (abrazar) to hug, embrace; **estrecharse** vr (reducirse) to narrow, grow narrow;

(*abrazarse*) to embrace; **~ la mano** to shake hands

estrechez [estre'tʃeθ] nf narrowness; (*de ropa*) tightness; **estrecheces** nfpl (*dificultades económicas*) financial difficulties

estrecho, -a [es'tretʃo, a] adj narrow; (*apretado*) tight; (*íntimo*) close, intimate; (*miserable*) mean ▷ nm strait; **~ de miras** narrow-minded

estrella [es'treʎa] nf star; **estrella de mar**(Zool) starfish; **estrella fugaz** shooting star

estrellar [estre'ʎar] vt (*hacer añicos*) to smash to pieces; (*huevos*) to fry; **estrellarse** vr to smash; (*chocarse*) to crash; (*fracasar*) to fail

estremecer [estreme'θer] vt to shake; **estremecerse** vr to shake, tremble

estrenar [estre'nar] vt (*vestido*) to wear for the first time; (*casa*) to move into; (*película, obra de teatro*) to première; **estrenarse** vr (*persona*) to make one's début; **estreno** nm (*Cine etc*) première

estreñido, -a [estre'ɲiðo, a] adj constipated

estreñimiento [estreɲi'mjento] nm constipation

estrepitoso, -a [estrepi'toso, a] adj noisy; (*fiesta*) rowdy

estrés [es'tres] nm stress

estría [es'tria] nf groove

estribar [estri'βar] vi: **~ en** to lie on

estribillo [estri'βiʎo] nm (*Literatura*) refrain; (*Mús*) chorus

estribo [es'triβo] nm (*de jinete*) stirrup; (*de coche, tren*) step; (*de puente*) support; (*Geo*) spur; **perder los ~s** to lose the handle

estribor [estri'βor] nm (*Náut*) starboard

estricto, -a [es'trikto, a] adj (*riguroso*) strict; (*severo*) severe

estridente [estri'ðente] adj (*color*) loud; (*voz*) raucous

estropajo [estro'paxo] nm scourer

estropear [estrope'ar] vt to spoil; (*dañar*) to damage; **estropearse** vr (*objeto*) to get damaged; (*persona, piel*) to be ruined

estructura [estruk'tura] nf structure

estrujar [estru'xar] vt (*apretar*) to squeeze; (*aplastar*) to crush; (*fig*) to drain, bleed

estuario [es'twarjo] nm estuary

estuche [es'tutʃe] nm box, case

estudiante [estu'ðjante] nmf student; **estudiantil** adj student cpd

estudiar [estu'ðjar] vt to study

estudio [es'tuðjo] nm study; (*Cine, Arte, Radio*) studio; **estudios** nmpl studies; (*erudición*) learning sg; **estudioso, -a** adj studious

estufa [es'tufa] nf heater, fire

estupefaciente [estupefa'θjente] nm drug, narcotic

estupefacto, -a [estupe'fakto, a] adj speechless, thunderstruck

estupendo, -a [estu'pendo, a] adj wonderful, terrific; (*fam*) great; **¡~!** that's great!, fantastic!

estupidez [estupi'ðeθ] nf (*torpeza*) stupidity; (*acto*) stupid thing (to do)

estúpido, -a [es'tupiðo, a] adj stupid, silly

estuve etc vb V **estar**

ETA ['eta] (Esp) nf abr (= Euskadi ta Askatasuna) ETA

etapa [e'tapa] nf (*de viaje*) stage; (*Deporte*) leg; (*parada*) stopping place; (*fase*) stage, phase

etarra [e'tarra] nmf member of ETA

etc. abr (= etcétera) etc

etcétera [eθ'θetera] adv etcetera

eternidad [eterni'ðað] nf eternity; **eterno, -a** adj eternal, everlasting

ética ['etika] nf ethics pl

ético, -a ['etiko, a] adj ethical

etiqueta [eti'keta] nf (*modales*) etiquette; (*rótulo*) label, tag

Eucaristía [eukaris'tia] nf Eucharist

euforia [eu'forja] nf euphoria

euro ['euro] nm (*moneda*) euro

eurodiputado, -a [euroðipu'taðo, a] nm/f Euro MP, MEP

Europa [eu'ropa] nf Europe; **europeo, -a** adj, nm/f European

Euskadi [eus'kaði] nm the Basque Country o Provinces pl

euskera [eus'kera] nm (Ling) Basque

evacuación [eβakwa'θjon] nf evacuation

evacuar [eβa'kwar] vt to evacuate

evadir [eβa'ðir] vt to evade, avoid; **evadirse** vr to escape

evaluar [eβa'lwar] vt to evaluate

evangelio [eβan'xeljo] nm gospel

evaporar [eβapo'rar] vt to evaporate; **evaporarse** vr to vanish

evasión [eβa'sjon] nf escape, flight; (fig) evasion; **evasión de capitales** flight of capital

evasiva [eβa'siβa] nf (pretexto) excuse

evento [e'βento] nm event

eventual [eβen'twal] adj possible, conditional (upon circumstances); (trabajador) casual, temporary

No confundir **eventual** con la palabra inglesa eventual.

evidencia [eβi'ðenθja] nf evidence, proof

evidente [eβi'ðente] adj obvious, clear, evident

evitar [eβi'tar] vt (evadir) to avoid; (impedir) to prevent; **~ hacer algo** to avoid doing sth

evocar [eβo'kar] vt to evoke, call forth

evolución [eβolu'θjon] nf (desarrollo) evolution, development; (cambio) change; (Mil) manoeuvre; **evolucionar** vi to evolve; to manoeuvre

ex [eks] adj ex-; **el ~ ministro** the former minister, the ex-minister

exactitud [eksakti'tuð] nf exactness; (precisión) accuracy; (puntualidad) punctuality; **exacto, -a** adj exact; accurate; punctual; **¡exacto!** exactly!

exageración [eksaxera'θjon] nf exaggeration

exagerar [eksaxe'rar] vt, vi to exaggerate

exaltar [eksal'tar] vt to exalt, glorify; **exaltarse** vr (excitarse) to get excited o worked up

examen [ek'samen] nm examination; **examen de conducir** driving test; **examen de ingreso** entrance examination

examinar [eksami'nar] vt to examine; **examinarse** vr to be examined, take an examination

excavadora [ekskaβa'ðora] nf excavator

excavar [ekska'βar] vt to excavate

excedencia [eksθe'ðenθja] nf: **estar en ~** to be on leave; **pedir o solicitar la ~** to ask for leave

excedente [eksθe'ðente] adj, nm excess, surplus

exceder [eksθe'ðer] vt to exceed, surpass; **excederse** vr (extralimitarse) to go too far

excelencia [eksθe'lenθja] nf excellence; **su E~** his Excellency; **excelente** adj excellent

excéntrico, -a [eks'θentriko, a] adj, nm/f eccentric

excepción [eksθep'θjon] nf exception; **a ~ de** with the exception of, except for; **excepcional** adj exceptional

excepto [eks'θepto] adv excepting, except (for)

exceptuar [eksθep'twar] vt to except, exclude

excesivo, -a [eksθe'siβo, a] adj excessive

exceso [eks'θeso] nm (gen) excess; (Com) surplus; **exceso de equipaje/ peso** excess luggage/weight; **exceso de velocidad** speeding

excitado, -a [eksθi'taðo, a] adj excited; (emociones) aroused

excitar [eksθi'tar] vt to excite; (incitar) to urge; **excitarse** vr to get excited

exclamación [eksklama'θjon] nf

exclamation

exclamar [ekskla'mar] vi to exclaim

excluir [eksklu'ir] vt to exclude; (dejar fuera) to shut out; (descartar) to reject

exclusiva [eksklu'siβa] nf (Prensa) exclusive, scoop; (Com) sole right

exclusivo, -a [eksklu'siβo, a] adj exclusive; **derecho ~** sole o exclusive right

Excmo. abr = **excelentísimo**

excomulgar [ekskomul'ɣar] vt (Rel) to excommunicate

excomunión [ekskomu'njon] nf excommunication

excursión [ekskur'sjon] nf excursion, outing; **excursionista** nmf (turista) sightseer

excusa [eks'kusa] nf excuse; (disculpa) apology; **excusar** [eksku'sar] vt to excuse

exhaustivo, -a [eksaus'tiβo, a] adj (análisis) thorough; (estudio) exhaustive

exhausto, -a [ek'sausto, a] adj exhausted

exhibición [eksiβi'θjon] nf exhibition, display, show

exhibir [eksi'βir] vt to exhibit, display, show

exigencia [eksi'xenθja] nf demand, requirement; **exigente** adj demanding

exigir [eksi'xir] vt (gen) to demand, require; **~ el pago** to demand payment

exiliado, -a [eksi'ljaðo, a] adj exiled ▷ nm/f exile

exilio [ek'siljo] nm exile

eximir [eksi'mir] vt to exempt

existencia [eksis'tenθja] nf existence; **existencias** nfpl stock(s) pl

existir [eksis'tir] vi to exist, be

éxito ['eksito] nm (triunfo) success; (Mús etc) hit; **tener ~** to be successful
  No confundir **éxito** con la palabra inglesa exit.

exorbitante [eksorβi'tante] adj (precio) exorbitant; (cantidad) excessive

exótico, -a [ek'sotiko, a] adj exotic

expandir [ekspan'dir] vt to expand

expansión [ekspan'sjon] nf expansion

expansivo, -a [ekspan'siβo, a] adj: **onda expansiva** shock wave

expatriarse [ekspa'trjarse] vr to emigrate; (Pol) to go into exile

expectativa [ekspekta'tiβa] nf (espera) expectation; (perspectiva) prospect

expedición [ekspeði'θjon] nf (excursión) expedition

expediente [ekspe'ðjente] nm expedient; (Jur: procedimiento) action, proceedings pl; (: papeles) dossier, file, record

expedir [ekspe'ðir] vt (despachar) to send, forward; (pasaporte) to issue

expensas [eks'pensas] nfpl: **a ~ de** at the expense of

experiencia [ekspe'rjenθja] nf experience

experimentado, -a [eksperimen'taðo, a] adj experienced

experimentar [eksperimen'tar] vt (en laboratorio) to experiment with; (probar) to test, try out; (notar, observar) to experience; (deterioro, pérdida) to suffer; **experimento** nm experiment

experto, -a [eks'perto, a] adj expert, skilled ▷ nm/f expert

expirar [ekspi'rar] vi to expire

explanada [ekspla'naða] nf (llano) plain

explayarse [ekspla'jarse] vr (en discurso) to speak at length; **~ con algn** to confide in sb

explicación [eksplika'θjon] nf explanation

explicar [ekspli'kar] vt to explain; **explicarse** vr to explain (o.s.)

explícito, -a [eks'pliθito, a] adj explicit

explique etc vb V **explicar**

explorador, a [eksplora'ðor, a] nm/f (pionero) explorer; (Mil) scout ▷ nm (Med) probe; (Tec) (radar) scanner

explorar [eksplo'rar] vt to explore; (Med) to probe; (radar) to scan

explosión [eksplo'sjon] *nf*
explosion; **explosivo, -a** *adj* explosive

explotación [eksplota'θjon] *nf*
exploitation; *(de planta etc)* running

explotar [eksplo'tar] *vt* to exploit to
run, operate ▷ *vi* to explode

exponer [ekspo'ner] *vt* to expose;
(cuadro) to display; *(vida)* to risk;
(idea) to explain; **exponerse** *vr*: **~se
a (hacer) algo** to run the risk of
(doing) sth

exportación [eksporta'θjon] *nf*
(acción) export; *(mercancías)* exports *pl*

exportar [ekspor'tar] *vt* to export

exposición [eksposi'θjon] *nf (gen)*
exposure; *(de arte)* show, exhibition;
(explicación) explanation; *(declaración)*
account, statement

expresamente [ekspresa'mente]
adv (decir) clearly; *(a propósito)* expressly

expresar [ekspre'sar] *vt* to express;
expresión *nf* expression

expresivo, -a [ekspre'siβo, a] *adj*
(persona, gesto, palabras) expressive;
(cariñoso) affectionate

expreso, -a [eks'preso, a] *pp de*
expresar ▷ *adj (explícito)* express;
(claro) specific, clear; *(tren)* fast
▷ *adv*: **enviar ~** to send by express
(delivery)

express [eks'pres] *(LAM) adv*: **enviar
algo ~** to send sth special delivery

exprimidor [eksprimi'ðor] *nm*
squeezer

exprimir [ekspri'mir] *vt (fruta)* to
squeeze; *(zumo)* to squeeze out

expuesto, -a [eks'pwesto, a] *pp de*
exponer ▷ *adj* exposed; *(cuadro etc)* on
show, on display

expulsar [ekspul'sar] *vt (echar)* to
eject, throw out; *(alumno)* to expel;
(despedir) to sack, fire; *(Deporte)* to
send off; **expulsión** *nf* expulsion;
sending-off

exquisito, -a [ekski'sito, a] *adj*
exquisite; *(comida)* delicious

éxtasis ['ekstasis] *nm* ecstasy

extender [eksten'der] *vt* to extend;

(los brazos) to stretch out, hold out;
(mapa, tela) to spread (out), open (out);
(mantequilla) to spread; *(certificado)*
to issue; *(cheque, recibo)* to make out;
(documento) to draw up; **extenderse**
vr (gen) to extend; *(persona: en el suelo)*
to stretch out; *(epidemia)* to spread;
extendido, -a *adj (abierto)* spread out,
open; *(brazos)* outstretched; *(costumbre)*
widespread

extensión [eksten'sjon] *nf (de
terreno, mar)* expanse, stretch;
(de tiempo) length, duration; *(Tel)*
extension; **en toda la ~ de la palabra**
in every sense of the word

extenso, -a [eks'tenso, a] *adj*
extensive

exterior [ekste'rjor] *adj (de fuera)*
external; *(afuera)* outside, exterior;
(apariencia) outward; *(deuda, relaciones)*
foreign ▷ *nm (gen)* exterior, outside;
(aspecto) outward appearance;
(Deporte) wing(er); *(países extranjeros)*
abroad; **en el ~** abroad; **al ~** outwardly,
on the surface

exterminar [ekstermi'nar] *vt* to
exterminate

externo, -a [eks'terno, a] *adj*
(exterior) external, outside; *(superficial)*
outward ▷ *nm/f* day pupil

extinguir [ekstin'gir] *vt (fuego)* to
extinguish, put out; *(raza, población)* to
wipe out; **extinguirse** *vr (fuego)* to go
out; *(Bio)* to become extinct

extintor [ekstin'tor] *nm* (fire)
extinguisher

extirpar [ekstir'par] *vt (Med)* to
remove (surgically)

extra ['ekstra] *adj inv (tiempo)* extra;
(chocolate, vino) good-quality ▷ *nmf*
extra ▷ *nm* extra; *(bono)* bonus

extracción [ekstrak'θjon] *nf*
extraction; *(en lotería)* draw

extracto [eks'trakto] *nm* extract

extradición [ekstraði'θjon] *nf*
extradition

extraer [ekstra'er] *vt* to extract,
take out

extraescolar [ekstraesko'lar] *adj*: **actividad ~** extracurricular activity

extranjero, -a [ekstran'xero, a] *adj* foreign ▷ *nm/f* foreigner ▷ *nm* foreign countries *pl*; **en el ~** abroad
No confundir **extranjero** con la palabra inglesa *stranger*.

extrañar [ekstra'ɲar] *vt* (*sorprender*) to find strange o odd; (*echar de menos*) to miss; **extrañarse** *vr* (*sorprenderse*) to be amazed, be surprised; **me extraña** I'm surprised

extraño, -a [eks'traɲo, a] *adj* (*extranjero*) foreign; (*raro, sorprendente*) strange, odd

extraordinario, -a [ekstraorði'narjo, a] *adj* extraordinary; (*edición, número*) special ▷ *nm* (*de periódico*) special edition; **horas extraordinarias** overtime *sg*

extrarradio [ekstra'rraðjo] *nm* suburbs

extravagante [ekstraβa'ɣante] *adj* (*excéntrico*) eccentric; (*estrafalario*) outlandish

extraviado, -a [ekstra'βjaðo, a] *adj* lost, missing

extraviar [ekstra'βjar] *vt* (*persona: desorientar*) to mislead, misdirect; (*perder*) to lose, misplace; **extraviarse** *vr* to lose one's way, get lost

extremar [ekstre'mar] *vt* to carry to extremes

extremaunción [ekstremaun'θjon] *nf* extreme unction

extremidad [ekstremi'ðað] *nf* (*punta*) extremity; **extremidades** *nfpl* (Anat) extremities

extremo, -a [eks'tremo, a] *adj* extreme; (*último*) last ▷ *nm* end; (*límite, grado sumo*) extreme; **en último ~** as a last resort

extrovertido, -a [ekstroβer'tiðo, a] *adj, nm/f* extrovert

exuberante [eksuβe'rante] *adj* exuberant; (*fig*) luxuriant, lush

eyacular [ejaku'lar] *vt, vi* to ejaculate

ejaculate
o lose one's way, get lost
extremar [ekstre'mar] *vt* to carry to extremes
extremaunción [ekstremaun'θjon] *nf* extreme unction
extremidad [ekstremi'ðað] *nf* (*punta*) extremity; **extremidades** *nfpl* (Anat) extremities
extremo, -a [eks'tremo, a] *adj* extreme; (*último*) last ▷ *nm* end; (*límite, grado sumo*) extreme; **en último ~** as a last resort
extrovertido, -a [ekstroβer'tiðo, a] *adj, nm/f* extrovert
exuberante [eksuβe'rante] *adj* exuberant; (*fig*) luxuriant, lush
eyacular [ejaku'lar] *vt, vi* to ejaculate

f

fa [fa] nm (Mús) fa, F

fabada [faˈβaða] nf bean and sausage stew

fábrica [ˈfaβrika] nf factory; **marca de ~** trademark; **precio de ~** factory price

No confundir **fábrica** con la palabra inglesa *fabric*.

fabricación [faβrikaˈθjon] nf (manufactura) manufacture; (producción) production; **de ~ casera** home-made; **fabricación en serie** mass production

fabricante [faβriˈkante] nmf manufacturer

fabricar [faβriˈkar] vt (manufacturar) to manufacture, make; (construir) to build; (cuento) to fabricate, devise

fábula [ˈfaβula] nf (cuento) fable; (chisme) rumour; (mentira) fib

fabuloso, -a [faβuˈloso, a] adj (oportunidad, tiempo) fabulous, great

facción [fakˈθjon] nf (Pol) faction; **facciones** nfpl (de rostro) features

faceta [faˈθeta] nf facet

facha [ˈfatʃa] (fam) nf (aspecto) look; (cara) face

fachada [faˈtʃaða] nf (Arq) façade, front

fácil [ˈfaθil] adj (simple) easy; (probable) likely

facilidad [faθiliˈðað] nf (capacidad) ease; (sencillez) simplicity; (de palabra) fluency; **facilidades** nfpl facilities; **facilidades de pago** credit facilities

facilitar [faθiliˈtar] vt (hacer fácil) to make easy; (proporcionar) to provide

factor [fakˈtor] nm factor

factura [fakˈtura] nf (cuenta) bill; **facturación** nf (de equipaje) check-in; **facturar** vt (Com) to invoice, charge for; (equipaje) to check in

facultad [fakulˈtað] nf (aptitud, Escol etc) faculty; (poder) power

faena [faˈena] nf (trabajo) work; (quehacer) task, job

faisán [faiˈsan] nm pheasant

faja [ˈfaxa] nf (para la cintura) sash; (de mujer) corset; (de tierra) strip

fajo [ˈfaxo] nm (de papeles) bundle; (de billetes) wad

falda [ˈfalda] nf (prenda de vestir) skirt; **falda pantalón** culottes pl, split skirt

falla [ˈfaʎa] nf (defecto) fault, flaw; **falla humana** (LAM) human error

fallar [faˈʎar] vt (Jur) to pronounce sentence on ▷ vi (memoria) to fail; (motor) to miss

Fallas [ˈfaʎas] nfpl Valencian celebration of the feast of St Joseph

○ **FALLAS**
○
○ In the week of 19 March (the feast
○ of San José), Valencia honours its
○ patron saint with a spectacular
○ fiesta called **Las Fallas**. The **Fallas**
○ are huge papier-mâché, cardboard
○ and wooden sculptures which
○ are built by competing teams
○ throughout the year. They depict
○ politicians and well-known public
○ figures and are thrown onto

● bonfires and set alight once a jury
● has judged them – only the best
● sculpture escapes the flames.

fallecer [faʎeˈθer] vi to pass away,
die; **fallecimiento** nm decease,
demise

fallido, -a [faˈʎiðo, a] adj (gen)
frustrated, unsuccessful

fallo [ˈfaʎo] nm (Jur) verdict, ruling;
(fracaso) failure; **fallo cardíaco** heart
failure; **fallo humano**(ESP) human
error

falsificar [falsifiˈkar] vt (firma etc) to
forge; (moneda) to counterfeit

falso, -a [ˈfalso, a] adj false;
(documento, moneda) fake; **en ~**
falsely

falta [ˈfalta] nf (defecto) fault, flaw;
(privación) lack, want; (ausencia)
absence; (carencia) shortage;
(equivocación) mistake; (Deporte) foul;
echar en ~ to miss; **hacer ~ hacer algo**
to be necessary to do sth; **me hace
~ una pluma** I need a pen; **falta de
educación** bad manners pl; **falta de
ortografía** spelling mistake

faltar [falˈtar] vi (escasear) to be
lacking, be wanting; (ausentarse) to
be absent, be missing; **faltan 2 horas
para llegar** there are 2 hours to go
till arrival; **~ al respeto a algn** to be
disrespectful to sb; **¡no faltaba más!**
(no hay de qué) don't mention it

fama [ˈfama] nf (renombre) fame;
(reputación) reputation

familia [faˈmilja] nf family; **familia
numerosa** large family; **familia
política** in-laws pl

familiar [famiˈljar] adj (relativo a la
familia) family cpd; (conocido, informal)
familiar ▷ nm relative, relation

famoso, -a [faˈmoso, a] adj
(renombrado) famous

fan [fan] (pl ~s) nm/f fan

fanático, -a [faˈnatiko, a] adj
fanatical ▷ nm/f fanatic; (Cine,
Deporte) fan

fanfarrón, -ona [fanfaˈrron, ona]
adj boastful

fango [ˈfango] nm mud

fantasía [fantaˈsia] nf fantasy,
imagination; **joyas de ~** imitation
jewellery sg

fantasma [fanˈtasma] nm (espectro)
ghost, apparition; (fanfarrón) show-off

fantástico, -a [fanˈtastiko, a] adj
fantastic

farmacéutico, -a [farmaˈθeutiko,
a] adj pharmaceutical ▷ nm/f
chemist (BRIT), pharmacist

farmacia [farˈmaθja] nf chemist's
(shop) (BRIT), pharmacy; **farmacia de
guardia** all-night chemist

fármaco [ˈfarmako] nm drug

faro [ˈfaro] nm (Náut: torre)
lighthouse; (Auto) headlamp;
faros antiniebla fog lamps; **faros
delanteros/traseros** headlights/rear
lights

farol [faˈrol] nm lantern, lamp

farola [faˈrola] nf street lamp (BRIT),
o light (US)

farra [ˈfarra] (LAM: fam) nf party; **ir de
~** to go on a binge

farsa [ˈfarsa] nf (gen) farce

farsante [farˈsante] nmf fraud, fake

fascículo [fasˈθikulo] nm (de revista)
part, instalment

fascinar [fasθiˈnar] vt (gen) to
fascinate

fascismo [fasˈθismo] nm fascism;
fascista adj, nmf fascist

fase [ˈfase] nf phase

fashion [ˈfaʃon] adj (fam) trendy

fastidiar [fastiˈðjar] vt (molestar)
to annoy, bother; (estropear) to spoil;
fastidiarse vr: **¡que se fastidie!** (fam)
he'll just have to put up with it!

fastidio [fasˈtiðjo] nm (molestia)
annoyance; **fastidioso, -a** adj
(molesto) annoying

fatal [faˈtal] adj (gen) fatal;
(desgraciado) ill-fated; (fam: malo,
pésimo) awful; **fatalidad** nf (destino)
fate; (mala suerte) misfortune

fatiga [fa'tixa] nf (cansancio) fatigue, weariness

fatigar [fati'xar] vt to tire, weary

fatigoso, -a [fati'xoso, a] adj (cansador) tiring

fauna ['fauna] nf fauna

favor [fa'βor] nm favour; **estar a ~ de** to be in favour of; **haga el ~ de ...** would you be so good as to ..., kindly ...; **por ~** please; **favorable** adj favourable

favorecer [faβore'θer] vt to favour; (vestido etc) to become, flatter; **este peinado le favorece** this hairstyle suits him

favorito, -a [faβo'rito, a] adj, nm/f favourite

fax [faks] nm inv fax; **mandar por ~** to fax

fe [fe] nf (Rel) faith; (documento) certificate; **actuar con buena/mala ~** to act in good/bad faith

febrero [fe'βrero] nm February

fecha ['fetʃa] nf date; **con ~ adelantada** postdated; **en ~ próxima** soon; **hasta la ~** to date, so far; **poner ~ to date**; **fecha de caducidad** (de producto alimenticio) sell-by date; (de contrato etc) expiry date; **fecha de nacimiento** date of birth; **fecha límite** o **tope** deadline

fecundo, -a [fe'kundo, a] adj (fértil) fertile; (fig) prolific; (productivo) productive

federación [feðera'θjon] nf federation

felicidad [feliθi'ðað] nf happiness; **¡~es!** (deseos) best wishes, congratulations!; (en cumpleaños) happy birthday!

felicitación [feliθita'θjon] nf (tarjeta) greeting(s) card

felicitar [feliθi'tar] vt to congratulate

feliz [fe'liθ] adj happy

felpudo [fel'puðo] nm doormat

femenino, -a [feme'nino, a] adj, nm feminine

feminista [femi'nista] adj, nmf feminist

fenómeno [fe'nomeno] nm phenomenon; (fig) freak, accident ▷ adj great ▷ excl great!, marvellous!; **fenomenal** adj =**fenómeno**

feo, -a ['feo, a] adj (gen) ugly; (desagradable) bad, nasty

féretro ['feretro] nm (ataúd) coffin; (sarcófago) bier

feria ['ferja] nf (gen) fair; (descanso) holiday, rest day; (MÉX: cambio) small o loose change; (cs: mercado) village market

feriado [fe'rjaðo] (LAM) nm holiday

fermentar [fermen'tar] vi to ferment

feroz [fe'roθ] adj (cruel) cruel; (salvaje) fierce

férreo, -a ['ferreo, a] adj iron

ferretería [ferrete'ria] nf (tienda) ironmonger's (shop) (BRIT), hardware store (US); **ferretero** [ferre'tero] nm ironmonger

ferrocarril [ferroka'rril] nm railway

ferroviario, -a [ferro'βjarjo, a] adj rail cpd

ferry ['ferri] (pl **~s** o **ferries**) nm ferry

fértil ['fertil] adj (productivo) fertile; (rico) rich; **fertilidad** af (gen) fertility; (productividad) fruitfulness

fervor [fer'βor] nm fervour

festejar [feste'xar] vt (celebrar) to celebrate

festejo [fes'texo] nm celebration; **festejos** nmpl (fiestas) festivals

festín [fes'tin] nm feast, banquet

festival [festi'βal] nm festival

festividad [festiβi'ðað] nf festivity

festivo, -a [fes'tiβo, a] adj (de fiesta) festive; (Cine, Literatura) humorous; **día ~** holiday

feto ['feto] nm foetus

fiable ['fjaβle] adj (persona) trustworthy; (máquina) reliable

fiambre ['fjambre] nm cold meat

fiambrera [fjam'brera] nf (para almuerzo) lunch box

fianza ['fjanθa] nf surety;

(Jur): libertad bajo ~ release on bail

fiar [fi'ar] *vt* (*salir garante de*) to guarantee; (*vender a crédito*) to sell on credit ▷ *vi* to trust; **fiarse** *vr* to trust (in), rely on; **~ a** (*secreto*) to confide (to); **~se de algn** to rely on sb

fibra ['fiβra] *nf* fibre; **fibra óptica** optical fibre

ficción [fik'θjon] *nf* fiction

ficha ['fitʃa] *nf* (*Tel*) token; (*en juegos*) counter, marker; (*tarjeta*) (index) card; **fichaje** nm (*Deporte*) signing; **fichar** *vt* (*archivar*) to file, index; (*Deporte*) to sign; **estar fichado** to have a record; **fichero** nm box file; (*Inform*) file

ficticio, -a [fik'tiθjo, a] *adj* (*imaginario*) fictitious; (*falso*) fabricated

fidelidad [fiðeli'ðað] *nf* (*lealtad*) fidelity, loyalty; **alta ~** high fidelity, hi-fi

fideos [fi'ðeos] *nmpl* noodles

fiebre ['fjeβre] *nf* (*Med*) fever; (*fig*) fever, excitement; **tener ~** to have a temperature; **fiebre aftosa** foot-and-mouth disease

fiel [fjel] *adj* (*leal*) faithful, loyal; (*fiable*) reliable; (*exacto*) accurate, faithful ▷ *nm*: **los ~es** the faithful

fieltro ['fjeltro] *nm* felt

fiera ['fjera] *nf* (*animal feroz*) wild animal o beast; (*fig*) dragon; V tb **fiero**

fiero, -a ['fjero, a] *adj* (*cruel*) cruel; (*feroz*) fierce; (*duro*) harsh

fierro ['fjerro] (LAM) *nm* (*hierro*) iron

fiesta ['fjesta] *nf* party; (*de pueblo*) festival; (*vacaciones*: tb: **~s**) holiday sg; **fiesta mayor** annual festival; **fiesta patria** (LAM) independence day

○ **FIESTAS**
○
○ **Fiestas** can be official public
○ holidays or holidays set by each
○ autonomous region, many of
○ which coincide with religious
○ festivals. There are also many
○ **fiestas** all over Spain for a local
○ patron saint or the Virgin Mary.

○ These often last several days and
○ can include religious processions,
○ carnival parades, bullfights and
○ dancing.

figura [fi'ɣura] *nf* (*gen*) figure; (*forma, imagen*) shape, form; (*Naipes*) face card

figurar [fiɣu'rar] *vt* (*representar*) to represent; (*fingir*) to figure ▷ *vi* to figure; **figurarse** *vr* (*imaginarse*) to imagine; (*suponer*) to suppose

fijador [fixa'ðor] *nm* (*Foto etc*) fixative; (*de pelo*) gel

fijar [fi'xar] *vt* (*gen*) to fix; (*estampilla*) to affix, stick (on); **fijarse** *vr*: **~se en** to notice

fijo, -a ['fixo, a] *adj* (*gen*) fixed; (*firme*) firm; (*permanente*) permanent ▷ *adv*: **mirar ~** to stare

fila ['fila] *nf* row; (*Mil*) rank; **ponerse en ~** to line up, get into line; **fila india** single file

filatelia [fila'telja] *nf* philately, stamp collecting

filete [fi'lete] *nm* (*de carne*) fillet steak; (*de pescado*) fillet

filiación [filja'θjon] *nf* (*Pol*) affiliation

filial [fi'ljal] *adj* filial ▷ *nf* subsidiary

Filipinas [fili'pinas] *nfpl*: **las (Islas) ~** the Philippines; **filipino, -a** *adj, nm/f* Philippine

filmar [fil'mar] *vt* to film, shoot

filo ['filo] *nm* (*gen*) edge; **sacar ~ a** to sharpen; **al ~ del mediodía** at about midday; **de doble ~** double-edged

filología [filolo'xia] *nf* philology; **filología inglesa** (*Univ*) English Studies

filón [fi'lon] *nm* (*Minería*) vein, lode; (*fig*) goldmine

filosofía [filoso'fia] *nf* philosophy; **filósofo, -a** *nm/f* philosopher

filtrar [fil'trar] *vt, vi* to filter, strain; **filtrarse** *vr* to filter; **filtro** *nm* (*Tec, utensilio*) filter

fin [fin] *nm* end; (*objetivo*) aim, purpose; **al ~ y al cabo** when all's said and done; **a ~ de** in order to; **por ~**

finally; **en ~** in short; **fin de semana** weekend

final [fiˈnal] adj final ▷ nm end, conclusion ▷ nf final; **al ~** in the end; **a ~es de** at the end of; **finalidad** nf (propósito) purpose, intention; **finalista** nmf finalist; **finalizar** vt to end, finish; (Inform) to log out o off ▷ vi to end, come to an end

financiar [finanˈθjar] vt to finance; **financiero, -a** adj financial ▷ nm/f financier

finca [ˈfinka] nf (casa de campo) country house; (ESP: bien inmueble) property, land; (LAM: granja) farm

finde [ˈfinde] nm abr (fam: fin de semana) weekend

fingir [finˈxir] vt (simular) to simulate, feign ▷ vi (aparentar) to pretend

finlandés, -esa [finlanˈdes, esa] adj Finnish ▷ nm/f Finn ▷ nm (Ling) Finnish

Finlandia [finˈlandja] nf Finland

fino, -a [ˈfino, a] adj fine; (delgado) slender; (de buenas maneras) polite, refined; (jerez) fino, dry

firma [ˈfirma] nf signature; (Com) firm, company

firmamento [firmaˈmento] nm firmament

firmar [firˈmar] vt to sign

firme [ˈfirme] adj firm; (estable) stable; (sólido) solid; (constante) steady; (decidido) resolute ▷ nm road (surface); **firmeza** nf firmness; (constancia) steadiness; (solidez) solidity

fiscal [fisˈkal] adj fiscal ▷ nmf public prosecutor; **año ~** tax o fiscal year

fisgonear [fisɣoneˈar] vt to poke one's nose into ▷ vi to pry, spy

física [ˈfisika] nf physics sg; V tb **físico**

físico, -a [ˈfisiko, a] adj physical ▷ nm physique ▷ nm/f physicist

fisura [fiˈsura] nf crack; (Med) fracture

flác(c)ido, -a [ˈfla(k)θiðo, a] adj flabby

flaco, -a [ˈflako, a] adj (muy delgado) skinny, thin; (débil) weak, feeble

flagrante [flaˈɣrante] adj flagrant

flama [ˈflama] (MÉX) nf flame; **flamable** (MÉX) adj flammable

flamante [flaˈmante] (fam) adj brilliant; (nuevo) brand-new

flamenco, -a [flaˈmenko, a] adj (de Flandes) Flemish; (baile, música) flamenco ▷ nm (baile, música) flamenco; (Zool) flamingo

flamingo [flaˈmingo] (MÉX) nm flamingo

flan [flan] nm creme caramel

No confundir **flan** con la palabra inglesa flan.

flash [flaʃ] (pl ~ o ~es) nm (Foto) flash

flauta [ˈflauta] nf (Mús) flute

flecha [ˈfletʃa] nf arrow

flechazo [fleˈtʃaθo] nm love at first sight

fleco [ˈfleko] nm fringe

flema [ˈflema] nm phlegm

flequillo [fleˈkiʎo] nm (pelo) fringe

flexible [flekˈsiβle] adj flexible

flexión [flekˈsjon] nf press-up

flexo [ˈflekso] nm adjustable table-lamp

flirtear [flirteˈar] vi to flirt

flojera [floˈxera] (LAM: fam) nf: **me da ~** I can't be bothered

flojo, -a [ˈfloxo, a] adj (gen) loose; (sin fuerzas) limp; (débil) weak

flor [flor] nf flower; **a ~ de** on the surface of; **flora** nf flora; **florecer** vi (Bot) to flower, bloom; (fig) to flourish; **florería** (LAM) nf florist's (shop); **florero** nm vase; **floristería** nf florist's (shop)

flota [ˈflota] nf fleet

flotador [flotaˈðor] nm (gen) float; (para nadar) rubber ring

flotar [floˈtar] vi (gen) to float; **flote** nm: **a flote** afloat; **salir a flote** (fig) to get back on one's feet

fluidez [fluiˈðeθ] nf fluidity; (fig) fluency

fluido, -a [ˈfluiðo, a] adj, nm fluid

fluir [fluˈir] vi to flow

flujo [ˈfluxo] nm flow; **flujo y reflujo**

ebb and flow

lúor ['fluor] nm fluoride

luorescente [flwores'θente] adj fluorescent ▷ nm fluorescent light

luvial [flu'βjal] adj (navegación, cuenca) fluvial, river cpd

obia ['fobja] nf phobia; **fobia a las alturas** fear of heights

oca ['foka] nf seal

oco ['foko] nm focus; (Elec) floodlight; (Méx: bombilla) (light) bulb

ofo, -a ['fofo, a] adj soft, spongy; (carnes) flabby

ogata [fo'ɤata] nf bonfire

ogón [fo'ɤon] nm (de cocina) ring, burner

olio ['foljo] nm folio, page

ollaje [fo'ʎaxe] nm foliage

olleto [fo'ʎeto] nm (Pol) pamphlet

ollón [fo'ʎon] (esp: fam) nm (lío) mess; (conmoción) fuss; **armar un ~** to kick up a row

omentar [fomen'tar] vt (Med) to foment

onda ['fonda] nf inn

ondo ['fondo] nm (de mar) bottom; (de coche, sala) back; (Arte etc) background; (reserva) fund; **fondos** nmpl (Com) funds, resources; **una investigación a ~** a thorough investigation; **en el ~** at bottom, deep down

onobuzón [fonoβu'θon] nm voice mail

ontanería [fontane'ria] nf plumbing; **fontanero, -a** nm/f plumber

ooting ['futin] nm jogging; **hacer ~** to jog, go jogging

orastero, -a [foras'tero, a] nm/f stranger

orcejear [forθexe'ar] vi (luchar) to struggle

orense [fo'rense] nmf pathologist

orma ['forma] nf (figura) form, shape; (Med) fitness; (método) way, means; **las ~s** the conventions; **estar en ~** to be fit; **de ~ que ...** so that ...; **de**

todas ~s in any case

formación [forma'θjon] nf (gen) formation; (educación) education; **formación profesional** vocational training

formal [for'mal] adj (gen) formal; (fig: serio) serious; (: de fiar) reliable; **formalidad** nf formality; seriousness; reliability; seriousness; **formalizar** vt (Jur) to formalize; (situación) to put in order, regularize; **formalizarse** vr (situación) to be put in order, be regularized

formar [for'mar] vt (componer) to form, shape; (constituir) to make up, constitute; (Escol) to train, educate; **formarse** vr (Escol) to be trained, educated; (cobrar forma) to form, take form; (desarrollarse) to develop

formatear [formate'ar] vt to format

formato [for'mato] nm format

formidable [formi'ðaβle] adj (temible) formidable; (estupendo) tremendous

fórmula ['formula] nf formula

formulario [formu'larjo] nm form

fornido, -a [for'niðo, a] adj well-built

foro ['foro] nm (Pol, Inform etc) forum

forrar [fo'rrar] vt (abrigo) to line; (libro) to cover; **forro** nm (de cuaderno) cover; (Costura) lining; (de sillón) upholstery; **forro polar** fleece

fortalecer [fortale'θer] vt to strengthen

fortaleza [forta'leθa] nf (Mil) fortress, stronghold; (fuerza) strength; (determinación) resolution

fortuito, -a [for'twito, a] adj accidental

fortuna [for'tuna] nf (suerte) fortune, (good) luck; (riqueza) fortune, wealth

forzar [for'θar] vt (puerta) to force (open); (compeler) to compel

forzoso, -a [for'θoso, a] adj necessary

fosa ['fosa] nf (sepultura) grave; (en tierra) pit; **fosas nasales** nostrils

fósforo ['fosforo] nm (Quím)

phosphorus; (cerilla) match

fósil ['fosil] nm fossil

foso ['foso] nm ditch; (Teatro) pit; (Auto) inspection pit

foto ['foto] nf photo, snap(shot); **sacar una ~** to take a photo o picture; **foto (de) carné** passport(-size) photo

fotocopia [foto'kopja] nf photocopy; **fotocopiadora** nf photocopier; **fotocopiar** vt to photocopy

fotografía [fotoɣra'fia] nf (Arte) photography; (una fotografía) photograph; **fotografiar** vt to photograph

fotógrafo, -a [fo'toɣrafo, a] nm/f photographer

fotomatón [fotoma'ton] nm photo booth

FP (ESP) nf abr (= Formación Profesional) vocational courses for 14- to 18-year-olds

fracasar [fraka'sar] vi (gestión) to fail

fracaso [fra'kaso] nm failure

fracción [frak'θjon] nf fraction

fractura [frak'tura] nf fracture, break

fragancia [fra'ɣanθja] nf (olor) fragrance, perfume

frágil ['fraxil] adj (débil) fragile; (Com) breakable

fragmento [fraɣ'mento] nm (pedazo) fragment

fraile ['fraile] nm (Rel) friar; (: monje) monk

frambuesa [fram'bwesa] nf raspberry

francés, -esa [fran'θes, esa] adj French ▷ nm/f Frenchman(-woman) ▷ nm (Ling) French

Francia ['franθja] nf France

franco, -a ['franko, a] adj (cándido) frank, open; (Com: exento) free ▷ nm (moneda) franc

francotirador, a [frankotira'ðor, a] nm/f sniper

franela [fra'nela] nf flannel

franja ['franxa] nf fringe

franquear [franke'ar] vt (camino) to clear; (carta, paquete postal) to frank,

stamp; (obstáculo) to overcome

franqueo [fran'keo] nm postage

franqueza [fran'keθa] nf (candor) frankness

frasco ['frasko] nm bottle, flask

frase ['frase] nf sentence; **frase hecha** set phrase; (pey) stock phrase

fraterno, -a [fra'terno, a] adj brotherly, fraternal

fraude ['frauðe] nm (cualidad) dishonesty; (acto) fraud

frazada [fra'saða] (LAM) nf blanket

frecuencia [fre'kwenθja] nf frequency; **con ~** frequently, often

frecuentar [frekwen'tar] vt to frequent

frecuente [fre'kwente] adj (gen) frequent

fregadero [freɣa'ðero] nm (kitchen) sink

fregar [fre'ɣar] vt (frotar) to scrub; (platos) to wash (up); (LAM: fam: fastidiar) to annoy; (: malograr) to screw up

fregona [fre'ɣona] nf mop

freír [fre'ir] vt to fry

frenar [fre'nar] vt to brake; (fig) to check

frenazo [fre'naθo] nm: **dar un ~** to brake sharply

frenesí [frene'si] nm frenzy

freno ['freno] nm (Tec, Auto) brake; (de cabalgadura) bit; (fig) check; **freno de mano** handbrake

frente ['frente] nm (Arq, Pol) front; (de objeto) front part ▷ nf forehead, brow; **~ a** in front of; (en situación opuesta de) opposite; **al ~ de** (fig) at the head of; **chocar de ~** to crash head-on; **hacer ~ a** to face up to

fresa ['fresa] (ESP) nf strawberry

fresco, -a ['fresko, a] adj (nuevo) fresh; (frío) cool; (descarado) cheeky ▷ nm (aire) fresh air; (Arte) fresco; (LAM: jugo) fruit drink ▷ nm/f (fam): **ser un ~** to have a nerve; **tomar el ~** to get some fresh air; **frescura** nf freshness; (descaro) cheek, nerve

frialdad [frial'dað] nf (gen) coldness;

(indiferencia) indifference

frigidez [frixi'ðeθ] nf frigidity

frigo ['frixo] nm fridge

frigorífico [friɣo'rifiko] nm refrigerator

frijol [fri'xol] nm kidney bean

frío, -a etc ['frio, a] vb V **freír** ▷ adj cold; (indiferente) indifferent ▷ nm cold; (indiferencia) indifference; **hace ~** it's cold; **tener ~** to be cold

frito, -a ['frito, a] adj fried; **me trae ~ ese hombre** I'm sick and tired of that man; **fritos** nmpl fried food

frívolo, -a ['friβolo, a] adj frivolous

frontal [fron'tal] adj frontal; **choque ~** head-on collision

frontera [fron'tera] nf frontier

fronterizo, -a adj frontier cpd; (contiguo) bordering

frontón [fron'ton] nm (Deporte: cancha) pelota court; (: juego) pelota

frotar [fro'tar] vt to rub; **frotarse** vr: **~se las manos** to rub one's hands

fructífero, -a [fruk'tifero, a] adj fruitful

fruncir [frun'θir] vt to pucker; (Costura) to pleat; **~ el ceño** to knit one's brow

frustrar [frus'trar] vt to frustrate

fruta ['fruta] nf fruit; **frutería** nf fruit shop; **frutero, -a** adj fruit cpd ▷ nm/f fruiterer ▷ nm fruit bowl

frutilla [fru'tiʎa] (cs) nf strawberry

fruto ['fruto] nm fruit; (fig: resultado) result; (: beneficio) benefit; **frutos secos** nuts and dried fruit pl

fucsia ['fuksja] nf fuchsia

fue [fwe] vb V **ser**; **ir**

fuego ['fwexo] nm (gen) fire; **a ~ lento** on a low heat; **¿tienes ~?** have you (got) a light?; **fuego amigo** friendly fire; **fuegos artificiales** fireworks

fuente ['fwente] nf fountain; (manantial: fig) spring; (origen) source; (plato) large dish

fuera etc ['fwera] vb V **ser**; **ir** ▷ adv out(side); (en otra parte) away; (excepto, salvo) except, save ▷ prep: **~ de** outside;

(fig) besides; **~ de sí** beside o.s.; **por ~** (on the) outside

fuera-borda [fwera'βorða] nm speedboat

fuerte ['fwerte] adj strong; (golpe) hard; (ruido) loud; (comida) rich; (lluvia) heavy; (dolor) intense ▷ adv strongly; hard; loud(ly); **ser ~ en** to be good at

fuerza etc ['fwerθa] vb V **forzar** ▷ nf (fortaleza) strength; (Tec, Elec) power; (coacción) force; (Mil, Pol) force; **a ~ de** by dint of; **cobrar ~s** to recover one's strength; **tener ~s para** to have the strength to; **a la ~** forcibly, by force; **por ~** of necessity; **fuerza de voluntad** willpower; **fuerzas aéreas** air force sg; **fuerzas armadas** armed forces

fuga ['fuɣa] nf (huida) flight, escape; (de gas etc) leak

fugarse [fu'xarse] vr to flee, escape

fugaz [fu'xaθ] adj fleeting

fugitivo, -a [fuxi'tiβo, a] adj, nm/f fugitive

fui [fwi] vb V **ser**; **ir**

fulano, -a [fu'lano, a] nm/f so-and-so, what's-his-name/what's-her-name

fulminante [fulmi'nante] adj (fig: mirada) fierce; (Med: enfermedad, ataque) sudden; (fam: éxito, golpe) sudden

fumador, a [fuma'ðor, a] nm/f smoker

fumar [fu'mar] vt, vi to smoke; **~ en pipa** to smoke a pipe

función [fun'θjon] nf function; (en trabajo) duties pl; (espectáculo) show; **entrar en funciones** to take up one's duties

funcionar [funθjo'nar] vi (gen) to function; (máquina) to work; **"no funciona"** "out of order"

funcionario, -a [funθjo'narjo, a] nm/f civil servant

funda ['funda] nf (gen) cover; (de almohada) pillowcase

fundación [funda'θjon] nf foundation

fundamental [fundamen'tal] adj

fundamental, basic

fundamento [funda'mento] *nm*
(*base*) foundation

fundar [fun'dar] *vt* to found;
fundarse *vr*: **~se en** to be founded on

fundición [fundi'θjon] *nf* fusing;
(*fábrica*) foundry

fundir [fun'dir] *vt* (*gen*) to fuse;
(*metal*) to smelt, melt down; (*nieve
etc*) to melt; (*Com*) to merge; (*estatua*)
to cast; **fundirse** *vr* (*colores etc*) to
merge, blend; (*unirse*) to fuse together;
(*Elec*: *fusible, lámpara etc*) to fuse, blow;
(*nieve etc*) to melt

fúnebre ['funeβre] *adj* funeral *cpd*,
funereal

funeral [fune'ral] *nm* funeral;
funeraria *nf* undertaker's

funicular [funiku'lar] *nm* (*tren*)
funicular; (*teleférico*) cable car

furgón [fur'xon] *nm* wagon;
furgoneta *nf* (*Auto, Com*) (transit) van
(*BRIT*), pick-up (truck) (*US*)

furia ['furja] *nf* (*ira*) fury; (*violencia*)
violence; **furioso, -a** *adj* (*iracundo*)
furious; (*violento*) violent

furtivo, -a [fur'tiβo, a] *adj* furtive
▷ *nm* poacher

fusible [fu'siβle] *nm* fuse

fusil [fu'sil] *nm* rifle; **fusilar** *vt* to
shoot

fusión [fu'sjon] *nf* (*gen*) melting;
(*unión*) fusion; (*Com*) merger

fútbol ['futβol] *nm* football (*BRIT*),
soccer (*US*); **fútbol americano**
American football (*BRIT*), football
(*US*); **fútbol sala** indoor football (*BRIT*)
o soccer (*US*); **futbolín** *nm* table
football; **futbolista** *nmf* footballer

futuro, -a [fu'turo, a] *adj, nm* future

g

gabardina [gaβar'ðina] *nf* raincoat,
gabardine

gabinete [gaβi'nete] *nm* (*Pol*)
cabinet; (*estudio*) study; (*de abogados
etc*) office

gachas ['gatʃas] *nfpl* porridge *sg*

gafas ['gafas] *nfpl* glasses; **gafas de
sol** sunglasses

gafe ['gafe] (*ESP*) *nm* jinx

gaita ['gaita] *nf* bagpipes *pl*

gajes ['gaxes] *nmpl*: **~ del oficio**
occupational hazards

gajo ['gaxo] *nm* (*de naranja*) segment

gala ['gala] *nf* (*traje de etiqueta*) full
dress; **galas** *nfpl* (*ropa*) finery *sg*; **estar
de ~** to be in one's best clothes; **hacer
~ de** to display

galápago [ga'lapaxo] *nm* (*Zool*)
turtle

galardón [galar'ðon] *nm* award,
prize

galaxia [ga'laksja] *nf* galaxy

galera [ga'lera] *nf* (*nave*) galley; (*carro*)
wagon; (*Imprenta*) galley

galería [gale'ria] *nf* (*gen*) gallery;

(balcón) veranda(h); (pasillo) corridor;
galería comercial shopping mall

Gales ['gales] nm (tb: **País de ~**)
Wales; **galés, -esa** adj Welsh ▷ nm/f
Welshman(-woman) ▷ nm (Ling)
Welsh

galgo, -a ['galγo, a] nm/f greyhound
gallego, -a [ga'λeγo, a] adj, nm/f
Galician

galleta [ga'λeta] nf biscuit (BRIT),
cookie (US)

gallina [ga'λina] nf hen ▷ nmf
(fam: cobarde) chicken; **gallinero** nm
henhouse; (Teatro) top gallery

gallo ['gaλo] nm cock, rooster
galopar [galo'par] vi to gallop
gama ['gama] nf (fig) range
gamba ['gamba] nf prawn (BRIT),
shrimp (US)

gamberro, -a [gam'berro, a] (ESP)
nm/f hooligan, lout

gamuza [ga'muθa] nf chamois
gana ['gana] nf (deseo) desire,
wish; (apetito) appetite; (voluntad)
will; (añoranza) longing; **de buena ~**
willingly; **de mala ~** reluctantly; **me
da ~s de** I feel like, I want to; **no me
da la ~** I don't feel like it; **tener ~s de**
to feel like

ganadería [ganaðe'ria] nf (ganado)
livestock; (ganado vacuno) cattle pl; (cría,
comercio) cattle raising

ganadero, -a [gana'ðero, a] (ESP)
nm/f (hacendado) rancher

ganado [ga'naðo] nm livestock;
ganado porcino pigs pl

ganador, -a [gana'ðor, a] adj
winning ▷ nm/f winner

ganancia [ga'nanθja] nf (lo ganado)
gain; (aumento) increase; (beneficio)
profit; **ganancias** nfpl (ingresos)
earnings; (beneficios) profit sg,
winnings

ganar [ga'nar] vt (obtener) to get,
obtain; (sacar ventaja) to gain; (salario
etc) to earn; (Deporte, premio) to win;
(derrotar a) to beat; (alcanzar) to reach
▷ vi (Deporte) to win; **ganarse** vr: **~se**

la vida to earn one's living

ganchillo [gan'tʃiλo] nm crochet
gancho ['gantʃo] nm (gen) hook;
(colgador) hanger

gandul, a [gan'dul, a] adj, nm/f
good-for-nothing, layabout

ganga ['ganga] nf bargain
gangrena [gaŋ'grena] nf gangrene
ganso, -a ['ganso, a] nm/f (Zool)
goose; (fam) idiot

ganzúa [gan'θua] nf skeleton key
garabato [gara'βato] nm (escritura)
scrawl, scribble

garaje [ga'raxe] nm garage; **garajista**
[gara'xista] nmf mechanic

garantía [garan'tia] nf guarantee
garantizar [garanti'θar] vt to
guarantee

garbanzo [gar'βanθo] nm chickpea
(BRIT), garbanzo (US)

garfio ['garfjo] nm grappling iron
garganta [gar'γanta] nf (Anat)
throat; (de botella) neck; **gargantilla**
nf necklace

gárgaras ['garγaras] nfpl: **hacer ~**
to gargle

gargarear [garγare'ar] (LAM) vi to
gargle

garita [ga'rita] nf cabin, hut; (Mil)
sentry box

garra ['garra] nf (de gato, Tec) claw; (de
ave) talon; (fam: mano) hand, paw

garrafa [ga'rrafa] nf carafe, decanter
garrapata [garra'pata] nf tick
gas [gas] nm gas; **gases
lacrimógenos** tear gas sg

gasa ['gasa] nf gauze
gaseosa [gase'osa] nf lemonade
gaseoso, -a [gase'oso, a] adj gassy,
fizzy

gasoil [ga'soil] nm diesel (oil)
gasóleo [ga'soleo] nm = **gasoil**
gasolina [gaso'lina] nf petrol (BRIT),
gas(oline) (US); **gasolinera** nf petrol
(BRIT) o gas (US) station

gastado, -a [gas'taðo, a] adj (dinero)
spent; (ropa) worn out; (usado: frase
etc) trite

gastar [gas'tar] vt (dinero, tiempo) to spend; (fuerzas) to use up; (desperdiciar) to waste; (llevar) to wear; **gastarse** vr to wear out; (estropearse) to waste; **~ en** to spend on; **~ bromas** to crack jokes; **¿qué número gastas?** what size (shoe) do you take?

gasto ['gasto] nm (desembolso) expenditure, spending; (consumo, uso) use; **gastos** nmpl (desembolsos) expenses; (cargos) charges, costs

gastronomía [gastrono'mia] nf gastronomy

gatear [gate'ar] vi (andar a gatas) to go on all fours

gatillo [ga'tiʎo] nm (de arma de fuego) trigger; (de dentista) forceps

gato, -a ['gato, a] nm/f cat ▷ nm (Tec) jack; **andar a gatas** to go on all fours

gaucho ['gautʃo] nm gaucho

○ **GAUCHO**
○
○ **Gauchos** are the herdsmen or
○ riders of the Southern Cone plains.
○ Although popularly associated
○ with Argentine folklore, **gauchos**
○ belong equally to the cattle-
○ raising areas of Southern Brazil
○ and Uruguay. **Gauchos'** traditions
○ and clothing reflect their mixed
○ ancestry and cultural roots. Their
○ baggy trousers are Arabic in
○ origin, while the horse and guitar
○ are inherited from the Spanish
○ conquistadors; the poncho, maté
○ and **boleadoras** (strips of leather
○ weighted at either end with
○ stones) form part of the Indian
○ tradition.

gaviota [ga'βjota] nf seagull
gay [ge] adj inv, nm gay, homosexual
gazpacho [gaθ'patʃo] nm gazpacho
gel [xel] nm: **~ de baño/ducha** bath/shower gel
gelatina [xela'tina] nf jelly; (polvos

etc) gelatine
gema ['xema] nf gem
gemelo, -a [xe'melo, a] adj, nm/f twin; **gemelos** nmpl (de camisa) cufflinks; (prismáticos) field glasses, binoculars
gemido [xe'miðo] nm (quejido) moan, groan; (aullido) howl
Géminis ['xeminis] nm Gemini
gemir [xe'mir] vi (quejarse) to moan, groan; (aullar) to howl
generación [xenera'θjon] nf generation
general [xene'ral] adj general ▷ nm general; **por lo o en ~** in general; **Generalitat** nf Catalan parliament; **generalizar** vt to generalize; **generalizarse** vr to become generalized, spread
generar [xene'rar] vt to generate
género ['xenero] nm (clase) kind, sort; (tipo) type; (Bio) genus; (Ling) gender; (Com) material; **género humano** human race
generosidad [xeneɾosi'ðað] nf generosity; **generoso, -a** adj generous
genial [xe'njal] adj inspired; (idea) brilliant; (estupendo) wonderful
genio ['xenjo] nm (carácter) nature, disposition; (humor) temper; (facultad creadora) genius; **de mal ~** bad-tempered
genital [xeni'tal] adj genital; **genitales** nmpl genitals
genoma [xe'noma] nm genome
gente ['xente] nf (personas) people pl; (parientes) relatives pl
gentil [xen'til] adj (elegante) graceful; (encantador) charming

▌No confundir **gentil** con la palabra inglesa *gentle*.

genuino, -a [xe'nwino, a] adj genuine
geografía [xeoɣra'fia] nf geography
geología [xeolo'xia] nf geology
geometría [xeome'tria] nf geometry
gerente [xe'rente] nmf (supervisor)

manager; (jefe) director

eriatría [xeria'tria] nf (Med) geriatrics sg

ermen ['xermen] nm germ

esticular [xestiku'lar] vi to esticulate; (hacer muecas) to grimace; **esticulación** nf gesticulation; (mueca) grimace

estión [xes'tjon] nf management; diligencia, acción) negotiation

esto ['xesto] nm (mueca) grimace; además) gesture

braltar [xiβral'tar] nm Gibraltar; **ibraltareño, -a** adj, nm/f ibraltarian

gante [xi'ɣante] adj, nmf giant; **igantesco, -a** adj gigantic

lipollas [xili'poʎas] (fam) adj inv aft ⊳nmf inv wally

mnasia [xim'nasja] nf gymnastics l; **gimnasio** nm gymnasium; **imnasta** nmf gymnast; **gimnástica** xim'nastika] nf inv gymnastics sg

nebra [xi'neβra] nf gin

necólogo, -a [xine'koloɣo, a] m/f gynaecologist

ra [xira] nf tour, trip

rar [xi'rar] vt (dar la vuelta) to urn (around); (: rápidamente) to spin; Com: giro postal) to draw; (: letra de ambio) to issue ⊳vi to turn (round); rápido) to spin

rasol [xira'sol] nm sunflower

ratorio, -a [xira'torjo, a] adj evolving

ro ['xiro] nm (movimiento) turn, evolution; (Ling) expression; (Com) raft; **giro bancario/postal** bank raft/money order

s [xis] (MÉX) nm chalk

tano, -a [xi'tano, a] adj, nm/f ypsy

acial [gla'θjal] adj icy, freezing

aciar [gla'θjar] nm glacier

ándula ['glandula] nf gland

obal [glo'βal] adj global; **obalización** nf globalization

obo ['gloβo] nm (esfera) globe,

sphere; (aerostato, juguete) balloon

glóbulo ['gloβulo] nm globule; (Anat) corpuscle

gloria ['glorja] nf glory

glorieta [glo'rjeta] nf (de jardín) bower, arbour; (plazoleta) roundabout (BRIT), traffic circle (us)

glorioso, -a [glo'rjoso, a] adj glorious

glotón, -ona [glo'ton, ona] adj gluttonous, greedy ⊳nm/f glutton

glucosa [glu'kosa] nf glucose

gobernador, a [goβerna'ðor, a] adj governing ⊳nm/f governor; **gobernante** adj governing

gobernar [goβer'nar] vt (dirigir) to guide, direct; (Pol) to rule, govern ⊳vi to govern; (Náut) to steer

gobierno etc [go'βjerno] vb V **gobernar** ⊳nm (Pol) government; (dirección) guidance, direction; (Náut) steering

goce etc ['goθe] vb V **gozar** ⊳nm enjoyment

gol [gol] nm goal

golf [golf] nm golf

golfa ['golfa] (fam!) nf (mujer) slut, whore

golfo, -a ['golfo, a] nm (Geo) gulf ⊳nm/f (fam: niño) urchin; (gamberro) lout

golondrina [golon'drina] nf swallow

golosina [golo'sina] nf (dulce) sweet; **goloso, -a** adj sweet-toothed

golpe ['golpe] nm blow; (de mano) smack; (de puño) punch; (de remo) stroke; (fig: choque) clash; **no dar ~** to be bone idle; **de un ~** with one blow; **de ~** suddenly; **golpe (de estado)** coup (d'état); **golpear** vt, vi to strike, knock; (asestar) to beat; (de puño) to punch; (golpetear) to tap

goma ['goma] nf (caucho) rubber; (elástico) elastic; (una goma) elastic band; **goma de borrar** eraser, rubber (BRIT); **goma espuma** foam rubber

gomina [go'mina] nf hair gel

gomita [go'mita] (RPL) nf rubber band

gordo, -a ['goɾðo, a] adj (gen) fat; (fam) enormous; **el (premio) ~** (en lotería) first prize

gorila [go'rila] nm gorilla

gorra ['goɾra] nf cap; (de bebé) bonnet; (militar) bearskin; **entrar de ~** (fam) to gatecrash; **ir de ~** to sponge

gorrión [go'rrjon] nm sparrow

gorro ['goɾro] nm (gen) cap; (de bebé, mujer) bonnet

gorrón, -ona [go'rron, ona] nm/f scrounger; **gorronear** (fam) vi to scrounge

gota ['gota] nf (gen) drop; (de sudor) bead; (Med) gout; **gotear** vi to drip; (llovizna) to drizzle; **gotera** nf leak

gozar [go'θaɾ] vi to enjoy o.s.; **~ de** (disfrutar) to enjoy; (poseer) to possess

gr. abr (= gramo, gramos) g

grabación [gɾaβa'θjon] nf recording

grabado [gɾa'βaðo] nm print, engraving

grabadora [gɾaβa'ðoɾa] nf tape-recorder; **grabadora de CD/DVD** CD/DVD writer

grabar [gɾa'βaɾ] vt to engrave; (discos, cintas) to record

gracia [gɾa'θja] nf (encanto) grace, gracefulness; (humor) humour, wit; **¡(muchas) ~s!** thanks (very much!); **~s a** thanks to; **dar las ~s a algn por algo** to thank sb for sth; **tener ~** (chiste etc) to be funny; **no me hace ~** I am not keen; **gracioso, -a** adj (divertido) funny, amusing; (cómico) comical ▷ nm/f (Teatro) comic character

grada ['gɾaða] nf (de escalera) step; (de anfiteatro) tier, row; **gradas** nfpl (Deporte: de estadio) terraces

grado ['gɾaðo] nm degree; (de aceite, vino) grade; (grada) step; (Mil) rank; **de buen ~** willingly; **grado centígrado/Fahrenheit** degree centigrade/Fahrenheit

graduación [gɾaðwa'θjon] nf (del alcohol) proof, strength; (Escol)

graduation; (Mil) rank

gradual [gɾa'ðwal] adj gradual

graduar [gɾa'ðwaɾ] vt (gen) to graduate; (Mil) to commission; **graduarse** vr to graduate; **~se la vista** to have one's eyes tested

gráfica ['gɾafika] nf graph

gráfico, -a ['gɾafiko, a] adj graphic ▷ nm diagram; **gráficos** nmpl (Inform) graphics

grajo ['gɾaxo] nm rook

gramática [gɾa'matika] nf gramma

gramo ['gɾamo] nm gramme (BRIT), gram (US)

gran [gɾan] adj V **grande**

grana ['gɾana] nf (color, tela) scarlet

granada [gɾa'naða] nf pomegranate; (Mil) grenade

granate [gɾa'nate] adj deep red

Gran Bretaña [-bɾe'taɲa] nf Great Britain

grande ['gɾande] (antes de nmsg **gran**) adj (de tamaño) big, large; (alto) tall; (distinguido) great; (impresionante) gran ▷ nm grandee

granel [gɾa'nel]: **a ~** adv (Com) in bulk

granero [gɾa'neɾo] nm granary, barn

granito [gɾa'nito] nm (Agr) small grain; (roca) granite

granizado [gɾani'θaðo] nm iced drink

granizar [gɾani'θaɾ] vi to hail; **granizo** nm hail

granja ['gɾanxa] nf (gen) farm; **granjero, -a** nm/f farmer

grano ['gɾano] nm grain; (semilla) seed; (de café) bean; (Med) pimple, spot

granuja [gɾa'nuxa] nm/f rogue; (golfillo) urchin

grapa ['gɾapa] nf staple; (Tec) clamp; **grapadora** nf stapler

grasa ['gɾasa] nf (gen) grease; (de cocinar) fat, lard; (sebo) suet; (mugre) filth; **grasiento, -a** adj greasy; (de aceite) oily; **graso, -a** adj (leche, queso, carne) fatty; (pelo, piel) greasy

gratinar [gɾati'naɾ] vt to cook au gratin

ratis ['gratis] adv free

rato, -a ['grato, a] adj (agradable) pleasant, agreeable

ratuito, -a [gra'twito, a] adj (gratis) free; (sin razón) gratuitous

rave ['graβe] adj heavy; (serio) grave, serious; **gravedad** nf gravity

recia ['greθja] nf Greece

remio ['gremjo] nm trade, industry

riego, -a ['grjeɣo, a] adj, nm/f Greek

rieta ['grjeta] nf crack

rifo ['grifo] (ESP) nm tap (BRIT), faucet (US)

rillo ['griʎo] nm (Zool) cricket

ripa ['gripa] (MÉX) nf flu, influenza

ripe ['gripe] nf flu, influenza; **gripe aviar** bird flu

ris [gris] adj (color) grey

ritar [gri'tar] vt, vi to shout, yell; **grito** nm shout, yell; (de horror) scream

rosella [gro'seʎa] nf (red)currant

rosero, -a [gro'sero, a] adj (poco cortés) rude, bad-mannered; (ordinario) vulgar, crude

rosor [gro'sor] nm thickness

rúa ['grua] nf (Tec) crane; (de petróleo) derrick

rueso, -a ['grweso, a] adj thick; (persona) stout ⊳ nm bulk; **el ~ de** the bulk of

rulla [gruʎa] nf crane

rumo ['grumo] nm clot, lump

ruñido [gru'niðo] nm grunt; (de persona) grumble

ruñir [gru'nir] vi (animal) to growl; (persona) to grumble

rupo ['grupo] nm group; (Tec) unit, set; **grupo de presión** pressure group; **grupo sanguíneo** blood group

ruta ['gruta] nf grotto

uacho, -a [gwa'tʃo, a] (cs) nm/f homeless child

uajolote [gwaxo'lote] (MÉX) nm turkey

uante ['gwante] nm glove; **guantes de goma** rubber gloves; **guantera** nf glove compartment

uapo, -a ['gwapo, a] ['gwapo, a] adj good-looking, attractive; (elegante) smart

guarda ['gwarða] nmf (persona) guard, keeper ⊳ nf (acto) guarding; (custodia) custody; **guarda jurado** (armed) security guard; **guardabarros** nm inv mudguard (BRIT), fender (US); **guardabosques** nm inv gamekeeper; **guardacostas** nm inv coastguard vessel ⊳ nmf guardian, protector; **guardaespaldas** nmf inv bodyguard; **guardameta** nmf goalkeeper; **guardar** vt (gen) to keep; (vigilar) to guard, watch over; (dinero: ahorrar) to save; **guardarse** vr (preservarse) to protect o.s.; (evitar) to avoid; **guardar cama** to stay in bed; **guardarropa** nm (armario) wardrobe; (en establecimiento público) cloakroom

guardería [gwarðe'ria] nf nursery

guardia ['gwarðja] nf (Mil) guard; (cuidado) care, custody ⊳ nmf guard; (policía) policeman(-woman); **estar de ~** to be on guard; **montar la ~** to mount guard; **Guardia Civil** Civil Guard

guardián, -ana [gwar'ðjan, ana] nm/f (gen) guardian, keeper

guarida [gwa'riða] nf (de animal) den, lair; (refugio) refuge

guarnición [gwarni'θjon] nf (de vestimenta) trimming; (de piedra) mount; (Culin) garnish; (arneses) harness; (Mil) garrison

guarro, -a ['gwarro, a] nm/f pig

guasa ['gwasa] nf joke; **guasón, -ona** adj (bromista) joking ⊳ nm/f wit; joker

Guatemala [gwate'mala] nf Guatemala

guay [gwai] (fam) adj super, great

güero, -a ['gwero, a] (MÉX) adj blond(e)

guerra ['gerra] nf war; **dar ~** to annoy; **guerra civil** civil war; **guerra fría** cold war; **guerrero, -a** adj fighting; (carácter) warlike ⊳ nm/f warrior

guerrilla [ge'rriʎa] nf guerrilla warfare; (tropas) guerrilla band o group

guía etc ['gia] vb V **guiar** ⊳ nmf

(*persona*) guide; (*nf*: *libro*) guidebook;
guía telefónica telephone directory;
guía turística tourist guide
guiar [gi'ar] *vt* to guide, direct; (*Auto*)
to steer; **guiarse** *vr*: **~se por** to be
guided by
guinda ['ginda] *nf* morello cherry
guindilla [gin'diʎa] *nf* chilli pepper
guiñar [gi'ɲar] *vt* to wink
guión [gi'on] *nm* (*Ling*) hyphen,
dash; (*Cine*) script; **guionista** *nmf*
scriptwriter
guiri ['giri] (*ESP*: *fam*, *pey*) *nmf*
foreigner
guirnalda [gir'nalda] *nf* garland
guisado [gi'saðo] *nm* stew
guisante [gi'sante] *nm* pea
guisar [gi'sar] *vt*, *vi* to cook; **guiso**
nm cooked dish
guitarra [gi'tarra] *nf* guitar
gula ['gula] *nf* gluttony, greed
gusano [gu'sano] *nm* worm; (*lombriz*)
earthworm
gustar [gus'tar] *vt* to taste, sample
▷ *vi* to please, be pleasing; **~ de algo**
to like o enjoy sth; **me gustan las uvas** I
like grapes; **le gusta nadar** she likes o
enjoys swimming
gusto ['gusto] *nm* (*sentido*, *sabor*)
taste; (*placer*) pleasure; **tiene ~ a
menta** it tastes of mint; **tener buen
~** to have good taste; **coger el o
tomar ~ a algo** to take a liking to sth;
sentirse a ~ to feel at ease; **mucho ~
(en conocerle)** pleased to meet you;
el ~ es mío the pleasure is mine; **con ~**
willingly, gladly

ha *vb* V **haber**
haba ['aβa] *nf* bean
Habana [a'βana] *nf*: **la ~** Havana
habano [a'βano] *nm* Havana cigar
habéis *vb* V **haber**

○ **PALABRA CLAVE**

haber [a'βer] *vb aux* 1 (*tiempos
compuestos*) to have; **había comido** I
had eaten; **antes/después de haberlo
visto** before seeing/after seeing o
having seen it
2: **¡haberlo dicho antes!** you should
have said so before!
3: **haber de**: **he de hacerlo** I have to
do it; **ha de llegar mañana** it should
arrive tomorrow
▷ *vb impers* 1 (*existencia*: *sg*) there is;
(: *pl*) there are; **hay un hermano/dos
hermanos** there is one brother/there
are two brothers; **¿cuánto hay de
aquí a Sucre?** how far is it from here
to Sucre?
2 (*obligación*): **hay que hacer algo**

something must be done; **hay que apuntarlo para acordarse** you have to write it down to remember

3: **¡hay que ver!** well I never!

4: **¡no hay de o por** (LAM) **qué!** don't mention it!, not at all!

5: **¿qué hay?** (¿qué pasa?) what's up?, what's the matter?; (¿qué tal?) how's it going?

▷ vt: **he aquí unas sugerencias** here are some suggestions; **no hay cintas blancas pero sí las hay rojas** there aren't any white ribbons but there are some red ones

▷ nm (en cuenta) credit side; **haberes** nmpl assets; **¿cuánto tengo en el haber?** how much do I have in my account?; **tiene varias novelas en su haber** he has several novels to his credit

haberse vr: **habérselas con algn** to have it out with sb

abichuela [aβiˈtʃwela] nf kidney bean

ábil [ˈaβil] adj (listo) clever, smart; (capaz) fit, capable; (experto) expert; **día - working** day; **habilidad** nf skill, ability

abitación [aβitaˈθjon] nf (cuarto) room; (Bio: morada) habitat; **habitación doble o matrimonio** double room; **habitación individual o sencilla** single room

abitante [aβiˈtante] nmf inhabitant

abitar [aβiˈtar] vt (residir en) to inhabit; (ocupar) to occupy ▷ vi to live

ábito [ˈaβito] nm habit

abitual [aβiˈtwal] adj usual

abituar [aβiˈtwar] vt to accustom; **abituarse** vr: **~se a** to get used to

abla [ˈaβla] nf (capacidad de hablar) speech; (idioma) language; (dialecto) dialect; **perder el ~** to become speechless; **de ~ francesa** French-speaking; **estar al ~** to be in contact; **¡González al ~!** (Tel) González speaking!

ablador, a [aβlaˈðor, a] adj

talkative ▷ nm/f chatterbox

habladuría [aβlaðuˈria] nf rumour; **habladurías** nfpl gossip sg

hablante [aˈβlante] adj speaking ▷ nmf speaker

hablar [aˈβlar] vt to speak, talk ▷ vi to speak; **hablarse** vr to speak to each other; **~ con** to speak to; **~ de** to speak of o about; **¡ni ~!** it's out of the question!; **"se habla inglés"** "English spoken here"

habré etc [aˈβre] vb V **haber**

hacendado [aθenˈdaðo] (LAM) nm rancher, farmer

hacendoso, -a [aθenˈdoso, a] adj industrious

○ **PALABRA CLAVE**

hacer [aˈθer] vt 1 (fabricar, producir) to make; (construir) to build; **hacer una película/un ruido** to make a film/noise; **el guisado lo hice yo** I made o cooked the stew

2 (ejecutar: trabajo etc) to do; **hacer la colada** to do the washing; **hacer la comida** to do the cooking; **¿qué haces?** what are you doing?; **hacer el malo** o **el papel del malo** (Teatro) to play the villain

3 (estudios, algunos deportes) to do; **hacer español/economics** to do o study Spanish/economics; **hacer yoga/gimnasia** to go to yoga/go to the gym

4 (transformar, incidir en): **esto lo hará más difícil** this will make it more difficult; **salir te hará sentir mejor** going out will make you feel better

5 (cálculo): **2 y 2 hacen 4** 2 and 2 make 4; **éste hace 100** this one makes 100

6 (+ sub): **esto hará que ganemos** this will make us win; **harás que no quiera venir** you'll stop him wanting to come

7 (como sustituto de vb) to do; **él bebió y yo hice lo mismo** he drank and I did likewise

8 **no hace más que criticar** all he does is criticize

hacha | 142

▷ *vb semi-aux* (*directo*): **hacer +infin: les hice venir** I made o had them come; **hacer trabajar a los demás** to get others to work

▷ *vi* 1 **haz como que no lo sabes** act as if you don't know

2 (*ser apropiado*): **si os hace** if it's alright with you

3 **hacer de: hacer de Otelo** to play Othello

▷ *vb impers* 1 **hace calor/frío** it's hot/cold; V tb **bueno, sol, tiempo**

2 (*tiempo*): **hace 3 años** 3 years ago; **hace un mes que voy/no voy** I've been going/I haven't been for a month

3 **¿cómo has hecho para llegar tan rápido?** how did you manage to get here so quickly?

hacerse *vr* 1 (*volverse*) to become; **se hicieron amigos** they became friends

2 (*acostumbrarse*): **hacerse a** to get used to

3 **se hace con huevos y leche** it's made out of eggs and milk; **eso no se hace** that's not done

4 (*obtener*): **hacerse de** o **con algo** to get hold of sth

5 (*fingirse*): **hacerse el sueco** to turn a deaf ear

hacha ['atʃa] *nf* axe; (*antorcha*) torch

hachís [a'tʃis] *nm* hashish

hacia ['aθja] *prep* (*en dirección de*) towards; (*cerca de*) near; (*actitud*) towards; **~ adelante/atrás** forwards/backwards; **~ arriba/abajo** up(wards)/down(wards); **~ mediodía/las cinco** about noon/five

hacienda [a'θjenda] *nf* (*propiedad*) property; (*finca*) farm; (LAM: *rancho*) ranch; **(Ministerio de H~** (BRIT), Treasury Department (US); **hacienda pública** public finance

hada ['aða] *nf* fairy

hago *etc vb* V **hacer**

Haití [ai'ti] *nm* Haiti

halagar [ala'ɣar] *vt* to flatter

halago [a'laɣo] *nm* flattery

halcón [al'kon] *nm* falcon, hawk

hallar [a'ʎar] *vt* (*gen*) to find; (*descubrir*) to discover; (*toparse con*) to run into; **hallarse** *vr* to be (situated)

halterofilia [altero'filja] *nf* weightlifting

hamaca [a'maka] *nf* hammock

hambre ['ambre] *nf* hunger; (*plaga*) famine; (*deseo*) longing; **tener ~** to be hungry; **¡me muero de ~!** I'm starving!; **hambriento, -a** *adj* hungry, starving

hamburguesa [ambur'ɣesa] *nf* hamburger; **hamburguesería** *nf* burger bar

hámster ['amster] *nm* hamster

han *vb* V **haber**

harapos [a'rapos] *nmpl* rags

haré *vb* V **hacer**

harina [a'rina] *nf* flour; **harina de maíz** cornflour (BRIT), cornstarch (US); **harina de trigo** wheat flour

hartar [ar'tar] *vt* to satiate, glut; (*fig*) to tire, sicken; **hartarse** *vr* (*de comida*) to fill o.s., gorge o.s.: (*cansarse*): **~se (de)** to get fed up (with); **harto, -a** *adj* (*lleno*) full; (*cansado*) fed up ▷ *adv* (*bastante*) enough; (*muy*) very; **estar harto de hacer algo/de algn** to be fed up of doing sth/with sb

has *vb* V **haber**

hasta ['asta] *adv* even ▷ *prep* (*alcanzando a*) as far as; up to; down to; (*de tiempo: a tal hora*) till, until; (*antes de*) before ▷ *conj*: **~ que …** until; **~ luego/el sábado** see you soon/on Saturday; **~ ahora** (*al despedirse*) see you in a minute; **~ pronto** see you soon

hay *vb* V **haber**

Haya ['aja] *nf*: **la ~** The Hague

haya *etc* ['aja] *vb* V **haber** ▷ *nf* beech tree

haz [aθ] *vb* V **hacer** ▷ *nm* (*de luz*) beam

hazaña [a'θaɲa] *nf* feat, exploit

hazmerreír [aθmerre'ir] *nm inv* laughing stock

he *vb* V **haber**

hebilla [e'βiʎa] *nf* buckle, clasp

ebra ['eβra] nf thread; (Bot: fibra) fibre, grain

ebreo, -a [e'βreo, a] adj, nm/f Hebrew ▷ nm (Ling) Hebrew

echizar [etʃi'θar] vt to cast a spell on, bewitch

echizo [e'tʃiθo] nm witchcraft, magic; (acto de magia) spell, charm

echo, -a ['etʃo, a] pp de **hacer** ▷ adj (carne) done; (Costura) ready-to-wear ▷ nm deed, act; (dato) fact; (cuestión) matter; (suceso) event ▷ excl agreed!, done!; **de ~** in fact, as a matter of fact; **~ el es que ...** the fact is that ...; **¡bien ~!** well done!

echura [e'tʃura] nf (forma) form, shape; (de persona) build

ectárea [ek'tarea] nf hectare

elada [e'laða] nf frost

eladera [ela'ðera] (LAM) nf (refrigerador) refrigerator

elado, -a [e'laðo, a] adj frozen; (glacial) icy; (fig) chilly, cold ▷ nm ice cream

elar [e'lar] vt to freeze, ice (up); (dejar atónito) to amaze; (desalentar) to discourage ▷ vi to freeze; **helarse** vr to freeze

elecho [e'letʃo] nm fern

élice [e'liθe] nf (Tec) propeller

elicóptero [eli'koptero] nm helicopter

embra ['embra] nf (Bot, Zool) female; (mujer) woman; (Tec) nut

emorragia [emo'rraxja] nf haemorrhage

emorroides [emo'rroiðes] nfpl haemorrhoids, piles

emos vb V **haber**

eno ['eno] nm hay

eredar [ere'ðar] vt to inherit; **heredero, -a** nm/f heir(ess)

ereje [e'rexe] nm heretic

erencia [e'renθja] nf inheritance

erida [e'riða] nf wound, injury; V **herido**

erido, -a [e'riðo, a] adj injured, wounded ▷ nm/f casualty

herir [e'rir] vt to wound, injure; (fig) to offend

hermanación [ermanaθ'on] nf (of towns) twinning

hermanado [erma'naðo] adj (town) twinned

hermanastro, -a [erma'nastro, a] nm/f stepbrother/sister

hermandad [erman'dað] nf brotherhood

hermano, -a [er'mano, a] nm/f brother/sister; **hermano(-a) gemelo(-a), twin brother/sister; **hermano(-a) político(-a), brother-in-law/sister-in-law

hermético, -a [er'metiko, a] adj hermetic; (fig) watertight

hermoso, -a [er'moso, a] adj beautiful, lovely; (estupendo) splendid; (guapo) handsome; **hermosura** nf beauty

hernia ['ernja] nf hernia; **hernia discal** slipped disc

héroe ['eroe] nm hero

heroína [ero'ina] nf (mujer) heroine; (droga) heroin

herradura [erra'ðura] nf horseshoe

herramienta [erra'mjenta] nf tool

herrero [e'rrero] nm blacksmith

hervidero [erβi'ðero] nm (fig) swarm; (Pol etc) hotbed

hervir [er'βir] vi to boil; (burbujear) to bubble; **~ a fuego lento** to simmer; **hervor** nm boiling; (fig) ardour, fervour

heterosexual [eterosek'swal] adj heterosexual

hice etc vb V **hacer**

hidratante [iðra'tante] adj: **crema ~** moisturizing cream, moisturizer; **hidratar** vt (piel) to moisturize; **hidrato** nm hydrate; **hidratos de carbono** carbohydrates

hidráulico, -a [i'ðrauliko, a] adj hydraulic

hidro... [iðro] prefijo hydro..., water-...; **hidrodeslizador** nm hovercraft; **hidroeléctrico, -a**

h

adj hydroelectric; **hidrógeno** *nm* hydrogen

hiedra [ˈjeðra] *nf* ivy

hiel [jel] *nf* gall, bile; *(fig)* bitterness

hiela *etc vb* V **helar**

hielo [ˈjelo] *nm (gen)* ice; *(escarcha)* frost; *(fig)* coldness, reserve

hiena [ˈjena] *nf* hyena

hierba [ˈjerβa] *nf (pasto)* grass; *(Culin, Med: planta)* herb; **mala ~** weed; *(fig)* evil influence; **hierbabuena** *nf* mint

hierro [ˈjerro] *nm (metal)* iron; *(objeto)* iron object

hígado [ˈiɣaðo] *nm* liver

higiene [iˈxjene] *nf* hygiene; **higiénico, -a** *adj* hygienic

higo [ˈiɣo] *nm* fig; **higo seco** dried fig; **higuera** *nf* fig tree

hijastro, -a [iˈxastro, a] *nm/f* stepson/daughter

hijo, -a [ˈixo, a] *nm/f* son/daughter, child; **hijos** *nmpl* children, sons and daughters; **hijo adoptivo** adopted child; **hijo de papá/mamá** daddy's/mummy's boy; **hijo de puta** *(fam!)* bastard (!), son of a bitch (!); **hijo/a político/a** son-/daughter-in-law; **hijo único** only child

hilera [iˈlera] *nf* row, file

hilo [ˈilo] *nm* thread; *(Bot)* fibre; *(metal)* wire; *(de agua)* trickle, thin stream

hilvanar [ilβaˈnar] *vt (Costura)* to tack (ʙʀɪᴛ), baste (us); *(fig)* to do hurriedly

himno [ˈimno] *nm* hymn; **himno nacional** national anthem

hincapié [inkaˈpje] *nm*: **hacer ~ en** to emphasize

hincar [inˈkar] *vt* to drive (in), thrust (in)

hincha [ˈintʃa] *(fam)* *nmf* fan

hinchado, -a [inˈtʃaðo, a] *adj (gen)* swollen; *(persona)* pompous

hinchar [inˈtʃar] *vt (gen)* to swell; *(inflar)* to blow up, inflate; *(fig)* to exaggerate; **hincharse** *vr (inflarse)* to swell up; *(fam: de comer)* to stuff o.s.; **hinchazón** *nf (Med)* swelling; *(altivez)*

arrogance

hinojo [iˈnoxo] *nm* fennel

hipermercado [ipermerˈkaðo] *nm* hypermarket, superstore

hípico, -a [ˈipiko, a] *adj* horse *cpd*

hipnotismo [ipnoˈtismo] *nm* hypnotism; **hipnotizar** *vt* to hypnotize

hipo [ˈipo] *nm* hiccups *pl*

hipocresía [ipokreˈsia] *nf* hypocrisy; **hipócrita** *adj* hypocritical ▷ *nmf* hypocrite

hipódromo [iˈpoðromo] *nm* racetrack

hipopótamo [ipoˈpotamo] *nm* hippopotamus

hipoteca [ipoˈteka] *nf* mortgage

hipótesis [iˈpotesis] *nf inv* hypothesis

hispánico, -a [isˈpaniko, a] *adj* Hispanic

hispano, -a [isˈpano, a] *adj* Hispanic, Spanish, Hispano- ▷ *nm/f* Spaniard; **Hispanoamérica** *nf* Latin America; **hispanoamericano, -a** *adj, nm/f* Latin American

histeria [isˈterja] *nf* hysteria

historia [isˈtorja] *nf* history; *(cuento)* story, tale; **historias** *nfpl (chismes)* gossip *sg*; **dejarse de ~s** to come to the point; **pasar a la ~** to go down in history; **historiador, a** *nm/f* historian; **historial** *nm (profesional)* curriculum vitae, C.V.; *(Med)* case history; **histórico, -a** *adj* historical; *(memorable)* historic

historieta [istoˈrjeta] *nf* tale, anecdote; *(dibujos)* comic strip

hito [ˈito] *nm (fig)* landmark

hizo *vb* V **hacer**

hocico [oˈθiko] *nm* snout

hockey [ˈxokei] *nm* hockey; **hockey sobre hielo/patines** ice/roller hockey

hogar [oˈɣar] *nm* fireplace, hearth; *(casa)* home; *(vida familiar)* home life; **hogareño, -a** *adj* home *cpd*; *(persona)* home-loving

hoguera [oˈɣera] *nf (gen)* bonfire

hoja ['oxa] nf (gen) leaf; (de flor) petal; (de papel) sheet; (página) page; **hoja de afeitar** (LAM) razor blade; **hoja de solicitud** application form; **hoja electrónica** o **de cálculo** spreadsheet; **hoja informativa** leaflet, handout

hojalata [oxa'lata] nf tin(plate)

hojaldre [o'xaldre] nm (Culin) puff pastry

hojear [oxe'ar] vt to leaf through, turn the pages of

hojuela [o'xwela] nf (MÉX) nf flake

hola ['ola] excl hello!

holá [o'la] (RPL) excl hello!

Holanda [o'landa] nf Holland; **holandés, -esa** adj Dutch ▷ nm/f Dutchman(-woman) ▷ nm (Ling) Dutch

holgado, -a [ol'yaðo, a] adj (ropa) loose, baggy; (rico) comfortable

holgar [ol'yar] vi (descansar) to rest; (sobrar) to be superfluous

holgazán, -ana [olya'θan, ana] adj idle, lazy ▷ nm/f loafer

hollín [o'ʎin] nm soot

hombre ['ombre] nm (gen) man; (raza humana): **el ~** man(kind) ▷ excl: **¡sí ~!** (claro) of course!; (para énfasis) man, old boy; **hombre de negocios** businessman; **hombre de pro** honest man; **hombre-rana** frogman

hombrera [om'brera] nf shoulder strap

hombro ['ombro] nm shoulder

homenaje [ome'naxe] nm (gen) homage; (tributo) tribute

homicida [omi'θiða] adj homicidal ▷ nmf murderer; **homicidio** nm murder, manslaughter

homologar [omolo'yar] vt (Com: productos, tamaños) to standardize

homólogo, -a [o'moloyo, a] nm/f: **su** etc **~** his etc counterpart o opposite number

homosexual [omosek'swal] adj, nmf homosexual

onda ['onda] (cs) nf catapult

hondo, -a ['ondo, a] adj deep; **lo ~** the depth(s) pl, the bottom; **hondonada** nf hollow, depression; (cañón) ravine

Honduras [on'duras] nf Honduras

hondureño, -a [ondu'reɲo, a] adj, nm/f Honduran

honestidad [onesti'ðað] nf purity, chastity; (decencia) decency; **honesto, -a** adj chaste; decent; honest; (justo) just

hongo ['ongo] nm (Bot: gen) fungus; (: comestible) mushroom; (: venenoso) toadstool

honor [o'nor] nm (gen) honour; **en ~ a la verdad** to be fair; **honorable** adj honourable

honorario, -a [ono'rarjo, a] adj honorary; **honorarios** nmpl fees

honra ['onra] nf (gen) honour; (renombre) good name; **honradez** nf honesty; (de persona) integrity; **honrado, -a** adj honest, upright; **honrar** [on'rar] vt to honour

hora ['ora] nf (una hora) hour; (tiempo) time; **¿qué ~ es?** what time is it?; **¿a qué ~?** at what time?; **media ~** half an hour; **a la ~ de recreo** at playtime; **a primera ~** first thing (in the morning); **a última ~** at the last moment; **a altas ~s** in the small hours; **¡a buena ~!** about time too!; **pedir ~** to make an appointment; **dar la ~** to strike the hour; **horas de oficina/trabajo** office/working hours; **horas de visita** visiting times; **horas extras** o **extraordinarias** overtime sg; **horas pico** (LAM) rush o peak hours; **horas punta** (ESP) rush hours

horario, -a [o'rarjo, a] adj hourly, hour cpd ▷ nm timetable; **horario comercial** business hours pl

horca ['orka] nf gallows sg

horcajadas [orka'xaðas]: **a ~** adv astride

horchata [or'tʃata] nf cold drink made from tiger nuts and water, tiger nut milk

horizontal [oriθon'tal] adj

horizonte | 146

horizontal

horizonte [oriˈθonte] *nm* horizon

horma [ˈorma] *nf* mould

hormiga [orˈmiɣa] *nf* ant; **hormigas** *nfpl* (*Med*) pins and needles

hormigón [ormiˈɣon] *nm* concrete; **hormigón armado/pretensado** reinforced/prestressed concrete; **hormigonera** *nf* cement mixer

hormigueo [ormiˈɣeo] *nm* (*comezón*) itch

hormona [orˈmona] *nf* hormone

hornillo [orˈniʎo] *nm* (*cocina*) portable stove; **hornillo de gas** gas ring

horno [ˈorno] *nm* (*Culin*) oven; (*Tec*) furnace; **alto ~** blast furnace

horóscopo [oˈroskopo] *nm* horoscope

horquilla [orˈkiʎa] *nf* hairpin; (*Agr*) pitchfork

horrendo, -a [oˈrrendo, a] *adj* horrendous, frightful

horrible [oˈrriβle] *adj* horrible, dreadful

horripilante [orripiˈlante] *adj* hair-raising, horrifying

horror [oˈrror] *nm* horror, dread; (*atrocidad*) atrocity; **¡qué ~!** (*fam*) how awful!; **horrorizar** *vt* to horrify, frighten; **horrorizarse** *vr* to be horrified; **horroroso, -a** *adj* horrifying, ghastly

hortaliza [ortaˈliθa] *nf* vegetable

hortelano, -a [orteˈlano, a] *nm/f* (market) gardener

hortera [orˈtera] (*fam*) *adj* tacky

hospedar [ospeˈðar] *vt* to put up; **hospedarse** *vr* to stay, lodge

hospital [ospiˈtal] *nm* hospital

hospitalario, -a [ospitaˈlarjo, a] *adj* (*acogedor*) hospitable; **hospitalidad** *nf* hospitality

hostal [osˈtal] *nm* small hotel

hostelería [osteleˈria] *nf* hotel business o trade

hostia [ˈostja] *nf* (*Rel*) host, consecrated wafer; (*fam!: golpe*) whack, punch ▷ *excl* (*fam!*) **¡~(s)!** damn!

hostil [osˈtil] *adj* hostile

hotdog [otˈdoɡ] (*LAM*) *nm* hot dog

hotel [oˈtel] *nm* hotel; **hotelero, -a** *adj* hotel *cpd* ▷ *nm/f* hotelier

● HOTEL

● In Spain you can choose from
● the following categories of
● accommodation, in descending
● order of quality and price: **hotel**
● (from 5 stars to 1), **hostal**, **pensión**,
● **casa de huéspedes**, **fonda**. The
● State also runs luxury hotels called
● **paradores**, which are usually sited
● in places of particular historical
● interest and are often historic
● buildings themselves.

hoy [oi] *adv* (*este día*) today; (*la actualidad*) now(adays) ▷ *nm* present time; **~ (en) día** now(adays)

hoyo [ˈojo] *nm* hole, pit

hoz [oθ] *nf* sickle

hube etc *vb* V **haber**

hucha [ˈutʃa] *nf* money box

hueco, -a [ˈweko, a] *adj* (*vacío*) hollow, empty; (*resonante*) booming ▷ *nm* hollow, cavity

huelga etc [ˈwelɣa] *vb* V **holgar** ▷ *nf* strike; **declararse en ~** to go on strike, come out on strike; **huelga de hambre** hunger strike; **huelga general** general strike

huelguista [welˈɣista] *nmf* striker

huella [ˈweʎa] *nf* (*pisada*) tread; (*marca del paso*) footprint, footstep; (: *de animal, máquina*) track; **huella dactilar** fingerprint

huelo etc *vb* V **oler**

huérfano, -a [ˈwerfano, a] *adj* orphan(ed) ▷ *nm/f* orphan

huerta [ˈwerta] *nf* market garden; (*en Murcia y Valencia*) irrigated region

huerto [ˈwerto] *nm* kitchen garden; (*de árboles frutales*) orchard

hueso [ˈweso] *nm* (*Anat*) bone; (*de fruta*) stone

nuésped ['wespeð] nmf guest

hueva ['weβa] nf roe

huevera [we'βera] nf eggcup

huevo ['weβo] nm eg; **huevo a la copa** (cs) soft-boiled egg; **huevo duro/escalfado** hard-boiled/poached egg; **huevo estrellado** (LAM) fried egg; **huevo frito** (ESP) fried egg; **huevo pasado por agua** soft-boiled egg; **huevos revueltos** scrambled eggs; **huevo tibio** (MÉX) soft-boiled egg

huida [u'iða] nf escape, flight

huir [u'ir] vi (escapar) to flee, escape; (evitar) to avoid

hule ['ule] nm oilskin; (MÉX: goma) rubber

hulera [u'lera] (MÉX) nf catapult

humanidad [umani'ðað] nf (género humano) man(kind); (cualidad) humanity

humanitario, -a [umani'tarjo, a] adj humanitarian

humano, -a [u'mano, a] adj (gen) human; (humanitario) humane ⊳ nm human; **ser ~** human being

humareda [uma'reða] nf cloud of smoke

humedad [ume'ðað] nf (de clima) humidity; (de pared etc) dampness; **a prueba de ~** damp-proof; **humedecer** vt to moisten, wet; **humedecerse** vr to get wet

húmedo, -a ['umeðo, a] adj (mojado) damp, wet; (tiempo etc) humid

humilde [u'milde] adj humble, modest

humillación [umiʎa'θjon] nf humiliation; **humillante** adj humiliating

humillar [umi'ʎar] vt to humiliate

humo ['umo] nm (de fuego) smoke; (gas nocivo) fumes pl; (vapor) steam, vapour; **humos** nmpl (fig) conceit sg

humor [u'mor] nm (disposición) mood, temper; (lo que divierte) humour; **de buen/mal ~** in a good/bad mood; **humorista** nmf comic; **humorístico, -a** adj funny, humorous

hundimiento [undi'mjento] nm (gen) sinking; (colapso) collapse

hundir [un'dir] vt to sink; (edificio, plan) to ruin, destroy; **hundirse** vr to sink, collapse

húngaro, -a ['ungaro, a] adj, nm/f Hungarian

Hungría [un'gria] nf Hungary

huracán [ura'kan] nm hurricane

huraño, -a [u'raɲo, a] adj (antisocial) unsociable

hurgar [ur'xar] vt to poke, jab; (remover) to stir (up); **hurgarse** vr: **~se (las narices)** to pick one's nose

hurón, -ona [u'ron, ona] nm (Zool) ferret

hurtadillas [urta'ðiʎas]: **a ~** adv stealthily, on the sly

hurtar [ur'tar] vt to steal; **hurto** nm theft, stealing

husmear [usme'ar] vt (oler) to sniff out, scent; (fam) to pry into

huyo etc vb V **huir**

i

iba etc vb V **ir**

ibérico, -a [i'βeriko, a] adj Iberian

iberoamericano, -a
[iβeroameri'kano, a] adj, nm/f Latin
American

Ibiza [i'βiθa] nf Ibiza

iceberg [iθe'βer] nm iceberg

icono [i'kono] nm ikon, icon

ida ['iða] nf going, departure; **~ y
vuelta** round trip, return

idea [i'ðea] nf idea; **no tengo la
menor ~** I haven't a clue

ideal [iðe'al] adj, nm ideal; **idealista**
nmf idealist; **idealizar** vt to idealize

ídem ['iðem] pron ditto

idéntico, -a [i'ðentiko, a] adj
identical

identidad [iðenti'ðað] nf identity

identificación [iðentifika'θjon] nf
identification

identificar [iðentifi'kar] vt to
identify; **identificarse** vr: **~se con** to
identify with

ideología [iðeolo'xia] nf ideology

idilio [i'ðiljo] nm love-affair

idioma [i'ðjoma] nm (gen) language
▌ No confundir **idioma** con la palabra
▌ inglesa *idiom*.

idiota [i'ðjota] adj idiotic ▷ nmf idiot

ídolo ['iðolo] nm (tb fig) idol

idóneo, -a [i'ðoneo, a] adj suitable

iglesia [i'ɣlesja] nf church

ignorante [iɣno'rante] adj ignorant,
uninformed ▷ nmf ignoramus

ignorar [iɣno'rar] vt not to know, be
ignorant of; (no hacer caso a) to ignore

igual [i'ɣwal] adj (gen) equal; (similar)
like, similar; (mismo) (the) same;
(constante) constant; (temperatura)
even ▷ nmf equal; **~ que** like, the same
as; **me da o es ~** I don't care; **son ~es**
they're the same; **al ~ que** (prep, conj)
like, just like

igualar [iɣwa'lar] vt (gen) to equalize,
make equal; (allanar, nivelar) to level
(off), even (out); **igualarse** vr (platos de
balanza) to balance out

igualdad [iɣwal'dað] nf equality;
(similaridad) sameness; (uniformidad)
uniformity

igualmente [iɣwal'mente] adv
equally; (también) also, likewise ▷ excl
the same to you!

ilegal [ile'ɣal] adj illegal

ilegítimo, -a [ile'xitimo, a] adj
illegitimate

ileso, -a [i'leso, a] adj unhurt

ilimitado, -a [ilimi'taðo, a] adj
unlimited

iluminación [ilumina'θjon] nf
illumination; (alumbrado) lighting

iluminar [ilumi'nar] vt to
illuminate, light (up); (fig) to enlighten

ilusión [ilu'sjon] nf illusion; (quimera)
delusion; (esperanza) hope; **hacerse
ilusiones** to build up one's hopes;
ilusionado, -a adj excited; **ilusionar**
vi: **le ilusiona ir de vacaciones** he's
looking forward to going on holiday;
ilusionarse vr: **ilusionarse (con)** to
get excited (about)

iluso, -a [i'luso, a] adj easily
deceived ▷ nm/f dreamer

ilustración [ilustraˈθjon] nf
illustration; (saber) learning, erudition;
la l- the Enlightenment; **ilustrado, -a**
adj illustrated; learned

ilustrar [ilusˈtrar] vt to illustrate;
(instruir) to instruct; (explicar) to
explain, make clear

ilustre [iˈlustre] adj famous,
illustrious

imagen [iˈmaxen] nf (gen) image;
(dibujo) picture

imaginación [imaxinaˈθjon] nf
imagination

imaginar [imaxiˈnar] vt (gen) to
imagine; (idear) to think up; (suponer) to
suppose; **imaginarse** vr to imagine;
imaginario, -a adj imaginary;
imaginativo, -a adj imaginative

imán [iˈman] nm magnet

imbécil [imˈbeθil] nmf imbecile, idiot

imitación [imitaˈθjon] nf imitation;
de - imitation cpd

imitar [imiˈtar] vt to imitate;
(parodiar, remedar) to mimic, ape

impaciente [impaˈθjente] adj
impatient; (nervioso) anxious

impacto [imˈpakto] nm impact

impar [imˈpar] adj odd

imparcial [imparˈθjal] adj impartial,
fair

impecable [impeˈkaβle] adj
impeccable

impedimento [impeðiˈmento] nm
impediment, obstacle

impedir [impeˈðir] vt (obstruir) to
impede, obstruct; (estorbar) to prevent;
- a algn hacer o **que algn haga algo**
to prevent sb (from) doing sth, stop
sb doing sth

imperativo, -a [imperaˈtiβo, a] adj
(urgente, Ling) imperative

imperdible [imperˈðiβle] nm
safety pin

imperdonable [imperðoˈnaβle] adj
unforgivable, inexcusable

imperfecto, -a [imperˈfekto, a] adj
imperfect

imperio [imˈperjo] nm empire;

(autoridad) rule, authority; (fig) pride,
haughtiness

impermeable [impermeˈaβle] adj
waterproof ▷ nm raincoat, mac (BRIT)

impersonal [impersoˈnal] adj
impersonal

impertinente [impertiˈnente] adj
impertinent

ímpetu [ˈimpetu] nm (impulso)
impetus, impulse; (impetuosidad)
impetuosity; (violencia) violence

implantar [implanˈtar] vt to
introduce

implemento [impleˈmento] nm (LAM)
tool, implement

implicar [impliˈkar] vt to involve;
(entrañar) to imply

implícito, -a [imˈpliθito, a] adj
(tácito) implicit; (sobreentendido)
implied

imponente [impoˈnente] adj
(impresionante) impressive, imposing;
(solemne) solemn

imponer [impoˈner] vt (gen) to
impose; (exigir) to exact; **imponerse**
vr to assert o.s.; (prevalecer) to prevail;
imponible adj (Com) taxable

impopular [impopuˈlar] adj
unpopular

importación [importaˈθjon] nf
(acto) importing; (mercancías)
imports pl

importancia [imporˈtanθja] nf
importance; (valor) value, significance;
(extensión) size, magnitude; **no**
tiene - it's nothing; **importante** adj
important; valuable, significant

importar [imporˈtar] vt (del
extranjero) to import; (costar) to amount
to ▷ vi to be important, matter; **me**
importa un rábano I couldn't care
less; **no importa** it doesn't matter;
¿le importa que fume? do you mind
if I smoke?

importe [imˈporte] nm (total)
amount; (valor) value

imposible [impoˈsiβle] adj (gen)
impossible; (insoportable) unbearable,

intolerable

imposición [imposi'θjon] nf
imposition; (Com: impuesto) tax;
(: inversión) deposit

impostor, a [impos'tor, a] nm/f
impostor

impotencia [impo'tenθja] nf
impotence; **impotente** adj impotent

impreciso, -a [impre'θiso, a] adj
imprecise, vague

impregnar [imɣre'nar] vt to
impregnate; **impregnarse** vr to
become impregnated

imprenta [im'prenta] nf (acto)
printing; (aparato) press; (casa)
printer's; (letra) print

imprescindible [impresθin'diβle]
adj essential, vital

impresión [impre'sjon] nf (gen)
impression; (Imprenta) printing;
(edición) edition; (Foto) print; (marca)
imprint; **impresión digital** fingerprint

impresionante [impresjo'nante]
adj impressive; (tremendo) tremendous;
(maravilloso) great, marvellous

impresionar [impresjo'nar] vt
(conmover) to move; (afectar) to impress,
strike; (película fotográfica) to expose;
impresionarse vr to be impressed;
(conmoverse) to be moved

impreso, -a [im'preso, a] pp de
imprimir ⊳ adj printed; **impresos**
nmpl printed matter; **impresora** nf
printer

imprevisto, -a [impre'βisto, a]
adj (gen) unforeseen; (inesperado)
unexpected

imprimir [impri'mir] vt to imprint,
impress, stamp; (textos) to print;
(Inform) to output, print out

improbable [impro'βaβle] adj
improbable; (inverosímil) unlikely

impropio, -a [im'propjo, a] adj
improper

improvisado, -a [improβi'saðo, a]
adj improvised

improvisar [improβi'sar] vt to
improvise

improviso, -a [impro'βiso, a] adj: **de**
~ unexpectedly, suddenly

imprudencia [impru'ðenθja] nf
imprudence; (indiscreción) indiscretion;
(descuido) carelessness; **imprudente**
adj unwise, imprudent; (indiscreto)
indiscreet

impuesto, -a [im'pwesto, a] adj
imposed ⊳ nm tax; **impuesto al valor
agregado o añadido** (LAM) value added
tax (BRIT) = sales tax (US); **impuesto
sobre el valor añadido** (ESP) value
added tax (BRIT) = sales tax (US)

impulsar [impul'sar] vt to drive;
(promover) to promote, stimulate

impulsivo, -a [impul'siβo, a] adj
impulsive; **impulso** nm impulse;
(fuerza, empuje) thrust, drive;
(fig: sentimiento) urge, impulse

impureza [impu'reθa] nf impurity;
impuro, -a adj impure

inaccesible [inakθe'siβle] adj
inaccessible

inaceptable [inaθep'taβle] adj
unacceptable

inactivo, -a [inak'tiβo, a] adj
inactive

inadecuado, -a [inaðe'kwaðo, a]
adj (insuficiente) inadequate; (inapto)
unsuitable

inadvertido, -a [inaðβer'tiðo, a] adj
(no visto) unnoticed

inaguantable [inaɣwan'taβle] adj
unbearable

inanimado, -a [inani'maðo, a] adj
inanimate

inaudito, -a [inau'ðito, a] adj
unheard-of

inauguración [inauɣura'θjon] nf
inauguration; opening

inaugurar [inauɣu'rar] vt to
inaugurate; (exposición) to open

inca [inka] nmf Inca

incalculable [inkalku'laβle] adj
incalculable

incandescente [inkandes'θente]
adj incandescent

incansable [inkan'saβle] adj

tireless, untiring

incapacidad [inkapaθi'ðað] nf incapacity; (incompetencia) incompetence; **incapacidad física/mental** physical/mental disability

incapacitar [inkapaθi'tar] vt (inhabilitar) to incapacitate, render unfit; (descalificar) to disqualify

incapaz [inka'paθ] adj incapable

incautarse [inkau'tarse] vr: ~ **de** to seize, confiscate

incauto, -a [in'kauto, a] adj (imprudente) incautious, unwary

incendiar [inθen'djar] vt to set fire to; (fig) to inflame; **incendiarse** vr to catch fire; **incendiario, -a** adj incendiary

incendio [in'θendjo] nm fire

incentivo [inθen'tiβo] nm incentive

incertidumbre [inθerti'ðumbre] nf (inseguridad) uncertainty; (duda) doubt

incesante [inθe'sante] adj incessant

incesto [in'θesto] nm incest

incidencia [inθi'ðenθja] nf (Mat) incidence

incidente [inθi'ðente] nm incident

incidir [inθi'ðir] vi (influir) to influence; (afectar) to affect

incienso [in'θjenso] nm incense

incierto, -a [in'θjerto, a] adj uncertain

incineración [inθinera'θjon] nf incineration; (de cadáveres) cremation

incinerar [inθine'rar] vt to burn; (cadáveres) to cremate

incisión [inθi'sjon] nf incision

incisivo, -a [inθi'siβo, a] adj sharp, cutting; (fig) incisive

incitar [inθi'tar] vt to incite, rouse

inclemencia [inkle'menθja] nf (severidad) harshness, severity; (del tiempo) inclemency

inclinación [inklina'θjon] nf (gen) inclination; (de tierras) slope, incline; (de cabeza) nod, bow; (fig) leaning, bent

inclinar [inkli'nar] vt (cabeza) to nod, bow ▷ vi to lean, slope; **inclinarse** vr to bow; (encorvarse) to

stoop; **~se a** (parecerse a) to take after, resemble; **~se ante** to bow down to; **me inclino a pensar que ...** I'm inclined to think that ...

incluir [inklu'ir] vt to include; (incorporar) to incorporate; (meter) to enclose

inclusive [inklu'siβe] adv inclusive ▷ prep including

incluso [in'kluso] adv even

incógnita [in'koɣnita] nf (Mat) unknown quantity

incógnito [in'koɣnito] nm: **de ~** incognito

incoherente [inkoe'rente] adj incoherent

incoloro, -a [inko'loro, a] adj colourless

incomodar [inkomo'ðar] vt to inconvenience; (molestar) to bother, trouble; (fastidiar) to annoy

incomodidad [inkomoði'ðað] nf inconvenience; (fastidio, enojo) annoyance; (de vivienda) discomfort

incómodo, -a [in'komoðo, a] adj (inconfortable) uncomfortable; (molesto) annoying; (inconveniente) inconvenient

incomparable [inkompa'raβle] adj incomparable

incompatible [inkompa'tiβle] adj incompatible

incompetente [inkompe'tente] adj incompetent

incompleto, -a [inkom'pleto, a] adj incomplete, unfinished

incomprensible [inkompren'siβle] adj incomprehensible

incomunicado, -a [inkomuni'kaðo, a] adj (aislado) cut off, isolated; (confinado) in solitary confinement

incondicional [inkondiθjo'nal] adj unconditional; (apoyo) wholehearted; (partidario) staunch

inconfundible [inkonfun'diβle] adj unmistakable

incongruente [inkon'grwente] adj incongruous

inconsciente [inkons'θjente] adj

unconscious; thoughtless

inconsecuente [inkonse'kwente] *adj* inconsistent

inconstante [inkons'tante] *adj* inconstant

incontable [inkon'taβle] *adj* countless, innumerable

inconveniencia [inkombe'njenθja] *nf* unsuitability, inappropriateness; (*descortesía*) impoliteness; **inconveniente** *adj* unsuitable; impolite ▷ *nm* obstacle; (*desventaja*) disadvantage; **el inconveniente es que ...** the trouble is that ...

incordiar [inkor'ðjar] (*fam*) *vt* to bug, annoy

incorporar [inkorpo'rar] *vt* to incorporate; **incorporarse** *vr* to sit up; **-se a** to join

incorrecto, -a [inko'rrekto, a] *adj* (*gen*) incorrect, wrong; (*comportamiento*) bad-mannered

incorregible [inkorre'xiβle] *adj* incorrigible

incrédulo, -a [in'kreðulo, a] *adj* incredulous, unbelieving; sceptical

increíble [inkre'iβle] *adj* incredible

incremento [inkre'mento] *nm* increment; (*aumento*) rise, increase

increpar [inkre'par] *vt* to reprimand

incruento, -a [in'krwento, a] *adj* bloodless

incrustar [inkrus'tar] *vt* to incrust; (*piedras: en joya*) to inlay

incubar [inku'βar] *vt* to incubate

inculcar [inkul'kar] *vt* to inculcate

inculto, -a [in'kulto, a] *adj* (*persona*) uneducated; (*grosero*) uncouth ▷ *nm/f* ignoramus

incumplimiento [inkumpli'mjento] *nm* non-fulfilment; **incumplimiento de contrato** breach of contract

incurrir [inku'rrir] *vi*: **~ en** to incur; (*crimen*) to commit

indagar [inda'ɣar] *vt* to investigate; to search; (*averiguar*) to ascertain

indecente [inde'θente] *adj* indecent,

improper; (*lascivo*) obscene

indeciso, -a [inde'θiso, a] *adj* (*por decidir*) undecided; (*vacilante*) hesitant

indefenso, -a [inde'fenso, a] *adj* defenceless

indefinido, -a [indefi'niðo, a] *adj* indefinite; (*vago*) vague, undefined

indemne [in'demne] *adj* (*objeto*) undamaged; (*persona*) unharmed, unhurt

indemnizar [indemni'θar] *vt* to indemnify; (*compensar*) to compensate

independencia [indepen'denθja] *nf* independence

independiente [indepen'djente] *adj* (*libre*) independent; (*autónomo*) self-sufficient

indeterminado, -a [indetermi'naðo, a] *adj* indefinite; (*desconocido*) indeterminate

India ['indja] *nf*: **la ~** India

indicación [indika'θjon] *nf* indication; (*señal*) sign; (*sugerencia*) suggestion, hint

indicado, -a [indi'kaðo, a] *adj* (*momento, método*) right; (*tratamiento*) appropriate; (*solución*) likely

indicador [indika'ðor] *nm* indicator; (*Tec*) gauge, meter

indicar [indi'kar] *vt* (*mostrar*) to indicate, show; (*termómetro etc*) to read, register; (*señalar*) to point to

índice ['indiθe] *nm* index; (*catálogo*) catalogue; (*Anat*) index finger, forefinger; **índice de materias** table of contents

indicio [in'diθjo] *nm* indication, sign; (*en pesquisa etc*) clue

indiferencia [indife'renθja] *nf* indifference; (*apatía*) apathy; **indiferente** *adj* indifferent

indígena [in'dixena] *adj* indigenous, native ▷ *nm/f* native

indigestión [indixes'tjon] *nf* indigestion

indigesto, -a [indi'xesto, a] *adj* (*alimento*) indigestible; (*fig*) turgid

indignación [indiɣna'θjon] *nf*

indignation

indignar [indiɣ'nar] vt to anger, make indignant; **indignarse** vr: **~se por** to get indignant about

indigno, -a [in'diɣno, a] adj (despreciable) low, contemptible; (inmerecido) unworthy

indio, -a ['indjo, a] adj, nm/f Indian

indirecta [indi'rekta] nf insinuation, innuendo; (sugerencia) hint

indirecto, -a [indi'rekto, a] adj indirect

indiscreción [indiskre'θjon] nf (imprudencia) indiscretion; (irreflexión) tactlessness; (acto) gaffe, faux pas

indiscreto, -a [indis'kreto, a] adj indiscreet

indiscutible [indisku'tiβle] adj indisputable, unquestionable

indispensable [indispen'saβle] adj indispensable, essential

indispuesto, -a [indis'pwesto, a] adj (enfermo) unwell, indisposed

indistinto, -a [indis'tinto, a] adj indistinct; (vago) vague

individual [indiβi'ðwal] adj individual; (habitación) single ▷ nm (Deporte) singles sg

individuo, -a [indi'βiðwo, a] adj, nm individual

índole ['indole] nf (naturaleza) nature; (clase) sort, kind

inducir [indu'θir] vt to induce; (inferir) to infer; (persuadir) to persuade

indudable [indu'ðaβle] adj undoubted; (incuestionable) unquestionable

indultar [indul'tar] vt (perdonar) to pardon, reprieve; (librar de pago) to exempt; **indulto** nm pardon; exemption

industria [in'dustrja] nf industry; (habilidad) skill; **industrial** adj industrial ▷ nm industrialist

inédito, -a [in'eðito, a] adj (texto) unpublished; (nuevo) new

ineficaz [inefi'kaθ] adj (inútil) ineffective; (ineficiente) inefficient

ineludible [inelu'ðiβle] adj inescapable, unavoidable

ineptitud [inepti'tuð] nf ineptitude, incompetence; **inepto, -a** adj inept, incompetent

inequívoco, -a [ine'kiβoko, a] adj unequivocal; (inconfundible) unmistakable

inercia [in'erθja] nf inertia; (pasividad) passivity

inerte [in'erte] adj inert; (inmóvil) motionless

inesperado, -a [inespe'raðo, a] adj unexpected, unforeseen

inestable [ines'taβle] adj unstable

inevitable [ineβi'taβle] adj inevitable

inexacto, -a [inek'sakto, a] adj inaccurate; (falso) untrue

inexperto, -a [inek'sperto, a] adj (novato) inexperienced

infalible [infa'liβle] adj infallible; (plan) foolproof

infame [in'fame] adj infamous; (horrible) dreadful; **infamia** nf infamy; (deshonra) disgrace

infancia [in'fanθja] nf infancy, childhood

infantería [infante'ria] nf infantry

infantil [infan'til] adj (pueril, aniñado) infantile; (cándido) childlike; (literatura, ropa etc) children's

infarto [in'farto] nm (tb: **~ de miocardio**) heart attack

infatigable [infati'ɣaβle] adj tireless, untiring

infección [infek'θjon] nf infection; **infeccioso, -a** adj infectious

infectar [infek'tar] vt to infect; **infectarse** vr to become infected

infeliz [infe'liθ] adj unhappy, wretched ▷ nmf wretch

inferior [infe'rjor] adj inferior; (situación) lower ▷ nmf inferior, subordinate

inferir [infe'rir] vt (deducir) to infer, deduce; (causar) to cause

infidelidad [infiðeli'ðað] nf (gen)

infidelity, unfaithfulness

infiel [in'fjel] *adj* unfaithful, disloyal; (*erróneo*) inaccurate ▷ *nm/f* infidel, unbeliever

infierno [in'fjerno] *nm* hell

infiltrarse [infil'trarse] *vr*: ~ **en** to infiltrate in(to); (*persona*) to work one's way in(to)

ínfimo, -a ['infimo, a] *adj* (*más bajo*) lowest; (*despreciable*) vile, mean

infinidad [infini'ðað] *nf* infinity; (*abundancia*) great quantity

infinito, -a [infi'nito, a] *adj, nm* infinite

inflación [infla'θjon] *nf* (*hinchazón*) swelling; (*monetaria*) inflation; (*fig*) conceit

inflamable [infla'maßle] *adj* flammable

inflamar [infla'mar] *vt* (*Med*: *fig*) to inflame; **inflamarse** *vr* to catch fire; to become inflamed

inflar [in'flar] *vt* (*hinchar*) to inflate, blow up; (*fig*) to exaggerate; **inflarse** *vr* to swell (up); (*fig*) to get conceited

inflexible [inflek'siβle] *adj* inflexible; (*fig*) unbending

influencia [influ'enθja] *nf* influence

influir [influ'ir] *vt* to influence

influjo [in'fluxo] *nm* influence

influya *etc vb* V **influir**

influyente [influ'jente] *adj* influential

información [informa'θjon] *nf* information; (*noticias*) news *sg*; (*Jur*) inquiry; **I~** (*oficina*) Information Office; (*mostrador*) Information Desk; (*Tel*) Directory Enquiries

informal [infor'mal] *adj* (*gen*) informal

informar [infor'mar] *vt* (*gen*) to inform; (*revelar*) to reveal, make known ▷ *vi* (*Jur*) to plead; (*denunciar*) to inform; (*dar cuenta de*) to report on; **informarse** *vr* to find out; **~se de** to inquire into

informática [infor'matika] *nf* computer science, information technology

informe [in'forme] *adj* shapeless ▷ *nm* report

infracción [infrak'θjon] *nf* infraction, infringement

infravalorar [infrabalo'rar] *vt* to undervalue, underestimate

infringir [infrin'xir] *vt* to infringe, contravene

infundado, -a [infun'daðo, a] *adj* groundless, unfounded

infundir [infun'dir] *vt* to infuse, instil

infusión [infu'sjon] *nf* infusion; **infusión de manzanilla** camomile tea

ingeniería [inxenje'ria] *nf* engineering; **ingeniería genética** genetic engineering; **ingeniero, -a** *nm/f* engineer; **ingeniero civil o de caminos** civil engineer

ingenio [in'xenjo] *nm* (*talento*) talent; (*agudeza*) wit; (*habilidad*) ingenuity, inventiveness; **ingenio azucarero** (*LAM*) sugar refinery; **ingenioso, -a** [inxe'njoso, a] *adj* ingenious, clever; (*divertido*) witty; **ingenuo, -a** *adj* ingenuous

ingerir [inxe'rir] *vt* to ingest; (*tragar*) to swallow; (*consumir*) to consume

Inglaterra [ingla'terra] *nf* England

ingle ['ingle] *nf* groin

inglés, -esa [in'gles, esa] *adj* English ▷ *nm/f* Englishman(-woman) ▷ *nm* (*Ling*) English

ingrato, -a [in'grato, a] *adj* (*gen*) ungrateful

ingrediente [ingre'ðjente] *nm* ingredient

ingresar [ingre'sar] *vt* (*dinero*) to deposit ▷ *vi* to come in; **~ en el hospital** to go into hospital

ingreso [in'greso] *nm* (*entrada*) entry; (*en hospital etc*) admission; **ingresos** *nmpl* (*dinero*) income *sg*; (*Com*) takings *pl*

inhabitable [inaβi'taβle] *adj* uninhabitable

inhalar [ina'lar] *vt* to inhale

inhibir [ini'βir] *vt* to inhibit

inhóspito, -a [i'nospito, a] adj
(región, paisaje) inhospitable
inhumano, -a [inu'mano, a] adj
inhuman
inicial [ini'θjal] adj, nf initial
iniciar [ini'θjar] vt (persona) to
initiate; (empezar) to begin, commence;
(conversación) to start up
iniciativa [iniθja'tiβa] nf initiative;
iniciativa privada private enterprise
ininterrumpido, -a
[ininterrum'piðo, a] adj
uninterrupted
injertar [inxer'tar] vt to graft;
injerto nm graft
injuria [in'xurja] nf (agravio, ofensa)
offence; (insulto) insult
    No confundir **injuria** con la palabra
    inglesa injury.
injusticia [inxus'tiθja] nf injustice
injusto, -a [in'xusto, a] adj unjust,
unfair
inmadurez [inmaðu'reθ] nf
immaturity
inmediaciones [inmeðja'θjones]
nfpl neighbourhood sg, environs
inmediato, -a [inme'ðjato, a]
adj immediate; (contiguo)
adjoining; (rápido) prompt; (próximo)
neighbouring, next; **de ~** immediately
inmejorable [inmexo'raβle] adj
unsurpassable; (precio) unbeatable
inmenso, -a [in'menso, a] adj
immense, huge
inmigración [inmiɣra'θjon] nf
immigration
inmobiliaria [inmoβi'ljarja] nf
estate agency
inmolar [inmo'lar] vt to immolate,
sacrifice
inmoral [inmo'ral] adj immoral
inmortal [inmor'tal] adj immortal;
inmortalizar vt to immortalize
inmóvil [in'moβil] adj immobile
inmueble [in'mweβle] adj: **bienes
~s** real estate, landed property ▷ nm
property
inmundo, -a [in'mundo, a] adj

filthy
inmune [in'mune] adj: **~ (a)** (Med)
immune (to)
inmunidad [inmuni'ðað] nf
immunity
inmutarse [inmu'tarse] vr to turn
pale; **no se inmutó** he didn't turn a hair
innato, -a [in'nato, a] adj innate
innecesario, -a [inneθe'sarjo, a] adj
unnecessary
innovación [innoβa'θjon] nf
innovation
innovar [inno'βar] vt to introduce
inocencia [ino'θenθja] nf innocence
inocentada [inoθen'taða] nf
practical joke
inocente [ino'θente] adj (ingenuo)
naive, innocent; (inculpable) innocent;
(sin malicia) harmless ▷ nm/f simpleton;
el día de los (Santos) I~s ≈ April
Fools' Day

> **DÍA DE LOS (SANTOS)
> INOCENTES**
>
> The 28th December, el **día de los
> (Santos) Inocentes**, is when
> the Church commemorates the
> story of Herod's slaughter of the
> innocent children of Judaea.
> On this day Spaniards play
> **inocentadas** (practical jokes) on
> each other, much like our April
> Fool's Day pranks.

inodoro [ino'ðoro] nm toilet,
lavatory (BRIT)
inofensivo, -a [inofen'siβo, a] adj
inoffensive, harmless
inolvidable [inolβi'ðaβle] adj
unforgettable
inoportuno, -a [inopor'tuno, a] adj
untimely; (molesto) inconvenient
inoxidable [inoksi'ðaβle] adj: **acero
~** stainless steel
inquietar [inkje'tar] vt to worry,
trouble; **inquietarse** vr to worry,
get upset; **inquieto, -a** adj anxious,

worried; **inquietud** nf anxiety, worry

inquilino, -a [inki'lino, a] nm/f tenant

insaciable [insa'θjaβle] adj insatiable

inscribir [inskri'βir] vt to inscribe; **~ a algn en** (lista) to put sb on; (censo) to register sb on

inscripción [inskrip'θjon] nf inscription; (Escol etc) enrolment; (en censo) registration

insecticida [insekti'θiða] nm insecticide

insecto [in'sekto] nm insect

inseguridad [inseɣuri'ðað] nf insecurity; **inseguridad ciudadana** lack of safety in the streets

inseguro, -a [inse'ɣuro, a] adj insecure; (inconstante) unsteady; (incierto) uncertain

insensato, -a [insen'sato, a] adj foolish, stupid

insensible [insen'siβle] adj (gen) insensitive; (movimiento) imperceptible; (sin sentido) numb

insertar [inser'tar] vt to insert

inservible [inser'βiβle] adj useless

insignia [in'siɣnja] nf (señal distintiva) badge; (estandarte) flag

insignificante [insiɣnifi'kante] adj insignificant

insinuar [insi'nwar] vt to insinuate, imply

insípido, -a [in'sipiðo, a] adj insipid

insistir [insis'tir] vi to insist; **~ en algo** to insist on sth; (enfatizar) to stress sth

insolación [insola'θjon] nf (Med) sunstroke

insolente [inso'lente] adj insolent

insólito, -a [in'solito, a] adj unusual

insoluble [inso'luβle] adj insoluble

insomnio [in'somnjo] nm insomnia

insonorizado, -a [insonori'θaðo, a] adj (cuarto etc) soundproof

insoportable [insopor'taβle] adj unbearable

inspección [inspek'θjon] nf inspection, check; **inspeccionar** vt (examinar) to inspect, examine; (controlar) to check

inspector, a [inspek'tor, a] nm/f inspector

inspiración [inspira'θjon] nf inspiration

inspirar [inspi'rar] vt to inspire; (Med) to inhale; **inspirarse** vr: **~se en** to be inspired by

instalación [instala'θjon] nf (equipo) fittings pl, equipment; **instalación eléctrica** wiring

instalar [insta'lar] vt (establecer) to instal; (erguir) to set up, erect; **instalarse** vr to establish o.s.; (en una vivienda) to move into

instancia [ins'tanθja] nf (Jur) petition; (ruego) request; **en última ~** as a last resort

instantáneo, -a [instan'taneo, a] adj instantaneous; **café ~** instant coffee

instante [ins'tante] nm instant, moment; **al ~** right now

instar [ins'tar] vt to press, urge

instaurar [instau'rar] vt (costumbre) to establish; (normas, sistema) to bring in, introduce; (gobierno) to instal

instigar [insti'ɣar] vt to instigate

instinto [ins'tinto] nm instinct; **por ~** instinctively

institución [institu'θjon] nf institution, establishment

instituir [institu'ir] vt to establish; (fundar) to found; **instituto** nm (gen) institute; (Esp Escol) ≈ comprehensive (BRIT) o high (US) school

institutriz [institu'triθ] nf governess

instrucción [instruk'θjon] nf instruction

instructor [instruk'tor] nm instructor

instruir [instru'ir] vt (gen) to instruct; (enseñar) to teach, educate

instrumento [instru'mento] nm (gen) instrument; (herramienta) tool,

implement

insubordinarse [insuβorði'narse] vr to rebel

insuficiente [insufi'θjente] adj (gen) insufficient; (Escol: calificación) unsatisfactory

insular [insu'lar] adj insular

insultar [insul'tar] vt to insult; **insulto** nm insult

insuperable [insupe'raβle] adj (excelente) unsurpassable; (problema etc) insurmountable

insurrección [insurrek'θjon] nf insurrection, rebellion

intachable [inta'tʃaβle] adj irreproachable

intacto, -a [in'takto, a] adj intact

integral [inte'yral] adj integral; (completo) complete; **pan ~** wholemeal (BRIT) o wholewheat (US) bread

integrar [inte'yrar] vt to make up, compose; (Mat: fig) to integrate

integridad [inteyri'ðað] nf wholeness; (carácter) integrity

íntegro, -a [in'teyro, a] adj whole, entire; (honrado) honest

intelectual [intelek'twal] adj, nmf intellectual

inteligencia [inteli'xenθja] nf intelligence; (ingenio) ability

inteligente [inteli'xente] adj intelligent

intemperie [intem'perje] nf: **a la ~** out in the open, exposed to the elements

intención [inten'θjon] nf (gen) intention, purpose; **con segundas intenciones** maliciously; **con ~** deliberately

intencionado, -a [intenθjo'naðo, a] adj deliberate; **mal ~** ill-disposed, hostile

intensidad [intensi'ðað] nf (gen) intensity; (Elec, Tec) strength; **llover con ~** to rain hard

intenso, -a [in'tenso, a] adj intense; (sentimiento) profound, deep

intentar [inten'tar] vt (tratar) to try, attempt; **intento** nm attempt

interactivo, -a [interak'tiβo, a] adj (Inform) interactive

intercalar [interka'lar] vt to insert

intercambio [inter'kambjo] nm exchange, swap

interceder [interθe'ðer] vi to intercede

interceptar [interθep'tar] vt to intercept

interés [inte'res] nm (gen) interest; (parte) share, part; (pey) self-interest; **intereses creados** vested interests

interesado, -a [intere'saðo, a] adj interested; (prejuiciado) prejudiced; (pey) mercenary, self-seeking

interesante [intere'sante] adj interesting

interesar [intere'sar] vt, vi to interest, be of interest to; **interesarse** vr: **~se en** o **por** to take an interest in

interferir [interfe'rir] vt to interfere with; (Tel) to jam ▷ vi to interfere

interfón [inter'fon] (MÉX) nm entry phone

interino, -a [inte'rino, a] adj temporary ▷ nm/f temporary holder of a post; (Med) locum; (Escol) supply teacher

interior [inte'rjor] adj inner, inside; (Com) domestic, internal ▷ nm interior, inside; (fig) soul, mind; **Ministerio del I~** ≈ Home Office (BRIT) ≈ Department of the Interior (US); **interiorista** (ESP) nmf interior designer

interjección [interxek'θjon] nf interjection

interlocutor, a [interloku'tor, a] nm/f speaker

intermedio, -a [inter'meðjo, a] adj intermediate ▷ nm interval

interminable [intermi'naβle] adj endless

intermitente [intermi'tente] adj intermittent ▷ nm (Auto) indicator

internacional [internaθjo'nal] adj international

internado [inter'naðo] nm boarding

school

internar [inter'nar] vt to intern; (en un manicomio) to commit; **internarse** vr (penetrar) to penetrate

internauta [inter'nauta] nmf web surfer, Internet user

Internet, internet [inter'net] nm of Internet

interno, -a [in'terno, a] adj internal, interior; (Pol etc) domestic ▷ nm/f (alumno) boarder

interponer [interpo'ner] vt to interpose, put in; **interponerse** vr to intervene

interpretación [interpreta'θjon] nf interpretation

interpretar [interpre'tar] vt to interpret; (Teatro, Mús) to perform, play; **intérprete** nmf (Ling) interpreter, translator; (Mús, Teatro) performer, artist(e)

interrogación [interroxa'θjon] nf interrogation; (Ling: tb: **signo de ~**) question mark

interrogar [interro'xar] vt to interrogate, question

interrumpir [interrum'pir] vt to interrupt

interrupción [interrup'θjon] nf interruption

interruptor [interrup'tor] nm (Elec) switch

intersección [intersek'θjon] nf intersection

interurbano, -a [interur'βano, a] adj: **llamada interurbana** long-distance call

intervalo [inter'βalo] nm interval; (descanso) break

intervenir [interβe'nir] vt (controlar) to control, supervise; (Med) to operate on ▷ vi (participar) to take part, participate; (mediar) to intervene

interventor, a [interβen'tor, a] nm/f inspector; (Com) auditor

intestino [intes'tino] nm (Med) intestine

intimar [inti'mar] vi to become

friendly

intimidad [intimi'ðað] nf intimacy; (familiaridad) familiarity; (vida privada) private life; (Jur) privacy

íntimo, -a [ˈintimo, a] adj intimate

intolerable [intoleˈraβle] adj intolerable, unbearable

intoxicación [intoksikaˈθjon] nf poisoning; **intoxicación alimenticia** food poisoning

intranet [intraˈnet] nf intranet

intranquilo, -a [intranˈkilo, a] adj worried

intransitable [intransiˈtaβle] adj impassable

intrépido, -a [inˈtrepiðo, a] adj intrepid

intriga [inˈtrixa] nf intrigue; (plan) plot; **intrigar** vt, vi to intrigue

intrínseco, -a [inˈtrinseko, a] adj intrinsic

introducción [introðukˈθjon] nf introduction

introducir [introðuˈθir] vt (gen) to introduce; (moneda etc) to insert; (Inform) to input, enter

intromisión [intromiˈsjon] nf interference, meddling

introvertido, -a [introβerˈtiðo, a] adj, nm/f introvert

intruso, -a [inˈtruso, a] adj intrusive ▷ nm/f intruder

intuición [intwiˈθjon] nf intuition

inundación [inundaˈθjon] nf flood(ing); **inundar** vt to flood; (fig) to swamp, inundate

inusitado, -a [inusiˈtaðo, a] adj unusual, rare

inútil [inˈutil] adj useless; (esfuerzo) vain, fruitless

inutilizar [inutiliˈθar] vt to make o render useless

invadir [imbaˈðir] vt to invade

inválido, -a [imˈbaliðo, a] adj invalid ▷ nm/f invalid

invasión [imbaˈsjon] nf invasion

invasor, a [imbaˈsor, a] adj invading ▷ nm/f invader

invención [imben'θjon] *nf* invention

inventar [imben'tar] *vt* to invent

inventario [imben'tarjo] *nm* inventory

invento [im'bento] *nm* invention

inventor, a [imben'tor, a] *nm/f* inventor

invernadero [imberna'ðero] *nm* greenhouse

inverosímil [imbero'simil] *adj* implausible

inversión [imber'sjon] *nf* (Com) investment

inverso, -a [im'berso, a] *adj* inverse, opposite; **en el orden ~** in reverse order; **a la inversa** inversely, the other way round

inversor, a [imber'sor, a] *nm/f* (Com) investor

invertir [imber'tir] *vt* (Com) to invest; (volcar) to turn upside down; (tiempo etc) to spend

investigación [imbestixa'θjon] *nf* investigation; (Escol) research; **investigación y desarrollo** research and development

investigar [imbesti'xar] *vt* to investigate; (Escol) to do research into

invierno [im'bjerno] *nm* winter

invisible [imbi'siβle] *adj* invisible

invitación [imbita'θjon] *nf* invitation

invitado, -a [imbi'taðo, a] *nm/f* guest

invitar [imbi'tar] *vt* to invite; (incitar) to entice; (pagar) to buy, pay for

invocar [imbo'kar] *vt* to invoke, call on

involucrar [imbolu'krar] *vt*: **~ en** to involve in; **involucrarse** *vr* (persona): **~se en** to get mixed up in

involuntario, -a [imbolun'tarjo, a] *adj* (movimiento, gesto) involuntary; (error) unintentional

inyección [injek'θjon] *nf* injection

inyectar [injek'tar] *vt* to inject

iPod® ['ipoð] (*pl* **-s**) *nm* iPod®

○ **PALABRA CLAVE**

ir [ir] *vi* 1 to go; (*a pie*) to walk; (*viajar*) to travel; **ir caminando** to walk; **fui en tren** I went o travelled by train; **¡(ahora) voy!** (I'm just) coming!
2: **ir (a) por**: **ir (a) por el médico** to fetch the doctor
3 (*progresar: persona, cosa*) to go; **el trabajo va muy bien** work is going very well; **¿cómo te va?** how are things going?; **me va muy bien** I'm getting on very well; **le fue fatal** it went awfully badly for him
4 (*funcionar*): **el coche no va muy bien** the car isn't running very well
5: **te va estupendamente ese color** that colour suits you fantastically well
6 (*locuciones*): **¿vino? - ¡que va!** did he come? - of course not!; **vamos, no llores** come on, don't cry; **¡vaya coche!** what a car!, that's some car!
7: **no vaya a ser: tienes que correr, no vaya a ser que pierdas el tren** you'll have to run so as not to miss the train
8 (+ *pp*): **iba vestido muy bien** he was very well dressed
9: **ni me** *etc* **va ni me** *etc* **viene** I *etc* don't care
▷ *vb aux* 1 **ir a**: **voy/iba a hacerlo hoy** I am/was going to do it today
2 (+ *gerundio*): **iba anocheciendo** it was getting dark; **todo se me iba aclarando** everything was gradually becoming clearer to me
3 (+ *pp* = *pasivo*): **van vendidos 300 ejemplares** 300 copies have been sold so far

irse *vr* 1: **¿por dónde se va al zoológico?** which is the way to the zoo?
2 (*marcharse*) to leave; **ya se habrán ido** they must already have left o gone

ira ['ira] *nf* anger, rage

Irak [i'rak] nm = **Iraq**

Irán [i'ran] nm Iran; **iraní** adj, nmf Iranian

Iraq [i'rak] nm Iraq; **iraquí** adj, nmf Iraqi

iris ['iris] nm inv (tb: **arco ~**) rainbow; (Anat) iris

Irlanda [ir'landa] nf Ireland; **Irlanda del Norte** Northern Ireland; **irlandés, -esa** adj Irish ▷ nm/f Irishman(-woman); **los irlandeses** the Irish

ironía [iro'nia] nf irony; **irónico, -a** adj ironic(al)

IRPF nm abr (= Impuesto sobre la Renta de las Personas Físicas) (personal) income tax

irreal [irre'al] adj unreal

irregular [irreɣu'lar] adj (gen) irregular; (situación) abnormal

irremediable [irreme'ðjaβle] adj irremediable; (vicio) incurable

irreparable [irrepa'raβle] adj (daños) irreparable; (pérdida) irrecoverable

irrespetuoso, -a [irrespe'twoso, a] adj disrespectful

irresponsable [irrespon'saβle] adj irresponsible

irreversible [irreβer'sible] adj irreversible

irrigar [irri'ɣar] vt to irrigate

irrisorio, -a [irri'sorjo, a] adj derisory, ridiculous

irritar [irri'tar] vt to irritate, annoy

irrupción [irrup'θjon] nf irruption; (invasión) invasion

isla ['isla] nf island

Islam [is'lam] nm Islam; **las enseñanzas del ~** the teachings of Islam; **islámico, -a** adj Islamic

islandés, -esa [islan'des, esa] adj Icelandic ▷ nm/f Icelander

Islandia [is'landja] nf Iceland

isleño, -a [is'leɲo, a] adj island cpd ▷ nm/f islander

Israel [isra'el] nm Israel; **israelí** adj, nmf Israeli

istmo ['istmo] nm isthmus

Italia [i'talja] nf Italy; **italiano, -a** adj, nm/f Italian

itinerario [itine'rarjo] nm itinerary, route

ITV (ESP) nf abr (= inspección técnica de vehículos) roadworthiness test, = MOT (BRIT)

IVA ['iβa] nm abr (= impuesto sobre el valor añadido) VAT

izar [i'θar] vt to hoist

izdo, -a abr (= izquierdo, a) l

izquierda [iθ'kjerda] nf left; (Pol) left (wing); **a la ~** (estar) on the left; (torcer etc) (to the) left

izquierdo, -a [iθ'kjerðo, a] adj left

J

jabalí [xaβa'li] nm wild boar
jabalina [xaβa'lina] nf javelin
jabón [xa'βon] nm soap
jaca ['xaka] nf pony
jacal [xa'kal] (MÉX) nm shack
jacinto [xa'θinto] nm hyacinth
jactarse [xak'tarse] vr to boast, brag
jadear [xaðe'ar] vi to pant, gasp
for breath
jaguar [xa'ɣwar] nm jaguar
jaiba ['xaiβa] (LAM) nf crab
jalar [xa'lar] (LAM) vt to pull
jalea [xa'lea] nf jelly
jaleo [xa'leo] nm racket, uproar;
armar un ~ to kick up a racket
jalón [xa'lon] (LAM) nm tug
jamás [xa'mas] adv never
jamón [xa'mon] nm ham; **jamón**
dulce o **de York** cooked ham; **jamón**
serrano cured ham
Japón [xa'pon] nm Japan; **japonés,**
-esa adj, nm/f Japanese ▷ nm (Ling)
Japanese
jaque ['xake] nm (Ajedrez) check;
jaque mate checkmate

jaqueca [xa'keka] nf (very bad)
headache, migraine
jarabe [xa'raβe] nm syrup
jardín [xar'ðin] nm garden; **jardín**
infantil o **de infancia** nursery (school);
jardinería nf gardening; **jardinero, -a**
nm/f gardener
jardinaje [xarði'naxe] nm gardening
jarra ['xarra] nf jar; (jarro) jug
jarro ['xarro] nm jug
jarrón [xa'rron] nm vase
jaula ['xaula] nf cage
jauría [xau'ria] nf pack of hounds
jazmín [xaθ'min] nm jasmine
J.C. abr (=Jesucristo) J.C.
jeans [jins, dʒins] (LAM) nmpl jeans,
denims; **unos ~** a pair of jeans
jefatura [xefa'tura] nf (tb: **~ de**
policía) police headquarters sg
jefe, -a ['xefe, a] nm/f (gen) chief,
head; (patrón) boss; **jefe de cocina**
chef; **jefe de estación** stationmaster;
jefe de Estado head of state; **jefe de**
estudios (Escol) director of studies;
jefe de gobierno head of government
jengibre [xen'xiβre] nm ginger
jeque ['xeke] nm sheik
jerárquico, -a [xe'rarkiko, a] adj
hierarchic(al)
jerez [xe'reθ] nm sherry
jerga ['xerxa] nf jargon
jeringa [xe'ringa] nf syringe;
(LAM: molestia) annoyance, bother;
jeringuilla nf syringe
jeroglífico [xero'xlifiko] nm
hieroglyphic
jersey [xer'sei] (pl **~s**) nm jersey,
pullover, jumper
Jerusalén [xerusa'len] n Jerusalem
Jesucristo [xesu'kristo] nm Jesus
Christ
jesuita [xe'swita] adj, nm Jesuit
Jesús [xe'sus] nm Jesus; **¡~!** good
heavens!; (al estornudar) bless you!
jinete [xi'nete] nmf
horseman(-woman), rider
jipijapa [xipi'xapa] (LAM) nm straw
hat

jirafa [xi'rafa] *nf* giraffe
jirón [xi'ron] *nm* rag, shred
jitomate [xito'mate] (*MÉX*) *nm* tomato
joder [xo'ðer] (*fam!*) *vt, vi* to fuck (!)
jogging ['joxin] (*RPL*) *nm* tracksuit (*BRIT*), sweat suit (*US*)
jornada [xor'naða] *nf* (*viaje de un día*) day's journey; (*camino o viaje entero*) journey; (*día de trabajo*) working day
jornal [xor'nal] *nm* (day's) wage; **jornalero** *nm* (day) labourer
joroba [xo'roβa] *nf* hump, hunched back; **jorobado, -a** *adj* hunchbacked ▷ *nm/f* hunchback
jota ['xota] *nf* (*the letter*) J; (*danza*) Aragonese dance; **no saber ni** ~ to have no idea
joven ['xoβen] (*pl* **jóvenes**) *adj* young ▷ *nm* young man, youth ▷ *nf* young woman, girl
joya ['xoja] *nf* jewel, gem; (*fig: persona*) gem; **joyas de fantasía** costume o imitation jewellery; **joyería** *nf* (*joyas*) jewellery; (*tienda*) jeweller's (shop); **joyero** *nm* (*persona*) jeweller; (*caja*) jewel case
juanete [xwa'nete] *nm* (*del pie*) bunion
jubilación [xuβila'θjon] *nf* (*retiro*) retirement
jubilado, -a [xuβi'laðo, a] *adj* retired ▷ *nm/f* pensioner (*BRIT*), senior citizen
jubilar [xuβi'lar] *vt* to pension off, retire; (*fam*) to discard; **jubilarse** *vr* to retire
júbilo ['xuβilo] *nm* joy, rejoicing; **jubiloso, -a** *adj* jubilant
judía [xu'ðia] *nf* (*Culin*) bean; **judía blanca/verde** haricot/French bean; V tb **judío**
judicial [xuði'θjal] *adj* judicial
judío, -a [xu'ðio, a] *adj* Jewish ▷ *nm/f* Jew(ess)
judo ['juðo] *nm* judo
juego *etc* ['xweɣo] *vb* V **jugar** ▷ *nm* (*gen*) play; (*pasatiempo, partido*) game; (*en casino*) gambling; (*conjunto*) set;

fuera de ~ (*Deporte: persona*) offside; (: *pelota*) out of play; **juego de mesa** board game; **juego de palabras** pun, play on words; **Juegos Olímpicos** Olympic Games
juerga ['xwerɣa] (*ESP: fam*) *nf* binge; (*fiesta*) party; **ir de ~** to go out on a binge
jueves ['xweβes] *nm inv* Thursday
juez [xweθ] *nm/f* judge; **juez de instrucción** examining magistrate; **juez de línea** linesman; **juez de salida** starter
jugada [xu'ɣaða] *nf* play; **buena ~** good move o shot o stroke *etc*
jugador, a [xuɣa'ðor, a] *nm/f* player; (*en casino*) gambler
jugar [xu'ɣar] *vt, vi* to play; (*en casino*) to gamble; (*apostar*) to bet; **~ al fútbol** to play football
juglar [xu'ɣlar] *nm* minstrel
jugo ['xuɣo] *nm* (*Bot*) juice; (*fig*) essence, substance; **jugo de naranja** (*LAM*) orange juice; **jugoso, -a** *adj* juicy; (*fig*) substantial, important
juguete [xu'ɣete] *nm* toy; **juguetear** *vi* to play; **juguetería** *nf* toyshop
juguetón, -ona [xuɣe'ton, ona] *adj* playful
juicio [xwiθjo] *nm* judgement; (*razón*) sanity, reason; (*opinión*) opinion
julio ['xuljo] *nm* July
jumper ['dʒumper] (*LAM*) *nm* pinafore dress (*BRIT*), jumper (*US*)
junco ['xunko] *nm* rush, reed
jungla ['xuŋgla] *nf* jungle
junio ['xunjo] *nm* June
junta ['xunta] *nf* (*asamblea*) meeting, assembly; (*comité, consejo*) council, committee; (*Com, Finanzas*) board; (*Tec*) joint; **junta directiva** board of directors
juntar [xun'tar] *vt* to join, unite; (*maquinaria*) to assemble, put together; (*dinero*) to collect; **juntarse** *vr* to join, meet; (*reunirse: personas*) to meet, assemble; (*arrimarse*) to approach, draw closer; **~se con algn** to join sb

junto, -a ['xunto, a] *adj* joined; (*unido*) united; (*anexo*) near, close; (*contiguo, próximo*) next, adjacent ▷ *adv*: **todo ~** all at once; **~s** together; **~ a** near (to), next to; **~ con** (together) with

jurado [xu'raðo] *nm* (Jur: *individuo*) juror; (: *grupo*) jury; (*de concurso*: *grupo*) panel (of judges); (: *individuo*) member of a panel

juramento [xura'mento] *nm* oath; (*maldición*) oath, curse; **prestar ~** to take the oath; **tomar ~ a** to swear in, administer the oath to

jurar [xu'rar] *vt, vi* to swear; **~ en falso** to commit perjury; **tenérsela jurada a algn** to have it in for sb

jurídico, -a [xu'riðiko, a] *adj* legal

jurisdicción [xurisðik'θjon] *nf* (*poder, autoridad*) jurisdiction; (*territorio*) district

justamente [xusta'mente] *adv* justly, fairly; (*precisamente*) just, exactly

justicia [xus'tiθja] *nf* justice; (*equidad*) fairness, justice

justificación [xustifika'θjon] *nf* justification; **justificar** *vt* to justify

justo, -a ['xusto, a] *adj* (*equitativo*) just, fair, right; (*preciso*) exact, correct; (*ajustado*) tight ▷ *adv* (*precisamente*) exactly, precisely; (LAM: *apenas a tiempo*) just in time

juvenil [xuße'nil] *adj* youthful

juventud [xußen'tuð] *nf* (*adolescencia*) youth; (*jóvenes*) young people *pl*

juzgado [xuθ'ɣaðo] *nm* tribunal; (Jur) court

juzgar [xuθ'ɣar] *vt* to judge; **a ~ por ...** to judge by ..., judging by ...

k

kárate ['karate] *nm* karate

kg *abr* (= *kilogramo*) kg

kilo ['kilo] *nm* kilo; **kilogramo** *nm* kilogramme; **kilometraje** *nm* distance in kilometres = mileage; **kilómetro** *nm* kilometre; **kilovatio** *nm* kilowatt

kiosco ['kjosko] *nm* = **quiosco**

kleenex® [kli'neks] *nm* paper handkerchief, tissue

Kosovo [ko'soβo] *nm* Kosovo

km *abr* (= *kilómetro*) km

kv *abr* (= *kilovatio*) kw

l *abr* (= litro) l

la [la] *art def* the ▷ *pron* her; (Ud.) you; (cosa) it ▷ *nm* (Mús) la; **~ del sombrero rojo** the girl in the red hat; V *tb* **el**

laberinto [laβe'rinto] *nm* labyrinth

labio ['laβjo] *nm* lip

labor [la'βor] *nf* labour; (Agr) farm work; (tarea) job, task; (Costura) needlework; **labores domésticas** o **del hogar** household chores; **laborable** *adj* (Agr) workable; **día laborable** working day; **laboral** *adj* (accidente) at work; (jornada) working

laboratorio [laβora'torjo] *nm* laboratory

laborista [laβo'rista] *adj*: **Partido L~** Labour Party

labrador, a [laβra'ðor, a] *adj* farming *cpd* ▷ *nm/f* farmer

labranza [la'βranθa] *nf* (Agr) cultivation

labrar [la'βrar] *vt* (gen) to work; (madera etc) to carve; (fig) to cause, bring about

laca ['laka] *nf* lacquer

lacio, -a ['laθjo, a] *adj* (pelo) straight

lacón [la'kon] *nm* shoulder of pork

lactancia [lak'tanθja] *nf* lactation

lácteo, -a ['lakteo, a] *adj*: **productos ~s** dairy products

ladear [laðe'ar] *vt* to tip, tilt ▷ *vi* to tilt; **ladearse** *vr* to lean

ladera [la'ðera] *nf* slope

lado ['laðo] *nm* (gen) side; (fig) protection; (Mil) flank; **al ~ de** beside; **poner de ~** to put on its side; **poner a un ~** to put aside; **por todos ~s** on all sides, all round (BRIT)

ladrar [la'ðrar] *vi* to bark; **ladrido** *nm* bark, barking

ladrillo [la'ðriʎo] *nm* (gen) brick; (azulejo) tile

ladrón, -ona [la'ðron, ona] *nm/f* thief

lagartija [laɣar'tixa] *nf* (Zool) (small) lizard

lagarto [la'ɣarto] *nm* (Zool) lizard

lago ['laɣo] *nm* lake

lágrima ['laɣrima] *nf* tear

laguna [la'ɣuna] *nf* (lago) lagoon; (hueco) gap

lamentable [lamen'taβle] *adj* lamentable, regrettable; (miserable) pitiful

lamentar [lamen'tar] *vt* (sentir) to regret; (deplorar) to lament; **lamentarse** *vr* to lament; **lo lamento mucho** I'm very sorry

lamer [la'mer] *vt* to lick

lámina ['lamina] *nf* (plancha delgada) sheet; (para estampar, estampa) plate

lámpara ['lampara] *nf* lamp; **lámpara de alcohol/gas** spirit/gas lamp; **lámpara de pie** standard lamp

lana ['lana] *nf* wool

lancha ['lantʃa] *nf* launch; **lancha motora** motorboat, speedboat

langosta [laŋ'gosta] *nf* (crustáceo) lobster; (: de río) crayfish; **langostino** *nm* Dublin Bay prawn

lanza ['lanθa] *nf* (arma) lance, spear

lanzamiento [lanθa'mjento] *nm* (gen) throwing; (Náut, Com) launch;

launching; **lanzamiento de peso** putting the shot

lanzar [lan'θar] vt (gen) to throw; (Deporte: pelota) to bowl; (Náut, Com) to launch; (Jur) to evict; **lanzarse** vr to throw o.s.

lapa ['lapa] nf limpet

lapicero [lapi'θero] (CAM) nm (boligrafo) ballpoint pen, Biro®

lápida ['lapiða] nf stone; **lápida mortuoria** headstone

lápiz ['lapiθ] nm pencil; **lápiz de color** coloured pencil; **lápiz de labios** lipstick; **lápiz de ojos** eyebrow pencil

largar [lar'ɣar] vt (soltar) to release; (aflojar) to loosen; (lanzar) to launch; (fam) to let fly; (velas) to unfurl; (LAM: lanzar) to throw; **largarse** vr (fam) to beat it; **~se a** (cs: empezar) to start to

largo, -a ['larɣo, a] adj (longitud) long; (tiempo) lengthy; (fig) generous ▷ nm length; (Mús) largo; **dos años ~s** two long years; **tiene 9 metros de ~** it is 9 metres long; **a la larga** in the long run; **a lo ~ de** along; (tiempo) all through; throughout

No confundir **largo** con la palabra inglesa large.

largometraje nm feature film

laringe [la'rinxe] nf larynx; **laringitis** nf laryngitis

las [las] art def the ▷ pron them; **~ que cantan** the ones o women o girls who sing; V tb **el**

lasaña [la'saɲa] nf lasagne, lasagna

láser ['laser] nm laser

lástima ['lastima] nf (pena) pity; **dar ~** to be pitiful; **es una ~ que ...** it's a pity that ...; **¡qué ~!** what a pity!; **está hecha una ~** she looks pitiful

lastimar [lasti'mar] vt (herir) to wound; (ofender) to offend; **lastimarse** vr to hurt o.s.

lata ['lata] nf (metal) tin; (caja) tin (BRIT), can; (fam) nuisance; **en ~** tinned (BRIT), canned; **dar la ~** to be a nuisance

latente [la'tente] adj latent

lateral [late'ral] adj side cpd, lateral ▷ nm (Teatro) wings

latido [la'tiðo] nm (de corazón) beat

latifundio [lati'fundjo] nm large estate

latigazo [lati'ɣaθo] nm (golpe) lash; (sonido) crack

látigo ['latiɣo] nm whip

latín [la'tin] nm Latin

latino, -a [la'tino, a] adj Latin; **latinoamericano, -a** adj, nm/f Latin-American

latir [la'tir] vi (corazón, pulso) to beat

latitud [lati'tuð] nf (Geo) latitude

latón [la'ton] nm brass

laurel [lau'rel] nm (Bot) laurel; (Culin) bay

lava ['laβa] nf lava

lavabo [la'βaβo] nm (pila) washbasin; (tb: **~s**) toilet

lavado [la'βaðo] nm washing; (de ropa) laundry; (Arte) wash; **lavado de cerebro** brainwashing; **lavado en seco** dry-cleaning

lavadora [laβa'ðora] nf washing machine

lavanda [la'βanda] nf lavender

lavandería [laβande'ria] nf laundry; (automática) launderette

lavaplatos [laβa'platos] nm inv dishwasher

lavar [la'βar] vt to wash; (borrar) to wipe away; **lavarse** vr to wash o.s.; **~se las manos** to wash one's hands; **~se los dientes** to brush one's teeth; **~ y marcar** (pelo) to shampoo and set; **~ en seco** to dry-clean; **~ los platos** to wash the dishes

lavarropas [laβa'rropas] (RPL) nm inv washing machine

lavavajillas [laβaβa'xiʎas] nm inv dishwasher

laxante [lak'sante] nm laxative

lazarillo [laθa'riʎo] nm (tb: **perro ~**) guide dog

lazo [la'θo] nm knot; (lazada) bow; (para animales) lasso; (trampa) snare;

(vínculo) tie

le [le] pron (directo) him (o her); (: usted) you; (indirecto) him (o her o it); (: usted) to you

leal [le'al] adj loyal; **lealtad** nf loyalty

lección [lek'θjon] nf lesson

leche ['letʃe] nf milk; **tiene mala ~** (fam!) he's a swine (!); **leche condensada** condensed milk; **leche desnatada** skimmed milk

lechería [letʃe'ria] nf dairy

lecho ['letʃo] nm (cama: de río) bed; (Geo) layer

lechón [le'tʃon] nm sucking (BRIT) o suckling (US) pig

lechoso, -a [le'tʃoso, a] adj milky

lechuga [le'tʃuɣa] nf lettuce

lechuza [le'tʃuθa] nf owl

lector, a [lek'tor, a] nm/f reader ▷ nm: **~ de discos compactos** CD player

lectura [lek'tura] nf reading

leer [le'er] vt to read

legado [le'ɣaðo] nm (don) bequest; (herencia) legacy; (enviado) legate

legajo [le'ɣaxo] nm file

legal [le'ɣal] adj (gen) legal; (persona) trustworthy; **legalizar** [leɣaliθar] vt to legalize; (documento) to authenticate

legaña [le'ɣaɲa] nf sleep (in eyes)

legión [le'xjon] nf legion; **legionario, -a** adj legionary ▷ nm legionnaire

legislación [lexisla'θjon] nf legislation

legislar [lexis'lar] vi to legislate

legislatura [lexisla'tura] nf (Pol) period of office

legítimo, -a [le'xitimo, a] adj (genuino) authentic; (legal) legitimate

legua ['leɣwa] nf league

legumbres [le'ɣumbres] nfpl pulses

leído, -a [le'iðo, a] adj well-read

lejanía [lexa'nia] nf distance; **lejano, -a** adj far-off; (en el tiempo) distant; (fig) remote

lejía [le'xia] nf bleach

lejos ['lexos] adv far, far away; **a lo ~** in the distance; **de o desde ~** from afar;

~ de far from

lema ['lema] nm motto; (Pol) slogan

lencería [lenθe'ria] nf linen, drapery

lengua ['lengwa] nf tongue; (Ling) language; **morderse la ~** to hold one's tongue

lenguado [len'gwaðo] nm sole

lenguaje [len'gwaxe] nm language; **lenguaje de programación** program(m)ing language

lengüeta [len'gweta] nf (Anat) epiglottis; (zapatos) tongue; (Mús) reed

lente ['lente] nf lens; (lupa) magnifying glass; **lentes** nfpl lenses ▷ nmpl (LAM: gafas) glasses; **lentes bifocales/de sol** (LAM) bifocals/sunglasses; **lentes de contacto** contact lenses

lenteja [len'texa] nf lentil; **lentejuela** nf sequin

lentilla [len'tiλa] nf contact lens

lentitud [lenti'tuð] nf slowness; **con ~** slowly

lento, -a ['lento, a] adj slow

leña ['leɲa] nf firewood; **leñador, a** nm/f woodcutter

leño ['leɲo] nm (trozo de árbol) log; (madero) timber; (fig) blockhead

Leo ['leo] nm Leo

león [le'on] nm lion; **león marino** sea lion

leopardo [leo'parðo] nm leopard

leotardos [leo'tarðos] nmpl tights

lepra ['lepra] nf leprosy; **leproso, -a** nm/f leper

les [les] pron (directo) them; (: ustedes) you; (indirecto) to them; (: ustedes) to you

lesbiana [les'βjana] adj, nf lesbian

lesión [le'sjon] nf wound, lesion; (Deporte) injury; **lesionado, -a** adj injured ▷ nm/f injured person

letal [le'tal] adj lethal

letanía [leta'nia] nf litany

letra ['letra] nf letter; (escritura) handwriting; (Mús) lyrics pl; **letra de cambio** bill of exchange; **letra de imprenta** print; **letrado, -a**

learned ▷ nm/f lawyer; **letrero** nm (cartel) sign; (etiqueta) label

letrina [le'trina] nf latrine

leucemia [leu'θemja] nf leukaemia

levadura [leβa'ðura] nf (para el pan) yeast; (de cerveza) brewer's yeast

levantar [leβan'tar] vt (gen) to raise; (del suelo) to pick up; (hacia arriba) to lift (up); (plan) to make, draw up; (mesa) to clear; (campamento) to strike; (fig) to cheer up, hearten; **levantarse** vr to get up; (enderezarse) to straighten up; (rebelarse) to rebel; **el ánimo** to cheer up

levante [le'βante] nm east coast; **el L~** region of Spain extending from Castellón to Murcia

leve [leβe] adj light; (fig) trivial

levita [le'βita] nf frock coat

léxico ['leksiko] nm (vocabulario) vocabulary

ley [lei] nf (gen) law; (metal) standard

leyenda [le'jenda] nf legend

leyó etc vb V **leer**

liar [li'ar] vt to tie (up); (unir) to bind; (envolver) to wrap (up); (enredar) to confuse; (cigarrillo) to roll; **liarse** vr (fam) to get involved; **~se a palos** to get involved in a fight

Líbano ['liβano] nm: **el ~** the Lebanon

libélula [li'βelula] nf dragonfly

liberación [liβera'θjon] nf liberation; (de la cárcel) release

liberal [liβe'ral] adj, nmf liberal

liberar [liβe'rar] vt to liberate

libertad [liβer'tað] nf liberty, freedom; **libertad bajo fianza** bail; **libertad bajo palabra** parole; **libertad condicional** probation; **libertad de culto/de prensa/de comercio** freedom of worship/of the press/of trade

libertar [liβer'tar] vt (preso) to set free; (de una obligación) to release; (eximir) to exempt

libertino, -a [liβer'tino, a] adj permissive ▷ nm/f permissive person

libra ['liβra] nf pound; **L~** (Astrología) Libra; **libra esterlina** pound sterling

libramiento [liβra'mjento] (MÉX) nm ring road (BRIT), beltway (US)

librar [li'βrar] vt (de peligro) to save; (batalla) to wage, fight; (de impuestos) to exempt; (cheque) to make out; (Jur) to exempt; **librarse** vr: **~se de** to escape from, free o.s. from

libre ['liβre] adj free; (lugar) unoccupied; (asiento) vacant; (de deudas) free of debts; **~ de impuestos** free of tax; **tiro ~** free kick; **los 100 metros ~s** the 100 metres free-style (race); **al aire ~** in the open air

librería [liβre'ria] nf (tienda) bookshop

> No confundir **librería** con la palabra inglesa *library*.

librero, -a nm/f bookseller

libreta [li'βreta] nf notebook

libro ['liβro] nm book; **libro de bolsillo** paperback; **libro de texto** textbook; **libro electrónico** e-book

Lic. abr = **licenciado, a**

licencia [li'θenθja] nf (gen) licence; (permiso) permission; **licencia de caza** game licence; **licencia por enfermedad** (MÉX, RPL) sick leave; **licenciado, -a** adj licensed ▷ nm/f graduate; **licenciar** vt (empleado) to dismiss; (permitir) to permit, allow; (soldado) to discharge; (estudiante) to confer a degree upon; **licenciarse** vr: **licenciarse en Derecho** to graduate in law

licenciatura [liθenθja'tura] nf (título) degree; (estudios) degree course

lícito, -a ['liθito, a] adj (legal) lawful; (justo) fair, just; (permisible) permissible

licor [li'kor] nm spirits pl (BRIT), liquor (US); (de frutas etc) liqueur

licuadora [likwa'ðora] nf blender

líder ['liðer] nmf leader; **liderato** nm leadership; **liderazgo** nm leadership

lidia [liðja] nf bullfighting; (una lidia) bullfight; **toros de ~** fighting bulls; **lidiar** vt, vi to fight

liebre | 116

liebre ['ljeβre] nf hare

lienzo ['ljenθo] nm linen; (Arte) canvas; (Arq) wall

liga ['liɣa] nf (de medias) garter, suspender; (LAM: goma) rubber band; (confederación) league

ligadura [liɣa'ðura] nf bond, tie; (Med, Mús) ligature

ligamento [liɣa'mento] nm ligament

ligar [li'ɣar] vt (atar) to tie; (unir) to join; (Med) to bind up; (Mús) to slur ▷ vi to mix, blend; (fam) **(él) liga mucho** he pulls a lot of women; **ligarse** vr to commit o.s.

ligero, -a [li'ɣero, a] adj (de peso) light; (tela) thin; (rápido) swift, quick; (ágil) agile, nimble; (de importancia) slight; (de carácter) flippant, superficial ▷ adv: **a la ligera** superficially

liguero [li'ɣero] nm suspender (BRIT) o garter (US) belt

lija ['lixa] nf (Zool) dogfish; (tb: **papel de ~**) sandpaper

lila ['lila] nf lilac

lima ['lima] nf file; (Bot) lime; **lima de uñas** nailfile; **limar** vt to file

limitación [limita'θjon] nf limitation, limit

limitar [limi'tar] vt to limit; (reducir) to reduce, cut down ▷ vi: **~ con** to border on; **limitarse** vr: **~se a** to limit o.s. to

límite ['limite] nm (gen) limit; (fin) end; (frontera) border; **límite de velocidad** speed limit

limítrofe [li'mitrofe] adj neighbouring

limón [li'mon] nm lemon ▷ adj: **amarillo ~** lemon-yellow; **limonada** nf lemonade

limosna [li'mosna] nf alms pl; **vivir de ~** to live on charity

limpiador, a [limpja'ðor] (MÉX) nm = **limpiaparabrisas**

limpiaparabrisas [limpjapara'βrisas] nm inv windscreen (BRIT) o windshield (US) wiper

limpiar [lim'pjar] vt to clean; (con trapo) to wipe; (quitar) to wipe away; (zapatos) to shine, polish; (Inform) to debug; (fig) to clean up

limpieza [lim'pjeθa] nf (estado) cleanliness; (acto) cleaning; (: de las calles) cleansing; (: de zapatos) polishing; (habilidad) skill; (fig: Policía) clean-up; (pureza) purity; (Mil) **operación de ~** mopping-up operation; **limpieza en seco** dry cleaning

limpio, -a ['limpjo, a] adj clean; (moralmente) pure; (Com) clear, net; (fam) honest ▷ adv: **jugar ~** to play fair; **pasar a** (ESP) **o en** (LAM) **~** to make a clean copy of

lince ['linθe] nm lynx

linchar [lin'tʃar] vt to lynch

lindar [lin'dar] vi to adjoin; **~ con** to border on

lindo, -a ['lindo, a] adj pretty, lovely ▷ adv: **nos divertimos de lo ~** we had a marvellous time; **canta muy ~** (LAM) she sings beautifully

línea ['linea] nf (gen) line; **en ~** (Inform) on line; **línea aérea** airline; **línea de meta** goal line; (en carrera) finishing line; **línea discontinua** (Auto) broken line; **línea recta** straight line

lingote [lin'ɣote] nm ingot

lingüista [lin'ɣwista] nmf linguist; **lingüística** nf linguistics sg

lino ['lino] nm linen; (Bot) flax

linterna [lin'terna] nf torch (BRIT), flashlight (US)

lío ['lio] nm bundle; (fam) fuss; (desorden) muddle, mess; **armar un ~** to make a fuss

liquen ['liken] nm lichen

liquidación [likiða'θjon] nf liquidation; **venta de ~** clearance sale

liquidar [liki'ðar] vt (mercancías) to liquidate; (deudas) to pay off; (empresa) to wind up

líquido, -a ['likiðo, a] adj liquid; (ganancia) net ▷ nm liquid; **líquido imponible** net taxable income

lira ['lira] nf (Mús) lyre; (moneda) lira

lírico, -a ['liriko, a] *adj* lyrical

lirio ['lirjo] *nm* (Bot) iris

lirón [li'ron] *nm* (Zool) dormouse; (fig) sleepyhead

Lisboa [lis'βoa] *n* Lisbon

lisiar [li'sjar] *vt* to maim

liso, -a ['liso, a] *adj* (terreno) flat; (cabello) straight; (superficie) even; (tela) plain

lisonja [li'soŋxa] *nf* flattery

lista ['lista] *nf* list; (de alumnos) school register; (de libros) catalogue; (de platos) menu; (de precios) price list; **pasar ~** to call the roll; **tela de ~s** striped material; **lista de espera** waiting list; **lista de precios** price list; **listín** (*tb*: **listín telefónico** *o* **de teléfonos**) telephone directory

listo, -a ['listo, a] *adj* (perspicaz) smart, clever; (preparado) ready

listón [lis'ton] *nm* (de madera, metal) strip

litera [li'tera] *nf* (en barco, tren) berth; (en dormitorio) bunk, bunk bed

literal [lite'ral] *adj* literal

literario, -a [lite'rarjo, a] *adj* literary

literato, -a [lite'rato, a] *adj* literary ▷ *nm/f* writer

literatura [litera'tura] *nf* literature

litigio [li'tixjo] *nm* (Jur) lawsuit; (fig): **en ~ con** in dispute with

litografía [litoɣra'fia] *nf* lithography; (una litografía) lithograph

litoral [lito'ral] *adj* coastal ▷ *nm* coast, seaboard

litro ['litro] *nm* litre

lívido, -a [li'βiðo, a] *adj* livid

llaga ['ʎaɣa] *nf* wound

llama ['ʎama] *nf* flame; (Zool) llama

llamada [ʎa'maða] *nf* call; **llamada a cobro revertido** reverse-charge (BRIT) *o* collect (US) call; **llamada al orden** call to order; **llamada de atención** warning; **llamada local** (LAM) local call; **llamada metropolitana** (ESP) local call; **llamada por cobrar** (MÉX) reverse-charge (BRIT) *o* collect (US) call

llamamiento [ʎama'mjento] *nm* call

llamar [ʎa'mar] *vt* to call; (atención) to attract ▷ *vi* (por teléfono) to telephone; (a la puerta) to knock (o ring); (por señas) to beckon; (Mil) to call up; **llamarse** *vr* to be called, be named; **¿cómo se llama (usted)?** what's your name?

llamativo, -a [ʎama'tiβo, a] *adj* showy; (color) loud

llano, -a ['ʎano, a] *adj* (superficie) flat; (persona) straightforward; (estilo) clear ▷ *nm* plain, flat ground

llanta ['ʎanta] *nf* (ESP) (wheel) rim; **llanta de goma** (LAM: neumático) tyre; (: cámara) inner (tube); **llanta de repuesto** (LAM) spare tyre

llanto ['ʎanto] *nm* weeping

llanura [ʎa'nura] *nf* plain

llave ['ʎaβe] *nf* key; (del agua) tap; (Mecánica) spanner; (de la luz) switch; (Mús) key; **echar la ~** to lock up; **llave de contacto** (ESP Auto) ignition key; **llave de encendido** (LAM Auto) ignition key; **llave de paso** stopcock; **llave inglesa** monkey wrench; **llave maestra** master key; **llavero** *nm* keyring

llegada [ʎe'ɣaða] *nf* arrival

llegar [ʎe'ɣar] *vi* to arrive; (alcanzar) to reach; (bastar) to be enough; **llegarse** *vr*: **~se a** to approach; **~ a** to manage to, to succeed in; **~ a saber** to find out; **~ a ser** to become; **~ a las manos de** to come into the hands of

llenar [ʎe'nar] *vt* to fill; (espacio) to cover; (formulario) to fill in *o* up; (fig) to heap

lleno, -a ['ʎeno, a] *adj* full, filled; (repleto) full up ▷ *nm* (Teatro) full house; **dar de ~ contra un muro** to hit a wall head-on

llevadero, -a [ʎeβa'ðero, a] *adj* bearable, tolerable

llevar [ʎe'βar] *vt* to take; (ropa) to wear; (cargar) to carry; (quitar) to take away; (en coche) to drive; (transportar) to transport; (traer: dinero) to carry; (conducir) to lead; (Mat) to carry ▷ *vi* (suj: camino etc): **~ a** to lead to; **llevarse**

vt to carry off, take away; **llevamos dos días aquí** we have been here for two days; **él me lleva 2 años** he's 2 years older than me; **~ los libros** (*Com*) to keep the books; **~se bien** to get on well (together)

llorar [ʎo'rar] *vt, vi* to cry, weep; **~ de risa** to cry with laughter

llorón, -ona [ʎo'ron, ona] *adj* tearful ▷ *nm/f* cry-baby

lloroso, -a [ʎo'roso, a] *adj* (*gen*) weeping, tearful; (*triste*) sad, sorrowful

llover [ʎo'βer] *vi* to rain

llovizna [ʎo'βiθna] *nf* drizzle; **lloviznar** *vi* to drizzle

llueve etc *vb* V **llover**

lluvia ['ʎuβja] *nf* rain; **lluvia radioactiva** (radioactive) fallout; **lluvioso, -a** *adj* rainy

lo [lo] *art def*: **~ bel-** the beautiful, what is beautiful, that which is beautiful ▷ *pron* (*persona*) him; (*cosa*) it; **~ que sea** whatever; V tb **el**

loable [lo'aβle] *adj* praiseworthy

lobo ['loβo] *nm* wolf; **lobo de mar** (*fig*) sea dog

lóbulo ['loβulo] *nm* lobe

local [lo'kal] *adj* local ▷ *nm* place, site; (*oficinas*) premises *pl*; **localidad** *nf* (*barrio*) locality; (*lugar*) location; (*Teatro*) seat, ticket; **localizar** *vt* (*ubicar*) to locate, find; (*restringir*) to localize; (*situar*) to place)

loción [lo'θjon] *nf* lotion

loco, -a ['loko, a] *adj* mad ▷ *nm/f* lunatic, mad person; **estar ~ con o por algo/por algn** to be mad about sth/sb

locomotora [lokomo'tora] *nf* engine, locomotive

locuaz [lo'kwaθ] *adj* loquacious

locución [loku'θjon] *nf* expression

locura [lo'kura] *nf* madness; (*acto*) crazy act

locutor, a [loku'tor, a] *nm/f* (*Radio*) announcer; (*comentarista*) commentator; (*TV*) newsreader

locutorio [loku'torjo] *nm* (*en telefónica*) telephone booth

lodo ['loðo] *nm* mud

lógica ['loxika] *nf* logic

lógico, -a [lo'xiko, a] *adj* logical

login [lo'xin] *nm* login

logística [lo'xistika] *nf* logistics *sg*

logotipo [logo'tipo] *nm* logo

logrado, -a [lo'ðraðo, a] *adj* (*interpretación, reproducción*) polished, excellent

lograr [lo'xrar] *vt* to achieve; (*obtener*) to get, obtain; **~ hacer** to manage to do; **~ que algn venga** to manage to get sb to come

logro ['loxro] *nm* achievement, success

lóker ['loker] (*LAM*) *nm* locker

loma ['loma] *nf* hillock (*BRIT*), small hill

lombriz [lom'briθ] *nf* worm

lomo ['lomo] *nm* (*de animal*) back; (*Culin: de cerdo*) pork loin; (: *de vaca*) rib steak; (*de libro*) spine

lona ['lona] *nf* canvas

loncha ['lontʃa] *nf* = **lonja**

lonchería [lontʃe'ria] (*LAM*) *nf* snack bar, diner (*US*)

Londres ['londres] *n* London

longaniza [longa'niθa] *nf* pork sausage

longitud [lonxi'tuð] *nf* length; (*Geo*) longitude; **tener 3 metros de ~** to be 3 metres long; **longitud de onda** wavelength

lonja ['lonxa] *nf* slice; (*de tocino*) rasher; **lonja de pescado** fish market

loro ['loro] *nm* parrot

los [los] *art def* the ▷ *pron* them; (*ustedes*) you; **mis libros y ~ tuyos** my books and yours; V tb **el**

losa ['losa] *nf* stone

lote ['lote] *nm* portion; (*Com*) lot

lotería [lote'ria] *nf* lottery; (*juego*) lotto

⊜ LOTERÍA

⊜
⊜ Millions of pounds are spent
⊜ on lotteries each year in Spain,
⊜ two of which are state-run: the

Lotería Primitiva and the **Lotería Nacional**, with money raised going directly to the government.
● One of the most famous lotteries is run by the wealthy and influential society for the blind, "la ONCE".

loza ['loθa] nf crockery
lubina [lu'βina] nf sea bass
lubricante [luβri'kante] nm lubricant
lubricar [luβri'kar] vt to lubricate
lucha ['lutʃa] nf fight, struggle; **lucha de clases** class struggle; **lucha libre** wrestling; **luchar** vi to fight
lúcido, -a ['luθiðo, a] adj (persona) lucid; (mente) logical; (idea) crystal-clear
luciérnaga [lu'θjernaɣa] nf glow-worm
lucir [lu'θir] vt to illuminate, light (up); (ostentar) to show off ▷ vi (brillar) to shine; **lucirse** vr (irónico) to make a fool of o.s.
lucro ['lukro] nm profit, gain
lúdico, -a ['luðiko, a] adj (aspecto, actividad) play cpd
luego ['lweɣo] adv (después) next; (más tarde) later, afterwards
lugar [lu'ɣar] nm place; (sitio) spot; **en primer ~** in the first place, firstly; **en ~ de** instead of; **hacer ~** to make room; **fuera de ~** out of place; **sin ~ a dudas** without doubt, undoubtedly; **dar ~ a** to give rise to; **tener ~** to take place; **yo en su ~** if I were him; **lugar común** commonplace
lúgubre ['luɣuβre] adj mournful
lujo ['luxo] nm luxury; (fig) profusion, abundance; **de ~** luxury cpd, de luxe; **lujoso, -a** adj luxurious
lujuria [lu'xurja] nf lust
lumbre ['lumbre] nf fire; (para cigarrillo) light
luminoso, -a [lumi'noso, a] adj luminous, shining
luna ['luna] nf moon; (de un espejo) glass; (de gafas) lens; (fig) crescent; **estar en la ~** to have one's head in the

clouds; **luna de miel** honeymoon; **luna llena/nueva** full/new moon
lunar [lu'nar] adj lunar ▷ nm (Anat) mole; **tela de ~es** spotted material
lunes ['lunes] nm inv Monday
lupa ['lupa] nf magnifying glass
lustre ['lustre] nm polish; (fig) lustre; **dar ~ a** to polish
luto ['luto] nm mourning; **llevar el o vestirse de ~** to be in mourning
Luxemburgo [luksem'burɣo] nm Luxembourg
luz [luθ] (pl **luces**) nf light; **dar a ~ un niño** to give birth to a child; **sacar a la ~** to bring to light; **dar o encender** (ESP) o **prender** (LAM)/**apagar la ~** to switch the light on/off; **tener pocas luces** to be dim o stupid; **traje de luces** bullfighter's costume; **luces de tráfico** traffic lights; **luz de freno** brake light; **luz roja/verde** red/green light

m

m *abr* (= *metro*) m; (= *minuto*) m

macana [ma'kana] (*MÉX*) *nf* truncheon (*BRIT*), billy club (*US*)

macarrones [maka'rrones] *nmpl* macaroni *sg*

macedonia [maθe'ðonja] *nf* (tb: **~ de frutas**) fruit salad

maceta [ma'θeta] *nf* (*de flores*) pot of flowers; (*para plantas*) flowerpot

machacar [matʃa'kar] *vt* to crush, pound ▷ *vi* (*insistir*) to go on, keep on

machete [ma'tʃete] *nm* machete, (large) knife

machetear [matʃete'ar] (*MÉX*) *vt* to swot (*BRIT*), grind away (*US*)

machismo [ma'tʃismo] *nm* male chauvinism; **machista** *adj, nm* sexist

macho ['matʃo] *adj* male; (*fig*) virile ▷ *nm* male; (*fig*) he-man

macizo, -a [ma'θiθo, a] *adj* (*grande*) massive; (*fuerte, sólido*) solid ▷ *nm* mass, chunk

madeja [ma'ðexa] *nf* (*de lana*) skein, hank; (*de pelo*) mass, mop

madera [ma'ðera] *nf* wood; (*fig*) nature, character; **una ~** a piece of wood

madrastra [ma'ðrastra] *nf* stepmother

madre ['maðre] *adj* mother *cpd* ▷ *nf* mother; (*de vino etc*) dregs *pl*; **madre política/soltera** mother-in-law/ unmarried mother

Madrid [ma'ðrið] *n* Madrid

madriguera [maðri'ɣera] *nf* burrow

madrileño, -a [maðri'leɲo, a] *adj* of o from Madrid ▷ *nm/f* native of Madrid

madrina [ma'ðrina] *nf* godmother; (*Arq*) prop, shore; (*Tec*) brace; (*de boda*) bridesmaid

madrugada [maðru'ɣaða] *nf* early morning; (*alba*) dawn, daybreak

madrugador, a [maðruɣa'ðor, a] *adj* early-rising

madrugar [maðru'ɣar] *vi* to get up early; (*fig*) to get ahead

madurar [maðu'rar] *vt, vi* (*fruta*) to ripen; (*fig*) to mature; **madurez** *nf* ripeness; maturity; **maduro, -a** *adj* ripe; mature

maestra [ma'estra] *nf* V **maestro**

maestría [maes'tria] *nf* mastery; (*habilidad*) skill, expertise

maestro, -a [ma'estro, a] *adj* masterly; (*principal*) main ▷ *nm/f* master/mistress; (*profesor*) teacher ▷ *nm* (*autoridad*) authority; (*Mús*) maestro; (*experto*) master; **maestro albañil** master mason

magdalena [maɣða'lena] *nf* fairy cake

magia ['maxja] *nf* magic; **mágico, -a** *adj* magic(al) ▷ *nm/f* magician

magisterio [maxis'terjo] *nm* (*enseñanza*) teaching; (*profesión*) teaching profession; (*maestros*) teachers *pl*

magistrado [maxis'traðo] *nm* magistrate

magistral [maxis'tral] *adj* magisterial; (*fig*) masterly

magnate [maɣ'nate] *nm* magnate, tycoon

magnético, -a [maɣ'netiko, a] *adj*
magnetic

magnetofón [maɣneto'fon] *nm*
tape recorder

magnetófono [maɣne'tofono] *nm* =
magnetofón

magnífico, -a [maɣ'nifiko, a] *adj*
splendid, magnificent

magnitud [maɣni'tuð] *nf*
magnitude

mago, -a ['maɣo, a] *nm/f* magician;
los Reyes M~s the Three Wise Men

magro, -a ['maɣro, a] *adj* (*carne*) lean

mahonesa [mao'nesa] *nf*
mayonnaise

maître ['metre] *nm* head waiter

maíz [ma'iθ] *nm* maize (BRIT), corn
(US); sweet corn

majestad [maxes'tað] *nf* majesty

majo, -a ['maxo, a] *adj* nice; (*guapo*)
attractive, good-looking; (*elegante*)
smart

mal [mal] *adv* badly; (*equivocadamente*)
wrongly ▷ *adj* = **malo** ▷ *nm* evil;
(*desgracia*) misfortune; (*daño*) harm,
damage; (*Med*) illness; **~ que bien**
rightly or wrongly; **ir de ~ en peor** to
get worse and worse

malabarista [malaβa'rista] *nmf*
juggler

malaria [ma'larja] *nf* malaria

malcriado, -a [mal'krjaðo, a] *adj*
spoiled

maldad [mal'dað] *nf* evil,
wickedness

maldecir [malde'θir] *vt* to curse

maldición [maldi'θjon] *nf* curse

maldito, -a [mal'dito, a] *adj*
(*condenado*) damned; (*perverso*) wicked;
¡~ sea! damn it!

malecón [male'kon] (LAM) *nm* sea
front, promenade

maleducado, -a [maleðu'kaðo, a]
adj bad-mannered, rude

malentendido [malenten'diðo] *nm*
misunderstanding

malestar [males'tar] *nm* (*gen*)
discomfort; (*fig: inquietud*) uneasiness;

(*Pol*) unrest

maleta [ma'leta] *nf* case, suitcase;
(*Auto*) boot (BRIT), trunk (US); **hacer las
~s** to pack; **maletero** *nm* (*Auto*) boot
(BRIT), trunk (US); **maletín** *nm* small
case, bag

maleza [ma'leθa] *nf* (*malas hierbas*)
weeds *pl*; (*arbustos*) thicket

malgastar [malɣas'tar] *vt* (*tiempo,
dinero*) to waste; (*salud*) to ruin

malhechor, -a [male'tʃor, a] *nm/f*
delinquent

malhumorado, -a [malumo'raðo,
a] *adj* bad-tempered

malicia [ma'liθja] *nf* (*maldad*)
wickedness; (*astucia*) slyness, guile;
(*mala intención*) malice, spite; (*carácter
travieso*) mischievousness

maligno, -a [ma'liɣno, a] *adj* evil;
(*malévolo*) malicious; (*Med*) malignant

malla ['maʎa] *nf* mesh; (*de baño*)
swimsuit; (*de ballet, gimnasia*) leotard;
mallas *nfpl* tights; **malla de alambre**
wire mesh

Mallorca [ma'ʎorka] *nf* Majorca

malo, -a ['malo, a] *adj* bad, false
▷ *nm/f* villain; **estar ~** to be ill

malograr [malo'ɣrar] *vt* to spoil;
(*plan*) to upset; (*ocasión*) to waste

malparado, -a [malpa'raðo, a]
adj: **salir ~** to come off badly

malpensado, -a [malpen'saðo, a]
adj nasty

malteada [malte'aða] (LAM) *nf*
milkshake

maltratar [maltra'tar] *vt* to ill-treat,
mistreat

malvado, -a [mal'βaðo, a] *adj* evil,
villainous

Malvinas [mal'βinas] *nfpl* (*tb*: **Islas
~**) Falklands, Falkland Islands

mama ['mama] *nf* (*de animal*) teat; (*de
mujer*) breast

mamá [ma'ma] (*pl* **~s**) (*fam*) *nf* mum,
mummy

mamar [ma'mar] *vt, vi* to suck

mamarracho [mama'ratʃo] *nm*
sight, mess

mameluco [mameluko] (RPL) nm dungarees pl (BRIT), overalls pl (US)

mamífero [ma'mifero] nm mammal

mampara [mam'para] nf (entre habitaciones) partition; (biombo) screen

mampostería [mamposte'ria] nf masonry

manada [ma'naða] nf (Zool) herd; (: de leones) pride; (: de lobos) pack

manantial [manan'tjal] nm spring

mancha ['mantʃa] nf stain, mark; (Zool) patch; **manchar** vt (gen) to stain, mark; (ensuciar) to soil, dirty

manchego, -a [man'tʃexo, a] adj of o from La Mancha

manco, -a ['manko, a] adj (de un brazo) one-armed; (de una mano) one-handed; (fig) defective, faulty

mancuernas [man'kwernas] (MÉX) nfpl cufflinks

mandado [man'daðo] (LAM) nm errand

mandamiento [manda'mjento] nm (orden) order, command; (Rel) commandment

mandar [man'dar] vt (ordenar) to order; (dirigir) to lead, command; (enviar) to send; (pedir) to order, ask for ▷ vi to be in charge; (pey) to be bossy; **¿mande?** (MÉX: ¿cómo dice?) pardon?, excuse me?; ~ **hacer un traje** to have a suit made

mandarina [manda'rina] (ESP) nf tangerine, mandarin (orange)

mandato [man'dato] nm (orden) order; (Pol: período) term of office; (: territorio) mandate

mandíbula [man'diβula] nf jaw

mandil [man'dil] nm apron

mando ['mando] nm (Mil) command; (de país) rule; (el primer lugar) lead; (Pol) term of office; (Tec) control; ~ **a la izquierda** left-hand drive; **mando a distancia** remote control

mandón, -ona [man'don, ona] adj bossy, domineering

manejar [mane'xar] vt to manage; (máquina) to work, operate; (caballo etc) to handle; (casa) to run, manage; (LAM: coche) to drive; **manejarse** vr (comportarse) to act, behave; (arreglárselas) to manage; **manejo** nm (de bicicleta) handling; (de negocio) management, running; (LAM Auto) driving; (facilidad de trato) ease, confidence; **manejos** nmpl (intrigas) intrigues

manera [ma'nera] nf way, manner, fashion; **maneras** nfpl (modales) manners; **su ~ de ser** the way he is; (aire) his manner; **de ninguna** ~ no way, by no means; **de otra** ~ otherwise; **de todas ~s** at any rate; **no hay ~ de persuadirle** there's no way of convincing him

manga ['manga] nf (de camisa) sleeve; (de riego) hose

mango ['mango] nm handle; (Bot) mango

manguera [man'gera] nf hose

maní [ma'ni] (LAM) nm peanut

manía [ma'nia] nf (Med) mania; (fig: moda) rage, craze; (disgusto) dislike; (malicia) spite; **coger ~ a algn** to take a dislike to sb; **tener ~ a algn** to dislike sb; **maníaco, -a** adj maniac(al) ▷ nm/f maniac

maniático, -a [ma'njatiko, a] adj maniac(al) ▷ nm/f maniac

manicomio [mani'komjo] nm mental hospital (BRIT), insane asylum (US)

manifestación [manifesta'θjon] nf (declaración) statement, declaration; (de emoción) show, display; (Pol: desfile) demonstration; (: concentración) mass meeting

manifestar [manifes'tar] vt to show, manifest; (declarar) to state, declare; **manifiesto, -a** adj clear, manifest ▷ nm manifesto

manillar [mani'ʎar] nm handlebars pl

maniobra [ma'njoβra] nf manoeuvre; **maniobras** nfpl (Mil) manoeuvres; **maniobrar** vt to manoeuvre

manipulación [manipula'θjon] *nf* manipulation

manipular [manipu'lar] *vt* to manipulate; *(manejar)* to handle

maniquí [mani'ki] *nm* dummy ▷ *nmf* model

manivela [mani'βela] *nf* crank

manjar [man'xar] *nm* (tasty) dish

mano ['mano] *nf* hand; *(Zool)* foot, paw; *(de pintura)* coat; *(serie)* lot, series; **a ~** by hand; **a ~ derecha/izquierda** on the right/left-hand side); **de primera ~** (at) first hand; **de segunda ~** (at) second hand; **robo a ~ armada** armed robbery; **estrechar la ~ a algn** to shake sb's hand; **mano de obra** labour, manpower; **manos libres** *adj inv* (teléfono, dispositivo) hands-free ▷ *nm inv* hands-free kit

manojo [ma'noxo] *nm* handful, bunch; *(de llaves)* bunch

manopla [ma'nopla] *nf* mitten

manosear [manose'ar] *vt (tocar)* to handle, touch; *(desordenar)* to mess up, rumple; *(insistir en)* to overwork; *(LAM: acariciar)* to caress, fondle

manotazo [mano'taθo] *nm* slap, smack

mansalva [man'salβa]: **a ~** *adv* indiscriminately

mansión [man'sjon] *nf* mansion

manso, -a ['manso, a] *adj* gentle, mild; *(animal)* tame

manta ['manta] *nf* blanket

manteca [man'teka] *nf* fat; *(cs: mantequilla)* butter; **manteca de cerdo** lard

mantecado [mante'kaðo] (ESP) *nm* Christmas sweet made from flour, almonds and lard

mantel [man'tel] *nm* tablecloth

mantendré *etc vb* V **mantener**

mantener [mante'ner] *vt* to support, maintain; *(alimentar)* to sustain; *(conservar)* to keep; *(Tec)* to maintain, service; **mantenerse** *vr (seguir de pie)* to be still standing; *(no ceder)* to hold one's ground;

(subsistir) to sustain o.s., keep going; **mantenimiento** *nm* maintenance; sustenance; *(sustento)* support

mantequilla [mante'kiʎa] *nf* butter

mantilla [man'tiʎa] *nf* mantilla; **mantillas** *nfpl (de bebé)* baby clothes

manto ['manto] *nm (capa)* cloak; *(de ceremonia)* robe, gown

mantuve *etc vb* V **mantener**

manual [ma'nwal] *adj* manual ▷ *nm* manual, handbook

manuscrito, -a [manus'krito, a] *adj* handwritten ▷ *nm* manuscript

manutención [manuten'θjon] *nf* maintenance; *(sustento)* support

manzana [man'θana] *nf* apple; *(Arq)* block (of houses)

manzanilla [manθa'niʎa] *nf (planta)* camomile; *(infusión)* camomile tea

manzano [man'θano] *nm* apple tree

maña ['maɲa] *nf (gen)* skill, dexterity; *(pey)* guile; *(destreza)* trick, knack

mañana [ma'ɲana] *adv* tomorrow ▷ *nm* future ▷ *nf* morning; **de o por la ~** in the morning; **¡hasta ~!** I see you tomorrow!; **por la ~** tomorrow morning

mapa ['mapa] *nm* map

maple ['maple] (LAM) *nm* maple

maqueta [ma'keta] *nf (scale)* model

maquiladora [makila'ðora] (MÉX) *nf (Com)* bonded assembly plant

maquillaje [maki'ʎaxe] *nm* make-up; *(acto)* making up

maquillar [maki'ʎar] *vt* to make up; **maquillarse** *vr* to put on (some) make-up

máquina ['makina] *nf* machine; *(de tren)* locomotive, engine; *(Foto)* camera; *(fig)* machinery; **escrito a ~** typewriter; **máquina de afeitar** electric razor; **máquina de coser** sewing machine; **máquina de escribir** typewriter; **máquina fotográfica** camera

maquinaria [maki'narja] *nf (máquinas)* machinery; *(mecanismo)* mechanism, works *pl*

maquinilla [maki'niʎa] (ESP) *nf*

(tb: **~ de afeitar**) razor
maquinista [maki'nista] nmf (de
tren) engine driver; (Tec) operator;
(Náut) engineer
mar [mar] nm of sea; **~ adentro** out
at sea; **en alta ~** on the high seas; **la
~ de** (fam) lots of; **el Mar Negro/Báltico**
the Black/Baltic Sea
maraña [ma'raɲa] nf (maleza)
thicket; (confusión) tangle
maravilla [mara'βiʎa] nf marvel,
wonder; (Bot) marigold; **maravillar**
vt to astonish, amaze; **maravillarse**
vr to be astonished, be amazed;
maravilloso, -a adj wonderful,
marvellous
marca ['marka] nf (gen) mark;
(sello) stamp; (Com) make, brand; **de
~ excellent**, outstanding; **marca de
fábrica** trademark; **marca registrada**
registered trademark
marcado, -a [mar'kaðo, a] adj
marked, strong
marcador [marka'ðor] nm (Deporte)
scoreboard; (: persona) scorer
marcapasos [marka'pasos] nm inv
pacemaker
marcar [mar'kar] vt (gen) to mark;
(número de teléfono) to dial; (gol) to
score; (números) to record, keep a tally
of; (pelo) to set ▷ vi (Deporte) to score;
(Tel) to dial
marcha ['martʃa] nf march; (Tec)
running, working; (Auto) gear;
(velocidad) speed; (fig) progress;
(dirección) course; **poner en ~** to put
into gear; (fig) to set in motion, get
going; **dar ~ atrás** to reverse, put into
reverse; **estar en ~** to be under way,
be in motion
marchar [mar'tʃar] vi (ir) to go;
(funcionar) to work, go; **marcharse** vr
to go (away), leave
marchitar [martʃi'tar] vt to whither,
dry up; **marchitarse** vr (Bot) to wither;
(fig) to fade away; **marchito, -a** adj
withered, faded; (fig) in decline
marciano, -a [mar'θjano, a] adj,

nm/f Martian
marco ['marko] nm frame; (moneda)
mark; (fig) framework
marea [ma'rea] nf tide; **marea negra**
oil slick
marear [mare'ar] vt (fig) to annoy,
upset; (Med): **~ a algn** to make
sb feel sick; **marearse** vr (tener
náuseas) to feel sick; (desvanecerse)
to feel faint; (aturdirse) to feel dizzy;
(fam: emborracharse) to get tipsy
maremoto [mare'moto] nm tidal
wave
mareo [ma'reo] nm (náusea) sick
feeling; (en viaje) travel sickness;
(aturdimiento) dizziness; (fam: lata)
nuisance
marfil [mar'fil] nm ivory
margarina [marɣa'rina] nf
margarine
margarita [marɣa'rita] nf (Bot)
daisy; (Tip) daisywheel
margen ['marxen] nm (borde) edge,
border; (fig) margin, space ▷ nf (de
río etc) bank; **dar ~ para** to give an
opportunity for; **mantenerse al ~** to
keep out (of things)
marginar [marxi'nar] vt
(socialmente) to marginalize, ostracize
mariachi [ma'rjatʃi] nm (persona)
mariachi musician; (grupo) mariachi
band

MARIACHI

Mariachi music is the musical style
most characteristic of Mexico.
From the state of Jalisco in the 19th
century, this music spread rapidly
throughout the country, until each
region had its own particular style
of the Mariachi "sound". A Mariachi
band can be made up of several
singers, up to eight violins, two
trumpets, guitars, a "vihuela" (an
old form of guitar), and a harp. The
dance associated with this music
is called the "zapateado".

marica [ma'rika] (fam) nm sissy

maricón [mari'kon] (fam) nm queer

marido [ma'riðo] nm husband

marihuana [mari'wana] nf marijuana, cannabis

marina [ma'rina] nf navy; **marina mercante** merchant navy

marinero, -a [mari'nero, a] adj sea cpd ▷ nm sailor, seaman

marino, -a [ma'rino, a] adj sea cpd, marine ▷ nm sailor

marioneta [marjo'neta] nf puppet

mariposa [mari'posa] nf butterfly

mariquita [mari'kita] nf ladybird (BRIT), ladybug (US)

marisco [ma'risko] (ESP) nm shellfish inv, seafood; **mariscos** (LAM) nmpl = **marisco**

marítimo, -a [ma'ritimo, a] adj sea cpd, maritime

mármol ['marmol] nm marble

marqués, -esa [mar'kes, esa] nm/f marquis/marchioness

marrón [ma'rron] adj brown

marroquí [marro'ki] adj, nmf Moroccan ▷ nm Morocco (leather)

Marruecos [ma'rrwekos] nm Morocco

martes ['martes] nm inv Tuesday; **~ y trece** ≈ Friday 13th

MARTES Y TRECE

According to Spanish superstition Tuesday is an unlucky day, even more so if it falls on the 13th of the month.

martillo [mar'tiʎo] nm hammer

mártir ['martir] nmf martyr; **martirio** nm martyrdom; (fig) torture, torment

marxismo [mark'sismo] nm Marxism

marzo ['marθo] nm March

PALABRA CLAVE

más [mas] adj, adv **1 más (que o de)** (compar) more (than), ...+ er (than); **más grande/inteligente** bigger/more intelligent; **trabaja más (que yo)** he works more (than me); V tb **cada**
2 (superl): **el más** the most, ...+ est; **el más grande/inteligente (de)** the biggest/most intelligent (in)
3 (negativo): **no tengo más dinero** I haven't got any more money; **no viene más por aquí** he doesn't come here any more
4 (adicional): **no le veo más solución que ...** I see no other solution than to ...; **¿alguien más?** anybody else?
5 (+ adj: valor intensivo): **¡qué perro más sucio!** what a filthy dog!; **¡es más tonto!** he's so stupid!
6 (locuciones): **más o menos** more or less; **los más** most people; **es más** furthermore; **más bien** rather; **¡qué más da!** what does it matter!; V tb **no**
7: **por más: por más que te esfuerces** no matter how hard you try; **por más que quisiera ...** much as I should like to ...
8: **de más: veo que aquí estoy de más** I can see I'm not needed here; **tenemos uno de más** we've got one extra
▷ prep: **2 más 2 son 4** 2 and 2 are 4
▷ nm inv: **este trabajo tiene sus más y sus menos** this job's got its good points and its bad points

mas [mas] conj but

masa ['masa] nf (mezcla) dough; (volumen) volume, mass; (Física) mass; **en ~** en masse; **las ~s** (Pol) the masses

masacre [ma'sakre] nf massacre

masaje [ma'saxe] nm massage

máscara ['maskara] nf mask; **máscara antigás/de oxígeno** gas/oxygen mask; **mascarilla** nf (de *belleza, Med)* mask

masculino, -a [masku'lino, a] *adj* masculine; *(Bio)* male

masía [ma'sia] *nf* farmhouse

masivo, -a [ma'siβo, a] *adj* mass *cpd*

masoquista [maso'kista] *nmf* masochist

máster ['master] *(ESP)* nm master

masticar [masti'kar] *vt* to chew

mástil [ˈmastil] *nm (de navío)* mast; *(de guitarra)* neck

mastín [mas'tin] *nm* mastiff

masturbarse [mastur'βarse] *vr* to masturbate

mata ['mata] *nf (arbusto)* bush, shrub; *(de hierba)* tuft

matadero [mata'ðero] *nm* slaughterhouse, abattoir

matador, a [mata'ðor, a] *adj* killing ▷ *nm/f* killer ▷ *nm (Taur)* matador, bullfighter

matamoscas [mata'moskas] *nm inv (pala)* fly swat

matanza [ma'tanθa] *nf* slaughter

matar [ma'tar] *vt, vi* to kill; **matarse** *vr (suicidarse)* to kill o.s., commit suicide; *(morir)* to be o get killed; **~ el hambre** to stave off hunger

matasellos [mata'seʎos] *nm inv* postmark

mate ['mate] *adj* matt ▷ *nm (en ajedrez)* (check)mate; *(LAM: hierba)* maté; *(: vasija)* gourd

matemáticas [mate'matikas] *nfpl* mathematics; **matemático, -a** *adj* mathematical ▷ *nm/f* mathematician

materia [ma'terja] *nf (gen)* matter; *(Tec)* material; *(Escol)* subject; **en ~ de** on the subject of; **materia prima** raw material; **material** *adj* material ▷ *nm (Tec)* equipment; **materialista** *adj* materialist(ic); **materialmente** *adv* materially; *(fig)* absolutely

maternal [mater'nal] *adj* motherly, maternal

maternidad [materni'ðað] *nf* motherhood, maternity; **materno, -a**

adj maternal; *(lengua)* mother *cpd*

matinal [mati'nal] *adj* morning *cpd*

matiz [ma'tiθ] *nm* shade; **matizar** *vt (variar)* to vary; *(Arte)* to blend; **matizar de** to tinge with

matón [ma'ton] *nm* bully

matorral [mato'rral] *nm* thicket

matrícula [ma'trikula] *nf (registro)* register; *(Auto)* registration number; *(: placa)* number plate; **matrícula de honor** *(Univ)* top marks in a subject at university with the right to free registration the following year; **matricular** *vt* to register, enrol

matrimonio [matri'monjo] *nm (pareja)* (married) couple; *(unión)* marriage

matriz [ma'triθ] *nf (Anat)* womb; *(Tec)* mould

matrona [ma'trona] *nf (persona de edad)* matron; *(comadrona)* midwife

matufia [ma'tufja] *(RPL: fam)* nf put-up job

maullar [mau'ʎar] *vi* to mew, miaow

maxilar [maksi'lar] *nm* jaw(bone)

máxima [ˈmaksima] *nf* maxim

máximo, -a ['maksimo, a] *adj* maximum; *(más alto)* highest; *(más grande)* greatest ▷ *nm* maximum; **como ~** at most

mayo ['majo] *nm* May

mayonesa [majo'nesa] *nf* mayonnaise

mayor [ma'jor] *adj* main, chief; *(adulto)* adult; *(de edad avanzada)* elderly; *(Mús)* major; *(compar: de tamaño)* bigger; *(: de edad)* older; *(superl: de tamaño)* biggest; *(: de edad)* oldest ▷ *nm (adulto)* adult; **mayores** *nmpl (antepasados)* ancestors; **al por ~** wholesale; **mayor de edad** adult

mayoral [majo'ral] *nm* foreman

mayordomo [major'ðomo] *nm* butler

mayoría [majo'ria] *nf* majority, greater part

mayorista [majo'rista] *nmf* wholesaler

mayoritario, -a [majori'tarjo, a]
adj majority *cpd*

mayúscula [ma'juskula] *nf* capital
letter

mazapán [maθa'pan] *nm* marzipan

mazo ['maθo] *nm* (*martillo*) mallet; (*de flores*) bunch; (*Deporte*) bat

me [me] *pron* (*directo*) me; (*indirecto*)
(to) me; (*reflexivo*) (to) myself; **¡dá-lo!**
give it to me!

mear [me'ar] (*fam*) *vi* to pee, piss (!)

mecánica [me'kanika] *nf* (*Escol*)
mechanics *sg*; (*mecanismo*) mechanism;
V tb **mecánico**

mecánico, -a [me'kaniko, a] *adj*
mechanical ▷ *nm/f* mechanic

mecanismo [meka'nismo] *nm*
mechanism; (*marcha*) gear

mecanografía [mekanoɣra'fia]
nf typewriting; **mecanógrafo, -a**
nm/f typist

mecate [me'kate] (*MÉX, CAM*) *nm* rope

mecedora [meθe'ðora] *nf* rocking
chair

mecer [me'θer] *vt* (*cuna*) to rock;
mecerse *vr* to rock; (*rama*) to sway

mecha ['metʃa] *nf* (*de vela*) wick; (*de
bomba*) fuse

mechero [me'tʃero] *nm* (*cigarette*)
lighter

mechón [me'tʃon] *nm* (*gen*) tuft; (*de
pelo*) lock

medalla [me'ðaʎa] *nf* medal

media ['meðja] *nf* stocking;
(*LAM: calcetín*) sock; (*promedio*) average;
medias [me'ðjas] *nfpl* (*ropa interior*)
tights

mediado, -a [me'ðjaðo, a] *adj* half-
full; (*trabajo*) half-completed; **a ~s de**
in the middle of, halfway through

mediano, -a [me'ðjano, a] *adj*
(*regular*) medium, average; (*mediocre*)
mediocre

medianoche [meðja'notʃe] *nf*
midnight

mediante [me'ðjante] *adv* by
(means of), through

mediar [me'ðjar] *vi* (*interceder*) to

mediate, intervene

medicamento [meðika'mento] *nm*
medicine, drug

medicina [meði'θina] *nf* medicine

médico, -a ['meðiko, a] *adj* medical
▷ *nm/f* doctor

medida [me'ðiða] *nf* measure;
(*medición*) measurement; (*prudencia*)
moderation, prudence; **en cierta/
gran ~** up to a point/to a great extent;
un traje a la ~ a made-to-measure
suit; **~ de cuello** collar size; **a ~ de**
in proportion to; (*de acuerdo con*) in
keeping with; **a ~ que** (*conforme*) as;
medidor (*LAM*) *nm* meter

medio, -a ['meðjo, a] *adj* half (a);
(*punto*) mid, middle; (*promedio*) average
▷ *adv* half ▷ *nm* (*centro*) middle,
centre; (*promedio*) average; (*método*)
means, way; (*ambiente*) environment;
medios *nmpl* means, resources;
~ litro half a litre; **las tres y media**
half past three; **a ~ terminar** half
finished; **pagar a medias** to share the
cost; **medio ambiente** environment;
medio de transporte means of
transport; **Medio Oriente** Middle East;
medios de comunicación media;
medioambiental *adj* (*política, efectos*)
environmental

mediocre [me'ðjokre] *adj*
mediocre

mediodía [meðjo'ðia] *nm* midday,
noon

medir [me'ðir] *vt, vi* (*gen*) to measure

meditar [meði'tar] *vt* to ponder,
think over, meditate on; (*planear*) to
think out

mediterráneo, -a [meðite'rraneo,
a] *adj* Mediterranean ▷ *nm*: **el M~** the
Mediterranean

médula ['meðula] *nf* (*Anat*) marrow;
médula espinal spinal cord

medusa [me'ðusa] (*ESP*) *nf* jellyfish

megáfono [me'ɣafono] *nm*
megaphone

megapíxel [meɣa'piksel] (*pl*
megapixels *or* **~es**) *nm* megapixel

mejicano, -a [mexi'kano, a] *adj*, *nm/f* Mexican

Méjico ['mexiko] *nm* Mexico

mejilla [me'xiʎa] *nf* cheek

mejillón [mexi'ʎon] *nm* mussel

mejor [me'xor] *adj*, *adv* (*compar*) better; (*superl*) best; **a lo ~** probably; (*quizá*) maybe; **~ dicho** rather; **tanto ~** so much the better

mejora [me'xora] *nf* improvement; **mejorar** *vt* to improve, make better ▷ *vi* to improve, get better; **mejorarse** *vr* to improve, get better

melancólico, -a [melan'koliko, a] *adj* (*triste*) sad, melancholy; (*soñador*) dreamy

melena [me'lena] *nf* (*de persona*) long hair; (*Zool*) mane

mellizo, -a [me'ʎiθo, a] *adj*, *nm/f* twin

melocotón [meloko'ton] (*ESP*) *nm* peach

melodía [melo'ðia] *nf* melody, tune

melodrama [melo'ðrama] *nm* melodrama; **melodramático, -a** *adj* melodramatic

melón [me'lon] *nm* melon

membrete [mem'brete] *nm* letterhead

membrillo [mem'briʎo] *nm* quince; **(carne de) ~** quince jelly

memoria [me'morja] *nf* (*gen*) memory; **memorias** *nfpl* (*de autor*) memoirs; **memorizar** *vt* to memorize

menaje [me'naxe] *nm* (*tb*: **artículos de ~**) household items

mencionar [menθjo'nar] *vt* to mention

mendigo, -a [men'diɣo, a] *nm/f* beggar

menear [mene'ar] *vt* to move; **menearse** *vr* to shake; (*balancearse*) to sway; (*moverse*) to move; (*fig*) to get a move on

menestra [me'nestra] *nf* (*tb*: **~ de verduras**) vegetable stew

menopausia [meno'pausja] *nf* menopause

menor [me'nor] *adj* (*más pequeño: compar*) smaller; (*: superl*) smallest; (*más joven: compar*) younger; (*: superl*) youngest; (*Mús*) minor ▷ *nmf* (*joven*) young person, juvenile; **no tengo la ~ idea** I haven't the faintest idea; **al por ~** retail; **menor de edad** person under age

Menorca [me'norka] *nf* Minorca

○ **PALABRA CLAVE**

menos [menos] *adj* **1**: **menos (que o de: compar: cantidad)** less (than); (*: número*) fewer (than); **con menos entusiasmo** with less enthusiasm; **menos gente** fewer people; *V tb* **cada**

2 (*superl*): **es el que menos culpa tiene** he is the least to blame
▷ *adv* **1** (*compar*): **menos (que o de)** less (than); **me gusta menos que el otro** I like it less than the other one
2 (*superl*): **es el menos listo (de su clase)** he's the least bright in his class; **de todas ellas es la que menos me agrada** out of all of them she's the one I like least

3 (*locuciones*): **no quiero verle y menos visitarle** I don't want to see him, let alone visit him; **tenemos siete de menos** we're seven short; **(por) lo menos** at (the very) least; **¡menos mal!** thank goodness!
▷ *prep* except; (*cifras*) minus; **todos menos él** everyone except (for) him; **5 menos 2** 5 minus 2; **las 7 menos 10 (hora)** 10 to 7
▷ *conj*: **a menos que: a menos que venga mañana** unless he comes tomorrow

menospreciar [menospre'θjar] *vt* to underrate, undervalue; (*despreciar*) to scorn, despise

mensaje [men'saxe] *nm* message; **enviar un ~ a algn** (*por móvil*) to text sb, send sb a text message; **mensaje**

de texto text message; **mensaje electrónico** email; **mensajero, -a** *nm/f* messenger

menso, -a ['menso, a] (*MÉX: fam*) *adj* stupid

menstruación [menstrua'θjon] *nf* menstruation

mensual [men'swal] *adj* monthly; **100 euros ~es** 100 euros a month; **mensualidad** *nf* (*salario*) monthly salary; (*Com*) monthly payment, monthly instalment

menta ['menta] *nf* mint

mental [men'tal] *adj* mental; **mentalidad** *nf* mentality; **mentalizar** *vt* (*sensibilizar*) to make aware; (*convencer*) to convince; (*padres*) to prepare (mentally); **mentalizarse** *vr* (*concienciarse*) to become aware; **mentalizarse (de)** to get used to the idea (of); **mentalizarse de que ...** (*convencerse*) to get it into one's head that ...

mente ['mente] *nf* mind

mentir [men'tir] *vi* to lie

mentira [men'tira] *nf* (*una mentira*) lie; (*acto*) lying; (*invención*) fiction; **parece mentira que ...** it seems incredible that ..., I can't believe that ...; **mentiroso, -a** [menti'roso, a] *adj* lying ⊳ *nm/f* liar

menú [me'nu] (*pl* **-s**) *nm* menu; **menú del día** set menu; **menú turístico** tourist menu

menudencias [menu'ðenθjas] (*LAM*) *nfpl* giblets

menudo, -a [me'nuðo, a] *adj* (*pequeño*) small, tiny; (*sin importancia*) petty, insignificant; **¡~ negocio!** (*fam*) some deal!; **a ~** often, frequently

meñique [me'nike] *nm* little finger

mercadillo [merka'ðiʎo] (*ESP*) *nm* flea market

mercado [mer'kaðo] *nm* market; **mercado de pulgas** (*LAM*) flea market

mercancía [merkan'θia] *nf* commodity; **mercancías** *nfpl* goods, merchandise *sg*

mercenario, -a [merθe'narjo, a] *adj, nm* mercenary

mercería [merθe'ria] *nf* haberdashery (*BRIT*), notions *pl* (*US*); (*tienda*) haberdasher's (*BRIT*), notions store (*US*)

mercurio [mer'kurjo] *nm* mercury

merecer [mere'θer] *vt* to deserve, merit ⊳ *vi* to be deserving, be worthy; **merece la pena** it's worthwhile; **merecido, -a** *adj* (well) deserved; **llevar su merecido** to get one's deserts

merendar [meren'dar] *vt* to have for tea ⊳ *vi* to have tea; (*en el campo*) to have a picnic; **merendero** *nm* open-air cafe

merengue [me'renge] *nm* meringue

meridiano [meri'ðjano] *nm* (*Geo*) meridian

merienda [me'rjenda] *nf* (light) tea, afternoon snack; (*de campo*) picnic

mérito ['merito] *nm* merit; (*valor*) worth, value

merluza [mer'luθa] *nf* hake

mermelada [merme'laða] *nf* jam

mero, -a ['mero, a] *adj* mere; (*MÉX, CAM: fam*) very

merodear [meroðe'ar] *vi*: **~ por** to prowl about

mes [mes] *nm* month

mesa ['mesa] *nf* table; (*de trabajo*) desk; (*Geo*) plateau; **poner/quitar la ~** to lay/clear the table; **mesa electoral** officials in charge of a polling station; **mesa redonda** (*reunión*) round table; **mesero, -a** (*LAM*) *nm/f* waiter/waitress

meseta [me'seta] *nf* (*Geo*) plateau, tableland

mesilla [me'siʎa] *nf* (*tb*: **~ de noche**) bedside table

mesón [me'son] *nm* inn

mestizo, -a [mes'tiθo, a] *adj* half-caste, of mixed race ⊳ *nm/f* half-caste

meta ['meta] *nf* goal; (*de carrera*) finish

metabolismo [metaβo'lismo] *nm* metabolism

metáfora | 182

metáfora [me'tafora] nf metaphor
metal [me'tal] nm (materia) metal;
(Mús) brass; **metálico, -a** adj metallic;
(de metal) metal; ⊳ nm (dinero contante)
cash
meteorología [meteorolo'xia] nf
meteorology
meter [me'ter] vt (colocar) to put,
place; (introducir) to put in, insert;
(involucrar) to involve; (causar) to make,
cause; **meterse** vr: **~se en** to go into,
enter; (fig) to interfere in, meddle
in; **~se a** to start; **~se a escritor** to
become a writer; **~se con uno** to
provoke sb, pick a quarrel with sb
meticuloso, -a [metiku'loso, a] adj
meticulous, thorough
metódico, -a [me'toðiko, a] adj
methodical
método ['metoðo] nm method
metralleta [metra'ʎeta] nf sub-
machine-gun
métrico, -a ['metriko, a] adj metric
metro ['metro] nm metre; (tren)
underground (BRIT), subway (US)
metrosexual [metrosek'swal] adj,
nm metrosexual
mexicano, -a [mexi'kano, a] adj,
nm/f Mexican
México ['mexiko] nm Mexico;
Ciudad de ~ Mexico City
mezcla ['meθkla] nf mixture;
mezcladora (MÉX) nf (tb: **mezcladora
de cemento**) cement mixer; **mezclar**
vt to mix (up); **mezclarse** vr to mix,
mingle; **mezclarse en** to get mixed up
in, get involved in
mezquino, -a [meθ'kino, a] adj
mean
mezquita [meθ'kita] nf mosque
mg. abr (= miligramo) mg
mi [mi] adj pos my ⊳ nm (Mús) E
mí [mi] pron me; myself
mía pron V **mío**
michelín [mitʃe'lin] (fam) nm (de
grasa) spare tyre
microbio [mi'kroβjo] nm microbe
micrófono [mi'krofono] nm

microphone
microondas [mikro'ondas] nm inv
(tb: **horno ~**) microwave (oven)
microscopio [mikro'skopjo] nm
microscope
miedo ['mjeðo] nm fear; (nerviosismo)
apprehension, nervousness; **tener ~** to
be afraid; **de ~** wonderful, marvellous;
hace un frío de ~ (fam) it's terribly cold;
miedoso, -a adj fearful, timid
miel [mjel] nf honey
miembro ['mjembro] nm limb;
(socio) member; **miembro viril** penis
mientras ['mjentras] conj while;
(duración) as long as ⊳ adv meanwhile;
~ tanto meanwhile
miércoles ['mjerkoles] nm inv
Wednesday
mierda ['mjerða] (fam!) nf shit (!)
miga ['mixa] nf crumb; (fig: meollo)
essence; **hacer buenas ~s** (fam) to
get on well
mil [mil] num thousand; **dos ~ libras**
two thousand pounds
milagro [mi'laxro] nm miracle;
milagroso, -a adj miraculous
milésima [mi'lesima] nf (de segundo)
thousandth
mili ['mili] (ESP: fam) nf: **hacer la ~** to
do one's military service
milímetro [mi'limetro] nm
millimetre
militante [mili'tante] adj militant
militar [mili'tar] adj military ⊳ nmf
soldier ⊳ vi (Mil) to serve; (en un
partido) to be a member
milla ['miʎa] nf mile
millar [mi'ʎar] nm thousand
millón [mi'ʎon] num million;
millonario, -a nm/f millionaire
milusos [mi'lusos] (MÉX) nm inv
odd-job man
mimar [mi'mar] vt to spoil, pamper
mimbre ['mimbre] nm wicker
mímica ['mimika] nf (para
comunicarse) sign language; (imitación)
mimicry
mimo ['mimo] nm (caricia) caress; (de

niño) spoiling; (Teatro) mime; (: actor) mime artist

mina ['mina] nf mine

mineral [mine'ral] adj mineral ▷ nm (Geo) mineral; (mena) ore

minero, -a [mi'nero, a] adj mining cpd ▷ nm/f miner

miniatura [minja'tura] adj inv, nf miniature

minidisco [mini'disko] nm MiniDisc®

minifalda [mini'falda] nf miniskirt

mínimo, -a ['minimo, a] adj, nm minimum

minino, -a [mi'nino, a] (fam) nm/f puss, pussy

ministerio [minis'terjo] nm Ministry; **Ministerio de Hacienda/de Asuntos Exteriores** Treasury (BRIT), Treasury Department (US)/Foreign Office (BRIT), State Department (US)

ministro, -a [mi'nistro, a] nm/f minister

minoría [mino'ria] nf minority

minúscula [mi'nuskula] nf small letter

minúsculo, -a [mi'nuskulo, a] adj tiny, minute

minusválido, -a [minus'βaliðo, a] adj (physically) handicapped ▷ nm/f (physically) handicapped person

minuta [mi'nuta] nf (de comida) menu

minutero [minu'tero] nm minute hand

minuto [mi'nuto] nm minute

mío, -a ['mio, a] pron: **el ~/la mía** mine; **un amigo ~** a friend of mine; **lo ~** what is mine

miope [mi'ope] adj short-sighted

mira ['mira] nf (de arma) sight(s) (pl); (fig) aim, intention

mirada [mi'raða] nf look, glance; (expresión) look, expression; **clavar la ~ en** to stare at; **echar una ~ a** to glance at

mirado, -a [mi'raðo, a] adj (sensato) sensible; (considerado) considerate;

bien/mal ~ (estimado) well/not well thought of; **bien ~ ...** all things considered ...

mirador [mira'ðor] nm viewpoint, vantage point

mirar [mi'rar] vt to look at; (observar) to watch; (considerar) to consider, think over; (vigilar, cuidar) to watch, look after ▷ vi to look; (Arq) to face; **mirarse** vr (dos personas) to look at each other; **~ bien/mal** to think highly of/have a poor opinion of; **~se al espejo** to look at o.s. in the mirror

mirilla [mi'riλa] nf spyhole, peephole

mirlo ['mirlo] nm blackbird

misa ['misa] nf mass

miserable [mise'raβle] adj (avaro) mean, stingy; (nimio) miserable, paltry; (lugar) squalid; (fam) vile, despicable ▷ nmf (malvado) rogue

miseria [mi'serja] nf (pobreza) poverty; (tacañería) meanness, stinginess; (condiciones) squalor; **una ~ pittance**

misericordia [miseri'korðja] nf (compasión) compassion, pity; (piedad) mercy

misil [mi'sil] nm missile

misión [mi'sjon] nf mission; **misionero, -a** nm/f missionary

mismo, -a ['mismo, a] adj (semejante) same; (después de pron) -self; (para énfasis) very ▷ adv: **aquí/hoy ~** right here/this very day; **ahora ~** right now ▷ conj: **lo ~ que** just like it as; **el ~ traje** the same suit; **en ese ~ momento** at that very moment; **vino el ~ ministro** the minister himself came; **yo ~ lo vi** I saw it myself; **lo ~** the same (thing); **da lo ~** it's all the same; **quedamos en las mismas** we're no further forward; **por lo ~** for the same reason

misterio [mis'terjo] nm mystery; **misterioso, -a** adj mysterious

mitad [mi'tað] nf (medio) half; (centro) middle; **a ~ de precio** (at) half-price; **en o a ~ del camino** halfway along the road; **cortar por la ~** to cut through the middle

mitin ['mitin] (pl **mítines**) nm meeting

mito ['mito] nm myth

mixto, -a ['miksto, a] adj mixed

ml. abr (= mililitro) ml

mm. abr (= milímetro) mm

mobiliario [moβi'ljarjo] nm furniture

mochila [mo'tʃila] nf rucksack (BRIT), back-pack

moco ['moko] nm mucus; **mocos** nmpl (fam) snot; **limpiarse los ~s de la nariz** (fam) to wipe one's nose

moda ['moða] nf fashion; (estilo) style; **a la o de ~** in fashion, fashionable; **pasado de ~** out of fashion

modales [mo'ðales] nmpl manners

modelar [moðe'lar] vt to model

modelo [mo'ðelo] adj inv, nmf model

módem ['moðem] nm (Inform) modem

moderado, -a [moðe'raðo, a] adj moderate

moderar [moðe'rar] vt to moderate; (violencia) to restrain, control; (velocidad) to reduce; **moderarse** vr to restrain o.s., control o.s.

modernizar [moðerni'θar] vt to modernize

moderno, -a [mo'ðerno, a] adj modern; (actual) present-day

modestia [mo'ðestja] nf modesty; **modesto, -a** adj modest

modificar [moðifi'kar] vt to modify

modisto, -a [mo'ðisto, a] nm/f (diseñador) couturier, designer; (que confecciona) dressmaker

modo ['moðo] nm way, manner; (Mús) mode; **modos** nmpl manners; **de ningún ~** in no way; **de todos ~s** at any rate; **modo de empleo** directions pl (for use)

mofarse [mo'farse] vr: **~ de** to mock, scoff at

mofle ['mofle] (MÉX, CAM) nm silencer (BRIT), muffler (US)

mogollón [moɣo'ʎon] (ESP: fam) adv a hell of a lot

moho ['moo] nm mould, mildew; (en metal) rust

mojar [mo'xar] vt to wet; (humedecer) to damp(en), moisten; (calar) to soak; **mojarse** vr to get wet

molcajete [molka'xete] (MÉX) nm mortar

molde ['molde] nm mould; (Costura) pattern; (fig) model; **moldeado** nm soft perm; **moldear** vt to mould

mole ['mole] nf mass, bulk; (edificio) pile

moler [mo'ler] vt to grind, crush

molestar [moles'tar] vt to bother; (fastidiar) to annoy; (incomodar) to inconvenience, put out ▷ vi to be a nuisance; **molestarse** vr to bother; (incomodarse) to go to trouble; (ofenderse) to take offence; **¿(no) te molesta si ...?** do you mind if...?

No confundir **molestar** con la palabra inglesa **molest**.

molestia [mo'lestja] nf bother, trouble; (incomodidad) inconvenience; (Med) discomfort; **es una ~** it's a nuisance; **molesto, -a** adj (que fastidia) annoying; (incómodo) inconvenient; (inquieto) uncomfortable, ill at ease; (enfadado) annoyed

molido, -a [mo'liðo, a] adj: **estar ~** (fig) to be exhausted o dead beat

molinillo [moli'niʎo] nm hand mill; **molinillo de café** coffee grinder

molino [mo'lino] nm (edificio) mill; (máquina) grinder

momentáneo, -a [momen'taneo, a] adj momentary

momento [mo'mento] nm moment; **de ~** at o for the moment

momia ['momja] nf mummy

monarca [mo'narka] nmf monarch, ruler; **monarquía** nf monarchy

monasterio [monas'terjo] nm monastery

mondar [mon'dar] vt to peel; **mondarse** vr (ESP): **~ de risa** (fam) to split one's sides laughing

mondongo [mon'dongo] (LAM) nm tripe

moneda [mo'neða] nf (tipo de dinero) currency, money; (pieza) coin; **una ~ de 2 euros** a 2 euro piece; **monedero** nm purse

monitor, a [moni'tor, a] nm/f instructor, coach ▷ nm (TV) set; (Inform) monitor

monja ['monxa] nf nun

monje ['monxe] nm monk

mono, -a ['mono, a] adj (bonito) lovely, pretty; (gracioso) nice, charming ▷ nm/f monkey, ape ▷ nm dungarees pl; (overoles) overalls pl

monopatín [monopa'tin] nm skateboard

monopolio [mono'poljo] nm monopoly; **monopolizar** vt to monopolize

monótono, -a [mo'notono, a] adj monotonous

monstruo ['monstrwo] nm monster ▷ adj inv fantastic; **monstruoso, -a** adj monstrous

montaje [mon'taxe] nm assembly; (Teatro) décor; (Cine) montage

montaña [mon'taɲa] nf (monte) mountain; (sierra) mountains pl, mountainous area; **montaña rusa** roller coaster; **montañero, -a** nm/f mountaineer; **montañismo** nm mountaineering

montar [mon'tar] vt (subir a) to mount, get on; (Tec) to assemble, put together; (negocio) to set up; (arma) to cock; (colocar) to lift on to; (Culin) to beat ▷ vi to mount, get on; (sobresalir) to overlap; **~ en bicicleta** to ride a bicycle; **~ en cólera** to get angry; **~ a caballo** to ride, go horseriding

monte ['monte] nm (montaña) mountain; (bosque) woodland; (área sin cultivar) wild area, wild country; **monte de piedad** pawnshop

montón [mon'ton] nm heap, pile; (fig) **un ~ de** heaps or lots of

monumento [monu'mento] nm monument

moño ['moɲo] nm bun

moqueta [mo'keta] nf fitted carpet

mora ['mora] nf blackberry; V tb **moro**

morado, -a [mo'raðo, a] adj purple, violet ▷ nm bruise

moral [mo'ral] adj moral ▷ nf (ética) ethics pl; (moralidad) morals pl, morality; (ánimo) morale

moraleja [mora'lexa] nf moral

morboso, -a [mor'βoso, a] adj morbid

morcilla [mor'θiʎa] nf blood sausage ≈ black pudding (BRIT)

mordaza [mor'ðaθa] nf (para la boca) gag; (Tec) clamp

morder [mor'ðer] vt to bite; (fig: consumir) to eat away, eat into; **mordisco** nm bite

moreno, -a [mo'reno, a] adj (color) (dark) brown; (de tez) dark; (de pelo moreno) dark-haired; (negro) black

morfina [mor'fina] nf morphine

moribundo, -a [mori'βundo, a] adj dying

morir [mo'rir] vi to die; (fuego) to die down; (luz) to go out; **morirse** vr to die; (fig) to be dying; **murió en un accidente** he was killed in an accident; **~se por algo** to be dying for sth

moro, -a ['moro, a] adj Moorish ▷ nm/f Moor

moroso, -a [mo'roso, a] nm/f bad debtor, defaulter

morralla [mo'rraʎa] (MÉX) nf (cambio) small o loose change

morro ['morro] nm (Zool) snout, nose; (Auto, Aviac) nose

morsa ['morsa] nf walrus

mortadela [morta'ðela] nf mortadella

mortal [mor'tal] adj mortal; (golpe) deadly; **mortalidad** nf mortality

mortero [mor'tero] nm mortar

mosca [ˈmoska] *nf* fly

Moscú [mosˈku] *n* Moscow

mosquearse [moskeˈarse] *(fam)* *vr*
(enojarse) to get cross; *(ofenderse)* to
take offence

mosquitero [moskiˈtero] *nm*
mosquito net

mosquito [mosˈkito] *nm* mosquito

mostaza [mosˈtaθa] *nf* mustard

mosto [ˈmosto] *nm* (unfermented)
grape juice

mostrador [mostraˈðor] *nm (de
tienda)* counter; *(de café)* bar

mostrar [mosˈtrar] *vt* to show;
(exhibir) to display, exhibit; *(explicar)* to
explain; **mostrarse** *vr:* **~se amable**
to be kind; to prove to be kind; **no se
muestra muy inteligente** he doesn't
seem (to be) very intelligent

mota [ˈmota] *nf* speck, tiny piece; *(en
diseño)* dot

mote [ˈmote] *nm* nickname

motín [moˈtin] *nm (del pueblo)* revolt,
rising; *(del ejército)* mutiny

motivar [motiˈβar] *vt (causar)*
to cause, motivate; *(explicar)* to
explain, justify; **motivo** *nm* motive,
reason

moto [ˈmoto] *(fam)* *nf* = **motocicleta**

motocicleta [motoθiˈkleta] *nf*
motorbike *(BRIT)*, motorcycle

motociclista [motoθiˈklista] *nmf*
motorcyclist, biker

motoneta [motoˈneta] *(cs)* *nf*
scooter

motor [moˈtor] *nm* motor, engine;
**motor a chorro de reacción/de
explosión** jet engine/internal
combustion engine

motora [moˈtora] *nf* motorboat

movedizo, -a *adj* V **arena**

mover [moˈβer] *vt* to move; *(cabeza)*
to shake; *(accionar)* to drive; *(fig)* to
cause, provoke; **moverse** *vr* to move;
(fig) to get a move on

móvil [ˈmoβil] *adj* mobile; *(pieza de
máquina)* moving; *(mueble)* movable
▷ *nm (motivo)* motive; *(teléfono)*

mobile; *(us)* cellphone

movimiento [moβiˈmjento] *nm*
movement; *(Tec)* motion; *(actividad)*
activity

mozo, -a [ˈmoθo, a] *adj (joven)*
young ▷ *nm/f* youth, young man/girl;
(cs: mesero) waiter/waitress

MP3 *nm* MP3; **reproductor (de) ~**
MP3 player

mucama [muˈkama] *(RPL)* *nf* maid

muchacho, -a [muˈtʃatʃo, a] *nm/f*
(niño) boy/girl; *(criado)* servant; *(criada)*
maid

muchedumbre [mutʃeˈðumbre]
nf crowd

○ **PALABRA CLAVE**

mucho, -a [ˈmutʃo, a] *adj* 1 *(cantidad)*
a lot of, much; *(número)* lots of, a lot of,
many; **mucho dinero** a lot of money;
hace mucho calor it's very hot;
muchas amigas lots o a lot of friends
2 *(sg: grande):* **ésta es mucha casa
para él** this house is much too big
for him
▷ *pron:* **tengo mucho que hacer** I've
got a lot to do; **muchos dicen que ...** a
lot of people say that ...; V *tb* **tener**
▷ *adv* 1 **me gusta mucho** I like it a
lot; **lo siento mucho** I'm very sorry;
come mucho he eats a lot; **¿te vas a
quedar mucho?** are you going to be
staying long?
2 *(respuesta)* very; **¿estás cansado?
– ¡mucho!** are you tired? – very!
3 *(locuciones):* **como mucho** at (the)
most; **con mucho: el mejor con
mucho** by far the best; **ni mucho
menos: no es rico ni mucho menos**
he's far from being rich
4: **por mucho que: por mucho que le
creas** no matter how o however much
you believe her

muda [ˈmuða] *nf* change of clothes

mudanza [muˈðanθa] *nf (de casa)*
move

mudar [mu'ðar] vt to change; (Zool) to shed ▷ vi to change; **mudarse** vr (ropa) to change; **~se de casa** to move house

mudo, -a ['muðo, a] adj dumb; (callado, Cine) silent

mueble ['mweβle] nm piece of furniture; **muebles** nmpl furniture sg

mueca ['mweka] nf face, grimace; **hacer ~ a** to make faces at

muela ['mwela] nf back tooth; **muela del juicio** wisdom tooth

muelle ['mweʎe] nm spring; (Náut) wharf; (malecón) pier

muero etc vb V **morir**

muerte ['mwerte] nf death; (homicidio) murder; **dar ~ a** to kill

muerto, -a ['mwerto, a] pp de **morir** ▷ adj dead ▷ nm/f dead man/woman; (difunto) deceased; (cadáver) corpse; **estar ~ de cansancio** to be dead tired; **Día de los Muertos** (MÉX) All Souls' Day

○ **DÍA DE LOS MUERTOS**
○
○ All Souls' Day (or "Day of the Dead")
○ in Mexico coincides with All
○ Saints' Day, which is celebrated
○ in the Catholic countries of Latin
○ America on November 1st and
○ 2nd. All Souls' Day is actually
○ a celebration which begins
○ in the evening of October 31st
○ and continues until November
○ 2nd. It is a combination of the
○ Catholic tradition of honouring
○ the Christian saints and martyrs,
○ and the ancient Mexican or Aztec
○ traditions, in which death was not
○ something sinister. For this reason
○ all the dead are honoured by
○ bringing offerings of food, flowers
○ and candles to the cemetery.

muestra ['mwestra] nf (señal) indication, sign; (demostración) demonstration; (prueba) proof; (estadística) sample; (modelo) model,

pattern; (testimonio) token

muestro etc vb V **mostrar**

muevo etc vb V **mover**

mugir [mu'xir] vi (vaca) to moo

mugre ['muxre] nf dirt, filth

mujer [mu'xer] nf woman; (esposa) wife; **mujeriego** nm womanizer

mula ['mula] nf mule

muleta [mu'leta] nf (para andar) crutch; (Taur) stick with red cape attached

multa ['multa] nf fine; **poner una ~ a** to fine; **multar** vt to fine

multicines [multi'θines] nmpl multiscreen cinema sg

multinacional [multinaθjo'nal] nf multinational

múltiple ['multiple] adj multiple; (pl) many, numerous

multiplicar [multipli'kar] vt (Mat) to multiply; (fig) to increase; **multiplicarse** vr (Bio) to multiply; (fig) to be everywhere at once

multitud [multi'tuð] nf (muchedumbre) crowd; **~ de** lots of

mundial [mun'djal] adj world-wide, universal; (guerra, récord) world cpd

mundo ['mundo] nm world; **todo el ~** everybody; **tener ~** to be experienced, know one's way around

munición [muni'θjon] nf ammunition

municipal [muniθi'pal] adj municipal, local

municipio [muni'θipjo] nm (ayuntamiento) town council, corporation; (territorio administrativo) town, municipality

muñeca [mu'neka] nf (Anat) wrist; (juguete) doll

muñeco [mu'neko] nm (figura) figure; (marioneta) puppet; (fig) puppet, pawn

mural [mu'ral] adj mural, wall cpd ▷ nm mural

muralla [mu'raʎa] nf (city) wall(s) (pl)

murciélago [mur'θjelaxo] nm bat

murmullo [mur'muʎo] nm

murmur(ing); (cuchicheo) whispering
murmurar [murmu'rar] vi to
murmur, whisper; (cotillear) to gossip
muro ['muro] nm wall
muscular [musku'lar] adj muscular
músculo ['muskulo] nm muscle
museo [mu'seo] nm museum; **museo
de arte** art gallery
musgo ['musɣo] nm moss
música ['musika] nf music; V tb
músico
músico, -a ['musiko, a] adj musical
▷ nm/f musician
muslo ['muslo] nm thigh
musulmán, -ana [musul'man,
ana] nm/f Moslem
mutación [muta'θjon] nf (Bio)
mutation; (cambio) (sudden) change
mutilar [muti'lar] vt to mutilate; (a
una persona) to maim
mutuo, -a ['mutwo, a] adj mutual
muy [mwi] adv very; (demasiado) too;
M~ Señor mío Dear Sir; **~ de noche**
very late at night; **eso es ~ de él** that's
just like him

N abr (= norte) N
nabo ['naβo] nm turnip
nacer [na'θer] vi to be born; (de huevo)
to hatch; (vegetal) to sprout; (río) to
rise; **nací en Barcelona** I was born
in Barcelona; **nacido, -a** adj born;
recién nacido newborn; **nacimiento**
nm birth; (de Navidad) Nativity; (de
río) source
nación [na'θjon] nf nation; **nacional**
adj national; **nacionalismo** nm
nationalism
nacionalidad [naθjonali'ðað] nf
nationality
nada ['naða] pron nothing ▷ adv
not at all, in no way; **no decir ~** to say
nothing, not to say anything; **~ más**
nothing else; **de ~** don't mention it
nadador, a [naða'ðor, a] nm/f
swimmer
nadar [na'ðar] vi to swim
nadie ['naðje] pron nobody, no-one;
~ habló nobody spoke; **no había ~**
there was nobody there, there wasn't
anybody there

nado ['naðo] **a nado:** *adv:* **pasar a ~** to swim across

nafta ['nafta] (*RPL*) *nf* petrol (*BRIT*), gas (*US*)

naipe ['naipe] *nm* (playing) card; **naipes** *nmpl* cards

nalgas ['nalɣas] *nfpl* buttocks

nalguear [nalɣe'ar] (*MÉX, CAM*) *vt* to spank

nana ['nana] (*ESP*) *nf* lullaby

naranja [na'ranxa] *adj inv, nf* orange; **media ~** (*fam*) better half; **naranjada** *nf* orangeade; **naranjo** *nm* orange tree

narciso [nar'θiso] *nm* narcissus

narcótico, -a [nar'kotiko, a] *adj, nm* narcotic; **narcotizar** *vt* to drug; **narcotráfico** *nm* drug trafficking o running

nariz [na'riθ] *nf* nose; **nariz chata/respingona** snub/turned-up nose

narración [narra'θjon] *nf* narration

narrar [na'rrar] *vt* to narrate, recount; **narrativa** *nf* narrative

nata ['nata] *nf* cream; **nata montada** whipped cream

natación [nata'θjon] *nf* swimming

natal [na'tal] *adj:* **ciudad ~** home town; **natalidad** *nf* birth rate

natillas [na'tiʎas] *nfpl* custard *sg*

nativo, -a [na'tiβo, a] *adj, nm/f* native

natural [natu'ral] *adj* natural; (*fruta etc*) fresh ▷ *nmf* native ▷ *nm* (*disposición*) nature

naturaleza [natura'leθa] *nf* nature; (*género*) nature, kind; **naturaleza muerta** still life

naturalmente [natural'mente] *adv* (*de modo natural*) in a natural way; **¡~!** of course!

naufragar [naufra'ɣar] *vi* to sink; **naufragio** *nm* shipwreck

nauseabundo, -a [nausea'βundo, a] *adj* nauseating, sickening

náuseas ['nauseas] *nfpl* nausea *sg*; **me da ~** it makes me feel sick

náutico, -a ['nautiko, a] *adj* nautical

navaja [na'βaxa] *nf* knife; (*de barbero, peluquero*) razor

naval [na'βal] *adj* naval

Navarra [na'βarra] *n* Navarre

nave ['naβe] *nf* (*barco*) ship, vessel; (*Arq*) nave; **nave espacial** spaceship; **nave industrial** factory premises *pl*

navegador [naβeɣa'ðor] *nm* (*Inform*) browser

navegante [naβe'ɣante] *nmf* navigator

navegar [naβe'ɣar] *vi* (*barco*) to sail; (*avión*) to fly; **~ por Internet** to surf the Net

Navidad [naβi'ðað] *nf* Christmas; **Navidades** *nfpl* Christmas time; **¡Feliz ~!** Merry Christmas!; **navideño, -a** *adj* Christmas *cpd*

nazca *etc vb V* **nacer**

nazi ['naθi] *adj, nmf* Nazi

NE *abr* (= *nor(d)este*) NE

neblina [ne'βlina] *nf* mist

necesario, -a [neθe'sarjo, a] *adj* necessary

neceser [neθe'ser] *nm* toilet bag; (*bolsa grande*) holdall

necesidad [neθesi'ðað] *nf* need; (*lo inevitable*) necessity; (*miseria*) poverty; **en caso de ~** in case of need o emergency; **hacer sus ~es** to relieve o.s.

necesitado, -a [neθesi'taðo, a] *adj* needy, poor; **~ de** in need of

necesitar [neθesi'tar] *vt* to need, require

necio, -a [ne'θjo, a] *adj* foolish

nectarina [nekta'rina] *nf* nectarine

nefasto, -a [ne'fasto, a] *adj* ill-fated, unlucky

negación [neɣa'θjon] *nf* negation; (*rechazo*) refusal, denial

negar [ne'ɣar] *vt* (*renegar, rechazar*) to refuse; (*prohibir*) to refuse, deny; (*desmentir*) to deny; **negarse** *vr:* **~se a** to refuse to

negativa [neɣa'tiβa] *nf* negative; (*rechazo*) refusal, denial

negativo, -a [neɣa'tiβo, a] *adj, nm*

negative

negligente [neɣliˈxente] *adj* negligent

negociación [neɣoθjaˈθjon] *nf* negotiation

negociante [neɣoˈθjante] *nmf* businessman/woman

negociar [neɣoˈθjar] *vt, vi* to negotiate; **~ en** to deal or trade in

negocio [neˈɣoθjo] *nm* (Com) business; (asunto) affair, business; (operación comercial) deal, transaction; (lugar) place of business; **los ~s** business *sg*; **hacer ~** to do business

negra [ˈneɣra] *nf* (Mús) crotchet; V *tb* **negro**

negro, -a [ˈneɣro, a] *adj* black; (suerte) awful ▷ *nm* black ▷ *nm/f* black man/woman

nene, -a [ˈnene, a] *nm/f* baby, small child

neón [neˈon] *nm*: **luces/lámpara de ~** neon lights/lamp

neoyorquino, -a [neojorˈkino, a] *adj* (of) New York

nervio [ˈnerβjo] *nm* nerve; **nerviosismo** *nm* nervousness, nerves *pl*; **nervioso, -a** *adj* nervous

neto, -a [ˈneto, a] *adj* net

neumático, -a [neuˈmatiko, a] *adj* pneumatic ▷ *nm* (ESP) tyre (BRIT), tire (US); **neumático de recambio** spare tyre

neurólogo, -a [neuˈroloxo, a] *nm/f* neurologist

neurona [neuˈrona] *nf* nerve cell

neutral [neuˈtral] *adj* neutral; **neutralizar** *vt* to neutralize; (contrarrestar) to counteract

neutro, -a [ˈneutro, a] *adj* (Bio, Ling) neuter

neutrón [neuˈtron] *nm* neutron

nevada [neˈβaða] *nf* snowstorm; (caída de nieve) snowfall

nevar [neˈβar] *vi* to snow

nevera [neˈβera] (ESP) *nf* refrigerator (BRIT), icebox (US)

nevería [neβeˈria] (MÉX) *nf* ice-cream

parlour

nexo [ˈnekso] *nm* link, connection

ni [ni] *conj* nor, neither; (tb: **~ siquiera**) not... even; **~ aunque que** not even if; **~ blanco ~ negro** neither white nor black

Nicaragua [nikaˈraɣwa] *nf* Nicaragua; **nicaragüense** *adj, nmf* Nicaraguan

nicho [ˈnitʃo] *nm* niche

nicotina [nikoˈtina] *nf* nicotine

nido [ˈniðo] *nm* nest

niebla [ˈnjeβla] *nf* fog; (neblina) mist

niego *etc vb* V **negar**

nieto, -a [ˈnjeto, a] *nm/f* grandson/daughter; **nietos** *nmpl* grandchildren

nieve *etc* V **nevar** ▷ *nf* snow; (MÉX: helado) ice cream

NIF *nm abr* (= Número de Identificación Fiscal) personal identification number used for financial and tax purposes

ninfa [ˈninfa] *nf* nymph

ningún *adj* V **ninguno**

ninguno, -a [ninˈguno, a] (adj **ningún**) *no pron* (nadie) nobody; (ni uno) none, not one; (ni uno ni otro) neither; **de ninguna manera** by no means, not at all

niña [ˈnina] *nf* (Anat) pupil; V *tb* **niño**

niñera [niˈnera] *nf* nursemaid, nanny

niñez [niˈneθ] *nf* childhood; (infancia) infancy

niño, -a [ˈnino, a] *adj* (joven) young; (inmaduro) immature ▷ *nm/f* child, boy/girl

nipón, -ona [niˈpon, ona] *adj, nm/f* Japanese

níquel [ˈnikel] *nm* nickel

níspero [ˈnispero] *nm* medlar

nítido, -a [ˈnitiðo, a] *adj* clear; sharp

nitrato [niˈtrato] *nm* nitrate

nitrógeno [niˈtroxeno] *nm* nitrogen

nivel [niˈβel] *nm* (Geo) level; (norma) level, standard; (altura) height; **nivel de aceite** oil level; **nivel de aire** spirit level; **nivel de vida** standard of living; **nivelar** *vt* to level out; (fig) to even up; (Com) to balance

no [no] adv no; not; (con verbo) not ▷ excl no!; **~ tengo nada** I don't have anything, I have nothing; **~ es el mío** it's not mine; **ahora ~** not now; **¿~ lo sabes?** don't you know?; **~ mucho** not much; **~ bien termine, lo entregaré** as soon as I finish, I'll hand it over; **~ más: ayer ~ más** just yesterday; **¡pase ~ más!** come in!; **¡a que ~ lo sabes!** I bet you don't know!; **¡cómo ~!** of course!; **la ~ intervención** non-intervention

noble ['noβle] adj, nmf noble; **nobleza** nf nobility

noche ['notʃe] nf night, night-time; (la tarde) evening; **de ~, por la ~** at night; **es de ~** it's dark; **Noche de San Juan** see note

● **NOCHE DE SAN JUAN**
●
● The **Noche de San Juan** on the
● 24th June is a **fiesta** coinciding
● with the summer solstice and
● which has taken the place of
● other ancient pagan festivals.
● Traditionally fire plays a major
● part in these festivities with
● celebrations and dancing taking
● place around bonfires in towns
● and villages across the country.

nochebuena [notʃe'βwena] nf Christmas Eve

● **NOCHEBUENA**
●
● Traditional Christmas
● celebrations in Spanish-speaking
● countries mainly take place
● on the night of **Nochebuena**,
● Christmas Eve. Families gather
● together for a large meal and the
● more religiously inclined attend
● Midnight Mass. While presents are
● traditionally given by **los Reyes**
● **Magos** on the 6th January, more
● and more people are exchanging
● gifts on Christmas Eve.

nochevieja [notʃe'βjexa] nf New Year's Eve

nocivo, -a [no'θiβo, a] adj harmful

noctámbulo, -a [nok'tambulo, a] nm/f sleepwalker

nocturno, -a [nok'turno, a] adj (de la noche) nocturnal, night cpd; (de la tarde) evening cpd ▷ nm nocturne

nogal [no'ɣal] nm walnut tree

nómada [no'maða] adj nomadic ▷ nmf nomad

nombrar [nom'brar] vt (designar) to name; (mencionar) to mention; (dar puesto a) to appoint

nombre ['nombre] nm name; (sustantivo) noun; **~ y apellidos** in full; **poner ~ a** to call, name; **nombre común/propio** common/proper noun; **nombre de pila/de soltera** Christian/maiden name

nómina ['nomina] nf (lista) payroll; (hoja) payslip

nominal [nomi'nal] adj nominal

nominar [nomi'nar] vt to nominate

nominativo, -a [nomina'tiβo, a] adj (Com): **cheque ~ a X** cheque made out to X

nordeste [nor'ðeste] adj north-east, north-eastern, north-easterly ▷ nm north-east

nórdico, -a [norðiko, a] adj Nordic

noreste [no'reste] adj, nm = **nordeste**

noria ['norja] nf (Agr) waterwheel; (de carnaval) big (BRIT) o Ferris (US) wheel

norma ['norma] nf rule (of thumb)

normal [nor'mal] adj (corriente) normal; (habitual) usual, natural; **normalizarse** vr to return to normal; **normalmente** adv normally

normativa [norma'tiβa] nf (set of) rules pl, regulations pl

noroeste [noro'este] adj north-west, north-western, north-westerly ▷ nm north-west

norte ['norte] adj north, northern, northerly ▷ nm north; (fig) guide

norteamericano, -a [norteameri'kano, a] adj, nm/f

(North) American

Noruega [noˈrweɣa] nf Norway

noruego, -a [noˈrweɣo, a] adj, nm/f Norwegian

nos [nos] pron (directo) us; (indirecto) us; to us; for us; from us; (reflexivo) (to) ourselves; (recíproco) (to) each other; **~ levantamos a las 7** we get up at 7

nosotros, -as [noˈsotros, as] pron (sujeto) we; (después de prep) us

nostalgia [nosˈtalxja] nf nostalgia

nota [ˈnota] nf note; (Escol) mark

notable [noˈtaβle] adj notable; (Escol) outstanding

notar [noˈtar] vt to notice, note; **notarse** vr to be obvious; **se nota que ...** one observes that ...

notario [noˈtarjo] nm notary

noticia [noˈtiθja] nf (información) piece of news; **las ~s** the news sg; **tener ~s de algn** to hear from sb

⚠ No confundir **noticia** con la palabra inglesa *notice*.

noticiero [notiˈθjero] (LAM) nm news bulletin

notificar [notifiˈkar] vt to notify, inform

notorio, -a [noˈtorjo, a] adj (público) well-known; (evidente) obvious

novato, -a [noˈβato, a] adj inexperienced ▷ nm/f beginner, novice

novecientos, -as [noβeˈθjentos, as] num nine hundred

novedad [noβeˈðað] nf (calidad de nuevo) newness; (noticia) piece of news; (cambio) change, (new) development

novel [noˈβel] adj new; (inexperto) inexperienced ▷ nm/f beginner

novela [noˈβela] nf novel

noveno, -a [noˈβeno, a] adj ninth

noventa [noˈβenta] num ninety

novia [ˈnoβja] nf V **novio**

noviazgo [noˈβjaθɣo] nm engagement

novicio, -a [noˈβiθjo, a] nm/f novice

noviembre [noˈβjembre] nm November

novillada [noβiˈʎaða] nf (Taur) bullfight with young bulls; **novillero** nm novice bullfighter; **novillo** nm young bull, bullock; **hacer novillos** (fam) to play truant

novio, -a [ˈnoβjo, a] nm/f boyfriend/ girlfriend; (prometido) fiancé/fiancée; (recién casado) bridegroom/bride; **los ~s** the newly-weds

nube [ˈnuβe] nf cloud

nublado, -a [nuˈβlaðo, a] adj cloudy; **nublarse** vr to grow dark

nubosidad [nuβosiˈðað] nf cloudiness; **había mucha ~** it was very cloudy

nuboso, -a [nuˈβoso] adj cloudy

nuca [ˈnuka] nf nape of the neck

nuclear [nukleˈar] adj nuclear

núcleo [ˈnukleo] nm (centro) core; (Física) nucleus; **núcleo urbano** city centre

nudillo [nuˈðiʎo] nm knuckle

nudista [nuˈðista] adj nudist

nudo [ˈnuðo] nm knot; (de carreteras) junction

nuera [ˈnwera] nf daughter-in-law

nuestro, -a [ˈnwestro, a] adj pos our ▷ pron ours; **~ padre** our father; **un amigo ~** a friend of ours; **es el ~** it's ours

Nueva York [-ˈjork] n New York

Nueva Zelanda [-θeˈlanda] nf New Zealand

nueve [ˈnweβe] num nine

nuevo, -a [ˈnweβo, a] adj (gen) new; **de ~** again

nuez [nweθ] nf walnut; (Anat) Adam's apple; **nuez moscada** nutmeg

nulo, -a [ˈnulo, a] adj (inepto, torpe) useless; (inválido) (null and) void; (Deporte) drawn, tied

núm. abr (= número) no.

numerar [numeˈrar] vt to number

número [ˈnumero] nm (gen) number; (tamaño: de zapato) size; (ejemplar: de diario) number, issue; **sin ~** numberless, unnumbered; **número atrasado** back number; **número de matrícula/**

teléfono registration/telephone number; **número impar/par** odd/even number; **número romano** Roman numeral

numeroso, -a [nume'roso, a] *adj* numerous

nunca ['nunka] *adv* (*jamás*) never; ~ **lo pensé** I never thought it; **no viene** ~ he never comes; ~ **más** never again; **más que** ~ more than ever

nupcias ['nupθjas] *nfpl* wedding *sg*, nuptials

nutria ['nutrja] *nf* otter

nutrición [nutri'θjon] *nf* nutrition

nutrir [nu'trir] *vt* (*alimentar*) to nourish; (*dar de comer*) to feed; (*fig*) to strengthen; **nutritivo, -a** *adj* nourishing, nutritious

nylon [ni'lon] *nm* nylon

ñango, -a ['nango, a] (*MÉX*) *adj* puny

ñapa ['napa] (*LAM*) *nf* extra

ñata ['nata] (*LAM*: *fam*) *nf* nose; V *tb* **ñato**

ñato, -a ['nato, a] (*LAM*) *adj* snub-nosed

ñoñería [none'ria] *nf* insipidness

ñoño, -a ['nono, a] *adj* (*fam*: *tonto*) silly, stupid; (*soso*) insipid; (*persona*) spineless; (*ESP*: *película, novela*) sentimental

O

O abr (= oeste) W

o [o] conj or; **o ... o** either ... or

oasis [o'asis] nm inv oasis

obcecarse [oβθe'karse] vr to get o become stubborn

obedecer [oβeðe'θer] vt to obey; **obediente** adj obedient

obertura [oβer'tura] nf overture

obeso, -a [o'βeso, a] adj obese

obispo [o'βispo] nm bishop

obituario [oβi'twarjo] (LAM) nm obituary

objetar [oβxe'tar] vt, vi to object

objetivo, -a [oβxe'tiβo, a] adj, nm objective

objeto [oβ'xeto] nm (cosa) object; (fin) aim

objetor, a [oβxe'tor, a] nm/f objector

obligación [oβliɣa'θjon] nf obligation; (Com) bond

obligar [oβli'ɣar] vt to force; **obligarse** vr to bind o.s.; **obligatorio, -a** adj compulsory, obligatory

oboe [o'βoe] nm oboe

obra ['oβra] nf work; (Arq) construction, building; (Teatro) play; **por ~ de** thanks to (the efforts of); **obra maestra** masterpiece; **obras públicas** public works; **obrar** vt to work; (tener efecto) to have an effect on ▷ vi to act, behave; (tener efecto) to have an effect; **la carta obra en su poder** the letter is in his/her possession

obrero, -a [o'βrero, a] adj (clase) working; (movimiento) labour cpd ▷ nm/f (gen) worker; (sin oficio) labourer

obsceno, -a [oβs'θeno, a] adj obscene

obscu... = **oscu...**

obsequiar [oβse'kjar] vt (ofrecer) to present with; (agasajar) to make a fuss of, lavish attention on; **obsequio** nm (regalo) gift; (cortesía) courtesy, attention

observación [oβserβa'θjon] nf observation; (reflexión) remark

observador, a [oβserβa'ðor, a] nm/f observer

observar [oβser'βar] vt to observe; (anotar) to notice; **observarse** vr to keep to, observe

obsesión [oβse'sjon] nf obsession; **obsesivo, -a** adj obsessive

obstáculo [oβs'takulo] nm obstacle; (impedimento) hindrance, drawback

obstante [oβs'tante]: **no ~** adv nevertheless

obstinado, -a [oβsti'naðo, a] adj obstinate, stubborn

obstinarse [oβsti'narse] vr to be obstinate; **~ en** to persist in

obstruir [oβstru'ir] vt to obstruct

obtener [oβte'ner] vt (premio) to obtain; (premio) to win

obturador [oβtura'ðor] nm (Foto) shutter

obvio, -a ['oββjo, a] adj obvious

oca ['oka] nf (animal) goose; (juego) ≈ snakes and ladders

ocasión [oka'sjon] nf (oportunidad) opportunity, chance; (momento) occasion, time; (causa) cause; **de ~**

secondhand; **ocasionar** vt to cause
ocaso [o'kaso] nm (fig) decline
occidente [okθi'ðente] nm west
OCDE nf abr (= Organización de
Cooperación y Desarrollo Económico)
OECD
océano [o'θeano] nm ocean; **Océano
Índico** Indian Ocean
ochenta [o'tʃenta] num eighty
ocho ['otʃo] num eight; **dentro de ~
días** within a week
ocio ['oθjo] nm (tiempo) leisure; (pey)
idleness
octavilla [okta'viʎa] nf leaflet,
pamphlet
octavo, -a [ok'taβo, a] adj eighth
octubre [ok'tuβre] nm October
oculista [oku'lista] nmf oculist
ocultar [okul'tar] vt (esconder) to
hide; (callar) to conceal; **oculto, -a** adj
hidden; (fig) secret
ocupación [okupa'θjon] nf
occupation
ocupado, -a [oku'paðo, a] adj
(persona) busy; (plaza) occupied, taken;
(teléfono) engaged; **ocupar** vt (gen) to
occupy; **ocuparse** vr: **ocuparse de**
(gen) to concern o.s. with; (cuidar)
to look after
ocurrencia [oku'rrenθja] nf (idea)
bright idea
ocurrir [oku'rrir] vi to happen;
ocurrirse vr: **se me ocurrió que ...** it
occurred to me that ...
odiar [o'ðjar] vt to hate; **odio** nm
hate, hatred; **odioso, -a** adj (gen)
hateful; (malo) nasty
odontólogo, -a [oðon'toloxo, a]
nm/f dentist, dental surgeon
oeste [o'este] nm west; **una película
del ~** a western
ofender [ofen'der] vt (agraviar) to
offend; (insultar) to insult; **ofenderse**
vr to take offence; **ofensa** nf offence;
ofensiva nf offensive; **ofensivo, -a**
adj offensive
oferta [o'ferta] nf offer; (propuesta)
proposal; **la ~ y la demanda** supply

and demand; **artículos en ~** goods
on offer
oficial [ofi'θjal] adj official ⊳ nm
(Mil) officer
oficina [ofi'θina] nf office; **oficina
de correos** post office; **oficina de
información** information bureau;
oficina de turismo tourist office;
oficinista nmf clerk
oficio [o'fiθjo] nm (profesión)
profession; (puesto) post; (Rel) service;
ser de ~ to be an old hand; **tener
mucho ~** to have a lot of experience;
oficio de difuntos funeral service
ofimática [ofi'matika] nf office
automation
ofrecer [ofre'θer] vt (dar) to offer;
(proponer) to propose; **ofrecerse**
vr (persona) to offer o.s., volunteer;
(situación) to present itself; **¿qué se le
ofrece?, ¿se le ofrece algo?** what can I
do for you?, can I get you anything?
ofrecimiento [ofreθi'mjento]
nm offer
oftalmólogo, -a [oftal'moloxo, a]
nm/f ophthalmologist
oída [o'iða] nf: **de ~s** by hearsay
oído [o'iðo] nm (Anat) ear; (sentido)
hearing
oigo etc vb V **oír**
oír [o'ir] vt (gen) to hear; (atender a)
to listen to; **¡oiga!** listen!; **~ misa** to
attend mass
OIT nf abr (= Organización Internacional
del Trabajo) ILO
ojal [o'xal] nm buttonhole
ojalá [oxa'la] excl if only (it were so)!,
some hope! ⊳ conj if only ...!, would
that ...!; **~ (que) venga hoy** I hope he
comes today
ojeada [oxe'aða] nf glance
ojera [o'xera] nf: **tener ~s** to have bags
under one's eyes
ojo ['oxo] nm eye; (de puente) span;
(de cerradura) keyhole ⊳ nm carefull;
tener ~ para to have an eye for; **ojo de
buey** porthole
okey ['okei] (LAM) excl O.K.

okupa [o'kupa] (ESP: fam) nmf squatter

ola ['ola] nf wave

olé [o'le] excl bravo!, olé!

oleada [ole'aða] nf big wave, swell; (fig) wave

oleaje [ole'axe] nm swell

óleo ['oleo] nm oil; **oleoducto** nm (oil) pipeline

oler [o'ler] vt (gen) to smell; (inquirir) to pry into; (fig: sospechar) to sniff out ▷ vi to smell; **~ a** to smell of

olfatear [olfate'ar] vt to smell; (inquirir) to pry into; **olfato** nm sense of smell

olimpiada [olim'piaða] nf: **las O~s** the Olympics; **olímpico, -a** [o'limpiko, a] adj Olympic

oliva [o'liβa] nf (aceituna) olive; **aceite de ~** olive oil; **olivo** nm olive tree

olla ['oʎa] nf pan; (comida) stew; **olla exprés o a presión** (ESP) pressure cooker; **olla podrida** type of Spanish stew

olmo ['olmo] nm elm (tree)

olor [o'lor] nm smell; **oloroso, -a** adj scented

olvidar [olβi'ðar] vt to forget; (omitir) to omit; **olvidarse** vr (fig) to forget o.s.; **se me olvidó** I forgot

olvido [ol'βiðo] nm oblivion; (despiste) forgetfulness

ombligo [om'bliɣo] nm navel

omelette [ome'lete] (LAM) nf omelet(te)

omisión [omi'sjon] nf (abstención) omission; (descuido) neglect

omiso, -a [o'miso, a] adj: **hacer caso ~ de** to ignore, pass over

omitir [omi'tir] vt to omit

omnipotente [omnipo'tente] adj omnipotent

omóplato [o'moplato] nm shoulder blade

OMS nf abr (= Organización Mundial de la Salud) WHO

once ['onθe] num eleven; **onces** (CS) nfpl tea break sg

onda ['onda] nf wave; **onda corta/larga/media** short/long/medium wave; **ondear** vt, vi to wave; (tener ondas) to be wavy; (agua) to ripple

ondulación [ondula'θjon] nf undulation; **ondulado, -a** adj wavy

ONG nf abr (= organización no gubernamental) NGO

ONU ['onu] nf abr (= Organización de las Naciones Unidas) UNO

opaco, -a [o'pako, a] adj opaque

opción [op'θjon] nf (gen) option; (derecho) right, option

OPEP ['opep] nf abr (= Organización de Países Exportadores de Petróleo) OPEC

ópera ['opera] nf opera; **ópera bufa o cómica** comic opera

operación [opera'θjon] nf (gen) operation; (Com) transaction, deal

operador, a [opera'ðor, a] nm/f operator; (Cine: de proyección) projectionist; (: de rodaje) cameraman

operar [ope'rar] vt (producir) to produce, bring about; (Med) to operate on ▷ vi (Com) to operate, deal; **operarse** vr to occur; (Med) to have an operation

opereta [ope'reta] nf operetta

opinar [opi'nar] vt to think ▷ vi to give one's opinion; **opinión** nf (creencia) belief; (criterio) opinion

opio ['opjo] nm opium

oponer [opo'ner] vt (resistencia) to put up, offer; **oponerse** vr (objetar) to object; (estar frente a frente) to be opposed; (dos personas) to oppose each other; **~ A a B** set A against B; **me opongo a pensar que ...** I refuse to believe o think that ...

oportunidad [oportuni'ðað] nf (ocasión) opportunity; (posibilidad) chance

oportuno, -a [opor'tuno, a] adj (en su tiempo) opportune, timely; (respuesta) suitable; **en el momento ~** at the right moment

oposición [oposi'θjon] nf opposition; **oposiciones** nfpl (Escol) public examinations

opositor, a [oposi'tor, a] nm/f (adversario) opponent; (candidato): ~ **(a)** candidate (for)

opresión [opre'sjon] nf oppression; **opresor, a** nm/f oppressor

oprimir [opri'mir] vt to squeeze; (fig) to oppress

optar [op'tar] vi (elegir) to choose; ~ **por** to opt for; **optativo, -a** adj optional

óptico, -a ['optiko, a] adj optic(al) ▷ nm/f optician; **óptica** nf optician's (shop); **desde esta óptica** from this point of view

optimismo [opti'mismo] nm optimism; **optimista** nmf optimist

opuesto, -a [o'pwesto, a] adj (contrario) opposite; (antagónico) opposing

oración [ora'θjon] nf (Rel) prayer; (Ling) sentence

orador, a [ora'ðor, a] nm/f (conferenciante) speaker, orator

oral [o'ral] adj oral

orangután [orangu'tan] nm orangutan

orar [o'rar] vi to pray

oratoria [ora'torja] nf oratory

órbita ['orβita] nf orbit

orden ['orðen] nm (gen) order ▷ nf (gen) order; (Inform) command; **en ~ de prioridad** in order of priority; **orden del día** agenda

ordenado, -a [orðe'naðo, a] adj (metódico) methodical; (arreglado) orderly

ordenador [orðena'ðor] nm computer; **ordenador central** mainframe computer

ordenar [orðe'nar] vt (mandar) to order; (poner orden) to put in order, arrange; **ordenarse** vr (Rel) to be ordained

ordeñar [orðe'ɲar] vt to milk

ordinario, -a [orði'narjo, a] adj (común) ordinary, usual; (vulgar) vulgar, common

orégano [o'reɣano] nm oregano

oreja [o'rexa] nf ear; (Mecánica) lug, flange

orfanato [orfa'nato] nm orphanage

orfebrería [orfeβre'ria] nf gold/silver work

orgánico, -a [or'ɣaniko, a] adj organic

organismo [orɣa'nismo] nm (Bio) organism; (Pol) organization

organización [orɣaniθa'θjon] nf organization; **organizar** vt to organize

órgano [or'ɣano] nm organ

orgasmo [or'ɣasmo] nm orgasm

orgía [or'xia] nf orgy

orgullo [or'ɣuʎo] nm pride; **orgulloso, -a** adj (gen) proud; (altanero) haughty

orientación [orjenta'θjon] nf (posición) position; (dirección) direction

oriental [orjen'tal] adj eastern; (del Extremo Oriente) oriental

orientar [orjen'tar] vt (situar) to orientate; (señalar) to point; (dirigir) to direct; (guiar) to guide; **orientarse** vr to get one's bearings

oriente [o'rjente] nm east; **el O~ Medio** the Middle East; **el Próximo/Extremo O~** the Near/Far East

origen [o'rixen] nm origin

original [orixi'nal] adj (nuevo) original; (extraño) odd, strange; **originalidad** nf originality

originar [orixi'nar] vt to start, cause; **originarse** vr to originate; **originario, -a** adj (que origina); **originario de** native of

orilla [o'riʎa] nf (borde) border; (de río) bank; (de bosque, tela) edge; (de mar) shore

orina [o'rina] nf urine; **orinal** nm (chamber) pot; **orinar** vi to urinate; **orinarse** vr to wet o.s.

oro ['oro] nm gold; **oros** nmpl (Naipes) hearts

orquesta [or'kesta] nf orchestra; **orquesta sinfónica** symphony orchestra

orquídea [or'kiðea] nf orchid

ortiga [or'tiɣa] nf nettle

ortodoxo, -a [orto'ðokso, a] adj orthodox

ortografía [ortoɣra'fia] nf spelling

ortopedia [orto'peðja] nf orthopaedics sg; **ortopédico, -a** adj orthopaedic

oruga [o'ruɣa] nf caterpillar

orzuelo [or'θwelo] nm stye

os [os] pron (gen) you; (a vosotros) to you

osa ['osa] nf (she-)bear; **Osa Mayor/ Menor** Great/Little Bear

osadía [osa'ðia] nf daring

osar [o'sar] vi to dare

oscilación [osθila'θjon] nf (movimiento) oscillation; (fluctuación) fluctuation

oscilar [osθi'lar] vi to oscillate; to fluctuate

oscurecer [oskure'θer] vt to darken ▷ vi to grow dark; **oscurecerse** vr to grow o get dark

oscuridad [oskuri'ðað] nf obscurity; (tinieblas) darkness

oscuro, -a [os'kuro, a] adj dark; (fig) obscure; **a oscuras** in the dark

óseo, -a [o'seo, a] adj bone cpd

oso ['oso] nm bear; **oso de peluche** teddy bear; **oso hormiguero** anteater

ostentar [osten'tar] vt (gen) to show; (pey) to flaunt, show off; (poseer) to have, possess

ostión [os'tjon] (MÉX) nm = **ostra**

ostra ['ostra] nf oyster

OTAN ['otan] nf abr (= Organización del Tratado del Atlántico Norte) NATO

otitis [o'titis] nf earache

otoñal [oto'ɲal] adj autumnal

otoño [o'toɲo] nm autumn

otorgar [otor'ɣar] vt (conceder) to concede; (dar) to grant

otorrino, -a [oto'rrino, a], **otorrinolaringólogo, -a** [otorrinolarin'ɣoloɣo, a] nm/f ear,

nose and throat specialist

○ **PALABRA CLAVE**

otro, -a ['otro, a] adj **1** (distinto: sg) another; (: pl) other; **con otros amigos** with other o different friends
2 (adicional): **tráigame otro café (más), por favor** can I have another coffee please; **otros diez días más** another ten days
▷ pron **1 el otro** the other one; **(los) otros** (the) others; **de otro** somebody else's; **que lo haga otro** let somebody else do it
2 (recíproco): **se odian (la) una a (la) otra** they hate one another o each other
3: **otro tanto**: **comer otro tanto** to eat the same o as much again; **recibió una decena de telegramas y otras tantas llamadas** he got about ten telegrams and as many calls

ovación [oβa'θjon] nf ovation

oval [o'βal] adj oval; **ovalado, -a** adj oval; **óvalo** nm oval

ovario [o'βarjo] nm ovary

oveja [o'βexa] nf sheep

overol [oβe'rol] (LAM) nm overalls pl

ovillo [o'βiʎo] nm (de lana) ball of wool

OVNI ['oβni] nm abr (= objeto volante no identificado) UFO

ovulación [oβula'θjon] nf ovulation; **óvulo** nm ovum

oxidación [oksiða'θjon] nf rusting

oxidar [oksi'ðar] vt to rust; **oxidarse** vr to go rusty

óxido ['oksiðo] nm oxide

oxigenado, -a [oksixe'naðo, a] adj (Quím) oxygenated; (pelo) bleached

oxígeno [ok'sixeno] nm oxygen

oyente [o'jente] nmf listener

oyes etc vb V **oír**

ozono [o'θono] nm ozone

P

pabellón [paβe'ʎon] nm bell tent; (Arq) pavilion; (de hospital etc) block, section; (bandera) flag

pacer [pa'θer] vi to graze

paciencia [pa'θjenθja] nf patience

paciente [pa'θjente] adj, nmf patient

pacificación [paθifika'θjon] nf pacification

pacífico, -a [pa'θifiko, a] adj (persona) peaceable; (existencia) peaceful; **el (Océano) P~** the Pacific (Ocean)

pacifista [paθi'fista] nmf pacifist

pacotilla [pako'tiʎa] nf: **de ~** (actor, escritor) third-rate

pactar [pak'tar] vt to agree to on ▷ vi to come to an agreement

pacto ['pakto] nm (tratado) pact; (acuerdo) agreement

padecer [paðe'θer] vt (sufrir) to suffer; (soportar) to endure, put up with; **padecimiento** nm suffering

padrastro [pa'ðrastro] nm stepfather

padre ['paðre] nm father ▷ adj (fam): **un éxito ~** a tremendous success; **padres** nmpl parents; **padre político** father-in-law

padrino [pa'ðrino] nm (Rel) godfather; (tb: **~ de boda**) best man; (fig) sponsor, patron; **padrinos** nmpl godparents

padrón [pa'ðron] nm (censo) census, roll

padrote [pa'ðrote] (MÉX: fam) nm pimp

paella [pa'eʎa] nf paella, dish of rice with meat, shellfish etc

paga ['paɣa] nf (pago) payment; (sueldo) pay, wages pl

pagano, -a [pa'ɣano, a] adj, nm/f pagan, heathen

pagar [pa'ɣar] vt to pay; (las compras, crimen) to pay for; (fig: favor) to repay ▷ vi to pay; **~ al contado/a plazos** to pay (in) cash/in instalments

pagaré [paɣa're] nm I.O.U.

página ['paxina] nf page; **página de inicio** (Inform) home page; **página web** (Inform) web page

pago ['paɣo] nm (dinero) payment; **en ~ de** in return for; **pago anticipado/a cuenta/contra reembolso/en especie** advance payment/payment on account/cash on delivery/payment in kind

pág(s). abr (= página(s)) p(p).

pague etc vb V **pagar**

país [pa'is] nm (gen) country; (región) land; **los P~es Bajos** the Low Countries; **el P~ Vasco** the Basque Country

paisaje [pai'saxe] nm landscape, scenery

paisano, -a [pai'sano, a] adj of the same country ▷ nm/f (compatriota) fellow countryman/woman; **vestir de ~** (soldado) to be in civvies; (guardia) to be in plain clothes

paja ['paxa] nf straw; (fig) rubbish (BRIT), trash (US)

pajarita [paxa'rita] nf (corbata) bow tie

pájaro ['paxaro] *nm* bird; **pájaro carpintero** woodpecker

pajita [pa'xita] *nf* (drinking) straw

pala ['pala] *nf* spade, shovel; (*raqueta etc*) bat; (*: de tenis*) racquet; (*Culin*) slice; **pala mecánica** power shovel

palabra [pa'laβra] *nf* word; (*facultad*) (power of) speech; (*derecho de hablar*) right to speak; **tomar la ~** (*en mitin*) to take the floor

palabrota [pala'βrota] *nf* swearword

palacio [pa'laθjo] *nm* palace; (*mansión*) mansion, large house; **palacio de justicia** courthouse; **palacio municipal** town o city hall

paladar [pala'ðar] *nm* palate; **paladear** *vt* to taste

palanca [pa'lanka] *nf* lever; (*fig*) pull, influence

palangana [palaŋ'gana] *nf* washbasin

palco ['palko] *nm* box

Palestina [pales'tina] *nf* Palestine; **palestino, -a** *nm/f* Palestinian

paleta [pa'leta] *nf* (*de pintor*) palette; (*de albañil*) trowel; (*de ping-pong*) bat; (*MÉX, CAM: helado*) ice lolly (*BRIT*), Popsicle® (*US*)

palidecer [paliðe'θer] *vi* to turn pale; **palidez** *nf* paleness; **pálido, -a** *adj* pale

palillo [pa'liʎo] *nm* (*mondadientes*) toothpick; (*para comer*) chopstick

palito [pa'lito] (*RPL*) *nm* (*helado*) ice lolly (*BRIT*), Popsicle® (*US*)

paliza [pa'liθa] *nf* beating, thrashing

palma ['palma] *nf* (*Anat*) palm; (*árbol*) palm tree; **batir** o **dar ~s** to clap, applaud; **palmada** *nf* slap; **palmadas** *nfpl* clapping *sg*, applause *sg*

palmar [pal'mar] (*fam*) *vi* (*tb*: **-la**) to die, kick the bucket

palmear [palme'ar] *vi* to clap

palmera [pal'mera] *nf* (*Bot*) palm tree

palmo ['palmo] *nm* (*medida*) span; (*fig*) small amount; **~ a ~** inch by inch

palo ['palo] *nm* stick; (*poste*) post; (*tienda de campaña*) pole; (*mango*) handle, shaft; (*golpe*) blow, hit; (*de golf*) club; (*de béisbol*) bat; (*Náut*) mast; (*Naipes*) suit

paloma [pa'loma] *nf* dove, pigeon

palomitas [palo'mitas] *nfpl* popcorn *sg*

palpar [pal'par] *vt* to touch, feel

palpitar [palpi'tar] *vi* to palpitate; (*latir*) to beat

palta ['palta] (*CS*) *nf* avocado

paludismo [palu'ðismo] *nm* malaria

pamela [pa'mela] *nf* picture hat, sun hat

pampa ['pampa] *nf* pampas, prairie

pan [pan] *nm* bread; (*una barra*) loaf; **pan integral** wholemeal (*BRIT*) o wholewheat (*US*) bread; **pan rallado** breadcrumbs *pl*; **pan tostado** (*MÉX: tostada*) toast

pana ['pana] *nf* corduroy

panadería [panaðe'ria] *nf* baker's (shop); **panadero, -a** *nm/f* baker

Panamá [pana'ma] *nm* Panama; **panameño, -a** *adj* Panamanian

pancarta [pan'karta] *nf* placard, banner

panceta [pan'θeta] (*ESP, RPL*) *nf* bacon

pancho ['pantʃo] (*RPL*) *nm* hot dog

pancito [pan'θito] *nm* (*bread*) roll

panda ['panda] *nm* (*Zool*) panda

pandereta [pande'reta] *nf* tambourine

pandilla [pan'diʎa] *nf* set, group; (*de criminales*) gang; (*pey: camarilla*) clique

panecillo [pane'θiʎo] (*ESP*) *nm* (*bread*) roll

panel [pa'nel] *nm* panel; **panel solar** solar panel

panfleto [pan'fleto] *nm* pamphlet

pánico ['paniko] *nm* panic

panorama [pano'rama] *nm* panorama; (*vista*) view

panqueque [pan'keke] (*LAM*) *nm* pancake

pantalla [pan'taʎa] *nf* (*de cine*) screen; (*de lámpara*) lampshade

pantalón [panta'lon] nm trousers;
pantalones nmpl trousers;
pantalones cortes shorts

pantano [pan'tano] nm (ciénaga)
marsh, swamp; (de agua)
reservoir; (fig) jam, difficulty

panteón [pante'on] nm (monumento)
pantheon

pantera [pan'tera] nf panther

pantimedias [panti'meðjas] (MÉX)
nfpl = **pantis**

pantis ['pantis] nmpl tights (BRIT),
pantyhose (US)

pantomima [panto'mima] nf
pantomime

pantorrilla [panto'rriʎa] nf calf
(of the leg)

pants [pants] (MÉX) nmpl tracksuit
(BRIT), sweat suit (US)

pantufla [pan'tufla] nf slipper

panty(s) ['panti(s)] nm(pl) tights
(BRIT), pantyhose (US)

panza ['panθa] nf belly, paunch

pañal [pa'nal] nm nappy (BRIT),
diaper (US); **pañales** nmpl (fig) early
stages, infancy sg

paño ['paɲo] nm (tela) cloth; (pedazo de
tela) (piece of) cloth; (trapo) duster, rag;
paños menores underclothes

pañuelo [pa'nwelo] nm
handkerchief, hanky; (fam: para la
cabeza) (head)scarf

papa ['papa] nm: **el P~** the Pope ▷ nf
(LAM: patata) potato; **papas fritas** (LAM)
French fries, chips (BRIT); (de bolsa)
crisps (BRIT), potato chips (US)

papá [pa'pa] (fam) nm dad(dy), pa (US)

papada [pa'paða] nf double chin

papagayo [papa'ɣajo] nm parrot

papalote [papa'lote] (MÉX, CAM)
nm kite

papanatas [papa'natas] (fam) nm
inv simpleton

papaya [pa'paja] nf papaya

papear [pape'ar] (fam) vt, vi to scoff

papel [pa'pel] nm paper; (hoja de
papel) sheet of paper; (Teatro: fig) role;
papel de aluminio aluminium (BRIT)

o aluminum (US) foil; **papel de arroz/
envolver/fumar** rice/wrapping/
cigarette paper; **papel de estaño**
platatinfoil; **papel de lija** sandpaper;
papel higiénico toilet paper; **papel
moneda** paper money; **papel pintado**
wallpaper; **papel secante** blotting
paper

papeleo [pape'leo] nm red tape

papelera [pape'lera] nf wastepaper
basket; (en la calle) litter bin; **papelera
(de reciclaje)** (Inform) wastebasket

papelería [papele'ria] nf stationer's
(shop)

papeleta [pape'leta] (ESP) nf (Pol)
ballot paper

paperas [pa'peras] nfpl mumps sg

papilla [pa'piʎa] nf (de bebé) baby
food

paquete [pa'kete] nm (de cigarrillos
etc) packet; (Correos etc) parcel

par [par] adj (igual) like, equal; (Mat)
even ▷ nm equal; (de guantes) pair; (de
veces) couple; (Pol) peer; (Golf, Com) par;
abrir de ~ en ~ to open wide

para ['para] prep for; **no es ~ comer**
it's not for eating; **decir ~ sí** to say to
o.s.; **¿~ qué lo quieres?** what do you
want it for?; **se casaron ~ separarse
otra vez** they married only to separate
again; **lo tendré ~ mañana** I'll have
it (for) tomorrow; **ir ~ casa** to go
home, head for home; **~ profesor es
muy estúpido** he's very stupid for a
teacher; **¿quién es usted ~ gritar así?**
who are you to shout like that?; **tengo
bastante ~ vivir** I have enough to live
on; V tb **con**

parabién [para'βjen] nm
congratulations pl

parábola [pa'raβola] nf parable;
(Mat) parabola; **parabólica** nf
(tb: **antena parabólica**) satellite dish

parabrisas [para'βrisas] nm inv
windscreen (BRIT), windshield (US)

paracaídas [paraka'iðas] nm
inv parachute; **paracaidista** nmf
parachutist; (Mil) paratrooper

parachoques [para'tʃokes] nm inv
(Auto) bumper; (Mecánica etc) shock
absorber

parada [pa'raða] nf stop; (acto)
stopping; (de industria) shutdown,
stoppage; (lugar) stopping place;
parada de autobús bus stop; **parada
de taxis** taxi stand o rank (BRIT)

paradero [para'ðero] nm stopping-
place; (situación) whereabouts

parado, -a [pa'raðo, a] adj (persona)
motionless, standing still; (fábrica)
closed, at a standstill; (coche) stopped;
(LAM: de pie) standing (up); (ESP: sin
empleo) unemployed, idle

paradoja [para'ðoxa] nf paradox

parador [para'ðor] nm parador,
state-run hotel

paragolpes [para'golpes] (RPL) nm
inv (Auto) bumper, fender (us)

paraguas [pa'raɣwas] nm inv
umbrella

Paraguay [paraɣwai] nm Paraguay;
paraguayo, -a adj, nm/f Paraguayan

paraíso [para'iso] nm paradise,
heaven

paraje [pa'raxe] nm place, spot

paralelo, -a [para'lelo, a] adj
parallel

parálisis [pa'ralisis] nf inv paralysis;
paralítico, -a adj, nm/f paralytic

paralizar [parali'θar] vt to paralyse;
paralizarse vr to become paralysed;
(fig) to come to a standstill

páramo [paramo] nm bleak plateau

paranoico, -a [para'noiko, a] nm/f
paranoiac

parapente [para'pente] nm (deporte)
paragliding; (aparato) paraglider

parapléjico, -a [para'plexiko, a] adj,
nm/f paraplegic

parar [pa'rar] vt to stop; (golpe) to
ward off ▷ vi to stop; **pararse** vr to
stop; (LAM: ponerse de pie) to stand up;
ha parado de llover it has stopped
raining; **van a ir a ~ a comisaría**
they're going to end up in the police
station; **~se en** to pay attention to

pararrayos [para'rrajos] nm inv
lightning conductor

parásito, -a [pa'rasito, a] nm/f
parasite

parasol [para'sol] nm parasol,
sunshade

parcela [par'θela] nf plot, piece of
ground

parche [partʃe] nm (gen) patch

parchís [par'tʃis] nm ludo

parcial [par'θjal] adj (pago) part-;
(eclipse) partial; (Jur) prejudiced, biased;
(Pol) partisan

parecer [pare'θer] nm (opinión)
opinion, view; (aspecto) looks pl
▷ vi (tener apariencia) to seem, look;
(asemejarse) to look o seem like;
(aparecer, llegar) to appear; **parecerse**
vr to look alike, resemble each
other; **al ~** apparently; **según parece**
evidently, apparently; **~se a** to look
like, resemble; **me parece que** I think
(that), it seems to me

parecido, -a [pare'θiðo, a] adj
similar ▷ nm similarity, likeness,
resemblance; **bien ~** good-looking,
nice-looking

pared [pa'reð] nf wall

pareja [pa'rexa] nf (par) pair; (dos
personas) couple; (otro: de un par) other
one (of a pair); (persona) partner

parentesco [paren'tesko] nm
relationship

paréntesis [pa'rentesis] nm inv
parenthesis; (en escrito) bracket

parezco etc vb V **parecer**

pariente [pa'rjente] nmf relative,
relation

▌ No confundir **pariente** con la
palabra inglesa **parent**.

parir [pa'rir] vt to give birth to ▷ vi
(mujer) to give birth, have a baby

París [pa'ris] n Paris

parka ['parka] (LAM) nf anorak

parking [parkin] nm car park (BRIT),
parking lot (us)

parlamentar [parlamen'tar] vi
to parley

parlamentario, -a [parlamen'tarjo, a] *adj* parliamentary ▷ *nm/f* member of parliament

parlamento [parla'mento] *nm* parliament

parlanchín, -ina [parlan'tʃin, ina] *adj* indiscreet ▷ *nm/f* chatterbox

parlar [par'lar] *vi* to chatter (away)

paro ['paro] *nm* (huelga) stoppage (of work), strike; (MÉX: desempleo) unemployment; (: subsidio) unemployment benefit; **estar en ~** (ESP) to be unemployed; **paro cardíaco** cardiac arrest

parodia [pa'roðja] *nf* parody; **parodiar** *vt* to parody

parpadear [parpaðe'ar] *vi* (ojos) to blink; (luz) to flicker

párpado ['parpaðo] *nm* eyelid

parque ['parke] *nm* (lugar verde) park; (MÉX: munición) ammunition; **parque de atracciones** fairground; **parque de bomberos** (ESP) fire station; **parque infantil/temático/zoológico** playground/theme park/zoo

parqué [par'ke] *nm* parquet (flooring)

parquímetro [par'kimetro] *nm* parking meter

parra ['parra] *nf* (grape)vine

párrafo ['parrafo] *nm* paragraph; **echar un ~** (fam) to have a chat

parranda [pa'rranda] (fam) *nf* spree, binge

parrilla [pa'rriʎa] *nf* (Culin) grill; (de coche) grille; **(carne a la) ~** barbecue; **parrillada** *nf* barbecue

párroco ['parroko] *nm* parish priest

parroquia [pa'rrokja] *nf* parish; (iglesia) parish church; (Com) clientele, customers pl; **parroquiano, -a** *nm/f* parishioner; (Com) client, customer

parte ['parte] *nm* message; (informe) report ▷ *nf* part; (lado, cara) side; (de reparto) share; (Jur) party; **en alguna ~ de Europa** somewhere in Europe; **en o por todas ~s** everywhere; **en gran ~** to a large extent; **la mayor ~**

de los españoles most Spaniards; **de un tiempo a esta ~** for some time past; **de ~ de algn** on sb's behalf; **¿de ~ de quién?** (Tel) who is speaking?; **por ~ de** on the part of; **yo por mi ~** I for my part; **por otra ~** on the other hand; **dar ~** to inform; **tomar ~** to take part; **parte meteorológico** weather forecast o report

participación [partiθipa'θjon] *nf* (acto) participation, taking part; (parte, Com) share; (de lotería) shared prize; (aviso) notice, notification

participante [partiθi'pante] *nmf* participant

participar [partiθi'par] *vt* to notify, inform ▷ *vi* to take part, participate

partícipe [par'tiθipe] *nmf* participant

particular [partiku'lar] *adj* (especial) particular, special; (individual, personal) private, personal ▷ *nm* (punto, asunto) particular, point; (individuo) individual; **tiene coche ~** he has a car of his own

partida [par'tiða] *nf* (salida) departure; (Com) entry, item; (juego) game; (grupo de personas) band, group; **mala ~** dirty trick; **partida de nacimiento/matrimonio/defunción** (ESP) birth/marriage/death certificate

partidario, -a [parti'ðarjo, a] *adj* partisan ▷ *nm/f* supporter, follower

partido [par'tiðo] *nm* (Pol) party; (Deporte) game, match; **sacar ~ de** to profit o benefit from; **tomar ~** to take sides

partir [par'tir] *vt* (dividir) to split, divide; (compartir, distribuir) to share (out), distribute; (romper) to break open, split open; (rebanada) to cut (off) ▷ *vi* (ponerse en camino) to set off o out; (comenzar) to start (off o out); **partirse** *vr* to crack o split o break (in two etc); **a ~ de** (starting) from

partitura [parti'tura] *nf* (Mús) score

parto ['parto] *nm* birth; (fig) product, creation; **estar de ~** to be in labour

parvulario [parβu'larjo] (ESP) *nm*

nursery school, kindergarten

pasa ['pasa] *nf* raisin; **pasa de Corinto** currant

pasacintas [pasa'θintas] (LAM) *nm* cassette player

pasada [pa'saða] *nf* passing, passage; **de ~** in passing, incidentally; **una mala ~** a dirty trick

pasadizo [pasa'ðiθo] *nm* (*pasillo*) passage, corridor; (*callejuela*) alley

pasado, -a [pa'saðo, a] *adj* past; (*malo: comida, fruta*) bad; (*muy cocido*) overdone; (*anticuado*) out of date ▷ *nm* past; **~ mañana** the day after tomorrow; **el mes ~** last month

pasador [pasa'ðor] *nm* (*cerrojo*) bolt; (*de pelo*) hair slide; (*horquilla*) grip

pasaje [pa'saxe] *nm* (*pago de viaje*) fare; (*los pasajeros*) passengers *pl*; (*pasillo*) passageway

pasajero, -a [pasa'xero, a] *adj* passing; (*situación, estado*) temporary; (*amor, enfermedad*) brief ▷ *nm/f* passenger

pasamanos [pasa'manos] *nm inv* balaclava helmet

pasamontañas [pasamon'taɲas] *nm inv* balaclava helmet

pasaporte [pasa'porte] *nm* passport

pasar [pa'sar] *vt* to pass; (*tiempo*) to spend; (*desgracias*) to suffer, endure; (*noticia*) to give, pass on; (*río*) to cross; (*barrera*) to pass through; (*falta*) to overlook, tolerate; (*contrincante*) to surpass, do better than; (*coche*) to overtake; (*Cine*) to show; (*enfermedad*) to give, infect with; **~ la aspiradora** to do the vacuuming, to hoover o do the hoovering ▷ *vi* (*gen*) to pass; (*terminarse*) to be over; (*ocurrir*) to happen; **pasarse** *vr* (*flores*) to fade; (*comida*) to go bad o off; (*fig*) to overdo it, go too far; **~ de** to go beyond, exceed; **~ por** (LAM) to fetch; **-lo bien/mal** to have a good/bad time; **¡pase!** come in!; **hacer ~** to show in; **lo que pasa es que ...** the thing is ...; **~se al enemigo** to go over to the enemy; **se me pasó** I forgot; **no se le pasa nada** he misses nothing; **pase lo que pase**

come what may; **¿qué pasa?** what's going on o, what's up?; **¿qué te pasa?** what's wrong?

pasarela [pasa'rela] *nf* footbridge; (*en barco*) gangway

pasatiempo [pasa'tjempo] *nm* pastime, hobby

Pascua [pa'skwa] *nf* (*en Semana Santa*) Easter; **Pascuas** *nfpl* Christmas (time); **¡felices ~s!** Merry Christmas!

pase ['pase] *nm* pass; (*Cine*) performance, showing

pasear [pase'ar] *vt* to take for a walk; (*exhibir*) to parade, show off ▷ *vi* to walk, go for a walk; **pasearse** *vr* to walk, go for a walk; **~ en coche** to go for a drive; **paseo** *nm* (*avenida*) avenue; (*distancia corta*) walk, stroll; **dar un o ir de paseo** to go for a walk; **paseo marítimo** (ESP) promenade

pasillo [pa'siʎo] *nm* passage, corridor

pasión [pa'sjon] *nf* passion

pasivo, -a [pa'siβo, a] *adj* passive; (*inactivo*) inactive ▷ *nm* (*Com*) liabilities *pl*, debts *pl*

pasmoso, -a [pas'moso, a] *adj* amazing, astonishing

paso, -a ['paso, a] *adj* dried ▷ *nm* step; (*modo de andar*) walk; (*huella*) footprint; (*rapidez*) speed, pace, rate; (*camino accesible*) way through, passage; (*cruce*) crossing; (*pasaje*) passing, passage; (*Geo*) pass; (*estrecho*) strait; **a ese ~** (*fig*) at that rate; **salir al ~ de o** to waylay; **estar de ~** to be passing through; **prohibido el ~** no entry; **ceda el ~** give way; **paso a nivel** (Ferro) level-crossing; **paso (de) cebra** (ESP) zebra crossing; **paso de peatones** pedestrian crossing; **paso elevado** flyover

pasota [pa'sota] (ESP: *fam*) *adj, nmf* ≈ dropout; **ser un ~** to be a bit of a dropout; (*ser indiferente*) not to care about anything

pasta ['pasta] *nf* paste; (*Culin: masa*) dough; (: *de bizcochos etc*) pastry; (*fam*) dough; **pastas** *nfpl* (*bizcochos*) pastries, small cakes; (fideos, espaguetis etc) pasta; **pasta dentífrica** o **de dientes** toothpaste

pastar [pas'tar] vt, vi to graze

pastel [pas'tel] nm (dulce) cake; (Arte) pastel; **pastel de carne** meat pie; **pastelería** nf cake shop

pastilla [pas'tiʎa] nf (de jabón, chocolate) bar; (píldora) tablet, pill

pasto ['pasto] nm (hierba) grass; (lugar) pasture, field; **pastor, a** [pas'tor, a] nm/f shepherd/ess ▷ nm (Rel) clergyman, pastor; **pastor alemán** Alsatian

pata ['pata] nf (pierna) leg; (pie) foot; (de muebles) leg; **~s arriba** upside down; **metedura de ~** (fam) gaffe; **meter la ~** (fam) to put one's foot in it; **tener buena/mala ~** to be lucky/unlucky; **pata de cabra** (Tec) crowbar; **patada** nf kick; (en el suelo) stamp

patata [pa'tata] nf potato; **patatas fritas** chips, French fries; (de bolsa) crisps

paté [pa'te] nm pâté

patente [pa'tente] adj obvious, evident; (Com) patent ▷ nf patent

paternal [pater'nal] adj fatherly, paternal; **paterno, -a** adj paternal

patético, -a [pa'tetiko, a] adj pathetic, moving

patilla [pa'tiʎa] nf (de gafas) side(piece); **patillas** nfpl sideburns

patín [pa'tin] nm skate; (de trineo) runner; **patín de ruedas** roller skate; **patinaje** nm skating; **patinar** vi to skate; (resbalarse) to skid, slip; (fam) to slip up, blunder

patineta [pati'neta] nf (MÉX: patinete) scooter; (cs: monopatín) skateboard

patinete [pati'nete] nm scooter

patio ['patjo] nm (de casa) patio, courtyard; **patio de recreo** playground

pato ['pato] nm duck; **pagar el ~** (fam) to take the blame, carry the can

patoso, -a [pa'toso, a] (fam) adj clumsy

patotero [pato'tero] (cs) nm

hooligan, lout

patraña [pa'traɲa] nf story, fib

patria ['patrja] nf native land, mother country

patrimonio [patri'monjo] nm inheritance; (fig) heritage

patriota [pa'trjota] nmf patriot

patrocinar [patroθi'nar] vt to sponsor

patrón, -ona [pa'tron, ona] nm/f (jefe) boss, chief, master(mistress); (propietario) landlord/lady; (Rel) patron saint ▷ nm (Tec, Costura) pattern

patronato [patro'nato] nm sponsorship; (acto) patronage; (fundación benéfica) trust, foundation

patrulla [pa'truʎa] nf patrol

pausa ['pausa] nf pause, break

pauta ['pauta] nf line, guide line

pava ['paβa] (RPL) nf kettle

pavimento [paβi'mento] nm (de losa) pavement, paving

pavo ['paβo] nm turkey; **pavo real** peacock

payaso, -a [pa'jaso, a] nm/f clown

payo, -a ['pajo, a] nm/f non-gipsy

paz [paθ] nf peace; (tranquilidad) peacefulness, tranquillity; **hacer las paces** to make peace; (fig) to make up; **¡déjame en ~!** leave me alone!

PC nm PC, personal computer

P.D. abr (= posdata) P.S., p.s.

peaje [pe'axe] nm toll

peatón [pea'ton] nm pedestrian; **peatonal** adj pedestrian

peca ['peka] nf freckle

pecado [pe'kaðo] nm sin; **pecador, a** adj sinful ▷ nm/f sinner

pecaminoso, -a [pekami'noso, a] adj sinful

pecar [pe'kar] vi (Rel) to sin; **peca de generoso** he is generous to a fault

pecera [pe'θera] nf fish tank; (redonda) goldfish bowl

pecho ['petʃo] nm (Anat) chest; (de mujer) breast; **dar el ~ a** to breast-feed; **tomar algo a ~** to take sth to heart

pechuga [pe'tʃuxa] nf breast

peculiar [pekuˈljar] *adj* special, peculiar; (*característico*) typical, characteristic

pedal [peˈðal] *nm* pedal; **pedalear** *vi* to pedal

pédalo [ˈpedalo] *nm* pedalo, pedal boat

pedante [peˈðante] *adj* pedantic ▷*nmf* pedant

pedazo [peˈðaθo] *nm* piece, bit; **hacerse ~s** to smash, shatter

pediatra [peˈðjatra] *nmf* paediatrician

pedido [peˈðiðo] *nm* (Com) order; (*petición*) request

pedir [peˈðir] *vt* to ask for, request; (*comida, Com: mandar*) to order; (*necesitar*) to need, demand, require ▷*vi* to ask; **me pidió que cerrara la puerta** he asked me to shut the door; **¿cuánto piden por el coche?** how much are they asking for the car?

pedo [ˈpeðo] (*fam!*) *nm* fart

pega [ˈpeɣa] *nf* snag; **poner ~s (a)** to complain about

pegadizo, -a [peɣaˈðiθo, a] *adj* (*Mús*) catchy

pegajoso, -a [peɣaˈxoso, a] *adj* sticky, adhesive

pegamento [peɣaˈmento] *nm* gum, glue

pegar [peˈɣar] *vt* (*papel, sellos*) to stick (on); (*cartel*) to stick up; (*coser*) to sew (on); (*unir: partes*) to join, fix together; (*Comput*) to paste; (*Med*) to give, infect with; (*dar: golpe*) to give, deal ▷*vi* (*adherirse*) to stick, adhere; (*ir juntos: colores*) to match, go together; (*golpear*) to hit; (*quemar: el sol*) to strike hot, burn; **pegarse** *vr* (*gen*) to stick; (*dos personas*) to hit each other, fight; (*fam*): **~ un grito** to let out a yell; **~ un salto** to jump (with fright); **~ en** to touch; **~se un tiro** to shoot o.s.; **~ fuego** to catch fire

pegatina [peɣaˈtina] *nf* sticker

pegote [peˈɣote] (*fam*) *nm* eyesore, sight

peinado [peiˈnaðo] *nm* hairstyle

peinar [peiˈnar] *vt* to comb; (*hacer estilo*) to style; **peinarse** *vr* to comb one's hair

peine [ˈpeine] *nm* comb; **peineta** *nf* ornamental comb

p.ej. *abr* (= *por ejemplo*) e.g.

Pekín [peˈkin] *n* Pekin(g)

pelado, -a [peˈlaðo, a] *adj* (*fruta, patata etc*) peeled; (*cabeza*) shorn; (*campo, fig*) bare; (*fam: sin dinero*) broke

pelar [peˈlar] *vt* (*fruta, patatas etc*) to peel; (*cortar el pelo a*) to cut the hair of; (*quitar la piel: animal*) to skin; **pelarse** *vr* (*la piel*) to peel off; **voy a ~me** I'm going to get my hair cut

peldaño [pelˈdaɲo] *nm* step

pelea [peˈlea] *nf* (*lucha*) fight; (*discusión*) quarrel, row; **peleado, -a** [peleˈaðo, a] *adj*: **estar peleado (con algn)** to have fallen out (with sb); **pelear** [peleˈar] *vi* to fight; **pelearse** *vr* to fight; (*reñirse*) to fall out, quarrel

pelela [peˈlela] (*cs*) *nf* potty

peletería [peleteˈria] *nf* furrier's, fur shop

pelícano [peˈlikano] *nm* pelican

película [peˈlikula] *nf* film; (*cobertura ligera*) thin covering; (*Foto: rollo*) roll o reel of film; **película de dibujos (animados)** cartoon; **película del oeste** western

peligro [peˈliɣro] *nm* danger; (*riesgo*) risk; **correr ~ de** to run the risk of; **peligroso, -a** *adj* dangerous; risky

pelirrojo, -a [peliˈrroxo, a] *adj* red-haired, red-headed ▷*nm/f* redhead

pellejo [peˈʎexo] *nm* (*de animal*) skin, hide

pellizcar [peʎiθˈkar] *vt* to pinch, nip

pelma [ˈpelma] (*ESP: fam*) *nmf* pain (in the neck)

pelmazo [pelˈmaθo] (*fam*) *nm* = **pelma**

pelo [ˈpelo] *nm* (*cabellos*) hair; (*de barba, bigote*) whisker; (*de animal: pellejo*) hair, fur, coat; **venir al ~** to be exactly what one needs; **un**

hombre de ~ en pecho a brave man;
por los ~s by the skin of one's teeth; **no tener ~s en la lengua** to be outspoken, not to mince one's words; **con ~s y señales** in minute detail; **tomar el ~ a algn** to pull sb's leg

pelota [pe'lota] *nf* ball; **en ~** stark naked; **hacer la ~ (a algn)** (ESP: fam) to creep (to sb); **pelota vasca** pelota

pelotón [pelo'ton] *nm* (Mil) squad, detachment

peluca [pe'luka] *nf* wig

peluche [pe'lutʃe] *nm*: **oso/muñeco de ~** teddy bear/soft toy

peludo, -a [pe'luðo, a] *adj* hairy, shaggy

peluquería [peluke'ria] *nf* hairdresser's; **peluquero, -a** *nm/f* hairdresser

pelusa [pe'lusa] *nf* (Bot) down; (en tela) fluff

pena ['pena] *nf* (congoja) grief, sadness; (remordimiento) regret; (dificultad) trouble; (dolor) pain; (Jur) sentence; **merecer** o **valer la ~** to be worthwhile; **a duras ~s** with great difficulty; **¡qué ~!** what a shame!; **pena capital** capital punishment; **pena de muerte** death penalty

penal [pe'nal] *adj* penal ▷ *nm* (cárcel) prison

penalidad [penali'ðað] *nf* (problema, dificultad) trouble, hardship; (Jur) penalty, punishment; **penalidades** *nfpl* trouble *sg*, hardship *sg*

penalti [pe'nalti] *nm* = **penalty**

penalty [pe'nalti] (*pl* **~s** o **penalties**) *nm* penalty (kick)

pendiente [pen'djente] *adj* pending, unsettled ▷ *nm* earring ▷ *nf* hill, slope

pene ['pene] *nm* penis

penetrante [pene'trante] *adj* (herida) deep; (persona, arma) sharp; (sonido) penetrating, piercing; (mirada) searching; (viento, crítica) biting

penetrar [pene'trar] *vt* to penetrate, pierce; (entender) to grasp ▷ *vi* to penetrate, go in; (entrar) to enter, go in;

(líquido) to soak in; (fig) to pierce

penicilina [peniθi'lina] *nf* penicillin

península [pe'ninsula] *nf* peninsula; **peninsular** *adj* peninsular

penique [pe'nike] *nm* penny

penitencia [peni'tenθja] *nf* penance

penoso, -a [pe'noso, a] *adj* (lamentable) distressing; (difícil) arduous, difficult

pensador, a [pensa'ðor, a] *nm/f* thinker

pensamiento [pensa'mjento] *nm* thought; (mente) mind; (idea) idea

pensar [pen'sar] *vt* to think; (considerar) to think over, think out; (proponerse) to intend, plan; (imaginarse) to think up, invent ▷ *vi* to think; **~ en** to aim at, aspire to; **pensativo, -a** *adj* thoughtful, pensive

pensión [pen'sjon] *nf* (casa) boarding o guest house; (dinero) pension; (cama y comida) board and lodging; **media ~** half-board; **pensión completa** full board; **pensionista** *nm/f* (jubilado) (old-age) pensioner; (huésped) lodger

penúltimo, -a [pe'nultimo, a] *adj* penultimate, last but one

penumbra [pe'numbra] *nf* half-light

peña ['pena] *nf* (roca) rock; (cuesta) cliff, crag; (grupo) group, circle; (LAM: club) folk club

peñasco [pe'nasko] *nm* large rock, boulder

peñón [pe'non] *nm* wall of rock; **el P~** the Rock (of Gibraltar)

peón [pe'on] *nm* labourer; (LAM Agr) farm labourer, farmhand; (Ajedrez) pawn

peonza [pe'onθa] *nf* spinning top

peor [pe'or] *adj* (comparativo) worse; (superlativo) worst ▷ *adv* worse; worst; **de mal en ~** from bad to worse

pepinillo [pepi'niʎo] *nm* gherkin

pepino [pe'pino] *nm* cucumber; **(no) me importa un ~** I don't care one bit

pepita [pe'pita] *nf* (Bot) pip; (Minería) nugget

pepito [pe'pito] (ESP) *nm* (tb: **~ de**

ternera) steak sandwich

pequeño, -a [pe'keɲo, a] adj small, little

pera ['pera] nf pear; **peral** nm pear tree

percance [per'kanθe] nm setback, misfortune

percatarse [perka'tarse] vr: **~ de** to notice, take note of

percebe [per'θeβe] nm barnacle

percepción [perθep'θjon] nf (vista) perception; (idea) notion, idea

percha ['pertʃa] nf (coat)hanger; (ganchos) coat hooks pl; (de ave) perch

percibir [perθi'βir] vt to perceive, notice; (Com) to earn, get

percusión [perku'sjon] nf percussion

perdedor, -a [perðe'ðor, a] adj losing ▷ nm/f loser

perder [per'ðer] vt to lose; (tiempo, palabras) to waste; (oportunidad) to lose, miss; (tren) to miss ▷ vi to lose; **perderse** vr (extraviarse) to get lost; (desaparecer) to disappear, be lost to view; (arruinarse) to be ruined; **echar a ~ (comida)** to spoil, ruin; (oportunidad) to waste

pérdida ['perðiða] nf loss; (de tiempo) waste; **pérdidas** nfpl (Com) losses

perdido, -a [per'ðiðo, a] adj lost

perdiz [per'ðiθ] nf partridge

perdón [per'ðon] nm (disculpa) pardon, forgiveness; (clemencia) mercy; **¡~!** sorry!, I beg your pardon!; **perdonar** vt to pardon, forgive; (la vida) to spare; (excusar) to exempt, excuse; **¡perdone (usted)!** sorry!, I beg your pardon!

perecedero, -a [pereθe'ðero, a] adj perishable

perecer [pere'θer] vi to perish, die

peregrinación [pereɣrina'θjon] nf (Rel) pilgrimage

peregrino, -a [pere'ɣrino, a] adj (idea) strange, absurd ▷ nm/f pilgrim

perejil [pere'xil] nm parsley

perenne [pe'renne] adj everlasting, perennial

pereza [pe'reθa] nf laziness, idleness; **perezoso, -a** adj lazy, idle

perfección [perfek'θjon] nf perfection; **perfeccionar** vt to perfect; (mejorar) to improve; (acabar) to complete, finish

perfecto, -a [per'fekto, a] adj perfect; (total) complete

perfil [per'fil] nm profile; (contorno) silhouette, outline; (Arq) (cross) section; **perfiles** nmpl features

perforación [perfora'θjon] nf perforation; (con taladro) drilling; **perforadora** nf punch

perforar [perfo'rar] vt to perforate; (agujero) to drill, bore; (papel) to punch a hole in ▷ vi to drill, bore

perfume [per'fume] nm perfume, scent

periferia [peri'ferja] nf periphery; (de ciudad) outskirts pl

periférico [peri'feriko] (LAM) nm ring road (BRIT), beltway (US)

perilla [pe'riʎa] nf (barba) goatee; (LAM: de puerta) doorknob, door handle

perímetro [pe'rimetro] nm perimeter

periódico, -a [pe'rjoðiko, a] adj periodic(al) ▷ nm newspaper

periodismo [perjo'ðismo] nm journalism; **periodista** nmf journalist

periodo [pe'rjoðo] nm period

período [pe'rjoðo] nm = **periodo**

periquito [peri'kito] nm budgerigar, budgie

perito, -a [pe'rito, a] adj (experto) expert; (diestro) skilled, skilful ▷ nm/f expert; skilled worker; (técnico) technician

perjudicar [perxuði'kar] vt (gen) to damage, harm; **perjudicial** adj damaging, harmful; (en detrimento) detrimental; **perjuicio** nm damage, harm

perjurar [perxu'rar] vi to commit perjury

perla ['perla] nf pearl; **me viene de ~s** it suits me fine

permanecer [permane'θer] vi
(*quedarse*) to stay, remain; (*seguir*) to
continue to be

permanente [perma'nente] adj
permanent, constant ▷ nf perm

permiso [per'miso] nm permission;
(*licencia*) permit, licence (*us*); **con** - excuse
me; **estar de** ~ (*Mil*) on leave;
permiso de conducir driving licence
(*BRIT*), driver's license (*US*); **permiso
por enfermedad** (*LAM*) sick leave

permitir [permi'tir] vt to permit,
allow

pernera [per'nera] nf trouser leg

pero ['pero] conj but; (*aún*) yet ▷ nm
(*defecto*) flaw, defect; (*reparo*) objection

perpendicular [perpendiku'lar] adj
perpendicular

perpetuo, -a [per'petwo, a] adj
perpetual

perplejo, -a [per'plexo, a] adj
perplexed, bewildered

perra ['perra] nf (*Zool*) bitch; **estar sin
una** ~ (*ESP: fam*) to be flat broke

perrera [pe'rrera] nf kennel

perrito [pe'rrito] nm (tb: ~ **caliente**)
hot dog

perro ['perro] nm dog

persa ['persa] adj, nmf Persian

persecución [perseku'θjon] nf
pursuit, chase; (*Rel, Pol*) persecution

perseguir [perse'xir] vt to pursue,
hunt; (*cortejar*) to chase after; (*molestar*)
to pester, annoy; (*Rel, Pol*) to persecute

persiana [per'sjana] nf (Venetian)
blind

persistente [persis'tente] adj
persistent

persistir [persis'tir] vi to persist

persona [per'sona] nf person;
persona mayor elderly person

personaje [perso'naxe] nm
important person, celebrity; (*Teatro
etc*) character

personal [perso'nal] adj (*particular*)
personal; (*para una persona*) single, for
one person ▷ nm personnel, staff;
personalidad nf personality

personarse [perso'narse] vr to
appear in person

personificar [personifi'kar] vt to
personify

perspectiva [perspek'tiβa] nf
perspective; (*vista, panorama*) view,
panorama; (*posibilidad futura*) outlook,
prospect

persuadir [perswa'ðir] vt (*gen*) to
persuade; (*convencer*) to convince;
persuadirse vr to become convinced;
persuasión nf persuasion

pertenecer [pertene'θer] vi to
belong; (*fig*) to concern; **perteneciente**
adj: **perteneciente a** belonging
to; **pertenencia** nf ownership;
pertenencias nfpl (*bienes*)
possessions, property sg

pertenezca etc vb V **pertenecer**

pértiga [per'tixa] nf: **salto de** ~
pole vault

pertinente [perti'nente] adj
relevant, pertinent; (*apropiado*)
appropriate; ~ **a** concerning, relevant
to

perturbación [perturβa'θjon]
nf (*Pol*) disturbance; (*Med*) upset,
disturbance

Perú [pe'ru] nm Peru; **peruano, -a**
adj, nm/f Peruvian

perversión [perβer'sjon] nf
perversion; **perverso, -a** adj perverse;
(*depravado*) depraved

pervertido, -a [perβer'tiðo, a] adj
perverted ▷ nm/f pervert

pervertir [perβer'tir] vt to pervert,
corrupt

pesa ['pesa] nf weight; (*Deporte*) shot

pesadez [pesa'ðeθ] nf (*peso*)
heaviness; (*lentitud*) slowness;
(*aburrimiento*) tediousness

pesadilla [pesa'ðiʎa] nf nightmare,
bad dream

pesado, -a [pe'saðo, a] adj heavy;
(*lento*) slow; (*difícil, duro*) tough, hard;
(*aburrido*) boring, tedious; (*tiempo*)
sultry

pésame ['pesame] nm expression of

condolence, message of sympathy; **dar el ~** to express one's condolences

pesar [pe'sar] vt to weigh ▷ vi to weigh; (ser pesado) to weigh a lot, be heavy; (fig: opinión) to carry weight; **no pesa mucho** it's not very heavy ▷ nm (arrepentimiento) regret; (pena) grief, sorrow; **a ~ de** o **pese a (que)** in spite of, despite

pesca ['peska] nf (acto) fishing; (lo pescado) catch; **ir de ~** to go fishing

pescadería [peskaðe'ria] nf fish shop, fishmonger's (BRIT)

pescadilla [peska'ðiʎa] nf whiting

pescado [pes'kaðo] nm fish

pescador, a [peska'ðor, a] nm/f fisherman/woman

pescar [pes'kar] vt (tomar) to catch; (intentar tomar) to fish for; (conseguir: trabajo) to manage to get ▷ vi to fish, go fishing

pesebre [pe'seβre] nm manger

peseta [pe'seta] nf (Hist) peseta

pesimista [pesi'mista] adj pessimistic ▷ nmf pessimist

pésimo, -a ['pesimo, a] adj awful, dreadful

peso ['peso] nm weight; (balanza) scales pl; (moneda) peso; **vender al ~** to sell by weight; **peso bruto/neto** gross/net weight; **peso pesado/pluma** heavyweight/featherweight

pesquero, -a [pes'kero, a] adj fishing cpd

pestaña [pes'taɲa] nf (Anat) eyelash; (borde) rim

peste ['peste] nf plague; (mal olor) stink, stench

pesticida [pesti'θiða] nm pesticide

pestillo [pes'tiʎo] nm (cerrojo) bolt; (picaporte) door handle

petaca [pe'taka] nf (de cigarros) cigarette case; (de pipa) tobacco pouch; (MÉX: maleta) suitcase

pétalo ['petalo] nm petal

petardo [pe'tarðo] nm firework, firecracker

petición [peti'θjon] nf (pedido)

request, plea; (memorial) petition; (Jur) plea

peto ['peto] (ESP) nm dungarees pl, overalls pl (US)

petróleo [pe'troleo] nm oil, petroleum; **petrolero, -a** adj petroleum cpd ▷ nm (oil) tanker

peyorativo, -a [pejora'tiβo, a] adj pejorative

pez [peθ] nm fish; **pez dorado/de colores** goldfish; **pez espada** swordfish

pezón [pe'θon] nm teat, nipple

pezuña [pe'θuɲa] nf hoof

pianista [pja'nista] nmf pianist

piano ['pjano] nm piano

piar [pjar] vi to cheep

pibe, -a ['piβe, a] (RPL) nm/f boy/girl

picadero [pika'ðero] nm riding school

picadillo [pika'ðiʎo] nm mince, minced meat

picado, -a [pi'kaðo, a] adj pricked, punctured; (Culin) minced, chopped; (mar) choppy; (diente) bad; (tabaco) cut; (enfadado) cross

picador [pika'ðor] nm (Taur) picador; (minero) faceworker

picadura [pika'ðura] nf (pinchazo) puncture; (de abeja) sting; (de mosquito) bite; (tabaco picado) cut tobacco

picante [pi'kante] adj hot; (comentario) racy, spicy

picaporte [pika'porte] nm (manija) doorhandle; (pestillo) latch

picar [pi'kar] vt (agujerear, perforar) to prick, puncture; (abeja) to sting; (mosquito, serpiente) to bite; (Culin) to mince, chop; (incitar) to incite, goad; (dañar, irritar) to annoy, bother; (quemar: lengua) to burn, sting ▷ vi (pez) to bite, take the bait; (sol) to burn, scorch; (abeja, Med) to sting; (mosquito) to bite; **picarse** vr (agriarse) to turn sour, go off; (ofenderse) to take offence

picardía [pikar'ðia] nf villainy; (astucia) slyness, craftiness; (una picardía) dirty trick; (palabra) rude/bad word o expression

pícaro, -a ['pikaro, a] *adj* (*malicioso*) villainous; (*travieso*) mischievous ▷ *nm* (*astuto*) crafty sort; (*sinvergüenza*) rascal, scoundrel

pichi ['pitʃi] (ESP) *nm* pinafore dress (BRIT), jumper (US)

pichón [pi'tʃon] *nm* young pigeon

pico ['piko] *nm* (*de ave*) beak; (*punta*) sharp point; (*Tec*) pick, pickaxe; (*Geo*) peak, summit; **y ~** and a bit; **las seis y ~** six and a bit

picor [pi'kor] *nm* itch

picoso, -a [pi'koso, a] (MÉX) *adj* (*comida*) hot

picudo, -a [pi'kuðo, a] *adj* pointed, with a point

pidió *etc vb* V **pedir**

pido *etc vb* V **pedir**

pie [pje] (*pl* **~s**) *nm* foot; (*fig: motivo*) motive, basis; (: *fundamento*) foothold; **ir a ~** to go on foot, walk; **estar de ~** to be standing (up); **ponerse de ~** to stand up; **de ~ a cabeza** from top to bottom; **al ~ de la letra** (*citar*) literally, verbatim; (*copiar*) exactly, word for word; **en ~ de guerra** on a war footing; **dar ~ a** to give cause for; **hacer ~** (*en el agua*) to touch (the) bottom

piedad [pje'ðað] *nf* (*lástima*) pity, compassion; (*clemencia*) mercy; (*devoción*) piety, devotion

piedra ['pjeðra] *nf* stone; (*roca*) rock; (*de mechero*) flint; (*Meteorología*) hailstone; **piedra preciosa** precious stone

piel [pjel] *nf* (*Anat*) skin; (*Zool*) skin, hide, fur; (*cuero*) leather; (*Bot*) skin, peel

pienso *etc vb* V **pensar**

pierdo *etc vb* V **perder**

pierna ['pjerna] *nf* leg

pieza ['pjeθa] *nf* piece; (*habitación*) room; **pieza de recambio o repuesto** spare (part)

pigmeo, -a [pix'meo, a] *adj, nm/f* pigmy

pijama [pi'xama] *nm* pyjamas *pl* (BRIT), pajamas *pl* (US)

pila ['pila] *nf* (*Elec*) battery; (*montón*) heap, pile; (*lavabo*) sink

píldora ['pildora] *nf* pill; **la ~ (anticonceptiva)** the (contraceptive) pill

pileta [pi'leta] (RPL) *nf* (*fregadero*) (kitchen) sink; (*piscina*) swimming pool

pillar [pi'ʎar] *vt* (*saquear*) to pillage, plunder; (*fam: coger*) to catch; (: *agarrar*) to grasp, seize; (: *entender*) to grasp, catch on to; **pillarse** *vr*: **~se un dedo con la puerta** to catch one's finger in the door

pillo, -a ['piʎo, a] *adj* villainous; (*astuto*) sly, crafty ▷ *nm/f* rascal, rogue, scoundrel

piloto [pi'loto] *nm* pilot; (*de aparato*) (pilot) light; (*Auto: luz*) tail o rear light; (: *conductor*) driver; **piloto automático** automatic pilot

pimentón [pimen'ton] *nm* paprika

pimienta [pi'mjenta] *nf* pepper

pimiento [pi'mjento] *nm* pepper, pimiento

pin [pin] (*pl* **~s**) *nm* badge

pinacoteca [pinako'teka] *nf* art gallery

pinar [pi'nar] *nm* pine forest (BRIT), pine grove (US)

pincel [pin'θel] *nm* paintbrush

pinchadiscos [pintʃa'ðiskos] (ESP) *nmf inv* disc-jockey, DJ

pinchar [pin'tʃar] *vt* (*perforar*) to prick, pierce; (*neumático*) to puncture; (*fig*) to prod; (*Inform*) to click

pinchazo [pin'tʃaθo] *nm* (*perforación*) prick; (*de neumático*) puncture; (*fig*) prod

pincho ['pintʃo] *nm* savoury (snack); **pincho de tortilla** small slice of omelette; **pincho moruno** shish kebab

ping-pong ['pin'pon] *nm* table tennis

pingüino [pin'gwino] *nm* penguin

pino ['pino] *nm* pine (tree)

pinta ['pinta] *nf* spot; (*de líquidos*) spot, drop; (*aspecto*) appearance, look(s) (*pl*); **pintado, -a** *adj* spotted; (*de colores*) colourful; **pintadas** *nfpl* graffiti sg

pintalabios [pinta'laβjos] (ESP) nm
inv lipstick

pintar [pin'tar] vt to paint ⊳vi to
paint; (fam) to count, be important;
pintarse vr to put on make-up

pintor, a [pin'tor, a] nm/f painter

pintoresco, -a [pinto'resko, a] adj
picturesque

pintura [pin'tura] nf painting;
pintura al óleo oil painting

pinza ['pinθa] nf (Zool) claw; (para
colgar ropa) clothes peg; (Tec) pincers
pl; **pinzas** nfpl (para depilar etc)
tweezers pl

piña ['pina] nf (de pino) pine cone;
(fruta) pineapple; (fig) group

piñata [pi'nata] nf container hung up
at parties to be beaten with sticks until
sweets or presents fall out

○ **PIÑATA**
●
● **Piñata** is a very popular party
● game in Mexico. The **piñata** itself
● is a hollow figure made of papier
● maché, or traditionally, from
● adobe, in the shape of an object,
● a star, a person or an animal. It is
● filled with either sweets and toys,
● or fruit and yam beans. The game
● consists of hanging the **piñata**
● from the ceiling, and beating it
● with a stick, blindfolded, until it
● breaks and the presents fall out.

piñón [pi'non] nm (fruto) pine nut;
(Tec) pinion

pío, -a ['pio, a] adj (devoto) pious,
devout; (misericordioso) merciful

piojo ['pjoxo] nm louse

pipa ['pipa] nf pipe; **pipas** nfpl (Bot)
(edible) sunflower seeds

pipí [pi'pi] (fam) nm: **hacer ~** to have
a wee(-wee) (BRIT), have to go (wee-
wee) (US)

pique ['pike] nm (resentimiento)
pique, resentment; (rivalidad)

rivalry, competition; **irse a ~** to sink;
(esperanza, familia) to be ruined

piqueta [pi'keta] nf pick(axe)

piquete [pi'kete] nm (Mil) squad,
party; (de obreros) picket; (MÉX: de
insecto) bite; **piquetear** (LAM) vt to
picket

pirado, -a [pi'raðo, a] (fam) adj
round the bend ⊳nm/f nutter

piragua [pi'raxwa] nf canoe;
piragüismo nm canoeing

pirámide [pi'ramiðe] nf pyramid

pirata [pi'rata] adj, nmf pirate; **pirata
informático** hacker

Pirineo(s) [piri'neo(s)] nm(pl)
Pyrenees pl

pirómano, -a [pi'romano, a] nm/f
(Med, Jur) arsonist

piropo [pi'ropo] nm compliment,
(piece of) flattery

pirueta [pi'rweta] nf pirouette

piruleta [piru'leta] (ESP) nf lollipop

pis [pis] (fam) nm pee, piss; **hacer ~** to
have a pee; (para niños) to wee-wee

pisada [pi'saða] nf (paso) footstep;
(huella) footprint

pisar [pi'sar] vt (caminar sobre) to walk
on, tread on; (apretar con el pie) to press;
(fig) to trample on, walk all over ⊳vi to
tread, step, walk

piscina [pis'θina] nf swimming pool

Piscis ['pisθis] nm Pisces

piso ['piso] nm (suelo, planta)
floor; (ESP: apartamento) flat (BRIT),
apartment; **primer ~** (ESP) first floor;
(LAM: planta baja) ground floor

pisotear [pisote'ar] vt to trample (on
○ underfoot)

pista ['pista] nf track, trail; (indicio)
clue; **pista de aterrizaje** runway; **pista
de baile** dance floor; **pista de hielo** ice
rink; **pista de tenis** (ESP) tennis court

pistola [pis'tola] nf pistol; (Tec)
spray-gun

pistón [pis'ton] nm (Tec) piston;
(Mús) key

pitar [pi'tar] vt (silbato) to blow;
(rechiflar) to whistle at, boo ⊳vi to

whistle; (*Auto*) to sound o toot one's
horn; (*LAM: fumar*) to smoke

pitillo [pi'tiʎo] *nm* cigarette

pito ['pito] *nm* whistle; (*de coche*) horn

pitón [pi'ton] *nm* (*Zool*) python

pitonisa [pito'nisa] *nf* fortune-teller

pitorreo [pito'rreo] *nm* joke; **estar
de ~** to be joking

píxel ['piksel] (*pl* **pixels** *or* **-es**) *nm*
pixel

piyama [pi'jama] (*LAM*) *nm* pyjamas
pl (*BRIT*), pajamas *pl* (*US*)

pizarra [pi'θarra] *nf* (*piedra*)
slate; (*ESP: encerado*) blackboard;
pizarra blanca whiteboard; **pizarra
interactiva** interactive whiteboard

pizarrón [piθa'rron] (*LAM*) *nm*
blackboard

pizca ['piθka] *nf* pinch, spot; (*fig*)
spot, speck; **ni ~** not a bit

placa ['plaka] *nf* plate; (*distintivo*)
badge, insignia; **placa de matrícula**
(*LAM*) number plate

placard [pla'kar] (*RPL*) *nm* cupboard

placer [pla'θer] *nm* pleasure ▷*vt*
to please

plaga ['plaxa] *nf* pest; (*Med*) plague;
(*abundancia*) abundance

plagio ['plaxjo] *nm* plagiarism

plan [plan] *nm* (*esquema, proyecto*)
plan; (*idea, intento*) idea, intention;
tener ~ (*fam*) to have a date; **tener un ~**
(*fam*) to have an affair; **en ~ económico**
(*fam*) on the cheap; **vamos en ~ de
turismo** we're going as tourists; **si
te pones en ese ~ ...** if that's your
attitude ...

plana ['plana] *nf* sheet (of paper),
page; (*Tec*) trowel; **en primera ~** on the
front page

plancha ['plantʃa] *nf* (*para planchar*)
iron; (*rótulo*) plate, sheet; (*Náut*)
gangway; **a la ~** (*Culin*) grilled;
planchar *vt* to iron ▷*vi* to do the
ironing

planear [plane'ar] *vt* to plan ▷*vi*
to glide

planeta [pla'neta] *nm* planet

plano, -a ['plano, a] *adj* flat, level,
even ▷*nm* (*Mat, Tec*) plane; (*Foto*) shot;
(*Arq*) plan; (*Geo*) map; (*de ciudad*) map,
street plan; **primer ~** close-up

planta ['planta] *nf* (*Bot, Tec*) plant;
(*Anat*) sole of the foot; foot; (*piso*)
floor; (*LAM: personal*) staff; **planta baja**
ground floor

plantar [plan'tar] *vt* (*Bot*) to plant;
(*levantar*) to erect, set up; **plantarse** *vr*
to stand firm; **~ a algn en la calle** to
throw sb out; **dejar plantado a algn**
(*fam*) to stand sb up

plantear [plante'ar] *vt* (*problema*) to
pose; (*dificultad*) to raise

plantilla [plan'tiʎa] *nf* (*de zapato*)
insole; (*ESP: personal*) personnel; **ser de
~** (*ESP*) to be on the staff

plantón [plan'ton] *nm* (*Mil*) guard,
sentry; (*fam*) long wait; **dar (un) ~ a
algn** to stand sb up

plasta ['plasta] (*ESP: fam*) *adj inv*
boring ▷*nmf* bore

plástico, -a ['plastiko, a] *adj* plastic
▷*nm* plastic

Plastilina® [plasti'lina] *nf*
Plasticine®

plata ['plata] *nf* (*metal*) silver; (*cosas
hechas de plata*) silverware; (*cs: dinero*)
cash, dough

plataforma [plata'forma] *nf*
platform; **plataforma de
lanzamiento/perforación**
launch(ing) pad/drilling rig

plátano ['platano] *nm* (*fruta*) banana;
(*árbol*) plane tree; banana tree

platea [pla'tea] *nf* (*Teatro*) pit

plática ['platika] *nf* talk, chat;
platicar *vi* to talk, chat

platillo [pla'tiʎo] *nm* saucer; **platillos**
nmpl (*Mús*) cymbals; **platillo volante**
flying saucer

platino [pla'tino] *nm* platinum;
platinos *nmpl* (*Auto*) contact points

plato ['plato] *nm* plate, dish; (*comida*)
course; (*comida*) dish; **primer
~** first course; **plato combinado** set
main course (*served on one plate*); **plato**

fuerte main course
playa ['plaja] *nf* beach; *(costa)*
seaside; **playa de estacionamiento**
(cs) car park *(BRIT)*, parking lot *(US)*
playera [pla'jera] *nf (MÉX: camiseta)*
T-shirt; **playeras** *nfpl (zapatos)* canvas
shoes
plaza ['plaθa] *nf* square; *(mercado)*
market *(plaza)*; *(sitio)* room, space; *(de
vehículo)* seat, place; *(colocación)* post,
job; **plaza de toros** bullring
plazo ['plaθo] *nm (lapso de tiempo)*
time, period; *(fecha de vencimiento)*
expiry date; *(pago parcial)* instalment;
a corto/largo ~ short-/long-term;
comprar algo a ~s to buy sth on hire
purchase *(BRIT)* o on time *(US)*
plazoleta [plaθo'leta] *nf* small
square
plebeyo, -a [ple'βejo, a] *adj*
plebeian; *(pey)* coarse, common
plegable [ple'xaβle] *adj* collapsible;
(silla) folding
pleito ['pleito] *nm (Jur)* lawsuit, case;
(fig) dispute, feud
plenitud [pleni'tuð] *nf* plenitude,
fullness; *(abundancia)* abundance
pleno, -a ['pleno, a] *adj* full;
(completo) complete ▷ *nm* plenum; **en
~ día** in broad daylight; **en ~ verano** at
the height of summer; **en plena cara**
full in the face
pliego *etc* ['pljexo] *vb* V **plegar**
▷ *nm (hoja)* sheet (of paper); *(carta)*
sealed letter/document; **pliego de
condiciones** details *pl*, specifications
pl
pliegue *etc* ['pljexe] *vb* V **plegar** ▷ *nm*
fold, crease; *(de vestido)* pleat
plomería [plome'ria] *(LAM) nf*
plumbing; **plomero** *(LAM) nm* plumber
plomo ['plomo] *nm (metal)* lead; *(Elec)*
fuse; **sin ~** unleaded
pluma ['pluma] *nf* feather; *(para
escribir)*: **~ (estilográfica)** ink pen; **~
fuente** *(LAM)* fountain pen
plumero [plu'mero] *nm (para el polvo)*
feather duster

plumón [plu'mon] *nm (de ave)* down
plural [plu'ral] *adj* plural
pluriempleo [pluriem'pleo] *nm*
having more than one job
plus [plus] *nm* bonus
población [poβla'θjon] *nf*
population; *(pueblo, ciudad)* town, city
poblado, -a [po'βlaðo, a] *adj*
inhabited ▷ *nm (aldea)* village; *(pueblo*
(small) town; **densamente ~** densely
populated
poblador, a [poβla'ðor, a] *nm/f*
settler, colonist
pobre [poβre] *adj* poor ▷ *nmf* poor
person; **pobreza** *nf* poverty
pocilga [po'θilxa] *nf* pigsty

○ **PALABRA CLAVE**

poco, -a ['poko, a] *adj* 1 *(sg)* little,
not much; **poco tiempo** little o not
much time; **de poco interés** little
interest, not very interesting; **poca
cosa** not much
2 *(pl)* few, not many; **unos pocos** a
few, some; **pocos niños comen lo que
les conviene** few children eat what
they should
▷ *adv* 1 little, not much; **cuesta poco** it
doesn't cost much
2 (+ *adj*: *negativo, antónimo*): **poco
amable/inteligente** not very nice/
intelligent
3: **por poco me caigo** I almost fell
4: **a poco: a poco de haberse casado**
shortly after getting married
5: **poco a poco** little by little
▷ *nm* a little, a bit; **un poco triste/de
dinero** a little sad/money

podar [po'ðar] *vt* to prune
podcast ['poðkast] *nm* podcast;
podcastear [poðkaste'ar] *vi* to
podcast

○ **PALABRA CLAVE**

poder [po'ðer] *vi* 1 *(tener capacidad)*

can, be able to; **no puedo hacerlo** I can't do it, I'm unable to do it
2 (tener permiso) can, may, be allowed to; **¿se puede?** may I (o we)?; **puedes irte ahora** you may go now; **no se puede fumar en este hospital** smoking is not allowed in this hospital
3 (tener posibilidad) may, might, could; **puede llegar mañana** he may (o might) arrive tomorrow; **pudiste haberte hecho daño** you might o could have hurt yourself; **¡podías habérmelo dicho antes!** you might have told me before!
4: **puede ser** perhaps; **puede ser que lo sepa Tomás** Tomás may o might know
5: **¡no puedo más!** I've had enough!; **es tonto a más no poder** he's as stupid as they come
6: **poder con: no puedo con este crío** this kid's too much for me
  ▷ *nm* power; **detentar** o **ocupar** o **estar en el poder** to be in power; **poder adquisitivo/ejecutivo/ legislativo** purchasing/executive/ legislative power; **poder judicial** judiciary

poderoso, -a [poˈðeroso, a] *adj* (político, país) powerful
podio [ˈpoðjo] *nm* (Deporte) podium
podium [ˈpoðjum] = **podio**
podrido, -a [poˈðriðo, a] *adj* rotten, bad; (fig) rotten, corrupt
podrir [poˈðrir] = **pudrir**
poema [poˈema] *nm* poem
poesía [poeˈsia] *nf* poetry
poeta [poˈeta] *nmf* poet; **poético, -a** *adj* poetic(al)
poetisa [poeˈtisa] *nf* (woman) poet
póker [ˈpoker] *nm* poker
polaco, -a [poˈlako, a] *adj* Polish
  ▷ *nm/f* Pole
polar [poˈlar] *adj* polar
polea [poˈlea] *nf* pulley
polémica [poˈlemika] *nf* polemics

sg; (una polémica) controversy, polemic
polen [ˈpolen] *nm* pollen
policía [poliˈθia] *nmf* policeman/ woman ▷ *nf* police; **policíaco, -a** *adj* police *cpd*: **novela policíaca** detective story; **policial** *adj* police *cpd*
polideportivo [poliðeporˈtiβo] *nm* sports centre o complex
polígono [poˈliɣono] *nm* (Mat) polygon; **polígono industrial** (ESP) industrial estate
polilla [poˈliʎa] *nf* moth
polio [ˈpoljo] *nf* polio
política [poˈlitika] *nf* politics *sg*; (económica, agraria etc) policy; V tb **político**
político, -a [poˈlitiko, a] *adj* political; (discreto) tactful; (de familia) ...-in-law ▷ *nm/f* politician; **padre ~** father-in-law
póliza [ˈpoliθa] *nf* certificate, voucher; (impuesto) tax stamp; **póliza de seguro(s)** insurance policy
polizón [poliˈθon] *nm* stowaway
pollera [poˈʎera] (cs) *nf* skirt
pollo [ˈpoʎo] *nm* chicken
polo [ˈpolo] *nm* (Geo, Elec) pole; (helado) ice lolly (BRIT), Popsicle® (US); (Deporte) polo; (suéter) polo-neck; **polo Norte/Sur** North/South Pole
Polonia [poˈlonja] *nf* Poland
poltrona [polˈtrona] *nf* easy chair
polución [poluˈθjon] *nf* pollution
polvera [polˈβera] *nf* powder compact
polvo [ˈpolβo] *nm* dust; (Quím, Culin, Med) powder; **polvos** *nmpl* (maquillaje) powder *sg*; **en ~** powdered; **quitar el ~ to** dust; **estar hecho ~** (fam) to be worn out o exhausted; **polvos de talco** talcum powder *sg*
pólvora [ˈpolβora] *nf* gunpowder
polvoriento, -a [polβoˈrjento, a] *adj* (superficie) dusty; (sustancia) powdery
pomada [poˈmaða] *nf* cream, ointment

pomelo [po'melo] nm grapefruit

pómez ['pomeθ] nf: **piedra ~** pumice stone

pomo ['pomo] nm doorknob

pompa ['pompa] nf 1 (burbuja) bubble; (bomba) pump; (esplendor) pomp, splendour

pómulo ['pomulo] nm cheekbone

pon [pon] vb V **poner**

ponchadura [pontʃa'dura] (MÉX) nf puncture (BRIT), flat (US); **ponchar** (MÉX) vt (llanta) to puncture

ponche ['pontʃe] nm punch

poncho ['pontʃo] nm poncho

pondré etc vb V **poner**

🔵 **PALABRA CLAVE**

poner [po'ner] vt 1 (colocar) to put; (telegrama) to send; (obra de teatro) to put on; (película) to show; **ponlo más fuerte** turn it up; **¿qué ponen en el Excelsior?** what's on at the Excelsior?

2 (tienda) to open; (instalar: gas etc) to put in; (radio, TV) to switch o turn on

3 (suponer): **pongamos que ...** let's suppose that ...

4 (contribuir): **el gobierno ha puesto otro millón** the government has contributed another million

5 (Tel): **póngame con el Sr. López** can you put me through to Mr. López?

6: **poner de: le han puesto de director general** they've appointed him general manager

7 (+ adj) to make; **me estás poniendo nerviosa** you're making me nervous

8 (dar nombre): **al hijo le pusieron Diego** they called their son Diego

▷ vi (gallina) to lay

ponerse vr 1 (colocarse): **se puso a mi lado** he came and stood beside me; **tú ponte en esa silla** you go and sit on that chair; **ponerse en camino** to set off

2 (vestido, cosméticos) to put on; **¿por qué no te pones el vestido nuevo?**

why don't you put on o wear your new dress?

3 (+ adj) to turn; to get, become; **se puso muy serio** he got very serious; **después de lavarla la tela se puso azul** after washing it the material turned blue

4: **ponerse a: se puso a llorar** she started to cry; **tienes que ponerte a estudiar** you must get down to studying

pongo etc vb V **poner**

poniente [po'njente] nm (occidente) west; (viento) west wind

pontífice [pon'tifiθe] nm pope, pontiff

pop [pop] adj inv, nm (Mus) pop

popa ['popa] nf stern

popote [po'pote] (MÉX) nm straw

popular [popu'lar] adj (cultura) of the people, folk cpd; **popularidad** nf popularity

🔵 **PALABRA CLAVE**

por [por] prep 1 (objetivo) for; **luchar por la patria** to fight for one's country

2 (+ infin): **por no llegar tarde** so as not to arrive late; **por citar unos ejemplos** to give a few examples

3 (causa) out of, because of; **por escasez de fondos** through o for lack of funds

4 (tiempo): **por la mañana/noche** in the morning/at night; **se queda por una semana** she's staying (for) a week

5 (lugar): **pasar por Madrid** to pass through Madrid; **ir a Guayaquil por Quito** to go to Guayaquil via Quito; **caminar por la calle** to walk along the street; **¿Hay un banco por aquí?** Is there a bank near here?; V tb **todo**

6 (cambio, precio): **te doy uno nuevo por el que tienes** I'll give you a new one (in return) for the one you've got

7 (valor distributivo): **6 euros por**

hora/cabeza 6 euros an o per hour/a
o per head
8 (*modo, medio*) by; **por correo/avión**
by post/air; **entrar por la entrada
principal** to go in through the main
entrance
g: **10 por 10 son 100** 10 times 10 is 100
10 (*en lugar de*): **vino él por su jefe** he
came instead of his boss
m: **por mí que revienten** as far as I'm
concerned they can drop dead
na: **¿por qué?** why?; **¿por qué no?**
why not?

orcelana [porθe'lana] *nf* porcelain;
(*china*) china
orcentaje [porθen'taxe] *nm*
percentage
orción [por'θjon] *nf* (*parte*) portion,
share; (*cantidad*) quantity, amount
orfiar [por'fjar] *vi* to persist, insist;
(*disputar*) to argue stubbornly
ormenor [porme'nor] *nm* detail,
particular
ornografía [pornoɣra'fia] *nf*
pornography
oro ['poro] *nm* pore
ororó [poro'ro] (RPL) *nm* popcorn
oroso, -a [po'roso, a] *adj* porous
oroto [po'roto] (CS) *nm* bean
orque ['porke] *conj* (*a causa de*)
because; (*ya que*) since; (*con el fin de*) so
that, in order that
orqué [por'ke] *nm* reason, cause
orquería [porke'ria] *nf* (*suciedad*)
filth, dirt; (*acción*) dirty trick; (*objeto*)
small thing, trifle; (*fig*) rubbish
orra ['porra] (ESP) *nf* (*arma*) stick,
club
orrazo [po'rraθo] *nm* blow, bump
orro ['porro] (*fam*) *nm* (*droga*) joint
(*fam*)
orrón [po'rron] *nm* glass wine jar with
long spout
ortaaviones [porta'(a)βjones] *nm
inv* aircraft carrier
ortada [por'taða] *nf* (*de revista*)
cover

portador, a [porta'ðor, a] *nm/f*
carrier, bearer; (Com) bearer, payee
portaequipajes [portaeki'paxes]
nm inv (Auto: *maletero*) boot; (: *baca*)
luggage rack
portafolio [porta'foljo] (LAM) *nm*
briefcase
portal [por'tal] *nm* (*entrada*)
vestibule, hall; (*portada*) porch,
doorway; (*puerta de entrada*) main door;
(*Internet*) portal; **portales** *nmpl* (LAM)
arcade sg
portamaletas [portama'letas]
nm inv (Auto: *maletero*) boot; (: *baca*)
roof rack
portamonedas [portamo'neðas]
nm inv purse
portarse [por'tarse] *vr* to behave,
conduct o.s.
portátil [por'tatil] *adj* portable;
(ordenador) portátil laptop computer
portavoz [porta'βoθ] *nmf*
spokesman/woman
portazo [por'taθo] *nm*: **dar un ~** to
slam the door
porte ['porte] *nm* (Com) transport;
(*precio*) transport charges *pl*
portentoso, -a [porten'toso, a] *adj*
marvellous, extraordinary
porteño, -a [por'teɲo, a] *adj* of o
from Buenos Aires
portería [porte'ria] *nf* (*oficina*)
porter's office; (*Deporte*) goal
portero, -a [por'tero, a] *nm/f* porter;
(*conserje*) caretaker; (*ujier*) doorman;
(*Deporte*) goalkeeper; **portero
automático**(ESP) entry phone
pórtico [portiko] *nm* (*patio*) portico,
porch; (*fig*) gateway; (*arcada*) arcade
portorriqueño, -a [portorri'keɲo,
a] *adj* Puerto Rican
Portugal [portu'ɣal] *nm* Portugal;
portugués, -esa *adj*, *nm/f* Portuguese
▷ *nm* (Ling) Portuguese
porvenir [porβe'nir] *nm* future
pos [pos] *prep*: **en ~ de** after, in
pursuit of
posaderas [posa'ðeras] *nfpl*

P

backside sg, buttocks

posar [po'sar] vt (en el suelo) to lay down, put down; (la mano) to place, put gently ▷ vi (modelo) to sit, pose; **posarse** vr to settle; (pájaro) to perch; (avión) to land, come down

posavasos [posa'βasos] nm inv coaster; (para cerveza) beermat

posdata [pos'ðata] nf postscript

pose ['pose] nf pose

poseedor, -a [posee'ðor, a] nm/f owner, possessor; (de récord, puesto) holder

poseer [pose'er] vt to possess, own; (ventaja) to enjoy; (récord, puesto) to hold

posesivo, -a [pose'siβo, a] adj possessive

posibilidad [posiβili'ðað] nf possibility; (oportunidad) chance; **posibilitar** vt to make possible; (hacer realizable) to make feasible

posible [po'siβle] adj possible; (realizable) feasible; **de ser ~** if possible; **en lo ~** as far as possible

posición [posi'θjon] nf position; (rango social) status

positivo, -a [posi'tiβo, a] adj positive

poso ['poso] nm sediment; (heces) dregs pl

posponer [pospo'ner] vt (relegar) to put behind/below; (aplazar) to postpone

posta ['posta] nf: **a ~** deliberately, on purpose

postal [pos'tal] adj postal ▷ nf postcard

poste ['poste] nm (de telégrafos etc) post, pole; (columna) pillar

póster ['poster] (pl **-es, ~s**) nm poster

posterior [poste'rjor] adj back, rear; (siguiente) following, subsequent; (más tarde) later

postgrado [post'graðo] nm = **posgrado**

postizo, -a [pos'tiθo, a] adj false, artificial ▷ nm hairpiece

postre ['postre] nm sweet, dessert

póstumo, -a ['postumo, a] adj posthumous

postura [pos'tura] nf (del cuerpo) posture, position; (fig) attitude, position

potable [po'taβle] adj drinkable; **agua ~** drinking water

potaje [po'taxe] nm thick vegetable soup

potencia [po'tenθja] nf power; **potencial** [poten'θjal] adj, nm potential

potente [po'tente] adj powerful

potro, -a ['potro, a] nm/f (Zool) colt/ filly ▷ nm (de gimnasia) vaulting horse

pozo ['poθo] nm well; (de río) deep pool; (de mina) shaft

PP (ESP) nm abr = **Partido Popular**

práctica ['praktika] nf practice; (método) method; (arte, capacidad) skill; **en la ~** in practice

practicable [prakti'kaβle] adj practicable; (camino) passable

practicante [prakti'kante] nmf (Med: ayudante de doctor) medical assistant; (: enfermero) nurse; (quien practica algo) practitioner ▷ adj practising

practicar [prakti'kar] vt to practise; (Deporte) to play; (realizar) to carry out, perform

práctico, -a ['praktiko, a] adj practical; (instruido: persona) skilled, expert

practique etc vb V **practicar**

pradera [pra'ðera] nf meadow; (us etc) prairie

prado ['praðo] nm (campo) meadow, field; (pastizal) pasture

Praga ['praxa] n Prague

pragmático, -a [prax'matiko, a] adj pragmatic

precario, -a [pre'karjo, a] adj precarious

precaución [prekau'θjon] nf (medida preventiva) preventive measure, precaution; (prudencia) caution, wariness

precedente [preθe'ðente] *adj*
preceding; (*anterior*) former ▷ *nm*
precedent

preceder [preθe'ðer] *vt, vi* to
precede, go before, come before

precepto [pre'θepto] *nm* precept

recinto [pre'θinto] *nm* (*tb*: ~ **de
garantía**) seal

recio ['preθjo] *nm* price; (*costo*)
cost; (*valor*) value, worth; (*de viaje*)
fare; **precio al contado/de coste/de
oportunidad** cash/cost/bargain
price; **precio al por menor** retail price;
precio de ocasión bargain price;
precio de venta al público retail price;
precio tope top price

reciosidad [preθjosi'ðað] *nf* (*valor*)
(high) value, (great) worth; (*encanto*)
charm; (*cosa bonita*) beautiful thing; **es
una ~** it's lovely, it's really beautiful

recioso, -a [pre'θjoso, a] *adj*
precious; (*de mucho valor*) valuable;
(*fam*) lovely, beautiful

recipicio [preθi'piθjo] *nm* cliff,
precipice; (*fig*) abyss

recipitación [preθipita'θjon] *nf*
haste; (*lluvia*) rainfall

recipitado, -a [preθipi'taðo, a] *adj*
(*conducta*) hasty, rash; (*salida*) hasty,
sudden

recipitar [preθipi'tar] *vt* (*arrojar*) to
hurl down, throw; (*apresurar*) to hasten;
(*acelerar*) to speed up, accelerate;
precipitarse *vr* to throw o.s.;
(*apresurarse*) to rush; (*actuar sin pensar*)
to act rashly

recisamente [preθisa'mente]
adv precisely; (*exactamente*) precisely,
exactly

recisar [preθi'sar] *vt* (*necesitar*)
to need, require; (*fijar*) to determine
exactly, fix; (*especificar*) to specify

recisión [preθi'sjon] *nf* (*exactitud*)
precision

reciso, -a [pre'θiso, a] *adj* (*exacto*)
precise; (*necesario*) necessary, essential

reconcebido, -a [prekonθe'βiðo,

a] *adj* preconceived

precoz [pre'koθ] *adj* (*persona*)
precocious; (*calvicie etc*) premature

predecir [preðe'θir] *vt* to predict,
forecast

predestinado, -a [preðesti'naðo, a]
adj predestined

predicar [preði'kar] *vt, vi* to preach

predicción [preðik'θjon] *nf*
prediction

predilecto, -a [preði'lekto, a] *adj*
favourite

predisposición [preðisposi'θjon] *nf*
inclination; prejudice, bias

predominar [preðomi'nar] *vt* to
dominate ▷ *vi* to predominate;
(*prevalecer*) to prevail; **predominio** *nm*
predominance; prevalence

preescolar [pre(e)sko'lar] *adj*
preschool

prefabricado, -a [prefaβri'kaðo, a]
adj prefabricated

prefacio [pre'faθjo] *nm* preface

preferencia [prefe'renθja] *nf*
preference; **de ~** preferably, for
preference

preferible [prefe'riβle] *adj* preferable

preferido, -a [prefe'riðo, a] *adj, nm/f*
favourite, favorite (*us*)

preferir [prefe'rir] *vt* to prefer

prefiero *etc vb* V **preferir**

prefijo [pre'fixo] *nm* (*Tel*) (dialling)
code

pregunta [pre'xunta] *nf* question;
hacer una ~ to ask a question;
preguntas frecuentes FAQs,
frequently asked questions

preguntar [prexun'tar] *vt* to
ask; (*cuestionar*) to question ▷ *vi* to
ask; **preguntarse** *vr* to wonder;
preguntar por algn to ask for sb;
preguntón, -ona [prexun'ton, ona]
adj inquisitive

prehistórico, -a [preis'toriko, a] *adj*
prehistoric

prejuicio [pre'xwiθjo] *nm* (*acto*)
prejudgement; (*idea preconcebida*)
preconception; (*parcialidad*) prejudice,

bias

preludio [pre'luðjo] nm prelude

prematuro, -a [prema'turo, a] adj premature

premeditar [premeði'tar] vt to premeditate

premiar [pre'mjar] vt to reward; (en un concurso) to give a prize to

premio ['premjo] nm reward; prize; (Com) premium

prenatal [prena'tal] adj antenatal, prenatal

prenda ['prenda] nf (ropa) garment, article of clothing; (garantía) pledge; **prendas** nfpl (talentos) talents, gifts

prender [pren'der] vt (captar) to catch, capture; (detener) to arrest; (Costura) to pin, attach; (sujetar) to fasten ▷ vi to catch; (arraigar) to take root; **prenderse** vr (encenderse) to catch fire

prendido, -a [pren'diðo, a] (LAM) adj (luz etc) on

prensa ['prensa] nf press; **la ~** the press

preñado, -a [pre'ɲaðo, a] adj pregnant; **~ de** pregnant with, full of

preocupación [preokupa'θjon] nf worry, concern; (ansiedad) anxiety

preocupado, -a [preoku'paðo, a] adj worried, concerned; (ansioso) anxious

preocupar [preoku'par] vt to worry; **preocuparse** vr to worry; **~se de algo** (hacerse cargo) to take care of sth

preparación [prepara'θjon] nf (acto) preparation; (estado) readiness; (entrenamiento) training

preparado, -a [prepa'raðo, a] adj (dispuesto) prepared; (Culin) ready (to serve) ▷ nm preparation

preparar [prepa'rar] vt (disponer) to prepare, get ready; (Tec: tratar) to prepare, process; (entrenar) to teach, train; **prepararse** vr: **~se a o para** to prepare to o for; **preparativo, -a** adj preparatory, preliminary; **preparativos** nmpl

preparations; **preparatoria**(MÉX) nf sixth-form college (BRIT), senior high school (US)

presa ['presa] nf (cosa apresada) catch; (víctima) victim; (de animal) prey; (de agua) dam

presagiar [presa'xjar] vt to presage, forebode; **presagio** nm omen

prescindir [presθin'dir] vi: **~ de** (privarse de) to do o go without; (descartar) to dispense with

prescribir [preskri'βir] vt to prescribe

presencia [pre'senθja] nf presence; **presenciar** vt to be present at; (asistir a) to attend; (ver) to see, witness

presentación [presenta'θjon] nf presentation; (introducción) introduction

presentador, a [presenta'ðor, a] nm/f presenter, compère

presentar [presen'tar] vt to present; (ofrecer) to offer; (mostrar) to show, display; (a una persona) to introduce; **presentarse** vr (llegar inesperadamente) to appear, turn up; (ofrecerse: como candidato) to run, stand; (aparecer) to show, appear; (solicitar empleo) to apply

presente [pre'sente] adj present ▷ nm present; **hacer ~** to state, declare; **tener ~** to remember, bear in mind

presentimiento [presenti'mjento] nm premonition, presentiment

presentir [presen'tir] vt to have a premonition of

preservación [preserβa'θjon] nf protection, preservation

preservar [preser'βar] vt to protect, preserve; **preservativo** nm sheath, condom

presidencia [presi'ðenθja] nf presidency; (de comité) chairmanship

presidente [presi'ðente] nmf president; (de comité) chairman/woman

presidir [presi'ðir] vt (dirigir) to preside at, preside over; (: comité) to take the chair at; (dominar) to

dominate, rule ▷vi to preside; to take the chair
presión [pre'sjon] nf pressure; **presión atmosférica** atmospheric o air pressure; **presionar** vt to press; (fig) to press, put pressure on ▷ vi: **presionar para** to press for
preso, -a ['preso, a] nm/f prisoner; **tomar** o **llevar ~ a algn** to arrest sb, take sb prisoner
prestación [presta'θjon] nf service; (subsidio) benefit; **prestaciones** nfpl (Tec, Auto) performance features
prestado, -a [pres'taðo, a] adj on loan; **pedir ~** to borrow
prestamista [presta'mista] nmf moneylender
préstamo ['prestamo] nm loan; **préstamo hipotecario** mortgage
prestar [pres'tar] vt to lend, loan; (atención) to pay; (ayuda) to give
prestigio [pres'tixjo] nm prestige; **prestigioso, -a** adj (honorable) (famoso, renombrado) renowned, famous
presumido, -a [presu'miðo, a] adj ▷vi (tener aires) to be conceited; **presunto, -a** adj (supuesto) supposed, presumed; (así llamado) so-called; **presuntuoso, -a** adj conceited, presumptuous
presupuesto [presu'pwesto] pp de **presuponer** ▷nm (Finanzas) budget; (estimación: de costo) estimate
pretencioso, -a [preten'θjoso, a] adj pretentious
pretender [preten'der] vt (intentar) o try to, seek to; (reivindicar) to claim; buscar) to seek, try for; (cortejar) to woo, court; **~ que** to expect that
☐ No confundir **pretender** con la palabra inglesa pretend.
pretendiente nmf (amante) suitor; (al trono) pretender; **pretensión** nf (aspiración) aspiration; (reivindicación) claim; (orgullo) pretension

pretexto [pre'teksto] nm pretext; (excusa) excuse
prevención [preβen'θjon] nf prevention; (precaución) precaution
prevenido, -a [preβe'niðo, a] adj prepared, ready; (cauteloso) cautious
prevenir [preβe'nir] vt (impedir) to prevent; (predisponer) to prejudice, bias; (avisar) to warn; (preparar) to prepare, get ready; **prevenirse** vr to get ready, prepare; **~se contra** to take precautions against; **preventivo, -a** adj preventive, precautionary
prever [pre'βer] vt to foresee
previo, -a ['preβjo, a] adj (anterior) previous; (preliminar) preliminary ▷ prep: **~ acuerdo de los otros** subject to the agreement of the others
previsión [preβi'sjon] nf (perspicacia) foresight; (predicción) forecast; **previsto, -a** adj anticipated, forecast
prima ['prima] nf (Com) bonus; (de seguro) premium; V tb **primo**
primario, -a [pri'marjo, a] adj primary
primavera [prima'βera] nf spring(-time)
primera [pri'mera] nf (Auto) first gear; (Ferro: tb: **~ clase**) first class; **de ~** (fam) first-class, first-rate
Primer Ministro [pri'mer-] nm Prime Minister
primero, -a [pri'mero, a] adj (adj **primer**) first; (principal) prime adv first; (más bien) sooner, rather; **primera plana** front page
primitivo, -a [primi'tiβo, a] adj primitive; (original) original
primo, -a ['primo, a] adj prime ▷nm/f cousin; (fam) fool, idiot; **materias primas** raw materials; **primo hermano** first cousin
primogénito, -a [primo'xenito, a] adj first-born
primoroso, -a [primo'roso, a] adj exquisite, delicate
princesa [prin'θesa] nf princess
principal [prinθi'pal] adj principal,

main ▷ nm (jefe) chief, principal

príncipe [ˈprinθipe] nm prince

principiante [prinθiˈpjante] nmf beginner

principio [prinˈθipjo] nm (comienzo) beginning, start; (origen) origin; (primera etapa) rudiment, basic idea; (moral) principle; **desde el ~** from the first; **en un ~** at first; **a ~s de** at the beginning of

pringue [ˈpriŋge] nm (grasa) grease, fat, dripping

prioridad [prioriˈðað] nf priority

prisa [ˈprisa] nf (apresuramiento) hurry, haste; (rapidez) speed; (urgencia) (sense of) urgency; **a ~ de ~** quickly; **correr ~** to be urgent; **darse ~** to hurry up; **tener ~** to be in a hurry

prisión [priˈsjon] nf (cárcel) prison; (período de cárcel) imprisonment; **prisionero, -a** nm/f prisoner

prismáticos [prisˈmatikos] nmpl binoculars

privado, -a [priˈβaðo, a] adj private

privar [priˈβar] vt to deprive; **privativo, -a** adj exclusive

privilegiar [priβileˈxjar] vt to grant a privilege to; (favorecer) to favour

privilegio [priβiˈlexjo] nm privilege; (concesión) concession

pro [pro] nm o f profit, advantage ▷ prep: **asociación ~ ciegos** association for the blind ▷ prefijo: **~ americano** pro-American; **en ~ de** on behalf of, for; **los ~s y los contras** the pros and cons

proa [ˈproa] nf bow, prow; **de ~** bow cpd, fore

probabilidad [proβaβiliˈðað] nf probability, likelihood; (oportunidad, posibilidad) chance, prospect; **probable** adj probable, likely

probador [proβaˈðor] nm (en tienda) fitting room

probar [proˈβar] vt (demostrar) to prove; (someter a prueba) to test, try out; (ropa) to try on; (comida) to taste ▷ vi to try; **~se un traje** to try on a suit

probeta [proˈβeta] nf test tube

problema [proˈβlema] nm problem

procedente [proθeˈðente] adj (razonable) reasonable; (conforme a derecho) proper, fitting; **~ de** coming from, originating in

proceder [proθeˈðer] vi (avanzar) to proceed; (actuar) to act; (ser correcto) to be right (and proper), be fitting ▷ nm (comportamiento) behaviour, conduct; **~ de** to come from, originate in; **procedimiento** nm procedure; (proceso) process; (método) means pl, method

procesador [proθesaˈðor] nm processor; **procesador de textos** word processor

procesar [proθeˈsar] vt to try, put on trial

procesión [proθeˈsjon] nf procession

proceso [proˈθeso] nm process; (Jur) trial

proclamar [proklaˈmar] vt to proclaim

procrear [prokreˈar] vt, vi to procreate

procurador, a [prokuraˈðor, a] nm/f attorney

procurar [prokuˈrar] vt (intentar) to try, endeavour; (conseguir) to get, obtain; (asegurar) to secure; (producir) to produce

prodigio [proˈðixjo] nm prodigy; (milagro) wonder, marvel; **prodigioso, -a** adj prodigious, marvellous

pródigo, -a [ˈproðixo, a] adj: **hijo ~** prodigal son

producción [proðukˈθjon] nf (gen) production; (producto) output; **producción en serie** mass production

producir [proðuˈθir] vt to produce; (causar) to cause, bring about; **producirse** vr (cambio) to come about; (accidente) to take place; (problema etc) to arise; (hacerse) to be produced, be made; (estallar) to break out

productividad [proðuktiβiˈðað] nf productivity; **productivo, -a** adj

productive; (*provechoso*) profitable
producto [pro'ðukto] *nm* product
productor, a [proðuk'tor, a] *adj*
productive, producing ▷ *nm/f* producer
proeza [pro'eθa] *nf* exploit, feat
profano, -a [pro'fano, a] *adj* profane
▷ *nm/f* layman/woman
profecía [profe'θia] *nf* prophecy
profesión [profe'sjon] *nf* profession;
(*en formulario*) occupation; **profesional**
adj professional
profesor, a [profe'sor, a] *nm/f*
teacher; **profesorado** *nm* teaching
profession
profeta [pro'feta] *nm* prophet
prófugo, -a ['profuxo, a] *nm/f*
fugitive; (*Mil: desertor*) deserter
profundidad [profundi'ðað] *nf*
depth; **profundizar** *vi*: **profundizar
en** to go deeply into; **profundo, -a** *adj*
deep; (*misterio, pensador*) profound
progenitor [proxeni'tor] *nm*
ancestor; **progenitores** *nmpl* (*padres*)
parents
programa [pro'xrama] *nm*
programme (BRIT), program (US);
programa de estudios curriculum,
syllabus; **programación** *nf*
programming; **programador, a**
nm/f programmer; **programar** *vt* to
program
progresar [proxre'sar] *vi* to
progress, make progress; **progresista**
adj, nmf progressive; **progresivo,
-a** *adj* progressive; (*gradual*) gradual;
(*continuo*) continuous; **progreso** *nm*
progress
prohibición [proiβi'θjon] *nf*
prohibition, ban
prohibir [proi'βir] *vt* to prohibit, ban,
forbid; **prohibido** o **se prohíbe fumar**
no smoking; **"prohibido el paso"**
"no entry"
prójimo, -a ['proximo, a] *nm/f*
fellow man; (*vecino*) neighbour
prólogo ['proloxo] *nm* prologue
prolongar [prolon'xar] *vt* to extend;
(*reunión etc*) to prolong; (*calle, tubo*)

to extend
promedio [pro'meðjo] *nm* average;
(*de distancia*) middle, mid-point
promesa [pro'mesa] *nf* promise
prometer [prome'ter] *vt* to promise
▷ *vi* to show promise; **prometerse** *vr*
(*novios*) to get engaged; **prometido,
-a** *adj* promised; engaged ▷ *nm/f*
fiancé/fiancée
prominente [promi'nente] *adj*
prominent
promoción [promo'θjon] *nf*
promotion
promotor [promo'tor] *nm* promoter;
(*instigador*) instigator
promover [promo'βer] *vt* to
promote; (*causar*) to cause; (*instigar*) to
instigate, stir up
promulgar [promul'xar] *vt* to
promulgate; (*anunciar*) to proclaim
pronombre [pro'nombre] *nm*
pronoun
pronosticar [pronosti'kar] *vt* to
predict, foretell, forecast; **pronóstico**
nm prediction, forecast; **pronóstico
del tiempo** weather forecast
pronto, -a ['pronto, a] *adj* (*rápido*)
prompt, quick; (*preparado*) ready ▷ *adv*
quickly, promptly; (*en seguida*) at once,
right away; (*dentro de poco*) soon;
(*temprano*) early ▷ *nm*: **tiene unos
~s muy malos** he gets ratty all of a
sudden (*inf*); **de ~** suddenly; **por lo ~**
meanwhile, for the present
pronunciación [pronunθja'θjon] *nf*
pronunciation
pronunciar [pronun'θjar] *vt* to
pronounce; (*discurso*) to make, deliver;
pronunciarse *vr* to revolt, rebel;
(*declararse*) to declare o.s.
propagación [propaxa'θjon] *nf*
propagation
propaganda [propa'xanda] *nf* (*Pol*)
propaganda; (*Com*) advertising
propenso, -a [pro'penso, a] *adj*
inclined to; **ser ~ a** to be inclined to,
have a tendency to
propicio, -a [pro'piθjo, a] *adj*

P

favourable, propitious

propiedad [propje'ðað] nf property; (posesión) possession, ownership; **propiedad particular** private property

propietario, -a [propje'tarjo, a] nm/f owner, proprietor

propina [pro'pina] nf tip

propio, -a ['propjo, a] adj own, of one's own; (característico) characteristic, typical; (debido) proper; (mismo) selfsame, very; **el ~ ministro** the minister himself; **¿tienes casa propia?** have you a house of your own?

proponer [propo'ner] vt to propose, put forward; (problema) to pose; **proponerse** vr to propose, intend

proporción [propor'θjon] nf proportion; (Mat) ratio; **proporciones** nfpl (dimensiones) dimensions; (fig) size sg; **proporcionado, -a** adj proportionate; (regular) medium, middling; (justo) just right; **proporcionar** vt (dar) to give, supply, provide

proposición [proposi'θjon] nf proposition; (propuesta) proposal

propósito [pro'posito] nm purpose; (intento) aim, intention ▷ adv: **a ~** by the way, incidentally; (a posta) on purpose, deliberately; **a ~ de** about, with regard to

propuesta [pro'pwesta] vb V **proponer** ▷ nf proposal

propulsar [propul'sar] vt to drive, propel; (fig) to promote, encourage; **propulsión** nf propulsion; **propulsión a chorro por reacción** jet propulsion

prórroga ['prorroxa] nf extension; (Jur) stay; (Com) deferment; (Deporte) extra time; **prorrogar** vt (período) to extend; (decisión) to defer, postpone

prosa ['prosa] nf prose

proseguir [prose'xir] vt to continue, carry on ▷ vi to continue, go on

prospecto [pros'pekto] nm prospectus

prosperar [prospe'rar] vi to prosper, thrive, flourish; **prosperidad** nf prosperity; (éxito) success; **próspero,**

-a adj prosperous, flourishing; (que tiene éxito) successful

prostíbulo [pros'tiβulo] nm brothel (BRIT), house of prostitution (US)

prostitución [prostitu'θjon] nf prostitution

prostituir [prosti'twir] vt to prostitute; **prostituirse** vr to prostitute o.s., become a prostitute

prostituta [prosti'tuta] nf prostitute

protagonista [protaɣo'nista] nmf protagonist

protección [protek'θjon] nf protection

protector, a [protek'tor, a] adj protective, protecting ▷ nm/f protector

proteger [prote'xer] vt to protect; **protegido, -a** nm/f protégé/protégée

proteína [prote'ina] nf protein

protesta [pro'testa] nf protest; (declaración) protestation

protestante [protes'tante] adj Protestant

protestar [protes'tar] vt to protest, declare ▷ vi to protest

protocolo [proto'kolo] nm protocol

prototipo [proto'tipo] nm prototype

provecho [pro'βetʃo] nm advantage, benefit; (Finanzas) profit; **¡buen ~!** bon appétit!; **en ~ de** to the benefit of; **sacar ~ de** to benefit from, profit by

provenir [proβe'nir] vi: **~ de** to come o stem from

proverbio [pro'βerβjo] nm proverb

providencia [proβi'ðenθja] nf providence

provincia [pro'βinθja] nf province

provisión [proβi'sjon] nf provision; (abastecimiento) provision, supply; (medida) measure, step

provisional [proβisjo'nal] adj provisional

provocar [proβo'kar] vt to provoke; (alentar) to tempt, invite; (causar) to bring about, lead to; (promover) to promote; (estimular) to rouse, stimulate; **¿te provoca un café?** (CAM) would you like a coffee?; **provocativo,**

-a adj provocative

proxeneta [prokse'neta] nm pimp

próximamente [proksima'mente] adv shortly, soon

proximidad [proksimi'ðað] nf closeness, proximity; **próximo, -a** adj near, close; (vecino) neighbouring; (siguiente) next

proyectar [projek'tar] vt (objeto) to hurl, throw; (luz) to cast, shed; (Cine) to screen, show; (planear) to plan

proyectil [projek'til] nm projectile, missile

proyecto [pro'jekto] nm plan; (estimación de gastos) detailed estimate

proyector [projek'tor] nm (Cine) projector

prudencia [pru'ðenθja] nf (sabiduría) wisdom; (cuidado) care; **prudente** adj sensible, wise; (conductor) careful

prueba etc [ˈprweβa] vb V **probar** ▷ nf proof; (ensayo) test, trial; (degustación) tasting, sampling; (de ropa) fitting; **a ~ on trial**; **a ~ de** proof against; **a ~ de agua/fuego** waterproof/fireproof; **someter a ~** to put to the test

psico- [siko] prefijo psycho...; **psicología** nf psychology; **psicológico, -a** adj psychological; **psicólogo, -a** nm/f psychologist; **psicópata** nmf psychopath; **psicosis** nf inv psychosis

psiquiatra [si'kjatra] nmf psychiatrist; **psiquiátrico, -a** adj psychiatric

PSOE [pe'soe] (ESP) nm abr = **Partido Socialista Obrero Español**

púa [ˈpua] nf (Bot, Zool) prickle, spine; (para guitarra) plectrum (BRIT), pick (US); **alambre de ~** barbed wire

pubertad [puβer'tað] nf puberty

publicación [puβlika'θjon] nf publication

publicar [puβli'kar] vt (editar) to publish; (hacer público) to publicize; (divulgar) to make public, divulge

publicidad [puβliθi'ðað] nf publicity; (Com: propaganda)

advertising; **publicitario, -a** adj publicity cpd; advertising cpd

público, -a [ˈpuβliko, a] adj public ▷ nm public; (Teatro etc) audience

puchero [pu'tʃero] nm (Culin: guiso) stew; (: olla) cooking pot; **hacer ~s** to pout

pucho [ˈputʃo] (cs: fam) nm cigarette, fag (BRIT)

pude etc vb V **poder**

pudiente [pu'ðjente] adj (rico) wealthy, well-to-do

pudiera etc vb V **poder**

pudor [pu'ðor] nm modesty

pudrir [pu'ðrir] vt to rot; **pudrirse** vr to rot, decay

pueblo [ˈpweβlo] nm people; (nación) nation; (aldea) village

puedo etc vb V **poder**

puente [ˈpwente] nm bridge; **hacer ~** (fam) to take extra days off work between 2 public holidays; to take a long weekend; **puente aéreo** shuttle service; **puente colgante** suspension bridge; **puente levadizo** drawbridge

> **HACER PUENTE**
>
> When a public holiday in Spain
> falls on a Tuesday or Thursday it is
> common practice for employers
> to make the Monday or Friday
> a holiday as well and to give
> everyone a four-day weekend. This
> is known as **hacer puente**. When
> a named public holiday such as the
> **Día de la Constitución** falls on a
> Tuesday or Thursday, people refer
> to the whole holiday period as e.g.
> the **puente de la Constitución**.

puerco, -a [ˈpwerko, a] nm/f pig/ sow ▷ adj (sucio) dirty, filthy; (obsceno) disgusting; **puerco espín** porcupine

pueril [pweˈril] adj childish

puerro [ˈpwerro] nm leek

puerta [ˈpwerta] nf door; (de jardín) gate; (portal) doorway; (fig) gateway;

(*portería*) goal: **a la ~** at the door; **a ~ cerrada** behind closed doors; **puerta giratoria** revolving door

puerto ['pwerto] *nm* port; (*paso*) pass; (*fig*) haven, refuge

Puerto Rico [pwerto'riko] *nm* Puerto Rico; **puertorriqueño, -a** *adj, nm/f* Puerto Rican

pues [pwes] *adv* (*entonces*) then; (*bueno*) well, well then; (*así que*) so ⊳ *conj* (*ya que*) since; **¡~ sí!** yes!, certainly!

puesta *nf* (*apuesta*) bet, stake; **puesta al día** updating; **puesta a punto** fine tuning; **puesta de sol** sunset; **puesta en marcha** starting

puesto, -a ['pwesto, a] *pp de* **poner** ⊳ *adj*: **tener algo ~** to have sth on, be wearing sth ⊳ *nm* (*lugar, posición*) place; (*trabajo*) post, job; (*Com*) stall ⊳ *conj*: **~ que** since, as

púgil ['puxil] *nm* boxer

pulga ['pulγa] *nf* flea

pulgada [pul'γaða] *nf* inch

pulgar [pul'γar] *nm* thumb

pulir [pu'lir] *vt* to polish; (*alisar*) to smooth; (*fig*) to polish up, touch up

pulmón [pul'mon] *nm* lung; **pulmonía** *nf* pneumonia

pulpa ['pulpa] *nf* pulp; (*de fruta*) flesh, soft part

pulpería [pulpe'ria] (*LAM*) *nf* (*tienda*) small grocery store

púlpito ['pulpito] *nm* pulpit

pulpo ['pulpo] *nm* octopus

pulque ['pulke] *nm* pulque

○ **PULQUE**
○
○ **Pulque** is a thick, white, alcoholic
○ drink which is very popular in
○ Mexico. In ancient times it was
○ considered sacred by the Aztecs.
○ It is produced by fermenting the
○ juice of the **maguey**, a Mexican
○ cactus similar to the agave. It can
○ be drunk by itself or mixed with
○ fruit or vegetable juice.

pulsación [pulsa'θjon] *nf* beat; **pulsaciones** pulse rate

pulsar [pul'sar] *vt* (*tecla*) to touch, tap; (*Mús*) to play; (*botón*) to press, push ⊳ *vi* to pulsate; (*latir*) to beat, throb

pulsera [pul'sera] *nf* bracelet

pulso ['pulso] *nm* (*Anat*) pulse; (*fuerza*) strength; (*firmeza*) steadiness, steady hand

pulverizador [pulβeriθa'ðor] *nm* spray, spray gun

pulverizar [pulβeri'θar] *vt* to pulverize; (*líquido*) to spray

puna ['puna] (*CAM*) *nf* mountain sickness

punta ['punta] *nf* point, tip; (*extremo*) end; (*fig*) touch, trace; **horas ~** peak o rush hours; **sacar ~ a** to sharpen

puntada [pun'taða] *nf* (*Costura*) stitch

puntal [pun'tal] *nm* prop, support

puntapié [punta'pje] *nm* kick

puntería [punte'ria] *nf* (*de arma*) aim, aiming; (*destreza*) marksmanship

puntero, -a [pun'tero, a] *adj* leading ⊳ *nm* (*palo*) pointer

puntiagudo, -a [puntja'xuðo, a] *adj* sharp, pointed

puntilla [pun'tiʎa] *nf* (*encaje*) lace edging o trim; **(andar) de ~s** (to walk) on tiptoe

punto ['punto] *nm* (*gen*) point; (*señal diminuta*) spot, dot; (*Costura, Med*) stitch; (*lugar*) spot, place; (*momento*) point, moment; **a ~** ready: **estar a ~ de** to be on the point of o about to; **en ~** on the dot; **hasta cierto ~** to some extent; **hacer ~** (*ESP: tejer*) to knit; **dos ~s** (*Ling*) colon; **punto de interrogación** question mark; **punto de vista** point of view, viewpoint; **punto final** full stop (*BRIT*), period (*US*); **punto muerto** dead center; (*Auto*) neutral (gear); **punto y aparte** (*en dictado*) full stop, new paragraph; **punto y coma** semicolon

puntocom [punto'kom] *adj inv, nf inv* dotcom

puntuación [puntwa'θjon] nf punctuation; (puntos: en examen) mark(s) (pl); (Deporte) score

puntual [pun'twal] adj (a tiempo) punctual; (exacto) exact, accurate; **puntualidad** nf punctuality; exactness, accuracy

puntuar [pun'twar] vi (Deporte) to score, count

punzante [pun'θante] adj (dolor) shooting, sharp; (herramienta) sharp

puñado [pu'naðo] nm handful

puñal [pu'nal] nm dagger; **puñalada** nf stab

puñetazo [pune'taθo] nm punch

puño ['puno] nm (Anat) fist; (cantidad) fistful, handful; (Costura) cuff; (de herramienta) handle

pupila [pu'pila] nf pupil

pupitre [pu'pitre] nm desk

puré [pu're] nm purée; (sopa) (thick) soup; **puré de papas** (LAM) mashed potatoes; **puré de patatas** (ESP) mashed potatoes

purga ['purxa] nf purge; **purgante** adj, nm purgative

purgatorio [purxa'torjo] nm purgatory

purificar [purifi'kar] vt to purify; (refinar) to refine

puritano, -a [puri'tano, a] adj (actitud) puritanical; (iglesia, tradición) puritan ▷ nm/f puritan

puro, -a ['puro, a] adj pure; (verdad) simple, plain ▷ nm cigar

púrpura ['purpura] nf purple

pus [pus] nm pus

puse etc vb V **poder**

pusiera etc vb V **poder**

puta ['puta] (fam!) nf whore, prostitute

putrefacción [putrefak'θjon] nf rotting, putrefaction

▷PV nm abr (= precio de venta al público) RRP

▷yme, PYME ['pime] nf abr (= Pequeña y Mediana Empresa) SME

○ PALABRA CLAVE

que [ke] conj 1 (con oración subordinada: muchas veces no se traduce) that; **dijo que vendría** he said (that) he would come; **espero que lo encuentres** I hope (that) you find it; V tb **el**

2 (en oración independiente): **¡que entre!** send him in; **¡que aproveche!** enjoy your meal!; **¡que se mejore tu padre!** I hope your father gets better

3 (enfático): **¿me quieres? – ¡que sí!** do you love me? – of course!

4 (consecutivo: muchas veces no se traduce) that; **es tan grande que no lo puedo levantar** it's so big (that) I can't lift it

5 (comparaciones) than; **yo que tú/él** if I were you/him; V tb **más, menos, mismo**

6 (valor disyuntivo): **que le guste o no** whether he likes it or not; **que venga o que no venga** whether he comes or not

7(*porque*): **no puedo, que tengo que quedarme en casa** I can't, I've got to stay in
▷ *pron* **1**(*cosa*) that, which; (+ *prep*) which; **el sombrero que te compraste** the hat (that or which) you bought; **la cama en que dormí** the bed (that (that or which) I slept in
2(*persona: suj*) that, who; (: *objeto*) that, whom; **el amigo que me acompañó al museo** the friend that or who went to the museum with me; **la chica que invité** the girl (that or whom) I invited

qué [ke] *adj* what?, which? ▷ *pron* what?; **¡~ divertido!** how funny!; **¿~ edad tienes?** how old are you?; **¿de ~ me hablas?** what are you saying to me?; **¿~ tal?** how are you?, how are things?; **¿~ hay (de nuevo)?** what's new?

quebrado, -a [ke'βraðo, a] *adj* (*roto*) broken ▷ *nm/f* bankrupt ▷ *nm* (*Mat*) fraction

quebrantar [keβran'tar] *vt* (*infringir*) to violate, transgress

quebrar [ke'βrar] *vt* to break, smash ▷ *vi* to go bankrupt

quedar [ke'ðar] *vi* to stay, remain; (*encontrarse: sitio*) to be; (*haber aún*) to remain, be left; **quedarse** *vr* to remain, stay (behind); **~se (con) algo** to keep sth; **~ en** (*acordar*) to agree on/to; **~ en nada** to come to nothing; **~ por hacer** to be still to do; **~ ciego/mudo** to be left blind/dumb; **no te queda bien ese vestido** that dress doesn't suit you; **eso queda muy lejos** that's a long way (away); **quedamos a las seis** we agreed to meet at six

quedo, -a [ke'ðo, a] *adj* still ▷ *adv* softly, gently

quehacer [kea'θer] *nm* task, job; **quehaceres (domésticos)** *nmpl* household chores

queja [kexa] *nf* complaint; **quejarse** *vr* (*enfermo*) to moan, groan; (*protestar*) to complain; **quejarse de que** to

complain (about the fact) that;
quejido *nm* moan

quemado, -a [ke'maðo, a] *adj* burnt

quemadura [kema'ðura] *nf* burn, scald

quemar [ke'mar] *vt* to burn; (*fig: malgastar*) to burn up, squander ▷ *vi* to be burning hot; **quemarse** *vr* (*consumirse*) to burn (up); (*del sol*) to get sunburnt

quemarropa [kema'rropa]: **a ~** *adv* point-blank

quepo *etc vb V* **caber**

querella [ke'reʎa] *nf* (*Jur*) charge; (*disputa*) dispute

○ **PALABRA CLAVE**

querer [ke'rer] *vt* **1** (*desear*) to want; **quiero más dinero** I want more money; **quisiera** o **querría un té** I'd like a tea; **sin querer** unintentionally; **quiero ayudar/que vayas** I want to help/you to go
2(*preguntas: para pedir algo*): **¿quiere abrir la ventana?** could you open the window?; **¿quieres echarme una mano?** can you give me a hand?
3(*amar*) to love; (*tener cariño a*) to be fond of; **te quiero** I love you; **quiere mucho a sus hijos** he's very fond of his children
4 le pedí que me dejara ir pero no quiso I asked him to let me go but he refused

querido, -a [ke'riðo, a] *adj* dear ▷ *nm/f* darling; (*amante*) lover

queso [keso] *nm* cheese; **queso crema** (LAM) cream cheese; **queso de untar** (ESP) cream cheese; **queso manchego** sheep's milk cheese made in La Mancha; **queso rallado** grated cheese

quicio [kiθjo] *nm* hinge; **sacar a algn de ~** to get on sb's nerves

quiebra [kjeβra] *nf* break, split; (*Com*) bankruptcy; (*Econ*) slump

quiebro [kjeβro] *nm* (*del cuerpo*)

swerve

quien [kjen] _pron_ who; **hay ~ piensa
que** there are those who think that; **no
hay ~ lo haga** no-one will do it

quién [kjen] _pron_ who, whom; **¿~ es?**
who's there?

quienquiera [kjen'kjera] (_pl_
quienesquiera) _pron_ whoever

quiero _etc vb_ V **querer**

quieto, -a ['kjeto, a] _adj_ still;
(_carácter_) placid

⬛ No confundir **quieto** con la palabra
inglesa _quiet_.

quietud _nf_ stillness

quilate [ki'late] _nm_ carat

químico, -a ['kimiko, a] _adj_
chemical ▷ _nm/f_ chemist ▷ _nf_
chemistry

quincalla [kin'kaʎa] _nf_ hardware,
ironmongery (_BRIT_)

quince ['kinθe] _num_ fifteen; **~ días**
a fortnight; **quinceañero, -a** _nm/f_
teenager; **quincena** _nf_ fortnight;
(_pago_) fortnightly pay; **quincenal** _adj_
fortnightly

quiniela [ki'njela] _nf_ football pools
_pl_; **quinielas** _nfpl_ (_impreso_) pools
coupon _sg_

quinientos, -as [ki'njentos, as] _adj_,
num five hundred

quinto, -a ['kinto, a] _adj_ fifth ▷ _nf_
country house; (_Mil_) call-up, draft

quiosco ['kjosko] _nm_ (_de música_)
bandstand; (_de periódicos_) news stand

quirófano [ki'rofano] _nm_ operating
theatre

quirúrgico, -a [ki'rurxiko, a] _adj_
surgical

quise _etc vb_ V **querer**

quisiera _etc vb_ V **querer**

quisquilloso, -a [kiski'ʎoso, a]
adj (_susceptible_) touchy; (_meticuloso_)
pernickety

quiste [kiste] _nm_ cyst

quitaesmalte [kitaes'malte] _nm_
nail-polish remover

quitamanchas [kita'mantʃas] _nm_
inv stain remover

quitanieves [kita'njeβes] _nm inv_
snowplough (_BRIT_), snowplow (_US_)

quitar [ki'tar] _vt_ to remove, take
away; (_ropa_) to take off; (_dolor_) to
relieve; **¡quita de ahí!** get away!;
quitarse _vr_ to withdraw; (_ropa_) to
take off; **se quitó el sombrero** he took
off his hat

Quito ['kito] _n_ Quito

quizá(s) [ki'θa(s)] _adv_ perhaps,
maybe

q

r

rábano [ˈraβano] nm radish; **me importa un ~** I don't give a damn

rabia [ˈraβja] nf (Med) rabies sg; (ira) fury, rage; **rabiar** vi to have rabies; to rage, be furious; **rabiar por algo** to long for sth

rabieta [raˈβjeta] nf tantrum, fit of temper

rabino [raˈβino] nm rabbi

rabioso, -a [raˈβjoso, a] adj rabid; (fig) furious

rabo [ˈraβo] nm tail

racha [ˈratʃa] nf gust of wind; **buena/mala ~** spell of good/bad luck

racial [raˈθjal] adj racial, race cpd

racimo [raˈθimo] nm bunch

ración [raˈθjon] nf portion; **raciones** nfpl rations

racional [raθjoˈnal] adj (razonable) reasonable; (lógico) rational

racionar [raθjoˈnar] vt to ration (out)

racismo [raˈθismo] nm racism; **racista** adj, nm racist

radar [raˈðar] nm radar

radiador [raðjaˈðor] nm radiator

radiante [raˈðjante] adj radiant

radical [raðiˈkal] adj, nmf radical

radicar [raðiˈkar] vi: **~ en** (dificultad, problema) to lie in; (solución) to consist in

radio [ˈraðjo] nf radio; (aparato) radio (set) ▷ nm (Mat) radius; (Quím) radium; **radioactividad** nf radioactivity; **radioactivo, -a** adj radioactive; **radiografía** nf X-ray; **radioterapia** nf radiotherapy; **radioyente** nmf listener

ráfaga [ˈrafaɣa] nf gust; (de luz) flash; (de tiros) burst

raíz [raˈiθ] nf root; **a ~ de** as a result of; **raíz cuadrada** square root

raja [ˈraxa] nf (de melón etc) slice; (grieta) crack; **rajar** vt to split; (fam) to slash; **rajarse** vr to split, crack; **rajarse de** to back out of

rajatabla [raxaˈtaβla]: **a ~** adv (estrictamente) strictly, to the letter

rallador [raʎaˈðor] nm grater

rallar [raˈʎar] vt to grate

rama [ˈrama] nf branch; **ramaje** nm branches pl, foliage; **ramal** nm (de cuerda) strand; (Ferro) branch line (BRIT); (Auto) branch (road) (BRIT)

rambla [ˈrambla] nf (avenida) avenue

ramo [ˈramo] nm branch; (sección) department, section

rampa [ˈrampa] nf ramp; **rampa de acceso** entrance ramp

rana [ˈrana] nf frog; **salto de ~** leapfrog

ranchero [ranˈtʃero] (MÉX) nm (hacendado) rancher; smallholder

rancho [ˈrantʃo] nm (grande) ranch; (pequeño) small farm

rancio, -a [ˈranθjo, a] adj (comestibles) rancid; (vino) aged, mellow; (fig) ancient

rango [ˈrango] nm rank, standing

ranura [raˈnura] nf groove; (de teléfono etc) slot

rapar [raˈpar] vt to shave; (los cabellos) to crop

rapaz [raˈpaθ] nf (~a) nmf young

boy/girl ▷ adj (Zool) predatory
rape ['rape] nm (pez) monkfish; **al ~** cropped
rapidez [rapi'ðeθ] nf speed, rapidity; **rápido, -a** adj fast, quick ▷ adv quickly ▷ nm (Ferro) express; **rápidos** nmpl rapids
rapiña [ra'piɲa] nm robbery; **ave de ~** bird of prey
raptar [rap'tar] vt to kidnap; **rapto** nm kidnapping; (impulso) sudden impulse; (éxtasis) ecstasy, rapture
raqueta [ra'keta] nf racquet
raquítico, -a [ra'kitiko, a] adj stunted; (fig) poor, inadequate
rareza [ra'reθa] nf rarity; (fig) eccentricity
raro, -a ['raro, a] adj (poco común) rare; (extraño) odd, strange; (excepcional) remarkable
ras [ras] nm: **a ~ de** level with; **a ~ de tierra** at ground level
rasar [ra'sar] vt (igualar) to level
rascacielos [raska'θjelos] nm inv skyscraper
rascar [ras'kar] vt (con las uñas etc) to scratch; (raspar) to scrape; **rascarse** vr to scratch (o.s.)
rasgar [ras'xar] vt to tear, rip (up)
rasgo ['rasxo] nm (con pluma) stroke; **rasgos** nmpl (facciones) features, characteristics; **a grandes ~s** in outline, broadly
rasguño [ras'xuɲo] nm scratch
raso, -a ['raso, a] adj (liso) flat, level; (a baja altura) very low ▷ nm satin; **cielo ~** clear sky
raspadura [raspa'ðura] nf (acto) scrape, scraping; (marca) scratch; **raspaduras** nfpl (de papel etc) scrapings
raspar [ras'par] vt to scrape; (arañar) to scratch; (limar) to file
rastra ['rastra] nf (Agr) rake; **a ~s by** dragging; (fig) unwillingly
rastrear [rastre'ar] vt (seguir) to track
rastrero, -a [ras'trero, a] adj (Bot,

Zool) creeping; (fig) despicable, mean
rastrillo [ras'triʎo] nm rake
rastro ['rastro] nm (Agr) rake; (pista) track, trail; (vestigio) trace; **el R~** (ESP) the Madrid fleamarket
rasurado [rasu'raðo] (MÉX) nm shaving; **rasuradora** [rasura'ðora] (MÉX) nf electric shaver; **rasurar** [rasu'rar] (MÉX) vt to shave; **rasurarse** vr to shave
rata ['rata] nf rat
ratear [rate'ar] vt (robar) to steal
ratero, -a [ra'tero, a] adj light-fingered ▷ nm/f (carterista) pickpocket; (ladrón) petty thief
rato ['rato] nm while, short time; **a ~s** from time to time; **hay para ~** there's still a long way to go; **al poco ~** soon afterwards; **pasar el ~** to kill time; **pasar un buen/mal ~** to have a good/rough time; **en mis ~s libres** in my spare time
ratón [ra'ton] nm mouse; **ratonera** nf mousetrap
raudal [rau'ðal] nm torrent; **a ~es** in abundance
raya ['raja] nf line; (marca) scratch; (en tela) stripe; (de pelo) parting; (límite) boundary; (pez) ray; (puntuación) dash; **a ~s** striped; **pasarse de la ~** to go too far; **tener a ~** to keep in check; **rayar** vt to line; to scratch; (subrayar) to underline ▷ vi: **rayar en o con** to border on
rayo ['rajo] nm (del sol) ray, beam; (de luz) shaft; (en una tormenta) (flash of) lightning; **rayos X** X-rays
raza ['raθa] nf race; **raza humana** human race
razón [ra'θon] nf reason; (justicia) right, justice; (razonamiento) reasoning; (motivo) reason, motive; (Mat) ratio: **a ~ de 10 cada día** at the rate of 10 a day; **en ~ de** with regard to; **dar ~ a algn** to agree that sb is right; **tener ~** to be right; **razón de ser** raison d'être; **razón directa/inversa** direct/inverse proportion; **razonable**

adj reasonable; (*justo, moderado*) fair; **razonamiento** *nm* (*juicio*) judg(e)ment; (*argumento*) reasoning; **razonar** *vt*, *vi* to reason, argue

re [re] *nm* (*Mús*) D

reacción [reak'θjon] *nf* reaction; **avión a ~** jet plane; **reacción en cadena** chain reaction; **reaccionar** *vi* to react

reacio, -a [re'aθjo, a] *adj* stubborn

reactivar [reakti'βar] *vt* to revitalize

reactor [reak'tor] *nm* reactor

real [re'al] *adj* real; (*del rey, fig*) royal

realidad [reali'ðað] *nf* reality, fact; (*verdad*) truth

realista [rea'lista] *nmf* realist

realización [realiθa'θjon] *nf* fulfilment

realizador, a [realiθa'ðor, a] *nm/f* film-maker

realizar [reali'θar] *vt* (*objetivo*) to achieve; (*plan*) to carry out; (*viaje*) to make, undertake; **realizarse** *vr* to come about, come true

realmente [real'mente] *adv* really, actually

realzar [real'θar] *vt* to enhance; (*acentuar*) to highlight

reanimar [reani'mar] *vt* to revive; (*alentar*) to encourage; **reanimarse** *vr* to revive

reanudar [reanu'ðar] *vt* (*renovar*) to renew; (*historia, viaje*) to resume

reaparición [reapari'θjon] *nf* reappearance

rearme [re'arme] *nm* rearmament

rebaja [re'βaxa] *nf* (*Com*) reduction; (: *descuento*) discount; **rebajas** *nfpl* (*Com*) sale; **rebajar** *vt* (*bajar*) to lower; (*reducir*) to reduce; (*disminuir*) to lessen; (*humillar*) to humble

rebanada [reβa'naða] *nf* slice

rebañar [reβa'ɲar] *vt* (*comida*) to scrape up; (*plato*) to scrape clean

rebaño [re'βaɲo] *nm* herd; (*de ovejas*) flock

rebatir [reβa'tir] *vt* to refute

rebeca [re'βeka] *nf* cardigan

rebelarse [reβe'larse] *vr* to rebel, revolt

rebelde [re'βelde] *adj* rebellious; (*niño*) unruly ▷ *nmf* rebel; **rebeldía** *nf* rebelliousness; (*desobediencia*) disobedience

rebelión [reβe'ljon] *nf* rebellion

reblandecer [reβlande'θer] *vt* to soften

rebobinar [reβoβi'nar] *vt* (*cinta, película de video*) to rewind

rebosante [reβo'sante] *adj* overflowing

rebosar [reβo'sar] *vi* (*líquido, recipiente*) to overflow; (*abundar*) to abound, be plentiful

rebotar [reβo'tar] *vt* to bounce; (*rechazar*) to repel ▷ *vi* (*pelota*) to bounce; (*bala*) to ricochet; **rebote** *nm* rebound; **de rebote** on the rebound

rebozado, -a [reβo'θaðo, a] *adj* fried in batter o breadcrumbs

rebozar [reβo'θar] *vt* to wrap up; (*Culin*) to fry in batter o breadcrumbs

rebuscado, -a [reβus'kaðo, a] *adj* (*amanerado*) affected; (*palabra*) recherché; (*idea*) far-fetched

rebuscar [reβus'kar] *vi*: ~ **(en/por)** to search carefully (in/for)

recado [re'kaðo] *nm* (*mensaje*) message; (*encargo*) errand; **tomar un ~** (*Tel*) to take a message

recaer [reka'er] *vi* to relapse; **~ en** to fall to o on; (*criminal etc*) to fall back into, relapse into; **recaída** *nf* relapse

recalcar [rekal'kar] *vt* (*fig*) to stress, emphasize

recalentar [rekalen'tar] *vt* (*volver a calentar*) to reheat; (*calentar demasiado*) to overheat

recámara [re'kamara] (MÉX) *nf* bedroom

recambio [re'kambjo] *nm* spare; (*de pluma*) refill

recapacitar [rekapaθi'tar] *vi* to reflect

recargado, -a [rekar'xaðo, a] *adj* overloaded

recargar [rekar'ɣar] vt to overload; (batería) to recharge; **~ el saldo de** (Tel) to top up; **recargo** nm surcharge; (aumento) increase

recatado, -a [reka'taðo, a] adj (modesto) modest, demure; (prudente) cautious

recaudación [rekauða'θjon] nf (acción) collection; (cantidad) takings pl; (en deporte) gate; **recaudador, a** nm/f tax collector

recelar [reθe'lar] vt: **~ que ...** (sospechar) to suspect that ...; (temer) to fear that ... ▷ vi: **~ de** to distrust; **recelo** nm distrust, suspicion

recepción [reθep'θjon] nf reception; **recepcionista** nmf receptionist

receptor, a [reθep'tor, a] nm/f recipient ▷ nm (Tel) receiver

recesión [reθe'sjon] nf (Com) recession

receta [re'θeta] nf (Culin) recipe; (Med) prescription

> No confundir **receta** con la palabra inglesa receipt.

rechazar [retʃa'θar] vt to reject; (oferta) to turn down; (ataque) to repel

rechazo [re'tʃaθo] nm rejection

rechinar [retʃi'nar] vi to creak; (dientes) to grind

rechistar [retʃis'tar] vi: **sin ~** without a murmur

rechoncho, -a [re'tʃontʃo, a] (fam) adj thickset (BRIT), heavy-set (US)

rechupete [retʃu'pete]: **de ~** adj (comida) delicious, scrumptious

recibidor [reθiβi'ðor] nm entrance hall

recibimiento [reθiβi'mjento] nm reception, welcome

recibir [reθi'βir] vt to receive; (dar la bienvenida) to welcome ▷ vi to entertain; **recibo** nm receipt

reciclable [reθi'klaβle] adj recyclable

reciclar [reθi'klar] vt to recycle

recién [re'θjen] adv recently, newly; **los ~ casados** the newly-weds; **el ~ llegado** the newcomer; **el ~ nacido** the

newborn child

reciente [re'θjente] adj recent; (fresco) fresh

recinto [re'θinto] nm enclosure; (área) area, place

recio, -a ['reθjo, a] adj strong, tough; (voz) loud ▷ adv hard, loud(ly)

recipiente [reθi'pjente] nm receptacle

recíproco, -a [re'θiproko, a] adj reciprocal

recital [reθi'tal] nm (Mús) recital; (Literatura) reading

recitar [reθi'tar] vt to recite

reclamación [reklama'θjon] nf claim, demand; (queja) complaint; **libro de reclamaciones** complaints book

reclamar [rekla'mar] vt to claim, demand ▷ vi: **~ contra** to complain about; **reclamo** nm (anuncio) advertisement; (tentación) attraction

reclinar [rekli'nar] vt to recline, lean; **reclinarse** vr to lean back

reclusión [reklu'sjon] nf (prisión) prison; (refugio) seclusion

recluta [re'kluta] nmf recruit ▷ nf recruitment; **reclutar** vt (datos) to collect; (dinero) to collect up; **reclutamiento** nm recruitment

recobrar [reko'βrar] vt (salud) to recover; (rescatar) to get back; **recobrarse** vr to recover

recodo [re'koðo] nm (de río, camino) bend

recogedor [rekoxe'ðor] nm dustpan

recoger [reko'xer] vt to collect; (Agr) to harvest; (levantar) to pick up; (juntar) to gather; (pasar a buscar) to come for, get; (dar asilo) to give shelter to; (faldas) to gather up; (pelo) to put up; **recogerse** vr (retirarse) to retire; **recogido, -a** adj (lugar) quiet, secluded; (pequeño) small ▷ nf (Correos) collection; (Agr) harvest

recolección [rekolek'θjon] nf (Agr) harvesting; (colecta) collection

recomendación [rekomenda'θjon] nf (sugerencia) suggestion, recommendation; (*referencia*) reference

recomendar [rekomen'dar] *vt* to suggest, recommend; (*confiar*) to entrust

recompensa [rekom'pensa] *nf* reward, recompense; **recompensar** *vt* to reward, recompense

reconciliación [rekonθilja'θjon] *nf* reconciliation

reconciliar [rekonθi'ljar] *vt* to reconcile; **reconciliarse** *vr* to become reconciled

recóndito, -a [re'kondito, a] *adj* (*lugar*) hidden, secret

reconocer [rekono'θer] *vt* to recognize; (*registrar*) to search; (*Med*) to examine; **reconocido, -a** *adj* recognized; (*agradecido*) grateful; **reconocimiento** *nm* recognition; search; examination; gratitude; (*confesión*) admission

reconquista [rekon'kista] *nf* reconquest; **la R~** the Reconquest (of Spain)

reconstituyente [rekonstitu'jente] *nm* tonic

reconstruir [rekonstru'ir] *vt* to reconstruct

reconversión [rekonβer'sjon] *nf* (*reestructuración*) restructuring; **reconversión industrial** industrial rationalization

recopilación [rekopila'θjon] *nf* (*resumen*) summary; (*compilación*) compilation; **recopilar** *vt* to compile

récord ['rekorð] (*pl* **-s**) *adj inv, nm* record

recordar [rekor'ðar] *vt* (*acordarse de*) to remember; (*acordar a otro*) to remind ▷ *vi* to remember

> No confundir **recordar** con la palabra inglesa *record*.

recorrer [reko'rrer] *vt* (*país*) to cross, travel through; (*distancia*) to cover; (*registrar*) to search; (*repasar*) to look over; **recorrido** *nm* run, journey; **tren de largo recorrido** main-line train

recortar [rekor'tar] *vt* to cut out;

recorte *nm* (*acción, de prensa*) cutting; (*de telas, chapas*) trimming; **recorte presupuestario** budget cut

recostar [rekos'tar] *vt* to lean; **recostarse** *vr* to lie down

recoveco [reko'βeko] *nm* (*de camino, río etc*) bend; (*en casa*) cubby hole

recreación [rekrea'θjon] *nf* recreation

recrear [rekre'ar] *vt* (*entretener*) to entertain; (*volver a crear*) to recreate; **recreativo, -a** *adj* recreational; **recreo** *nm* recreation; (*Escol*) break, playtime

recriminar [rekrimi'nar] *vt* to reproach ▷ *vi* to recriminate; **recriminarse** *vr* to reproach each other

recrudecer [rekruðe'θer] *vt, vi* to worsen; **recrudecerse** *vr* to worsen

recta ['rekta] *nf* straight line

rectángulo, -a [a rek'tangulo, a] *adj* rectangular ▷ *nm* rectangle

rectificar [rektifi'kar] *vt* to rectify; (*volverse recto*) to straighten ▷ *vi* to correct o.s.

rectitud [rekti'tuð] *nf* straightness

recto, -a ['rekto, a] *adj* straight; (*persona*) honest, upright; **siga todo ~** go straight on ▷ *nm* rectum

rector, a [rek'tor, a] *adj* governing

recuadro [re'kwaðro] *nm* box; (*Tip*) inset

recubrir [reku'βrir] *vt*: **~ (con)** (*pintura, crema*) to cover (with)

recuento [re'kwento] *nm* inventory; **hacer el ~ de** to count o reckon up

recuerdo [re'kwerðo] *nm* souvenir; **recuerdos** *nmpl* (*memorias*) memories; **¡~s a tu madre!** give my regards to your mother!

recular [reku'lar] *vi* to back down

recuperación [rekupera'θjon] *nf* recovery

recuperar [rekupe'rar] *vt* to recover; (*tiempo*) to make up; **recuperarse** *vr* to recuperate

recurrir [reku'rrir] *vi* (*Jur*) to appeal;

~ a to resort to; (persona) to turn to;
recurso nm resort; (medios) means pl,
resources pl; (Jur) appeal

red [reð] nf net, mesh; (Ferro etc)
network; (trampa) trap; **la R~** (Internet)
the Net

redacción [reðak'θjon] nf (acción)
editing; (personal) editorial staff; (Escol)
essay, composition

redactar [reðak'tar] vt to draw up,
draft; (periódico) to edit

redactor, a [reðak'tor, a] nm/f
editor

redada [re'ðaða] nf (de policía) raid,
round-up

rededor [reðe'ðor] nm: **al** o **en ~**
around, round about

redoblar [reðo'βlar] vt to redouble
▷ vi (tambor) to roll

redonda [re'ðonda] nf: **a la ~** around,
round about

redondear [reðonde'ar] vt to round,
round off

redondel [reðon'del] nm (círculo)
circle; (Taur) bullring, arena

redondo, -a [re'ðondo, a] adj
(circular) round; (completo) complete

reducción [reðuk'θjon] nf reduction

reducido, -a [reðu'θiðo, a] adj
reduced; (limitado) limited; (pequeño)
small

reducir [reðu'θir] vt to reduce; to
limit; **reducirse** vr to diminish

redundancia [reðun'danθja] nf
redundancy

reembolsar [re(e)mbol'sar] vt
(persona) to reimburse; (dinero) to
repay, pay back; (depósito) to refund;
reembolso nm reimbursement;
refund

reemplazar [re(e)mpla'θar] vt to
replace; **reemplazo** nm replacement;
de reemplazo (Mil) reserve

reencuentro [re(e)n'kwentro] nm
reunion

reescribible [reeskri'βiβle] adj
rewritable

refacción [refak'θjon] nf (MÉX)

spare (part)

referencia [refe'renθja] nf reference;
con ~ a with reference to

referéndum [refe'rendum] (pl **~s**)
nm referendum

referente [refe'rente] adj: **~ a**
concerning, relating to

réferi ['referi] (LAM) nmf referee

referir [refe'rir] vt (contar) to tell,
recount; (relacionar) to refer, relate;
referirse vr: **~se a** to refer to

refilón [refi'lon]: **de ~** adv obliquely

refinado, -a [refi'naðo, a] adj
refined

refinar [refi'nar] vt to refine;
refinería nf refinery

reflejar [refle'xar] vt to reflect;
reflejo, -a adj reflected; (movimiento)
reflex ▷ nm reflection; (Anat) reflex

reflexión [reflek'sjon] nf reflection

reflexionar vt to reflect on ▷ vi to
reflect; (detenerse) to pause (to think)

reflexivo, -a [reflek'siβo, a] adj
thoughtful; (Ling) reflexive

reforma [re'forma] nf reform; (Arq
etc) repair; **reforma agraria** agrarian
reform

reformar [refor'mar] vt to reform;
(modificar) to change, alter; (Arq)
to repair; **reformarse** vr to mend
one's ways

reformatorio [reforma'torjo] nm
reformatory

reforzar [refor'θar] vt to strengthen;
(Arq) to reinforce; (fig) to encourage

refractario, -a [refrak'tarjo, a] adj
(Tec) heat-resistant

refrán [re'fran] nm proverb, saying

refregar [refre'ɣar] vt to scrub

refrescante [refres'kante] adj
refreshing, cooling

refrescar [refres'kar] vt to refresh
▷ vi to cool down; **refrescarse** vr to
get cooler; (tomar aire fresco) to go
out for a breath of fresh air; (beber) to
have a drink

refresco [re'fresko] nm soft drink,
cool drink; **"~s"** "refreshments"

refriega [re'frjexa] nf scuffle, brawl

refrigeración [refrixera'θjon] nf refrigeration; (de sala) air-conditioning

refrigerador [refrixera'ðor] nm refrigerator (BRIT), icebox (US)

refrigerar [refrixe'rar] vt to refrigerate; (sala) to air-condition

refuerzo [re'fwerθo] nm reinforcement; (Tec) support

refugiado, -a [refu'xjaðo, a] nm/f refugee

refugiarse [refu'xjarse] vr to take refuge, shelter

refugio [re'fuxjo] nm refuge; (protección) shelter

refunfuñar [refunfu'nar] vi to grunt, growl; (quejarse) to grumble

regadera [reɣa'ðera] nf watering can

regadío [reɣa'ðio] nm irrigated land

regalado, -a [reɣa'laðo, a] adj comfortable, luxurious; (gratis) free, for nothing

regalar [reɣa'lar] vt (dar) to give (as a present); (entregar) to give away; (mimar) to pamper, make a fuss of

regaliz [reɣa'liθ] nm liquorice

regalo [re'ɣalo] nm (obsequio) gift, present; (gusto) pleasure

regañadientes [reɣana'ðjentes]: **a ~** adv reluctantly

regañar [reɣa'nar] vt to scold ▷ vi to grumble; **regañón, -ona** adj nagging

regar [re'ɣar] vt to water, irrigate; (fig) to scatter, sprinkle

regatear [reɣate'ar] vt (Com) to bargain over; (escatimar) to be mean with ▷ vi to bargain, haggle; (Deporte) to dribble; **regateo** nm bargaining; (del cuerpo) swerve, dodge

regazo [re'ɣaθo] nm lap

regenerar [rexene'rar] vt to regenerate

régimen ['reximen] (pl **regímenes**) nm regime; (Med) diet

regimiento [rexi'mjento] nm regiment

regio, -a ['rexjo, a] adj royal, regal; (fig: suntuoso) splendid; (cs: fam) great,

terrific

región [re'xjon] nf region

regir [re'xir] vt to govern, rule; (dirigir) to manage, run ▷ vi to apply, be in force

registrar [rexis'trar] vt (buscar) to search; (: en cajón) to look through; (inspeccionar) to inspect; (anotar) to register, record; (Inform) to log; **registrarse** vr to register; (ocurrir) to happen

registro [re'xistro] nm (acto) registration; (Mús, libro) register; (inspección) inspection, search; **registro civil** registry office

regla ['reɣla] nf (ley) rule, regulation; (de medir) ruler, rule; (Med: período) period; **en ~** in order

reglamentación [reɣlamenta'θjon] nf (acto) regulation; (lista) rules pl

reglamentar [reɣlamen'tar] vt to regulate; **reglamentario, -a** adj statutory; **reglamento** nm rules pl, regulations pl

regocijarse [reɣoθi'xarse] vr (alegrarse) to rejoice; **regocijo** nm joy, happiness

regrabadora [reɣraβa'ðora] nf rewriter; **regrabadora de DVD** DVD rewriter

regresar [reɣre'sar] vi to come back, go back, return; **regreso** nm return

reguero [re'ɣero] nm (de sangre etc) trickle; (de humo) trail

regulador [reɣula'ðor] nm regulator; (de radio etc) knob, control

regular [reɣu'lar] adj regular; (normal) normal, usual; (común) ordinary; (organizado) regular, orderly; (mediano) average; (fam) not bad, so-so ▷ adv so-so, alright ▷ vt (controlar) to control, regulate; (Tec) to adjust; **por lo ~ as a rule; **regularidad** nf regularity; **regularizar** vt to regularize

rehabilitación [reaβilita'θjon] nf rehabilitation; (Arq) restoration

rehabilitar [reaβili'tar] vt to rehabilitate; (Arq) to restore; (reintegrar)

to reinstate
rehacer [rea'θer] vt (reparar) to mend, repair; (volver a hacer) to redo, repeat; **rehacerse** vr (Med) to recover
rehén [re'en] nm hostage
rehuir [reu'ir] vt to avoid, shun
rehusar [reu'sar] vt, vi to refuse
reina ['reina] nf queen; **reinado** nm reign
reinar [rei'nar] vi to reign
reincidir [reinθi'ðir] vi to relapse
reincorporarse [reinkorpo'rarse] vr: ~ **a** to rejoin
reino ['reino] nm kingdom; **reino animal/vegetal** animal/plant kingdom; **el Reino Unido** the United Kingdom
reintegrar [reinte'ɣrar] vt (reconstituir) to reconstruct; (persona) to reinstate; (dinero) to refund, pay back; **reintegrarse** vr: ~ **a** to return to
reír [re'ir] vi to laugh; **reírse** vr to laugh; ~**se de** to laugh at
reiterar [reite'rar] vt to reiterate
reivindicación [reiβindika'θjon] nf (demanda) claim, demand; (justificación) vindication
reivindicar [reiβindi'kar] vt to claim
reja ['rexa] nf (de ventana) grille, bars pl; (en la calle) grating
rejilla [re'xiʎa] nf grating, grille; (muebles) wickerwork; (de ventilación) vent; (de coche etc) luggage rack
rejoneador [rexonea'ðor] nm mounted bullfighter
rejuvenecer [rexuβene'θer] vt, vi to rejuvenate
relación [rela'θjon] nf relation, relationship; (Mat) ratio; (narración) report; **con ~ a, en ~ con** in relation to; **relaciones públicas** public relations; **relacionar** vt to relate, connect; **relacionarse** vr to be connected, be linked
relajación [relaxa'θjon] nf relaxation
relajar [rela'xar] vt to relax; **relajarse** vr to relax

relamerse [rela'merse] vr to lick one's lips
relámpago [re'lampaɣo] nm flash of lightning; **visita ~** lightning visit
relatar [rela'tar] vt to tell, relate
relativo, -a [rela'tiβo, a] adj relative; **en lo ~ a** concerning
relato [re'lato] nm (narración) story, tale
relegar [rele'ɣar] vt to relegate
relevante [rele'βante] adj eminent, outstanding
relevar [rele'βar] vt (sustituir) to relieve; **relevarse** vr to relay; ~ **a algn de un cargo** to relieve sb of his post
relevo [re'leβo] nm relief; **carrera de ~s** relay race
relieve [re'ljeβe] nm (Arte, Tec) relief; (fig) prominence, importance; **bajo ~** bas-relief
religión [reli'xjon] nf religion; **religioso, -a** adj religious ▷ nm/f monk/nun
relinchar [relin'tʃar] vi to neigh
reliquia [re'likja] nf relic; **reliquia de familia** heirloom
rellano [re'ʎano] nm (Arq) landing
rellenar [reʎe'nar] vt (llenar) to fill up; (Culin) to stuff; (Costura) to pad; **relleno, -a** adj full up; stuffed ▷ nm stuffing; (de tapicería) padding
reloj [re'lo(x)] nm clock; **poner el ~ (en hora)** to set one's watch (o the clock); **reloj (de pulsera)** wristwatch; **reloj despertador** alarm (clock); **reloj digital** digital watch; **relojero, -a** nm/f clockmaker; watchmaker
reluciente [relu'θjente] adj brilliant, shining
relucir [relu'θir] vi to shine; (fig) to excel
remachar [rema'tʃar] vt to rivet; (fig) to hammer home, drive home; **remache** nm rivet
remangar [reman'gar] vt to roll up
remanso [re'manso] nm pool
remar [re'mar] vi to row
rematado, -a [rema'taðo, a] adj

complete, utter

rematar [rema'tar] vt to finish off; (Com) to sell off cheap ▷ vi to end, finish off; (Deporte) to shoot

remate [re'mate] nm end, finish; (punta) tip; (Deporte) shot; (Arq) top; **de o para** to crown it all (BRIT), to top it off

remedar [reme'ðar] vt to imitate

remediar [reme'ðjar] vt to remedy; (subsanar) to make good, repair; (evitar) to avoid

remedio [re'meðjo] nm remedy; (alivio) relief, help; (Jur) recourse, remedy; **poner ~ a** to correct, stop; **no tener más ~** to have no alternative; **¡qué ~!** there's no choice!; **sin ~** hopeless

remendar [remen'dar] vt to repair; (con parche) to patch

remiendo [re'mjendo] nm mend; (con parche) patch; (cosido) darn

remilgado, -a [remil'ɣaðo, a] adj prim; (afectado) affected

remiso, -a [re'miso, a] adj slack, slow

remite [re'mite] nm (en sobre) name and address of sender

remitir [remi'tir] vt to remit, send ▷ vi to slacken; (en carta): **remite: X** sender: X; **remitente** nmf sender

remo ['remo] nm (de barco) oar; (Deporte) rowing

remojar [remo'xar] vt to steep, soak; (galleta etc) to dip, dunk

remojo [re'moxo] nm: **dejar la ropa en ~** to leave clothes to soak

remolacha [remo'latʃa] nf beet, beetroot

remolcador [remolka'ðor] nm (Náut) tug; (Auto) breakdown lorry

remolcar [remol'kar] vt to tow

remolino [remo'lino] nm eddy; (de agua) whirlpool; (de viento) whirlwind; (de gente) crowd

remolque [re'molke] nm tow, towing; (cuerda) towrope; **llevar a ~ to** tow

remontar [remon'tar] vt to mend; **remontarse** vr to soar; **~se a** (Com) to amount to; **~ el vuelo** to soar

remorder [remor'ðer] vt to distress, disturb; **~le la conciencia a algn** to make sb feel guilty; **remordimiento** nm remorse

remoto, -a [re'moto, a] adj remote

remover [remo'ßer] vt to stir; (tierra) to turn over; (objetos) to move round

remuneración [remunera'θjon] nf remuneration

remunerar [remune'rar] vt to remunerate; (premiar) to reward

renacer [rena'θer] vi to be reborn; (fig) to revive; **renacimiento** nm rebirth; **el Renacimiento** the Renaissance

renacuajo [rena'kwaxo] nm (Zool) tadpole

renal [re'nal] adj renal, kidney cpd

rencilla [ren'θiʎa] nf quarrel

rencor [ren'kor] nm rancour, bitterness; **rencoroso, -a** adj spiteful

rendición [rendi'θjon] nf surrender

rendido, -a [ren'diðo, a] adj (sumiso) submissive; (cansado) worn-out, exhausted

rendija [ren'dixa] nf (hendedura) crack, cleft

rendimiento [rendi'mjento] nm (producción) output; (Tec, Com) efficiency

rendir [ren'dir] vt (vencer) to defeat; (producir) to produce; (dar beneficio) to yield; (agotar) to exhaust ▷ vi to pay; **rendirse** vr (someterse) to surrender; (cansarse) to wear o.s. out; **~ homenaje o culto a** to pay homage to

renegar [rene'ɣar] vi (renunciar) to renounce; (blasfemar) to blaspheme; (quejarse) to complain

RENFE ['renfe] nf abr (= Red Nacional de los Ferrocarriles Españoles)

renglón [ren'glon] nm (línea) line; (Com) item, article; **a ~ seguido** immediately after

renombre [re'nombre] nm renown

renovación [renoβa'θjon] nf (de contrato) renewal; (Arq) renovation

renovar [reno'βar] vt to renew; (Arq) to renovate

renta ['renta] nf (ingresos) income; (beneficio) profit; (alquiler) rent; **renta vitalicia** annuity; **rentable** adj profitable

renuncia [re'nunθja] nf resignation; **renunciar** [renun'θjar] vt to renounce; (tabaco, alcohol etc): **renunciar a** to give up; (oferta, oportunidad) to turn down; (puesto) to resign ▷ vi to resign

reñido, -a [re'niðo, a] adj (batalla) bitter, hard-fought; **estar ~ con algn** to be on bad terms with sb

reñir [re'nir] vt (regañar) to scold ▷ vi (estar peleado) to quarrel, fall out; (combatir) to fight

reo ['reo] nmf culprit, offender; (acusado) accused, defendant

reojo [re'oxo]: **de ~** adv out of the corner of one's eye

reparación [repara'θjon] nf (acto) mending, repairing; (Tec) repair; (fig) amends pl, reparation

reparador, a [repara'ðor] adj refreshing; (comida) fortifying ▷ nm repairer

reparar [repa'rar] vt to repair; (fig) to make amends for; (observar) to observe ▷ vi: **~ en** (darse cuenta de) to notice; (prestar atención a) to pay attention to

reparo [re'paro] nm (advertencia) observation; (duda) doubt; (dificultad) difficulty; **poner ~s (a)** to raise objections (to)

repartidor, a [reparti'ðor] nm/f distributor

repartir [repar'tir] vt to distribute, share out; (Correos) to deliver; **reparto** nm distribution; delivery; (Teatro, Cine) cast; (cam: urbanización) housing estate (brit), real estate development (us)

repasar [repa'sar] vt (Escol) to revise; (Mecánica) to check, overhaul; (Costura) to mend; **repaso** nm revision

overhaul, checkup; mending

repecho [re'petʃo] nm steep incline

repelente [repe'lente] adj repellent, repulsive

repeler [repe'ler] vt to repel

repente [re'pente] nm: **de ~** suddenly

repentino, -a [repen'tino, a] adj sudden

repercusión [reperku'sjon] nf repercussion

repercutir [reperku'tir] vi (objeto) to rebound; (sonido) to echo; **~ en** (fig) to have repercussions on

repertorio [reper'torjo] nm list; (Teatro) repertoire

repetición [repeti'θjon] nf repetition

repetir [repe'tir] vt to repeat; (plato) to have a second helping of ▷ vi to repeat; (sabor) to come back; **repetirse** vr (volver sobre un tema) to repeat o.s.

repetitivo, -a [repeti'tiβo, a] adj repetitive, repetitious

repique [re'pike] nm pealing, ringing; **repiqueteo** nm pealing; (de tambor) drumming

repisa [re'pisa] nf ledge, shelf; (de ventana) windowsill; **la ~ de la chimenea** the mantelpiece

repito etc vb V **repetir**

replantearse [replante'arse] vr: **~ un problema** to reconsider a problem

repleto, -a [re'pleto, a] adj replete, full up

réplica ['replika] nf answer; (Arte) replica

replicar [repli'kar] vi to answer; (objetar) to argue, answer back

repliegue [re'pljeɣe] nm (Mil) withdrawal

repoblación [repoβla'θjon] nf repopulation; (de río) restocking; **repoblación forestal** reafforestation

repoblar [repo'βlar] vt to repopulate; (con árboles) to reafforest

repollito [repo'ʎito] (cs) nm: **~s de Bruselas** (Brussels) sprouts

repollo [re'poʎo] nm cabbage

reponer [repo'ner] vt to replace, put back; (Teatro) to revive; **reponerse** vr to recover; **~ que ...** to reply that ...

reportaje [repor'taxe] nm report, article

reportero, -a [repor'tero, a] nm/f reporter

reposacabezas [reposaka'βeθas] nm inv headrest

reposar [repo'sar] vt to rest, repose

reposera [repo'sera] (RPL) nf deck chair

reposición [reposi'θjon] nf replacement; (Cine) remake

reposo [re'poso] nm rest

repostar [repos'tar] vt to replenish; (Auto) to fill up (with petrol (BRIT) o gasoline (US))

repostería [reposte'ria] nf confectioner's (shop)

represa [re'presa] nf dam; (lago artificial) lake, pool

represalia [repre'salja] nf reprisal

representación [representa'θjon] nf representation; (Teatro) performance; **representante** nmf representative; performer

representar [represen'tar] vt to represent; (Teatro) to perform; (edad) to look; **representarse** vr to imagine; **representativo, -a** adj representative

represión [repre'sjon] nf repression

reprimenda [repri'menda] nf reprimand, rebuke

reprimir [repri'mir] vt to repress

reprobar [repro'βar] vt to censure, reprove

reprochar [repro'tʃar] vt to reproach; **reproche** nm reproach

reproducción [reproðuk'θjon] nf reproduction

reproducir [reproðu'θir] vt to reproduce; **reproducirse** vr to breed; (situación) to recur

reproductor, a [reproðuk'tor, a] adj reproductive ▷nm player; **reproductor de CD** CD player

reptil [rep'til] nm reptile

república [re'puβlika] nf republic; **República Dominicana** Dominican Republic; **republicano, -a** adj, nm republican

repudiar [repu'ðjar] vt to repudiate; (fe) to renounce

repuesto [re'pwesto] nm (pieza de recambio) spare (part); (abastecimiento) supply; **rueda de ~** spare wheel

repugnancia [repuɣ'nanθja] nf repugnance; **repugnante** adj repugnant, repulsive

repugnar [repuɣ'nar] vt to disgust

repulsa [re'pulsa] nf rebuff

repulsión [repul'sjon] nf repulsion, aversion; **repulsivo, -a** adj repulsive

reputación [reputa'θjon] nf reputation

requerir [reke'rir] vt (pedir) to ask, request; (exigir) to require; (llamar) to send for, summon

requesón [reke'son] nm cottage cheese

requete... [re'kete] prefijo extremely

réquiem ['rekjem] (pl ~s) nm requiem

requisito [reki'sito] nm requirement, requisite

res [res] nf beast, animal

resaca [re'saka] nf (de mar) undertow, undercurrent; (fam) hangover

resaltar [resal'tar] vi to project, stick out; (fig) to stand out

resarcir [resar'θir] vt to compensate; **resarcirse** vr to make up for

resbaladero [resβala'ðero] (MÉX) nm slide

resbaladizo, -a [resβala'ðiθo, a] adj slippery

resbalar [resβa'lar] vi to slip, slide; (fig) to slip (up); **resbalarse** vr to slip, slide; to slip (up); **resbalón** nm (acción) slip

rescatar [reska'tar] vt (salvar) to save, rescue; (objeto) to get back, recover; (cautivos) to ransom

rescate [res'kate] nm rescue; (de objeto) recovery; **pagar un ~** to pay a ransom

rescindir [resθin'dir] *vt* to rescind

rescisión [resθi'sjon] *nf* cancellation

resecar [rese'kar] *vt* to dry
thoroughly; (*Med*) to cut out, remove;
resecarse *vr* to dry up

reseco, -a [re'seko, a] *adj* very dry;
(*fig*) skinny

resentido, -a [resen'tiðo, a] *adj*
resentful

resentimiento [resenti'mjento] *nm*
resentment, bitterness

resentirse [resen'tirse] *vr*
(*debilitarse: persona*) to suffer; **~ de**
(*consecuencias*) to feel the effects of; **~
de** (*o por*) **algo** to resent sth, to be bitter
about sth

reseña [re'seɲa] *nf* (*cuenta*) account;
(*informe*) report; (*Literatura*) review

reseñar [rese'ɲar] *vt* to describe;
(*Literatura*) to review

reserva [re'serβa] *nf* reserve;
(*reservación*) reservation

reservación [reserβaθjon] *nf*
reservation

reservado, -a [reser'βaðo, a] *adj*
reserved; (*retraído*) cold, distant ⊳ *nm*
private room

reservar [reser'βar] *vt* (*guardar*) to
keep; (*habitación, entrada*) to reserve;
reservarse *vr* to save o.s.; (*callar*) to
keep to o.s.

resfriado [resfri'aðo] *nm* cold;
resfriarse *vr* to cool; (*Med*) to catch
a cold

resguardar [resɣwar'ðar] *vt* to
protect, shield; **resguardarse** *vr*: **~se
de** to guard against; **resguardo**
nm defence; (*vale*) voucher; (*recibo*)
receipt, slip

residencia [resi'ðenθja] *nf*
residence; **residencia de ancianos**
residential home, old people's
home; **residencia universitaria**
hall of residence; **residencial** *nf*
(*urbanización*) housing estate

residente [resi'ðente] *adj, nmf*
resident

residir [resi'ðir] *vi* to reside, live; **~ en**
to reside in, lie in

residuo [re'siðwo] *nm* residue

resignación [resiɣna'θjon] *nf*
resignation; **resignarse** *vr*: **resignarse
a o con** to resign o.s. to, be resigned to

resina [re'sina] *nf* resin

resistencia [resis'tenθja] *nf* (*dureza*)
endurance, strength; (*oposición, Elec*)
resistance; **resistente** *adj* strong,
hardy; resistant

resistir [resis'tir] *vt* (*soportar*) to bear;
(*oponerse a*) to resist, oppose; (*aguantar*)
to put up with ⊳ *vi* to resist; (*aguantar*)
to last, endure; **resistirse** *vr*: **~se a** to
refuse to, resist

resoluto, -a [reso'luto, a] *adj*
resolute

resolver [resol'βer] *vt* to resolve;
(*solucionar*) to solve, resolve; (*decidir*) to
decide, settle; **resolverse** *vr* to make
up one's mind

resonar [reso'nar] *vi* to ring, echo

resoplar [reso'plar] *vi* to snort;
resoplido *nm* heavy breathing

resorte [re'sorte] *nm* spring; (*fig*)
lever

resortera [resor'tera] (*MÉX*) *nf*
catapult

respaldar [respal'dar] *vt* to back
(up), support; **respaldarse** *vr* to lean
back; **~se con o en** (*fig*) to take one's
stand on; **respaldo** *nm* (*de sillón*) back;
(*fig*) support, backing

respectivo, -a [respek'tiβo, a] *adj*
respective; **en lo ~ a** with regard to

respecto [res'pekto] *nm*: **al ~** on this
matter; **con ~ a, ~ de** with regard to,
in relation to

respetable [respe'taβle] *adj*
respectable

respetar [respe'tar] *vt* to respect;
respeto *nm* respect; (*acatamiento*)
deference; **respetos** *nmpl* respects;
respetuoso, -a *adj* respectful

respingo [res'pingo] *nm* start, jump

respiración [respira'θjon] *nf*
breathing; (*Med*) respiration;

respirar | 242

(ventilación) ventilation; **respiración asistida** artificial respiration (by machine)

respirar [respi'rar] vi to breathe; **respiratorio, -a** adj respiratory; **respiro** nm breathing; *(fig: descanso)* respite

resplandecer [resplande'θer] vi to shine; **resplandeciente** adj resplendent, shining; **resplandor** nm brilliance, brightness; *(de luz, fuego)* blaze

responder [respon'der] vt to answer ▷ vi to answer; *(fig)* to respond; *(pey)* to answer back; **~ de o por** to answer for; **respondón, -ona** adj cheeky

responsabilidad [responsaβili'ðað] nf responsibility

responsabilizarse [responsaβili'θarse] vr to make o.s. responsible, take charge

responsable [respon'saβle] adj responsible

respuesta [res'pwesta] nf answer, reply

resquebrajar [reskeβra'xar] vt to crack, split; **resquebrajarse** vr to crack, split

resquicio [res'kiθjo] nm chink; *(hendedura)* crack

resta ['resta] nf *(Mat)* remainder

restablecer [restaβle'θer] vt to re-establish, restore; **restablecerse** vr to recover

restante [res'tante] adj remaining; **lo ~** the remainder

restar [res'tar] vt *(Mat)* to subtract; *(fig)* to take away ▷ vi to remain, be left

restauración [restaura'θjon] nf restoration

restaurante [restau'rante] nm restaurant

restaurar [restau'rar] vt to restore

restituir [restitu'ir] vt *(devolver)* to return, give back; *(rehabilitar)* to restore

resto ['resto] nm *(residuo)* rest, remainder; *(apuesta)* stake; **restos** nmpl remains

restorán [resto'ran] nm *(Lam)* restaurant

restregar [restre'ɣar] vt to scrub, rub

restricción [restrik'θjon] nf restriction

restringir [restrin'xir] vt to restrict, limit

resucitar [resuθi'tar] vt, vi to resuscitate, revive

resuelto, -a [re'swelto, a] pp de **resolver** ▷ adj resolute, determined

resultado [resul'taðo] nm result; *(conclusión)* outcome; **resultante** adj resulting, resultant

resultar [resul'tar] vi *(ser)* to be; *(llegar a ser)* to turn out to be; *(salir bien)* to turn out well; *(Com)* to amount to; **~ de** to stem from; **me resulta difícil hacerlo** it's difficult for me to do it

resumen [re'sumen] *(pl* **resúmenes**) nm summary, résumé; **en ~** in short

resumir [resu'mir] vt to sum up; *(cortar)* to abridge, cut down; *(condensar)* to summarize

⎸ No confundir **resumir** con la
⎸ palabra inglesa resume.

resurgir [resur'xir] vi *(reaparecer)* to reappear

resurrección [resurre(k)'θjon] nf resurrection

retablo [re'taβlo] nm altarpiece

retaguardia [reta'ɣwarðja] nf rearguard

retahíla [reta'ila] nf series, string

retal [re'tal] nm remnant

retar [re'tar] vt to challenge; *(desafiar)* to defy, dare

retazo [re'taθo] nm snippet *(BRIT)*, fragment

retención [reten'θjon] nf *(tráfico)* hold-up; **retención fiscal** deduction for tax purposes

retener [rete'ner] vt *(intereses)* to withhold

reticente [reti'θente] adj *(tono)* insinuating; *(postura)* reluctant; **ser ~ a hacer algo** to be reluctant o unwilling to do sth

retina [re'tina] nf retina

retintín [retin'tin] nm jangle, jingle

retirada [reti'raða] nf (Mil, refugio) retreat; (de dinero) withdrawal; (de embajador) recall; **retirado, -a** adj (lugar) remote; (vida) quiet; (jubilado) retired

retirar [reti'rar] vt to withdraw; (quitar) to remove; (jubilar) to retire, pension off; **retirarse** vr to retreat, withdraw; to retire; (acostarse) to retire, go to bed; **retiro** nm retreat; retirement; (pago) pension

reto ['reto] nm dare, challenge

retocar [reto'kar] vt (fotografía) to touch up, retouch

retoño [re'toɲo] nm sprout, shoot; (fig) offspring, child

retoque [re'toke] nm retouching

retorcer [retor'θer] vt to twist; (manos, lavado) to wring; **retorcerse** vr to become twisted; (mover el cuerpo) to writhe

retorcido, -a [retor'θiðo, a] adj (persona) devious

retorcijón [retorθi'xon] (LAM) nm (tb: ~ de tripas) stomach cramp

retórica [re'torika] nf rhetoric; (pey) affectedness

retorno [re'torno] nm return

retortijón [retorti'xon] (ESP) nm (tb: ~ de tripas) stomach cramp

retozar [reto'θar] vi (juguetear) to frolic, romp; (saltar) to gambol

retracción [retrak'θjon] nf retraction

retraerse [retra'erse] vr to retreat, withdraw; **retraído, -a** adj shy, retiring; **retraimiento** nm retirement; (timidez) shyness

retransmisión [retransmi'sjon] nf repeat (broadcast)

retransmitir [retransmi'tir] vt (mensaje) to relay; (TV etc) to repeat, retransmit; (: en vivo) to broadcast live

retrasado, -a [retra'saðo, a] adj late; (Med) mentally retarded; (país etc) backward, underdeveloped

retrasar [retra'sar] vt (demorar) to postpone, put off; (retardar) to slow down ▷ vi (atrasarse) to be late; (reloj) to be slow; (producción) to fall (off); (quedarse atrás) to lag behind; **retrasarse** vr to be late; to be slow; to fall (off); to lag behind

retraso [re'traso] nm (demora) delay; (lentitud) slowness; (tardanza) lateness; (atraso) backwardness; **retrasos** nmpl (Finanzas) arrears; **llegar con ~** to arrive late; **retraso mental** mental deficiency

retratar [retra'tar] vt (Arte) to paint the portrait of; (fotografiar) to photograph; (fig) to depict, describe; **retrato** nm portrait; (fig) likeness; **retrato-robot** (ESP) nm Identikit®

retrete [re'trete] nm toilet

retribuir [retriβwir] vt (recompensar) to reward; (pagar) to pay

retro... ['retro] prefijo retro...

retroceder [retroθe'ðer] vi (echarse atrás) to move back(wards); (fig) to back down

retroceso [retro'θeso] nm backward movement; (Med) relapse; (fig) backing down

retrospectivo, -a [retrospek'tiβo, a] adj retrospective

retrovisor [retroβi'sor] nm (tb: espejo ~) rear-view mirror

retumbar [retum'bar] vi to echo, resound

reúma [re'uma], **reuma** ['reuma] nm rheumatism

reunión [reu'njon] nf (asamblea) meeting; (fiesta) party

reunir [reu'nir] vt (juntar) to reunite, join (together); (recoger) to gather (together); (personas) to get together; (cualidades) to combine; **reunirse** vr (personas: en asamblea) to meet, gather

revalidar [reβali'ðar] vt (ratificar) to confirm, ratify

revalorizar [reβalori'θar] vt to revalue, reassess

revancha [re'βantʃa] nf revenge

revelación [reβela'θjon] nf
revelation

revelado [reβe'laðo] nm developing

revelar [reβe'lar] vt to reveal; *(Foto)*
to develop

reventa [re'βenta] nf *(de
entradas: para concierto)* touting

reventar [reβen'tar] vt to burst,
explode

reventón [reβen'ton] nm *(Auto)*
blow-out (BRIT), flat (US)

reverencia [reβe'renθja] nf
reverence; **reverenciar** vt to revere

reverendo, -a [reβe'rendo, a] adj
reverend

reverente [reβe'rente] adj reverent

reversa [re'βersa] *(MÉX, CAM)* nf
reverse *(gear)*

reversible [reβer'siβle] adj *(prenda)*
reversible

reverso [re'βerso] nm back, other
side; *(de moneda)* reverse

revertir [reβer'tir] vi to revert

revés [re'βes] nm back, wrong
side; *(fig)* reverse, setback; *(Deporte)*
backhand; **al ~** the wrong way round;
(de arriba abajo) upside down; *(ropa)*
inside out; **volver algo del ~** to turn
sth round; *(ropa)* to turn sth inside out

revisar [reβi'sar] vt *(examinar)* to
check; *(texto etc)* to review; **revisión**
nf revision; **revisión salarial** wage
review

revisor, a [reβi'sor, a] nm/f
inspector; *(Ferro)* ticket collector

revista [re'βista] nf magazine,
review; *(Teatro)* revue; *(inspección)*
inspection; **pasar ~ a** to review,
inspect; **revista del corazón** magazine
featuring celebrity gossip and real-life
romance stories

revivir [reβi'βir] vi to revive

revolcarse [reβol'karse] vr to roll
about

revoltijo [reβol'tixo] nm mess, jumble

revoltoso, -a [reβol'toso, a] adj
(travieso) naughty, unruly

revolución [reβolu'θjon] nf

revolution; **revolucionario, -a** adj,
nm/f revolutionary

revolver [reβol'βer] vt *(desordenar)*
to disturb, mess up; *(mover)* to move
about ▷ vi: **~ en** to go through,
rummage (about) in; **revolverse** vr
(volver contra) to turn on o against

revólver [re'βolβer] nm revolver

revuelo [re'βwelo] nm fluttering; *(fig)*
commotion

revuelta [re'βwelta] nf *(motín)* revolt;
(agitación) commotion

revuelto, -a [re'βwelto, a] pp de
revolver ▷ adj *(mezclado)* mixed-up,
in disorder

rey [rei] nm king; **Día de R~es** Twelfth
Night; **los R~es Magos** the Three Wise
Men, the Magi

● **REYES MAGOS**
●
● On the night before the 6th
● January (the Epiphany), children
● go to bed expecting **los Reyes**
● **Magos** (the Three Wise Men) to
● bring them presents. Twelfth
● Night processions, known as
● **cabalgatas**, take place that
● evening when 3 people dressed
● as **los Reyes Magos** arrive in the
● town by land or sea to the delight
● of the children.

reyerta [re'jerta] nf quarrel, brawl

rezagado, -a [reθa'ɣaðo, a] nm/f
straggler

rezar [re'θar] vi to pray; **~ con** *(fam)*
to concern, have to do with; **rezo**
nm prayer

rezumar [reθu'mar] vt to ooze

ría ['ria] nf estuary

riada [ri'aða] nf flood

ribera [ri'βera] nf *(de río)* bank; (: *área*)
riverside

ribete [ri'βete] nm *(de vestido)* border;
(fig) addition

ricino [ri'θino] nm: **aceite de ~**
castor oil

rico, -a ['riko, a] *adj* rich; *(adinerado)* wealthy, rich; *(lujoso)* luxurious; *(comida)* delicious; *(niño)* lovely, cute ▷ *nm/f* rich person

ridiculez [riðiku'leθ] *nf* absurdity

ridiculizar [riðikuli'θar] *vt* to ridicule

ridículo, -a [ri'ðikulo, a] *adj* ridiculous; **hacer el ~** to make a fool of o.s.; **poner a algn en ~** to make a fool of sb

riego ['rjexo] *nm (aspersión)* watering; *(irrigación)* irrigation; **riego sanguíneo** blood flow o circulation

riel [rjel] *nm* rail

rienda ['rjenda] *nf* rein; **dar ~ suelta a** to give free rein to

riesgo ['rjesxo] *nm* risk; **correr el ~ de** to run the risk of

rifa ['rifa] *nf (lotería)* raffle; **rifar** *vt* to raffle

rifle ['rifle] *nm* rifle

rigidez [rixi'ðeθ] *nf* rigidity, stiffness; *(fig)* strictness; **rígido, -a** *adj* rigid, stiff; strict, inflexible

rigor [ri'xor] *nm* strictness, rigour; *(inclemencia)* harshness; **de ~** de rigueur, essential; **riguroso, -a** *adj* rigorous; harsh; *(severo)* severe

rimar [ri'mar] *vi* to rhyme

rimbombante [rimbom'bante] *adj* pompous

rímel ['rimel] *nm* mascara

rímmel ['rimel] *nm* = **rímel**

rin [rin] *(MÉX)* *nm (wheel)* rim

rincón [rin'kon] *nm* corner *(inside)*

rinoceronte [rinoθe'ronte] *nm* rhinoceros

riña ['riɲa] *nf (disputa)* argument; *(pelea)* brawl

riñón [ri'ɲon] *nm* kidney

río *etc* ['rio] *vb* V **reír** ▷ *nm* river; *(fig)* torrent, stream; **río abajo/arriba** downstream/upstream; **Río de la Plata** River Plate

rioja [ri'oxa] *nf (vino)* rioja (wine)

rioplatense [riopla'tense] *adj* of o from the River Plate region

riqueza [ri'keθa] *nf* wealth, riches *pl*;

(cualidad) richness

risa ['risa] *nf* laughter; *(una risa)* laugh; **¡qué ~!** what a laugh!

risco ['risko] *nm* crag, cliff

ristra ['ristra] *nf* string

risueño, -a [ri'sweɲo, a] *adj* *(sonriente)* smiling; *(contento)* cheerful

ritmo ['ritmo] *nm* rhythm; **a ~ lento** slowly; **trabajar a ~ lento** to go slow; **ritmo cardíaco** heart rate

rito ['rito] *nm* rite

ritual [ri'twal] *adj, nm* ritual

rival [ri'βal] *adj, nm/f* rival; **rivalidad** *nf* rivalry; **rivalizar** *vi*: **rivalizar con** to rival, vie with

rizado, -a [ri'θaðo, a] *adj* curly ▷ *nm* curls *pl*

rizar [ri'θar] *vt* to curl; **rizarse** *vr (pelo)* to curl; *(agua)* to ripple; **rizo** *nm* curl; ripple

RNE *nf abr* = **Radio Nacional de España**

robar [ro'βar] *vt* to rob; *(objeto)* to steal; *(casa etc)* to break into; *(Naipes)* to draw

roble ['roβle] *nm* oak; **robledal** o **robledo** *nm* oakwood

robo ['roβo] *nm* robbery, theft

robot [ro'βot] *nm* robot; **robot (de cocina)** *(ESP)* food processor

robustecer [roβuste'θer] *vt* to strengthen

robusto, -a [ro'βusto, a] *adj* robust, strong

roca ['roka] *nf* rock

roce ['roθe] *nm (caricia)* brush; *(Tec)* friction; *(en la piel)* graze; **tener ~ con** to be in close contact with

rociar [ro'θjar] *vt* to spray

rocín [ro'θin] *nm* nag, hack

rocío [ro'θio] *nm* dew

rocola [ro'kola] *(LAM)* *nf* jukebox

rocoso, -a [ro'koso, a] *adj* rocky

rodaballo [roða'βaʎo] *nm* turbot

rodaja [ro'ðaxa] *nf* slice

rodaje [ro'ðaxe] *nm (Cine)* shooting, filming; *(Auto)*: **en ~** running in

rodar [ro'ðar] *vt (vehículo)* to wheel (along); *(escalera)* to roll down; *(viajar)*

rodear [roðe'ar] vt to surround ▷ vi to go round; (Cine) to shoot, film

rodear [roðe'ar] vt to surround ▷ vi to go round; **rodearse** vr: **~se de amigos** to surround o.s. with friends

rodeo [ro'ðeo] nm (ruta indirecta) detour; (evasión) evasion; (Deporte) rodeo; **hablar sin ~s** to come to the point, speak plainly

rodilla [ro'ðiʎa] nf knee; **de ~s** kneeling; **ponerse de ~s** to kneel (down)

rodillo [ro'ðiʎo] nm roller; (Culin) rolling-pin

roedor, a [roe'ðor, a] adj gnawing ▷ nm rodent

roer [ro'er] vt (masticar) to gnaw; (corroer, fig) to corrode

rogar [ro'xar] vt, vi (pedir) to ask for; (suplicar) to beg, plead; **se ruega no fumar** please do not smoke

rojizo, -a [ro'xiθo, a] adj reddish

rojo, -a ['roxo, a] adj, nm red; **al ~ vivo** red-hot

rol [rol] nm list, roll; (papel) role

rollito [ro'ʎito] nm (tb: **~ de primavera**) spring roll

rollizo, -a [ro'ʎiθo, a] adj (objeto) cylindrical; (persona) plump

rollo ['roʎo] nm roll; (de cuerda) coil; (madera) log; (Esp: fam) bore; **¡qué ~! (Esp: fam)** what a carry-on!

Roma ['roma] n Rome

romance [ro'manθe] nm (amoroso) romance; (Literatura) ballad

romano, -a [ro'mano, a] adj, nm/f Roman; **a la romana** in batter

romanticismo [romanti'θismo] nm romanticism

romántico, -a [ro'mantiko, a] adj romantic

rombo ['rombo] nm (Geom) rhombus

romería [rome'ria] nf (Rel) pilgrimage; (excursión) trip, outing

○ **ROMERÍA**
○
○ Originally a pilgrimage to a shrine
○ or church to express devotion to
○ the Virgin Mary or a local Saint,
○ the **romería** has also become a
○ rural festival which accompanies
○ the pilgrimage. People come from
○ all over to attend, bringing their
○ own food and drink, and spend the
○ day in celebration.

romero, -a [ro'mero, a] nm/f pilgrim ▷ nm rosemary

romo, -a ['romo, a] adj blunt; (fig) dull

rompecabezas [rompeka'βeθas] nm inv riddle, puzzle; (juego) jigsaw (puzzle)

rompehuelgas [rompe'welɣas] (LAM) nm inv strikebreaker, scab

rompeolas [rompe'olas] nm inv breakwater

romper [rom'per] vt to break; (hacer pedazos) to smash; (papel, tela etc) to tear, rip ▷ vi (olas) to break; (sol, diente) to break through; **romperse** vr to break; **~ un contrato** to start a contract; **~ a** (empezar a) to start (suddenly) to; **~ a llorar** to burst into tears; **~ con algn** to fall out with sb

ron [ron] nm rum

roncar [ron'kar] vi to snore

ronco, -a ['ronko, a] adj (afónico) hoarse; (áspero) raucous

ronda ['ronda] nf (gen) round; (patrulla) patrol; **rondar** vt to patrol ▷ vi to patrol; (fig) to prowl round

ronquido [ron'kiðo] nm snore, snoring

ronronear [ronrone'ar] vi to purr

roña ['roɲa] nf (Veterinaria) mange; (mugre) dirt, grime; (óxido) rust

roñoso, -a [ro'ɲoso, a] adj (mugriento) filthy; (tacaño) mean

ropa ['ropa] nf clothes pl, clothing; **ropa blanca** linen; **ropa de cama** bed linen; **ropa de color** coloureds pl; **ropa interior** underwear; **ropa sucia** dirty washing; **ropaje** nm gown, robes pl

ropero [ro'pero] nm linen cupboard; (guardarropa) wardrobe

rosa ['rosa] adj pink ▷ nf rose

rosado, -a [ro'saðo, a] adj pink
▷ nm rosé

rosal [ro'sal] nm rosebush

rosario [ro'sarjo] nm (Rel) rosary;
rezar el ~ to say the rosary

rosca ['roska] nf (de tornillo) thread;
(de humo) coil, spiral; (pan, postre) ring-
shaped roll/pastry

rosetón [rose'ton] nm rosette; (Arq)
rose window

rosquilla [ros'kiʎa] nf doughnut-
shaped fritter

rostro ['rostro] nm (cara) face

rotativo, -a [rota'tiβo, a] adj rotary

roto, -a ['roto, a] pp de **romper** ▷ adj
broken

rotonda [ro'tonda] nf roundabout

rótula ['rotula] nf kneecap; (Tec) ball-
and-socket joint

rotulador [rotula'ðor] nm felt-tip
pen

rótulo ['rotulo] nm heading, title;
label; (letrero) sign

rotundamente [rotunda'mente]
adv (negar) flatly; (responder, afirmar)
emphatically; **rotundo, -a** adj round;
(enfático) emphatic

rotura [ro'tura] nf (acto) breaking;
(Med) fracture

rozadura [roθa'ðura] nf abrasion,
graze

rozar [ro'θar] vt (frotar) to rub;
(arañar) to scratch; (tocar ligeramente)
to shave, touch lightly; **rozarse** vr to
rub (together); **~se con** (fam) to rub
shoulders with

rte. abr (= remite, remitente) sender

RTVE nf abr = **Radiotelevisión
Española**

rubí [ru'βi] nm ruby; (de reloj) jewel

rubio, -a ['ruβjo, a] adj fair-haired,
blond(e) ▷ nm/f blond/blonde;
tabaco ~ Virginia tobacco

rubor [ru'βor] nm (sonrojo) blush;
(timidez) bashfulness; **ruborizarse**
vr to blush

rúbrica ['ruβrika] nf (de la firma)

flourish; **rubricar** vt (firmar) to sign
with a flourish; (concluir) to sign
and seal

rudimentario, -a [ruðimen'tarjo,
a] adj rudimentary

rudo, -a ['ruðo, a] adj (sin pulir)
unpolished; (grosero) coarse; (violento)
violent; (sencillo) simple

rueda ['rweða] nf wheel; (círculo)
ring, circle; (rodaja) slice, round; **rueda
de auxilio** (RPL) spare tyre; **rueda
delantera/trasera/de repuesto**
front/back/spare wheel; **rueda de
prensa** press conference; **rueda
gigante** (LAM) big (BRIT) o Ferris (US)
wheel

ruedo ['rweðo] nm (círculo) circle;
(Taur) arena, bullring

ruego etc ['rwexo] vb V **rogar** ▷ nm
request

rugby ['ruxβi] nm rugby

rugido [ru'xiðo] nm roar

rugir [ru'xir] vi to roar

rugoso, -a [ru'xoso, a] adj (arrugado)
wrinkled; (áspero) rough; (desigual)
ridged

ruido ['rwiðo] nm noise; (sonido)
sound; (alboroto) racket, row;
(escándalo) commotion, rumpus;
ruidoso, -a adj noisy, loud; (fig)
sensational

ruin [rwin] adj contemptible, mean

ruina ['rwina] nf ruin; (colapso)
collapse; (de persona) ruin, downfall

ruinoso, -a [rwi'noso, a] adj
ruinous; (destartalado) dilapidated,
tumbledown; (Com) disastrous

ruiseñor [rwise'nor] nm nightingale

rulero [ru'lero] (RPL) nm roller

ruleta [ru'leta] nf roulette

rulo ['rulo] nm (para el pelo) curler

Rumanía [ruma'nia] nf Rumania

rumba ['rumba] nf rumba

rumbo ['rumbo] nm (ruta) route,
direction; (ángulo de dirección) course,
bearing; (fig) course of events; **ir con ~
a** to be heading for

rumiante [ru'mjante] nm ruminant

rumiar [ru'mjar] vt to chew; (fig) to chew over ▷ vi to chew the cud

rumor [ru'mor] nm (ruido sordo) low sound; (murmuración) murmur, buzz; **rumorearse** vr: **se rumorea que ...** it is rumoured that ...

rupestre [ru'pestre] adj rock cpd

ruptura [rup'tura] nf rupture

rural [ru'ral] adj rural

Rusia ['rusja] nf Russia; **ruso, -a** adj, nm/f Russian

rústico, -a ['rustiko, a] adj rustic; (ordinario) coarse, uncouth ▷ nm/f yokel

ruta ['ruta] nf route

rutina [ru'tina] nf routine

S

S abr (= santo, a) St; (= sur) S

s. abr (= siglo) C.; (= siguiente) foll

S.A. abr (= Sociedad Anónima) Ltd. (BRIT), Inc. (US)

sábado ['saβaðo] nm Saturday

sábana ['saβana] nf sheet

sabañón [saβa'ɲon] nm chilblain

saber [sa'βer] vt to know; (llegar a conocer) to find out, learn; (tener capacidad de) to know how to ▷ vi: **~ a** to taste of, taste like ▷ nm knowledge, learning; **a ~** namely; **¿sabes conducir/nadar?** can you drive/swim?; **¿sabes francés?** do you speak French?; **~ de memoria** to know by heart; **hacer ~ algo a algn** to inform sb of sth, let sb know sth

sabiduría [saβiðu'ria] nf (conocimientos) wisdom; (instrucción) learning

sabiendas [sa'βjendas]: **a ~** adv knowingly

sabio, -a ['saβjo, a] adj (docto) learned; (prudente) wise, sensible

sabor [sa'βor] nm taste, flavour;

saborear [saβoˈrear] vt to taste, savour; (fig) to relish

sabotaje [saβoˈtaxe] nm sabotage

sabré etc vb V **saber**

sabroso, -a [saˈβroso, a] adj tasty; (fig: fam) racy, salty

sacacorchos [sakaˈkortʃos] nm inv corkscrew

sacapuntas [sakaˈpuntas] nm inv pencil sharpener

sacar [saˈkar] vt to take out; (fig: extraer) to get (out); (quitar) to remove, get out; (hacer salir) to bring out; (conclusión) to draw; (novela etc) to publish, bring out; (ropa) to take off; (obra) to make; (premio) to receive; (entradas) to get; (Tenis) to serve; ~ adelante (niño) to bring up; (negocio) to carry on, go on with; ~ a algn a bailar to get sb up to dance; ~ una foto to take a photo; ~ la lengua to stick out one's tongue; ~ buenas/malas notas to get good/bad marks

sacarina [sakaˈrina] nf saccharin(e)

sacerdote [saθerˈðote] nm priest

saciar [saˈθjar] vt (hambre, sed) to satisfy; **saciarse** vr (de comida) to get full up

saco [ˈsako] nm bag; (grande) sack; (su contenido) bagful; (LAM: chaqueta) jacket; **saco de dormir** sleeping bag

sacramento [sakraˈmento] nm sacrament

sacrificar [sakrifiˈkar] vt to sacrifice; **sacrificio** nm sacrifice

sacristía [sakrisˈtia] nf sacristy

sacudida [sakuˈðiða] nf (agitación) shake, shaking; (sacudimiento) jolt, bump; **sacudida eléctrica** electric shock

sacudir [sakuˈðir] vt to shake; (golpear) to hit

Sagitario [saxiˈtarjo] nm Sagittarius

sagrado, -a [saˈɣraðo, a] adj sacred, holy

Sáhara [ˈsaara] nm: **el ~** the Sahara (desert)

sal [sal] vb V **salir** ▷ nf salt; **sales de**

baño bath salts

sala [ˈsala] nf room; (tb: ~ de estar) living room; (Teatro) house, auditorium; (de hospital) ward; **sala de espera** waiting room; **sala de estar** living room; **sala de fiestas** dance hall

salado, -a [saˈlaðo, a] adj salty; (fig) witty, amusing; **agua salada** salt water

salar [saˈlar] vt to salt, add salt to

salariado [salaˈrjaðo] adj (empleado) salaried

salario [saˈlarjo] nm wage, pay

salchicha [salˈtʃitʃa] nf (pork) sausage; **salchichón** nm (salami-type) sausage

saldo [ˈsaldo] nm (pago) settlement; (de una cuenta) balance; (lo restante) remnant(s) (pl), remainder; (de móvil) credit; **saldos** nmpl (en tienda) sale

saldré etc vb V **salir**

salero [saˈlero] nm salt cellar

salgo etc vb V **salir**

salida [saˈliða] nf (puerta etc) exit, way out; (acto) leaving, going out; (de tren, Aviac) departure; (Tec) output, production; (fig) way out; (Com) opening; (Geo, válvula) outlet; (de gas) leak; **calle sin ~** cul-de-sac; **salida de baño** (RPL) bathrobe; **salida de emergencia/incendios** emergency exit/fire escape

○ **PALABRA CLAVE**

salir [saˈlir] vi 1 (partir: tb: **salir de**) to leave; **Juan ha salido** Juan is out; **salió de la cocina** he came out of the kitchen

2 (aparecer) to appear; (disco, libro) to come out; **anoche salió en la tele** she appeared o was on TV last night; **salió en todos los periódicos** it was in all the papers

3 (resultar): **la muchacha nos salió muy trabajadora** the girl turned out to be a very hard worker; **la comida te ha salido exquisita** the food was

delicious; **sale muy caro** it's very expensive

4: salirle a uno algo: la entrevista que hice me salió bien/mal the interview I did went o turned out well/badly

5: salir adelante: no sé como haré para salir adelante I don't know how I'll get by

salirse *vr* (*líquido*) to spill; (*animal*) to escape

saliva [sa'liβa] *nf* saliva

salmo ['salmo] *nm* psalm

salmón [sal'mon] *nm* salmon

salmonete [salmo'nete] *nm* red mullet

salón [sa'lon] *nm* (*de casa*) living room, lounge; (*muebles*) lounge suite; **salón de actos** assembly hall; **salón de baile** dance hall; **salón de belleza** beauty parlour

salpicadera [salpika'ðera] (*MÉX*) *nf* mudguard (*BRIT*), fender (*US*)

salpicadero [salpika'ðero] *nm* (*Auto*) dashboard

salpicar [salpi'kar] *vt* (*rociar*) to sprinkle, spatter; (*esparcir*) to scatter

salpicón [salpi'kon] *nm* (*tb*: **~ de marisco**) seafood salad

salsa ['salsa] *nf* sauce; (*con carne asada*) gravy; (*fig*) spice

saltamontes [salta'montes] *nm inv* grasshopper

saltar [sal'tar] *vt* to jump (over), leap (over); (*dejar de lado*) to skip, miss out ▷ *vi* to jump, leap; (*pelota*) to bounce; (*al aire*) to fly up; (*quebrarse*) to break; (*al agua*) to dive; (*fig*) to explode, blow up

salto ['salto] *nm* jump, leap; (*al agua*) dive; **salto de agua** waterfall; **salto de altura/longitud** high/long jump

salud [sa'luð] *nf* health; **¡(a su) ~!** cheers!, good health!; **saludable** *adj* (*de buena salud*) healthy; (*provechoso*) good, beneficial

saludar [salu'ðar] *vt* to greet; (*Mil*) to salute; **saludo** greeting;

"saludos" (*en carta*) "best wishes", "regards"

salvación [salβa'θjon] *nf* salvation; (*rescate*) rescue

salvado [sal'βaðo] *nm* bran

salvaje [sal'βaxe] *adj* wild; (*tribu*) savage

salvamanteles [salβaman'teles] *nm inv* table mat

salvamento [salβa'mento] *nm* rescue

salvapantallas [salβapan'taʎas] *nm inv* screen saver

salvar [sal'βar] *vt* (*rescatar*) to save, rescue; (*resolver*) to overcome, resolve; (*cubrir distancias*) to cover, travel; (*hacer excepción*) to except, exclude; (*barco*) to salvage

salvavidas [salβa'βiðas] *adj inv*: **bote/chaleco ~** lifeboat/life jacket

salvo, -a ['salβo, a] *adj* safe ▷ *adv* except (for), save; **a ~** out of danger; **~ que** unless

san [san] *adj* saint; **S~ Juan** St John

sanar [sa'nar] *vt* (*herida*) to heal; (*persona*) to cure ▷ *vi* (*persona*) to get well, recover; (*herida*) to heal

sanatorio [sana'torjo] *nm* sanatorium

sanción [san'θjon] *nf* sanction

sancochado, -a [sanko'tʃaðo, a] (*MÉX*) *adj* Culin underdone, rare

sandalia [san'dalja] *nf* sandal

sandía [san'dia] *nf* watermelon

sandwich ['sandwitʃ] (*pl* **~s, ~es**) *nm* sandwich

sanfermines [sanfer'mines] *nmpl* festivities in celebration of San Fermín (Pamplona)

● **SANFERMINES**
●
● The **Sanfermines** is a week-long
● festival in Pamplona made famous
● by Ernest Hemingway. From the
● 7th July, the feast of "San Fermín",
● crowds of mainly young people
● take to the streets drinking,

singing and dancing. Early in the morning bulls are released along the narrow streets leading to the bullring, and young men risk serious injury to show their bravery by running out in front of them, a custom which is also typical of many Spanish villages.

sangrar [saŋ'grar] vt, vi to bleed; **sangre** nf blood

sangría [saŋ'gria] nf sangria, sweetened drink of red wine with fruit

sangriento, -a [saŋ'grjento, a] adj bloody

sanguíneo, -a [saŋ'gineo, a] adj blood cpd

sanidad [sani'ðað] nf (tb: ~ **pública**) public health

San Isidro [sani'siðro] nm patron saint of Madrid

⬤ **SAN ISIDRO**
⬤
⬤ **San Isidro** is the patron saint of
⬤ Madrid, and gives his name to
⬤ the week-long festivities which
⬤ take place around the 15th May.
⬤ Originally an 18th-century trade
⬤ fair, the **San Isidro** celebrations
⬤ now include music, dance, a
⬤ famous **romería**, theatre and
⬤ bullfighting.

sanitario, -a [sani'tarjo, a] adj health cpd; **sanitarios** nmpl toilets (BRIT), washroom (US)

sano, -a ['sano, a] adj healthy; (sin daños) sound; (comida) wholesome; (entero) whole, intact; ~ **y salvo** safe and sound

⚠ No confundir **sano** con la palabra inglesa **sane**.

Santiago [san'tjaxo] nm ~ **(de Chile)** Santiago

santiamén [santja'men] nm: **en un ~** in no time at all

santidad [santi'ðað] nf holiness,

sanctity

santiguarse [santi'ɣwarse] vr to make the sign of the cross

santo, -a ['santo, a] adj holy; (fig) wonderful, miraculous ▷ nm/f saint ▷ nm saint's day; ~ **y seña** password

santuario [san'twarjo] nm sanctuary, shrine

sapo ['sapo] nm toad

saque ['sake] nm (Tenis) service, serve; (Fútbol) throw-in; **saque de esquina** corner (kick)

saquear [sake'ar] vt (Mil) to sack; (robar) to loot, plunder; (fig) to ransack

sarampión [saram'pjon] nm measles sg

sarcástico, -a [sar'kastiko, a] adj sarcastic

sardina [sar'ðina] nf sardine

sargento [sar'xento] nm sergeant

sarmiento [sar'mjento] nm (Bot) vine shoot

sarna ['sarna] nf itch; (Med) scabies

sarpullido [sarpu'ʎiðo] nm (Med) rash

sarro ['sarro] nm (en dientes) tartar, plaque

sartén [sar'ten] nf frying pan

sastre ['sastre] nm tailor; **sastrería** nf (arte) tailoring; (tienda) tailor's (shop)

Satanás [sata'nas] nm Satan

satélite [sa'telite] nm satellite

sátira ['satira] nf satire

satisfacción [satisfak'θjon] nf satisfaction

satisfacer [satisfa'θer] vt to satisfy; (gastos) to meet; (pérdida) to make good; **satisfacerse** vr to satisfy o.s., be satisfied; (vengarse) to take revenge; **satisfecho, -a** adj satisfied; (contento) content(ed), happy; (tb: **satisfecho de sí mismo**) self-satisfied, smug

saturar [satu'rar] vt to saturate; **saturarse** vr (mercado, aeropuerto) to reach saturation point

sauce ['sauθe] nm willow; **sauce llorón** weeping willow

S

sauna ['sauna] nf sauna

savia ['saβja] nf sap

saxofón [sakso'fon] nm saxophone

sazonar [saθo'nar] vt to ripen; (Culin) to flavour, season

scooter [e'skuter] (ESP) nf scooter

Scotch® [skotʃ] (LAM) nm Sellotape® (BRIT), Scotch tape® (US)

SE abr (= sudeste) SE

○ **PALABRA CLAVE**

se [se] pron 1 (reflexivo: sg: m) himself; (: f) herself; (: pl) themselves; (: cosa) itself; (: deVd) yourself; (: deVds) yourselves; **se está preparando** she's preparing herself

2 (con complemento indirecto) to him; to her; to them; to it; to you; **a usted se lo dije ayer** I told you yesterday; **se compró un sombrero** he bought himself a hat; **se rompió la pierna** he broke his leg

3 (uso recíproco) each other, one another; **se miraron (el uno al otro)** they looked at each other o one another

4 (en oraciones pasivas): **se han vendido muchos libros** a lot of books have been sold

5 (impers): **se dice que ...** people say that ..., it is said that ...; **allí se come muy bien** the food there is very good, you can eat very well there

sé etc [se] vb V **saber**; **ser**

sea etc vb V **ser**

sebo ['seβo] nm fat, grease

secador [seka'ðor] nm: **~ de pelo** hair-dryer

secadora [seka'ðora] nf tumble dryer

secar [se'kar] vt to dry; **secarse** vr to dry (off); (río, planta) to dry up

sección [sek'θjon] nf section

seco, -a ['seko, a] adj dry; (carácter) cold; (respuesta) sharp, curt; **parar en ~** to stop dead; **decir algo a secas** to say sth curtly

secretaría [sekreta'ria] nf secretariat

secretario, -a [sekre'tarjo, a] nm/f secretary

secreto, -a [se'kreto, a] adj secret; (persona) secretive ▷ nm secret; (calidad) secrecy

secta ['sekta] nf sect

sector [sek'tor] nm sector

secuela [se'kwela] nf consequence

secuencia [se'kwenθja] nf sequence

secuestrar [sekwes'trar] vt to kidnap; (bienes) to seize, confiscate; **secuestro** nm kidnapping; seizure, confiscation

secundario, -a [sekun'darjo, a] adj secondary

sed [seð] nf thirst; **tener ~** to be thirsty

seda ['seða] nf silk

sedal [se'ðal] nm fishing line

sedán [se'ðan] (LAM) nm saloon (BRIT), sedan (US)

sedante [se'ðante] nm sedative

sede ['seðe] nf (de gobierno) seat; (de compañía) headquarters pl; **Santa S~** Holy See

sedentario, -a [seðen'tarjo, a] adj sedentary

sediento, -a [se'ðjento, a] adj thirsty

sedimento [seði'mento] nm sediment

seducción [seðuk'θjon] nf seduction

seducir [seðu'θir] vt to seduce; (cautivar) to charm, fascinate; (atraer) to attract; **seductor, a** adj seductive; charming, fascinating; attractive ▷ nm/f seducer

segar [se'ɣar] vt (mies) to reap, cut; (hierba) to mow, cut

seglar [se'ɣlar] adj secular, lay

seguida [se'ɣiða] nf: **en ~** at once, right away

seguido, -a [se'ɣiðo, a] adj (continuo) continuous, unbroken; (recto) straight ▷ adv (directo) straight (on); (después) after; (LAM: a menudo) often; **~s**

consecutive, successive; **5 días ~s** 5
days running, 5 days in a row
seguir [se'ɣir] vt to follow; (venir
después) to follow on, come after;
(proseguir) to continue; (perseguir) to
chase, pursue ▷ vi (gen) to follow;
(continuar) to continue, carry o go
on; **seguirse** vr to follow; **sigo sin
comprender** I still don't understand;
sigue lloviendo it's still raining
según [se'ɣun] prep according to
▷ adv: **¿irás? - ~** are you going? – it all
depends ▷ conj as; **~ caminamos**
while we walk
segundo, -a [se'ɣundo, a] adj
second ▷ nm second ▷ nf second
meaning; **de segunda mano** secondhand; **segunda** (clase) second class;
segunda (marcha) (Auto) second
(gear)
seguramente [seɣura'mente] adv
surely; (con certeza) for sure, with
certainty
seguridad [seɣuri'ðað] nf safety;
(del estado, de casa etc) security;
(certidumbre) certainty; (confianza)
confidence; (estabilidad) stability;
seguridad social social security
seguro, -a [se'ɣuro, a] adj (cierto)
sure, certain; (fiel) trustworthy; (libre
de peligro) safe; (bien defendido, firme)
secure ▷ adv for sure, certainly ▷ nm
(Com) insurance; **seguro contra
terceros/a todo riesgo** third party/
comprehensive insurance; **seguros
sociales** social security sg
seis [seis] num six
seísmo [se'ismo] nm tremor,
earthquake
selección [selek'θjon] nf selection;
seleccionar vt to pick, choose, select
selectividad [selektiβi'ðað] (ESP) nf
university entrance examination
electo, -a [se'lekto, a] adj select,
choice; (escogido) selected
ellar [se'ʎar] vt (documento oficial) to
seal; (pasaporte, visado) to stamp
ello ['seʎo] nm stamp; (precinto) seal

selva ['selβa] nf (bosque) forest,
woods pl; (jungla) jungle
semáforo [se'maforo] nm (Auto)
traffic lights pl; (Ferro) signal
semana [se'mana] nf week; **entre
~** during the week; **Semana Santa**
Holy Week; **semanal** adj weekly;
semanario nm weekly magazine

sembrar [sem'brar] vt to sow;
(objetos) to sprinkle, scatter about;
(noticias etc) to spread
semejante [seme'xante] adj
(parecido) similar ▷ nm fellow man,
fellow creature; **~s** alike, similar;
nunca hizo cosa ~ he never did any
such thing; **semejanza** nf similarity,
resemblance
semejar [seme'xar] vi to seem like,
resemble; **semejarse** vr to look alike,
be similar
semen ['semen] nm semen
semestral [semes'tral] adj half-
yearly, bi-annual
semicírculo [semi'θirkulo] nm
semicircle
semidesnatado, -a
[semiðesna'taðo, a] adj semi-

skimmed

semifinal [semifi'nal] nf semifinal

semilla [se'miʎa] nf seed

seminario [semi'narjo] nm (Rel) seminary; (Escol) seminar

sémola ['semola] nf semolina

senado [se'naðo] nm senate; **senador, a** nm/f senator

sencillez [senθi'ʎeθ] nf simplicity; (de persona) naturalness; **sencillo, -a** adj simple; natural, unaffected

senda ['senda] nf path, track

senderismo [sende'rismo] nm hiking

sendero [sen'dero] nm path, track

sendos, -as ['sendos, as] adj pl: **les dio ~ golpes** he hit both of them

senil [se'nil] adj senile

seno ['seno] nm (Anat) bosom, bust; (fig) bosom; **~s** breasts

sensación [sensa'θjon] nf sensation; (sentido) sense; (sentimiento) feeling; **sensacional** adj sensational

sensato, -a [sen'sato, a] adj sensible

sensible [sen'sible] adj sensitive; (apreciable) perceptible, appreciable; (pérdida) considerable

> No confunda **sensible** con la palabra inglesa sensible.

sensiblero, a adj sentimental

sensitivo, -a [sensi'tiβo, a] adj sense cpd

sensorial [senso'rjal] adj sensory

sensual [sen'swal] adj sensual

sentada [sen'taða] nf sitting; (protesta) sit-in

sentado, -a [sen'taðo, a] adj: **estar ~** to sit, be sitting (down); **dar por ~** to take for granted, assume

sentar [sen'tar] vt to sit, seat; (fig) to establish ▷ vi (vestido) to suit; (alimento): **~ bien/mal a** to agree/ disagree with; **sentarse** vr (persona) to sit, sit down; (los depósitos) to settle

sentencia [sen'tenθja] nf (máxima) maxim, saying; (Jur) sentence; **sentenciar** vt to sentence

sentido, -a [sen'tiðo, a] adj (pérdida)

regrettable; (carácter) sensitive ▷ nm sense; (sentimiento) feeling; (significado) sense, meaning; (dirección) direction; **mi más ~ pésame** my deepest sympathy; **tener ~** to make sense; **sentido común** common sense; **sentido del humor** sense of humour; **sentido único** one-way (street)

sentimental [sentimen'tal] adj sentimental; **vida ~** love life

sentimiento [senti'mjento] nm feeling

sentir [sen'tir] vt to feel; (percibir) to perceive, sense; (lamentar) to regret, be sorry for ▷ vi (tener la sensación) to feel; (lamentarse) to feel sorry ▷ nm opinion, judgement; **~se bien/mal** to feel well/ill; **lo siento** I'm sorry

seña ['seɲa] nf sign; (Mil) password; **señas** nfpl (dirección) address sg; **señas personales** personal description sg

señal [se'ɲal] nf sign; (síntoma) symptom; (Ferro, Tel) signal; (marca) mark; (Com) deposit; **en ~ de** as a token of sign of; **señalar** vt to mark; (indicar) to point out, indicate

señor [se'ɲor] nm (hombre) man; (caballero) gentleman; (dueño) owner. master; (trato: antes de nombre propio) Mr; (: hablando directamente) sir; **muy ~ mío** Dear Sir; **el ~ alcalde/presidente** the mayor/president

señora [se'ɲora] nf (dama) lady; (trato: antes de nombre propio) Mrs; (: hablando directamente) madam; (esposa) wife; **Nuestra S~** Our Lady

señorita [seɲo'rita] nf (con nombre y/o apellido) Miss; (mujer joven) young lady

señorito [seɲo'rito] nm young gentleman; (pey) rich kid

sepa etc vb V **saber**

separación [separa'θjon] nf separation; (división) division; (hueco) gap

separar [sepa'rar] vt to separate; (dividir) to divide; **separarse** vr (parte) to come away; (partes) to come apart;

(persona) to leave, go away; (matrimonio) to separate; **separatismo** nm separatism

sepia ['sepja] nf cuttlefish

septentrional [septentrjo'nal] adj northern

se(p)tiembre [sep'tjembre] nm September

séptimo, -a ['septimo, a] adj, nm seventh

sepulcral [sepul'kral] adj (fig: silencio, atmósfera) deadly; **sepulcro** nm tomb, grave

sepultar [sepul'tar] vt to bury; **sepultura** nf (acto) burial; (tumba) grave, tomb

sequía [se'kia] nf drought

séquito ['sekito] nm (de rey etc) retinue; (seguidores) followers pl

○ **PALABRA CLAVE**

ser [ser] vi 1 (descripción) to be; **es médica/muy alta** she's a doctor/very tall; **la familia es de Cuzco** his (o her etc) family is from Cuzco; **soy Ana** (Tel) Ana speaking o here

2 (propiedad): **es de Joaquín** it's Joaquín's, it belongs to Joaquín

3 (horas, fechas, números): **es la una** it's one o'clock; **son las seis y media** it's half-past six; **es el 1 de junio** it's the first of June; **somos/son seis** there are six of us/them

4 (en oraciones pasivas): **ha sido descubierto ya** it's already been discovered

5: **es de esperar que ...** it is to be hoped o I etc hope that ...

6 (locuciones con sub): **o sea** that is to say; **sea él sea su hermana** either him or his sister

7: **a no ser por él ...** but for him ...

8: **a no ser que: a no ser que tenga uno ya** unless he's got one already ▷ nm being; **ser humano** human being

sereno, -a [se'reno, a] adj (persona) calm, unruffled; (el tiempo) fine, settled; (ambiente) calm, peaceful ▷ nm night watchman

serial [se'rjal] nm serial

serie ['serje] nf series; (cadena) sequence, succession; **fuera de ~** out of order; (fig) special, out of the ordinary; **fabricación en ~** mass production

seriedad [serje'ðað] nf seriousness; (formalidad) reliability; **serio, -a** adj serious; reliable, dependable; grave, serious; **en serio** adv seriously

serigrafía [serixra'fia] nf silk-screen printing

sermón [ser'mon] nm (Rel) sermon

seropositivo, -a [seroposi'tiβo] adj HIV positive

serpentear [serpente'ar] vi to wriggle; (camino, río) to wind, snake

serpentina [serpen'tina] nf streamer

serpiente [ser'pjente] nf snake; **serpiente de cascabel** rattlesnake

serranía [serra'nia] nf mountainous area

serrar [se'rrar] vt =**aserrar**

serrín [se'rrin] nm sawdust

serrucho [se'rrutʃo] nm saw

service ['serβis] (RPL) nm service; (Auto) service

servicio [ser'βiθjo] nm service; (LAM Auto) service; **servicios** nmpl (ESP) toilet(s); **servicio incluido** service charge included; **servicio militar** military service

servidumbre [serβi'ðumbre] nf (sujeción) servitude; (criados) servants pl, staff

servil [ser'βil] adj servile

servilleta [serβi'ʎeta] nf serviette, napkin

servir [ser'βir] vt to serve ▷ vi to serve; (tener utilidad) to be of use, be useful; **servirse** vr to serve o help o.s.; **~se de algo** to make use of sth, use sth; **sírvase pasar** please come in

sesenta [se'senta] *num* sixty

sesión [se'sjon] *nf* (*Pol*) session, sitting; (*Cine*) showing

seso ['seso] *nm* brain; **sesudo, -a** *adj* sensible, wise

seta ['seta] *nf* mushroom; **seta venenosa** toadstool

setecientos, -as [sete'θjentos, as] *adj, num* seven hundred

setenta [se'tenta] *num* seventy

seto ['seto] *nm* hedge

severo, -a [se'βero, a] *adj* severe

Sevilla [se'βiʎa] *n* Seville; **sevillano, -a** *adj* of o from Seville ▷ *nm/f* native o inhabitant of Seville

sexo ['sekso] *nm* sex

sexto, -a ['seksto, a] *adj, nm* sixth

sexual [sek'swal] *adj* sexual; **vida ~** sex life

si [si] *conj* if ▷ *nm* (*Mús*) B; **me pregunto ~ ...** I wonder if o whether ...

sí [si] *adv* yes ▷ *nm* consent ▷ *pron* (*uso impersonal*) oneself; (*sg: m*) himself; (*: f*) herself; (*: de cosa*) itself; (*de usted*) yourself; (*pl*) themselves; (*de ustedes*) yourselves; (*recíproco*) each other; **él no quiere pero yo ~** he doesn't want to but I do; **ella ~ vendrá** she will certainly come, she is sure to come; **claro que ~** of course; **creo que ~** I think so

siamés, -esa [sja'mes, esa] *adj, nm/f* Siamese

SIDA ['siða] *nm abr* (= *Síndrome de Inmunodeficiencia Adquirida*) AIDS

siderúrgico, -a [siðe'rurxico, a] *adj* iron and steel *cpd*

sidra ['siðra] *nf* cider

siembra ['sjembra] *nf* sowing

siempre ['sjempre] *adv* always; (*todo el tiempo*) all the time; **~ que** (*cada vez*) whenever; (*dado que*) provided that; **como ~** as usual; **para ~** for ever

sien [sjen] *nf* temple

siento *etc vb* V **sentar**; **sentir**

sierra ['sjerra] *nf* (*Tec*) saw; (*cadena de montañas*) mountain range

siervo, -a ['sjerβo, a] *nm/f* slave

siesta ['sjesta] *nf* siesta, nap; **echar la ~** to have an afternoon nap o a siesta

siete ['sjete] *num* seven

sifón [si'fon] *nm* syphon

sigla ['siɣla] *nf* abbreviation; acronym

siglo ['siɣlo] *nm* century; (*fig*) age

significado [siɣnifi'kaðo] *nm* (*de palabra etc*) meaning

significar [siɣnifi'kar] *vt* to mean, signify; (*notificar*) to make known, express

significativo, -a [siɣnifika'tiβo, a] *adj* significant

signo ['siɣno] *nm* sign; **signo de admiración o exclamación** exclamation mark; **signo de interrogación** question mark

sigo *etc vb* V **seguir**

siguiente [si'ɣjente] *adj* next, following

siguió *etc vb* V **seguir**

sílaba ['silaβa] *nf* syllable

silbar [sil'βar] *vt, vi* to whistle; **silbato** *nm* whistle; **silbido** *nm* whistle, whistling

silenciador [silenθja'ðor] *nm* silencer

silenciar [silen'θjar] *vt* (*persona*) to silence; (*escándalo*) to hush up; **silencio** *nm* silence, quiet; **silencioso, -a** *adj* silent, quiet

silla ['siʎa] *nf* (*asiento*) chair; (*tb: ~ de montar*) saddle; **silla de ruedas** wheelchair

sillón [si'ʎon] *nm* armchair, easy chair

silueta [si'lweta] *nf* silhouette; (*de edificio*) outline; (*figura*) figure

silvestre [sil'βestre] *adj* wild

simbólico, -a [sim'boliko, a] *adj* symbolic(al)

simbolizar [simboli'θar] *vt* to symbolize

símbolo ['simbolo] *nm* symbol

similar [simi'lar] *adj* similar

simio ['simjo] *nm* ape

simpatía [simpa'tia] *nf* liking; (*afecto*) affection; (*amabilidad*) kindness;

simpático, -a adj nice, pleasant; kind No confundir **simpático** con la palabra inglesa *sympathetic*.

simpatizante [simpati'θante] nmf sympathizer

simpatizar [simpati'θar] vi: **~ con** to get on well with

simple ['simple] adj simple; (*elemental*) simple, easy; (*mero*) mere; (*puro*) pure, sheer ▷ nmf simpleton; **simpleza** nf simpleness; (*necedad*) silly thing; **simplificar** vt to simplify

simposio [sim'posjo] nm symposium

simular [simu'lar] vt to simulate

simultáneo, -a [simul'taneo, a] adj simultaneous

sin [sin] prep without; **la ropa está ~ lavar** the clothes are unwashed; **~ que** without; **~ embargo** however, still

sinagoga [sina'xoɣa] nf synagogue

sinceridad [sinθeri'ðað] nf sincerity; **sincero, -a** adj sincere

sincronizar [sinkroni'θar] vt to synchronize

sindical [sindi'kal] adj union cpd, trade-union cpd; **sindicalista** adj, nmf trade unionist

sindicato [sindi'kato] nm (*de trabajadores*) trade(s) union; (*de negociantes*) syndicate

síndrome ['sindrome] nm (Med) syndrome; **síndrome de abstinencia** (Med) withdrawal symptoms; **síndrome de la clase turista** (Med) economy-class syndrome

sinfín [sin'fin] nm: **un ~ de** a great many, no end of

sinfonía [sinfo'nia] nf symphony

singular [singu'lar] adj singular; (*fig*) outstanding, exceptional; (*raro*) peculiar, odd

siniestro, -a [si'njestro, a] adj sinister ▷ nm (*accidente*) accident

sinnúmero [sin'numero] nm = **sinfín**

sino ['sino] nm fate, destiny ▷ conj (*pero*) but; (*salvo*) except, save

sinónimo, -a [si'nonimo, a] adj

synonymous ▷ nm synonym

síntesis ['sintesis] nf synthesis; **sintético, -a** adj synthetic

sintió vb V **sentir**

síntoma ['sintoma] nm symptom

sintonía [sinto'nia] nf (Radio, Mús: de programa) tuning; **sintonizar** vt (Radio: emisora) to tune (in)

sinvergüenza [simber'xwenθa] nmf rogue, scoundrel; **¡es un ~!** he's got a nerve!

siquiera [si'kjera] conj even if, even though ▷ adv at least; **ni ~** not even

Siria ['sirja] nf Syria

sirviente, -a [sir'βjente, a] nm/f servant

sirvo etc vb V **servir**

sistema [sis'tema] nm system; (*método*) method; **sistema educativo** education system; **sistemático, -a** adj systematic

● **SISTEMA EDUCATIVO**
●
● The reform of the Spanish **sistema**
● **educativo** (education system)
● begun in the early 90s has replaced
● the courses **EGB**, **BUP** and **COU**
● with the following: "Primaria" a
● compulsory 6 years; "Secundaria"
● a compulsory 4 years and
● "Bachillerato" an optional 2-year
● secondary school course, essential
● for those wishing to go on to higher
● education.

sitiar [si'tjar] vt to besiege, lay siege to

sitio ['sitjo] nm (*lugar*) place; (*espacio*) room, space; (Mil) siege; **sitio de taxis** (MÉX: *parada*) taxi stand or rank (BRIT); **sitio web** (Inform) website

situación [sitwa'θjon] nf situation, position; (*estatus*) position, standing

situado, -a [situ'aðo] adj situated, placed

situar [si'twar] vt to place, put; (*edificio*) to locate, situate

slip [slip] *nm* pants *pl*, briefs *pl*

smoking ['smokin, es'mokin] (*pl* **~s**) *nm* dinner jacket (*BRIT*), tuxedo (*US*)
　No confundir **smoking** con la palabra inglesa **smoking**.

SMS *nm* (*mensaje*) text message, SMS message

snob [es'nob] = **esnob**

SO *abr* (= *suroeste*) SW

sobaco [so'βako] *nm* armpit

sobar [so'βar] *vt* (*ropa*) to rumple; (*comida*) to play around with

soberanía [soβera'nia] *nf* sovereignty; **soberano, -a** *adj* sovereign; (*fig*) supreme ▷ *nm/f* sovereign

soberbia [so'βerβja] *nf* pride; haughtiness, arrogance; magnificence

soberbio, -a [so'βerβjo, a] *adj* (*orgulloso*) proud; (*altivo*) arrogant; (*estupendo*) magnificent, superb

sobornar [soβor'nar] *vt* to bribe; **soborno** *nm* bribe

sobra ['soβra] *nf* excess, surplus; **sobras** *nfpl* left-overs, scraps; **de ~** surplus, extra; **tengo de ~** I've more than enough; **sobrado, -a** *adj* (*más que suficiente*) more than enough; (*superfluo*) excessive; **sobrante** *adj* remaining, extra ▷ *nm* surplus, remainder

sobrar [so'βrar] *vt* to exceed, surpass ▷ *vi* (*tener de más*) to be more than enough; (*quedar*) to remain, be left (over)

sobrasada [soβra'saða] *nf* pork sausage spread

sobre ['soβre] *prep* (*gen*) on; (*encima*) on (top of); (*por encima de, arriba de*) over, above; (*más que*) more than; (*además*) in addition to, besides; (*alrededor de*) about ▷ *nm* envelope; **~ todo** above all

sobrecama [soβre'kama] *nf* bedspread

sobrecargar [soβrekar'xar] *vt* (*camión*) to overload; (*Com*) to surcharge

sobredosis [soβre'ðosis] *nf inv* overdose

sobreentender [soβre(e)nten'der] *vt* to deduce, infer; **sobreentenderse** *vr*: **se sobreentiende que ...** it is implied that ...

sobrehumano, -a [soβreu'mano, a] *adj* superhuman

sobrellevar [soβreλe'βar] *vt* to bear, endure

sobremesa [soβre'mesa] *nf*: **durante la ~** after dinner

sobrenatural [soβrenatu'ral] *adj* supernatural

sobrenombre [soβre'nombre] *nm* nickname

sobrepasar [soβrepa'sar] *vt* to exceed, surpass

sobreponerse [soβrepo'nerse] *vr*: **~ a** to overcome

sobresaliente [soβresa'ljente] *adj* outstanding, excellent

sobresalir [soβresa'lir] *vi* to project, jut out; (*fig*) to stand out, excel

sobresaltar [soβresal'tar] *vt* (*asustar*) to scare, frighten; (*sobrecoger*) to startle; **sobresalto** *nm* (*movimiento*) start; (*susto*) scare; (*turbación*) sudden shock

sobretodo [soβre'toðo] *nm* overcoat

sobrevenir [soβreβe'nir] *vi* (*ocurrir*) to happen (unexpectedly); (*resultar*) to follow, ensue

sobrevivir [soβreβi'βir] *vi* to survive

sobrevolar [soβreβo'lar] *vt* to fly over

sobriedad [soβrje'ðað] *nf* sobriety, soberness; (*moderación*) moderation, restraint

sobrino, -a [so'βrino, a] *nm/f* nephew/niece

sobrio, -a ['soβrjo, a] *adj* sober; (*moderado*) moderate, restrained

socarrón, -ona [soka'rron, ona] *adj* (*sarcástico*) sarcastic, ironic(al)

socavón [soka'βon] *nm* (*hoyo*) hole

sociable [so'θjaβle] *adj* (*persona*) sociable, friendly; (*animal*) social

social [so'θjal] adj social; (Com) company cpd

socialdemócrata [soθjalde'mokrata] nmf social democrat

socialista [soθja'lista] adj, nm socialist

socializar [soθjali'θar] vt to socialize

sociedad [soθje'ðað] nf society; (Com) company; **sociedad anónima** limited company; **sociedad de consumo** consumer society

socio, -a ['soθjo, a] nm/f (miembro) member; (Com) partner

sociología [soθjolo'xia] nf sociology;

sociólogo, -a nm/f sociologist

socorrer [soko'rrer] vt to help;

socorrista nmf first aider; (en piscina, playa) lifeguard; **socorro** nm (ayuda) help, aid; (Mil) relief; **socorro!** help!

soda ['soða] nf (sosa) soda; (bebida) soda (water)

sofá [so'fa] (pl ~s) nm sofa, settee; **sofá-cama** nm studio couch; sofa bed

sofocar [sofo'kar] vt to suffocate; (apagar) to smother, put out; **sofocarse** vr to suffocate; (fig) to blush, feel embarrassment; **sofoco** nm suffocation; embarrassment

sofreír [sofre'ir] vt (Culin) to fry lightly

software ['sofwer] nm (Inform) software

soga ['soxa] nf rope

sois etc vb V **ser**

soja ['soxa] nf soya

sol [sol] nm sun; (luz) sunshine, sunlight; (Mús) G; **hace ~** it's sunny

solamente [sola'mente] adv only, just

solapa [so'lapa] nf (de chaqueta) lapel; (de libro) jacket

solapado, -a [sola'paðo, a] adj (intenciones) underhand; (gestos, movimiento) sly

solar [so'lar] adj solar, sun cpd; (terreno) plot of (ground)

soldado [sol'daðo] nm soldier; **soldado raso** private

soldador [solda'ðor] nm soldering iron; (persona) welder

soldar [sol'dar] vt to solder, weld

soleado, -a [sole'aðo, a] adj sunny

soledad [sole'ðað] nf solitude; (estado infeliz) loneliness

solemne [so'lemne] adj solemn

soler [so'ler] vi to be in the habit of, be accustomed to; **suele salir a las ocho** she usually goes out at eight o'clock

solfeo [sol'feo] nm solfa

solicitar [soliθi'tar] vt (permiso) to ask for, seek; (puesto) to apply for; (votos) to canvass for; (atención) to attract

solícito, -a [so'liθito, a] adj (diligente) diligent; (cuidadoso) careful; **solicitud** nf (calidad) great care; (petición) request; (a un puesto) application

solidaridad [soliðari'ðað] nf solidarity; **solidario, -a** adj (participación) joint, common; (compromiso) mutually binding

sólido, -a ['soliðo, a] adj solid

soliloquio [soli'lokjo] nm soliloquy

solista [so'lista] nmf soloist

solitario, -a [soli'tarjo, a] adj (persona) lonely, solitary; (lugar) lonely, desolate ▷ nm/f (recluso) recluse; (en la sociedad) loner ▷ nm solitaire

sollozar [soλo'θar] vi to sob; **sollozo** nm sob

solo, -a ['solo, a] adj (único) single, sole; (sin compañía) alone; (solitario) lonely; **hay una sola dificultad** there is just one difficulty; **a solas** alone, by oneself

sólo ['solo] adv only, just

solomillo [solo'miλo] nm sirloin

soltar [sol'tar] vt (dejar ir) to let go of; (desprender) to unfasten, loosen; (librar) to release, set free; (risa etc) to let out

soltero, -a [sol'tero, a] adj single, unmarried ▷ nm/f bachelor/single woman; **solterón, -ona** nm/f old bachelor/spinster

soltura [sol'tura] nf looseness,

slackness; (de los miembros) agility, ease of movement; (en el hablar) fluency, ease

soluble [so'luβle] adj (Quím) soluble; (problema) solvable; ~ **en agua** soluble in water

solución [solu'θjon] nf solution; **solucionar** vt (problema) to solve; (asunto) to settle, resolve

solventar [solβen'tar] vt (pagar) to settle, pay; (resolver) to resolve; **solvente** adj (Econ: empresa, persona) solvent

sombra ['sombra] nf shadow; (como protección) shade; **sombras** nfpl (oscuridad) darkness sg, shadows; **tener buena/mala** ~ to be lucky/unlucky

sombrero [som'brero] nm hat

sombrilla [som'briλa] nf parasol, sunshade

sombrío, -a [som'brio, a] adj (oscuro) dark; (triste) sombre, sad; (persona) gloomy

someter [some'ter] vt (país) to conquer; (persona) to subject to one's will; (informe) to present, submit; **someterse** vr to give in, yield, submit; ~ **a** to subject to

somier [so'mjer] (pl ~**s**) n spring mattress

somnífero [som'nifero] nm sleeping pill

somos vb V **ser**

son [son] vb V **ser** ⊳nm sound

sonaja [so'naxa] (méx) nf = **sonajero**

sonajero [sona'xero] nm (baby's) rattle

sonambulismo [sonambu'lismo] nm sleepwalking; **sonámbulo, -a** nm/f sleepwalker

sonar [so'nar] vt to ring ⊳vi to sound; (hacer ruido) to make a noise; (pronunciarse) to be sounded, be pronounced; (ser conocido) to sound familiar; (campana) to ring; (reloj) to strike, chime; **sonarse** vr: ~**se (las narices)** to blow one's nose; **me suena ese nombre** that name rings a bell

sonda ['sonda] nf (Náut) sounding; (Tec) bore, drill; (Med) probe

sondear [sonde'ar] vt to sound; to bore (into), drill; to probe, sound; (fig) to sound out; **sondeo** nm sounding; boring, drilling; (fig) poll, enquiry

sonido [so'niðo] nm sound

sonoro, -a [so'noro, a] adj sonorous; (resonante) loud, resonant

sonreír [sonre'ir] vi to smile; **sonreírse** vr to smile; **sonriente** adj smiling; **sonrisa** nf smile

sonrojarse [sonro'xarse] vr to blush, go red; **sonrojo** nm blush

soñador, a [sona'ðor, a] nm/f dreamer

soñar [so'nar] vt, vi to dream; ~ **con** to dream about o of

soñoliento, -a [sono'ljento, a] adj sleepy, drowsy

sopa ['sopa] nf soup

soplar [so'plar] vt (polvo) to blow away, blow off; (inflar) to blow up; (vela) to blow out ⊳vi to blow; **soplo** nm blow, puff; (de viento) puff, gust

soplón, -ona [so'plon, ona] (fam) nm/f (niño) telltale; (: de policía) grass (fam)

soporífero [sopo'rifero] nm sleeping pill

soportable [sopor'taβle] adj bearable

soportar [sopor'tar] vt to bear, carry; (fig) to bear, put up with

> ⬛ No confundir **soportar** con la palabra inglesa support.

soporte nm support; (fig) pillar, support

soprano [so'prano] nf soprano

sorber [sor'βer] vt (chupar) to sip; (absorber) to soak up, absorb

sorbete [sor'βete] nm iced fruit drink

sorbo ['sorβo] nm (trago: grande) gulp, swallow; (: pequeño) sip

sordera [sor'ðera] nf deafness

sórdido, -a [sorðiðo, a] adj dirty, squalid

sordo, -a ['sorðo, a] adj (persona) deaf

▷ *nm/f* deaf person; **sordomudo, -a** *adj* deaf and dumb

sorna ['sorna] *nf* sarcastic tone

soroche [so'rotʃe] (CAM) *nm* mountain sickness

sorprendente [sorpren'dente] *adj* surprising

sorprender [sorpren'der] *vt* to surprise; **sorpresa** *nf* surprise

sortear [sorte'ar] *vt* to draw lots for; (*rifar*) to raffle; (*dificultad*) to avoid; **sorteo** *nm* (*en lotería*) draw; (*rifa*) raffle

sortija [sor'tixa] *nf* ring; (*rizo*) ringlet, curl

sosegado, -a [sose'xaðo, a] *adj* quiet, calm

sosiego [so'sjexo] *nm* quiet(ness), calm(ness)

soso, -a ['soso, a] *adj* (*Culin*) tasteless; (*aburrido*) dull, uninteresting

sospecha [sos'petʃa] *nf* suspicion; **sospechar** *vt* to suspect; **sospechoso, -a** *adj* suspicious; (*testimonio, opinión*) suspect ▷ *nm/f* suspect

sostén [sos'ten] *nm* (*apoyo*) support; (*sujetador*) bra; (*alimentación*) sustenance, food

sostener [soste'ner] *vt* to support; (*mantener*) to keep up, maintain; (*alimentar*) to sustain, keep going; **sostenerse** *vr* to support o.s.; (*seguir*) to continue, remain; **sostenido, -a** *adj* continuous, sustained; (*prolongado*) prolonged

sotana [so'tana] *nf* (*Rel*) cassock

sótano ['sotano] *nm* basement

soy [soi] *vb* V **ser**

soya ['soja] (LAM) *nf* soya (BRIT), soy (US)

Sr. *abr* (= Señor) Mr

Sra. *abr* (= Señora) Mrs

Sras. *abr* (= Señoras) Mrs

Sres. *abr* (= Señores) Messrs

Srta. *abr* (= Señorita) Miss

Sta. *abr* (= Santa) St

Sto. *abr* (= Santo) St

su [su] *pron* (*de él*) his; (*de ella*) her; (*de

una cosa*) its; (*de ellos, ellas*) their; (*de usted, ustedes*) your

suave ['swaβe] *adj* gentle; (*superficie*) smooth; (*trabajo*) easy; (*música, voz*) soft, sweet; **suavidad** *nf* gentleness; smoothness; softness, sweetness; **suavizante** *nm* (*de ropa*) softener; (*del pelo*) conditioner; **suavizar** *vt* to soften; (*quitar la aspereza*) to smooth (out)

subasta [su'βasta] *nf* auction; **subastar** *vt* to auction (off)

subcampeón, -ona [suβkampe'on, ona] *nm/f* runner-up

subconsciente [suβkon'sθjente] *adj, nm* subconscious

subdesarrollado, -a [suβðesarro'ʎaðo, a] *adj* underdeveloped

subdesarrollo [suβðesa'rroʎo] *nm* underdevelopment

subdirector, a [suβðirek'tor, a] *nm/f* assistant director

súbdito, -a ['suβðito, a] *nm/f* subject

subestimar [suβesti'mar] *vt* to underestimate, underrate

subida [su'βiða] *nf* (*de montaña etc*) ascent, climb; (*de precio*) rise, increase; (*pendiente*) slope, hill

subir [su'βir] *vt* (*objeto*) to raise, lift up; (*cuesta, calle*) to go up; (*colina, montaña*) to climb; (*precio*) to raise, put up ▷ *vi* to go up, come up; (*a un coche*) to get in; (*a un autobús, tren o avión*) to get on, board; (*precio*) to rise, go up; (*río, marea*) to rise: **subirse** *vr* to get up, climb

súbito, -a ['suβito, a] *adj* (*repentino*) sudden; (*imprevisto*) unexpected

subjetivo, -a [suβxe'tiβo, a] *adj* subjective

sublevar [suβle'βar] *vt* to rouse to revolt; **sublevarse** *vr* to revolt, rise

sublime [su'βlime] *adj* sublime

submarinismo [suβmari'nismo] *nm* scuba diving

submarino, -a [suβma'rino, a] *adj*

underwater ⊳ nm submarine

subnormal [suβnor'mal] adj subnormal ⊳ nmf subnormal person

subordinado, -a [suβorði'naðo, a] adj, nm/f subordinate

subrayar [suβra'jar] vt to underline

subsanar [suβsa'nar] vt to rectify

subsidio [suβ'siðjo] nm (ayuda) aid, financial help; (subvención) subsidy, grant; (de enfermedad, paro etc) benefit, allowance

subsistencia [suβsis'tenθja] nf subsistence

subsistir [suβsis'tir] vi to subsist; (sobrevivir) to survive, endure

subte ['suβte] (RPL) nm underground (BRIT), subway (US)

subterráneo, -a [suβte'traneo, a] adj underground, subterranean ⊳ nm underpass, underground passage

subtitulado [suβtitu'laðo] adj subtitled

subtítulo [suβ'titulo] nm (Cine) subtitle

suburbio [su'βurβjo] nm (barrio) slum quarter

subvención [suββen'θjon] nf (Econ) subsidy, grant; **subvencionar** vt to subsidize

sucedáneo, -a [suθe'ðaneo, a] adj substitute ⊳ nm substitute (food)

suceder [suθe'ðer] vt, vi to happen; (seguir) to succeed, follow; **lo que sucede es que ...** the fact is that ...; **sucesión** nf succession; (serie) sequence, series

sucesivamente [suθesiβa'mente] adv: **y así** ~ and so on

sucesivo, -a [suθe'siβo, a] adj successive, following; **en lo** ~ in future, from now on

suceso [su'θeso] nm (hecho) event, happening; (incidente) incident

🔲 No confundir **suceso** con la palabra inglesa success.

suciedad [suθje'ðað] nf (estado) dirtiness; (mugre) dirt, filth

sucio, -a ['suθjo, a] adj dirty

suculento, -a [suku'lento, a] adj succulent

sucumbir [sukum'bir] vi to succumb

sucursal [sukur'sal] nf branch (office)

sudadera [suða'ðera] nf sweatshirt

Sudáfrica [suð'afrika] nf South Africa

Sudamérica [suða'merika] nf South America; **sudamericano, -a** adj, nm/f South American

sudar [su'ðar] vt, vi to sweat

sudeste [su'ðeste] nm south-east

sudoeste [suðo'este] nm south-west

sudoku [su'ðoku] nm sudoku

sudor [su'ðor] nm sweat; **sudoroso, -a** adj sweaty, sweating

Suecia ['sweθja] nf Sweden; **sueco, -a** adj Swedish ⊳ nm/f Swede

suegro, -a ['swexro, a] nm/f father-/mother-in-law

suela ['swela] nf sole

sueldo ['sweldo] nm pay, wage(s) (pl)

suele etc vb V **soler**

suelo ['swelo] nm (tierra) ground; (de casa) floor

suelto, -a ['swelto, a] adj loose; (libre) free; (separado) detached; (ágil) quick, agile ⊳ nm (loose) change, small change

sueñito [swe'ɲito] (LAM) nm nap

sueño etc ['sweɲo] vb V **soñar** ⊳ nm sleep; (somnolencia) sleepiness, drowsiness; (lo soñado, fig) dream; **tener** ~ to be sleepy

suero ['swero] nm (Med) serum; (de leche) whey

suerte ['swerte] nf (fortuna) luck; (azar) chance; (destino) fate, destiny; (especie) sort, kind; **tener** ~ to be lucky

suéter ['sweter] nm sweater

suficiente [sufi'θjente] adj enough, sufficient ⊳ nm (Escol) pass

sufragio [su'fraxjo] nm (voto) vote; (derecho de voto) suffrage

sufrido, -a [su'friðo, a] adj (persona) tough; (paciente) long-suffering, patient

sufrimiento [sufri'mjento] nm
(dolor) suffering

sufrir [su'frir] vt (padecer) to suffer;
(soportar) to bear, put up with; (apoyar)
to hold up, support ▷ vi to suffer

sugerencia [suxe'renθja] nf
suggestion

sugerir [suxe'rir] vt to suggest;
(sutilmente) to hint

sugestión [suxes'tjon] nf
suggestion; (sutil) hint; **sugestionar**
vt to influence

sugestivo, -a [suxes'tiβo, a] adj
stimulating; (fascinante) fascinating

suicida [sui'θiða] adj suicidal ▷ nmf
suicidal person; (muerto) suicide,
person who has committed suicide;
suicidarse vr to commit suicide, kill
o.s.; **suicidio** nm suicide

Suiza ['swiθa] nf Switzerland; **suizo,
-a** adj, nm/f Swiss

sujeción [suxe'θjon] nf subjection

sujetador [suxeta'ðor] nm (sostén)
bra

sujetar [suxe'tar] vt (fijar) to fasten;
(detener) to hold down; **sujetarse** vr to
subject o.s.; **sujeto, -a** adj fastened,
secure ▷ nm subject; (individuo)
individual; **sujeto a** subject to

suma ['suma] nf (cantidad) total,
sum; (de dinero) sum; (acto) adding (up),
addition; **en ~** in short

sumamente [suma'mente] adv
extremely, exceedingly

sumar [su'mar] vt to add (up) ▷ vi
to add up

sumergir [sumer'xir] vt to
submerge; (hundir) to sink

suministrar [sumini'strar] vt to
supply, provide; **suministro** nm
supply; (acto) supplying, providing

sumir [su'mir] vt to sink, submerge;
(fig) to plunge

sumiso, -a [su'miso, a] adj
submissive, docile

sumo, -a ['sumo, a] adj great,
extreme; (autoridad) highest, supreme

suntuoso, -a [sun'twoso, a] adj
sumptuous, magnificent

supe etc vb V **saber**

super... [super] prefijo super..., over...

superbueno, -a [super'bweno, a]
adj great, fantastic

súper ['super] nf (gasolina) four-star
(petrol)

superar [supe'rar] vt (sobreponerse
a) to overcome; (rebasar) to surpass,
do better than; (pasar) to go beyond;
superarse vr to excel o.s.

superficial [superfi'θjal] adj
superficial; (medida) surface cpd, of
the surface

superficie [super'fiθje] nf surface;
(área) area

superfluo, -a [su'perflwo, a] adj
superfluous

superior [supe'rjor] adj (piso, clase)
upper; (temperatura, número, nivel)
higher; (mejor: calidad, producto)
superior, better ▷ nmf superior;
superioridad nf superiority

supermercado [supermer'kaðo] nm
supermarket

superponer [superpo'ner] vt to
superimpose

superstición [supersti'θjon] nf
superstition; **supersticioso, -a** adj
superstitious

supervisar [superβi'sar] vt to
supervise

supervivencia [superβi'βenθja]
nf survival

superviviente [superβi'βjente] adj
surviving

supiera etc vb V **saber**

suplantar [suplan'tar] vt to
supplant

suplementario, -a
[suplemen'tarjo, a] adj
supplementary

suplemento [suple'mento] nm
supplement

suplente [su'plente] adj, nm
substitute

supletorio, -a [suple'torjo, a] adj
supplementary ▷ nm supplement;

teléfono ~ extension
súplica ['suplika] nf request; (Jur) petition
suplicar [supli'kar] vt (cosa) to beg (for), plead for; (persona) to beg, plead with
suplicio [su'pliθjo] nm torture
suplir [su'plir] vt (compensar) to make good, make up for; (reemplazar) to replace, substitute ▷ vi: ~ **a** to take the place of, substitute for
supo etc vb V **saber**
suponer [supo'ner] vt to suppose; **suposición** nf supposition
suprimir [supri'mir] vt to suppress; (derecho, costumbre) to abolish; (palabra etc) to delete; (restricción) to cancel, lift
supuesto, -a [su'pwesto, a] pp de **suponer** ▷ adj (hipotético) supposed ▷ nm assumption, hypothesis; ~ **que** since; **por** ~ of course
sur [sur] nm south
suramericano, -a [surameri'kano, a] adj South American ▷ nm/f South American
surcar [sur'kar] vt to plough; **surco** nm (en metal, disco) groove; (Agr) furrow
surfear [surfe'ar] vt: ~ **el Internet** to surf the internet
surgir [sur'xir] vi to arise, emerge; (dificultad) to come up, crop up
suroeste [suro'este] nm south-west
surtido, -a [sur'tiðo, a] adj mixed, assorted ▷ nm (selección) selection, stock; **surtidor** nm (tb: **surtidor de gasolina**) petrol pump (BRIT), gas pump (US)
surtir [sur'tir] vt to supply, provide ▷ vi to spout, spurt
susceptible [susθep'tiβle] adj susceptible; (sensible) sensitive; ~ **de** capable of
suscitar [susθi'tar] vt to cause, provoke; (interés, sospechas) to arouse
suscribir [suskri'βir] vt (firmar) to sign; (respaldar) to endorse; **suscribirse** vr to subscribe;

suscripción nf subscription
susodicho, -a [suso'ðitʃo, a] adj above-mentioned
suspender [suspen'der] vt (objeto) to hang (up), suspend; (trabajo) to stop, suspend; (Escol) to fail; (interrumpir) to adjourn; (atrasar) to postpone
suspense [sus'pense] (ESP) nm suspense; **película/novela de** ~ thriller
suspensión [suspen'sjon] nf suspension; (fig) stoppage, suspense
suspenso, -a [sus'penso, a] adj hanging, suspended; (ESP Escol) failed ▷ nm (ESP Escol) fail; **película o novela de** ~ (LAM) thriller; **quedar o estar en** ~ to be pending
suspicaz [suspi'kaθ] adj suspicious, distrustful
suspirar [suspi'rar] vi to sigh; **suspiro** nm sigh
sustancia [sus'tanθja] nf substance
sustento [sus'tento] nm support; (alimento) sustenance, food
sustituir [sustitu'ir] vt to substitute, replace; **sustituto, -a** nm/f substitute, replacement
susto ['susto] nm fright, scare
sustraer [sustra'er] vt to remove, take away; (Mat) to subtract
susurrar [susu'rrar] vi to whisper; **susurro** nm whisper
sutil [su'til] adj (aroma, diferencia) subtle; (tenue) thin; (inteligencia, persona) sharp
suyo, -a ['sujo, a] (con artículo o después del verbo ser) adj (de él) his; (de ella) hers; (de ellos, ellas) theirs; (de Ud, Uds) yours; **un amigo** ~ a friend of his (o hers o theirs o yours)

t

Tabacalera [taβaka'lera] *nf* Spanish state tobacco monopoly

tabaco [ta'βako] *nm* tobacco; (ESP: *fam*) cigarettes *pl*

tabaquería [tabake'ria] (LAM) *nf* tobacconist's (shop) (BRIT), smoke shop (US); **tabaquero, -a** (LAM) *nm/f* tobacconist

taberna [ta'βerna] *nf* bar, pub (BRIT)

tabique [ta'βike] *nm* partition (wall)

tabla ['taβla] *nf* (*de madera*) plank; (*estante*) shelf; (*de vestido*) pleat; (Arte) panel; **tablas** *nfpl*: **estar** o **quedar en ~s** to draw; **tablado** *nm* (*plataforma*) platform; (Teatro) stage

tablao [ta'βlao] *nm* (*tb*: **~ flamenco**) flamenco show

tablero [ta'βlero] *nm* (*de madera*) plank, board; (*de ajedrez, damas*) board; **tablero de mandos** (LAM Auto) dashboard

tableta [ta'βleta] *nf* (Med) tablet; (*de chocolate*) bar

tablón [ta'βlon] *nm* (*de suelo*) plank; (*de techo*) beam; **tablón de anuncios** notice (BRIT) o bulletin (US) board

tabú [ta'βu] *nm* taboo

taburete [taβu'rete] *nm* stool

tacaño, -a [ta'kaɲo, a] *adj* mean

tacha ['tatʃa] *nf* flaw; (Tec) stud; **tachar** *vt* (*borrar*) to cross out; **tachar de** to accuse of

tacho ['tatʃo] (CS) *nm* (*balde*) bucket; **tacho de la basura** rubbish bin (BRIT), trash can (US)

taco ['tako] *nm* (Billar) cue; (*de billetes*) book; (CS: *de zapato*) heel; (*tarugo*) peg; (*palabrota*) swear word

tacón [ta'kon] *nm* heel; **de ~ alto** high-heeled

táctica ['taktika] *nf* tactics *pl*

táctico, -a ['taktiko, a] *adj* tactical

tacto ['takto] *nm* touch; (*fig*) tact

tajada [ta'xaða] *nf* slice

tajante [ta'xante] *adj* sharp

tajo ['taxo] *nm* (*corte*) cut; (Geo) cleft

tal [tal] *adj* such ▷ *pron* (*persona*) someone, such a one; (*cosa*) something, such a thing ▷ *adv*: **~ como** (*igual*) just as ▷ *conj*: **con ~ de que** provided that; **~ cual** (*como es*) just as it is; **~ vez** perhaps; **~ como** such as; **~ para cual** (*dos iguales*) two of a kind; **¿qué ~?** how are things?; **¿qué ~ te gusta?** how do you like it?

taladrar [tala'ðrar] *vt* to drill; **taladro** *nm* drill

talante [ta'lante] *nm* (*humor*) mood; (*voluntad*) will, willingness

talar [ta'lar] *vt* to fell, cut down; (*devastar*) to devastate

talco ['talko] *nm* (*polvos*) talcum powder

talento [ta'lento] *nm* talent; (*capacidad*) ability

TALGO ['talɣo] (ESP) *nm abr* (= *tren articulado ligero Goicoechea-Oriol*) ≈ HST (BRIT)

talismán [talis'man] *nm* talisman

talla ['taʎa] *nf* (*estatura, fig, Med*) height, stature; (*palo*) measuring rod; (Arte) carving; (*medida*) size

tallar [ta'ʎar] *vt* (*madera*) to carve;

(metal etc) to engrave; *(medir)* to measure

tallarines [taʎa'rines] *nmpl* noodles

talle ['taʎe] *nm (Anat)* waist; *(fig)* appearance

taller [ta'ʎer] *nm (Tec)* workshop; *(de artista)* studio

tallo ['taʎo] *nm (de planta)* stem; *(de hierba)* blade; *(brote)* shoot

talón [ta'lon] *nm (Anat)* heel; *(Com)* counterfoil; *(cheque)* cheque (BRIT), check (US)

talonario [talo'narjo] *nm (de cheques)* chequebook (BRIT), checkbook (US); *(de recibos)* receipt book

tamaño, -a [ta'maɲo, a] *adj (tan grande)* such a big; *(tan pequeño)* such a small ▷ *nm* size; **de ~ natural** full-size

tamarindo [tama'rindo] *nm* tamarind

tambalearse [tambale'arse] *vr (persona)* to stagger; *(vehículo)* to sway

también [tam'bjen] *adv (igualmente)* also, too, as well; *(además)* besides

tambor [tam'bor] *nm* drum; *(Anat)* eardrum; **tambor del freno** brake drum

Támesis ['tamesis] *nm* Thames

tamizar [tami'θar] *vt* to sieve

tampoco [tam'poko] *adv* nor, neither; **yo ~ lo compré** I didn't buy it either

tampón [tam'pon] *nm* tampon

tan [tan] *adv* so; **~ es así que ...** so much so that ...

tanda ['tanda] *nf (gen)* series; *(turno)* shift

tangente [tan'xente] *nf* tangent

tangerina [tanxe'rina] (LAM) *nf* tangerine

tangible [tan'xiβle] *adj* tangible

tanque ['tanke] *nm (cisterna, Mil)* tank; *(Auto)* tanker

tantear [tante'ar] *vt (calcular)* to reckon (up); *(medir)* to take the measure of; *(probar)* to test, try out; *(tomar la medida: persona)* to take the measurements of; *(situación)* to weigh up; *(persona: opinión)* to sound out ▷ *vi (Deporte)* to score; **tanteo** *nm (cálculo)*

(rough) calculation; *(prueba)* test, trial; *(Deporte)* scoring

tanto, -a ['tanto, a] *adj (cantidad)* so much, as much ▷ *adv (cantidad)* so much, as much; *(tiempo)* so long, as long ▷ *nm (suma)* certain amount; *(proporción)* so much; *(punto)* point; *(gol)* goal; **un ~ perezoso** somewhat lazy ▷ *pron:* **cada uno paga ~** each one pays so much; **~s** so many, as many; **20 y ~s** 20-odd; **hasta ~ (que)** until such time as; **~ tú como yo** both you and I; **~ como eso** as much as that; **~ más ... cuanto que** all the more ... because; **~ mejor/peor** so much the better/the worse; **~ si viene como si va** whether he comes or whether he goes; **~ es así que** so much so that; **por (lo) ~** therefore; **entre ~** meanwhile; **estar al ~** to be up to date; **me he vuelto ronco de o con ~ hablar** I have become hoarse with so much talking; **a ~s de agosto** on such and such a day in August

tapa ['tapa] *nf (de caja, olla)* lid; *(de botella)* top; *(de libro)* cover; *(comida)* snack

tapadera [tapa'ðera] *nf* lid, cover

tapar [ta'par] *vt (cubrir)* to cover; *(envolver)* to wrap o cover up; *(la vista)* to obstruct; *(persona, falta)* to conceal; *(MÉX, CAM: diente)* to fill; **taparse** *vr* to wrap o.s. up

taparrabo [tapa'rraβo] *nm* loincloth

tapete [ta'pete] *nm* table cover

tapia ['tapja] *nf (garden)* wall

tapicería [tapiθe'ria] *nf* tapestry; *(para muebles)* upholstery; *(tienda)* upholsterer's *(shop)*

tapiz [ta'piθ] *nm (alfombra)* carpet; *(tela tejida)* tapestry; **tapizar** *vt (muebles)* to upholster

tapón [ta'pon] *nm (de botella)* top; *(de lavabo)* plug; **tapón de rosca** screw-top

taquigrafía [takixra'fia] *nf* shorthand; **taquígrafo, -a** *nm/f* shorthand writer, stenographer

taquilla [ta'kiʎa] *nf (donde se*

compra) booking office; (suma recogida) takings pl

tarántula [ta'rantula] nf tarantula

tararear [tarare'ar] vi to hum

tardar [tar'ðar] vi (tomar tiempo) to take a long time; (llegar tarde) to be late; (demorar) to delay; **¿tarda mucho el tren?** does the train take (very) long?; **a más ~** at the latest; **no tardes en venir** come soon

tarde [tarðe] adv late ⊳ nf (de día) afternoon; (al anochecer) evening; **de ~ en ~** from time to time; **¡buenas ~s!** good afternoon!; **a o por la ~** in the afternoon; in the evening

tardío, -a [tar'ðio, a] adj (retrasado) late; (lento) slow (to arrive)

tarea [ta'rea] nf task; (faena) chore; (Escol) homework

tarifa [ta'rifa] nf (lista de precios) price list; (precio) tariff

tarima [ta'rima] nf (plataforma) platform

tarjeta [tar'xeta] nf card; **tarjeta de crédito/de Navidad/postal/ telefónica** credit card/Christmas card/postcard/phonecard; **tarjeta de embarque** boarding pass; **tarjeta de memoria** memory card; **tarjeta prepago** top-up card; **tarjeta SIM** SIM card

tarro ['tarro] nm jar, pot

tarta ['tarta] nf (pastel) cake; (de base dura) tart

tartamudear [tartamuðe'ar] vi to stammer; **tartamudo, -a** adj stammering ⊳ nm/f stammerer

tártaro, -a ['tartaro, a] adj: **salsa tártara** tartar(e) sauce

tasa ['tasa] nf (precio) fixed price, rate; (valoración) valuation; (medida, norma) measure, standard; **tasa de cambio/interés** exchange/interest rate; **tasas de aeropuerto** airport tax; **tasas universitarias** university fees

tasar [ta'sar] vt (arreglar el precio) to fix a price for; (valorar) to value, assess

tasca ['taska] (fam) nf pub

tatarabuelo, -a [tatara'βwelo, a] nm/f great-great-grandfather/mother

tatuaje [ta'twaxe] nm (dibujo) tattoo; (acto) tattooing

tatuar [ta'twar] vt to tattoo

taurino, -a [tau'rino, a] adj bullfighting cpd

Tauro ['tauro] nm Taurus

tauromaquia [tauro'makja] nf tauromachy, (art of) bullfighting

taxi ['taksi] nm taxi; **taxista** [tak'sista] nmf taxi driver

taza ['taθa] nf (de retrete) bowl; **~ para café** coffee cup; **taza de café** cup of coffee; **tazón** nm (taza grande) mug, large cup; (de fuente) basin

te [te] pron (complemento de objeto) you; (complemento indirecto) (to) you; (reflexivo) (to) yourself; **¿- duele mucho el brazo?** does your arm hurt a lot?; **~ equivocas** you're wrong; **¡cálma~!** calm down!

té [te] nm tea

teatral [tea'tral] adj theatre cpd; (fig) theatrical

teatro [te'atro] nm theatre; (Literatura) plays pl, drama

tebeo [te'βeo] nm comic

techo ['tetʃo] nm (externo) roof; (interno) ceiling; **techo corredizo** sunroof

tecla ['tekla] nf key; **teclado** nm keyboard; **teclear** vi (Mús) to strum; (con los dedos) to tap ⊳ vt (Inform) to key in

técnica ['teknika] nf technique; (tecnología) technology; V tb **técnico**

técnico, -a ['tekniko, a] adj technical ⊳ nm/f technician; (experto) expert

tecnología [teknolo'xia] nf technology; **tecnológico, -a** adj technological

tecolote [teko'lote] (MÉX) nm owl

tedioso, -a [te'ðjoso, a] adj boring, tedious

teja ['texa] nf tile; (Bot) lime (tree); **tejado** nm (tiled) roof

tejanos [te'xanos] nmpl (vaqueros) jeans

tejemaneje [texema'nexe] nm (lío) fuss; (intriga) intrigue

tejer [te'xer] vt to weave; (hacer punto) to knit; (fig) to fabricate; **tejido** nm (tela) material, fabric; (telaraña) web; (Anat) tissue

tel [tel] abr (= teléfono) tel

tela ['tela] nf (tejido) material; (telaraña) web; (en líquido) skin; **telar** nm (máquina) loom

telaraña [tela'raɲa] nf cobweb

tele ['tele] (fam) nf telly (BRIT), tube (US)

tele... ['tele] prefijo tele...; **telebasura** nf trash TV; **telecomunicación** nf telecommunication; **telediario** nm television news; **teledirigido, -a** adj remote-controlled

teleférico [tele'feriko] nm (de esquí) ski-lift

telefonear [telefone'ar] vi to telephone

telefónico, -a [tele'foniko, a] adj telephone cpd

telefonillo [telefo'niʎo] nm (de puerta) intercom

telefonista [telefo'nista] nmf telephonist

teléfono [te'lefono] nm (tele)phone; **estar hablando al ~** to be on the phone; **llamar a algn por ~** to ring sb (up) o phone sb (up); **teléfono celular** (LAM) mobile phone; **teléfono con cámara** camera phone; **teléfono inalámbrico** cordless phone; **teléfono móvil** (ESP) mobile phone

telégrafo [te'leɣrafo] nm telegraph

telegrama [tele'ɣrama] nm telegram

tele: **telenovela** nf soap (opera); **teleobjetivo** nm telephoto lens; **telepatía** nf telepathy; **telepático, -a** adj telepathic; **telerrealidad** nf reality TV; **telescopio** nm telescope; **telesilla** nm chairlift; **telespectador, a** nm/f viewer; **telesquí** nm ski-lift; **teletarjeta** nf phonecard; **teletexto** nm textext; **teletipo** nm teletype; **teletrabajador, a** nm/f teleworker;

teletrabajo nm teleworking; **televentas** nfpl telesales

televidente [teleβi'ðente] nmf viewer

televisar [teleβi'sar] vt to televise

televisión [teleβi'sjon] nf television; **televisión digital** digital television

televisor [teleβi'sor] nm television set

télex ['teleks] nm inv telex

telón [te'lon] nm curtain; **telón de acero** (Pol) iron curtain; **telón de fondo** backcloth, background

tema [tema] nm (asunto) subject, topic; (Mús) theme; **temático, -a** adj thematic

temblar [tem'blar] vi to shake, tremble; (por frío) to shiver; **temblor** nm (temblón); (de tierra) earthquake; **tembloroso, -a** adj trembling

temer [te'mer] vt to fear ▸ vi to be afraid; **temo que llegue tarde** I am afraid he may be late

temible [te'miβle] adj fearsome

temor [te'mor] nm (miedo) fear; (duda) suspicion

témpano ['tempano] nm (tb: ~ de hielo) ice-floe

temperamento [tempera'mento] nm temperament

temperatura [tempera'tura] nf temperature

tempestad [tempes'taθ] nf storm

templado, -a [tem'plaðo, a] adj (moderado) moderate; (frugal) frugal; (agua) lukewarm; (clima) mild; (Mús) well-tuned; **templanza** nf moderation; mildness

templar [tem'plar] vt (moderar) to moderate; (furia) to restrain; (calor) to reduce; (afinar) to tune (up); (acero) to temper; (tuerca) to tighten up; **temple** nm (ajuste) tempering; (afinación) tuning; (pintura) tempera

templo ['templo] nm (iglesia) church; (pagano etc) temple

temporada [tempo'raða] nf time, period; (estación) season

temporal [tempo'ral] *adj* (*no permanente*) temporary ▷ *nm* storm

temprano, -a [tem'prano, a] *adj* early; (*demasiado pronto*) too soon, too early

ten *vb* V **tener**

tenaces [te'naθes] *adj pl* V **tenaz**

tenaz [te'naθ] *adj* (*material*) tough; (*persona*) tenacious; (*creencia, resistencia*) stubborn

tenaza(s) [te'naθa(s)] *nf(pl)* (*Med*) forceps; (*Tec*) pliers; (*Zool*) pincers

tendedero [tende'ðero] *nm* (*para ropa*) drying place; (*cuerda*) clothes line

tendencia [ten'denθja] *nf* tendency; **tener ~ a** to tend to, have a tendency to

tender [ten'der] *vt* (*extender*) to spread out; (*colgar*) to hang out; (*vía férrea, cable*) to lay; (*estirar*) to stretch ▷ *vi*: **~ a** to tend to, have a tendency towards; **tenderse** *vr* to lie down; **~ la cama/mesa** (*LAM*) to make the bed/lay (*BRIT*) o set (*us*) the table

tenderete [tende'rete] *nm* (*puesto*) stall; (*exposición*) display of goods

tendero, -a [ten'dero, a] *nm/f* shopkeeper

tendón [ten'don] *nm* tendon

tendré *etc vb* V **tener**

tenebroso, -a [tene'βroso, a] *adj* (*oscuro*) dark; (*fig*) gloomy

tenedor [tene'ðor] *nm* (*Culin*) fork

tenencia [te'nenθja] *nf* (*de casa*) tenancy; (*de oficio*) tenure; (*de propiedad*) possession

🔑 **PALABRA CLAVE**

tener [te'ner] *vt* **1** (*poseer, gen*) to have; (*en la mano*) to hold; **¿tienes un boli?** have you got a pen?; **va a tener un niño** she's going to have a baby; **¡ten** (*o* **tenga**)**!, ¡aquí tienes** (*o* **tiene**)**!** here you are!

2 (*edad, medidas*) to be: **tiene 7 años** she's 7 (years old); **tiene 15 cm de largo** it's 15 cm long; V **calor; hambre** etc

3 (*considerar*): **lo tengo por brillante** I

consider him to be brilliant; **tener en mucho a algn** to think very highly of sb

4 (+ *pp*: = *pretérito*): **tengo terminada ya la mitad del trabajo** I've done half the work already

5: **tener que hacer algo** to have to do sth; **tengo que acabar este trabajo hoy** I have to finish this job today

6: **¿qué tienes, estás enfermo?** what's the matter with you, are you ill?

tenerse *vr* **1 tenerse en pie** to stand up

2 tenerse por to think o.s.

tengo *etc vb* V **tener**

tenia ['tenja] *nf* tapeworm

teniente [te'njente] *nm* (*rango*) lieutenant; (*ayudante*) deputy

tenis ['tenis] *nm* tennis; **tenis de mesa** table tennis; **tenista** *nmf* tennis player

tenor [te'nor] *nm* (*sentido*) meaning; (*Mús*) tenor; **a ~ de** on the lines of this

tensar [ten'sar] *vt* to tighten; (*arco*) to draw

tensión [ten'sjon] *nf* tension; (*Tec*) stress; **tener la ~ alta** to have high blood pressure; **tensión arterial** blood pressure

tenso, -a ['tenso, a] *adj* tense

tentación [tenta'θjon] *nf* temptation

tentáculo [ten'takulo] *nm* tentacle

tentador, a [tenta'ðor, a] *adj* tempting

tentar [ten'tar] *vt* (*seducir*) to tempt; (*atraer*) to attract

tentempié [tentem'pje] *nm* snack

tenue ['tenwe] *adj* (*delgado*) thin, slender; (*neblina*) light; (*lazo, vínculo*) slight

teñir [te'nir] *vt* to dye; (*fig*) to tinge; **teñirse** *vr* to dye; **~se el pelo** to dye one's hair

teología [teolo'xia] *nf* theology

teoría [teo'ria] *nf* theory; **en ~** in theory; **teórico, -a** *adj* theoretic(al) ▷ *nm/f* theoretician, theorist; **teorizar**

vi to theorize

terapéutico, -a [tera'peutiko, a] *adj* therapeutic

terapia [te'rapja] *nf* therapy

tercer *adj* V **tercero**

tercermundista [terθermun'dista] *adj* Third World *cpd*

tercero, -a [ter'θero, a] (*delante de nmsg*: **tercer**) *adj* third ▷ *nm* (*Jur*) third party

terceto [ter'θeto] *nm* trio

terciar [ter'θjar] *vi* (*participar*) to take part; (*hacer de árbitro*) to mediate; **terciario, -a** *adj* tertiary

tercio [ter'θjo] *nm* third

terciopelo [terθjo'pelo] *nm* velvet

terco, -a ['terko, a] *adj* obstinate

tergal ® [ter'ɣal] *nm* type of polyester

tergiversar [terxiβer'sar] *vt* to distort

termal [ter'mal] *adj* thermal

termas [termas] *nfpl* hot springs

térmico, -a ['termiko, a] *adj* thermal

terminal [termi'nal] *adj, nm, nf* terminal

terminante [termi'nante] *adj* (*final*) final, definitive; (*tajante*) categorical; **terminantemente** *adv*: **terminantemente prohibido** strictly forbidden

terminar [termi'nar] *vt* (*completar*) to complete, finish; (*concluir*) to end ▷ *vi* (*llegar a su fin*) to end; (*parar*) to stop; (*acabar*) to finish; **terminarse** to come to an end; **~ por hacer algo** to end up (by) doing sth

término ['termino] *nm* end, conclusion; (*parada*) terminus; (*límite*) boundary; **en último ~** (*a fin de cuentas*) in the last analysis; (*como último recurso*) as a last resort; **término medio** average; (*fig*) middle way

termómetro [ter'mometro] *nm* thermometer

termo(s) ® ['termo(s)] *nm* Thermos ®

termostato [termo'stato] *nm* thermostat

ternero, -a [ter'nero, a] *nm/f* (*animal*) calf ▷ *nf* (*carne*) veal, beef

ternura [ter'nura] *nf* (*trato*) tenderness; (*palabra*) endearment; (*cariño*) fondness

terrado [te'rraðo] *nm* terrace

terraplén [terra'plen] *nm* embankment

terrateniente [terrate'njente] *nmf* landowner

terraza [te'rraθa] *nf* (*balcón*) balcony; (*tejado*) (flat) roof; (*Agr*) terrace

terremoto [terre'moto] *nm* earthquake

terrenal [terre'nal] *adj* earthly

terreno [te'rreno] *nm* (*tierra*) land; (*parcela*) plot; (*suelo*) soil; (*fig*) field; **un ~** a piece of land

terrestre [te'rrestre] *adj* terrestrial; (*ruta*) land *cpd*

terrible [te'rriβle] *adj* terrible, awful

territorio [terri'torjo] *nm* territory

terrón [te'rron] *nm* (*de azúcar*) lump; (*de tierra*) clod, lump

terror [te'rror] *nm* terror; **terrorífico, -a** *adj* terrifying; **terrorista** *adj, nmf* terrorist; **terrorista suicida** suicide bomber

terso, -a ['terso, a] *adj* (*liso*) smooth; (*pulido*) polished

tertulia [ter'tulja] *nf* (*reunión informal*) social gathering; (*grupo*) group, circle

tesis ['tesis] *nf inv* thesis

tesón [te'son] *nm* (*firmeza*) firmness; (*tenacidad*) tenacity

tesorero, -a [teso'rero, a] *nm/f* treasurer

tesoro [te'soro] *nm* treasure; (*Com, Pol*) treasury

testamento [testa'mento] *nm* will

testarudo, -a [testa'ruðo, a] *adj* stubborn

testículo [tes'tikulo] *nm* testicle

testificar [testifi'kar] *vt* to testify; (*fig*) to attest ▷ *vi* to give evidence

testigo [tes'tiɣo] *nmf* witness; **testigo de cargo/descargo** witness for the prosecution/defence; **testigo ocular** eye witness

testimonio [testiˈmonjo] *nm* testimony

teta [ˈteta] *nf (de biberón)* teat; *(Anat: fam)* breast

tétanos [ˈtetanos] *nm* tetanus

tetera [teˈtera] *nf* teapot

tétrico, -a [ˈtetriko, a] *adj* gloomy, dismal

textear [teksteˈar] *vt* to text

textil [teksˈtil] *adj* textile

texto [ˈteksto] *nm* text; **textual** *adj* textual

textura [teksˈtura] *nf (de tejido)* texture

tez [teθ] *nf (cutis)* complexion

ti [ti] *pron* you; *(reflexivo)* yourself

tía [ˈtia] *nf (pariente)* aunt; *(fam)* chick, bird

tibio, -a [ˈtiβjo, a] *adj* lukewarm

tiburón [tiβuˈron] *nm* shark

tic [tik] *nm (ruido)* click; *(de reloj)* tick; *(Med)*: **~ nervioso** nervous tic

tictac [tikˈtak] *nm (de reloj)* tick tock

tiempo [ˈtjempo] *nm* time; *(época, período)* age, period; *(Meteorología)* weather; *(Ling)* tense; *(Deporte)* half; **a ~** in time; **a un o al mismo ~** at the same time; **al poco ~** very soon (after); **se quedó poco ~** he didn't stay very long; **hace poco ~** not long ago; **mucho ~** a long time; **de ~ en ~** from time to time; **hace buen/mal ~** the weather is fine/bad; **estar a ~** to be in time; **hace ~** some time ago; **hacer ~** to while away the time; **motor de 2 ~s** two-stroke engine; **primer ~** first half

tienda [ˈtjenda] *nf* shop, store; **tienda de abarrotes** *(MÉX, CAM)* grocer's, grocery store *(US)*; **tienda de alimentación** o **comestibles** grocer's *(BRIT)*, grocery store *(US)*; **tienda de campaña** tent

tienes *etc vb V* **tener**

tienta *etc* [ˈtjenta] *vb V* **tentar** ⊳ *nf*: **andar a ~s** to grope one's way along

tiento *etc* [ˈtjento] *vb V* **tentar** ⊳ *nm*

(tacto) touch; *(precaución)* wariness

tierno, -a [ˈtjerno, a] *adj (blando)* tender; *(fresco)* fresh; *(amable)* sweet

tierra [ˈtjerra] *nf* earth; *(suelo)* soil; *(mundo)* earth, world; *(país)* country, land; **~ adentro** inland

tieso, -a [ˈtjeso, a] *adj (rígido)* rigid; *(duro)* stiff; *(fam: orgulloso)* conceited

tiesto [ˈtjesto] *nm* flowerpot

tifón [tiˈfon] *nm* typhoon

tifus [ˈtifus] *nm* typhus

tigre [ˈtiɣre] *nm* tiger

tijera [tiˈxera] *nf* scissors *pl*; *(Zool)* claw; **tijeras** *nfpl* scissors; *(para plantas)* shears

tila [ˈtila] *nf* lime blossom tea

tildar [tilˈdar] *vt*: **~ de** to brand as

tilde [ˈtilde] *nf (Tip)* tilde

tilín [tiˈlin] *nm* tinkle

timar [tiˈmar] *vt (estafar)* to swindle

timbal [timˈbal] *nm* small drum

timbre [ˈtimbre] *nm (sello)* stamp; *(campanilla)* bell; *(tono)* timbre; *(Com)* stamp duty

timidez [timiˈðeθ] *nf* shyness; **tímido, -a** *adj* shy

timo [ˈtimo] *nm* swindle

timón [tiˈmon] *nm* helm, rudder; **timonel** *nm* helmsman

tímpano [ˈtimpano] *nm (Anat)* eardrum; *(Mús)* small drum

tina [ˈtina] *nf* tub; *(baño)* bath(tub); **tinaja** *nf* large jar

tinieblas [tiˈnjeβlas] *nfpl* darkness *sg*; *(sombras)* shadows

tino [ˈtino] *nm (habilidad)* skill; *(juicio)* insight

tinta [ˈtinta] *nf* ink; *(Tec)* dye; *(Arte)* colour

tinte [ˈtinte] *nm* dye

tintero [tinˈtero] *nm* inkwell

tinto [ˈtinto] *nm* red wine

tintorería [tintoreˈria] *nf* dry cleaner's

tío [ˈtio] *nm (pariente)* uncle; *(fam: individuo)* bloke *(BRIT)*, guy

tiovivo [tioˈβiβo] *nm* merry-go-round

típico, -a ['tipiko, a] *adj* typical

tipo ['tipo] *nm* (*clase*) type, kind; (*hombre*) fellow; (*Anat: de hombre*) build; (: *de mujer*) figure; (*Imprenta*) type; **tipo bancario/de descuento/de interés/ de cambio** bank/discount/interest/ exchange rate

tipografía [tipoɣraˈfia] *nf* printing *cpd*

tíquet ['tiket] (*pl* -s) *nm* ticket; (*en tienda*) cash slip

tiquismiquis [tikisˈmikis] *nm inv* fussy person ▷ *nmpl* (*querellas*) squabbling *sg*; (*escrúpulos*) silly scruples

tira ['tira] *nf* strip; (*fig*) abundance; **tira y afloja** give and take

tirabuzón [tiraβuˈθon] *nm* (*rizo*) curl

tirachinas [tiraˈtʃinas] *nm inv* catapult

tirada [tiˈraða] *nf* (*acto*) cast, throw; (*serie*) series; (*Tip*) printing, edition; **de una ~** at one go

tirado, -a [tiˈraðo, a] *adj* (*barato*) dirt-cheap; (*fam: fácil*) very easy

tirador [tiraˈðor] *nm* (*mango*) handle

tirano, -a [tiˈrano, a] *adj* tyrannical ▷ *nm/f* tyrant

tirante [tiˈrante] *adj* (*cuerda etc*) tight, taut; (*relaciones*) strained ▷ *nm* (*Arq*) brace; (*Tec*) stay; **tirantes** *nmpl* (*de pantalón*) braces (BRIT), suspenders (US); **tirantez** *nf* tightness; (*fig*) tension

tirar [tiˈrar] *vt* to throw; (*dejar caer*) to drop; (*volcar*) to upset; (*derribar*) to knock down o over; (*desechar*) to throw out o away; (*dinero*) to squander; (*imprimir*) to print ▷ *vi* (*disparar*) to shoot; (*de la puerta etc*) to pull; (*fam: andar*) to go; (*tender a, buscar realizar*) to tend to; (*Deporte*) to shoot; **tirarse** *vr* (*arrojarse*) to throw o.s.; **~ abajo** to bring down, destroy; **tira más a su padre** he takes more after his father; **ir tirando** to manage

tirita [tiˈrita] *nf* (*sticking*) plaster (BRIT), Bandaid® (US)

tiritar [tiriˈtar] *vi* to shiver

tiro ['tiro] *nm* (*lanzamiento*) throw; (*disparo*) shot; (*Deporte*) shot; (*Golf, Tenis*) drive; (*alcance*) range; **caballo de ~** cart-horse; **tiro al blanco** target practice

tirón [tiˈron] *nm* (*sacudida*) pull, tug; **de un ~** in one go, all at once

tiroteo [tiroˈteo] *nm* exchange of shots, shooting

tisis ['tisis] *nf inv* consumption, tuberculosis

títere ['titere] *nm* puppet

titubear [tituβeˈar] *vi* to stagger; to stammer; (*fig*) to hesitate; **titubeo** *nm* staggering; stammering; hesitation

titulado, -a [tituˈlaðo, a] *adj* (*libro*) entitled; (*persona*) titled

titular [tituˈlar] *adj* titular ▷ *nmf* holder ▷ *nm* headline ▷ *vt* to title; **titularse** *vr* to be entitled; **título** *nm* title; (*de diario*) headline; (*certificado*) professional qualification; (*universitario*) (university) degree; **a título de** in the capacity of

tiza ['tiθa] *nf* chalk

toalla [toˈaʎa] *nf* towel

tobillo [toˈβiʎo] *nm* ankle

tobogán [toβoˈɣan] *nm* (*montaña rusa*) roller-coaster; (*de niños*) chute, slide

tocadiscos [tokaˈðiskos] *nm inv* record player

tocado, -a [toˈkaðo, a] *adj* (*fam*) touched ▷ *nm* headdress

tocador [tokaˈðor] *nm* (*mueble*) dressing table; (*cuarto*) boudoir; (*fam*) ladies' toilet (BRIT) o room (US)

tocar [toˈkar] *vt* to touch; (*Mús*) to play; (*referirse a*) to allude to; (*timbre*) to ring ▷ *vi* (*a la puerta*) to knock (on o at the door); (*ser de turno*) to fall to, be the turn of; (*ser hora*) to be due; **tocarse** *vr* (*cubrirse la cabeza*) to cover one's head; (*tener contacto*) to touch; **por lo que a mí me toca** as far as I am concerned; **te toca a ti** it's your turn

tocayo, -a [toˈkajo, a] *nm/f* namesake

tocino [to'θino] nm bacon

todavía [toða'βia] adv (aun) even; (aún) still, yet; **~ más** yet more; **~ no** not yet

○ **PALABRA CLAVE**

todo, -a ['toðo, a] adj 1(con artículo sg) all; **toda la carne** all the meat; **toda la noche** all night, the whole night; **todo el libro** the whole book; **toda una botella** a whole bottle; **todo lo contrario** quite the opposite; **está toda sucia** she's all dirty; **por todo el país** throughout the whole country
2(con artículo pl) all; every; **todos los libros** all the books; **todas las noches** every night; **todos los que quieran salir** all those who want to leave
▷ pron 1everything, all; **todos** everyone, everybody; **lo sabemos todo** we know everything; **todos querían más tiempo** everybody o everyone wanted more time; **nos marchamos todos** all of us left
2 con todo: **con todo él me sigue gustando** even so I still like him
▷ adv all; **vaya todo seguido** keep straight on o ahead
▷ nm: **como un todo** as a whole; **del todo: no me agrada del todo** I don't entirely like it

todopoderoso, -a [toðopoðe'roso, a] adj all powerful; (Rel) almighty

todoterreno [toðote'rreno] sm inv four-wheel drive, SUV (ESP US)

toga ['toɣa] nf toga; (Escol) gown

Tokio ['tokjo] n Tokyo

toldo ['toldo] nm (para el sol) sunshade (BRIT), parasol; (tienda) marquee

tolerancia [tole'ranθja] nf tolerance; **tolerante** adj (sociedad) liberal; (persona) open-minded

tolerar [tole'rar] vt to tolerate; (resistir) to endure

toma ['toma] nf (acto) taking; (Med) dose; **toma de corriente** socket; **toma de tierra** earth (wire); **tomacorriente** (LAM) nm socket

tomar [to'mar] vt to take; (aspecto) to take on; (beber) to drink ▷ vi to take; (LAM: beber) to drink; **tomarse** vr to take; **~se por** to consider o.s. to be; **~ a bien/mal** to take well/badly; **~ en serio** to take seriously; **~ el pelo a algn** to pull sb's leg; **~la con algn** to pick a quarrel with sb; **¡tome!** here you are!; **~ el sol** to sunbathe

tomate [to'mate] nm tomato

tomillo [to'miλo] nm thyme

tomo ['tomo] nm (libro) volume

ton [ton] abr = **tonelada** ▷ nm: **sin ~ ni son** without rhyme or reason

tonalidad [tonali'ðað] nf tone

tonel [to'nel] nm barrel

tonelada [tone'laða] nf ton; **tonelaje** nm tonnage

tónica [tonika] nf (Mús) tonic; (fig) keynote

tónico, -a [toniko, a] adj tonic ▷ nm (Med) tonic

tono ['tono] nm tone; **fuera de ~** inappropriate; **tono de llamada** ringtone

tontería [tonte'ria] nf (estupidez) foolishness; (cosa) stupid thing; (acto) foolish act; **tonterías** nfpl (disparates) rubbish sg, nonsense sg

tonto, -a ['tonto, a] adj stupid, silly ▷ nm/f fool

topar [to'par] vi: **~ contra** o **en** to run into; **~ con** to run up against

tope ['tope] adj maximum ▷ nm (fin) end; (límite) limit; (Ferro) buffer; (Auto) bumper; **al ~** end to end

tópico, -a ['topiko, a] adj topical ▷ nm platitude

topo ['topo] nm (Zool) mole; (fig) blunderer

toque etc ['toke] vb V **tocar** ▷ nm touch; (Mús) beat; (de campana) peal; **dar un ~ a** to warn; **toque de queda** curfew

toqué etc vb V **tocar**

toquetear [tokete'ar] vt to finger

toquilla [to'kiʎa] nf (pañuelo) headscarf; (chal) shawl

tórax ['toraks] nm thorax

torbellino [torβe'ʎino] nm whirlwind; (fig) whirl

torcedura [torθe'ðura] nf twist; (Med) sprain

torcer [tor'θer] vt to twist; (la esquina) to turn; (Med) to sprain ▷ vi (desviar) to turn off; **torcerse** vr (ladearse) to bend; (desviarse) to go astray; (fracasar) to go wrong; **torcido, -a** adj twisted; (fig) crooked ▷ nm curl

tordo, -a ['torðo, a] adj dappled ▷ nm thrush

torear [tore'ar] vt (fig: evadir) to avoid; (jugar con) to tease ▷ vi to fight bulls; **toreo** nm bullfighting; **torero, -a** nm/f bullfighter

tormenta [tor'menta] nf storm; (fig: confusión) turmoil

tormento [tor'mento] nm torture; (fig) anguish

tornar [tor'nar] vt (devolver) to return, give back; (transformar) to transform ▷ vi to go back

tornasolado, -a [tornaso'laðo, a] adj (brillante) iridescent; (reluciente) shimmering

torneo [tor'neo] nm tournament

tornillo [tor'niʎo] nm screw

torniquete [torni'kete] nm (Med) tourniquet

torno ['torno] nm (Tec) winch; (tambor) drum; (Tec: de banco) lathe; en ~ a round, about

toro ['toro] nm bull; (fam) he-man; **los ~s** bullfighting

toronja [to'ronxa] nf grapefruit

torpe ['torpe] adj (poco hábil) clumsy, awkward; (necio) dim; (lento) slow

torpedo [tor'peðo] nm torpedo

torpeza [tor'peθa] nf (falta de agilidad) clumsiness; (lentitud) slowness; (error) mistake

torre ['torre] nf tower; (de petróleo) derrick

torrefacto, -a [torre'fakto, a] adj roasted

torrente [to'rrente] nm torrent

torrija [to'rrixa] nf French toast

torsión [tor'sjon] nf twisting

torso ['torso] nm torso

torta ['torta] nf cake; (fam) slap

tortícolis [tor'tikolis] nm inv stiff neck

tortilla [tor'tiʎa] nf omelette; (LAM: de maíz) maize pancake; **tortilla de papas** (LAM) potato omelette; **tortilla de patatas** (ESP) potato omelette; **tortilla francesa** (ESP) plain omelette

tórtola ['tortola] nf turtledove

tortuga [tor'tuɣa] nf tortoise

tortuoso, -a [tor'twoso, a] adj winding

tortura [tor'tura] nf torture; **torturar** vt to torture

tos [tos] nf cough; **tos ferina** whooping cough

toser [to'ser] vi to cough

tostada [tos'taða] nf piece of toast; **tostado, -a** adj toasted; (por el sol) dark brown; (piel) tanned

tostador [tosta'ðor] (ESP) nm toaster; **tostadora** (LAM) nf = **tostador**

tostar [tos'tar] vt (pan) to toast; (café) to roast; (persona) to tan; **tostarse** vr to get brown

total [to'tal] adj total ▷ adv in short; (al fin y al cabo) when all is said and done ▷ nm total; **en ~** in all; **~ que ...** to cut (BRIT) o make (US) a long story short ...

totalidad [totali'ðað] nf whole

totalitario, -a [totali'tarjo, a] adj totalitarian

tóxico, -a ['toksiko, a] adj toxic ▷ nm poison; **toxicómano, -a** nm/f drug addict

toxina [to'ksina] nf toxin

tozudo, -a [to'θuðo, a] adj obstinate

trabajador, a [traβaxa'ðor, a] adj hard-working ▷ nm/f worker; **trabajador autónomo** o **por cuenta propia** self-employed person

trabajar [traβa'xar] vt to work; (Agr) to till; (empeñarse en) to work at; (convencer) to persuade ▷ vi to work; (esforzarse) to strive; **trabajo** nm work; (tarea) task; (Pol) labour; (fig) effort; **tomarse el trabajo de** to take the trouble to; **trabajo a destajo** piecework; **trabajo en equipo** teamwork; **trabajo por turnos** shift work; **trabajos forzados** hard labour sg

trabalenguas [traβa'lengwas] nm inv tongue twister

tracción [trak'θjon] nf traction; **tracción delantera/trasera** front-wheel/rear-wheel drive

tractor [trak'tor] nm tractor

tradición [traði'θjon] nf tradition; **tradicional** adj traditional

traducción [traðuk'θjon] nf translation

traducir [traðu'θir] vt to translate; **traductor, a** nm/f translator

traer [tra'er] vt to bring; (llevar) to carry; (llevar puesto) to wear; (incluir) to carry; (causar) to cause; **traerse: ~se algo** to be up to sth

traficar [trafi'kar] vi to trade

tráfico ['trafiko] nm (Com) trade; (Auto) traffic

tragaluz [traɣa'luθ] nm skylight

tragamonedas [traɣamo'neðas] (LAM) nf inv slot machine

tragaperras [traɣa'perras] (ESP) nf inv slot machine

tragar [tra'ɣar] vt to swallow; (devorar) to devour, bolt down; **tragarse** vr to swallow

tragedia [tra'xeðja] nf tragedy; **trágico, -a** adj tragic

trago ['traɣo] nm (líquido) drink; (bocado) gulp; (fam: de bebida) swig; (desgracia) blow; **echar un ~** to have a drink

traición [trai'θjon] nf treachery; (Jur) treason; (una traición) act of treachery; **traicionar** vt to betray

traidor, a [trai'ðor, a] adj

treacherous ▷ nm/f traitor

traigo etc vb V **traer**

traje ['traxe] vb V **traer** ▷ nm (de hombre) suit; (de mujer) dress; (vestido típico) costume; **traje de baño/chaqueta** swimsuit/suit; **traje de etiqueta** dress suit; **traje de luces** bullfighter's costume

trajera etc vb V **traer**

trajín [tra'xin] nm (fam: movimiento) bustle; **trajinar** vi (moverse) to bustle about

trama ['trama] nf (intriga) plot; (de tejido) weft (BRIT), woof (US); **tramar** vt to plot; (Tec) to weave

tramitar [trami'tar] vt (asunto) to transact; (negociar) to negotiate

trámite ['tramite] nm (paso) step; (Jur) transaction; **trámites** nmpl (burocracia) procedure sg; (Jur) proceedings

tramo ['tramo] nm (de tierra) plot; (de escalera) flight; (de vía) section

trampa ['trampa] nf trap; (en el suelo) trapdoor; (truco) trick; (engaño) fiddle; **trampear** vt, vi to cheat

trampolín [trampo'lin] nm (de piscina etc) diving board

tramposo, -a [tram'poso, a] adj crooked, cheating ▷ nm/f crook, cheat

tranca ['tranka] nf (palo) stick; (de puerta, ventana) bar; **trancar** vt to bar

trance ['tranθe] nm (momento difícil) difficult moment o juncture; (estado hipnotizado) trance

tranquilidad [trankili'ðað] nf (calma) calmness, stillness; (paz) peacefulness

tranquilizar [trankili'θar] vt (calmar) to calm (down); (asegurar) to reassure; **tranquilizarse** vr to calm down; **tranquilo, -a** adj (calmado) calm; (apacible) peaceful; (mar) calm; (mente) untroubled

transacción [transak'θjon] nf transaction

transbordador [transβorða'ðor] nm ferry

transbordo [trans'βorðo] *nm* transfer; **hacer ~** to change (trains *etc*)

transcurrir [transku'rrir] *vi* (*tiempo*) to pass; (*hecho*) to take place

transcurso [trans'kurso] *nm*: **~ del tiempo** lapse (of time)

transeúnte [transe'unte] *nmf* passer-by

transferencia [transfe'renθja] *nf* transference; (*Com*) transfer

transferir [transfe'rir] *vt* to transfer

transformación [transforma'θjon] *nf* transformation

transformador [transforma'ðor] *nm* (*Elec*) transformer

transformar [transfor'mar] *vt* to transform; (*convertir*) to convert

transfusión [transfu'sjon] *nf* transfusion

transgénico, -a [trans'xeniko, a] *adj* genetically modified, GM

transición [transi'θjon] *nf* transition

transigir [transi'xir] *vi* to compromise, make concessions

transitar [transi'tar] *vi* to go (from place to place); **tránsito** *nm* transit; (*Auto*) traffic; **transitorio, -a** *adj* transitory

transmisión [transmi'sjon] *nf* (*Tec*) transmission; (*transferencia*) transfer; **transmisión exterior/en directo** outside/live broadcast

transmitir [transmi'tir] *vt* to transmit; (*Radio, TV*) to broadcast

transparencia [transpa'renθja] *nf* transparency; (*claridad*) clearness, clarity; (*foto*) slide

transparentar [transparen'tar] *vt* to reveal ▷ *vi* to be transparent; **transparente** *adj* transparent; (*claro*) clear

transpirar [transpi'rar] *vi* to perspire

transportar [transpor'tar] *vt* to transport; (*llevar*) to carry; **transporte** *nm* transport; (*Com*) haulage

transversal [transβer'sal] *adj* transverse, cross

tranvía [tram'bia] *nm* tram

trapeador [trapea'ðor] (LAM) *nm* mop; **trapear**(LAM) *vt* to mop

trapecio [tra'peθjo] *nm* trapeze; **trapecista** *nmf* trapeze artist

trapero, -a [tra'pero, a] *nm/f* ragman

trapicheo [trapi'tʃeo] (*fam*) *nm* scheme, fiddle

trapo ['trapo] *nm* (*tela*) rag; (*de cocina*) cloth

tráquea [trakea] *nf* windpipe

traqueteo [trake'teo] *nm* rattling

tras [tras] *prep* (*detrás de*) behind; (*después*) after

trasatlántico [trasat'lantiko] *nm* (*barco*) (cabin) cruiser

trascendencia [trasθen'denθja] *nf* (*importancia*) importance; (*Filosofía*) transcendence

trascendental [trasθenden'tal] *adj* important; (*Filosofía*) transcendental

trasero, -a [tra'sero, a] *adj* back, rear ▷ *nm* (*Anat*) bottom

trasfondo [tras'fondo] *nm* background

trasgredir [trasγre'ðir] *vt* to contravene

trashumante [trasu'mante] *adj* (*animales*) migrating

trasladar [trasla'ðar] *vt* to move; (*persona*) to transfer; (*postergar*) to postpone; (*copiar*) to copy; **trasladarse** *vr* (*mudarse*) to move; **traslado** *nm* move; (*mudanza*) move, removal

traslucir [traslu'θir] *vt* to show

trasluz [tras'luθ] *nm* reflected light; **al ~** against or up to the light

trasnochador, a [trasnotʃa'ðor, a] *nm/f* night owl

trasnochar [trasno'tʃar] *vi* (*acostarse tarde*) to stay up late

traspapelar [traspape'lar] *vt* (*documento, carta*) to mislay, misplace

traspasar [traspa'sar] *vt* (*suj: bala etc*) to pierce, go through; (*propiedad*) to sell, transfer; (*calle*) to cross over; (*límites*) to go beyond; (*ley*) to break; **traspaso** *nm* (*venta*) transfer, sale

traspatio [tras'patjo] (LAM) nm
backyard

traspié [tras'pje] nm (tropezón) trip;
(error) blunder

trasplantar [trasplan'tar] vt to
transplant

traste ['traste] nm (Mús) fret; **dar al ~
con algo** to ruin sth

trastero [tras'tero] nm storage room

trastienda [tras'tjenda] nf back
of shop

trasto ['trasto] nm (pey) (cosa) piece of
junk; (persona) dead loss

trastornado, -a [trastor'naðo, a]
adj (loco) mad, crazy

trastornar [trastor'nar] vt
(fig: planes) to disrupt; (: nervios) to
shatter; (: persona) to drive crazy;
trastornarse vr (volverse loco) to go
mad o crazy; **trastorno** nm (acto)
overturning; (confusión) confusion

tratable [tra'taβle] adj friendly

tratado [tra'taðo] nm (Pol) treaty;
(Com) agreement

tratamiento [trata'mjento] nm
treatment; **tratamiento de textos**
(Inform) word processing cpd

tratar [tra'tar] vt (ocuparse de) to
treat; (manejar, Tec) to handle; (Med) to
treat; (dirigirse a: persona) to address
▷ vi: **~ de** (hablar sobre) to deal with,
be about; (intentar) to try to; **tratarse**
vr to treat each other; **~ con** (Com) to
trade in; (negociar) to negotiate with;
(tener contactos) to have dealings with;
¿de qué se trata? what's it about?;
trato nm dealings pl; (relaciones)
relationship; (comportamiento) manner;
(Com) agreement

trauma ['trauma] nm trauma

través [tra'βes] nm (fig): **al ~**
across, crossways; **a ~ de** across; (sobre)
over; (por) through

travesaño [traβe'saɲo] nm (Arq)
crossbeam; (Deporte) crossbar

travesía [traβe'sia] nf (calle) cross-
street; (Náut) crossing

travesura [traβe'sura] nf (broma)

prank; (ingenio) wit

travieso, -a [tra'βjeso, a] adj (niño)
naughty

trayecto [tra'jekto] nm (ruta) road,
way; (viaje) journey; (tramo) stretch;
trayectoria nf trajectory; (fig) path

traza ['traθa] nf (aspecto) looks pl;
(señal) sign; **trazado, -a** adj: **bien
trazado** shapely, well-formed ▷ nm
(Arq) plan, design; (fig) outline

trazar [tra'θar] vt (Arq) to plan; (Arte)
to sketch; (fig) to trace; (plan) to draw
up; **trazo** nm (línea) line; (bosquejo)
sketch

trébol ['treβol] nm (Bot) clover

trece ['treθe] num thirteen

trecho ['tretʃo] nm (distancia)
distance; (tiempo) while

tregua ['trexwa] nf (Mil) truce; (fig)
respite

treinta ['treinta] num thirty

tremendo, -a [tre'mendo, a] adj
(terrible) terrible; (imponente: cosa)
imposing; (fam: fabuloso) tremendous

tren [tren] nm train; **tren de
aterrizaje** undercarriage; **tren de
cercanías** suburban train

trenca ['trenka] nf duffel coat

trenza ['trenθa] nf (de pelo) plait
(BRIT), braid (US)

trepadora [trepa'ðora] nf (Bot)
climber

trepar [tre'par] vt, vi to climb

tres [tres] num three

tresillo [tre'siʎo] nm three-piece
suite; (Mús) triplet

treta ['treta] nf trick

triángulo ['trjangulo] nm triangle

tribu ['triβu] nf tribe

tribuna [tri'βuna] nf (plataforma)
platform; (Deporte) (grand)stand

tribunal [triβu'nal] nm (Jur) court;
(comisión, fig) tribunal; **~ popular** jury

tributo [tri'βuto] nm (Com) tax

trigal [tri'xal] nm wheat field

trigo ['trixo] nm wheat

trigueño, -a [tri'xeɲo, a] adj (pelo)
corn-coloured

t

trillar [tri'ʎar] vt (Agr) to thresh

trimestral [trimes'tral] adj quarterly; (Escol) termly

trimestre [tri'mestre] nm (Escol) term

trinar [tri'nar] vi (pájaros) to sing; (rabiar) to fume, be angry

trinchar [trin'tʃar] vt to carve

trinchera [trin'tʃera] nf (fosa) trench

trineo [tri'neo] nm sledge

trinidad [trini'ðað] nf trio; (Rel): **la T~** the Trinity

tripa ['tripa] nf (Anat) intestine; (fam: tb: **~s**) insides pl

triple ['triple] adj triple

triplicado, -a [tripli'kaðo, a] adj: **por~** in triplicate

tripulación [tripula'θjon] nf crew

tripulante [tripu'lante] nmf crewman/woman

tripular [tripu'lar] vt (barco) to man; (Auto) to drive

triquiñuela [triki'nwela] nf trick

tris [tris] nm inv crack

triste ['triste] adj sad; (lamentable) sorry, miserable; **tristeza** nf (aflicción) sadness; (melancolía) melancholy

triturar [tritu'rar] vt (moler) to grind; (mascar) to chew

triunfar [trjun'far] vi (tener éxito) to triumph; (ganar) to win; **triunfo** nm triumph

trivial [tri'βjal] adj trivial

triza ['triθa] nf: **hacer~s** to smash to bits; (papel) to tear to shreds

trocar [tro'kar] vt (carne, manzana) to cut up, cut into pieces

trocha ['trotʃa] nf short cut

trofeo [tro'feo] nm (premio) trophy; (éxito) success

tromba ['tromba] nf downpour

trombón [trom'bon] nm trombone

trombosis [trom'bosis] nf inv thrombosis

trompa ['trompa] nf horn; (trompo) humming top; (hocico) snout; (fam): **cogerse una~** to get tight

trompazo [trom'paθo] nm bump, bang

trompeta [trom'peta] nf trumpet; (clarín) bugle

trompicón [trompi'kon]: **a trompicones** adv in fits and starts

trompo ['trompo] nm spinning top

trompón [trom'pon] nm bump

tronar [tro'nar] vt (MÉX, CAM: fusilar) to shoot; (MÉX: examen) to flunk ▷ vi to thunder; (fig) to rage

tronchar [tron'tʃar] vt (árbol) to chop down; (fig: vida) to cut short; (: esperanza) to shatter; (persona) to tire out; **troncharse** vr to fall down

tronco ['tronko] nm (de árbol, Anat) trunk

trono ['trono] nm throne

tropa ['tropa] nf (Mil) troop; (soldados) soldiers pl

tropezar [trope'θar] vi to trip, stumble; (errar) to slip up; **~con** to run into; (topar con) to bump into; **tropezón** nm trip; (fig) blunder

tropical [tropi'kal] adj tropical

trópico ['tropiko] nm tropic

tropiezo [tro'pjeθo] vb V **tropezar** ▷ nm (error) slip, blunder; (desgracia) misfortune; (obstáculo) snag

trotamundos [trota'mundos] nm inv globetrotter

trotar [tro'tar] vi to trot; **trote** nm trot; (fam) travelling; **de mucho trote** hard-wearing

trozar [tro'θar] vt (LAM) to cut up, cut into pieces

trozo ['troθo] nm bit, piece

trucha ['trutʃa] nf trout

truco ['truko] nm (habilidad) knack; (engaño) trick

trueno ['trweno] nm thunder; (estampido) bang

trueque etc ['trweke] vb V **trocar** ▷ nm exchange; (Com) barter

trufa ['trufa] nf (Bot) truffle

truhán, -ana [tru'an, ana] nm/f rogue

truncar [trun'kar] vt (cortar) to truncate; (fig: la vida etc) to cut short; (: el desarrollo) to stunt

tu [tu] *adj* your

tú [tu] *pron* you

tubérculo [tu'βerkulo] *nm* (Bot) tuber

tuberculosis [tuβerku'losis] *nf inv* tuberculosis

tubería [tuβe'ria] *nf* pipes *pl*; (conducto) pipeline

tubo ['tuβo] *nm* tube, pipe; **tubo de ensayo** test tube; **tubo de escape** exhaust (pipe)

tuerca ['twerka] *nf* nut

tuerto, -a ['twerto, a] *adj* blind in one eye ▷ *nm/f* one-eyed person

tuerza *etc vb* V **torcer**

tuétano ['twetano] *nm* marrow; (Bot) pith

tufo ['tufo] *nm* (hedor) stench

tul [tul] *nm* tulle

tulipán [tuli'pan] *nm* tulip

tullido, -a [tu'ʎiðo, a] *adj* crippled

tumba ['tumba] *nf* (sepultura) tomb

tumbar [tum'bar] *vt* to knock down; **tumbarse** *vr* (echarse) to lie down; (extenderse) to stretch out

tumbo ['tumbo] *nm*: **dar ~s** to stagger

tumbona [tum'bona] *nf* (butaca) easy chair; (de playa) deckchair (BRIT), beach chair (US)

tumor [tu'mor] *nm* tumour

tumulto [tu'multo] *nm* turmoil

tuna ['tuna] *nf* (Mús) student music group; V tb **tuno**

● **TUNA**
●
● A **tuna** is a musical group made
● up of university students or
● former students who dress up
● in costumes from the "Edad de
● Oro", the Spanish Golden Age.
● These groups go through the
● town playing their guitars, lutes
● and tambourines and serenade
● the young ladies in the halls of
● residence or make impromptu
● appearances at weddings or
● parties singing traditional
● Spanish songs for a few coins.

tunante [tu'nante] *nmf* rascal

tunear [tune'ar] *vt* (Auto) to style, mod (inf)

túnel ['tunel] *nm* tunnel

tuning ['tunin] *nm* (Auto) car styling, modding (inf)

tuno, -a ['tuno, a] *nm/f* (fam) rogue ▷ *nm* member of student music group

tupido, -a [tu'piðo, a] *adj* (denso) dense; (tela) close-woven

turbante [tur'βante] *nm* turban

turbar [tur'βar] *vt* (molestar) to disturb; (incomodar) to upset

turbina [tur'βina] *nf* turbine

turbio, -a ['turβjo, a] *adj* cloudy; (tema etc) confused

turbulencia [turβu'lenθja] *nf* turbulence; (fig) restlessness; **turbulento, -a** *adj* turbulent; (fig: intranquilo) restless; (: ruidoso) noisy

turco, -a ['turko, a] *adj* Turkish ▷ *nm/f* Turk

turismo [tu'rismo] *nm* tourism; (coche) car; **turista** *nmf* tourist; **turístico, -a** *adj* tourist *cpd*

turnar [tur'nar] *vi* to take (it in) turns; **turnarse** *vr* to take (it in) turns; **turno** *nm* (de trabajo) shift; (en juegos etc) turn

turquesa [tur'kesa] *nf* turquoise

Turquía [tur'kia] *nf* Turkey

turrón [tu'rron] *nm* (dulce) nougat

tutear [tute'ar] *vt* to address as familiar "tú"; **tutearse** *vr* to be on familiar terms

tutela [tu'tela] *nf* (legal) guardianship; **tutelar** *adj* tutelary ▷ *vt* to protect

tutor, a [tu'tor, a] *nm/f* (legal) guardian; (Escol) tutor

tuve *etc vb* V **tener**

tuviera *etc vb* V **tener**

tuyo, -a ['tujo, a] *adj* yours, of yours ▷ *pron* yours; **un amigo ~** a friend of yours; **los ~s** (fam) your relations o family

TV *nf abr* (= televisión) TV

TVE *nf abr* = **Televisión Española**

u

u [u] *conj* or

ubicar [uβi'kar] *vt* to place, situate; (*LAM: encontrar*) to find; **ubicarse** *vr* (*LAM: encontrarse*) to lie, be located

ubre ['uβre] *nf* udder

UCI *nf abr* (= *Unidad de Cuidados Intensivos*) ICU

Ud(s) *abr* = **usted(es)**

UE *nf abr* (= *Unión Europea*) EU

ufanarse [ufa'narse] *vr* to boast; **ufano, -a** *adj* (*arrogante*) arrogant; (*presumido*) conceited

UGT (*ESP*) *nf abr* = **Unión General de Trabajadores**

úlcera ['ulθera] *nf* ulcer

ulterior [ulte'rjor] *adj* (*más allá*) farther, further; (*subsecuente, siguiente*) subsequent

últimamente ['ultimamente] *adv* (*recientemente*) lately, recently

ultimar [ulti'mar] *vt* to finish; (*finalizar*) to finalize; (*LAM: matar*) to kill

ultimátum [ulti'matum] (*pl* **-s**) *nm* ultimatum

último, -a ['ultimo, a] *adj* last; (*más*

reciente) latest, most recent; (*más bajo*) bottom; (*más alto*) top; **en las últimas** on one's last legs; **por ~** finally

ultra ['ultra] *adj* ultra ▷ *nmf* extreme right-winger

ultraje [ul'traxe] *nm* outrage; insult

ultramar [ultra'mar] *nm*: **de** o **en ~** abroad, overseas

ultramarinos [ultrama'rinos] *nmpl* groceries; **tienda de ~** grocer's (shop)

ultranza [ul'tranθa]: **a ~** *adv* (*a todo trance*) at all costs; (*completo*) outright

umbral [um'bral] *nm* (*gen*) threshold

○ **PALABRA CLAVE**

un, una [un, 'una] *art indef* a; (*antes de vocal*) an; **una mujer/naranja** a woman/an orange
▷ *adj*: **unos** (o **unas**): **hay unos regalos para ti** there are some presents for you; **hay unas cervezas en la nevera** there are some beers in the fridge

unánime [u'nanime] *adj* unanimous; **unanimidad** *nf* unanimity

undécimo, -a [un'deθimo, a] *adj* eleventh

ungir [un'xir] *vt* to anoint

ungüento [un'gwento] *nm* ointment

único, -a ['uniko, a] *adj* only, sole; (*sin par*) unique

unidad [uni'ðað] *nf* unity; (*Com, Tec etc*) unit

unido, -a [u'niðo, a] *adj* joined, linked; (*fig*) united

unificar [unifi'kar] *vt* to unite, unify

uniformar [unifor'mar] *vt* to make uniform, level up; (*persona*) to put into uniform

uniforme [uni'forme] *adj* uniform, equal; (*superficie*) even ▷ *nm* uniform

unilateral [unilate'ral] *adj* unilateral

unión [u'njon] *nf* union; (*acto*) uniting, joining; (*unidad*) unity; (*Tec*) joint; **Unión Europea** European Union

unir [u'nir] *vt* (*juntar*) to join, unite;

(atar) to tie, fasten; (combinar) to combine; **unirse** vr to join together, unite; (empresas) to merge

unísono [u'nisono] nm: **al ~** in unison

universal [uniβer'sal] adj universal; (mundial) world cpd

universidad [uniβersi'ðað] nf university

universitario, -a [uniβersi'tarjo, a] adj university cpd ▷ nm/f (profesor) lecturer; (estudiante) (university) student; (graduado) graduate

universo [uni'βerso] nm universe

○ **PALABRA CLAVE**

uno, -a ['uno, a] adj one; **unos pocos** a few; **unos cien** about a hundred
▷ pron 1one; **quiero sólo uno** I only want one; **uno de ellos** one of them
2(alguien) somebody, someone;
conozco a uno que se te parece I know somebody o someone who looks like you; **uno mismo** oneself; **unos querían quedarse** some (people) wanted to stay
3 (los) **unos ... (los) otros ...** some ... others
▷ nf one; **es la una** it's one o'clock
▷ nm (number) one

untar [un'tar] vt (mantequilla) to spread; (engrasar) to grease, oil

uña ['uɲa] nf (Anat) nail; (garra) claw; (casco) hoof; (arrancaclavos) claw

uranio [u'ranjo] nm uranium

urbanización [urβaniθa'θjon] nf (barrio, colonia) housing estate

urbanizar [urβani'θar] vt (zona) to develop, urbanize

urbano, -a [ur'βano, a] adj (de ciudad) urban; (cortés) courteous, polite

urbe ['urβe] nf large city

urdir [ur'ðir] vt to warp; (complot) to plot, contrive

urgencia [ur'xenθja] nf urgency; (prisa) haste, rush; (emergencia) emergency; **servicios de ~** emergency

services; "**U~s**" "Casualty"; **urgente** adj urgent

urgir [ur'xir] vi to be urgent; **me urge** I'm in a hurry for it

urinario, -a [uri'narjo, a] adj urinary ▷ nm urinal

urna ['urna] nf urn; (Pol) ballot box

urraca [u'rraka] nf magpie

URSS [urs] nf (Hist): **la URSS** the USSR

Uruguay [uru'ɣwai] nm (tb: **el ~**) Uruguay; **uruguayo, -a** adj, nm/f Uruguayan

usado, -a [u'saðo, a] adj used; (de segunda mano) secondhand

usar [u'sar] vt to use; (ropa) to wear; (tener costumbre) to be in the habit of; **usarse** vr to be used; **uso** nm use; wear; (costumbre) usage, custom; (moda) fashion; **al uso** in keeping with custom; **al uso de** in the style of; **de uso externo** (Med) for external use

usted [us'teð] pron (sg) you sg; (pl): **~es** you pl

usual [u'swal] adj usual

usuario, -a [usu'arjo, a] nm/f user

usura [u'sura] nf usury; **usurero, -a** nm/f usurer

usurpar [usur'par] vt to usurp

utensilio [uten'siljo] nm tool; (Culin) utensil

útero ['utero] nm uterus, womb

útil ['util] adj useful ▷ nm tool; **utilidad** nf usefulness; (Com) profit; **utilizar** vt to use, utilize

utopía [uto'pia] nf Utopia; **utópico, -a** adj Utopian

uva ['uβa] nf grape

● **LAS UVAS**
●
● In Spain **Las uvas** play a big part on
● New Year's Eve (**Nochevieja**), when
● on the stroke of midnight people
● gather at home, in restaurants or
● in the **plaza mayor** and eat a grape
● for each stroke of the clock of the
● **Puerta del Sol** in Madrid. It is said
● to bring luck for the following year.

V

v *abr* (= voltio) v

va *vb* V **ir**

vaca [ˈbaka] *nf* (*animal*) cow; **carne de ~** beef

vacaciones [bakaˈθjones] *nfpl* holidays

vacante [baˈkante] *adj* vacant, empty ▷ *nf* vacancy

vaciar [baˈθjar] *vt* to empty out; (*ahuecar*) to hollow out; (*moldear*) to cast; **vaciarse** *vr* to empty

vacilar [baθiˈlar] *vi* to be unsteady; (*al hablar*) to falter; (*dudar*) to hesitate, waver; (*memoria*) to fail

vacío, -a [baˈθio, a] *adj* empty; (*puesto*) vacant; (*desocupado*) idle; (*vano*) vain ▷ *nm* emptiness; (*Física*) vacuum; (*un vacío*) (empty) space

vacuna [baˈkuna] *nf* vaccine; **vacunar** *vt* to vaccinate

vacuno, -a [baˈkuno, a] *adj* cow *cpd*; **ganado ~** cattle

vadear [baðeˈar] *vt* (*río*) to ford; **vado** *nm* ford; **'vado permanente'** 'keep clear'

vagabundo, -a [baɣaˈβundo, a] *adj* wandering ▷ *nm* tramp

vagancia [baˈɣanθja] *nf* (*pereza*) idleness, laziness

vagar [baˈɣar] *vi* to wander; (*no hacer nada*) to idle

vagina [baˈxina] *nf* vagina

vago, -a [ˈbaɣo, a] *adj* vague; (*perezoso*) lazy ▷ *nm/f* (*vagabundo*) tramp; (*flojo*) lazybones *sg*, idler

vagón [baˈɣon] *nm* (*Ferro: de pasajeros*) carriage; (*: de mercancías*) wagon

vaho [ˈbao] *nm* (*vapor*) vapour, steam; (*respiración*) breath

vaina [ˈbaina] *nf* sheath

vainilla [baiˈniʎa] *nf* vanilla

vais *vb* V **ir**

vaivén [baiˈβen] *nm* to-and-fro movement; (*de tránsito*) coming and going; **vaivenes** *nmpl* (*fig*) ups and downs

vajilla [baˈxiʎa] *nf* crockery, dishes *pl*; (*juego*) service, set

valdré *etc vb* V **valer**

vale [ˈbale] *nm* voucher; (*recibo*) receipt; (*pagaré*) IOU

valedero, -a [baleˈðero, a] *adj* valid

valenciano, -a [balenˈθjano, a] *adj* Valencian

valentía [balenˈtia] *nf* courage, bravery

valer [baˈler] *vt* to be worth; (*Mat*) to equal; (*costar*) to cost ▷ *vi* (*ser útil*) to be useful; (*ser válido*) to be valid; **valerse** *vr* to take care of oneself; **~se de** to make use of, take advantage of; **~ la pena** to be worthwhile; **¿vale?** (*ESP*) OK?; **más vale que nos vayamos** we'd better go; **¡eso sí me vale!** (*MÉX: fam: no importar*) I couldn't care less about that

valeroso, -a [baleˈroso, a] *adj* brave, valiant

valgo *etc vb* V **valer**

valía [baˈlia] *nf* worth, value

validar [baliˈðar] *vt* to validate; **validez** *nf* validity; **válido, -a** *adj* valid

valiente [ba'ljente] adj brave, valiant
▷ nm hero

valija [ba'lixa] (cs) nf (suit)case

valioso, -a [ba'ljoso, a] adj valuable

valla ['baʎa] nf fence; (Deporte) hurdle;
valla publicitaria hoarding; **vallar** vt
to fence in

valle ['baʎe] nm valley

valor [ba'lor] nm value, worth;
(precio) price; (valentía) valour, courage;
(importancia) importance; **valores**
nmpl (Com) securities; **valorar** vt
to value

vals [bals] nm inv waltz

válvula ['balβula] nf valve

vamos vb V **ir**

vampiro, -resa [bam'piro, 'resa]
nm/f vampire

van vb V **ir**

vanguardia [ban'gwardja] nf
vanguard; (Arte etc) avant-garde

vanidad [bani'ðað] nf vanity;
vanidoso, -a adj vain, conceited

vano, -a ['bano, a] adj vain

vapor [ba'por] nm vapour; (vaho)
steam; **al ~** (Culin) steamed; **vapor de
agua** water vapour; **vaporizador** nm
atomizer; **vaporizar** vt to vaporize;
vaporoso, -a adj vaporous

vaquero, -a [ba'kero, a] adj cattle
cpd ▷ nm cowboy; **vaqueros** nmpl
(pantalones) jeans

vaquilla [ba'kiʎa] nf (Zool) heifer

vara ['bara] nf stick; (Tec) rod

variable [ba'rjaβle] adj, nf variable

variación [barja'θjon] nf variation

variar [bar'jar] vt to vary; (modificar)
to modify; (cambiar de posición) to
switch around ▷ vi to vary

varicela [bari'θela] nf chickenpox

varices [ba'riθes] nfpl varicose veins

variedad [barje'ðað] nf variety

varilla [ba'riʎa] nf stick; (Bot) twig;
(Tec) rod; (de rueda) spoke

vario, -a ['barjo, a] adj varied; **~s**
various, several

varita [ba'rita] nf (tb: **~ mágica**)
magic wand

varón [ba'ron] nm male, man; **varonil**
adj manly, virile

Varsovia [bar'soβja] n Warsaw

vas vb V **ir**

vasco, -a ['basko, a] adj,
nm/f Basque; **vascongado, -a**
[baskon'gaðo, a] adj Basque; **las
Vascongadas** the Basque Country

vaselina [base'lina] nf Vaseline®

vasija [ba'sixa] nf container, vessel

vaso ['baso] nm glass, tumbler;
(Anat) vessel

▌ No confundir **vaso** con la palabra
inglesa **vase**.

vástago ['bastaxo] nm (Bot) shoot;
(Tec) rod; (fig) offspring

vasto, -a ['basto, a] adj vast, huge

Vaticano [bati'kano] nm: **el ~** the
Vatican

vatio ['batjo] nm (Elec) watt

vaya etc vb V **ir**

Vd(s) abr = **usted(es)**

ve [be] vb V **ir; ver**

vecindad [beθin'dað] nf
neighbourhood; (habitantes) residents
pl

vecindario [beθin'darjo] nm
neighbourhood; residents pl

vecino, -a [be'θino, a] adj
neighbouring ▷ nm/f neighbour;
(residente) resident

veda ['beða] nf prohibition; **vedar**
[be'ðar] vt (prohibir) to ban, prohibit;
(impedir) to stop, prevent

vegetación [bexeta'θjon] nf
vegetation

vegetal [bexe'tal] adj, nm vegetable

vegetariano, -a [bexeta'rjano, a]
adj, nm/f vegetarian

vehículo [be'ikulo] nm vehicle;
(Med) carrier

veía etc vb V **ver**

veinte ['beinte] num twenty

vejar [be'xar] vt (irritar) to annoy, vex;
(humillar) to humiliate

vejez [be'xeθ] nf old age

vejiga [be'xixa] nf (Anat) bladder

vela ['bela] nf (de cera) candle; (Náut)

velado | 284

sail; (insomnio) sleeplessness; (vigilia)
vigil; (Mil) sentry duty; **estar a dos ~s**
(fam: sin dinero) to be skint
velado, -a [be'laðo, a] adj veiled;
(sonido) muffled; (Foto) blurred ▷ nf
soirée
velar [be'lar] vt (vigilar) to keep watch
over ▷ vi to stay awake; **~ por** to watch
over, look after
velatorio [bela'torjo] nm (funeral)
wake
velero [be'lero] nm (Náut) sailing
ship; (Aviac) glider
veleta [be'leta] nf weather vane
veliz [be'lis] (MÉX) nm (suit)case
vello ['beʎo] nm down, fuzz
velo ['belo] nm veil
velocidad [beloθi'ðað] nf speed; (Tec,
Auto) gear
velocímetro [belo'θimetro] nm
speedometer
velorio [be'lorjo] (LAM) nm (funeral)
wake
veloz [be'loθ] adj fast
ven vb V venir
vena ['bena] nf vein
venado [be'naðo] nm deer
vencedor, a [benθe'ðor, a] adj
victorious ▷ nm/f victor, winner
vencer [ben'θer] vt (dominar) to
defeat, beat; (derrotar) to vanquish;
(superar, controlar) to overcome,
master ▷ vi (triunfar) to win (through),
triumph; (plazo) to expire; **vencido,
-a** adj (derrotado) defeated, beaten;
(Com) due ▷ adv: **pagar vencido** to
pay in arrears
venda ['benda] nf bandage; **vendaje**
nm bandage, dressing; **vendar** vt to
bandage; **vendar los ojos** to blindfold
vendaval [benda'βal] nm (viento)
gale
vendedor, a [bende'ðor, a] nm/f
seller
vender [ben'der] vt to sell; **venderse**
vr (estar a la venta) to be on sale; **~ al
contado/al por mayor/al por menor**
to sell for cash/wholesale/retail; **"se

vende" "for sale"
vendimia [ben'dimja] nf grape
harvest
vendré etc vb V venir
veneno [be'neno] nm poison; (de
serpiente) venom; **venenoso, -a** adj
poisonous; venomous
venerable [bene'raβle] adj
venerable; **venerar** vt (respetar) to
revere; (adorar) to worship
venéreo, -a [be'nereo, a]
adj: **enfermedad venérea** venereal
disease
venezolano, -a [beneθo'lano, a] adj
Venezuelan
Venezuela [bene'θwela] nf
Venezuela
venganza [ben'ganθa] nf
vengeance, revenge; **vengar** vt to
avenge; **vengarse** vr to take revenge;
vengativo, -a adj (persona) vindictive
vengo etc vb V venir
venia ['benja] nf (perdón) pardon;
(permiso) consent
venial [be'njal] adj venial
venida [be'niða] nf (llegada) arrival;
(regreso) return
venidero, -a [beni'ðero, a] adj
coming, future
venir [be'nir] vi to come; (ocurrir)
to arrive; (ocurrir) to happen; (fig): **~
de** to stem from; **~ bien/mal** to be
suitable/unsuitable; **el año que viene**
next year; **~se abajo** to collapse
venta ['benta] nf (Com) sale; **"en
~"** "for sale"; **estar a la o en ~** to be
(up) for sale o on the market; **venta a
domicilio** door-to-door selling; **venta
a plazos** hire purchase; **venta al
contado** cash sale; **venta al por mayor/al por menor**
cash sale/wholesale/retail
ventaja [ben'taxa] nf advantage;
ventajoso, -a adj advantageous
ventana [ben'tana] nf window;
ventanilla nf (de taquilla) window (of
booking office etc)
ventilación [bentila'θjon] nf
ventilation; (corriente) draught

ventilador [bentila'ðor] nm fan

ventilar [benti'lar] vt to ventilate; (para secar) to put out to dry; (asunto) to air, discuss

ventisca [ben'tiska] nf blizzard

ventrílocuo, -a [ben'trilokwo, a] nm/f ventriloquist

ventura [ben'tura] nf (felicidad) happiness; (buena suerte) luck; (destino) fortune; **a la (buena) ~** at random; **venturoso, -a** adj happy; (afortunado) lucky, fortunate

veoetc vb V **ver**

ver [ber] vt to see; (mirar) to look at, watch; (entender) to understand; (investigar) to look into ▷ vi to see; to understand; **verse** vr (encontrarse) to meet; (dejarse ver) to be seen; (hallarse: en un apuro) to find o.s., be; **(vamos) a ~** let's see; **no tener nada que ~ con** to have nothing to do with; **a mi modo de ~** as I see it; **ya ~emos** we'll see

vera ['bera] nf edge, verge; (de río) bank

veraneante [berane'ante] nm/f holidaymaker, (summer) vacationer (us)

veranear [berane'ar] vi to spend the summer; **veraneo** nm summer holiday; **veraniego, -a** adj summer cpd

verano [be'rano] nm summer

veras ['beras] nfpl truth sg; **de ~** really, truly

verbal [ber'βal] adj verbal

verbena [ber'βena] nf (baile) open-air dance

verbo ['berβo] nm verb

verdad [ber'ðað] nf truth; (fiabilidad) reliability; **de ~** real, proper; **a decir ~** to tell the truth; **verdadero, -a** (veraz) true, truthful; (fiable) reliable; (fig) real

verde ['berðe] adj green; (chiste) blue, dirty ▷ nm green; **viejo ~** dirty old man; **verdear** vi to turn green; **verdor** nm greenness

verdugo [ber'ðuɣo] nm executioner

verdulero, -a [berðu'lero, a] nm/f greengrocer

verduras [ber'ðuras] nfpl (Culin) greens

vereda [be'reða] nf path; (cs: acera) pavement (BRIT), sidewalk (us)

veredicto [bere'ðikto] nm verdict

vergonzoso, -a [berɣon'θoso, a] adj shameful; (tímido) timid, bashful

vergüenza [ber'ɣwenθa] nf shame, sense of shame; (timidez) bashfulness; (pudor) modesty; **me da ~** I'm ashamed

verídico, -a [be'riðiko, a] adj true, truthful

verificar [berifi'kar] vt to check; (corroborar) to verify; (llevar a cabo) to carry out; **verificarse** vr (predicción) to prove to be true

verja ['berxa] nf (cancela) iron gate; (valla) iron railings pl; (de ventana) grille

vermut [ber'mut] (pl **~s**) nm vermouth

verosímil [bero'simil] adj likely, probable; (relato) credible

verruga [be'rruɣa] nf wart

versátil [ber'satil] adj versatile

versión [ber'sjon] nf version

verso ['berso] nm verse; **un ~** a line of poetry

vértebra [bertéβra] nf vertebra

verter [ber'ter] vt (líquido: adrede) to empty, pour (out); (: sin querer) to spill; (basura) to dump ▷ vi to flow

vertical [berti'kal] adj vertical

vértice [berti'θe] nm vertex, apex

vertidos [ber'tiðos] nmpl waste sg

vertiente [ber'tjente] nf slope; (fig) aspect

vértigo [bertiɣo] nm vertigo; (mareo) dizziness

vesícula [be'sikula] nf blister

vespino® [bes'pino] nm o nf moped

vestíbulo [bes'tiβulo] nm hall; (de teatro) foyer

vestido [bes'tiðo] nm (ropa) clothes pl, clothing; (de mujer) dress, frock ▷ pp de **vestir**; **~ de azul/marinero** dressed

vestidor | 286

in blue/as a sailor

vestidor [besti'ðor] (MÉX) nm (Deporte) changing (BRIT) o locker (US) room

vestimenta [besti'menta] nf clothing

vestir [bes'tir] vt (poner: ropa) to put on; (llevar: ropa) to wear; (proveer de ropa a) to clothe; (sastre) to make clothes for ▷ vi to dress; (verse bien) to look good; **vestirse** vr to get dressed, dress o.s.

vestuario [bes'twarjo] nm clothes pl, wardrobe; (Teatro: cuarto) dressing room; (Deporte) changing (BRIT) o locker (US) room

vetar [be'tar] vt to veto

veterano, -a [bete'rano, a] adj, nm veteran

veterinaria [beteri'narja] nf veterinary science; V tb **veterinario**

veterinario, -a [beteri'narjo, a] nm/f vet(erinary surgeon)

veto ['beto] nm veto

vez [beθ] nf (tiempo; (turno) turn; **a la ~ que** at the same time as; **a su ~** in its turn; **otra ~** again; **una ~** once; **de una ~** in one go; **de una ~ para siempre** once and for all; **de ~ en cuando** from time to time; **7 veces 9** 7 times 9; **hacer las veces de** to stand in for; **tal ~** perhaps

vía ['bia] nf track, route; (Ferro) line; (fig) way; (Anat) passage, tube ▷ prep via, by way of; **por ~ judicial** by legal means; **en ~s de** in the process of; **vía aérea** airway; **Vía Láctea** Milky Way; **vía pública** road o thoroughfare

viable ['bjaβle] adj (solución, plan, alternativa) feasible

viaducto [bja'ðukto] nm viaduct

viajante [bja'xante] nm commercial traveller

viajar [bja'xar] vi to travel; **viaje** nm journey; (gira) tour; (Náut) voyage; **estar de viaje** to be on a trip; **viaje de ida y vuelta** round trip; **viaje**

de novios honeymoon; **viajero, -a** adj travelling; (Zool) migratory ▷ nm/f (quien viaja) traveller; (pasajero) passenger

víbora ['biβora] nf (Zool) viper; (; (MÉX: venenoso) poisonous snake

vibración [biβra'θjon] nf vibration

vibrar [bi'βrar] vt, vi to vibrate

vicepresidente [biθepresi'ðente] nmf vice-president

viceversa [biθe'βersa] adv vice versa

vicio ['biθjo] nm vice; (mala costumbre) bad habit; **vicioso, -a** adj (muy malo) vicious; (corrompido) depraved ▷ nm/f depraved person

víctima ['biktima] nf victim

victoria [bik'torja] nf victory; **victorioso, -a** adj victorious

vid [bið] nf vine

vida ['biða] nf (gen) life; (duración) lifetime; **de por ~** for life; **en la o mi ~** never; **estar con ~** to be still alive; **ganarse la ~** to earn one's living

video ['biðeo] nm video ▷ adj inv: **película de ~** video film; **videocámara** nf camcorder; **videocasete** nm video cassette; **videotape; videoclub** nm video club; **videojuego** nm video game; **videollamada** nf video call; **videoteléfono** nf videophone

vidrio ['biðrjo] nm glass

vieira ['bjeira] nf scallop

viejo, -a ['bjexo, a] adj ▷ nm/f old man/woman; **hacerse ~** to get old

Viena ['bjena] n Vienna

vienes etc vb V **venir**

vienés, -esa [bje'nes, esa] adj Viennese

viento ['bjento] nm wind; **hacer ~** to be windy

vientre ['bjentre] nm belly; (matriz) womb

viernes ['bjernes] nm inv Friday; **Viernes Santo** Good Friday

Vietnam [bjet'nam] nm Vietnam; **vietnamita** adj Vietnamese

viga ['biɣa] nf beam, rafter; (de metal)

girder

vigencia [bi'xenθja] *nf* validity; **estar en ~** to be in force; **vigente** *adj* valid, in force; (*imperante*) prevailing

vigésimo, -a [bi'xesimo, a] *adj* twentieth

vigía [bi'xia] *nm* look-out

vigilancia [bixi'lanθja] *nf* vigilance; **tener a algn bajo ~** to keep watch on sb

vigilar [bixi'lar] *vt* to watch over ▷ *vi* (*gen*) to be vigilant; (*hacer guardia*) to keep watch; **~ por** to take care of

vigilia [bi'xilja] *nf* wakefulness, being awake; (*Rel*) fast

vigor [bi'xor] *nm* vigour, vitality; **en ~** in force; **entrar/poner en ~** to come/put into effect; **vigoroso, -a** *adj* vigorous

VIH *nm abr* (= *virus de la inmunodeficiencia humana*) HIV; **VIH negativo/positivo** HIV-negative/-positive

vil [bil] *adj* vile, low

villa ['biʎa] *nf* (*casa*) villa; (*pueblo*) small town; (*municipalidad*) municipality

villancico [biʎan'θiko] *nm* (Christmas) carol

vilo ['bilo]: **en ~** *adv* in the air, suspended; (*fig*) on tenterhooks, in suspense

vinagre [bi'naɣre] *nm* vinegar

vinagreta [bina'ɣreta] *nf* vinaigrette, French dressing

vinculación [binkula'θjon] *nf* (*lazo*) link, bond; (*acción*) linking

vincular [binku'lar] *vt* to link, bind; **vínculo** *nm* link, bond

vine *etc vb* V **venir**

vinicultor, a [binikul'tor] *nm/f* wine grower

vinicultura [binikul'tura] *nf* wine growing

viniera *etc vb* V **venir**

vino ['bino] *vb* V **venir** ▷ *nm* wine; **vino blanco/tinto** white/red wine

viña ['biɲa] *nf* vineyard; **viñedo** *nm* vineyard

viola ['bjola] *nf* viola

violación [bjola'θjon] *nf* violation; (*sexual*) rape

violar [bjo'lar] *vt* to violate; (*sexualmente*) to rape

violencia [bjo'lenθja] *nf* violence, force; (*incomodidad*) embarrassment; (*acto injusto*) unjust act; **violentar** *vt* to force; (*casa*) to break into; (*agredir*) to assault; (*violar*) to violate; **violento, -a** *adj* violent; (*furioso*) furious; (*situación*) embarrassing; (*acto*) forced, unnatural

violeta [bjo'leta] *nf* violet

violín [bjo'lin] *nm* violin

violón [bjo'lon] *nm* double bass

virar [bi'rar] *vi* to change direction

virgen ['birxen] *adj*, *nf* virgin

Virgo ['birxo] *nm* Virgo

viril [bi'ril] *adj* virile; **virilidad** *nf* virility

virtud [bir'tuð] *nf* virtue; **en ~ de** by virtue of; **virtuoso, -a** *adj* virtuous ▷ *nm/f* virtuoso

viruela [bi'rwela] *nf* smallpox

virulento, -a [biru'lento, a] *adj* virulent

virus ['birus] *nm inv* virus

visa ['bisa] (*LAM*) *nf* = **visado**

visado [bi'saðo] (*ESP*) *nm* visa

víscera [bi'sθera] *nf* (*Anat, Zool*) gut, bowel; **vísceras** *nfpl* entrails

visceral [bisθe'ral] *adj* (*odio*) intense; **reacción ~** gut reaction

visera [bi'sera] *nf* visor

visibilidad [bisiβili'ðað] *nf* visibility; **visible** *adj* visible; (*fig*) obvious

visillos [bi'siʎos] *nmpl* lace curtains

visión [bi'sjon] *nf* (*Anat*) vision, (eye)sight; (*fantasía*) vision, fantasy

visita [bi'sita] *nf* call, visit; (*persona*) visitor; **hacer una ~** to pay a visit; **visitar** [bisi'tar] *vt* to visit, call on

visitante [bisi'tante] *adj* visiting ▷ *nmf* visitor

visón [bi'son] *nm* mink

visor [bi'sor] *nm* (*Foto*) viewfinder

víspera ['bispera] *nf*: **la ~ de** the day before ...

vista ['bista] nf sight, vision; (capacidad de ver) (eye)sight; (mirada) look(s) (pl); **a primera ~** at first glance; **hacer la ~ gorda** to turn a blind eye; **volver la ~** to look back; **está a la ~ que** it's obvious that; **en ~ de** in view of; **en ~ de que** in view of the fact that; **¡hasta la ~!** so long!, see you!; **con ~s a** with a view to; **vistazo** nm glance; **dar** o **echar un vistazo a** to glance at

visto, -a ['bisto, a] pp de **ver** ▷ vb V tb **vestir** ▷ adj seen; (considerado) considered ▷ nm: **~ bueno** approval; **por lo ~** apparently; **está ~ que** it's clear that; **está bien/mal ~** it's acceptable/unacceptable; **~ que** since, considering that

vistoso, -a [bis'toso, a] adj colourful

visual [bi'swal] adj visual

vital [bi'tal] adj life cpd, living cpd; (fig) vital; (persona) lively, vivacious; **vitalicio, -a** adj for life; **vitalidad** nf energy; (de ciudad) liveliness

vitamina [bita'mina] nf vitamin

vitorear [bitore'ar] vt to cheer, acclaim

vitrina [bi'trina] nf show case; (LAM: escaparate) shop window

viudo, -a ['bjuðo, a] nm/f widower/ widow

viva ['biβa] excl hurrah!; **¡~ el rey!** long live the king!

vivaracho, -a [biβa'ratʃo, a] adj jaunty, lively; (ojos) bright, twinkling

vivaz [bi'βaθ] adj lively

víveres ['biβeres] nmpl provisions

vivero [bi'βero] nm (para plantas) nursery; (para peces) fish farm; (fig) hotbed

viveza [bi'βeθa] nf liveliness; (agudeza: mental) sharpness

vivienda [bi'βjenda] nf housing; (una vivienda) house; (piso) flat (BRIT), apartment (us)

viviente [bi'βjente] adj living

vivir [bi'βir] vt, vi to live ▷ nm life, living

vivo, -a ['biβo, a] adj living, alive; (fig: descripción) vivid; (persona: astuto) smart, clever; **en ~** (transmisión etc) live

vocablo [bo'kaβlo] nm (palabra) word; (término) term

vocabulario [bokaβu'larjo] nm vocabulary

vocación [boka'θjon] nf vocation; **vocacional** (LAM) nf ≈ technical college

vocal [bo'kal] adj vocal ▷ nf vowel; **vocalizar** vt to vocalize

vocero [bo'θero] (LAM) nm spokesman/woman

voces ['boθes] pl de **voz**

vodka ['boðka] nm o f vodka

vol abr = **volumen**

volado [bo'laðo] (MÉX) adv in a rush, hastily

volador, a [bola'ðor, a] adj flying

volandas [bo'landas]: **en ~** adv in the air

volante [bo'lante] adj flying ▷ nm (de coche) steering wheel; (de reloj) balance

volar [bo'lar] vt (edificio) to blow up ▷ vi to fly

volátil [bo'latil] adj volatile

volcán [bol'kan] nm volcano; **volcánico, -a** adj volcanic

volcar [bol'kar] vt to upset, overturn; (tumbar, derribar) to knock over; (vaciar) to empty out ▷ vi to overturn; **volcarse** vr to tip over

voleibol [bolei'βol] nm volleyball

volqué etc vb V **volcar**

voltaje [bol'taxe] nm voltage

voltear [bolte'ar] vt to turn over; (volcar) to turn upside down

voltereta [bolte'reta] nf somersault

voltio [bol'tjo] nm volt

voluble [bo'luβle] adj fickle

volumen [bo'lumen] (pl **volúmenes**) nm volume; **voluminoso, -a** adj voluminous; (enorme) massive

voluntad [bolun'taɒ] nf will; (resolución) willpower; (deseo) desire, wish

voluntario, -a [bolun'tarjo, a] *adj*
voluntary ▷ *nm/f* volunteer

volver [bol'βer] *vt* (*gen*) to turn; (*dar
vuelta a*) to turn (over); (*voltear*) to turn
round, turn upside down; (*poner al
revés*) to turn inside out; (*devolver*) to
return ▷ *vi* to return, go back, come
back; **volverse** *vr* to turn round; **~ la
espalda** to turn one's back; **~ triste** *etc*
a algn to make sb sad *etc*; **~ a hacer**
to do again; **~ en sí** to come to; **~se
insoportable/muy caro** to get o
become unbearable/very expensive;
~se loco to go mad

vomitar [bomi'tar] *vt, vi* to vomit;
vómito *nm* vomit

voraz [bo'raθ] *adj* voracious

vos [bos] (*LAM*) *pron* you

vosotros, -as [bo'sotros, as] (*ESP*)
pron you; (*reflexivo*): **entre/para ~**
among/for yourselves

votación [bota'θjon] *nf* (*acto*) voting;
(*voto*) vote

votar [bo'tar] *vi* to vote; **voto** *nm*
vote; (*promesa*) vow; **votos** *nmpl*
(good) wishes

voy *vb* V **ir**

voz [boθ] *nf* voice; (*grito*) shout;
(*rumor*) rumour; (*Ling*) word; **dar voces**
to shout, yell; **de viva ~** verbally; **en ~
alta** aloud; **en ~ baja** in a low voice, in
a whisper; **voz de mando** command

vuelco ['bwelko] *vb* V **volcar** ▷ *nm*
spill, overturning

vuelo ['bwelo] *vb* V **volar** ▷ *nm*
flight; (*encaje*) lace, frill; **coger al ~** to
catch in flight; **vuelo chárter/regular**
charter/scheduled flight; **vuelo libre**
(*Deporte*) hang-gliding

vuelquec *etc* *vb* V **volcar**

vuelta ['bwelta] *nf* (*gen*) turn; (*curva*)
bend, curve; (*regreso*) return; (*revolución*)
revolution; (*de circuito*) lap; (*de papel,
tela*) reverse; (*cambio*) change; **a la ~**
on one's return; **a la ~ (de la esquina)**
round the corner; **a ~ de correo** by
return of post; **dar ~s** (*cabeza*) to spin;
dar(se) la ~ (*volverse*) to turn round;

dar ~s a una idea to turn over an idea
(in one's head); **estar de ~** to be back;
dar una ~ to go for a walk; (*en coche*) to
go for a drive; **vuelta ciclista** (*Deporte*)
(cycle) tour

vuelto ['bwelto] *pp de* **volver**

vuelvo *etc* *vb* V **volver**

vuestro, -a ['bwestro, a] *adj pos*
your; **un amigo ~** a friend of yours
▷ *pron*: **el ~/la vuestra, los ~s/las
vuestras** yours

vulgar [bul'ɣar] *adj* (*ordinario*)
vulgar; (*común*) common; **vulgaridad**
nf commonness; (*acto*) vulgarity;
(*expresión*) coarse expression

vulnerable [bulne'raβle] *adj*
vulnerable

vulnerar [bulne'rar] *vt* (*ley, acuerdo*)
to violate, breach; (*derechos, intimidad*)
to violate; (*reputación*) to damage

W X

walkie-talkie [walki-'talki] (pl **~s**) nm walkie-talkie
Walkman® ['walkman] nm Walkman®
wáter ['bater] nm (taza) toilet; (LAM: lugar) toilet (BRIT), rest room (US)
web [web] nm o f (página) website; (red) (World Wide) Web; **webcam** nf webcam; **webmaster** nmf webmaster; **website** nm website
western ['western] (pl **~s**) nm western
whisky ['wiski] nm whisky, whiskey
wifi [waɪfaɪ] nm Wi-Fi
windsurf ['winsurf] nm windsurfing; **hacer ~** to go windsurfing

xenofobia [kseno'foβja] nf xenophobia
xilófono [ksi'lofono] nm xylophone
xocoyote, -a [ksoko'yote, a] (MÉX) nm/f baby of the family, youngest child

yogur(t) [joˈɣur(t)] *nm* yoghurt
yuca [ˈjuka] *nf* (*alimento*) cassava, manioc root
Yugoslavia [juɣosˈlaβja] *nf* (*Hist*) Yugoslavia
yugular [juɣuˈlar] *adj* jugular
yunque [ˈjunke] *nm* anvil
yuyo [ˈjujo] (*RPL*) *nm* (*mala hierba*) weed

y [i] *conj* and; (*tiempo*) **la una y cinco** five past one
ya [ja] *adv* (*gen*) already; (*ahora*) now; (*en seguida*) at once; (*pronto*) soon ▷ *excl* all right! ▷ *conj* (*ahora que*) now that; **~ lo sé!** I know; **~ que ...** since; **¡~ está bien!** that's (quite) enough!; **¡~ voy!** coming!
yacaré [jakaˈre] (*CS*) *nm* cayman
yacer [jaˈθer] *vi* to lie
yacimiento [jaθiˈmjento] *nm* (*de mineral*) deposit; (*arqueológico*) site
yanqui [ˈjanki] *adj, nmf* Yankee
yate [ˈjate] *nm* yacht
yazco *etc vb V* **yacer**
yedra [ˈjeðra] *nf* ivy
yegua [ˈjeɣwa] *nf* mare
yema [ˈjema] *nf* (*del huevo*) yolk; (*Bot*) leaf bud; (*fig*) best part; **yema del dedo** fingertip
yerno [ˈjerno] *nm* son-in-law
yeso [ˈjeso] *nm* plaster
yo [jo] *pron* I; **soy ~** it's me
yodo [ˈjoðo] *nm* iodine
yoga [ˈjoɣa] *nm* yoga

Z

zafar [θa'far] vt (soltar) to untie; (superficie) to clear; **zafarse** vr (escaparse) to escape; (Tec) to slip off

zafiro [θa'firo] nm sapphire

zaga ['θaɣa] nf: **a la ~** behind

zaguán [θa'ɣwan] nm hallway

zalamero, -a [θala'mero, a] adj flattering; (cobista) suave

zamarra [θa'marra] nf (chaqueta) sheepskin jacket

zambullirse [θambu'ʎirse] vr to dive

zampar [θam'par] vt to gobble down

zanahoria [θana'orja] nf carrot

zancadilla [θanka'ðiʎa] nf trip

zanco ['θanko] nm stilt

zanja ['θanxa] nf (ditch; **zanjar** vt (resolver) to resolve

zapata [θa'pata] nf (Mecánica) shoe

zapatería [θapate'ria] nf (oficio) shoemaking; (tienda) shoe shop; (fábrica) shoe factory; **zapatero, -a** nm/f shoemaker

zapatilla [θapa'tiʎa] nf slipper; **zapatilla de deporte** training shoe

zapato [θa'pato] nm shoe

zapping ['θapin] nm channel-hopping; **hacer ~** to channel-hop

zar [θar] nm tsar, czar

zarandear [θarande'ar] (fam) vt to shake vigorously

zarpa ['θarpa] nf (garra) claw

zarpar [θar'par] vi to weigh anchor

zarza ['θarθa] nf (Bot) bramble; **zarzamora** nf blackberry

zarzuela [θar'θwela] nf Spanish light opera

zigzag [θiɣ'θaɣ] nm zigzag

zinc [θink] nm zinc

zíper ['θiper] (MÉX, CAM) nm zip (fastener) (BRIT), zipper (US)

zócalo ['θokalo] nm (Arq) plinth, base; (de pared) skirting board (BRIT), baseboard (US); (MÉX: plaza) main o public square

zoclo ['θoklo] (MÉX) nm skirting board (BRIT), baseboard (US)

zodíaco [θo'ðiako] nm zodiac

zona ['θona] nf zone; **zona fronteriza** border area; **zona roja** (LAM) red-light district

zonzo, -a [ˈθonθo, a] (LAM: fam) adj silly ▷ nm/f fool

zoo ['θoo] nm zoo

zoología [θoolo'xia] nf zoology; **zoológico, -a** adj zoological ▷ nm (tb: **parque zoológico**) zoo; **zoólogo, -a** nm/f zoologist

zoom [θum] nm zoom lens

zopilote [θopi'lote] (MÉX, CAM) nm buzzard

zoquete [θo'kete] nm (fam) blockhead

zorro, -a ['θorro, a] adj crafty ▷ nm/f fox/vixen

zozobrar [θoθo'βrar] vi (hundirse) to capsize; (fig) to fail

zueco ['θweko] nm clog

zumbar [θum'bar] vt (golpear) to hit ▷ vi to buzz; **zumbido** nm buzzing

zumo ['θumo] nm juice

zurcir [θur'θir] vt (coser) to darn

zurdo, -a ['θurðo, a] adj left-handed

zurrar [θu'rrar] (fam) vt to wallop

Phrasefinder

Guía del viajero

TOPICS | TEMAS

TOPICS | TEMAS

Hello!	¡Buenos días!
Good evening!	¡Buenas tardes!
Good night!	¡Buenas noches!
Goodbye!	¡Adiós!
What's your name?	¿Cómo se llama usted?
My name is ...	Me llamo ...
This is ...	Le presento a ...
my wife.	*mi mujer.*
my husband.	*mi marido.*
my partner.	*mi pareja.*
Where are you from?	¿De dónde es usted?
I come from ...	Soy de ...
How are you?	¿Cómo está usted?
Fine, thanks.	Bien, gracias.
And you?	¿Y usted?
Do you speak English?	¿Habla usted inglés?
I don't understand Spanish.	No entiendo el español.
Thanks very much!	¡Muchas gracias!

Asking the Way | ¿Cómo ir hasta …?

Where is the nearest …?	¿Dónde está el/la … más próximo(-a)?
How do I get to …?	¿Cómo voy hasta el/la …?
Is it far?	¿Está muy lejos?
How far is it to there?	¿Qué distancia hay hasta allí?
Is this the right way to …?	¿Es éste el camino correcto para ir al/a la/a …?
I'm lost.	Me he perdido.
Can you show me on the map?	¿Me lo puede señalar en el mapa?
You have to turn round.	Tiene que dar la vuelta.
Go straight on.	Siga todo recto.
Turn left/right.	Tuerza a la izquierda/ a la derecha.
Take the second street on the left/right.	Tome la segunda calle a la izquierda/a la derecha.

Car Hire | Alquiler de coches

I want to hire …	Quisiera alquilar …
a car.	*un coche.*
a moped.	*una motocicleta.*
a motorbike.	*una moto.*
How much is it for …?	¿Cuánto cuesta por …?
one day	*un día*
a week	*una semana*
I'd like a child seat for a … -year-old child.	Quisiera un asiento infantil para un niño de … años.
What do I do if I have an accident/if I break down?	¿Qué debo hacer en caso de accidente/de avería?

Breakdowns | Averías

My car has broken down.	Tengo una avería.
Where is the next garage?	¿Dónde está el taller más próximo?
The exhaust	El escape
The gearbox	El cambio
... is broken.	... está roto.
The brakes	Los frenos
The headlights	Las luces
The windscreen wipers	Los limpiaparabrisas
... are not working.	... no funcionan.
The battery is flat.	La batería está descargada.
The car won't start.	El motor no arranca.
The engine is overheating.	El motor se recalienta.
I have a flat tyre.	He tenido un pinchazo.
Can you repair it?	¿Puede repararlo?
When will the car be ready?	¿Cuándo estará listo el coche?

Parking | Aparcamiento

Can I park here?	¿Puedo aparcar aquí?
Do I need to buy a (car-parking) ticket?	¿Tengo que sacar un ticket de estacionamiento?
Where is the ticket machine?	¿Dónde está el expendedor de tickets de estacionamiento?
The ticket machine isn't working.	El expendedor de tickets de estacionamiento no funciona.

Petrol Station | Gasolinera

Where is the nearest petrol station?	¿Dónde está la gasolinera más próxima?
Fill it up, please.	Lleno, por favor.

30 euros' worth of ..., please.	30 euros de ...
diesel	*diesel.*
(unleaded) economy petrol	*gasolina normal.*
premium unleaded	*súper.*
Pump number ... please.	Número ..., por favor.
Please check ...	Por favor, compruebe ...
the tyre pressure.	*la presión de los neumáticos.*
the oil.	*el aceite.*
the water.	*el agua.*

Accident | Accidentes

Please call ...	Por favor, llame ...
the police.	*a la policía.*
the emergency doctor.	*al médico de urgencia.*
Here are my insurance details.	Éstos son los datos de mi seguro.
Give me your insurance details, please.	Por favor, deme los datos de su seguro.
Can you be a witness for me?	¿Puede ser usted mi testigo?
You were driving too fast.	Usted conducía muy rápido.
It wasn't your right of way.	Usted no tenía preferencia.

Travelling by Car | Viajando en coche

What's the best route to ...?	¿Cuál es el mejor camino para ir a ...?
I'd like a motorway tax sticker ...	Quisiera un indicativo de pago de peaje ...
for a week.	*para una semana.*
for a year.	*para un año.*
Do you have a road map of this area?	¿Tiene un mapa de carreteras de esta zona?

Cycling	En bicicleta
Where is the cycle path to ...?	¿Dónde está el carril-bici para ir a ...?
Can I keep my bike here?	¿Puedo dejar aquí mi bicicleta?
My bike has been stolen.	Me han robado la bicicleta.
Where is the nearest bike repair shop?	¿Dónde hay por aquí un taller de bicicletas?
The brake isn't/the gears aren't working.	El freno/el cambio de marchas no funciona.
The chain is broken.	La cadena se ha roto.
I've got a flat tyre.	He tenido un pinchazo.
I need a puncture repair kit.	Necesito una caja de parches.

Train	Ferrocarril
A single to ..., please.	Un billete sencillo para ..., por favor.
I would like to travel first/second class.	Me gustaría viajar en primera/segunda clase.
Two returns to ..., please.	Dos billetes de ida y vuelta para ..., por favor.
Is there a reduction ...?	¿Hay descuento ...?
for students	para estudiantes
for pensioners	para pensionistas
for children	para niños
with this pass	con este carnet

I'd like to reserve a seat on the train to ... please.	Una reserva para el tren que va a ..., por favor.
Non smoking/smoking, please.	No fumadores/fumadores, por favor.
I want to book a couchette/a berth to ...	Quisiera reservar una litera/coche-cama para ...
When is the next train to ...?	¿Cuándo sale el próximo tren para ...?
Is there a supplement to pay?	¿Tengo que pagar suplemento?
Do I need to change?	¿Hay que hacer transbordo?
Where do I change?	¿Dónde tengo que hacer transbordo?
Is this the train for ...?	¿Es éste el tren que va a ...?
Excuse me, that's my seat.	Perdone, éste es mi asiento.
I have a reservation.	Tengo una reserva.
Is this seat free?	¿Está libre este asiento?
Please let me know when we get to ...	¿Por favor, avíseme cuando lleguemos a ...?
Where is the buffet car?	¿Dónde está el coche restaurante?
Where is coach number ...?	¿Cuál es el vagón número ...?

Ferry — Transbordador

Is there a ferry to ...?	¿Sale algún transbordador para ...?
When is the next ferry to ...?	¿Cuándo sale el próximo transbordador para ...?
How much is it for a car/camper with ... people?	¿Cuánto cuesta transportar el coche/coche caravana con ... personas?

How long does the crossing take?	¿Cuánto dura la travesía?
Where is ...?	¿Dónde está ...?
the restaurant	el restaurante
the bar	el bar
the duty-free shop	la tienda de duty-free
Where is cabin number ...?	¿Dónde está la cabina número ...?
Do you have anything for seasickness?	¿Tienen algo para el mareo?

Plane — Avión

Where is the luggage for the flight from ...?	¿Dónde está el equipaje procedente de...?
Where is ...?	¿Dónde está ...?
the taxi rank	la parada de taxis
the bus stop	la parada del bus
the information office	la oficina de información
My luggage hasn't arrived.	Mi equipaje no ha llegado.
Can you page ...?	¿Puede llamar por el altavoz a ...?
Where do I check in for the flight to ...?	¿Dónde hay que facturar para el vuelo a ...?
Which gate for the flight to ...?	¿Cuál es la puerta de embarque del vuelo para ...?
When is the latest I can check in?	¿Hasta qué hora como máximo se puede facturar?
When does boarding begin?	¿Cuándo es el embarque?
Window/aisle, please.	Ventanilla/pasillo, por favor.
I've lost my boarding pass/ my ticket.	He perdido la tarjeta de embarque/el billete.

Local Public Transport	Transporte público de cercanías
How do I get to ...?	¿Cómo se llega al/a la/hasta ...?
Where is the nearest ...?	¿Dónde está la próxima ...?
bus stop	parada del bus
underground station	estación de metro
Where is the bus station?	¿Dónde está la estación de autobuses?
A ticket to ..., please.	Un billete a ..., por favor.
Is there a reduction ...?	¿Hay descuento ...?
for students	para estudiantes
for pensioners	para pensionistas
for children	para niños
for the unemployed	para desempleados
with this card	con este carnet
How does the (ticket) machine work?	¿Cómo funciona la máquina (de billetes)?
Please tell me when to get off.	¿Puede decirme cuándo tengo que bajar?
What is the next stop?	¿Cuál es la próxima parada?
Can I get past, please?	¿Me deja pasar?

Taxi	Taxi
Where can I get a taxi?	¿Dónde puedo coger un taxi?
Call me a taxi, please.	¿Puede llamar a un taxi?
To the airport/station, please.	Al aeropuerto/a la estación, por favor.
To this address, please.	A esta dirección, por favor.
I'm in a hurry.	Tengo mucha prisa.
How much is it?	¿Cuánto cuesta el trayecto?
I need a receipt.	Necesito un recibo.
Keep the change.	Quédese con el cambio.
Stop here, please.	Pare aquí, por favor.

Camping | Camping

Is there a campsite here?	¿Hay un camping por aquí?
We'd like a site for ...	Quisiéramos un lugar para ...
a tent.	*una tienda de campaña.*
a caravan.	*una caravana.*
We'd like to stay one night/... nights.	Queremos quedarnos una noche/... noches.
How much is it per night?	¿Cuánto es por noche?
Where are ...?	¿Dónde están ...?
the toilets	*los lavabos*
the showers	*las duchas*
Where is ...?	¿Dónde está ...?
the site office	*la oficina de administración*
Can we camp/park here overnight?	¿Podemos acampar/aparcar aquí esta noche?

Self-Catering | Vivienda para las vacaciones

Where do we get the key for the apartment/house?	¿Dónde nos dan la llave para el piso/la casa?
Do we have to pay extra for electricity/gas?	¿Hay que pagar aparte la luz/ el gas?
How does the heating work?	¿Cómo funciona la calefacción?
Whom do I contact if there are any problems?	¿Con quién debo hablar si hubiera algún problema?
We need ...	Necesitamos ...
a second key.	*otra copia de la llave.*
more sheets.	*más sábanas.*
The gas has run out.	Ya no queda gas.
There is no electricity.	No hay corriente.
Do we have to clean the apartment/the house before we leave?	¿Hay que limpiar el piso/ la casa antes de marcharnos?

Hotel	Hotel
Do you have a ... for tonight?	¿Tienen una ... para esta noche?
single room	*habitación individual*
double room	*habitación doble*
with bath	con baño
with shower	con ducha
I want to stay for one night/ ... nights.	Quisiera pasar una noche/ ... noches.
I booked a room in the name of ...	Tengo reservada una habitación a nombre de ...
I'd like another room.	Quisiera otra habitación.
What time is breakfast?	¿Cuándo sirven el desayuno?
Can I have breakfast in my room?	¿Podrían traerme el desayuno a la habitación?
Where is ...?	¿Dónde está ...?
the gym	*el gimnasio*
I'd like an alarm call for tomorrow morning at ...	Por favor, despiértenme mañana a las ...
I'd like to get these things washed/cleaned.	¿Puede lavarme/limpiarme esto?
Please bring me ...	Por favor, tráigame ...
... doesn't work.	... no funciona.
Room number ...	Número de habitación ...
Are there any messages for me?	¿Hay mensajes para mí?

I'd like ...	Quisiera ...
Do you have ...?	¿Tienen ...?
Do you have this ...?	¿Lo tiene ...?
in another size	*en otra talla*
in another colour	*en otro color*
I take size ...	Mi talla es la ...
I'm a size $5^1/_2$.	Calzo un cuarenta.
I'll take it.	Me lo quedo.
Do you have anything else?	¿Tienen alguna otra cosa distinta?
That's too expensive.	Es demasiado caro.
I'm just looking.	Sólo estaba mirando.
Do you take credit cards?	¿Aceptan tarjetas de crédito?

Food Shopping / Alimentos

Where is the nearest ...?	¿Dónde hay por aquí cerca ...?
supermarket	*un supermercado*
baker's	*una panadería*
butcher's	*una carnicería*
Where is the market?	¿Dónde está el mercado?
When is the market on?	¿Cuándo hay mercado?
a kilo/pound of ...	un kilo/medio kilo de ...
200 grams of ...	doscientos gramos de ...
... slices of ...	... lonchas de ...
a litre of ...	un litro de ...
a bottle/packet of ...	una botella/un paquete de ...

Post Office / Correos

Where is the nearest post office?	¿Dónde queda la oficina de Correos más cercana?
When does the post office open?	¿Cuándo abre Correos?
Where can I buy stamps?	¿Dónde puedo comprar sellos?

I'd like ... stamps for postcards/letters to Britain/the United States.	Quisiera ... sellos para postales/cartas a Gran Bretaña/Estados Unidos.
I'd like to post/send ...	Quisiera entregar ...
this letter.	esta carta.
this parcel.	este paquete.
By airmail/express mail/ registered mail.	Por avión/por correo urgente/ certificado.
Is there any mail for me?	¿Tengo correo?
Where is the nearest postbox?	¿Dónde hay un buzón de correos por aquí cerca?

Photos and Videos — Vídeo y fotografía

A colour film/slide film, please.	Un carrete en color/un carrete para diapositivas, por favor.
With twenty-four/thirty-six exposures.	De veinticuatro/treinta y seis fotos.
Can I have batteries for this camera, please?	Quisiera pilas para esta cámara, por favor.
The camera is sticking.	La cámara se atasca.
Can you develop this film, please?	Quisiera revelar este carrete.
I'd like the photos ...	Las fotos las quiero ...
matt.	en mate.
glossy.	en brillo.
ten by fifteen centimetres.	en formato de diez por quince.
When will the photos be ready?	¿Cuándo puedo pasar a recoger las fotos?
How much do the photos cost?	¿Cuánto cuesta el revelado?
Could you take a photo of us, please?	¿Podría sacarnos una foto?

Sightseeing	Visitas turísticas
Where is the tourist office?	¿Dónde está la oficina de turismo?
Do you have any leaflets about ...?	¿Tienen folletos sobre ...?
Are there any sightseeing tours of the town?	¿Se organizan visitas por la ciudad?
When is ... open?	¿Cuándo está abierto(-a) ...?
the museum	*el museo*
the church	*la iglesia*
the castle	*el palacio*
How much does it cost to get in?	¿Cuánto cuesta la entrada?
Are there any reductions ...?	¿Hay descuento ...?
for students	*para estudiantes*
for children	*para niños*
for pensioners	*para pensionistas*
for the unemployed	*para desempleados*
Is there a guided tour in English?	¿Hay alguna visita guiada en inglés?
Can I take photos here?	¿Puedo sacar fotos?
Can I film here?	¿Puedo filmar?

Entertainment	Ocio
What is there to do here?	¿Qué se puede hacer por aquí?
Where can we ...?	¿Dónde se puede ...?
go dancing	*bailar*
hear live music	*escuchar música en directo*
Where is there ...?	¿Dónde hay ... ?
a nice bar	*un buen bar*
a good club	*una buena discoteca*
What's on tonight ...?	¿Qué dan esta noche ...?

at the cinema	*en el cine*
at the theatre	*en el teatro*
at the opera	*en la ópera*
at the concert hall	*en la sala de conciertos*
Where can I buy tickets for ...?	¿Dónde puedo comprar entradas para ...?
the theatre	*el teatro*
the concert	*el concierto*
the opera	*la ópera*
the ballet	*el ballet*
How much is it to get in?	¿Cuánto cuesta la entrada?
I'd like a ticket/... tickets for ...	Quisiera una entrada/... entradas para ...
Are there any reductions for ...?	¿Hay descuento para ...?
children	*niños*
pensioners	*pensionistas*
students	*estudiantes*
the unemployed	*desempleados*

At the Beach | En la playa

How deep is the water?	¿Qué profundidad tiene el agua?
Is it safe to swim here?	¿Se puede nadar aquí sin peligro?
Is there a lifeguard?	¿Hay socorrista?
Where can you ...?	¿Dónde se puede ... por aquí?
go surfing	*hacer surf*
go waterskiing	*practicar esquí acuático*
go diving	*bucear*
go paragliding	*hacer parapente*

I'd like to hire ...	*Quisiera alquilar ...*
a deckchair.	*una tumbona.*
a sunshade.	*una sombrilla.*
a surfboard.	*una tabla de surf.*
a jet-ski.	*una moto acuática.*
a rowing boat.	*un bote de remos.*
a pedal boat.	*un patín a pedales.*

Sport | Deporte

Where can we ...?	*¿Dónde se puede ...?*
play tennis/golf	*jugar a tenis/golf*
go swimming	*ir a nadar*
go riding	*montar a caballo*
go fishing	*ir a pescar*
How much is it per hour?	*¿Cuánto cuesta la hora?*
Where can I book a court?	*¿Dónde puedo reservar una pista?*
Where can I hire rackets?	*¿Dónde puedo alquilar raquetas de tenis?*
Where can I hire a rowing boat/a pedal boat?	*¿Dónde puedo alquilar un bote de remos/ un patín a pedales?*
Do you need a fishing permit?	*¿Se necesita un permiso de pesca?*

Skiing | Esquí

Where can I hire skiing equipment?	*¿Dónde puedo alquilar un equipo de esquí?*
I'd like to hire ...	*Quisiera alquilar ...*
downhill skis.	*unos esquís (de descenso).*
cross-country skis.	*unos esquís de fondo.*
ski boots.	*unas botas de esquí.*
ski poles.	*unos bastones de esquí.*

Can you tighten my bindings, please?	¿Podría ajustarme la fijación, por favor?
Where can I buy a ski pass?	¿Dónde puedo comprar el forfait?
I'd like a ski pass ...	Quisiera un forfait ...
for a day.	para un día.
for five days.	para cinco días.
for a week.	para una semana.
How much is a ski pass?	¿Cuánto cuesta el forfait?
When does the first/ last chair-lift leave?	¿Cuándo sale el primer/ el último telesilla?
Do you have a map of the ski runs?	¿Tiene un mapa de las pistas?
Where are the beginners' slopes?	¿Dónde están las pistas para principiantes?
How difficult is this slope?	¿Cuál es la dificultad de esta pista?
Is there a ski school?	¿Hay una escuela de esquí?
Where is the nearest mountain rescue service post?	¿Dónde se encuentra la unidad más próxima de servicio de salvamento?
Where is the nearest mountain hut?	¿Dónde se encuentra el refugio más próximo?
What's the weather forecast?	¿Cuál es el pronóstico del tiempo?
What is the snow like?	¿Cómo es el estado de la nieve?
Is there a danger of avalanches?	¿Hay peligro de aludes?

RESTAURANT	AL RESTAURANTE
A table for ... people, please.	Una mesa para ... personas, por favor.
The ... please.	Por favor, ...
menu	*la carta*
wine list	*la carta de vinos.*
What do you recommend?	¿Qué me recomienda?
Do you have ...?	¿Sirven ...?
any vegetarian dishes	*platos vegetarianos*
children's portions	*raciones para niños*
Does that contain ...?	¿Tiene esto ...?
peanuts	*cacahuetes*
alcohol	*alcohol*
Can you bring (more) ... please?	Por favor, traiga (más) ...
I'll have ...	Para mí ...
The bill, please.	La cuenta, por favor.
All together, please.	Cóbrelo todo junto.
Separate bills, please.	Haga cuentas separadas, por favor.
Keep the change.	Quédese con el cambio.
I didn't order this.	Yo no he pedido esto.
The bill is wrong.	La cuenta está mal.
The food is cold/too salty.	La comida está fría/ demasiado salada.

Where can I make a phone call?	¿Dónde puedo hacer una llamada por aquí cerca?
Where is the nearest card phone?	¿Dónde hay un teléfono de tarjetas cerca de aquí?
Where is the nearest coin box?	¿Dónde hay un teléfono de monedas cerca de aquí?
I'd like a twenty-five euro phone card.	Quisiera una tarjeta de teléfono de veinticinco euros.
I'd like some coins for the phone, please.	Necesito monedas para llamar por teléfono.
I'd like to make a reverse charge call.	Quisiera hacer una llamada a cobro revertido.
Hello.	Hola.
This is ...	Soy ...
Who's speaking, please?	¿Con quién hablo?
Can I speak to Mr/Ms ..., please?	¿Puedo hablar con el señor/la señora ...?
Extension ..., please.	Por favor, póngame con el número ...
I'll phone back later.	Volveré a llamar más tarde.
Can you text me your answer?	¿Puede contestarme con mensaje de móvil?
Where can I charge my mobile phone?	¿Dónde puedo cargar la batería del móvil?
I need a new battery.	Necesito una batería nueva.
Where can I buy a top-up card?	¿Dónde venden tarjetas para móviles?
I can't get a network.	No hay cobertura.

Passport/Customs | Pasaporte/Aduana

Here is ...	Aquí tiene ...
my passport.	mi pasaporte.
my identity card.	mi documento de identidad.
my driving licence.	mi permiso de conducir.
my green card.	mi carta verde.
Here are my vehicle documents.	Aquí tiene la documentación de mi vehículo.
The children are on this passport.	Los niños están incluidos en este pasaporte.
Do I have to pay duty on this?	¿Tengo que declararlo?
This is ...	Esto es ...
a present.	un regalo.
a sample.	una muestra.
This is for my own personal use.	Es para consumo propio.
I'm on my way to ...	Estoy de paso para ir a ...

At the Bank | En el banco

Where can I change money?	¿Dónde puedo cambiar dinero?
Is there a bank/bureau de change here?	¿Hay por aquí un banco/ una casa de cambio?
When is the bank/bureau de change open?	¿Cuándo está abierto el banco/ abierta la casa de cambio?
I'd like ... euros.	Quisiera ... euros.
I'd like to cash these traveller's cheques/ eurocheques.	Quisiera cobrar estos cheques de viaje/eurocheques.

What's the commission?	¿Cuánto cobran de comisión?
Can I use my credit card to get cash?	¿Puedo sacar dinero en efectivo con mi tarjeta de crédito?
Where is the nearest cash machine?	¿Dónde hay por aquí un cajero automático?
The cash machine swallowed my card.	El cajero automático no me ha devuelto la tarjeta.
Can you give me some change, please.	Deme cambio en monedas, por favor.

Repairs / Reparaciones

Where can I get this repaired?	¿Dónde pueden repararme esto?
Can you repair ...?	¿Puede reparar ...?
these shoes	*estos zapatos*
this watch	*este reloj*
this jacket	*esta chaqueta*
Is it worth repairing?	¿Vale la pena repararlo?
How much will the repairs cost?	¿Cuánto cuesta la reparación?
Where can I have my shoes reheeled?	¿Dónde me pueden poner tacones nuevos?
When will it be ready?	¿Cuándo estará listo?
Can you do it straight away?	¿Puede hacerlo ahora mismo?

Emergency Services	Servicios de urgencia
Help!	¡Socorro!
Fire!	¡Fuego!
Please call ...	Por favor, llame a ...
the emergency doctor.	un médico de urgencia.
the fire brigade.	los bomberos.
the police.	la policía.
I need to make an urgent phone call.	Tengo que hacer una llamada urgente.
I need an interpreter.	Necesito un intérprete.
Where is the police station?	¿Dónde está la comisaría?
Where is the nearest hospital?	¿Dónde está el hospital más cercano?
I want to report a theft.	Quisiera denunciar un robo.
... has been stolen.	Han robado ...
There's been an accident.	Ha habido un accidente.
There are ... people injured.	Hay ... heridos.
My location is ...	Estoy en ...
I've been ...	Me han ...
robbed.	robado.
attacked.	atracado.
raped.	violado.
I'd like to phone my embassy.	Quisiera hablar con mi embajada.

Pharmacy | Farmacia

Where is the nearest pharmacy?	¿Dónde hay por aquí una farmacia?
Which pharmacy provides emergency service?	¿Qué farmacia está de guardia?
I'd like something for ...	Quisiera algo para ...
diarrhoea.	*la diarrea.*
a temperature.	*la fiebre.*
travel sickness.	*el mareo.*
a headache.	*el dolor de cabeza.*
a cold.	*el resfriado.*
I'd like ...	Quisiera ...
plasters.	*tiritas.*
a bandage.	*un vendaje.*
some paracetamol.	*paracetamol.*
I can't take ...	Soy alérgico(-a) a la ...
aspirin.	*aspirina.*
penicillin.	*penicilina.*
Is is safe to give to children?	¿Pueden tomarlo los niños?
How should I take it?	¿Cómo tengo que tomarlo?

At the Doctor's | En la consulta médica

I need a doctor.	Necesito que me atienda un médico.
Where is casualty?	¿Dónde está Urgencias?
I have a pain here.	Me duele aquí.
I feel ...	Tengo ...
hot.	*mucho calor.*
cold.	*frío.*
I feel sick.	Me siento mal.
I feel dizzy.	Tengo mareos.

I'm allergic to ...	Tengo alergia a ...
I am ...	Yo ...
pregnant.	*estoy embarazada.*
diabetic.	*soy diabético(-a).*
HIV-positive.	*soy seropositivo(-a).*
I'm on this medication.	Estoy tomando este medicamento.
My blood group is ...	Mi grupo sanguíneo es ...

At the Hospital | En el hospital

Which ward is ... in?	¿En qué unidad está ...?
When are visiting hours?	¿Cuándo son las horas de visita?
I'd like to speak to ...	Quisiera hablar con ...
a doctor.	*un médico.*
a nurse.	*una enfermera.*
When will I be discharged?	¿Cuándo me van a dar de alta?

At the Dentist's | En el dentista

I need a dentist.	Tengo que ir al dentista.
This tooth hurts.	Me duele este diente.
One of my fillings has fallen out.	Se me ha caído un empaste.
I have an abscess.	Tengo un absceso.
I want/don't want an injection for the pain.	Quiero/no quiero que me ponga una inyección para calmar el dolor.
Can you repair my dentures?	¿Me puede reparar la dentadura?
I need a receipt for the insurance.	Necesito un recibo para mi seguro.

Business Travel | Viajes de negocios

I'd like to arrange a meeting with ...	Quisiera concertar hora para una reunión con ...
I have an appointment with Mr/Ms ...	Tengo una cita con el señor/ la señora ...
Here is my card.	Aquí tiene mi tarjeta.
I work for ...	Trabajo para ...
How do I get to ...?	¿Cómo se llega ...?
your office	*a su despacho*
I need an interpreter.	Necesito un intérprete.
Can you copy that for me, please?	Por favor, hágame una copia de eso.
May I use ...?	¿Puedo usar ...?
your phone	*su teléfono*
your computer	*su ordenador*

Disabled Travellers | Minusválidos

Is it possible to visit ... with a wheelchair?	¿La visita a ... es posible también para personas en silla de ruedas?
Where is the wheelchair-accessible entrance?	¿Por dónde se puede entrar con la silla de ruedas?
Is your hotel accessible to wheelchairs?	¿Tiene su hotel acceso para minusválidos?
I need a room ...	Necesito una habitación ...
on the ground floor.	*en la planta baja.*
with wheelchair access.	*con acceso para minusuálidos.*
Do you have a lift for wheelchairs?	¿Tienen ascensor para minusválidos?
Do you have wheelchairs?	¿Tienen sillas de ruedas?

Where is the disabled toilet?	¿Dónde está el lavabo para minusválidos?
Can you help me get on/ off please?	¿Podría ayudarme a subir/ bajar, por favor?
A tyre has burst.	Se ha reventado un neumático.
The battery is flat.	La batería está descargada.
The wheels lock.	Las ruedas se bloquean.

Travelling with children | Viajando con niños

Are children allowed in too?	¿Pueden entrar niños?
Is there a reduction for children?	¿Hay descuento para niños?
Do you have children's portions?	¿Sirven raciones para niños?
Do you have ...?	¿Tienen ...?
a high chair	*una sillita*
a cot	*una cama infantil*
a child's seat	*un asiento infantil*
a baby's changing table	*una mesa para cambiar al bebé*
Where can I change the baby?	¿Dónde puedo cambiar al bebé?
Where can I breast-feed the baby?	¿Dónde puedo dar el pecho al niño?
Can you warm this up, please?	¿Puede calentarlo, por favor?
What is there for children to do?	¿Qué pueden hacer aquí los niños?
Is there a child-minding service?	¿Hay aquí un servicio de guardería?
My son/daughter is ill.	Mi hijo/mi hija está enfermo(-a).

bangers and mash salchichas con puré de patatas, cebolla frita y salsa hecha con jugo de carne asada

banoffee pie tarta rellena de plátano, caramelo y nata

BLT (sandwich) sándwich de bacón, lechuga, tomate y mayonesa

butternut squash variedad de calabaza de color amarillo y sabor dulce, que a menudo se sirve asada

Caesar salad ensalada César

chocolate brownie brownie: pastelito de chocolate y nueces

chowder guiso de pescado

chicken Kiev pollo a la Kiev

chicken nuggets croquetas de pollo

club sandwich sándwich caliente de tres pisos; normalmente relleno de carne, queso, lechuga, tomate y cebollas

cottage pie pastel de carne picada y verduras, cubierto con puré de patatas y queso

English breakfast desayuno inglés: huevos, bacón, salchichas, alubias cocidas, pan frito y champiñones

filo pastry masa de hojaldre

haggis plato escocés a base de hígado y corazón de cordero, avena y otros condimentos, hervidos en una bolsa formada por el estómago del animal

hash browns trocitos de patata sofritos con cebolla, que a menudo se sirven con el desayuno

hotpot estofado de carne, verdura y patatas

Irish stew estofado irlandés, a base de cordero, patatas y cebolla

monkfish rape

oatcake galleta de avellana

pavlova pastel de merengue con frutas y nata

ploughman's lunch almuerzo de pub a base de pan, queso y encurtidos

purée puré

Quorn® proteína vegetal usada como sustituto de carne

Savoy cabbage col rizada

sea bass lubina

Scotch broth sopa de carne, cebada y verduras

Scotch egg huevo duro envuelto en carne de salchicha y rebozado

COMIDA Y BEBIDA

spare ribs costillas de cerdo
spring roll rollito de primavera
Stilton Stilton: queso azul
  inglés
sundae sundae: helado con
  jarabe, nueces y nata
Thousand Island dressing
  salsa rosa
toad in the hole salchichas
  horneadas en una masa de
  huevos, leche y harina

Waldorf salad ensalada
  Waldorf: manzanas
  troceadas, apio, nueces
  y mayonesa
Welsh rarebit tostada
  cubierta con queso derretido
  y huevo
Yorkshire pudding buñuelo,
  a veces relleno de verduras,
  que se sirve acompañando
  al rosbif

adobo, ... en marinated

ajillo, ... al with garlic

arroz negro black rice (with squid in its own ink)

asadillo roasted sliced red peppers in olive oil and garlic

bandeja de quesos cheese platter

brasa, ... a la barbecued

buñuelos type of fritter. Savoury ones are filled with cheese, ham, mussels or prawns. Sweet ones can be filled with fruit

caldereta stew/casserole

cazuela de fideos bean, meat and noodle stew

chilindrón, ... al sauce made with pepper, tomato, fried onions and meat pork or lamb

chistorra spicy sausage from Navarra

chorizo spicy red sausage

chuletón large steak

churros fried batter sticks sprinkled with sugar, usually eaten with thick hot chocolate.

crema catalana similar to crème brûlée

cuajada cream-based dessert like junket, served with honey or sugar

dulces cakes and pastries

empanadilla pasty/small pie filled with meat or fish

empanado breadcrumbed and fried

ensalada de la casa lettuce, tomato and onion salad (may include tuna)

fritura de pescado fried assortment of fish

gazpacho traditional cold tomato soup of southern Spain. Basic ingredients are water, tomatoes, garlic, fresh bread-crumbs, salt, vinegar and olive oil

horno, ...al baked (in oven)

ibéricos traditional Spanish gourmet products; a surtido de ibéricos means assorted products such as cured ham, cheese, chorizo and salchichón

jamón serrano dark red cured ham

leche frita very thick custard dipped into an egg and breadcrumb mixture, fried and served hot

mariscada mixed shellfish

medallón thick steak (medallion)

mollejas sweetbreads

moros y cristianos rice, black beans and onions with garlic sausage

paella Paella varies from region to region but usually consists of rice, chicken, shellfish, vegetables, garlic and saffron. Paella Valenciana contains rabbit, chicken and sometimes eel

parrilla, ... a la grilled

patatas bravas fried diced potatoes mixed with a garlic, oil and vinegar dressing and flavoured with tomatoes and red chilli peppers

pepitoria de pavo/pollo turkey/chicken fricassée

pimientos morrones sweet red peppers

pote thick soup with beans and sausage which has many regional variations

puchero hotpot made from meat or fish

revuelto scrambled eggs often cooked with another ingredient

romesco sauce made traditionally with olive oil, red pepper and bread. Other ingredients are often added, such as almonds and garlic

salsa verde garlic, olive oil and parsley sauce

sofrito basic sauce made with slowly fried onions, garlic and tomato

tapas Bar snacks. A larger portion of tapas is called a ración. A pincho is a tapa on a cocktail stick.

tortilla (española) traditional potato and onion omelette, often served as a tapa

zarzuela de mariscos mixed seafood with wine and saffron

A [eɪ] n (Mus) la m

○ KEYWORD

a [ə] (before vowel or silent h: an) indef art
1 un(a); **a book** un libro; **an apple** una manzana; **she's a doctor** (ella) es médica
2 (instead of the number "one") un(a); **a year ago** hace un año; **a hundred/thousand** etc **pounds** cien/mil etc libras
3 (in expressing ratios, prices etc): **3 a day/week** 3 al día/a la semana; **10 km an hour** 10 km por hora; **£5 a person** £5 por persona; **30p a kilo** 30p el kilo

A2 (BRIT: Scol) n segunda parte de los "A levels"

A.A. n abbr (BRIT: = Automobile Association) ≈ RACE m (SP); (= Alcoholics Anonymous) Alcohólicos Anónimos

A.A.A. (US) n abbr (= American Automobile Association) ≈ RACE m (SP)

aback [əˈbæk] adv: **to be taken ~**
quedar desconcertado

abandon [əˈbændən] vt abandonar; (give up) renunciar a

abattoir [ˈæbətwɑː*] (BRIT) n matadero

abbey [ˈæbɪ] n abadía

abbreviation [əˌbriːvɪˈeɪʃən] n (short form) abreviatura

abdomen [ˈæbdəmən] n abdomen m

abduct [æbˈdʌkt] vt raptar, secuestrar

abide [əˈbaɪd] vt: **I can't ~ it/him** no lo/le puedo ver; **abide by** vt fus atenerse a

ability [əˈbɪlɪtɪ] n habilidad f, capacidad f; (talent) talento

able [ˈeɪbl] adj capaz; (skilled) hábil; **to be ~ to do sth** poder hacer algo

abnormal [æbˈnɔːməl] adj anormal

aboard [əˈbɔːd] adv a bordo ▷ prep a bordo de

abolish [əˈbɒlɪʃ] vt suprimir, abolir

abolition [æbəuˈlɪʃən] n supresión f, abolición f

abort [əˈbɔːt] vt, vi abortar; **abortion** [əˈbɔːʃən] n aborto; **to have an abortion** abortar, hacerse abortar

○ KEYWORD

about [əˈbaut] adv 1 (approximately) más o menos, aproximadamente; **about a hundred/thousand** etc unos(unas) cien/mil etc; **it takes about 10 hours** se tarda unas o más o menos 10 horas; **at about 2 o'clock** sobre las dos; **I've just about finished** casi he terminado
2 (referring to place) por todas partes; **to leave things lying about** dejar las cosas (tiradas) por ahí; **to run about** correr por todas partes; **to walk about** pasearse, ir y venir
3: **to be about to do sth** estar a punto de hacer algo
▷ prep 1 (relating to) de, sobre, acerca de; **a book about London** un libro sobre o acerca de Londres; **what is it**

about? ¿de qué se trata?; **we talked about it** hablamos de eso or ello; **what or how about doing this?** ¿qué tal si hacemos esto?
2 (referring to place) por; **to walk about the town** caminar por la ciudad

above [ə'bʌv] adv encima, por encima, arriba ▷ prep encima de; (greater than: in number) más de; (: in rank) superior a; **mentioned ~** susodicho; **~ all** sobre todo

abroad [ə'brɔːd] adv (to be) en el extranjero; (to go) al extranjero

abrupt [ə'brʌpt] adj (sudden) brusco; (curt) áspero

abscess ['æbses] n absceso

absence ['æbsəns] n ausencia

absent ['æbsənt] adj ausente; **absent-minded** adj distraído

absolute ['æbsəluːt] adj absoluto; **absolutely** [-'luːtlɪ] adv (totally) totalmente; (certainly!) ¡por supuesto (que sí)!

absorb [əb'zɔːb] vt absorber; **to be ~ed in a book** estar absorto en un libro; **absorbent cotton** (us) n algodón m hidrófilo; **absorbing** adj absorbente

abstain [əb'steɪn] vi: **to ~ (from)** abstenerse de

abstract ['æbstrækt] adj abstracto

absurd [əb'səːd] adj absurdo

abundance [ə'bʌndəns] n abundancia

abundant [ə'bʌndənt] adj abundante

abuse [n ə'bjuːs, vb ə'bjuːz] n (insults) insultos mpl, injurias fpl; (ill-treatment) malos tratos mpl; (misuse) abuso ▷ vt insultar; maltratar; abusar de; **abusive** adj ofensivo

abysmal [ə'bɪzməl] adj pésimo; (failure) garrafal; (ignorance) supino

academic [ækə'demɪk] adj académico, universitario; (pej: issue) puramente teórico ▷ n estudioso/a, profesor(a) m/f universitario/a; **academic year** n (Univ) año m

académico; (Scol) año m escolar

academy [ə'kædəmɪ] n (learned body) academia; (school) instituto, colegio; **~ of music** conservatorio

accelerate [æk'seləreɪt] vt, vi acelerar; **acceleration** [æksələ'reɪʃən] n aceleración f; **accelerator** (BRIT) n acelerador m

accent ['æksent] n acento; (fig) énfasis m

accept [ək'sept] vt aceptar; (responsibility, blame) admitir; **acceptable** adj aceptable; **acceptance** n aceptación f

access ['æksɛs] n acceso; **to have ~ to** tener libre acceso a; **accessible** [-'sɛsəbl] adj (place, person) accesible; (knowledge etc) asequible

accessory [æk'sɛsərɪ] n accesorio; (Law): **~ to** cómplice m

accident ['æksɪdənt] n accidente m; (chance event) casualidad f; **by ~** (unintentionally) sin querer; (by chance) por casualidad; **accidental** [æksɪ'dentl] adj accidental, fortuito; **accidentally** [-'dentəlɪ] adv sin querer; por casualidad; **Accident and Emergency Department** n (BRIT) Urgencias fpl; **accident insurance** n seguro contra accidentes

acclaim [ə'kleɪm] vt aclamar, aplaudir ▷ n aclamación f, aplausos mpl

accommodate [ə'kɔmədeɪt] vt (person) alojar, hospedar; (: car, hotel etc) tener cabida para; (oblige, help) complacer

accommodation [əkɔmə'deɪʃən] (us **accommodations**) n alojamiento

accompaniment [ə'kʌmpənɪmənt] n acompañamiento

accompany [ə'kʌmpənɪ] vt acompañar

accomplice [ə'kʌmplɪs] n cómplice mf

accomplish [ə'kʌmplɪʃ] vt (finish) concluir; (achieve) lograr; **accomplishment** n (skill: gen pl)

talento; (*completion*) realización f
accord [əˈkɔːd] n acuerdo
▷vt conceder; **of his own ~**
espontáneamente; **accordance**
n: **in accordance with** de acuerdo
con; **according to** according **to** prep
según; (*in accordance with*) conforme
a; **accordingly** adv (*appropriately*)
de acuerdo con esto; (*as a result*) en
consecuencia
account [əˈkaunt] n (*Comm*)
cuenta; (*report*) informe m; **accounts**
npl (*Comm*) cuentas fpl; **of no ~** de
ninguna importancia; **on ~** a cuenta;
on no ~ bajo ningún concepto; **on ~
of** a causa de, por motivo de; **to take
into ~, take ~ of** tener en cuenta;
account for vt fus (*explain*) explicar;
(*represent*) representar; **accountable**
adj; **accountable (to)** responsable
(ante); **accountant** n contable mf,
contador(a) m/f; **account number** n
(*at bank etc*) número de cuenta
accumulate [əˈkjuːmjuleɪt] vt
acumular ▷vi acumularse
accuracy [ˈækjurəsɪ] n (*of total*)
exactitud f; (*of description etc*)
precisión f
accurate [ˈækjurɪt] adj (*total*) exacto;
(*description*) preciso; (*person*) cuidadoso;
(*device*) de precisión; **accurately** adv
con precisión
accusation [ækjuˈzeɪʃən] n
acusación f
accuse [əˈkjuːz] vt: **to ~ sb (of sth)**
acusar a algn (de algo); **accused** n
(*Law*) acusado/a
accustomed [əˈkʌstəmd] adj: **~ to**
acostumbrado a
ace [eɪs] n as m
ache [eɪk] n dolor m ▷vi doler; **my
head ~s** me duele la cabeza
achieve [əˈtʃiːv] vt (*aim, result*)
alcanzar; (*success*) lograr, conseguir;
achievement n (*completion*)
realización f; (*success*) éxito
acid [ˈæsɪd] adj ácido; (*taste*) agrio ▷n
(*Chem, inf: LSD*) ácido

acknowledge [əkˈnɒlɪdʒ] vt
(*letter: also:* **~ receipt of**) acusar recibo
de; (*fact, situation, person*) reconocer;
acknowledgement n acuse m de
recibo
acne [ˈæknɪ] n acné m
acorn [ˈeɪkɔːn] n bellota
acoustic [əˈkuːstɪk] adj acústico
acquaintance [əˈkweɪntəns] n
(*person*) conocido/a; (*with person,
subject*) conocimiento
acquire [əˈkwaɪə*] vt adquirir;
acquisition [ækwɪˈzɪʃən] n
adquisición f
acquit [əˈkwɪt] vt absolver, exculpar;
to ~ o.s. well salir con éxito
acre [ˈeɪkə*] n acre m
acronym [ˈækrənɪm] n siglas fpl
across [əˈkrɒs] prep (*on the other side
of*) al otro lado de, del otro lado de;
(*crosswise*) a través de ▷adv de un lado
a otro, de una parte a otra; a través,
través; (*measurement*): **the road is 10m
~** la carretera tiene 10m de ancho; **to
run/swim ~** atravesar corriendo/
nadando; **~ from** enfrente de
acrylic [əˈkrɪlɪk] adj acrílico ▷n
acrílica
act [ækt] n acto, acción f; (*of play*)
acto; (*in music hall etc*) número;
(*Law*) decreto, ley f ▷vi (*behave*)
comportarse; (*have effect: drug,
chemical*) hacer efecto; (*Theatre*) actuar;
(*pretend*) fingir; (*take action*) obrar ▷vt
(*part*) hacer el papel de; **in the ~ of:
catch sb in the ~ of ...** pillar a algn en
el momento en que ...; **to ~ as** actuar
or hacer de; **act up** (inf) vi (*person*)
portarse mal; **acting** adj suplente
▷n (*activity*) actuación f; (*profession*)
profesión f de actor
action [ˈækʃən] n acción f, acto;
(*Mil*) acción f, batalla; (*Law*) proceso,
demanda; **out of ~** (*person*) fuera de
combate; (*thing*) estropeado; **to take ~**
tomar medidas; **action replay** n (*TV*)
repetición f
activate [ˈæktɪveɪt] vt activar

active ['æktɪv] adj activo, enérgico; (volcano) en actividad; **actively** adv (participate) activamente; (discourage, dislike) enérgicamente

activist ['æktɪvɪst] n activista m/f

activity [-'tɪvɪtɪ] n actividad f; **activity holiday** n vacaciones con actividades organizadas

actor ['æktə*] n actor m, actriz f

actress ['æktrɪs] n actriz f

actual ['æktjuəl] adj verdadero, real; (emphatic use) propiamente dicho

> ▌ Be careful not to translate **actual** by the Spanish word actual.

actually ['æktjuəlɪ] adv realmente, en realidad; (even) incluso

> ▌ Be careful not to translate **actually** by the Spanish word actualmente.

acupuncture ['ækjupʌŋktʃə*] n acupuntura

acute [ə'kju:t] adj agudo

ad [æd] n abbr = **advertisement**

A.D. adv abbr (= anno Domini) DC

adamant ['ædəmənt] adj firme, inflexible

adapt [ə'dæpt] vt adaptar ▷ vi: to ~ (to) adaptarse (a), ajustarse (a); **adapter** (us **adaptor**) n (Elec) adaptador m; (for several plugs) ladrón m

add [æd] vt añadir, agregar; **add up** (figures) sumar ▷ vi (fig): **it doesn't add up** no tiene sentido; **add up to** vt fus (Math) sumar, ascender a; (fig: mean) querer decir, venir a ser

addict ['ædɪkt] n adicto/a; (enthusiast) entusiasta mf; **addicted** [ə'dɪktɪd] adj: **to be addicted to** ser adicto a, ser fanático de; **addiction** [ə'dɪkʃən] n (to drugs etc) adicción f; **addictive** [ə'dɪktɪv] adj que causa adicción

addition [ə'dɪʃən] n (adding up) adición f; (thing added) añadidura, añadido; **in ~** además, por añadidura; **in ~ to** además de; **additional** adj adicional

additive ['ædɪtɪv] n aditivo

address [ə'drɛs] n dirección f, señas

fpl; (speech) discurso ▷ vt (letter) dirigir; (speak to) dirigirse a, dirigir la palabra a; (problem) tratar; **address book** n agenda (de direcciones)

adequate ['ædɪkwɪt] adj (satisfactory) adecuado; (enough) suficiente

adhere [əd'hɪə*] vi: **to ~ to** (stick to) pegarse a; (fig: abide by) observar; (: belief etc) ser partidario de

adhesive [əd'hi:zɪv] n adhesivo; **adhesive tape** n (BRIT) cinta adhesiva; (us Med) esparadrapo

adjacent [ə'dʒeɪsənt] adj: **~ to** contiguo a, inmediato a

adjective ['ædʒɛktɪv] n adjetivo

adjoining [ə'dʒɔɪnɪŋ] adj contiguo, vecino

adjourn [ə'dʒə:n] vt aplazar ▷ vi suspender

adjust [ə'dʒʌst] vt (change) modificar; (clothing) arreglar; (machine) ajustar ▷ vi: **to ~ (to)** adaptarse (a); **adjustable** adj ajustable; **adjustment** n adaptación f; (to machine, prices) ajuste m

administer [əd'mɪnɪstə*] vt administrar; **administration** [-'treɪʃən] n (management) administración f; (government) gobierno; **administrative** [-trətɪv] adj administrativo

administrator [əd'mɪnɪstreɪtə*] n administrador(a) m/f

admiral ['ædmərəl] n almirante m

admiration [ædmə'reɪʃən] n admiración f

admire [əd'maɪə*] vt admirar; **admirer** n (fan) admirador(a) m/f

admission [əd'mɪʃən] n (to university, club) ingreso; (entry fee) entrada; (confession) confesión f

admit [əd'mɪt] vt confesar; (permit to enter) dejar entrar, dar entrada a; (to club, organization) admitir; (accept: defeat) reconocer; **to be ~ted to hospital** ingresar en el hospital; **admit to** vt fus confesarse culpable de; **admittance** n entrada; **admittedly** adv es cierto que

adolescent [ædəʊˈlɛsnt] adj, n adolescente mf

adopt [əˈdɒpt] vt adoptar; **adopted** adj adoptivo; **adoption** [əˈdɒpʃən] n adopción f

adore [əˈdɔː*] vt adorar

adorn [əˈdɔːn] vt adornar

Adriatic [eɪdrɪˈætɪk] n: **the ~ (Sea)** el (Mar) Adriático

adrift [əˈdrɪft] adv a la deriva

ADSL abbr (= asymmetrical digital subscriber line) ADSL m

adult [ˈædʌlt] n adulto/a ▷ adj (grown-up) adulto; (for adults) para adultos; **adult education** n educación f para adultos

adultery [əˈdʌltərɪ] n adulterio

advance [ədˈvɑːns] n (progress) adelanto, progreso; (money) anticipo, préstamo; (Mil) avance n ▷ adj: **~ booking** venta anticipada; **~ warning** previo aviso ▷ vt (money) anticipar; (theory, idea) proponer (para la discusión) ▷ vi avanzar, adelantarse; **to make ~s (to sb)** hacer proposiciones (a algn); **in ~** por adelantado; **advanced** adj avanzado; (Scol: studies) superior

advantage [ədˈvɑːntɪdʒ] n (also Tennis) ventaja; **to take ~ of** (person) aprovecharse de; (opportunity) aprovechar

advent [ˈædvənt] n advenimiento; **A~** Adviento

adventure [ədˈvɛntʃə*] n aventura; **adventurous** [-tʃərəs] adj atrevido; aventurero

adverb [ˈædvəːb] n adverbio

adversary [ˈædvəsərɪ] n adversario, contrario

adverse [ˈædvəːs] adj adverso, contrario

advert [ˈædvəːt] (BRIT) n abbr = **advertisement**

advertise [ˈædvətaɪz] vi anunciar, hacer publicidad; **to ~ for** buscar por

medio de anuncios ▷ vt anunciar; **advertisement** [ədˈvəːtɪsmənt] n (Comm) anuncio; **advertiser** n anunciante mf; **advertising** n publicidad f, anuncios mpl; (industry) industria publicitaria

advice [ədˈvaɪs] n consejo, consejos mpl; (notification) aviso; **a piece of ~** un consejo; **to take legal ~** consultar con un abogado

advisable [ədˈvaɪzəbl] adj aconsejable, conveniente

advise [ədˈvaɪz] vt aconsejar; (inform) to ~ **sb of sth** informar a algn de algo; **to ~ sb against sth/doing sth** desaconsejar algo a algn/aconsejar a algn que no haga algo; **adviser, advisor** n consejero/a; (consultant) asesor/a m/f; **advisory** adj consultivo

advocate [vb ˈædvəkeɪt, n -kɪt] vt abogar por ▷ n (lawyer) abogado/a; (supporter): **~ of** defensor/a m/f de

Aegean [iːˈdʒiːən] n: **the ~ (Sea)** el (Mar) Egeo

aerial [ˈɛərɪəl] n antena ▷ adj aéreo

aerobics [ɛəˈrəʊbɪks] n aerobic m

aeroplane [ˈɛərəpleɪn] (BRIT) n avión m

aerosol [ˈɛərəsɒl] n aerosol m

affair [əˈfɛə*] n asunto; (also: love ~) aventura (amorosa)

affect [əˈfɛkt] vt (influence) afectar, influir en; (afflict, concern) afectar; (move) conmover; **affected** adj afectado; **affection** n afecto, cariño; **affectionate** adj afectuoso, cariñoso

afflict [əˈflɪkt] vt afligir

affluent [ˈæfluənt] adj (wealthy) acomodado; **the ~ society** la sociedad opulenta

afford [əˈfɔːd] vt (provide) proporcionar; **can we ~ (to buy) it?** ¿tenemos bastante dinero para comprarlo?; **affordable** adj asequible

Afghanistan [æfˈɡænɪstæn] n Afganistán m

afraid [əˈfreɪd] adj: **to be ~ of** (person) tener miedo a; (thing) tener miedo de;

to be ~ to tener miedo de, temer; **I am ~ that** me temo que; **I am ~ not/so** lo siento, pero no/es así

Africa ['æfrɪkə] *n* África; **African** *adj, n* africano/a *m/f*; **African-American** *adj, n* afroamericano/a

after ['ɑːftə*] *prep (time)* después de; *(place, order)* detrás de, tras ▷ *adv* después ▷ *conj* después (de) que; **what/who are you ~?** ¿qué/a quién busca usted?; **~ having done/he left** después de haber hecho/después de que se marchó; **to name sb ~ sb** llamar a algn por algn; **it's twenty ~ eight** *(us)* son las ocho y veinte; **to ask ~ sb** preguntar por algn; **~ all** después de todo, al fin y al cabo; **~ you!** ¡pase usted!; **after-effects** *npl* consecuencias *fpl*, efectos *mpl*; **aftermath** *n* consecuencias *fpl*, resultados *mpl*; **afternoon** *n* tarde *f*; **after-shave (lotion)** *n* aftershave *m*; **aftersun (lotion/cream)** *n* loción *f*/crema para después del sol, aftersun *m*; **afterwards** *(us* afterward*)* *adv* después, más tarde

again [ə'gɛn] *adv* otra vez, de nuevo; **to do sth ~** volver a hacer algo; **~ and ~** una y otra vez

against [ə'gɛnst] *prep (in opposition to)* en contra de; *(leaning on, touching)* contra, junto a

age [eɪdʒ] *n* edad *f; (period)* época ▷ *vi* envejecer(se) ▷ *vt* envejecer; **she is 20 years of ~** tiene 20 años; **to come of ~** llegar a la mayoría de edad; **it's been ~s since I saw you** hace siglos que no te veo; **~d 10** de 10 años de edad; **age group** *n*: **to be in the same age group** tener la misma edad; **age limit** *n* edad *f* mínima (or máxima)

agency ['eɪdʒənsɪ] *n* agencia

agenda [ə'dʒɛndə] *n* orden *m* del día
  Be careful not to translate **agenda** by the Spanish word *agenda*.

agent ['eɪdʒənt] *n* agente *mf; (Comm: holding concession)* representante *mf*, delegado/a; *(Chem,*

fig) agente *m*

aggravate ['ægrəveɪt] *vt (situation)* agravar; *(person)* irritar

aggression [ə'grɛʃən] *n* agresión *f*

aggressive [ə'grɛsɪv] *adj (belligerent)* agresivo; *(assertive)* enérgico

agile ['ædʒaɪl] *adj* ágil

agitated ['ædʒɪteɪtɪd] *adj* agitado

AGM *n abbr (= annual general meeting)* asamblea anual

ago [ə'gəu] *adv*: **2 days ~** hace 2 días; **not long ~** hace poco; **how long ~?** ¿hace cuánto tiempo?

agony ['ægənɪ] *n (pain)* dolor *m* agudo; *(distress)* angustia; **to be in ~** retorcerse de dolor

agree [ə'griː] *vt (price, date)* acordar, quedar en ▷ *vi (have same opinion)*: **to ~ (with/that)** estar de acuerdo (con/que); *(correspond)* coincidir, concordar; *(consent)* acceder; **to ~ with** *(person)* estar de acuerdo con, ponerse de acuerdo con; *(: food)* sentar bien a; *(Ling)* concordar con; **to ~ to sth/to do sth** consentir en algo/aceptar hacer algo; **to ~ that** *(admit)* estar de acuerdo en que; **agreeable** *adj (sensation)* agradable; *(person)* simpático; *(willing)* de acuerdo, conforme; **agreed** *adj (time, place)* convenido; **agreement** *n* acuerdo; *(contract)* contrato; **in agreement** de acuerdo, conforme

agricultural [ægrɪ'kʌltʃərəl] *adj* agrícola

agriculture ['ægrɪkʌltʃə*] *n* agricultura

ahead [ə'hɛd] *adv (in front)* delante; *(into the future)*: **she had no time to think ~** no tenía tiempo de hacer planes para el futuro; **~ of** delante de; *(in advance of)* antes de; **~ of time** antes de la hora; **go right** *or* **straight ~** *(direction)* siga adelante; *(permission)* hazlo (*or* hágalo)

aid [eɪd] *n* ayuda, auxilio; *(device)* aparato ▷ *vt* ayudar, auxiliar; **in ~ of** a beneficio de

aide [eɪd] *n (person, also Mil)* ayudante

mf

AIDS [eɪdz] n abbr (= acquired immune deficiency syndrome) SIDA m

ailing ['eɪlɪŋ] adj (person, economy) enfermizo

ailment ['eɪlmənt] n enfermedad f, achaque m

aim [eɪm] vt (gun, camera) apuntar; (missile, remark) dirigir; (blow) asestar ▷ vi (also: **take** ~) apuntar ▷ n (in shooting: skill) puntería; (objective) propósito, meta; **to** ~ **at** (with weapon) apuntar a; (objective) aspirar a, pretender; **to** ~ **to do** tener la intención de hacer

ain't [eɪnt] (inf) = **am not; aren't; isn't**

air [ɛəʳ] n (appearance) aspecto ▷ vt (room) ventilar; (clothes, ideas) airear ▷ cpd aéreo; **to throw sth into the** ~ (ball etc) lanzar algo al aire; **by** ~ (travel) en avión; **to be on the** ~ (Radio, TV) estar en antena; **airbag** n airbag m inv; **airbed** (BRIT) n colchón m neumático; **airborne** adj (in the air) en el aire; **as soon as the plane was airborne** tan pronto como el avión estuvo en el aire; **air-conditioned** adj climatizado; **air conditioning** n aire acondicionado; **aircraft** n inv avión m; **airfield** n campo de aviación; **Air Force** n fuerzas fpl aéreas, aviación f; **air hostess** (BRIT) n azafata; **airing cupboard** n (BRIT) armario m para oreo; **airlift** n puente m aéreo; **airline** n línea aérea; **airliner** n avión m de pasajeros; **airmail** n: **by airmail** por avión; **airplane** (US) n avión m; **airport** n aeropuerto; **air raid** n ataque m aéreo; **airsick** adj: **to be airsick** marearse (en avión); **airspace** n espacio aéreo; **airstrip** n pista de aterrizaje; **air terminal** n terminal f; **airtight** adj hermético; **air-traffic controller** n controlador(a) m/f aéreo/a; **airy** adj (room) bien ventilado; (fig: manner) desenfadado

aisle [aɪl] n (of church) nave f; (of theatre, supermarket) pasillo; **aisle seat**

n (on plane) asiento de pasillo

ajar [ə'dʒɑːʳ] adj entreabierto

à la carte [a:la:'kɑːt] adv a la carta

alarm [ə'lɑːm] n (in shop, bank) alarma; (anxiety) inquietud f ▷ vt asustar, inquietar; **alarm call** n (in hotel etc) alarma; **alarm clock** n despertador m; **alarmed** adj (person) alarmado, asustado; (house, car etc) con alarma; **alarming** adj alarmante

Albania [æl'beɪnɪə] n Albania

albeit [ɔːl'biːɪt] conj aunque

album ['ælbəm] n álbum m; (L.P.) elepé m

alcohol ['ælkəhɒl] n alcohol m; **alcohol-free** adj sin alcohol; **alcoholic** [-'hɒlɪk] adj, n alcohólico/a m/f

alcove ['ælkəʊv] n nicho, hueco

ale [eɪl] n cerveza

alert [ə'lɜːt] adj (attentive) atento; (to danger, opportunity) alerta ▷ n alerta m, alarma ▷ vt poner sobre aviso; **to be on the** ~ (also Mil) estar alerta or sobre aviso

algebra ['ældʒɪbrə] n álgebra

Algeria [æl'dʒɪərɪə] n Argelia

alias ['eɪlɪəs] adv alias, conocido por ▷ n (of criminal) apodo; (of writer) seudónimo

alibi ['ælɪbaɪ] n coartada

alien ['eɪlɪən] n (foreigner) extranjero; a; (extraterrestrial) extraterrestre mf ▷ adj: ~ **to** ajeno a; **alienate** vt enajenar, alejar

alight [ə'laɪt] adj ardiendo; (eyes) brillante ▷ vi (person) apearse, bajar; (bird) posarse

align [ə'laɪn] vt alinear

alike [ə'laɪk] adj semejantes, iguales ▷ adv igualmente, del mismo modo; **to look** ~ parecerse

alive [ə'laɪv] adj vivo; (lively) alegre

○ KEYWORD

all [ɔːl] adj (sg) todo/a; (pl) todos/as; **all day** todo el día; **all night** toda la noche; **all men** todos los hombres;

Allah | 300

all five came vinieron los cinco; **all the books** todos los libros; **all his life** toda su vida
▷ *pron* 1 todo; **I ate it all, I ate all of it** me lo comí todo; **all of us went** fuimos todos; **all the boys went** fueron todos los chicos; **is that all?** ¿eso es todo?, ¿algo más?; (*in shop*) ¿algo más?, ¿alguna cosa más?
2 (*in phrases*): **above all** sobre todo; por encima de todo; **after all** después de todo; **at all**: **not at all** (*in answer to question*) en absoluto; (*in answer to thanks*) ¡de nada!, ¡no hay de qué!; **I'm not at all tired** no estoy nada cansado/a; **anything at all will do** cualquier cosa viene bien; **all in all** a fin de cuentas
▷ *adv*: **all alone** completamente solo/a; **it's not as hard as all that** no es tan difícil como lo pintas; **all the more/the better** tanto más/mejor; **all but** casi; **the score is 2 all** están empatados a 2

Allah ['ælə] *n* Alá *m*
allegation [ælɪ'geɪʃən] *n* alegato *m*
alleged [ə'ledʒd] *adj* supuesto, presunto; **allegedly** *adv* supuestamente, según se afirma
allegiance [ə'liːdʒəns] *n* lealtad *f*
allergic [ə'lɜːdʒɪk] *adj*: ~ **to** alérgico a
allergy ['ælədʒɪ] *n* alergia *f*
alleviate [ə'liːvɪeɪt] *vt* aliviar
alley ['ælɪ] *n* callejuela
alliance [ə'laɪəns] *n* alianza
allied ['ælaɪd] *adj* aliado
alligator ['ælɪgeɪtə*] *n* (*Zool*) caimán *m*
all-in (*BRIT*) ['ɔːlɪn] *adj*, *adv* (*charge*) todo incluido
allocate ['æləkeɪt] *vt* (*money etc*) asignar
allot [ə'lɒt] *vt* asignar
all-out ['ɔːlaut] *adj* (*effort etc*) supremo
allow [ə'lau] *vt* permitir, dejar; (*a claim*) admitir; (*sum, time etc*)

dar, conceder; (*concede*): **to ~ that** reconocer que; **to ~ sb to do** permitir a algn hacer; **he is ~ed to ...** se le permite ...; **allow for** *vt fus* tener en cuenta;
allowance *n* subvención *f*; (*welfare payment*) subsidio, pensión *f*; (*pocket money*) dinero de bolsillo; (*tax allowance*) desgravación *f*; **to make allowances for** (*person*) disculpar a; (*thing*) tener en cuenta
all right *adv* bien; (*as answer*) ¡conforme!, ¡está bien!
ally ['ælaɪ] *n* aliado ▷ *vt*: **to ~ o.s. with** aliarse con
almighty [ɔːl'maɪtɪ] *adj* todopoderoso; (*row etc*) imponente
almond ['ɑːmənd] *n* almendra
almost ['ɔːlməust] *adv* casi
alone [ə'ləun] *adj*, *adv* solo; **to leave sb** – dejar a algn en paz; **to leave sth** – no tocar algo, dejar sin tocar; **let** – ... y mucho menos ...
along [ə'lɒŋ] *prep* a lo largo de, por ▷ *adv*: **is he coming ~ with us?** ¿viene con nosotros?; **he was limping** ~ iba cojeando; ~ **with** junto con; **all** – (*all the time*) desde el principio; **alongside** *prep* al lado de ▷ *adv* al lado
aloof [ə'luːf] *adj* reservado ▷ *adv*: **to stand** ~ mantenerse apartado
aloud [ə'laud] *adv* en voz alta
alphabet ['ælfəbet] *n* alfabeto
Alps [ælps] *npl*: **the** ~ los Alpes
already [ɔːl'redɪ] *adv* ya
alright ['ɔːl'raɪt] (*BRIT*) *adv* = **all right**
also ['ɔːlsəu] *adv* también, además
altar ['ɔltə*] *n* altar *m*
alter ['ɔltə*] *vt* cambiar, modificar ▷ *vi* cambiar; **alteration** [ɔltə'reɪʃən] *n* cambio; (*to clothes*) arreglo; (*to building*) arreglos *mpl*
alternate [*adj* ɔl'tɜːnɪt, *vb* 'ɔltəːneɪt] *adj* (*actions etc*) alternativo; (*events*) alterno; (*us*) = **alternative** ▷ *vi*: **to ~ (with)** alternar (con); **on ~ days** un día sí y otro no
alternative [ɔl'tɜːnətɪv] *adj* alternativo ▷ *n* alternativa; ~

medicine medicina alternativa;
alternatively adv: **alternatively one
could ...** por otra parte se podría ...
although [ɔːlˈðəu] conj aunque
altitude [ˈæltɪtjuːd] n altura
altogether [ɔːltəˈgeðəˈ] adv
completamente, del todo; (on the
whole) en total, en conjunto
aluminium [æljuˈmɪnɪəm] (BRIT),
aluminum [əˈluːmɪnəm] (US) n
aluminio
always [ˈɔːlweɪz] adv siempre
Alzheimer's (disease)
[ˈæltshaɪməz-] n enfermedad f de
Alzheimer
am [æm] vb see be
amalgamate [əˈmælɡəmeɪt] vi
amalgamarse ▷ vt amalgamar, unir
amass [əˈmæs] vt amontonar,
acumular
amateur [ˈæmətəˈ] n aficionado/a,
amateur mf
amaze [əˈmeɪz] vt asombrar, pasmar;
to be ~d (at) quedar pasmado (de);
amazed adj asombrado; **amazement**
n asombro, sorpresa; **amazing** adj
extraordinario; (fantastic) increíble
Amazon [ˈæmɜzən] n (Geo)
Amazonas m
ambassador [æmˈbæsədəˈ] n
embajador(a) m/f
amber [ˈæmbəˈ] n ámbar m; **at ~**
(BRIT Aut) (en) el amarillo
ambiguous [æmˈbɪɡjuəs] adj
ambiguo
ambition [æmˈbɪʃən] n ambición f;
ambitious [-ʃəs] adj ambicioso
ambulance [ˈæmbjuləns] n
ambulancia
ambush [ˈæmbuʃ] n emboscada ▷ vt
tender una emboscada a
amen [ɑːˈmen] excl amén
amend [əˈmend] vt enmendar; **to
make ~s** dar cumplida satisfacción;
amendment n enmienda
amenities [əˈmiːnɪtɪz] npl
comodidades fpl
America [əˈmerɪkə] n (USA)

Estados mpl Unidos; **American** adj, n
norteamericano/a; estadounidense
mf; **American football** n (BRIT) fútbol
m americano
amicable [ˈæmɪkəbl] adj amistoso,
amigable
amid(st) [əˈmɪd(st)] prep entre, en
medio de
ammunition [æmjuˈnɪʃən] n
municiones fpl
amnesty [ˈæmnɪstɪ] n amnistía
among(st) [əˈmʌŋ(st)] prep entre,
en medio de
amount [əˈmaunt] n (gen) cantidad
f; (of bill etc) suma, importe m ▷ vi: **to
~ to** sumar; (be same as) equivaler a,
significar
amp(ère) [ˈæmp(ɛəˈ)] n amperio
ample [ˈæmpl] adj (large) grande;
(abundant) abundante; (enough)
bastante, suficiente
amplifier [ˈæmplɪfaɪəˈ] n
amplificador m
amputate [ˈæmpjuteɪt] vt amputar
Amtrak [ˈæmtræk] (US) n empresa
nacional de ferrocarriles de los EEUU
amuse [əˈmjuːz] vt divertir; (distract)
distraer, entretener; **amusement**
n diversión f; (pastime) pasatiempo;
(laughter) risa; **amusement arcade** n
salón m de juegos; **amusement park** n
parque m de atracciones
amusing [əˈmjuːzɪŋ] adj divertido
an [æn] indef art see a
anaemia [əˈniːmɪə] (US anemia) n
anemia
anaemic [əˈniːmɪk] (US anemic) adj
anémico; (fig) soso, insípido
anaesthetic [ænɪsˈθetɪk] (US
anesthetic) n anestesia
analog(ue) [ˈænəlɔɡ] adj (computer,
watch) analógico
analogy [əˈnælədʒɪ] n analogía
analyse [ˈænəlaɪz] (US analyze)
vt analizar; **analysis** [əˈnæləsɪs] (pl
analyses) n análisis m inv; **analyst**
[-lɪst] n (political analyst, psychoanalyst)
analista mf

analyze ['ænəlaɪz] (US) vt = **analyse**

anarchy ['ænəkɪ] n anarquía, desorden m

anatomy [ə'nætəmɪ] n anatomía

ancestor ['ænsɪstə*] n antepasado

anchor ['æŋkə*] n ancla, áncora ▷ vi (also: **to drop ~**) anclar ▷ vt anclar; **to weigh ~** levar anclas

anchovy ['æntʃəvɪ] n anchoa

ancient ['eɪnʃənt] adj antiguo

and [ænd] conj y; (before i-, hi- + consonant) e; **men ~ women** hombres y mujeres; **father ~ son** padre e hijo; **trees ~ grass** árboles y hierba; **~ so on** etcétera, y así sucesivamente; **try ~ come** procura venir; **he talked ~ talked** habló sin parar; **better ~ better** cada vez mejor

Andes ['ændiːz] npl: **the ~** los Andes

Andorra [æn'dɔːrə] n Andorra

anemia etc [ə'niːmɪə] (US) = **anaemia** etc

anesthetic [ænɪs'θetɪk] (US) = **anaesthetic**

angel ['eɪndʒəl] n ángel m

anger ['æŋgə*] n cólera

angina [æn'dʒaɪnə] n angina (del pecho)

angle ['æŋgl] n ángulo; **from their ~** desde su punto de vista

angler ['æŋglə*] n pescador(a) m/f (de caña)

Anglican ['æŋglɪkən] adj, n anglicano/a m/f

angling ['æŋglɪŋ] n pesca con caña

angrily ['æŋgrɪlɪ] adv coléricamente, airadamente

angry ['æŋgrɪ] adj enfadado, airado; (wound) inflamado; **to be ~ with sb/at sth** estar enfadado con algn/por algo; **to get ~** enfadarse, enojarse

anguish ['æŋgwɪʃ] n (physical) tormentos mpl; (mental) angustia

animal ['ænɪməl] n animal m; (pej: person) bestia ▷ adj animal

animated [-meɪtɪd] adj animado

animation [ænɪ'meɪʃən] n animación f

aniseed ['ænɪsiːd] n anís m

ankle ['æŋkl] n tobillo

annex [n 'æneks, vb ə'neks] n (BRIT: also: **-e**: building) edificio anexo ▷ vt (territory) anexionar

anniversary [ænɪ'vɜːsərɪ] n aniversario

announce [ə'nauns] vt anunciar; **announcement** n anuncio; (official) declaración f; **announcer** n (Radio) locutor(a) m/f; (TV) presentador(a) m/f

annoy [ə'nɔɪ] vt molestar, fastidiar; **don't get ~ed!** ¡no se enfade!; **annoying** adj molesto, fastidioso; (person) pesado

annual ['ænjuəl] adj anual ▷ n (Bot) anual m; (book) anuario; **annually** adv anualmente, cada año

annum ['ænəm] n see **per**

anonymous [ə'nɒnɪməs] adj anónimo

anorak ['ænəræk] n anorak m

anorexia [ænə'reksɪə] n (Med: also: **~ nervosa**) anorexia

anorexic [ænə'reksɪk] adj, n anoréxico/a m/f

another [ə'nʌðə*] adj (one more, a different one) otro ▷ pron otro; see **one**

answer ['ɑːnsə*] n contestación f, respuesta; (to problem) solución f ▷ vi contestar, responder ▷ vt (reply to) contestar a, responder a; (problem) resolver; (prayer) escuchar; **in ~ to your letter** contestando or en contestación a su carta; **to ~ the phone** contestar or coger el teléfono; **to ~ the bell** or **the door** acudir a la puerta; **answer back** vi replicar, ser respondón/ ona; **answerphone** n (esp BRIT) contestador m (automático)

ant [ænt] n hormiga

Antarctic [ænt'ɑːktɪk] n: **the ~** el Antártico

antelope ['æntɪləup] n antílope m

antenatal ['æntɪ'neɪtl] adj antenatal, prenatal

antenna [æn'tenə, pl -niː] (pl **antennae**) n antena

anthem [ˈænθəm] n: **national ~**
himno nacional

anthology [ænˈθɒlədʒɪ] n
antología

anthrax [ˈænθræks] n ántrax m

anthropology [ænθrəˈpɒlədʒɪ] n
antropología

anti [ˈæntɪ] prefix anti; **antibiotic**
[-baɪˈɒtɪk] n antibiótico; **antibody**
[ˈæntɪbɒdɪ] n anticuerpo

anticipate [ænˈtɪsɪpeɪt] vt prever;
(expect) esperar, contar con; (look
forward to) esperar con ilusión; (do
first) anticiparse a, adelantarse a;
anticipation [-ˈpeɪʃən] n (expectation)
previsión f; (eagerness) ilusión f,
expectación f

anticlimax [æntɪˈklaɪmæks] n
decepción f

anticlockwise [æntɪˈklɒkwaɪz]
(BRIT) adv en dirección
contraria a la de las agujas
del reloj

antics [ˈæntɪks] npl gracias
fpl

anti: antidote [ˈæntɪdəʊt] n
antídoto; **antifreeze** [ˈæntɪfriːz] n
anticongelante m; **antihistamine**
[-ˈhɪstəmiːn] n antihistamínico;
antiperspirant [ˈæntɪpɜːspɪrənt] n
antitranspirante m

antique [ænˈtiːk] n antigüedad f
▷ adj antiguo; **antique shop** n tienda
de antigüedades

antiseptic [æntɪˈsɛptɪk] adj, n
antiséptico

antisocial [æntɪˈsəʊʃəl] adj
antisocial

antivirus [æntɪˈvaɪərəs] adj (program,
software) antivirus inv

antlers [ˈæntləz] npl cuernas fpl,
cornamenta sg

anxiety [æŋˈzaɪətɪ] n inquietud
f; (Med) ansiedad f; **~ to do** deseo
de hacer

anxious [ˈæŋkʃəs] adj inquieto,
preocupado; (worrying) preocupante;
(keen): **to be ~ to do** tener muchas

ganas de hacer

○ **KEYWORD**

any [ˈɛnɪ] adj ₁ (in questions etc)
algún/alguna; **have you any butter/**
children? ¿tienes mantequilla/
hijos?; **if there are any tickets left** si
quedan billetes, si queda algún
billete

₂ (with negative): **I haven't any money/**
books no tengo dinero/libros

₃ (no matter which) cualquier; **any**
excuse will do valdrá or servirá
cualquier excusa; **choose any book**
you like escoge el libro que quieras

₄ (in phrases): **in any case** de todas
formas, en cualquier caso; **any day**
now cualquier día (de estos); **at any**
moment en cualquier momento, de
un momento a otro; **at any rate** en
todo caso; **any time: come (at) any**
time ven cuando quieras; **he might**
come (at) any time podría llegar de un
momento a otro

▷ pron ₁ (in questions etc): **have you got**
any? ¿tienes alguno(s)/a(s)?; **can any**
of you sing? ¿sabe cantar alguno de
vosotros/ustedes?

₂ (with negative): **I haven't any (of**
them) no tengo ninguno

₃ (no matter which one(s)): **take any of**
those books (you like) toma el libro
que quieras de ésos

▷ adv ₁ (in questions etc): **do you**
want any more soup/sandwiches?
¿quieres más sopa/bocadillos?; **are**
you feeling any better? ¿te sientes
algo mejor?

₂ (with negative): **I can't hear him any**
more ya no le oigo; **don't wait any**
longer no esperes más

any: anybody pron cualquiera;
(in interrogative sentences) alguien;
(in negative sentences): **I don't see**
anybody no veo a nadie; **if anybody**
should phone ... si llama alguien

...; **anyhow** adv (at any rate) de todos modos, de todas formas; (haphazard): **to do it anyhow you like** hazlo como quieras; **she leaves things just anyhow** deja las cosas como quiera or de cualquier modo; **I shall go anyhow** de todos modos iré; **anyone** pron = **anybody**; **anything** pron (in questions etc) algo, alguna cosa; (with negative) nada; **can you see anything?** ¿ves algo?; **if you happens to me** ... si algo me ocurre...; (no matter what): **you can say anything you like** puedes decir lo que quieras; **anything will do** vale todo or cualquier cosa; **he'll eat anything** come de todo or lo que sea; **anytime** adv (at any moment) en cualquier momento, de un momento a otro; (whenever) no importa cuándo, cuando quiera; **anyway** adv (at any rate) de todos modos, de todas formas; **I shall go anyway** iré de todos modos; (besides): **anyway, I couldn't come even if I wanted to** además, no podría venir aunque quisiera; **why are you phoning, anyway?** ¿entonces, por qué llamas?, ¿por qué llamas, pues?; **anywhere** adv (in questions etc): **can you see him anywhere?** ¿le ves por algún lado?; **are you going anywhere?** ¿vas a algún sitio?; (with negative): **I can't see him anywhere** no le veo por ninguna parte; **anywhere in the world** en cualquier parte (del mundo); **put the books down anywhere** deja los libros donde quieras

apart [ə'pɑːt] adv (aside) aparte; (situation): **~ (from)** separado (de); (movement): **to pull ~** separar; **10 miles ~** separados por 10 millas; **to take ~** desmontar; **~ from** prep aparte de

apartment [ə'pɑːtmənt] n (us) piso (sp), departamento (LAM), apartamento; (room) cuarto; **apartment building** (us) n edificio de apartamentos

apathy ['æpəθɪ] n apatía,

indiferencia

ape [eɪp] n mono ▷ vt imitar, remedar

aperitif [ə'perɪtɪf] n aperitivo

aperture ['æpətʃjuə*] n rendija, resquicio; (Phot) abertura

APEX ['eɪpeks] n abbr (= Advanced Purchase Excursion Fare) tarifa f APEX

apologize [ə'pɒlədʒaɪz] vi: **to ~ (for sth to sb)** disculparse (con algn de algo)

apology [ə'pɒlədʒɪ] n disculpa, excusa

> Be careful not to translate **apology** by the Spanish word *apología*.

apostrophe [ə'pɒstrəfɪ] n apóstrofo

appal [ə'pɔːl] (us **appall**) vt horrorizar, espantar; **appalling** adj espantoso; (awful) pésimo

apparatus [æpə'reɪtəs] n (equipment) equipo; (organization) aparato; (in gymnasium) aparatos mpl

apparent [ə'pærənt] adj aparente; (obvious) evidente; **apparently** adv aparentemente; por lo visto, al parecer

appeal [ə'piːl] vi (Law) apelar ▷ n (Law) apelación f; (request) llamamiento; (plea) petición f; (charm) atractivo; **to ~ for** reclamar; **to ~ to** (be attractive to) atraer; **it doesn't ~ to me** no me atrae, no me llama la atención; **appealing** adj (attractive) atractivo

appear [ə'pɪə*] vi aparecer, presentarse; (Law) comparecer; (publication) salir (a luz), publicarse; (seem) parecer; **to ~ on TV/in "Hamlet"** salir por la tele/hacer un papel en "Hamlet"; **it would ~ that** parecería que; **appearance** n aparición f; (look) apariencia, aspecto

appendices [ə'pendɪsiːz] npl of **appendix**

appendicitis [əpendɪ'saɪtɪs] n apendicitis f

appendix [ə'pendɪks] (pl **appendices**) n apéndice m

appetite ['æpɪtaɪt] n apetito; (fig) deseo, anhelo

appetizer [ˈæpɪtaɪzəʳ] n (drink) aperitivo; (food) tapas fpl (SP)

applaud [əˈplɔːd] vt, vi aplaudir

applause [əˈplɔːz] n aplausos mpl

apple [ˈæpl] n manzana; **apple pie** n pastel m de manzana, pay m de manzana (LAM)

appliance [əˈplaɪəns] n aparato

applicable [əˈplɪkəbl] adj (relevant): **to be ~ (to)** referirse (a)

applicant [ˈæplɪkənt] n candidato/ a; solicitante mf

application [æplɪˈkeɪʃən] n aplicación f; (for a job etc) solicitud f, petición f; **application form** n solicitud f

apply [əˈplaɪ] vt (paint etc) poner; (law etc: put into practice) poner en vigor ▷ vi: **to ~ to** (ask) dirigirse a; (be applicable) ser aplicable a; **to ~ for** (permit, grant, job) solicitar; **to ~ o.s. to** aplicarse a, dedicarse a

appoint [əˈpɔɪnt] vt (to post) nombrar a

> Be careful not to translate **appoint** by the Spanish word **apuntar**.

appointment n (with client) cita; (act) nombramiento; (post) puesto; (at hairdresser etc): **to have an appointment** tener hora; **to make an appointment (with sb)** citarse (con algn)

appraisal [əˈpreɪzl] n valoración f

appreciate [əˈpriːʃieɪt] vt apreciar, tener en mucho; (be grateful for) agradecer; (be aware) comprender ▷ vi (Comm) aumentar(se) en valor; **appreciation** [-ˈeɪʃən] n apreciación f; (gratitude) reconocimiento, agradecimiento; (Comm) aumento en valor

apprehension [æprɪˈhenʃən] n (fear) aprensión f

apprehensive [æprɪˈhensɪv] adj aprensivo

apprentice [əˈprentɪs] n aprendiz(a) m/f

approach [əˈprəʊtʃ] vi acercarse

▷ vt acercarse a; (ask, apply to) dirigirse a; (situation, problem) abordar ▷ n acercamiento; (access) acceso; (to problem, situation): **~ (to)** actitud f (ante)

appropriate [adj əˈprəʊprɪɪt, vb əˈprəʊprɪeɪt] adj apropiado, conveniente ▷ vt (take) apropiarse de

approval [əˈpruːvəl] n aprobación f, visto bueno; (permission) consentimiento; **on ~** (Comm) a prueba

approve [əˈpruːv] vt aprobar; **approve of** vt fus (thing) aprobar; (person): **they don't approve of her** (ella) no les parece bien

approximate [əˈprɒksɪmɪt] adj aproximado; **approximately** adv aproximadamente, más o menos

Apr. abbr (= April) abr

apricot [ˈeɪprɪkɒt] n albaricoque m, chabacano (MEX), damasco (RPL)

April [ˈeɪprəl] n abril m; **April Fools' Day** n el primero de abril, ≈ día m de los Inocentes (28 December)

apron [ˈeɪprən] n delantal m

apt [æpt] adj acertado, apropiado; (likely): **~ to do** propenso a hacer

aquarium [əˈkwɛərɪəm] n acuario

Aquarius [əˈkwɛərɪəs] n Acuario

Arab [ˈærəb] adj, n árabe mf

Arabia [əˈreɪbiə] n Arabia; **Arabian** adj árabe; **Arabic** [ˈærəbɪk] adj árabe; (numerals) arábigo ▷ n árabe m

arbitrary [ˈɑːbɪtrərɪ] adj arbitrario

arbitration [ɑːbɪˈtreɪʃən] n arbitraje m

arc [ɑːk] n arco

arcade [ɑːˈkeɪd] n (round a square) soportales mpl; (shopping mall) galería comercial

arch [ɑːtʃ] n arco; (of foot) arco del pie ▷ vt arquear

archaeology [ɑːkɪˈɒlədʒɪ] (US **archeology**) n arqueología

archbishop [ɑːtʃˈbɪʃəp] n arzobispo

archeology [ɑːkɪˈɒlədʒɪ] (US) = **archaeology**

architect [ˈɑːkɪtekt] n arquitecto/a;

architectural [ɑːkɪˈtɛktʃərəl] adj arquitectónico; **architecture** n arquitectura

archive [ˈɑːkaɪv] n (often pl: also Comput) archivo

Arctic [ˈɑːktɪk] adj ártico ▷ n: **the ~** el Ártico

are [ɑː*] vb see **be**

area [ˈɛərɪə] n área, región f; (part of place) zona; (Math etc) área, superficie f; (in room: e.g. dining area) parte f; (of knowledge, experience) campo; **area code** (us) n (Tel) prefijo

arena [əˈriːnə] n estadio; (of circus) pista

aren't [ɑːnt] = **are not**

Argentina [ɑːdʒənˈtiːnə] n Argentina; **Argentinian** [-ˈtɪnɪən] adj, n argentino/a m/f

arguably [ˈɑːgjʊəblɪ] adv posiblemente

argue [ˈɑːgjuː] vi (quarrel) discutir, pelearse; (reason) razonar, argumentar; **to ~ that** sostener que

argument [ˈɑːgjʊmənt] n discusión f, pelea; (reasons) argumento

Aries [ˈɛərɪz] n Aries m

arise [əˈraɪz] (pt **arose**, pp **arisen**) vi surgir, presentarse

arithmetic [əˈrɪθmətɪk] n aritmética

arm [ɑːm] n brazo ▷ vt armar; **arms** npl armas fpl; **~ in ~** cogidos del brazo; **armchair** [ˈɑːmtʃɛə*] n sillón m, butaca

armed [ɑːmd] adj armado; **armed robbery** n robo a mano armada

armour [ˈɑːmə*] (us **armor**) n armadura; (Mil: tanks) blindaje m

armpit [ˈɑːmpɪt] n sobaco, axila

armrest [ˈɑːmrɛst] n apoyabrazos m inv

army [ˈɑːmɪ] n ejército; (fig) multitud f

A road n (BRIT) ≈ carretera f nacional

aroma [əˈrəʊmə] n aroma m, fragancia; **aromatherapy** n aromaterapia

arose [əˈrəʊz] pt of **arise**

around [əˈraʊnd] adv alrededor; (in the area): **there is no one else ~** no hay nadie más por aquí ▷ prep alrededor de

arouse [əˈraʊz] vt despertar; (anger) provocar

arrange [əˈreɪndʒ] vt arreglar, ordenar; (organize) organizar; **to ~ to do sth** quedar en hacer algo; **arrangement** n arreglo; (agreement) acuerdo; **arrangements** npl (preparations) preparativos mpl

array [əˈreɪ] n: **~ of** (things) serie f de; (people) conjunto de

arrears [əˈrɪəz] npl atrasos mpl; **to be in ~ with one's rent** estar retrasado en el pago del alquiler

arrest [əˈrɛst] vt detener; (sb's attention) llamar ▷ n detención f; **under ~** detenido

arrival [əˈraɪvl] n llegada; **new ~** recién llegado/a; (baby) recién nacido

arrive [əˈraɪv] vi llegar; (baby) nacer; **arrive at** vt fus (decision, solution) llegar a

arrogance [ˈærəgəns] n arrogancia, prepotencia (LAM)

arrogant [ˈærəgənt] adj arrogante

arrow [ˈærəʊ] n flecha

arse [ɑːs] (BRIT: inf!) n culo, trasero

arson [ˈɑːsn] n incendio premeditado

art [ɑːt] n arte m; (skill) destreza; **art college** n escuela f de Bellas Artes

artery [ˈɑːtərɪ] n arteria

art gallery n pinacoteca; (saleroom) galería de arte

arthritis [ɑːˈθraɪtɪs] n artritis f

artichoke [ˈɑːtɪtʃəʊk] n alcachofa; **Jerusalem ~** aguaturma

article [ˈɑːtɪkl] n artículo

articulate [adj ɑːˈtɪkjʊlɪt, vb ɑːˈtɪkjʊleɪt] adj claro, bien expresado ▷ vt expresar

artificial [ɑːtɪˈfɪʃəl] adj artificial; (affected) afectado

artist [ˈɑːtɪst] n artista mf; (Mus) intérprete mf; **artistic** [ɑːˈtɪstɪk] adj

artístico
art school n escuela de bellas artes

○ **KEYWORD**

as [æz] conj 1 (referring to time)
cuando, mientras; a medida que; **as
the years went by** con el paso de los
años; **he came in as I was leaving**
entró cuando me marchaba; **as
from tomorrow** desde or a partir de
mañana
2 (in comparisons): **as big as** tan grande
como; **twice as big as** el doble de
grande que; **as much money/many
books as** tanto dinero/tantos libros
como; **as soon as** en cuanto
3 (since, because) como, ya que; **he left
early as he had to be home by 10** se
fue temprano ya que tenía que estar en
casa a las 10
4 (referring to manner, way): **do as you
wish** haz lo que quieras; **as she said**
como dijo; **he gave it to me as a
present** me lo dio de regalo
5 (in the capacity of): **he works as
a barman** trabaja de barman; **as
chairman of the company, he ...**
como presidente de la compañía ...
6 (concerning): **as for or to that** por or en
lo que respecta a eso
7: **as if or though** como si; **he looked
as if he was ill** parecía como si
estuviera enfermo, tenía aspecto de
enfermo; *see also* **long**; **such**; **well**

a.s.a.p. abbr (= as soon as possible)
cuanto antes
asbestos [æz'bestəs] n asbesto,
amianto
ascent [ə'sent] n subida; (slope)
cuesta, pendiente f
ash [æʃ] n ceniza; (tree) fresno
ashamed [ə'feɪmd] adj avergonzado,
apenado (LAM); **to be ~ of** avergonzarse
de
ashore [ə'ʃɔ:ʳ] adv en tierra; (swim
etc) a tierra

ashtray ['æʃtreɪ] n cenicero
Ash Wednesday n miércoles m
de Ceniza
Asia ['eɪʃə] n Asia; **Asian** adj, n
asiático/a m/f
aside [ə'saɪd] adv a un lado ▷ n
aparte m
ask [ɑ:sk] vt (question) preguntar;
(invite) invitar; **to ~ sb sth/to do sth**
preguntar algo a algn/pedir a algn que
haga algo; **to ~ sb about sth** preguntar
algo a algn; **to ~ (sb) a question** hacer
una pregunta (a algn); **to ~ sb out to
dinner** invitar a cenar a algn; **ask for** vt
fus pedir; (trouble) buscar
asleep [ə'sli:p] adj dormido; **to fall ~**
dormirse, quedarse dormido
asparagus [əs'pærəgəs] n (plant)
espárrago; (food) espárragos mpl
aspect ['æspekt] n aspecto,
apariencia; (direction in which a building
etc faces) orientación f
aspirations [æspə'reɪʃənz] npl
aspiraciones fpl; (ambition) ambición f
aspire [əs'paɪəʳ] vi: **to ~ to** aspirar a,
ambicionar
aspirin ['æsprɪn] n aspirina
ass [æs] n asno, burro; (inf: idiot)
imbécil m/f; (us: infl) culo, trasero
assassin [ə'sæsɪn] n asesino/a;
assassinate vt asesinar
assault [ə'sɔ:lt] n asalto; (Law)
agresión f ▷ vt asaltar, atacar;
(sexually) violar
assemble [ə'sembl] vt reunir, juntar;
(Tech) montar ▷ vi reunirse, juntarse
assembly [ə'semblɪ] n reunión f,
asamblea; (parliament) parlamento;
(construction) montaje m
assert [ə'sɜ:t] vt afirmar; (authority)
hacer valer; **assertion** [-ʃən] n
afirmación f
assess [ə'ses] vt valorar, calcular;
(tax, damages) fijar; (for tax) gravar;
assessment n valoración f; (for tax)
gravamen m
asset ['æset] n ventaja; **assets**
npl (Comm) activo; (property, funds)

fondos *mpl*

assign [ə'saɪn] *vt*: **to ~ (to)** (*date*) fijar (para); (*task*) asignar (a); (*resources*) destinar (a); **assignment** *n* tarea

assist [ə'sɪst] *vt* ayudar; **assistance** *n* ayuda, auxilio; **assistant** *n* ayudante *mf*; (BRIT: *also*: **shop assistant**) dependiente/a *m/f*

associate [*adj, n* ə'səʊʃɪɪt, *vb* ə'səʊʃɪeɪt] *adj* asociado ⊳ *n* (*at work*) colega *mf* ⊳ *vt* asociar; (*ideas*) relacionar ⊳ *vi*: **to ~ with sb** tratar con algn

association [əsəʊsɪ'eɪʃən] *n* asociación *f*

assorted [ə'sɔːtɪd] *adj* surtido, variado

assortment [ə'sɔːtmənt] *n* (*of shapes, colours*) surtido; (*of books*) colección *f*; (*of people*) mezcla

assume [ə'sjuːm] *vt* suponer; (*responsibilities*) asumir; (*attitude*) adoptar, tomar

assumption [ə'sʌmpʃən] *n* suposición *f*, presunción *f*; (*of power etc*) toma

assurance [ə'ʃʊərəns] *n* garantía, promesa; (*confidence*) confianza, aplomo; (*insurance*) seguro

assure [ə'ʃʊə*] *vt* asegurar

asterisk ['æstərɪsk] *n* asterisco

asthma ['æsmə] *n* asma

astonish [ə'stɒnɪʃ] *vt* asombrar, pasmar; **astonished** *adj* estupefacto, pasmado; **to be astonished (at)** asombrarse (de); **astonishing** *adj* asombroso, pasmoso; **I find it astonishing that ...** me asombra or pasma que ...; **astonishment** *n* asombro, sorpresa

astound [ə'staʊnd] *vt* asombrar, pasmar

astray [ə'streɪ] *adv*: **to go ~** extraviarse; **to lead ~** (*morally*) llevar por mal camino

astrology [æs'trɒlədʒɪ] *n* astrología

astronaut ['æstrənɔːt] *n* astronauta *mf*

astronomer [əs'trɒnəmə*] *n* astrónomo/a

astronomical [æstrə'nɒmɪkəl] *adj* astronómico

astronomy [æs'trɒnəmɪ] *n* astronomía

astute [əs'tjuːt] *adj* astuto

asylum [ə'saɪləm] *n* (*refuge*) asilo; (*mental hospital*) manicomio

○ **KEYWORD**

at [æt] *prep* **1** (*referring to position*) en; (*direction*) a; **at the top** en lo alto; **at home/school** en casa/la escuela; **to look at sth/sb** mirar algo/a algn

2 (*referring to time*): **at 4 o'clock** a las 4; **at night** por la noche; **at Christmas** en Navidad; **at times** a veces

3 (*referring to rates, speed etc*): **at £1 a kilo** a una libra el kilo; **two at a time** de dos en dos; **at 50 km/h** a 50 km/h

4 (*referring to manner*): **at a stroke** de un golpe; **at peace** en paz

5 (*referring to activity*): **to be at work** estar trabajando; (*in the office etc*) estar en el trabajo; **to play at cowboys** jugar a los vaqueros; **to be good at sth** ser bueno en algo

6 (*referring to cause*): **shocked/ surprised/annoyed at sth** asombrado/sorprendido/fastidiado por algo; **I went at his suggestion** fui a instancias suyas

7 (*symbol*) arroba

ate [eɪt] *pt of* **eat**

atheist ['eɪθɪɪst] *n* ateo/a

Athens ['æθɪnz] *n* Atenas

athlete ['æθliːt] *n* atleta *mf*

athletic [æθ'lɛtɪk] *adj* atlético; **athletics** *n* atletismo

Atlantic [ət'læntɪk] *adj* atlántico ⊳ *n*: **the ~ (Ocean)** el (Océano) Atlántico

atlas ['ætləs] *n* atlas *m inv*

A.T.M. *n abbr* (= *automated telling*

machine) cajero automático

atmosphere [ˈætməsfɪəʳ] n
atmósfera; (of place) ambiente m

atom [ˈætəm] n átomo; **atomic**
[əˈtɒmɪk] adj atómico; **atom(ic)
bomb** n bomba atómica

A to Z® n (map) callejero

atrocity [əˈtrɒsɪtɪ] n atrocidad f

attach [əˈtætʃ] vt (fasten) atar;
(join) unir, sujetar; (document, email,
letter) adjuntar; (importance etc)
dar, conceder; **to be ~ed to sb/sth**
(to like) tener cariño a algn/algo;
attachment (tool) n accesorio;
(Comput) archivo, documento adjunto;
(love): **attachment (to)** apego (a)

attack [əˈtæk] vt (Mil) atacar;
(criminal) agredir, asaltar; (criticize)
criticar; (task) emprender ▷ n ataque
m, asalto; (on sb's life) atentado;
(fig: criticism) crítica; (of illness) ataque
m; **heart ~** infarto (de miocardio);
attacker n agresor(a) m/f, asaltante
mf

attain [əˈteɪn] vt (also: **~ to**) alcanzar;
(achieve) lograr, conseguir

attempt [əˈtɛmpt] n tentativa,
intento; (attack) atentado ▷ vt
intentar

attend [əˈtɛnd] vt asistir a; (patient)
atender; **attend to** vt fus ocuparse
de; (customer, patient) atender a;
attendance n asistencia, presencia;
(people present) concurrencia;
attendant n ayudante mf; (in garage
etc) encargado/a ▷ adj (dangers)
concomitante

attention [əˈtɛnʃən] n atención
f; (care) atenciones fpl ▷ excl (Mil)
¡firme(s)!; **for the ~ of ...** (Admin)
atención ...

attic [ˈætɪk] n desván m

attitude [ˈætɪtjuːd] n actitud f;
(disposition) disposición f

attorney [əˈtɜːnɪ] n (lawyer)
abogado/a; **Attorney General** n
(BRIT) ≈ Presidente m del Consejo del
Poder Judicial (SP); (US) ≈ ministro

de Justicia

attract [əˈtrækt] vt atraer; (sb's
attention) llamar; **attraction**
[əˈtrækʃən] n encanto; (gen
pl: amusements) diversiones fpl;
(Physics) atracción f; (fig: towards sb,
sth) atractivo; **attractive** adj guapo;
(interesting) atrayente

attribute [n ˈætrɪbjuːt, vb əˈtrɪbjuːt]
n atributo ▷ vt: **to ~ sth to** atribuir
algo a

aubergine [ˈəʊbəʒiːn] n (BRIT)
berenjena; (colour) morado

auburn [ˈɔːbən] adj color castaño
rojizo

auction [ˈɔːkʃən] n (also: **sale by ~**)
subasta ▷ vt subastar

audible [ˈɔːdɪbl] adj audible, que se
puede oír

audience [ˈɔːdɪəns] n público; (Radio)
radioescuchas mpl; (TV)
telespectadores mpl; (interview)
audiencia

audit [ˈɔːdɪt] vt revisar, intervenir

audition [ɔːˈdɪʃən] n audición f

auditor [ˈɔːdɪtəʳ] n interventor(a)
m/f, censor/a m/f de cuentas

auditorium [ɔːdɪˈtɔːrɪəm] n
auditorio

Aug. abbr (= August) ag

August [ˈɔːgəst] n agosto

aunt [ɑːnt] n tía; **auntie** n diminutive
of **aunt**; **aunty** n diminutive of **aunt**

au pair [ˈəʊˈpɛəʳ] n (also: **~ girl**)
(chica) au pair f

aura [ˈɔːrə] n aura; (atmosphere)
ambiente m

austerity [ɔˈstɛrɪtɪ] n austeridad f

Australia [ɔsˈtreɪlɪə] n Australia;
Australian adj, n australiano/a m/f

Austria [ˈɒstrɪə] n Austria; **Austrian**
adj, n austríaco/a m/f

authentic [ɔˈθɛntɪk] adj auténtico

author [ˈɔːθəʳ] n autor(a) m/f

authority [ɔːˈθɒrɪtɪ] n autoridad f;
(official permission) autorización f; **the
authorities** npl las autoridades

authorize [ˈɔːθəraɪz] vt autorizar

auto ['ɔ:təʊ] (us) n coche m (SP), carro (LAM), automóvil m

auto: autobiography [ɔ:təbaɪ'ɔgrəfɪ] n autobiografía; **autograph** ['ɔ:təgrɑ:f] n autógrafo ▷ vt (photo etc) dedicar; (programme) firmar; **automatic** [ɔ:tə'mætɪk] adj automático ▷ n (gun) pistola automática; (car) coche m automático; **automatically** adv automáticamente; **automobile** ['ɔ:təməbi:l] (us) n coche m (SP), carro m (LAM), automóvil m; **autonomous** [ɔ:'tɔnəməs] adj autónomo; **autonomy** [ɔ:'tɔnəmɪ] n autonomía

autumn ['ɔ:təm] n otoño

auxiliary [ɔ:g'zɪlɪərɪ] adj, n auxiliar mf

avail [ə'veɪl] vt: **to ~ o.s. of** aprovechar(se) de ▷ n: **to no ~** en vano, sin resultado

availability [əveɪlə'bɪlɪtɪ] n disponibilidad f

available [ə'veɪləbl] adj disponible; (unoccupied) libre; (person: unattached) soltero y sin compromiso

avalanche ['ævəlɑ:nʃ] n alud m, avalancha

Ave. abbr = **avenue**

avenue ['ævənju:] n avenida; (fig) camino

average ['ævərɪdʒ] n promedio, término medio ▷ adj medio, de término medio; (ordinary) regular, corriente ▷ vt sacar un promedio de; **on ~** por regla general

avert [ə'vɜ:t] vt prevenir; (blow) desviar; (one's eyes) apartar

avid ['ævɪd] adj ávido

avocado [ævə'kɑ:dəʊ] n (also BRIT: **~ pear**) aguacate m, palta (SC)

avoid [ə'vɔɪd] vt evitar, eludir

await [ə'weɪt] vt esperar, aguardar

awake [ə'weɪk] (pt **awoke**, pp **awoken** or **awaked**) adj despierto ▷ vt despertar ▷ vi despertarse; **to be ~** estar despierto

award [ə'wɔ:d] n premio;

(Law: damages) indemnización f ▷ vt otorgar, conceder; (Law: damages) adjudicar

aware [ə'weə*] adj: **~ (of)** consciente (de); **to become ~ of/that** (realize) darse cuenta de/de que; (learn) enterarse de/de que; **awareness** n conciencia; (knowledge) conocimiento

away [ə'weɪ] adv fuera; (movement): **she went ~** se marchó; **far ~** lejos; **two kilometres ~** a dos kilómetros de distancia; **two hours ~ by car** a dos horas en coche; **the holiday was two weeks ~** faltaban dos semanas para las vacaciones; **he's ~ for a week** estará ausente una semana; **to take ~ (from)** quitar (a); (subtract) substraer (de); **to work/pedal ~** seguir trabajando/pedaleando; **to fade ~** (colour) desvanecerse; (sound) apagarse

awe [ɔ:] n admiración f respetuosa; **awesome** ['ɔ:səm] (us) adj (excellent) formidable

awful ['ɔ:fəl] adj horroroso; (quantity): **an ~ lot (of)** cantidad (de); **awfully** adv (very) terriblemente

awkward ['ɔ:kwəd] adj desmañado, torpe; (shape) incómodo; (embarrassing) delicado, difícil

awoke [ə'wəʊk] pt of **awake**

awoken [ə'wəʊkən] pp of **awake**

axe [æks] (us **ax**) n hacha ▷ vt (project) cortar; (jobs) reducir

axle ['æksl] n eje m, árbol m

ay(e) [aɪ] excl sí

azalea [ə'zeɪlɪə] n azalea

b

B [biː] n (Mus) si m

B.A. abbr = **Bachelor of Arts**

baby ['beɪbɪ] n bebé mf; (us: inf: darling) mi amor; **baby carriage** (us) n cochecito; **baby-sit** vi hacer de canguro; **baby-sitter** n canguro/a; **baby wipe** n toallita húmeda (para bebés)

bachelor ['bætʃələ*] n soltero; **B~ of Arts/Science** licenciado/a en Filosofía y Letras/Ciencias

back [bæk] n (of person) espalda; (of animal) lomo; (of hand) dorso; (as opposed to front) parte f de atrás; (of chair) respaldo; (of page) reverso; (of book) final m; (Football) defensa m; (of crowd): **the ones at the ~** los del fondo ▷ vt (candidate: also: **~ up**) respaldar, apoyar; (horse: at races) apostar a; (car etc) dar marcha atrás a or con ▷ vi (car etc) ir (or salir or entrar) marcha atrás ▷ adj (payment, rent) atrasado; (seats, wheels) de atrás ▷ adv (not forward) (hacia) atrás; (returned): **he's ~** está de vuelta, ha vuelto; **he ran ~** volvió corriendo;

(restitution): **throw the ball ~** devuelve la pelota; **can I have it ~?** ¿me lo devuelve?; (again): **he called ~** llamó de nuevo; **back down** vi echarse atrás; **back out** vi (of promise) volverse atrás; **back up** vt (person) apoyar, respaldar; (theory) defender; (Comput) hacer una copia preventiva or de reserva; **backache** n dolor m de espalda; **backbencher** (BRIT) n miembro del parlamento sin cargo relevante; **backbone** n columna vertebral; **back door** n puerta f trasera; **backfire** vi (Aut) petardear; (plans) fallar, salir mal; **backgammon** n backgammon m; **background** n fondo; (of events) antecedentes mpl; (basic knowledge) bases fpl; (experience) conocimientos mpl, educación f; **family background** origen m, antecedentes mpl; **backing** n (fig) apoyo, respaldo; **backlog** n: **backlog of work** trabajo atrasado; **backpack** n mochila; **backpacker** n mochilero/a; **backslash** n pleca, barra inversa; **backstage** adv entre bastidores; **backstroke** n espalda; **backup** adj suplementario; (Comput) de reserva n (support) apoyo; (also: **backup file**) copia preventiva or de reserva; **backward** adj (person, country) atrasado; **backwards** adv hacia atrás; (read a list) al revés; (fall) de espaldas; **backyard** n traspatio

bacon ['beɪkən] n tocino, beicon m

bacteria [bæk'tɪərɪə] npl bacterias fpl

bad [bæd] adj malo; (mistake, accident) grave; (food) podrido, pasado; **his ~ leg** su pierna lisiada; **to go ~** (food) pasarse

badge [bædʒ] n insignia; (policeman's) chapa, placa

badger ['bædʒə*] n tejón m

badly ['bædlɪ] adv mal; **to reflect ~ on sb** influir negativamente en la reputación de algn; **~ wounded** gravemente herido; **he needs it ~** le hace gran falta; **to be ~ off (for money)** andar mal de dinero

bad-mannered ['bæd'mænəd] adj

mal educado

badminton ['bædmɪntən] n
bádminton m

bad-tempered ['bæd'tempəd] adj
de mal genio or carácter; (temporarily)
de mal humor

bag [bæg] n bolsa; (handbag) bolso;
(satchel) mochila; (case) maleta; **~s
of** (inf) un montón de; **baggage** n
equipaje m; **baggage allowance** n
límite m de equipaje; **baggage
reclaim** n recogida de equipajes;
baggy adj amplio; **bagpipes** npl
gaita

bail [beɪl] n fianza ▷ vt
(prisoner: gen: grant bail to) poner en
libertad bajo fianza; (boat: also: **~ out**)
achicar; **on ~** (prisoner) bajo fianza; **to
~ sb out** obtener la libertad de algn
bajo fianza

bait [beɪt] n cebo ▷ vt poner cebo en;
(tease) tomar el pelo a

bake [beɪk] vt cocer (al horno) ▷ vi
cocerse; **baked beans** npl judías fpl
en salsa de tomate; **baked potato** n
patata f al horno; **baker** n panadero;
bakery n panadería; (for cakes)
pastelería; **baking** n (act) amasar m;
(batch) hornada; **baking powder** n
levadura (en polvo)

balance ['bæləns] n equilibrio;
(Comm: sum) balance m; (remainder)
resto; (scales) balanza ▷ vt equilibrar;
(budget) nivelar; (account) saldar;
(make equal) equilibrar; **~ of trade/
payments** balanza de comercio/
pagos; **balanced** adj (personality, diet)
equilibrado; (report) objetivo; **balance
sheet** n balance m

balcony ['bælkənɪ] n (open) balcón m;
(closed) galería; (in theatre) anfiteatro

bald [bɔːld] adj calvo; (tyre) liso

Balearics [bælɪ'ærɪks] npl: **the ~** las
Baleares

ball [bɔːl] n (football) balón m;
(of wool, string) ovillo; (dance) baile m; **to
play ~** (fig) cooperar

ballerina [bælə'riːnə] n bailarina

ballet ['bæleɪ] n ballet m; **ballet
dancer** n bailarín/ina m/f

balloon [bə'luːn] n globo

ballot ['bælət] n votación f

ballpoint (pen) ['bɔːlpɔɪnt-] n
bolígrafo

ballroom ['bɔːlrum] n salón m
de baile

Baltic ['bɔːltɪk] n: **the ~ (Sea)** el (Mar)
Báltico

bamboo [bæm'buː] n bambú m

ban [bæn] n prohibición f,
proscripción f ▷ vt prohibir, proscribir

banana [bə'nɑːnə] n plátano, banana
(LAM), banano (CAM)

band [bænd] n grupo; (strip) faja, tira;
(stripe) lista; (Mus: jazz) orquesta; (: rock)
grupo; (Mil) banda

bandage ['bændɪdʒ] n venda,
vendaje m ▷ vt vendar

Band-Aid® ['bændeɪd] (us) n tirita

bandit ['bændɪt] n bandido

bang [bæŋ] n (of gun, exhaust)
estallido, detonación f; (of door)
portazo; (blow) golpe m ▷ vt (door)
cerrar de golpe; (one's head) golpear ▷ vi
estallar; (door) cerrar de golpe

Bangladesh [bæŋglə'deʃ] n
Bangladesh n

bangle ['bæŋgl] n brazalete m,
ajorca

bangs [bæŋz] (us) npl flequillo

banish ['bænɪʃ] vt desterrar

banister(s) ['bænɪstə(z)] n(pl)
barandilla, pasamanos m inv

banjo ['bændʒəʊ] (pl **~es** or **~s**) n
banjo

bank [bæŋk] n (Comm) banco; (of river,
lake) ribera, orilla; (of earth) terraplén
m ▷ vi (Aviat) ladearse; **bank on** vt fus
contar con; **bank account** n cuenta
de banco; **bank balance** n saldo;
bank card n tarjeta bancaria; **bank
charges** npl comisión fsg; **banker** n
banquero; **bank holiday** n (BRIT) día m
festivo or de fiesta; **banking** n banca;
bank manager n director(a) m/f
(de sucursal) de banco; **banknote** n

billete *m* de banco

El término **bank holiday** se aplica en el Reino Unido a todo día festivo oficial en el que cierran bancos y comercios. Los más importantes son en Navidad, Semana Santa, finales de mayo y finales de agosto y, al contrario que en los países de tradición católica, no coinciden necesariamente con una celebración religiosa.

bankrupt ['bæŋkrʌpt] *adj* quebrado, insolvente; **to go ~** hacer bancarrota; **to be ~** estar en quiebra; **bankruptcy** *n* quiebra

bank statement *n* balance *m* or detalle *m* de cuenta

banner ['bænə*] *n* pancarta

bannister(s) ['bænɪstə(z)] *n(pl)* = **banister(s)**

banquet ['bæŋkwɪt] *n* banquete *m*

baptism ['bæptɪzəm] *n* bautismo; (*act*) bautizo

baptize ['bæptaɪz] *vt* bautizar

bar [bɑː*] *n* (*pub*) bar *m*; (*counter*) mostrador *m*; (*rod*) barra; (*of window, cage*) reja; (*of soap*) pastilla; (*of chocolate*) tableta; (*fig: hindrance*) obstáculo; (*prohibition*) proscripción *f*; (*Mus*) barra ▷ *vt* (*road*) obstruir; (*person*) excluir; (*activity*) prohibir; **the B~** (*Law*) la abogacía; **behind ~s** entre rejas; **~ none** sin excepción

barbaric [bɑː'bærɪk] *adj* bárbaro

barbecue ['bɑːbɪkjuː] *n* barbacoa

barbed wire ['bɑːbd-] *n* alambre *m* de púas

barber ['bɑːbə*] *n* peluquero, barbero; **barber's (shop)** (*us* **barber (shop)**) *n* peluquería

bar code *n* código de barras

bare [beə*] *adj* desnudo; (*trees*) sin hojas; (*necessities etc*) básico ▷ *vt* desnudar; (*teeth*) enseñar; **barefoot**

adj, adv descalzo; **barely** *adv* apenas

bargain ['bɑːgɪn] *n* pacto, negocio; (*good buy*) ganga ▷ *vi* negociar; (*haggle*) regatear; **into the ~** además, por añadidura; **bargain for** *vt fus*: **he got more than he bargained for** le resultó peor de lo que esperaba

barge [bɑːdʒ] *n* barcaza; **barge in** *vi* irrumpir; (*interrupt: conversation*) interrumpir

bark [bɑːk] *n* (*of tree*) corteza; (*of dog*) ladrido ▷ *vi* ladrar

barley ['bɑːlɪ] *n* cebada

barmaid ['bɑːmeɪd] *n* camarera

barman ['bɑːmən] (*irreg*) *n* camarero, barman *m*

barn [bɑːn] *n* granero

barometer [bə'rɒmɪtə*] *n* barómetro

baron ['bærən] *n* barón *m*; (*press baron etc*) magnate *m*; **baroness** *n* baronesa

barracks ['bærəks] *npl* cuartel *m*

barrage ['bærɑːʒ] *n* (*Mil*) descarga, bombardeo; (*dam*) presa; (*of criticism*) lluvia, aluvión *m*

barrel ['bærəl] *n* barril *m*; (*of gun*) cañón *m*

barren ['bærən] *adj* estéril

barrette [bə'ret] (*us*) *n* pasador *m* (*LAM*, *US*), broche *m* (*MEX*)

barricade [bærɪ'keɪd] *n* barricada

barrier ['bærɪə*] *n* barrera

barring ['bɑːrɪŋ] *prep* excepto, salvo

barrister ['bærɪstə*] (*BRIT*) *n* abogado/a

barrow ['bærəʊ] *n* (*cart*) carretilla (de mano)

bartender ['bɑːtendə*] (*us*) *n* camarero, barman *m*

base [beɪs] *n* base *f* ▷ *vt*: **to ~ sth on** basar or fundar algo en ▷ *adj* bajo, infame

baseball ['beɪsbɔːl] *n* béisbol *m*; **baseball cap** *n* gorra *f* de béisbol

basement ['beɪsmənt] *n* sótano

bases[1] ['beɪsɪz] *npl of* **basis**

bases[2] ['beɪsiːz] *npl of* **base**

bash [bæʃ] (*inf*) *vt* golpear

basic ['beɪsɪk] adj básico; **basically**
adv fundamentalmente, en el fondo;
(simply) sencillamente; **basics** npl: **the
basics** los fundamentos

basil ['bæzl] n albahaca

basin ['beɪsn] n cuenco, tazón m;
(Geo) cuenca; (also: **wash~**) lavabo

basis ['beɪsɪs] (pl **bases**) n base f; **on a
part-time/trial ~** a tiempo parcial/a
prueba

basket ['bɑːskɪt] n cesta, cesto;
canasta; **basketball** n baloncesto

bass [beɪs] n (Mus: instrument) bajo;
(double bass) contrabajo; (singer) bajo

bastard ['bɑːstəd] n bastardo; (inf!)
hijo de puta (!)

bat [bæt] n (Zool) murciélago; (for ball
games) palo; (BRIT: for table tennis) pala
▷ vt **he didn't ~ an eyelid** ni pestañeó

batch [bætʃ] n (of bread) hornada; (of
letters etc) lote m

bath [bɑːθ, pl bɑːðz] n (action) baño;
(bathtub) bañera (SP), tina (LAM),
bañadera (RPL) ▷ vt bañar; **to have a ~**
bañarse, tomar un baño; see also **baths**

bathe [beɪð] vi bañarse ▷ vt (wound)
lavar

bathing ['beɪðɪŋ] n el bañarse;
bathing costume (US **bathing suit**) n
traje m de baño

bath: **bathrobe** n (man's) batín
m; (woman's) bata; **bathroom** n
(cuarto de) baño; **baths** [bɑːðz] npl
(also: **swimming baths**) piscina; **bath
towel** n toalla de baño; **bathtub**
n bañera

baton ['bætən] n (Mus) batuta;
(Athletics) testigo; (weapon) porra

batter ['bætə*] vt maltratar; (rain
etc) azotar ▷ n masa (para rebozar);
battered adj (hat, pan) estropeado

battery ['bætərɪ] n (Aut) batería; (of
torch) pila; **battery farming** n cría
intensiva

battle ['bætl] n batalla; (fig) lucha
▷ vi luchar; **battlefield** n campo m
de batalla

bay [beɪ] n (Geo) bahía; **B~ of Biscay**

= mar Cantábrico; **to hold sb at ~**
mantener a algn a raya

bazaar [bə'zɑː*] n bazar m; (fete) venta
con fines benéficos

B. & B. n abbr = **bed and breakfast**;
(place) pensión f; (terms) cama y
desayuno

BBC n abbr (= British Broadcasting
Corporation) cadena de radio y televisión
estatal británica

B.C. adv abbr (= before Christ) a. de C.

○ KEYWORD

be [biː] (pt **was**, **were**, pp **been**) aux
vb 1 (with present participle: forming
continuous tenses): **what are you
doing?** ¿qué estás haciendo?, ¿qué
haces?; **they're coming tomorrow**
vienen mañana; **I've been waiting for
you for** hours llevo horas esperándote
2 (with pp: forming passives) ser (but
often replaced by active or reflexive
constructions); **to be murdered** ser
asesinado; **the box had been opened**
habían abierto la caja; **the thief was
nowhere to be seen** no se veía al
ladrón por ninguna parte
3 (in tag questions): **it was fun, wasn't
it?** fue divertido, ¿no? or ¿verdad?; **he's
good-looking, isn't he?** es guapo, ¿no
te parece?; **she's back again, is she?**
entonces, ¿ha vuelto?
4 (+to +infin): **the house is to be sold**
(necessity) hay que vender la casa;
(future) van a vender la casa; **he's
not to open it** no tiene que abrirlo
▷ vb +complement 1 (with n or num
complement, but see also 3, 4, 5 and impers
vb below) ser; **he's a doctor** es médico;
2 and 2 are 4 2 y 2 son 4
2 (with adj complement: expressing
permanent or inherent quality) ser;
(: expressing state seen as temporary
or reversible) estar; **I'm English** soy
inglés/esa; **she's tall/pretty** es
alta/bonita; **he's young** es joven; **be
careful/good/quiet** ten cuidado/

315 | **bed**

pórtate bien/cállate; **I'm tired** estoy cansado/a; **it's dirty** está sucio/a **3** (of health) estar; **how are you?** ¿cómo estás?; **he's very ill** está muy enfermo; **I'm better now** ya estoy mejor **4** (of age) tener; **how old are you?** ¿cuántos años tienes?; **I'm sixteen (years old)** tengo dieciséis años **5** (cost) costar; ser; **how much was the meal?** ¿cuánto fue or costó la comida?; **that'll be £5.75, please** son £5.75, por favor; **this shirt is £17** esta camisa cuesta £17 ▷ *vi* **1** (exist, occur etc) existir, haber; **the best singer that ever was** el mejor cantante que existió jamás; **is there a God?** ¿hay un Dios?, ¿existe Dios?; **be that as it may** sea como sea; **so be it** así sea **2** (referring to place) estar; **I won't be here tomorrow** no estaré aquí mañana **3** (referring to movement): **where have you been?** ¿dónde has estado? ▷ *impers vb* **1** (referring to time): **it's 5 o'clock** son las 5; **it's the 28th of April** estamos a 28 de abril **2** (referring to distance): **it's 10 km to the village** el pueblo está a 10 km **3** (referring to the weather): **it's too hot/cold** hace demasiado calor/frío; **it's windy today** hace viento hoy **4** (emphatic): **it's me** soy yo; **it was Maria who paid the bill** fue María la que pagó la cuenta

beach [biːtʃ] *n* playa ▷ *vt* varar
beacon ['biːkən] *n* (lighthouse) faro; (marker) guía
bead [biːd] *n* cuenta; (of sweat etc) gota; **beads** *npl* (necklace) collar *m*
beak [biːk] *n* pico
beam [biːm] *n* (Arch) viga, travesaño; (of light) rayo, haz *m* de luz ▷ *vi* brillar; (smile) sonreír
bean [biːn] *n* judía; **runner/broad ~** habichuela/haba; **coffee ~** grano de café; **beansprouts** *npl* brotes

mpl de soja

bear [bɛəʳ] (*pt* **bore**, *pp* **borne**) *n* oso ▷ *vt* (weight etc) llevar; (cost) pagar; (responsibility) tener; (endure) soportar, aguantar; (children) parir, tener; (fruit) dar ▷ *vi*: **to ~ right/left** torcer a la derecha/izquierda
beard [biəd] *n* barba
bearer ['bɛərəʳ] *n* portador(a) *m/f*
bearing ['bɛərɪŋ] *n* porte *m*, comportamiento; (connection) relación *f*
beast [biːst] *n* bestia; (inf) bruto, salvaje *m*
beat [biːt] (*pt* ~, *pp* **beaten**) *n* (of heart) latido; (Mus) ritmo, compás *m*; (of policeman) ronda ▷ *vt* pegar, golpear; (eggs) batir; (defeat: opponent) vencer, derrotar; (: record) sobrepasar ▷ *vi* (heart) latir; (drum) redoblar; (rain, wind) azotar; **off the ~en track** aislado; **to ~ it** (inf) largarse; **beat up** *vt* (attack) dar una paliza a; **beating** *n* paliza
beautiful ['bjuːtɪful] *adj* precioso, hermoso, bello; **beautifully** *adv* maravillosamente
beauty ['bjuːtɪ] *n* belleza; **beauty parlour** (*us* **beauty parlor**) *n* salón *m* de belleza; **beauty salon** *n* salón *m* de belleza; **beauty spot** *n* (Tourism) lugar *m* pintoresco
beaver ['biːvəʳ] *n* castor *m*
became [bɪ'keɪm] *pt of* **become**
because [bɪ'kɔz] *conj* porque; **~ of** debido a, a causa de
beckon ['bɛkən] *vt* (also: **~ to**) llamar con señas
become [bɪ'kʌm] (*pt* **became**, *pp* ~) *vt* favorecer, sentar bien a ▷ *vi* (+ *n*) hacerse, llegar a ser; (+ *adj*) ponerse, volverse; **to ~ fat** engordar
bed [bɛd] *n* cama; (of flowers) macizo; (of coal, clay) capa; (of river) lecho; (of sea) fondo; **to go to ~** acostarse; **bed and breakfast** *n* (place) pensión *f*; (terms) cama y desayuno; **bedclothes** *npl* ropa de cama; **bedding** *n* ropa de cama; **bed linen** *n* (BRIT) ropa *f*

bed | 316

de cama

● **BED AND BREAKFAST**
●
● Se llama **bed and breakfast** a una
● forma de alojamiento, en el campo
● o la ciudad, que ofrece cama y
● desayuno a precios inferiores a
● los de un hotel. El servicio se suele
● anunciar con carteles en los que
● a menudo se usa únicamente la
● abreviatura **B. & B.**

bed: bedroom n dormitorio; **bedside**
n: **at the bedside of** a la cabecera de;
bedside lamp n lámpara de noche;
bedside table n mesilla de noche;
bedsit(ter) (BRIT) n cuarto de alquiler;
bedspread n cubrecama m, colcha;
bedtime n hora de acostarse
bee [biː] n abeja
beech [biːtʃ] n haya
beef [biːf] n carne f de vaca; **roast ~**
rosbif m; **beefburger** n hamburguesa;
Beefeater n alabardero de la Torre
de Londres
been [biːn] pp of **be**
beer [bɪə*] n cerveza; **beer garden**
n (BRIT) terraza f de verano, jardín m
(de un bar)
beet [biːt] (us) (also: **red ~**)
remolacha
beetle [biːtl] n escarabajo
beetroot ['biːtruːt] (BRIT) n
remolacha
before [bɪ'fɔː*] prep (of time) antes
de; (of space) delante de ▷ conj antes
(de) que ▷ adv antes, anteriormente;
delante, adelante; **~ going** antes
de marcharse; **~ she goes** antes de que se
vaya; **the week ~** la semana anterior;
I've never seen it ~ no lo he visto
nunca; **beforehand** adv de antemano,
con anticipación
beg [beg] vi pedir limosna ▷ vt pedir,
rogar; (entreat) suplicar; **to ~ sb to
do sth** rogar a algn que haga algo; see
also **pardon**

began [bɪ'gæn] pt of **begin**
beggar ['begə*] n mendigo
begin [bɪ'gɪn] (pt **began**, pp **begun**) vt,
vi empezar, comenzar; **to ~ doing** or **to
do sth** empezar a hacer algo; **beginner**
n principiante mf; **beginning**
n principio, comienzo
begun [bɪ'gʌn] pp of **begin**
behalf [bɪ'hɑːf] n: **on ~ of** en nombre
de, por; (for benefit of) en beneficio de;
on my/his ~ por mí/él
behave [bɪ'heɪv] vi (person)
portarse, comportarse; (well: also:
~ o.s.) portarse bien; **behaviour**
(us **behavior**) n comportamiento,
conducta
behind [bɪ'haɪnd] prep detrás de;
(supporting): **to be ~ sb** apoyar a
algn ▷ adv detrás, por detrás, atrás
▷ n trasero; **to be ~ (schedule)** ir
retrasado; **~ the scenes** (fig) entre
bastidores
beige [beɪʒ] adj color beige
Beijing [beɪ'dʒɪŋ] n Pekín m
being ['biːɪŋ] n ser m; (existence): **in ~**
existente; **to come into ~** aparecer
belated [bɪ'leɪtɪd] adj atrasado,
tardío
belch [beltʃ] vi eructar ▷ vt (gen: belch
out: smoke etc) arrojar
Belgian ['beldʒən] adj, n belga mf
Belgium ['beldʒəm] n Bélgica
belief [bɪ'liːf] n opinión f; (faith) fe f
believe [bɪ'liːv] vt, vi creer; **to ~ in**
creer en; believer n partidario/a; (Rel)
creyente mf, fiel mf
bell [bel] n campana; (small)
campanilla; (on door) timbre m
bellboy ['belbɔɪ] (BRIT) n botones
m inv
bellhop ['belhɒp] (us) n = **bellboy**
bellow ['beləʊ] vi bramar; (person)
rugir
bell pepper n (esp us) pimiento,
pimentón m (LAM)
belly ['beli] n barriga, panza; **belly
button** (inf) n ombligo
belong [bɪ'lɒŋ] vi: **to ~ to** pertenecer

a; (club etc) ser socio de; **this book ~s
here** este libro va aquí; **belongings** npl
pertenencias fpl
beloved [bɪˈlʌvɪd] adj querido/a
below [bɪˈləu] prep bajo, debajo de;
(less than) inferior a ▷ adv abajo, (por)
debajo; **see ~** véase más abajo
belt [bɛlt] n cinturón m; (Tech) correa,
cinta ▷ vt (thrash) pegar con correa;
beltway (us) n (Aut) carretera de
circunvalación
bemused [bɪˈmjuːzd] adj perplejo
bench [bɛntʃ] n banco; (BRIT Pol): **the
Government/Opposition ~es**
(los asientos que) los miembros del
Gobierno/de la Oposición; **the B~**
(Law: judges) magistratura
bend [bɛnd] (pt, pp bent) vt doblar
▷ vi inclinarse ▷ n (in road, river)
curva; (in pipe) codo; **bend down** vi
inclinarse; **doblarse; bend over** vi
inclinarse
beneath [bɪˈniːθ] prep bajo, debajo
de; (unworthy) indigno de ▷ adv abajo,
(por) debajo
beneficial [bɛnɪˈfɪʃəl] adj beneficioso
benefit [ˈbɛnɪfɪt] n beneficio;
(allowance of money) subsidio ▷ vt
beneficiar ▷ vi: **he'll ~ from it** le sacará
provecho
benign [bɪˈnaɪn] adj benigno; (smile)
afable
bent [bɛnt] pt, pp of **bend** ▷ n
inclinación f ▷ adj: **to be ~ on** estar
empeñado en
bereaved [bɪˈriːvd] npl: **the ~** los
íntimos de una persona afligidos por su
muerte
beret [ˈbɛreɪ] n boina
Berlin [bəːˈlɪn] n Berlín
Bermuda [bəːˈmjuːdə] n las
Bermudas
berry [ˈbɛrɪ] n baya
berth [bəːθ] n (bed) litera; (cabin)
camarote m; (for ship) amarradero ▷ vi
atracar, amarrar
beside [bɪˈsaɪd] prep junto a, al lado
de; **to be ~ o.s. with anger** estar fuera

de sí; **that's ~ the point** eso no tiene
nada que ver; **besides** adv además
▷ prep además de
best [bɛst] adj (el/la) mejor ▷ adv
(lo) mejor; **the ~ part of** (quantity) la
mayor parte de; **at ~** en el mejor de
los casos; **to make the ~ of sth** sacar
el mejor partido de algo; **to do one's
~** hacer todo lo posible; **to the ~ of
my knowledge** que yo sepa; **to the
~ of my ability** como mejor puedo;
best-before date n fecha de consumo
preferente; **best man** (irreg) n padrino
de boda; **bestseller** n éxito de librería,
bestseller m
bet [bɛt] (pt, pp ~ or ~ted) n apuesta
▷ vt: **to ~ money on** apostar dinero
por ▷ vi apostar; **to ~ sb sth** apostar
algo a algn
betray [bɪˈtreɪ] vt traicionar; (trust)
faltar a
better [ˈbɛtə*] adj, adv mejor ▷ vt
superar ▷ n: **to get the ~ of sb** quedar
por encima de algn; **you had ~ do it**
más vale que lo hagas; **he thought ~
of it** cambió de parecer; **to get ~** (Med)
mejorar(se)
betting [ˈbɛtɪŋ] n juego, el apostar;
betting shop (BRIT) n agencia de
apuestas
between [bɪˈtwiːn] prep entre ▷ adv
(time) mientras tanto; (place) en medio
beverage [ˈbɛvərɪdʒ] n bebida
beware [bɪˈwɛə*] vt, vi: **to ~ (of)** tener
cuidado (con); **"~ of the dog"** "perro
peligroso"
bewildered [bɪˈwɪldəd] adj aturdido,
perplejo
beyond [bɪˈjɔnd] prep más allá
de; (past: understanding) fuera de;
(after: date) después de, más allá de;
(above) superior a ▷ adv (in space)
más allá; (in time) posteriormente; **~
doubt** fuera de toda duda; **~ repair**
irreparable
bias [ˈbaɪəs] n (prejudice) prejuicio,
pasión f; (preference) predisposición f;
bias(s)ed adj parcial

bib [bɪb] n babero
Bible ['baɪbl] n Biblia
bicarbonate of soda [baɪ'kɑ:bənɪt-] n bicarbonato sódico
biceps ['baɪseps] n bíceps m
bicycle ['baɪsɪkl] n bicicleta; **bicycle pump** n bomba de bicicleta
bid [bɪd] (pt **bade** or ~, pp **bidden** or ~) n oferta, postura; (in tender) licitación f; (attempt) tentativa, conato ▷ vi hacer una oferta ▷ vt (offer) ofrecer; **to ~ sb good day** dar a algn los buenos días; **bidder** n: **the highest bidder** el mejor postor
bidet [bi:'deɪ] n bidet m
big [bɪg] adj grande; (brother, sister) mayor; **bigheaded** adj engreído; **big toe** n dedo gordo (del pie)
bike [baɪk] n bici f; **bike lane** n carril-bici m
bikini [bɪ'ki:nɪ] n bikini m
bilateral [baɪ'lætərəl] adj (agreement) bilateral
bilingual [baɪ'lɪŋgwəl] adj bilingüe
bill [bɪl] n cuenta; (invoice) factura; (Pol) proyecto de ley; (us: banknote) billete m; (of bird) pico; (of show) programa m; **"post no ~s"** prohibido fijar carteles; **to fit** or **fill the ~** (fig) cumplir con los requisitos; **billboard** (us) n cartelera; **billfold** ['bɪlfəuld] (us) n cartera
billiards ['bɪljədz] n billar m
billion ['bɪljən] n (BRIT) billón m (millón de millones); (us) mil millones mpl
bin [bɪn] n (for rubbish) cubo or bote m (MEX) or tacho (sc) de la basura; (container) recipiente m
bind [baɪnd] (pt, pp **bound**) vt atar; (book) encuadernar; (oblige) obligar ▷ n (inf: nuisance) lata
binge [bɪndʒ] (inf) n: **to go on a ~** ir de juerga
bingo ['bɪŋgəu] n bingo m
binoculars [bɪ'nɔkjuləz] npl prismáticos mpl
bio... [baɪə] prefix: **biochemistry** n

bioquímica; **biodegradable** [baɪəudɪ'greɪdəbl] adj biodegradable; **biography** [baɪ'ɔgrəfɪ] n biografía; **biological** [baɪə'lɔdʒɪkl] adj biológico; **biology** [baɪ'ɔlədʒɪ] n biología; **biometric** [baɪə'metrɪk] adj biométrico
birch [bə:tʃ] n (tree) abedul m
bird [bə:d] n ave f, pájaro; (BRIT: inf: girl) chica; **bird flu** n gripe f aviar; **bird of prey** n ave f de presa; **birdwatching** n: **he likes to go birdwatching on Sundays** los domingos le gusta ir a ver pájaros
Biro® ['baɪrəu] n boli m
birth [bə:θ] n nacimiento; **to give ~ to** parir, dar a luz; **birth certificate** n partida de nacimiento; **birth control** n (policy) control m de natalidad; (methods) métodos mpl anticonceptivos; **birthday** n cumpleaños m inv ▷ cpd (cake, card etc) de cumpleaños; **birthmark** n antojo, marca de nacimiento; **birthplace** n lugar m de nacimiento
biscuit ['bɪskɪt] (BRIT) n galleta
bishop ['bɪʃəp] n obispo; (Chess) alfil m
bistro ['bi:strəu] n café-bar m
bit [bɪt] pt of **bite** ▷ n trozo, pedazo, pedacito; (Comput) bit m, bitio; (for horse) freno, bocado; **a ~ of** un poco de; **a ~ mad** un poco loco; **~ by ~** poco a poco
bitch [bɪtʃ] n perra; (infl: woman) zorra (!)
bite [baɪt] (pt **bit**, pp **bitten**) vt, vi morder; (insect etc) picar ▷ n (insect bite) picadura; (mouthful) bocado; **to ~ one's nails** comerse las uñas; **let's have a ~ (to eat)** (inf) vamos a comer algo
bitten ['bɪtn] pp of **bite**
bitter ['bɪtə*] adj amargo; (wind) cortante, penetrante; (battle) encarnizado ▷ n (BRIT: beer) cerveza típica británica a base de lúpulos
bizarre [bɪ'zɑ:*] adj raro, extraño
black [blæk] adj negro; (tea, coffee) solo ▷ n color m negro; (person): **B~**

negro/a ▷ vt (BRIT Industry) boicotear; **to give sb a ~ eye** ponerle a algn el ojo morado; **~ and blue** (bruised) amoratado; **to be in the ~** (bank account) estar en números negros; **black out** vi (faint) desmayarse; **blackberry** n zarzamora; **blackbird** n mirlo; **blackboard** n pizarra; **black coffee** n café m solo; **blackcurrant** n grosella negra; **black ice** n hielo invisible en la carretera; **blackmail** n chantaje m ▷ vt chantajear; **black market** n mercado negro; **blackout** n (Mil) oscurecimiento; (power cut) apagón m; (TV, Radio) interrupción f de programas; (fainting) desvanecimiento; **black pepper** n pimienta f negra; **black pudding** n morcilla; **Black Sea** n: **the Black Sea** el Mar Negro

bladder ['blædə*] n vejiga

blade [bleɪd] n hoja; (of propeller) paleta; **a ~ of grass** una brizna de hierba

blame [bleɪm] n culpa ▷ vt: **to ~ sb for sth** echar a algn la culpa de algo; **to be to ~ (for)** tener la culpa de algo

bland [blænd] adj (music, taste) soso

blank [blæŋk] adj en blanco; (look) sin expresión ▷ n (of memory): **my mind is a ~** no puedo recordar nada; (on form) blanco, espacio en blanco; (cartridge) cartucho sin bala or de fogueo

blanket ['blæŋkɪt] n manta (SP), cobija (LAM); (of snow) capa; (of fog) manto

blast [blɑːst] n (of wind) ráfaga, soplo; (of explosive) explosión f ▷ vt (blow up) volar

blatant ['bleɪtənt] adj descarado

blaze [bleɪz] n (fire) fuego; (fig: of colour) despliegue m; (: of glory) esplendor m ▷ vi arder en llamas; (fig) brillar ▷ vt: **to ~ a trail** (fig) abrir un camino; **in a ~ of publicity** con gran publicidad

blazer ['bleɪzə*] n chaqueta de uniforme de colegial o de socio de club

bleach [bliːtʃ] n (also: household ~)

lejía ▷ vt blanquear; **bleachers** (US) npl (Sport) gradas fpl al sol

bleak [bliːk] adj (countryside) desierto; (prospect) poco prometedor; (weather) crudo; (smile) triste

bled [bled] pt, pp of **bleed**

bleed [bliːd] (pt, pp **bled**) vt, vi sangrar; **my nose is ~ing** me está sangrando la nariz

blemish ['blemɪʃ] n marca, mancha; (on reputation) tacha

blend [blend] n mezcla ▷ vt mezclar; (colours etc) combinar, mezclar ▷ vi (colours etc: also: **~ in**) combinarse, mezclarse; **blender** n (Culin) batidora

bless [bles] (pt, pp **~ed** or **blest**) vt bendecir; **~ you!** (after sneeze) ¡Jesús!; **blessing** n (approval) aprobación f; (godsend) don m del cielo, bendición f; (advantage) beneficio, ventaja

blew [bluː] pt of **blow**

blight [blaɪt] vt (hopes etc) frustrar, arruinar

blind [blaɪnd] adj ciego; (fig): **~ (to)** ciego (a) ▷ n (for window) persiana ▷ vt cegar; (dazzle) deslumbrar; (deceive): **to ~ sb to ...** cegar a algn a ...; **the blind** npl los ciegos; **blind alley** n callejón m sin salida; **blindfold** n venda ▷ adv con los ojos vendados ▷ vt vendar los ojos a

blink [blɪŋk] vi parpadear, pestañear; (light) oscilar

bliss [blɪs] n felicidad f

blister ['blɪstə*] n ampolla ▷ vi (paint) ampollarse

blizzard ['blɪzəd] n ventisca

bloated ['bləutɪd] adj hinchado; (person: full) ahíto

blob [blɒb] n (drop) gota; (indistinct object) bulto

block [blɒk] n bloque m; (in pipes) obstáculo; (of buildings) manzana (SP), cuadra (LAM) ▷ vt obstruir, cerrar; (progress) estorbar; **~ of flats** (BRIT) bloque m de pisos; **mental ~** bloqueo mental; **block up** vt tapar, obstruir; (pipe) atascar; **blockade**

blog | 320

[-'keɪd] n bloqueo ▷ vt bloquear; **blockage** n estorbo, obstrucción f; **blockbuster** n (book) bestseller m; (film) éxito de público: **block capitals** npl mayúsculas fpl; **block letters** npl mayúsculas fpl

blog [blɒg] n blog m

bloke [bləʊk] n (BRIT: inf) tipo, tío

blond(e) [blɒnd] adj, n rubio/a m/f

blood [blʌd] n sangre f; **blood donor** n donante m/f de sangre; **blood group** n grupo sanguíneo; **blood poisoning** n envenenamiento m en la sangre; **blood pressure** n presión f sanguínea; **bloodshed** n derramamiento de sangre; **bloodshot** adj inyectado en sangre; **bloodstream** n corriente f sanguínea; **blood test** n análisis m inv de sangre; **blood transfusion** n transfusión f de sangre; **blood type** n grupo sanguíneo; **blood vessel** n vaso sanguíneo; **bloody** adj sangriento; (nose etc) lleno de sangre; (BRIT: infl): **this bloody ...** este condenado o puñetero ... (!) ▷ adv: **bloody strong/good** (BRIT: infl) terriblemente fuerte/bueno

bloom [bluːm] n flor f ▷ vi florecer

blossom ['blɒsəm] n flor f ▷ vi florecer

blot [blɒt] n borrón m; (fig) mancha ▷ vt (stain) manchar

blouse [blaʊz] n blusa

blow [bləʊ] (pt blew, pp blown) n golpe m; (with sword) espadazo ▷ vi soplar; (dust, sand etc) volar; (fuse) fundirse ▷ vt (wind) llevar; (fuse) quemar; (instrument) tocar; **to ~ one's nose** sonarse; **blow away** vi llevarse, arrancar; **blow out** vi apagarse; **blow up** vi estallar ▷ vt inflar; (tyre) inflar; (Phot) ampliar; **blow-dry** n moldeado (con secador)

blown [bləʊn] pp of **blow**

blue [bluː] adj azul; (depressed) deprimido; **~ film/joke** película/chiste m verde; **out of the ~** (fig) de repente; **bluebell** n campanilla, campánula

azul; **blueberry** n arándano; **blue cheese** n queso azul; **blues** npl: **the blues** (Mus) el blues; **to have the blues** estar triste; **bluetit** n herrerillo m (común)

bluff [blʌf] vi tirarse un farol, farolear ▷ n farol m; **to call sb's ~** coger a algn la palabra

blunder ['blʌndə*] n patinazo, metedura de pata ▷ vi cometer un error, meter la pata

blunt [blʌnt] adj (pencil) despuntado; (knife) desafilado, romo; (person) franco, directo

blur [bləː*] n (shape): **to become a ~** hacerse borroso ▷ vt (vision) enturbiar; (distinction) borrar; **blurred** adj borroso

blush [blʌʃ] vi ruborizarse, ponerse colorado ▷ n rubor m; **blusher** n colorete m

board [bɔːd] n (cardboard) cartón m; (wooden) tabla, tablero; (on wall) tablón m; (for chess etc) tablero; (committee) junta, consejo; (in firm) mesa or junta directiva; (Naut, Aviat): **on ~** a bordo ▷ vt (ship) embarcarse en; (train) subir a; **full ~** (BRIT) pensión completa; **half ~** (BRIT) media pensión; **to go by the ~** (fig) ser abandonado u olvidado; **board game** n juego de tablero; **boarding card** (BRIT) n tarjeta de embarque; **boarding pass** (US) n = **boarding card**; **boarding school** n internado; **board room** n sala de juntas

boast [bəʊst] vi: **to ~ (about or of)** alardear (de)

boat [bəʊt] n barco, buque m; (small) barca, bote m

bob [bɒb] vi (also: **~ up and down**) menearse, balancearse

bobby pin ['bɒbɪ-] (US) n horquilla

body ['bɒdɪ] n cuerpo; (corpse) cadáver m; (of car) caja, carrocería; (fig: group) grupo; (: organization) organismo; **body-building** n culturismo; **bodyguard** n guardaespaldas m inv; **bodywork** n carrocería

bog [bɒg] n pantano, ciénaga ▷ vt: **to get ~ged down** (fig) empantanarse, atascarse

bogus ['bəugəs] adj falso, fraudulento

boil [bɔɪl] vt (water) hervir; (eggs) pasar por agua, cocer ▷ vi hervir; (fig: with anger) estar furioso; (: with heat) asfixiarse ▷ n (Med) furúnculo, divieso; **to come to the ~, to come to a ~** (us) comenzar a hervir; **to ~ down to** (fig) reducirse a; **boil over** vi salirse, rebosar; (anger etc) llegar al colmo; **boiled egg** n (soft) huevo tibio (MEX) or pasado por agua or a la copa (SC); (hard) huevo duro; **boiled potatoes** npl patatas fpl (SP) or papas fpl (LAM) cocidas; **boiler** n caldera; **boiling** ['bɔɪlɪŋ] adj: **I'm boiling (hot)** (inf) estoy asado; **boiling point** n punto de ebullición

bold [bəuld] adj valiente, audaz; (pej) descarado; (colour) llamativo

Bolivia [bə'lɪvɪə] n Bolivia; **Bolivian** adj, n boliviano/a m/f

bollard ['bɒləd] (BRIT) n (Aut) poste m

bolt [bəult] n (lock) cerrojo; (with nut) perno, tornillo ▷ adv: **~ upright** rígido, erguido ▷ vt (door) echar el cerrojo a; (also: **~ together**) sujetar con tornillos; (food) engullir ▷ vi fugarse; (horse) desbocarse

bomb [bɒm] n bomba ▷ vt bombardear; **bombard** [bɒm'bɑ:d] vt bombardear; (fig) asediar; **bomber** n (Aviat) bombardero; **bomb scare** n amenaza de bomba

bond [bɒnd] n (promise) fianza; (Finance) bono; (link) vínculo, lazo; (Comm): **in ~** en depósito bajo fianza; **bonds** npl (chains) cadenas fpl

bone [bəun] n hueso; (of fish) espina ▷ vt deshuesar; quitar las espinas a

bonfire ['bɒnfaɪə*] n hoguera, fogata

bonnet ['bɒnɪt] n gorra; (BRIT: of car) capó m

bonus ['bəunəs] n (payment) paga extraordinaria, plus m; (fig) bendición f

boo [bu:] excl ¡uh! ▷ vt abuchear,

rechiflar

book [buk] n libro; (of tickets) taco; (of stamps etc) librito ▷ vt (ticket) sacar; (seat, room) reservar; **books** npl (Comm) cuentas fpl, contabilidad f; **book in** vi (at hotel) registrarse; **book up** vt: **to be booked up** (hotel) estar completo; **bookcase** n librería, estante m para libros; **booking** n reserva; **booking office** n (BRIT Rail) despacho de billetes (SP) or boletos (LAM); (Theatre) taquilla (SP), boletería (LAM); **book-keeping** n contabilidad f; **booklet** n folleto; **bookmaker** n corredor m de apuestas; **bookmark** n (also Comput) marcador; **bookseller** n librero; **bookshelf** n estante m (para libros); **bookshop, book store** n librería

boom [bu:m] n (noise) trueno, estampido; (in prices etc) alza rápida; (Econ, in population) boom m ▷ vi (cannon) hacer gran estruendo, retumbar; (Econ) estar en alza

boost [bu:st] n estímulo, empuje m ▷ vt estimular, empujar

boot [bu:t] n bota; (BRIT: of car) maleta, maletero ▷ vt (Comput) arrancar; **to ~** (in addition) además, por añadidura

booth [bu:ð] n (telephone booth, voting booth) cabina

booze [bu:z] (inf) n bebida

border ['bɔ:də*] n borde m, margen m; (of a country) frontera; (for flowers) arriate m ▷ vt (road) bordear; (another country: also: **~ on**) lindar con; **borderline** n: **on the borderline** en el límite

bore [bɔ:*] pt of bear ▷ vt (hole) hacer un agujero en; (well) perforar; (person) aburrir ▷ n (person) pelmazo, pesado; (of gun) calibre m; **bored** adj aburrido; **he's bored to tears** or **to death** or **stiff** está aburrido como una ostra, está muerto de aburrimiento; **boredom** n aburrimiento

boring ['bɔ:rɪŋ] adj aburrido

born [bɔ:n] adj: **to be ~** nacer; **I was ~**

in 1960 nací en 1960

borne [bɔ:n] *pp* of **bear**

borough [ˈbʌrə] *n* municipio *m*

borrow [ˈbɔrəu] *vt*: **to ~ sth (from sb)** tomar algo prestado (a algn)

Bosnia(-Herzegovina) [ˈbɔːsnɪə(hɜːzəˈɡəuvɪːnə)] *n* Bosnia(-Herzegovina); **Bosnian** [ˈbɔznɪən] *adj, n* bosnio/a

bosom [ˈbuzəm] *n* pecho

boss [bɔs] *n* jefe *m* ▷ *vt* (also: **~ about** **or around**) mangonear; **bossy** *adj* mandón/ona

both [bəuθ] *adj, pron* ambos/as, los dos (*las* dos); **~ of us went, we ~ went** fuimos los dos, ambos fuimos ▷ *adv*: **~ A and B** tanto A como B

bother [ˈbɔðəʳ] *vt* (worry) preocupar; (disturb) molestar, fastidiar ▷ *vi* (also: **~ o.s.**) molestarse ▷ *n* (trouble) dificultad *f*; (nuisance) molestia, lata; **to ~ doing** tomarse la molestia de hacer

bottle [ˈbɔtl] *n* botella; (small) frasco; (baby's) biberón *m* ▷ *vt* embotellar; **bottle bank** *n* contenedor *m* de vidrio; **bottle-opener** *n* abrebotellas *m inv*

bottom [ˈbɔtəm] *n* (of box, sea) fondo; (buttocks) trasero, culo; (of page) pie *m*; (of list) final *m*; (of class) último/a ▷ *adj* (lowest) más bajo; (last) último

bought [bɔːt] *pt, pp* of **buy**

boulder [ˈbəuldəʳ] *n* canto rodado

bounce [bauns] *vi* (ball) (re)botar; (cheque) ser rechazado ▷ *vt* hacer (re)botar ▷ *n* (rebound) (re)bote *m*; **bouncer** (*inf*) *n* gorila *m* (que echa a los alborotadores de un bar, club etc)

bound [baund] *pt, pp* of **bind** ▷ *n* (leap) salto; (gen pl: limit) límite *m* ▷ *vi* (leap) saltar ▷ *vt* (border) rodear ▷ *adj*: **~ by** rodeado de; **to be ~ to do sth** (obliged) tener el deber de hacer algo; **he's ~ to come** es seguro que vendrá; **out of ~s** prohibido el paso; **~ for** con destino a

boundary [ˈbaundrɪ] *n* límite *m*

bouquet [ˈbukeɪ] *n* (of flowers) ramo

bourbon [ˈbuəbən] (US) *n* (also: **~ whiskey**) whisky *m* americano, bourbon *m*

bout [baut] *n* (of malaria etc) ataque *m*; (of activity) período; (Boxing etc) combate *m*, encuentro

boutique [buːˈtiːk] *n* boutique *f*, tienda de ropa

bow¹ [bəu] *n* (knot) lazo; (weapon, Mus) arco

bow² [bau] *n* (of the head) reverencia; (Naut: also: **~s**) proa ▷ *vi* inclinarse, hacer una reverencia

bowels [bauəlz] *npl* intestinos *mpl*, vientre *m*; (fig) entrañas *fpl*

bowl [bəul] *n* tazón *m*, cuenco; (ball) bola ▷ *vi* (Cricket) arrojar la pelota; *see also* **bowls**; **bowler** *n* (Cricket) lanzador *m* (de la pelota); (BRIT: also: **bowler hat**) hongo, bombín *m*; **bowling** *n* (game) bochas *fpl*, bolos *mpl*; **bowling alley** *n* bolera; **bowling green** *n* pista para bochas; **bowls** *n* juego de las bochas, bolos *mpl*

bow tie [ˈbəu-] *n* corbata de lazo, pajarita

box [bɔks] *n* (also: **cardboard ~**) caja, cajón *m*; (Theatre) palco ▷ *vt* encajonar ▷ *vi* (Sport) boxear; **boxer** [ˈbɔksəʳ] *n* (person) boxeador *m*; **boxer shorts** [ˈbɔksəʃɔːts] *pl n* bóxers; **a pair of boxer shorts** unos bóxers; **boxing** [ˈbɔksɪŋ] *n* (Sport) boxeo; **Boxing Day** (BRIT) *n* día en que se dan los aguinaldos, 26 de diciembre; **boxing gloves** *npl* guantes *mpl* de boxeo; **boxing ring** *n* ring *m*, cuadrilátero; **box office** *n* taquilla (SP), boletería (LAM)

boy [bɔɪ] *n* (young) niño; (older) muchacho, chico; (son) hijo; **boy band** *n* boy band *m* (grupo musical de chicos)

boycott [ˈbɔɪkɔt] *n* boicot *m* ▷ *vt* boicotear

boyfriend [ˈbɔɪfrend] *n* novio

bra [brɑː] *n* sostén *m*, sujetador *m*

brace [breɪs] *n* (BRIT: also: **~s: on teeth**) corrector *m*, aparato; (tool) berbiquí *m* ▷ *vt* (knees, shoulders) tensionar; **braces** *npl* (BRIT) tirantes *mpl*; **to ~ o.s.** (fig) prepararse

bracelet ['breɪslɪt] n pulsera, brazalete m

bracket ['brækɪt] n (Tech) soporte m, puntal m; (group) clase f, categoría; (also: **brace ~**) soporte m, abrazadera; (also: **round ~**) paréntesis m inv; (also: **square ~**) corchete m ▷ vt (word etc) poner entre paréntesis

brag [bræg] vi jactarse

braid [breɪd] n (trimming) galón m; (of hair) trenza

brain [breɪn] n cerebro; **brains** npl sesos mpl; **she's got ~s** es muy lista

braise [breɪz] vt cocer a fuego lento

brake [breɪk] n (on vehicle) freno ▷ vi frenar; **brake light** n luz f de frenado

bran [bræn] n salvado

branch [brɑːntʃ] n rama; (Comm) sucursal f; **branch off** vi: **a small road branches off to the right** hay una carretera pequeña que sale hacia la derecha; **branch out** vi (fig) extenderse

brand [brænd] n marca; (fig: type) tipo ▷ vt (cattle) marcar con hierro candente; **brand name** n marca; **brand-new** adj flamante, completamente nuevo

brandy ['brændɪ] n coñac m

brash [bræʃ] adj (forward) descarado

brass [brɑːs] n latón m; **the ~** (Mus) los cobres; **brass band** n banda de metal

brat [bræt] (pej) n mocoso/a

brave [breɪv] adj valiente, valeroso ▷ vt (face up to) desafiar; **bravery** n valor m, valentía

brawl [brɔːl] n pelea, reyerta

Brazil [brə'zɪl] n (el) Brasil; **Brazilian** adj, n brasileño/a m/f

breach [briːtʃ] vt abrir brecha en ▷ n (gap) brecha; (breaking): **~ of contract** infracción f de contrato; **~ of the peace** perturbación f del órden público

bread [brɛd] n pan m; **breadbin** n panera; **breadbox** (US) n panera; **breadcrumbs** npl migajas fpl; (Culin) pan rallado

breadth [brɛtθ] n anchura; (fig) amplitud f

break [breɪk] (pt **broke**, pp **broken**) vt romper; (promise) faltar a; (law) violar, infringir; (record) batir ▷ vi romperse, quebrarse; (storm) estallar; (weather) cambiar; (dawn) despuntar; (news etc) darse a conocer ▷ n (gap) abertura; (fracture) fractura; (time interval; (: at school) (período de recreo; (chance) oportunidad f; **to ~ the news to sb** comunicar la noticia a algn; **break down** vt (figures, data) analizar, descomponer ▷ vi (machine) estropearse; (Aut) averiarse; (person) romper a llorar; (talks) fracasar; **break in** vt (horse etc) domar ▷ vi (burglar) forzar una entrada; (interrupt) interrumpir; **break into** vt fus (house) forzar; **break off** vi (speaker) pararse, detenerse; (branch) partir; **break out** vi estallar; (prisoner) escaparse; **to break out in spots** salirle a algn granos; **break up** vi (ship) hacerse pedazos; (crowd, meeting) disolverse; (marriage) deshacerse; (Scol) terminar (el curso); (line) cortarse ▷ vt (rocks etc) partir; (journey) partir; (fight etc) acabar con; **the line's** or **you're breaking up** se corta; **breakdown** n (Aut) avería; (in communications) interrupción f; (Med: also: **nervous breakdown**) colapso, crisis f nerviosa; (of marriage, talks) fracaso; (of statistics) análisis m inv; **breakdown truck**, **breakdown van** n (camión m) grúa

breakfast ['brɛkfəst] n desayuno

break: **break-in** n robo con allanamiento de morada;
breakthrough n (also fig) avance m

breast [brɛst] n (of woman) pecho, seno; (chest) pecho; (of bird) pechuga; **breast-feed** (pt, pp **breast-fed**) vt, vi amamantar, criar a los pechos; **breast-stroke** n braza (de pecho)

breath [brɛθ] n aliento, respiración f; **to take a deep ~** respirar hondo; **out of ~** sin aliento, sofocado

Breathalyser® ['breθəlaɪzə*] (BRIT)
n alcoholímetro
breathe [bri:ð] vt, vi respirar;
breathe in vt, vi aspirar; **breathe
out** vt, vi espirar; **breathing** n
respiración f
breath: breathless adj sin aliento,
jadeante; **breathtaking** adj
imponente, pasmoso; **breath test** n
prueba de la alcoholemia
bred [bred] pt, pp of **breed**
breed [bri:d] (pt, pp **bred**) vt criar ▷ vi
reproducirse, procrear ▷ n (Zool) raza,
casta; (type) tipo
breeze [bri:z] n brisa
breezy ['bri:zi] adj de mucho viento,
ventoso; (person) despreocupado
brew [bru:] vt (tea) hacer; (beer)
elaborar ▷ vi (fig: trouble) prepararse;
(storm) amenazar; **brewery** n fábrica
de cerveza, cervecería
bribe [braɪb] n soborno ▷ vt
sobornar, cohechar; **bribery** n
soborno, cohecho
bric-a-brac ['brɪkəbræk] n inv
baratijas fpl
brick [brɪk] n ladrillo; **bricklayer** n
albañil m
bride [braɪd] n novia; **bridegroom** n
novio; **bridesmaid** n dama de honor
bridge [brɪdʒ] n puente m; (Naut)
puente m de mando; (of nose) caballete
m; (Cards) bridge m ▷ vt (fig): **to ~ a gap**
llenar un vacío
bridle ['braɪdl] n brida, freno
brief [bri:f] adj breve, corto ▷ n (Law)
escrito; (task) cometido, encargo
▷ vt informar; **briefs** npl (for men)
calzoncillos mpl; (for women) bragas fpl;
briefcase n cartera (SP), portafolio
(LAM); **briefing** n (Press) informe m;
briefly adv (glance) fugazmente; (say)
en pocas palabras
brigadier [brɪgə'dɪə*] n general m
de brigada
bright [braɪt] adj brillante; (room)
luminoso; (day) de sol; (person: clever)
listo, inteligente; (: lively) alegre;

(colour) vivo; (future) prometedor(a)
brilliant ['brɪljənt] adj brillante; (inf)
fenomenal
brim [brɪm] n borde m; (of hat) ala
brine [braɪn] n (Culin) salmuera
bring [brɪŋ] (pt, pp **brought**) vt (thing,
person: with you) traer; (: to sb) llevar,
conducir; (trouble, satisfaction) causar;
bring about vt ocasionar, producir;
bring back vt volver a traer; (return)
devolver; **bring down** vt (government,
plane) derribar; (price) rebajar; **bring
in** vt (harvest) recoger; (person) hacer
entrar o pasar; (object) traer; (Pol: bill,
law) presentar; (produce: income)
producir, rendir; **bring on** vt (illness,
attack) producir, causar; (player,
substitute) sacar (de la reserva), hacer
salir; **bring out** vt sacar; (book etc)
publicar; (meaning) subrayar; **bring
up** vt subir; (person) educar, criar;
(question) sacar a colación; (food: vomit)
devolver, vomitar
brink [brɪŋk] n borde m
brisk [brɪsk] adj (abrupt: tone) brusco;
(person) enérgico, vigoroso; (pace)
rápido; (trade) activo
bristle ['brɪsl] n cerda ▷ vi: **to ~ in
anger** temblar de rabia
Brit [brɪt] n abbr (inf: = British person)
británico/a
Britain ['brɪtən] n (also: **Great ~**)
Gran Bretaña
British ['brɪtɪʃ] adj británico
▷ npl: **the ~** los británicos; **British Isles**
npl: **the British Isles** las Islas Británicas
Briton ['brɪtən] n británico/a
brittle ['brɪtl] adj quebradizo, frágil
broad [brɔ:d] adj ancho; (range)
amplio; (smile) abierto; (general: outlines
etc) general; (accent) cerrado; **in ~
daylight** en pleno día; **broadband** n
banda ancha; **broad bean** n haba;
broadcast (pt, pp ~) n emisión f
▷ vt (Radio) emitir; (TV) transmitir
▷ vi emitir; transmitir; **broaden** vt
ampliar ▷ vi ensancharse; **to broaden
one's mind** hacer más tolerante a

algn; **broadly** adv en general; **broad-minded** adj tolerante, liberal

broccoli ['brɒkəlɪ] n brécol m

brochure ['brəʊʃjʊə*] n folleto m

broil [brɔɪl] vt (Culin) asar a la parrilla

broiler ['brɔɪlə*] n (grill) parrilla f

broke [brəʊk] pt of **break** ▷ adj (inf) pelado, sin blanca

broken ['brəʊkən] pp of **break** ▷ adj roto; (machine: also: ~) averiado; **~ leg** pierna rota; **in ~ English** en un inglés imperfecto

broker ['brəʊkə*] n agente mf, bolsista mf; (insurance broker) agente de seguros

bronchitis [brɒŋ'kaɪtɪs] n bronquitis f

bronze [brɒnz] n bronce m

brooch [brəʊtʃ] n prendedor m, broche m

brood [bru:d] n camada, cría ▷ vi (person) dejarse obsesionar

broom [brum] n escoba; (Bot) retama

Bros. abbr (= Brothers) Hnos

broth [brɒθ] n caldo

brothel ['brɒθəl] n burdel m

brother ['brʌðə*] n hermano; **brother-in-law** n cuñado

brought [brɔːt] pt, pp of **bring**

brow [braʊ] n (forehead) frente m; (eyebrow) ceja; (of hill) cumbre f

brown [braʊn] adj (colour) marrón m; (hair) castaño; (tanned) bronceado, moreno ▷ n (colour) color m marrón or pardo ▷ vt (Culin) dorar; **brown bread** n pan integral

Brownie ['braʊnɪ] n niña exploradora

brown rice n arroz m integral

brown sugar n azúcar m terciado

browse [braʊz] vi (through book) hojear; (in shop) mirar; **browser** n (Comput) navegador m

bruise [bru:z] n cardenal m (SP), moretón m ▷ vt magullar

brunette [bru:'net] n morena

brush [brʌʃ] n cepillo; (for painting, shaving etc) brocha; (artist's) pincel m;

(with police etc) roce m ▷ vt (sweep) barrer; (groom) cepillar; (also: ~ against) rozar al pasar

Brussels ['brʌslz] n Bruselas

Brussels sprout n col f de Bruselas

brutal ['bru:tl] adj brutal

B.Sc. abbr (= Bachelor of Science) licenciado en Ciencias

BSE n abbr (= bovine spongiform encephalopathy) encefalopatía f espongiforme bovina

bubble ['bʌbl] n burbuja ▷ vi burbujear, borbotar; **bubble bath** n espuma para el baño; **bubble gum** n chicle m de globo; **bubblejet printer** ['bʌbldʒet-] n impresora de inyección por burbujas

buck [bʌk] n (rabbit) conejo macho; (deer) gamo; (us: inf) dólar m ▷ vi corcovear; **to pass the ~ (to sb)** echar (a algn) el muerto

bucket ['bʌkɪt] n cubo, balde m

buckle ['bʌkl] n hebilla ▷ vt abrochar con hebilla ▷ vi combarse

bud [bʌd] n (of plant) brote m, yema; (of flower) capullo ▷ vi brotar, echar brotes

Buddhism ['budɪzm] n Budismo

Buddhist ['budɪst] adj, n budista m/f

buddy ['bʌdɪ] (us) n compañero, compinche m

budge [bʌdʒ] vt mover; (fig) hacer ceder ▷ vi moverse, ceder

budgerigar ['bʌdʒərɪgɑ:*] n periquito

budget ['bʌdʒɪt] n presupuesto ▷ vi: **to ~ for sth** presupuestar algo

budgie ['bʌdʒɪ] n = **budgerigar**

buff [bʌf] adj (colour) color de ante ▷ n (inf: enthusiast) entusiasta mf

buffalo ['bʌfələʊ] (pl ~ or ~es) n (BRIT) búfalo; (us: bison) bisonte m

buffer ['bʌfə*] n (Comput) memoria intermedia; (Rail) tope m

buffet[1] ['bufeɪ] vt golpear

buffet[2] ['bufeɪ] n (BRIT: in station) bar m, cafetería; (food) buffet m; **buffet car** (BRIT) n (Rail) coche-comedor m

bug [bʌg] n (esp us: insect) bicho, sabandija; (Comput) error m; (germ) microbio, bacilo; (spy device) micrófono oculto ⊳ vt (inf: annoy) fastidiar; (room) poner micrófono oculto en

buggy ['bʌgɪ] n cochecito de niño

build [bɪld] (pt, pp **built**) n (of person) tipo ⊳ vt construir, edificar; **build up** vt (morale, forces, production) acrecentar; (stocks) acumular; **builder** n (contractor) contratista mf; **building** n construcción f; (structure) edificio; **building site** (BRIT) n obra; **building society** (BRIT) n sociedad f inmobiliaria

built [bɪlt] pt, pp of **build**; **built-in** adj (cupboard) empotrado; (device) interior, incorporado; **built-up** adj (area) urbanizado

bulb [bʌlb] n (Bot) bulbo; (Elec) bombilla, foco (MEX), bujía (CAM), bombita (RPL)

Bulgaria [bʌl'geərɪə] n Bulgaria; **Bulgarian** adj n búlgaro/a m/f

bulge [bʌldʒ] n bulto, protuberancia ⊳ vi bombearse, pandearse; (pocket etc): **to ~ (with)** rebosar (de)

bulimia [bə'lɪmɪə] n bulimia

bulimic [bjuː'lɪmɪk] adj, n bulímico/a m/f

bulk [bʌlk] n masa, mole f; **in ~** (Comm) a granel; **the ~ of** la mayor parte de; **bulky** adj voluminoso, abultado

bull [bul] n toro; (male elephant, whale) macho

bulldozer ['buldəuzə*] n bulldozer m

bullet ['bulɪt] n bala

bulletin ['bulɪtɪn] n anuncio, parte m; (journal) boletín m; **bulletin board** n (US) tablón m de anuncios; (Comput) tablero de noticias

bullfight ['bulfaɪt] n corrida de toros; **bullfighter** n torero; **bullfighting** n los toros, el toreo

bully ['bulɪ] n valentón m, matón m ⊳ vt intimidar, tiranizar

bum [bʌm] n (inf: backside) culo; (esp us: tramp) vagabundo

bumblebee ['bʌmblbiː] n abejorro

bump [bʌmp] n (blow) tope m, choque m; (jolt) sacudida; (on road etc) bache m; (on head etc) chichón m ⊳ vt (strike) chocar contra; **bump into** vt fus chocar contra, tropezar con; (person) topar con; **bumper** n (Aut) parachoques m inv ⊳ adj: **bumper crop or harvest** cosecha abundante; **bumpy** adj (road) lleno de baches

bun [bʌn] n (BRIT: cake) pastel m; (us: bread) bollo; (of hair) moño

bunch [bʌntʃ] n (of flowers) ramo; (of keys) manojo; (of bananas) piña; (of people) grupo; (pej) pandilla; **bunches** npl (in hair) coletas fpl

bundle ['bʌndl] n bulto, fardo; (of sticks) haz m; (of papers) legajo ⊳ vt (also: **~ up**) atar, envolver; **to ~ sth/sb into** meter algo/a algn precipitadamente en

bungalow ['bʌŋgələu] n bungalow m, chalé m

bungee jumping ['bʌndʒiːˈdʒʌmpɪŋ] n puenting m, banyi m

bunion ['bʌnjən] n juanete m

bunk [bʌŋk] n litera; **bunk beds** npl literas fpl

bunker ['bʌŋkə*] n (coal store) carbonera; (Mil) refugio; (Golf) bunker m

bunny ['bʌnɪ] n (inf: also: **~ rabbit**) conejito

buoy [bɔɪ] n boya; **buoyant** adj (ship) capaz de flotar; (economy) boyante; (person) optimista

burden ['bəːdn] n carga ⊳ vt cargar

bureau [bjuəˈrəu] (pl **-x**) n (BRIT: writing desk) escritorio, buró m; (us: chest of drawers) cómoda; (office) oficina, agencia

bureaucracy [bjuəˈrɔkrəsɪ] n burocracia

bureaucrat ['bjuərəkræt] n burócrata m/f

bureau de change [-dəˈʒɑ̃ʒ] (pl **bureaux de change**) n caja f de cambio

bureaux ['bjuərəuz] npl of **bureau**

burger ['bɜːgə'] *n* hamburguesa

burglar ['bɜːglə'] *n* ladrón/ona *m/f*; **burglar alarm** *n* alarma *f* antirrobo; **burglary** *n* robo con allanamiento, robo de una casa

burial ['berɪəl] *n* entierro

burn [bɜːn] (*pt, pp* **-ed** *or* **-t**) *vt* quemar; (*house*) incendiar ▷ *vi* quemarse, arder; incendiarse; (*sting*) escocer ▷ *n* quemadura; **burn down** *vt* incendiar; **burn out** *vt* (*writer etc*): **to burn o.s. out** agotarse; **burning** *adj* (*building etc*) en llamas; (*hot: sand etc*) abrasador(a); (*ambition*) ardiente

Burns' Night [bɜːnz-] *n* ver recuadro

● **BURNS' NIGHT**
●
● Cada veinticinco de enero los
● escoceses celebran la llamada
● **Burns' Night** (noche de Burns),
● en honor al poeta escocés Robert
● Burns (1759–1796). Es tradición
● hacer una cena en la que, al son
● de la música de la gaita escocesa,
● se sirve "haggis", plato tradicional
● de asadura de cordero cocida
● en el estómago del animal,
● acompañado de nabos y puré de
● patatas. Durante la misma se
● recitan poemas del autor y varios
● discursos conmemorativos de
● carácter festivo.

burnt [bɜːnt] *pt, pp of* **burn**

burp [bɜːp] (*inf*) *n* eructo ▷ *vi* eructar

burrow ['bʌrəʊ] *n* madriguera ▷ *vi* hacer una madriguera; (*rummage*) hurgar

burst [bɜːst] (*pt, pp* **-**) *vt* reventar; (*river: banks etc*) romper ▷ *vi* reventarse; (*tyre*) pincharse ▷ *n* (*of gunfire*) ráfaga; (*also: ~ pipe*) reventón *m*; **a ~ of energy/speed/enthusiasm** una explosión de energía/un ímpetu de velocidad/un arranque de entusiasmo; **to ~ into flames**

estallar en llamas; **to ~ into tears** deshacerse en lágrimas; **to ~ out laughing** soltar la carcajada; **to ~ open** abrirse de golpe; **to be ~ing with** (*container*) estar lleno a rebosar de; (*: person*) reventar por *or* de; **burst into** *vt fus* (*room etc*) irrumpir en

bury ['berɪ] *vt* enterrar; (*body*) enterrar, sepultar

bus [bʌs] (*pl* **-es**) *n* autobús *m*; **bus conductor** *n* cobrador(a) *m/f*

bush [bʊʃ] *n* arbusto; (*scrub land*) monte *m*; **to beat about the ~** andar(se) con rodeos

business ['bɪznɪs] *n* (*matter*) asunto; (*trading*) comercio, negocios *mpl*; (*firm*) empresa, casa; (*occupation*) oficio; **to be away on ~** estar en viaje de negocios; **it's my ~ to ...** me toca *or* corresponde ...; **it's none of my ~** yo no tengo nada que ver; **he means ~** habla en serio; **business class** *n* (*Aer*) clase *f* preferente; **businesslike** *adj* eficiente; **businessman** (*irreg*) *n* hombre *m* de negocios; **business trip** *n* viaje *m* de negocios; **businesswoman** (*irreg*) *n* mujer *f* de negocios

busker ['bʌskə'] (*BRIT*) *n* músico/a ambulante

bus: bus pass *n* bonobús; **bus shelter** *n* parada cubierta; **bus station** *n* estación *f* de autobuses; **bus-stop** *n* parada de autobús

bust [bʌst] *n* (*Anat*) pecho; (*sculpture*) busto ▷ *adj* (*inf: broken*) roto, estropeado; **to go ~** quebrar

bustling ['bʌslɪŋ] *adj* (*town*) animado, bullicioso

busy ['bɪzɪ] *adj* ocupado, atareado; (*shop, street*) concurrido, animado; (*Tel: line*) comunicando ▷ *vt*: **to ~ o.s. with** ocuparse en; **busy signal** (*US*) *n* (*Tel*) señal *f* de comunicado

○ **KEYWORD**

but [bʌt] *conj* 1 pero; **he's not very bright, but he's hard-working** no es muy inteligente, pero es trabajador

2 (in direct contradiction) sino: **he's not English but French** no es inglés sino francés; **he didn't sing but he shouted** no cantó sino que gritó

3 (showing disagreement, surprise etc): **but that's far too expensive!** ¡pero eso es carísimo!; **but it does work!** ¡(pero) sí que funciona!

▷ prep (apart from, except) menos, salvo: **we've had nothing but trouble** no hemos tenido más que problemas; **no-one but him can do it** nadie más que él puede hacerlo; **who but a lunatic would do such a thing?** ¿sólo un loco haría una cosa así!; **but for you/your help** si no fuera por ti/tu ayuda; **anything but that** cualquier cosa menos eso

▷ adv (just, only): **she's but a child** no es más que una niña; **had I but known** si lo hubiera sabido; **I can but try** al menos lo puedo intentar; **it's all but finished** está casi acabado

butcher | ˈbutʃə* | n carnicero ▷ vt hacer una carnicería con; (cattle etc) matar; **butcher's (shop)** n carnicería

butler | ˈbʌtlə* | n mayordomo

butt | bʌt | n (barrel) tonel m; (of gun) culata; (of cigarette) colilla; (BRIT: fig: target) blanco ▷ vt dar cabezadas contra, top(et)ar

butter | ˈbʌtə* | n mantequilla ▷ vt untar con mantequilla; **buttercup** n botón m de oro

butterfly | ˈbʌtəflaɪ | n mariposa; (Swimming: also: ~ **stroke**) braza de mariposa

buttocks | ˈbʌtəks | npl nalgas fpl

button | ˈbʌtn | n botón m; (US) placa, chapa ▷ vt (also: ~ **up**) abotonar, abrochar ▷ vi abrocharse

buy | baɪ | (pt, pp **bought**) vt comprar ▷ n compra: **to ~ sb sth/sth from sb** comprarle algo a algn; **to ~ sb a drink** invitar a algn a tomar algo; **buy out** vt

(partner) comprar la parte de; **buy up** vt (property) acaparar; (stock) comprar todas las existencias de; **buyer** n comprador(a) m/f

buzz | bʌz | n zumbido; (inf: phone call) llamada (por teléfono) ▷ vi zumbar; **buzzer** n timbre m

○ **KEYWORD**

by | baɪ | prep 1 (referring to cause, agent) por; de; **killed by lightning** muerto por un relámpago; **a painting by Picasso** un cuadro de Picasso

2 (referring to method, manner, means): **by bus/car/train** en autobús/coche/tren; **to pay by cheque** pagar con un cheque; **by moonlight/candlelight** a la luz de la luna/una vela; **by saving hard he ...** ahorrando ...

3 (via, through) por; **we came by Dover** vinimos por Dover

4 (close to, past): **the house by the river** la casa junto al río; **she rushed by me** pasó a mi lado como una exhalación; **I go by the post office every day** paso por delante de Correos todos los días

5 (time: not later than) para; (: during): **by daylight** de día; **by 4 o'clock** para las cuatro; **by this time tomorrow** mañana a estas horas; **by the time I got here it was too late** cuando llegué ya era demasiado tarde

6 (amount): **by the metre/kilo** por metro/kilo; **paid by the hour** pagado por hora

7 (Math, measure): **to divide/multiply by 3** dividir/multiplicar por 3; **a room 3 metres by 4** una habitación de 3 metros por 4; **it's broader by a metre** es un metro más ancho

8 (according to) según, de acuerdo con; **it's 3 o'clock by my watch** según mi reloj, son las tres; **it's all right by me** por mí, está bien

9: **(all) by oneself** etc todo solo; **he did it (all) by himself** lo hizo él solo;

he was standing **(all) by himself** in a corner estaba de pie solo en un rincón

10: by the way a propósito, por cierto; **this wasn't my idea, by the way** pues, no fue idea mía
▷ *adv* 1 *see* **go; pass** *etc*

2: by and by finalmente; **they'll come back by and by** acabarán volviendo; **by and large** en líneas generales, en general

bye(-bye) ['baɪ('baɪ)] *excl* adiós, hasta luego

by-election (BRIT) *n* elección *f* parcial

bypass ['baɪpɑːs] *n* carretera de circunvalación; (Med) (operación *f* de) by-pass *f* ▷ *vt* evitar

byte [baɪt] *n* (Comput) byte *m*, octeto

C

C [siː] *n* (Mus) do *m*

cab [kæb] *n* taxi *m*; (of truck) cabina

cabaret ['kæbəreɪ] *n* cabaret *m*

cabbage ['kæbɪdʒ] *n* col *f*, berza

cabin ['kæbɪn] *n* cabaña; (on ship) camarote *m*; (on plane) cabina; **cabin crew** *n* tripulación *f* de cabina

cabinet ['kæbɪnɪt] *n* (Pol) consejo de ministros; (furniture) armario; (also: **display ~**) vitrina; **cabinet minister** *n* ministro/a (del gabinete)

cable ['keɪbl] *n* cable *m* ▷ *vt* cablegrafiar; **cable car** *n* teleférico; **cable television** *n* televisión *f* por cable

cactus ['kæktəs] (pl **cacti**) *n* cacto

café ['kæfeɪ] *n* café *m*

cafeteria [kæfɪ'tɪərɪə] *n* cafetería

caffein(e) ['kæfiːn] *n* cafeína

cage [keɪdʒ] *n* jaula

cagoule [kə'guːl] *n* chubasquero

cake [keɪk] *n* (Culin: large) tarta; (: small) pastel *m*; (of soap) pastilla

calcium ['kælsɪəm] *n* calcio

calculate ['kælkjuleɪt] *vt* calcular;

calculation [-'leɪʃən] n cálculo, cómputo; **calculator** n calculadora

calendar ['kæləndə*] n calendario

calf [kɑːf] (pl **calves**) n (of cow) ternero, becerro; (of other animals) cría; (also: **~skin**) piel f de becerro; (Anat) pantorrilla

calibre ['kælɪbə*] (US **caliber**) n calibre m

call [kɔːl] vt llamar; (meeting) convocar ▷ vi (shout) llamar; (Tel) llamar (por teléfono); (visit: also: **~ in, ~ round**) hacer una visita ▷ n llamada; (of bird) canto; **to be ~ed** llamarse; **on ~** (on duty) de guardia; **call back** vi (return) volver; (Tel) volver a llamar; **call for** vt fus (demand) pedir, exigir; (fetch) pasar a recoger; **call in** vt (doctor, expert, police) llamar; **call off** vt (cancel: meeting, race) cancelar; (: deal) anular; (: strike) desconvocar; **call on** vt fus (visit) visitar; (turn to) acudir a; **call out** vi gritar; **call up** vt (Mil) llamar al servicio militar; (Tel) llamar; **callbox** (BRIT) n cabina telefónica; **call centre** (US **call center**) n centro de atención al cliente; **caller** n visita; (Tel) usuario/a

callous ['kæləs] adj insensible, cruel

calm [kɑːm] adj tranquilo; (sea) liso, en calma ▷ n calma, tranquilidad f ▷ vt calmar, tranquilizar; **calm down** vi calmarse, tranquilizarse ▷ vt calmar, tranquilizar; **calmly** ['kɑːmlɪ] adv tranquilamente, con calma

Calor gas® ['kælə*-] n butano

calorie ['kælərɪ] n caloría

calves [kɑːvz] npl of **calf**

camcorder ['kæmkɔːdə*] n videocámara

came [keɪm] pt of **come**

camel ['kæməl] n camello

camera ['kæmərə] n máquina fotográfica; (Cinema, TV) cámara; **in ~** (Law) a puerta cerrada; **cameraman** (irreg) n cámara m; **camera phone** n teléfono con cámara

camouflage ['kæməflɑːʒ] n camuflaje m ▷ vt camuflar

camp [kæmp] n campamento, camping m; (Mil) campamento; (for prisoners) campo; (fig: faction) bando ▷ vi acampar ▷ adj afectado, afeminado

campaign [kæm'peɪn] n (Mil, Pol etc) campaña ▷ vi hacer campaña; **campaigner** n: **campaigner for** defensor(a) m/f de

camp: campbed (BRIT) n cama de campaña; **camper** n campista mf; (vehicle) caravana; **campground** (US) n camping m, campamento; **camping** n camping m; **to go camping** hacer camping; **campsite** n camping m

campus ['kæmpəs] n ciudad f universitaria

can¹ [kæn] n (of oil, water) bidón m; (tin) lata, bote m ▷ vt enlatar

○ KEYWORD

can² [kæn] (negative **cannot, can't**, conditional and pt **could**) aux vb 1 (be able to) poder; **you can do it if you try** puedes hacerlo si lo intentas; **I can't see you** no te veo

2 (know how to) saber; **I can swim/play tennis/drive** sé nadar/jugar al tenis/conducir; **can you speak French?** ¿hablas or sabes hablar francés?

3 (may) poder; **can I use your phone?** ¿me dejas or puedo usar tu teléfono?

4 (expressing disbelief, puzzlement etc): **it can't be true!** ¡no puede ser (verdad)!; **what can he want?** ¿qué querrá?

5 (expressing possibility, suggestion etc): **he could be in the library** podría estar en la biblioteca; **she could have been delayed** pudo haberse retrasado

Canada ['kænədə] n (el) Canadá; **Canadian** [kə'neɪdɪən] adj, n canadiense mf

canal [kə'næl] n canal m

canary [kə'neərɪ] n canario

Canary Islands [kə'neərɪ'aɪləndz]

npl: **the ~** las (Islas) Canarias
cancel ['kænsəl] vt cancelar; (train)
suprimir; (cross out) tachar, borrar;
cancellation [-'leɪʃən] n cancelación
f; supresión f
Cancer ['kænsə*] n (Astrology)
Cáncer m
cancer ['kænsə*] n cáncer m
candidate ['kændɪdeɪt] n
candidato/a
candle ['kændl] n vela; (in church)
cirio; **candlestick** n (single) candelero,
(low) palmatoria; (bigger, ornate)
candelabro
candy ['kændɪ] n azúcar m cande;
(us) caramelo; **candy bar** (us) n
barrita (dulce); **candyfloss**(BRIT) n
algodón m (azucarado)
cane [keɪn] n (Bot) caña; (stick) vara,
palmeta; (for furniture) mimbre f ▷ vt
(BRIT: Scol) castigar (con vara)
canister ['kænɪstə*] n bote m, lata;
(of gas) bombona
cannabis ['kænəbɪs] n marijuana
canned [kænd] adj en lata, de lata
cannon ['kænən] (pl ~ or ~s) n
cañón m
cannot ['kænɔt] = **can not**
canoe [kə'nu:] n canoa; (Sport)
piragua; **canoeing** n piragüismo
canon ['kænən] n (clergyman)
canónigo; (standard) canon m
can-opener ['kænəupnə*] n
abrelatas m inv
can't [kænt] = **can not**
canteen [kæn'ti:n] n (eating place)
cantina; (BRIT: of cutlery) juego
canter ['kæntə*] vi ir a medio galope
canvas ['kænvəs] n (material) lona;
(painting) lienzo; (Naut) velas fpl
canvass ['kænvəs] vi (Pol): **to ~
for** solicitar votos por ▷ vt (Comm)
sondear
canyon ['kænjən] n cañón m
cap [kæp] n (hat) gorra; (of pen)
capuchón m; (of bottle) tapa, tapón m;
(contraceptive) diafragma m; (for toy gun)
cápsula ▷ vt (outdo) superar; (limit)

recortar
capability [keɪpə'bɪlɪtɪ] n capacidad
f
capable ['keɪpəbl] adj capaz
capacity [kə'pæsɪtɪ] n capacidad f;
(position) calidad f
cape [keɪp] n capa; (Geo) cabo
caper ['keɪpə*] n (Culin: gen pl)
alcaparra; (prank) broma
capital ['kæpɪtl] n (also: ~ **city**)
capital f; (money) capital m; (also:
~ **letter**) mayúscula; **capitalism**
n capitalismo; **capitalist** adj, n
capitalista mf; **capital punishment** n
pena de muerte
Capitol ['kæpɪtl] n ver recuadro

CAPITOL

El Capitolio **(Capitol)** es el edificio
del Congreso **(Congress)** de
los Estados Unidos, situado en
la ciudad de Washington. Por
extensión, también se suele llamar
así al edificio en el que tienen lugar
las sesiones parlamentarias de
la cámara de representantes de
muchos de los estados.

Capricorn ['kæprɪkɔ:n] n
Capricornio
capsize [kæp'saɪz] vt volcar, hacer
zozobrar ▷ vi volcarse, zozobrar
capsule ['kæpsju:l] n cápsula
captain ['kæptɪn] n capitán m
caption ['kæpʃən] n (heading) título;
(to picture) leyenda
captivity [kæp'tɪvɪtɪ] n cautiverio
capture ['kæptʃə*] vt prender,
apresar; (animal, Comput) capturar;
(place) tomar; (attention) captar, llamar
▷ n apresamiento; captura; toma;
(data capture) formulación f de datos
car [kɑ:*] n coche m, carro (LAM),
automóvil m; (us Rail) vagón m
carafe [kə'ræf] n jarra
caramel ['kærəməl] n caramelo
carat ['kærət] n quilate m

caravan ['kærəvæn] n (BRIT)
caravana, rulof; (in desert) caravana;
caravan site (BRIT) n camping m para
caravanas

carbohydrate [kɑːbəʊ'haɪdreɪt] n
hidrato de carbono; (food) fécula

carbon ['kɑːbən] n carbono; **carbon
dioxide** n dióxido de carbono,
anhídrido carbónico; **carbon
footprint** n huella de carbono;
carbon monoxide n monóxido de
carbono

car boot sale n mercadillo organizado
en un aparcamiento, en el que se exponen
las mercancías en el maletero del coche

carburettor [kɑːbju'retə*] (US
carburetor) n carburador

card [kɑːd] n (material) cartulina;
(index card etc) ficha; (playing card) carta,
naipe m; (visiting card, greetings card etc)
tarjeta; **cardboard** n cartón m; **card
game** n juego de naipes o cartas

cardigan ['kɑːdɪgən] n rebeca

cardinal ['kɑːdɪnl] adj cardinal;
(importance, principal) esencial ▷ n
cardenal m

cardphone ['kɑːdfəʊn] n cabina que
funciona con tarjetas telefónicas

care [kεə*] n cuidado; (worry)
inquietud f; (charge) cargo, custodia
▷ vi: **to ~ about** (person, animal) tener
cariño a; (thing, idea) preocuparse por; **~
of** en casa de, al cuidado de; **in sb's ~** a
cargo de algn; **to take ~ to** cuidarse de,
tener cuidado de; **to take ~ of** cuidar;
(problem etc) ocuparse de; **I don't ~** no
me importa; **I couldn't ~ less** eso me
trae sin cuidado; **care for** vt fus cuidar
a; (like) querer

career [kə'rɪə*] n profesión f; (in work,
school) carrera ▷ vi (also: **~ along**)
correr a toda velocidad

care: **carefree** adj despreocupado;
careful adj cuidadoso; (cautious)
cauteloso; **(be) careful!** ¡tenga
cuidado!; **carefully** adv con cuidado,
con cuidado; **caregiver** (US) n (professional)
enfermero/a m/f; (unpaid) persona que

cuida a un pariente o vecino; **careless**
adj descuidado; (heedless) poco
atento; **carelessness** n descuido,
falta de atención; **carer** ['kεərə*] n
(professional) enfermero/a m/f; (unpaid)
persona que cuida a un pariente o vecino

caretaker n portero/a, conserje mf

car-ferry ['kɑːferɪ] n transbordador
m para coches

cargo ['kɑːgəʊ] (pl **-es**) n
cargamento, carga

car hire n alquiler m de automóviles

Caribbean [kærɪ'biːən] n: **the ~ (Sea)**
el (Mar) Caribe

caring ['kεərɪŋ] adj humanitario;
(behaviour) afectuoso

carnation [kɑː'neɪʃən] n clavel m

carnival ['kɑːnɪvəl] n carnaval m;
(US: tenfair) parque m de atracciones

carol ['kærəl] n: (Christmas) **~**
villancico

carousel [kærə'sεl] (US) n tiovivo,
caballitos mpl

car park (BRIT) n aparcamiento,
parking m

carpenter ['kɑːpɪntə*] n
carpintero/a

carpet ['kɑːpɪt] n alfombra; (fitted)
moqueta ▷ vt alfombrar

car rental n alquiler m de coches

carriage ['kærɪdʒ] n (BRIT Rail) vagón
m; (horse-drawn) coche m; (of goods)
transporte m; (: cost) porte m, flete m;
carriageway (BRIT) n (part of road)
calzada

carrier ['kærɪə*] n (transport company)
transportista, empresa de transportes;
(Med) portador(a) m/f; **carrier bag**
(BRIT) n bolsa de papel o plástico

carrot ['kærət] n zanahoria

carry ['kærɪ] vt (person)
llevar; (transport) transportar;
(involve: responsibilities etc) entrañar,
implicar; (Med) ser portador de ▷ vi
(sound) oírse; **to get carried away** (fig)
entusiasmarse; **carry on** vi (continue)
seguir (adelante), continuar ▷ vt
proseguir, continuar; **carry out** vt

(orders) cumplir; (investigation) llevar a cabo, realizar

cart [kɑːt] n carro, carreta ▷ vt (inf: transport) acarrear

carton ['kɑːtən] n (box) caja (de cartón); (of milk etc) bote m; (of yogurt) tarrina

cartoon [kɑː'tuːn] n (Press) caricatura; (comic strip) tira cómica; (film) dibujos mpl animados

cartridge ['kɑːtrɪdʒ] n cartucho; (of pen) recambio

carve [kɑːv] vt (meat) trinchar; (wood, stone) cincelar, esculpir; (initials etc) grabar; **carving** n (object) escultura; (design) talla; (art) tallado

car wash n lavado de coches

case [keɪs] n (container) caja; (Med) caso; (for jewels etc) estuche m; (Law) causa, proceso; (BRIT: also: **suit~**) maleta; **in ~ of** en caso de; **in any ~** en todo caso; **just in ~** por si acaso

cash [kæʃ] n dinero en efectivo, dinero contante ▷ vt cobrar, hacer efectivo; **to pay (in) ~** pagar al contado; **~ on delivery** cóbrese al entregar; **cashback** n (discount) devolución f; (at supermarket etc) retirada de dinero en efectivo en el establecimiento donde se ha pagado con tarjeta; también dinero retirado; **cash card** n tarjeta f dinero; **cash desk** (BRIT) n caja; **cash dispenser** n cajero automático

cashew [kæ'ʃuː] n (also: **~ nut**) anacardo

cashier [kæ'ʃɪə*] n cajero/a

cashmere ['kæʃmɪə*] n cachemira

cash point n cajero automático

cash register n caja

casino [kə'siːnəu] n casino

casket ['kɑːskɪt] n cofre m, estuche m; (US: coffin) ataúd m

casserole ['kæsərəul] n (food, pot) cazuela

cassette [kæ'set] n casete f; **cassette player, cassette recorder** n casete m

cast [kɑːst] (pt, pp **~~**) vt (throw) echar, arrojar, lanzar; (glance, eyes) dirigir;

(Theatre): **to ~ sb as Othello** dar a algn el papel de Otelo ▷ vi (Fishing) lanzar ▷ n (Theatre) reparto; (also: **plaster ~**) vaciado; (Knitting): **to ~ off** vi (Naut) desamarrar; (Knitting) cerrar (los puntos)

castanets [kæstə'nets] npl castañuelas fpl

caster sugar ['kɑːstə*] (BRIT) n azúcar m extrafino

Castile [kæs'tiːl] n Castilla; **Castilian** adj, n castellano m/f

cast-iron ['kɑːstaɪən] adj (lit) (hecho) de hierro fundido; (fig: case) irrebatible

castle ['kɑːsl] n castillo; (Chess) torre f

casual ['kæʒjul] adj fortuito; (irregular: work etc) eventual, temporero; (unconcerned) despreocupado; (clothes) informal

Be careful not to translate **casual** by the Spanish word casual.

casualty ['kæʒjultɪ] n víctima, herido/a; (dead) muerto/a; (Med: department) urgencias fpl

cat [kæt] n gato; (big cat) felino

Catalan ['kætəlæn] adj, n catalán/ ana m/f

catalogue ['kætəlɒg] (US **catalog**) n catálogo ▷ vt catalogar

Catalonia [kætə'ləunɪə] n Cataluña

catalytic converter [kætə'lɪtɪkən'vɜːtə*] n catalizador m

cataract ['kætərækt] n (Med) cataratas fpl

catarrh [kə'tɑː*] n catarro

catastrophe [kə'tæstrəfɪ] n catástrofe f

catch [kætʃ] (pt, pp **caught**) vt coger (SP), agarrar (LAM); (arrest) detener; (grasp) asir; (breath) contener; (surprise: person) sorprender; (attract: attention) captar; (hear) oír; (Med) contagiarse de, coger; (also: **~ up**) alcanzar ▷ vi (fire) encenderse; (in branches etc) enredarse ▷ n (fish etc) pesca; (act of catching) cogida; (hidden problem) dificultad f; (game) category | 334

pilla-pilla; (of lock) pestillo, cerradura;
to ~ fire encenderse; **to ~ sight of**
divisar; **catch up** vi (fig) ponerse al
día; **catching** ['kætʃɪŋ] adj (Med)
contagioso

category ['kætɪɡərɪ] n categoría,
clase f

cater ['keɪtə*] vi: **to ~ for** (BRIT)
abastecer a; (needs) atender a;
(Comm: parties etc) proveer comida a

caterpillar ['kætəpɪlə*] n oruga,
gusano

cathedral [kə'θiːdrəl] n catedral f

Catholic ['kæθəlɪk] adj, n (Rel)
católico/a m/f

Catseye® ['kæts'aɪ] (BRIT) n (Aut)
catafoto

cattle ['kætl] npl ganado

catwalk ['kætwɔːk] n pasarela

caught [kɔːt] pt, pp of **catch**

cauliflower ['kɒlɪflauə*] n coliflor f

cause [kɔːz] n causa, motivo, razón f;
(principle: also Pol) causa ▷ vt causar

caution ['kɔːʃən] n cautela,
prudencia; (warning) advertencia,
amonestación f ▷ vt amonestar;
cautious adj cauteloso, prudente,
precavido

cave [keɪv] n cueva, caverna; **cave in**
vi (roof etc) derrumbarse, hundirse

caviar(e) ['kævɪɑː*] n caviar m

cavity ['kævɪtɪ] n hueco, cavidad f

cc abbr (= cubic centimetres) c.c.; (= carbon
copy) copia hecha con papel de carbón

CCTV n abbr (= closed-circuit television)
circuito cerrado de televisión

CD n abbr (= compact disc) CD m; (player)
(reproductor m de) CD; **CD player** n
reproductor m de CD; **CD-ROM**
[siːdiː'rɔm] n abbr CD-ROM m; **CD
writer** n grabadora m de CD

cease [siːs] vt, vi cesar; **ceasefire** n
alto m el fuego

cedar ['siːdə*] n cedro

ceilidh ['keɪlɪ] n baile con música y
danzas tradicionales escocesas o irlandesas

ceiling ['siːlɪŋ] n techo; (fig) límite m

celebrate ['selɪbreɪt] vt celebrar ▷ vi

divertirse; **celebration** [-'breɪʃən] n
fiesta, celebración f

celebrity [sɪ'lebrɪtɪ] n celebridad f

celery ['selərɪ] n apio

cell [sel] n celda; (Biol) célula; (Elec)
elemento

cellar ['selə*] n sótano; (for wine)
bodega

cello ['tʃeləu] n violoncelo

Cellophane® ['seləfeɪn] n celofán m

cellphone ['selfəun] n móvil

Celsius ['selsɪəs] adj centígrado

Celtic ['keltɪk] adj celta

cement [sə'ment] n cemento

cemetery ['semɪtrɪ] n cementerio

censor ['sensə*] n censor m ▷ vt (cut)
censurar; **censorship** n censura

census ['sensəs] n censo

cent [sent] n (unit of dollar) centavo,
céntimo; (unit of euro) céntimo; see
also **per**

centenary [sen'tiːnərɪ] n
centenario

centennial [sen'tenɪəl] (US) n
centenario

center ['sentə*] (US) = **centre**

centi... ['sentɪ] prefix: **centigrade**
adj centígrado; **centimetre** (US
['sentɪmiːtə] n centímetro; **centipede**
['sentɪpiːd] n ciempiés m inv

central ['sentrəl] adj central; (of
house etc) céntrico; **Central America**
n Centroamérica; **central heating**
n calefacción f central; **central
reservation** n (BRIT Aut) mediana

centre ['sentə*] (US **center**) n centro;
(fig) núcleo ▷ vt centrar; **centre-
forward** n (Sport) delantero centro;
centre-half n (Sport) medio centro

century ['sentjurɪ] n siglo; **20th ~**
siglo veinte

CEO n abbr = **chief executive officer**

ceramic [sɪ'ræmɪk] adj cerámico

cereal ['siːrɪəl] n cereal m

ceremony ['serɪmənɪ] n ceremonia;
to stand on ~ hacer ceremonias, estar
de cumplido

certain ['sɜːtən] adj seguro;

(person): **a ~** Mr Smith un tal Sr. Smith; (particular, some) cierto; **for ~** a ciencia cierta; **certainly** adv (undoubtedly) ciertamente; (of course) desde luego, por supuesto; **certainty** n certeza, certidumbre f, seguridad f; (inevitability) certeza

certificate [səˈtɪfɪkɪt] n certificado m; **certify** [ˈsɜːtɪfaɪ] vt certificar; (award diploma to) conceder un diploma a; (declare insane) declarar loco

cf. abbr (= compare) cfr

CFC n abbr (= chlorofluorocarbon) CFC m

chain [tʃeɪn] n cadena; (of mountains) cordillera; (of events) sucesión f ▷ vt (also: ~ up) encadenar; **chain-smoke** vi fumar un cigarrillo tras otro

chair [tʃeə*] n silla; (armchair) sillón m, butaca; (of university) cátedra; (of meeting etc) presidencia ▷ vt (meeting) presidir; **chairlift** n telesilla; **chairman** (irreg) n presidente m; **chairperson** n presidente/a m/f; **chairwoman** (irreg) n presidenta

chalet [ˈʃæleɪ] n chalet m (de madera)

chalk [tʃɔːk] n (Geo) creta; (for writing) tiza, gis m (MEX); **chalkboard** (US) n pizarrón (LAM), pizarra (SP)

challenge [ˈtʃælɪndʒ] n desafío, reto ▷ vt desafiar, retar; (statement, right) poner en duda; **to ~ sb to do sth** retar a algn a que haga algo; **challenging** adj exigente; (tone) desafío

chamber [ˈtʃeɪmbə*] n cámara, sala; (Pol) cámara; (BRIT Law: gen pl) despacho; **~ of commerce** cámara de comercio; **chambermaid** n camarera

champagne [ʃæmˈpeɪn] n champaña m, champán m

champion [ˈtʃæmpɪən] n campeón/ona m/f; (of cause) defensor(a) m/f; **championship** n campeonato

chance [tʃɑːns] n (opportunity) ocasión f, oportunidad f; (likelihood) posibilidad f; (risk) riesgo ▷ vt arriesgar, probar ▷ adj fortuito, casual; **to ~ it** arriesgarse, intentarlo; **to take a ~** arriesgarse; **by ~** por

casualidad

chancellor [ˈtʃɑːnsələ*] n canciller m; **Chancellor of the Exchequer** (BRIT) n Ministro de Hacienda

chandelier [ʃændəˈlɪə*] n araña (de luces)

change [tʃeɪndʒ] vt cambiar; (replace) cambiar, reemplazar; (gear, clothes, job) cambiar de; (transform) transformar ▷ vi cambiar(se); (change trains) hacer transbordo; (traffic lights) cambiar de color; (be transformed): **to ~ into** transformarse en ▷ n cambio; (alteration) modificación f; (transformation) transformación f; (of clothes) muda; (coins) suelto, sencillo; (money returned) vuelta; **for a ~** para variar; **change over** vi (from sth to sth) cambiar; (players etc) cambiar(se) ▷ vt cambiar; **changeable** adj (weather) cambiable; **change machine** n máquina de cambio; **changing room** (BRIT) n vestuario

channel [ˈtʃænl] n (TV) canal m; (of river) cauce m; (groove) conducto; (fig: medium) medio ▷ vt (river etc) encauzar; **the (English) C~** el Canal (de la Mancha); **the C~ Islands** las Islas Normandas; **Channel Tunnel** n: **the Channel Tunnel** el túnel del Canal de la Mancha, el Eurotúnel

chant [tʃɑːnt] n (of crowd) gritos mpl; (Rel) canto ▷ vt (slogan, word) repetir a gritos

chaos [ˈkeɪɒs] n caos m

chaotic [keɪˈɒtɪk] adj caótico

chap [tʃæp] (BRIT: inf) n (man) tío, tipo

chapel [ˈtʃæpl] n capilla

chapped [tʃæpt] adj agrietado

chapter [ˈtʃæptə*] n capítulo

character [ˈkærɪktə*] n carácter m, naturaleza, índole f; (moral strength, personality) carácter; (in novel, film) personaje m; **characteristic** [-ˈrɪstɪk] adj característico ▷ n característica; **characterize** [ˈkærɪktəraɪz] vt caracterizar

charcoal ['tʃɑːkəʊl] n carbón m vegetal; (Art) carboncillo

charge [tʃɑːdʒ] n (Law) cargo, acusación f; (cost) precio, coste m; (responsibility) cargo ▷ vt (Law): **to ~ (with)** acusar de; (battery) cargar; (price) pedir; (customer) cobrar ▷ vi precipitarse; (Mil) cargar, atacar; **charge card** n tarjeta de cuenta; **charger** n (also: **battery charger**) cargador m (de baterías)

charismatic [kærɪzˈmætɪk] adj carismático

charity ['tʃærɪtɪ] n caridad f; (organization) sociedad f benéfica; (money, gifts) limosnas fpl; **charity shop** n (BRIT) tienda de artículos de segunda mano que dedica su recaudación a causas benéficas

charm [tʃɑːm] n encanto, atractivo; (talisman) hechizo; (on bracelet) dije m ▷ vt encantar; **charming** adj encantador(a)

chart [tʃɑːt] n (diagram) cuadro; (graph) gráfica; (map) carta de navegación ▷ vt (course) trazar; (progress) seguir; **charts** npl (Top 40): **the ~s** los 40 principales (SP)

charter ['tʃɑːtə*] vt (plane) alquilar; (ship) fletar ▷ n (document) carta; (of university, company) estatutos mpl; **chartered accountant** (BRIT) n contable m/f diplomado/a; **charter flight** n vuelo chárter

chase [tʃeɪs] vt (pursue) perseguir; (also: **~ away**) ahuyentar ▷ n persecución f

chat [tʃæt] vi (also: **have a ~**) charlar; (on Internet) chatear ▷ n charla; **chat up** vt (inf: girl) ligar con, enrollarse con; **chat room** n (Internet) chat m, canal m de charla; **chat show** (BRIT) n programa m de entrevistas

chatter ['tʃætə*] vi (person) charlar; (teeth) castañetear ▷ n (of birds) parloteo; (of people) charla, cháchara

chauffeur ['ʃəʊfə*] n chófer m

chauvinist ['ʃəʊvɪnɪst] n (male chauvinist) machista m; (nationalist) chovinista mf

cheap [tʃiːp] adj barato; (joke) de mal gusto; (poor quality) de mala calidad ▷ adv barato; **cheap day return** n billete de ida y vuelta el mismo día; **cheaply** adv barato, a bajo precio

cheat [tʃiːt] vi hacer trampa ▷ vt: **to ~ sb (out of sth)** estafar (algo) a algn ▷ n (person) tramposo/a; **cheat on** vt fus engañar

Chechnya [tʃɪtʃˈnjɑː] n Chechenia

check [tʃek] vt (examine) controlar; (facts) comprobar; (halt) parar, detener; (restrain) refrenar, restringir ▷ n (inspection) control m, inspección f; (curb) freno; (us: bill) nota, cuenta; (us) = **cheque**; (pattern: gen pl) cuadro; **check in** vi (at hotel) firmar el registro; (at airport) facturar el equipaje ▷ vt (luggage) facturar; **check off** vt (esp us: check) comprobar; (cross off) tachar; **check out** vi (of hotel) marcharse; **check up** vi: **to check up on sth** comprobar algo; **to check up on sb** investigar a algn; **checkbook** (us) = **chequebook**; **checked** adj a cuadros; **checkers** (us) n juego de damas; **check-in** n (also: **check-in desk**: at airport) mostrador m de facturación; **checking account** (us) n cuenta corriente; **checklist** n lista (de control); **checkmate** n jaque m mate; **checkout** n caja; **checkpoint** n (punto de) control m; **checkroom** (us) n consigna; **checkup** n (Med) reconocimiento general

cheddar ['tʃedə*] n (also: **~ cheese**) queso m cheddar

cheek [tʃiːk] n mejilla; (impudence) descaro; **what a ~!** ¡qué cara!; **cheekbone** n pómulo; **cheeky** adj fresco, descarado

cheer [tʃɪə*] vt vitorear, aplaudir; (gladden) alegrar, animar ▷ vi dar vivas ▷ n viva m; **cheer up** vi animarse ▷ vt alegrar, animar; **cheerful** adj alegre

cheerio [tʃɪərɪ'əʊ] (BRIT) excl ¡hasta luego!

cheerleader ['tʃɪəliːdə*] n animador(a) m/f

cheese [tʃiːz] n queso; **cheeseburger** n hamburguesa con queso; **cheesecake** n pastel m de queso

chef [ʃef] n jefe/a m/f de cocina

chemical ['kemɪkəl] adj químico ▷n producto químico

chemist ['kemɪst] n (BRIT: pharmacist) farmacéutico/a; (scientist) químico/a; **chemistry** n química; **chemist's (shop)** (BRIT) n farmacia

cheque [tʃek] (us **check**) n cheque m; **chequebook** n talonario de cheques (sp), chequera (LAM); **cheque card** n tarjeta de cheque

cherry ['tʃerɪ] n cereza; (also: **~ tree**) cerezo

chess [tʃes] n ajedrez m

chest [tʃest] n (Anat) pecho; (box) cofre m, cajón m

chestnut ['tʃesnʌt] n castaña; (also: **~ tree**) castaño

chest of drawers n cómoda

chew [tʃuː] vt mascar, masticar; **chewing gum** n chicle m

chic [ʃiːk] adj elegante

chick [tʃɪk] n pollito, polluelo/a; (inf: girl) chica

chicken ['tʃɪkɪn] n gallina, pollo; (food) pollo; (inf: coward) gallina mf; **chicken out** (inf) vi rajarse; **chickenpox** n varicela

chickpea ['tʃɪkpiː] n garbanzo

chief [tʃiːf] n jefe/a m/f ▷ adj principal; **chief executive (officer)** n director(a) m/f general; **chiefly** adv principalmente

child [tʃaɪld] (pl **~ren**) n niño/a; (offspring) hijo/a m/f; **child abuse** n (with violence) malos tratos mpl a niños; (sexual) abuso m sexual de niños; **child benefit** n (BRIT) subsidio por cada hijo pequeño; **childbirth** n parto; **child-care** n cuidado de los niños; **childhood** n niñez f, infancia; **childish**

adj pueril, aniñado; **child minder** (BRIT) n madre f de día; **children** ['tʃɪldrən] npl of **child**

Chile ['tʃɪlɪ] n Chile m; **Chilean** adj, n chileno/a m/f

chill [tʃɪl] n frío; (Med) resfriado ▷vt enfriar; (Culin) congelar; **chill out** vi (esp us: inf) tranquilizarse

chil(l)i ['tʃɪlɪ] (BRIT) n chile m, ají m (SC)

chilly ['tʃɪlɪ] adj frío

chimney ['tʃɪmnɪ] n chimenea

chimpanzee [tʃɪmpæn'ziː] n chimpancé m

chin [tʃɪn] n mentón m, barbilla

China ['tʃaɪnə] n China

china ['tʃaɪnə] n porcelana; (crockery) loza

Chinese [tʃaɪ'niːz] adj chino ▷n inv chino/a m/f; (Ling) chino

chip [tʃɪp] n (gen pl: Culin: BRIT) patata (SP) or papa (LAM) frita; (: us: also: **potato ~**) patata or papa frita; (of wood) astilla; (of glass, stone) lasca; (at poker) ficha; (Comput) chip m ▷vt (cup, plate) desconchar; **chip shop** pescadería (donde se vende principalmente pescado rebozado y patatas fritas)

chiropodist [kɪ'rɔpədɪst] (BRIT) n pedicuro/a, callista m/f

chisel ['tʃɪzl] n (for wood) escoplo; (for stone) cincel m

chives [tʃaɪvz] npl cebollinos mpl

chlorine ['klɔːriːn] n cloro

choc-ice ['tʃɔkaɪs] n (BRIT) helado m cubierto de chocolate

chocolate ['tʃɔklɪt] n chocolate m; (sweet) bombón m

choice [tʃɔɪs] n elección f, selección f; (option) opción f; (preference) preferencia ▷adj escogido

choir ['kwaɪə*] n coro

choke [tʃəʊk] vi ahogarse; (on food) atragantarse ▷vt estrangular, ahogar; (block): **to be ~d with** estar atascado de ▷n (Aut) estárter m

cholesterol [kə'lestərʊl] n colesterol m

choose [tʃuːz] (pt **chose**, pp **chosen**)

chop vt escoger, elegir; (team) seleccionar; **to ~ to do sth** optar por hacer algo

chop [tʃɒp] n (wood) cortar, tajar; (Culin: also: **~ up**) picar ▷ n (Culin) chuleta; **chop down** vt (tree) talar; **chop off** vt cortar (de un tajo); **chopsticks** [ˈtʃɒpstɪks] npl palillos mpl

chord [kɔːd] n (Mus) acorde m

chore [tʃɔːʳ] n faena, tarea; (routine task) trabajo rutinario

chorus [ˈkɔːrəs] n coro; (repeated part of song) estribillo

chose [tʃəuz] pt of **choose**

chosen [ˈtʃəuzn] pp of **choose**

Christ [kraɪst] n Cristo

christen [ˈkrɪsn] vt bautizar; **christening** n bautizo

Christian [ˈkrɪstɪən] adj, n cristiano/a m/f; **Christianity** [-ˈænɪtɪ] n cristianismo; **Christian name** n nombre m de pila

Christmas [ˈkrɪsməs] n Navidad f; **Merry ~!** ¡Felices Pascuas!; **Christmas card** n crismas m inv, tarjeta de Navidad; **Christmas carol** n villancico m; **Christmas Day** n día m de Navidad; **Christmas Eve** n Nochebuena; **Christmas pudding** (esp BRIT) pudin m de Navidad; **Christmas tree** n árbol m de Navidad

chrome [krəum] n cromo

chronic [ˈkrɒnɪk] adj crónico

chrysanthemum [krɪˈsænθəməm] n crisantemo

chubby [ˈtʃʌbɪ] adj regordete

chuck [tʃʌk] (inf) vt lanzar, arrojar; (BRIT: also: **~ up**) abandonar; **chuck out** vt (person) echar (fuera); (rubbish etc) tirar

chuckle [ˈtʃʌkl] vi reírse entre dientes

chum [tʃʌm] n compañero/a

chunk [tʃʌŋk] n pedazo, trozo

church [tʃəːtʃ] n iglesia; **churchyard** n cementerio

churn [tʃəːn] n (for butter) mantequera; (for milk) lechera

chute [ʃuːt] n (also: **rubbish ~**) vertedero; (for coal etc) rampa de caída

chutney [ˈtʃʌtnɪ] n condimento a base de frutas de la India

CIA (US) n abbr (= Central Intelligence Agency) CIA f

CID (BRIT) n abbr (= Criminal Investigation Department) ≈ B.I.C. f (SP)

cider [ˈsaɪdəʳ] n sidra

cigar [sɪˈɡɑːʳ] n puro

cigarette [sɪɡəˈrɛt] n cigarrillo; **cigarette lighter** n mechero

cinema [ˈsɪnəmə] n cine m

cinnamon [ˈsɪnəmən] n canela

circle [ˈsəːkl] n círculo; (in theatre) anfiteatro ▷ vi dar vueltas ▷ vt (surround) rodear, cercar; (move round) dar la vuelta a

circuit [ˈsəːkɪt] n circuito; (tour) pista; (track) pista; (lap) vuelta

circular [ˈsəːkjuləʳ] adj circular ▷ n circular f

circulate [ˈsəːkjuleɪt] vi circular; (person: at party etc) hablar con los invitados ▷ vt poner en circulación; **circulation** [-ˈleɪʃən] n circulación f; (of newspaper) tirada

circumstances [ˈsəːkəmstənsɪz] npl circunstancias fpl; (financial condition) situación f económica

circus [ˈsəːkəs] n circo

cite [saɪt] vt citar

citizen [ˈsɪtɪzn] n (Pol) ciudadano/a; (of city) vecino/a, habitante mf; **citizenship** n ciudadanía; (BRIT: Scol) civismo

citrus fruits [ˈsɪtrəs-] npl agrios mpl

city [ˈsɪtɪ] n ciudad f; **the C~** centro financiero de Londres; **city centre** (BRIT) n centro de la ciudad; **city technology college** n centro de formación profesional (centro de enseñanza secundaria que da especial importancia a la ciencia y tecnología.)

civic [ˈsɪvɪk] adj cívico; (authorities) municipal

civil [ˈsɪvɪl] adj civil; (polite) atento, cortés; **civilian** [sɪˈvɪlɪən] adj civil (no militar) ▷ n civil mf, paisano/a

civilization [sɪvɪlaɪˈzeɪʃən] n civilización f

civilized [ˈsɪvɪlaɪzd] adj civilizado

civil: civil law n derecho civil; **civil rights** npl derechos mpl civiles; **civil servant** n funcionario/a del Estado; **Civil Service** n administración f pública; **civil war** n guerra civil

CJD n abbr (= Creutzfeldt-Jakob disease) enfermedad de Creutzfeldt-Jakob

claim [kleɪm] vt exigir, reclamar; (rights etc) reivindicar; (assert) pretender ▷ vi (for insurance) reclamar ▷ n reclamación f; pretensión f; **claim form** n solicitud f

clam [klæm] n almeja

clamp [klæmp] n abrazadera, grapa ▷ vt (two things together) cerrar fuertemente; (sth to sth) sujetar, afianzar (con abrazadera); (Aut: wheel) poner el cepo a

clan [klæn] n clan m

clap [klæp] vi aplaudir

claret [ˈklærət] n burdeos m inv

clarify [ˈklærɪfaɪ] vt aclarar

clarinet [klærɪˈnet] n clarinete m

clarity [ˈklærɪtɪ] n claridad f

clash [klæʃ] n enfrentamiento; choque m; desacuerdo; estruendo ▷ vi (fight) enfrentarse; (beliefs) chocar; (disagree) estar en desacuerdo; (colours) desentonar; (two events) coincidir

clasp [klɑːsp] n (hold) apretón m; (of necklace, bag) cierre m ▷ vt apretar; abrazar

class [klɑːs] n clase f ▷ vt clasificar

classic [ˈklæsɪk] adj, n clásico; **classical** adj clásico

classification [klæsɪfɪˈkeɪʃən] n clasificación f

classify [ˈklæsɪfaɪ] vt clasificar

classmate [ˈklɑːsmeɪt] n compañero/a de clase

classroom [ˈklɑːsrʊm] n aula; **classroom assistant** n profesor(a) m/f de apoyo

classy [ˈklɑːsɪ] adj (inf) elegante, con estilo

clatter [ˈklætə*] n estrépito ▷ vi hacer ruido or estrépito

clause [klɔːz] n cláusula; (Ling) oración f

claustrophobic [klɔːstrəˈfəʊbɪk] adj claustrofóbico; **I feel ~** me entra claustrofobia

claw [klɔː] n (of cat) uña; (of bird of prey) garra; (of lobster) pinza

clay [kleɪ] n arcilla

clean [kliːn] adj limpio; (record, reputation) bueno, intachable; (joke) decente ▷ vt limpiar; (hands etc) lavar; **clean up** vt limpiar, asear; **cleaner** n (person) asistenta; (substance) producto para la limpieza; **cleaner's** n tintorería; **cleaning** n limpieza

cleanser [ˈklenzə*] n (for face) crema limpiadora

clear [klɪə*] adj claro; (road, way) libre; (conscience) limpio, tranquilo; (skin) terso; (sky) despejado ▷ vt (space) despejar, limpiar; (Law: suspect) absolver; (obstacle) salvar, saltar por encima de; (cheque) aceptar ▷ vi (fog etc) despejarse ▷ adv: **~ of** a distancia de; **to ~ the table** recoger or levantar la mesa; **clear away** vt (things, clothes etc) quitar (de en medio); (dishes) retirar; **clear up** vt limpiar; (mystery) aclarar, resolver; **clearance** n (removal) despeje m; (permission) acreditación f; **clear-cut** adj bien definido, nítido; **clearing** n (in wood) claro; **clearly** adv claramente; (evidently) sin duda; **clearway** (BRIT) n carretera donde no se puede parar

clench [klentʃ] vt apretar, cerrar

clergy [ˈklɜːdʒɪ] n clero

clerk [klɑːk, (US) klɜːrk] n (BRIT) oficinista mf; (US) dependiente/a m/f

clever [ˈklevə*] adj (intelligent) inteligente, listo; (skilful) hábil; (device, arrangement) ingenioso

cliché [ˈkliːʃeɪ] n cliché m, frase f hecha

click [klɪk] vt (tongue) chasquear; (heels) taconear ▷ vi (Comput) hacer clic; **to ~ on an icon** hacer clic en un icono

client ['klaɪənt] n cliente m/f

cliff [klɪf] n acantilado

climate ['klaɪmɪt] n clima m; **climate change** n cambio climático

climax ['klaɪmæks] n (of battle, career) apogeo; (of film, book) punto culminante; (sexual) orgasmo

climb [klaɪm] vi subir; (plant) trepar; (move with effort): **to ~ over a wall/into a car** trepar a una tapia/subir a un coche ▷vt (stairs) subir; (tree) trepar a; (mountain) escalar ▷n subida; **climb down** vi (fig) volverse atrás; **climber** n alpinista m/f (SP, MEX), andinista m/f (LAM); **climbing** n alpinismo m (SP, MEX), andinismo (LAM)

clinch [klɪntʃ] vt (deal) cerrar; (argument) remachar

cling [klɪŋ] (pt, pp **clung**) vi: **to ~ to** agarrarse a; (clothes) pegarse a

Clingfilm® ['klɪŋfɪlm] n plástico adherente

clinic ['klɪnɪk] n clínica

clip [klɪp] n (for hair) horquilla; (also: **paper ~**) sujetapapeles m inv, clip m; (TV, Cinema) fragmento ▷vt (cut) cortar; (also: **~ together**) unir; **clipping** n (newspaper) recorte m

cloak [kləuk] n capa, manto ▷vt (fig) encubrir, disimular; **cloakroom** n guardarropa; (BRIT: WC) lavabo (SP), aseos mpl (SP), baño (LAM)

clock [klɔk] n reloj m; **clock in** or **clock on** vi (with card) fichar, picar; (start work) entrar a trabajar; **clock off** or **clock out** vi (with card) fichar or picar la salida; (leave work) salir del trabajar; **clockwise** adv en el sentido de las agujas del reloj; **clockwork** n aparato de relojería ▷adj (toy) de cuerda

clog [klɔg] n zueco, chanclo ▷vt atascar ▷vi (also: **~ up**) atascarse

clone [kləun] n clon m ▷vt clonar

close¹ [kləus] adj (near): **~ (to)** cerca (de); (friend) íntimo; (connection) estrecho; (examination) detallado,

minucioso; (weather) bochornoso ▷adv cerca; **~ by, ~ at hand** muy cerca; **to have a ~ shave** (fig) escaparse por un pelo

close² [kləuz] vt (shut) cerrar; (end) concluir, terminar ▷vi (shop etc) cerrarse; (end) concluirse, terminarse ▷n (end) fin m, final m, conclusión f; **close down** vi cerrarse definitivamente; **closed** adj (shop etc) cerrado

closely ['kləuslɪ] adv (study) con detalle; (watch) de cerca; (resemble) estrechamente

closet ['klɔzɪt] n armario

close-up ['kləusʌp] n primer plano

closing time n hora de cierre

closure ['kləuʒə*] n cierre m

clot [klɔt] n (gen) coágulo; (inf: idiot) imbécil m/f ▷vi (blood) coagularse

cloth [klɔθ] n (material) tela, paño; (rag) trapo

clothes [kləuðz] npl ropa; **clothes line** n cuerda (para tender la ropa); **clothes peg** (us **clothes pin**) n pinza

clothing ['kləuðɪŋ] n = **clothes**

cloud [klaud] n nube f; **cloud over** vi (also fig) nublarse; **cloudy** adj nublado, nubloso; (liquid) turbio

clove [kləuv] n clavo; **~ of garlic** diente de ajo

clown [klaun] n payaso ▷vi (also: **~ about, ~ around**) hacer el payaso

club [klʌb] n (society) club m; (weapon) porra, cachiporra; (also: **golf ~**) palo ▷vt aporrear ▷vi: **to ~ together** (for gift) comprar entre todos; **clubs** npl (Cards) tréboles mpl; **club class** n (Aviat) clase f preferente

clue [klu:] n pista; (in crosswords) indicación f; **I haven't a ~** no tengo ni idea

clump [klʌmp] n (of trees) grupo

clumsy ['klʌmzɪ] adj (person) torpe, desmañado; (tool) difícil de manejar; (movement) desgarbado

clung [klʌŋ] pt, pp of **cling**

cluster ['klʌstə*] n grupo ▷vi

agruparse, apiñarse
clutch [klʌtʃ] *n* (Aut) embrague *m*; (grasp): **~es** garras *fpl* ▷ *vt* asir; agarrar
cm *abbr* (= centimetre) cm
Co. *abbr* = county; company
c/o *abbr* (= care of) c/a, a/c
coach [kəʊtʃ] *n* autocar *m* (SP), coche *m* de línea; (horse-drawn) coche *m*; (of train) vagón *m*, coche *m*; (Sport) entrenador(a) *m/f*, instructor(a) *m/f*; (tutor) profesor(a) *m/f* particular ▷ *vt* (Sport) entrenar; (student) preparar, enseñar; **coach station** *n* (BRIT) estación *f* de autobuses *etc*; **coach trip** *n* excursión *f* en autocar
coal [kəʊl] *n* carbón *m*
coalition [kəʊəˈlɪʃən] *n* coalición *f*
coarse [kɔːs] *adj* basto, burdo; (vulgar) grosero, ordinario
coast [kəʊst] *n* costa, litoral *m* ▷ *vi* (Aut) ir en punto muerto; **coastal** *adj* costero, costanero; **coastguard** *n* guardacostas *m inv*; **coastline** *n* litoral *m*
coat [kəʊt] *n* abrigo; (of animal) pelaje *m*, lana; (of paint) mano *f*, capa ▷ *vt* cubrir, revestir; **coat hanger** *n* percha (SP), gancho (LAM); **coating** *n* capa, baño
coax [kəʊks] *vt* engatusar
cob [kɒb] *n* see **corn**
cobbled [ˈkɒbld] *adj*: **~ street** calle *f* empedrada, calle *f* adoquinada
cobweb [ˈkɒbwɛb] *n* telaraña
cocaine [kəˈkeɪn] *n* cocaína
cock [kɒk] *n* (rooster) gallo; (male bird) macho ▷ *vt* (gun) amartillar; **cockerel** *n* gallito
cockney [ˈkɒknɪ] *n* habitante *m* de ciertos barrios de Londres
cockpit [ˈkɒkpɪt] *n* cabina
cockroach [ˈkɒkrəʊtʃ] *n* cucaracha
cocktail [ˈkɒkteɪl] *n* coctel *m*, cóctel *m*
cocoa [ˈkəʊkəʊ] *n* cacao; (drink) chocolate *m*
coconut [ˈkəʊkənʌt] *n* coco
cod [kɒd] *n* bacalao

C.O.D. *abbr* (= cash on delivery) C.A.E.
code [kəʊd] *n* código; (cipher) clave *f*; (dialling code) prefijo; (post code) código postal
coeducational [kəʊɛdjuːˈkeɪʃənl] *adj* mixto
coffee [ˈkɒfɪ] *n* café *m*; **coffee bar** *n* (BRIT) cafetería; **coffee bean** *n* grano de café; **coffee break** *n* descanso (para tomar café); **coffee maker** *n* máquina de hacer café, cafetera; **coffeepot** *n* cafetera; **coffee shop** *n* café *m*; **coffee table** *n* mesita (para servir el café)
coffin [ˈkɒfɪn] *n* ataúd *m*
cog [kɒg] *n* (wheel) rueda dentada; (tooth) diente *m*
cognac [ˈkɒnjæk] *n* coñac *m*
coherent [kəʊˈhɪərənt] *adj* coherente
coil [kɔɪl] *n* rollo; (Elec) bobina, carrete *m*; (contraceptive) espiral *f* ▷ *vt* enrollar
coin [kɔɪn] *n* moneda ▷ *vt* (word) inventar, idear
coincide [kəʊɪnˈsaɪd] *vi* coincidir; (agree) estar de acuerdo; **coincidence** [kəʊˈɪnsɪdəns] *n* casualidad *f*
Coke® [kəʊk] *n* Coca-Cola®
coke [kəʊk] *n* (coal) coque *m*
colander [ˈkɒləndə*] *n* colador *m*, escurridor *m*
cold [kəʊld] *adj* frío ▷ *n* frío; (Med) resfriado; **it's ~** hace frío; **to be ~** (person) tener frío; **to catch (a) ~** resfriarse; **in ~ blood** a sangre fría; **cold sore** *n* herpes *mpl* or *fpl*
coleslaw [ˈkəʊlslɔː] *n* especie de ensalada de col
colic [ˈkɒlɪk] *n* cólico
collaborate [kəˈlæbəreɪt] *vi* colaborar
collapse [kəˈlæps] *vi* hundirse, derrumbarse; (Med) sufrir un colapso ▷ *n* hundimiento, derrumbamiento; (Med) colapso
collar [ˈkɒlə*] *n* (of coat, shirt) cuello; (of dog etc) collar; **collarbone** *n* clavícula

colleague [ˈkɒliːg] n colega mf; (at work) compañero/a

collect [kəˈlekt] vt (litter, mail etc) recoger; (as a hobby) coleccionar; (BRIT: call and pick up) recoger; (debts, subscriptions etc) recaudar ▷ vi reunirse; (dust) acumularse; **to call ~** (US Tel) llamar a cobro revertido;

collection [kəˈlekʃən] n colección f, (of mail, for charity) recogida; **collective** [kəˈlektɪv] adj colectivo; **collector** n coleccionista m

college [ˈkɒlɪdʒ] n colegio mayor; (of agriculture, technology) escuela universitaria

collide [kəˈlaɪd] vi chocar

collision [kəˈlɪʒən] n choque m

cologne [kəˈləʊn] n (also: **eau de ~**) (agua de) colonia

Colombia [kəˈlɒmbɪə] n Colombia; **Colombian** adj, n colombiano/a

colon [ˈkəʊlən] n (sign) dos puntos; (Med) colon m

colonel [ˈkɜːnl] n coronel m

colonial [kəˈləʊnɪəl] adj colonial

colony [ˈkɒlənɪ] n colonia

colour etc [ˈkʌlə*] (US **color** etc) n color m ▷ vt color(e)ar; (dye) teñir; (fig: account) adornar; (: judgement) distorsionar ▷ vi (blush) sonrojarse; **colour in** vt colorear; **colour-blind** adj daltónico; **coloured** adj de color; (photo) en color; **colour film** n película en color; **colourful** adj lleno de color; (story) fantástico; (person) excéntrico; **colouring** n (complexion) tez f; (in food) colorante m; **colour television** n televisión f en color

column [ˈkɒləm] n columna

coma [ˈkəʊmə] n coma m

comb [kəʊm] n peine m; (ornamental) peineta ▷ vt (hair) peinar; (area) registrar a fondo

combat [ˈkɒmbæt] n combate m ▷ vt combatir

combination [kɒmbɪˈneɪʃən] n combinación f

combine [vb kəmˈbaɪn, n ˈkɒmbaɪn]

vt combinar; (qualities) reunir ▷ vi combinarse ▷ n (Econ) cartel m

🔑 **KEYWORD**

come [kʌm] (pt **came**, pp **come**) vi
1 (movement towards) venir; **to come running** venir corriendo
2 (arrive) llegar; **he's come here to work** ha venido aquí para trabajar; **to come home** volver a casa
3 (reach): **to come to** llegar a; **the bill came to £40** la cuenta ascendía a cuarenta libras
4 (occur): **an idea came to me** se me ocurrió una idea
5 (be, become): **to come loose/undone** etc aflojarse/desabrocharse/desatarse etc; **I've come to like him** por fin ha llegado a gustarme

come across vt fus (person) topar con; (thing) dar con

come along vi (BRIT: progress) ir

come back vi (return) volver

come down vi (price) bajar; (tree, building) ser derribado

come from vt fus (place, source) ser de

come in vi (visitor) entrar; (train, report) llegar; (fashion) ponerse de moda; (on deal etc) entrar

come off vi (button) soltarse, desprenderse; (attempt) salir bien

come on vi (pupil) progresar; (work, project) desarrollarse; (lights) encenderse; (electricity) volver; **come on!** ¡vamos!

come out vi (fact) salir a la luz; (book, sun) salir; (stain) quitarse

come round vi (after faint, operation) volver en sí

come to vi (wake) volver en sí

come up vi (sun) salir; (problem) surgir; (event) aproximarse; (in conversation) mencionarse

come up with vt fus (idea) sugerir; (money) conseguir

comeback [ˈkʌmbæk] n: **to make a ~**

(Theatre) volver a las tablas

comedian [kə'miːdɪən] n humorista mf

comedy ['kɒmɪdɪ] n comedia; (humour) comicidad f

comet ['kɒmɪt] n cometa m

comfort ['kʌmfət] n bienestar m; (relief) alivio ▷ vt consolar; **comfortable** adj cómodo; (financially) acomodado; (easy) fácil; **comfort station** (us) n servicios mpl

comic ['kɒmɪk] adj (also: **~al**) cómico ▷ n (comedian) cómico; (BRIT: for children) tebeo; (BRIT: for adults) comic m; **comic book** (us) n libro m de cómics; **comic strip** n tira cómica

comma ['kɒmə] n coma

command [kə'mɑːnd] n orden f, mandato; (Mil: authority) mando; (mastery) dominio ▷ vt (troops) mandar; (give orders to): **to ~ sb to do** mandar or ordenar a algn hacer; **commander** n (Mil) comandante mf, jefe/a m/f

commemorate [kə'meməreɪt] vt conmemorar

commence [kə'mens] vt, vi comenzar, empezar; **commencement** (us) n (Univ) (ceremonia de) graduación f

commend [kə'mend] vt elogiar, alabar; (recommend) recomendar

comment ['kɒment] n comentario ▷ vi: **to ~ on** hacer comentarios sobre; **"no ~"** (written) "sin comentarios"; (spoken) "no tengo nada que decir"; **commentary** ['kɒmənterɪ] n comentario; **commentator** ['kɒmənteɪtə*] n comentarista mf

commerce ['kɒmɜːs] n comercio

commercial [kə'mɜːʃəl] adj comercial ▷ n (TV, Radio) anuncio; **commercial break** n intermedio para publicidad

commission [kə'mɪʃən] n (committee, fee) comisión f ▷ vt (work of art) encargar; **out of ~** fuera de servicio; **commissioner** n (Police)

comisario de policía

commit [kə'mɪt] vt (act) cometer; (resources) dedicar; (to sb's care) entregar; **to ~ o.s. (to do)** comprometerse (a hacer); **to ~ suicide** suicidarse; **commitment** n compromiso; (to ideology etc) entrega

committee [kə'mɪtɪ] n comité m

commodity [kə'mɒdɪtɪ] n mercancía

common ['kɒmən] adj común; (pej) ordinario ▷ n campo común; **commonly** adv comúnmente; **commonplace** adj de lo más común; **Commons** (BRIT) npl (Pol): **the Commons** (la Cámara de) los Comunes; **common sense** n sentido común; **Commonwealth** n: **the Commonwealth** la Commonwealth

communal ['kɒmjuːnl] adj (property) comunal; (kitchen) común

commune [n 'kɒmjuːn, vb kə'mjuːn] n (group) comuna ▷ vi: **to ~ with** comulgar or conversar con

communicate [kə'mjuːnɪkeɪt] vt comunicar ▷ vi: **to ~ (with)** comunicarse (con); (in writing) estar en contacto (con)

communication [kəmjuːnɪ'keɪʃən] n comunicación f

communion [kə'mjuːnɪən] n (also: **Holy ~**) comunión f

communism ['kɒmjunɪzəm] n comunismo; **communist** adj, n comunista mf

community [kə'mjuːnɪtɪ] n comunidad f; (large group) colectividad f; **community centre** (us **community center**) n centro social; **community service** n trabajo m comunitario (prestado en lugar de cumplir una pena de prisión)

commute [kə'mjuːt] vi viajar a diario de la casa al trabajo ▷ vt conmutar; **commuter** n persona que viaja a diario de la casa al trabajo

compact [adj kəm'pækt, n 'kɒmpækt] adj compacto ▷ n (also: **powder ~**)

polvera; **compact disc** n compact
disc m; **compact disc player** n
reproductor m de disco compacto,
compact disc m

companion [kəm'pænɪən] n
compañero/a

company ['kʌmpənɪ] n compañía;
(Comm) sociedad f, compañía; **to keep
sb ~** acompañar a algn; **company car**
n coche m de la empresa; **company
director** n director(a) m/f de empresa

comparable ['kɒmpərəbl] adj
comparable

comparative [kəm'pærətɪv]
adj relativo; (study) comparativo;
comparatively adv (relatively)
relativamente

compare [kəm'pɛə*] vt: **to ~ sth/sb
with** or **to** comparar algo/a algn
con ▷ vi: **to ~ (with)** compararse
(con); **comparison** [-'pærɪsn] n
comparación f

compartment [kəm'pɑːtmənt] n
(also: Rail) compartim(i)ento

compass ['kʌmpəs] n brújula;
compasses npl (Math) compás m

compassion [kəm'pæʃən] n
compasión f

compatible [kəm'pætɪbl] adj
compatible

compel [kəm'pɛl] vt obligar;
compelling adj (fig: argument)
convincente

compensate ['kɒmpənseɪt] vt
compensar ▷ vi: **to ~ for** compensar;
compensation [-'seɪʃən] n (for loss)
indemnización f

compete [kəm'piːt] vi (take part)
tomar parte, concurrir; (vie with): **to ~
with** competir con, hacer competencia
a

competent ['kɒmpɪtənt] adj
competente, capaz

competition [kɒmpɪ'tɪʃə
n] n (contest) concurso; (rivalry)
competencia

competitive [kəm'pɛtɪtɪv] adj (Econ,
Sport) competitivo

competitor [kəm'pɛtɪtə*] n (rival)
competidor(a) m/f; (participant)
concursante mf

complacent [kəm'pleɪsənt] adj
autocomplaciente

complain [kəm'pleɪn] vi quejarse;
(Comm) reclamar; **complaint** n queja;
reclamación f; (Med) enfermedad f

complement [n 'kɒmplɪmənt,
vb 'kɒmplɪment] n complemento;
(esp of ship's crew) dotación
f ▷ vt (enhance) complementar;
complementary [kɒmplɪ'mɛntərɪ]
adj complementario

complete [kəm'pliːt] adj (full)
completo; (finished) acabado ▷ vt
(fulfil) completar; (finish) acabar;
(a form) llenar; **completely** adv
completamente; **completion**
[-'pliːʃən] n terminación f; (of contract)
realización f

complex ['kɒmplɛks] adj, n complejo

complexion [kəm'plɛkʃən] n (of
face) tez f, cutis m

compliance [kəm'plaɪəns] n
(submission) sumisión f; (agreement)
conformidad f; **in ~ with** de acuerdo
con

complicate ['kɒmplɪkeɪt] vt
complicar; **complicated** adj
complicado; **complication** [-'keɪʃən]
n complicación f

compliment ['kɒmplɪmənt] n
(formal) cumplido ▷ vt felicitar;
complimentary [-'mɛntərɪ] adj
lisonjero; (free) de favor

comply [kəm'plaɪ] vi: **to ~ with**
cumplir con

component [kəm'pəʊnənt] n
componente ▷ n (Tech) pieza

compose [kəm'pəʊz] vt: **to be ~d of**
componerse de; (music etc) componer;
to ~ o.s. tranquilizarse; **composer** n
(Mus) compositor(a) m/f; **composition**
[kɒmpə'zɪʃən] n composición f

composure [kəm'pəʊʒə*] n
serenidad f, calma

compound ['kɒmpaʊnd] n (Chem)

compuesto; (Ling) palabra compuesta; (enclosure) recinto ▷ adj compuesto; (fracture) complicado

comprehension [ˌkɒmprɪˈhenʃən] n comprensión f

comprehensive [ˌkɒmprɪˈhensɪv] adj exhaustivo; (Insurance) contra todo riesgo; **comprehensive (school)** n centro estatal de enseñanza secundaria ≈ Instituto Nacional de Bachillerato (SP)

compress [vb kəmˈpres, n ˈkɒmpres] vt comprimir; (information) condensar ▷ n (Med) compresa

comprise [kəmˈpraɪz] vt (also: **be ~d of**) comprender, constar de; (constitute) constituir

compromise [ˈkɒmprəmaɪz] n (agreement) arreglo ▷ vt comprometer ▷ vi transigir

compulsive [kəmˈpʌlsɪv] adj compulsivo; (viewing, reading) obligado

compulsory [kəmˈpʌlsərɪ] adj obligatorio

computer [kəmˈpjuːtə*] n ordenador m, computador m, computadora; **computer game** n juego para ordenador; **computer-generated** adj realizado por ordenador, creado por ordenador; **computerize** vt (data) computerizar; (system) informatizar; **we're computerized now** ya nos hemos informatizado; **computer programmer** n programador(a) m/f; **computer programming** n programación f; **computer science** n informática; **computer studies** npl informática fsg, computación fsg (LAM); **computing** n (activity, science) informática

con [kɒn] vt (deceive) engañar; (cheat) estafar ▷ n estafa

conceal [kənˈsiːl] vt ocultar

concede [kənˈsiːd] vt (point, argument) reconocer; (territory) ceder; **to ~ (defeat)** darse por vencido; **to ~ that** admitir que

conceited [kənˈsiːtɪd] adj presumido

conceive [kənˈsiːv] vt, vi concebir

concentrate [ˈkɒnsəntreɪt] vi concentrarse ▷ vt concentrar

concentration [ˌkɒnsənˈtreɪʃən] n concentración f

concept [ˈkɒnsept] n concepto

concern [kənˈsɜːn] n (matter) asunto; (Comm) empresa; (anxiety) preocupación f ▷ vt (worry) preocupar; (involve) afectar; (relate to) tener que ver con; **to be ~ed (about)** interesarse (por), preocuparse (por); **concerning** prep sobre, acerca de

concert [ˈkɒnsət] n concierto; **concert hall** n sala de conciertos

concerto [kənˈtʃɜːtəu] n concierto

concession [kənˈseʃən] n concesión f; **tax ~** privilegio fiscal

concise [kənˈsaɪs] adj conciso

conclude [kənˈkluːd] vt concluir; (treaty etc) firmar; (agreement) llegar a; (decide) llegar a la conclusión de; **conclusion** [-ˈkluːʒən] n conclusión f; firma

concrete [ˈkɒnkriːt] n hormigón m ▷ adj de hormigón; (fig) concreto

concussion [kənˈkʌʃən] n conmoción f cerebral

condemn [kənˈdem] vt condenar; (building) declarar en ruina

condensation [ˌkɒndenˈseɪʃən] n condensación f

condense [kənˈdens] vi condensarse ▷ vt condensar, abreviar

condition [kənˈdɪʃən] n condición f, estado; (requirement) condición f ▷ vt condicionar; **on ~ that** a condición (de) que; **conditional** [kənˈdɪʃənl] adj condicional; **conditioner** n suavizante

condo [ˈkɒndəu] (us) n (inf) = **condominium**

condom [ˈkɒndəm] n condón m

condominium [ˌkɒndəˈmɪnɪəm] (us) n (building) bloque m de pisos or apartamentos (propiedad de quienes lo habitan), condominio (LAM); (apartment) piso or apartamento (en propiedad),

condominio (LAM)
condone [kən'dəʊn] vt condonar
conduct [n 'kɒndʌkt, vb kən'dʌkt]
n conducta, comportamiento ▷ vt
(lead) conducir; (manage) llevar a
cabo, dirigir; (Mus) dirigir ▷ vi
comportarse; **conducted tour** (BRIT)
n visita acompañada; **conductor** n
(of orchestra) director m; (us: on train)
revisor(a) m/f; (on bus) cobrador m;
(Elec) conductor m
cone [kəʊn] n cono; (pine cone)
piña; (on road) pivote m; (for ice-cream)
cucurucho
confectionery [kən'fekʃənrɪ] n
dulces mpl
confer [kən'fəː*] vt: **to ~ sth on**
otorgar algo a ▷ vi **to ~ with**
conferenciar
conference ['kɒnfərəns] n (meeting)
reunión f; (convention) congreso
confess [kən'fes] vt confesar ▷ vi
admitir; **confession** [-'feʃən] n
confesión f
confide [kən'faɪd] vi: **to ~ in** confiar
en
confidence ['kɒnfɪdns] n (also: self-
~) confianza; (secret) confidencia; **in ~**
(speak, write) en confianza; **confident**
adj seguro de sí mismo; (certain)
seguro; **confidential** [kɒnfɪ'denʃəl]
adj confidencial
confine [kən'faɪn] vt (limit) limitar;
(shut up) encerrar; **confined** adj (space)
reducido
confirm [kən'fəːm] vt confirmar;
confirmation [kɒnfə'meɪʃən] n
confirmación f
confiscate ['kɒnfɪskeɪt] vt confiscar
conflict [n 'kɒnflɪkt, vb kən'flɪkt]
n conflicto ▷ vi (opinions) chocar
conform [kən'fɔːm] vi conformarse;
to ~ to ajustarse a
confront [kən'frʌnt] vt (problems)
hacer frente a; (enemy, danger)
enfrentarse con; **confrontation**
[kɒnfrən'teɪʃən] n enfrentamiento
confuse [kən'fjuːz] vt (perplex)
aturdir, desconcertar; (mix up)

confundir; (complicate) complicar;
confused adj confuso; (person)
perplejo; **confusing** adj confuso;
confusion [-'fjuːʒən] n confusión f
congestion [kən'dʒestʃən] n
congestión f
congratulate [kən'grætjuleɪt]
vt: **to ~ sb (on)** felicitar a algn (por);
congratulations [-'leɪʃənz] npl
felicitaciones fpl; **congratulations!**
¡enhorabuena!
congregation [-'geɪʃən] n (of a
church) feligreses mpl
congress ['kɒŋgres] n congreso;
(us): **C~** Congreso; **congressman**
(irreg: us) n miembro del Congreso;
congresswoman (irreg:us) n
diputada, miembro del Congreso
conifer ['kɒnɪfə*] n conífera
conjugate ['kɒndʒugeɪt] vt conjugar
conjugation [kɒndʒə'geɪʃən] n
conjugación f
conjunction [kən'dʒʌŋkʃən] n
conjunción f; **in ~ with** junto con
conjure ['kʌndʒə*] vi hacer juegos
de manos
connect [kə'nekt] vt juntar, unir;
(Elec) conectar; (Tel: subscriber) poner;
(: caller) poner al habla; (fig) relacionar,
asociar ▷ vi: **to ~ with** (train) enlazar
con; **to be ~ed with** (associated) estar
relacionado con; **connecting flight** n
vuelo m de enlace; **connection**
[-ʃən] n juntura, unión f; (Elec)
conexión f; (Rail) enlace m; (Tel)
comunicación f; (fig) relación f
conquer ['kɒŋkə*] vt (territory)
conquistar; (enemy, feelings) vencer
conquest ['kɒŋkwest] n conquista
cons [kɒnz] npl see **convenience;
pro; mod**
conscience ['kɒnʃəns] n conciencia
conscientious [kɒnʃɪ'enʃəs] adj
concienzudo; (objection) de conciencia
conscious ['kɒnʃəs] adj (deliberate)
deliberado; (awake, aware) consciente;
consciousness n conciencia; (Med)
conocimiento

consecutive [kən'sɛkjutɪv] *adj* consecutivo; **on 3 ~ occasions** en 3 ocasiones consecutivas

consensus [kən'sɛnsəs] *n* consenso

consent [kən'sɛnt] *n* consentimiento ▷ *vi*: **to ~ (to)** consentir (en)

consequence ['kɒnsɪkwəns] *n* consecuencia; *(significance)* importancia

consequently ['kɒnsɪkwəntlɪ] *adv* por consiguiente

conservation [kɒnsə'veɪʃən] *n* conservación *f*

conservative [kən'sə:vətɪv] *adj* conservador(a); *(estimate etc)* cauteloso; **Conservative** (BRIT) *adj, n* (Pol) conservador(a) *m/f*

conservatory [kən'sə:vətrɪ] *n* invernadero; *(Mus)* conservatorio

consider [kən'sɪdə*] *vt* considerar; *(take into account)* tener en cuenta; *(study)* estudiar, examinar; **to ~ doing sth** pensar en (la posibilidad de) hacer algo; **considerable** *adj* considerable; **considerably** *adv* notablemente; **considerate** *adj* considerado; **consideration** [-'reɪʃə] *n* consideración *f*; *(factor)* factor *m*; **to give sth further consideration** estudiar algo más a fondo; **considering** *prep* teniendo en cuenta

consignment [kən'saɪnmənt] *n* envío

consist [kən'sɪst] *vi*: **~ of** consistir en

consistency [kən'sɪstənsɪ] *n* *(of argument etc)* coherencia; consecuencia; *(thickness)* consistencia

consistent [kən'sɪstənt] *adj* *(person)* consecuente; *(argument etc)* coherente

consolation [kɒnsə'leɪʃən] *n* consuelo

console[1] [kən'səul] *vt* consolar

console[2] ['kɒnsəul] *n* consola

consonant ['kɒnsənənt] *n* consonante *f*

conspicuous [kən'spɪkjuəs] *adj*

(visible) visible

conspiracy [kən'spɪrəsɪ] *n* conjura, complot *m*

constable ['kʌnstəbl] (BRIT) *n* policía *mf*; **chief ~** = jefe *m* de policía

constant ['kɒnstənt] *adj* constante; **constantly** *adv* constantemente

constipated ['kɒnstɪpeɪtəd] *adj* estreñido

> Be careful not to translate **constipated** by the Spanish word *constipado*.

constipation [kɒnstɪ'peɪʃən] *n* estreñimiento

constituency [kən'stɪtjuənsɪ] *n* *(Pol: area)* distrito electoral; *(: electors)* electorado

constitute ['kɒnstɪtjuːt] *vt* constituir

constitution [kɒnstɪ'tjuːʃən] *n* constitución *f*

constraint [kən'streɪnt] *n* obligación *f*; *(limit)* restricción *f*

construct [kən'strʌkt] *vt* construir; **construction** [-ʃən] *n* construcción *f*; **constructive** *adj* constructivo

consul ['kɒnsl] *n* cónsul *mf*; **consulate** ['kɒnsjulɪt] *n* consulado

consult [kən'sʌlt] *vt* consultar; **consultant** *n* (BRIT Med) especialista *mf*; *(other specialist)* asesor(a) *m/f*; **consultation** [kɒnsəl'teɪʃən] *n* consulta; **consulting room** (BRIT) *n* consultorio

consume [kən'sjuːm] *vt* *(eat)* comerse; *(drink)* beberse; *(fire etc, Comm)* consumir; **consumer** *n* consumidor(a) *m/f*

consumption [kən'sʌmpʃən] *n* consumo

cont. *abbr* (= *continued*) sigue

contact ['kɒntækt] *n* contacto; *(person)* contacto; *(: pej)* enchufe *m* ▷ *vt* ponerse en contacto con; **contact lenses** *npl* lentes *fpl* de contacto

contagious [kən'teɪdʒəs] *adj* contagioso

contain [kən'teɪn] *vt* contener;

to ~ o.s. contenerse; **container**
n recipiente m; (for shipping etc)
contenedor m

contaminate [kən'tæmɪneɪt] vt
contaminar

cont'd abbr (=continued) sigue

contemplate ['kɒntəmpleɪt] vt
contemplar; (reflect upon) considerar

contemporary [kən'tempərərɪ] adj,
n contemporáneo/a m/f

contempt [kən'tempt] n desprecio;
~ of court (Law) desacato (a los
tribunales)

contend [kən'tend] vt (argue) afirmar
▷ vi: **to ~ with/for** luchar contra/por

content [adj, vb kən'tent, n
'kɒntent] adj (happy) contento;
(satisfied) satisfecho ▷ vt contentar;
satisfacer ▷ n contenido; **contents**
npl contenido; **(table of) ~s** índice m
de materias; **contented** adj contento;
satisfecho

contest [n 'kɒntest, vb kən'test] n
lucha; (competition) concurso m;
(dispute) impugnar; (Pol) presentarse
como candidato/a en

> Be careful not to translate **contest**
> by the Spanish word contestar.

contestant [kən'testənt] n
concursante mf; (in fight) contendiente
mf

context ['kɒntekst] n contexto

continent ['kɒntɪnənt] n continente
m; **the C~** (BRIT) el continente
europeo; **continental** [-'nentl] adj
continental; **continental breakfast** n
desayuno estilo europeo; **continental
quilt** (BRIT) n edredón m

continual [kən'tɪnjuəl] adj
continuo; **continually** adv
constantemente

continue [kən'tɪnjuː] vi, vt seguir,
continuar

continuity [kɒntɪ'njuːɪtɪ] n (also
Cine) continuidad f

continuous [kən'tɪnjuəs] adj
continuo; **continuous assessment**
n (BRIT) evaluación f continua;

continuously adv continuamente

contour ['kɒntuə*] n contorno; (also:
~ line) curva de nivel

contraception [kɒntrə'sepʃən] n
contracepción f

contraceptive [kɒntrə'septɪv] adj, n
anticonceptivo

contract [n 'kɒntrækt, vb kən'trækt]
n contrato ▷ vi (Comm): **to ~ to do
sth** comprometerse por contrato a
hacer algo; (become smaller) contraerse,
encogerse ▷ vt contraer; **contractor**
n contratista mf

contradict [kɒntrə'dɪkt] vt
contradecir; **contradiction** [-ʃən] n
contradicción f

contrary[1] ['kɒntrərɪ] adj contrario
▷ n lo contrario; **on the ~** al contrario;
unless you hear to the ~ a no ser que
le digan lo contrario

contrary[2] [kən'treərɪ] adj (perverse)
terco

contrast [n 'kɒntrɑːst, vt kən'trɑːst]
n contraste m ▷ vt comparar; **in ~ to**
en contraste con

contribute [kən'trɪbjuːt] vi
contribuir ▷ vt: **to ~ £10/an article to**
contribuir con 10 libras/un artículo
a; **to ~** (to charity) donar a; (newspaper)
escribir para; (discussion) intervenir en;
contribution [kɒntrɪ'bjuːʃən]
n (donation) donativo; (BRIT: for social
security) cotización f; (to debate)
intervención f; (to journal) colaboración
f; **contributor** n contribuyente mf; (to
newspaper) colaborador(a) m/f

control [kən'trəul] vt controlar;
(process etc) dirigir; (machinery)
manejar; (temper) dominar; (disease)
contener ▷ n control m; **controls** npl
(of vehicle) instrumentos mpl de mando;
(of radio) controles mpl; (governmental)
medidas fpl de control; **under ~** bajo
control; **to be in ~ of** tener el mando
de; **the car went out of ~** se perdió
el control del coche; **control tower** n
(Aviat) torre f de control

controversial [kɒntrə'vɜːʃl]

polémico

controversy ['kɔntrəvə:sɪ] n polémica

convenience [kən'vi:nɪəns] n (easiness) comodidad f; (suitability) idoneidad f; (advantage) ventaja f; **at your ~** cuando le sea conveniente; **all modern ~s, all mod cons** (BRIT) todo confort

convenient [kən'vi:nɪənt] adj (useful) útil; (place, time) conveniente

convent ['kɔnvənt] n convento

convention [kən'venʃən] n convención f; (meeting) asamblea; (agreement) convenio; **conventional** adj convencional

conversation [kɔnvə'seɪʃən] n conversación f

conversely [-'və:slɪ] adv a la inversa

conversion [kən'və:ʃən] n conversión f

convert [vb kən'və:t, n 'kɔnvə:t] vt (Rel, Comm) convertir; (alter): **to ~ sth into/to** transformar algo en/convertir algo a ▷ n converso/a; **convertible** adj convertible ▷ n descapotable m

convey [kən'veɪ] vt llevar; (thanks) comunicar; (idea) expresar; **conveyor belt** n cinta transportadora

convict [vb kən'vɪkt, n 'kɔnvɪkt] vt (find guilty) declarar culpable a ▷ n presidiario/a; **conviction** [-ʃən] n condena; (belief, certainty) convicción f

convince [kən'vɪns] vt convencer; **convinced** adj: **convinced of/that** convencido de/de que; **convincing** adj convincente

convoy ['kɔnvɔɪ] n convoy m

cook [kuk] vt (stew etc) guisar; (meal) preparar ▷ vi cocer; (person) cocinar ▷ n cocinero/a; **cook book** n libro de cocina; **cooker** n cocina; **cookery** n cocina; **cookery book** (BRIT) = **cook book**; **cookie** n galleta; **cooking** n cocina

cool [ku:l] adj fresco; (not afraid) tranquilo; (unfriendly) frío ▷ vt enfriar ▷ vi enfriarse; **cool down** vi enfriarse;

(fig: person, situation) calmarse; **cool off** vi (become calmer) calmarse, apaciguarse; (lose enthusiasm) perder (el) interés, enfriarse

cop [kɔp] (inf) n poli m f (SP), tira m f (MEX)

cope [kəup] vi: **to ~ with** (problem) hacer frente a

copper ['kɔpə*] n (metal) cobre m; (BRIT: inf) poli m f, tira m f (MEX)

copy ['kɔpɪ] n copia; (of book etc) ejemplar m ▷ vt copiar; **copyright** n derechos mpl de autor

coral ['kɔrəl] n coral m

cord [kɔ:d] n cuerda; (Elec) cable m; (fabric) pana; **cords** npl (trousers) pantalones mpl de pana; **cordless** adj sin hilos

corduroy ['kɔ:dərɔɪ] n pana

core [kɔ:*] n centro, núcleo; (of fruit) corazón m; (of problem) meollo ▷ vt quitar el corazón de

coriander [kɔrɪ'ændə*] n culantro

cork [kɔ:k] n corcho; (tree) alcornoque m; **corkscrew** n sacacorchos m inv

corn [kɔ:n] n (BRIT: cereal crop) trigo; (us: maize) maíz m; (on foot) callo; **~ on the cob** (Culin) mazorca, elote m (MEX), choclo (SC)

corned beef ['kɔ:nd-] n carne f acecinada (en lata)

corner ['kɔ:nə*] n (outside) esquina; (inside) rincón m; (in road) curva; (Football) córner m; (Boxing) esquina ▷ vt (trap) arrinconar; (Comm) acaparar ▷ vi (in car) tomar las curvas; **corner shop** (BRIT) tienda de la esquina

cornflakes ['kɔ:nfleɪks] npl copos mpl de maíz, cornflakes mpl

cornflour ['kɔ:nflauə*] (BRIT) n harina de maíz

cornstarch ['kɔ:nstɑ:tʃ] (us) n = **cornflour**

Cornwall ['kɔ:nwəl] n Cornualles m

coronary ['kɔrənərɪ] n (also: ~ **thrombosis**) infarto

coronation [kɔrə'neɪʃən] n coronación f

coroner ['kɒrənə*] n juez mf de
instrucción

corporal ['kɔ:pərl] n cabo ▷ adj: ~
punishment castigo corporal

corporate ['kɔ:pərɪt] adj (action,
ownership) colectivo; (finance, image)
corporativo

corporation [kɔ:pə'reɪʃən] n
(of town) ayuntamiento m; (Comm)
corporación f

corps [kɔ:*, pl kɔ:z] n inv cuerpo;
diplomatic ~ cuerpo diplomático;
press ~ gabinete m de prensa

corpse [kɔ:ps] n cadáver m

correct [kə'rekt] adj justo, exacto;
(proper) correcto ▷ vt corregir; (exam)
corregir, calificar; **correction**
[-ʃən] n (act) corrección f; (instance)
rectificación f

correspond [kɒrɪs'pɒnd] vi
(write): **to ~ (with)** escribirse (con); (be
equivalent to): **to ~ (to)** corresponder
(a); (be in accordance): **to ~ (with)**
corresponder (con); **correspondence**
n correspondencia; **correspondent**
n corresponsal mf; **corresponding** adj
correspondiente

corridor ['kɒrɪdɔ:*] n pasillo

corrode [kə'rəud] vt corroer ▷ vi
corroerse

corrupt [kə'rʌpt] adj (person)
corrupto; (Comput) corrompido
▷ vt corromper; (Comput) degradar;
corruption n corrupción f; (of data)
alteración f

Corsica ['kɔ:sɪkə] n Córcega

cosmetic [kɒz'metɪk] adj, n
cosmético; **cosmetic surgery** n
cirugía f estética

cosmopolitan [kɒzmə'pɒlɪtn] adj
cosmopolita

cost [kɒst] (pt, pp ~) n (price) precio
▷ vi costar, valer ▷ vt preparar el
presupuesto de; **how much does it ~?**
¿cuánto cuesta?; **to ~ sb time/effort**
costarle a algn tiempo/esfuerzo; **it ~**
him his life le costó la vida; **at all ~s**
cueste lo que cueste; **costs** npl (Comm)

costes mpl; (Law) costas fpl

co-star ['kəustɑ:*] n coprotagonista

Costa Rica [kɒstə'ri:kə] n
Costa Rica; **Costa Rican** adj, n
costarriqueño/a

costly ['kɒstlɪ] adj costoso

cost of living n costo or coste m (Sp)
de la vida

costume ['kɒstju:m] n traje m;
(BRIT: also: **swimming ~**) traje de baño

cosy ['kəuzɪ] (us **cozy**) adj (person)
cómodo; (room) acogedor(a)

cot [kɒt] n (BRIT: child's) cuna;
(us: campbed) cama de campaña

cottage ['kɒtɪdʒ] n casita de campo;
(rustic) barraca; **cottage cheese** n
requesón m

cotton ['kɒtn] n algodón m; (thread)
hilo; **cotton on** vi (inf): **to cotton on**
(to sth) caer en la cuenta (de algo);
cotton bud n (BRIT) bastoncillo m
de algodón; **cotton candy** (us) n
algodón m (azucarado); **cotton wool**
(BRIT) n algodón m (hidrófilo)

couch [kautʃ] n sofá m; (doctor's etc)
diván m

cough [kɒf] vi toser ▷ n tos f; **cough**
mixture n jarabe m para la tos

could [kud] pt of **can²**; **couldn't** =
could not

council ['kaunsl] n consejo; **city** or
town ~ consejo municipal; **council**
estate (BRIT) n urbanización de
viviendas municipales de alquiler; **council**
house (BRIT) n vivienda municipal de
alquiler; **councillor** (us **councilor**) n
concejal(a) m/f; **council tax** n (BRIT)
contribución f municipal (dependiente
del valor de la vivienda)

counsel ['kaunsl] n (advice) consejo;
(lawyer) abogado/a ▷ vt aconsejar;
counselling (us **counseling**) n (Psych)
asistencia f psicológica; **counsellor** (us
counselor) n consejero/a, abogado/a

count [kaunt] vt contar; (include)
incluir ▷ vi contar ▷ n cuenta;
(of votes) escrutinio; (level) nivel m;

(nobleman) conde m; **count in** (inf)
vt: **to count sb in on sth** contar con
algn para algo; **count on** vt fus contar
con; **countdown** n cuenta atrás
counter ['kauntə*] n (in shop)
mostrador m; (in games) ficha ▷ vt
contrarrestar ▷ adv: **to run ~ to** ser
contrario a, ir en contra de; **counter
clockwise** (us) adv en sentido
contrario al de las agujas del reloj
counterfeit ['kauntəfɪt] n
falsificación f, simulación f ▷ vt
falsificar ▷ adj falso, falsificado
counterpart ['kauntəpɑːt] n
homólogo/a
countess ['kauntɪs] n condesa
countless ['kauntlɪs] adj
innumerable
country ['kʌntrɪ] n país m; (native
land) patria; (as opposed to town) campo;
(region) región f, tierra; **country and
western (music)** n música country;
country house n casa de campo;
countryside n campo
county ['kauntɪ] n condado
coup [kuː] (pl ~s) n (also: ~ **d'état**)
golpe m (de estado); (achievement) éxito
couple ['kʌpl] n (of things) par m;
(of people) pareja; (married couple)
matrimonio; **a ~ of** un par de
coupon ['kuːpɔn] n cupón m;
(voucher) valé m
courage ['kʌrɪdʒ] n coraje m, valentía;
courageous [kə'reɪdʒəs] adj valiente
courgette [kuə'ʒet] (BRIT) n
calabacín m, calabaza (MEX)
courier ['kurɪə*] n mensajero/a; (for
tourists) guía mf (de turismo)
course [kɔːs] n (direction) dirección
f; (of river, Scol) curso; (process)
transcurso; (Med): **~ of treatment**
tratamiento; (of meal) plato; (Golf) campo; **of ~** desde
luego, naturalmente; **of ~!** ¡claro!
court [kɔːt] n (royal) corte f; (Law)
tribunal m, juzgado; (Tennis etc) pista,
cancha ▷ vt (woman) cortejar a; **to
take to ~** demandar

courtesy ['kɔːtəsɪ] n cortesía; **(by)
~ of** por cortesía de; **courtesy bus,
courtesy coach** n autobús m gratuito
court: **court-house** ['kɔːthaus] (us) n
palacio de justicia; **courtroom**
['kɔːtrum] n sala de justicia;
courtyard ['kɔːtjɑːd] n patio
cousin ['kʌzn] n primo/a; **first ~**
primo/a carnal, primo/a hermano/a
cover ['kʌvə*] vt cubrir; (feelings,
mistake) ocultar; (with lid) tapar; (book
etc) forrar; (distance) recorrer; (include)
abarcar; (protect: also: Insurance) cubrir;
(Press) investigar; (discuss) tratar
▷ n cubierta; (lid) tapa; (for chair etc)
funda; (envelope) sobre m; (for book)
forro; (of magazine) portada; (shelter)
abrigo; (Insurance) cobertura; (of spy)
cobertura; **covers** npl (on bed) sábanas;
mantas; **to take ~** (shelter) protegerse,
resguardarse; **under ~** (indoors) bajo
techo; **under ~ of darkness** al amparo
de la oscuridad; **under separate ~**
(Comm) por separado; **cover up** vi: **to
cover up for sb** encubrir a algn;
coverage n (TV, Press) cobertura;
cover charge n precio del cubierto;
cover-up n encubrimiento
cow [kau] n vaca; (inf: woman) bruja
▷ vt intimidar
coward ['kauəd] n cobarde mf;
cowardly adj cobarde
cowboy ['kaubɔɪ] n vaquero
cozy ['kəuzɪ] (us) adj =**cosy**
crab [kræb] n cangrejo
crack [kræk] n grieta; (noise) crujido;
(drug) crack m ▷ vt agrietar, romper;
(nut) cascar; (solve: problem) resolver;
(: code) descifrar; (whip etc) chasquear;
(knuckles) crujir; (joke) contar ▷ adj
(expert) de primera; **crack down on** vt
fus adoptar fuertes medidas contra;
cracked adj (cup, window) rajado;
(wall) resquebrajado; **cracker** n
(biscuit) crácker m; (Christmas cracker)
petardo sorpresa
crackle ['krækl] vi crepitar
cradle ['kreɪdl] n cuna

craft [krɑːft] n (skill) arte m; (trade) oficio; (cunning) astucia; (boat: pl inv) barco; (plane: pl inv) avión m; **craftsman** (irreg) n artesano; **craftsmanship** n (quality) destreza

cram [kræm] vt (fill): **to ~ sth with** llenar algo (a reventar) de; (put): **to ~ sth into** meter algo a la fuerza en ▷ vi (for exams) empollar

cramp [kræmp] n (Med) calambre m; **cramped** adj apretado, estrecho

cranberry [ˈkrænbərɪ] n arándano agrio

crane [kreɪn] n (Tech) grúa; (bird) grulla

crap [kræp] n (inf!) mierda (!)

crash [kræʃ] n (noise) estrépito; (of cars etc) choque m; (of plane) accidente m de aviación; (Comm) quiebra ▷ vt (car, plane) estrellar ▷ vi (car, plane) estrellarse; (two cars) chocar; (Comm) quebrar; **crash course** n curso acelerado; **crash helmet** n casco (protector)

crate [kreɪt] n cajón m de embalaje; (for bottles) caja

crave [kreɪv] vt, vi: **to ~ (for)** ansiar, anhelar

crawl [krɔːl] vi (drag o.s.) arrastrarse; (child) andar a gatas, gatear; (vehicle) avanzar (lentamente) ▷ n (Swimming) crol m

crayfish [ˈkreɪfɪʃ] n inv (freshwater) cangrejo de río; (saltwater) cigala

crayon [ˈkreɪən] n lápiz m de color

craze [kreɪz] n (fashion) moda

crazy [ˈkreɪzɪ] adj (person) loco; (idea) disparatado; (inf: keen): **~ about sb/sth** loco por algn/algo

creak [kriːk] vi (floorboard) crujir; (hinge etc) chirriar, rechinar

cream [kriːm] n (of milk) nata, crema; (lotion) crema; (fig) flor f y nata ▷ adj (colour) color crema; **cream cheese** n queso blanco; **creamy** adj cremoso

crease [kriːs] n (fold) pliegue m; (in trousers) raya; (wrinkle) arruga ▷ vt (wrinkle) arrugar ▷ vi (wrinkle up)

arrugarse

create [kriːˈeɪt] vt crear; **creation** [-ʃən] n creación f; **creative** adj creativo; **creator** n creador(a) m/f

creature [ˈkriːtʃə*] n (animal) animal m, bicho; (person) criatura

crèche [kreʃ] n guardería (infantil)

credentials [krɪˈdenʃlz] npl (references) referencias fpl; (identity papers) documentos mpl de identidad

credibility [kredrˈbɪlɪtɪ] n credibilidad f

credible [ˈkredɪbl] adj creíble; (trustworthy) digno de confianza

credit [ˈkredɪt] n crédito; (merit) honor m, mérito ▷ vt (Comm) abonar; (believe: also: **give ~ to**) creer, prestar fe a ▷ adj crediticio; **credits** npl (Cinema) fichas fpl técnicas; **to be in ~** (person) tener saldo a favor; **to ~ sb with** (fig) reconocer a algn el mérito de; **credit card** n tarjeta de crédito; **credit crunch** n crisis f crediticia

creek [kriːk] n cala, ensenada; (us) riachuelo

creep [kriːp] (pt, pp **crept**) vi arrastrarse

cremate [krɪˈmeɪt] vt incinerar

crematorium [kremə'tɔːrɪəm] (pl **crematoria**) n crematorio

crept [krept] pt, pp of **creep**

crescent [ˈkresnt] n media luna; (street) calle f (en forma de semicírculo)

cress [kres] n berro

crest [krest] n (of bird) cresta; (of hill) cima, cumbre f; (of coat of arms) blasón m

crew [kruː] n (of ship etc) tripulación f; (TV, Cinema) equipo; **crew-neck** n cuello a la caja

crib [krɪb] n cuna ▷ vt (inf) plagiar

cricket [ˈkrɪkɪt] n (insect) grillo; (game) críquet m; **cricketer** n jugador(a) m/f de críquet

crime [kraɪm] n (no pl: illegal activities) crimen m; (illegal action) delito; **criminal** [ˈkrɪmɪnl] n criminal mf, delincuente mf ▷ adj criminal; (illegal) delictivo; (law) penal

crimson ['krɪmzn] adj carmesí

cringe [krɪndʒ] vi agacharse, encogerse

cripple ['krɪpl] n lisiado/a, cojo/a ▷ vt lisiar, mutilar

crisis ['kraɪsɪs] (pl **crises**) n crisis f inv

crisp [krɪsp] adj fresco; (vegetables etc) crujiente; (manner) seco; **crispy** adj crujiente

criterion [kraɪ'tɪərɪən] (pl **criteria**) n criterio

critic ['krɪtɪk] n crítico/a; **critical** adj crítico; (illness) grave; **criticism** ['krɪtɪsɪzm] n crítica; **criticize** ['krɪtɪsaɪz] vt criticar

Croat ['krəuæt] adj, n = **Croatian**

Croatia [krəu'eɪʃə] n Croacia; **Croatian** adj, n croata m/f ▷ n (Ling) croata m

crockery ['krɔkərɪ] n loza, vajilla

crocodile ['krɔkədaɪl] n cocodrilo

crocus ['krəukəs] n croco, crocus m

croissant ['krwasɑ̃] n croissant m, medialuna (esp LAM)

crook [kruk] n ladrón/ona m/f; (of shepherd) cayado; **crooked** ['krukɪd] adj torcido; (dishonest) nada honrado

crop [krɔp] n (produce) cultivo; (amount produced) cosecha; (riding crop) látigo de montar ▷ vt cortar, recortar; **crop up** vi surgir, presentarse

cross [krɔs] n cruz f; (hybrid) cruce m ▷ vt (street etc) cruzar, atravesar ▷ adj de mal humor, enojado; **cross off** vt tachar; **cross out** vt tachar; **cross over** vi cruzar; **cross-Channel ferry** ['krɔs'tʃænl-] n transbordador m que cruza el Canal de la Mancha; **crosscountry (race)** n carrera a campo traviesa, cross m; **crossing** n (sea passage) travesía; (also: **pedestrian crossing**) paso para peatones; **crossing guard** (us) n persona encargada de ayudar a los niños a cruzar la calle; **crossroads** n cruce m, encrucijada; **crosswalk** (us) n paso de peatones; **crossword** n crucigrama m

crotch [krɔtʃ] n (Anat, of garment) entrepierna

crouch [krautʃ] vi agacharse, acurrucarse

crouton ['kru:tɔn] n cubito de pan frito

crow [krəu] n (bird) cuervo; (of cock) canto, cacareo ▷ vi (cock) cantar

crowd [kraud] n muchedumbre f, multitud f ▷ vt (fill) llenar ▷ vi (gather): **to ~ round** reunirse en torno a; (cram): **to ~ in** entrar en tropel; **crowded** adj (full) atestado; (densely populated) superpoblado

crown [kraun] n corona; (of head) coronilla; (for tooth) funda; (of hill) cumbre f ▷ vt coronar; (fig) completar, rematar; **crown jewels** npl joyas fpl reales

crucial ['kru:ʃl] adj decisivo

crucifix ['kru:sɪfɪks] n crucifijo

crude [kru:d] adj (materials) bruto; (fig: basic) tosco; (: vulgar) ordinario; **crude (oil)** n (petróleo) crudo

cruel ['kruəl] adj cruel; **cruelty** n crueldad f

cruise [kru:z] n crucero ▷ vi (ship) hacer un crucero; (car) ir a la velocidad de crucero

crumb [krʌm] n miga, migaja

crumble ['krʌmbl] vt desmenuzar ▷ vi (building, also fig) desmoronarse

crumpet ['krʌmpɪt] n ≈ bollo para tostar

crumple ['krʌmpl] vt (paper) estrujar; (material) arrugar

crunch [krʌntʃ] vt (with teeth) mascar; (underfoot) hacer crujir ▷ n (fig) hora o momento de la verdad; **crunchy** adj crujiente

crush [krʌʃ] n (crowd) aglomeración f; (infatuation): **to have a ~ on sb** estar loco por algn; (drink): **lemon ~** limonada ▷ vt aplastar; (paper) estrujar; (cloth) arrugar; (fruit) exprimir; (opposition) aplastar; (hopes) destruir

crust [krʌst] n corteza; (of snow, ice) costra; **crusty** adj (bread) crujiente;

(person) de mal carácter

crutch [krʌtʃ] n muleta

cry [kraɪ] vi llorar ▷ n (shriek) chillido; (shout) grito; **cry off** vi (call out, shout) lanzar un grito, echar un grito ▷ vt gritar

crystal ['krɪstl] n cristal m

cub [kʌb] n cachorro m; (also: **~ scout**) niño explorador

Cuba ['kju:bə] n Cuba; **Cuban** adj, n cubano/a m/f

cube [kju:b] n cubo ▷ vt (Math) cubicar

cubicle ['kju:bɪkl] n (at pool) caseta; (for bed) cubículo

cuckoo ['kuku:] n cuco

cucumber ['kju:kʌmbə*] n pepino

cuddle ['kʌdl] vt abrazar ▷ vi abrazarse

cue [kju:] n (snooker cue) taco; (Theatre etc) señal f

cuff [kʌf] n (of sleeve) puño; (us: of trousers) vuelta; (blow) bofetada ▷ **off the ~** adv de improviso; **cufflinks** npl gemelos mpl

cuisine [kwɪˈzi:n] n cocina

cul-de-sac ['kʌldəsæk] n callejón m sin salida

cull [kʌl] vt (idea) sacar ▷ n (of animals) matanza selectiva

culminate ['kʌlmɪneɪt] vi: **to ~ in** terminar en

culprit ['kʌlprɪt] n culpable mf

cult [kʌlt] n culto

cultivate ['kʌltɪveɪt] vt cultivar

cultural ['kʌltʃərəl] adj cultural

culture ['kʌltʃə*] n (also fig) cultura; (Biol) cultivo

cumin ['kʌmɪn] n (spice) comino

cunning ['kʌnɪŋ] n astucia ▷ adj astuto

cup [kʌp] n taza; (as prize) copa

cupboard ['kʌbəd] n armario; (in kitchen) alacena

cup final n (Football) final f de copa

curator [kjuə'reɪtə*] n director(a) m/f

curb [kə:b] vt refrenar; (person)

reprimir ▷ n freno; (us) bordillo

curdle ['kə:dl] vi cuajarse

cure [kjuə*] vt curar ▷ n cura, curación f; (fig: solution) remedio

curfew ['kə:fju:] n toque m de queda

curiosity [kjuərɪˈɒsɪtɪ] n curiosidad f

curious ['kjuərɪəs] adj curioso; (person: interested): **to be ~** sentir curiosidad

curl [kə:l] n rizo ▷ vt (hair) rizar ▷ vi rizarse; **curl up** vi (person) hacerse un ovillo; **curler** n rulo; **curly** adj rizado

currant ['kʌrnt] n pasa (de Corinto); (blackcurrant, redcurrant) grosella

currency ['kʌrnsɪ] n moneda; **to gain ~** (fig) difundirse

current ['kʌrnt] n corriente f ▷ adj (accepted) corriente; (present) actual; **current account** (BRIT) n cuenta corriente; **current affairs** npl noticias fpl de actualidad; **currently** adv actualmente

curriculum [kə'rɪkjuləm] (pl **~s** or **curricula**) n plan m de estudios; **curriculum vitae** n currículum m

curry ['kʌrɪ] n curry m ▷ vt: **to ~ favour with** buscar favores con; **curry powder** n curry m en polvo

curse [kə:s] vi soltar tacos vi maldecir n maldición f; (swearword) palabrota, taco

cursor ['kə:sə*] n (Comput) cursor m

curt [kə:t] adj corto, seco

curtain ['kə:tn] n cortina; (Theatre) telón m

curve [kə:v] n curva ▷ vi (road) hacer una curva; (line etc) curvarse; **curved** adj curvo

cushion ['kuʃən] n cojín m; (of air) colchón m ▷ vt (shock) amortiguar

custard ['kʌstəd] n natillas fpl

custody ['kʌstədɪ] n custodia; **to take into ~** detener

custom ['kʌstəm] n costumbre f; (Comm) clientela

customer ['kʌstəmə*] n cliente m/f

customized ['kʌstəmaɪzd] adj (car etc) hecho a encargo

customs ['kʌstəmz] *npl* aduana; **customs officer** *n* aduanero/a

cut [kʌt] (*pt, pp* **~**) *vt* cortar; (*price*) rebajar; (*text, programme*) acortar; (*reduce*) reducir ▷ *vi* cortar ▷ *n* (*of garment*) corte *m*; (*in skin*) cortadura; (*in salary etc*) rebaja; (*in spending*) reducción *f*, recorte *m*; (*slice of meat*) tajada; **to ~ a tooth** echar un diente; **to ~ and paste** (*Comput*) cortar y pegar; **cut back** *vt* (*plants*) podar; (*production, expenditure*) reducir; **cut down** *vt* (*tree*) derribar; (*reduce*) reducir; **cut off** *vt* cortar; (*person, place*) aislar; (*Tel*) desconectar; **cut out** *vt* (*shape*) recortar; (*stop: activity etc*) dejar; (*remove*) quitar; **cut up** *vt* cortar (en pedazos); **cutback** *n* reducción *f*

cute [kju:t] *adj* mono

cutlery ['kʌtlərɪ] *n* cubiertos *mpl*

cutlet ['kʌtlɪt] *n* chuleta; (*nut etc cutlet*) plato vegetariano hecho con nueces y verdura en forma de chuleta

cut-price ['kʌt'praɪs] (*BRIT*) *adj* a precio reducido

cut-rate ['kʌt'reɪt] (*US*) *adj* = **cut-price**

cutting ['kʌtɪŋ] *adj* (*remark*) mordaz ▷ *n* (*BRIT: from newspaper*) recorte *m*; (*from plant*) esqueje *m*

CV *n abbr* = **curriculum vitae**

cwt *abbr* = **hundredweight(s)**

cybercafé ['saɪbəkæfeɪ] *n* cibercafé *m*

cyberspace ['saɪbəspeɪs] *n* ciberespacio

cycle ['saɪkl] *n* ciclo; (*bicycle*) bicicleta ▷ *vi* ir en bicicleta; **cycle hire** *n* alquiler *m* de bicicletas; **cycle lane** *n* carril-bici *m*; **cycle path** *n* carril-bici *m*; **cycling** *n* ciclismo; **cyclist** *n* ciclista *mf*

cyclone ['saɪkləun] *n* ciclón *m*

cylinder ['sɪlɪndə*] *n* cilindro; (*of gas*) bombona

cymbal ['sɪmbl] *n* címbalo, platillo

cynical ['sɪnɪkl] *adj* cínico

Cypriot ['sɪprɪət] *adj, n* chipriota *m/f*

Cyprus ['saɪprəs] *n* Chipre *f*

cyst [sɪst] *n* quiste *m*; **cystitis** [-'taɪtɪs] *n* cistitis *f*

czar [zɑ:*] *n* zar *m*

Czech [tʃɛk] *adj, n* checo/a *m/f*; **Czech Republic** *n*: **the Czech Republic** la República Checa

d

D [di:] n (Mus) re m

dab [dæb] vt (eyes, wound) tocar (ligeramente); (paint, cream) poner un poco de

dad [dæd] n = **daddy**

daddy ['dædɪ] n papá m

daffodil ['dæfədɪl] n narciso

daft [dɑ:ft] adj tonto

dagger ['dægə*] n puñal m, daga

daily ['deɪlɪ] adj diario, cotidiano ▷ n (shop) lechería; (curse) ▷ adv todos los días, cada día

dairy ['dɛərɪ] n diario, cotidiano ▷ n (shop) lechería; (on farm) vaquería; **dairy produce** n productos mpl lácteos

daisy ['deɪzɪ] n margarita

dam [dæm] n presa ▷ vt construir una presa sobre, represar

damage ['dæmɪdʒ] n lesión f; daño; (dents etc) desperfectos mpl; (fig) perjuicio ▷ vt dañar, perjudicar; (spoil, break) estropear; **damages** npl (Law) daños mpl y perjuicios

damn [dæm] vt condenar; (curse) maldecir ▷ n (inf): **I don't give a ~** me importa un pito ▷ adj (inf: also: **~ed**)

maldito; **~ (it)!** ¡maldito sea!

damp [dæmp] adj húmedo, mojado ▷ n humedad f ▷ vt (also: **~en**: cloth, rag) mojar; (: enthusiasm) enfriar

dance [dɑ:ns] n baile m ▷ vi bailar; **dance floor** n pista f de baile; **dancer** n bailador(a) m/f; (professional) bailarín/ina m/f; **dancing** n baile m

dandelion ['dændɪlaɪən] n diente m de león

dandruff ['dændrəf] n caspa

Dane [deɪn] n danés/esa m/f

danger ['deɪndʒə*] n peligro; (risk) riesgo; **~!** (on sign) ¡peligro de muerte!; **to be in ~ of** correr riesgo de; **dangerous** adj peligroso

dangle ['dæŋɡl] vt colgar ▷ vi pender, colgar

Danish ['deɪnɪʃ] adj danés/esa ▷ n (Ling) danés m

dare [dɛə*] vt: **to ~ sb to do** desafiar a algn a hacer ▷ vi: **to ~ (to) do sth** atreverse a hacer algo; **I ~ say** (I suppose) puede ser (que); **daring** adj atrevido, osado ▷ n atrevimiento, osadía

dark [dɑ:k] adj oscuro; (hair, complexion) moreno ▷ n: **in the ~** a oscuras; **to be in the ~ about** (fig) no saber nada de; **after ~** después del anochecer; **darken** vt (colour) hacer más oscuro ▷ vi oscurecerse; **darkness** n oscuridad f; **darkroom** n cuarto oscuro

darling ['dɑ:lɪŋ] adj, n querido/a m/f

dart [dɑ:t] n dardo; (in sewing) sisa ▷ vi precipitarse; **dartboard** n diana; **darts** n (game) dardos mpl

dash [dæʃ] n (small quantity: of liquid) gota, chorrito; (sign) raya ▷ vt (throw) tirar; (hopes) defraudar ▷ vi precipitarse, ir de prisa

dashboard ['dæʃbɔ:d] n (Aut) salpicadero

data ['deɪtə] npl datos mpl; **database** n base f de datos; **data processing** n proceso de datos

date [deɪt] n (day) fecha; (with

friend) cita; (*fruit*) dátil m ▷ vt fechar; (*person*) salir con; **~ of birth** fecha de nacimiento; **to ~** adv hasta la fecha; **dated** adj anticuado

daughter ['dɔːtə*] n hija; **daughter-in-law** n nuera, hija política

daunting ['dɔːntɪŋ] adj desalentador(a)

dawn [dɔːn] n alba, amanecer m; (*fig*) nacimiento ▷ vi (*day*) amanecer; (*fig*): **it ~ed on him that ...** cayó en la cuenta de que ...

day [deɪ] n día m; (*working day*) jornada; (*heyday*) tiempos mpl, días mpl; **the ~ before/after** el día anterior/siguiente; **the ~ after tomorrow** pasado mañana; **the ~ before yesterday** anteayer; **the following ~** el día siguiente; **by ~** de día; **day-care centre** ['deɪkeə-] n centro de día; (*for children*) guardería infantil; **daydream** vi soñar despierto; **daylight** n luz f (del día); **day return** (BRIT) n billete m de ida y vuelta (en un día); **daytime** n día m; **day-to-day** adj cotidiano; **day trip** n excursión f (de un día)

dazed [deɪzd] adj aturdido

dazzle ['dæzl] vt deslumbrar; **dazzling** adj (*light, smile*) deslumbrante; (*colour*) fuerte

DC abbr (= *direct current*) C.C.

dead [dɛd] adj muerto; (*limb*) dormido; (*telephone*) cortado; (*battery*) agotado ▷ adv (*completely*) totalmente; (*exactly*) exactamente; **to shoot sb ~** matar a algn a tiros; **~ tired** muerto (de cansancio); **to stop ~** parar en seco; **dead end** n callejón m sin salida; **deadline** n fecha (or hora) tope; **deadly** adj mortal, fatal; **Dead Sea** n: **the Dead Sea** el Mar Muerto

deaf [dɛf] adj sordo; **deafen** vt ensordecer; **deafening** adj ensordecedor/a

deal [diːl] (*pt, pp* **~t**) n (*agreement*) pacto, convenio; (*business deal*) trato ▷ vt dar; (*card*) repartir; **a great ~ (of)** bastante, mucho; **deal with**

vt fus (*people*) tratar con; (*problem*) ocuparse de; (*subject*) tratar de; **dealer** n comerciante m/f; (*Cards*) mano f; **dealings** npl (*Comm*) transacciones fpl; (*relations*) relaciones fpl

dealt [dɛlt] pt, pp of **deal**

dean [diːn] n (*Rel*) deán m; (*Scol*: BRIT) decano; (: US) decano; rector m

dear [dɪə*] adj querido; (*expensive*) caro ▷ n: **my ~** mi querido/a ▷ excl: **me!** ¡Dios mío!; **D~ Sir/Madam** (*in letter*) Muy Señor Mío, Estimado Señor/Estimada Señora; **D~ Mr/Mrs X** Estimado/a Señor(a) X; **dearly** adv (*love*) mucho; (*pay*) caro

death [dɛθ] n muerte f; **death penalty** n pena de muerte; **death sentence** n condena a muerte

debate [dɪ'beɪt] n debate m ▷ vt discutir

debit ['dɛbɪt] n debe m ▷ vt: **to ~ a sum to sb or to sb's account** cargar una suma en cuenta a algn; **debit card** n tarjeta f de débito

debris ['dɛbriː] n escombros mpl

debt [dɛt] n deuda; **to be in ~** tener deudas

debug [diː'bʌg] vt (*Comput*) limpiar

debut ['deɪbjuː] n presentación f

Dec. abbr (= *December*) dic.

decade ['dɛkeɪd] n decenio, década

decaffeinated [dɪ'kæfɪneɪtɪd] adj descafeinado

decay [dɪ'keɪ] n (*of building*) desmoronamiento; (*of tooth*) caries f inv ▷ vi (*rot*) pudrirse

deceased [dɪ'siːst] n: **the ~** el(la) difunto/a

deceit [dɪ'siːt] n engaño; **deceive** [dɪ'siːv] vt engañar

December [dɪ'sɛmbə*] n diciembre m

decency ['diːsənsɪ] n decencia

decent ['diːsənt] adj (*proper*) decente; (*person: kind*) amable, bueno

deception [dɪ'sɛpʃən] n engaño
Be careful not to translate **deception** by the Spanish word *decepción*.

deceptive [dɪ'sɛptɪv] adj engañoso

decide [dɪˈsaɪd] vt (person) decidir; (question, argument) resolver ▷vi decidir; **to ~ to do/that** decidir hacer/que; **to ~ on sth** decidirse por algo

decimal [ˈdesɪməl] adj decimal ▷n decimal m

decision [dɪˈsɪʒən] n decisión f

decisive [dɪˈsaɪsɪv] adj decisivo; (person) decidido

deck [dek] n (Naut) cubierta; (of bus) piso; (record deck) platina; (of cards) baraja; **deckchair** n tumbona

declaration [dekləˈreɪʃən] n declaración f

declare [dɪˈklɛəʳ] vt declarar

decline [dɪˈklaɪn] n disminución f, descenso ▷vt rehusar ▷vi (person, business) decaer; (strength) disminuir

decorate [ˈdekəreɪt] vt (adorn): **to ~ (with)** adornar (de), decorar (de); (paint) pintar; (paper) empapelar; **decoration** [-ˈreɪʃən] n adorno; (act) decoración f; (medal) condecoración f; **decorator** n (workman) pintor m (decorador)

decrease [n ˈdiːkriːs, vb diˈkriːs] n: **~ (in)** disminución f (de) ▷vt disminuir, reducir ▷vi reducirse

decree [dɪˈkriː] n decreto

dedicate [ˈdedɪkeɪt] vt dedicar; **dedicated** adj dedicado; (Comput) especializado; **dedicated word processor** procesador m de textos especializado or dedicado; **dedication** [-ˈkeɪʃən] n (devotion) dedicación f; (in book) dedicatoria

deduce [dɪˈdjuːs] vt deducir

deduct [dɪˈdʌkt] vt restar; descontar; **deduction** [dɪˈdʌkʃən] n (amount deducted) descuento; (conclusion) deducción f, conclusión f

deed [diːd] n hecho, acto; (feat) hazaña; (Law) escritura

deem [diːm] vt (formal) juzgar, considerar

deep [diːp] adj profundo; (expressing measurements) de profundidad; (voice) bajo; (breath) profundo; (colour) intenso

▷adv: **the spectators stood 20 ~** los espectadores se formaron de 20 en fondo; **to be 4 metres ~** tener 4 metros de profundidad; **deep-fry** vt freír en aceite abundante; **deeply** adv (breathe) a pleno pulmón; (interested, moved, grateful) profundamente, hondamente

deer [dɪəʳ] n inv ciervo

default [dɪˈfɔːlt] n: **by ~** (win) por incomparecencia ▷adj (Comput) por defecto

defeat [dɪˈfiːt] n derrota ▷vt derrotar, vencer

defect [n ˈdiːfekt, vb dɪˈfekt] n defecto ▷vi: **to ~ to the enemy** pasarse al enemigo; **defective** [dɪˈfektɪv] adj defectuoso

defence [dɪˈfens] (us **defense**) n defensa

defend [dɪˈfend] vt defender; (accusation) n acusado/a; (in civil case) demandado/a; **defender** n defensor(a) m/f; (Sport) defensa mf

defense [dɪˈfens] (us) = **defence**

defensive [dɪˈfensɪv] adj defensivo ▷n: **on the ~** a la defensiva

defer [dɪˈfəːʳ] vt aplazar

defiance [dɪˈfaɪəns] n desafío; **in ~ of** en contra de; **defiant** [dɪˈfaɪənt] adj (challenging) desafiante, retador(a)

deficiency [dɪˈfɪʃənsɪ] n (lack) falta; (defect) defecto; **deficient** [dɪˈfɪʃənt] adj deficiente

deficit [ˈdefɪsɪt] n déficit m

define [dɪˈfaɪn] vt (word etc) definir; (limits etc) determinar

definite [ˈdefɪnɪt] adj (fixed) determinado; (obvious) claro; (certain) indudable; **he was ~ about it** no dejó lugar a dudas (sobre ello); **definitely** adv desde luego, por supuesto

definition [defɪˈnɪʃən] n definición f; (clearness) nitidez f

deflate [diːˈfleɪt] vt desinflar

deflect [dɪˈflekt] vt desviar

defraud [dɪˈfrɔːd] vt: **to ~ sb of sth** estafar algo a algn

defrost [diːˈfrɒst] vt descongelar

defuse [diːˈfjuːz] vt desactivar; (situation) calmar

defy [dɪˈfaɪ] vt (resist) oponerse a; (challenge) desafiar; (fig): **it defies description** resulta imposible describirlo

degree [dɪˈgriː] n grado; (Scol) título; **to have a ~ in maths** tener una licenciatura en matemáticas; **by ~s** (gradually) poco a poco, por etapas; **to some ~** hasta cierto punto

dehydrated [diːhaɪˈdreɪtɪd] adj deshidratado; (milk) en polvo

de-icer [diːˈaɪsəʳ] n descongelador m

delay [dɪˈleɪ] vt demorar, aplazar; (person) entretener; (train) retrasar ▷ vi tardar ▷ n demora, retraso; **to be ~ed** retrasarse; **without ~** en seguida, sin tardar

delegate [n ˈdelɪgɪt, vb ˈdelɪgeɪt] n delegado/a ▷ vt (powers) delegar en; (task) delegar

delete [dɪˈliːt] vt suprimir, tachar

deli [ˈdelɪ] n = **delicatessen**

deliberate [adj dɪˈlɪbərɪt, vb dɪˈlɪbəreɪt] adj (intentional) intencionado; (slow) pausado, lento ▷ vi deliberar; **deliberately** adv (on purpose) a propósito

delicacy [ˈdelɪkəsɪ] n delicadeza; (choice food) manjar m

delicate [ˈdelɪkɪt] adj delicado; (fragile) frágil

delicatessen [delɪkəˈtesn] n ultramarinos mpl finos

delicious [dɪˈlɪʃəs] adj delicioso

delight [dɪˈlaɪt] n (feeling) placer m, deleite m; (person, experience etc) encanto, delicia ▷ vt encantar, deleitar; **to take ~ in** deleitarse en; **delighted** adj: **delighted (at or with/to do)** encantado (con/de hacer); **delightful** adj encantador(a), delicioso

delinquent [dɪˈlɪŋkwənt] adj, n delincuente mf

deliver [dɪˈlɪvəʳ] vt (distribute)

repartir; (hand over) entregar; (message) comunicar; (speech) pronunciar; (Med) asistir al parto de; **delivery** n reparto; entrega; (of speaker) modo de expresarse; (Med) parto, alumbramiento; **to take delivery of** recibir

delusion [dɪˈluːʒən] n ilusión f, engaño

de luxe [dəˈlʌks] adj de lujo

delve [delv] vi: **to ~ into** hurgar en

demand [dɪˈmɑːnd] vt (gen) exigir; (rights) reclamar ▷ n exigencia; (claim) reclamación f; (Econ) demanda; **to be in ~** ser muy solicitado; **on ~** a solicitud; **demanding** adj (boss) exigente; (work) absorbente

demise [dɪˈmaɪz] n (death) fallecimiento

demo [ˈdeməu] (inf) n abbr (= demonstration) manifestación f

democracy [dɪˈmɔkrəsɪ] n democracia; **democrat** [ˈdeməkræt] n demócrata mf; **democratic** [deməˈkrætɪk] adj democrático; (us) demócrata

demolish [dɪˈmɔlɪʃ] vt derribar, demoler; (fig: argument) destruir

demolition [deməˈlɪʃən] n derribo, demolición f

demon [ˈdiːmən] n (evil spirit) demonio

demonstrate [ˈdemənstreɪt] vt demostrar; (skill, appliance) mostrar ▷ vi manifestarse; **demonstration** [-ˈstreɪʃən] n (Pol) manifestación f; (proof, exhibition) demostración f; **demonstrator** n (Pol) manifestante mf; (Comm) demostrador(a) m/f; vendedor(a) m/f

demote [dɪˈməut] vt degradar

den [den] n (of animal) guarida; (room) habitación f

denial [dɪˈnaɪəl] n (refusal) negativa; (of report etc) negación f

denim [ˈdenɪm] n tela vaquera; **denims** npl vaqueros mpl

Denmark [ˈdenmɑːk] n Dinamarca

denomination [dɪnɒmɪˈneɪʃən] n
valor m; (Rel) confesión f

denounce [dɪˈnauns] vt denunciar

dense [dɛns] adj (crowd) denso; (thick)
espeso; (: foliage etc) tupido; (inf: stupid)
torpe

density [ˈdɛnsɪtɪ] n densidad f
▷ **single/double-~ disk** n (Comput)
disco de densidad sencilla/de doble
densidad

dent [dɛnt] n abolladura ▷ vt
(also: **make a ~ in**) abollar

dental [ˈdɛntl] adj dental; **dental
floss** [-flɒs] n seda dental; **dental
surgery** n clínica f dental, consultorio
m dental

dentist [ˈdɛntɪst] n dentista mf

dentures [ˈdɛntʃəz] npl dentadura (
(postiza)

deny [dɪˈnaɪ] vt negar; (charge)
rechazar

deodorant [diːˈəudərənt] n
desodorante m

depart [dɪˈpɑːt] vi irse, marcharse;
(train) salir; **to ~ from** (fig: differ from)
apartarse de

department [dɪˈpɑːtmənt] n
(Comm) sección f; (Scol) departamento;
(Pol) ministerio; **department store** n
gran almacén m

departure [dɪˈpɑːtʃə*] n partida, ida;
(of train) salida; (of employee) marcha;
a new ~ un nuevo rumbo; **departure
lounge** n (at airport) sala de embarque

depend [dɪˈpɛnd] vi: **to ~ on** depender
de; (rely on) contar con; **it ~s** depende,
según; **~ing on the result** según el
resultado; **dependant** n dependiente
mf; **dependent** adj: **to be dependent
on** ▷ n = **dependant**

depict [dɪˈpɪkt] vt (in picture) pintar;
(describe) representar

deport [dɪˈpɔːt] vt deportar

deposit [dɪˈpɒzɪt] n depósito; (Chem)
sedimento; (of ore, oil) yacimiento ▷ vt
(gen) depositar; **deposit account** (BRIT)
n cuenta de ahorros

depot [ˈdɛpəu] n (storehouse)

depósito; (for vehicles) parque m; (US)
estación f

depreciate [dɪˈpriːʃɪeɪt] vi
depreciarse, perder valor

depress [dɪˈprɛs] vt deprimir; (wages
etc) hacer bajar; (press down) apretar;
depressed adj deprimido; **depressing**
adj deprimente; **depression**
[dɪˈprɛʃən] n depresión f

deprive [dɪˈpraɪv] vt: **to ~ sb of** privar
a algn de; **deprived** adj necesitado

dept. abbr (= department) dto

depth [dɛpθ] n profundidad f; (of
cupboard) fondo; **to be in the ~s of
despair** sentir la mayor desesperación;
to be out of one's ~ (in water) no hacer
pie; (fig) sentirse totalmente perdido

deputy [ˈdɛpjutɪ] adj, n cabeza ▷ **~
head** subdirector(a) m/f ▷ n sustituto/a,
suplente mf; (US Pol) diputado/a;
(US: also: **~ sheriff**) agente m del sheriff

derail [dɪˈreɪl] vt: **to be ~ed**
descarrilarse

derelict [ˈdɛrɪlɪkt] adj abandonado

derive [dɪˈraɪv] vt (benefit etc) obtener
▷ vi: **to ~ from** derivarse de

descend [dɪˈsɛnd] vt, vi descender,
bajar; **to ~ from** descender de; **to
~ to** rebajarse a; **descendant** n
descendiente mf

descent [dɪˈsɛnt] n descenso; (origin)
descendencia

describe [dɪsˈkraɪb] vt describir;
description [-ˈkrɪpʃən] n descripción
f; (sort) clase f, género

desert [n ˈdɛzət, vb dɪˈzəːt] n desierto
▷ vt abandonar ▷ vi (Mil) desertar;
deserted [dɪˈzəːtɪd] adj desierto

deserve [dɪˈzəːv] vt merecer, ser
digno de

design [dɪˈzaɪn] n (sketch) bosquejo;
(layout, shape) diseño; (pattern) dibujo;
(intention) intención f ▷ vt diseñar;
design and technology (BRIT: Scol) n
= dibujo y tecnología

designate [vb ˈdɛzɪgneɪt, adj
ˈdɛzɪgnɪt] vt (appoint) nombrar;
(destine) designar ▷ adj designado

designer [dɪˈzaɪnə*] n diseñador(a) m/f; (fashion designer) modisto/a, diseñador(a) m/f de moda

desirable [dɪˈzaɪərəbl] adj (proper) deseable; (attractive) atractivo

desire [dɪˈzaɪə*] n deseo ▷ vt desear

desk [dɛsk] n (in office) escritorio; (for pupil) pupitre m; (in hotel, at airport) recepción f; (BRIT: in shop, restaurant) caja; **desk-top publishing** [ˈdɛsktɔp-] n autoedición f

despair [dɪsˈpɛə*] n desesperación f ▷ vi: **to ~ of** perder la esperanza de

despatch [dɪsˈpætʃ] n, vt = **dispatch**

desperate [ˈdɛspərɪt] adj desesperado; (fugitive) peligroso; **to be ~ for sth/to do sth** necesitar urgentemente algo/hacer; **desperately** adv desesperadamente; (very) terriblemente, gravemente

desperation [dɛspəˈreɪʃən] n desesperación f; **in (sheer) ~** (absolutamente) desesperado

despise [dɪsˈpaɪz] vt despreciar

despite [dɪsˈpaɪt] prep a pesar de, pese a

dessert [dɪˈzəːt] n postre m; **dessertspoon** n cuchara (de postre)

destination [dɛstɪˈneɪʃən] n destino

destined [ˈdɛstɪnd] adj: **~ for London** con destino a Londres

destiny [ˈdɛstɪnɪ] n destino

destroy [dɪsˈtrɔɪ] vt destruir; (animal) sacrificar

destruction [dɪsˈtrʌkʃən] n destrucción f

destructive [dɪsˈtrʌktɪv] adj destructivo, destructor(a)

detach [dɪˈtætʃ] vt separar; (unstick) despegar; **detached** adj (attitude) imparcial; **detached house** n = chalé m, chalet m

detail [ˈdiːteɪl] n detalle m; (no pl; (: in picture etc) detalles mpl; (trifle) pequeñez f ▷ vt detallar; (Mil) destacar; **in ~** = detalladamente; **detailed** adj detallado

detain [dɪˈteɪn] vt retener; (in captivity) detener

detect [dɪˈtɛkt] vt descubrir; (Med, Police) identificar; (Mil, Radar, Tech) detectar; **detection** [dɪˈtɛkʃən] n descubrimiento; identificación f;

detective n detective m/f; **detective story** n novela policíaca

detention [dɪˈtɛnʃən] n detención f, arresto; (Scol) castigo

deter [dɪˈtəː*] vt (dissuade) disuadir

detergent [dɪˈtəːdʒənt] n detergente m

deteriorate [dɪˈtɪərɪəreɪt] vi deteriorarse

determination [dɪtəːmɪˈneɪʃən] n resolución f

determine [dɪˈtəːmɪn] vt determinar; **determined** adj (person) resuelto, decidido; **determined to do** resuelto a hacer

deterrent [dɪˈtɛrənt] n (Mil) fuerza de disuasión

detest [dɪˈtɛst] vt aborrecer

detour [ˈdiːtuə*] n (gen, us Aut) desviación f

detract [dɪˈtrækt] vt: **to ~ from** quitar mérito a, desvirtuar

detrimental [dɛtrɪˈmɛntl] adj: **~ (to)** perjudicial (a)

devastating [ˈdɛvəsteɪtɪŋ] adj devastador(a); (fig) arrollador(a)

develop [dɪˈvɛləp] vt desarrollar; (Phot) revelar; (disease) coger; (habit) adquirir; (fault) empezar a tener ▷ vi desarrollarse; (advance) progresar; (facts, symptoms) aparecer; **developing country** n país m en desarrollo; **development** n desarrollo; (advance) progreso; (of affair, case) desenvolvimiento; (of land) urbanización f

device [dɪˈvaɪs] n (apparatus) aparato, mecanismo

devil [ˈdɛvl] n diablo, demonio

devious [ˈdiːvɪəs] adj taimado

devise [dɪˈvaɪz] vt idear, inventar

devote [dɪˈvəut] vt: **to ~ sth** dedicar algo a; **devoted** adj (loyal)

devour | 362

leal, fiel; **to be devoted to sb** querer
con devoción a algn; **the book is
devoted to politics** el libro trata de
la política; **devotion** n dedicación f;
(Rel) devoción f

devour [dɪ'vauə*] vt devorar

devout [dɪ'vaut] adj devoto

dew [dju:] n rocío

diabetes [daɪə'biːtiːz] n diabetes f

diabetic [daɪə'betɪk] adj, n
diabético/a m/f

diagnose ['daɪəgnəuz] vt
diagnosticar

diagnosis [daɪəg'nəusɪs] (pl -ses) n
diagnóstico

diagonal [daɪ'ægənl] adj, n
diagonal f

diagram ['daɪəgræm] n diagrama m,
esquema m

dial ['daɪəl] n esfera (SP), cara (LAM);
(on radio etc) dial m; (of phone) disco ▷ vt
(number) marcar

dialect ['daɪəlekt] n dialecto

dialling code ['daɪəlɪŋ-] n prefijo

dialling tone (US **dial tone**) n (BRIT)
señal f or tono de marcar

dialogue ['daɪəlɔg] (US **dialog**) n
diálogo

diameter [daɪ'æmɪtə*] n diámetro

diamond ['daɪəmənd] n diamante m;
(shape) rombo; **diamonds** npl (Cards)
diamantes mpl

diaper ['daɪəpə*] (US) n pañal m

diarrhoea [daɪə'riːə] (US **diarrhea**)
n diarrea

diary ['daɪərɪ] n (daily account) diario;
(book) agenda

dice [daɪs] n inv dados mpl ▷ vt (Culin)
cortar en cuadritos

dictate [dɪk'teɪt] vt dictar;
(conditions) imponer; **dictation**
[-'teɪʃən] n dictado; (giving of orders)
órdenes fpl

dictator [dɪk'teɪtə*] n dictador m

dictionary ['dɪkʃənrɪ] n diccionario

did [dɪd] pt of **do**

didn't ['dɪdənt] = **did not**

die [daɪ] vi morir; (fig: fade)

desvanecerse, desaparecer; **to be
dying for sth/to do sth** morirse por
algo/de ganas de hacer algo; **die down**
vi apagarse; (wind) amainar; **die out** vi
desaparecer

diesel ['diːzəl] n vehículo con motor
Diesel

diet ['daɪət] n dieta; (restricted food)
régimen m ▷ vi (also: **be on a ~**) estar a
dieta, hacer régimen

differ ['dɪfə*] vi: **to ~ (from)** (be
different) ser distinto (a), diferenciarse
(de); (disagree) discrepar (de);
difference n diferencia; (disagreement)
desacuerdo; **different** adj diferente,
distinto; **differentiate** [-'renʃieɪt]
vi: **to differentiate (between)**
distinguir (entre); **differently** adv de
otro modo, en forma distinta

difficult ['dɪfɪkəlt] adj difícil;
difficulty n dificultad f

dig [dɪg] (pt, pp **dug**) vt (hole,
ground) cavar ▷ n (prod) empujón m;
(archaeological) excavación f; (remark)
indirecta; **to ~ one's nails into** clavar
las uñas en; **dig up** vt (information)
desenterrar; (plant) desarraigar

digest [vb daɪ'dʒest, n 'daɪdʒest]
vt (food) digerir; (facts) asimilar ▷ n
resumen m; **digestion** [dɪ'dʒestʃən]
n digestión f

digit ['dɪdʒɪt] n (number) dígito;
(finger) dedo; **digital** adj digital;
digital camera n cámara digital;
digital TV n televisión digital

dignified ['dɪgnɪfaɪd] adj grave,
solemne

dignity ['dɪgnɪtɪ] n dignidad f

digs [dɪgz] (BRIT: inf) npl pensión f,
alojamiento

dilemma [daɪ'lemə] n dilema m

dill [dɪl] n eneldo

dilute [daɪ'luːt] vt diluir

dim [dɪm] adj (light) débil; (outline)
indistinto; (room) oscuro; (inf: stupid)
lerdo ▷ vt (light) bajar

dime [daɪm] (US) n moneda de diez
centavos

dimension [dɪ'mɛnʃən] n dimensión f

diminish [dɪ'mɪnɪʃ] vt, vi disminuir

din [dɪn] n estruendo, estrépito

dine [daɪn] vi cenar; **diner** n (person) comensal m

dinghy ['dɪŋgɪ] n bote m; (also: **rubber ~**) lancha (neumática)

dingy ['dɪndʒɪ] adj (room) sombrío; (colour) sucio

dining car ['daɪnɪŋ-] n (BRIT) (Rail) coche-comedor m

dining room ['daɪnɪŋ-] n comedor m

dining table n mesa f de comedor

dinner ['dɪnə*] n (evening meal) cena; (lunch) comida; (public) cena, banquete m; **dinner jacket** n smoking m; **dinner party** n cena; **dinner time** n (evening) hora de cenar; (midday) hora de comer

dinosaur ['daɪnəsɔ:*] n dinosaurio

dip [dɪp] n (slope) pendiente m; (in sea) baño; (Culin) salsa ▷ vt (in water) mojar; (ladle etc) meter; (BRIT Aut): to ~ **one's lights** poner luces de cruce ▷ vi (road etc) descender, bajar

diploma [dɪ'pləumə] n diploma m

diplomacy [dɪ'pləuməsɪ] n diplomacia

diplomat ['dɪpləmæt] n diplomático/a; **diplomatic** [dɪplə'mætɪk] adj diplomático

dipstick ['dɪpstɪk] (BRIT) n (Aut) varilla de nivel (del aceite)

dire [daɪə*] adj calamitoso

direct [daɪ'rɛkt] adj directo; (challenge) claro; (person) franco ▷ vt dirigir; (order): to ~ **sb to do sth** mandar a algn hacer algo ▷ adv derecho; **can you ~ me to ...?** ¿puede indicarme dónde está ...?; **direct debit** (BRIT) n domiciliación f bancaria de recibos

direction [dɪ'rɛkʃən] n dirección f; **sense of ~** sentido de la dirección; **directions** npl (instructions) instrucciones fpl; **~s for use** modo de empleo

directly [dɪ'rɛktlɪ] adv (in straight line)

directamente; (at once) en seguida

director [dɪ'rɛktə*] n director(a) m/f

directory [dɪ'rɛktərɪ] n (Tel) guía (telefónica); (Comput) directorio; **directory enquiries** (US **directory assistance**) n (servicio de) información f

dirt [də:t] n suciedad f; (earth) tierra; **dirty** adj sucio; (joke) verde, colorado (MEX) ▷ vt ensuciar; (stain) manchar

disability [dɪsə'bɪlɪtɪ] n incapacidad f

disabled [dɪs'eɪbld] adj: **to be physically ~** ser minusválido/a; **to be mentally ~** ser deficiente mental

disadvantage [dɪsəd'vɑ:ntɪdʒ] n desventaja, inconveniente m

disagree [dɪsə'gri:] vi (differ) discrepar; **to ~ (with)** no estar de acuerdo (con); **disagreeable** adj desagradable; (person) antipático; **disagreement** n desacuerdo m

disappear [dɪsə'pɪə*] vi desaparecer; **disappearance** n desaparición f

disappoint [dɪsə'pɔɪnt] vt decepcionar, defraudar; **disappointed** adj decepcionado; **disappointing** adj decepcionante; **disappointment** n decepción f

disapproval [dɪsə'pru:vəl] n desaprobación f

disapprove [dɪsə'pru:v] vi: **to ~ of** ver mal

disarm [dɪs'ɑ:m] vt desarmar; **disarmament** [dɪs'ɑ:məmənt] n desarme m

disaster [dɪ'zɑ:stə*] n desastre m; **disastrous** [dɪ'zɑ:strəs] adj desastroso

disbelief [dɪsbə'li:f] n incredulidad f

disc [dɪsk] n disco; (Comput) = **disk**

discard [dɪs'kɑ:d] vt (old things) tirar; (fig) descartar

discharge [vb dɪs'tʃɑ:dʒ, n 'dɪstʃɑ:dʒ] vt (task, duty) cumplir; (waste) verter; (patient) dar de alta; (employee) despedir; (soldier) licenciar; (defendant) poner en libertad ▷ n (Elec)

discipline | 364

descarga; *(Med)* supuración *f*; *(dismissal)*
despedida; *(of duty)* desempeño *m*; *(of debt)* pago, descargo

discipline ['dɪsɪplɪn] *n* disciplina
▷ *vt* disciplinar; *(punish)* castigar

disc jockey *n* pinchadiscos *mf inv*

disclose [dɪs'kləuz] *vt* revelar

disco ['dɪskəu] *n abbr* discoteca

discoloured [dɪs'kʌləd] *(us* **discolored)** *adj* descolorido

discomfort [dɪs'kʌmfət] *n* incomodidad *f*; *(unease)* inquietud *f*; *(physical)* malestar *m*

disconnect [dɪskə'nekt] *vt* separar; *(Elec etc)* desconectar

discontent [dɪskən'tent] *n* descontento

discontinue [dɪskən'tɪnjuː] *vt* interrumpir; *(payments)* suspender; **"-d"** *(Comm)* "ya no se fabrica"

discount [*n* 'dɪskaunt, *vb* dɪs'kaunt] *n* descuento ▷ *vt* descontar

discourage [dɪs'kʌrɪdʒ] *vt* desalentar; *(advise against)* desaconsejar: **to ~ sb from doing** disuadir a algn de hacer

discover [dɪs'kʌvə*] *vt* descubrir; *(error)* darse cuenta de; **discovery** *n* descubrimiento

discredit [dɪs'kredɪt] *vt* desacreditar

discreet [dɪs'kriːt] *adj (tactful)* discreto; *(careful)* prudente

discrepancy [dɪs'krepənsɪ] *n* diferencia

discretion [dɪs'kreʃən] *n (tact)* discreción *f*; **at the ~ of** a criterio de

discriminate [dɪs'krɪmɪneɪt] *vi:* **to ~ between** distinguir entre; **to ~ against** discriminar contra; **discrimination** [-'neɪʃən] *n (discernment)* perspicacia; *(bias)* discriminación *f*

discuss [dɪs'kʌs] *vt* discutir; *(a theme)* tratar; **discussion** [dɪs'kʌʃən] *n* discusión *f*

disease [dɪ'ziːz] *n* enfermedad *f*

disembark [dɪsɪm'baːk] *vt, vi* desembarcar

disgrace [dɪs'greɪs] *n* ignominia;

(shame) vergüenza, escándalo
▷ *vt* deshonrar; **disgraceful** *adj* vergonzoso

disgruntled [dɪs'grʌntld] *adj* disgustado, descontento

disguise [dɪs'gaɪz] *n* disfraz *m* ▷ *vt* disfrazar; **in ~** disfrazado

disgust [dɪs'gʌst] *n* repugnancia ▷ *vt* repugnar, dar asco a
> Be careful not to translate **disgust** by the Spanish word *disgustar*.

disgusted [dɪs'gʌstɪd] *adj* indignado
> Be careful not to translate **disgusted** by the Spanish word *disgustado*.

disgusting [dɪs'gʌstɪŋ] *adj* repugnante, asqueroso; *(behaviour etc)* vergonzoso

dish [dɪʃ] *n (gen)* plato; **to do** or **wash the -es** fregar los platos; **dishcloth** *n* estropajo

dishonest [dɪs'ɔnɪst] *adj (person)* poco honrado, tramposo; *(means)* fraudulento

dishtowel ['dɪʃtauəl] *(us)* *n* estropajo

dishwasher ['dɪʃwɔʃə*] *n* lavaplatos *m inv*

disillusion [dɪsɪ'luːʒən] *vt* desilusionar

disinfectant [dɪsɪn'fektənt] *n* desinfectante *m*

disintegrate [dɪs'ɪntɪgreɪt] *vi* disgregarse, desintegrarse

disk [dɪsk] *n (esp us)* = **disc**; *(Comput)* disco, disquete *m*; **single-/double-sided** ~ disco de una cara/dos caras; **disk drive** ~ disco drive *m*; **diskette** *n* = **disk**

dislike [dɪs'laɪk] *n* antipatía, aversión *f* ▷ *vt* tener antipatía a

dislocate ['dɪsləkeɪt] *vt* dislocar

disloyal [dɪs'lɔɪəl] *adj* desleal

dismal ['dɪzml] *adj (gloomy)* deprimente, triste; *(very bad)* malísimo, fatal

dismantle [dɪs'mæntl] *vt* desmontar, desarmar

dismay [dɪs'meɪ] n consternación f
▷ vt consternar

dismiss [dɪs'mɪs] vt (worker)
despedir; (pupils) dejar marchar;
(soldiers) dar permiso para irse; (idea,
Law) rechazar; (possibility) descartar;
dismissal n despido

disobedient [dɪsə'biːdɪənt] adj
desobediente

disobey [dɪsə'beɪ] vt desobedecer

disorder [dɪs'ɔːdə*] n desorden m;
(rioting) disturbios mpl; (Med) trastorno

disorganized [dɪs'ɔːgənaɪzd] adj
desorganizado

disown [dɪs'əʊn] vt (action) renegar
de; (person) negar cualquier tipo de
relación con

dispatch [dɪs'pætʃ] vt enviar ▷ n
(sending) envío; (Press) informe m; (Mil)
parte m

dispel [dɪs'pel] vt disipar

dispense [dɪs'pens] vt (medicines)
preparar; **dispense with** vt fus
prescindir de; **dispenser** n (container)
distribuidor m automático

disperse [dɪs'pəːs] vt dispersar ▷ vi
dispersarse

display [dɪs'pleɪ] n (in shop window)
escaparate m; (exhibition) exposición
f; (Comput) visualización f; (of feeling)
manifestación f ▷ vt exponer;
manifestar; (ostentatiously) lucir

displease [dɪs'pliːz] vt (offend)
ofender; (annoy) fastidiar

disposable [dɪs'pəʊzəbl] adj
desechable; (income) disponible

disposal [dɪs'pəʊzl] n (of rubbish)
destrucción f; **at one's ~** a su
disposición

dispose [dɪs'pəʊz] vi: **to ~ of**
(unwanted goods) deshacerse de;
(problem etc) resolver; **disposition**
[dɪspə'zɪʃən] n (nature)
temperamento; (inclination)
propensión f

disproportionate [dɪsprə'pɔːʃənət]
adj desproporcionado

dispute [dɪs'pjuːt] n disputa; (also:

industrial ~) conflicto (laboral) ▷ vt
(argue) disputar, discutir; (question)
cuestionar

disqualify [dɪs'kwɔlɪfaɪ] vt (Sport)
desclasificar; **to ~ sb for sth/from
doing sth** incapacitar a algn para
algo/hacer algo

disregard [dɪsrɪ'gɑːd] vt (ignore) no
hacer caso de

disrupt [dɪs'rʌpt] vt (plans)
desbaratar, trastornar; (conversation)
interrumpir; **disruption**
[dɪs'rʌpʃən] n trastorno,
desbaratamiento; interrupción f

dissatisfaction [dɪssætɪs'fækʃən] n
disgusto, descontento

dissatisfied [dɪs'sætɪsfaɪd] adj
insatisfecho

dissect [dɪ'sekt] vt disecar

dissent [dɪ'sent] n disensión f

dissertation [dɪsə'teɪʃən] n tesina

dissolve [dɪ'zɔlv] vt disolver
▷ vi disolverse; **to ~ in(to) tears**
deshacerse en lágrimas

distance ['dɪstəns] n distancia; **in
the ~** a lo lejos

distant ['dɪstənt] adj lejano; (manner)
reservado, frío

distil [dɪs'tɪl] (us **distill**) vt destilar;
distillery n destilería

distinct [dɪs'tɪŋkt] adj (different)
distinto; (clear) claro; (unmistakeable)
inequívoco; **as ~ from** a diferencia
de; **distinction** [dɪs'tɪŋkʃən] n
distinción f; (honour) honor m; (in
exam) sobresaliente m; **distinctive** adj
distintivo

distinguish [dɪs'tɪŋgwɪʃ] vt
distinguir; **to ~ o.s.** destacarse;
distinguished adj (eminent)
distinguido

distort [dɪs'tɔːt] vt distorsionar;
(shape, image) deformar

distract [dɪs'trækt] vt distraer;
distracted adj distraído; **distraction**
[dɪs'trækʃən] n distracción f;
(confusion) aturdimiento

distraught [dɪs'trɔːt] adj loco de

inquietud

distress [dɪs'tres] n (anguish)
angustia, aflicción f ▷ vt afligir;
distressing adj angustioso; doloroso

distribute [dɪs'trɪbjuːt] vt distribuir;
(share out) repartir; **distribution**
[-'bjuːʃən] n distribución f, reparto m;
distributor n (Aut) distribuidor m;
(Comm) distribuidora f

district ['dɪstrɪkt] n (of country)
zona, región f; (of town) barrio; (Admin)
distrito; **district attorney** (US) n
fiscal mf

distrust [dɪs'trʌst] n desconfianza
▷ vt desconfiar de

disturb [dɪs'təːb] vt (person: bother,
interrupt) molestar; (: upset)
perturbar, inquietar; (disorganize)
alterar; **disturbance** n (upheaval)
perturbación f; (political etc: gen
pl) disturbio; (of mind) trastorno;
disturbed adj (worried, upset)
preocupado, angustiado; **emotionally
disturbed** trastornado; (childhood)
inseguro; **disturbing** adj inquietante,
perturbador(a)

ditch [dɪtʃ] n zanja; (irrigation ditch)
acequia ▷ vt (inf: partner) deshacerse
de; (: plan, car etc) abandonar

ditto ['dɪtəu] adv ídem, lo mismo

dive [daɪv] n (from board) salto;
(underwater) buceo; (of submarine)
sumersión f ▷ vi (underwater) bucear;
saltar; (: under water) zambullirse,
bucear; (fish, submarine) sumergirse;
(bird) lanzarse en picado; **to ~ into** (bag
etc) meter la mano en; (place) meterse
de prisa en; **diver** n (underwater) buzo

diverse [daɪ'vəːs] adj diversos/as,
varios/as

diversion [daɪ'vəːʃən] n (BRIT Aut)
desviación f; (distraction, Mil) diversión
f; (of funds) distracción f

diversity [daɪ'vəːsɪtɪ] n diversidad f

divert [daɪ'vəːt] vt (turn aside) desviar

divide [dɪ'vaɪd] vt dividir; (separate)
separar ▷ vi dividirse; (road)
bifurcarse; **divided highway** (US) n

carretera de doble calzada

divine [dɪ'vaɪn] adj (also fig) divino

diving ['daɪvɪŋ] n (Sport) salto;
(underwater) buceo; **diving board** n
trampolín m

division [dɪ'vɪʒən] n división f;
(sharing out) reparto m; (disagreement)
diferencias fpl; (Comm) sección f

divorce [dɪ'vɔːs] n divorcio
▷ vt divorciarse de; **divorced** adj
divorciado; **divorcee** [-'siː] n
divorciado/a

D.I.Y. (BRIT) adj, n abbr = **do-it-
yourself**

dizzy ['dɪzɪ] adj (spell) de mareo; **to
feel ~** marearse

DJ n abbr = **disc jockey**

DNA n abbr (= deoxyribonucleic acid)
ADN m

○ KEYWORD

do [duː] (pt **did**, pp **done**) n (inf: party
etc): **we're having a little do on
Saturday** damos una fiestecita el
sábado; **it was rather a grand do** fue
un acontecimiento a lo grande
▷ aux vb 1 (in negative constructions: not
translated): **I don't understand** no
entiendo
2 (to form questions: not translated):
didn't you know? ¿no lo sabías?; **what
do you think?** ¿qué opinas?
3 (for emphasis, in polite expressions):
**people do make mistakes
sometimes** sí que se cometen errores
a veces; **she does seem rather late**
a mí también me parece que se ha
retrasado; **do sit down/help yourself**
siéntate/sírvete por favor; **do take
care!** ¡ten cuidado(, te pido)!
4 (used to avoid repeating vb): **she sings
better than I do** canta mejor que yo;
do you agree? – yes, I do/no, I don't
¿estás de acuerdo? – sí (lo estoy)/no
(lo estoy); **she lives in Glasgow – so
do I** vivo en Glasgow – yo también; **he
didn't like it and neither did we** no

le gustó y a nosotros tampoco; **who made the mess?** – I did ¿quién hizo esta chapuza? – yo; **he asked me to help him** and **I did** me pidió que le ayudara y lo hice

5 *(in question tags):* **you like him, don't you?** te gusta, ¿verdad? or ¿no?; **I don't know him, do I?** creo que no lo conozco

▷ vt 1 *(gen, carry out, perform etc):* **what are you doing tonight?** ¿qué haces esta noche?; **what can I do for you?** ¿en qué puedo servirle?; **to do the washing-up/cooking** fregar los platos/cocinar; **to do one's teeth/hair/nails** lavarse los dientes/ arreglarse el pelo/arreglarse las uñas

2 *(Aut etc):* **the car was doing 100** el coche iba a 100; **we've done 200 km already** ya hemos hecho 200 km; **he can do 100 in that car** puede ir a 100 en ese coche

▷ vi 1 *(act, behave)* hacer; **do as I do** haz como yo

2 *(get on, fare):* **he's doing well/badly at school** le va bien/mal en la escuela; **the firm is doing well** la empresa anda or va bien; **how do you do?** mucho gusto; *(less formal)* ¿qué tal?

3 *(suit):* **will it do?** ¿sirve?, ¿está or así está bien?

4 *(be sufficient)* bastar; **will £10 do?** ¿será bastante con £10?; **that'll do!** *(in annoyance)* ¡ya está bien!, ¡basta ya!; **to make do (with)** arreglárselas (con)

do up vt *(laces)* atar; *(zip, dress, shirt)* abrochar; *(renovate: room, house)* renovar

do with vt fus *(need):* **I could do with a drink/some help** no me vendría mal un trago/un poco de ayuda; *(be connected)* tener que ver con; **what has it got to do with you?** ¿qué tiene que ver contigo?

do without vi pasar sin; **if you're late for tea then you'll do without** si llegas tarde tendrás que quedarte

sin cenar

▷ vt fus pasar sin; **I can do without a car** puedo pasar sin coche

dock [dɔk] n *(Naut)* muelle m; *(Law)* banquillo (de los acusados) ▷ vi *(enter dock)* atracar (la) muelle; *(Space)* acoplarse; **docks** npl *(Naut)* muelles mpl, puerto sg

doctor ['dɔktə*] n médico/a; *(Ph. D. etc)* doctor(a) m/f ▷ vt *(drink etc)* adulterar; **Doctor of Philosophy** n Doctor en Filosofía y Letras

document ['dɔkjumənt] n documento; **documentary** [-'mentərɪ] adj documental ▷ n documental m; **documentation** [-men'teɪʃən] n documentación f

dodge [dɔdʒ] n *(fig)* truco ▷ vt evadir; *(blow)* esquivar

dodgy ['dɔdʒɪ] adj *(inf: uncertain)* dudoso; *(suspicious)* sospechoso; *(risky)* arriesgado

does [dʌz] vb see **do**

doesn't ['dʌznt] = **does not**

dog [dɔg] n perro ▷ vt seguir los pasos de; *(bad luck)* perseguir; **doggy bag** ['dɔgɪ-] n bolsa para llevarse las sobras de la comida

do-it-yourself ['du:ɪtjɔ:'self] n bricolaje m

dole [dəʊl] *(BRIT)* n *(payment)* subsidio de paro; **on the** ~ parado

doll [dɔl] n muñeca; *(us: inf: woman)* muñeca, gachí f

dollar ['dɔlə*] n dólar m

dolphin ['dɔlfɪn] n delfín m

dome [dəʊm] n *(Arch)* cúpula

domestic [də'mestɪk] adj *(animal, duty)* doméstico; *(flight, policy)* nacional; **domestic appliance** n aparato m doméstico, aparato m de uso doméstico

dominant ['dɔmɪnənt] adj dominante

dominate ['dɔmɪneɪt] vt dominar

domino ['dɔmɪnəʊ] *(pl* **-es***)* n ficha de dominó; **dominoes** n *(game)* dominó

donate [də'neɪt] vt donar; **donation** [də'neɪʃən] n donativo

done [dʌn] pp of **do**

donkey ['dɔŋkɪ] n burro

donor ['dəʊnə*] n donante mf; **donor card** n carnet m de donante

don't [dəʊnt] = **do not**

doodle ['duːdl] vi hacer dibujitos or garabatos

doom [duːm] n (fate) suerte f ▷ vt: **to be ~ed to failure** estar condenado al fracaso

door [dɔː*] n puerta; **doorbell** n timbre m; **door handle** n tirador m; (of car) manija; **doorknob** n pomo m de la puerta, manilla f (LAM); **doorstep** n peldaño; **doorway** n entrada, puerta

dope [dəʊp] n (inf: illegal drug) droga; (: person) imbécil mf ▷ vt (horse etc) drogar

dormitory ['dɔːmɪtrɪ] n (BRIT) dormitorio; (US) colegio mayor

DOS n abbr (= disk operating system) DOS m

dosage ['dəʊsɪdʒ] n dosis f inv

dose [dəʊs] n dosis f inv

dot [dɔt] n punto ▷ vi: ~**ted with** salpicado de; **on the ~** en punto; **dotcom** [dɔt'kɔm] n puntocom f inv; **dotted line** ['dɔtɪd-] n: **to sign on the dotted line** firmar

double ['dʌbl] adj doble ▷ adv (twice): **to cost** ~ costar el doble ▷ n doble m ▷ vt doblar ▷ vi doblarse; **on the ~**, **at the ~** (BRIT) corriendo; **double back** vi (person) volver sobre sus pasos; **double bass** n contrabajo; **double bed** n cama de matrimonio; **double-check** vt volver a revisar ▷ vi: **I'll double-check** voy a revisarlo otra vez; **double-click** vi (Comput) hacer doble clic; **double-cross** vt (trick) engañar; (betray) traicionar; **doubledecker** n autobús m de dos pisos; **double glazing** n doble acristalamiento; **double room** n habitación f doble; **doubles** n (Tennis)

juego de dobles; **double yellow lines** npl (BRIT: Aut) línea doble amarilla de prohibido aparcar, ≈ línea fsg amarilla continua

doubt [daʊt] n duda ▷ vt dudar; (suspect) dudar de; **to ~ that** dudar que; **doubtful** adj dudoso; (person): **to be doubtful about sth** tener dudas sobre algo; **doubtless** adv sin duda

dough [dəʊ] n masa, pasta; **doughnut** (US **donut**) n ≈ rosquilla

dove [dʌv] n paloma

down [daʊn] n (feathers) plumón m, flojel m ▷ adv (downwards) abajo, hacia abajo; (on the ground) por o en tierra ▷ prep abajo ▷ vt (inf: drink) beberse; ~ **with X!** ¡abajo X!; **down-and-out** n vagabundo/a; **downfall** n caída, ruina; **downhill** adv: **to go downhill** (also fig) ir cuesta abajo

Downing Street ['daʊnɪŋ-] n (BRIT) Downing Street f

down: download n (Comput) bajar; **downloadable** adj (Comput) descargable; **downright** adj (nonsense, lie) manifiesto; (refusal) terminante

Down's syndrome ['daʊnz-] n síndrome m de Down

down: downstairs adv (below) (en el piso de) abajo; (downwards) escaleras abajo; **down-to-earth** adj práctico; **downtown** adv en el centro de la ciudad; **down under** adv en Australia (or Nueva Zelanda); **downward** [-wəd] adj, adv hacia abajo; **downwards** [-wədz] adv hacia abajo

doz. abbr = **dozen**

doze [dəʊz] vi dormitar

dozen ['dʌzn] n docena; **a ~ books** una docena de libros; ~**s of** cantidad de

Dr. abbr = **doctor**; **drive**

drab [dræb] adj gris, monótono

draft [drɑːft] n (first copy) borrador m; (Pol: of bill) anteproyecto; (US: call-up) quinta ▷ vt (plan) preparar; (write roughly) hacer un borrador de; see also **draught**

drag [dræg] vt arrastrar; (river) dragar,

rastrear ▷ vi (time) pasar despacio; (play, film etc) hacerse pesado ▷ n (inf) lata; (women's clothing): **in ~** vestido de travesti; **to ~ and drop** (Comput) arrastrar y soltar

dragon ['drægən] n dragón m

dragonfly ['drægənflaɪ] n libélula

drain [dreɪn] n desaguadero; (in street) sumidero; (source of loss): **to be a ~ on** consumir, agotar ▷ vt (land, marshes) desaguar; (reservoir) desecar; (vegetables) escurrir ▷ vi escurrirse; **drainage** n (act) desagüe m; (Med, Agr) drenaje m; (sewage) alcantarillado; **drainpipe** n tubo de desagüe

drama ['drɑːmə] n (art) teatro; (play) drama m; (excitement) emoción f; **dramatic** [drə'mætɪk] adj dramático; (sudden, marked) espectacular

drank [dræŋk] pt of **drink**

drape [dreɪp] vt (cloth) colocar; (flag) colgar; **drapes** npl (us) cortinas fpl

drastic ['dræstɪk] adj (measure) severo; (change) radical, drástico

draught [drɑːft] (us **draft**) n (of air) corriente f de aire; (Naut) calado; **on ~** (beer) de barril; **draught beer** n cerveza de barril; **draughts** (BRIT) n (game) juego de damas

draw [drɔː] (pt **drew**, pp **drawn**) vt (picture) dibujar; (cart) tirar de; (curtain) correr; (take out) sacar; (attract) atraer; (money) retirar; (wages) cobrar ▷ vi (Sport) empatar ▷ n (Sport) empate m; (lottery) sorteo; **draw out** vi (lengthen) alargarse ▷ vt sacar; **draw up** vi (stop) pararse ▷ vt (chair) acercar; (document) redactar; **drawback** n inconveniente m, desventaja

drawer [drɔːʳ] n cajón m

drawing ['drɔːɪŋ] n dibujo; **drawing pin** (BRIT) n chincheta; **drawing room** n salón m

drawn [drɔːn] pp of **draw**

dread [dred] n pavor m, terror m ▷ vt temer, tener miedo o pavor a; **dreadful** adj horroroso

dream [driːm] n (pt, pp **-ed** o **-t**) n

sueño ▷ vt, vi soñar; **dreamer** n soñador(a) m/f

dreamt [dremt] pt, pp of **dream**

dreary ['drɪərɪ] adj monótono

drench [drentʃ] vt empapar

dress [dres] n (clothing) ropa ▷ vt vestir; (wound) vendar ▷ vi vestirse; **to get ~ed** vestirse; **dress up** vi vestirse de etiqueta; (in fancy dress) disfrazarse; **dress circle** (BRIT) n principal m; **dresser** n (furniture) aparador m; (: us) cómoda (con espejo); **dressing** n (Med) vendaje m; (Culin) aliño; **dressing gown** (BRIT) n bata; **dressing room** n (Theatre) camarín m; (Sport) vestuario; **dressing table** n tocador m; **dressmaker** n modista, costurera

drew [druː] pt of **draw**

dribble ['drɪbl] vi (baby) babear ▷ vt (ball) regatear

dried [draɪd] adj (fruit) seco; (milk) en polvo

drier ['draɪəʳ] n = **dryer**

drift [drɪft] n (of current etc) flujo; (of snow) ventisquero; (meaning) significado ▷ vi (boat) ir a la deriva; (sand, snow) amontonarse

drill [drɪl] n (drill bit) broca; (tool for DIY etc) taladro; (of dentist) fresa; (for mining etc) perforadora, barrena; (Mil) instrucción f ▷ vt perforar, taladrar; (troops) enseñar la instrucción a ▷ vi (for oil) perforar

drink [drɪŋk] (pt **drank**, pp **drunk**) n bebida; (sip) trago ▷ vt, vi beber; **to have a ~** tomar algo; tomar una copa o un trago; **a ~ of water** un trago de agua; **drink-driving** n: **to be charged with drink-driving** ser acusado de conducir borracho o en estado de embriaguez; **drinker** n bebedor(a) m/f; **drinking water** n agua potable

drip [drɪp] n (act) goteo; (one drip) gota; (Med) gota a gota m ▷ vi gotear

drive [draɪv] (pt **drove**, pp **driven**) n (journey) viaje m (en coche); (also: **~way**) entrada; (energy) energía, vigor m; (Comput: also: **disk ~**) drive m ▷ vt (car) conducir (SP), manejar (LAM); (nail) clavar; (push) empujar; (Tech: motor) impulsar ▷ vi (Aut: at controls) conducir; (: travel) pasearse en coche; **left-/right-hand ~** conducción f a la izquierda/derecha; **to ~ sb mad** volverle loco a algn; (drive out) vt (force out) expulsar, echar; **drive-in** adj (esp US): **drive-in cinema** autocine m

driven ['drɪvn] pp of **drive**

driver ['draɪvə*] n conductor(a) m/f (SP), chofer mf (LAM); (of taxi, bus) taxista mf(SP), chofer mf(LAM); **driver's license** (US) n carnet m de conducir

driveway ['draɪvweɪ] n entrada

driving ['draɪvɪŋ] n el conducir (SP), el manejar (LAM); **driving instructor** n profesor(a) m/f de autoescuela (SP), instructor(a) m/f de manejo (LAM); **driving lesson** n clase f de conducir (SP) or manejar (LAM); **driving licence** (BRIT) n licencia de manejo (LAM), carnet m de conducir (SP); **driving test** n examen m de conducir (SP) or manejar (LAM)

drizzle ['drɪzl] n llovizna

droop [druːp] vi (flower) marchitarse; (shoulders) encorvarse; (head) inclinarse

drop [drɔp] n (of water) gota; (lessening) baja; (fall) caída ▷ vt dejar caer; (voice, eyes, price) bajar; (passenger) dejar; (omit) omitir ▷ vi (object) caer; (wind) amainar; **drop in** vi (inf: visit): **to drop in (on)** pasar por casa (de); **drop off** vi (sleep) dormirse ▷ vt (passenger) dejar; **drop out** vi (withdraw) retirarse

drought [draut] n sequía

drove [drəuv] pt of **drive**

drown [draun] vt ahogar ▷ vi ahogarse

drowsy ['drauzɪ] adj soñoliento; **to be ~** tener sueño

drug [drʌg] n medicamento; (narcotic) droga ▷ vt drogar; **to be on ~s** drogarse; **drug addict** n drogadicto/a; **drug dealer** n traficante mf de drogas; **druggist** (US) n farmacéutico;

drugstore (US) n farmacia

drum [drʌm] n tambor m; (for oil, petrol) bidón m; **drums** npl batería; **drummer** n tambor m

drunk [drʌŋk] pp of **drink** ▷ adj borracho ▷ n (also: **~ard**) borracho/a; **drunken** adj borracho; (laughter, party) de borrachos

dry [draɪ] adj seco; (day) sin lluvia; (climate) árido, seco ▷ vt secar; (tears) enjuagarse ▷ vi secarse; **dry off** vi secarse ▷ vt secar; **dry up** vi (river) secarse; **dry-cleaner's** n tintorería; **dry-cleaning** n lavado en seco; **dryer** n (for hair) secador m; (US: for clothes) secadora

DSS n abbr = **Department of Social Security**

D & T (BRIT: Scol) n abbr (= design and technology) = dibujo y tecnología

DTP n abbr (= desk-top publishing) autoedición f

dual ['djuːəl] adj doble; **dual carriageway** (BRIT) n carretera de doble calzada

dubious ['djuːbɪəs] adj indeciso; (reputation, company) sospechoso

duck [dʌk] n pato ▷ vi agacharse

due [djuː] adj (owed): **he is ~ £10** se le deben 10 libras; (expected: event): **the meeting is ~ on Wednesday** la reunión tendrá lugar el miércoles; (: arrival): **the train is ~ at 8am** el tren tiene su llegada para las 8; (proper) debido ▷ n: **to give sb his (or her) ~** ser justo con algn ▷ adv: **~ north** derecho al norte

duel ['djuːəl] n duelo

duet [djuːˈɛt] n dúo

dug [dʌg] pt, pp of **dig**

duke [djuːk] n duque m

dull [dʌl] adj (light) débil; (stupid) torpe; (boring) pesado; (sound, pain) sordo; (weather, day) gris ▷ vt (pain, grief) aliviar; (mind, senses) entorpecer

dumb [dʌm] adj mudo; (pej: stupid) estúpido

dummy ['dʌmɪ] n (tailor's dummy)

maniquí m; (*mock-up*) maqueta; (BRIT: *for baby*) chupete m ▷ *adj* falso, postizo

dump [dʌmp] n (*also*: **rubbish ~**) basurero, vertedero; (*inf*: *place*) cuchitril m ▷ *vt* (*put down*) dejar; (*get rid of*) deshacerse de; (*Comput*: *data*) transferir

dumpling ['dʌmplɪŋ] n bola de masa hervida

dune [dju:n] n duna

dungarees [dʌŋgə'ri:z] *npl* mono

dungeon ['dʌndʒən] n calabozo

duplex ['dju:pleks] n dúplex m

duplicate [n 'dju:plɪkət, vb 'dju:plɪkeɪt] n duplicado ▷ *vt* duplicar; (*photocopy*) fotocopiar; (*repeat*) repetir; **in ~** por duplicado

durable ['djuərəbl] *adj* duradero

duration [djuə'reɪʃən] n duración f

during ['djuarɪŋ] *prep* durante

dusk [dʌsk] n crepúsculo, anochecer m

dust [dʌst] n polvo ▷ *vt* quitar el polvo a, desempolvar; (*cake etc*): **to ~ with** espolvorear de; **dustbin** (BRIT) n cubo or bote m (MEX) or tacho (SC) de la basura; **duster** n paño, trapo; **dustman** (BRIT: *irreg*) n basurero; **dustpan** n cogedor m; **dusty** *adj* polvoriento

Dutch [dʌtʃ] *adj* holandés/esa ▷ n (*Ling*) holandés m; **the Dutch** *npl* los holandeses; **to go ~** (*inf*) pagar cada uno lo suyo; **Dutchman** (*irreg*) n holandés m; **Dutchwoman** (*irreg*) n holandésa

duty ['dju:tɪ] n deber m; (*tax*) derechos *mpl* de aduana; **on ~** de servicio; (*at night etc*) de guardia; **off ~** libre (de servicio); **duty-free** *adj* libre de impuestos

duvet ['du:veɪ] (BRIT) n edredón m

DVD n *abbr* (= *digital versatile or video disc*) DVD m; **DVD player** n lector m de DVD; **DVD writer** n grabadora de DVD

dwarf [dwɔ:f] (*pl* **dwarves**) n enano/a ▷ *vt* empequeñecer

dwell [dwɛl] (*pt, pp* **dwelt**) *vi* morar; **dwell on** *vt fus* explayarse en

dwelt [dwɛlt] *pt, pp of* **dwell**

dwindle ['dwɪndl] *vi* disminuir

dye [daɪ] n tinte m ▷ *vt* teñir

dying ['daɪɪŋ] *adj* moribundo

dynamic [daɪ'næmɪk] *adj* dinámico

dynamite ['daɪnəmaɪt] n dinamita

dyslexia [dɪs'lɛksɪə] n dislexia

dyslexic [dɪs'lɛksɪk] *adj*, n disléxico/a m/f

E [i:] n (Mus) mi m

E111 n abbr (= form E111) impreso E111

each [i:tʃ] adj cada inv ▷ pron cada
uno; ~ **other** el uno a otro; **they
hate** ~ **other** se odian (entre ellos or
mutuamente); **they have 2 books** ~
tienen 2 libros por persona

eager ['i:gə*] adj (keen)
entusiasmado; **to be** ~ **to do sth**
tener muchas ganas de hacer algo,
impacientarse por hacer algo; **to be** ~
for tener muchas ganas de

eagle ['i:gl] n águila

ear [ɪə*] n oreja; oído; (of corn) espiga;
earache n dolor m de oídos; **eardrum**
n tímpano

earl [ə:l] n conde m

earlier ['ə:lɪə*] adj anterior ▷ adv
antes

early ['ə:lɪ] adv temprano; (before
time) con tiempo, con anticipación
▷ adj temprano; (settlers etc) primitivo;
(death, departure) prematuro; (reply)
pronto; **to have an** ~ **night** acostarse
temprano; **in the** ~ **or** ~ **in the**

spring/19th century a principios de
primavera/del siglo diecinueve; **early
retirement** n jubilación f anticipada

earmark ['ɪəmɑ:k] vt: **to** ~ **(for)**
reservar (para), destinar (a)

earn [ə:n] vt (salary) percibir; (interest)
devengar; (praise) merecerse

earnest ['ə:nɪst] adj (wish) fervoroso;
(person) serio, formal; **in** ~ en serio

earnings ['ə:nɪŋz] npl (personal)
sueldo, ingresos mpl; (company)
ganancias fpl

ear: earphones npl auriculares mpl;
earplugs npl tapones mpl para los
oídos; **earring** n pendiente m, arete m

earth [ə:θ] n tierra; (BRIT Elec) cable
m de toma de tierra ▷ vt (BRIT Elec)
conectar a tierra; **earthquake** n
terremoto

ease [i:z] n facilidad f; (comfort)
comodidad f ▷ vt (lessen: problem)
mitigar; (: pain) aliviar; (: tension)
reducir; **to** ~ **sth in/out** meter/sacar
algo con cuidado; **at** ~! (Mil)
¡descansen!

easily ['i:zɪlɪ] adv fácilmente

east [i:st] n este m ▷ adj del este,
oriental; (wind) este ▷ adv al este,
hacia el este; **the E~** el Oriente; (Pol)
los países del Este; **eastbound** adj en
dirección este

Easter ['i:stə*] n Pascua (de
Resurrección); **Easter egg** n huevo
de Pascua

eastern ['i:stən] adj del este,
oriental; (oriental) oriental

Easter Sunday n Domingo de
Resurrección

easy ['i:zɪ] adj fácil; (simple) sencillo;
(comfortable) holgado, cómodo;
(relaxed) tranquilo ▷ adv: **to take it** or
things ~ (not worry) tomarlo con calma;
(rest) descansar; **easy-going** adj
acomodadizo

eat [i:t] (pt **ate**, pp **eaten**) vt comer;
eat out vi comer fuera

eavesdrop ['i:vzdrɔp] vi: **to** ~ **(on)**
escuchar a escondidas

e-book ['iːbʊk] n libro electrónico
e-business ['iːbɪznɪs] n (company) negocio electrónico; (commerce) comercio electrónico
EC n abbr (= European Community) CE f
eccentric [ɪk'sɛntrɪk] adj, n excéntrico/a m/f
echo ['ɛkəʊ] (pl **~es**) n eco ▷ vt (sound) repetir ▷ vi resonar, hacer eco
eclipse [ɪ'klɪps] n eclipse m
eco-friendly [iːkəʊ'frɛndlɪ] adj ecológico
ecological [iːkə'lɔdʒɪkl] adj ecológico
ecology [ɪ'kɔlədʒɪ] n ecología
e-commerce n abbr comercio electrónico
economic [iːkə'nɔmɪk] adj económico; (business etc) rentable;
economical adj económico;
economics n (Scol) economía ▷ npl (of project etc) rentabilidad f
economist [ɪ'kɔnəmɪst] n economista m/f
economize [ɪ'kɔnəmaɪz] vi economizar, ahorrar
economy [ɪ'kɔnəmɪ] n economía;
economy class n (Aviat) clase f económica; **economy class syndrome** n síndrome m de la clase turista
ecstasy ['ɛkstəsɪ] n éxtasis m inv; (drug) éxtasis m inv; **ecstatic** [ɛks'tætɪk] adj extático
eczema ['ɛksɪmə] n eczema m
edge [ɛdʒ] n (of knife) filo; (of object) borde m; (of lake) orilla ▷ vt (Sewing) ribetear; **on ~** (fig) = **edgy**; **to ~ away from** alejarse poco a poco de
edgy ['ɛdʒɪ] adj nervioso, inquieto
edible ['ɛdɪbl] adj comestible
Edinburgh ['ɛdɪnbərə] n Edimburgo
edit ['ɛdɪt] vt (be editor of) dirigir; (text, report) corregir, preparar; **edition** [ɪ'dɪʃən] n edición f; **editor** n (of newspaper) director a m/f; (of column): **foreign/political editor** n encargado de la sección de extranjero/política; (of book) redactor a m/f;

editorial [-'tɔːrɪəl] adj editorial ▷ n editorial m
educate ['ɛdjʊkeɪt] vt (gen) educar; (instruct) instruir; **educated** ['ɛdjʊkeɪtɪd] adj culto
education [ɛdjʊ'keɪʃən] n educación f; (schooling) enseñanza; (Scol) pedagogía; **educational** adj (policy etc) educacional; (experience) docente; (toy) educativo
eel [iːl] n anguila
eerie ['ɪərɪ] adj misterioso
effect [ɪ'fɛkt] n efecto ▷ vt efectuar, llevar a cabo; **to take ~** (law) entrar en vigor or vigencia; (drug) surtir efecto; **in ~** en realidad; **effects** npl (property) efectos mpl; **effective** adj eficaz; (actual) verdadero; **effectively** adv eficazmente; (in reality) efectivamente
efficiency [ɪ'fɪʃənsɪ] n eficiencia; rendimiento
efficient [ɪ'fɪʃənt] adj eficiente; (machine) de buen rendimiento; **efficiently** adv eficientemente, de manera eficiente
effort ['ɛfət] n esfuerzo; **effortless** adj sin ningún esfuerzo; (style) natural
e.g. adv abbr (= exempli gratia) p. ej.
egg [ɛg] n huevo; **hard-boiled/soft-boiled ~** huevo duro/pasado por agua; **eggcup** n huevera; **eggplant** (esp us) n berenjena; **eggshell** n cáscara de huevo; **egg white** n clara de huevo; **egg yolk** n yema de huevo
ego ['iːgəʊ] n ego
Egypt ['iːdʒɪpt] n Egipto; **Egyptian** [ɪ'dʒɪpʃən] adj, n egipcio/a m/f
eight [eɪt] num ocho; **eighteen** num diez y ocho, dieciocho; **eighteenth** adj decimoctavo; **the eighteenth floor** la planta dieciocho; **the eighteenth of August** el dieciocho de agosto; **eighth** num octavo; **eightieth** ['eɪtɪɪθ] adj octogésimo
eighty ['eɪtɪ] num ochenta
Eire ['ɛərə] n Eire m
either ['aɪðə*] adj cualquiera de los dos; (both, each) cada ▷ pron: **~ (of**

them) cualquiera (de los dos) ▷ adv tampoco ▷ conj: **~ yes or no** o sí o no; **on ~ side** en ambos lados; **I don't like ~** no me gusta ninguno/a de la(s) dos; **no, I don't ~** yo tampoco

eject [ɪ'dʒɛkt] vt echar, expulsar; (tenant) desahuciar

elaborate [adj ɪ'læbərɪt, vb ɪ'læbəreɪt] adj (complex) complejo ▷ vt (expand) ampliar; (refine) refinar ▷ vi explicar con más detalles

elastic [ɪ'læstɪk] n elástico ▷ adj elástico; (fig) flexible; **elastic band** (BRIT) n gomita

elbow ['ɛlbəu] n codo

elder ['ɛldə*] adj mayor ▷ n. (tree) saúco; (person) mayor; **elderly** adj de edad, mayor ▷ npl: **the elderly** los mayores

eldest ['ɛldɪst] adj, n el/la mayor

elect [ɪ'lɛkt] vt elegir ▷ adj: **the president ~** el presidente electo; **to ~ to do** optar por hacer; **election** n elección f; **electoral** adj electoral; **electorate** n electorado

electric [ɪ'lɛktrɪk] adj eléctrico; **electrical** adj eléctrico; **electric blanket** n manta eléctrica; **electric fire** n estufa eléctrica; **electrician** [ɪlɛk'trɪʃən] n electricista mf; **electricity** [ɪlɛk'trɪsɪtɪ] n electricidad f; **electric shock** n electrochoque m; **electrify** [ɪ'lɛktrɪfaɪ] vt (Rail) electrificar; (fig: audience) electrizar

electronic [ɪlɛk'trɔnɪk] adj electrónico; **electronic mail** n correo electrónico; **electronics** n electrónica

elegance ['ɛlɪɡəns] n elegancia

elegant ['ɛlɪɡənt] adj elegante

element ['ɛlɪmənt] n elemento; (of kettle etc) resistencia

elementary [ɛlɪ'mɛntərɪ] adj elemental; (primitive) rudimentario; **elementary school** (US) n escuela de enseñanza primaria

elephant ['ɛlɪfənt] n elefante m

elevate ['ɛlɪveɪt] vt (gen) elevar; (in rank) ascender

elevator ['ɛlɪveɪtə*] (US) n ascensor m; (in warehouse etc) montacargas m inv

eleven [ɪ'lɛvn] num once; **eleventh** adj undécimo

eligible ['ɛlɪdʒəbl] adj: **an ~ young man/woman** un buen partido; **to be ~ for sth** llenar los requisitos para algo

eliminate [ɪ'lɪmɪneɪt] vt (suspect, possibility) descartar

elm [ɛlm] n olmo

eloquent ['ɛləkwənt] adj elocuente

else [ɛls] adv: **something ~** otra cosa; **somewhere ~** en otra parte; **everywhere ~** en todas partes menos aquí; **where ~?** ¿dónde más?, ¿en qué otra parte?; **there was little ~ to do** apenas quedaba otra cosa que hacer; **nobody ~ spoke** no habló nadie más; **elsewhere** adv (be) en otra parte; (go) a otra parte

elusive [ɪ'lu:sɪv] adj esquivo; (quality) difícil de encontrar

email ['i:meɪl] n abbr (= electronic mail) correo electrónico, e-mail m; **email address** n dirección f electrónica, email m

embankment [ɪm'bæŋkmənt] n terraplén m

embargo [ɪm'bɑ:gəu] (pl **~es**) n (Comm, Naut) embargo; (prohibition) prohibición f; **to put an ~ on** poner un embargo en algo

embark [ɪm'bɑ:k] vi embarcarse ▷ vt embarcar; **to ~ on** (journey) emprender; (course of action) lanzarse a

embarrass [ɪm'bærəs] vt avergonzar; (government etc) dejar en mal lugar; **embarrassed** adj (laugh, silence) embarazoso

> ┃ Be careful not to translate
> ┃ **embarrassed** by the Spanish word
> ┃ embarazada.

embarrassing adj (situation) violento; (question) embarazoso; **embarrassment** n (shame) vergüenza; (problem) lo que es embarrassment for sb poner en un aprieto a algn

embassy ['ɛmbəsɪ] n embajada
embrace [ɪmˈbreɪs] vt abrazar, dar un abrazo a; (include) abarcar ⊳ vi abrazarse ⊳ n abrazo
embroider [ɪmˈbrɔɪdə*] vt bordar; **embroidery** n bordado
embryo ['ɛmbrɪəʊ] n embrión m
emerald ['ɛmərəld] n esmeralda
emerge [ɪˈmɜːdʒ] vi salir; (arise) surgir
emergency [ɪˈmɜːdʒənsɪ] n crisis f inv; **in an ~** en caso de urgencia; **state of ~** estado de emergencia; **emergency brake** (us) n freno de mano; **emergency exit** n salida de emergencia; **emergency landing** n aterrizaje m forzoso; **emergency room** (us: Med) n sala f de urgencias; **emergency services** npl (fire, police, ambulance) servicios mpl de urgencia
emigrate ['ɛmɪɡreɪt] vi emigrar; **emigration** [ɛmɪˈɡreɪʃən] n emigración f
eminent ['ɛmɪnənt] adj eminente
emissions [ɪˈmɪʃənz] npl emisión f
emit [ɪˈmɪt] vt emitir; (smoke) arrojar; (smell) despedir; (sound) producir
emoticon [ɪˈməʊtɪkɒn] n emoticon m
emotion [ɪˈməʊʃən] n emoción f; **emotional** adj (needs) emocional; (person) sentimental; (scene) conmovedor(a), emocionante; (speech) emocionado
emperor ['ɛmpərə*] n emperador m
emphasis ['ɛmfəsɪs] (pl **-ses**) n énfasis m inv
emphasize ['ɛmfəsaɪz] vt (word, point) subrayar, recalcar; (feature) hacer resaltar
empire ['ɛmpaɪə*] n imperio m
employ [ɪmˈplɔɪ] vt emplear; **employee** [-'iː] n empleado/a; **employer** n patrón/ona m/f; **employment** n (work) trabajo; **employment agency** n agencia de colocaciones
empower [ɪmˈpaʊə*] vt: **to ~ sb to do sth** autorizar a algn para hacer algo
empress ['ɛmprɪs] n emperatriz f

emptiness ['ɛmptɪnɪs] n vacío; (of life etc) vaciedad f
empty ['ɛmptɪ] adj vacío; (place) desierto; (house) desocupado; (threat) vano ⊳ vt vaciar; (place) dejar vacío ⊳ vi vaciarse; (house etc) quedar desocupado; **empty-handed** adj con las manos vacías
EMU n abbr (= European Monetary Union) UME f
emulsion [ɪˈmʌlʃən] n emulsión f; (also: **~ paint**) pintura emulsión
enable [ɪˈneɪbl] vt: **to ~ sb to do sth** permitir a algn hacer algo
enamel [ɪˈnæməl] n esmalte m; (also: **~ paint**) pintura esmaltada
enchanting [ɪnˈtʃɑːntɪŋ] adj encantador(a)
encl. abbr (= enclosed) adj
enclose [ɪnˈkləʊz] vt (land) cercar; (letter etc) adjuntar; **please find ~d** le mandamos adjunto
enclosure [ɪnˈkləʊʒə*] n cercado, recinto
encore [ɒŋˈkɔː*] excl ¡otra!, ¡bis! ⊳ n bis m
encounter [ɪnˈkaʊntə*] n encuentro ⊳ vt encontrar, encontrarse con; (difficulty) tropezar con
encourage [ɪnˈkʌrɪdʒ] vt alentar, animar; (activity) fomentar; (growth) estimular; **encouragement** n estímulo; (of industry) fomento
encouraging [ɪnˈkʌrɪdʒɪŋ] adj alentador(a)
encyclop(a)edia [ɛnsaɪkləʊˈpiːdɪə] n enciclopedia
end [ɛnd] n fin m; (of table) extremo; (of street) final m; (Sport) lado ⊳ vt terminar, acabar; (also: **bring to an ~**, **put an ~ to**) acabar con ⊳ vi terminar, acabar; **in the ~** al fin; **on ~** (object) de punta, de cabeza; **to stand on ~** (hair) erizarse; **for hours on ~** hora tras hora; **end up** vi: **to end up in** terminar en; (place) ir a parar en
endanger [ɪnˈdeɪndʒə*] vt poner en peligro; **an ~ed species** una especie en

peligro de extinción

endearing [ɪn'dɪərɪŋ] *adj* simpático, atractivo

endeavour [ɪn'devə*] (*US* **endeavor**) *n* esfuerzo; (*attempt*) tentativa ▷ *vi*: **to ~ to do** esforzarse por hacer; (*try*) procurar hacer

ending ['endɪŋ] *n* (*of book*) desenlace *m*; (*Ling*) terminación *f*

endless ['endlɪs] *adj* interminable, inacabable

endorse [ɪn'dɔːs] *vt* (*cheque*) endosar; (*approve*) aprobar; **endorsement** *n* (*on driving licence*) nota de inhabilitación *f*

endurance [ɪn'djuərəns] *n* resistencia

endure [ɪn'djuə*] *vt* (*bear*) aguantar, soportar ▷ *vi* (*last*) durar

enemy ['enəmɪ] *adj, n* enemigo/a *m/f*

energetic [enə'dʒetɪk] *adj* enérgico

energy ['enədʒɪ] *n* energía

enforce [ɪn'fɔːs] *vt* (*Law*) hacer cumplir

engaged [ɪn'geɪdʒd] *adj* (*BRIT: busy, in use*) ocupado; (*betrothed*) prometido; **to get ~** prometerse; **engaged tone** (*BRIT*) *n* (*Tel*) señal *f* de comunicando

engagement [ɪn'geɪdʒmənt] *n* (*appointment*) compromiso, cita; (*booking*) contratación *f*; (*to marry*) compromiso; (*period*) noviazgo; **engagement ring** *n* anillo de prometida

engaging [ɪn'geɪdʒɪŋ] *adj* atractivo

engine ['endʒɪn] *n* (*Aut*) motor *m*; (*Rail*) locomotora

engineer [endʒɪ'nɪə*] *n* ingeniero; (*BRIT: for repairs*) mecánico; (*on ship, US Rail*) maquinista *m*; **engineering** *n* ingeniería

England ['ɪŋɡlənd] *n* Inglaterra

English ['ɪŋɡlɪʃ] *adj* inglés/esa ▷ *n* (*Ling*) inglés *m*; **the English** *npl* los ingleses *mpl*; **English Channel** *n*: **the English Channel** (el Canal de) la Mancha; **Englishman** (*irreg*) *n* inglés *m*; **Englishwoman** (*irreg*) *n* inglesa

engrave [ɪn'greɪv] *vt* grabar

engraving [ɪn'greɪvɪŋ] *n* grabado

enhance [ɪn'hɑːns] *vt* (*gen*) aumentar; (*beauty*) realzar

enjoy [ɪn'dʒɔɪ] *vt* (*health, fortune*) disfrutar de, gozar de; (*like*) gustarle a algn; **to ~ o.s.** divertirse; **enjoyable** *adj* agradable; (*amusing*) divertido; **enjoyment** *n* (*joy*) placer *m*; (*activity*) diversión *f*

enlarge [ɪn'lɑːdʒ] *vt* aumentar; (*broaden*) extender; (*Phot*) ampliar ▷ *vi*: **to ~ on** (*subject*) tratar con más detalles; **enlargement** *n* (*Phot*) ampliación *f*

enlist [ɪn'lɪst] *vt* alistar; (*support*) conseguir ▷ *vi* alistarse

enormous [ɪ'nɔːməs] *adj* enorme

enough [ɪ'nʌf] *adj*: **~ time/books** bastante tiempo/bastantes libros ▷ *pron* bastante(s) ▷ *adv*: **big ~** bastante grande; **he has not worked ~** no ha trabajado bastante; **have you got ~?** ¿tiene usted bastante(s)?; **~ to eat** (lo) suficiente or (lo) bastante para comer; **~!** ¡basta ya!; **that's ~, thanks** con eso basta, gracias; **I've had ~ of him** estoy harto de él; **... which, funnily or oddly ~ ...** ... lo que, por extraño que parezca ...

enquire [ɪn'kwaɪə*] *vt, vi* = **inquire**

enquiry [ɪn'kwaɪərɪ] *n* (*official investigation*) investigación

enrage [ɪn'reɪdʒ] *vt* enfurecer

enrich [ɪn'rɪtʃ] *vt* enriquecer

enrol [ɪn'rəul] (*US* **enroll**) *vt* (*members*) inscribir; (*Scol*) matricular ▷ *vi* inscribirse; matricularse; **enrolment**; (*US* **enrollment**) *n* inscripción *f*; matriculación *f*

en route [ɔn'ruːt] *adv* durante el viaje

en suite [ɔn'swiːt] *adj*: **with ~ bathroom** con baño

ensure [ɪn'ʃuə*] *vt* asegurar

entail [ɪn'teɪl] *vt* suponer

enter ['entə*] *vt* (*room*) entrar en; (*club*) hacerse socio de; (*army*) alistarse en; (*sb for a competition*) inscribir; (*write*

down) anotar, apuntar; (*Comput*) meter
▷ *vi* entrar

enterprise ['entəpraɪz] *n*
empresa; (*spirit*) iniciativa; **free
~** la libre empresa; **private ~** la
iniciativa privada; **enterprising** *adj*
emprendedor(a)

entertain [entə'teɪn] *vt* (*amuse*)
divertir; (*invite: guest*) invitar (a casa);
(*idea*) abrigar; **entertainer** *n* artista
mf; **entertaining** *adj* divertido,
entretenido; **entertainment** *n*
(*amusement*) diversión *f*; (*show*)
espectáculo

enthusiasm [ɪn'θuːzɪæzəm] *n*
entusiasmo

enthusiast [ɪn'θuːzɪæst] *n*
entusiasta *mf*; **enthusiastic** [-'æstɪk]
adj entusiasta; **to be enthusiastic
about** entusiasmarse por

entire [ɪn'taɪə*] *adj* entero; **entirely**
adv totalmente

entitle [ɪn'taɪtl] *vt*: **to ~ sb to sth** dar
a algn derecho a algo; **entitled** *adj*
(*book*) titulado; **to be entitled to do**
tener derecho a hacer

entrance [*n* 'entrəns, *vb* ɪn'trɑːns] *n*
entrada ▷ *vt* encantar, hechizar; **to
gain ~ to** (*university etc*) ingresar en;
entrance examination *n* examen
m de ingreso; **entrance fee** *n* cuota;
entrance ramp (*us*) *n* (*Aut*) rampa
de acceso

entrant ['entrənt] *n* (*in race,
competition*) participante *mf*; (*in
examination*) candidato/a

entrepreneur [ɒntrəprə'nəː] *n*
empresario

entrust [ɪn'trʌst] *vt*: **to ~ sth to sb**
confiar algo a algn

entry ['entrɪ] *n* entrada; (*in
competition*) participación *f*; (*in
register*) apunte *m*; (*in account*) partida;
(*in reference book*) artículo; **"no ~"**
"prohibido el paso"; (*Aut*) "dirección
prohibida"; **entry phone** *n* portero
automático

envelope ['envələup] *n* sobre *m*

envious ['envɪəs] *adj* envidioso; (*look*)
de envidia

environment [ɪn'vaɪərnmənt] *n*
(*surroundings*) entorno; (*natural world*):
the ~ el medio ambiente;
environmental [-'mentl] *adj*
ambiental; medioambiental;
environmentally [-'mentəlɪ]
adv: **environmentally sound/friendly**
ecológico

envisage [ɪn'vɪzɪdʒ] *vt* prever

envoy ['envɔɪ] *n* enviado

envy ['envɪ] *n* envidia ▷ *vt* tener
envidia a; **to ~ sb sth** envidiar algo
a algn

epic ['epɪk] *n* épica ▷ *adj* épico

epidemic [epɪ'demɪk] *n* epidemia

epilepsy ['epɪlepsɪ] *n* epilepsia

epileptic [epɪ'leptɪk] *adj*, *n*
epiléptico/a *m/f*; **epileptic fit**
[epɪˈleptɪk-] *n* ataque *m* de epilepsia,
acceso *m* epiléptico

episode ['epɪsəud] *n* episodio

equal ['iːkwl] *adj* igual; (*treatment*)
equitativo ▷ *n* igual *mf* ▷ *vt* ser igual
a; (*fig*) igualar; **to be ~ to** (*task*) estar
a la altura de; **equality** [iːˈkwɒlɪtɪ]
n igualdad *f*; **equalize** *vi* (*Sport*)
empatar; **equally** *adv* igualmente;
(*share etc*) a partes iguales

equation [ɪ'kweɪʒən] *n* (*Math*)
ecuación *f*

equator [ɪ'kweɪtə*] *n* ecuador *m*

equip [ɪ'kwɪp] *vt* equipar; (*person*)
proveer; **to be well ~ped** estar bien
equipado; **equipment** *n* equipo;
(*tools*) avíos *mpl*

equivalent [ɪ'kwɪvələnt] *adj*: **~ (to)**
equivalente (a) ▷ *n* equivalente *m*

ER *abbr* (*BRIT*: = *Elizabeth Regina*) la reina
Isabel; (*us*: *Med*) = **emergency room**

era ['ɪərə] *n* era, época

erase [ɪ'reɪz] *vt* borrar; **eraser** *n*
goma de borrar

erect [ɪ'rekt] *adj* erguido ▷ *vt* erigir,
levantar; (*assemble*) montar; **erection**
[-ʃən] *n* construcción *f*; (*assembly*)
montaje *m*; (*Physiol*) erección *f*

ERM n abbr (= Exchange Rate Mechanism) tipo de cambio europeo

erode [ɪ'rəʊd] vt (Geo) erosionar; (metal) corroer, desgastar; (fig) desgastar

erosion [ɪ'rəʊʒən] n erosión f; desgaste m

erotic [ɪ'rɒtɪk] adj erótico

errand ['ɛrnd] n recado (SP), mandado (LAM)

erratic [ɪ'rætɪk] adj desigual, poco uniforme

error ['ɛrə*] n error m, equivocación f

erupt [ɪ'rʌpt] vi entrar en erupción; (fig) estallar; **eruption** [ɪ'rʌpʃən] n erupción f; (of war) estallido

escalate ['ɛskəleɪt] vi extenderse, intensificarse

escalator ['ɛskəleɪtə*] n escalera móvil

escape [ɪ'skeɪp] n fuga ▷ vi escaparse; (flee) huir, evadirse; (leak) fugarse ▷ vt (responsibility etc) evitar, eludir; (consequences) escapar a; (elude): **his name ~s me** no me sale su nombre; **to ~ from** (place) escaparse de; (person) escaparse a

escort [n 'ɛskɔːt, vb ɪ'skɔːt] n acompañante mf; (Mil) escolta mf ▷ vt acompañar

especially [ɪ'spɛʃlɪ] adv (above all) sobre todo; (particularly) en particular, especialmente

espionage ['ɛspɪɒnɑːʒ] n espionaje m

essay ['ɛseɪ] n (Literature) ensayo; (Scol: short) redacción f; (: long) trabajo

essence ['ɛsns] n esencia

essential [ɪ'sɛnʃl] adj (necessary) imprescindible; (basic) esencial; **essentially** adv esencialmente; **essentials** npl lo imprescindible, lo esencial

establish [ɪ'stæblɪʃ] vt establecer; (prove) demostrar; (relations) entablar; (reputation) ganarse; **establishment** n establecimiento; **the Establishment**

la clase dirigente

estate [ɪ'steɪt] n (land) finca, hacienda; (inheritance) herencia; (BRIT: also: **housing ~**) urbanización f; **estate agent** (BRIT) n agente mf inmobiliario/a; **estate car** (BRIT) n furgoneta

estimate [n 'ɛstɪmət, vb 'ɛstɪmeɪt] n estimación f, apreciación f; (assessment) tasa, cálculo; (Comm) presupuesto ▷ vt estimar, tasar; calcular

etc abbr (= et cetera) etc

eternal [ɪ'tɜːnl] adj eterno

eternity [ɪ'tɜːnɪtɪ] n eternidad f

ethical ['ɛθɪkl] adj ético; **ethics** ['ɛθɪks] n ética ▷ npl moralidad f

Ethiopia [iː'θɪəʊpɪə] n Etiopía

ethnic ['ɛθnɪk] adj étnico; **ethnic minority** n minoría étnica

e-ticket ['iːtɪkɪt] n billete m electrónico (SP), boleto electrónico (LAM)

etiquette ['ɛtɪkɛt] n etiqueta

EU n abbr (= European Union) UE f

euro n euro

Europe ['juərəp] n Europa; **European** [-'piːən] adj, n europeo/a m/f; **European Community** n Comunidad f Europea; **European Union** n Unión f Europea

Eurostar® ['juərəʊstɑː*] n Eurostar® m

evacuate [ɪ'vækjueɪt] vt (people) evacuar; (place) desocupar

evade [ɪ'veɪd] vt evitar, eludir

evaluate [ɪ'væljueɪt] vt evaluar; (value) tasar; (evidence) interpretar

evaporate [ɪ'væpəreɪt] vi evaporarse; (fig) desvanecerse

eve [iːv] n: **on the ~ of** en vísperas de

even ['iːvn] adj (level) llano; (smooth) liso; (speed, temperature) uniforme; (number) par ▷ adv hasta, incluso; (introducing a comparison) aún, todavía; **~ if, ~ though** aunque +subjun; **~ more** aún más; **~ so** aun así; **not ~** ni siquiera; **~ he was there** hasta él estuvo allí; **~ on Sundays** incluso los domingos; **to get ~ with sb** ajustar cuentas con algn

evening ['iːvnɪŋ] *n* tarde *f*; *(late)* noche *f*; **in the ~** por la tarde; **evening class** *n* clase *f* nocturna; **evening dress** *n* *(no pl: formal clothes)* traje *m* de etiqueta; *(woman's)* traje *m* de noche

event [ɪ'vɛnt] *n* suceso, acontecimiento *m*; *(Sport)* prueba; **in the ~ of** en caso de; **eventful** *adj* *(life)* activo; *(day)* ajetreado

eventual adv *(finally)* finalmente; *(in time)* con el tiempo

Be careful not to translate **eventual** by the Spanish word **eventual**.

eventually adv *(finally)* finalmente; *(in time)* con el tiempo

ever ['ɛvə*] adv *(at any time)* nunca, jamás; *(at all times)* siempre; *(in question)*: **why ~ not?** ¿por qué no?; **the best ~** lo nunca visto; **have you ~ seen it?** ¿lo ha visto alguna vez?; **better than ~** mejor que nunca; **~ since** adv desde entonces ▷ *conj* después de que; **evergreen** *n* árbol *m* de hoja perenne

every: everybody *pron* = **everyone; everyday** *adj* *(daily)* cotidiano, de todos los días; *(usual)* acostumbrado; **everyone** *pron* todos/as, todo el mundo; **everything** *pron* todo; **this shop sells everything** esta tienda vende de todo; **everywhere** *adv*: **I've been looking for you everywhere** te he estado buscando por todas partes; **everywhere you go you meet ...** en todas partes encuentras ...

evict [ɪ'vɪkt] *vt* desahuciar

evidence ['ɛvɪdəns] *n* *(proof)* prueba; *(of witness)* testimonio; *(sign)* indicios *mpl*; **to give ~** prestar declaración, dar testimonio

evident ['ɛvɪdənt] *adj* evidente, manifiesto; **evidently** *adv* por lo visto

evil ['iːvl] *adj* malo; *(influence)* funesto ▷ *n* mal *m*

evoke [ɪ'vəuk] *vt* evocar

evolution [iːvə'luːʃən] *n* evolución *f*

evolve [ɪ'vɔlv] *vt* desarrollar ▷ *vi* evolucionar, desarrollarse

ewe [juː] *n* oveja

ex [ɛks] *(inf)* *n*: **my ~** mi ex

ex- [ɛks] *prefix* ex

○ KEYWORD

every ['ɛvrɪ] *adj* **1** *(each)* cada; **every one of them** *(persons)* todos ellos/as; *(objects)* cada uno de ellos/as; **every shop in the town was closed** todas las tiendas de la ciudad estaban cerradas

2 *(all possible)* todo/a; **I gave you every assistance** te di toda la ayuda posible; **I have every confidence in him** tengo toda mi confianza; **we wish you every success** te deseamos toda suerte de éxitos

3 *(showing recurrence)* todo/a; **every day/week** todos los días/todas las semanas; **every other car had been broken into** habían forzado uno de cada dos coches; **she visits me every other/third day** me visita cada dos/tres días; **every now and then** de vez en cuando

exact [ɪg'zækt] *adj* exacto; *(person)* meticuloso ▷ *vt*: **to ~ sth (from)** exigir algo (de); **exactly** *adv* exactamente; *(indicating agreement)* exacto

exaggerate [ɪg'zædʒəreɪt] *vt, vi* exagerar; **exaggeration** [-'reɪʃən] *n* exageración *f*

exam [ɪg'zæm] *n abbr* *(Scol)* = **examination**

examination [ɪgzæmɪ'neɪʃən] *n* examen *m*; *(Med)* reconocimiento

examine [ɪg'zæmɪn] *vt* examinar; *(inspect)* inspeccionar, escudriñar; *(Med)* reconocer; **examiner** *n* examinador(a) *m/f*

example [ɪg'zɑːmpl] *n* ejemplo; **for ~** por ejemplo

exasperated [ɪg'zɑːspəreɪtɪd] *adj* exasperado

excavate ['ɛkskəveɪt] *vt* excavar

exceed [ɪk'siːd] *vt* *(amount)* exceder;

(number) pasar de; (speed limit) sobrepasar; (powers) excederse en; (hopes) superar; **exceedingly** adv sumamente, sobremanera

excel [ɪkˈsɛl] vi sobresalir; **to ~ o.s** lucirse

excellence [ˈɛksələns] n excelencia

excellent [ˈɛksələnt] adj excelente

except [ɪkˈsɛpt] prep (also: **~ for, ~ing**) excepto, salvo ▷ vt exceptuar, excluir; **~ if/when** excepto si/cuando; **~ that** salvo que; **exception** [ɪkˈsɛpʃən] n excepción f; **to take exception to** ofenderse por; **exceptional** [ɪkˈsɛpʃənl] adj excepcional; **exceptionally** [ɪkˈsɛpʃənəlɪ] adv excepcionalmente, extraordinariamente

excerpt [ˈɛksəːpt] n extracto

excess [ɪkˈsɛs] n exceso; **excess baggage** n exceso de equipaje; **excessive** adj excesivo

exchange [ɪksˈtʃeɪndʒ] n intercambio; (conversation) diálogo; (also: **telephone ~**) central f (telefónica) ▷ vt: **to ~ (for)** cambiar (por); **exchange rate** n tipo de cambio

excite [ɪkˈsaɪt] vt (stimulate) estimular; (arouse) excitar; **excited** adj: **to get excited** emocionarse; **excitement** n (agitation) excitación f; (exhilaration) emoción f; **exciting** adj emocionante

exclaim [ɪksˈkleɪm] vi exclamar; **exclamation** [ɛksklə'meɪʃən] n exclamación f; **exclamation mark** n punto de admiración; **exclamation point** (us) = **exclamation mark**

exclude [ɪksˈkluːd] vt excluir; exceptuar

excluding [ɪksˈkluːdɪŋ] prep: **~ VAT** IVA no incluido

exclusion [ɪksˈkluːʒən] n exclusión f; **to the ~ of** con exclusión de

exclusive [ɪksˈkluːsɪv] adj exclusivo; (club, district) selecto; **~ of tax** excluyendo impuestos; **exclusively** adv únicamente

excruciating [ɪkˈskruːʃɪeɪtɪŋ] adj (pain) agudísimo, atroz; (noise, embarrassment) horrible

excursion [ɪkˈskəːʃən] n (tourist excursion) excursión f

excuse n [ɪkˈskjuːs], vb [ɪkˈskjuːz] n disculpa, excusa; (pretext) pretexto ▷ vt (justify) justificar; (forgive) disculpar, perdonar; **to ~ sb from doing sth** dispensar a algn de hacer algo; **~ me!** (attracting attention) ¡por favor!; (apologizing) ¡perdón!; **if you will ~ me** con su permiso

ex-directory [ˈɛksdɪˈrɛktərɪ] (BRIT) adj que no consta en la guía

execute [ˈɛksɪkjuːt] vt (plan) realizar; (order) cumplir; (person) ajusticiar, ejecutar; **execution** [-ˈkjuːʃən] n realización f; cumplimiento; ejecución f

executive [ɪɡˈzɛkjutɪv] n (person, committee) ejecutivo; (Pol: committee) poder m ejecutivo ▷ adj ejecutivo

exempt [ɪɡˈzɛmpt] adj: **~ from** exento de ▷ vt: **to ~ sb from** eximir a algn de

exercise [ˈɛksəsaɪz] n ejercicio ▷ vt (patience) usar de; (right) valerse de; (dog) llevar de paseo; (mind) preocupar ▷ vi (also: **to take ~**) hacer ejercicio(s); **exercise book** n cuaderno

exert [ɪɡˈzəːt] vt ejercer; **to ~ o.s.** esforzarse; **exertion** [-ʃən] n esfuerzo

exhale [ɛksˈheɪl] vt, vi despedir ▷ vi exhalar

exhaust [ɪɡˈzɔːst] n (Aut: also: **~ pipe**) escape m; (: fumes) gases mpl de escape ▷ vt agotar; **exhausted** adj agotado; **exhaustion** [ɪɡˈzɔːstʃən] n agotamiento; **nervous exhaustion** postración f nerviosa

exhibit [ɪɡˈzɪbɪt] n (Art) obra expuesta; (Law) objeto expuesto ▷ vt (show: emotions) manifestar; (: courage, skill) demostrar; (paintings) exponer; **exhibition** [ɛksɪ'bɪʃən] n exposición f; (of talent etc) demostración f

exhilarating [ɪɡˈzɪləreɪtɪŋ] adj estimulante, tónico

...ksail] n exilio; (person)
...a ▷ vt desterrar, exiliar
...zist] vi existir; (live) vivir;
...e n existencia; **existing** adj
...] actual
...is; (Comput) salir (del

...ful not to translate **exit** by
...ish word éxito.
...us) n (Aut) vía de acceso
...otik] adj exótico
...spænd] vt ampliar;
...entar ▷ vi (population)
...rade etc) crecer
...se
...ik'spænʃən] n (of
...mento; (of trade)

...ekt] vt esperar;
...con; (suppose) suponer
...(pregnant woman)
...nda; **expectation**
...n (hope) esperanza;
...iva
...kspə'diʃən] n

...t arrojar; (from place)

...ks'penditʃə*] n
...bolso; consumo
...s] n gasto, gastos
...ta; **expenses** npl
...; **at the ~ of** a costa
...unt n cuenta de

...nsiv] adj caro,

...iəriəns] n
...perimentar;
...enced adj

...erimənt] n
...cer experimentos,
...ntl] n
...ocess is still at
...age el proceso
...a

expert ['ekspə:t] adj experto, perito
▷ n experto/a, perito/a; (specialist)
especialista mf; **expertise** [-'ti:z] n
pericia

expire [ik'spaiə*] vi caducar, vencer;
expiry n vencimiento; **expiry date**
n (of medicine, food item) fecha de
caducidad

explain [ik'splein] vt explicar;
explanation [eksplə'neiʃən] n
explicación f

explicit [ik'splisit] adj explícito

explode [ik'spləud] vi estallar,
explotar; (population) crecer
rápidamente; (with anger) reventar

exploit [n 'eksplɔit, vb ik'splɔit] n
hazaña ▷ vt explotar; **exploitation**
[-'teiʃən] n explotación f

explore [ik'splɔ:*] vt examinar; investigar; (fig)
examinar; investigar; **explorer** n
explorador(a) m/f

explosion [ik'spləuʒən] n explosión
f; **explosive** [iks'pləusiv] adj, n
explosivo

export [vb ek'spɔ:t, n, cpd 'ekspɔ:t]
vt exportar ▷ n (process) exportación
f; (product) producto de exportación
▷ cpd de exportación; **exporter** n
exportador m

expose [ik'spəuz] vt exponer;
(unmask) desenmascarar; **exposed**
adj expuesto

exposure [ik'spəuʒə*] n exposición
f; (publicity) publicidad f; (Phot: speed)
velocidad f de obturación; (: shot)
fotografía; **to die from ~** (Med) morir
de frío

express [ik'spres] adj (definite)
expreso, explícito; (BRIT: letter etc)
urgente ▷ n (train) rápido ▷ vt
expresar; **expression** [ik'spreʃən] n
expresión f; (of actor etc) sentimiento;
expressway (us) n (urban motorway)
autopista

exquisite [ek'skwizit] adj exquisito

extend [ik'stend] vt (visit, street)
prolongar; (building) ampliar;
(invitation) ofrecer ▷ vi (land)

extenderse; (*period of time*) prolongarse
extension [ɪkˈstɛnʃən] *n* extensión
f; (*building*) ampliación *f*; (*of time*)
prolongación *f*; (Tel: *in private house*)
línea derivada; (: *in office*) extensión
f; **extension lead** *n* alargador *m*,
alargadera
extensive [ɪkˈstɛnsɪv] *adj* extenso;
(*damage*) importante; (*knowledge*)
amplio
extent [ɪkˈstɛnt] *n* (*breadth*)
extensión *f*; (*scope*) alcance *m*; **to some**
~ hasta cierto punto; **to the** ~ **of** ...
hasta el punto de ...; **to such an** ~ **that**
... hasta tal punto que ...; **to what** ~?
¿hasta qué punto?
exterior [ɛkˈstɪərɪə*] *adj* exterior,
externo ▷ *n* exterior *m*
external [ɛkˈstɔːnl] *adj* externo
extinct [ɪkˈstɪŋkt] *adj* (*volcano*)
extinguido; (*race*) extinto; **extinction**
n extinción *f*
extinguish [ɪkˈstɪŋgwɪʃ] *vt*
extinguir, apagar
extra [ˈɛkstrə] *adj* adicional ▷ *adv* (*in
addition*) de más ▷ *n* (*luxury, addition*)
extra *m*; (Cinema, Theatre) extra *mf*,
comparsa *mf*
extract [*vb* ɪkˈstrækt, *n* ˈɛkstrækt] *vt*
sacar; (*tooth*) extraer; (*money, promise*)
obtener ▷ *n* extracto
extradite [ˈɛkstrədaɪt] *vt* extraditar
extraordinary [ɪkˈstrɔːdnrɪ] *adj*
extraordinario; (*odd*) raro
extravagance [ɪkˈstrævəgəns] *n*
derroche *m*, despilfarro; (*thing bought*)
extravagancia
extravagant [ɪkˈstrævəgənt]
adj (*lavish: person*) pródigo; (: *gift*)
(demasiado) caro; (*wasteful*)
despilfarrador(a)
extreme [ɪkˈstriːm] *adj* extremo,
extremado ▷ *n* extremo; **extremely**
adv sumamente, extremadamente
extremist [ɪkˈstriːmɪst] *adj, n*
extremista *m/f*
extrovert [ˈɛkstrəvɜːt] *n*
extrovertido/a

eye [aɪ] *n* ojo ▷ *vt* mirar de soslayo,
ojear; **to keep an** ~ **on** vigilar; **eyeball**
n globo ocular; **eyebrow** *n* ceja;
eyedrops *npl* gotas *fpl* para los ojos,
colirio; **eyelash** *n* pestaña; **eyelid**
n párpado; **eyeliner** *n* delineador *m* (
ojos); **eyeshadow** *n* sombreador *n*
ojos; **eyesight** *n* vista; **eye witnes**
testigo *mf* presencial

f

F [ɛf] n (Mus) fa m

fabric ['fæbrɪk] n tejido, tela
Be careful not to translate **fabric** by
the Spanish word *fábrica*.

fabulous ['fæbjuləs] adj fabuloso

face [feɪs] n (Anat) cara, rostro;
(of clock) esfera (SP), cara (LAM); (of
mountain) cara, ladera; (of building)
fachada ▷ vt (direction) estar de cara
a; (situation) hacer frente a; (facts)
aceptar; **~ down** (person, card) boca
abajo; **to lose ~** desprestigiarse; **to
make** or **pull a ~** hacer muecas; **in the
~ of** (difficulties etc) ante; **on the ~ of it**
a primera vista; **to ~ up to** cara a cara; **face
up to** vt fus hacer frente a, arrostrar;
face cloth (BRIT) n manopla; **face
pack** n (BRIT) mascarilla

facial ['feɪʃəl] adj de la cara ▷ n
(also: **beauty ~**) tratamiento facial,
limpieza

facilitate [fə'sɪlɪteɪt] vt facilitar

facilities [fə'sɪlɪtɪz] npl (buildings)
instalaciones fpl; (equipment) servicios
mpl; **credit ~** facilidades fpl de crédito

fact [fækt] n hecho; **in ~** en realidad

faction ['fækʃən] n facción f

factor ['fæktə*] n factor m

factory ['fæktərɪ] n fábrica

factual ['fæktjuəl] adj basado en
los hechos

faculty ['fækəltɪ] n facultad f;
(US: teaching staff) personal m docente

fad [fæd] n novedad f, moda

fade [feɪd] vi desteñirse; (sound, smile)
desvanecerse; (light) apagarse; (flower)
marchitarse; (hope, memory) perderse;
fade away vi (sound) apagarse

fag [fæg] (BRIT: inf) n (cigarette) pitillo
(SP), cigarro

Fahrenheit ['fɑːrənhaɪt] n
Fahrenheit m

fail [feɪl] vt (candidate, test) suspender
(SP), reprobar (LAM); (memory etc) fallar a
▷ vi suspender (SP), reprobar (LAM); (be
unsuccessful) fracasar; (strength, brakes)
fallar; (light) acabarse; **to ~ to do sth**
(neglect) dejar de hacer algo; (be unable)
no poder hacer algo; **without ~** sin
falta; **failing** n falta, defecto ▷ prep a
falta de; **failure** ['feɪljə*] n fracaso;
(person) fracasado/a; (mechanical
etc) fallo

faint [feɪnt] adj débil; (recollection)
vago; (mark) apenas visible ▷ n
desmayo ▷ vi desmayarse; **to feel ~**
estar mareado, marearse; **faintest**
adj: **I haven't the faintest idea** no
tengo la más remota idea; **faintly** adv
débilmente; (vaguely) vagamente

fair [fɛə*] adj justo; (hair, person) rubio;
(weather) bueno; (good enough) regular;
(considerable) considerable ▷ adv
(play) limpio ▷ n feria; (BRIT: funfair)
parque m de atracciones; **fairground** n
recinto ferial; **fair-haired** adj (person)
rubio; **fairly** adv (justly) con justicia;
(quite) bastante; **fair trade** n comercio
justo; **fairway** n (Golf) calle f

fairy ['fɛərɪ] n hada; **fairy tale** n
cuento de hadas

faith [feɪθ] n fe f; (trust) confianza;
(sect) religión f; **faithful** adj

(loyal: troops etc) leal; (spouse) fiel;
(account) exacto; **faithfully** adv
fielmente; **yours faithfully** (BRIT: in
letters) le saluda atentamente
fake [feɪk] n (painting etc) falsificación
f; (person) impostor(a) m/f ▷ adj falso
▷ vt fingir; (painting etc) falsificar
falcon ['fɔːlkən] n halcón m
fall [fɔːl] (pt **fell**, pp **fallen**) n caída;
(in price etc) descenso; (us) otoño ▷ vi
caer(se); (price) bajar, descender; **falls**
npl (waterfall) cascada, salto de agua;
to ~ flat (on one's face) caerse (boca
abajo); (plan) fracasar; (joke, story) no
hacer gracia; **fall apart** vi deshacerse;
fall down vi (person) caerse; (building,
hopes) derrumbarse; **fall for** vt fus
(trick) dejarse engañar por; (person)
enamorarse de; **fall off** vi caerse;
(diminish) disminuir; **fall out** vi (friends
etc) reñir; (hair, teeth) caerse; **fall over**
vi caer(se); **fall through** vi (plan,
project) fracasar
fallen ['fɔːlən] pp of **fall**
fallout ['fɔːlaut] n lluvia radioactiva
false [fɔːls] adj falso; **under ~
pretences** con engaños; **false alarm**
n falsa alarma; **false teeth** (BRIT) npl
dentadura postiza
fame [feɪm] n fama
familiar [fə'mɪlɪə*] adj conocido,
familiar; (tone) de confianza; **to
be ~ with** (subject) conocer (bien);
familiarize [fə'mɪlɪəraɪz] vt: **to
familiarize o.s. with** familiarizarse
con
family ['fæmɪlɪ] n familia; **family
doctor** n médico/a de cabecera;
family planning n planificación f
familiar
famine ['fæmɪn] n hambre f,
hambruna
famous ['feɪməs] adj famoso, célebre
fan [fæn] n abanico; (Elec) ventilador
m; (of pop star) fan m/f; (Sport) hincha m/f
▷ vt abanicar; (fire, quarrel) atizar
fanatic [fə'nætɪk] n fanático/a
fan belt n correa del ventilador

fan club n club m de fans
fancy ['fænsɪ] n (whim) capricho,
antojo; (imagination) imaginación f
▷ adj (luxury) lujoso, de lujo ▷ vt (feel
like, want) tener ganas de; (imagine)
imaginarse; (think) creer ▷ vt: **to take a ~ to
sb** tomar cariño a algn; **he fancies her**
(inf) le gusta (ella) mucho; **fancy dress**
n disfraz m
fan heater n calefactor m de aire
fantasize ['fæntəsaɪz] vi fantasear,
hacerse ilusiones
fantastic [fæn'tæstɪk] adj (enormous)
enorme; (strange, wonderful) fantástico
fantasy ['fæntəzɪ] n (dream) sueño;
(unreality) fantasía
fanzine ['fænziːn] n fanzine m
FAQs abbr (= frequently asked questions)
preguntas frecuentes
far [fɑː*] adj (distant) lejano ▷ adv
lejos; (much, greatly) mucho; **~ away,** **~
off** (a lo) lejos; **~ better** mucho mejor;
~ from lejos de; **by ~** con mucho; **go as
~ as the farm** vaya hasta la granja; **as
~ as I know** que yo sepa; **how ~?** ¿hasta
dónde?; (fig) ¿hasta qué punto?
farce [fɑːs] n farsa
fare [fɛə*] n (on trains, buses) precio
(del billete); (in taxi: cost) tarifa; (food)
comida; **half ~** medio pasaje m; **full ~**
pasaje completo
Far East n: **the ~** el Extremo Oriente
farewell [fɛə'wɛl] excl, n adiós m
farm [fɑːm] n cortijo (SP), hacienda
(LAM), rancho (MEX), estancia (RPL)
▷ vt cultivar; **farmer** n granjero,
hacendado (LAM), ranchero (MEX),
estanciero (RPL); **farmhouse** n granja,
casa del hacendado (LAM), rancho
(MEX), casco de la estancia (RPL);
farming n agricultura; (of crops)
cultivo; (of animals) cría; **farmyard** n
corral m
far-reaching [fɑː'riːtʃɪŋ] adj (reform,
effect) de gran alcance
fart [fɑːt] (inf!) vi tirarse un pedo (!)
farther ['fɑːðə*] adv más lejos, más
allá ▷ adj más lejano

farthest ['fɑːðɪst] *superlative of* **far**

fascinate ['fæsɪneɪt] *vt* fascinar; **fascinated** *adj* fascinado

fascinating ['fæsɪneɪtɪŋ] *adj* fascinante

fascination [-'neɪʃən] *n* fascinación *f*

fascist ['fæʃɪst] *adj, n* fascista *m/f*

fashion ['fæʃən] *n* moda; (*fashion industry*) industria de la moda; (*manner*) manera *f* ▷ *vt* formar; **in ~** a la moda; **out of ~** pasado de moda; **fashionable** *adj* de moda; **fashion show** *n* desfile *m* de modelos

fast [fɑːst] *adj* rápido; (*dye, colour*) resistente; (*clock*): **to be ~** estar adelantado ▷ *adv* rápidamente, de prisa; (*stuck, held*) firmemente ▷ *n* ayuno ▷ *vi* ayunar; **~ asleep** profundamente dormido

fasten ['fɑːsn] *vt* atar, sujetar; (*coat, belt*) abrochar ▷ *vi* atarse; abrocharse

fast food *n* comida rápida, platos *mpl* preparados

fat [fæt] *adj* gordo; (*book*) grueso; (*profit*) grande, pingüe ▷ *n* grasa; (*on person*) carnes *fpl*; (*lard*) manteca *f*

fatal ['feɪtl] *adj* (*mistake*) fatal; (*injury*) mortal; **fatality** [fə'tælɪtɪ] *n* (*road death etc*) víctima; **fatally** *adv* fatalmente; mortalmente

fate [feɪt] *n* destino; (*of person*) suerte *f*

father ['fɑːðə*] *n* padre *m*; **Father Christmas** *n* Papá *m* Noel; **father-in-law** *n* suegro

fatigue [fə'tiːg] *n* fatiga, cansancio

fattening ['fætnɪŋ] *adj* (*food*) que hace engordar

fatty ['fætɪ] *adj* (*food*) graso ▷ *n* (*inf*) gordito/a, gordinflón/ona *m/f*

faucet ['fɔːsɪt] (*US*) *n* grifo (*SP*), llave *f*, canilla (*RPL*)

fault [fɔːlt] *n* (*blame*) culpa; (*defect: in person, machine*) defecto; (*Geo*) falla ▷ *vt* criticar; **it's my ~** es culpa mía; **to find ~ with** criticar, poner peros a; **at ~** culpable; **faulty** *adj* defectuoso

fauna ['fɔːnə] *n* fauna

favour *etc* ['feɪvə*] (*US* **favor** *etc*) *n* favor *m*; (*approval*) aprobación *f* ▷ *vt* (*proposition*) estar a favor de, aprobar; (*assist*) ser propicio a; **to do sb a ~** hacer un favor a algn; **to find ~ with sb** caer en gracia a algn; **in ~ of** a favor de; **favourable** *adj* favorable; **favourite** ['feɪvrɪt] *adj, n* favorito, preferido

fawn [fɔːn] *n* cervato ▷ *adj* (*also:* **~-coloured**) color de cervato, leonado ▷ *vi*: **to ~ (up)on** adular

fax [fæks] *n* (*document*) fax *m*; (*machine*) telefax *m* ▷ *vt* mandar por telefax

FBI (*US*) *n abbr* (= *Federal Bureau of Investigation*) ≈ BIC *f* (*SP*)

fear [fɪə*] *n* miedo, temor *m* ▷ *vt* tener miedo de, temer; **for ~ of** por si; **fearful** *adj* temeroso, miedoso; (*awful*) terrible; **fearless** *adj* audaz

feasible ['fiːzəbl] *adj* factible

feast [fiːst] *n* banquete *m*; (*Rel: also:* **~ day**) fiesta ▷ *vi* festejar

feat [fiːt] *n* hazaña

feather ['feðə*] *n* pluma

feature ['fiːtʃə*] *n* característica; (*article*) artículo de fondo ▷ *vt* (*film*) presentar ▷ *vi*: **to ~ in** tener un papel destacado en; **features** *npl* (*of face*) facciones *fpl*; **feature film** *n* largometraje *m*

Feb. *abbr* (= *February*) feb

February ['februərɪ] *n* febrero

fed [fed] *pt, pp of* **feed**

federal ['fedərəl] *adj* federal

federation [fedə'reɪʃən] *n* federación *f*

fed up ['fedʌp] *adj*: **to be ~ (with)** estar harto de

fee [fiː] *n* pago; (*professional*) derechos *mpl*, honorarios *mpl*; (*of club*) cuota; **school ~s** matrícula

feeble ['fiːbl] *adj* débil; (*excuse*) flojo

feed [fiːd] (*pt, pp* **fed**) *n* comida; (*of animal*) pienso; (*on printer*) dispositivo de alimentación ▷ *vt* alimentar; (*BRIT: baby: breastfeed*) dar el pecho a; (*animal*) dar de comer a; (*data,*

information): **to ~ into** meter en;
feedback n reacción f; feedback m

feel [fiːl] (*pt, pp* **felt**) n (*sensation*)
sensación f; (*sense of touch*) tacto;
(*impression*): **to have the ~ of** parecerse
a ▷ vt tocar; (*pain etc*) sentir; (*think,
believe*) creer; **to ~ hungry/cold** tener
hambre/frío; **to ~ lonely/better**
sentirse solo/mejor; **I don't ~ well**
no me siento bien; **it ~s soft** es suave
al tacto; **to ~ like** (*want*) tener ganas
de; **feeling** n (*physical*) sensación f;
(*foreboding*) presentimiento; (*emotion*)
sentimiento

feet [fiːt] *npl of* **foot**

feign [feɪn] vt fingir

fell [fel] *pt of* **fall** ▷ vt (*tree*) talar

fellow ['fɛləu] n tipo, tío (SP);
(*comrade*) compañero; (*of learned
society*) socio/a; **fellow citizen** n
conciudadano/a; **fellow countryman**
(*irreg*) n compatriota m; **fellow men**
npl semejantes *mpl*; **fellowship** n
compañerismo; (*grant*) beca

felony ['fɛlənɪ] n crimen m

felt [fɛlt] *pt, pp of* **feel** ▷ n fieltro;
felt-tip ~ (*also:* **felt-tip pen**)
rotulador m

female ['fiːmeɪl] n (*pej: woman*) mujer
f, tía; (*Zool*) hembra ▷ *adj* femenino;
hembra

feminine ['fɛmɪnɪn] *adj* femenino

feminist ['fɛmɪnɪst] n feminista

fence [fɛns] n valla, cerca ▷ vt (*also:* **~
in**) cercar ▷ vi (*Sport*) hacer esgrima;
fencing n esgrima f

fend [fɛnd] vi: **to ~ for o.s.** valerse por
sí mismo; **fend off** vt (*attack*) rechazar;
(*questions*) evadir

fender ['fɛndə*] (US) n guardafuego;
(*Aut*) parachoques m inv

fennel ['fɛnl] n hinojo

ferment [vb fə'mɛnt, 'fɜːmɛnt] vi
fermentar ▷ n (*fig*) agitación f

fern [fɜːn] n helecho

ferocious [fə'rəʊʃəs] *adj* feroz

ferret ['fɛrɪt] n hurón m

ferry ['fɛrɪ] n (*small*) barca (de pasaje),
balsa; (*large: also:* **~boat**) transbordador

m, ferry m ▷ vt transportar

fertile ['fɜːtaɪl] *adj* fértil; (*Biol*)
fecundo; **fertilize** ['fɜːtɪlaɪz] vt (*Biol*)
fecundar; (*Agr*) abonar; **fertilizer** n
abono

festival ['fɛstɪvəl] n (*Rel*) fiesta; (*Art,
Mus*) festival m

festive ['fɛstɪv] *adj* festivo; **the ~
season** (*BRIT: Christmas*) las Navidades

fetch [fɛtʃ] vt ir a buscar; (*sell for*)
venderse por

fête [feɪt] n fiesta

fetus ['fiːtəs] (US) n = **foetus**

feud [fjuːd] n (*hostility*) enemistad f;
(*quarrel*) disputa

fever ['fiːvə*] n fiebre f; **feverish**
adj febril

few [fjuː] *adj* (*not many*) pocos ▷ *pron*
pocos; algunos; **a ~** *adj* unos pocos,
algunos; **fewer** *adj* menos; **fewest** *adj*
los(las) menos

fiancé [fɪ'ɑːnseɪ] n novio, prometido;
fiancée n novia, prometida

fiasco [fɪ'æskəu] n fiasco

fib [fɪb] n mentirilla

fibre ['faɪbə*] (US **fiber**) n fibra;
fibreglass (US **Fiberglass**®) n fibra
de vidrio

fickle ['fɪkl] *adj* inconstante

fiction ['fɪkʃən] n ficción f; **fictional**
adj novelesco

fiddle ['fɪdl] n (*Mus*) violín m;
(*cheating*) trampa ▷ vt (*also: accounts*)
falsificar; **fiddle with** vt fus juguetear
con

fidelity [fɪ'dɛlɪtɪ] n fidelidad f

field [fiːld] n campo; (*fig*) campo,
esfera; (*Sport*) campo (SP), cancha (LAM);
field marshal n mariscal m

fierce [fɪəs] *adj* feroz; (*wind, heat*)
fuerte; (*fighting, enemy*) encarnizado

fifteen [fɪf'tiːn] num quince;
fifteenth *adj* decimoquinto; **the
fifteenth floor** la planta quince;
the fifteenth of August el quince
de agosto

fifth [fɪfθ] num quinto

fiftieth ['fɪftɪɪθ] *adj* quincuagésimo

-fifty

...uena)
...apropiado
...bien a;
...(gen)
...(ggle) lucha
...con
...ace
...alcoholism)
...(Med)
...entar ganar;
...pelear, luchar;
for
...derse; (after illness)
...(tears) contener;
...attack, attacker) rechazar;
...p, urge) luchar contra;
...n combate m, pelea

figa*] n (Drawing, Geom)
...a, dibujo; (number, cipher) cifra;
...dy, outline) tipo; (personality) figura
▷ vt (esp US) imaginar ▷ vi (appear)
figurar; **figure out** vt (work out)
resolver

file [faɪl] n (tool) lima; (dossier)
expediente m; (folder) carpeta;
(Comput) fichero; (row) fila ▷ vt limar;
(Law: claim) presentar; (store) archivar;
filing cabinet n fichero, archivador m

Filipino [fɪlɪˈpiːnəʊ] adj filipino ▷ n
(person) filipino/a m/f; (Ling) tagalo

fill [fɪl] vt (space): **to ~ (with)** llenar
(de); (vacancy, need) cubrir ▷ n: **to eat
one's ~** llenarse; **fill in** vt rellenar; **fill
out** vt (form, receipt) rellenar; **fill up** vt
llenar (hasta el borde) ▷ vi (Aut) poner
gasolina

fillet [ˈfɪlɪt] n filete m; **fillet steak** n
filete m de ternera

filling [ˈfɪlɪŋ] n (Culin) relleno; (for
tooth) empaste m; **filling station** n
estación f de servicio

film [fɪlm] n película ▷ vt (scene)
filmar ▷ vi rodar (una película); **film
star** n astro, estrella de cine

filter [ˈfɪltə*] n filtro ▷ vt filtrar; **filter
lane** (BRIT) n carril m de selección

filth [fɪlθ] n suciedad f; **filthy** adj
sucio; (language) obsceno

fin [fɪn] n (gen) aleta

final [ˈfaɪnl] adj (last) final, último;
(definitive) definitivo, terminante ▷ n

(BRIT Sport) final f; **finals** npl (Scol)
examen m final; (US Sport) final f

finale [fɪˈnɑːlɪ] n final m

final: finalist n (Sport) finalista mf;
finalize vt concluir, completar; **finally**
adv (lastly) por último, finalmente;
(eventually) por fin

finance [faɪˈnæns] n (money)
fondos mpl ▷ vt financiar; **finances**
npl finanzas fpl; (personal finances)
situación f económica; **financial**
[-ˈnænʃəl] adj financiero; **financial
year** n ejercicio (financiero)

find [faɪnd] (pt, pp **found**) vt
encontrar, hallar; (come upon) descubrir
▷ n hallazgo; descubrimiento; **to ~ sb
guilty** (Law) declarar culpable a algn;
find out vt averiguar; (truth, secret)
descubrir; **to find out about** (subject)
informarse sobre; (by chance) enterarse
de; **findings** npl (Law) veredicto, fallo;
(of report) recomendaciones fpl

fine [faɪn] adj excelente; (thin) fino
▷ adv (well) bien ▷ n (Law) multa ▷ vt
(Law) multar; **to be ~** (person) estar
bien; (weather) hacer buen tiempo; **fine
arts** npl bellas artes fpl

finger [ˈfɪŋɡə*] n dedo ▷ vt (touch)
manosear; **little/index ~** (dedo)
meñique m/índice m; **fingernail** n
uña; **fingerprint** n huella dactilar;
fingertip n yema del dedo

finish [ˈfɪnɪʃ] n (end) fin m; (Sport)
meta; (polish etc) acabado ▷ vt, vi
terminar; **to ~ doing sth** acabar de
hacer algo; **to ~ third** llegar el tercero;
finish off vt acabar, terminar; (kill)
acabar con; **finish up** vt acabar,
terminar ▷ vi ir a parar, terminar

Finland [ˈfɪnlənd] n Finlandia

Finn [fɪn] n finlandés/esa m/f;
Finnish adj finlandés/esa ▷ n (Ling)
finlandés m

fir [fəː*] n abeto

fire [ˈfaɪə*] n fuego; (in hearth) lumbre
f; (accidental) incendio; (heater) estufa
▷ vt (gun) disparar; (interest) despertar;
(inf: dismiss) despedir ▷ vi (shoot)

firm

disparar; **on ~** ardiendo, en llamas;
fire alarm n alarma de incendios;
firearm n arma de fuego; **fire brigade**
(us **fire department**) n (cuerpo de)
bomberos mpl; **fire engine** (BRIT)
coche m de bomberos; **fire escape**
n escalera de incendios; **fire exit** n
salida de incendios; **fire extinguisher**
n extintor m (de incendios); **fireman**
(irreg) n bombero; **fireplace** n
chimenea; **fire station** n parque m
de bomberos; **firetruck** (us) n = **fire
engine**; **firewall** n (Internet) firewall
m; **firewood** n leña; **fireworks** npl
fuegos mpl artificiales

firm [fə:m] adj firme; (look, voice)
resuelto ⊳ n firma, empresa; **firmly**
adv firmemente; resueltamente

first [fə:st] adj primero ⊳ adv (before
others) primero; (when listing reasons
etc) en primer lugar, primeramente
⊳ n (person: in race) primero/a; (Aut)
primera; (BRIT Scol) título de licenciado
con calificación de sobresaliente; **at ~** al
principio; **~ of all** ante todo; **first aid** n
primera ayuda, primeros auxilios mpl;
first-aid kit n botiquín m; **first-class**
adj (excellent) de primera (categoría);
(ticket etc) de primera clase; **first-hand**
adj de primera mano; **first lady** n
(esp us) primera dama; **firstly** adv en
primer lugar; **first name** n nombre m
(de pila); **first-rate** adj estupendo

fiscal ['fiskəl] adj fiscal; **fiscal year** n
año fiscal, ejercicio

fish [fɪʃ] n inv pez m; (food) pescado
⊳ vt, vi pescar; **to go ~ing** ir de pesca;
~ and chips pescado frito con patatas
fritas; **fisherman** (irreg) n pescador
m; **fish fingers** (BRIT) npl croquetas
fpl de pescado; **fishing** n pesca;
fishing boat n barca de pesca; **fishing
line** n sedal m; **fishmonger** (BRIT)
n pescadero/a; **fishmonger's (shop)**
(BRIT) n pescadería; **fish sticks** (us)
npl = **fish fingers**; **fishy** (inf) adj
sospechoso

fist [fɪst] n puño

fit [fɪt] adj (healthy) en (b
forma; (proper) adecuado,
⊳ vt (clothes) estar o senta
(instal) poner; (equip) provee
(facts) cuadrar o correspon
⊳ vi (clothes) sentar bien; (in s
gap) caber; (facts) coincidir ⊳ n
ataque m; **~ to** (ready) a punto d
apropiado para; **a ~ of anger/pr**
un arranque de cólera/orgullo; **th
dress is a good ~** este vestido me
sienta bien; **by ~s and starts** a rach
fit in vi (fig: person) llevarse bien
(con todos); **fitness** n (Med) salud
f; **fitted** adj (skirt, shirt) entallado;
(sheet) de cuatro picos; **fitted carpet**
n moqueta; **fitted kitchen** n cocina
amueblada; **fitting** adj apropiado ⊳ n
(of dress) prueba; (of piece of equipment)
instalación f; **fitting room** n probador
m; **fittings** npl instalaciones fpl

five [faɪv] num cinco; **fiver** (inf) n
(BRIT) billete m de cinco libras; (us)
billete m de cinco dólares

fix [fɪks] vt (secure) fijar, asegurar;
(mend) arreglar; (prepare) preparar
⊳ n: **to be in a ~** estar en un aprieto; **fix
up** vt (meeting) arreglar; **to fix sb up
with sth** proveer a algn de algo; **fixed**
adj (prices etc) fijo; **fixture** n (Sport)
encuentro

fizzy ['fɪzɪ] adj (drink) gaseoso

flag [flæg] n bandera; (stone) losa ⊳ vi
decaer ⊳ vt: **to ~ sb down** hacer señas
a algn para que se pare; **flagpole** n
asta de bandera

flair [fleə*] n aptitud f especial

flak [flæk] n (Mil) fuego antiaéreo;
(inf: criticism) lluvia de críticas

flake [fleɪk] n (of rust, paint) escama;
(of snow, soap powder) copo ⊳ vi (also: ~
off) desconcharse

flamboyant [flæm'bɔɪənt] adj
(dress) vistoso; (person)
extravagante

flame [fleɪm] n llama

flamingo [flə'mɪŋgəʊ] n flamenco

flammable ['flæməbl] adj

389 | flock

inflamable

flan [flæn] (BRIT) n tarta
◻ Be careful not to translate **flan** by the Spanish word *flan*.

flank [flæŋk] n (of animal) ijar m; (of army) flanco ▷ vt flanquear

flannel ['flænl] n (BRIT: also: **face ~**) manopla; (fabric) franela

flap [flæp] n (of pocket, envelope) solapa ▷ vt (wings, arms) agitar ▷ vi (sail, flag) ondear

flare [fleə*] n llamarada; (Mil) bengala; (in skirt etc) vuelo; **flares** npl (trousers) pantalones mpl de campana; **flare up** vi encenderse; (fig: person) encolerizarse; (: revolt) estallar

flash [flæʃ] n relámpago; (also: **news ~**) noticias fpl de última hora; (Phot) flash m ▷ vt (light, headlights) lanzar un destello con; (news, message) transmitir; (smile) lanzar ▷ vi brillar; (hazard light etc) lanzar destellos; **in a ~** en un instante; **he ~ed by** or **past** pasó como un rayo; **flashback** n (Cinema) flashback m; **flashbulb** n bombilla fusible; **flashlight** n linterna

flask [flɑːsk] n frasco; (also: **vacuum ~**) termo

flat [flæt] adj llano; (smooth) liso; (tyre) desinflado; (battery) descargado; (beer) muerto; (refusal etc) rotundo; (Mus) desafinado; (rate) fijo ▷ n (BRIT: apartment) piso sp; departamento (LAM), apartamento; (Aut) pinchazo; (Mus) bemol m; **to work ~ out** trabajar a toda mecha; **flatten** vt (also: **flatten out**) allanar; (smooth out) alisar; (building, plants) arrasar

flatter ['flætə*] vt adular, halagar; **flattering** adj halagüeño; (dress) que favorece

flaunt [flɔːnt] vt ostentar, lucir

flavour etc ['fleɪvə*] (US **flavor** etc) n sabor m, gusto ▷ vt sazonar, condimentar; **strawberry-flavoured** con sabor a fresa; **flavouring** n (in product) aromatizante m

flaw [flɔː] n defecto; **flawless** adj

impecable

flea [fliː] n pulga; **flea market** n rastro, mercadillo

flee [fliː] (pt, pp **fled**) vt huir de ▷ vi huir, fugarse

fleece [fliːs] n vellón m; (wool) lana; (top) forro polar ▷ vt (inf) desplumar

fleet [fliːt] n flota; (of lorries etc) escuadra

fleeting ['fliːtɪŋ] adj fugaz

Flemish ['flemɪʃ] adj flamenco

flesh [fleʃ] n carne f; (skin) piel f; (of fruit) pulpa

flew [fluː] pt of **fly**

flex [fleks] n cordón m ▷ vt (muscles) tensar; **flexibility** n flexibilidad f; **flexible** adj flexible; **flexitime** (US **flextime**) n horario flexible

flick [flɪk] n capirotazo; chasquido ▷ vt (with hand) dar un capirotazo a; (whip etc) chasquear; (switch) accionar; **flick through** vt fus hojear

flicker ['flɪkə*] vi (light) parpadear; (flame) vacilar

flies [flaɪz] npl of **fly**

flight [flaɪt] n vuelo; (escape) huida, fuga; (also: **~ of steps**) tramo (de escaleras); **flight attendant** n auxiliar mf de vuelo

flimsy ['flɪmzɪ] adj (thin) muy ligero; (building) endeble; (excuse) flojo

flinch [flɪntʃ] vi encogerse; **to ~ from** retroceder ante

fling [flɪŋ] (pt, pp **flung**) vt arrojar

flint [flɪnt] n pedernal m; (in lighter) piedra

flip [flɪp] vt dar la vuelta a; (switch: turn on) encender; (turn) apagar; (coin) echar a cara o cruz

flip-flops ['flɪpflɒps] npl (esp BRIT) chancletas fpl

flipper ['flɪpə*] n aleta

flirt [flɜːt] vi coquetear, flirtear ▷ n coqueta

float [fləʊt] n flotador m; (in procession) carroza; (money) reserva ▷ vi flotar; (swimmer) hacer la plancha

flock [flɒk] n (of sheep) rebaño; (of

flood | 390

birds) bandada ▷ *vi:* **to ~ to** acudir en tropel a

flood [flʌd] *n* inundación *f; (of letters, imports etc)* avalancha ▷ *vt* inundar ▷ *vi (place)* inundarse; *(people):* **to ~ into** inundar; **flooding** *n* inundaciones *fpl;* **floodlight** *n* foco

floor [flɔː*] *n* suelo; *(storey)* piso; *(of sea)* fondo ▷ *vt (question)* dejar sin respuesta; *(: blow)* derribar; **ground ~, first ~** *(us)* planta baja; **first ~, second ~** *(us)* primer piso; **floorboard** *n* tabla; **flooring** *n* suelo; *(material)* solería; **floor show** *n* cabaret *m*

flop [flɔp] *n* fracaso ▷ *vi (fail)* fracasar; *(fall)* derrumbarse; **floppy** *adj* flojo ▷ *n (Comput: also:* **floppy disk)** floppy *m*

flora [ˈflɔːrə] *n* flora

floral [ˈflɔːrl] *adj (pattern)* floreado

florist [ˈflɔrɪst] *n* florista *mf;* **florist's (shop)** *n* floristería

flotation [fləʊˈteɪʃən] *n (of shares)* emisión *f; (of company)* lanzamiento

flour [ˈflaʊə*] *n* harina

flourish [ˈflʌrɪʃ] *vi* florecer ▷ *n* además *m,* movimiento *(ostentoso)*

flow [fləʊ] *n (movement)* flujo; *(of traffic)* circulación *f; (tide)* corriente *f* ▷ *vi (river, blood)* fluir; *(traffic)* circular

flower [ˈflaʊə*] *n* flor *f* ▷ *vi* florecer; **flower bed** *n* macizo; **flowerpot** *n* tiesto

flown [fləʊn] *pp of* **fly**

fl. oz. *abbr* = **fluid ounce**

flu [fluː] *n:* **to have ~** tener la gripe

fluctuate [ˈflʌktjʊeɪt] *vi* fluctuar

fluent [ˈfluːənt] *adj (linguist)* que habla perfectamente; *(speech)* elocuente; **he speaks ~ French, he's ~ in French** domina el francés

fluff [flʌf] *n* pelusa; **fluffy** *adj* de pelo suave

fluid [ˈfluːɪd] *adj (movement)* fluido, líquido; *(situation)* inestable ▷ *n* fluido, líquido; **fluid ounce** *n* onza *f* líquida

fluke [fluːk] *(inf) n* chiripa

flung [flʌŋ] *pt, pp of* **fling**

fluorescent [fluəˈrɛsnt] *adj* fluorescente

fluoride [ˈfluəraɪd] *n* fluoruro

flurry [ˈflʌrɪ] *n (of snow)* temporal *m; ~ of activity* frenesí *m* de actividad

flush [flʌʃ] *n* rubor *m; (fig: of youth etc)* esplendor *m* ▷ *vt* limpiar con agua ▷ *vi* ruborizarse ▷ *adj:* **~ with** a ras de; **to ~ the toilet** hacer funcionar la cisterna

flute [fluːt] *n* flauta

flutter [ˈflʌtə*] *n (of wings)* revoloteo, aleteo; *(fig):* **a ~ of panic/excitement** una oleada de pánico/excitación ▷ *vi* revolotear

fly [flaɪ] *(pt* **flew***, pp* **flown***) n* mosca; *(on trousers: also:* **flies)** bragueta *f* ▷ *vt (plane)* pilot(e)ar; *(cargo)* transportar (en avión); *(distances)* recorrer (en avión) ▷ *vi volar; (passengers)* ir en avión; *(escape)* evadirse; *(flag)* ondear; **fly away, fly off** *vi* emprender el vuelo; **fly-drive** *n:* **fly-drive holiday** vacaciones que incluyen vuelo y alquiler de coche; **flying** *n (activity)* (el) volar; *(action)* vuelo ▷ *adj:* **flying visit** visita relámpago; **with flying colours** con lucimiento; **flying saucer** *n* platillo volante; **flyover** (BRIT) *n* paso a desnivel or superior

FM *abbr (Radio)* (= frequency modulation) FM

foal [fəʊl] *n* potro

foam [fəʊm] *n* espuma ▷ *vi* hacer espuma

focus [ˈfəʊkəs] *(pl* **~es***) n* foco; *(centre)* centro ▷ *vt (field glasses etc)* enfocar ▷ *vi:* **to ~ (on)** enfocar (a); *(issue etc)* centrarse en; **in/out of ~** enfocado/ desenfocado

foetus [ˈfiːtəs] *(us* **fetus)** *n* feto

fog [fɔg] *n* niebla; **foggy** *adj:* **it's foggy** hay niebla, está brumoso; **fog lamp** *(us* **fog light)** *(Aut) n* faro de niebla

foil [fɔɪl] *vt* frustrar ▷ *n* hoja; *(kitchen foil)* papel *m* (de) aluminio; *(complement)* complemento; *(Fencing)* florete *m*

fold [fəuld] n (bend, crease) pliegue m; (Agr) redil m ▷ vt doblar; (arms) cruzar; **fold up** vi plegarse, doblarse; (business) quebrar ▷ vt (map etc) plegar; **folder** n (for papers) carpeta; (Comput) directorio; **folding** adj (chair, bed) plegable

foliage ['fəuliɪdʒ] n follaje m

folk [fəuk] npl gente f ▷ adj popular, folklórico; **folks** npl (family) familia sg, parientes mpl; **folklore** ['fəuklɔːʳ] n folklore m; **folk music** n música folk; **folk song** n canción f popular

follow ['fɔləu] vt seguir ▷ vi seguir; (result) resultar; **to ~ suit** hacer lo mismo; **follow up** vt (letter, offer) responder a; (case) investigar; **follower** n (of person, belief) partidario/a; **following** adj siguiente ▷ n afición f, partidarios mpl; **follow-up** n continuación f

fond [fɔnd] adj (memory, smile etc) cariñoso; (hopes) ilusorio; **to be ~ of** tener cariño a; (pastime, food) ser aficionado a

food [fuːd] n comida; **food mixer** n batidora; **food poisoning** n intoxicación f alimenticia; **food processor** n robot m de cocina; **food stamp** (US) n vale m para comida

fool [fuːl] n tonto/a; (Culin) puré m de frutas con nata ▷ vt engañar ▷ vi (gen) bromear; **fool about, fool around** vi hacer el tonto; **foolish** adj tonto; (careless) imprudente; **foolproof** adj (plan etc) infalible

foot [fut] (pl **feet**) n pie m; (measure) pie m (= 304 mm); (of animal) pata ▷ vt (bill) pagar; **on ~** a pie; **footage** n (Cinema) imágenes fpl; **foot-and-mouth (disease)** [futənd'mauθ] n fiebre f aftosa; **football** n balón m; (game: BRIT) fútbol m; (: US) fútbol m americano; **footballer** (BRIT) = **football player**; **football match** n partido de fútbol; **football player** n (BRIT) futbolista mf; (US) jugador m de fútbol americano; **footbridge** n

puente m para peatones; **foothills** npl estribaciones fpl; **foothold** n pie m firme; **footing** n (fig) posición f; **to lose one's footing** perder el pie; **footnote** n nota (al pie de la página); **footpath** n sendero; **footprint** n huella, pisada; **footstep** n paso; **footwear** n calzado

○ **KEYWORD**

for [fɔːʳ] prep 1 (indicating destination, intention) para; **the train for London** el tren con destino a or de Londres; **he left for Rome** marchó para Roma; **he went for the paper** fue por el periódico; **is this for me?** ¿es esto para mí?; **it's time for lunch** es la hora de comer

2 (indicating purpose) para; **what's it for?** ¿para qué es(to)?; **to pray for peace** rezar por la paz

3 (on behalf of, representing): **the MP for Hove** el diputado por Hove; **he works for the government/a local firm** trabaja para el gobierno/en una empresa local; **I'll ask him for you** se lo pediré por ti; **G for George** G de Gerona

4 (because of) por esta razón; **for fear of being criticized** por temor a ser criticado

5 (with regard to) para; **it's cold for July** hace frío para julio; **he has a gift for languages** tiene don de lenguas

6 (in exchange for) por; **I sold it for £5** lo vendí por £5; **to pay 50 pence for a ticket** pagar 50 peniques por un billete

7 (in favour of): **are you for or against us?** ¿estás con nosotros o contra nosotros?; **I'm all for it** estoy totalmente a favor; **vote for X** vote (a) X

8 (referring to distance): **there are roadworks for 5 km** hay obras en 5 km; **we walked for miles** caminamos kilómetros y kilómetros

9 (referring to time): **he was away for two years** estuvo fuera (durante) dos

años; **it hasn't rained for 3 weeks** no ha llovido durante or en 3 semanas; **I have known her for years** la conozco desde hace años; **can you do it for tomorrow?** ¿lo podrás hacer para mañana?

10 (*with infinitive clauses*): **it is not for me to decide** la decisión no es cosa mía; **it would be best for you to leave** sería mejor que te fueras; **there is still time for you to do it** todavía te queda tiempo para hacerlo; **for this to be possible ...** para que esto sea posible ...

11 (*in spite of*) a pesar de; **for all his complaints** a pesar de sus quejas ▷ *conj* (*since, as: rather formal*) puesto que

forbid [fə'bɪd] (*pt* forbad(e), *pp* forbidden) *vt* prohibir; **to ~ sb to do sth** prohibir a algn hacer algo; **forbidden** *pt of* forbid ▷ *adj* (*food, area*) prohibido; (*word, subject*) tabú

force [fɔːs] *n* fuerza ▷ *vt* forzar; (*push*) meter a la fuerza; **to ~ o.s. to do** hacer un esfuerzo por hacer; **forced** *adj* forzado; **forceful** *adj* enérgico

ford [fɔːd] *n* vado

fore [fɔː*] *n*: **to come to the ~** empezar a destacar; **forearm** *n* antebrazo; **forecast** (*pt, pp* forecast) *n* pronóstico ▷ *vt* pronosticar; **forecourt** *n* patio; **forefinger** *n* (dedo) índice *m*; **forefront** *n*: **in the forefront of** en la vanguardia de; **foreground** *n* primer plano; **forehead** ['fɔrɪd] *n* frente *f*

foreign ['fɔrɪn] *adj* extranjero; (*trade*) exterior; (*object*) extraño; **foreign currency** *n* divisas *fpl*; **foreigner** *n* extranjero/a; **foreign exchange** *n* divisas *fpl*; **Foreign Office** (BRIT) *n* Ministerio de Asuntos Exteriores; **Foreign Secretary** (BRIT) *n* Ministro de Asuntos Exteriores

fore: **foreman** (*irreg*) *n* capataz *m*; (*in construction*) maestro de obras; **foremost** *adj* principal ▷ *adv*: **first**

and foremost ante todo; **forename** *n* nombre *m* (de pila)

forensic [fə'rɛnsɪk] *adj* forense

foresee [fɔː'siː] (*pt* foresaw, *pp* foreseen) *vt* prever; **foreseeable** *adj* previsible

forest ['fɔrɪst] *n* bosque *m*; **forestry** *n* silvicultura

forever [fə'rɛvə*] *adv* para siempre; (*endlessly*) constantemente

foreword ['fɔːwəːd] *n* prefacio

forfeit ['fɔːfɪt] *vt* perder

forgave [fə'geɪv] *pt of* **forgive**

forge [fɔːdʒ] *n* herrería ▷ *vt* (*signature, money*) falsificar; (*metal*) forjar; **forger** *n* falsificador(a) *m/f*; **forgery** *n* falsificación *f*

forget [fə'gɛt] (*pt* forgot, *pp* forgotten) *vt* olvidar ▷ *vi* olvidarse; **forgetful** *adj* despistado

forgive [fə'gɪv] (*pt* forgave, *pp* forgiven) *vt* perdonar; **to ~ sb for sth** perdonar algo a algn

forgot [fə'gɒt] *pt of* **forget**

forgotten [fə'gɒtn] *pp of* **forget**

fork [fɔːk] *n* (*for eating*) tenedor *m*; (*for gardening*) horca; (*of roads*) bifurcación *f* ▷ *vi* (*road*) bifurcarse

forlorn [fə'lɔːn] *adj* (*person*) triste, melancólico; (*place*) abandonado; (*attempt, hope*) desesperado

form [fɔːm] *n* forma; (BRIT Scol) clase *f*; (*document*) formulario ▷ *vt* formar; (*idea*) concebir; (*habit*) adquirir; **in top ~** en plena forma; **to ~ a queue** hacer cola

formal ['fɔːməl] *adj* (*offer, receipt*) por escrito; (*person etc*) correcto; (*occasion, dinner*) de etiqueta; (*dress*) correcto; (*garden*) (de estilo) clásico; **formality** [-'mælɪtɪ] *n* (*procedure*) trámite *m*; corrección *f*; etiqueta

format ['fɔːmæt] *n* formato ▷ *vt* (*Comput*) formatear

formation [fɔː'meɪʃən] *n* formación *f*

former ['fɔːmə*] *adj* anterior; (*earlier*) antiguo; (*ex*) ex; **the ~ ... the latter ...** aquél ... éste ...; **formerly** *adv* antes

formidable ['fɔːmɪdəbl] *adj* formidable

formula ['fɔːmjulə] *n* fórmula

fort [fɔːt] *n* fuerte *m*

forthcoming [fɔːθ'kʌmɪŋ] *adj* próximo, venidero; (help, information) disponible; (character) comunicativo

fortieth ['fɔːtɪɪθ] *adj* cuadragésimo

fortify ['fɔːtɪfaɪ] *vt* (city) fortificar; (person) fortalecer

fortnight ['fɔːtnaɪt] (BRIT) *n* quince días *mpl*; quincena; **fortnightly·** *adj* de cada quince días, quincenal ▷ *adv* cada quince días, quincenalmente

fortress ['fɔːtrɪs] *n* fortaleza

fortunate ['fɔːtʃənɪt] *adj* afortunado; **it is ~ that...** (es una) suerte que...; **fortunately** *adv* afortunadamente

fortune ['fɔːtʃən] *n* suerte *f*; (wealth) fortuna; **fortune-teller** *n* adivino *m*

forty ['fɔːtɪ] *num* cuarenta

forum ['fɔːrəm] *n* foro

forward ['fɔːwəd] *adj* (movement, position) avanzado; (front) delantero; (in time) adelantado; (not shy) atrevido ▷ *n* (Sport) delantero ▷ *vt* (letter) remitir; (career) promocionar; **to move ~** avanzar; **forwarding address** *n* destinatario; **forward(s)** *adv* (hacia) adelante; **forward slash** *n* barra diagonal

fossil ['fɔsl] *n* fósil *m*

foster ['fɔstə*] *vt* (child) acoger en una familia; fomentar; **foster child** *n* hijo/a adoptivo/a; **foster mother** *n* madre *f* adoptiva

fought [fɔːt] *pt, pp of* **fight**

foul [faul] *adj* (weather, smell etc) asqueroso; (language) grosero; (temper) malísimo ▷ *n* (Sport) falta ▷ *vt* (dirty) ensuciar; **foul play** *n* (Law) muerte *f* violenta

found [faund] *pt, pp of* **find** ▷ *vt* fundar; **foundation** [-'deɪʃən] *n* (act) fundación *f*; (basis) base *f*; (also: **foundation cream**) crema base; **foundations** *npl* (of building)

cimientos *mpl*

founder ['faundə*] *n* fundador(a) *m/f* ▷ *vi* hundirse

fountain ['fauntɪn] *n* fuente *f*; **fountain pen** *n* (pluma) estilográfica (SP), pluma-fuente *f* (LAM)

four [fɔː*] *num* cuatro; **on all ~s** a gatas; **four-letter word** *n* taco; **four-poster** *n* (also: **four-poster bed**) cama de columnas; **fourteen** *num* catorce; **fourteenth** *adj* decimocuarto; **fourth** *num* cuarto; **four-wheel drive** *n* tracción *f* a las cuatro ruedas

fowl [faul] *n* ave *f* (de corral)

fox [fɔks] *n* zorro ▷ *vt* confundir

foyer ['fɔɪeɪ] *n* vestíbulo

fraction ['frækʃən] *n* fracción *f*

fracture ['fræktʃə*] *n* fractura

fragile ['frædʒaɪl] *adj* frágil

fragment ['frægmənt] *n* fragmento

fragrance ['freɪgrəns] *n* fragancia

frail [freɪl] *adj* frágil; (person) débil

frame [freɪm] *n* (Tech) armazón *m*; (of person) cuerpo; (of picture, door etc) marco; (of spectacles: also: **~s**) montura ▷ *vt* enmarcar; **framework** *n* marco

France [frɑːns] *n* Francia

franchise ['fræntʃaɪz] *n* (Pol) derecho de votar, sufragio; (Comm) licencia, concesión *f*

frank [fræŋk] *adj* franco ▷ *vt* (letter) franquear; **frankly** *adv* francamente

frantic ['fræntɪk] *adj* (distraught) desesperado; (hectic) frenético

fraud [frɔːd] *n* fraude *m*; (person) impostor/a *m/f*

fraught [frɔːt] *adj*: **~ with** lleno de

fray [freɪ] *vi* deshilacharse

freak [friːk] *n* (person) fenómeno; (event) suceso anormal

freckle ['frekl] *n* peca

free [friː] *adj* libre; (gratis) gratuito ▷ *vt* (prisoner etc) poner en libertad; (jammed object) soltar; **~ (of charge), for ~** gratis; **freedom** *n* libertad *f*; **Freefone®** *n* número gratuito; **free gift** *n* prima; **free kick** *n* tiro libre; **freelance** *adj* independiente

▷ *adv* por cuenta propia; **freely** *adv*
libremente; (*liberally*) generosamente;
Freepost® *n* porte pagado;
free-range *adj* (*hen, eggs*) de granja;
freeway (*US*) *n* autopista; **free will** *n*
libre albedrío; **of one's own free will**
por su propia voluntad

freeze [friːz] (*pt* **froze**, *pp* **frozen**) *vi*
(*weather*) helar; (*liquid, pipe, person*)
helarse, congelarse ▷ *vt* helar; (*food,
prices, salaries*) congelar ▷ *n* helada; (*on
arms, wages*) congelación *f*; **freezer** *n*
congelador *m*, freezer *m* (*SC*)

freezing ['friːzɪŋ] *adj* helado; **three
degrees below** ~ tres grados bajo
cero; **freezing point** *n* punto de
congelación

freight [freɪt] *n* (*goods*) carga; (*money
charged*) flete *m*; **freight train** (*US*) *n*
tren *m* de mercancías

French [frɛntʃ] *adj* francés/esa ▷ *n*
(*Ling*) francés *m*; **the French** *npl* los
franceses; **French bean** *n* judía
verde; **French bread** *n* pan francés;
French dressing *n* (*Culin*) vinagreta;
French fried potatoes, French fries
(*US*) *npl* patatas *fpl* (*SP*) or papas *fpl*
(*LAM*) fritas; **Frenchman** (*irreg*) *n*
francés *m*; **Frenchwoman** (*irreg*) *n*
francesa; **French stick** *n* barra de pan;
French window *n* puerta de cristal

frenzy ['frɛnzɪ] *n* frenesí *m*

frequency ['friːkwənsɪ] *n* frecuencia

frequent [*adj* 'friːkwənt, *vb*
frɪ'kwɛnt] *adj* frecuente ▷ *vt*
frecuentar; **frequently** [~əntlɪ] *adv*
frecuentemente, a menudo

fresh [frɛʃ] *adj* fresco; (*bread*) tierno;
(*new*) nuevo; **freshen** *vi* (*wind, air*)
soplar más recio; **freshen up** *vi*
(*person*) arreglarse, lavarse; **fresher**
(*BRIT: inf*) *n* (*Univ*) estudiante *mf* de
primer año; **freshly** *adv* (*made, painted
etc*) recién; **freshman** (*US: irreg*) *n* =
fresher; **freshwater** *adj* (*fish*) de
agua dulce

fret [frɛt] *vi* inquietarse

Fri *abbr* (= *Friday*) vier

friction ['frɪkʃən] *n* fricción *f*

Friday ['fraɪdɪ] *n* viernes *m inv*

fridge [frɪdʒ] (*BRIT*) *n* frigorífico
(*SP*), nevera (*SP*), refrigerador *m* (*LAM*),
heladera (*RPL*)

fried [fraɪd] *adj* frito

friend [frɛnd] *n* amigo/a; **friendly**
adj simpático; (*government*) amigo;
(*place*) acogedor(a); (*match*) amistoso;
friendship *n* amistad *f*

fries [fraɪz] (*esp US*) *npl* = **French fried
potatoes**

frigate ['frɪgɪt] *n* fragata

fright [fraɪt] *n* (*terror*) terror *m*; (*scare*)
susto; **to take** ~ asustarse; **frighten**
vt asustar; **frightened** *adj* asustado;
frightening *adj* espantoso; **frightful**
adj espantoso, horrible

frill [frɪl] *n* volante *m*

fringe [frɪndʒ] *n* (*BRIT: of hair*)
flequillo; (*on lampshade etc*) flecos *mpl*;
(*of forest etc*) borde *m*, margen *m*

Frisbee® ['frɪzbɪ] *n* frisbee® *m*

fritter ['frɪtə*] *n* buñuelo

frivolous ['frɪvələs] *adj* frívolo

fro [frəʊ] *see* **to**

frock [frɒk] *n* vestido

frog [frɒg] *n* rana; **frogman** (*irreg*) *n*
hombre-rana *m*

○ **KEYWORD**

from [frɒm] *prep* **1** (*indicating starting
place*) de, desde; **where do you come
from?** ¿de dónde eres?; **from London
to Glasgow** de Londres a Glasgow;
to escape from sth/sb escaparse de
algo/algn

2 (*indicating origin etc*) de; **a letter/
telephone call from my sister** una
carta/llamada de mi hermana; **tell
him from me that ...** dígale de mi
parte que ...

3 (*indicating time*) from **one o'clock
to** *or* **until** *or* **till two** de(sde) la una a
or hasta las dos; **from January (on)** a
partir de enero

4 (*indicating distance*) de; **the hotel is**

1 km from the beach el hotel está a 1 km de la playa

5 (indicating price, number etc) de; **prices range from £10 to £50** los precios van desde £10 a/hasta £50; **the interest rate was increased from 9% to 10%** el tipo de interés fue incrementado en un 9% a un 10%

6 (indicating difference) de; **he can't tell red from green** no sabe distinguir el rojo del verde; **to be different from sb/sth** ser diferente a algn/algo

7 (because of, on the basis of): **from what he says** por lo que dice; **weak from hunger** debilitado por el hambre

front [frʌnt] n (foremost part) parte f delantera; (of house) fachada f; (of dress) delantero; (promenade: also: **sea ~**) paseo marítimo; (Mil, Pol, Meteorology) frente m; (fig: appearances) apariencias fpl ▷ adj (wheel, leg) delantero; (row, line) primero; **in ~ (of)** delante (de)

front door n puerta principal; **frontier** ['frʌntɪə*] n frontera; **front page** n primera plana; **front-wheel drive** n tracción f delantera

frost [frɔst] n helada; (also: **hoar~**) escarcha; **frostbite** n congelación f; **frosting** n (esp us: icing) glaseado; **frosty** adj (weather) de helada; (welcome etc) glacial

froth [frɔθ] n espuma

frown [fraun] vi fruncir el ceño

froze [frəuz] pt of **freeze**

frozen ['frəuzn] pp of **freeze**

fruit [fru:t] n inv fruta; (fig) fruto; resultados mpl; **fruit juice** n zumo (SP) or jugo (LAM) de fruta; **fruit machine** (BRIT) n máquina f tragaperras; **fruit salad** n macedonia (SP) or ensalada (LAM) de frutas

frustrate [frʌs'treɪt] vt frustrar; **frustrated** adj frustrado

fry [fraɪ] (pt, pp **fried**) vt freír; **small ~** gente f menuda; **frying pan** n sartén f

ft. abbr = **foot; feet**

fudge [fʌdʒ] n (Culin) caramelo blando

fuel [fjuəl] n (for heating) combustible m; (coal) carbón m; (wood) leña; (for engine) carburante m; **fuel tank** n depósito de combustible

fulfil [ful'fɪl] vt (function) cumplir con; (condition) satisfacer; (wish, desire) realizar

full [ful] adj lleno; (fig) pleno; (complete) completo; (maximum) máximo; (information) detallado; (price) íntegro; (skirt) amplio ▷ adv: **to know ~ well that** saber perfectamente que; **I'm ~ (up)** no puedo más; **~ employment** pleno empleo; **a ~ two hours** dos horas completas; **at ~ speed** a máxima velocidad; **in ~** (reproduce, quote) íntegramente; **full-length** adj (novel etc) entero; (coat) largo; (portrait) de cuerpo entero; **full moon** n luna llena; **full-scale** adj (attack, war) en gran escala; (model) de tamaño natural; **full stop** n punto; **full-time** adj (work) de tiempo completo ▷ adv: **to work full-time** trabajar a tiempo completo; **fully** adv completamente; (at least) por lo menos

fumble ['fʌmbl] vi: **to ~ with** manejar torpemente

fume [fju:m] vi (rage) estar furioso; **fumes** npl humo, gases mpl

fun [fʌn] n (amusement) diversión f; **to have ~** divertirse; **for ~** en broma; **to make ~ of** burlarse de

function ['fʌŋkʃən] n función f ▷ vi funcionar

fund [fʌnd] n fondo; (reserve) reserva; **funds** npl (money) fondos mpl

fundamental [fʌndə'mentl] adj fundamental

funeral ['fju:nərəl] n (burial) entierro; (ceremony) funerales mpl; **funeral director** n director(a) m/f de pompas fúnebres; **funeral parlour** (BRIT) n funeraria

funfair ['fʌnfɛə*] (BRIT) n parque m de atracciones

fungus ['fʌŋɡəs] (pl **fungi**) n hongo; (mould) moho

funnel ['fʌnl] n embudo; (of ship) chimenea

funny ['fʌnɪ] adj gracioso, divertido; (strange) curioso, raro

fur [fəː*] n piel f; (BRIT: in kettle etc) sarro; **fur coat** n abrigo de pieles

furious ['fjuərɪəs] adj furioso; (effort) violento

furnish ['fəːnɪʃ] vt amueblar; (supply) suministrar; (information) facilitar; **furnishings** npl muebles mpl

furniture ['fəːnɪtʃə*] n muebles mpl; **piece of ~** mueble m

furry ['fəːrɪ] adj peludo

further ['fəːðə*] adj (new) nuevo, adicional ▷ adv más lejos; (more) más; (moreover) además ▷ vt promover, adelantar; **further education** n educación f superior; **furthermore** adv además

furthest ['fəːðɪst] superlative of **far**

fury ['fjuərɪ] n furia

fuse [fjuːz] (us **fuze**) n fusible m; (for bomb etc) mecha ▷ vt (metal) fundir; (fig) fusionar ▷ vi fundirse; fusionarse; (BRIT Elec): **to ~ the lights** fundir los plomos; **fuse box** n caja de fusibles

fusion ['fjuːʒən] n fusión f

fuss [fʌs] n (excitement) conmoción f; (trouble) alboroto; **to make a ~** armar un lío or jaleo; **to make a ~ of sb** mimar a algn; **fussy** adj (person) exigente; (too ornate) recargado

future ['fjuːtʃə*] adj futuro; (coming) venidero ▷ n futuro; (prospects) porvenir m; **in ~** de ahora en adelante; **futures** npl (Comm) operaciones fpl a término, futuros mpl

fuze [fjuːz] (us) = **fuse**

fuzzy ['fʌzɪ] adj (Phot) borroso; (hair) muy rizado

g

G [dʒiː] n (Mus) sol m

g. abbr (= gram(s)) gr.

gadget ['gædʒɪt] n aparato

Gaelic ['geɪlɪk] adj, n (Ling) gaélico

gag [gæg] n (on mouth) mordaza; (joke) chiste m ▷ vt amordazar

gain [geɪn] n: ~ **(in)** aumento (de); (profit) ganancia ▷ vt ganar ▷ vi (watch) adelantarse; **to ~ from/by sth** sacar provecho de algo; **to ~ on sb** ganar terreno a algn; **to ~ 3 lbs (in weight)** engordar 3 libras

gal. abbr = **gallon**

gala ['gɑːlə] n fiesta

galaxy ['gæləksɪ] n galaxia

gale [geɪl] n (wind) vendaval m

gall bladder ['gɔːl-] n vesícula biliar

gallery ['gælərɪ] n (also: **art ~**: public) pinacoteca; (: private) galería de arte; (for spectators) tribuna

gallon ['gæln] n galón m (BRIT = 4.546 litros, US = 3.785 litros)

gallop ['gæləp] n galope m ▷ vi galopar

gallstone ['gɔːlstəun] n cálculo

biliario

gamble ['gæmbl] n (risk) riesgo ▷ vt jugar, apostar ▷ vi (take a risk) jugárselas; (bet) apostar; **to ~ on** apostar a; (success etc) contar con; **gambler** n jugador/a m/f; **gambling** n juego

game [geɪm] n juego; (match) partido; (of cards) partida; (Hunting) caza ▷ adj (willing): **to be ~ for anything** atreverse a todo; **big ~** caza mayor (contest) juegos; (BRIT: Scol) deportes mpl; **games console** [geɪmz-] n consola de juegos; **game show** n programa m concurso m, concurso

gammon ['gæmən] n (bacon) tocino ahumado; (ham) jamón m ahumado

gang [gæŋ] n (of criminals) pandilla; (of friends etc) grupo; (of workmen) brigada

gangster ['gæŋstə*] n gángster m

gap [gæp] n vacío (SP), hueco (LAM); (in trees, traffic) claro; (in time) intervalo; (difference): **~ (between)** diferencia (entre)

gape [geɪp] vi mirar boquiabierto; (shirt etc) abrirse (completamente)

gap year n año sabático (antes de empezar a estudiar en la universidad)

garage ['gærɑːʒ] n garaje m; (for repairs) taller m; **garage sale** n venta de objetos usados (en el jardín de una casa particular)

garbage ['gɑːbɪdʒ] (US) n basura; (inf: nonsense) tonterías fpl; **garbage can** n cubo o bote m (MEX) or tacho (SC) de la basura; **garbage collector** (US) n basurero/a

garden ['gɑːdn] n jardín m; **gardens** npl (park) parque m; **garden centre** (BRIT) n centro de jardinería; **gardener** n jardinero/a; **gardening** n jardinería

garlic ['gɑːlɪk] n ajo

garment ['gɑːmənt] n prenda (de vestir)

garnish ['gɑːnɪʃ] vt (Culin) aderezar

garrison ['gærɪsn] n guarnición f

gas [gæs] n gas m; (fuel) combustible m; (us: gasoline) gasolina ▷ vt asfixiar con gas; **gas cooker** (BRIT) n cocina de gas; **gas cylinder** n bombona de gas; **gas fire** n estufa de gas

gasket ['gæskɪt] n (Aut) junta de culata

gasoline ['gæsəliːn] (US) n gasolina

gasp [gɑːsp] n boqueada; (of shock etc) grito sofocado ▷ vi (pant) jadear

gas: gas pedal n (esp us) acelerador m; **gas station** (us) n gasolinera; **gas tank** (US) n (Aut) depósito (de gasolina)

gate [geɪt] n puerta; (iron gate) verja

gateau ['gætəu] (pl **~x**) n tarta

gatecrash ['geɪtkræʃ] (BRIT) vt colarse en

gateway ['geɪtweɪ] n puerta

gather ['gæðə*] vt (flowers, fruit) coger (SP), recoger; (assemble) reunir; (pick up) recoger; (Sewing) fruncir; (understand) entender ▷ vi (assemble) reunirse; **to ~ speed** ganar velocidad; **gathering** n reunión f, asamblea

gauge [geɪdʒ] n (instrument) indicador m ▷ vt medir; (fig) juzgar

gave [geɪv] pt of **give**

gay [geɪ] adj (homosexual) gay; (joyful) alegre; (colour) vivo

gaze [geɪz] n mirada fija ▷ vi: **to ~ at sth** mirar algo fijamente

GB abbr = **Great Britain**

GCSE (BRIT) n abbr (= General Certificate of Secondary Education) examen de reválida que se hace a los 16 años

gear [gɪə*] n equipo, herramientas fpl; (Tech) engranaje m; (Aut) velocidad f, marcha f; (fig: adapt): **to ~ sth to** adaptar or ajustar algo a; **top** or **high** (US)/**low** ~ cuarta/primera velocidad; **in ~** en marcha; **gear up** vi prepararse; **gear box** n caja de cambios; **gear lever** n palanca de cambio; **gear shift** (us) n = **gear lever**; **gear stick** n (BRIT) palanca de cambios

geese [giːs] npl of **goose**

gel [dʒɛl] n gel m

gem [dʒɛm] n piedra preciosa

Gemini ['dʒɛmɪnaɪ] n Géminis m, Gemelos mpl

gender ['dʒɛndə*] n género

gene [dʒiːn] n gen(e)m

general ['dʒɛnərl] n general m ▷ adj general; **in ~** en general; **general anaesthetic** (US **general anesthetic**) n anestesia general; **general election** n elecciones fpl generales; **generalize** vi generalizar; **generally** adv generalmente, en general; **general practitioner** n médico general; **general store** n tienda (que vende de todo) (LAM, SP), almacén m (SC, SP)

generate ['dʒɛnəreɪt] vt (Elec) generar; (jobs, profits) producir

generation [dʒɛnə'reɪʃən] n generación f

generator ['dʒɛnəreɪtə*] n generador m

generosity [dʒɛnə'rɔsɪtɪ] n generosidad f

generous ['dʒɛnərəs] adj generoso

genetic [dʒɪ'nɛtɪk] adj: **~ engineering** ingeniería f genética; **~ fingerprinting** identificación f genética; **genetically modified** adj transgénico; **genetics** n genética

genitals ['dʒɛnɪtlz] npl (órganos mpl) genitales mpl

genius ['dʒiːnɪəs] n genio

genome ['giːnəʊm] n genoma m

gent [dʒɛnt] n abbr (BRIT inf) =**gentleman**

gentle ['dʒɛntl] adj apacible, dulce; (animal) manso; (breeze, curve etc) suave
▌ Be careful not to translate **gentle** by the Spanish word gentil.

gentleman ['dʒɛntlmən] (irreg) n señor m; (well-bred man) caballero

gently ['dʒɛntlɪ] adv dulcemente, suavemente

gents [dʒɛnts] n aseos mpl (de caballeros)

genuine ['dʒɛnjuɪn] adj auténtico; (person) sincero; **genuinely** adv

sinceramente

geographic(al) [dʒɪə'græfɪk(l)] adj geográfico

geography [dʒɪ'ɔgrəfɪ] n geografía

geology [dʒɪ'ɔlədʒɪ] n geología

geometry [dʒɪ'ɔmətrɪ] n geometría

geranium [dʒɪ'reɪnjəm] n geranio

gerbil ['dʒɜːbɪl] n gerbo

geriatric [dʒɛrɪ'ætrɪk] adj, n geriátrico/a m/f

germ [dʒɜːm] n (microbe) microbio, bacteria; (seed, fig) germen m

German ['dʒɜːmən] adj alemán/ana
▷ n alemán/ana m/f; (Ling) alemán m; **German measles** n rubéola

Germany ['dʒɜːmənɪ] n Alemania

gesture ['dʒɛstjə*] n gesto; (symbol) muestra

⬡ KEYWORD

get [gɛt] (pt, pp **got**, pp **gotten** (US)) vi
1 (become, be) ponerse, volverse; **to get old/tired** envejecer/cansarse; **to get drunk** emborracharse; **to get dirty** ensuciarse; **when do I get paid?** ¿cuándo me pagan or se me paga?; **it's getting late** se está haciendo tarde
2 (go): **to get to/from** llegar a/de; **to get home** llegar a casa
3 (begin) empezar a; **to get to know sb** (llegar a) conocer a algn; **I'm getting to like him** me está empezando a gustar; **let's get going** or **started** ¡vamos (a empezar)!
4 (modal aux vb): **you've got to do it** tienes que hacerlo
▷ vt **1**: **to get sth done** (finish) terminar algo; (have done) mandar hacer algo; **to get one's hair cut** cortarse el pelo; **to get the car going** or **to go** arrancar el coche; **to get sb to do sth** conseguir or hacer que algn haga algo; **to get sth/sb ready** preparar algo/a algn
2 (obtain: money, permission, results) conseguir; (find: job, flat) encontrar; (fetch: person, doctor) buscar; (object) ir a buscar, traer; **to get sth for sb**

conseguir algo para algn; **get me Mr Jones, please** (Tel) póngame (SP) or comuníqueme (LAM) con el Sr. Jones, por favor; **can I get you a drink?** ¿quieres algo de beber?

3 (receive: present, letter) recibir; (acquire: reputation) alcanzar; (: prize) ganar; **what did you get for your birthday?** ¿qué te regalaron por tu cumpleaños?; **how much did you get for the painting?** ¿cuánto sacaste por el cuadro?

4 (catch) coger (SP), agarrar (LAM); (hit: target etc) dar en; **to get sb by the arm/throat** coger or agarrar a algn por el brazo/cuello; **get him!** ¡cógelo! (SP), ¡atrápalo! (LAM); **the bullet got him in the leg** la bala le dio en la pierna

5 (take, move) llevar; **to get sth to sb** hacer llegar algo a algn; **do you think we'll get it through the door?** ¿crees que lo podremos meter por la puerta?

6 (catch, take: plane, bus etc) coger (SP), tomar (LAM); **where do I get the train for Birmingham?** ¿dónde se coge or se toma el tren para Birmingham?

7 (understand) entender; (hear) oír; **I've got it!** ¡ya lo tengo!, ¡eureka!; **I don't get your meaning** no te entiendo; **I'm sorry, I didn't get your name** lo siento, no cogí tu nombre

8 (have, possess): **to have got** tener

get away vi marcharse; (escape) escaparse

get away with vt fus hacer impunemente

get back vi (return) volver ▷ vt recobrar

get in vi entrar; (train) llegar; (arrive home) volver a casa, regresar

get into vt fus entrar en; (vehicle) subir a; **to get into a rage** enfadarse

get off vi (from train etc) bajar; (depart: person, car) marcharse ▷ vt (remove) quitar ▷ vt fus (train, bus) bajar de

get on vi (at exam etc): **how are you getting on?** ¿cómo te va?; (agree): **to**

get on (with) llevarse bien (con) ▷ vt fus subir a

get out vi salir; (of vehicle) bajar ▷ vt sacar

get out of vt fus salir de; (duty etc) escaparse de

get over vt fus (illness) recobrarse de

get through vi (Tel) lograr comunicarse

get up vi (rise) levantarse ▷ vt fus subir

getaway ['getəweɪ] n fuga

Ghana ['gɑːnə] n Ghana

ghastly ['gɑːstlɪ] adj horrible

ghetto ['getəu] n gueto

ghost [gəust] n fantasma m

giant ['dʒaɪənt] n gigante mf ▷ adj gigantesco, gigante

gift [gɪft] n regalo; (ability) talento; **gifted** adj dotado; **gift shop** (US **gift store**) n tienda de regalos; **gift token**, **gift voucher** n vale m canjeable por un regalo

gig [gɪg] n (inf: concert) actuación f

gigabyte ['dʒɪgəbaɪt] n gigabyte m

gigantic [dʒaɪ'gæntɪk] adj gigantesco

giggle ['gɪgl] vi reírse tontamente

gills [gɪlz] npl (of fish) branquias fpl, agallas fpl

gilt [gɪlt] adj, n dorado

gimmick ['gɪmɪk] n truco

gin [dʒɪn] n ginebra

ginger ['dʒɪndʒə*] n jengibre m

gipsy ['dʒɪpsɪ] n = **gypsy**

giraffe [dʒɪ'rɑːf] n jirafa

girl [gəːl] n (small) niña; (young woman) chica, joven f, muchacha; (daughter) hija; **an English ~** una (chica) inglesa; **girl band** n (grupo musical de chicas); **girlfriend** n (of girl) amiga; (of boy) novia; **Girl Scout** (US) n = **Girl Guide**

gist [dʒɪst] n lo esencial

give [gɪv] (pt **gave**, pp **given**) vt dar; (deliver) entregar; (as gift) regalar ▷ vi (break) romperse; (stretch: fabric) dar

de sí; **to ~ sb sth**, **~ sth to sb** dar
algo a algn; **give away** vt (give free)
regalar; (betray) traicionar; (disclose)
revelar; **give back** vt devolver; **give
in** vi ceder ▷ vt entregar; **give out** vt
distribuir; **give up** vi rendirse, darse
por vencido ▷ vt renunciar a; **to give
up smoking** dejar de fumar; **to give
o.s. up** entregarse

given ['gɪvn] pp of **give** ▷ adj
(fixed: time, amount) determinado
▷ conj: **~ (that)** ... dado (que) ...; **~
the circumstances** ... dadas las
circunstancias ...

glacier ['glæsɪə*] n glaciar m

glad [glæd] adj contento; **gladly** ['-lɪ]
adv con mucho gusto

glamour ['glæmə*] (us **glamor**) n
encanto, atractivo; **glamorous** adj
encantador(a), atractivo

glance [glɑːns] n ojeada, mirada
▷ vi: **to ~ at** echar una ojeada a

gland [glænd] n glándula

glare [glɛə*] n (of anger) mirada feroz;
(of light) deslumbramiento, brillo; **to
be in the ~ of publicity** ser el foco de
la atención pública ▷ vi deslumbrar;
to ~ at mirar con odio a; **glaring** adj
(mistake) manifiesto

glass [glɑːs] n vidrio, cristal m;
(for drinking) vaso; (: with stem) copa;
glasses npl (spectacles) gafas fpl

glaze [gleɪz] vt (window) poner
cristales a; (pottery) vidriar ▷ n
vidriado

gleam [gliːm] vi brillar

glen [glen] n cañada

glide [glaɪd] vi deslizarse; (Aviat: birds)
planear; **glider** n (Aviat) planeador m

glimmer ['glɪmə*] n luz f tenue; (of
interest) muestra; (of hope) rayo

glimpse [glɪmps] n vislumbre m ▷ vt
vislumbrar, entrever

glint [glɪnt] vi centellear

glisten ['glɪsn] vi relucir, brillar

glitter ['glɪtə*] vi relucir, brillar

global ['gləʊbl] adj mundial;
globalization n globalización f;

global warming n (re)calentamiento
global or de la tierra

globe [gləʊb] n globo; (model) globo
terráqueo

gloom [gluːm] n oscuridad f; (sadness)
tristeza; **gloomy** adj (dark) oscuro;
(sad) triste; (pessimistic) pesimista

glorious ['glɔːrɪəs] adj glorioso;
(weather etc) magnífico

glory ['glɔːrɪ] n gloria

gloss [glɒs] n (shine) brillo; (paint)
pintura de aceite

glossary ['glɒsərɪ] n glosario

glossy ['glɒsɪ] adj lustroso; (magazine)
de lujo

glove [glʌv] n guante m; **glove
compartment** n (Aut) guantera

glow [gləʊ] vi brillar

glucose ['gluːkəʊs] n glucosa

glue [gluː] n goma (de pegar),
cemento ▷ vt pegar

GM adj abbr (= genetically modified)
transgénico

gm abbr (= gram) g

GMO n abbr (= genetically modified
organism) organismo transgénico

GMT abbr (= Greenwich Mean Time) GMT

gnaw [nɔː] vt roer

go [gəʊ] (pt **went**, pp **gone**, pl
~es) vi ir; (travel) viajar; (depart)
irse, marcharse; (work) funcionar,
marchar; (be sold) venderse; (time)
pasar; (fit, suit): **to ~ with** hacer juego
con; (become) ponerse; (break etc)
estropearse, romperse > n (try)
tentativa; (turn) turno; **to have a
~ (at)** probar suerte (con); **to be
on the ~** no parar; **whose ~ is it?** ¿a
quién le toca?; **he's ~ing to do it** va a
hacerlo; **to ~ for a walk** ir de paseo;
to ~ dancing ir a bailar; **how did it ~?**
¿qué tal salió or resultó?, ¿cómo ha ido?;
to ~ round the back pasar por detrás;
go ahead vi seguir adelante; **go away**
vi irse, marcharse; **go back** vi volver;
go by vi (time) pasar ▷ vt fus guiarse
por; **go down** vi bajar; (ship) hundirse;
(sun) ponerse ▷ vt fus bajar; **go for** vt
fus (fetch) ir por; (like) gustar; (attack)

atacar; **go in** vi entrar; **go into** vt fus entrar en; (*investigate*) investigar; (*embark on*) dedicarse a; **go off** vi irse, marcharse; (*food*) pasarse; (*explode*) estallar; (*event*) realizarse ▷ vt fus dejar de gustar; **I'm going off him/the idea** ya no me gusta tanto él/la idea; **go on** vi (*continue*) seguir, continuar; (*happen*) pasar, ocurrir; **to go on doing sth** seguir haciendo algo; **go out** vi salir; (*fire, light*) apagarse; **go over** vi (*ship*) zozobrar ▷ vt fus (*check*) revisar; **go past** vi, vt fus pasar; **go round** vi (*circulate: news, rumour*) correr; (*suffice*) alcanzar, bastar; (*revolve*) girar, dar vueltas; (*visit*): **to go round to sb's** pasar a ver (a algn); **to go round (by)** (*make a detour*) dar la vuelta (por); **go through** vt fus (*town etc*) atravesar; **go up** vi, vt fus subir; **go with** vt fus (*accompany*) ir con, acompañar a; **go without** vt fus pasarse sin

go-ahead ['gəuəhɛd] adj (*person*) dinámico; (*firm*) innovador(a) ▷ n luz f verde

goal [gəul] n meta; (*score*) gol m; **goalkeeper** n portero; **goal-post** n poste m (de la portería)

goat [gəut] n cabra

gobble ['gɔbl] vt (*also:* ~ **down**, ~ **up**) tragarse, engullir

God [gɔd] n Dios m; **godchild** n ahijado/a; **goddaughter** n ahijada; **goddess** n diosa; **godfather** n padrino; **godmother** n madrina; **godson** n ahijado

goggles ['gɔglz] npl gafas fpl

going ['gəuɪŋ] n (*conditions*) estado del terreno ▷ adj: **the ~ rate** la tarifa corriente or en vigor

gold [gəuld] n oro ▷ adj: de oro; **golden** adj (*made of gold*) de oro; (*gold in colour*) dorado; **goldfish** n pez m de colores; **goldmine** n (*also fig*) mina de oro; **gold-plated** adj chapado en oro

golf [gɔlf] n golf m; **golf ball** n (*for game*) pelota de golf; (*on typewriter*) esfera; **golf club** n club m de golf;

(*stick*) palo (de golf); **golf course** n campo de golf; **golfer** n golfista mf

gone [gɔn] pp of **go**

gong [gɔŋ] n gong m

good [gud] adj bueno; (*pleasant*) agradable; (*kind*) bueno, amable; (*well-behaved*) educado ▷ n bien m, provecho; **goods** npl (Comm) mercancías fpl; **~!** ¡qué bien!; **to be ~ at** tener aptitud para; **to be ~ for** servir para; **it's ~ for you** te hace bien; **would you be ~ enough to ...?** ¿podría hacerme el favor de ...?, ¿sería tan amable de ...?; **a ~ deal (of)** mucho; **a ~ many** muchos; **to make ~** reparar; **it's no ~ complaining** no vale la pena de quejarse; **for ~** para siempre, definitivamente; **~ morning/ afternoon!** ¡buenos días/buenas tardes!; **~ evening!** ¡buenas noches!; **~ night!** ¡buenas noches!

goodbye [gud'baɪ] excl ¡adiós!; **to say ~ (to)** (*person*) despedirse (de)

good: Good Friday n Viernes m Santo; **good-looking** adj guapo; **good-natured** adj amable, simpático; **goodness** n (*of person*) bondad f; **for goodness sake!** ¡por Dios!; **goodness gracious!** ¡Dios mío!; **goods train** (BRIT) n tren m de mercancías; **goodwill** n buena voluntad f

Google® ['gu:gəl] n Google® m ▷ vi hacer búsquedas en Internet ▷ vt buscar información en Internet sobre

goose [gu:s] (pl **geese**) n ganso, oca

gooseberry ['guzbərɪ] n grosella espinosa; **to play ~** hacer de carabina

goose bumps, goose pimples npl carne f de gallina

gorge [gɔːdʒ] n barranco ▷ vr: **to ~ o.s. (on)** atracarse (de)

gorgeous ['gɔːdʒəs] adj (*thing*) precioso; (*weather*) espléndido; (*person*) guapísimo

gorilla [gə'rɪlə] n gorila m

gosh [gɔʃ] (inf) excl ¡cielos!

gospel ['gɔspl] n evangelio

gossip ['gɔsɪp] n (*scandal*)

got | 402

cotilleo, chismes *mpl*; (*chat*) charla; (*scandalmonger*) cotilla *m/f*, chismoso/a ▷ *vi* cotillear; **gossip column** *n* ecos *mpl* de sociedad

got [gɒt] *pt, pp of* **get**

gotten (*US*) ['gɒtn] *pp of* **get**

gourmet ['guəmeɪ] *n* gastrónomo/a *m/f*

govern ['gʌvən] *vt* gobernar; (*influence*) dominar; **government** *n* gobierno; **governor** *n* gobernador/a *m/f*; (*of school etc*) miembro del consejo; (*of jail*) director(a) *m/f*

gown [gaun] *n* traje *m*; (*of teacher, BRIT: of judge*) toga

G.P. *n abbr* = **general practitioner**

grab [græb] *vt* coger (*SP*), agarrar (*LAM*), arrebatar ▷ *vi*: **to ~ at** intentar agarrar

grace [greɪs] *n* gracia ▷ *vt* honrar; (*adorn*) adornar; **5 days' ~** un plazo de 5 días; **graceful** *adj* grácil, ágil; (*style, shape*) elegante, gracioso; **gracious** ['greɪʃəs] *adj* amable

grade [greɪd] *n* (*quality*) clase *f*, calidad *f*; (*in hierarchy*) grado; (*Scol: mark*) nota; (*us: school class*) curso ▷ *vt* clasificar; **grade crossing** (*US*) *n* paso a nivel; **grade school** (*US*) *n* escuela primaria

gradient ['greɪdɪənt] *n* pendiente *f*

gradual ['grædjuəl] *adj* paulatino; **gradually** *adv* paulatinamente

graduate [*n* 'grædjuɪt, *vb* 'grædjueɪt] *n* (*us: of high school*) graduado/a; (*of university*) licenciado/a ▷ *vi* graduarse; licenciarse; **graduation** [-'eɪʃən] *n* (*ceremony*) entrega del título

graffiti [grə'fi:tɪ] *n* pintadas *fpl*

graft [grɑ:ft] *n* (*Agr, Med*) injerto; (*BRIT: inf*) trabajo duro; (*bribery*) corrupción *f* ▷ *vt* injertar

grain [greɪn] *n* (*single particle*) grano; (*corn*) granos *mpl*, cereales *mpl*; (*of wood*) fibra

gram [græm] *n* gramo

grammar ['græmə*] *n* gramática; **grammar school** (*BRIT*) *n* ≈ instituto

de segunda enseñanza, liceo (*SP*)

gramme [græm] *n* = **gram**

gran [græn] (*inf*) *n* (*BRIT*) abuelita

grand [grænd] *adj* magnífico, imponente; (*wonderful*) estupendo; (*gesture etc*) grandioso; **grandad** (*inf*) *n* = **granddad**; **grandchild** (*pl* **grandchildren**) *n* nieto/a *m/f*; **granddad** (*inf*) *n* yayo, abuelito; **granddaughter** *n* nieta; **grandfather** *n* abuelo; **grandma** (*inf*) *n* yaya, abuelita; **grandmother** *n* abuela; **grandpa** (*inf*) *n* = **granddad**; **grandparents** *npl* abuelos *mpl*; **grand piano** *n* piano de cola; **Grand Prix** ['grɑ̃:'pri:] *n* (*Aut*) gran premio, Grand Prix *m*; **grandson** *n* nieto

granite ['grænɪt] *n* granito

granny ['grænɪ] (*inf*) *n* abuelita, yaya

grant [grɑ:nt] *vt* (*concede*) conceder; (*admit*) reconocer *n* (*Scol*) beca; (*Admin*) subvención *f*; **to take sth/sb for ~ed** dar algo por sentado/no hacer ningún caso a algn

grape [greɪp] *n* uva

grapefruit ['greɪpfru:t] *n* pomelo (*SP, SC*), toronja (*LAM*)

graph [grɑ:f] *n* gráfica; **graphic** ['græfɪk] *adj* gráfico; **graphics** *n* artes *fpl* gráficas ▷ *npl* (*drawings*) dibujos *mpl*

grasp [grɑ:sp] *vt* agarrar, asir; (*understand*) comprender ▷ *n* (*grip*) asimiento; (*understanding*) comprensión *f*

grass [grɑ:s] *n* hierba; (*lawn*) césped *m*; **grasshopper** *n* saltamontes *m inv*

grate [greɪt] *n* parrilla de chimenea ▷ *vi*: **to ~ (on)** chirriar (sobre) ▷ *vt* (*Culin*) rallar

grateful ['greɪtful] *adj* agradecido

grater ['greɪtə*] *n* rallador *m*

gratitude ['grætɪtju:d] *n* agradecimiento

grave [greɪv] *n* tumba ▷ *adj* serio, grave

gravel ['grævl] *n* grava

gravestone ['greɪvstəun] *n* lápida

graveyard ['greɪvjɑːd] n cementerio

gravity ['grævɪtɪ] n gravedad f

gravy ['greɪvɪ] n salsa de carne

gray [greɪ] adj = **grey**

graze [greɪz] vi pacer ▷ vt (touch lightly) rozar; (scrape) raspar ▷ n (Med) abrasión f

grease [griːs] n (fat) grasa; (lubricant) lubricante m ▷ vt engrasar; lubrificar; **greasy** adj grasiento

great [greɪt] adj grande; (inf) magnífico, estupendo; **Great Britain** n Gran Bretaña; **great-grandfather** n bisabuelo; **great-grandmother** n bisabuela; **greatly** adv muy; (with verb) mucho

Greece [griːs] n Grecia

greed [griːd] n (also: ~iness) codicia, avaricia; (for food) gula; (for power etc) avidez f; **greedy** adj avaro; (for food) glotón/ona

Greek [griːk] adj griego ▷ n griego/a; (Ling) griego

green [griːn] adj (also Pol) verde; (inexperienced) novato ▷ n verde m; (stretch of grass) césped m; (Golf) green m **greens** npl (vegetables) verduras fpl; **green card** n (Aut) carta verde; (us: work permit) permiso de trabajo para los extranjeros en EE. UU.; **greengage** n (ciruela) claudia; **greengrocer** (BRIT) n verdulero/a; **greenhouse** n invernadero; **greenhouse effect** n efecto invernadero

Greenland ['griːnlənd] n Groenlandia

green salad n ensalada f (de lechuga, pepino, pimiento verde, etc)

greet [griːt] vt (welcome) dar la bienvenida a; (receive: news) recibir; **greeting** n (welcome) bienvenida; **greeting(s) card** n tarjeta de felicitación

grew [gruː] pt of **grow**

grey [greɪ] (us **gray**) adj gris; (weather) sombrío; **grey-haired** adj canoso; **greyhound** n galgo

grid [grɪd] n reja; (Elec) red f; **gridlock** n (traffic jam) retención f

grief [griːf] n dolor m, pena

grievance ['griːvəns] n motivo de queja, agravio

grieve [griːv] vi afligirse, acongojarse ▷ vt dar pena a; **to ~ for** llorar por

grill [grɪl] n (on cooker) parrilla; (also: mixed ~) parrillada ▷ vt (BRIT) asar a la parrilla; (inf: question) interrogar

grille [grɪl] n reja; (Aut) rejilla

grim [grɪm] adj (place) sombrío; (situation) triste; (person) ceñudo

grime [graɪm] n mugre f, suciedad f

grin [grɪn] n sonrisa abierta ▷ vi sonreír abiertamente

grind [graɪnd] (pt, pp **ground**) vt (coffee, pepper etc) moler; (us: meat) picar; (make sharp) afilar ▷ n (work) rutina

grip [grɪp] n (hold) asimiento; (control) control m, dominio; (of tyre etc): **to have a good/bad ~** agarrrar bien/mal; (handle) asidero; (holdall) maletín m ▷ vt agarrar; (viewer, reader) fascinar; **to get to ~s with** enfrentarse con; **gripping** adj absorbente

grit [grɪt] n (gravilla; (courage) valor m ▷ vt (road) poner gravilla en; **to ~ one's teeth** apretar los dientes

grits [grɪts] (us) npl maíz msg a medio moler

groan [grəun] n gemido; quejido ▷ vi gemir; quejarse

grocer ['grəusə*] n tendero (de ultramarinos (SP)); **groceries** npl comestibles mpl; **grocer's (shop)** n tienda de comestibles or (MEX, CAM) abarrotes, almacén (SC); **grocery** n (shop) tienda de ultramarinos

groin [grɔɪn] n ingle f

groom [gruːm] n mozo/a de cuadra; (also: **bride~**) novio ▷ vt (horse) almohazar; (fig): **to ~ sb for** preparar a algn para; **well-~ed** de buena presencia

groove [gruːv] n ranura, surco

grope [grəup] vi: **to ~ for** buscar a tientas

gross [grəus] adj (neglect, injustice) grave; (vulgar: behaviour) grosero;

(: *appearance*) de mal gusto; (*Comm*) bruto; **grossly** *adv* (*greatly*) enormemente

grotesque [grə'tɛsk] *adj* grotesco

ground [graʊnd] *pt, pp of* **grind**
▷ *n* suelo, tierra *f*; (*Sport*) campo, terreno; (*reason: gen pl*) causa, razón *f*; (*us: also:* **~ wire**) tierra ▷ *vt* (*plane*) mantener en tierra; (*us Elec*) conectar con tierra; **grounds** *npl* (*of coffee etc*) poso; (*gardens etc*) jardines *mpl*, parque *m*; **on the ~** en el suelo; **to the ~** al suelo; **to gain/lose ~** ganar/perder terreno; **ground floor** *n* (*BRIT*) planta baja; **groundsheet** (*BRIT*) *n* tela impermeable; suelo; **groundwork** *n* preparación *f*

group [gru:p] *n* grupo; (*musical*) conjunto ▷ *vt* (*also:* **~ together**) agrupar ▷ *vi* (*also:* **~ together**) agruparse

grouse [graʊs] *n inv* (*bird*) urogallo ▷ *vi* (*complain*) quejarse

grovel ['grɔvl] *vi* (*fig*): **to ~ before** humillarse ante

grow [grəʊ] (*pt* **grew**, *pp* **grown**) *vi* crecer; (*increase*) aumentar; (*expand*) desarrollarse; (*become*) volverse: **to ~ rich/weak** enriquecerse/debilitarse ▷ *vt* cultivar; (*hair, beard*) dejar crecer; **grow on** *vt fus*: **that painting is growing on me** ese cuadro me gusta cada vez más; **grow up** *vi* crecer, hacerse hombre/mujer

growl [graʊl] *vi* gruñir

grown [grəʊn] *pp of* **grow**; **grown-up** *n* adulto/a, mayor *mf*

growth [grəʊθ] *n* crecimiento, desarrollo; (*what has grown*) brote *m*; (*Med*) tumor *m*

grub [grʌb] *n* larva, gusano; (*inf: food*) comida

grubby ['grʌbɪ] *adj* sucio, mugriento

grudge [grʌdʒ] *n* (*motivo de*) rencor *m* ▷ *vt*: **to ~ sb sth** dar algo a algn de mala gana; **to bear sb a ~** guardar rencor a algn

gruelling ['grʊəlɪŋ] (*us* **grueling**) *adj*

penoso, duro

gruesome ['gru:səm] *adj* horrible

grumble ['grʌmbl] *vi* refunfuñar, quejarse

grumpy ['grʌmpɪ] *adj* gruñón/ona

grunt [grʌnt] *vi* gruñir

guarantee [gærən'ti:] *n* garantía ▷ *vt* garantizar

guard [gɑ:d] *n* (*squad*) guardia; (*one man*) guardia *mf*; (*BRIT Rail*) jefe *m* de tren; (*on machine*) dispositivo de seguridad; (*also:* **fire~**) rejilla de protección ▷ *vt* guardar; (*prisoner*) vigilar; **to be on one's ~** estar alerta; **guardian** ['gɑ:dɪən] *n* guardián/ana *m/f*; (*of minor*) tutor(a) *m/f*

guerrilla [gə'rɪlə] *n* guerrillero/a

guess [gɛs] *vi, vt* adivinar; (*us*) suponer ▷ *vt* adivinar; suponer ▷ *n* suposición *f*, conjetura; **to take** *or* **have a ~** tratar de adivinar

guest [gɛst] *n* invitado/a; (*in hotel*) huésped *mf*; **guest house** *n* casa de huéspedes, pensión *f*; **guest room** *n* cuarto de huéspedes

guidance ['gaɪdəns] *n* (*advice*) consejos *mpl*

guide [gaɪd] *n* (*person*) guía *mf*; (*book, fig*) guía; (*also:* **Girl ~**) guía ▷ *vt* (*round museum etc*) guiar; (*lead*) conducir; (*direct*) orientar; **guidebook** *n* guía; **guide dog** *n* perro *m* guía; **guided tour** *n* visita *f* con guía; **guidelines** *npl* (*advice*) directrices *fpl*

guild [gɪld] *n* gremio

guilt [gɪlt] *n* culpabilidad *f*; **guilty** *adj* culpable

guinea pig ['gɪnɪ-] *n* cobaya; (*fig*) conejillo de Indias

guitar [gɪ'tɑ:*] *n* guitarra; **guitarist** *n* guitarrista *m/f*

gulf [gʌlf] *n* golfo; (*abyss*) abismo

gull [gʌl] *n* gaviota

gulp [gʌlp] *vi* tragar saliva ▷ *vt* (*also:* **~ down**) tragarse

gum [gʌm] *n* (*Anat*) encía; (*glue*) goma, cemento; (*sweet*) caramelo de goma; (*also:* **chewing-~**) chicle *m* ▷ *vt* pegar con goma

gun [gʌn] n (small) pistola, revólver m; (shotgun) escopeta; (rifle) fusil m; (cannon) cañón m; **gunfire** n disparos mpl; **gunman** (irreg) n pistolero; **gunpoint** n: **at gunpoint** a mano armada; **gunpowder** n pólvora; **gunshot** n escopetazo

gush [gʌʃ] vi salir a raudales; (person) deshacerse en efusiones

gust [gʌst] n (of wind) ráfaga

gut [gʌt] n intestino; **guts** npl (Anat) tripas fpl; (courage) valor m

gutter ['gʌtə*] n (of roof) canalón m; (in street) cuneta

guy [gaɪ] n (also: **~-rope**) cuerda; (inf: man) tío (sp), tipo; (figure) monigote m

Guy Fawkes' Night [gaɪ'fɔ:ks-] n ver recuadro

gym [dʒɪm] n gimnasio; **gymnasium** n gimnasio mf; **gymnast** n gimnasta mf; **gymnastics** n gimnasia; **gym shoes** npl zapatillas fpl (de deporte)

gynaecologist [gaɪnɪ'kɔlədʒɪst] (us **gynecologist**) n ginecólogo/a

gypsy ['dʒɪpsɪ] n gitano/a

h

haberdashery [hæbə'dæʃərɪ] (BRIT) n mercería

habit ['hæbɪt] n hábito, costumbre f; (drug habit) adicción f; (costume) hábito

habitat ['hæbɪtæt] n hábitat m

hack [hæk] vt (cut) cortar; (slice) tajar ▷ n (pej: writer) escritor(a) m/fa sueldo; **hacker** n (Comput) pirata mf informático/a

had [hæd] pt, pp of **have**

haddock ['hædək] (pl **~** or **~s**) n especie de merluza

hadn't ['hædnt] = **had not**

haemorrhage ['hemərɪdʒ] (us **hemorrhage**) n hemorragia

haemorrhoids ['hemərɔɪdz] (us **hemorrhoids**) npl hemorroides fpl

haggle ['hægl] vi regatear

Hague [heɪg] n: **The ~** La Haya

hail [heɪl] n (also: (fig) lluvia ▷ vt saludar; (taxi) llamar a; (acclaim) ▷ vi granizar; **hailstone** n (piedra de) granizo

hair [heə*] n pelo, cabellos mpl; (one hair) pelo, cabello; (on legs etc) vello

to do one's ~ arreglarse el pelo; **to have grey ~** tener canas *fpl*; **hairband** *n* cinta; **hairbrush** *n* cepillo (para el pelo); **haircut** *n* corte *m* (de pelo); **hairdo** *n* peinado; **hairdresser** *n* peluquero/a; **hairdresser's** *n* peluquería; **hair dryer** *n* secador *m* de pelo; **hair gel** *n* fijador; **hair spray** *n* laca; **hairstyle** *n* peinado; **hairy** *adj* peludo; velludo; (*inf*: *frightening*) espeluznante

hake [heɪk] (*pl* ~ *or* ~**s**) *n* merluza

half [hɑːf] (*pl* **halves**) *n* mitad *f*; (*of beer*) = caña (*SP*), media pinta; (*Rail, Bus*) billete *m* de niño ▷ *adj* medio ▷ *adv* medio, a medias; **two and a ~** dos y media; **~ a dozen** media docena; **~ a pound** media libra; **to cut sth in ~** cortar algo por la mitad; **half board** *n* (*BRIT*: *in hotel*) media pensión; **half-brother** *n* hermanastro; **half day** *n* medio día *m*, media jornada; **half fare** *n* medio pasaje *m*; **half-hearted** *adj* indiferente, poco entusiasta; **half-hour** *n* media hora; **half-price** *adj, adv* a mitad de precio; **half term** *n* (*BRIT*) (*Scol*) vacaciones *fpl* de mediados del trimestre; **half-time** *n* descanso; **halfway** *adv* a medio camino; **halfway through** a mitad de

hall [hɔːl] *n* (*for concerts*) sala; (*entrance way*) hall *m*; vestíbulo

hallmark [ˈhɔːlmɑːk] *n* sello

hallo [haˈləu] *excl* = **hello**

hall of residence (*BRIT*) *n* residencia

Hallowe'en [hæləuˈiːn] *n* víspera de Todos los Santos

● HALLOWE'EN

● La tradición anglosajona dice que en la noche del 31 de octubre, **Hallowe'en**, víspera de Todos los Santos, es posible ver a brujas y fantasmas. En este día los niños se disfrazan y van de puerta en puerta llevando un farol hecho con una calabaza en forma de cabeza

humana. Cuando se les abre la puerta gritan "trick or treat", amenazando con gastar una broma a quien no les dé golosinas o algo de calderilla.

hallucination [həluːsɪˈneɪʃən] *n* alucinación *f*

hallway [ˈhɔːlweɪ] *n* vestíbulo

halo [ˈheɪləu] *n* (*of saint*) halo, aureola

halt [hɔːlt] *n* (*stop*) alto, parada ▷ *vt* parar; interrumpir ▷ *vi* pararse

halve [hɑːv] *vt* partir por la mitad

halves [hɑːvz] *npl of* **half**

ham [hæm] *n* jamón *m* (cocido)

hamburger [ˈhæmbəːgə*] *n* hamburguesa

hamlet [ˈhæmlɪt] *n* aldea

hammer [ˈhæmə*] *n* martillo ▷ *vt* (*nail*) clavar; (*force*): **to ~ an idea into sb/a message home** meter una idea en la cabeza a algn/machacar una idea ▷ *vi* dar golpes

hammock [ˈhæmək] *n* hamaca

hamper [ˈhæmpə*] *vt* estorbar ▷ *n* cesto

hamster [ˈhæmstə*] *n* hámster *m*

hamstring [ˈhæmstrɪŋ] *n* (*Anat*) tendón *m* de la corva

hand [hænd] *n* mano *f*; (*of clock*) aguja; (*writing*) letra; (*worker*) obrero ▷ *vt* dar, pasar; **to give** *or* **lend sb a ~** echar una mano a algn, ayudar a algn; **at ~** a mano; **in ~** (*time*) libre; (*job etc*) entre manos; **on ~** (*person, services*) a mano, al alcance; **to ~** (*information etc*) a mano; **on the one ~ ..., on the other ~ ...** por una parte ... por otra (parte) ...; **hand down** *vt* (*pass, bajar*; (*tradition*) transmitir; (*heirloom*) dejar en herencia; (*US*: *sentence, verdict*) imponer; **hand in** *vt* entregar; **hand out** *vt* distribuir; **hand over** *vt* (*deliver*) entregar; **handbag** *n* bolsa (*SP*), cartera (*LAM*), bolsa (*MEX*) **hand baggage** *n* = **hand luggage**; **handbook** *n* manual *m*; **handbrake** *n* freno de mano; **handcuffs** *npl* esposas *fpl*; **handful**

n puñado
handicap ['hændɪkæp] n
minusvalía; (disadvantage) desventaja;
(Sport) handicap m ▷ vt estorbar; **to be
mentally ~ped** ser mentalmente m/f
discapacitado; **to be physically ~ped**
ser minusválido/a
handkerchief ['hæŋkətʃɪf] n
pañuelo
handle ['hændl] n (of door etc)
tirador m; (of cup etc) asa; (of knife etc)
mango; (for winding) manivela ▷ vt
(touch) tocar; (deal with) encargarse de;
(treat: people) manejar; **"~ with care"**
"(manéjase) con cuidado"; **to fly off
the ~** perder los estribos; **handlebar(s)**
n(pl) manillar m
hand: **hand luggage** n equipaje m
de mano; **handmade** adj hecho a
mano; **handout** n (money etc) limosna;
(leaflet) folleto; **hands-free** adj (phone)
manos libres inv; **hands-free kit** n
manos libres m inv
handsome ['hænsəm] adj guapo;
(building) bello; (fig: profit) considerable
handwriting ['hændraɪtɪŋ] n letra
handy ['hændɪ] adj (close at hand)
a la mano; (tool etc) práctico; (skilful)
hábil, diestro
hang [hæŋ] (pt, pp **hung**) vt colgar;
(criminal: pt, pp **hanged**) ahorcar ▷ vi
(painting, coat etc) colgar; (hair, drapery)
caer; **to get the ~ of sth** (inf) lograr
dominar algo; **hang about** or **around**
vi haraganear; **hang down** vi colgar,
pender; **hang on** vi (wait) esperar;
hang out vt (washing) tender; colgar
▷ vi (inf: live) vivir; (spend time) pasar
el rato; **to hang out of sth** colgar
fuera de algo; **hang round** vi = **hang
around**; **hang up** vi (Tel) colgar ▷ vt
colgar
hanger ['hæŋə*] n percha
hang-gliding ['-glaɪdɪŋ] n vuelo
libre
hangover ['hæŋəuvə*] n (after
drinking) resaca
hankie, hanky ['hæŋkɪ] n abbr =

407 | harm

handkerchief
happen ['hæpən] vi suceder, ocurrir;
(chance): **he ~ed to hear/see** dió la
casualidad de que oyó/vió; **as it ~s** da
la casualidad de que
happily ['hæpɪlɪ] adv (luckily)
afortunadamente; (cheerfully)
alegremente
happiness ['hæpɪnɪs] n felicidad f;
(cheerfulness) alegría
happy ['hæpɪ] adj feliz; (cheerful)
alegre; **to be ~ (with)** estar contento
(con); **to be ~ to do** estar encantado de
hacer; **~ birthday!** ¡feliz cumpleaños!
harass ['hærəs] vt acosar, hostigar;
harassment n persecución f
harbour (us **harbor**) ['hɑːbə*] n
puerto ▷ vt (fugitive) dar abrigo a; (hope
etc) abrigar
hard [hɑːd] adj duro; (difficult) difícil;
(work) arduo; (person) severo; (fact)
innegable ▷ adv (work) mucho, duro;
(think) profundamente; **to look ~ at**
clavar los ojos en; **to try ~** esforzarse;
no ~ feelings! ¡sin rencor(es)!; **to be
~ of hearing** ser duro de oído; **to be
~ done by** ser tratado injustamente;
hardback n libro en cartoné;
hardboard n aglomerado m (de
madera); **hard disk** n (Comput) disco
duro or rígido; **harden** vt endurecer;
(fig) curtir ▷ vi endurecerse; curtirse
hardly ['hɑːdlɪ] adv apenas; **~ ever**
casi nunca
hard: **hardship** n privación f; **hard
shoulder** (BRIT) n (Aut) arcén m; **hard-
up** (inf) adj sin un duro (SP), pelado, sin
un centavo (MEX), pato (SC); **hardware**
n ferretería; (Comput) hardware m;
(Mil) armamento; **hardware shop** (us
hardware store) n ferretería; **hard-
working** adj trabajador(a)
hardy ['hɑːdɪ] adj fuerte; (plant)
resistente
hare [hɛə*] n liebre f
harm [hɑːm] n daño, mal m ▷ vt
(person) hacer daño a; (health, interests)
perjudicar; (thing) dañar; **out of ~'s**

way a salvo; **harmful** adj dañino; **harmless** adj (person) inofensivo; (joke etc) inocente

harmony ['hɑ:mənɪ] n armonía

harness ['hɑ:nɪs] n arreos mpl; (for child) arnés m; (safety harness) arneses mpl ▷ vt (horse) enjaezar; (resources) aprovechar

harp [hɑ:p] n arpa ▷ vi: **to ~ on (about)** machacar (con)

harsh [hɑ:ʃ] adj (cruel) duro, cruel; (severe) severo; (sound) áspero; (light) deslumbrador(a)

harvest ['hɑ:vɪst] n (harvest time) siega; (of cereals etc) cosecha; (of grapes) vendimia ▷ vt cosechar

has [hæz] vb see **have**

hasn't ['hæznt] = **has not**

hassle ['hæsl] (inf) n lata

haste [heɪst] n prisa; **hasten** ['heɪsn] vt acelerar ▷ vi darse prisa; **hastily** adv de prisa; precipitadamente; **hasty** adj apresurado; (rash) precipitado

hat [hæt] n sombrero

hatch [hætʃ] n (Naut: also: ~way) escotilla; (also: **service ~**) ventanilla ▷ vi (bird) salir del cascarón ▷ vt incubar; (plot) tramar; **5 eggs have ~ed** han salido 5 pollos

hatchback ['hætʃbæk] n (Aut) tres or cinco puertas m

hate [heɪt] vt odiar, aborrecer ▷ n odio; **hatred** ['heɪtrɪd] n odio

haul [hɔ:l] vt tirar ▷ n (of fish) redada; (of stolen goods etc) botín m

haunt [hɔ:nt] vt (ghost) aparecerse en; (obsess) obsesionar ▷ n guarida; **haunted** adj (castle etc) embrujado; (look) de angustia

○ **KEYWORD**

have [hæv] (pt, pp had) aux vb 1 (gen) haber; **to have arrived/eaten** haber llegado/comido; **having finished** or **when he had finished, he left** cuando hubo acabado, se fue

2 (in tag questions): **you've done it,**

haven't you? lo has hecho, ¿verdad? or ¿no?

3 (in short answers and questions): **I haven't!** no; **so I have** pues, es verdad; **we haven't paid – yes we have!** no hemos pagado – ¡sí que hemos pagado!; **I've been there before, have you?** he estado allí antes, ¿y tú?

▷ modal aux vb (be obliged): **to have (got) to do sth** tener que hacer algo; **you haven't to tell her** no hay que or no debes decírselo

▷ vt 1 (possess): **to have (got) blue eyes/dark hair** tiene los ojos azules/el pelo negro

2 (referring to meals etc): **to have breakfast/lunch/dinner** desayunar/ comer/cenar; **to have a drink/a cigarette** tomar algo/fumar un cigarrillo

3 (receive) recibir; (obtain) obtener; **may I have your address?** ¿puedes darme tu dirección?; **you can have it for £5** te lo puedes quedar por £5; **I must have it by tomorrow** lo necesito para mañana; **to have a baby** tener un niño or bebé

4 (maintain, allow): **I won't have it/this nonsense!** ¡no lo permitiré!/¡no permitiré estas tonterías!; **we can't have that** no podemos permitir eso

5 **to have sth done** hacer or mandar hacer algo; **to have one's hair cut** cortarse el pelo; **to have sb do sth** hacer que algn haga algo

6 (experience, suffer): **to have a cold/flu** tener un resfriado/la gripe; **she had her bag stolen/her arm broken** le robaron el bolso/se rompió un brazo; **to have an operation** operarse

7 (+ noun): **to have a swim/walk/ bath/rest** nadar/dar un paseo/darse un baño/descansar; **let's have a look** vamos a ver; **to have a meeting/ party** celebrar una reunión/una fiesta; **let me have a try** déjame intentarlo

haven ['heɪvn] n puerto; (fig) refugio

haven't ['hævnt] = **have not**

havoc ['hævək] n estragos mpl

Hawaii [hə'waɪiː] n (Islas fpl)
Hawaii fpl

hawk [hɔːk] n halcón m

hawthorn ['hɔːθɔːn] n espino

hay [heɪ] n heno; **hay fever** n fiebre f
del heno; **haystack** n almiar m

hazard ['hæzəd] n peligro ▷ vt
aventurar; **hazardous** adj peligroso;
hazard warning lights npl (Aut)
señales fpl de emergencia

haze [heɪz] n neblina

hazel ['heɪzl] n (tree) avellano ▷ adj
(eyes) color m de avellano; **hazelnut** n
avellana

hazy ['heɪzɪ] adj brumoso; (idea) vago

he [hiː] pron él; ~ **who ...** él que ...,
quien ...

head [hɛd] n cabeza; (leader) jefe/a
m/f; (of school) director(a) m/f ▷ vt
(list) encabezar; (group) capitanear;
(company) dirigir; **~s (or tails)** cara (o
cruz); **~ first** de cabeza; **~ over heels**
(in love) perdidamente; **to ~ the ball**
cabecear (la pelota); **head for** vt fus
dirigirse a; (disaster) ir camino de; **head
off** vt (threat, danger) evitar; **headache** n
dolor m de cabeza; **heading** n título;
headlamp (BRIT) n = **headlight**;
headlight n faro; **headline** n titular
m; **head office** n oficina central,
central f; **headphones** npl auriculares
mpl; **headquarters** npl sede f central;
(Mil) cuartel m general; **headroom** n
(in car) altura interior; (under bridge)
(límite m de) altura; **headscarf** n
pañuelo; **headset** n cascos mpl;
headteacher n director(directora);
head waiter n maître m

heal [hiːl] vt curar ▷ vi cicatrizarse

health [hɛlθ] n salud f; **health
care** n asistencia sanitaria; **health
centre** (BRIT) n ambulatorio, centro
médico; **health food** n alimentos mpl
orgánicos; **Health Service** (BRIT) n el
servicio de salud pública, = el Insalud
(SP); **healthy** adj sano, saludable

heap [hiːp] n montón m ▷ vt: **to
~ (up)** amontonar; **to ~ sth with**
llenar algo hasta arriba de; **~s of** un
montón de

hear [hɪə*] (pt, pp **~d**) vt (also Law) oír;
(news) saber ▷ vi oír; **to ~ about** oír
hablar de; **to ~ from sb** tener noticias
de algn

heard [hɜːd] pt, pp of **hear**

hearing ['hɪərɪŋ] n (sense) oído; (Law)
vista; **hearing aid** n audífono

hearse [hɜːs] n coche m fúnebre

heart [hɑːt] n corazón m; (fig) valor
m; (of lettuce) cogollo; **hearts** npl
(Cards) corazones mpl; **to lose/take
~** descorazonarse/cobrar ánimo; **at
~** en el fondo; **by ~** (learn, know) de
memoria; **heart attack** n infarto (de
miocardio); **heartbeat** n latido (del
corazón); **heartbroken** adj: **she was
heartbroken about it** esto le partió el
corazón; **heartburn** n acedía; **heart
disease** n enfermedad f cardíaca

hearth [hɑːθ] n (fireplace) chimenea

heartless ['hɑːtlɪs] adj despiadado

hearty ['hɑːtɪ] adj (person)
campechano; (laugh) sano; (dislike,
support) absoluto

heat [hiːt] n calor m; (Sport: also:
qualifying ~) prueba eliminatoria ▷ vt
calentar; **heat up** vi calentarse ▷ vt
calentar; **heated** adj caliente; (fig)
acalorado; **heater** n estufa; (in car)
calefacción f

heather ['hɛðə*] n brezo

heating ['hiːtɪŋ] n calefacción f

heatwave ['hiːtweɪv] n ola de calor

heaven ['hɛvn] n cielo; (fig) una
maravilla; **heavenly** adj celestial; (fig)
maravilloso

heavily ['hɛvɪlɪ] adv pesadamente;
(drink, smoke) con exceso; (sleep, sigh)
profundamente; (depend) mucho

heavy ['hɛvɪ] adj pesado; (work,
blow) duro; (sea, rain, meal) fuerte;
(drinker, smoker) grande; (responsibility)
grave; (schedule) ocupado; (weather)
bochornoso

Hebrew ['hiːbruː] *adj*, *n* (Ling) hebreo

hectare ['hɛktɑː*] *n* (BRIT) hectárea

hectic ['hɛktɪk] *adj* agitado

he'd [hiːd] = **he would; he had**

hedge [hɛdʒ] *n* seto ▷ *vi* contestar con evasivas; **to ~ one's bets** (*fig*) cubrirse

hedgehog ['hɛdʒhɔg] *n* erizo

heed [hiːd] *vt* (*also*: **take ~**: *pay attention to*) hacer caso de

heel [hiːl] *n* talón m; (*of shoe*) tacón m ▷ *vt* (*shoe*) poner tacón a

hefty ['hɛftɪ] *adj* (*person*) fornido; (*parcel, profit*) gordo

height [haɪt] *n* (*of person*) estatura; (*of building*) altura; (*high ground*) cerro; (*altitude*) altitud f; (*fig: of season*): **at the ~ of summer** en los días más calurosos del verano; (*: of power etc*) cúspide f; (*: of stupidity etc*) colmo; **heighten** *vt* elevar; (*fig*) aumentar

heir [ɛə*] *n* heredero; **heiress** *n* heredera

held [hɛld] *pt, pp of* **hold**

helicopter ['hɛlɪkɔptə*] *n* helicóptero

hell [hɛl] *n* infierno; **~!** (*inf*) ¡demonios!

he'll [hiːl] = **he will; he shall**

hello [hə'ləu] *excl* ¡hola!; (*to attract attention*) ¡oiga!; (*surprise*) ¡caramba!

helmet ['hɛlmɪt] *n* casco

help [hɛlp] *n* ayuda; (*cleaner etc*) criada, asistenta ▷ *vt* ayudar; **~!** ¡socorro!; **~ yourself** sírvete; **he can't ~ it** no es culpa suya; **help out** *vi* ayudar, echar una mano ▷ *vt*: **to help sb out** ayudar a algn, echar una mano a algn; **helper** *n* ayudante *mf*; **helpful** *adj* útil; (*person*) servicial; (*advice*) útil; **helping** *n* ración f; **helpless** *adj* (*incapable*) incapaz; (*defenceless*) indefenso; **helpline** *n* teléfono de asistencia al público

hem [hɛm] *n* dobladillo ▷ *vt* poner or coser el dobladillo de

hemisphere ['hɛmɪsfɪə*] *n* hemisferio

hemorrhage ['hɛmərɪdʒ] (US) *n* = **haemorrhage**

hemorrhoids ['hɛmərɔɪdz] (US) *npl* = **haemorrhoids**

hen [hɛn] *n* gallina; (*female bird*) hembra

hence [hɛns] *adv* (*therefore*) por lo tanto; **2 years ~** de aquí a 2 años

hen night, hen party *n* (*inf*) despedida de soltera

hepatitis [hɛpə'taɪtɪs] *n* hepatitis f

her [həː*] *pron* (*direct*) la; (*indirect*) le; (*stressed, after prep*) ella ▷ *adj* su; *see also* **me; my**

herb [həːb] *n* hierba; **herbal** *adj* de hierbas; **herbal tea** *n* infusión f de hierbas

herd [həːd] *n* rebaño

here [hɪə*] *adv* aquí; (*at this point*) en este punto; **~!** (*present*) ¡presente!; **~ is/are** aquí está/están; **~ she is** aquí está

hereditary [hɪ'rɛdɪtrɪ] *adj* hereditario

heritage ['hɛrɪtɪdʒ] *n* patrimonio

hernia ['həːnɪə] *n* hernia

hero ['hɪərəu] (*pl* **~es**) *n* héroe *m*; (*in book, film*) protagonista *m*; **heroic** [hɪ'rəuɪk] *adj* heroico

heroin ['hɛrəuɪn] *n* heroína

heroine ['hɛrəuɪn] *n* heroína; (*in book, film*) protagonista

heron ['hɛrən] *n* garza

herring ['hɛrɪŋ] *n* arenque *m*

hers [həːz] *pron* (el) suyo/(la) suya) *etc*; *see also* **mine[1]**

herself [həː'sɛlf] *pron* (*reflexive*) se; (*emphatic*) ella misma; (*after prep*) sí (misma); *see also* **oneself**

he's [hiːz] = **he is; he has**

hesitant ['hɛzɪtənt] *adj* vacilante

hesitate ['hɛzɪteɪt] *vi* vacilar; (*in speech*) titubear; (*be unwilling*) resistirse; **hesitation** [-'teɪʃən] *n* indecisión f; titubeo; dudas *fpl*

heterosexual [hɛtərəu'sɛksjuəl] *adj* heterosexual

hexagon ['hɛksəgən] *n* hexágono

hey [heɪ] *excl* ¡oye!, ¡oiga!

heyday ['heɪdeɪ] *n*: **the ~ of** el apogeo de

HGV *n abbr* (= heavy goods vehicle) vehículo pesado

hi [haɪ] *excl* ¡hola!; (to attract attention) ¡oiga!

hibernate ['haɪbəneɪt] *vi* invernar

hiccough ['hɪkʌp] = **hiccup**

hiccup ['hɪkʌp] *vi* hipar

hid [hɪd] *pt of* **hide**

hidden ['hɪdn] *pp of* **hide** ▷ *adj*: **~ agenda** plan *m* encubierto

hide [haɪd] (*pt* **hid**, *pp* **hidden**) *n* (skin) piel *f* ▷ *vt* esconder, ocultar ▷ *vi*: **to ~ (from sb)** esconderse or ocultarse (de algn)

hideous ['hɪdɪəs] *adj* horrible

hiding ['haɪdɪŋ] *n* (beating) paliza; **to be in ~** (concealed) estar escondido

hi-fi ['haɪfaɪ] *n* estéreo, hifi *m* ▷ *adj* de alta fidelidad

high [haɪ] *adj* alto; (speed, number) grande; (price) elevado; (wind) fuerte; (voice) agudo ▷ *adv* alto, a gran altura; **it is 20 m ~** tiene 20 m de altura; **~ in the air** en las alturas; **highchair** *n* silla alta; **high-class** *adj* (hotel) de lujo; (person) distinguido, de categoría; (food) de alta categoría; **higher education** *n* educación *f* or enseñanza superior; **high heels** *npl* (heels) tacones *mpl* altos; (shoes) zapatos *mpl* de tacón; **high jump** *n* (Sport) salto de altura; **the Highlands** ['haɪləndz] *npl* tierras *fpl* altas; **the Highlands** (in Scotland) las Tierras Altas de Escocia; **highlight** *n* (fig: of event) punto culminante ▷ *vt* subrayar; **highlights** *npl* (in hair) reflejos *mpl*; **highlighter** *n* rotulador; **highly** *adv* (paid) muy bien; (critical, confidential) sumamente; (a lot): **to speak/think highly of** hablar muy bien de/tener en mucho a; **highness** *n* altura; **Her/His Highness** Su Alteza; **high** *n* (also: **high-rise block**, **high-rise building**) torre *f* de pisos; **high school**

n = Instituto Nacional de Bachillerato (SP); **high season** (BRIT) *n* temporada alta; **high street** (BRIT) *n* calle *f* mayor; **high-tech** (inf) *adj* al-tec (inf), de alta tecnología; **highway** *n* carretera; (US) carretera nacional; autopista; **Highway Code** (BRIT) *n* código de la circulación

hijack ['haɪdʒæk] *vt* secuestrar; **hijacker** *n* secuestrador(a) *m/f*

hike [haɪk] *vi* (go walking) ir de excursión (a pie) ▷ *n* caminata; **hiker** *n* excursionista *mf*; **hiking** *n* senderismo

hilarious [hɪ'leərɪəs] *adj* divertidísimo

hill [hɪl] *n* (high) montaña; (slope) cuesta; **hillside** *n* ladera; **hill walking** *n* senderismo (de montaña); **hilly** *adj* montañoso

him [hɪm] *pron* (direct) le, lo; (indirect) le; (stressed, after prep) él; see also **me**; **himself** *pron* (reflexive) se; (emphatic) él mismo; (after prep) sí (mismo); see also **oneself**

hind [haɪnd] *adj* posterior

hinder ['hɪndə*] *vt* estorbar, impedir

hindsight ['haɪndsaɪt] *n*: **with ~** en retrospectiva

Hindu ['hɪnduː] *n* hindú *mf*; **Hinduism** *n* (Rel) hinduismo

hinge [hɪndʒ] *n* bisagra, gozne *m* ▷ *vi* (fig): **to ~ on** depender de

hint [hɪnt] *n* indirecta; (advice) consejo; (sign) dejo ▷ *vt*: **to ~ that** insinuar que ▷ *vi*: **to ~ at** hacer alusión a

hip [hɪp] *n* cadera

hippie ['hɪpɪ] *n* hippie *m/f*, jipi *m/f*

hippo ['hɪpəu] (*pl* **~s**) *n* hipopótamo

hippopotamus [hɪpə'pɔtəməs] (*pl* **~es** or **hippopotami**) *n* hipopótamo

hippy ['hɪpɪ] *n* = **hippie**

hire ['haɪə*] *vt* (BRIT: car, equipment) alquilar; (worker) contratar ▷ *n* alquiler *m*; for ~ se alquila; (taxi) libre; **hire(d) car** (BRIT) *n* coche *m* de alquiler; **hire purchase** (BRIT) *n* compra a plazos

his [hɪz] pron (el) suyo((la) suya) etc
▷ adj su; see also **mine¹**; **my**
Hispanic [hɪsˈpænɪk] adj hispánico
hiss [hɪs] vi silbar
historian [hɪˈstɔːrɪən] n
historiador(a) m/f
historic(al) [hɪˈstɔrɪk(l)] adj
histórico
history [ˈhɪstərɪ] n historia
hit [hɪt] (pt, pp ~) vt (strike) golpear,
pegar; (reach: target) alcanzar; (collide
with: car) chocar contra; (fig: affect)
afectar ▷ n golpe m; (success) éxito;
(on website) visita; (in web search)
correspondencia; **to ~ it off with
sb** llevarse bien con algn; **hit back**
vi defenderse; (fig) devolver golpe
por golpe
hitch [hɪtʃ] vt (fasten) atar, amarrar;
(also: ~ **up**) remangar ▷ n (difficulty)
dificultad f; **to ~ a lift** hacer
autostop
hitch-hike [ˈhɪtʃhaɪk] vi hacer
autostop; **hitch-hiker** n autostopista
m/f; **hitch-hiking** n autostop m
hi-tech [ˈhaɪˈtek] adj de alta
tecnología
hitman [ˈhɪtmæn] (irreg) n asesino
a sueldo
HIV n abbr (= human immunodeficiency
virus) VIH m; **~-negative/positive**
VIH negativo/positivo
hive [haɪv] n colmena
hoard [hɔːd] n (treasure) tesoro;
(stockpile) provisión f ▷ vt acumular;
(goods in short supply) acaparar
hoarse [hɔːs] adj ronco
hoax [həʊks] n trampa
hob [hɔb] n quemador m
hobble [ˈhɔbl] vi cojear
hobby [ˈhɔbɪ] n pasatiempo, afición
f
hobo [ˈhəʊbəʊ] (US) n vagabundo
hockey [ˈhɔkɪ] n hockey; **hockey
stick** n palo m de hockey
hog [hɔg] n cerdo, puerco ▷ vt
acaparar; **to go the whole ~** poner
toda la carne en el asador

Hogmanay [ˈhɔgməˈneɪ] n ver
recuadro

hoist [hɔɪst] n (crane) grúa ▷ vt
levantar, alzar; (flag, sail) izar
hold [həʊld] (pt, pp **held**) vt sostener;
(contain) contener; (have: power,
qualification) tener; (keep back) retener;
(believe) sostener; (consider) considerar;
(keep in position): **to ~ one's head up**
mantener la cabeza alta; (meeting)
celebrar ▷ vi (withstand pressure)
resistir; (be valid) valer ▷ n (grasp)
asimiento; (fig) dominio; **~ the line!**
(Tel) ¡no cuelgue!; **to ~ one's own** (fig)
defenderse; **to catch or get (a) ~ of**
agarrarse o asirse de; **hold back** vt
retener; (secret) ocultar; **hold on** vi
agarrarse bien; (wait) esperar; **hold
on!** (Tel) ¡(espere) un momento!; **hold
out** vt ofrecer ▷ vi (resist) resistir;
hold up vt (raise) levantar; (support)
apoyar; (delay) retrasar; (rob) asaltar;
holdall (BRIT) n bolsa; **holder** n
(container) receptáculo; (of ticket, record)
poseedor(a) m/f; (of office, title etc)
titular mf
hole [həʊl] n agujero
holiday [ˈhɔlɪdɪ] n vacaciones
fpl; (public holiday) (día m de) fiesta,
día m feriado; **on ~** de vacaciones;
holiday camp n (BRIT: also: **holiday
centre**) centro de vacaciones; **holiday

job n (BRIT) trabajillo extra para las vacaciones; **holiday-maker** (BRIT) n turista mf; **holiday resort** n centro turístico

Holland ['hɔlənd] n Holanda

hollow ['hɔləu] adj hueco; (claim) vacío; (eyes) hundido; (sound) sordo ▷ n hueco; (in ground) hoyo ▷ vt: **to ~ out** excavar

holly ['hɔlɪ] n acebo

Hollywood ['hɔlɪwud] n Hollywood m

holocaust ['hɔləkɔ:st] n holocausto

holy ['həulɪ] adj santo, sagrado; (water) bendito

home [həum] n casa; (country) patria; (institution) asilo ▷ cpd (domestic) casero, de casa; (Econ, Pol) nacional ▷ adv (direction) a casa; (right in: nail etc) a fondo; **at ~** en casa; (in country) en el país; (fig) como pez en el agua; **to go/come ~** ir/volver a casa; **make yourself at ~** ¡estás en tu casa!; **home address** n domicilio; **homeland** n tierra natal; **homeless** adj sin hogar, sin casa; **homely** adj (simple) sencillo; **home-made** adj casero; **home match** n partido en casa; **Home Office** (BRIT) n Ministerio del Interior; **home owner** n propietario/a m/f de una casa; **home page** n página de inicio; **Home Secretary** (BRIT) n Ministro del Interior; **homesick** adj: **to be homesick** tener morriña, sentir nostalgia; **home town** n ciudad f natal; **homework** n deberes mpl

homicide ['hɔmɪsaɪd] (US) n homicidio

homoeopathic [həumɪəˈpæθɪk] (US **homeopathic**) adj homeopático

homoeopathy [həumɪˈɔpəθɪ] (US **homeopathy**) n homeopatía

homosexual [hɔməuˈsɛksjuəl] adj, n homosexual mf

honest ['ɔnɪst] adj honrado; (sincere) franco, sincero; **honestly** adv honradamente; francamente; **honesty** n honradez f

honey ['hʌnɪ] n miel f; **honeymoon** n luna de miel; **honeysuckle** n madreselva

Hong Kong ['hɔŋ'kɔŋ] n Hong-Kong m

honorary ['ɔnərərɪ] adj (member, president) de honor; (title) honorífico; **~ degree** doctorado honoris causa

honour ['ɔnə*] (US **honor**) vt honrar; (commitment, promise) cumplir con ▷ n honor m, honra; **to graduate with ~s** = licenciarse con matrícula (de honor); **honourable** (US **honorable**) adj honorable; **honours degree** n (Scol) título de licenciado con calificación alta

hood [hud] n capucha; (BRIT Aut) capota; (US Aut) capó m; (of cooker) campana de humos; **hoodie** n (top) jersey m con capucha

hoof [hu:f] (pl **hooves**) n pezuña

hook [huk] n gancho; (on dress) corchete m, broche m; (for fishing) anzuelo ▷ vt enganchar; (fish) pescar

hooligan ['hu:lɪgən] n gamberro

hoop [hu:p] n aro

hooray [hu:'reɪ] excl = **hurray**

hoot [hu:t] (BRIT) vi (Aut) tocar el pito, pitar; (siren) hacer sonar; (owl) - ulular

Hoover® ['hu:və*] (BRIT) n aspiradora ▷ vt: **to hoover** pasar la aspiradora por

hooves [hu:vz] npl of **hoof**

hop [hɔp] vi saltar, brincar; (on one foot) saltar con un pie

hope [həup] vt, vi esperar ▷ n esperanza; **I ~ so/not** espero que sí/no; **hopeful** adj (person) optimista; (situation) prometedor(a); **hopefully** adv con esperanza; (one hopes): **hopefully he will recover** esperamos que se recupere; **hopeless** adj desesperado; (person): **to be hopeless** ser un desastre

hops [hɔps] npl lúpulo

horizon [həˈraɪzn] n horizonte m; **horizontal** [hɔrɪˈzɔntl] adj horizontal

hormone ['hɔ:məun] n hormona

horn [hɔ:n] n cuerno; (Mus: also:

French ~) trompa; (Aut) pito, claxon m
horoscope [ˈhɒrəskəup] n horóscopo
horrendous [hɒˈrɛndəs] adj horrendo
horrible [ˈhɒrɪbl] adj horrible
horrid [ˈhɒrɪd] adj horrible, horroroso
horrific [hɒˈrɪfɪk] adj (accident)
horroroso; (film) horripilante
horrifying [ˈhɒrɪfaɪɪŋ] adj horroroso
horror [ˈhɒrə*] n horror m; **horror
film** n película de horror
hors d'œuvre [ɔːˈdəːvrə] n
entremeses mpl
horse [hɔːs] n caballo; **horseback**
n: **on horseback** a caballo; **horse
chestnut** n (tree) castaño de indias;
(nut) castaña de indias; **horsepower**
n caballo (de fuerza); **horse-racing**
n carreras fpl de caballos; **horseradish**
n rábano picante; **horse riding** n (BRIT)
equitación f
hose [həuz] n manguera; **hosepipe** n
manguera
hospital [ˈhɒspɪtl] n hospital m
hospitality [hɒspɪˈtælɪtɪ] n
hospitalidad f
host [həust] n anfitrión m; (TV, Radio)
presentador m; (Rel) hostia; (large
number): **a ~ of** multitud de
hostage [ˈhɒstɪdʒ] n rehén m
hostel [ˈhɒstl] n hostal m; (youth) ~)
albergue m juvenil
hostess [ˈhəustɪs] n anfitriona;
(BRIT: air hostess) azafata; (TV, Radio)
presentadora
hostile [ˈhɒstaɪl] adj hostil
hostility [hɒˈstɪlɪtɪ] n hostilidad f
hot [hɒt] adj caliente; (weather)
caluroso, de calor; (as opposed to warm)
muy caliente; (spicy) picante; **to be
~** (person) tener calor; (object) estar
caliente; (weather) hacer calor; **hot dog**
n perro caliente
hotel [həuˈtɛl] n hotel m
hotspot [ˈhɒtspɒt] n (Comput):
wireless hotspot punto m de acceso
inalámbrico
hot-water bottle [hɒtˈwɔːtə*-] n
bolsa de agua caliente

hound [haund] vt acosar ▷ n perro
(de caza)
hour [ˈauə*] n hora; **hourly** adj (de)
cada hora
house [n haus, pl ˈhauzɪz, vb hauz] n
(gen, firm) casa; (Pol) cámara; (Theatre)
sala ▷ vt (person) alojar; (collection)
albergar; **on the ~** (fig) la casa invita;
household n familia; (home) casa;
householder n propietario/a; (head of
house) cabeza de familia; **housekeeper**
n ama de llaves; **housekeeping**
n (work) trabajos mpl domésticos;
housewife (irreg) n ama de casa;
house wine n vino m de la casa;
housework n faenas fpl (de la casa)
housing [ˈhauzɪŋ] n (act)
alojamiento; (houses) viviendas fpl;
**housing development,
housing estate** (BRIT) n urbanización f
hover [ˈhɒvə*] vi flotar (en el aire);
hovercraft n aerodeslizador m
how [hau] adv (in what way) cómo;
~ are you? ¿cómo estás?; **~ much milk/
many people?** ¿cuánta leche/gente?;
~ much does it cost? ¿cuánto cuesta?;
~ long have you been here? ¿cuánto
hace que estás aquí?; **~ old are you?**
¿cuántos años tienes?; **~ tall is he?**
¿cómo es de alto?; **~ is school?** ¿cómo
(te) va (en) la escuela?; **~ was the film?**
¿qué tal la película?; **~ lovely/awful!**
¡qué bonito/horror!
however [hauˈevə*] adv: **~ I do it** lo
haga como lo haga; **~ cold it is** por
mucho frío que haga; **~ did you do it?**
¿cómo lo hiciste? ▷ conj sin embargo,
no obstante
howl [haul] n aullido; (of animal) aullar;
(person) dar alaridos; (wind) ulular
H.P. n abbr = **hire purchase**
h.p. abbr = **horsepower**
HQ n abbr = **headquarters**
hr(s) abbr (= hour(s)) h
HTML n abbr (= hypertext markup
language) lenguaje m de hipertexto
hubcap [ˈhʌbkæp] n tapacubos m inv
huddle [ˈhʌdl] vi: **to ~ together**

acurrucarse

huff [hʌf] n: **in a ~** enojado

hug [hʌg] vt abrazar; (thing) apretar con los brazos

huge [hju:dʒ] adj enorme

hull [hʌl] n (of ship) casco

hum [hʌm] vt tararear, canturrear ▷ vi tararear, canturrear; (insect) zumbar

human ['hju:mən] adj, n humano

humane [hju:'meɪn] adj humano, humanitario

humanitarian [hju:mænɪ'teərɪən] adj humanitario

humanity [hju:'mænɪtɪ] n humanidad f

human rights npl derechos mpl humanos

humble ['hʌmbl] adj humilde

humid ['hju:mɪd] adj húmedo; **humidity** [-'mɪdɪtɪ] n humedad f

humiliate [hju:'mɪlɪeɪt] vt humillar

humiliating [hju:'mɪlɪeɪtɪŋ] adj humillante, vergonzoso

humiliation [hju:mɪlɪ'eɪʃən] n humillación f

hummus ['huməs] n paté de garbanzos

humorous ['hju:mərəs] adj gracioso, divertido

humour ['hju:mə*] (US **humor**) n humorismo, sentido del humor; (mood) humor m ▷ vt (person) complacer

hump [hʌmp] n (in ground) montículo; (camel's) giba

hunch [hʌntʃ] n (premonition) presentimiento

hundred ['hʌndrəd] num ciento; (before n) cien; **~s of** centenares de; **hundredth** [-ɪdθ] adj centésimo

hung [hʌŋ] pt, pp of **hang**

Hungarian [hʌŋ'geərɪən] adj, n húngaro/a m/f

Hungary ['hʌŋgərɪ] n Hungría

hunger ['hʌŋgə*] n hambre f ▷ vi: **to ~ for** (fig) tener hambre de, anhelar

hungry ['hʌŋgrɪ] adj: **~ (for)** hambriento (de); **to be ~** tener hambre

hunt [hʌnt] vt (seek) buscar; (Sport) cazar ▷ vi (search): **to ~ (for)** buscar; (Sport) cazar ▷ n búsqueda; caza, cacería; **hunter** n cazador/a m/f; **hunting** n caza

hurdle ['hə:dl] n (Sport) valla; (fig) obstáculo

hurl [hə:l] vt lanzar, arrojar

hurrah [hu'rɑ:] excl = **hurray**

hurray [hu'reɪ] excl ¡viva!

hurricane ['hʌrɪkən] n huracán m

hurry ['hʌrɪ] n prisa ▷ vt (also: **~ up**: person) dar prisa a; (: work) apresurar, hacer de prisa; **to be in a ~** tener prisa; **hurry up** vi darse prisa, apurarse (LAM)

hurt [hə:t] (pt, pp ~) vt hacer daño a ▷ vi doler ▷ adj lastimado

husband ['hʌzbənd] n marido

hush [hʌʃ] n silencio ▷ vt hacer callar; **~!** ¡chitón!, ¡cállate!

husky ['hʌskɪ] adj ronco ▷ n perro esquimal

hut [hʌt] n cabaña; (shed) cobertizo

hyacinth ['haɪəsɪnθ] n jacinto

hydrangea [haɪ'dreɪndʒə] n hortensia

hydrofoil ['haɪdrəfɔɪl] n aerodeslizador m

hydrogen ['haɪdrədʒən] n hidrógeno

hygiene ['haɪdʒi:n] n higiene f; **hygienic** [-'dʒi:nɪk] adj higiénico

hymn [hɪm] n himno

hype [haɪp] (inf) n bombardeo publicitario

hyperlink ['haɪpəlɪŋk] n hiperlink m

hyphen ['haɪfn] n guión m

hypnotize ['hɪpnətaɪz] vt hipnotizar

hypocrite ['hɪpəkrɪt] n hipócrita mf

hypocritical [hɪpə'krɪtɪkl] adj hipócrita

hypothesis [haɪ'pɔθɪsɪs] (pl **hypotheses**) n hipótesis f inv

hysterical [hɪ'sterɪkl] adj histérico; (funny) para morirse de risa

hysterics [hɪ'sterɪks] npl histeria; **to be in ~** (fig) morirse de risa

I [aɪ] *pron* yo

ice [aɪs] *n* hielo; (*ice cream*) helado ▷ *vt* (*cake*) alcorzar ▷ *vi* (*also:* **~ up**) helarse; **iceberg** *n* iceberg *m*; **ice cream** *n* helado; **ice cube** *n* cubito de hielo; **ice hockey** *n* hockey *m* sobre hielo

Iceland ['aɪslənd] *n* Islandia; **Icelander** *n* islandés/esa *m/f*; **Icelandic** [aɪs'lændɪk] *adj* islandés/esa ▷ *n* (*Ling*) islandés *m*

ice: ice lolly (BRIT) *n* polo; **ice rink** *n* pista de hielo; **ice skating** *n* patinaje *m* sobre hielo

icing ['aɪsɪŋ] *n* (*Culin*) alcorza; **icing sugar** (BRIT) *n* azúcar *m* glas(eado)

icon ['aɪkɔn] *n* icono

ICT (BRIT: *Scol*) *n abbr* (= *information and communications technology*) informática

icy ['aɪsɪ] *adj* helado

I'd [aɪd] = **I would; I had**

ID card *n* (*identity card*) DNI *m*

idea [aɪ'dɪə] *n* idea

ideal [aɪ'dɪəl] *n* ideal *m* ▷ *adj* ideal; **ideally** [-dɪəlɪ] *adv* idealmente;

they're ideally suited hacen una pareja ideal

identical [aɪ'dɛntɪkl] *adj* idéntico

identification [aɪdɛntɪfɪ'keɪʃə n] *n* identificación *f*; **(means of) ~** documentos *mpl* personales

identify [aɪ'dɛntɪfaɪ] *vt* identificar

identity [aɪ'dɛntɪtɪ] *n* identidad *f*; **identity card** *n* carnet *m* de identidad; **identity theft** *n* robo de identidad

ideology [aɪdɪ'ɔlədʒɪ] *n* ideología

idiom ['ɪdɪəm] *n* modismo; (*style of speaking*) lenguaje *m*

> Be careful not to translate **idiom** by the Spanish word **idioma**.

idiot ['ɪdɪət] *n* idiota *mf*

idle ['aɪdl] *adj* (*inactive*) ocioso; (*lazy*) holgazán/ana; (*unemployed*) parado, desocupado; (*machinery etc*) parado; (*talk etc*) frívolo ▷ *vi* (*machine*) marchar en vacío

idol ['aɪdl] *n* ídolo

idyllic [ɪ'dɪlɪk] *adj* idílico

i.e. *abbr* (= *that is*) esto es

if [ɪf] *conj* si; **~ necessary** si fuera necesario, si hiciese falta; **~ I were you** yo en tu lugar; **~ so/not** de ser así/si no; **~ only I could!** ¡ojalá pudiera!; *see also* **as; even**

ignite [ɪg'naɪt] *vt* (*set fire to*) encender ▷ *vi* encenderse

ignition [ɪg'nɪʃən] *n* (*Aut: process*) ignición *f*; (*: mechanism*) encendido; **to switch on/off the ~** arrancar/apagar el motor

ignorance ['ɪgnərəns] *n* ignorancia

ignorant ['ɪgnərənt] *adj* ignorante; **to be ~ of** ignorar

ignore [ɪg'nɔː] *vt* (*person, advice*) no hacer caso de; (*fact*) pasar por alto

I'll [aɪl] = **I will; I shall**

ill [ɪl] *adj* enfermo, malo ▷ *n* mal *m* ▷ *adv* mal; **to be taken ~** ponerse enfermo

illegal [ɪ'liːgl] *adj* ilegal

illegible [ɪ'lɛdʒɪbl] *adj* ilegible

illegitimate [ɪlɪ'dʒɪtɪmət] *adj*

ilegítimo

ill health n mala salud f; **to be in ~** estar mal de salud

illiterate [ɪ'lɪtərət] adj analfabeto

illness ['ɪlnɪs] n enfermedad f

illuminate [ɪ'luːmɪneɪt] vt (room, street) iluminar, alumbrar

illusion [ɪ'luːʒən] n ilusión f; (trick) truco

illustrate ['ɪləstreɪt] vt ilustrar

illustration [ɪlə'streɪʃən] n (act of illustrating) ilustración f; (example) ejemplo, ilustración f; (in book) lámina

I'm [aɪm] = **I am**

image ['ɪmɪdʒ] n imagen f

imaginary [ɪ'mædʒɪnərɪ] adj imaginario

imagination [ɪmædʒɪ'neɪʃən] n imaginación f; (inventiveness) inventiva

imaginative [ɪ'mædʒɪnətɪv] adj imaginativo

imagine [ɪ'mædʒɪn] vt imaginarse

imbalance [ɪm'bæləns] n desequilibrio

imitate ['ɪmɪteɪt] vt imitar

imitation [ɪmɪ'teɪʃən] n imitación f; (copy) copia

immaculate [ɪ'mækjulət] adj inmaculado

immature [ɪmə'tjuə*] adj (person) inmaduro

immediate [ɪ'miːdɪət] adj inmediato; (pressing) urgente, apremiante; (nearest: family) próximo; (: neighbourhood) inmediato;
immediately adv (at once) en seguida; (directly) inmediatamente;
immediately next to muy junto a

immense [ɪ'mɛns] adj inmenso, enorme; (importance) enorme;
immensely adv enormemente

immerse [ɪ'mɜːs] vt (submerge) sumergir; **to be ~d in** (fig) estar absorto en

immigrant ['ɪmɪɡrənt] n inmigrante mf; **immigration** [ɪmɪ'ɡreɪʃən] n inmigración f

imminent ['ɪmɪnənt] adj inminente

immoral [ɪ'mɒrəl] adj inmoral

immortal [ɪ'mɔːtl] adj inmortal

immune [ɪ'mjuːn] adj: **~ (to)** inmune (a); **immune system** n sistema m inmunitario

immunize ['ɪmjunaɪz] vt inmunizar

impact ['ɪmpækt] n impacto

impair [ɪm'pɛə*] vt perjudicar

impartial [ɪm'pɑːʃl] adj imparcial

impatience [ɪm'peɪʃəns] n impaciencia

impatient [ɪm'peɪʃənt] adj impaciente; **to get** or **grow ~** impacientarse

impeccable [ɪm'pɛkəbl] adj impecable

impending [ɪm'pɛndɪŋ] adj inminente

imperative [ɪm'pɛrətɪv] adj (tone) imperioso; (need) imprescindible

imperfect [ɪm'pɜːfɪkt] adj (goods etc) defectuoso ▷ n (Ling: also: **~ tense**) imperfecto

imperial [ɪm'pɪərɪəl] adj imperial

impersonal [ɪm'pɜːsənl] adj impersonal

impersonate [ɪm'pɜːsəneɪt] vt hacerse pasar por; (Theatre) imitar

impetus ['ɪmpətəs] n ímpetu m; (fig) impulso

implant [ɪm'plɑːnt] vt (Med) injertar, implantar; (fig: idea, principle) inculcar

implement [n 'ɪmplɪmənt, vb 'ɪmplɪmɛnt] n herramienta; (for cooking) utensilio ▷ vt (regulation) hacer efectivo; (plan) realizar

implicate ['ɪmplɪkeɪt] vt (compromise) comprometer; **to ~ sb in sth** comprometer a algn en algo

implication [ɪmplɪ'keɪʃən] n consecuencia; **by ~** indirectamente

implicit [ɪm'plɪsɪt] adj implícito; (belief, trust) absoluto

imply [ɪm'plaɪ] vt (involve) suponer; (hint) dar a entender que

impolite [ɪmpə'laɪt] adj mal educado

import [vb ɪmˈpɔːt, n ˈɪmpɔːt] vt importar ▷ n (Comm) importación f; (: article) producto importado; (meaning) significado, sentido

importance [ɪmˈpɔːtəns] n importancia

important [ɪmˈpɔːtənt] adj importante; **it's not ~** no importa, no tiene importancia

importer [ɪmˈpɔːtə*] n importador(a) m/f

impose [ɪmˈpəuz] vt imponer ▷ vi: **to ~ on sb** abusar de algn; **imposing** adj imponente, impresionante

impossible [ɪmˈpɔsɪbl] adj imposible; (person) insoportable

impotent [ˈɪmpətənt] adj impotente

impoverished [ɪmˈpɔvərɪʃt] adj necesitado

impractical [ɪmˈpræktɪkl] adj (person, plan) poco práctico

impress [ɪmˈpres] vt impresionar; (mark) estampar; **to ~ sth on sb** hacer entender algo a algn

impression [ɪmˈpreʃən] n impresión f; (imitation) imitación f; **to be under the ~ that** tener la impresión de que

impressive [ɪmˈpresɪv] adj impresionante

imprison [ɪmˈprɪzn] vt encarcelar; **imprisonment** n encarcelamiento; (term of imprisonment) cárcel f

improbable [ɪmˈprɔbəbl] adj improbable, inverosímil

improper [ɪmˈprɔpə*] adj (unsuitable: conduct etc) incorrecto; (: activities) deshonesto

improve [ɪmˈpruːv] vt mejorar; (foreign language) perfeccionar ▷ vi mejorarse; **improvement** n mejoramiento; perfección f; progreso

improvise [ˈɪmprəvaɪz] vt, vi improvisar

impulse [ˈɪmpʌls] n impulso; **to act on ~** obrar sin reflexión; **impulsive**

[ɪmˈpʌlsɪv] adj irreflexivo

○ **KEYWORD**

in [ɪn] prep 1 (indicating place, position, with place names) en; **in the house/garden** en (la) casa/el jardín; **in here/there** aquí/ahí o allí dentro; **in London/England** en Londres/Inglaterra

2 (indicating time) en; **in spring** en (la) primavera; **in the afternoon** por la tarde; **at 4 o'clock in the afternoon** a las 4 de la tarde; **I did it in 3 hours/days** lo hice en 3 horas/días; **I'll see you in 2 weeks** or **in 2 weeks' time** te veré dentro de 2 semanas

3 (indicating manner etc) en; **in a loud/soft voice** en voz alta/baja; **in pencil/ink** a lápiz/bolígrafo; **the boy in the blue shirt** el chico de la camisa azul

4 (indicating circumstances): **in the sun/shade/rain** al sol/a la sombra/bajo la lluvia; **a change in policy** un cambio de política

5 (indicating mood, state): **in tears** en lágrimas, llorando; **in anger/despair** enfadado/desesperado; **to live in luxury** vivir lujosamente

6 (with ratios, numbers): **1 in 10 households, 1 household in 10** una de cada 10 familias; **20 pence in the pound** 20 peniques por libra; **they lined up in twos** se alinearon de dos en dos

7 (referring to people, works) en; entre; **the disease is common in children** la enfermedad es común entre los niños; **in (the works of) Dickens** en (las obras de) Dickens

8 (indicating profession etc): **to be in teaching** estar en la enseñanza

9 (after superlative) de; **the best pupil in the class** el(la) mejor alumno/a de la clase

10 (with present participle): **in saying this** al decir esto

▷ adv: **to be in** (person: at home) estar en

casa; (at work) estar; (in train, ship, plane) haber llegado; (in fashion) estar de moda; **she'll be in later today** llegará más tarde hoy; **to ask sb in** hacer pasar a algn; **to run/limp etc in** entrar corriendo/cojeando etc
▷ n: **the ins and outs** (of proposal, situation etc) los detalles

inability [ɪnəˈbɪlɪtɪ] n: ~ **(to do)** incapacidad f (de hacer)

inaccurate [ɪnˈækjʊrət] adj inexacto, incorrecto

inadequate [ɪnˈædɪkwət] adj (income, reply etc) insuficiente; (person) incapaz

inadvertently [ɪnədˈvɜːtntlɪ] adv por descuido

inappropriate [ɪnəˈprəʊprɪət] adj inadecuado; (improper) poco oportuno

inaugurate [ɪˈnɔːɡjʊreɪt] vt inaugurar; (president, official) investir

Inc. (us) abbr (= incorporated) S.A.

incapable [ɪnˈkeɪpəbl] adj incapaz

incense [n ˈɪnsens, vb ɪnˈsens] n incienso ▷ vt (anger) indignar, encolerizar

incentive [ɪnˈsentɪv] n incentivo, estímulo

inch [ɪntʃ] n pulgada; **to be within an ~ of** estar a dos dedos de; **he didn't give an ~** no dio concesión alguna

incidence [ˈɪnsɪdns] n (of crime, disease) incidencia

incident [ˈɪnsɪdnt] n incidente m

incidentally [ɪnsɪˈdentəlɪ] adv (by the way) a propósito

inclination [ɪnklɪˈneɪʃən] n (tendency) tendencia, inclinación f; (desire) deseo; (disposition) propensión f

incline [n ˈɪnklaɪn, vb ɪnˈklaɪn] n pendiente m, cuesta ▷ vt (head) poner de lado e ▷ vi inclinarse; **to be ~d to** (tend) tener tendencia a hacer algo

include [ɪnˈkluːd] vt (incorporate) incluir; (in letter) adjuntar; **including** prep incluso, inclusive

inclusion [ɪnˈkluːʒən] n inclusión f

inclusive [ɪnˈkluːsɪv] adj inclusivo; ~ **of tax** incluidos los impuestos

income [ˈɪnkʌm] n (earned) ingresos mpl; (from property etc) renta; (from investment etc) rédito; **income support** n (Brit) ≈ ayuda familiar; **income tax** n impuesto sobre la renta

incoming [ˈɪnkʌmɪŋ] adj (flight, government) entrante

incompatible [ɪnkəmˈpætɪbl] adj incompatible

incompetence [ɪnˈkɒmpɪtəns] n incompetencia

incompetent [ɪnˈkɒmpɪtənt] adj incompetente

incomplete [ɪnkəmˈpliːt] adj (partial: achievement etc) incompleto; (unfinished: painting etc) inacabado

inconsistent [ɪnkənˈsɪstənt] adj (inconsequent: contradictory) incongruente; ~ **with** (que) no concuerda con

inconvenience [ɪnkənˈviːnjəns] n inconvenientes mpl; (trouble) molestia, incomodidad f ▷ vt incomodar

inconvenient [ɪnkənˈviːnjənt] adj incómodo, poco práctico; (time, place, visitor) inoportuno

incorporate [ɪnˈkɔːpəreɪt] vt incorporar; (contain) comprender; (add) agregar

incorrect [ɪnkəˈrekt] adj incorrecto

increase [n ˈɪnkriːs, vb ɪnˈkriːs] n aumento ▷ vi aumentar; (grow) crecer; (price) subir ▷ vt aumentar; (price) subir; **increasingly** adv cada vez más, más y más

incredible [ɪnˈkredɪbl] adj increíble; **incredibly** adv increíblemente

incur [ɪnˈkɜː*] vt (expenditure) incurrir; (loss) sufrir; (anger, disapproval) provocar

indecent [ɪnˈdiːsnt] adj indecente

indeed [ɪnˈdiːd] adv efectivamente, en realidad; (in fact) en efecto; (furthermore) es más; **yes ~!** ¡claro que sí!

indefinitely [ɪnˈdɛfɪnɪtlɪ] adv (wait) indefinidamente

independence [ɪndɪˈpɛndns] n independencia; **Independence Day** (US) n Día m de la Independencia

● **INDEPENDENCE DAY**

El cuatro de julio es **Independence Day**, la fiesta nacional de Estados Unidos, que se celebra en conmemoración de la Declaración de Independencia, escrita por Thomas Jefferson y aprobada en 1776. En ella se proclamaba la independencia total de Gran Bretaña de las trece colonias americanas que serían el origen de los Estados Unidos de América.

independent [ɪndɪˈpɛndnt] adj independiente; **independent school** n (BRIT) escuela f privada, colegio m privado

index [ˈɪndɛks] (pl **-es**) n (in book) índice m; (: in library etc) catálogo; (pl **indices**: ratio, sign) exponente m

India [ˈɪndɪə] n la India; **Indian** adj, n indio/a; **Red Indian** piel roja mf

indicate [ˈɪndɪkeɪt] vt indicar; **indication** [-ˈkeɪʃən] n indicio, señal f; **indicative** [ɪnˈdɪkətɪv] adj: **to be indicative of** indicar; **indicator** n indicador m; (Aut) intermitente m

indices [ˈɪndɪsiːz] npl of **index**

indict [ɪnˈdaɪt] vt acusar; **indictment** n acusación f

indifference [ɪnˈdɪfrəns] n indiferencia

indifferent [ɪnˈdɪfrənt] adj indiferente; (mediocre) regular

indigenous [ɪnˈdɪdʒɪnəs] adj indígena

indigestion [ɪndɪˈdʒɛstʃən] n indigestión f

indignant [ɪnˈdɪgnənt] adj: **to be ~ at sth/with sb** indignarse por

algo/con algn

indirect [ɪndɪˈrɛkt] adj indirecto

indispensable [ɪndɪˈspɛnsəbl] adj indispensable, imprescindible

individual [ɪndɪˈvɪdjuəl] n individuo ▷ adj individual; (personal) personal; (particular) particular; **individually** adv (singly) individualmente

Indonesia [ɪndəˈniːzɪə] n Indonesia

indoor [ˈɪndɔːʳ] adj (swimming pool) cubierto; (plant) de interior; (sport) bajo cubierta; **indoors** [ɪnˈdɔːz] adv dentro

induce [ɪnˈdjuːs] vt inducir, persuadir; (bring about) producir; (labour) provocar

indulge [ɪnˈdʌldʒ] vt (whim) satisfacer; (person) complacer; (child) mimar ▷ vi: **to ~ in** darse el gusto de; **indulgent** adj indulgente

industrial [ɪnˈdʌstrɪəl] adj industrial; **industrial estate** (BRIT) n polígono (SP) or zona (LAM) industrial; **industrialist** n industrial mf; **industrial park** (US) n = **industrial estate**

industry [ˈɪndəstrɪ] n industria; (diligence) aplicación f

inefficient [ɪnɪˈfɪʃənt] adj ineficaz, ineficiente

inequality [ɪnɪˈkwɒlɪtɪ] n desigualdad f

inevitable [ɪnˈɛvɪtəbl] adj inevitable; **inevitably** adv inevitablemente

inexpensive [ɪnɪkˈspɛnsɪv] adj económico

inexperienced [ɪnɪkˈspɪərɪənst] adj inexperto

inexplicable [ɪnɪkˈsplɪkəbl] adj inexplicable

infamous [ˈɪnfəməs] adj infame

infant [ˈɪnfənt] n niño/a; (baby) niño/a pequeño/a, bebé m/f; (pej) aniñado

infantry [ˈɪnfəntrɪ] n infantería

infant school (BRIT) n parvulario

infect [ɪnˈfɛkt] vt (wound) infectar; (food) contaminar; (person, animal) contagiar; **infection** [ɪnˈfɛkʃən] n infección f; (fig) contagio; **infectious**

[ɪnˈfɛkʃəs] adj (also fig) contagioso

infer [ɪnˈfəː*] vt deducir, inferir

inferior [ɪnˈfɪərɪə*] adj, n inferior mf

infertile [ɪnˈfəːtaɪl] adj estéril; (person) infecundo

infertility [ɪnfəˈtɪlɪtɪ] n esterilidad f; infecundidad f

infested [ɪnˈfɛstɪd] adj: ~ **with** plagado de

infinite [ˈɪnfɪnɪt] adj infinito; **infinitely** adv infinitamente

infirmary [ɪnˈfəːmərɪ] n hospital m

inflamed [ɪnˈfleɪmd] adj: **to become** ~ inflamarse

inflammation [ɪnfləˈmeɪʃən] n inflamación f

inflatable [ɪnˈfleɪtəbl] adj (ball, boat) inflable

inflate [ɪnˈfleɪt] vt (tyre, price etc) inflar; (fig) hinchar; **inflation** [ɪnˈfleɪʃən] n (Econ) inflación f

inflexible [ɪnˈflɛksəbl] adj (rule) rígido; (person) inflexible

inflict [ɪnˈflɪkt] vt: **to ~ sth on sb** infligir algo en algn

influence [ˈɪnfluəns] n influencia ▷ vt influir en, influenciar; **under the ~ of alcohol** en estado de embriaguez; **influential** [-ˈɛnʃl] adj influyente

influx [ˈɪnflʌks] n afluencia

info (inf) [ˈɪnfəu] n = **information**

inform [ɪnˈfɔːm] vt: **to ~ sb of sth** informar a algn sobre or de algo ▷ vi: **to ~ on sb** delatar a algn

informal [ɪnˈfɔːmal] adj (manner, tone) familiar; (dress, interview, occasion) informal; (visit, meeting) extraoficial

information [ɪnfəˈmeɪʃən] n información f; (knowledge) conocimientos mpl; **a piece of** ~ un dato; **information office** n información f; **information technology** n informática

informative [ɪnˈfɔːmətɪv] adj informativo

infra-red [ɪnfrəˈrɛd] adj infrarrojo

infrastructure [ˈɪnfrəstrʌktʃə*] n (of system etc) infraestructura

[ɪnˈfrɪːkwənt] adj infrecuente

infuriate [ɪnˈfjuərɪeɪt] vt: **to become ~d** ponerse furioso

infuriating [ɪnˈfjuərɪeɪtɪŋ] adj (habit, noise) enloquecedor(a)

ingenious [ɪnˈdʒiːnjəs] adj ingenioso

ingredient [ɪnˈgriːdɪənt] n ingrediente m

inhabit [ɪnˈhæbɪt] vt vivir en; **inhabitant** n habitante mf

inhale [ɪnˈheɪl] vt inhalar ▷ vi (breathe in) aspirar; (in smoking) tragar; **inhaler** n inhalador m

inherent [ɪnˈhɪərənt] adj: ~ **in** or **to** inherente a

inherit [ɪnˈhɛrɪt] vt heredar; **inheritance** n herencia f; (fig) patrimonio

inhibit [ɪnˈhɪbɪt] vt inhibir, impedir; **inhibition** [-ˈbɪʃən] n cohibición f

initial [ɪˈnɪʃl] adj primero ▷ n inicial f ▷ vt firmar con las iniciales; **initials** npl (as signature) iniciales fpl; (abbreviation) siglas fpl; **initially** adv al principio

initiate [ɪˈnɪʃɪeɪt] vt iniciar; **to ~ proceedings against sb** (Law) entablar proceso contra algn

initiative [ɪˈnɪʃɪətɪv] n iniciativa f

inject [ɪnˈdʒɛkt] vt inyectar; **to ~ sb with sth** inyectar algo a algn; **injection** [ɪnˈdʒɛkʃən] n inyección f

injure [ˈɪndʒə*] vt (hurt) herir, lastimar; (fig: reputation etc) perjudicar; **injured** adj (person, arm) herido, lastimado; **injury** n herida, lesión f; (wrong) perjuicio, daño

> Be careful not to translate **injury** by the Spanish word **injuria**.

injustice [ɪnˈdʒʌstɪs] n injusticia

ink [ɪŋk] n tinta; **ink-jet printer** [ˈɪŋkdʒɛt-] n impresora de chorro de tinta

inland [adj ˈɪnlənd, adv ɪnˈlænd] adj (waterway, port etc) interior ▷ adv tierra adentro; **Inland Revenue** (BRIT) n departamento de impuestos ≈

Hacienda (SP)

in-laws ['ɪnlɔːz] npl suegros mpl
inmate ['ɪnmeɪt] n (in prison) preso/a, presidiario/a; (in asylum) internado/a
inn [ɪn] n posada, mesón m
inner ['ɪnə*] adj (courtyard, calm) interior; (feelings) íntimo; **inner-city** adj (schools, problems) de las zonas céntricas pobres, de los barrios céntricos pobres
inning ['ɪnɪŋ] n (US: Baseball) inning m, entrada; **~s** (Cricket) entrada, turno
innocence ['ɪnəsns] n inocencia
innocent ['ɪnəsnt] adj inocente
innovation [ɪnəu'veɪʃən] n novedad f
innovative ['ɪnəu'veɪtɪv] adj innovador
in-patient ['ɪnpeɪʃənt] n paciente m/f interno/a
input ['ɪnput] n entrada; (of resources) inversión f; (Comput) entrada de datos
inquest ['ɪnkwest] n (coroner's) encuesta judicial
inquire [ɪn'kwaɪə*] vi preguntar ▷ vt: **to ~ whether** preguntar si; **to ~ about** (person) preguntar por; (fact) informarse de; **inquiry** n pregunta; (investigation) investigación f, pesquisa; **"Inquiries"** "Información"
ins. abbr = **inches**
insane [ɪn'seɪn] adj loco; (Med) demente
insanity [ɪn'sænɪtɪ] n demencia, locura
insect ['ɪnsekt] n insecto; **insect repellent** n loción f contra insectos
insecure [ɪnsɪ'kjuə*] adj inseguro
insecurity [ɪnsɪ'kjuərɪtɪ] n inseguridad f
insensitive [ɪn'sensɪtɪv] adj insensible
insert [vb ɪn'sɜːt, n 'ɪnsɜːt] vt (into sth) introducir ▷ n encarte m
inside ['ɪn'saɪd] n interior m ▷ adj interior, interno ▷ adv (be) (por) dentro; (go) hacia dentro ▷ prep dentro de; (of time): **~ 10 minutes** en menos

de 10 minutos; **inside lane** n (Aut: in Britain) carril m izquierdo; (: in US, Europe etc) carril m derecho; **inside out** adv (turn) al revés; (know) a fondo
insight ['ɪnsaɪt] n perspicacia
insignificant [ɪnsɪg'nɪfɪknt] adj insignificante
insincere [ɪnsɪn'sɪə*] adj poco sincero
insist [ɪn'sɪst] vi insistir; **to ~ on** insistir en; **to ~ that** insistir en que; (claim) exigir que; **insistent** adj insistente; (noise, action) persistente
insomnia [ɪn'sɒmnɪə] n insomnio
inspect [ɪn'spekt] vt inspeccionar, examinar; (troops) pasar revista a; **inspection** [ɪn'spekʃən] n inspección f, examen m; (of troops) revista; **inspector** n inspector/a m/f; (BRIT: on buses, trains) revisor/a m/f
inspiration [ɪnspə'reɪʃən] n inspiración f; **inspire** [ɪn'spaɪə*] vt inspirar; **inspiring** adj inspirador(a)
instability [ɪnstə'bɪlɪtɪ] n inestabilidad f
install [ɪn'stɔːl] (US **instal**) vt instalar; (official) nombrar; **installation** [ɪnstə'leɪʃən] n instalación f
instalment [ɪn'stɔːlmənt] (US **installment**) n plazo; (of story) entrega; (of TV serial etc) capítulo; **in ~s** (pay, receive) a plazos
instance ['ɪnstəns] n ejemplo, caso; **for ~** por ejemplo; **in the first ~** en primer lugar
instant ['ɪnstənt] n instante m, momento ▷ adj inmediato; (coffee etc) instantáneo; **instantly** adv en seguida; **instant messaging** n mensajería instantánea
instead [ɪn'sted] adv en cambio; **~ of** en lugar de, en vez de
instinct ['ɪnstɪŋkt] n instinto; **instinctive** adj instintivo
institute ['ɪnstɪtjuːt] n instituto; (professional body) colegio ▷ vt (begin) iniciar, empezar; (proceedings) entablar; (system, rule) establecer

institution [ɪnstɪˈtjuːʃən] *n*
institución *f*; (*Med: home*) asilo;
(*: asylum*) manicomio; (*of system etc*)
establecimiento *m*; (*of custom*)
iniciación *f*

instruct [ɪnˈstrʌkt] *vt*: **to ~ sb in**
instruir a algn en *o* sobre algo; **to ~ sb
to do sth** dar instrucciones a algn de
hacer algo; **instruction** [ɪnˈstrʌkʃən]
n (*teaching*) instrucción *f*; **instructions**
npl (*orders*) órdenes *fpl*; **instructions
(for use)** modo de empleo; **instructor**
n instructor(a) *m/f*

instrument [ˈɪnstrəmənt] *n*
instrumento; **instrumental** [-ˈmentl]
adj (*Mus*) instrumental; **to be
instrumental in** ser (el) artífice de

insufficient [ɪnsəˈfɪʃənt] *adj*
insuficiente

insulate [ˈɪnsjuleɪt] *vt* aislar;
insulation [-ˈleɪʃən] *n* aislamiento

insulin [ˈɪnsjulɪn] *n* insulina

insult [*n* ˈɪnsʌlt, *vb* ɪnˈsʌlt] *n* insulto
▷ *vt* insultar; **insulting** *adj* insultante

insurance [ɪnˈʃuərəns] *n* seguro;
fire/life ~ seguro contra incendios/
sobre la vida; **insurance company**
n compañía de seguros; **insurance
policy** *n* póliza (de seguros)

insure [ɪnˈʃuə*] *vt* asegurar

intact [ɪnˈtækt] *adj* íntegro,
(*unharmed*) intacto

intake [ˈɪnteɪk] *n* (*of food*) ingestión *f*;
(*of air*) consumo; (BRIT *Scol*): **an ~ of 200
a year** 200 matriculados al año

integral [ˈɪntɪɡrəl] *adj* (*whole*)
íntegro; (*part*) integrante

integrate [ˈɪntɪɡreɪt] *vt* integrar ▷ *vi*
integrarse

integrity [ɪnˈteɡrɪtɪ] *n* honradez *f*,
rectitud *f*

intellect [ˈɪntəlekt] *n* intelecto;
intellectual [-ˈlektjuəl] *adj, n*
intelectual *mf*

intelligence [ɪnˈtelɪdʒəns] *n*
inteligencia

intelligent [ɪnˈtelɪdʒənt] *adj*
inteligente

intend [ɪnˈtend] *vt* (*gift etc*): **to ~ sth
for** destinar algo a; **to ~ to do sth** tener
intención de *or* pensar hacer algo

intense [ɪnˈtens] *adj* intenso

intensify [ɪnˈtensɪfaɪ] *vt* intensificar;
(*increase*) aumentar

intensity [ɪnˈtensɪtɪ] *n* (*gen*)
intensidad *f*

intensive [ɪnˈtensɪv] *adj* intensivo;
intensive care *n*: **to be in intensive
care** estar bajo cuidados intensivos;
intensive care unit *n* unidad *f* de
vigilancia intensiva

intent [ɪnˈtent] *n* propósito, (*Law*)
premeditación *f* ▷ *adj* (*absorbed*)
absorto; (*attentive*) atento; **to all ~s
and purposes** prácticamente; **to
be ~ on doing sth** estar resuelto a
hacer algo

intention [ɪnˈtenʃən] *n* intención *f*,
propósito; **intentional** *adj* deliberado

interact [ɪntərˈækt] *vi* influirse
mutuamente; **interaction**
[ɪntərˈækʃən] *n* interacción *f*, acción
f recíproca; **interactive** *adj* (*Comput*)
interactivo

intercept [ɪntəˈsept] *vt* interceptar;
(*stop*) detener

interchange [ˈɪntətʃeɪndʒ] *n*
intercambio; (*on motorway*)
intersección *f*

intercourse [ˈɪntəkɔːs] *n* (*sexual*)
relaciones *fpl* sexuales

interest [ˈɪntrɪst] *n* (*also Comm*)
interés *m* ▷ *vt* interesar; **interested**
adj interesado; **to be interested
in** interesarse por; **interesting** *adj*
interesante; **interest rate** *n* tipo *or*
tasa de interés

interface [ˈɪntəfeɪs] *n* (*Comput*)
junción *f*

interfere [ɪntəˈfɪə*] *vi*: **to ~ in**
entrometerse en; **to ~ with** (*hinder*)
estorbar; (*damage*) estropear

interference [ɪntəˈfɪərəns] *n*
intromisión *f*; (*Radio, TV*) interferencia

interim [ˈɪntərɪm] *n*: **in the ~** en el
ínterin ▷ *adj* provisional

interior | 424

interior [ɪn'tɪərɪə*] n interior m ▷ adj interior; **interior design** n interiorismo, decoración f de interiores

intermediate [ɪntə'miːdɪət] adj intermedio

intermission [ɪntə'mɪʃən] n intermisión f; (Theatre) descanso

intern [vb ɪn'tɜːn, n 'ɪntɜːn] (us) vt internar ▷ n interno/a

internal [ɪn'tɜːnl] adj (layout, pipes, security) interior; (injury, structure, memo) internal; **Internal Revenue Service** (us) n departamento de impuestos, ≈ Hacienda (sp)

international [ɪntə'næʃənl] adj internacional ▷ n (BRIT: match) partido internacional

Internet ['ɪntənet] n: **the ~** Internet m or f; **Internet café** n cibercafé m; **Internet Service Provider** n proveedor m de (acceso a) Internet; **Internet user** n internauta mf

interpret [ɪn'tɜːprɪt] vt interpretar; (translate) traducir; (understand) entender ▷ vi hacer de intérprete; **interpretation** [ɪntɜːprɪ'teɪʃən] n interpretación f, traducción f; **interpreter** n intérprete mf

interrogate [ɪn'terəugeɪt] vt interrogar; **interrogation** [-'geɪʃən] n interrogatorio

interrogative [ɪntə'rɔgətɪv] adj interrogativo

interrupt [ɪntə'rʌpt] vt, vi interrumpir; **interruption** [-'rʌpʃən] n interrupción f

intersection [ɪntə'sekʃən] n (of roads) cruce m

interstate ['ɪntəsteɪt] (us) n carretera interestatal

interval ['ɪntəvl] n intervalo; (BRIT Theatre, Sport) descanso; (Scol) recreo; **at ~s** a ratos, de vez en cuando

intervene [ɪntə'viːn] vi intervenir; (event) interponerse; (time) transcurrir

interview ['ɪntəvjuː] n entrevista ▷ vt entrevistarse con; **interviewer** n entrevistador(a) m/f

intimate [adj 'ɪntɪmət, vb 'ɪntɪmeɪt] adj íntimo; (friendship) estrecho; (knowledge) profundo ▷ vt dar a entender

intimidate [ɪn'tɪmɪdeɪt] vt intimidar, amedrentar

intimidating [ɪn'tɪmɪdeɪtɪŋ] adj amedrentador, intimidante

into ['ɪntuː] prep en; (towards) a; (inside) hacia el interior de; **~ 3 pieces/ French** en 3 pedazos/al francés

intolerant [ɪn'tɔlərənt] adj: **~ (of)** intolerante (con or para)

intranet ['ɪntrənet] n intranet f

intransitive [ɪn'trænsɪtɪv] adj intransitivo

intricate ['ɪntrɪkət] adj (design, pattern) intrincado

intrigue [ɪn'triːg] n intriga ▷ vt fascinar; **intriguing** adj fascinante

introduce [ɪntrə'djuːs] vt introducir, meter; (speaker, TV show etc) presentar; **to ~ sb (to sb)** presentar a algn (a algn); **to ~ sb to** (pastime, technique) introducir a algn a; **introduction** [-'dʌkʃən] n introducción f; (of person) presentación f; **introductory** [-'dʌktərɪ] adj introductorio; (lesson, offer) de introducción

intrude [ɪn'truːd] vi (person) entrometerse; **to ~ on** estorbar; **intruder** n intruso/a

intuition [ɪntjuː'ɪʃən] n intuición f

inundate ['ɪnʌndeɪt] vt: **to ~ with** inundar de

invade [ɪn'veɪd] vt invadir

invalid [n 'ɪnvəlɪd, adj ɪn'vælɪd] n (Med) minusválido/a ▷ adj (not valid) inválido, nulo

invaluable [ɪn'væljuəbl] adj inestimable

invariably [ɪn'veərɪəblɪ] adv sin excepción, siempre; **she is ~ late** siempre llega tarde

invasion [ɪn'veɪʒən] n invasión f

invent [ɪn'vent] vt inventar; **invention** [ɪn'venʃən] n invento;

(lie) ficción f, mentira; **inventor** n
inventor(a) m/f

inventory [ˈɪnvəntrɪ] n inventario

inverted commas [ɪnˈvɜːtɪd-] (BRIT)
npl comillas fpl

invest [ɪnˈvest] vt invertir ▷ vi: **to ~ in**
(company etc) invertir dinero en; *(fig: sth
useful)* comprar

investigate [ɪnˈvestɪgeɪt] vt
investigar; **investigation** [-ˈgeɪʃən] n
investigación f, pesquisa

investigator [ɪnˈvestɪgeɪtə*]
n investigador(a) m/f; **private ~**
investigador(a) m/f privado/a

investment [ɪnˈvestmənt] n
inversión f

investor [ɪnˈvestə*] n inversionista
mf

invisible [ɪnˈvɪzɪbl] adj invisible

invitation [ɪnvɪˈteɪʃən] n invitación f

invite [ɪnˈvaɪt] vt invitar; *(opinions etc)*
solicitar, pedir; **inviting** adj atractivo;
(food) apetitoso

invoice [ˈɪnvɔɪs] n factura ▷ vt
facturar

involve [ɪnˈvɒlv] vt suponer,
implicar; tener que ver con; *(concern,
affect)* corresponder; **to ~ sb (in sth)**
comprometer a algn (con algo);
involved adj complicado; **to be
involved in** *(take part)* tomar parte
en; *(be engrossed)* estar muy metido
en; **involvement** n participación f,
dedicación f

inward [ˈɪnwəd] adj *(movement)*
interior, interno; *(thought, feeling)*
íntimo; **inward(s)** adv hacia dentro

iPod ® [ˈaɪpɒd] n iPod ® m

IQ n abbr *(= intelligence quotient)*
cociente m intelectual

IRA n abbr *(= Irish Republican Army)*
IRA m

Iran [ɪˈrɑːn] n Irán m; **Iranian**
[ɪˈreɪnɪən] adj, n iraní mf

Iraq [ɪˈrɑːk] n Iraq; **Iraqi** adj, n
iraquí mf

Ireland [ˈaɪələnd] n Irlanda

iris [ˈaɪrɪs] (pl **~es**) n *(Anat)* iris m;

(Bot) lirio

Irish [ˈaɪrɪʃ] adj irlandés/esa
▷ npl: **the ~** los irlandeses; **Irishman**
(irreg) n irlandés m; **Irishwoman** *(irreg)*
n irlandesa

iron [ˈaɪən] n hierro; *(for clothes)*
plancha ▷ cpd de hierro ▷ vt *(clothes)*
planchar

ironic(al) [aɪˈrɒnɪk(l)] adj irónico;
ironically adv irónicamente

ironing [ˈaɪənɪŋ] n *(activity)*
planchado; *(clothes: ironed)* ropa
planchada; *(: to be ironed)* ropa por
planchar; **ironing board** n tabla de
planchar

irony [ˈaɪrənɪ] n ironía

irrational [ɪˈræʃənl] adj irracional

irregular [ɪˈregjulə*] adj irregular;
(surface) desigual; *(action, event)*
anómalo; *(behaviour)* poco ortodoxo

irrelevant [ɪˈreləvənt] adj fuera de
lugar, inoportuno

irresistible [ɪrɪˈzɪstɪbl] adj
irresistible

irresponsible [ɪrɪˈspɒnsɪbl] adj *(act)*
irresponsable; *(person)* poco serio

irrigation [ɪrɪˈgeɪʃən] n riego

irritable [ˈɪrɪtəbl] adj *(person)* de
mal humor

irritate [ˈɪrɪteɪt] vt fastidiar; *(Med)*
picar; **irritating** adj fastidioso;
irritation [-ˈteɪʃən] n fastidio;
enfado; picazón f

IRS *(US)* n abbr = **Internal Revenue
Service**

is [ɪz] vb see **be**

ISDN n abbr *(= Integrated Services Digital
Network)* RDSI f

Islam [ˈɪzlɑːm] n Islam m; **Islamic**
[ɪzˈlæmɪk] adj islámico

island [ˈaɪlənd] n isla; **islander** n
isleño/a

isle [aɪl] n isla

isn't [ˈɪznt] = **is not**

isolated [ˈaɪsəleɪtɪd] adj aislado

isolation [aɪsəˈleɪʃən] n aislamiento

ISP n abbr = **Internet Service Provider**

Israel [ˈɪzreɪl] n Israel m; **Israeli**

[ız'reılı] *adj, n* israelí *mf*

issue ['ısju:] *n* (*problem, subject*)
cuestión *f*; (*outcome*) resultado; (*of banknotes etc*) emisión *f*; (*of newspaper etc*) edición *f* ▷ *vt* (*rations, equipment*) distribuir, repartir; (*orders*) dar; (*certificate, passport*) expedir; (*decree*) promulgar; (*magazine*) publicar; (*cheques*) extender; (*banknotes, stamps*) emitir; **at ~** en cuestión; **to take ~ with sb (over)** estar en desacuerdo con algn (sobre); **to make an ~ of sth** hacer una cuestión de algo

IT *n abbr* = **information technology**

○ **KEYWORD**

it [ıt] *pron* **1** (*specific subject: not generally translated*) él (ella); (: *direct object*) lo, la; (: *indirect object*) le; (*after prep*) él (ella); (*abstract concept*) ello; **it's on the table** está en la mesa; **I can't find it** no lo (or la) encuentro; **give it to me** dámelo (or dámela); **I spoke to him about it** le hablé del asunto; **what did you learn from it?** ¿qué aprendiste de él (or ella)?; **did you go to it?** (*party, concert etc*) ¿fuiste?
2 (*impersonal*): **it's raining** llueve, está lloviendo; **it's 6 o'clock/the 10th of August** son las 6/es el 10 de agosto; **how far is it?** - **it's 10 miles/2 hours on the train** ¿a qué distancia está? - a 10 millas/2 horas en tren; **who is it?** - **it's me** ¿quién es? - soy yo

Italian [ı'tæljən] *adj* italiano ▷ *n* italiano/a; (*Ling*) italiano

italics [ı'tælıks] *npl* cursiva

Italy ['ıtəlı] *n* Italia

itch [ıtʃ] *n* picazón *f* ▷ *vi* (*part of body*) picar; **to ~ to do sth** rabiar por hacer algo; **itchy** *adj*: **my hand is itchy** me pica la mano

it'd ['ıtd] = **it would; it had**

item ['aıtəm] *n* artículo; (*on agenda*) asunto (a tratar); (*also:* **news ~**) noticia

itinerary [aı'tınərərı] *n* itinerario

it'll ['ıtl] = **it will; it shall**

its [ıts] *adj* su; sus *pl*

it's [ıts] = **it is; it has**

itself [ıt'self] *pron* (*reflexive*) sí mismo/a; (*emphatic*) él mismo (ella misma)

ITV *n abbr* (BRIT: = Independent Television) cadena de televisión comercial independiente del Estado

I've [aıv] = **I have**

ivory ['aıvərı] *n* marfil *m*

ivy ['aıvı] *n* (Bot) hiedra

j

jab [dʒæb] vt: **to ~ sth into sth** clavar algo en algo ▷ n (inf: Med) pinchazo

jack [dʒæk] n (Aut) gato; (Cards) sota

jacket ['dʒækɪt] n chaqueta, americana (SP), saco (LAM); (of book) sobrecubierta; **jacket potato** n patata asada (con piel)

jackpot ['dʒækpɔt] n premio gordo

Jacuzzi® [dʒə'ku:zɪ] n jacuzzi® m

jagged ['dʒægɪd] adj dentado

jail [dʒeɪl] n cárcel f ▷ vt encarcelar; **jail sentence** n pena f de cárcel

jam [dʒæm] n mermelada; (also: **traffic ~**) embotellamiento; (inf: difficulty) apuro ▷ vt (passage etc) obstruir; (mechanism, drawer etc) atascar; (Radio) interferir ▷ vi atascarse, trabarse; **to ~ sth into sth** meter algo a la fuerza en algo

Jamaica [dʒə'meɪkə] n Jamaica

jammed [dʒæmd] adj atascado

Jan abbr (=January) ene

janitor ['dʒænɪtə*] n (caretaker) portero, conserje m

January ['dʒænjuərɪ] n enero

Japan [dʒə'pæn] n (el) Japón; **Japanese** [dʒæpə'ni:z] adj japonés/esa ▷ n inv japonés/esa m/f; (Ling) japonés m

jar [dʒɑ:*] n tarro, bote m ▷ vi (sound) chirriar; (colours) desentonar

jargon ['dʒɑ:gən] n jerga

javelin ['dʒævlɪn] n jabalina

jaw [dʒɔ:] n mandíbula

jazz [dʒæz] n jazz m

jealous ['dʒeləs] adj celoso; (envious) envidioso; **jealousy** n celos mpl; envidia

jeans [dʒi:nz] npl vaqueros mpl, tejanos mpl

Jello® ['dʒeləu] (US) n gelatina

jelly ['dʒelɪ] n (jam) jalea; (dessert etc) gelatina; **jellyfish** n inv medusa, aguaviva (RPL)

jeopardize ['dʒepədaɪz] vt arriesgar, poner en peligro

jerk [dʒɜ:k] n (jolt) sacudida; (wrench) tirón m; (inf) imbécil mf ▷ vt tirar bruscamente de ▷ vi (vehicle) traquetear

jersey ['dʒɜ:zɪ] n Jersey m

jersey ['dʒɜ:zɪ] n jersey m; (fabric) (tejido de) punto

Jesus ['dʒi:zəs] n Jesús m

jet [dʒet] n (of gas, liquid) chorro; (Aviat) avión m a reacción; **jet lag** n desorientación f después de un largo vuelo; **jet-ski** vi practicar el motociclismo acuático

jetty ['dʒetɪ] n muelle m, embarcadero

Jew [dʒu:] n judío/a

jewel ['dʒu:əl] n joya; (in watch) rubí m; **jeweller** (US **jeweler**) n joyero/a; **jeweller's (shop)** (US **jewelry store**) n joyería; **jewellery** (US **jewelry**) n joyas fpl, alhajas fpl

Jewish ['dʒu:ɪʃ] adj judío

jigsaw ['dʒɪgsɔ:] n (also: **~ puzzle**) rompecabezas m inv, puzle m

job [dʒɔb] n (task) tarea; (post) empleo; **it's not my ~** no me incumbe a mí; **it's a good ~ that ...** menos mal que

...; **just the ~!** ¡estupendo!; **job centre** (BRIT) n oficina estatal de colocaciones; **jobless** adj sin trabajo

jockey ['dʒɔkɪ] n jockey mf ▷ vi: **to ~ for position** maniobrar para conseguir una posición

jog [dʒɔg] vt empujar (ligeramente) ▷ vi (run) hacer footing; **to ~ sb's memory** refrescar la memoria a algn; **jogging** n footing m

join [dʒɔɪn] vt (things) juntar, unir; (club) hacerse socio de; (Pol: party) afiliarse a; (queue) ponerse en; (meet: people) reunirse con ▷ vi (roads) juntarse; (rivers) confluir ▷ n juntura; **join in** vi tomar parte, participar ▷ vt fus tomar parte or participar en; **join up** vi reunirse; (Mil) alistarse

joiner ['dʒɔɪnə*] (BRIT) n carpintero/a

joint [dʒɔɪnt] n (Tech) junta, unión f; (Anat) articulación f; (BRIT Culin) pieza de carne (para asar); (inf: place) tugurio; (: of cannabis) porro ▷ adj (common) común; (combined) combinado; **joint account** n (with bank etc) cuenta común; **jointly** adv (gen) en común; (together) conjuntamente

joke [dʒəuk] n chiste m; (also: **practical ~**) broma ▷ vi bromear; **to play a ~ on** gastar una broma a; **joker** n (Cards) comodín m

jolly ['dʒɔlɪ] adj (merry) alegre; (enjoyable) divertido ▷ adv (BRIT: inf) muy, terriblemente

jolt [dʒəult] n (jerk) sacudida; (shock) susto ▷ vt (physically) sacudir; (emotionally) asustar

Jordan ['dʒɔ:dən] n (country) Jordania; (river) Jordán m

journal ['dʒə:nl] n (magazine) revista; (diary) periódico, diario; **journalism** n periodismo; **journalist** n periodista mf, reportero/a

journey ['dʒə:nɪ] n viaje m; (distance covered) trayecto

joy [dʒɔɪ] n alegría; **joyrider** n gamberro que roba un coche para dar una vuelta y luego abandonarlo; **joy stick** n

(Aviat) palanca de mando; (Comput) palanca de control

Jr abbr = **junior**

judge [dʒʌdʒ] n juez mf; (fig: expert) perito ▷ vt juzgar; (consider) considerar

judo ['dʒu:dəu] n judo

jug [dʒʌg] n jarra

juggle ['dʒʌgl] vi hacer juegos malabares; **juggler** n malabarista mf

juice [dʒu:s] n zumo (sp), jugo (LAM); **juicy** adj jugoso

Jul abbr (= July) jul

July [dʒu:'laɪ] n julio

jumble ['dʒʌmbl] n revoltijo ▷ vt (also: **~ up**) revolver; **jumble sale** (BRIT) n venta de objetos usados con fines benéficos

JUMBLE SALE

Los **jumble sales** son unos mercadillos que se organizan con fines benéficos en los locales de un colegio, iglesia u otro centro público. En ellos puede comprarse todo tipo de artículos baratos de segunda mano, sobre todo ropa, juguetes, libros, vajillas o muebles.

jumbo ['dʒʌmbəu] n (also: **~ jet**) jumbo

jump [dʒʌmp] vi saltar, dar saltos; (with fear etc) pegar un bote; (increase) aumentar ▷ vt saltar ▷ n salto; aumento; **to ~ the queue** (BRIT) colarse

jumper ['dʒʌmpə*] n (BRIT: pullover) suéter m, jersey m; (us: dress) mandil m

jumper cables (US) npl = **jump leads**

jump leads npl cables mpl puente de batería

Jun. abbr = **junior**

junction ['dʒʌŋkʃən] n (BRIT: of roads) cruce m; (Rail) empalme m

June [dʒu:n] n junio

jungle ['dʒʌŋgl] n selva, jungla

junior ['dʒu:nɪə*] adj (in age) menor, más joven; (brother/sister etc): **seven**

K

years her ~ siete años menor que ella; *(position)* subalterno ▷ *n* menor *mf*, joven *mf*; **junior high school** *(us)* *n* centro de educación secundaria; see also **high school**; **junior school** *(BRIT)* *n* escuela primaria

junk [dʒʌŋk] *n (cheap goods)* baratijas *fpl; (rubbish)* basura; **junk food** *n* alimentos preparados y envasados de escaso valor nutritivo

junkie ['dʒʌŋkɪ] *(inf)* *n* drogadicto/a, yonqui *mf*

junk mail *n* propaganda de buzón

Jupiter ['dʒuːpɪtə*] *n (Mythology, Astrology)* Júpiter *m*

jurisdiction [dʒuərɪs'dɪkʃən] *n* jurisdicción *f*; **it falls** or **comes within/ outside our ~** es/no es de nuestra competencia

jury ['dʒuərɪ] *n* jurado

just [dʒʌst] *adj* justo ▷ *adv (exactly)* exactamente; *(only)* sólo, solamente; **he's ~ done it/left** acaba de hacerlo/ irse; **~ right** perfecto; **~ two o'clock** las dos en punto; **she's ~ as clever as you** (ella) es tan lista como tú; **~ as well that ...** menos mal que ...; **~ as he was leaving** en el momento en que se marchaba; **~ before/enough** justo antes/lo suficiente; **~ here** aquí mismo; **he ~ missed** ha fallado por poco; **~ listen to this** escucha esto un momento

justice ['dʒʌstɪs] *n* justicia; *(us: judge)* juez *mf*; **to do ~ to** *(fig)* hacer justicia a

justification [dʒʌstɪfɪ'keɪʃən] *n* justificación *f*

justify ['dʒʌstɪfaɪ] *vt* justificar; *(text)* alinear

jut [dʒʌt] *vi (also:* **~ out**) sobresalir

juvenile ['dʒuːvənaɪl] *adj (court)* de menores; *(humour, mentality)* infantil ▷ *n* menor *m* de edad

K *abbr* (= *one thousand*) mil; (= *kilobyte*) kilobyte *m*, kiloocteto

kangaroo [kæŋgə'ruː] *n* canguro

karaoke [kɑːrə'əʊkɪ] *n* karaoke *m*

karate [kə'rɑːtɪ] *n* karate *m*

kebab [kə'bæb] *n* pincho moruno

keel [kiːl] *n* quilla; **on an even ~** *(fig)* en equilibrio

keen [kiːn] *adj (interest, desire)* grande, vivo; *(eye, intelligence)* agudo; *(competition)* reñido; *(edge)* afilado; *(eager)* entusiasta; **to be ~ to do** or **on doing sth** tener muchas ganas de hacer algo; **to be ~ on sth/sb** interesarse por algo/algn

keep [kiːp] *(pt, pp* **kept**) *vt (preserve, store)* guardar; *(hold back)* quedarse con; *(maintain)* mantener; *(detain)* detener; *(shop)* ser propietario de; *(feed: family etc)* mantener; *(promise)* cumplir; *(chickens, bees etc)* criar; *(accounts)* llevar; *(diary)* escribir; *(prevent)*: **to ~ sb from doing sth** impedir a algn hacer algo ▷ *vi (food)* conservarse; *(remain)* seguir, continuar ▷ *n (of*

kennel | 430

castle) torreón m; (*food etc*) comida, subsistencia; (*interj*): **for ~s** para siempre; **to ~ doing sth** seguir haciendo algo; **to ~ sb happy** tener a algn contento; **to ~ a place tidy** mantener un lugar limpio; **to ~ sth to o.s.** guardar algo para sí mismo; **to ~ sth (back) from sb** ocultar algo a algn; **to ~ time** (*clock*) mantener la hora exacta; **keep away** *vt*: **to keep sth/sb away from sb** mantener algo/algn apartado de algn ▷ *vi*: **to keep away (from)** mantenerse apartado (de); **keep back** *vt* (*crowd, tears*) contener; (*money*) quedarse con; (*conceal: information*): **to keep sth back from sb** ocultar algo a algn ▷ *vi* hacerse a un lado; **keep off** *vt* (*dog, person*) mantener a distancia ▷ *vi*: **if the rain keeps off** si no llueve; **keep your hands off!** ¡no toques!; **"keep off the grass"** "prohibido pisar el césped"; **keep on** *vi*: **to keep on doing** seguir o continuar haciendo; **to keep on (about sth)** hablar (de algo); **keep out** *vi* (*stay out*) permanecer fuera; **"keep out"** "prohibida la entrada"; **keep up** *vt* mantener, conservar ▷ *vi* no retrasarse; **to keep up with** (*pace*) ir al paso de; (*level*) mantenerse a la altura de; **keeper** *n* guardián/ana *m/f*; **keeping** *n* (*care*) cuidado *m*; **in keeping with** de acuerdo con

kennel [ˈkɛnl] *n* perrera; **kennels** *npl* residencia canina

Kenya [ˈkɛnjə] *n* Kenia

kept [kɛpt] *pt, pp of* **keep**

kerb [kə:b] (*BRIT*) *n* bordillo

kerosene [ˈkɛrəsiːn] *n* keroseno

ketchup [ˈkɛtʃəp] *n* salsa de tomate, catsup *m*

kettle [ˈkɛtl] *n* hervidor *m* de agua

key [ki:] *n* llave *f*; (*Mus*) tono; (*of piano, typewriter*) tecla ▷ *adj* (*issue etc*) clave *inv* ▷ *vt* (*also*: **~ in**) teclear; **keyboard** *n* teclado; **keyhole** *n* ojo (de la cerradura); **keyring** *n* llavero

kg *abbr* (= *kilogram*) kg

khaki [ˈkɑːkɪ] *n* caqui

kick [kɪk] *vt* dar una patada o un puntapié a; (*inf: habit*) quitarse de ▷ *vi* (*horse*) dar coces ▷ *n* patada; puntapié *m*; (*of animal*) coz *f*; (*thrill*): **he does it for ~s** lo hace por pura diversión; **kick off** *vi* (*Sport*) hacer el saque inicial; **kick-off** *n* saque inicial; **the kick-off is at ten o'clock** el partido empieza a las diez

kid [kɪd] *n* (*inf: child*) chiquillo/a; (*animal*) cabrito; (*leather*) cabritilla ▷ *vi* (*inf*) bromear

kidnap [ˈkɪdnæp] *vt* secuestrar; **kidnapping** *n* secuestro

kidney [ˈkɪdnɪ] *n* riñón *m*; **kidney bean** *n* judía, alubia

kill [kɪl] *vt* matar; (*murder*) asesinar ▷ *n* matanza; **to ~ time** matar el tiempo; **killer** *n* asesino/a; **killing** *n* (*one*) asesinato; (*several*) matanza; **to make a killing** (*fig*) hacer su agosto

kiln [kɪln] *n* horno

kilo [ˈkiːləu] *n* kilo; **kilobyte** *n* (*Comput*) kilobyte *m*, kiloocteto; **kilogram(me)** *n* kilo, kilogramo; **kilometre** [ˈkɪləmiːtə*] (*US* **kilometer**) *n* kilómetro; **kilowatt** *n* kilovatio

kilt [kɪlt] *n* falda escocesa

kin [kɪn] *n see* **next-of-kin**

kind [kaɪnd] *adj* amable, atento ▷ *n* clase *f*, especie *f*; (*species*) género; **in ~ clase** (*Comm*) en especie; **a ~ of** una especie de; **to be two of a ~** ser tal para cual

kindergarten [ˈkɪndəgɑːtn] *n* jardín *m* de la infancia

kindly [ˈkaɪndlɪ] *adj* bondadoso, cariñoso ▷ *adv* bondadosamente, amablemente; **will you ~ ...** sea usted tan amable de ...

kindness [ˈkaɪndnɪs] *n* (*quality*) bondad *f*, amabilidad *f*; (*act*) favor *m*

king [kɪŋ] *n* rey *m*; **kingdom** *n* reino; **kingfisher** *n* martín *m* pescador; **king-size(d) bed** *n* cama de matrimonio extragrande

kiosk [ˈkiːɔsk] *n* quiosco; (*BRIT Tel*) cabina

kipper [ˈkɪpə*] *n* arenque *m* ahumado

kiss [kɪs] n beso ▷ vt besar; **to ~ (each other)** besarse; **kiss of life** n respiración f boca a boca

kit [kɪt] n (equipment) equipo; (tools etc) (caja de) herramientas fpl; (assembly kit) juego de armar

kitchen ['kɪtʃɪn] n cocina

kite [kaɪt] n (toy) cometa

kitten ['kɪtn] n gatito/a

kiwi ['kiːwiː] n (also: ~ **fruit**) kiwi m

km abbr (= kilometre) km

km/h abbr (= kilometres per hour) km/h

knack [næk] n: **to have the ~ of doing sth** tener el don de hacer algo

knee [niː] n rodilla; **kneecap** n rótula

kneel [niːl] (pt, pp **knelt**) vi (also: ~ **down**) arrodillarse

knelt [nɛlt] pt, pp of **kneel**

knew [njuː] pt of **know**

knickers ['nɪkəz] (BRIT) npl bragas fpl

knife [naɪf] (pl **knives**) n cuchillo ▷ vt acuchillar

knight [naɪt] n caballero; (Chess) caballo

knit [nɪt] vt tejer, tricotar ▷ vi hacer punto, tricotar; (bones) soldarse; **to ~ one's brows** fruncir el ceño; **knitting** n labor f de punto; **knitting needle** n aguja de hacer punto; **knitwear** n prendas fpl de punto

knives [naɪvz] npl of **knife**

knob [nɔb] n (of door) tirador m; (of stick) puño; (on radio, TV) botón m

knock [nɔk] vt (strike) golpear; (bump into) chocar contra; (inf) criticar ▷ vi (at door etc): **to ~ at/on** llamar a ▷ n golpe m; (on door) llamada; **knock down** vt atropellar; **knock off** (inf) vi (finish) salir del trabajo ▷ vt (from price) descontar; (inf: steal) birlar; **knock out** vt dejar sin sentido; (Boxing) poner fuera de combate, dejar K.O.; (in competition) eliminar; **knock over** vt (object) tirar; (person) atropellar; **knockout** n (Boxing) K.O. m, knockout m ▷ cpd (competition etc) eliminatorio

knot [nɔt] n nudo ▷ vt anudar

know [nəu] (pt **knew**, pp **known**) vt (facts) saber; (be acquainted with) conocer; (recognize) reconocer, conocer; **to ~ how to swim** saber nadar; **to ~ about or of sb/sth** saber de algn/algo; **know-all** n sabelotodo mf; **know-how** n conocimientos mpl; **knowing** adj (look) de complicidad; **knowingly** adv (purposely) adrede; (smile, look) con complicidad; **know-it-all** (us) n = **know-all**

knowledge ['nɔlɪdʒ] n conocimiento; (learning) saber m, conocimientos mpl; **knowledgeable** adj entendido

known [nəun] pp of **know** ▷ adj (thief, facts) conocido; (expert) reconocido

knuckle ['nʌkl] n nudillo

koala [kəu'aːlə] n (also: ~ **bear**) koala m

Koran [kɔ'raːn] n Corán m

Korea [kə'rɪə] n Corea; **Korean** adj, n coreano/a m/f

kosher ['kəuʃə*] adj autorizado por la ley judía

Kosovar ['kɔsəvaː*], **Kosovan** ['kɔːsəvan] adj kosovar

Kosovo ['kɔsəvəu] n Kosovo m

Kremlin ['krɛmlɪn] n: **the ~** el Kremlin

Kuwait [ku'weɪt] n Kuwait m

k

L

L (BRIT) abbr = **learner driver**

l. abbr (= litre) l

lab [læb] n abbr = **laboratory**

label ['leɪbl] n etiqueta ⊳vt poner etiqueta a

labor etc ['leɪbə*] (US) = **labour** etc

laboratory [lə'bɒrətərɪ] n laboratorio

Labor Day (US) n día m de los trabajadores (primer lunes de septiembre)

labor union (US) n sindicato

labour ['leɪbə*] (US **labor**) n (hard work) trabajo; (labour force) mano f de obra; (Med): **to be in ~** estar de parto ⊳vi: **to ~ (at sth)** trabajar (en algo) ⊳vt: **to ~ a point** insistir en un punto; **L~, the L~ party** (BRIT) el partido laborista, los laboristas mpl; **labourer** n peón m; **farm labourer** peón m (day labourer) jornalero

lace [leɪs] n encaje m; (of shoe etc) cordón m ⊳vt (shoes: also: **~ up**) atarse (los zapatos)

lack [læk] n (absence) falta ⊳vt faltarle a algn, carecer de; **through** or

for ~ of por falta de; **to be ~ing** faltar, no haber; **to be ~ing in sth** faltarle a algn algo

lacquer ['lækə*] n laca

lacy ['leɪsɪ] adj (of lace) de encaje; (like lace) como de encaje

lad [læd] n muchacho, chico

ladder ['lædə*] n escalera (de mano); (BRIT: in tights) carrera

ladle ['leɪdl] n cucharón m

lady ['leɪdɪ] n señora; (dignified, graceful) dama; **"ladies and gentlemen ..."** "señoras y caballeros ..."; **young ~** señorita; **the ladies' (room)** los servicios de señoras; **ladybird** (US **ladybug**) n mariquita

lag [læg] n retraso ⊳vi (also: **~ behind**) retrasarse, quedarse atrás ⊳vt (pipes) revestir

lager ['lɑːɡə*] n cerveza (rubia)

lagoon [lə'ɡuːn] n laguna

laid [leɪd] pt, pp of **lay**; **laid back** (inf) adj relajado

lain [leɪn] pp of **lie**

lake [leɪk] n lago

lamb [læm] n cordero; (meat) (carne f de) cordero

lame [leɪm] adj cojo; (excuse) poco convincente

lament [lə'mɛnt] n quejo ⊳vt lamentarse de

lamp [læmp] n lámpara; **lamppost** (BRIT) n (poste m de) farol m; **lampshade** n pantalla

land [lænd] n tierra; (country) país m; (piece of land) terreno; (estate) tierras fpl, finca ⊳vi (from ship) desembarcar; (Aviat) aterrizar; (fig: fall) caer, terminar ⊳vt (passengers, goods) desembarcar; **to ~ sb with sth** (inf) hacer cargar a algn con algo; **landing** n aterrizaje m; (of staircase) rellano; **landing card** n tarjeta de desembarque; **landlady** n (of rented house, pub etc) dueña; **landlord** n propietario; (of pub etc) patrón m; **landmark** n lugar m conocido; **to be a landmark** (fig) marcar un hito histórico; **landowner** n terrateniente mf; **landscape** n paisaje m; **landslide** n (Geo) corrimiento de tierras; (fig: Pol) victoria arrolladora

lane [leɪn] n (in country) camino; (Aut) carril m; (in race) calle f

language ['læŋgwɪdʒ] n lenguaje m; (national tongue) idioma m, lengua; **bad ~** palabrotas fpl; **language laboratory** n laboratorio de idiomas; **language school** n academia de idiomas

lantern ['læntn] n linterna, farol m

lap [læp] n (of track) vuelta; (of body) regazo ▷ vt (also: ~ **up**) beber a lengüetadas ▷ vi (waves) chapotear; **to sit on sb's ~** sentarse en las rodillas de algn

lapel [lə'pel] n solapa

lapse [læps] n fallo; (moral) desliz m; (of time) intervalo ▷ vi (expire) caducar; (time) pasar, transcurrir; **to ~ into bad habits** caer en malos hábitos

laptop (computer) ['læptɒp-] n (ordenador m) portátil m

lard [lɑːd] n manteca (de cerdo)

larder ['lɑːdə*] n despensa

large [lɑːdʒ] adj grande; **at ~** (free) en libertad; (generally) en general

⚠ Be careful not to translate **large** by the Spanish word largo.

largely adv (mostly) en su mayor parte; (introducing reason) en gran parte; **large-scale** adj (map) en gran escala; (fig) importante

lark [lɑːk] n (bird) alondra; (joke) broma

laryngitis [lærɪn'dʒaɪtɪs] n laringitis f

lasagne [lə'zænjə] n lasaña

laser ['leɪzə*] n láser m; **laser printer** n impresora (por) láser

lash [læʃ] n latigazo; (also: **eye~**) pestaña ▷ vt azotar; (tie): **to ~ to/ together** atar a/atar; **lash out** vi: **to lash out (at sb)** (hit) arremeter (contra algn); **to lash out against sb** lanzar invectivas contra algn

lass [læs] (BRIT) n chica

last [lɑːst] adj último; (end: of series

etc) final ▷ adv (most recently) la última vez; (finally) por último ▷ vi durar; (continue) continuar, seguir; **~ night** anoche; **~ week** la semana pasada; **at ~** por fin; **~ but one** penúltimo; **lastly** adv por último, finalmente; **last-minute** adj de última hora

latch [lætʃ] n pestillo; **latch onto** vt fus (person, group) pegarse a; (idea) agarrarse a

late [leɪt] adj (far on: in time, process etc) al final de; (not on time) tarde, atrasado; (dead) fallecido ▷ adv tarde; (behind time, schedule) con retraso; **of ~** últimamente; **~ at night** a última hora de la noche; **in ~ May** hacia fines de mayo; **the ~ Mr X** el difunto Sr X; **latecomer** n recién llegado/a; **lately** adv últimamente; **later** adj (date etc) posterior; (version etc) más reciente ▷ adv más tarde, después; **latest** ['leɪtɪst] adj último; **at the latest** a más tardar

lather ['lɑːðə*] n espuma (de jabón) ▷ vt enjabonar

Latin ['lætɪn] n latín m ▷ adj latino; **Latin America** n América latina; **Latin American** adj, n latinoamericano/a m/f

latitude ['lætɪtjuːd] n latitud f; (fig) libertad f

latter ['lætə*] adj (of two) segundo ▷ n: **the ~** el último, éste

laugh [lɑːf] n risa ▷ vi reír(se); **(to do sth) for a ~** (hacer algo) en broma; **laugh at** vt fus reírse de; **laughter** n risa

launch [lɔːntʃ] n lanzamiento; (boat) lancha ▷ vt (ship) botar; (rocket etc) lanzar; (fig) comenzar; **launch into** vt fus lanzarse a

launder ['lɔːndə*] vt lavar

Launderette® [lɔːn'dret] (BRIT) n lavandería (automática)

Laundromat® ['lɔːndrəmæt] (US) n = **Launderette**

laundry ['lɔːndrɪ] n (dirty) ropa sucia; (clean) colada; (room) lavadero

lava | 434

lava ['lɑ:və] n lava
lavatory ['lævətəri] n wáter m
lavender ['lævəndə*] n lavanda
lavish ['lævɪʃ] adj (amount) abundante; (person): ~ with pródigo en ▷ vt: to ~ sth on sb colmar a algn de algo
law [lɔ:] n ley f; (Scol) derecho; (a rule) regla; (professions connected with law) jurisprudencia; **lawful** adj legítimo, lícito; **lawless** adj (action) criminal
lawn [lɔ:n] n césped m; **lawnmower** n cortacésped m
lawsuit ['lɔ:su:t] n pleito
lawyer ['lɔ:jə*] n abogado/a; (for sales, wills etc) notario/a
lax [læks] adj laxo
laxative ['læksətɪv] n laxante m
lay [leɪ] (pt, pp **laid**) pt of **lie** ▷ adj laico; (not expert) lego ▷ vt (place) colocar; (eggs, table) poner; (cable) tender; (carpet) extender; **lay down** vt (pen etc) dejar; (rules etc) establecer; **to lay down the law** (pej) imponer las normas; **lay off** vt (workers) despedir; **lay on** vt (meal, facilities) proveer; **lay out** vt (spread out) disponer, exponer; **lay-by** n (BRIT Aut) área de aparcamiento
layer ['leɪə*] n capa
layman ['leɪmən] (irreg) n lego
layout ['leɪaʊt] n (design) plan m, trazado; (Press) composición f
lazy ['leɪzɪ] adj perezoso, vago; (movement) lento

lb. abbr = **pound** (weight)
lead¹ [li:d] (pt, pp **led**) n (front position) delantera; (clue) pista; (Elec) cable m; (for dog) correa; (Theatre) papel m principal ▷ vt (walk etc in front) ir a la cabeza de; (guide): **to ~ sb somewhere** conducir a algn a algún sitio; (be leader) dirigir; (start, guide: activity) protagonizar ▷ vi (road, pipe etc) conducir a; (Sport) ir primero; **to be in the ~** (Sport) llevar la delantera; (fig) ir a la cabeza; **to ~ the way** llevar la delantera; **lead up to** vt fus (events)

conducir a; (in conversation) preparar el terreno para
lead² [lɛd] n (metal) plomo; (in pencil) mina
leader ['li:də*] n jefe/a m, líder mf; (Sport) líder m; **leadership** n dirección f; (position) mando; (quality) iniciativa
lead-free ['lɛdfri:] adj sin plomo
leading ['li:dɪŋ] adj (main) principal; (first) primero; (front) delantero
lead singer [li:d-] n cantante mf
leaf [li:f] (pl **leaves**) n hoja ▷ vi: **to ~ through** hojear; **to turn over a new ~** reformarse
leaflet ['li:flɪt] n folleto
league [li:g] n sociedad f; (Football) liga; **to be in ~ with** haberse confabulado con
leak [li:k] n (of liquid, gas) escape m, fuga; (in pipe) agujero; (in roof) gotera; (in security) filtración f ▷ vi (shoes, ship) hacer agua; (pipe) tener (un) escape; (roof) gotear; (liquid, gas) escaparse, fugarse; (fig) divulgarse ▷ vt (fig) filtrar
lean [li:n] (pt, pp **~ed** o **~t**) adj (thin) flaco; (meat) magro ▷ vt: **to ~ sth on sth** apoyar algo en algo ▷ vi (slope) inclinarse; **to ~ against** apoyarse contra; **to ~ on** apoyarse en; **lean forward** vi inclinarse hacia adelante; **lean over** vi inclinarse; **leaning** n: **leaning (towards)** inclinación f (hacia)
leant [lɛnt] pt, pp of **lean**
leap [li:p] (pt, pp **~ed** o **~t**) n salto ▷ vi saltar
leapt [lɛpt] pt, pp of **leap**
leap year n año bisiesto
learn [lɜ:n] (pt, pp **~ed** o **~t**) vt aprender ▷ vi aprender; **to ~ about sth** enterarse de algo; **to do sth** aprender a hacer algo; **learner** n (BRIT also: **learner driver**) principiante mf; **learning** n el saber m, conocimientos mpl
learnt [lɜ:nt] pt, pp of **learn**
lease [li:s] n arriendo ▷ vt arrendar
leash [li:ʃ] n correa

least [li:st] *adj:* **the ~** (*slightest*) el menor, el más pequeño; (*smallest amount of*) mínimo ▷ *adv* (+ *vb*) menos; (+ *adj*): **the ~ expensive** el (la) menos costoso/a; **the ~ possible effort** el menor esfuerzo posible; **at ~** por lo menos, al menos; **you could at ~ have written** por lo menos podías haber escrito; **not in the ~** en absoluto

leather ['leðə'] *n* cuero

leave [li:v] (*pt, pp* **left**) *vt* dejar; (*go away from*) abandonar; (*place etc: permanently*) salir de ▷ *vi* irse; (*train etc*) salir ▷ *n* permiso; **to ~ sth to sb** (*money etc*) legar algo a algn; (*responsibility etc*) encargar algo de algo; **to be left** quedar, sobrar; **there's some milk left over** sobra or queda algo de leche; **on ~** de permiso; **leave behind** *vt* (*on purpose*) dejar; (*accidentally*) dejarse; **leave out** *vt* omitir

leaves [li:vz] *npl of* **leaf**

Lebanon ['lebənən] *n:* **the ~** el Líbano

lecture ['lektʃə'] *n* conferencia; (*Scol*) clase *f* ▷ *vi* dar una clase ▷ *vt* (*scold*): **to ~ sb on** *or* **about sth** echar una reprimenda a algn por algo; **to give a ~ on** dar una conferencia sobre; **lecture hall** *n* sala de conferencias; (*Univ*) aula; **lecturer** *n* conferenciante *mf*; (*BRIT: at university*) profesor/a *m/f*; **lecture theatre** *n* = **lecture hall**

led [led] *pt, pp of* **lead¹**

ledge [ledʒ] *n* repisa; (*of window*) alféizar *m*; (*of mountain*) saliente *m*

leek [li:k] *n* puerro

left [left] *pt, pp of* **leave** ▷ *adj* izquierdo; (*remaining*): **there are two ~** quedan dos ▷ *n* izquierda ▷ *adv* a la izquierda; **on** *or* **to the ~** a la izquierda; **the L~** (*Pol*) la izquierda; **left-hand** *adj:* **the left-hand side** la izquierda; **left-hand drive** *adj:* **a left-hand drive car** un coche con el volante a la izquierda; **left-handed** *adj* zurdo; **left-luggage locker** *n* (*BRIT*) consigna *f* automática; **left-luggage**

(office) (*BRIT*) *n* consigna; **left-overs** *npl* sobras *fpl*; **left-wing** *adj* (*Pol*) de izquierdas, izquierdista

leg [leg] *n* pierna; (*of animal, chair*) pata; (*trouser leg*) pernera; (*Culin: of lamb*) pierna; (*: of chicken*) pata; (*of journey*) etapa

legacy ['legəsɪ] *n* herencia

legal ['li:gl] *adj* (*permitted by law*) lícito; (*of law*) legal; **legal holiday** (*US*) *n* fiesta oficial; **legalize** *vt* legalizar; **legally** *adv* legalmente

legend ['ledʒənd] *n* (*also fig: person*) leyenda; **legendary** [-ərɪ] *adj* legendario

leggings ['legɪŋz] *npl* mallas *fpl*, leggins *mpl*

legible ['ledʒəbl] *adj* legible

legislation [ledʒɪs'leɪʃən] *n* legislación *f*

legislative ['ledʒɪslətɪv] *adj* legislativo

legitimate [lɪ'dʒɪtɪmət] *adj* legítimo

leisure ['leʒə'] *n* ocio, tiempo libre; **at ~** con tranquilidad; **leisure centre** (*BRIT*) *n* centro de recreo; **leisurely** *adj* sin prisa; lento

lemon ['lemən] *n* limón *m*; **lemonade** *n* (*fizzy*) gaseosa; **lemon tea** *n* té *m* con limón

lend [lend] (*pt, pp* **lent**) *vt:* **to ~ sth to sb** prestar algo a algn

length [leŋθ] *n* (*size*) largo, longitud *f*; (*distance*): **the ~ of** todo lo largo de; (*of swimming pool, cloth*) largo; (*of wood, string*) trozo; (*amount of time*) duración *f*; **at ~** (*at last*) por fin, finalmente; (*lengthily*) largamente; **lengthen** *vt* alargar ▷ *vi* alargarse; **lengthways** *adv* a lo largo; **lengthy** *adj* largo, extenso

lens [lenz] *n* (*of spectacles*) lente *f*; (*of camera*) objetivo

Lent [lent] *n* Cuaresma

lent [lent] *pt, pp of* **lend**

lentil ['lentl] *n* lenteja

Leo ['li:əu] *n* Leo

leopard ['lepəd] *n* leopardo

leotard [ˈliːətɑːd] n mallas fpl
leprosy [ˈleprəsɪ] n lepra
lesbian [ˈlezbɪən] n lesbiana
less [les] adj (in size, degree etc)
menor; (in quality) menos ▷ pron, adv
menos ▷ prep: ~ **tax/10% discount**
menos impuestos/el 10 por ciento
de descuento; ~ **than half** menos
de la mitad; ~ **than ever** menos que
nunca; ~ **and** ~ cada vez menos; **the**
~ **he works** ... cuanto menos trabaja
...; **lessen** vi disminuir, reducirse ▷ vt
disminuir, reducir; **lesser** [ˈlesə*] adj
menor; **to a lesser extent** en menor
grado
lesson [ˈlesn] n clase f; (warning)
lección f
let [let] (pt, pp ~) vt (allow) dejar,
permitir; (BRIT: lease) alquilar; **to ~**
sb do sth dejar que algn haga algo; **to ~**
sb know sth comunicar algo a algn;
~'s go ¡vamos!; ~ **him come** que venga;
"to ~" "se alquila"; **let down** vt (tyre)
desinflar; (disappoint) defraudar; **let in**
vt dejar entrar; (visitor etc) hacer pasar;
let off vt (culprit) dejar escapar; (gun)
disparar; (bomb) accionar; (firework)
hacer estallar; **let out** vt dejar salir;
(sound) soltar
lethal [ˈliːθl] adj (weapon) mortífero;
(poison, wound) mortal
letter [ˈletə*] n (of alphabet) letra;
(correspondence) carta; **letterbox** (BRIT)
n buzón m
lettuce [ˈletɪs] n lechuga
leukaemia [luːˈkiːmɪə] (US **leukemia**)
n leucemia
level [ˈlevl] adj (flat) llano ▷ adv: **to**
draw ~ with llegar a la altura de ▷ n
nivel m; (height) altura ▷ vt nivelar,
allanar; (destroy: building) derribar;
(: forest) arrasar; **to be ~ with** estar
a nivel de; **A ~s** (BRIT) ≈ exámenes
mpl de bachillerato superior, B.U.P.;
AS ~ (BRIT) asignatura aprobada entre
los "GCSEs" y los "A levels" ... on the ~
(fig: honest) serio; **level crossing** (BRIT)
n paso a nivel

lever [ˈliːvə*] n (also fig) palanca
▷ vt: **to ~ up** levantar con palanca;
leverage n (using bar etc)
apalancamiento; (fig: influence)
influencia
levy [ˈlevɪ] n impuesto ▷ vt exigir,
recaudar
liability [laɪəˈbɪlətɪ] n (pej: person,
thing) estorbo, lastre m; (Jur:
responsibility) responsabilidad f
liable [ˈlaɪəbl] adj (subject): ~ **to** sujeto
a; (responsible): ~ **for** responsable de;
(likely): ~ **to do** propenso a hacer
liaise [lɪˈeɪz] vi: **to ~ with** enlazar con
liar [ˈlaɪə*] n mentiroso/a
liberal [ˈlɪbərəl] adj liberal; (offer,
amount etc) generoso; **Liberal**
Democrat (BRIT) n demócrata m/f
liberal
liberate [ˈlɪbəreɪt] vt (people: from
poverty etc) liberar; (prisoner) libertar;
(country) liberar
liberation [lɪbəˈreɪʃən] n liberación f
liberty [ˈlɪbətɪ] n libertad f; **to be at**
~ (criminal) estar en libertad; **to be at**
~ **to do** estar libre para hacer; **to take**
the ~ of doing sth tomarse la libertad
de hacer algo
Libra [ˈliːbrə] n Libra
librarian [laɪˈbrɛərɪən] n
bibliotecario/a
library [ˈlaɪbrərɪ] n biblioteca

> Be careful not to translate **library**
> by the Spanish word **librería**.

Libya [ˈlɪbɪə] n Libia
lice [laɪs] npl of **louse**
licence [ˈlaɪsəns] (US **license**) n
licencia; (permit) permiso; (also: **driving**
~) carnet m de conducir (SP), licencia de
manejo (LAM)
license [ˈlaɪsəns] n (US) = **licence** ▷ vt
autorizar, dar permiso a; **licensed** adj
(for alcohol) autorizado para vender
bebidas alcohólicas; (car) matriculado;
license plate (US) n placa (de
matrícula); **licensing hours** (BRIT) npl
horas durante las cuales se permite la venta
y consumo de alcohol (en un bar etc)

lick [lɪk] vt lamer; (inf: defeat) dar una paliza a; **to ~ one's lips** relamerse

lid [lɪd] n (of box, case) tapa; (of pan) tapadera

lie [laɪ] (pt **lay**, pp **lain**) vi (rest) estar echado, estar acostado; (of object: be situated) estar, encontrarse; (tell lies: pt, pp **lied**) mentir ▷ n mentira; **to ~ low** (fig) mantenerse a escondidas; **lie about** oraround vi (things) estar tirado; (BRIT: people) estar tumbado; **lie down** vi echarse, tumbarse

Liechtenstein [ˈlɪktənstaɪn] n Liechtenstein m

lie-in [ˈlaɪɪn] (BRIT) n **to have a ~** quedarse en la cama

lieutenant [lɛfˈtɛnənt, US luːˈtɛnənt] n (Mil) teniente mf

life [laɪf] (pl **lives**) n vida; **to come to ~** animarse; **life assurance** (BRIT) n seguro de vida; **lifeboat** n lancha de socorro; **lifeguard** n vigilante mf, socorrista mf; **life insurance** = **life assurance**; **life jacket** n chaleco salvavidas; **lifelike** adj (model etc) que parece vivo; (realistic) realista; **life preserver** (US) n cinturón m/chaleco salvavidas; **life sentence** n cadena perpetua; **lifestyle** n estilo de vida; **lifetime** n (of person) vida; (of thing) período de vida

lift [lɪft] vt levantar; (end: ban, rule) levantar, suprimir ▷ vi (fog) disiparse ▷ n (BRIT: machine) ascensor m; **to give sb a ~** (BRIT) llevar a algn en el coche; **lift up** vt levantar; **lift-off** n despegue m

light [laɪt] (pt, pp **~ed** or **lit**) n luz f; (lamp) luz f, lámpara; (Aut) faro; (for cigarette etc): **have you got a ~?** ¿tienes fuego? ▷ vt (candle, cigarette, fire) encender (SP), prender (LAM); (room) alumbrar ▷ adj (colour) claro; (not heavy, also fig) ligero; (room) con mucha luz; (gentle, graceful) ágil; **lights** npl (traffic lights) semáforos mpl; **to come to ~** salir a luz; **in the ~ of** (new evidence etc) a la luz de; **light up** vi

(smoke) encender un cigarrillo; (face) iluminarse ▷ vt (illuminate) iluminar, alumbrar; (set fire to) encender; **light bulb** n bombilla (SP), foco (MEX), bujía (CAM), bombita (RPL); **lighten** vt (make less heavy) aligerar; **lighter** n (also: **cigarette lighter**) encendedor m, mechero; **light-hearted** adj (person) alegre; (remark etc) divertido; **lighthouse** n faro; **lighting** n (system) alumbrado; **lightly** adv ligeramente; (not seriously) con poca seriedad; **to get off lightly** ser castigado con poca severidad

lightning [ˈlaɪtnɪŋ] n relámpago, rayo

lightweight [ˈlaɪtweɪt] adj (suit) ligero ▷ n (Boxing) peso ligero

like [laɪk] vt gustarle a algn ▷ prep como ▷ adj parecido, semejante ▷ n: **and the ~** y otros por el estilo; **his ~s and dislikes** sus gustos y aversiones; **I would ~, I'd ~** me gustaría; (for purchase) quisiera; **would you ~ a coffee?** ¿te apetece un café?; **I ~ swimming** me gusta nadar; **she ~s apples** le gustan las manzanas; **to be or look ~ sb/sth** parecerse a algn/algo; **what does it look/taste/sound ~?** ¿cómo es/a qué sabe/cómo suena?; **that's just ~ him** es muy de él, es característico de él; **do it ~ this** hazlo así; **it is nothing ~ ...** no tiene nada parecido alguno con ...; **likeable** adj simpático, agradable

likelihood [ˈlaɪklɪhʊd] n probabilidad f

likely [ˈlaɪklɪ] adj probable; **he's ~ to leave** es probable que se vaya; **not ~!** ¡ni hablar!

likewise [ˈlaɪkwaɪz] adv igualmente; **to do ~** hacer lo mismo

liking [ˈlaɪkɪŋ] n: **~ (for)** (person) cariño (a); (thing) afición (a); **to be to sb's ~** ser del gusto de algn

lilac [ˈlaɪlək] n (tree) lilo; (flower) lila

Lilo® [ˈlaɪləʊ] n colchoneta inflable

lily [ˈlɪlɪ] n lirio, azucena; **~ of the**

valley lirio de los valles

limb [lɪm] n miembro

limbo ['lɪmbəu] n: **to be in ~** (fig) quedar a la expectativa

lime [laɪm] n (tree) limero; (fruit) lima; (Geo) cal f

limelight ['laɪmlaɪt] n: **to be in the ~** (fig) ser el centro de atención

limestone ['laɪmstəun] n piedra caliza

limit ['lɪmɪt] n límite m ▷ vt limitar; **limited** adj limitado; **to be limited to** limitarse a

limousine ['lɪməziːn] n limusina

limp [lɪmp] n: **to have a ~** tener cojera ▷ vi cojear ▷ adj flojo; (material) fláccido

line [laɪn] n línea; (rope) cuerda; (for fishing) sedal m; (wire) hilo; (row, series) fila, hilera; (of writing) renglón m, línea; (of song) verso; (on face) arruga; (Rail) vía ▷ vt (road etc) llenar; (Sewing) forrar; **to ~ the streets** llenar las aceras; **in ~ with** alineado con; (according to) de acuerdo con; **line up** vi hacer cola ▷ vt alinear; (prepare) preparar; organizar

linear ['lɪnɪə*] adj lineal

linen ['lɪnɪn] n ropa blanca; (cloth) lino

liner ['laɪnə*] n vapor m de línea, transatlántico; (for bin) bolsa (de basura)

line-up ['laɪnʌp] n (us: queue) cola; (Sport) alineación f

linger ['lɪŋgə*] vi retrasarse, tardar en marcharse; (smell, tradition) persistir

lingerie ['lænʒəriː] n lencería

linguist ['lɪŋgwɪst] n lingüista mf; **linguistic** adj lingüístico

lining ['laɪnɪŋ] n forro; (Anat) (membrana) mucosa

link [lɪŋk] n (of a chain) eslabón m; (relationship) relación f, vínculo; (Internet) link m, enlace m ▷ vt vincular, unir; (associate) **to ~ with** or **to** relacionar con; **links** npl (Golf) campo de golf; **link up** vt acoplar ▷ vi unirse

lion ['laɪən] n león m; **lioness** n leona

lip [lɪp] n labio; **lipread** vi leer los labios; **lip salve** n crema protectora para labios; **lipstick** n lápiz m de labios, carmín m

liqueur [lɪ'kjuə*] n licor m

liquid ['lɪkwɪd] adj, n líquido; **liquidizer** [-aɪzə*] n licuadora

liquor ['lɪkə*] n licor m, bebidas fpl alcohólicas; **liquor store** (us) n bodega, tienda de vinos y bebidas alcohólicas

Lisbon ['lɪzbən] n Lisboa

lisp [lɪsp] n ceceo ▷ vi cecear

list [lɪst] n lista ▷ vt (mention) enumerar; (put on a list) poner en una lista

listen ['lɪsn] vi escuchar, oír; **to ~ to sb/sth** escuchar a algn/algo; **listener** n oyente mf; (Radio) radioyente mf

lit [lɪt] pt, pp of **light**

liter ['liːtə*] (us) n = **litre**

literacy ['lɪtərəsɪ] n capacidad f de leer y escribir

literal ['lɪtərl] adj literal; **literally** adv literalmente

literary ['lɪtərərɪ] adj literario

literate ['lɪtərət] adj que sabe leer y escribir; (educated) culto

literature ['lɪtərɪtʃə*] n literatura; (brochures etc) folletos mpl

litre ['liːtə*] (us **liter**) n litro

litter ['lɪtə*] n (rubbish) basura; (young animals) camada, cría; **litter bin** (BRIT) n papelera; **littered** adj: **littered with** (scattered) lleno de

little ['lɪtl] adj (small) pequeño; (not much) poco ▷ adv poco; **a ~** un poco (de); **~ house/bird** casita/pajarito; **a ~ bit** un poquito; **by ~** poco a poco; **little finger** n dedo meñique

live¹ [laɪv] adj (animal) vivo; (wire) conectado; (broadcast) en directo; (shell) cargado

live² [lɪv] vi vivir; **live together** vi vivir juntos; **live up to** vt fus (fulfil) cumplir con

livelihood ['laɪvlɪhud] n sustento

lively ['laɪvlɪ] adj vivo;

(*interesting: place, book etc*) animado
liven up ['laɪvn-] *vt* animar ▷ *vi*
animarse
liver ['lɪvə*] *n* hígado
lives [laɪvz] *npl of* **life**
livestock ['laɪvstɔk] *n* ganado
living ['lɪvɪŋ] *adj* (*alive*) vivo ▷ *n*: **to**
earn *or* **make a ~** ganarse la vida;
living room *n* sala (de estar)
lizard ['lɪzəd] *n* lagarto; (*small*)
lagartija
load [ləud] *n* carga; (*weight*) peso ▷ *vt*
(*Comput*) cargar; (*also*: **~ up**): **to ~ (with)**
cargar (con *or* de); **a ~ of rubbish** (*inf*)
tonterías *fpl*; **a ~ of, ~s of** (*fig*) (gran
cantidad de, montones de; **loaded**
adj (*vehicle*): **to be loaded with** estar
cargado de
loaf [ləuf] (*pl* **loaves**) *n* (barra de)
pan *m*
loan [ləun] *n* préstamo ▷ *vt* prestar;
on ~ prestado
loathe [ləuð] *vt* aborrecer; (*person*)
odiar
loaves [ləuvz] *npl of* **loaf**
lobby ['lɔbɪ] *n* vestíbulo, sala de
espera; (*Pol: pressure group*) grupo de
presión ▷ *vt* presionar
lobster ['lɔbstə*] *n* langosta
local ['ləukl] *adj* local ▷ *n* (*in pub*) bar *m*;
the locals *npl* los vecinos, los del lugar;
local anaesthetic *n* (*Med*) anestesia
local; **local authority** *n* municipio,
ayuntamiento (*sp*); **local government**
n gobierno municipal; **locally** [-kəlɪ]
adv en la vecindad; por aquí
locate [ləu'keɪt] *vt* (*find*) localizar;
(*situate*) situar; **to be ~d in** estar situado en
location [ləu'keɪʃən] *n* situación *f*;
on ~ (*Cinema*) en exteriores
loch [lɔx] *n* lago
lock [lɔk] *n* (*of door, box*) cerradura;
(*of canal*) esclusa; (*of hair*) mechón *m*
▷ *vt* (*with key*) cerrar (con llave) ▷ *vi*
(*door etc*) cerrarse (con llave); (*wheels*)
trabarse; **lock in** *vt* encerrar; **lock out**
vt (*person*) cerrar la puerta a; **lock up**
vt (*criminal*) meter en la cárcel; (*mental*

patient) encerrar; (*house*) cerrar (con
llave) ▷ *vi* echar la llave
locker ['lɔkə*] *n* casillero; **locker-**
room (*us*) *n* (*Sport*) vestuario
locksmith ['lɔksmɪθ] *n* cerrajero/a
locomotive [ləukə'məutɪv] *n*
locomotora
lodge [lɔdʒ] *n* casita del (guarda)
▷ *vi* (*person*): **to ~ (with)** alojarse (en
casa de); (*bullet, bone*) incrustarse ▷ *vt*
presentar; **lodger** *n* huésped *mf*
lodging ['lɔdʒɪŋ] *n* alojamiento,
hospedaje *m*
loft [lɔft] *n* desván *m*
log [lɔg] *n* (*of wood*) leño, tronco;
(*written account*) diario ▷ *vt* anotar;
log in, log on *vi* (*Comput*) entrar en
el sistema, hacer un login; **log off, log**
out *vi* (*Comput*) salir del sistema
logic ['lɔdʒɪk] *n* lógica; **logical** *adj*
lógico
login ['lɔgɪn] *n* (*Comput*) login *m*
lollipop ['lɔlɪpɔp] *n* pirulí *m*; **lollipop**
man/lady(*BRIT: irreg*) *n* persona
encargada de ayudar a los niños a cruzar
la calle
lolly ['lɔlɪ] *n* (*inf: ice cream*) polo;
(*: lollipop*) piruleta; (*: money*) guita
London ['lʌndən] *n* Londres;
Londoner *n* londinense *mf*
lone [ləun] *adj* solitario
loneliness ['ləunlɪnɪs] *n* soledad *f*;
aislamiento
lonely ['ləunlɪ] *adj* (*situation*)
solitario; (*person*) solo; (*place*) aislado
long [lɔŋ] *adj* largo ▷ *adv* mucho
tiempo, largamente ▷ *vi*: **to ~ for sth**
anhelar algo; **so** *or* **as ~ as** mientras,
con tal que; **don't be ~!** ¡no tardes!,
¡vuelve pronto!; **how ~ is the street?**
¿cuánto tiene la calle de largo?; **how ~**
is the lesson? ¿cuánto dura la clase?;
6 metres ~ que mide 6 metros, de
6 metros de largo; **6 months ~** que
dura 6 meses, de 6 meses de duración;
all night ~ toda la noche; **he no ~er**
comes ya no viene; **I can't stand it**
any ~er ya no lo aguanto más; **~ before**

mucho antes; **before ~** (+ *future*) dentro de poco; (+ *past*) poco tiempo después; **at ~ last** al fin, por fin; **long-distance** *adj* (*race*) de larga distancia; (*call*) interurbano; **long-haul** *adj* (*flight*) de larga distancia; **longing** *n* anhelo, ansia; (*nostalgia*) nostalgia ▷ *adj* anhelante

longitude ['lɔŋgɪtjuːd] *n* longitud *f*

long *adj* **long jump** *n* salto de longitud; **long-life** *adj* (*batteries*) de larga duración; (*milk*) uperizado; **long-sighted** (BRIT) *adj* présbita; **long-standing** *adj* de mucho tiempo; **long-term** *adj* a largo plazo

loo [luː] (BRIT: *inf*) *n* váter *m*

look [luk] *vi* mirar; (*seem*) parecer; (*building etc*): **to ~ south/on to the sea** dar al sur/al mar ▷ *n* (*gen*): **to have a ~** mirar; (*glance*) mirada; (*appearance*) aire *m*, aspecto; **looks** *npl* (*good looks*) belleza; **~ (here)!** (*expressing annoyance etc*) ¡oye!; **~!** (*expressing surprise*) ¡mira!; **look after** *vt fus* (*care for*) cuidar a; (*deal with*) encargarse de; **look around** *vi* echar una mirada alrededor; **look at** *vt fus* mirar; (*read quickly*) echar un vistazo a; **look back** *vi* mirar hacia atrás; **look down on** *vt fus* (*fig*) despreciar, mirar con desprecio; **look for** *vt fus* buscar; **look forward to** *vt fus* esperar con ilusión; (*in letters*): **we look forward to hearing from you** quedamos a la espera de sus gratas noticias; **look into** *vt* investigar; **look out** *vi* (*beware*) tener cuidado (de); **look out for** *vt fus* (*seek*) buscar; (*await*) esperar; **look round** *vi* volver la cabeza; **look through** *vt fus* (*examine*) examinar; **look up** *vi* mirar hacia arriba; (*improve*) mejorar ▷ *vt* (*word*) buscar; **look up to** *vt fus* admirar; **lookout** *n* (*tower etc*) puesto de observación; (*person*) vigía *mf*; **to be on the lookout for sth** estar al acecho de algo

loom [luːm] *vi*: **~ (up)** (*threaten*) surgir, amenazar; (*event*: *approach*)

aproximarse

loony ['luːnɪ] (*inf*) *n*, *adj* loco/a *m/f*

loop [luːp] *n* lazo ▷ *vt*: **to ~ sth round sth** pasar algo alrededor de algo; **loophole** *n* escapatoria

loose [luːs] *adj* suelto; (*clothes*) ancho; (*morals*, *discipline*) relajado; **to be on the ~** estar en libertad; **to be at a ~ end** *or* **~ ends** (US) no saber qué hacer; **loosely** *adv* libremente, aproximadamente; **loosen** *vt* aflojar

loot [luːt] *n* botín *m* ▷ *vt* saquear

lop-sided ['lɔp'saɪdɪd] *adj* torcido

lord [lɔːd] *n* señor *m*; **L~ Smith** Lord Smith; **the L~** el Señor; **my ~** (*to bishop*) Ilustrísima; (*to noble etc*) Señor; **good L~!** ¡Dios mío!; **Lords** (BRIT: *Pol*): **the (House of) Lords** la Cámara de los Lores

lorry ['lɔrɪ] (BRIT) *n* camión *m*; **lorry driver** (BRIT) *n* camionero/a *m/f*

lose [luːz] (*pt*, *pp* **lost**) *vt* perder ▷ *vi* perder, ser vencido; **to ~ (time)** (*clock*) atrasarse; **lose out** *vi* salir perdiendo; **loser** *n* perdedor/a *m/f*

loss [lɔs] *n* pérdida; **heavy ~es** (*Mil*) grandes pérdidas; **to be at a ~** no saber qué hacer; **to make a ~** sufrir pérdidas

lost [lɔst] *pt*, *pp* of **lose** ▷ *adj* perdido; **lost property** (US **lost and found**) *n* objetos *mpl* perdidos

lot [lɔt] *n* (*group: of things*) grupo; (*at auctions*) lote *m*; **the ~** el todo, todos; **a ~** (*large number: of books etc*) muchos; (*a great deal*) muchos, bastante; **a ~ of**, **~s of** mucho(s) (*pl*); **I read a ~** leo bastante; **to draw ~s (for sth)** echar suertes (para decidir algo)

lotion ['ləuʃən] *n* loción *f*

lottery ['lɔtərɪ] *n* lotería

loud [laud] *adj* (*voice*, *sound*) fuerte; (*laugh*, *shout*) estrepitoso; (*condemnation etc*) enérgico; (*gaudy*) chillón/ona ▷ *adv* (*speak etc*) fuerte; **out ~** en voz alta; **loudly** *adv* (*noisily*) fuerte; (*aloud*) en voz alta; **loudspeaker** *n* altavoz *m*

lounge [laundʒ] *n* salón *m*, sala (de

estar); (at airport etc) sala; (BRIT: also: **~-bar**) salón-bar m ▷ vi (also: **~ about** or **around**) reposar, holgazanear

louse [laus] (pl **lice**) n piojo

lousy ['lauzɪ] (inf) adj (bad quality) malísimo, asqueroso; (ill) fatal

love [lʌv] n (romantic, sexual) amor m; (kind, caring) cariño ▷vt amar, querer; (thing, activity) encantarle a algn; **"~ from Anne"** (on letter) "un abrazo (de) Anne"; **to ~ to do** encantarle a algn hacer; **to be/fall in ~ with** estar enamorado/enamorarse de; **to make ~** hacer el amor; **for the ~ of** por amor de; **"15 ~"** (Tennis) "15 a cero"; **I ~ you** te quiero; **I ~ paella** me encanta la paella; **love affair** n aventura sentimental; **love life** n vida sentimental

lovely ['lʌvlɪ] adj (delightful) encantador(a); (beautiful) precioso

lover ['lʌvə*] n amante mf; (person in love) enamorado; (amateur): **a ~ of** un(a) aficionado/a or un(a) amante de

loving ['lʌvɪŋ] adj amoroso, cariñoso; (action) tierno

low [ləu] adj, adv bajo ▷n (Meteorology) área de baja presión; **to be ~ on** (supplies etc) andar mal de; **to feel ~** sentirse deprimido; **to turn (down) ~** bajar; **low-alcohol** adj bajo contenido en alcohol; **low-calorie** adj bajo en calorías

lower ['ləuə*] adj más bajo; (less important) menos importante ▷vt bajar; (reduce) reducir ▷vr: **to ~ o.s. to** (fig) rebajarse a

low-fat adj (milk, yoghurt) desnatado; (diet) bajo en calorías

loyal ['lɔɪəl] adj leal; **loyalty** n lealtad f; **loyalty card** n tarjeta cliente

L.P. n abbr (= long-playing record) elepé m

L-plates ['el-] (BRIT) npl placas fpl de aprendiz de conductor

L-PLATES

En el Reino Unido las personas que están aprendiendo a conducir

deben llevar en la parte delantera y trasera de su vehículo unas placas blancas con una L en rojo conocidas como **L-Plates** (de **learner**). No es necesario que asistan a clases teóricas sino que, desde el principio, se entrega un carnet de conducir provisional ("provisional driving licence") para que realicen sus prácticas, aunque no pueden circular por las autopistas y deben ir siempre acompañadas por un conductor con carnet definitivo ("full driving licence").

Lt abbr (= lieutenant) Tte.

Ltd abbr (= limited company) S.A.

luck [lʌk] n suerte f; **bad ~** mala suerte; **good ~!** ¡que tengas suerte!, ¡suerte!; **bad** or **hard** or **tough ~!** ¡qué pena!; **luckily** adv afortunadamente; **lucky** adj afortunado; (at cards etc) con suerte; (object) que trae suerte

lucrative ['lu:krətɪv] adj lucrativo

ludicrous ['lu:dɪkrəs] adj absurdo

luggage ['lʌgɪdʒ] n equipaje m; **luggage rack** n (on car) baca, portaequipajes m inv

lukewarm [lu:kwɔ:m] adj tibio

lull [lʌl] n tregua ▷vt: **to ~ sb to sleep** arrullar a algn; **to ~ sb into a false sense of security** dar a algn una falsa sensación de seguridad

lullaby ['lʌləbaɪ] n nana

lumber ['lʌmbə*] n (junk) trastos mpl viejos; (wood) maderos mpl

luminous ['lu:mɪnəs] adj luminoso

lump [lʌmp] n terrón m; (fragment) trozo; (swelling) bulto ▷vt (also: **~ together**) juntar; **lump sum** n suma global; **lumpy** adj (sauce) lleno de grumos; (mattress) lleno de bultos

lunatic ['lu:nətɪk] adj loco

lunch [lʌntʃ] n almuerzo, comida ▷vi almorzar; **lunch break, lunch hour** n hora del almuerzo; **lunch time** n hora de comer

lung [lʌŋ] n pulmón m
lure [luə*] n (attraction) atracción f
▷ vt tentar
lurk [lə:k] vi (person, animal) estar al
acecho; (fig) acechar
lush [lʌʃ] adj exuberante
lust [lʌst] n lujuria; (greed) codicia
Luxembourg ['lʌksəmbə:g] n
Luxemburgo
luxurious [lʌg'zjuəriəs] adj lujoso
luxury ['lʌkʃəri] n lujo ▷ cpd de lujo
Lycra® ['laikrə] n licra®
lying ['laiiŋ] n mentiras fpl ▷ adj
mentiroso
lyrics ['liriks] npl (of song) letra

m. abbr = **metre; mile; million**
M.A. abbr = **Master of Arts**
ma (inf) [mɑ:] n mamá
mac [mæk] (BRIT) n impermeable m
macaroni [mækə'rəuni] n
macarrones mpl
Macedonia [mæsɪ'dəuniə] n
Macedonia; **Macedonian** [-'dəuniən]
adj macedonio ▷ n macedonio/a;
(Ling) macedonio
machine [mə'ʃi:n] n máquina
▷ vt (dress etc) coser a máquina;
(Tech) hacer a máquina; **machine
gun** n ametralladora; **machinery**
n maquinaria; (fig) mecanismo;
machine washable adj lavable a
máquina
macho ['mætʃəu] adj machista
mackerel ['mækrl] n inv caballa
mackintosh ['mækintɔʃ] (BRIT) n
impermeable m
mad [mæd] adj loco; (idea)
disparatado; (angry) furioso; (keen): **to
be ~ about sth** volverle loco a algn algo
Madagascar [mædə'gæskə*] n

Madagascar m

madam ['mædəm] n señora

mad cow disease n encefalopatía espongiforme bovina

made [meɪd] pt, pp of **make**;
made-to-measure (BRIT) adj hecho a la medida; **made-up** ['meɪdʌp] adj (story) ficticio

madly ['mædlɪ] adv locamente

madman ['mædmən] (irreg) n loco

madness ['mædnɪs] n locura

Madrid [mə'drɪd] n Madrid m

Mafia ['mæfɪə] n Mafia

mag [mæg] n abbr (BRIT inf) = **magazine**

magazine [mægə'zi:n] n revista; (Radio, TV) programa m magazina

maggot ['mægət] n gusano

magic ['mædʒɪk] n magia ▷ adj mágico; **magical** adj mágico; **magician** [mə'dʒɪʃən] n mago/a; (conjurer) prestidigitador(a) m/f

magistrate ['mædʒɪstreɪt] n juez mf (municipal)

magnet ['mægnɪt] n imán m; **magnetic** [-'nɛtɪk] adj magnético; (personality) atrayente

magnificent [mæg'nɪfɪsənt] adj magnífico

magnify ['mægnɪfaɪ] vt (object) ampliar; (sound) aumentar; **magnifying glass** n lupa

magpie ['mægpaɪ] n urraca

mahogany [mə'hɔgənɪ] n caoba

maid [meɪd] n criada; mayor; **old ~** (pej) solterona

maiden name n nombre m de soltera

mail [meɪl] n correo; (letters) cartas fpl ▷ vt echar al correo; **mailbox** (US) n buzón m; **mailing list** n lista de direcciones; **mailman** (US: irreg) n cartero; **mail-order** n pedido postal

main [meɪn] adj principal, mayor ▷ n (pipe) cañería maestra; (US) red f eléctrica ▷ **the ~s** npl (BRIT Elec) la red eléctrica; **in the ~** en general; **main course** n (Culin) plato principal; **mainland** n tierra firme; **mainly**

adv principalmente; **main road** n carretera; **mainstream** n corriente f principal; **main street** n calle f mayor

maintain [meɪn'teɪn] vt mantener; **maintenance** ['meɪntənəns] n mantenimiento; (Law) manutención f

maisonette [meɪzə'nɛt] n dúplex m

maize [meɪz] (BRIT) n maíz m, choclo (SC)

majesty ['mædʒɪstɪ] n majestad f; (title): **Your M~** Su Majestad

major ['meɪdʒə*] n (Mil) comandante mf ▷ adj principal; (Mus) mayor

Majorca [mə'jɔːkə] n Mallorca

majority [mə'dʒɔrɪtɪ] n mayoría

make [meɪk] (pt, pp **made**) vt hacer; (manufacture) fabricar; (mistake) cometer; (speech) pronunciar; (cause to be): **to ~ sb sad** poner triste a algn; (force): **to ~ sb do sth** obligar a algn a hacer algo; (earn) ganar; (equal): **2 and 2 ~ 4** 2 y 2 son 4 ▷ n marca; **to ~ the bed** hacer la cama; **to ~ a fool of sb** poner a algn en ridículo; **to ~ a profit/loss** obtener ganancias/sufrir pérdidas; **to ~ it** (arrive) llegar; (achieve sth) tener éxito; **what time do you ~ it?** ¿qué hora tienes?; **to ~ do with** contentarse con; **make off** vi largarse; **make out** vt (decipher) descifrar; (understand) entender; (see) distinguir; (cheque) extender; **make up** vt (invent) inventar; (prepare) hacer; (constitute) constituir ▷ vi reconciliarse; (with cosmetics) maquillarse; **make up for** vt fus compensar; **makeover** ['meɪkəuvə*] n (by beautician) sesión f de maquillaje y peluquería; (change of image) lavado de cara; **maker** n fabricante m/f; (of film, programme) autor(a) m/f; **makeshift** adj improvisado; **make-up** n maquillaje m

making ['meɪkɪŋ] n (fig): **in the ~** en vías de formación; **to have the ~s of** (person) tener madera de

malaria [mə'lɛərɪə] n malaria

Malaysia [mə'leɪzɪə] n Malasia,

Malaysia

male [meɪl] n (Biol) macho ▷ adj (sex, attitude) masculino; (child etc) varón

malicious [məˈlɪʃəs] adj malicioso; rencoroso

malignant [məˈlɪɡnənt] adj (Med) maligno

mall [mɔːl] (US) n (also: **shopping ~**) centro comercial

mallet [ˈmælɪt] n mazo

malnutrition [mælnjuːˈtrɪʃən] n desnutrición f

malpractice [mælˈpræktɪs] n negligencia profesional

malt [mɔːlt] n malta; (whisky) whisky m de malta

Malta [ˈmɔːltə] n Malta; **Maltese** [-ˈtiːz] adj, n inv maltés/esa m/f

mammal [ˈmæml] n mamífero

mammoth [ˈmæməθ] n mamut m ▷ adj gigantesco

man [mæn] (pl **men**) n hombre m; (mankind) el hombre ▷ vt (Naut) tripular; (Mil) guarnecer; (operate: machine) manejar; **an old ~** un viejo; **~ and wife** marido y mujer

manage [ˈmænɪdʒ] vi arreglárselas, ir tirando ▷ vt (be in charge of) dirigir; (control: person) manejar; (: ship) gobernar; **manageable** adj manejable; **management** n dirección f; **manager** n director(a) m/f; (of pop star) mánager mf; (Sport) entrenador(a) m/f; **manageress** n directora, entrenadora; **managerial** adj directivo; **managing director** n director(a) m/f general

mandarin [ˈmændərɪn] n (also: **~ orange**) mandarina; (person) mandarín m

mandate [ˈmændeɪt] n mandato

mandatory [ˈmændətərɪ] adj obligatorio

mane [meɪn] n (of horse) crin f; (of lion) melena

maneuver [məˈnuːvə*] (US) = **manoeuvre**

mangetout [mɒnʒˈtuː] n tirabeque

m

mango [ˈmæŋɡəu] (pl **~es**) n mango

man: manhole n agujero de acceso; **manhood** n edad f viril; (state) virilidad f

mania [ˈmeɪnɪə] n manía; **maniac** [ˈmeɪnɪæk] n maníaco/a; (fig) maniático

manic [ˈmænɪk] adj frenético

manicure [ˈmænɪkjuə*] n manicura

manifest [ˈmænɪfest] vt manifestar, mostrar ▷ adj manifiesto

manifesto [mænɪˈfestəu] n manifiesto

manipulate [məˈnɪpjuleɪt] vt manipular

man: mankind [mænˈkaɪnd] n humanidad f, género humano; **manly** adj varonil; **man-made** adj artificial

manner [ˈmænə*] n manera, modo; (behaviour) conducta, manera de ser; (type): **all ~ of things** toda clase de cosas; **manners** npl (behaviour) modales mpl; **bad ~s** mala educación

manoeuvre [məˈnuːvə*] (US **maneuver**) vt, vi maniobrar ▷ n maniobra

manpower [ˈmænpauə*] n mano f de obra

mansion [ˈmænʃən] n palacio, casa grande

manslaughter [ˈmænslɔːtə*] n homicidio no premeditado

mantelpiece [ˈmæntlpiːs] n repisa, chimenea

manual [ˈmænjuəl] adj manual ▷ n manual m

manufacture [mænjuˈfæktʃə*] vt fabricar ▷ n fabricación f; **manufacturer** n fabricante mf

manure [məˈnjuə*] n estiércol m

manuscript [ˈmænjuskrɪpt] n manuscrito

many [ˈmenɪ] adj, pron muchos/as; **a great ~** muchísimos, un buen número de; **~ a time** muchas veces

map [mæp] n mapa m ▷ **to ~ out** vt proyectar

maple ['meɪpl] n arce m, maple m (LAM)

Mar abbr (= March) mar

mar [mɑː*] vt estropear

marathon ['mærəθən] n maratón m

marble ['mɑːbl] n mármol m; (toy) canica

March [mɑːtʃ] n marzo

march [mɑːtʃ] vi (Mil) marchar; (demonstrators) manifestarse ▷ n marcha; (demonstration) manifestación f

mare [mɛə*] n yegua

margarine [mɑːdʒəˈriːn] n margarina

margin ['mɑːdʒɪn] n margen m; (Comm: profit margin) margen m de beneficios; **marginal** adj marginal; **marginally** adv ligeramente

marigold ['mærɪɡəʊld] n caléndula

marijuana [mærɪˈwɑːnə] n marijuana

marina [məˈriːnə] n puerto deportivo

marinade [mærɪˈneɪd] n adobo

marinate ['mærɪneɪt] vt marinar

marine [məˈriːn] adj marino ▷ n soldado de marina

marital ['mærɪtl] adj matrimonial; **marital status** n estado m civil

maritime ['mærɪtaɪm] adj marítimo

marjoram ['mɑːdʒərəm] n mejorana

mark [mɑːk] n marca, señal f; (in snow, mud etc) huella; (stain) mancha; (BRIT Scol) nota ▷ vt marcar; manchar; (damage: furniture) rayar; (indicate: place etc) señalar; (BRIT Scol) calificar, corregir; **to ~ time** marcar el paso; (fig) marcar(se) un ritmo; **marked** adj (obvious) marcado, acusado; **marker** n (sign) marcador m; (bookmark) señal f (de libro)

market ['mɑːkɪt] n mercado ▷ vt (Comm) comercializar; **marketing** n márketing m; **marketplace** n mercado; **market research** n análisis m inv de mercados

marmalade ['mɑːməleɪd] n

mermelada de naranja

maroon [məˈruːn] vt: **to be ~ed** quedar aislado; (fig) quedar abandonado ▷ n (colour) granate m

marquee [mɑːˈkiː] n entoldado

marriage ['mærɪdʒ] n (relationship, institution) matrimonio; (wedding) boda; (act) casamiento; **marriage certificate** n partida de casamiento

married ['mærɪd] adj casado; (life, love) conyugal

marrow ['mærəʊ] n médula; (vegetable) calabacín m

marry ['mærɪ] vt casarse con; (father, priest etc) casar ▷ vi (also: **get married**) casarse

Mars [mɑːz] n Marte m

marsh [mɑːʃ] n pantano; (salt marsh) marisma

marshal ['mɑːʃl] n (Mil) mariscal m; (at sports meeting etc) oficial m; (us: of police, fire department) jefe/a m/f ▷ vt (thoughts etc) ordenar; (soldiers) formar

martyr ['mɑːtə*] n mártir m/f

marvel ['mɑːvl] n maravilla, prodigio ▷ vi: **to ~ (at)** maravillarse (de); **marvellous** (US **marvelous**) adj maravilloso

Marxism ['mɑːksɪzəm] n marxismo

Marxist ['mɑːksɪst] adj, n marxista m/f

marzipan ['mɑːtɪpæn] n mazapán m

mascara [mæsˈkɑːrə] n rímel m

mascot ['mæskət] n mascota

masculine ['mæskjʊlɪn] adj masculino

mash [mæʃ] vt machacar; **mashed potato(es)** n(pl) puré m de patatas (SP) or papas (LAM)

mask [mɑːsk] n máscara ▷ vt (cover): **to ~ one's face** ocultarse la cara; (hide: feelings) esconder

mason ['meɪsn] n (also: **stone~**) albañil m; (also: **free~**) masón m; **masonry** n (in building) mampostería

mass [mæs] n (gen) muchedumbre f; (of air, liquid etc) masa; (of detail, hair etc) gran cantidad f; (Rel) misa ▷ cpd masivo ▷ vi reunirse; concentrarse; **the masses** npl las masas; **~es of** (inf) montones de

massacre ['mæsəkə*] n masacre f

massage ['mæsɑːʒ] n masaje m ▷ vt dar masaje en

massive ['mæsɪv] adj enorme; (support, changes) masivo

mass media npl medios mpl de comunicación

mass-produce ['mæsprə'djuːs] vt fabricar en serie

mast [mɑːst] n (Naut) mástil m; (Radio etc) torre f

master ['mɑːstə*] n (of servant) amo; (of situation) dueño, maestro; (in primary school) maestro; (in secondary school) profesor m; (title for boys): **M~ X** Señorito X ▷ vt dominar; **mastermind** n inteligencia superior ▷ vt dirigir, planear; **Master of Arts/Science** n licenciatura superior en Letras/Ciencias; **masterpiece** n obra maestra

masturbate ['mæstəbeɪt] vi masturbarse

mat [mæt] n estera; (also: **door~**) felpudo; (also: **table~**) salvamanteles m inv, posavasos m inv ▷ adj = **matt**

match [mætʃ] n cerilla, fósforo; (game) partido; (equal) igual m/f ▷ vt (go well with) hacer juego con; (equal) igualar; (correspond to) corresponderse con; (pair: also: **~ up**) casar con ▷ vi hacer juego; **to be a good ~** hacer juego; **matchbox** n caja de cerillas; **matching** adj que hace juego

mate [meɪt] n (workmate) colega mf; (inf: friend) amigo/a; (animal) macho/hembra; (in merchant navy) segundo de a bordo ▷ vi acoplarse, aparearse ▷ vt aparear

material [mə'tɪərɪəl] n (substance) materia; (information) material m; (cloth) tela, tejido ▷ adj material; (important) esencial; **materials** npl materiales mpl

materialize [mə'tɪərɪəlaɪz] vi

materializarse

maternal [mə'təːnl] adj maternal

maternity [mə'təːnɪtɪ] n maternidad f; **maternity hospital** n hospital m de maternidad; **maternity leave** n baja por maternidad

math [mæθ] (US) n = **mathematics**

mathematical [mæθə'mætɪkl] adj matemático

mathematician [mæθəmə'tɪʃən] n matemático/a

mathematics [mæθə'mætɪks] n matemáticas fpl

maths [mæθs] (BRIT) n = **mathematics**

matinée ['mætɪneɪ] n sesión f de tarde

matron ['meɪtrən] n enfermera f jefe; (in school) ama de llaves

matt [mæt] adj mate

matter ['mætə*] n cuestión f, asunto; (Physics) sustancia, materia; (reading matter) material m; (Med: pus) pus m ▷ vi importar; **matters** npl (affairs) asuntos mpl, temas mpl; **it doesn't ~** no importa; **what's the ~?** ¿qué pasa?; **no ~ what** pase lo que pase; **as a ~ of course** por rutina; **as a ~ of fact** de hecho

mattress ['mætrɪs] n colchón m

mature [mə'tjuə*] adj maduro ▷ vi madurar; **mature student** n estudiante de más de 21 años; **maturity** n madurez f

maul [mɔːl] vt magullar

mauve [məuv] adj de color malva (SP) or guinda (LAM)

max abbr = **maximum**

maximize ['mæksɪmaɪz] vt (profits etc) llevar al máximo; (chances) maximizar

maximum ['mæksɪməm] (pl **maxima**) adj máximo ▷ n máximo

May [meɪ] n mayo

may [meɪ] (conditional **might**) vi (indicating possibility): **he ~ come** puede que venga; (be allowed to): **~ I smoke?** ¿puedo fumar?; (wishes): **~ God bless**

you! ¡que Dios le bendiga!; you ~ as
well go bien puedes irte
maybe ['meɪbɪ] adv quizá(s)
May Day n el primero de Mayo
mayhem ['meɪhem] n caos m total
mayonnaise [meɪə'neɪz] n
mayonesa
mayor [mɛə*] n alcalde m; mayoress
n alcaldesa
maze [meɪz] n laberinto
MD n abbr = managing director
me [miː] pron (direct) me; (stressed,
after prep) mí; can you hear ~? ¿me
oyes?; he heard ME ¡me oyó a mí!; it's
~ soy yo; give them to ~ dámelos/las;
with/without ~ conmigo/sin mí
meadow ['mɛdəʊ] n prado, pradera
meagre ['miːgə*] (US meager) adj
escaso, pobre
meal [miːl] n comida; (flour) harina;
mealtime n hora de comer
mean [miːn] (pt, pp ~t) adj (with
money) tacaño; (unkind) mezquino,
malo; (shabby) humilde; (average) medio
▷ vt (signify) querer decir, significar;
(refer to) referirse a; (intend): to ~ to
do sth pensar o pretender hacer algo
▷ n medio, término medio; (means)
npl (way) medio, manera; (money)
recursos mpl, medios mpl; by all ~s!
¡naturalmente!, ¡claro que sí!; do you ~
it? ¿lo dices en serio?; what do you ~?
¿qué quiere decir?; to be ~t for sb/sth
ser para algn/algo
meaning ['miːnɪŋ] n significado,
sentido; (purpose) sentido, propósito;
meaningful adj significativo;
meaningless adj sin sentido
meant [mɛnt] pt, pp of mean
meantime ['miːntaɪm] adv (also: in
the ~) mientras tanto
meanwhile ['miːnwaɪl] adv =
meantime
measles ['miːzlz] n sarampión m
measure ['mɛʒə*] vt, vi medir ▷ n
medida; (ruler) regla; measurement
['mɛʒəmənt] n (measure) medida;

(act) medición f; to take sb's
measurements tomar las medidas
a algn
meat [miːt] n carne f; cold ~ fiambre
m; meatball n albóndiga
Mecca ['mɛkə] n La Meca
mechanic [mɪ'kænɪk] n mecánico/
a; mechanical adj mecánico
mechanism ['mɛkənɪzəm] n
mecanismo
medal ['mɛdl] n medalla; medallist
(US medalist) n medallista mf
meddle ['mɛdl] vi: to ~ in
entrometerse en; to ~ with sth
manosear algo
media ['miːdɪə] npl medios mpl de
comunicación ▷ npl of medium
mediaeval [mɛdɪ'iːvl] adj =
medieval
mediate ['miːdɪeɪt] vi mediar
medical ['mɛdɪkl] adj médico ▷ n
reconocimiento médico; medical
certificate n certificado m médico
medicated ['mɛdɪkeɪtɪd] adj
medicinal
medication [mɛdɪ'keɪʃən] n
medicación f
medicine ['mɛdsɪn] n medicina;
(drug) medicamento
medieval [mɛdɪ'iːvl] adj medieval
mediocre [miːdɪ'əʊkə*] adj
mediocre
meditate ['mɛdɪteɪt] vi meditar
meditation [mɛdɪ'teɪʃən] n
meditación f
Mediterranean [mɛdɪtə'reɪnɪən]
adj mediterráneo; the ~ (Sea) el (Mar)
Mediterráneo
medium ['miːdɪəm] (pl media)
adj mediano, regular ▷ n (means)
medio; (pl mediums: person) médium
mf; medium-sized adj de tamaño
mediano; (clothes) de (la) talla mediana;
medium wave n onda media
meek [miːk] adj manso, sumiso
meet [miːt] (pt, pp met) vt encontrar;
(accidentally) encontrarse con,
tropezar con; (by arrangement) reunirse

m

con; *(for the first time)* conocer; *(go and fetch)* ir a buscar; *(opponent)* enfrentarse con; *(obligations)* cumplir; *(encounter: problem)* hacer frente a; *(need)* satisfacer ▷ vi encontrarse; *(in session)* reunirse; *(join: objects)* unirse; *(for the first time)* conocerse; **meet up** vi: **to meet up with sb** reunirse con algn; **meet with** vt fus *(difficulty)* tropezar con; **to meet with success** tener éxito; **meeting** n encuentro; *(arranged)* cita, compromiso; *(business meeting)* reunión f; *(Pol)* mítin m; **meeting place** n lugar m de reunión or encuentro

megabyte ['mɛgəbaɪt] n *(Comput)* megabyte m, megaocteto

megaphone ['mɛgəfəun] n megáfono

megapixel ['mɛgəpɪksl] n megapíxel m

melancholy ['mɛlənkəlɪ] n melancolía ▷ adj melancólico

melody ['mɛlədɪ] n melodía

melon ['mɛlən] n melón m

melt [mɛlt] vi *(metal)* fundirse; *(snow)* derretirse ▷ vt fundir

member ['mɛmbə*] n *(gen, Anat)* miembro m; *(of club)* socio/a; **Member of Congress** *(US)* n miembro m del Congreso; **Member of Parliament** *(BRIT)* diputado/a m/f, parlamentario/a m/f; **Member of the European Parliament** n diputado/a m/f del Parlamento Europeo, eurodiputado/a m/f; **Member of the Scottish Parliament** *(BRIT)* diputado/a del Parlamento escocés; **membership** n *(members)* número de miembros; *(state)* filiación f; **membership card** n carnet m de socio

memento [mə'mɛntəu] n recuerdo

memo ['mɛməu] n apunte m, nota

memorable ['mɛmərəbl] adj memorable

memorandum [mɛmə'rændəm] *(pl* memoranda) n apunte m, nota; *(official note)* acta

memorial [mɪ'mɔːrɪəl] n monumento conmemorativo ▷ adj conmemorativo

memorize ['mɛməraɪz] vt aprender de memoria

memory ['mɛmərɪ] n *(also: Comput)* memoria; *(instance)* recuerdo; *(of dead person)* **in ~ of** a la memoria de; **memory card** n tarjeta de memoria; **memory stick** n barra de memoria

men [mɛn] npl of **man**

menace ['mɛnəs] n amenaza ▷ vt amenazar

mend [mɛnd] vt reparar, arreglar; *(darn)* zurcir ▷ vi reponerse ▷ n arreglo, reparación f zurcido ▷ n: **to be on the ~** ir mejorando; **to ~ one's ways** enmendarse

meningitis [mɛnɪn'dʒaɪtɪs] n meningitis f

menopause ['mɛnəupɔːz] n menopausia

men's room *(US)* n: **the ~** el servicio de caballeros

menstruation [mɛnstru'eɪʃən] n menstruación f

menswear ['mɛnzwɛə*] n confección f de caballero

mental ['mɛntl] adj mental; **mental hospital** n *(hospital m)* psiquiátrico; **mentality** [mɛn'tælɪt] n mentalidad f; **mentally** adv: **to be mentally ill** tener una enfermedad mental

menthol ['mɛnθɔl] n mentol m

mention ['mɛnʃən] n mención f ▷ vt mencionar; *(speak)* hablar de; **don't ~ it!** ¡de nada!

menu ['mɛnjuː] n *(set menu)* menú m; *(printed)* carta; *(Comput)* menú m

MEP n abbr = **Member of the European Parliament**

mercenary ['məːsɪnərɪ] adj, n mercenario/a

merchandise ['məːtʃəndaɪz] n mercancías fpl

merchant ['məːtʃənt] n comerciante mf; **merchant navy** *(US)*, **merchant marine** n marina mercante

merciless ['mɜːsɪlɪs] *adj* despiadado
mercury ['mɜːkjʊrɪ] *n* mercurio
mercy ['mɜːsɪ] *n* compasión *f*; (Rel) misericordia; **at the ~ of** a la merced de
mere [mɪə*] *adj* simple, mero; **merely** *adv* simplemente, sólo
merge [mɜːdʒ] *vt* (join) unir ▷ *vi* unirse; (Comm) fusionarse; (colours etc) fundirse; **merger** *n* (Comm) fusión *f*
meringue [mə'ræŋ] *n* merengue *m*
merit ['mɛrɪt] *n* mérito ▷ *vt* merecer
mermaid ['mɜːmeɪd] *n* sirena
merry ['mɛrɪ] *adj* alegre; **M~ Christmas!** ¡Felices Pascuas!; **merry-go-round** *n* tiovivo
mesh [mɛʃ] *n* malla
mess [mɛs] *n* (muddle: of situation) confusión *f*; (: of room) revoltijo; (dirt) porquería; (Mil) comedor *m*; **mess about** or **around** (inf) *vi* perder el tiempo; (pass the time) entretenerse; **mess up** *vt* (spoil) estropear; (dirty) ensuciar; **mess with** (inf) *vt fus* (challenge, confront) meterse con (inf); (interfere with) interferir con
message ['mɛsɪdʒ] *n* recado, mensaje *m*
messenger ['mɛsɪndʒə*] *n* mensajero/a
Messrs *abbr* (on letters) (= Messieurs) Sres
messy ['mɛsɪ] *adj* (dirty) sucio; (untidy) desordenado
met [mɛt] *pt, pp of* **meet**
metabolism [mɛ'tæbəlɪzəm] *n* metabolismo
metal ['mɛtl] *n* metal *m*; **metallic** [-'tælɪk] *adj* metálico
metaphor ['mɛtəfə*] *n* metáfora
meteor ['miːtɪə*] *n* meteoro; **meteorite** [-aɪt] *n* meteorito
meteorology [miːtɪə'rɔlədʒɪ] *n* meteorología
meter ['miːtə*] *n* (instrument) contador *m*; (us: unit) = **metre** ▷ *vt* (us Post) franquear
method ['mɛθəd] *n* método; **methodical** [mɪ'θɔdɪkl] *adj* metódico

meths [mɛθs] *n* (BRIT) alcohol *m* metilado or desnaturalizado
meticulous [mɛ'tɪkjʊləs] *adj* meticuloso
metre ['miːtə*] (us **meter**) *n* metro
metric ['mɛtrɪk] *adj* métrico
metro ['mɛtrəu] *n* metro
metropolitan [mɛtrə'pɔlɪtən] *adj* metropolitano; **the M~ Police** (BRIT) la policía londinense
Mexican ['mɛksɪkən] *adj, n* mexicano/a, mejicano/a
Mexico ['mɛksɪkəu] *n* México, Méjico (sp)
mg *abbr* (= milligram) mg
mice [maɪs] *npl of* **mouse**
micro... [maɪkrəu] *prefix* micro...;
microchip *n* microplaqueta;
microphone *n* micrófono;
microscope *n* microscopio;
microwave *n* (also: **microwave oven**) horno microondas
mid [mɪd] *adj*: **in ~ May** a mediados de mayo; **in ~ afternoon** a media tarde; **in ~ air** en el aire; **midday** *n* mediodía *m*
middle ['mɪdl] *n* centro; (half-way point) medio; (waist) cintura ▷ *adj* de en medio; (course, way) intermedio; **in the ~ of the night** en plena noche; **middle-aged** *adj* de mediana edad; **Middle Ages** *npl*: **the Middle Ages** la Edad Media; **middle-class** *adj* de clase media; **the middle class(es)** la clase media; **Middle East** *n* Oriente *m* Medio; **middle name** *n* segundo nombre; **middle school** *n* (us) colegio para niños de doce a catorce años; (BRIT) colegio para niños de ocho o nueve a doce o trece años
midge [mɪdʒ] *n* mosquito
midget ['mɪdʒɪt] *n* enano/a
midnight ['mɪdnaɪt] *n* medianoche *f*
midst [mɪdst] *n*: **in the ~ of** (crowd) en medio de; (situation, action) en mitad de
midsummer [mɪd'sʌmə*] *n*: **in ~** en pleno verano
midway [mɪd'weɪ] *adj, adv*: **~ (between)** a medio camino (entre); **~**

through a la mitad (de)
midweek ['mɪd'wiːk] adv entre semana
midwife ['mɪdwaɪf] (irreg) n comadrona, partera
midwinter [mɪd'wɪntə*] n: **in** ~ en pleno invierno
might [maɪt] vb see **may** ▷ n fuerza, poder m; **mighty** adj fuerte, poderoso
migraine ['miːɡreɪn] n migraña
migrant ['maɪɡrənt] n, adj (bird) migratorio; (worker) emigrante
migrate [maɪ'ɡreɪt] vi emigrar
migration [maɪ'ɡreɪʃən] n emigración f
mike [maɪk] n abbr (= microphone) micro
mild [maɪld] adj (person) apacible; (climate) templado; (slight) ligero; (taste) suave; (illness) leve; **mildly** ['-lɪ] adv ligeramente; suavemente; **to put it mildly** para no decir más
mile [maɪl] n milla; **mileage** n número de millas ≈ kilometraje m; **mileometer** [maɪ'lɒmɪtə] n = cuentakilómetros m inv; **milestone** n mojón m
military ['mɪlɪtərɪ] adj militar
militia [mɪ'lɪʃə] n milicia
milk [mɪlk] n leche f ▷ vt (cow) ordeñar; (fig) chupar; **milk chocolate** n chocolate m con leche; **milkman** (irreg) n lechero; **milky** adj lechoso
mill [mɪl] n (windmill etc) molino; (coffee mill) molinillo; (factory) fábrica ▷ vt moler ▷ vi (also: ~ **about**) arremolinarse
millennium [mɪ'lenɪəm] (pl ~**s** or **millennia**) n milenio, milenario
milli... ['mɪlɪ] prefix: **milligram(me)** n miligramo; **millilitre** (us **milliliter**) ['mɪlɪliːtə*] n mililitro; **millimetre** (us **millimeter**) n milímetro
million ['mɪljən] n millón m; **a ~ times** un millón de veces; **millionaire** [-jə'nɛə*] n millonario/a; **millionth** [-θ] adj millonésimo
milometer [maɪ'lɒmɪtə*] (BRIT) n =

mileometer
mime [maɪm] n mímica; (actor) mimo/a ▷ vt remedar ▷ vi actuar de mimo
mimic ['mɪmɪk] n imitador(a) m/f ▷ adj mímico ▷ vt remedar, imitar
min. abbr = **minimum; minute(s)**
mince [mɪns] vt picar ▷ n (BRIT Culin) carne f picada; **mincemeat** n conserva de fruta picada; (us: meat) carne f picada; **mince pie** n empanadilla rellena de fruta picada
mind [maɪnd] n mente f; (intellect) intelecto; (contrasted with matter) espíritu m ▷ vt (attend to, look after) ocuparse de, cuidar; (be careful) tener cuidado con; (object to): **I don't ~ the noise** no me molesta el ruido; **it is on my ~** me preocupa; **to bear sth in mind** ~ tomar or tener algo en cuenta; **to make up one's ~** decidirse; **I don't ~** me es igual; **~ you ...** te advierto que ...; **never ~!** ¡es igual!, ¡no importa!; (don't worry) ¡no te preocupes!; **"~ the step"** "cuidado con el escalón"; **mindless** adj (crime) sin motivo; (work) de autómata
mine¹ [maɪn] pron el mío la mía etc; **a friend of ~** un(a) amigo/a mío/mía ▷ adj: **this book is ~** este libro es mío
mine² [maɪn] n mina ▷ vt (coal) extraer; (bomb: beach etc) minar; **minefield** n campo de minas; **miner** n minero/a
mineral ['mɪnərəl] adj mineral ▷ n mineral m; **mineral water** n agua mineral
mingle ['mɪŋɡl] vi: **to ~ with** mezclarse con
miniature ['mɪnətʃə*] adj (en) miniatura ▷ n miniatura
minibar ['mɪnibɑ:*] n minibar m
minibus ['mɪnɪbʌs] n microbús m
minicab ['mɪnɪkæb] n taxi m (que sólo puede pedirse por teléfono)
minimal ['mɪnɪml] adj mínimo
minimize ['mɪnɪmaɪz] vt minimizar; (play down) empequeñecer
minimum ['mɪnɪməm] (pl **minima**)

n, adj mínimo

mining ['maɪnɪŋ] n explotación f minera

miniskirt ['mɪnɪskɜːt] n minifalda

minister ['mɪnɪstə*] n (BRIT Pol) ministro/a (SP), secretario/a (LAM); (Rel) pastor m ▷ vi: **to ~ to** atender a

ministry ['mɪnɪstrɪ] n (BRIT Pol) ministerio, secretaría (MEX); (Rel) sacerdocio

minor ['maɪnə*] adj (repairs, injuries) leve; (poet, planet) menor; (Mus) menor ▷ n (Law) menor m de edad

Minorca [mɪ'nɔːkə] n Menorca

minority [maɪ'nɒrɪtɪ] n minoría

mint [mɪnt] n (plant) menta, hierbabuena; (sweet) caramelo de menta ▷ vt (coins) acuñar; **the (Royal) M~, the (US) M~** la Casa de la Moneda; **in ~ condition** en perfecto estado

minus ['maɪnəs] n (also: **~ sign**) signo de menos ▷ prep menos; **12 ~ 6 equals 6** 12 menos 6 son 6; **~ 24 °C** menos 24 grados

minute¹ ['mɪnɪt] n minuto; (fig) momento; **minutes** npl (of meeting) actas fpl; **at the last ~** a la última hora

minute² [maɪ'njuːt] adj diminuto; (search) minucioso

miracle ['mɪrəkl] n milagro

miraculous [mɪ'rækjʊləs] adj milagroso

mirage ['mɪrɑːʒ] n espejismo

mirror ['mɪrə*] n espejo; (in car) retrovisor m

misbehave [mɪsbɪ'heɪv] vi portarse mal

misc. abbr = **miscellaneous**

miscarriage ['mɪskærɪdʒ] n (Med) aborto; **~ of justice** error m judicial

miscellaneous [mɪsɪ'leɪnɪəs] adj varios/as, diversos/as

mischief ['mɪstʃɪf] n travesuras fpl, diabluras fpl; (maliciousness) malicia; **mischievous** [-ɪvəs] adj travieso

misconception [mɪskən'sɛpʃən] n idea equivocada; equivocación f

misconduct [mɪs'kɒndʌkt] n mala conducta; **professional ~** falta profesional

miser ['maɪzə*] n avaro/a

miserable ['mɪzərəbl] adj (unhappy) triste, desgraciado; (unpleasant, contemptible) miserable

misery ['mɪzərɪ] n tristeza; (wretchedness) miseria, desdicha

misfortune [mɪs'fɔːtʃən] n desgracia

misgiving [mɪs'gɪvɪŋ] n (apprehension) presentimiento; **to have ~s about sth** tener dudas acerca de algo

misguided [mɪs'gaɪdɪd] adj equivocado

mishap ['mɪshæp] n desgracia, contratiempo

misinterpret [mɪsɪn'tɜːprɪt] vt interpretar mal

misjudge [mɪs'dʒʌdʒ] vt juzgar mal

mislay [mɪs'leɪ] vt extraviar, perder

mislead [mɪs'liːd] vt llevar a conclusiones erróneas; **misleading** adj engañoso

misplace [mɪs'pleɪs] vt extraviar

misprint ['mɪsprɪnt] n errata, error m de imprenta

misrepresent [mɪsreprɪ'zɛnt] vt falsificar

Miss [mɪs] n Señorita

miss [mɪs] vt (train etc) perder; (fail to hit: target) errar; (regret the absence of): **I ~ him** (yo) le echo de menos or a faltar; (fail to see): **you can't ~ it** no tiene pérdida ▷ vi fallar ▷ n (shot) tiro fallido or perdido; **miss out** (BRIT) vt omitir; **miss out on** vt fus (fun, party, opportunity) perderse

missile ['mɪsaɪl] n (Aviat) mísil m; (object thrown) proyectil m

missing ['mɪsɪŋ] adj (pupil) ausente; (thing) perdido; (Mil): **~ in action** desaparecido en combate

mission ['mɪʃən] n misión f; (official representation) delegación f; **missionary** n misionero/a

misspell [mɪsˈspel] (pt, pp **misspelt** (BRIT) or **~ed**) vt escribir mal

mist [mɪst] n (light) neblina; (heavy) niebla; (at sea) bruma ▷ vi (eyes: also: ~ over, ~ up) llenarse de lágrimas; (BRIT: windows: also: ~ over, ~ up) empañarse

mistake [mɪsˈteɪk] (vt: irreg) n error m ▷ vt entender mal; **by ~** por equivocación; **to make a ~** equivocarse; **to ~ A for B** confundir A con B; **mistaken** pp of **mistake** ▷ adj equivocado; **to be mistaken** equivocarse, engañarse

mister [ˈmɪstə*] (inf) n señor m; see **Mr**

mistletoe [ˈmɪsltəu] n muérdago

mistook [mɪsˈtuk] pt of **mistake**

mistress [ˈmɪstrɪs] n (lover) amante f; (of house) señora (de la casa); (BRIT: in primary school) maestra; (in secondary school) profesora; (of situation) dueña

mistrust [mɪsˈtrʌst] vt desconfiar de

misty [ˈmɪstɪ] adj (day) de niebla; (glasses etc) empañado

misunderstand [mɪsʌndəˈstænd] (irreg) vt, vi entender mal; **misunderstanding** n malentendido

misunderstood [mɪsʌndəˈstud] pt, pp of **misunderstand** ▷ adj (person) incomprendido

misuse [n mɪsˈjuːs, vb mɪsˈjuːz] n mal uso; (of power) abuso; (of funds) malversación f ▷ vt abusar de; malversar

mitt(en) [ˈmɪt(n)] n manopla

mix [mɪks] vt mezclar; (combine) unir ▷ vi mezclarse; (people) llevarse bien ▷ n mezcla; **mix up** vt mezclar; (confuse) confundir; **mixed** adj mixto; (feelings etc) encontrado; **mixed grill** n (BRIT) parrillada mixta; **mixed salad** n ensalada mixta; **mixed-up** adj (confused) confuso, revuelto; **mixer** n (for food) licuadora; (for drinks) coctelera; (person): **he's a good mixer** tiene don de gentes; **mixture** n mezcla; (also: **cough mixture**) jarabe

m; **mix-up** n confusión f

ml abbr (= millilitre(s)) ml

mm abbr (= millimetre) mm

moan [məun] n gemido ▷ vi gemir; (inf: complain): **to ~ (about)** quejarse (de)

moat [məut] n foso

mob [mɔb] n multitud f ▷ vt acosar

mobile [ˈməubaɪl] adj móvil ▷ n móvil m; **mobile home** n caravana; **mobile phone** n teléfono móvil

mobility [məuˈbɪlɪtɪ] n movilidad f

mobilize [ˈməubɪlaɪz] vt movilizar

mock [mɔk] vt (ridicule) ridiculizar; (laugh at) burlarse de ▷ adj fingido; **~ exam** examen preparatorio antes de los exámenes oficiales (BRIT; Scol: inf) exámenes mpl de prueba; **mockery** n burla

mod cons [ˈmɔdˈkɔnz] npl abbr (= modern conveniences) see **convenience**

mode [məud] n modo

model [ˈmɔdl] n modelo; (fashion model, artist's model) modelo mf ▷ adj modelo ▷ vt (clothes) presentar; (copy): **to ~ o.s. on** tomar como modelo a ▷ vi ser modelo; **to ~ clothes** pasar modelos, ser modelo

modem [ˈməudəm] n modem m

moderate [adj ˈmɔdərət, vb ˈmɔdəreɪt] adj moderado/a ▷ vi moderarse, calmarse ▷ vt moderar

moderation [mɔdəˈreɪʃən] n moderación f; **in ~** con moderación

modern [ˈmɔdən] adj moderno; **modernize** vt modernizar; **modern languages** npl lenguas fpl modernas

modest [ˈmɔdɪst] adj modesto; (small) módico; **modesty** n modestia

modification [mɔdɪfɪˈkeɪʃən] n modificación f

modify [ˈmɔdɪfaɪ] vt modificar

module [ˈmɔdjuːl] n (unit, component, Space) módulo

mohair [ˈməuhεə*] n mohair m

Mohammed [məˈhæmed] n Mahoma m

moist [mɔɪst] adj húmedo; **moisture**
['mɔɪstʃə*] n humedad f; **moisturizer**
['mɔɪstʃəraɪzə*] n crema hidratante
mold etc [məʊld] n = **mould** etc
mole [məʊl] n (animal, spy) topo;
(spot) lunar m
molecule ['mɒlɪkjuːl] n molécula
molest [məʊ'lest] vt importunar;
(assault sexually) abusar sexualmente
de

> Be careful not to translate **molest**
> by the Spanish word molestar.

molten ['məʊltən] adj fundido;
(lava) líquido
mom [mɒm] (us) n = **mum**
moment ['məʊmənt] n momento;
at the ~ de momento, por ahora;
momentarily ['məʊməntrɪlɪ] adv
momentáneamente; (us: very soon) de
un momento a otro; **momentary** adj
momentáneo; **momentous** [-'mentə
s] adj trascendental, importante
momentum [məʊ'mentəm] n
momento; (fig) ímpetu m; **to gather ~**
cobrar velocidad; (fig) ganar fuerza
mommy ['mɒmɪ] (us) n = **mummy**
Mon abbr (= Monday) lun
Monaco ['mɒnəkəʊ] n Mónaco
monarch ['mɒnək] n monarca mf;
monarchy n monarquía
monastery ['mɒnəstərɪ] n
monasterio
Monday ['mʌndɪ] n lunes m inv
monetary ['mʌnɪtərɪ] adj monetario
money ['mʌnɪ] n dinero; (currency)
moneda; **to make ~** ganar dinero;
money belt n riñonera; **money
order** n giro
mongrel ['mʌŋɡrəl] n (dog) perro
mestizo
monitor ['mɒnɪtə*] n (Scol) monitor
m; (also: **television ~**) receptor m de
control; (of computer) monitor m ⊳ vt
controlar
monk [mʌŋk] n monje m
monkey ['mʌŋkɪ] n mono
monologue ['mɒnəlɒɡ] n monólogo
monopoly [mə'nɒpəlɪ] n monopolio

monosodium glutamate
[mɒnə'səʊdɪəm'ɡluːtəmeɪt] n
glutamato monosódico
monotonous [mə'nɒtənəs] adj
monótono
monsoon [mɒn'suːn] n monzón m
monster ['mɒnstə*] n monstruo
month [mʌnθ] n mes m; **monthly**
adj mensual ⊳ adv mensualmente
monument ['mɒnjumənt] n
monumento
mood [muːd] n humor m; (of crowd,
group) clima m; **to be in a good/bad ~**
estar de buen/mal humor; **moody** adj
(changeable) de humor variable; (sullen)
malhumorado
moon [muːn] n luna; **moonlight** n
luz f de la luna
moor [muə*] n páramo ⊳ vt (ship)
amarrar ⊳ vi echar las amarras
moose [muːs] n inv alce m
mop [mɒp] n fregona; (of hair)
greña, melena ⊳ vt fregar; **mop up**
vt limpiar
mope [məʊp] vi estar or andar
deprimido
moped ['məʊped] n ciclomotor m
moral ['mɒrl] adj moral ⊳ n
moraleja; **morals** npl moralidad f,
moral f
morale [mɔ'rɑːl] n moral f
morality [mə'rælɪt] n moralidad f
morbid ['mɔːbɪd] adj (interest)
morboso; (Med) mórbido

○ **KEYWORD**

more [mɔː*] adj 1 (greater in number
etc) más; **more people/work
than before** más gente/trabajo
que antes
2 (additional) más; **do you want
(some) more tea?** ¿quieres más té?; **is
there any more wine?** ¿queda vino?;
it'll take a few more weeks tardará
unas semanas más; **it's 2 kms more
to the house** faltan 2 kms para la casa;
more time/letters than we expected

más tiempo del que/más cartas de las que esperábamos
▷ *pron (greater amount, additional amount)* más; **more than 10** más de 10; **it cost more than the other one/than we expected** costó más que el otro/más de lo que esperábamos; **is there any more?** ¿hay más?; **many/much more** muchos(as)/ mucho(a) más
▷ *adv* más; **more dangerous/easily (than)** más peligroso/fácilmente (que); **more and more expensive** cada vez más caro; **more or less** más o menos; **more than ever** más que nunca

moreover [mɔːˈrəʊvə*] *adv* además, por otra parte
morgue [mɔːɡ] *n* depósito de cadáveres
morning [ˈmɔːnɪŋ] *n* mañana; *(early morning)* madrugada ▷ *cpd* matutino, de la mañana; **in the ~** por la mañana; **7 o'clock in the ~** las 7 de la mañana; **morning sickness** *n* náuseas *fpl* matutinas
Moroccan [məˈrɒkən] *adj, n* marroquí *m/f*
Morocco [məˈrɒkəʊ] *n* Marruecos *m*
moron [ˈmɔːrɒn] *(inf)* *n* imbécil *m/f*
morphine [ˈmɔːfiːn] *n* morfina
Morse [mɔːs] *n (also: ~ code)* (código) Morse
mortal [ˈmɔːtl] *adj, n* mortal *m*
mortar [ˈmɔːtə*] *n* argamasa
mortgage [ˈmɔːɡɪdʒ] *n* hipoteca ▷ *vt* hipotecar
mortician [mɔːˈtɪʃən] *(US) n* director/a *m/f* de pompas fúnebres
mortified [ˈmɔːtɪfaɪd] *adj*: **I was ~** me dio muchísima vergüenza
mortuary [ˈmɔːtjʊərɪ] *n* depósito de cadáveres
mosaic [məʊˈzeɪɪk] *n* mosaico
Moslem [ˈmɒzləm] *adj, n* = **Muslim**
mosque [mɒsk] *n* mezquita
mosquito [mɒsˈkiːtəʊ] *(pl ~es) n*

mosquito *(SP)*, zancudo *(LAM)*
moss [mɒs] *n* musgo
most [məʊst] *adj* la mayor parte de, la mayoría de ▷ *pron* la mayor parte, la mayoría ▷ *adv* el más; *(very)* muy; **the ~** *(also: + adj)* el más; **~ of them** la mayor parte de ellos; **I saw the ~** yo vi el que más; **at the (very) ~** a lo sumo, todo lo más; **to make the ~ of** aprovechar (al máximo); **a ~ interesting book** un libro interesantísimo; **mostly** *adv* en su mayor parte, principalmente
MOT *(BRIT) n abbr* = **Ministry of Transport**; **the ~ (test)** inspección *(anual)* obligatoria de coches y camiones
motel [məʊˈtel] *n* motel *m*
moth [mɒθ] *n* mariposa nocturna; *(clothes moth)* polilla
mother [ˈmʌðə*] *n* madre *f* ▷ *adj* materno ▷ *vt (care for)* cuidar (como una madre); **motherhood** *n* maternidad *f*; **mother-in-law** *n* suegra; **mother-of-pearl** *n* nácar *m*; **Mother's Day** *n* Día de la Madre; **mother-to-be** *n* futura madre *f*; **mother tongue** *n* lengua materna
motif [məʊˈtiːf] *n* motivo
motion [ˈməʊʃən] *n* movimiento; *(gesture)* ademán *m*, señal *f*; *(at meeting)* moción *f* ▷ *vt, vi*: **to ~ (to) sb to do sth** hacer señas a algn para que haga algo; **motionless** *adj* inmóvil; **motion picture** *n* película
motivate [ˈməʊtɪveɪt] *vt* motivar
motivation [məʊtɪˈveɪʃən] *n* motivación *f*
motive [ˈməʊtɪv] *n* motivo
motor [ˈməʊtə*] *n* motor *m*; *(BRIT: inf: vehicle)* coche *m (SP)*, carro *(LAM)*, automóvil *m* ▷ *adj* motor *(f: motora or motriz)*; **motorbike** *n* moto *f*; **motorboat** *n* lancha motora; **motorcar** *(BRIT) n* coche *m*, carro, automóvil *m*; **motorcycle** *n* motocicleta; **motorcyclist** *n* motociclista *m/f*; **motoring** *(BRIT) n* automovilismo; **motorist** *n* conductor(a) *m/f*, automovilista *m/f*;

motor racing (BRIT) n carreras fpl de coches, automovilismo; **motorway** (BRIT) n autopista

motto ['mɒtəʊ] (pl ~**es**) n lema m; (watchword) consigna

mould [məʊld] (US **mold**) n molde m; (mildew) moho ▷ vt moldear; (fig) formar; **mouldy** adj enmohecido

mound [maʊnd] n montón m, montículo

mount [maʊnt] n monte m ▷ vt montar, subir a; (jewel) engarzar; (picture) enmarcar; (exhibition etc) organizar ▷ vi (increase) aumentar; **mount up** vi aumentar

mountain ['maʊntɪn] n montaña ▷ cpd de montaña; **mountain bike** n bicicleta de montaña; **mountaineer** n alpinista mf (SP, MEX), andinista mf (LAM); **mountaineering** n alpinismo (SP, MEX), andinismo (LAM); **mountainous** adj montañoso; **mountain range** n sierra

mourn [mɔːn] vt llorar, lamentar ▷ vi: **to ~ for** llorar la muerte de; **mourner** n doliente mf; dolorido/a; **mourning** n luto; **in mourning** de luto

mouse [maʊs] (pl **mice**) n (Zool, Comput) ratón m; **mouse mat** n (Comput) alfombrilla

moussaka [mu'sɑːkə] n musaca

mousse [muːs] n (Culin) crema batida; (for hair) espuma (moldeadora)

moustache [məs'tɑːʃ] (US **mustache**) n bigote m

mouth [maʊθ, pl maʊðz] n boca; (of river) desembocadura; **mouthful** n bocado; **mouth organ** n armónica; **mouthpiece** n (of musical instrument) boquilla; (spokesman) portavoz mf; **mouthwash** n enjuague m

move [muːv] n (movement) movimiento; (in game) jugada; (: turn to play) turno; (change: of house) mudanza; (: of job) cambio de trabajo ▷ vt mover; (emotionally) conmover; (Pol: resolution etc) proponer ▷ vi moverse; (traffic)

circular; (also: **~ house**) trasladarse, mudarse; **to ~ sb to do sth** mover a algn a hacer algo; **to get a ~ on** darse prisa; **move back** vi retroceder; **move in** vi (to a house) instalarse; (police, soldiers) intervenir; **move off** vi ponerse en camino; **move on** vi ponerse en camino; **move out** vi (of house) mudarse; **move over** vi apartarse, hacer sitio; **move up** vi (employee) ser ascendido; **movement** n movimiento

movie ['muːvɪ] n película; **to go to the ~s** ir al cine; **movie theater** (US) n cine m

moving ['muːvɪŋ] adj (emotional) conmovedor(a); (that moves) móvil

mow [məʊ] (pt ~**ed**, pp **mowed** or **mown**) vt (grass, corn) cortar, segar; **mower** n (also: **lawnmower**) n cortacéspedes m inv

Mozambique [məʊzæm'biːk] n Mozambique m

MP n abbr = **Member of Parliament**

MP3 n MP3; **MP3 player** n reproductor m (de) MP3

mpg n abbr = **miles per gallon**

m.p.h. abbr = **miles per hour** (60 m.p.h. = 96 k.p.h.)

Mr ['mɪstə*] (US **Mr.**) n: **~ Smith** (el) Sr. Smith

Mrs ['mɪsɪz] (US **Mrs.**) n: **~ Smith** (la) Sra. Smith

Ms [mɪz] (US **Ms.**) n = **Miss** or **Mrs**; **~ Smith** (la) Srt(a). Smith

MSP n abbr = **Member of the Scottish Parliament**

Mt abbr (Geo) (= **mount**) m

much [mʌtʃ] adj mucho ▷ adv mucho; (before pp) muy ▷ n or pron mucho; **how ~ is it?** ¿cuánto es?, ¿cuánto cuesta?; **too ~** demasiado; **it's not ~** no es mucho; **as ~ as** tanto como; **however ~ he tries** por mucho que se esfuerce

muck [mʌk] n suciedad f; **muck up** (inf) vt arruinar, estropear; **mucky** adj (dirty) sucio

mucus ['mjuːkəs] n mucosidad f, moco

mud [mʌd] n barro, lodo

muddle ['mʌdl] n desorden m, confusión f; (mix-up) embrollo, lío ▷ vt (also: ~ up) embrollar, confundir

muddy ['mʌdɪ] adj fangoso, cubierto de lodo

mudguard ['mʌdgɑːd] n guardabarros m inv

muesli ['mjuːzlɪ] n muesli m

muffin ['mʌfɪn] n panecillo dulce

muffled ['mʌfld] adj (noise etc) amortiguado, apagado

muffler (US) ['mʌflə*] n (Aut) silenciador m

mug [mʌg] n taza grande (sin platillo); (for beer) jarra; (inf: face) jeta ▷ vt (assault) asaltar; **mugger** ['mʌgə*] n atracador(a) m/f; **mugging** n asalto

muggy ['mʌgɪ] adj bochornoso

mule [mjuːl] n mula

multicoloured ['mʌltɪkʌləd] (US), **multicolored** adj multicolor

multimedia ['mʌltɪ'miːdɪə] adj multimedia

multinational ['mʌltɪ'næʃənl] n multinacional f ▷ adj multinacional

multiple ['mʌltɪpl] adj múltiple ▷ n múltiplo; **multiple choice (test)** n examen m de tipo test; **multiple sclerosis** n esclerosis f múltiple

multiplex cinema ['mʌltɪpleks-] n multicines mpl

multiplication [mʌltɪplɪ'keɪʃən] n multiplicación f

multiply ['mʌltɪplaɪ] vt multiplicar ▷ vi multiplicarse

multistorey [mʌltɪ'stɔːrɪ] (BRIT) adj de muchos pisos

mum [mʌm] (BRIT: inf) n mamá ▷ adj: **to keep ~** mantener la boca cerrada

mumble ['mʌmbl] vt, vi hablar entre dientes, refunfuñar

mummy ['mʌmɪ] n (BRIT: mother) mamá; (embalmed) momia

mumps [mʌmps] n paperas fpl

munch [mʌntʃ] vt, vi mascar

municipal [mjuː'nɪsɪpl] adj municipal

mural ['mjuərl] n (pintura) mural m

murder ['məːdə*] n asesinato; (in law) homicidio ▷ vt asesinar, matar; **murderer** n asesino

murky ['məːkɪ] adj (water) turbio; (street, night) lóbrego

murmur ['məːmə*] n murmullo ▷ vt, vi murmurar

muscle ['mʌsl] n músculo; (fig: strength) garra, fuerza; **muscular** ['mʌskjulə*] adj muscular; (person) musculoso

museum [mjuː'zɪəm] n museo

mushroom ['mʌʃrum] n seta, hongo; (Culin) champiñón m ▷ vi crecer de la noche a la mañana

music ['mjuːzɪk] n música; **musical** adj musical; (sound) melodioso; (person) con talento musical ▷ n (show) comedia musical; **musical instrument** n instrumento musical; **musician** [-'zɪʃən] n músico/a

Muslim ['mʌzlɪm] adj, n, musulmán/ana m/f

muslin ['mʌzlɪn] n muselina

mussel ['mʌsl] n mejillón m

must [mʌst] aux vb (obligation): **I ~ do it** debo hacerlo, tengo que hacerlo; (probability): **he ~ be there by now** ya debe (de) estar allí ▷ n: **it's a ~** es imprescindible

mustache [mʌstæʃ] (US) n = **moustache**

mustard ['mʌstəd] n mostaza

mustn't ['mʌsnt] = **must not**

mute [mjuːt] adj, n mudo/a m/f

mutilate ['mjuːtɪleɪt] vt mutilar

mutiny ['mjuːtɪnɪ] n motín m ▷ vi amotinarse

mutter ['mʌtə*] vt, vi murmurar

mutton ['mʌtn] n carne f de cordero

mutual ['mjuːtʃuəl] adj mutuo; (interest) común

muzzle ['mʌzl] n hocico; (for dog) bozal m; (of gun) boca ▷ vt (dog) poner

un bozal a

my [maɪ] *adj* mi(s); **~ house/brother/
sisters** mi casa/mi hermano/mis
hermanas; **I've washed ~ hair/cut ~
finger** me he lavado el pelo/cortado un
dedo; **is this ~ pen or yours?** ¿es este
bolígrafo mío o tuyo?
myself [maɪ'sɛlf] *pron* (*reflexive*) me;
(*emphatic*) yo mismo; (*after prep*) mí
(mismo); *see also* **oneself**
mysterious [mɪs'tɪərɪəs] *adj*
misterioso
mystery ['mɪstərɪ] *n* misterio
mystical ['mɪstɪkl] *adj* místico
mystify ['mɪstɪfaɪ] *vt* (*perplex*) dejar
perplejo
myth [mɪθ] *n* mito; **mythology**
[mɪ'θɒlədʒɪ] *n* mitología

n/a *abbr* (= *not applicable*) no interesa
nag [næg] *vt* (*scold*) regañar
nail [neɪl] *n* (*human*) uña; (*metal*)
clavo ▷ *vt* clavar; **to ~ sth to sth**
clavar algo en algo; **to ~ sb down
to doing sth** comprometer a algn a
que haga algo; **nailbrush** *n* cepillo
para las uñas; **nailfile** *n* lima para las
uñas; **nail polish** *n* esmalte *m* or laca
para las uñas; **nail polish remover**
n quitaesmalte *m*; **nail scissors** *npl*
tijeras *fpl* para las uñas; **nail varnish**
(BRIT) *n* = **nail polish**
naïve [naɪ'iːv] *adj* ingenuo
naked ['neɪkɪd] *adj* (*nude*) desnudo;
(*flame*) expuesto al aire
name [neɪm] *n* nombre *m*; (*surname*)
apellido; (*reputation*) fama, renombre *m*
▷ *vt* (*child*) poner nombre a; (*criminal*)
identificar; (*price, date etc*) fijar; **what's
your ~?** ¿cómo se llama?; **by ~** de
nombre; **in the ~ of** en nombre de;
to give one's ~ and address dar sus
señas; **namely** *adv* a saber
nanny ['nænɪ] *n* niñera

nap [næp] n (sleep) sueñecito, siesta

napkin ['næpkɪn] n (also: **table ~**) servilleta

nappy ['næpɪ] n (BRIT) n pañal m

narcotics npl (illegal drugs) estupefacientes mpl, narcóticos mpl

narrative ['nærətɪv] n narrativa
▷ adj narrativo

narrator [nə'reɪtə*] n narrador(a) m/f

narrow ['nærəʊ] adj estrecho, angosto; (fig: majority etc) corto; (: ideas etc) estrecho ▷ vi (road) estrecharse; (diminish) reducirse; **to have a ~ escape** escaparse por los pelos;
narrow down vt (search, investigation, possibilities) restringir, limitar; (list) reducir; **narrowly** adv (miss) por poco; **narrow-minded** adj de miras estrechas

nasal ['neɪzl] adj nasal

nasty ['nɑːstɪ] adj (remark) feo; (person) antipático; (revolting: taste, smell) asqueroso; (wound, disease etc) peligroso, grave

nation ['neɪʃən] n nación f

national ['næʃənl] adj, n nacional m/f; **national anthem** n himno nacional; **national dress** n vestido nacional; **National Health Service** (BRIT) n servicio nacional de salud pública = Insalud m (SP); **National Insurance** (BRIT) n seguro social nacional; **nationalist** adj, n nacionalista mf; **nationality** [-'nælɪtɪ] n nacionalidad f; **nationalize** vt nacionalizar; **national park** (BRIT) n parque m nacional; **National Trust** n (BRIT) organización encargada de preservar el patrimonio histórico británico

nationwide ['neɪʃənwaɪd] adj en escala or a nivel nacional

native ['neɪtɪv] n (local inhabitant) natural mf, nacional mf ▷ adj (indigenous) indígena; (country) natal; (innate) natural, innato; **a ~ of Russia** un(a) natural mf de Rusia; **Native American** adj, n americano/a

indígena, amerindio/a; **native speaker** n hablante mf nativo/a

NATO ['neɪtəʊ] n abbr (= North Atlantic Treaty Organization) OTAN f

natural ['nætʃrəl] adj natural; **natural gas** n gas m natural; **natural history** n historia natural; **naturally** adv (speak etc) naturalmente; (of course) desde luego, por supuesto; **natural resources** npl recursos mpl naturales

nature ['neɪtʃə*] n (also: **N~**) naturaleza; (group, sort) género, clase f; (character) carácter m, genio; **by ~** por or de naturaleza; **nature reserve** n reserva natural

naughty ['nɔːtɪ] adj (child) travieso

nausea ['nɔːsɪə] n náuseas fpl

naval ['neɪvl] adj naval, de marina

navel ['neɪvl] n ombligo

navigate ['nævɪgeɪt] vt gobernar ▷ vi navegar; (Aut) ir de copiloto; **navigation** [-'geɪʃən] n (action) navegación f; (science) náutica

navy ['neɪvɪ] n marina de guerra; (ships) armada, flota

Nazi ['nɑːtsɪ] n nazi mf

NB abbr (= nota bene) nótese

near [nɪə*] adj (place, relation) cercano; (time) próximo ▷ adv cerca ▷ prep (also: **~ to**: space) cerca de a; (: time) cerca de ▷ vt acercarse a, aproximarse a; **nearby** [nɪə'baɪ] adj cercano, próximo ▷ adv cerca; **nearly** adv casi, por poco; **I nearly fell** por poco me caigo; **near-sighted** adj miope, corto de vista

neat [niːt] adj (place) ordenado, bien cuidado; (person) pulcro; (plan) ingenioso; (spirits) solo; **neatly** adv (tidily) con esmero; (skilfully) ingeniosamente

necessarily ['nɛsɪsrɪlɪ] adv necesariamente

necessary ['nɛsɪsrɪ] adj necesario, preciso

necessity [nɪ'sɛsɪtɪ] n necesidad f

neck [nɛk] n (of person, garment, bottle) cuello; (of animal) pescuezo ▷ vi (inf) besuquearse; **~ and ~** parejos;

necklace ['nɛklɪs] n collar m; **necktie** ['nɛktaɪ] n corbata

nectarine ['nɛktərɪn] n nectarina

need [niːd] n (lack) escasez f, falta; (necessity) necesidad f ▷ vt (require) necesitar; **I ~ to do it** tengo que or debo hacerlo; **you don't ~ to go** no hace falta que (te) vayas

needle ['niːdl] n aguja ▷ vt (fig: inf) picar, fastidiar

needless ['niːdlɪs] adj innecesario; **~ to say** huelga decir que

needlework ['niːdlwəːk] n (activity) costura, labor f de aguja

needn't ['niːdnt] = **need not**

needy ['niːdɪ] adj necesitado

negative ['nɛgətɪv] n (Phot) negativo; (Ling) negación f ▷ adj negativo

neglect [nɪ'glɛkt] vt (one's duty) faltar a, no cumplir con; (child) descuidar, desatender ▷ n (of house, garden etc) abandono; (of child) desatención f; (of duty) incumplimiento

negligee ['nɛglɪʒeɪ] n (nightdress) salto de cama

negotiate [nɪ'gəʊʃɪeɪt] vt (treaty, loan) negociar; (obstacle) franquear; (bend in road) tomar ▷ vi: **to ~ (with)** negociar (con)

negotiations [nɪgəʊʃɪ'eɪʃənz] pl n negociaciones

negotiator [nɪ'gəʊʃɪeɪtə*] n negociador(a) m/f

neighbour ['neɪbə*] (US **neighbor** etc) n vecino/a; **neighbourhood** n (place) vecindad f, barrio; (people) vecindario; **neighbouring** adj vecino

neither ['naɪðə*] adj ▷ conj: **I didn't move and ~ did John** no me he movido, ni Juan tampoco ▷ pron ninguno ▷ adv: **~ good nor bad** ni bueno ni malo; **~ is true** ninguno/a de los(las) dos es cierto/a

neon ['niːɔn] n neón m

Nepal [nɪ'pɔːl] n Nepal m

nephew ['nɛvjuː] n sobrino

nerve [nəːv] n (Anat) nervio; (courage) valor m; (impudence) descaro, frescura

(nervousness) nerviosismo msg; nervios mpl; **a fit of ~s** un ataque de nervios

nervous ['nəːvəs] adj (anxious, Anat) nervioso; (timid) tímido, miedoso; **nervous breakdown** n crisis f nerviosa

nest [nɛst] n (of bird) nido; (wasps' nest) avispero ▷ vi anidar

net [nɛt] n (gen) red f; (fabric) tul m ▷ adj (Comm) neto, líquido ▷ vt (catch sp) or agarrar (LAM) con red; (Sport) marcar; **netball** n balonred m

Netherlands ['nɛðələndz] npl: **the ~** los Países Bajos

nett [nɛt] adj = **net**

nettle ['nɛtl] n ortiga

network ['nɛtwəːk] n red f

neurotic [njuə'rɔtɪk] adj neurótico/a

neuter ['njuːtə*] adj (Ling) neutro ▷ vt castrar, capar

neutral ['njuːtrəl] adj (person) neutral; (colour etc, Elec) neutro ▷ n (Aut) punto muerto

never ['nɛvə*] adv nunca, jamás; **I ~ went** no fui nunca; **~ in my life** jamás en la vida; see also **mind**; **never-ending** adj interminable, sin fin; **nevertheless** [nɛvəðə'lɛs] adv sin embargo, no obstante

new [njuː] adj nuevo; (brand new) a estrenar; (recent) reciente; **New Age** n Nueva Era; **newborn** adj recién nacido; **newcomer** ['njuːkʌmə*] n recién venido/a or llegado/a; **newly** adv nuevamente, recién

news [njuːz] n noticias fpl; **a piece of ~** una noticia; **the ~** (Radio, TV) las noticias fpl; **news agency** n agencia de noticias; **newsagent** (BRIT) n vendedor(a) m/f de periódicos; **newscaster** n presentador(a) m/f, locutor(a) m/f; **news dealer** (US) n = **newsagent**; **newsletter** n hoja informativa, boletín m; **newspaper** n periódico, diario; **newsreader** n = **newscaster**

newt [njuːt] n tritón m

New Year n Año Nuevo; **New Year's**

Day n Día de Año Nuevo; **New Year's Eve** n Nochevieja

New Zealand [njuː'ziːlənd] n Nueva Zelanda; **New Zealander** n neozelandés/esa m/f

next [nɛkst] adj (house, room) vecino; (bus stop, meeting) próximo; (following: page etc) siguiente ▷ adv después; **the ~ day** el día siguiente; **~ time** la próxima vez; **~ year** el año próximo o que viene; **~ to** junto a, al lado de; **~ to nothing** casi nada; **~ please!** ¡el siguiente!; **next door** adv en la casa de al lado ▷ adj vecino, de al lado; **next-of-kin** n pariente m más cercano

NHS n abbr = **National Health Service**

nibble ['nɪbl] vt mordisquear, mordiscar

nice [naɪs] adj (likeable) simpático; (kind) amable; (pleasant) agradable; (attractive) bonito, lindo (LAM); **nicely** adv amablemente; bien

niche [niːʃ] n (Arch) nicho, hornacina

nick [nɪk] n (wound) rasguño; (cut, indentation) mella, muesca ▷ vt birlar, robar; **in the ~ of time** justo a tiempo

nickel ['nɪkl] n níquel m; (US) moneda de 5 centavos

nickname ['nɪkneɪm] n apodo, mote m ▷ vt apodar

nicotine ['nɪkətiːn] n nicotina

niece [niːs] n sobrina

Nigeria [naɪ'dʒɪərɪə] n Nigeria

night [naɪt] n noche f; (evening) tarde f; **the ~ before last** anteanoche; **at ~, by ~** de noche, por la noche; **night club** n cabaret m; **nightdress** (BRIT) n camisón m; **nightie** ['naɪtɪ] n =**nightdress**; **nightlife** n vida nocturna; **nightly** adj de todas las noches ▷ adv todas las noches, cada noche; **nightmare** n pesadilla; **night school** n clase(s) f(pl) nocturna(s); **night shift** n turno nocturno or de noche; **night-time** n noche f

nil [nɪl] (BRIT) n (Sport) cero, nada

nine [naɪn] num nueve; **nineteen** num diecinueve, diez y nueve; **nineteenth** [naɪn'tiːnθ] adj decimonoveno, decimonono; **ninetieth** ['naɪntɪɪθ] adj nonagésimo; **ninety** num noventa

ninth [naɪnθ] adj noveno

nip [nɪp] vt (pinch) pellizcar; (bite) morder

nipple ['nɪpl] n (Anat) pezón m

nitrogen ['naɪtrədʒən] n nitrógeno

⭘ **KEYWORD**

no [nəʊ] (pl **noes**) adv (opposite of "yes") no; **are you coming? ~ no (I'm not)** ¿vienes? - no; **would you like some more? ~ no thank you** ¿quieres más? - no gracias ▷ adj (not any): **I have no money/time/books** no tengo dinero/tiempo/libros; **no other man would have done it** ningún otro lo hubiera hecho; **"no entry"** "prohibido el paso"; **"no smoking"** "prohibido fumar" ▷ n no m

nobility [nəʊ'bɪlɪtɪ] n nobleza

noble ['nəʊbl] adj noble

nobody ['nəʊbədɪ] pron nadie

nod [nɔd] vi saludar con la cabeza; (in agreement) decir que sí con la cabeza; (doze) dar cabezadas ▷ vt: **to ~ one's head** inclinar la cabeza ▷ n inclinación f de cabeza; **nod off** vi dar cabezadas

noise [nɔɪz] n ruido; (din) escándalo, estrépito; **noisy** adj ruidoso; (child) escandaloso

nominal ['nɔmɪnl] adj nominal

nominate ['nɔmɪneɪt] vt (propose) proponer; (appoint) nombrar; **nomination** [nɔmɪ'neɪʃən] n propuesta; nombramiento; **nominee** [-'niː] n candidato/a

none [nʌn] pron ninguno/a ▷ adv de ninguna manera; **~ of you** ninguno de vosotros; **I've ~ left** no me queda ninguno/a; **he's ~ the worse for it** no le ha hecho ningún mal

nonetheless [nʌnðəˈles] adv sin embargo, no obstante

non-fiction [nɔnˈfɪkʃən] n literatura no novelesca

nonsense [ˈnɔnsəns] n tonterías fpl, disparates fpl; **~!** ¡qué tonterías!

non: non-smoker n no fumador(a) m/f; **non-smoking** adj (de) no fumador; **non-stick** adj (pan, surface) antiadherente

noodles [ˈnuːdlz] npl tallarines mpl

noon [nuːn] n mediodía m

no-one [ˈnʌwʌn] pron = **nobody**

nor [nɔː*] conj = **neither** ▷ adv see **neither**

norm [nɔːm] n norma

normal [ˈnɔːml] adj normal; **normally** adv normalmente

north [nɔːθ] n norte m ▷ adj del norte, norteño ▷ adv al or hacia el norte; **North America** n América del Norte; **North American** adj, n norteamericano a m/f; **northbound** [ˈnɔːθbaʊnd] adj (traffic) que se dirige al norte; (carriageway) de dirección al norte; **north-east** n nor(d)este m; **northeastern** adj nor(d)este, del nor(d)este; **northern** [ˈnɔːðən] adj norteño, del norte; **Northern Ireland** n Irlanda del Norte; **North Korea** n Corea del Norte; **North Pole** n Polo Norte; **North Sea** n Mar m del Norte; **north-west** n nor(d)oeste m; **northwestern** [ˈnɔːθˈwestən] adj noroeste, del noroeste

Norway [ˈnɔːweɪ] n Noruega; **Norwegian** [ˈwiːdʒən] adj noruego/a ▷ n noruego/a; (Ling) noruego

nose [nəʊz] n (Anat) nariz f; (Zool) hocico; (sense of smell) olfato ▷ vi: to **~ about** curiosear; **nosebleed** n hemorragia nasal; **nosey** (inf) adj curioso, fisgón/ona

nostalgia [nɔsˈtældʒɪə] n nostalgia

nostalgic [nɔsˈtældʒɪk] adj nostálgico

nostril [ˈnɔstrɪl] n ventana de la nariz

nosy [ˈnəʊzɪ] (inf) adj = **nosey**

not [nɔt] adv no; **~ that** ... no es que ...; **it's too late, isn't it?** es demasiado tarde, ¿verdad or no?; **~ yet/now** todavía/ahora no; **why ~?** ¿por qué no?; see also **all; only**

notable [ˈnəʊtəbl] adj notable; **notably** adv especialmente

notch [nɔtʃ] n muesca, corte m

note [nəʊt] n (Mus, record, letter) nota; (banknote) billete m; (tone) tono ▷ vt (observe) notar, observar; (write down) apuntar, anotar; **notebook** n libreta, cuaderno; **noted** [ˈnəʊtɪd] adj célebre, conocido; **notepad** n bloc m; **notepaper** n papel m para cartas

nothing [ˈnʌθɪŋ] n nada; (zero) cero; **he does ~** no hace nada; **~ new** nada nuevo; **~ much** no mucho; **for ~** (free) gratis, sin pago; (in vain) en balde

notice [ˈnəʊtɪs] n (announcement) anuncio; (warning) aviso; (dismissal) despido; (resignation) dimisión f; (period of time) plazo ▷ vt (observe) notar, observar; **to bring sth to sb's ~** (attention) llamar la atención de alguien sobre algo; **to take ~ of** tomar nota de, prestar atención a; **at short ~** con poca anticipación; **until further ~** hasta nuevo aviso; **to hand in one's ~** dimitir

> Be careful not to translate **notice** by the Spanish word noticia.

noticeable adj evidente, obvio

notify [ˈnəʊtɪfaɪ] vt: **to ~ sb (of sth)** comunicar (algo) a algn

notion [ˈnəʊʃən] n idea; (opinion) opinión f; **notions** npl (us) mercería

notorious [nəʊˈtɔːrɪəs] adj notorio

notwithstanding [nɔtwɪθˈstændɪŋ] adv no obstante, sin embargo; **~ this** a pesar de esto

nought [nɔːt] n cero

noun [naʊn] n nombre m, sustantivo

nourish [ˈnʌrɪʃ] vt nutrir; (fig) alimentar; **nourishment** n alimento, sustento

Nov. abbr (= November) nov

novel [ˈnɔvl] n novela ▷ adj (new)

nuevo, original; *(unexpected)* insólito;
novelist *n* novelista *mf*; **novelty** *n*
novedad *f*

November [nəʊˈvɛmbə*] *n*
noviembre *m*

novice [ˈnɒvɪs] *n (Rel)* novicio/a

now [naʊ] *adv (at the present time)*
ahora; *(these days)* actualmente, hoy
día ▷ *conj:* **~ (that)** ya que, ahora que;
right ~ ahora mismo; **by ~** ya; **just
~** ahora mismo; **~ and then, ~ and
again** de vez en cuando; **from ~ on** de
ahora en adelante; **nowadays** [ˈnaʊə
deɪz] *adv* hoy (en) día, actualmente

nowhere [ˈnaʊwɛə*] *adv (direction)*
a ninguna parte; *(location)* en ninguna
parte

nozzle [ˈnɒzl] *n* boquilla

nr *abbr (BRIT)* = **near**

nuclear [ˈnjuːklɪə*] *adj* nuclear

nucleus [ˈnjuːklɪəs] *(pl nuclei) n*
núcleo

nude [njuːd] *adj, n* desnudo/a *m/f*; **in
the ~** desnudo

nudge [nʌdʒ] *vt* dar un codazo a

nudist [ˈnjuːdɪst] *n* nudista *mf*

nudity [ˈnjuːdɪtɪ] *n* desnudez *f*

nuisance [ˈnjuːsns] *n* molestia,
fastidio; *(person)* pesado, latoso; **what
a ~!** ¡qué lata!

numb [nʌm] *adj:* **~ with cold/fear**
entumecido por el frío/paralizado
de miedo

number [ˈnʌmbə*] *n* número;
(quantity) cantidad *f* ▷ *vt (pages etc)*
numerar, poner número a; *(amount to)*
sumar, ascender a; *(be ~ed among*
figurar entre; **a ~ of** varios, algunos;
they were ten in ~ eran diez; **number
plate** *(BRIT) n* matrícula, placa;
Number Ten *n (BRIT:* 10 Downing
Street*)* residencia del primer ministro

numerical [njuːˈmɛrɪkl] *adj*
numérico

numerous [ˈnjuːmərəs] *adj*
numeroso

nun [nʌn] *n* monja, religiosa

nurse [nəːs] *n* enfermero/a; *(also:*

~maid) niñera ▷ *vt (patient)* cuidar,
atender

nursery [ˈnəːsərɪ] *n (institution)*
guardería infantil; *(room)* cuarto de los
niños; *(for plants)* criadero, semillero;
nursery rhyme *n* canción *f* infantil;
nursery school *n* parvulario, escuela
de párvulos; **nursery slope** *(BRIT) n
(Ski)* cuesta para principiantes

nursing [ˈnəːsɪŋ] *n (profession)*
profesión *f* de enfermera; *(care)*
asistencia, cuidado; **nursing home** *n*
clínica de reposo

nurture [ˈnəːtʃə*] *vt (child, plant)*
alimentar, nutrir

nut [nʌt] *n (Tech)* tuerca; *(Bot)* nuez *f*

nutmeg [ˈnʌtmɛg] *n* nuez *f* moscada

nutrient [ˈnjuːtrɪənt] *adj* nutritivo
▷ *n* elemento nutritivo

nutrition [njuːˈtrɪʃən] *n* nutrición *f*,
alimentación *f*

nutritious [njuːˈtrɪʃəs] *adj* nutritivo,
alimenticio

nuts [nʌts] *(inf) adj* loco

NVQ *n abbr (BRIT)* = **National
Vocational Qualification**

nylon [ˈnaɪlɔn] *n* nilón *m* ▷ *adj* de
nilón

O

oath [əʊθ] *n* juramento; (*swear word*) palabrota; **on** (BRIT) or **under ~** bajo juramento

oak [əʊk] *n* roble *m* ▷ *adj* de roble

O.A.P. (BRIT) *n, abbr* = **old-age pensioner**

oar [ɔ:*] *n* remo

oasis [əʊˈeɪsɪs] (*pl* **oases**) *n* oasis *m inv*

oath [əʊθ] *n* juramento; (*swear word*) palabrota; **on** (BRIT) or **under ~** bajo juramento

oatmeal [ˈəʊtmiːl] *n* harina de avena

oats [əʊts] *npl* avena

obedience [əˈbiːdɪəns] *n* obediencia

obedient [əˈbiːdɪənt] *adj* obediente

obese [əʊˈbiːs] *adj* obeso

obesity [əʊˈbiːsɪtɪ] *n* obesidad *f*

obey [əˈbeɪ] *vt* obedecer; (*instructions, regulations*) cumplir

obituary [əˈbɪtjʊərɪ] *n* necrología

object [*n* ˈɒbdʒɪkt, *vb* əbˈdʒɛkt] *n* objeto; (*purpose*) objeto, propósito; (*Ling*) complemento ▷ *vi*: **to ~ to** estar en contra de; (*proposal*) oponerse a; **to ~ that** objetar que; **expense is no**

~ no importa cuánto cuesta; **I ~!** ¡yo protesto!; **objection** [əbˈdʒɛkʃən] *n* protesta; **I have no objection to ...** no tengo inconveniente en que ...; **objective** *adj, n* objetivo

obligation [ɒblɪˈgeɪʃən] *n* obligación *f*; (*debt*) deber *m*; **without ~** sin compromiso

obligatory [əˈblɪgətərɪ] *adj* obligatorio

oblige [əˈblaɪdʒ] *vt* (*do a favour for*) complacer, hacer un favor a; **to ~ sb to do sth** forzar or obligar a algn a hacer algo; **to be ~d to sb for sth** estarle agradecido a algn por algo

oblique [əˈbliːk] *adj* oblicuo; (*allusion*) indirecto

obliterate [əˈblɪtəreɪt] *vt* borrar

oblivious [əˈblɪvɪəs] *adj*: **~ of** inconsciente de

oblong [ˈɒblɒŋ] *adj* rectangular ▷ *n* rectángulo

obnoxious [əbˈnɒkʃəs] *adj* odioso, detestable; (*smell*) nauseabundo

oboe [ˈəʊbəʊ] *n* oboe *m*

obscene [əbˈsiːn] *adj* obsceno

obscure [əbˈskjʊə*] *adj* oscuro ▷ *vt* oscurecer; (*hide: sun*) esconder

observant [əbˈzə:vnt] *adj* observador(a)

observation [ɒbzəˈveɪʃən] *n* observación *f*; (*Med*) examen *m*

observatory [əbˈzə:vətrɪ] *n* observatorio

observe [əbˈzə:v] *vt* observar; (*rule*) cumplir; **observer** *n* observador(a) *m/f*

obsess [əbˈsɛs] *vt* obsesionar; **obsession** [əbˈsɛʃən] *n* obsesión *f*; **obsessive** *adj* obsesivo; obsesionante

obsolete [ˈɒbsəliːt] *adj*: **to be ~** estar en desuso

obstacle [ˈɒbstəkl] *n* obstáculo; (*nuisance*) estorbo

obstinate [ˈɒbstɪnɪt] *adj* terco, porfiado; (*determined*) obstinado

obstruct [əbˈstrʌkt] *vt* obstruir; (*hinder*) estorbar, obstaculizar; **obstruction** [əbˈstrʌkʃən] *n* (*action*)

obstrucción f; (object) estorbo, obstáculo
obtain [əb'teɪn] vt obtener; (achieve)
conseguir
obvious ['ɒbvɪəs] adj obvio, evidente;
obviously adv evidentemente,
naturalmente; **obviously not** por
supuesto que no
occasion [ə'keɪʒən] n oportunidad
f, ocasión f; (event) acontecimiento;
occasional adj poco frecuente,
ocasional; **occasionally** adv de vez
en cuando
occult [ɒ'kʌlt] adj (gen) oculto
occupant ['ɒkjupənt] n (of house)
inquilino/a; (of car) ocupante mf
occupation [ɒkju'peɪʃən] n
ocupación f; (job) trabajo; (pastime)
ocupaciones fpl
occupy ['ɒkjupaɪ] vt (seat, post, time)
ocupar; (house) habitar; **to ~ o.s. in
doing** pasar el tiempo haciendo
occur [ə'kə:*] vi pasar, suceder; **to ~
to sb** ocurrírsele a algn; **occurrence**
[ə'kʌrəns] n acontecimiento;
(existence) existencia
ocean ['əuʃən] n océano
o'clock [ə'klɔk] adv: **it is 5 ~** son las 5
Oct. abbr (= October) oct
October [ɒk'təubə*] n octubre m
octopus ['ɒktəpəs] n pulpo
odd [ɒd] adj extraño, raro; (number)
impar, non; (sock, shoe etc) suelto; **60~** 60 y
pico; **at ~ times** de vez en cuando; **to
be the ~ one out** estar de más; **oddly**
adv curiosamente, extrañamente;
see also **enough; odds** npl (in betting)
puntos mpl de ventaja; **it makes no
odds** da lo mismo; **at odds** reñidos/as;
odds and ends minucias fpl
odometer [ɒ'dɒmɪtə*] (us) n
cuentakilómetros m inv
odour ['əudə*] (us **odor**) n olor m;
(unpleasant) hedor m

○ **KEYWORD**

of [ɒv, əv] prep 1 (gen) de; **a friend of
ours** un amigo nuestro; **a boy of 10** un

chico de 10 años; **that was kind of you**
eso fue muy amable por or de tu parte
2 (expressing quantity, amount, dates
etc) de; **a kilo of flour** un kilo de
harina; **there were three of them**
había tres; **three of us went** tres de
nosotros fuimos; **the 5th of july** el
5 de julio
3 (from, out of) de; **made of wood**
(hecho) de madera

off [ɒf] adj, adv (engine) desconectado;
(light) apagado; (tap) cerrado;
(BRIT: food: bad) pasado, malo, (: milk)
cortado; (cancelled) cancelado ▷ prep
de; **to be ~** (to leave) irse, marcharse;
to be ~ sick estar enfermo or de baja;
a day ~ un día libre or sin trabajar; **to
have an ~ day** tener un día malo; **he
had his coat ~** se había quitado el
abrigo; **10% ~** (Comm) (con el) 10% de
descuento; **5 km ~ (the road)** a 5 km
(de la carretera); **~ the coast** frente a la
costa; **I'm ~ meat** (no longer eat/like it)
paso de la carne; **on the ~ chance** por
si acaso; **~ and on** de vez en cuando

offence [ə'fɛns] (us **offense**) n (crime)
delito; **to take ~ at** ofenderse por
offend [ə'fɛnd] vt (person) ofender;
offender n delincuente mf
offense [ə'fɛns] (us) n = **offence**
offensive [ə'fɛnsɪv] adj repugnante;
(smell etc) repugnante ▷ n (Mil)
ofensiva
offer ['ɒfə*] n oferta, ofrecimiento;
(proposal) propuesta ▷ vt ofrecer;
(opportunity) facilitar; **"on ~"** (Comm)
"en oferta"
offhand [ɒf'hænd] adj informal ▷ adv
de improviso
office ['ɒfɪs] n (place) oficina; (room)
despacho; (position) carga, oficio;
doctor's ~ (us) consultorio; **to take
~** entrar en funciones; **office block**
(us), **office building** n bloque m de
oficinas; **office hours** npl horas fpl de
oficina; (us Med) horas fpl de consulta
officer ['ɒfɪsə*] n (Mil etc) oficial mf;

(also: **police ~**) agente mf de policía; (of organization) director(a) m/f

office worker n oficinista mf

official [əˈfɪʃl] adj oficial, autorizado ▸ n funcionario/a, oficial mf

off: **off-licence** (BRIT) n (shop) bodega tienda de vinos y bebidas alcohólicas; **off-line** adj, adv (Comput) fuera de línea; **off-peak** adj (electricity) de banda económica; (ticket) de precio reducido por viajar fuera de las horas punta; **off-putting** (BRIT) adj (person) asqueroso; (remark) desalentador; **off-season** adj, adv fuera de temporada

⬤ **OFF-LICENCE**

⬤ En el Reino Unido la venta
⬤ de bebidas alcohólicas está
⬤ estrictamente regulada
⬤ y se necesita una licencia
⬤ especial, que los cuentan
⬤ los bares, restaurantes y los
⬤ establecimientos de **off-licence**,
⬤ los únicos lugares en donde
⬤ se pueden adquirir bebidas
⬤ alcohólicas para su consumo
⬤ fuera del local, de donde viene
⬤ su nombre. También venden
⬤ bebidas no alcohólicas, tabaco,
⬤ chocolatinas, patatas fritas, etc.
⬤ y a menudo forman parte de una
⬤ cadena nacional.

offset [ˈɔfsɛt] vt contrarrestar, compensar

offshore [ɔfˈʃɔːˠ] adj (breeze, island) costera; (fishing) de bajura

offside [ˈɔfsaɪd] adj (Sport) fuera de juego; (Aut: in UK) del lado derecho; (: in US, Europe etc) del lado izquierdo

offspring [ˈɔfsprɪŋ] n inv descendencia

often [ˈɔfn] adv a menudo, con frecuencia; **how ~ do you go?** ¿cada cuánto vas?

oh [əu] excl ¡ah!

oil [ɔɪl] n aceite m; (petroleum) petróleo; (for heating) combustible ▸ vt engrasar; **oil filter** n (Aut) filtro de aceite; **oil painting** n pintura al óleo; **oil refinery** n refinería de petróleo; **oil rig** n torre f de perforación; **oil slick** n marea negra; **oil tanker** n petrolero; (truck) camión m cisterna; **oil well** n pozo de petróleo); **oily** adj aceitoso; (food) grasiento

ointment [ˈɔɪntmənt] n ungüento

O.K., okay [ˈəuˈkeɪ] (O.K.), ¡está bien!, ¡vale! (SP) ▸ adj bien ▸ vt dar el visto bueno a

old [əuld] adj viejo; (former) antiguo; **how ~ are you?** ¿cuántos años tienes?, ¿qué edad tienes?; **he's 10 years ~** tiene 10 años; **~er brother** hermano mayor; **old age** n vejez f; **old-age pension** n (BRIT) jubilación f, pensión f; **old-age pensioner** (BRIT) n jubilado/a; **old-fashioned** adj anticuado, pasado de moda; **old people's home** n (esp BRIT) residencia f de ancianos

olive [ˈɔlɪv] n (fruit) aceituna; (tree) olivo ▸ adj (also: **~-green**) verde oliva; **olive oil** n aceite m de oliva

Olympic [əuˈlɪmpɪk] adj olímpico; **the ~ Games, the ~s** las Olimpiadas

omelet(te) [ˈɔmlɪt] n tortilla francesa (SP), omelette f (LAM)

omen [ˈəumən] n presagio

ominous [ˈɔmɪnəs] adj de mal agüero, amenazador(a)

omit [əuˈmɪt] vt omitir

○ **KEYWORD**

on [ɔn] prep **1** (indicating position) en; sobre; **on the wall** en la pared; **it's on the table** está sobre or en la mesa; **on the left** a la izquierda

2 (indicating means, method, condition etc): **on foot** a pie; **on the train/**

plane (go) en tren/avión; (be) en el tren/el avión; **on the radio/television/telephone** por o en la radio/televisión/al teléfono; **to be on drugs** drogarse; (Med) estar a tratamiento; **to be on holiday/business** estar de vacaciones/en viaje de negocios
3 (referring to time): **on Friday** el viernes; **on Fridays** los viernes; **on June 20th** el 20 de junio; **a week on Friday** del viernes en una semana; **on arrival** al llegar; **on seeing this** al ver esto
4 (about, concerning) sobre, acerca de; **a book on physics** un libro de or sobre física
▷ adv **1** (referring to dress): **to have one's coat on** tener or llevar el abrigo puesto; **she put her gloves on** se puso los guantes
2 (referring to covering): **"screw the lid on tightly"** "cerrar bien la tapa"
3 (further, continuously): **to walk** etc **on** seguir caminando etc
▷ adj **1** (functioning, in operation: machine, radio, TV, light) encendido/a (SP), prendido/a (LAM); (: tap) abierto/a; (: brakes) echado/a, puesto/a; **is the meeting still on?** (in progress) ¿todavía continúa la reunión?; (not cancelled) ¿va a haber reunión al fin?; **there's a good film on at the cinema** ponen una buena película en el cine
2 **that's not on!** (inf: not possible) ¡eso ni hablar!; (: not acceptable) ¡eso no se hace!

once [wʌns] adv una vez; (formerly) antiguamente ▷ conj una vez que; **~ he had left/it was done** una vez que se había marchado/se hizo; **at ~** en seguida, inmediatamente; (simultaneously) a la vez; **~ a week** una vez por semana; **~ more** otra vez; **~ and for all** de una vez por todas; **~ upon a time** érase una vez
oncoming ['ɔnkʌmɪŋ] adj (traffic)

que viene de frente

○ **KEYWORD**

one [wʌn] num un(o)/una; **one hundred and fifty** ciento cincuenta; **one by one** uno a uno
▷ adj **1** (sole) único; **the one book which** el único libro que; **the one man who** el único que
2 (same) mismo/a; **they came in the one car** vinieron en un solo coche
▷ pron **1** **this one** éste(ésta); **that one** ése(ésa); (more remote) aquél(aquella); **I've already got a (red) one** ya tengo uno/a rojo/a; **one by one** uno/a por uno/a
2 **one another** os (SP), se (+ el uno al otro, unos a otros etc); **do you two ever see one another?** ¿vosotros dos os veis alguna vez? (SP), ¿se ven ustedes dos alguna vez?; **the boys didn't dare look at one another** los chicos no se atrevieron a mirarse (el uno al otro); **they all kissed one another** se besaron unos a otros
3 (impers): **one never knows** nunca se sabe; **to cut one's finger** cortarse el dedo; **one needs to eat** hay que comer
one-off [BRIT: inf] n (event) acontecimiento único

oneself [wʌn'sɛlf] pron (reflexive) se; (after prep) sí; (emphatic) uno mismo/a; **to hurt ~** hacerse daño; **to keep sth for ~** guardarse algo; **to talk to ~** hablar solo
one: **one-shot** [wʌn'ʃɔt] (US) n = **one-off**; **one-sided** adj (argument) parcial; **one-to-one** adj (relationship) de dos; **one-way** adj (street) de sentido único
ongoing ['ɔngəʊɪŋ] adj continuo
onion ['ʌnjən] n cebolla
on-line ['ɔnlaɪn] adj, adv (Comput) en línea
onlooker ['ɔnlʊkə*] n espectador(a) m/f

only ['əʊnlɪ] adv solamente, sólo
▷ adj único, solo ▷ conj solamente
que, pero; **an ~ child** un hijo único;
not ~ ... but also ... no sólo ... sino
también ...

on-screen [ɒn'skri:n] adj (Comput
etc) en pantalla; (romance, kiss)
cinematográfico

onset ['ɒnset] n comienzo

onto ['ɒntʊ] prep = **on to**

onward(s) ['ɒnwəd(z)] adv (move)
(hacia) adelante; **from that time ~**
desde entonces en adelante

oops [ups] excl (also: **~-a-daisy!**) ¡huy!

ooze [u:z] vi rezumar

opaque [əʊ'peɪk] adj opaco

open ['əʊpn] adj abierto; (car)
descubierto; (road, view) despejado;
(meeting) público; (admiration)
manifiesto ▷ vt abrir ▷ vi abrirse;
(book etc: commence) comenzar; **in the
~ (air)** al aire libre; **open up** vt abrir;
(blocked road) despejar ▷ vi abrirse,
empezar; **open-air** adj al aire libre;
opening n abertura; (start) comienzo;
(opportunity) oportunidad f; **opening
hours** npl horario de apertura; **open
learning** n enseñanza flexible a tiempo
parcial; **openly** adv abiertamente;
open-minded adj imparcial; **open-
necked** adj (shirt) desabrochado; sin
corbata; **open-plan** adj; **open-plan
office** gran oficina sin particiones; **Open
University** (BRIT) ≈ Universidad f
Nacional de Enseñanza a Distancia,
UNED f

● presentación de unos trabajos y la
● asistencia a los cursos de verano.

opera ['ɒpərə] n ópera; **opera house**
n teatro de la ópera; **opera singer** n
cantante m/f de ópera

operate ['ɒpəreɪt] vt (machine)
hacer funcionar; (company) dirigir ▷ vi
funcionar; **to ~ on sb** (Med) operar
a algn

operating room ['ɒpəreɪtɪŋ-] (US) n
quirófano, sala de operaciones

operating theatre (BRIT) n sala de
operaciones

operation [ɒpə'reɪʃən] n operación
f; (of machine) funcionamiento; **to
be in ~** estar funcionando or en
funcionamiento; **to have an ~**
(Med) ser operado; **operational** adj
operacional, en buen estado

operative ['ɒpərətɪv] adj en vigor

operator ['ɒpəreɪtə*] n (of machine)
maquinista mf, operario(a) m/f; (Tel)
operador(a) m/f, telefonista mf

opinion [ə'pɪnɪən] n opinión f; **in my
~** en mi opinión, a mi juicio; **opinion
poll** n encuesta, sondeo

opponent [ə'pəʊnənt] n adversario/
a, contrincante mf

opportunity [ɒpə'tju:nɪtɪ] n
oportunidad f; **to take the ~ of doing**
aprovechar la ocasión para hacer

oppose [ə'pəʊz] vt oponerse a; **to be
~d to sth** oponerse a algo; **as ~d to**
a diferencia de

opposite ['ɒpəzɪt] adj opuesto,
contrario a; (house etc) de enfrente
▷ adv en frente ▷ prep en frente de,
frente a ▷ n lo contrario

opposition [ɒpə'zɪʃən] n oposición f

oppress [ə'pres] vt oprimir

opt [ɒpt] vi: **to ~ for** optar por; **to ~ to
do** optar por hacer; **opt out** vi: **to opt
out of** optar por no hacer

optician [ɒp'tɪʃən] n óptico m/f

optimism ['ɒptɪmɪzəm] n
optimismo

optimist ['ɒptɪmɪst] n optimista mf;

optimistic [-'mɪstɪk] *adj* optimista
optimum ['ɒptɪməm] *adj* óptimo
option ['ɒpʃən] *n* opción *f*; **optional**
adj facultativo, discrecional
or [ɔː*] *conj* o; (*before o, no*) u; (*with
negative*): **he hasn't seen ~ heard
anything** no ha visto ni oído nada; **~
else** si no
oral ['ɔːrəl] *adj* oral ▷ *n* examen *m* oral
orange ['ɒrɪndʒ] *n* (*fruit*) naranja
▷ *adj* color naranja; **orange juice** *n*
jugo *m* de naranja, zumo *m* de naranja
(*sp*); **orange squash** *n* naranjada
orbit ['ɔːbɪt] *n* órbita ▷ *vt, vi* orbitar
orchard ['ɔːtʃəd] *n* huerto
orchestra ['ɔːkɪstrə] *n* orquesta;
(*us: seating*) platea
orchid ['ɔːkɪd] *n* orquídea
ordeal [ɔː'diːl] *n* experiencia
horrorosa
order ['ɔːdə*] *n* orden *m*; (*command*)
orden *f*; (*good order*) buen estado; (*Comm*) pedido *m* ▷ *vt* (*also: put in ~*)
arreglar, poner en orden; (*Comm*)
pedir; (*command*) mandar, ordenar;
in ~ en orden; (*of document*) en regla;
in (working) ~ en funcionamiento;
in ~ to do/that para hacer/que;
on ~ (*Comm*) pedido; **to be out of ~**
estar desordenado; (*not working*) no
funcionar; **to ~ sb to do sth** mandar
a algn hacer algo; **order form** *n* hoja
de pedido; **orderly** (*Mil*) ordenanza
m; (*Med*) enfermero/a (*auxiliar*) ▷ *adj*
ordenado
ordinary ['ɔːdnrɪ] *adj* corriente,
normal; (*pej*) común y corriente; **out of
the ~** fuera de lo común
ore [ɔː*] *n* mineral *m*
oregano [ɒrɪ'gɑːnəu] *n* orégano
organ ['ɔːgən] *n* órgano; **organic**
[ɔː'gænɪk] *adj* orgánico; **organism** *n*
organismo
organization [ɔːgənaɪ'zeɪʃən] *n*
organización *f*
organize ['ɔːgənaɪz] *vt* organizar;
organized ['ɔːgənaɪzd] *adj*
organizado; **organizer** *n*

organizador(a) *m/f*
orgasm ['ɔːgæzm] *n* orgasmo
orgy ['ɔːdʒɪ] *n* orgía
oriental [ɔːrɪ'entl] *adj* oriental
orientation [ɔːrɪen'teɪʃən] *n*
orientación *f*
origin ['ɒrɪdʒɪn] *n* origen *m*
original [ə'rɪdʒɪnl] *adj* original; (*first*)
primero; (*earlier*) primitivo ▷ *n* original
m; **originally** *adv* al principio
originate [ə'rɪdʒɪneɪt] *vi*: **to ~ from,
to ~ in** surgir de, tener su origen en
Orkneys ['ɔːknɪz] *npl*: **the ~** (*also*: **the
Orkney Islands**) las Orcadas
ornament ['ɔːnəmənt] *n* adorno;
(*trinket*) chuchería; **ornamental**
[-'mentl] *adj* decorativo, de adorno
ornate [ɔː'neɪt] *adj* muy ornado,
vistoso
orphan ['ɔːfn] *n* huérfano/a
orthodox ['ɔːθədɔks] *adj* ortodoxo
orthopaedic [ɔːθə'piːdɪk] (*us*
orthopedic) *adj* ortopédico
osteopath ['ɒstɪəpæθ] *n* osteópata
mf
ostrich ['ɒstrɪtʃ] *n* avestruz *m*
other ['ʌðə*] *adj* otro ▷ *pron*: **the ~
(one)** el(la) otro/a ▷ *adv*: **~ than** aparte
de; **otherwise** *adv* de otra manera
▷ *conj* (*if not*) si no
otter ['ɒtə*] *n* nutria
ouch [autʃ] *excl* ¡ay!
ought [ɔːt] (*pt ~*) *aux vb*: **I ~ to do
it** debería hacerlo; **this ~ to have
been corrected** esto debiera haberse
corregido; **he ~ to win** (*probability*)
debe o debiera ganar
ounce [auns] *n* onza (28.35g)
our ['auə*] *adj* nuestro; *see also* **my**;
ours *pron* (el) nuestro/(la) nuestra
etc; *see also* **mine[1]**; **ourselves** *pron pl*
(*reflexive, after prep*) nosotros; (*emphatic*)
nosotros mismos; *see also* **oneself**
oust [aust] *vt* desalojar
out [aut] *adv* fuera, afuera; (*not
at home*) fuera (de casa); (*light, fire*)
apagado; **~ there** allí (fuera); **he's ~**
(*absent*) no está, ha salido; **to be ~ in**

one's calculations equivocarse (en sus cálculos); **to run ~** salir corriendo; **~ loud** en alta voz; **~ of** (*outside*) fuera de; (*because of: anger etc*) por; **~ of petrol** sin gasolina; **"~ of order"** "no funciona"; **outback** n interior m; **outbound** adj (*flight*) de salida; (*flight: not return*) de ida; **outbreak** n (*of war*) comienzo m; (*of disease*) epidemia; (*of violence etc*) ola; **outburst** n explosión f, arranque m; **outcast** n paria mf; **outcome** n resultado; **outcry** n protestas fpl; **outdated** adj anticuado, fuera de moda; **outdoor** adj exterior, de aire libre; (*clothes*) de calle; **outdoors** adv al aire libre

outer ['autə*] adj exterior, externo; **outer space** n espacio exterior

outfit ['autfit] n (*clothes*) conjunto m

outgoing adj (*character*) extrovertido; (*retiring: president etc*) saliente; **outgoings** (BRIT) npl gastos mpl; **outhouse** n dependencia

outing ['autɪŋ] n excursión f, paseo m

out: outlaw n proscrito ▷ vt proscribir; **outlay** n inversión f; **outlet** n salida; (*of pipe*) desagüe m; (US *Elec*) toma de corriente; (*also*: **retail outlet**) punto de venta; **outline** n (*shape*) contorno, perfil m; (*sketch, plan*) esbozo ▷ vt (*plan etc*) esbozar; **in outline** (*fig*) a grandes rasgos; **outlook** n (*fig: prospects*) perspectivas fpl; (*: for weather*) pronóstico; **outnumber** vt superar en número; **out-of-date** adj (*passport*) caducado; (*clothes*) pasado de moda; **out-of-doors** adv al aire libre; **out-of-the-way** adj apartado; **out-of-town** adj (*shopping centre etc*) en las afueras; **outpatient** n paciente mf externo/a; **outpost** n puesto avanzado; **output** n (*volumen m de*) producción m, rendimiento; (*Comput*) salida

outrage ['autreɪdʒ] n escándalo m; (*atrocity*) atrocidad f ▷ vt ultrajar; **outrageous** [-'reɪdʒəs] adj monstruoso

outright [adv aut'raɪt, adj 'autraɪt] adv (*ask, deny*) francamente; (*refuse*) rotundamente; (*win*) de manera absoluta; (*be killed*) en el acto ▷ adj franco; rotundo

outset ['autset] n principio

outside [aut'saɪd] n exterior m ▷ adj exterior, externo ▷ adv fuera ▷ prep fuera de; (*beyond*) más allá de; **at the ~** (*fig*) a lo sumo; **outside lane** n (*Aut: in Britain*) carril m de la derecha; (*: in US, Europe etc*) carril m de la izquierda; **outside line** n (*Tel*) línea (exterior); **outsider** n (*stranger*) extraño, forastero

out: outsize adj (*clothes*) de talla grande; **outskirts** npl alrededores mpl, afueras fpl; **outspoken** adj muy franco; **outstanding** adj excepcional, destacado; (*remaining*) pendiente

outward ['autwəd] adj externo; (*journey*) de ida; **outwards** adv (*esp BRIT*) = **outward**

outweigh [aut'weɪ] vt pesar más que

oval ['əuvl] adj ovalado ▷ n óvalo

ovary ['əuvərɪ] n ovario

oven ['ʌvn] n horno; **oven glove** n guante m para el horno, manopla para el horno; **ovenproof** adj resistente al horno; **oven-ready** adj listo para el horno

over ['əuvə*] adv encima, por encima ▷ adj or adv (*finished*) terminado; (*surplus*) de sobra ▷ prep (*por*) encima de; (*above*) sobre; (*on the other side of*) al otro lado de; (*more than*) más de; (*during*) durante; **~ here** (*por*) aquí; **~ there** (*por*) allí or allá; **all ~** (*everywhere*) por todas partes; **~ and ~ (again)** una y otra vez; **~ and above** además de; **to ask sb ~** invitar a algn a casa; **to ~ inclinarse**

overall [adj, n 'əuvərɔːl, adv əuvər'ɔːl] adj (*length etc*) total; (*study*) de conjunto ▷ adv en conjunto ▷ n (BRIT) guardapolvo; **overalls** npl (*boiler suit*) mono (SP) or overol m (LAM) (*de trabajo*)

overboard ['əuvəbɔːd] adv (Naut) por la borda

overcame [əuvəˈkeɪm] pt of **overcome**

overcast [ˈəuvəkɑ:st] adj encapotado

overcharge [əuvəˈtʃɑ:dʒ] vt: **to ~ sb** cobrar un precio excesivo a algn

overcoat [ˈəuvəkəut] n abrigo, sobretodo

overcome [əuvəˈkʌm] vt vencer; (difficulty) superar

over: overcrowded adj atestado de gente; (city, country) superpoblado; **overdo** (irreg) vt exagerar; (overcook) cocer demasiado; **to overdo it** (work etc) pasarse; **overdone** [əuvəˈdʌn] adj (vegetables) recocido; (steak) demasiado hecho; **overdose** n sobredosis f inv; **overdraft** n saldo deudor; **overdrawn** adj (account) en descubierto; **overdue** adj retrasado; **overestimate** vt sobreestimar

overflow [vb əuvəˈfləu, n ˈəuvəfləu] vi desbordarse ▷ n (also: ~ **pipe**) (cañería de) desagüe m

overgrown [əuvəˈgrəun] adj (garden) invadido por la vegetación

overhaul [vb əuvəˈhɔ:l, n ˈəuvəhɔ:l] vt revisar, repasar ▷ n revisión f

overhead [adv əuvəˈhed, adj, n ˈəuvəhed] adv por arriba or encima ▷ adj (cable) aéreo ▷ n (us) **overheads**; **overhead projector** n retroproyector; **overheads** npl (expenses) gastos mpl generales

over: overhear (irreg) vt oír por casualidad; **overheat** vi (engine) recalentarse; **overland** adj, adv por tierra; **overlap** [əuvəˈlæp] vi traslaparse; **overleaf** adv al dorso; **overload** vt sobrecargar; **overlook** vt (have view of) dar a, tener vistas a; (miss: by mistake) pasar por alto; (excuse) perdonar

overnight [əuvəˈnaɪt] adv durante la noche; (fig) de la noche a la mañana ▷ adj de noche; **to stay ~** pasar la noche; **overnight bag** n fin m de semana, neceser m de viaje

overpass (us) [ˈəuvəpɑ:s] n paso superior

overpower [əuvəˈpauə*] vt dominar; (fig) embargar; **overpowering** adj (heat) agobiante; (smell) penetrante

over: overreact [əuvərɪˈækt] vi reaccionar de manera exagerada; **overrule** vt (decision) anular; (claim) denegar; **overrun** (irreg) vt (country) invadir; (time limit) rebasar, exceder

overseas [əuvəˈsi:z] adv (abroad: live) en el extranjero; (travel) al extranjero ▷ adj (trade) exterior; (visitor) extranjero

oversee [əuvəˈsi:] (irreg) vt supervisar

overshadow [əuvəˈʃædəu] vt: **to be ~ed by** estar a la sombra de

oversight [ˈəuvəsaɪt] n descuido

oversleep [əuvəˈsli:p] (irreg) vi quedarse dormido

overspend [əuvəˈspend] (irreg) vi gastar más de la cuenta; **we have overspent by 5 pounds** hemos excedido el presupuesto en 5 libras

overt [əuˈvə:t] adj abierto

overtake [əuvəˈteɪk] (irreg) vt sobrepasar; (BRIT Aut) adelantar

over: overthrow (irreg) vt (government) derrocar; **overtime** n horas fpl extraordinarias

overtook [əuvəˈtuk] pt of **overtake**

over: overturn vt volcar; (fig: plan) desbaratar; (: government) derrocar ▷ vi volcar; **overweight** adj demasiado gordo or pesado; **overwhelm** vt aplastar; (emotion) sobrecoger; **overwhelming** adj (victory, defeat) arrollador(a); (feeling) irresistible

ow [au] excl ¡ay!

owe [əu] vt: **to ~ sb sth, to ~ sth to sb** deber algo a algn; **owing to** prep debido a, por causa de

owl [aul] n búho, lechuza

own [əun] vt tener, poseer ▷ adj propio; **a house of my ~** una habitación propia; **to get one's ~ back** tomar revancha; **on one's ~** solo, a solas; **own up** vi confesar; **owner** n dueño/a;

ownership n posesión f
ox [ɔks] (pl ~**en**) n buey m
Oxbridge [ˈɔksbrɪdʒ] n universidades de Oxford y Cambridge
oxen [ˈɔksən] npl of **ox**
oxygen [ˈɔksɪdʒən] n oxígeno
oyster [ˈɔɪstə*] n ostra
oz. abbr = **ounce(s)**
ozone [ˈəʊzəʊn] n ozono; **ozone friendly** adj que no daña la capa de ozono; **ozone layer** n capa f de ozono

p

p [piː] abbr = **penny; pence**
P.A. n abbr = **personal assistant; public address system**
p.a. abbr = **per annum**
pace [peɪs] n paso ▷ vi: **to ~ up and down** pasearse de un lado a otro; **to keep ~ with** llevar el mismo paso que; **pacemaker** n (Med) regulador m cardíaco, marcapasos m inv; (Sport: also: **pacesetter**) liebre f
Pacific [pəˈsɪfɪk] n: **the ~ (Ocean)** el (Océano) Pacífico
pacifier [ˈpæsɪfaɪə*] (us) n (dummy) chupete m
pack [pæk] n (packet) paquete m; (of hounds) jauría; (of people) manada, bando; (of cards) baraja; (bundle) fardo; (us: of cigarettes) paquete m; (back pack) mochila ▷ vt (fill) llenar; (in suitcase etc) meter, poner; (cram) llenar, atestar; **to ~ (one's bags)** hacerse la maleta; **to ~ sb off** despachar a algn; **pack in** vi (watch, car) estropearse ▷ vt (inf) dejar; **pack it in!** ¡para!, ¡basta ya!; **pack up** vi (inf: machine) estropearse; (person) irse

▷ vt (belongings, clothes) recoger; (goods, presents) empaquetar, envolver

package ['pækɪdʒ] n paquete m; (bulky) bulto; (also: **~ deal**) acuerdo global; **package holiday** n vacaciones fpl organizadas; **package tour** n viaje m organizado

packaging ['pækɪdʒɪŋ] n envase m

packed [pækt] adj abarrotado; **packed lunch** n almuerzo frío

packet ['pækɪt] n paquete m

packing ['pækɪŋ] n embalaje m

pact [pækt] n pacto

pad [pæd] n (of paper) bloc m; (cushion) cojinete m; (inf: home) casa ▷ vt rellenar; **padded** adj (jacket) acolchado; (bra) reforzado

paddle ['pædl] n (oar) canalete m; (us: for table tennis) paleta ▷ vt impulsar con canalete ▷ vi (with feet) chapotear; **paddling pool** (BRIT) n estanque m de juegos

paddock ['pædək] n corral m

padlock ['pædlɔk] n candado

paedophile ['piːdəυfaɪl] (us **pedophile**) adj de pedófilos ▷ n pedófilo/a

page [peɪdʒ] n (of book) página; (of newspaper) plana; (also: **~ boy**) paje m ▷ vt (in hotel etc) llamar por altavoz a

pager ['peɪdʒə*] n (Tel) busca m

paid [peɪd] pt, pp of **pay** ▷ adj (work) remunerado; (holiday) pagado; (official etc) a sueldo; **to put ~ to** (BRIT) acabar con

pain [peɪn] n dolor m; **to be in ~** sufrir; **to take ~s to do sth** tomarse grandes molestias en hacer algo; **painful** adj doloroso; (difficult) penoso; (disagreeable) desagradable; **painkiller** n analgésico; **painstaking** ['peɪnzteɪkɪŋ] adj (person) concienzudo, esmerado

paint [peɪnt] n pintura ▷ vt pintar; **to ~ the door blue** pintar la puerta de azul; **paintbrush** n (of artist) pincel m; (of decorator) brocha; **painter** n pintor(a) m/f; **painting** n pintura

pair [pɛə*] n (of shoes, gloves etc) par m; (of people) pareja; **a ~ of scissors** unas tijeras; **a ~ of trousers** unos pantalones, un pantalón

pajamas [pə'dʒɑːməz] (us) npl pijama m

Pakistan [pɑːkɪ'stɑːn] n Paquistán m; **Pakistani** adj, n paquistaní mf

pal [pæl] (inf) n compinche mf, compañero/a

palace ['pæləs] n palacio

pale [peɪl] adj (gen) pálido; (colour) claro ▷ n: **to be beyond the ~** pasarse de la raya

Palestine ['pælɪstaɪn] n Palestina; **Palestinian** [-'tɪnɪən] adj, n palestino/a m/f

palm [pɑːm] n (Anat) palma; (also: **~ tree**) palmera, palma ▷ vt: **to ~ sth off on sb** (inf) encajar algo a algn

pamper ['pæmpə*] vt mimar

pamphlet ['pæmflət] n folleto

pan [pæn] n (also: **sauce~**) cacerola, cazuela, olla; (also: **frying ~**) sartén f

pancake ['pænkeɪk] n crepe f

panda ['pændə] n panda m

pane [peɪn] n cristal m

panel ['pænl] n (of wood etc) panel m; (Radio, TV) panel m de invitados

panhandler ['pænhændlə*] (us) n (inf) mendigo/a

panic ['pænɪk] n terror m pánico ▷ vi dejarse llevar por el pánico

panorama [pænə'rɑːmə] n panorama m

pansy ['pænzɪ] n (Bot) pensamiento; (inf, pej) maricón m

pant [pænt] vi jadear

panther ['pænθə*] n pantera

panties ['pæntɪz] npl bragas fpl, pantis mpl

pantomime ['pæntəmaɪm] (BRIT) n revista musical representada en Navidad, basada en cuentos de hadas

● **PANTOMIME**
●
● En época navideña se ponen en

escena en los teatros británicos las llamadas **pantomimes**, que son versiones libres de cuentos tradicionales como Aladino o El gato con botas. En ella nunca faltan personajes como la dama ("dame"), papel que siempre interpreta un actor, el protagonista joven ("principal boy"), normalmente interpretado por una actriz, y el malvado ("villain"). Es un espectáculo familiar en el que se anima al público a participar y aunque va dirigido principalmente a los niños, cuenta con grandes dosis de humor para adultos.

pants [pænts] n (BRIT: underwear: woman's) bragas fpl; (: man's) calzoncillos mpl; (US: trousers) pantalones mpl

paper ['peɪpə*] n papel m; (also: **news~**) periódico, diario; (academic essay) ensayo; (exam) examen m ▷ adj de papel ▷ vt empapelar, tapizar (MEX); **papers** npl (also: **identity ~s**) papeles mpl, documentos mpl; **paperback** n libro en rústica; **paper bag** n bolsa de papel; **paper clip** n clip m; **paper shop** (BRIT) n tienda de periódicos; **paperwork** n trabajo administrativo

paprika ['pæprɪkə] n pimentón m

par [pɑ:*] n par f; (Golf) par m; **to be on a ~ with** estar a la par con

paracetamol [pærə'si:təmɔl] (BRIT) n paracetamol m

parachute ['pærəʃu:t] n paracaídas m inv

parade [pə'reɪd] n desfile m ▷ vt (show) hacer alarde de ▷ vi desfilar; (Mil) pasar revista

paradise ['pærədaɪs] n paraíso

paradox ['pærədɔks] n paradoja

paraffin ['pærəfɪn] (BRIT) n (also: ~ oil) parafina

paragraph ['pærəgrɑ:f] n párrafo

parallel ['pærəlɛl] adj en paralelo;

(fig) semejante ▷ n (line) paralela; (fig, Geo) paralelo

paralysed ['pærəlaɪzd] adj paralizado

paralysis [pə'rælɪsɪs] n parálisis f inv

paramedic [pærə'mɛdɪk] n auxiliar m/f sanitario/a

paranoid ['pærənɔɪd] adj (person, feeling) paranoico

parasite ['pærəsaɪt] n parásito/a

parcel ['pɑ:sl] n paquete m ▷ vt (also: ~ up) empaquetar, embalar

pardon ['pɑ:dn] n (Law) indulto ▷ vt perdonar; **~ me!, I beg your ~!** (I'm sorry!) ¡perdone usted!; **(I beg your) ~?, ~ me?** (US: what did you say?) ¿cómo?

parent ['pɛərənt] n (mother) madre f; (father) padre m; **parents** npl padres mpl

Be careful not to translate **parent** by the Spanish word **pariente**.

parental [pə'rɛntl] adj paternal/ maternal

Paris ['pærɪs] n París

parish ['pærɪʃ] n parroquia

Parisian [pə'rɪzɪən] adj, n parisiense m/f

park [pɑ:k] n parque m ▷ vt aparcar, estacionar ▷ vi aparcar, estacionarse

parking ['pɑ:kɪŋ] n aparcamiento, estacionamiento; **"no ~"** "prohibido estacionarse"; **parking lot** (US) n parking m; **parking meter** n parquímetro; **parking ticket** n multa de aparcamiento

parkway ['pɑ:kweɪ] (US) n alameda

parliament ['pɑ:ləmənt] n parlamento; (Spanish) Cortes fpl; **parliamentary** [-'mɛntərɪ] adj parlamentario

PARLIAMENT

El Parlamento británico (**Parliament**) tiene como sede el palacio de Westminster, también llamado "Houses of Parliament" y consta de dos cámaras. La Cámara de los Comunes ("House of Commons"), compuesta por 650 diputados (**Members of Parliament**) elegidos por sufragio universal en su respectiva circunscripción electoral (**constituency**), se reúne 175 días al año y sus sesiones son moderadas por el Presidente de la Cámara (**Speaker**). La cámara alta es la Cámara de los Lores ("House of Lords") y está formada por miembros que han sido nombrados por el monarca o que han heredado su escaño. Su poder es limitado, aunque actúa como tribunal supremo de apelación, excepto en Escocia.

Parmesan [pɑːmɪˈzæn] n (also: **~ cheese**) queso parmesano

parole [pəˈrəʊl] n: **on ~** libre bajo palabra

parrot [ˈpærət] n loro, papagayo

parsley [ˈpɑːslɪ] n perejil m

parsnip [ˈpɑːsnɪp] n chirivía

parson [ˈpɑːsn] n cura m

part [pɑːt] n (gen, Mus) parte f; (bit) trozo; (of machine) pieza; (Theatre etc) papel m; (of serial) entrega; (us: in hair) raya ▷ adv ~ **partly** ▷ vt separar ▷ vi (people) separarse; (crowd) apartarse; **to take ~ in** tomar parte o participar en; **to take sth in good ~** tomar algo en buena parte; **to take sb's ~** defender a algn; **for my ~** por mi parte; **for the most ~** en su mayor parte; **to ~ one's hair** hacerse la raya; **part with** vt fus ceder, entregar; (money) pagar; **part of speech** n parte f de la oración, categoría f gramatical

partial [ˈpɑːʃl] adj parcial; **to be ~ to** ser aficionado a

participant [pɑːˈtɪsɪpənt] n (in competition) concursante mf; (in campaign etc) participante mf

participate [pɑːˈtɪsɪpeɪt] vi: **to ~ in** participar en

particle [ˈpɑːtɪkl] n partícula; (of dust) grano

particular [pəˈtɪkjʊlə*] adj (special) particular; (concrete) concreto; (given) determinado; (fussy) quisquilloso; (demanding) exigente; **in ~** en particular; **particularly** adv (in particular) sobre todo; (difficult, good etc) especialmente; **particulars** npl (information) datos mpl; (details) pormenores mpl

parting [ˈpɑːtɪŋ] n (act) separación f; (farewell) despedida; (BRIT: in hair) raya ▷ adj de despedida

partition [pɑːˈtɪʃən] n (Pol) división f; (wall) tabique m

partly [ˈpɑːtlɪ] adv en parte

partner [ˈpɑːtnə*] n (Comm) socio/a; (Sport, at dance) pareja; (spouse) cónyuge mf; (lover) compañero/a; **partnership** n asociación f; (Comm) sociedad f

partridge [ˈpɑːtrɪdʒ] n perdiz f

part-time [ˈpɑːtˈtaɪm] adj, adv a tiempo parcial

party [ˈpɑːtɪ] n (Pol) partido; (celebration) fiesta; (group) grupo; (Law) parte f interesada ▷ cpd (Pol) de partido

pass [pɑːs] vt (time, object) pasar; (place) pasar por; (overtake) rebasar; (exam) aprobar; (approve) aprobar ▷ vi pasar; (Scol) aprobar, ser aprobado ▷ n (permit) permiso; (membership card) carnet m; (in mountains) puerto, desfiladero; (Sport) pase m; (Scol: also: **~ mark**): **to get a ~** aprobar; **to ~ sth through sth** pasar algo por algo; **to make a ~ at sb** (inf) hacer proposiciones a algn; **pass away** vi fallecer; **pass by** vi pasar ▷ vt (ignore) pasar por alto; **pass on** vt transmitir; **pass out** vi desmayarse; **pass over** vi, vt omitir, pasar por alto; **pass up** vt (opportunity) renunciar a; **passable** adj (road) transitable; (tolerable) pasable

passage [ˈpæsɪdʒ] n (also: **~way**) pasillo; (act of passing) tránsito; (fare, in book) pasaje m; (by boat) travesía; (Anat) tubo

passenger ['pæsɪndʒə*] n pasajero/a, viajero/a

passer-by [pɑ:sə'baɪ] n transeúnte mf

passing place n (Aut) apartadero

passion ['pæʃən] n pasión f; **passionate** adj apasionado; **passion fruit** n fruta de la pasión, granadilla f

passive ['pæsɪv] adj (gen, also Ling) pasivo

passport ['pɑ:spɔ:t] n pasaporte m; **passport control** n control m de pasaporte; **passport office** n oficina de pasaportes

password ['pɑ:swɜ:d] n contraseña

past [pɑ:st] prep (in front of) por delante de; (further than) más allá de; (later than) después de ▷ adj pasado; (president etc) antiguo ▷ n (time) pasado; (of person) antecedentes mpl; **he's ~ forty** tiene más de cuarenta años; **ten/quarter ~ eight** las ocho y diez/cuarto; **for the ~ few/3 days** durante los últimos días/últimos 3 días; **to run ~ sb** pasar a algn corriendo

pasta ['pæstə] n pasta

paste [peɪst] n pasta; (glue) engrudo ▷ vt pegar

pastel ['pæstl] adj pastel; (painting) al pastel

pasteurized ['pæstəraɪzd] adj pasteurizado

pastime ['pɑ:staɪm] n pasatiempo

pastor ['pɑ:stə*] n pastor m

past participle [-'pɑ:tɪsɪpl] n (Ling) participio m (de) pasado or (de) pretérito or pasivo

pastry ['peɪstrɪ] n (dough) pasta; (cake) pastel m

pasture ['pɑ:stʃə*] n pasto

pasty¹ ['pæstɪ] n empanada

pasty² ['peɪstɪ] adj (complexion) pálido

pat [pæt] vt dar una palmadita a; (dog etc) acariciar

patch [pætʃ] n (of material,: eye patch) parche m; (mended part) remiendo; (of

land) terreno ▷ vt remendar; **(to go through) a bad ~** (pasar por) una mala racha; **patchy** adj desigual

pâté ['pæteɪ] n paté m

patent ['peɪtnt] n patente f ▷ vt patentar ▷ adj patente, evidente

paternal [pə'tɜ:nl] adj paternal; (relation) paterno

paternity leave [pə'tɜ:nɪtɪ-] n permiso m por paternidad, licencia por paternidad

path [pɑ:θ] n camino, sendero; (trail, track) pista; (of missile) trayectoria

pathetic [pə'θetɪk] adj patético, lastimoso; (very bad) malísimo

pathway ['pɑ:θweɪ] n sendero, vereda

patience ['peɪʃns] n paciencia; (BRIT Cards) solitario

patient ['peɪʃnt] n paciente mf ▷ adj paciente, sufrido

patio ['pætɪəu] n patio

patriotic [pætrɪ'ɒtɪk] adj patriótico

patrol [pə'trəul] n patrulla ▷ vt patrullar por; **patrol car** n coche m patrulla

patron ['peɪtrən] n (in shop) cliente mf; (of charity) patrocinador(a) m/f; **~ of the arts** mecenas m

patronizing ['pætrənaɪzɪŋ] adj condescendiente

pattern ['pætən] n (Sewing) patrón m; (design) dibujo; **patterned** adj (material) estampado

pause [pɔ:z] n pausa ▷ vi hacer una pausa

pave [peɪv] vt pavimentar; **to ~ the way for** preparar el terreno para

pavement ['peɪvmənt] (BRIT) n acera, banqueta (MEX), andén m (CAM), vereda (SC)

pavilion [pə'vɪlɪən] n (Sport) caseta

paving ['peɪvɪŋ] n pavimento, enlosado

paw [pɔ:] n pata

pawn [pɔ:n] n (Chess) peón m; (fig) instrumento ▷ vt empeñar; **pawn broker** n prestamista mf

pay | 476

pay [peɪ] (pt, pp **paid**) n (wage etc) sueldo, salario ▷ vt pagar ▷ vi (be profitable) rendir; **to ~ attention (to)** prestar atención (a); **to ~ sb a visit** hacer una visita a algn; **to ~ one's respects to sb** presentar sus respetos a algn; **pay back** vt (money) reembolsar; (person) pagar; **pay for** vt fus pagar; **pay in** vt ingresar; **pay off** vt saldar ▷ vi (scheme, decision) dar resultado; **pay out** vt (money) gastar, desembolsar; **pay up** vt pagar (de mala gana); **payable** adj: **payable to** pagadero a; **pay day** n día m de paga; **pay envelope** (US) n = **pay packet**; **payment** n pago; **monthly payment** mensualidad f; **payout** n pago; (in competition) premio en metálico; **pay packet** (BRIT) n sobre m (de paga); **pay phone** n teléfono público; **payroll** n nómina; **pay slip** n recibo de sueldo; **pay television** n televisión f de pago

PC n abbr = **personal computer**; (BRIT) (= police constable) policía mf ▷ adv abbr = **politically correct**

p.c. abbr = **per cent**

PDA n abbr (= personal digital assistant) agenda electrónica

PE n abbr (= physical education) ed. física

pea [pi:] n guisante m (SP), arveja (LAM), chícharo (MEX, CAM)

peace [pi:s] n paz f; (calm) paz f, tranquilidad f; **peaceful** adj (gentle) pacífico; (calm) tranquilo, sosegado

peach [pi:tʃ] n melocotón m (SP), durazno (LAM)

peacock ['pi:kɔk] n pavo real

peak [pi:k] n (of mountain) cumbre f, cima; (of cap) visera; (fig) cumbre f; **peak hours** npl horas fpl punta

peanut ['pi:nʌt] n cacahuete m (SP), maní m (LAM), cacahuate m (MEX); **peanut butter** n manteca de cacahuete or maní

pear [pɛə*] n pera

pearl [pə:l] n perla

peasant ['pɛznt] n campesino/a

peat [pi:t] n turba

pebble ['pɛbl] n guijarro

peck [pɛk] vt (also: **~ at**) picotear ▷ n picotazo; (kiss) besito; **peckish** (BRIT: inf) adj: **I feel peckish** tengo ganas de picar algo

peculiar [pɪˈkju:lɪə*] adj (odd) extraño, raro; (typical) propio, característico; **~ to** propio de

pedal ['pɛdl] n pedal m ▷ vi pedalear

pedalo ['pɛdələu] n patín m a pedal

pedestal ['pɛdəstl] n pedestal m

pedestrian [pɪˈdɛstrɪən] n peatón/ ona m/f ▷ adj pedestre; **pedestrian crossing** (BRIT) n paso de peatones; **pedestrianized** adj: **a pedestrianized street** una calle peatonal; **pedestrian precinct** (US **pedestrian zone**) n zona peatonal

pedigree ['pɛdɪɡri:] n genealogía; (of animal) raza, pedigrí m ▷ cpd (animal) de raza, de casta

pedophile ['pi:dəufaɪl] (US) n = **paedophile**

pee [pi:] (inf) vi mear

peek [pi:k] vi mirar a hurtadillas

peel [pi:l] n (of orange, lemon) cáscara; (: removed) peladuras fpl ▷ vt pelar ▷ vi (paint etc) desconcharse; (wallpaper) despegarse, desprenderse; (skin) pelar

peep [pi:p] n (BRIT: look) mirada furtiva; (sound) pío ▷ vi (BRIT: look) mirar furtivamente

peer [pɪə*] vi: **to ~ at** escudriñar ▷ n (noble) par m; (equal) igual m; (contemporary) contemporáneo/a

peg [pɛɡ] n (for coat etc) gancho, colgadero; (BRIT: also: **clothes ~**) pinza

pelican ['pɛlɪkən] n pelícano; **pelican crossing** (BRIT) n (Aut) paso de peatones señalizado

pelt [pɛlt] vt: **to ~ sb with sth** arrojarle algo a algn ▷ vi (rain) llover a cántaros; (inf: run) correr ▷ n pellejo

pelvis ['pɛlvɪs] n pelvis f

pen [pɛn] n (fountain pen) pluma; (ballpoint pen) bolígrafo; (for sheep) redil m

penalty ['penltɪ] n (gen) pena; (fine) multa

pence [pens] npl of **penny**

pencil ['pensl] n lápiz m; **pencil in** vt (appointment) apuntar con carácter provisional; **pencil case** n estuche m; **pencil sharpener** n sacapuntas m inv

pendant ['pendnt] n pendiente m

pending ['pendɪŋ] prep antes de ▷ adj pendiente

penetrate ['penɪtreɪt] vt penetrar

penfriend ['penfrend] (BRIT) n amigo/a por carta

penguin ['peŋgwɪn] n pingüino

penicillin [penɪ'sɪlɪn] n penicilina

peninsula [pə'nɪnsjulə] n península

penis ['pi:nɪs] n pene m

penitentiary [penɪ'tenʃərɪ] (US) n cárcel f, presidio

penknife ['pennaɪf] n navaja

penniless ['penɪlɪs] adj sin dinero

penny ['penɪ] (pl **pennies** or **pence**) (BRIT) n penique m; (US) centavo

penpal ['penpæl] n amigo/a por carta

pension ['penʃən] n (state benefit) jubilación f; **pensioner** (BRIT) n jubilado/a

pentagon ['pentəgən] (US) n: **the P~** (Pol) el Pentágono

- **PENTAGON**

  Se conoce como **Pentagon** al edificio de planta pentagonal que acoge las dependencias del Ministerio de Defensa estadounidense ("Department of Defense") en Arlington, Virginia. En lenguaje periodístico se aplica también a la dirección militar del país.

penthouse ['penthaus] n ático de lujo

penultimate [pe'nʌltɪmət] adj penúltimo

people ['pi:pl] npl gente f; (citizens) pueblo, ciudadanos mpl; (Pol): **the ~** el pueblo ▷ n (nation, race) pueblo, nación f; **several ~ came** vinieron varias personas; **~ say that ...** dice la gente que ...

pepper ['pepə*] n (spice) pimienta; (vegetable) pimiento ▷ vt: **to ~ with** (fig) salpicar de; **peppermint** n (sweet) pastilla de menta

per [pə:*] prep por; **~ day/~son** por día/persona; **~ annum** al año

perceive [pə'si:v] vt percibir; (realize) darse cuenta de

per cent n por ciento

percentage [pə'sentɪdʒ] n porcentaje m

perception [pə'sepʃən] n percepción f; (insight) perspicacia; (opinion etc) opinión f

perch [pə:tʃ] n (fish) perca; (for bird) percha ▷ vi: **to ~ (on)** posarse (en); (person) encaramarse (en)

percussion [pə'kʌʃən] n percusión f

perfect [adj, n 'pə:fɪkt, vb pə'fekt] adj perfecto ▷ n (also: **~ tense**) perfecto ▷ vt perfeccionar; **perfection** [pə'fekʃən] n perfección f; **perfectly** ['pə:fɪktlɪ] adv perfectamente

perform [pə'fɔ:m] vt (carry out) realizar, llevar a cabo; (Theatre) representar; (piece of music) interpretar ▷ vi (well, badly) funcionar; **performance** n (of a play) representación f; (of actor, athlete etc) actuación f; (of car, engine, company) rendimiento; (of economy) resultados mpl; **performer** n (actor) actor m, actriz f

perfume ['pə:fju:m] n perfume m

perhaps [pə'hæps] adv quizá(s), tal vez

perimeter [pə'rɪmɪtə*] n perímetro

period ['pɪərɪəd] n período; (Scol) clase f; (full stop) punto; (Med) regla ▷ adj (costume, furniture) de época; **periodical** [pɪərɪ'ɔdɪkl] n periódico; **periodically** adv de vez en cuando, cada cierto tiempo

perish ['perɪʃ] vi perecer; (decay) echarse a perder

perjury ['pɜːdʒərɪ] n (Law) perjurio

perk [pɜːk] n extra m

perm [pɜːm] n permanente f

permanent ['pɜːmənənt] adj permanente; **permanently** adv (lastingly) para siempre, de modo definitivo; (all the time) permanentemente

permission [pə'mɪʃən] n permiso

permit [n 'pɜːmɪt, vt pə'mɪt] n permiso, licencia ▷ vt permitir

perplex [pə'pleks] vt dejar perplejo

persecute ['pɜːsɪkjuːt] vt perseguir

persecution [pɜːsɪ'kjuːʃən] n persecución f

persevere [pɜːsɪ'vɪə*] vi persistir

Persian ['pɜːʃən] adj, n persa mf; **the ~ Gulf** el Golfo Pérsico

persist [pə'sɪst] vi: **to ~ (in doing sth)** persistir (en hacer algo); **persistent** adj persistente; (determined) porfiado

person ['pɜːsn] n persona; **in ~** en persona; **personal** adj personal; individual; (visit) personal; **personal assistant** n ayudante mf personal; **personal computer** n ordenador m personal; **personality** [-'nælɪtɪ] n personalidad f; **personally** adv personalmente; (in person) en persona; **to take sth personally** tomarse algo a mal; **personal organizer** n agenda; **personal stereo** n Walkman® m

personnel [pɜːsə'nel] n personal m

perspective [pə'spektɪv] n perspectiva

perspiration [pɜːspɪ'reɪʃən] n transpiración f

persuade [pə'sweɪd] vt: **to ~ sb to do sth** persuadir a algn para que haga algo

persuasion [pə'sweɪʒən] n persuasión f; (persuasiveness) persuasiva

persuasive [pə'sweɪsɪv] adj persuasivo

perverse [pə'vɜːs] adj perverso; (wayward) travieso

pervert [n 'pɜːvɜːt, vb pə'vɜːt] n pervertido/a ▷ vt pervertir; (truth, sb's words) tergiversar

pessimism ['pesɪmɪzəm] n pesimismo

pessimist ['pesɪmɪst] n pesimista mf; **pessimistic** [-'mɪstɪk] adj pesimista

pest [pest] n (insect) insecto nocivo; (fig) lata, molestia

pester ['pestə*] vt molestar, acosar

pesticide ['pestɪsaɪd] n pesticida m

pet [pet] n animal m doméstico ▷ cpd favorito ▷ vt acariciar; **teacher's ~** favorito/a (del profesor); **~ hate** manía

petal ['petl] n pétalo

petite [pə'tiːt] adj chiquita

petition [pə'tɪʃən] n petición f

petrified ['petrɪfaɪd] adj horrorizado

petrol ['petrəl] (BRIT) n gasolina

petroleum [pə'trəʊlɪəm] n petróleo

petrol: petrol pump (BRIT) n (in garage) surtidor m de gasolina; **petrol station** (BRIT) n gasolinera; **petrol tank** (BRIT) n depósito (de gasolina)

petticoat ['petɪkəʊt] n enaguas fpl

petty ['petɪ] adj (mean) mezquino; (unimportant) insignificante

pew [pjuː] n banco

pewter ['pjuːtə*] n peltre m

phantom ['fæntəm] n fantasma m

pharmacist ['fɑːməsɪst] n farmacéutico/a

pharmacy ['fɑːməsɪ] n farmacia

phase [feɪz] n fase f; **phase in** vt introducir progresivamente; **phase out** vt (machinery, product) retirar progresivamente; (job, subsidy) eliminar por etapas

Ph.D. abbr = **Doctor of Philosophy**

pheasant ['feznt] n faisán m

phenomena [fə'nɒmɪnə] npl of **phenomenon**

phenomenal [fɪ'nɒmɪnl] adj fenomenal, extraordinario

phenomenon [fə'nɒmɪnən] (pl **phenomena**) n fenómeno

Philippines ['fɪlɪpiːnz] npl: **the ~** las

Filipinas
philosopher [fɪ'lɒsəfə*] n filósofo/a
philosophical [fɪlə'sɒfɪkl] adj filosófico
philosophy [fɪ'lɒsəfɪ] n filosofía
phlegm [flem] n flema
phobia ['fəʊbjə] n fobia
phone [fəʊn] n teléfono ▷ vt telefonear, llamar por teléfono; **to be on the ~** tener teléfono; (be calling) estar hablando por teléfono; **phone back** vt, vi volver a llamar; **phone box** (BRIT) n = **phone booth**; **phone call** n llamada (telefónica); **phonecard** n teletarjeta; **phone number** n número de teléfono
phonetics [fə'netɪks] n fonética
phoney ['fəʊnɪ] adj falso
photo ['fəʊtəʊ] n foto f; **photo album** n álbum m de fotos; **photocopier** n fotocopiadora; **photocopy** n fotocopia ▷ vt fotocopiar
photograph ['fəʊtəgrɑːf] n fotografía f ▷ vt fotografiar; **photographer** [fə'tɒgrəfə*] n fotógrafo; **photography** [fə'tɒgrəfɪ] n fotografía
phrase [freɪz] n frase f ▷ vt expresar; **phrase book** n libro de frases
physical ['fɪzɪkl] adj físico; **physical education** n educación f física; **physically** adv físicamente
physician [fɪ'zɪʃən] n médico m
physicist ['fɪzɪsɪst] n físico/a
physics ['fɪzɪks] n física
physiotherapist [fɪzɪəʊ'θerəpɪst] n fisioterapeuta
physiotherapy [fɪzɪəʊ'θerəpɪ] n fisioterapia
physique [fɪ'ziːk] n físico
pianist ['piːənɪst] n pianista mf
piano [pɪ'ænəʊ] n piano
pick [pɪk] n (tool: also: **~-axe**) pico, piqueta ▷ vt (select) elegir, escoger; (gather) coger (SP), recoger; (remove, take out) sacar, quitar; (lock) abrir con

ganzúa; **take your ~** escoja lo que quiera; **the ~ of** lo mejor de; **to ~ one's nose/teeth** hurgarse las narices/ limpiarse los dientes; **to ~ a quarrel with sb** meterse con algn; **pick on** vt fus (person) meterse con; **pick out** vt escoger; (distinguish) identificar; **pick up** vi (improve: sales) ir mejor; (: patient) reponerse; (Finance) recobrarse ▷ vt recoger; (learn) aprender; (Police: arrest) detener; (person: for sex) ligar; (Radio) captar; **to pick up speed** acelerarse; **to pick o.s. up** levantarse
pickle ['pɪkl] n (also: **~s**: as condiment) escabeche m; (fig: mess) apuro ▷ vt encurtir
pickpocket ['pɪkpɒkɪt] n carterista mf
pick-up ['pɪkʌp] n (also: **~ truck**) furgoneta, camioneta
picnic ['pɪknɪk] n merienda ▷ vi ir de merienda; **picnic area** n zona de picnic; (Aut) área de descanso
picture ['pɪktʃə*] n cuadro; (painting) pintura; (photograph) fotografía; (TV) imagen f; (film) película; (fig: description) descripción f; (: situation) situación f ▷ vt (imagine) imaginar; **pictures** npl: **the ~s** (BRIT) el cine; **picture frame** n marco; **picture messaging** n (envío de) mensajes con imágenes
picturesque [pɪktʃə'resk] adj pintoresco
pie [paɪ] n pastel m; (open) tarta; (small: of meat) empanada
piece [piːs] n pedazo, trozo; (of cake) trozo; (item): **a ~ of clothing/ furniture/advice** una prenda (de vestir)/un mueble/un consejo ▷ vt: **to ~ together** juntar; (Tech) armar; **to take to ~s** desmontar
pie chart n gráfico de sectores or tarta
pier [pɪə*] n muelle m, embarcadero
pierce [pɪəs] vt perforar; **pierced** adj: **I've got pierced ears** tengo los agujeros hechos en las orejas
pig [pɪg] n cerdo, chancho (LAM);

P

(*pej: unkind person*) asqueroso; (*: greedy person*) glotón/ona *m/f*

pigeon ['pɪdʒən] *n* paloma; (*as food*) pichón *m*

piggy bank ['pɪgɪ-] *n* hucha (*en forma de cerdito*)

pigsty ['pɪgstaɪ] *n* pocilga

pigtail (*girl's*) trenza

pike [paɪk] *n* (*fish*) lucio

pilchard ['pɪltʃəd] *n* sardina

pile [paɪl] *n* montón *m*; (*of carpet, cloth*) pelo; **pile up** *vi +adv* (*accumulate: work*) amontonarse, acumularse ▷ *vt +adv* (*put in a heap: books, clothes*) apilar, amontonar; (*accumulate*) acumular; **piles** *npl* (*Med*) almorranas *fpl*, hemorroides *mpl*; **pile-up** *n* (*Aut*) accidente *m* múltiple

pilgrimage ['pɪlgrɪmɪdʒ] *n* peregrinación *f*, romería

pill [pɪl] *n* píldora; **the ~** la píldora

pillar ['pɪlə*] *n* pilar *m*

pillow ['pɪləu] *n* almohada; **pillowcase** *n* funda

pilot ['paɪlət] *n* piloto ▷ *cpd* (*scheme etc*) piloto ▷ *vt* pilotar; **pilot light** *n* piloto

pimple ['pɪmpl] *n* grano

PIN *n abbr* (= *personal identification number*) número personal

pin [pɪn] *n* alfiler *m* ▷ *vt* prender (con alfiler); **~s and needles** hormigueo; **to ~ sb down** (*fig*) hacer que algn concrete; **to ~ sth on sb** (*fig*) colgarle a algn el sambenito de algo

pinafore ['pɪnəfɔː*] *n* delantal *m*

pinch [pɪntʃ] *n* (*of salt etc*) pizca ▷ *vt* pellizcar; (*inf: steal*) birlar; **at a ~** en caso de apuro

pine [paɪn] *n* (*also: ~ tree*) pino ▷ *vi*: **to ~ for** suspirar por

pineapple ['paɪnæpl] *n* piña, ananás *m*

ping [pɪŋ] *n* (*noise*) sonido agudo; **ping-pong®** *n* pingpong *m*

pink [pɪŋk] *adj* rosado, (color de) rosa ▷ *n* (*colour*) rosa; (*Bot*) clavel *m*, clavellina

pinpoint ['pɪnpɔɪnt] *vt* precisar

pint [paɪnt] *n* pinta (BRIT = 568cc, US = 473cc); (BRIT: inf: of beer) pinta de cerveza ≈ jarra (SP)

pioneer [paɪə'nɪə*] *n* pionero/a

pious ['paɪəs] *adj* piadoso, devoto

pip [pɪp] *n* (*seed*) pepita; **the ~s** (BRIT) la señal

pipe [paɪp] *n* tubo, caño; (*for smoking*) pipa ▷ *vt* conducir en cañerías; **pipeline** (*for oil*) oleoducto; (*for gas*) gasoducto; **piper** *n* gaitero/a

pirate ['paɪərət] *n* pirata *mf* ▷ *vt* (*cassette, book*) piratear

Pisces ['paɪsiːz] *n* Piscis *m*

piss [pɪs] (*infl*) *vi* mear; **pissed** (*infl*) *adj* (*drunk*) borracho

pistol ['pɪstl] *n* pistola

piston ['pɪstən] *n* pistón *m*, émbolo

pit [pɪt] *n* hoyo; (*also: coal ~*) mina; (*in garage*) hoyo de inspección; (*also: orchestra ~*) platea ▷ *vt*: **to ~ one's wits against sb** medir fuerzas con algn

pitch [pɪtʃ] *n* (*Mus*) tono; (BRIT Sport) campo, terreno; (*fig*) punto; (*tar*) brea ▷ *vt* (*throw*) arrojar, lanzar ▷ *vi* (*fall*) caer(se); **to ~ a tent** montar una tienda (*de campaña*); **pitch-black** *adj* negro como boca de lobo

pitfall ['pɪtfɔːl] *n* riesgo

pith [pɪθ] *n* (*of orange*) médula

pitiful ['pɪtɪful] *adj* (*touching*) lastimoso, conmovedor(a)

pity ['pɪtɪ] *n* compasión *f*, piedad *f* ▷ *vt* compadecer(se de); **what a ~!** ¡qué pena!

pizza ['piːtsə] *n* pizza

placard ['plækɑːd] *n* letrero; (*in march etc*) pancarta

place [pleɪs] *n* lugar *m*, sitio; (*seat*) plaza, asiento; (*post*) puesto; (*home*) casa; **at/to his ~** en/a su casa; (*role: in society etc*) papel *m* ▷ *vt* (*object*) poner, colocar; (*identify*) reconocer; **to take ~** tener lugar; **to be ~d** (*in race, exam*) colocarse; **out of ~** (*not suitable*) fuera de lugar; **in the first ~** en primer lugar; **to change ~s with sb** cambiarse de sitio con algn: **~ of birth** lugar m de nacimiento; **place mat** n (wooden etc) salvamanteles m inv; (linen etc) mantel m individual; **placement** n (positioning) colocación f; (at work) emplazamiento

placid ['plæsɪd] adj apacible

plague [pleɪg] n plaga; (Med) peste f ▷ vt (fig) acosar, atormentar

plaice [pleɪs] n inv platija

plain [pleɪn] adj (unpatterned) liso; (clear) claro, evidente; (simple) sencillo; (not handsome) poco atractivo ▷ adv claramente ▷ n llano, llanura; **plain chocolate** n chocolate m amargo; **plainly** adv claramente

plaintiff ['pleɪntɪf] n demandante mf

plait [plæt] n trenza

plan [plæn] n (drawing) plano; (scheme) plan m, proyecto ▷ vt proyectar, planificar ▷ vi hacer proyectos; **to ~ to do** pensar hacer

plane [pleɪn] n (Aviat) avión m; (Math, fig) plano; (also: **~ tree**) plátano; (tool) cepillo

planet ['plænɪt] n planeta m

plank [plæŋk] n tabla

planning ['plænɪŋ] n planificación f; **family ~** planificación familiar

plant [plɑːnt] n planta; (machinery) maquinaria; (factory) fábrica ▷ vt plantar; (field) sembrar; (bomb) colocar

plantation [plæn'teɪʃən] n plantación f; (estate) hacienda

plaque [plæk] n placa

plaster ['plɑːstə*] n (for walls) yeso; (also: **~ of Paris**) yeso mate, escayola (SP); (BRIT: also: **sticking ~**) tirita (SP), curita (LAM) ▷ vt enyesar; (cover): **to ~ with** llenar or cubrir de; **plaster cast** n (Med) escayola; (model, statue) vaciado de yeso

plastic ['plæstɪk] n plástico ▷ adj de plástico; **plastic bag** n bolsa de plástico; **plastic surgery** n cirujía plástica

plate [pleɪt] n (dish) plato; (metal, in book) lámina; (dental plate) placa de

dentadura postiza

plateau ['plætəu] (pl **~s** or **~x**) n meseta, altiplanicie f

platform ['plætfɔːm] n (Rail) andén m; (stage, BRIT: on bus) plataforma; (at meeting) tribuna; (Pol) programa m (electoral)

platinum ['plætɪnəm] adj, n platino

platoon [plə'tuːn] n pelotón m

platter ['plætə*] n fuente f

plausible ['plɔːzɪbl] adj verosímil; (person) convincente

play [pleɪ] n (Theatre) obra, comedia ▷ vt (game) jugar; (compete against) jugar contra; (instrument) tocar; (part: in play etc) hacer el papel de; (tape, record) poner ▷ vi jugar; (band) tocar; (tape, record) sonar; **to ~ safe** ir a lo seguro; **play back** vt (tape) poner; **play up** vi (cause trouble to) dar guerra; **player** n jugador/a m/f; (Theatre) actor(actriz) m/f; (Mus) músico/a; **playful** adj juguetón/ona; **playground** n (in school) patio de recreo; (in park) parque m infantil; **playgroup** n jardín m de niños; **playing card** n naipe m, carta; **playing field** n campo de deportes; **playschool** n = **playgroup**; **playtime** n (Scol) recreo; **playwright** n dramaturgo/a

plc abbr (= public limited company) ≈ S.A.

plea [pliː] n súplica, petición f; (Law) alegato, defensa

plead [pliːd] vt (Law): **to ~ sb's case** defender a algn; (give as excuse) poner como pretexto ▷ vi (Law) declararse; (beg): **to ~ with sb** suplicar or rogar a algn

pleasant ['plɛznt] adj agradable

please [pliːz] excl ¡por favor! ▷ vt (give pleasure to) dar gusto a, agradar ▷ vi (think fit): **do as you ~** haz lo que quieras; **~ yourself!** (inf) ¡haz lo que quieras!, ¡como quieras!; **pleased** adj (happy) alegre, contento; **pleased (with)** satisfecho (de); **pleased to meet you** ¡encantado!, ¡tanto gusto!

pleasure ['plɛʒə*] n placer m, gusto;

"it's a ~" el gusto es mío"

pleat [pli:t] n pliegue m

pledge [pledʒ] n (promise) promesa, voto ▷ vt prometer

plentiful ['plentiful] adj copioso, abundante

plenty ['plenti] n: ~ of mucho(s)/a(s)

pliers ['plaɪəz] npl alicates mpl, tenazas fpl

plight [plaɪt] n situación f difícil

plod [plɔd] vi caminar con paso pesado; (fig) trabajar laboriosamente

plonk [plɔŋk] (inf) n (BRIT: wine) vino peleón ▷ vt: to ~ sth down dejar caer algo

plot [plɔt] n (scheme) complot m, conjura; (of story, play) argumento; (of land) terreno ▷ vt (mark out) trazar; (conspire) tramar, urdir ▷ vi conspirar

plough [plau] (us **plow**) n arado m; (earth) arar; to ~ money into invertir dinero en

plow [plau] (us) = **plough**

ploy [plɔɪ] n truco, estratagema

pluck [plʌk] vt (fruit) coger (SP), recoger (LAM); (musical instrument) puntear; (bird) desplumar; (eyebrows) depilar; to ~ up courage hacer de tripas corazón

plug [plʌg] n tapón m; (Elec) enchufe m, clavija; (Aut: also: **spark(ing) ~**) bujía ▷ vt (hole) tapar; (inf: advertise) dar publicidad a; **plug in** vt (Elec) enchufar; **plughole** n desagüe m

plum [plʌm] n (fruit) ciruela

plumber ['plʌmə*] n fontanero/a (SP, CAM), plomero/a (LAM)

plumbing ['plʌmɪŋ] n (trade) fontanería, plomería; (piping) cañería

plummet ['plʌmɪt] vi: to ~ (down) caer a plomo

plump [plʌmp] adj rechoncho, rollizo ▷ vi: to ~ for (inf: choose) optar por

plunge [plʌndʒ] n zambullida ▷ vt sumergir, hundir ▷ vi (fall) caer; (dive) saltar; (person) arrojarse; **to take the ~** lanzarse

plural ['pluərl] adj plural ▷ n plural m

plus [plʌs] n (also: ~ **sign**) signo más ▷ prep más, y, además de; **ten/twenty ~** más de diez/veinte

ply [plaɪ] vt (a trade) ejercer ▷ vi (ship) ir y venir ▷ n (of wool, rope) cabo; **to ~ sb with drink** insistir en ofrecer a algn muchas copas; **plywood** n madera contrachapada

P.M. n abbr = **Prime Minister**

p.m. adv abbr (= post meridiem) de la tarde or noche

PMS n abbr (= premenstrual syndrome) SPM m

PMT n abbr (= premenstrual tension) SPM m

pneumatic drill [nju:'mætɪk-] n martillo neumático

pneumonia [nju:'məunɪə] n pulmonía

poach [pəutʃ] vt (cook) escalfar; (steal) cazar (or pescar) en vedado ▷ vi cazar (or pescar) en vedado; **poached** adj escalfado

P.O. Box n abbr (= Post Office Box) apdo., aptdo.

pocket ['pɔkɪt] n bolsillo; (fig: small area) bolsa ▷ vt meter en el bolsillo; (steal) embolsar; **to be out of ~** (BRIT) salir perdiendo; **pocketbook** (us) n cartera; **pocket money** n asignación f

pod [pɔd] n vaina

podcast ['pɔdkɑ:st] n podcast m ▷ vi podcastear

podiatrist [pɔ'di:ətrɪst] (us) n pedicuro/a

podium ['pəudɪəm] n podio

poem ['pəuɪm] n poema m

poet ['pəuɪt] n poeta m/f; **poetic** [-'etɪk] adj poético; **poetry** n poesía

poignant ['pɔɪnjənt] adj conmovedor(a)

point [pɔɪnt] n punto; (tip) punta; (purpose) fin m, propósito; (use) utilidad f; (significant part) lo significativo; (moment) momento; (Elec) toma (de corriente); (also: **decimal ~**): **2 ~ 3 (2.3)** dos coma tres (2,3) ▷ vt señalar; (gun etc): **to ~ sth at sb** apuntar algo a algn ▷ vi: **to ~ at** señalar; **points** npl (Aut) contactos mpl; (Rail) agujas fpl; **to be on the ~ of doing sth** estar a punto de hacer algo; **to make a ~ of** poner empeño en; **to get/miss the ~** comprender/no comprender; **to come to the ~** ir al meollo; **there's no ~ (in doing)** no tiene sentido (hacer); **point out** vt señalar; **point-blank** adv (say, refuse) sin más hablar; (also: **at point-blank range**) a quemarropa; **pointed** adj (shape) puntiagudo, afilado; (remark) intencionado; **pointer** n (needle) aguja, indicador m; **pointless** adj sin sentido; **point of view** n punto de vista

poison ['pɔɪzn] n veneno ▷ vt envenenar; **poisonous** adj venenoso; (fumes etc) tóxico

poke [pəʊk] vt (jab with finger, stick etc) introducir algo en; **poke about** or **around** vi fisgonear; **poke out** vi (stick out) salir

poker ['pəʊkə*] n atizador m; (Cards) póker m

Poland ['pəʊlənd] n Polonia

polar ['pəʊlə*] adj polar; **polar bear** n oso polar

Pole [pəʊl] n polaco/a

pole [pəʊl] n palo; (fixed) poste m; (Geo) polo; **pole bean** (us) n ≈ judía verde; **pole vault** n salto con pértiga

police [pə'liːs] n policía ▷ vt vigilar; **police car** n coche-patrulla m; **police constable** (BRIT) n guardia m, policía m; **police force** n cuerpo de policía; **policeman** (irreg) n policía m, guardia m; **police officer** n policía m, guardia m; **police station** n comisaría; **policewoman** (irreg) n mujer f policía

policy ['pɔlɪsɪ] n política; (also: **insurance ~**) póliza

polio ['pəʊlɪəʊ] n polio f

Polish ['pəʊlɪʃ] adj polaco ▷ n (Ling) polaco

polish ['pɔlɪʃ] n (for shoes) betún m; (for floor) cera (de lustrar); (shine) brillo,

lustre m; (fig: refinement) educación f ▷ vt (shoes) limpiar; (make shiny) pulir, sacar brillo a; **polish off** vt (food) despachar; **polished** adj (fig: person) elegante

polite [pə'laɪt] adj cortés, atento; **politeness** n cortesía

political [pə'lɪtɪkl] adj político; **politically** adv políticamente; **politically correct** políticamente correcto

politician [pɔlɪ'tɪʃən] n político/a

politics ['pɔlɪtɪks] n política

poll [pəʊl] n (election) votación f; (also: **opinion ~**) sondeo, encuesta ▷ vt encuestar; (votes) obtener

pollen ['pɔlən] n polen m

polling station ['pəʊlɪŋ-] n centro electoral

pollute [pə'luːt] vt contaminar

pollution [pə'luːʃən] n polución f, contaminación f del medio ambiente

polo ['pəʊləʊ] n (sport) polo; **poloneck** adj de cuello vuelto ▷ n (sweater) suéter m de cuello vuelto; **polo shirt** n polo, niqui M

polyester [pɔlɪ'estə*] n poliéster m

polystyrene [pɔlɪ'staɪriːn] n poliestireno

polythene [pɔlɪθiːn] (BRIT) n politeno; **polythene bag** n bolsa de plástico

pomegranate ['pɔmɪɡrænɪt] n granada

pompous ['pɔmpəs] adj pomposo

pond [pɔnd] n (natural) charca; (artificial) estanque m

ponder ['pɔndə*] vt meditar

pony ['pəʊnɪ] n poni m; **ponytail** n coleta; **pony trekking** (BRIT) n excursión f a caballo

poodle ['puːdl] n caniche m

pool [puːl] n (natural) charca; (also: **swimming ~**) piscina, alberca (MEX), pileta (RPL); (fig: of light etc) charco; (Sport) chapolín m ▷ vt juntar; **pools** npl quinielas fpl

poor [puə*] adj pobre; (bad) de mala

calidad ▷ *npl*: **the ~** los pobres; **poorly**
adj mal, enfermo ▷ *adv* mal

pop [pɔp] *n* (*sound*) ruido seco; (*Mus*)
(música) pop *m*; (*inf*: *father*) papá *m*;
(*drink*) gaseosa ▷ *vt* (*put quickly*) meter
(de prisa) ▷ *vi* reventar; (*cork*) saltar;
pop in *vi* entrar un momento; **pop
out** *vi* salir un momento; **popcorn** *n*
palomitas *fpl*

poplar ['pɔplə*] *n* álamo

popper ['pɔpə*] (*BRIT*) *n* automático

poppy ['pɔpɪ] *n* amapola

Popsicle® ['pɔpsɪkl] (*US*) *n* polo

pop star *n* estrella del pop

popular ['pɔpjulə*] *adj* popular;
popularity [pɔpju'lærɪtɪ] *n*
popularidad *f*

population [pɔpju'leɪʃən] *n*
población *f*

pop-up ['pɔpʌp] (*Comput*) *adj* (*menu,
window*) emergente ▷ *n* ventana
emergente, (ventana*f*) pop-up *f*

porcelain ['pɔːslɪn] *n* porcelana

porch [pɔːtʃ] *n* pórtico, entrada; (*US*)
veranda

pore [pɔː*] *n* poro ▷ *vi*: **to ~ over**
engolfarse en

pork [pɔːk] *n* carne *f* de cerdo or
(*LAM*) chancho; **pork chop** *n* chuleta
de cerdo; **pork pie** *n* (*BRIT*: *Culin*)
empanada de carne de cerdo

porn [pɔːn] *adj* (*inf*) porno *inv* ▷ *n*
porno; **pornographic** [pɔːnə'græfɪk]
adj pornográfico; **pornography**
[pɔː'nɔɡrəfɪ] *n* pornografía

porridge ['pɔrɪdʒ] *n* gachas *fpl* de
avena

port [pɔːt] *n* puerto; (*Naut*: *left side*)
babor *m*; (*wine*) vino de Oporto; **~ of
call** puerto de escala

portable ['pɔːtəbl] *adj* portátil

porter ['pɔːtə*] *n* (*for luggage*)
maletero; (*doorkeeper*) portero/a,
conserje *m/f*

portfolio [pɔːt'fəulɪəu] *n* cartera

portion ['pɔːʃən] *n* porción *f*; (*of food*)
ración *f*

portrait ['pɔːtreɪt] *n* retrato

portray [pɔː'treɪ] *vt* retratar; (*actor*)
representar

Portugal ['pɔːtjuɡl] *n* Portugal *m*

Portuguese [pɔːtju'ɡiːz] *adj*
portugués/esa ▷ *n inv* portugués/esa
m/f; (*Ling*) portugués *m*

pose [pəuz] *n* postura, actitud *f* ▷ *vi*
(*pretend*): **to ~ as** hacerse pasar por ▷ *vt*
(*question*) plantear; **to ~ for** posar para

posh [pɔʃ] (*inf*) *adj* elegante, de lujo

position [pə'zɪʃən] *n* posición *f*;
(*job*) puesto; (*situation*) situación *f*
▷ *vt* colocar

positive ['pɔzɪtɪv] *adj* positivo;
(*certain*) seguro; (*definite*) definitivo;
positively *adv* (*affirmatively,
enthusiastically*) de forma positiva;
(*inf*: *really*) absolutamente

possess [pə'zɛs] *vt* poseer;
possession [pə'zɛʃən] *n* posesión
f; **possessions** *fpl* (*belongings*)
pertenencias *fpl*; **possessive** *adj*
posesivo

possibility [pɔsɪ'bɪlɪtɪ] *n* posibilidad
f

possible ['pɔsɪbl] *adj* posible; **as big
as ~** lo más grande posible; **possibly**
adv posiblemente; **I cannot possibly
come** me es imposible venir

post [pəust] *n* (*BRIT*: *system*) correos
mpl; (*BRIT*: *letters, delivery*) correo;
(*job, situation*) puesto; (*pole*) poste
m ▷ *vt* (*BRIT*: *send by post*) echar al
correo; (*BRIT*: *appoint*): **to ~ to** enviar a;
postage *n* porte *m*, franqueo; **postal**
adj postal, de correos; **postal order** *n*
giro postal; **postbox** (*BRIT*) *n* buzón *m*;
postcard *n* tarjeta postal; **postcode**
(*BRIT*) *n* código postal

poster ['pəustə*] *n* cartel *m*

postgraduate ['pəust'ɡrædjuət] *n*
posgraduado/a

postman ['pəustmən] (*BRIT*: *irreg*) *n*
cartero

postmark ['pəustmɑːk] *n*
matasellos *m inv*

post-mortem [-'mɔːtəm] *n*
autopsia

post office n (building) (oficina de) correos m; (organization): **the Post Office** Correos m inv (SP), Dirección f General de Correos (LAM)

postpone [pəs'pəun] vt aplazar

posture ['postʃə*] n postura, actitud f

postwoman ['pəustwumən] (BRIT: irreg) n cartera

pot [pot] n (for cooking) olla; (teapot) tetera; (coffeepot) cafetera; (for flowers) maceta; (for jam) tarro, pote m; (inf: marijuana) chocolate m ▷ vt (plant) poner en tiesto; **to go to ~** (inf) irse al traste

potato [pə'teɪtəu] (pl **~es**) n patata (SP), papa f (LAM); **potato peeler** n pelapatatas m inv

potent ['pəutnt] adj potente, poderoso; (drink) fuerte

potential [pə'tenʃl] adj potencial, posible ▷ n potencial m

pothole ['pothəul] n (in road) bache m; (BRIT: underground) gruta

pot plant ['potplɑːnt] n planta de interior

potter ['potə*] n alfarero/a ▷ vi: **to ~ around** or **about** (BRIT) hacer trabajitos; **pottery** n cerámica; (factory) alfarería

potty ['potɪ] n orinal m de niño

pouch [pautʃ] n (Zool) bolsa; (for tobacco) petaca

poultry ['pəultrɪ] n aves fpl de corral; (meat) pollo

pounce [pauns] vi: **to ~** precipitarse sobre

pound [paund] n libra (weight = 453g or 16oz; money = 100 pence) ▷ vt (beat) golpear; (crush) machacar ▷ vi (heart) latir; **pound sterling** n libra esterlina

pour [pɔː*] vt echar; (tea etc) servir ▷ vi correr, fluir; **to ~ sb a drink** servirle a algn una copa; **pour in** vi (people) entrar en tropel; **pour out** vi salir en tropel ▷ vt (drink) echar, servir; (fig): **to pour out one's feelings** desahogarse; **pouring** adj: **pouring rain** lluvia torrencial

pout [paut] vi hacer pucheros

poverty ['povətɪ] n pobreza, miseria

powder ['paudə*] n polvo; (also: **face ~**) polvos mpl ▷ vt polvorear; **to ~ one's face** empolvarse la cara; **powdered milk** n leche f en polvo

power ['pauə*] n poder m; (strength) fuerza; (nation, Tech) potencia; (drive) empuje m; (Elec) fuerza, energía ▷ vt impulsar; **to be in ~** (Pol) estar en el poder; **power cut** (BRIT) n apagón m; **power failure** n = **power cut**; **powerful** adj poderoso; (engine) potente; (speech etc) convincente; **powerless** adj: **powerless (to do)** incapaz (de hacer); **power point** n enchufe m; **power station** n central f eléctrica

p.p. abbr (= per procurationem); **p.p. J. Smith** p.p. (= por poder de) J. Smith; (= pages) págs

PR n abbr = **public relations**

practical ['præktɪkl] adj práctico; **practical joke** n broma pesada; **practically** adv (almost) casi

practice ['præktɪs] n (habit) costumbre f; (exercise) práctica, ejercicio; (training) adiestramiento; (Med: of profession) práctica, ejercicio, (Med, Law: business) consulta ▷ vt, vi (US) = **practise**; **in ~** (in reality) en la práctica; **out of ~** desentrenado

practise ['præktɪs] (US **practice**) vt (carry out) practicar; (profession) ejercer; (train at) practicar ▷ vi ejercer; (train) practicar; **practising** adj (Christian etc) practicante; (lawyer) en ejercicio

practitioner [præk'tɪʃənə*] n (Med) médico/a

pragmatic [præg'mætɪk] adj pragmático

prairie ['prɛərɪ] n pampa

praise [preɪz] n alabanza(s) f(pl), elogio(s) m(pl) ▷ vt alabar, elogiar

pram [præm] (BRIT) n cochecito de niño

prank [præŋk] n travesura

prawn [prɔːn] n gamba; **prawn**

cocktail n cóctel m de gambas

pray [preɪ] vi rezar; **prayer** [prɛə*] n oración f, rezo; (entreaty) ruego, súplica

preach [priːtʃ] vi predicar; **preacher** n predicador(a) m/f

precarious [prɪˈkɛərɪəs] adj precario

precaution [prɪˈkɔːʃən] n precaución f

precede [prɪˈsiːd] vt, vi preceder; **precedent** [ˈprɛsɪdənt] n precedente m; **preceding** [prɪˈsiːdɪŋ] adj anterior

precinct [ˈpriːsɪŋkt] n recinto

precious [ˈprɛʃəs] adj precioso

precise [prɪˈsaɪs] adj preciso, exacto; **precisely** adv precisamente, exactamente

precision [prɪˈsɪʒən] n precisión f

predator [ˈprɛdətə*] n depredador m

predecessor [ˈpriːdɪsɛsə*] n antecesor(a) m/f

predicament [prɪˈdɪkəmənt] n apuro

predict [prɪˈdɪkt] vt pronosticar; **predictable** adj previsible; **prediction** [-ˈdɪkʃən] n predicción f

predominantly [prɪˈdɔmɪnəntlɪ] adv en su mayoría

preface [ˈprɛfəs] n prefacio

prefect [ˈpriːfɛkt] (BRIT) n (in school) monitor(a) m/f

prefer [prɪˈfəː*] vt preferir; **to ~ doing** or **to do** preferir hacer; **preferable** [ˈprɛfrəbl] adj preferible; **preferably** [ˈprɛfrəblɪ] adv de preferencia; **preference** [ˈprɛfrəns] n preferencia; (priority) prioridad f

prefix [ˈpriːfɪks] n prefijo

pregnancy [ˈprɛgnənsɪ] n (of woman) embarazo; (of animal) preñez f

pregnant [ˈprɛgnənt] adj (woman) embarazada; (animal) preñada

prehistoric [ˈpriːhɪsˈtɔrɪk] adj prehistórico

prejudice [ˈprɛdʒudɪs] n prejuicio; **prejudiced** adj (person) predispuesto

preliminary [prɪˈlɪmɪnərɪ] adj preliminar

prelude [ˈprɛljuːd] n preludio

premature [ˈprɛmətʃuə*] adj prematuro

premier [ˈprɛmɪə*] adj primero, principal ▷ n (Pol) primer(a) ministro/a

première [ˈprɛmɪɛə*] n estreno

Premier League [prɛmɪəˈliːg] n primera división

premises [ˈprɛmɪsɪz] npl (of business etc) local m; **on the ~** en el lugar mismo

premium [ˈpriːmɪəm] n premio; (insurance) prima; **to be at a ~** ser muy solicitado

premonition [prɛməˈnɪʃən] n presentimiento

preoccupied [prɪˈɔkjupaɪd] adj ensimismado

prepaid [priːˈpeɪd] adj porte pagado

preparation [prɛpəˈreɪʃən] n preparación f; **preparations** npl preparativos mpl

preparatory school [prɪˈpærətərɪ-] n escuela preparatoria

prepare [prɪˈpɛə*] vt preparar, disponer; (Culin) preparar ▷ vi: **to ~ for** (action) prepararse or disponerse para; (event) hacer preparativos para; **~d to** dispuesto a; **~d for** listo para

preposition [prɛpəˈzɪʃən] n preposición f

prep school [prɛp-] n = **preparatory school**

prerequisite [priːˈrɛkwɪzɪt] n requisito

preschool [ˈpriːˈskuːl] adj preescolar

prescribe [prɪˈskraɪb] vt (Med) recetar

prescription [prɪˈskrɪpʃən] n (Med) receta

presence [ˈprɛzns] n presencia; **in sb's ~** en presencia de algn; **~ of mind** aplomo

present [adj, n ˈprɛznt, vb prɪˈzɛnt] adj (in attendance) presente; (current) actual ▷ n (gift) regalo; (actuality): **the ~** la actualidad, el presente ▷ vt (introduce, describe) presentar; (expound) exponer; (give) presentar, dar, ofrecer; (Theatre) representar; **to give sb a** ~ regalar algo a algn; **at** ~ actualmente; **presentable** [prɪ'zentəbl] *adj*: **to make o.s. presentable** arreglarse; **presentation** [-'teɪʃən] *n* presentación *f*; *(of report etc)* exposición *f*; *(formal ceremony)* entrega de un regalo; **present-day** *adj* actual; **presenter** [prɪ'zentə*] *n (Radio, TV)* locutor(a) *m/f*; **presently** *adv (soon)* dentro de poco; *(now)* ahora; **present participle** *n* participio (de) presente

preservation [prezə'veɪʃən] *n* conservación *f*

preservative [prɪ'zə:vətɪv] *n* conservante *m*

preserve [prɪ'zə:v] *vt (keep safe)* preservar, proteger; *(maintain)* mantener; *(food)* conservar ▷ *n (for game)* coto, vedado; *(often pl: jam)* conserva, confitura

preside [prɪ'zaɪd] *vi* presidir

president ['prezɪdənt] *n* presidente *m/f*; **presidential** [-'denʃl] *adj* presidencial

press [pres] *n (newspapers)*: **the P~** la prensa; *(printer's)* imprenta; *(of button)* pulsación *f* ▷ *vt* empujar; *(button etc)* apretar; *(clothes: iron)* planchar; *(put pressure on: person)* presionar; *(insist)*: **to ~ sth on sb** insistir en que algn acepte algo ▷ *vi (squeeze)* apretar; *(pressurize)*: **to ~ for** presionar por; **we are ~ed for time/money** estamos apurados de tiempo/dinero; **press conference** *n* rueda de prensa; **pressing** *adj* apremiante; **press stud** *n (BRIT)* botón *m* de presión; **press-up** *n (BRIT)* plancha

pressure ['preʃə*] *n* presión *f*; **to put ~ on sb** presionar a algn; **pressure cooker** *n* olla a presión; **pressure group** *n* grupo de presión

prestige [pres'tiːʒ] *n* prestigio

prestigious [pres'tɪdʒəs] *adj* prestigioso

presumably [prɪ'zjuːməbli] *adv* es de suponer que, cabe presumir que

presume [prɪ'zjuːm] *vt*: **to ~ (that)** presumir (que), suponer (que)

pretence [prɪ'tens] *(us* **pretense)** *n* fingimiento; **under false ~s** con engaños

pretend [prɪ'tend] *vt, vi (feign)* fingir
    Be careful not to translate **pretend** by the Spanish word *pretender*.

pretense [prɪ'tens] *(us) n* = **pretence**

pretentious [prɪ'tenʃəs] *adj* presumido; *(ostentatious)* ostentoso, aparatoso

pretext ['priːtekst] *n* pretexto

pretty ['prɪti] *adj* bonito, lindo (LAM) ▷ *adv* bastante

prevail [prɪ'veɪl] *vi (gain mastery)* prevalecer; *(be current)* predominar; **prevailing** *adj (dominant)* predominante

prevalent ['prevələnt] *adj (widespread)* extendido

prevent [prɪ'vent] *vt*: **to ~ sb from doing sth** impedir a algn hacer algo; **to ~ sth from happening** evitar que ocurra algo; **prevention** [prɪ'venʃə n] *n* prevención *f*; **preventive** *adj* preventivo

preview ['priːvjuː] *n (of film)* preestreno

previous ['priːvɪəs] *adj* previo, anterior; **previously** *adv* antes

prey [preɪ] *n* presa ▷ *vi*: **to ~ on** *(feed on)* alimentarse de; **it was ~ing on his mind** le preocupaba, le obsesionaba

price [praɪs] *n* precio ▷ *vt (goods)* fijar el precio de; **priceless** *adj* que no tiene precio; **price list** *n* tarifa

prick [prɪk] *n (sting)* picadura ▷ *vt* pinchar; *(hurt)* picar; **to ~ up one's ears** aguzar el oído

prickly ['prɪkli] *adj* espinoso; *(fig: person)* enojadizo

pride [praɪd] *n* orgullo; *(pej)* soberbia ▷ *vt*: **to ~ o.s. on** enorgullecerse de

priest [priːst] *n* sacerdote *m*

primarily ['praɪmərɪli] *adv* ante todo

primary ['praɪməri] *adj (first in importance)* principal ▷ *n (us Pol)*

elección f primaria; **primary school**
(BRIT) n escuela primaria
prime [praɪm] adj primero, principal;
(excellent) selecto, de primera clase
▷ n: **in the ~ of life** en la flor de la vida
▷ vt (wood: fig) preparar; **~ example**
ejemplo típico; **Prime Minister** n
primer(a) ministro/a
primitive ['prɪmɪtɪv] adj primitivo;
(crude) rudimentario
primrose ['prɪmrəʊz] n primavera,
prímula
prince [prɪns] n príncipe m
princess [prɪn'sɛs] n princesa
principal ['prɪnsɪpl] adj principal,
mayor ▷ n director(a) m/f; **principally**
adv principalmente
principle ['prɪnsɪpl] n principio; **in ~**
en principio; **on ~** por principio
print [prɪnt] n (footprint) huella;
(fingerprint) huella dactilar; (letters)
letra de molde; (fabric) estampado;
(Art) grabado; (Phot) impresión
f ▷ vt imprimir; (cloth) estampar;
(write in capitals) escribir en letras de
molde; **out of ~** agotado; **print out** vt
(Comput) imprimir; **printer** n (person)
impresor/a m/f; (machine) impresora;
printout n (Comput) impresión f
prior ['praɪə*] adj anterior, previo; **~**
to antes de
priority [praɪ'ɒrɪtɪ] n prioridad f; **to**
have ~ (over) tener prioridad (sobre)
prison ['prɪzn] n cárcel f, prisión f
▷ cpd carcelario; **prisoner** n (in prison)
preso/a; (captured person) prisionero;
prisoner-of-war n prisionero de
guerra
pristine ['prɪstiːn] adj prístino
privacy ['prɪvəsɪ] n intimidad f
private ['praɪvɪt] adj (personal)
particular; (property, industry, discussion
etc) privado; (person) reservado; (place)
tranquilo ▷ n soldado raso; **"~"** (on
envelope) "confidencial"; (on door)
"prohibido el paso"; **in ~** en privado;
privately adv en privado; (in o.s.)

en secreto; **private property** n
propiedad f privada; **private school** n
colegio particular
privatize ['praɪvɪtaɪz] vt privatizar
privilege ['prɪvɪlɪdʒ] n privilegio;
(prerogative) prerrogativa
prize [praɪz] n premio ▷ adj de
primera clase ▷ vt apreciar, estimar;
prize-giving n distribución f de
premios; **prizewinner** n premiado/a
pro [prəʊ] n (Sport) profesional mf
▷ prep a favor de; **the ~s and cons** los
pros y los contras
probability [prɒbə'bɪlɪtɪ] n
probabilidad f; **in all ~** con toda
probabilidad
probable ['prɒbəbl] adj probable
probably ['prɒbəblɪ] adv
probablemente
probation [prə'beɪʃən] n: **on ~**
(employee) a prueba; (Law) en libertad
condicional
probe [prəʊb] n (Med, Space) sonda;
(enquiry) encuesta, investigación f ▷ vt
sondar; (investigate) investigar
problem ['prɒbləm] n problema m
procedure [prə'siːdʒə*] n
procedimiento; (bureaucratic) trámites
mpl
proceed [prə'siːd] vi (do
afterwards): **to ~ to do sth** proceder
a hacer algo; (continue): **to ~ (with)**
continuar o seguir (con); **proceedings**
npl acto(s) (pl); (Law) proceso;
proceeds ['prəʊsiːdz] npl (money)
ganancias fpl, ingresos mpl
process ['prəʊsɛs] n proceso ▷ vt
tratar, elaborar
procession [prə'sɛʃən] n desfile m;
funeral ~ cortejo fúnebre
proclaim [prə'kleɪm] vt (announce)
anunciar
prod [prɒd] vt empujar ▷ n empujón
m
produce [n 'prɒdjuːs, vt prə'djuːs]
n (Agr) productos mpl agrícolas ▷ vt
producir; (play, film, programme)
presentar; **producer** n productor(a)

m/f; (of film, programme)
director(a) m/f; (of record) productor(a) m/f

product ['prɒdʌkt] n producto;
production [prə'dʌkʃən] n
producción f; (Theatre) presentación
f; **productive** [prə'dʌktɪv]
adj productivo; **productivity**
[prɒdʌk'tɪvɪtɪ] n productividad f

Prof. [prɒf] abbr (= professor) Prof

profession [prə'feʃən] n profesión
f; **professional** adj profesional ▷ n
profesional mf; (skilled person) perito

professor [prə'fesə*] n (BRIT)
catedrático/a; (US, CANADA) profesor(a)
m/f

profile ['prəufaɪl] n perfil m

profit ['prɒfɪt] n (Comm) ganancia
▷ vi: **to ~ by** or **from** aprovechar o sacar
provecho de; **profitable** adj (Econ)
rentable

profound [prə'faund] adj profundo

programme ['prəugræm] (us
program) n programa m ▷ vt
programar; **programmer** (us
programer) n programador(a) m/f;
programming (us **programing**) n
programación f

progress [n 'prəugres, vi prə'gres]
n progreso; (development) desarrollo
▷ vi progresar, avanzar; **in ~** en curso;
progressive [-'gresɪv] adj progresivo;
(person) progresista

prohibit [prə'hɪbɪt] vt prohibir; **to
~ sb from doing sth** prohibir a algn
hacer algo

project [n 'prɒdʒekt, vb
prə'dʒekt] n proyecto ▷ vt
proyectar ▷ vi (stick out) salir,
sobresalir; **projection**
[prə'dʒekʃən] n proyección f;
(overhang) saliente m; **projector**
[prə'dʒektə*] n proyector m

prolific [prə'lɪfɪk] adj prolífico

prolong [prə'lɒŋ] vt prolongar,
extender

prom [prɒm] n abbr = **promenade**
(us: ball) baile m de gala; **the P~s** ver

recuadro

● **PROM**

El ciclo de conciertos de música
clásica más conocido de Londres
es el llamado **the Proms**
(promenade concerts), que se
celebra anualmente en el Royal
Albert Hall. Su nombre se debe
a que originalmente el público
paseaba durante las actuaciones,
costumbre que en la actualidad
se mantiene de forma simbólica,
permitiendo que parte de los
asistentes permanezcan de
pie. En Estados Unidos se llama
prom a un baile de gala en un
centro de educación secundaria o
universitaria.

promenade [prɒmə'nɑːd] n (by sea)
paseo marítimo

prominent ['prɒmɪnənt] adj
(standing out) saliente; (important)
eminente, importante

promiscuous [prə'mɪskjuəs] adj
(sexually) promiscuo

promise ['prɒmɪs] n promesa
▷ vt, vi prometer; **promising** adj
prometedor(a)

promote [prə'məut] vt (employee)
ascender; (product, pop star) hacer
propaganda por; (ideas) fomentar;
promotion [-'məuʃən] n (advertising
campaign) campaña f de promoción; (in
rank) ascenso

prompt [prɒmpt] adj rápido ▷ adv: **at
6 o'clock ~** a las seis en punto ▷ n
(Comput) aviso ▷ vt (urge) mover,
incitar; (when talking) instar; (Theatre)
apuntar; **to ~ sb to do sth** instar
a algn a hacer algo; **promptly** adv
rápidamente; (exactly) puntualmente

prone [prəun] adj (lying) postrado; **~
to** propenso a

prong [prɒŋ] n diente m, punta

pronoun ['prəunaun] n pronombre

m

pronounce [prə'nauns] vt
pronunciar

pronunciation [prənʌnsɪ'eɪʃən] n
pronunciación f

proof [pruːf] n prueba ▷ adj: ~
against a prueba de

prop [prɔp] n apoyo; (fig) sostén m
accesorios mpl, at(t)rezzo msg; **prop up**
vt (roof, structure) apuntalar; (economy)
respaldar

propaganda [prɔpə'gændə] n
propaganda

propeller [prə'pɛlə*] n hélice f

proper [prɔpə*] adj (suited, right)
propio; (exact) justo; (seemly) correcto,
decente; (authentic) verdadero;
(referring to place): **the village ~**
el pueblo mismo; **properly** adv
(adequately) correctamente; (decently)
decentemente; **proper noun** n
nombre m propio

property ['prɔpətɪ] n propiedad f;
(personal) bienes mpl muebles

prophecy ['prɔfɪsɪ] n profecía

prophet ['prɔfɪt] n profeta m

proportion [prə'pɔːʃən] n
proporción f; (share) parte f;
proportions npl (size) dimensiones fpl;
proportional adj: **proportional (to)**
en proporción (con)

proposal [prə'pəuzl] n (offer of
marriage) oferta de matrimonio; (plan)
proyecto

propose [prə'pəuz] vt proponer ▷ vi
declararse; **to ~ to do** tener intención
de hacer

proposition [prɔpə'zɪʃən] n
propuesta

proprietor [prə'praɪətə*] n
propietario/a, dueño/a

prose [prəuz] n prosa

prosecute ['prɔsɪkjuːt] vt (Law)
procesar; **prosecution** [-'kjuːʃən]
n proceso, causa; (accusing
side) acusación f; **prosecutor** n
acusador(a) m/f; (also: **public
prosecutor**) fiscal mf

prospect [n 'prɔspɛkt, vb
prə'spɛkt] n (possibility) posibilidad
f; (outlook) perspectiva ▷ vi: **to ~
for** buscar; **prospects** npl (for work
etc) perspectivas fpl; **prospective**
[prə'spɛktɪv] adj futuro

prospectus [prə'spɛktəs] n
prospecto

prosper ['prɔspə*] vi prosperar;
prosperity [-'spɛrɪtɪ] n prosperidad f;
prosperous adj próspero

prostitute ['prɔstɪtjuːt] n
prostituta; (male) hombre que se dedica a
la prostitución

protect [prə'tɛkt] vt proteger;
protection [-'tɛkʃən] n protección f;
protective adj protector(a)

protein ['prəutiːn] n proteína

protest [n 'prəutɛst, vb prə'tɛst] n
protesta ▷ vi: **to ~ about** or **at/against**
protestar de/contra ▷ vt (insist): **to ~
(that)** insistir en (que)

Protestant ['prɔtɪstənt] adj, n
protestante m/f

protester [prə'tɛstə*] n
manifestante mf

protractor [prə'træktə*] n (Geom)
transportador m

proud [praud] adj orgulloso; (pej)
soberbio, altanero

prove [pruːv] vt probar; (show)
demostrar ▷ vi: **to ~ (to be) correct**
resultar correcto; **~ o.s.** probar
su valía

proverb ['prɔvəːb] n refrán m

provide [prə'vaɪd] vt proporcionar,
dar; **to ~ sb with sth** proveer a algn
de algo; **provide for** vt fus (person)
mantener a; (problem etc) tener en
cuenta; **provided (that)** conj: **provided
(that)** a tal de que, a condición
de que; **providing (that)**
conj: **providing (that)** a condición de
que, con tal de que

province ['prɔvɪns] n provincia; (fig)
esfera; **provincial** [prə'vɪnʃəl] adj
provincial; (pej) provinciano

provision [prə'vɪʒən] n (supplying)

suministro, abastecimiento; (of contract etc) disposición f; **provisions** npl (food) comestibles mpl; **provisional** adj provisional

provocative [prə'vɒkətɪv] adj provocativo

provoke [prə'vəuk] vt (cause) provocar, incitar; (anger) enojar

prowl [praul] vi (also: ~ **about**, ~ **around**) merodear ▷ n: **on the** ~ de merodeo

proximity [prɒk'sɪmɪtɪ] n proximidad f

proxy ['prɒksɪ] n: **by** ~ por poderes

prudent ['pru:dənt] adj prudente

prune [pru:n] n ciruela pasa ▷ vt podar

pry [praɪ] vi: **to** ~ **(into)** entrometerse (en)

PS n abbr (= postscript) P.D.

pseudonym ['sju:dəunɪm] n seudónimo

PSHE (BRIT: Scol) n abbr (= personal, social and health education) formación social y sanitaria

psychiatric [saɪkɪ'ætrɪk] adj psiquiátrico

psychiatrist [saɪ'kaɪətrɪst] n psiquiatra mf

psychic ['saɪkɪk] adj (also: ~**al**) psíquico

psychoanalysis [saɪkəuə'nælɪsɪs] n psicoanálisis m inv

psychological [saɪkə'lɒdʒɪkl] adj psicológico

psychologist [saɪ'kɒlədʒɪst] n psicólogo/a

psychology [saɪ'kɒlədʒɪ] n psicología

psychotherapy [saɪkəu'θerəpɪ] n psicoterapia

pt abbr = **pint(s); point(s)**

PTO abbr (= please turn over) sigue

pub [pʌb] n abbr (= public house) pub m, bar m

puberty ['pju:bətɪ] n pubertad f

public ['pʌblɪk] adj público ▷ n: **the** ~ el público; **in** ~ en público; **to make** ~

hacer público

publication [pʌblɪ'keɪʃən] n publicación f

public: public company n sociedad f anónima; **public convenience** (BRIT) n aseos mpl públicos (SP), sanitarios mpl (LAM); **public holiday** n (día m de) fiesta (SP), (día m) feriado (LAM); **public house** (BRIT) n bar m, pub m

publicity [pʌb'lɪsɪtɪ] n publicidad f

publicize ['pʌblɪsaɪz] vt publicitar

public: public limited company n sociedad f anónima (S.A.); **publicly** adv públicamente, en público; **public opinion** n opinión f pública; **public relations** n relaciones fpl públicas; **public school** n (BRIT) escuela privada; (US) instituto; **public transport** n transporte m público

publish ['pʌblɪʃ] vt publicar; **publisher** n (person) editor(a) m/f; (firm) editorial f; **publishing** n (industry) industria del libro

pub lunch n almuerzo que se sirve en un pub; **to go for a** ~ almorzar o comer en un pub

pudding ['pudɪŋ] n pudín m; (BRIT: dessert) postre m; **black** ~ morcilla

puddle ['pʌdl] n charco

Puerto Rico [pwɛːtəuˈriːkəu] n Puerto Rico

puff [pʌf] n (of smoke, air) bocanada; (of breathing) resoplido ▷ vt: **to** ~ **one's pipe** chupar la pipa ▷ vi (pant) jadear; **puff pastry** n hojaldre m

pull [pul] n (tug): **to give sth a** ~ dar un tirón a algo ▷ vt tirar de; (press: trigger) apretar; (haul) tirar, arrastrar; (close: curtain) echar ▷ vi tirar; **to** ~ **to pieces** hacer pedazos; **not to** ~ **one's punches** no andarse con bromas; **to** ~ **one's weight** hacer su parte; **to** ~ **o.s. together** sobreponerse; **to** ~ **sb's leg** tomar el pelo a algn; **pull apart** vt (break) romper; **pull away** vi (vehicle: move off) salir, arrancar; (draw back) apartarse bruscamente; **pull back** vt (lever etc)

tirar hacia sí; (*curtains*) descorrer ▷ vi
(*refrain*) contenerse; (*Mil: withdraw*)
retirarse; **pull down** vt (*building*)
derribar; **pull in** vi (*car etc*) parar
(junto a la acera); (*train*) llegar a la
estación; **pull off** vt (*deal etc*) cerrar;
pull out vi (*car, train etc*) salir ▷ vt
sacar, arrancar; **pull over** vi (*Aut*)
hacerse a un lado; **pull up** vi (*stop*)
parar ▷ vt (*raise*) levantar; (*uproot*)
arrancar, desarraigar
pulley ['pulɪ] n polea
pullover ['puləuvə*] n jersey m,
suéter m
pulp [pʌlp] n (*of fruit*) pulpa
pulpit ['pulpɪt] n púlpito
pulse [pʌls] n (*Anat*) pulso; (*rhythm*)
pulsación f; (*Bot*) legumbre f; **pulses** pl
n legumbres
puma ['pju:mə] n puma m
pump [pʌmp] n bomba; (*shoe*)
zapatilla ▷ vt sacar con una bomba;
pump up vt inflar
pumpkin ['pʌmpkɪn] n calabaza
pun [pʌn] n juego de palabras
punch [pʌntʃ] n (*blow*) golpe m,
puñetazo; (*tool*) punzón m; (*drink*)
ponche m ▷ vt (*hit*): **to ~ sb/sth** dar
un puñetazo a o golpear a algn/algo;
punch-up n (*BRIT: inf*) n riña
punctual ['pʌŋktjuəl] adj puntual
punctuation [pʌŋktju'eɪʃən] n
puntuación f
puncture ['pʌŋktʃə*] (*BRIT*) n
pinchazo ▷ vt pinchar
punish ['pʌnɪʃ] vt castigar;
punishment n castigo
punk [pʌŋk] n (*also: ~ rocker*)
punki mf; (*also: ~ rock*) música punk;
(*us: inf: hoodlum*) rufián m
pup [pʌp] n cachorro
pupil ['pju:pl] n alumno/a; (*of eye*)
pupila
puppet ['pʌpɪt] n títere m
puppy ['pʌpɪ] n cachorro, perrito
purchase ['pə:tʃɪs] n compra ▷ vt
comprar
pure [pjuə*] adj puro; **purely** adv

puramente
purify ['pjuərɪfaɪ] vt purificar,
depurar
purity ['pjuərɪtɪ] n pureza
purple ['pə:pl] adj purpúreo; morado
purpose ['pə:pəs] n propósito; **on ~** a
propósito, adrede
purr [pə:*] vi ronronear
purse [pə:s] n monedero; n
(*us: handbag*) bolso (*SP*), cartera (*LAM*),
bolsa (*MEX*) ▷ vt fruncir
pursue [pə'sju:] vt seguir
pursuit [pə'sju:t] n (*chase*) caza;
(*occupation*) actividad f
pus [pʌs] n pus m
push [puʃ] n empuje m, empujón
m; (*of button*) presión f; (*drive*) empuje
m ▷ vt empujar; (*button*) apretar;
(*promote*) promover ▷ vi empujar;
(*demand*): **to ~ for** luchar por; **push in**
vi colarse; **push off** (*inf*) vi largarse;
push on vi seguir adelante; **push over**
vt (*cause to fall*) hacer caer, derribar;
(*knock over*) volcar; **push through** vt
(*crowd*) abrirse paso a empujones ▷ vt
(*measure*) despachar; **pushchair** (*BRIT*)
n sillita de ruedas; **pusher** n (*drug
pusher*) traficante mf de drogas; **push-
up** (*us*) n plancha
pussy(-cat) ['pusɪ-] (*inf*) n minino
(*inf*)
put [put] (*pt, pp* ~) vt (*place*) poner,
colocar; (*put into*) meter; (*say*) expresar;
(*a question*) hacer; (*estimate*) estimar;
put aside vt (*lay down: book etc*) dejar
or poner a un lado; (*save*) ahorrar; (*in
shop*) guardar; **put away** vt (*store*)
guardar; **put back** vt (*replace*) devolver
a su lugar; (*postpone*) aplazar; **put by**
vt (*money*) guardar; **put down** vt (*on
ground*) poner en el suelo; (*animal*)
sacrificar; (*in writing*) apuntar; (*revolt
etc*) sofocar; **to put sth
down to** atribuir algo a; **put forward**
vt (*ideas*) presentar, proponer; **put
in** vt (*complaint*) presentar; (*time*)
dedicar; **put off** vt (*postpone*) aplazar;
(*discourage*) desanimar; **put on** vt

ponerse; (*light etc*) encender; (*play etc*)
presentar; (*gain*): **to put on weight**
engordar; (*brake*) echar; (*record, kettle
etc*) poner; (*assume*) adoptar; **put out**
vt (*fire, light*) apagar; (*rubbish etc*) sacar;
(*cat etc*) echar; (*one's hand*) alargar;
(*inf: person*): **to be put out** alterarse;
put through *vt* (*Tel*) poner; (*plan etc*)
hacer aprobar; **put together** *vt* unir,
reunir; (*assemble: furniture*) armar,
montar; (*meal*) preparar; **put up** *vt*
(*raise*) levantar, alzar; (*hang*) colgar;
(*build*) construir; (*increase*) aumentar;
(*accommodate*) alojar; **put up with** *vt
fus* aguantar
putt [pʌt] *n* putt *m*, golpe *m* corto;
putting green *n* green *m*; minigolf *m*
puzzle ['pʌzl] *n* rompecabezas *m
inv*; (*also:* **crossword ~**) crucigrama
m; (*mystery*) misterio ▷ *vt* dejar
perplejo, confundir ▷ *vi*: **to ~ over sth**
devanarse los sesos con algo; **puzzled**
adj perplejo; **puzzling** *adj* misterioso,
extraño
pyjamas [pɪ'dʒɑːməz] (*BRIT*) *npl*
pijama *m*
pylon ['paɪlən] *n* torre *f* de
conducción eléctrica
pyramid ['pɪrəmɪd] *n* pirámide *f*

q

quack [kwæk] *n* graznido; (*pej: doctor*)
curandero/a
quadruple [kwɒ'drupl] *vt, vi*
cuadruplicar
quail [kweɪl] *n* codorniz *f* ▷ *vi*: **to ~ at**
or **before** amedrentarse ante
quaint [kweɪnt] *adj* extraño;
(*picturesque*) pintoresco
quake [kweɪk] *vi* temblar ▷ *n abbr* =
earthquake
qualification [kwɒlɪfɪ'keɪʃən] *n*
(*ability*) capacidad *f*; (*often pl: diploma
etc*) título; (*reservation*) salvedad *f*
qualified ['kwɒlɪfaɪd] *adj*
capacitado; (*professionally*) titulado;
(*limited*) limitado
qualify ['kwɒlɪfaɪ] *vt* (*make competent*)
capacitar; (*modify*) modificar ▷ *vi* (*in
competition*): **to ~ (for)** calificarse
(para); (*pass examination*): **to ~ (as)**
calificarse (de), graduarse (en); (*be
eligible*): **to ~ (for)** reunir los requisitos
(para)
quality ['kwɒlɪtɪ] *n* calidad *f*; (*of
person*) cualidad *f*

qualm [kwɑːm] n escrúpulo
quantify ['kwɒntɪfaɪ] vt cuantificar
quantity ['kwɒntɪtɪ] n cantidad f; **in ~** en grandes cantidades
quarantine ['kwɒrəntiːn] n cuarentena
quarrel ['kwɒrl] n riña, pelea ▷ vi reñir, pelearse
quarry ['kwɒrɪ] n cantera
quart [kwɔːt] n ≈ litro
quarter ['kwɔːtə*] n cuarto, cuarta parte f; (us: coin) moneda de 25 centavos; (of year) trimestre m; (district) barrio ▷ vt dividir en cuartos; (Mil: lodge) alojar; **quarters** npl (barracks) cuartel m; (living quarters) alojamiento; **a ~ of an hour** un cuarto de hora; **quarter final** n cuarto de final; **quarterly** adj trimestral ▷ adv cada 3 meses, trimestralmente
quartet(te) [kwɔː'tɛt] n cuarteto
quartz [kwɔːts] n cuarzo
quay [kiː] n (also: **~side**) muelle m
queasy ['kwiːzɪ] adj: **to feel ~** tener náuseas
queen [kwiːn] n reina; (Cards etc) dama
queer [kwɪə*] adj raro, extraño ▷ n (inf: highly offensive) maricón m
quench [kwɛntʃ] vt: **to ~ one's thirst** apagar la sed
query ['kwɪərɪ] n (question) pregunta ▷ vt dudar de
quest [kwɛst] n busca, búsqueda
question ['kwɛstʃən] n pregunta; (doubt) duda; (matter) asunto, cuestión f ▷ vt (doubt) dudar de; (interrogate) interrogar, hacer preguntas a; **beyond ~** fuera de toda duda; **out of the ~** imposible; ni hablar; **questionable** adj dudoso; **question mark** n punto de interrogación; **questionnaire** [-'nɛə*] n cuestionario
queue [kjuː] (BRIT) n cola ▷ vi (also: **~ up**) hacer cola
quiche [kiːʃ] n quiche m
quick [kwɪk] adj rápido; (agile) ágil; (mind) listo ▷ n: **cut to the ~** (fig) herido

en lo vivo; **be ~!** ¡date prisa!; **quickly** adv rápidamente, de prisa
quid [kwɪd] (BRIT: inf) n inv libra
quiet ['kwaɪət] adj (voice, music etc) bajo; (person, place) tranquilo; (ceremony) íntimo ▷ n silencio; (calm) tranquilidad f ▷ vt, vi (us) = **quieten**

> Be careful not to translate **quiet** by the Spanish word **quieto**.

quietly adv tranquilamente; (silently) silenciosamente
quilt [kwɪlt] n edredón m
quirky ['kwɜːkɪ] adj raro, estrafalario
quit [kwɪt] (pt, pp ~ or **~ted**) vt dejar, abandonar; (premises) desocupar ▷ vi (give up) renunciar; (resign) dimitir
quite [kwaɪt] adv (rather) bastante; (entirely) completamente; **that's not ~ big enough** no acaba de ser lo bastante grande; **~ a few of them** un buen número de ellos; **~ (so)!** ¡así es!, ¡exactamente!
quits [kwɪts] adj: **~ (with)** en paz (con); **let's call it ~** dejémoslo en tablas
quiver ['kwɪvə*] vi estremecerse
quiz [kwɪz] n concurso ▷ vt interrogar
quota ['kwəʊtə] n cuota
quotation [kwəʊ'teɪʃən] n cita; (estimate) presupuesto; **quotation marks** npl comillas fpl
quote [kwəʊt] n cita; (estimate) presupuesto ▷ vt citar; (price) cotizar ▷ vi: **to ~ from** citar de; **quotes** npl (inverted commas) comillas fpl

r

rabbi ['ræbaɪ] n rabino
rabbit ['ræbɪt] n conejo
rabies ['reɪbiːz] n rabia
RAC (BRIT) n abbr (= Royal Automobile Club) ≈ RACE m
rac(c)oon [rə'kuːn] n mapache m
race [reɪs] n carrera; (species) raza ▷ vt (horse) hacer correr; (engine) acelerar ▷ vi (compete) competir; (run) correr; (pulse) latir a ritmo acelerado; **race car** (US) n = **racing car**; **racecourse** n hipódromo; **racehorse** n caballo de carreras; **racetrack** n pista; (for cars) autódromo
racial ['reɪʃl] adj racial
racing ['reɪsɪŋ] n carreras fpl; **racing car** (BRIT) n coche m de carreras; **racing driver** (BRIT) n piloto mf de carreras
racism ['reɪsɪzəm] n racismo; **racist** [-sɪst] adj, n racista mf
rack [ræk] n (also: **luggage ~**) rejilla; (shelf) estante m; (also: **roof ~**) baca, portaequipajes m inv; (dish rack) escurreplatos m inv; (clothes rack)

percha ▷ vt atormentar; **to ~ one's brains** devanarse los sesos
racket ['rækɪt] n (for tennis) raqueta; (noise) ruido, estrépito; (swindle) estafa, timo
racquet ['rækɪt] n raqueta
radar ['reɪdɑː*] n radar m
radiation [reɪdɪ'eɪʃən] n radiación f
radiator ['reɪdɪeɪtə*] n radiador m
radical ['rædɪkl] adj radical
radio ['reɪdɪəu] n radio f; **on the ~** por radio; **radioactive** adj radioactivo; **radio station** n emisora
radish ['rædɪʃ] n rábano
RAF n abbr (= Royal Air Force) las Fuerzas Aéreas Británicas
raffle ['ræfl] n rifa, sorteo
raft [rɑːft] n balsa; (also: **life ~**) balsa salvavidas
rag [ræg] n (piece of cloth) trapo; (torn cloth) harapo; (pej: newspaper) periodicucho; (for charity) actividades estudiantiles benéficas; **rags** npl (torn clothes) harapos mpl
rage [reɪdʒ] n rabia, furor m ▷ vi (person) rabiar, estar furioso; (storm) bramar; **it's all the ~** (very fashionable) está muy de moda
ragged ['rægɪd] adj (edge) desigual, mellado; (appearance) andrajoso, harapiento
raid [reɪd] n (Mil) incursión f; (criminal) asalto; (by police) redada ▷ vt invadir, atacar; asaltar
rail [reɪl] n (on stair) barandilla, pasamanos m inv; (on bridge, balcony) pretil m; (of ship) barandilla; (also: **towel ~**) toallero; **railcard** n (BRIT) tarjeta para obtener descuentos en el tren; **railing(s)** n (npl) vallado; **railroad** (US) n = **railway**; **railway** (BRIT) n ferrocarril m, vía férrea; **railway line** (BRIT) n línea (de ferrocarril); **railway station** (BRIT) n estación f de ferrocarril
rain [reɪn] n lluvia ▷ vi llover; **in the ~** bajo la lluvia; **it's ~ing** llueve, está lloviendo; **rainbow** n arco iris;

raincoat n impermeable m; **raindrop** n gota de lluvia; **rainfall** n lluvia; **rainforest** n selvas fpl tropicales; **rainy** adj lluvioso

raise [reɪz] n aumento ▷ vt levantar; (increase) aumentar; (improve: morale) subir; (: standards) mejorar; (doubts) suscitar; (a question) plantear; (cattle, family) criar; (crop) cultivar; (army) reclutar; (loan) obtener; **to ~ one's voice** alzar la voz

raisin ['reɪzn] n pasa de Corinto

rake [reɪk] n (tool) rastrillo; (person) libertino m ▷ vt (garden) rastrillar

rally ['rælɪ] n (Pol etc) reunión f, mitin m; (Aut) rallye m; (Tennis) peloteo ▷ vt reunir ▷ vi recuperarse

RAM [ræm] n abbr (= random access memory) RAM f

ram [ræm] n carnero; (also: battering ~) ariete m ▷ vt (crash into) dar contra, chocar con; (push: fist etc) empujar con fuerza

Ramadan [ræmə'dæn] n ramadán m

ramble ['ræmbl] n caminata, excursión f en el campo ▷ vi (pej: also: ~ on) divagar; **rambler** n excursionista mf; (Bot) trepadora; **rambling** adj (speech) inconexo; (house) laberíntico; (Bot) trepador(a)

ramp [ræmp] n rampa; **on/off ~** (Aut) vía de acceso/salida

rampage [ræm'peɪdʒ] n: **to be on the ~** desmandarse ▷ vi: **they went rampaging through the town** recorrieron la ciudad armando alboroto

ran [ræn] pt of **run**

ranch [rɑːntʃ] n hacienda, estancia

random ['rændəm] adj fortuito, sin orden; (Comput, Math) aleatorio ▷ n: **at ~** al azar

rang [ræŋ] pt of **ring**

range [reɪndʒ] n (of mountains) cadena de montañas, cordillera; (of missile) alcance m; (of voice) registro; (series) serie f; (of products) surtido; (Mil: also: **shooting ~**) campo de tiro;

(also: **kitchen ~**) fogón m ▷ vt (place) colocar; (arrange) arreglar ▷ vi: **to ~ over** (extend) extenderse por; **to ~ from ... to ...** oscilar entre ... y ...

ranger [reɪndʒə*] n guardabosques mf inv

rank [ræŋk] n (row) fila; (Mil) rango; (status) categoría; (BRIT: also: **taxi ~**) parada de taxis ▷ vi: **to ~ among** figurar entre ▷ adj fétido, rancio; **the ~ and file** (fig) la base

ransom ['rænsəm] n rescate m; **to hold to ~** (fig) hacer chantaje a

rant [rænt] vi divagar, desvariar

rap [ræp] vt golpear, dar un golpecito en ▷ n (music) rap m

rape [reɪp] n violación f; (Bot) colza ▷ vt violar

rapid ['ræpɪd] adj rápido; **rapidly** adv rápidamente; **rapids** npl (Geo) rápidos mpl

rapist ['reɪpɪst] n violador m

rapport [ræ'pɔ:*] n simpatía

rare [rɛə*] adj raro, poco común; (Culin: steak) poco hecho; **rarely** adv pocas veces

rash [ræʃ] adj imprudente, precipitado; n (Med) sarpullido, erupción f (cutánea); (of events) serie f

rasher ['ræʃə*] n lonja

raspberry ['rɑːzbərɪ] n frambuesa

rat [ræt] n rata

rate [reɪt] n (ratio) razón f; (price) precio; (: of hotel etc) tarifa; (of interest) tipo; (speed) velocidad f ▷ vt tasar; (estimate) estimar; **rates** npl (BRIT: property tax) impuesto municipal; (fees) tarifa; **to ~ sth/sb as** considerar algo/a algn como

rather ['rɑːðə*] adv: **it's ~ expensive** es algo caro; (too much) es demasiado caro; (to some extent) más bien; **there's a lot** hay bastante; **I would ~ or I'd ~ go** preferiría ir; **or ~** mejor dicho

rating ['reɪtɪŋ] n tasación f; (score) índice m; (of ship) clase f; **ratings** npl (Radio, TV) niveles mpl de audiencia

ratio ['reɪʃɪəʊ] n razón f; **in the ~ of**

100 to 1 a razón de 100 a 1

ration ['ræʃən] n ración f ▷ vt racionar; **rations** npl víveres mpl

rational ['ræʃənl] adj (solution, reasoning) lógico, razonable; (person) cuerdo, sensato

rattle ['rætl] n golpeteo; (of train etc) traqueteo; (for baby) sonaja, sonajero ▷ vi castañetear; (car, bus): **to ~ along** traquetear ▷ vt hacer sonar agitando

rave [reɪv] vi (in anger) encolerizarse; (with enthusiasm) entusiasmarse; (Med) delirar, desvariar ▷ n (inf: party) rave m

raven ['reɪvən] n cuervo

ravine [rə'viːn] n barranco

raw [rɔː] adj crudo; (not processed) bruto; (sore) vivo; (inexperienced) novato, inexperto; **~ materials** materias primas

ray [reɪ] n rayo; **~ of hope** (rayo de) esperanza

razor ['reɪzə*] n (open) navaja; (safety razor) máquina de afeitar; (electric razor) máquina (eléctrica) de afeitar; **razor blade** n hoja de afeitar

Rd abbr = **road**

RE n abbr (BRIT) = **religious education**

re [riː] prep con referencia a

reach [riːtʃ] n alcance m; (of river etc) extensión f entre dos recodos ▷ vt alcanzar, llegar a; (achieve) lograr ▷ vi extenderse; **within ~** al alcance (de la mano); **out of ~** fuera del alcance; **reach out** vt (hand) tender ▷ vi: **to reach out for sth** alargar or tender la mano para tomar algo

react [riː'ækt] vi reaccionar; **reaction** [-'ækʃən] n reacción f; **reactor** [riː'æktə*] n (also: **nuclear reactor**) reactor m (nuclear)

read [riːd, pt, pp read] (pt, pp ~) vi leer ▷ vt leer; (understand) entender; (study) estudiar; **read out** vt leer en alta voz; **reader** n lector(a) m/f; (BRIT: at university) profesor(a) m/f adjunto/a

readily ['rɛdɪlɪ] adv (willingly) de buena gana; (easily) fácilmente; (quickly) en seguida

reading ['riːdɪŋ] n lectura; (on instrument) indicación f

ready ['rɛdɪ] adj listo, preparado; (willing) dispuesto; (available) disponible ▷ adv: **~-cooked** listo para comer ▷ n: **at the ~** (Mil) listo para tirar; **to get ~** vi prepararse ▷ **to get ~** vt preparar; **ready-made** adj confeccionado

real [rɪəl] adj verdadero, auténtico; **in ~ terms** en términos reales; **real ale** n cerveza elaborada tradicionalmente; **real estate** n bienes mpl raíces; **realistic** [-'lɪstɪk] adj realista; **reality** [riː'ælɪtɪ] n realidad f; **reality TV** n telerrealidad f

realization [rɪəlaɪ'zeɪʃən] n comprensión f; (fulfilment, Comm) realización f

realize ['rɪəlaɪz] vt (understand) darse cuenta de

really ['rɪəlɪ] adv realmente; (for emphasis) verdaderamente; (actually): **what ~ happened** lo que pasó en realidad; **~?** ¿de veras?; **~!** (annoyance) ¡vamos!, ¡por favor!

realm [rɛlm] n reino; (fig) esfera

realtor ['rɪəltɔː*] (US) n agente mf inmobiliario/a

reappear [riːə'pɪə*] vi reaparecer

rear [rɪə*] adj trasero ▷ n parte f trasera ▷ vt (cattle, family) criar ▷ vi (also: **~ up**: animal) encabritarse

rearrange [riːə'reɪndʒ] vt ordenar or arreglar de nuevo

rear: **rear-view mirror** n (Aut) (espejo) retrovisor m; **rear-wheel drive** n tracción f trasera

reason ['riːzn] n razón f ▷ vi: **to ~ with sb** tratar de que algn entre en razón; **it stands to ~ that …** es lógico que …; **reasonable** adj razonable; (sensible) sensato; **reasonably** adv razonablemente; **reasoning** n razonamiento, argumentos mpl

reassurance [riːə'ʃuərəns] n consuelo

reassure [riːə'ʃuə*] vt tranquilizar,

alentar; **to ~ sb that ...** tranquilizar a algn asegurando que ...

rebate ['ri:beit] n (on tax etc) desgravación f

rebel [n 'rebl, vi ri'bel] n rebelde mf ▷ vi rebelarse, sublevarse; **rebellion** [ri'beljən] n rebelión f, sublevación f; **rebellious** [ri'beljəs] adj rebelde; (child) revoltoso

rebuild [ri:'bild] vt reconstruir

recall [vb ri'kɔ:l, n 'ri:kɔl] vt (remember) recordar; (ambassador etc) retirar ▷ n recuerdo; retirada

rec'd abbr (= received) rdbo

receipt [ri'si:t] n (document) recibo; (for parcel etc) acuse m de recibo; (act of receiving) recepción f; **receipts** npl (Comm) ingresos mpl

Be careful not to translate **receipt** with the Spanish word **receta**.

receive [ri'si:v] vt recibir; (guest) acoger; (wound) sufrir; **receiver** n (Tel) auricular m; (Radio) receptor m; (of stolen goods) perista mf; (Comm) administrador m jurídico

recent ['ri:snt] adj reciente; **recently** adv recientemente; **recently arrived** recién llegado

reception [ri'sepʃən] n recepción f; (welcome) acogida; **reception desk** n recepción f; **receptionist** n recepcionista mf

recession [ri'sɛʃən] n recesión f

recharge [ri:'tʃɑ:dʒ] vt (battery) recargar

recipe ['resipi] n receta; (for disaster, success) fórmula

recipient [ri'sipiənt] n recibidor(a) m/f; (of letter) destinatario/a

recital [ri'saitl] n recital m

recite [ri'sait] vt (poem) recitar

reckless ['rekləs] adj temerario, imprudente; (driving, driver) peligroso

reckon ['rekən] vt calcular; (consider) considerar; (think): **I ~ that ...** me parece que ...

reclaim [ri'kleim] vt (land, waste) recuperar; (land: from sea) rescatar;

(demand back) reclamar

recline [ri'klain] vi reclinarse

recognition [rekəg'niʃən] n reconocimiento; **transformed beyond ~** irreconocible

recognize [ri'kəgnaiz] vt: **to ~ (by/as)** reconocer (por/como)

recollection [rekə'lekʃən] n recuerdo

recommend [rekə'mend] vt recomendar; **recommendation** [rekəmen'deiʃən] n recomendación f

reconcile ['rekənsail] vt (two people) reconciliar; (two facts) compaginar; **to ~ o.s. to sth** conformarse a algo

reconsider [ri:kən'sidə*] vt repensar

reconstruct [ri:kən'strʌkt] vt reconstruir

record [n, adj 'rekɔːd, vt ri'kɔːd] n (Mus) disco; (of meeting etc) acta; (register) registro, partida; (file) archivo; (also: **criminal ~**) antecedentes mpl; (written) expediente m; (Sport, Comput) récord m ▷ adj récord, sin precedentes ▷ vt registrar; (Mus: song etc) grabar; **in ~ time** en un tiempo récord; **off the ~** adj no oficial ▷ adv confidencialmente; **recorded delivery** (BRIT) n (Post) entrega con acuse de recibo; **recorder** n (Mus) flauta de pico; **recording** n (Mus) grabación f; **record player** n tocadiscos m inv

recount [ri'kaunt] vt contar

recover [ri'kʌvə*] vt recuperar ▷ vi (from illness, shock) recuperarse; **recovery** n recuperación f

recreate [ri:kri'eit] vt recrear

recreation [rekri'eiʃən] n recreo; **recreational vehicle** (us) n caravan or rulota pequeña; **recreational drug** n droga recreativa

recruit [ri'kru:t] n recluta mf ▷ vt reclutar; (staff) contratar; **recruitment** n reclutamiento

rectangle ['rektæŋgl] n rectángulo; **rectangular** [-'tæŋgjulə*] adj rectangular

rectify ['rektifai] vt rectificar

rector ['rɛktə*] n (Rel) párroco
recur [rɪ'kə:*] vi repetirse; (pain, illness) producirse de nuevo; **recurring** adj (problem) repetido, constante
recyclable [ri:'saɪkləbl] adj reciclable
recycle [ri:'saɪkl] vt reciclar
recycling [ri:'saɪklɪŋ] n reciclaje
red [rɛd] n rojo ▷ adj rojo; (hair) pelirrojo; (wine) tinto; **to be in the ~** (account) estar en números rojos; (business) tener un saldo negativo; **to give sb the ~ carpet treatment** recibir a algn con todos los honores; **Red Cross** n Cruz f Roja; **redcurrant** n grosella roja
redeem [rɪ'di:m] vt redimir; (promises) cumplir; (sth in pawn) desempeñar; (fig, also Rel) rescatar
red: red-haired adj pelirrojo; **redhead** n pelirrojo/a; **red-hot** adj candente; **red light** n: **to go through a red light** (Aut) pasar la luz roja; **red-light district** n barrio chino
red meat n carne f roja
reduce [rɪ'dju:s] vt reducir; **to ~ sb to tears** hacer llorar a algn; **"~ speed now"** (Aut) "reduzca la velocidad"; **reduced** (decreased) reducido, rebajado; **at a reduced price** con rebaja o descuento; **"greatly reduced prices"** "grandes rebajas"; **reduction** [rɪ'dʌkʃən] n reducción f; (of price) rebaja; (discount) descuento; (smaller-scale copy) copia reducida
redundancy [rɪ'dʌndənsɪ] n (dismissal) despido; (unemployment) desempleo
redundant [rɪ'dʌndnt] adj (BRIT: worker) parado, sin trabajo; (detail, object) superfluo; **to be made ~** quedar(se) sin trabajo
reed [ri:d] n (Bot) junco, caña; (Mus) lengüeta
reef [ri:f] n (at sea) arrecife m
reel [ri:l] n carrete m, bobina; (of film) rollo; (dance) baile escocés ▷ vt (also: **~ up**) devanar; (also: **~ in**) sacar ▷ vi

(sway) tambalear(se)
ref [rɛf] (inf) n abbr = **referee**
refectory [rɪ'fɛktərɪ] n comedor m
refer [rɪ'fə:*] vt (send: patient) referir; (: matter) remitir ▷ vi: **to ~ to** (allude to) referirse a, aludir a; (apply to) relacionarse con; (consult) consultar
referee [rɛfə'ri:] n árbitro; (BRIT: for job application): **to be a ~ for sb** proporcionar referencias a algn ▷ vt (match) arbitrar en
reference ['rɛfrəns] n referencia; (for job application: letter) carta de recomendación; **with ~ to** (Comm: in letter) me remito a, **reference number** n número de referencia
refill [vt rɪ'fɪl, n 'ri:fɪl] vt rellenar ▷ n repuesto, recambio
refine [rɪ'faɪn] vt refinar; **refined** adj (person) fino; **refinery** n refinería
reflect [rɪ'flɛkt] vt reflejar ▷ vi (think) reflexionar, pensar; **it ~s badly/well on him** le perjudica/le hace honor; **reflection** [-'flɛkʃən] n (act) reflexión f; (image) reflejo; (criticism) crítica; **on reflection** pensándolo bien
reflex ['ri:flɛks] adj, n reflejo
reform [rɪ'fɔ:m] n reforma ▷ vt reformar
refrain [rɪ'freɪn] vi: **to ~ from doing** abstenerse de hacer ▷ n estribillo
refresh [rɪ'frɛʃ] vt refrescar; **refreshing** adj refrescante; **refreshments** npl refrescos mpl
refrigerator [rɪ'frɪdʒəreɪtə*] n frigorífico (SP), nevera (SP), refrigerador m (LAM), heladera (RPL)
refuel [ri:'fjuəl] vi repostar (combustible)
refuge ['rɛfju:dʒ] n refugio, asilo; **to take ~ in** refugiarse en; **refugee** [rɛfju'dʒi:] n refugiado/a
refund [n 'ri:fʌnd, vb rɪ'fʌnd] n reembolso ▷ vt devolver, reembolsar
refurbish [ri:'fə:bɪʃ] vt restaurar, renovar
refusal [rɪ'fju:zəl] n negativa; **to have first ~ on** tener la primera

opción a

refuse¹ ['refju:s] n basura

refuse² [rɪ'fju:z] vt rechazar; (invitation) declinar; (permission) denegar ▷ vi: **to ~ to do sth** negarse a hacer algo; (horse) rehusar

regain [rɪ'geɪn] vt recobrar, recuperar

regard [rɪ'gɑːd] n mirada; (esteem) respeto; (attention) consideración f ▷ vt (consider) considerar; **to give one's ~s to** saludar de su parte a; **"with kindest ~s"** "con muchos recuerdos"; **as ~s, with ~ to** con respecto a, en cuanto a; **regarding** prep con respecto a, en cuanto a; **regardless** adv a pesar de todo; **regardless of** sin reparar en

regenerate [rɪ'dʒenəreɪt] vt regenerar

reggae ['regeɪ] n reggae m

regiment ['redʒɪmənt] n regimiento

region ['riːdʒən] n región f; **in the ~ of** (fig) alrededor de; **regional** adj regional

register ['redʒɪstə*] n registro ▷ vt registrar; (birth) declarar; (car) matricular; (letter) certificar; (instrument) marcar, indicar ▷ vi (at hotel) registrarse; (as student) matricularse; (make impression) producir impresión; **registered** adj (letter, parcel) certificado

registrar ['redʒɪstrɑː*] n secretario/a (del registro civil)

registration [redʒɪs'treɪʃən] n (act) declaración f; (Aut: also: ~ number) matrícula

registry office ['redʒɪstrɪ-] n (BRIT) registro civil; **to get married in a ~** casarse por lo civil

regret [rɪ'gret] n sentimiento, pesar m ▷ vt sentir, lamentar; **regrettable** adj lamentable

regular ['regjulə*] adj regular; (soldier) profesional; (usual) habitual; (: doctor) de cabecera ▷ n (client etc) cliente a m/f; habitual; **regularly** adv con regularidad; (often) repetidas veces

regulate ['regjuleɪt] vt controlar;

regulation [-'leɪʃən] n (rule) regla, reglamento

rehabilitation ['riːəbɪlɪ'teɪʃən] n rehabilitación f

rehearsal [rɪ'həːsəl] n ensayo

rehearse [rɪ'həːs] vt ensayar

reign [reɪn] n reinado; (fig) predominio ▷ vi reinar; (fig) imperar

reimburse [riːɪm'bəːs] vt reembolsar

rein [reɪn] n (for horse) rienda

reincarnation [riːɪnkɑː'neɪʃən] n reencarnación f

reindeer ['reɪndɪə*] n inv reno

reinforce [riːɪn'fɔːs] vt reforzar; **reinforcements** npl (Mil) refuerzos mpl

reinstate [riːɪn'steɪt] vt reintegrar; (tax, law) reinstaurar

reject [n 'riːdʒekt, vb rɪ'dʒekt] n (thing) desecho ▷ vt rechazar; (suggestion) descartar; (coin) expulsar; **rejection** [rɪ'dʒekʃən] n rechazo

rejoice [rɪ'dʒɔɪs] vi: **to ~ at** or **over** regocijarse or alegrarse de

relate [rɪ'leɪt] vt (tell) contar, relatar; (connect) relacionar ▷ vi relacionarse; **related** adj afín; (person) emparentado; **related to** (subject) relacionado con; **relating to** prep referente a

relation [rɪ'leɪʃən] n (person) familiar mf, pariente mf; (link) relación f; **relations** npl (relatives) familiares mpl; **relationship** n relación f; (personal) relaciones fpl; (also: **family relationship**) parentesco

relative ['relətɪv] n pariente mf, familiar mf ▷ adj relativo; **relatively** adv (comparatively) relativamente

relax [rɪ'læks] vi descansar; (unwind) relajarse ▷ vt (one's grip) soltar, aflojar; (control) relajar; (mind, person) descansar; **relaxation** [riːlæk'seɪʃən] n descanso; (of rule, control) relajamiento; (entertainment) diversión f; **relaxed** adj relajado; (tranquil) tranquilo; **relaxing** adj relajante

relay ['riːleɪ] n (race) carrera de relevos

▷ vt (Radio, TV) retransmitir
release [rɪ'liːs] n (liberation)
liberación f; (from prison) puesta en
libertad; (of gas etc) escape m; (of film
etc) estreno; (of record) lanzamiento
▷ vt (prisoner) poner en libertad; (gas)
despedir, arrojar; (from wreckage)
soltar; (catch, spring etc) desenganchar;
(film) estrenar; (book) publicar; (news)
difundir
relegate ['relɪgeɪt] vt relegar; (BRIT
Sport): **to be ~d to** bajar a
relent [rɪ'lent] vi ablandarse;
relentless adj implacable
relevant ['reləvənt] adj (fact)
pertinente; **~ to** relacionado con
reliable [rɪ'laɪəbl] adj (person, firm)
de confianza, de fiar; (method, machine)
seguro; (source) fidedigno
relic ['relɪk] n (Rel) reliquia f; (of the
past) vestigio
relief [rɪ'liːf] n (from pain, anxiety)
alivio; (help, supplies) socorro, ayuda;
(Art, Geo) relieve m
relieve [rɪ'liːv] vt (pain) aliviar; (bring
help to) ayudar, socorrer; (take over from)
sustituir; (: guard) relevar; **to ~ sb of
sth** quitar algo a algn; **to ~ o.s.** hacer
sus necesidades; **relieved** adj: **to be
relieved** sentir un gran alivio
religion [rɪ'lɪdʒən] n religión f
religious [rɪ'lɪdʒəs] adj religioso;
religious education n educación f
religiosa
relish ['relɪʃ] n (Culin) salsa;
(enjoyment) entusiasmo ▷ vt (food
etc) saborear; (enjoy): **to ~ sth** hacerle
mucha ilusión a algn algo
relocate [riːləʊ'keɪt] vt cambiar de
lugar, mudar ▷ vi mudarse
reluctance [rɪ'lʌktəns] n renuencia
reluctant [rɪ'lʌktənt] adj renuente;
reluctantly adv de mala gana
rely on [rɪ'laɪ-] vt fus depender de;
(trust) contar con
remain [rɪ'meɪn] vi (survive) quedar; (be
left) sobrar; (continue) quedar(se),
permanecer; **remainder** n resto;

remaining adj que queda(n);
(surviving) restante(s); **remains** npl
restos mpl
remand [rɪ'mɑːnd] n: **on ~** detenido
(bajo custodia) ▷ vt: **to be ~ed in
custody** quedar detenido bajo
custodia
remark [rɪ'mɑːk] n comentario
▷ vt comentar; **remarkable** adj
(outstanding) extraordinario
remarry [riː'mærɪ] vi volver a casarse
remedy ['remədɪ] n remedio ▷ vt
remediar, curar
remember [rɪ'membə*] vt recordar,
acordarse de; (bear in mind) tener
presente; (send greetings to): **~ me
to him** dale recuerdos de mi parte;
Remembrance Day n ≈ día en el
que se recuerda a los caídos en las dos
guerras mundiales

● **REMEMBRANCE DAY**
●
● En el Reino Unido el domingo
● más próximo al 11 de noviembre
● se conoce como **Remembrance
● Sunday** o **Remembrance
● Day**, aniversario de la firma del
● armisticio de 1918 que puso fin a
● la Primera Guerra Mundial. Ese
● día, a las once de la mañana (hora
● en que se firmó el armisticio), se
● recuerda a los que murieron en
● las dos guerras mundiales con
● dos minutos de silencio ante los
● monumentos a los caídos. Allí se
● colocan coronas de amapolas,
● flor que también se suele llevar
● prendida en el pecho tras pagar un
● donativo destinado a los inválidos
● de guerra.

remind [rɪ'maɪnd] vt: **to ~ sb to do
sth** recordar a algn que haga algo; **to ~
sb of sth** (of fact) recordar algo a algn;
she ~s me of her mother me recuerda
a su madre; **reminder** n notificación f;
(memento) recuerdo

reminiscent [remɪˈnɪsnt] *adj*: **to be ~ of sth** recordar algo

remnant [ˈremnənt] *n* resto; (*of cloth*) retal *m*

remorse [rɪˈmɔːs] *n* remordimientos *mpl*

remote [rɪˈməʊt] *adj* (*distant*) lejano; (*person*) distante; **remote control** *n* telecontrol *m*; **remotely** *adv* remotamente; (*slightly*) levemente

removal [rɪˈmuːvəl] *n* (*taking away*) el quitar; (*BRIT: from house*) mudanza; (*from office: dismissal*) destitución *f*; (*Med*) extirpación *f*; **removal man** (*irreg*) *n* (*BRIT*) mozo de mudanzas; **removal van** (*BRIT*) *n* camión *m* de mudanzas

remove [rɪˈmuːv] *vt* quitar; (*employee*) destituir; (*name: from list*) tachar, borrar; (*doubt*) disipar; (*abuse*) suprimir, acabar con; (*Med*) extirpar

Renaissance [rɪˈneɪsãs] *n*: **the ~** el Renacimiento

rename [riːˈneɪm] *vt* poner nuevo nombre a

render [ˈrendə*] *vt* (*thanks*) dar; (*aid*) proporcionar, prestar; (*make*) : **to ~ sth useless** hacer algo inútil

rendezvous [ˈrɒndɪvuː] *n* cita

renew [rɪˈnjuː] *vt* renovar; (*resume*) reanudar; (*loan etc*) prorrogar; **renewable** *adj* (*energy*) renovable

renovate [ˈrenəveɪt] *vt* renovar

renowned [rɪˈnaʊnd] *adj* renombrado

rent [rent] *n* (*for house*) arriendo, renta ▷ *vt* alquilar; **rental** *n* (*for television, car*) alquiler *m*

reorganize [riːˈɔːɡənaɪz] *vt* reorganizar

rep [rep] *n abbr* = **representative**

repair [rɪˈpɛə*] *n* reparación *f*, compostura ▷ *vt* reparar, componer; (*shoes*) remendar; **in good/bad** = en buen/mal estado; **repair kit** *n* caja de herramientas

repay [riːˈpeɪ] *vt* (*money*) devolver, reembolsar; (*person*) pagar; (*debt*)

liquidar; (*sb's efforts*) devolver, corresponder a; **repayment** *n* reembolso, devolución *f*; (*sum of money*) recompensa

repeat [rɪˈpiːt] *n* (*Radio, TV*) reposición *f* ▷ *vt* repetir ▷ *vi* repetirse; **repeatedly** *adv* repetidas veces; **repeat prescription** *n* (*BRIT*) receta renovada

repellent [rɪˈpelənt] *adj* repugnante ▷ *n*: **insect ~** crema *or* loción *f* anti-insectos

repercussions [riːpəˈkʌʃənz] *npl* consecuencias *fpl*

repetition [repɪˈtɪʃən] *n* repetición *f*

repetitive [rɪˈpetɪtɪv] *adj* repetitivo

replace [rɪˈpleɪs] *vt* (*put back*) devolver a su sitio; (*take the place*) reemplazar, sustituir; **replacement** *n* (*act*) reposición *f*; (*thing*) recambio; (*person*) suplente *mf*

replay [ˈriːpleɪ] *n* (*Sport*) desempate *m*; (*of tape, film*) repetición *f*

replica [ˈreplɪkə] *n* copia, reproducción *f* (*exacta*)

reply [rɪˈplaɪ] *n* respuesta, contestación *f* ▷ *vi* contestar, responder

report [rɪˈpɔːt] *n* informe *m*; (*Press etc*) reportaje *m*; (*BRIT: also*: **school ~**) boletín *m* escolar; (*of gun*) estallido ▷ *vt* informar de; (*Press etc*) hacer un reportaje sobre; (*notify: accident, culprit*) denunciar ▷ *vi* (*make a report*) presentar un informe; (*present o.s.*): **to ~ (to sb)** presentarse (ante algn); **report card** *n* (*US, SCOTTISH*) cartilla escolar; **reportedly** *adv* según se dice; **reporter** *n* periodista *mf*

represent [reprɪˈzent] *vt* representar; (*Comm*) ser agente de; (*describe*): **to ~ sth as** describir algo como; **representation** [-ˈteɪʃən] *n* representación *f*; **representative** *n* representante *mf*; (*US Pol*) diputado *m/f* ▷ *adj* representativo

repress [rɪˈpres] *vt* reprimir; **repression** [-ˈpreʃən] *n* represión *f*

reprimand [ˈreprɪmɑːnd] *n*

reprimenda ▷vt reprender

reproduce [ˌriːprə'djuːs] vt reproducir ▷vi reproducirse; **reproduction** [-'dʌkʃən] n reproducción f

reptile ['reptaɪl] n reptil m

republic [rɪ'pʌblɪk] n república; **republican** adj, n republicano/a m/f

reputable ['repjutəbl] adj (make etc) de renombre

reputation [repju'teɪʃən] n reputación f

request [rɪ'kwest] n petición f; (formal) solicitud f ▷ vt: **to ~ sth of** or **from sb** solicitar algo a algn; **request stop** (BRIT) n parada discrecional

require [rɪ'kwaɪə*] vt (need: person) necesitar, tener necesidad de; (: thing, situation) exigir; (want) pedir; **to ~ sb to do sth** pedir a algn que haga algo; **requirement** n requisito; (need) necesidad f

resat [riː'sæt] pt, pp of **resit**

rescue ['reskjuː] n rescate m ▷ vt rescatar

research [rɪ'sɜːtʃ] n investigaciones fpl ▷ vt investigar

resemblance [rɪ'zembləns] n parecido

resemble [rɪ'zembl] vt parecerse a

resent [rɪ'zent] vt tomar a mal; **resentful** adj resentido; **resentment** n resentimiento

reservation [rezə'veɪʃən] n reserva; **reservation desk** (US) n (in hotel) recepción f

reserve [rɪ'zɜːv] n reserva; (Sport) suplente mf ▷ vt (seats etc) reservar; **reserved** adj reservado

reservoir ['rezəvwɑː*] n (artificial lake) embalse m, tank; (small) depósito

residence ['rezɪdəns] n (formal: home) domicilio; (length of stay) permanencia; **residence permit** (BRIT) n permiso de permanencia

resident ['rezɪdənt] n (of area) vecino/a; (in hotel) huésped mf ▷ adj (population) permanente; (doctor)

residente; **residential** [-'denʃəl] adj residencial

residue ['rezɪdjuː] n resto

resign [rɪ'zaɪn] vt renunciar a ▷ vi dimitir; **to ~ o.s. to** (situation) resignarse a; **resignation** [rezɪg'neɪʃən] n dimisión f; (state of mind) resignación f

resin ['rezɪn] n resina

resist [rɪ'zɪst] vt resistir, oponerse a; **resistance** n resistencia

resit [riː'sɪt] (BRIT) (pt, pp **resat**) vt (exam) volver a presentarse a; (subject) recuperar, volver a examinarse de (SP)

resolution [rezə'luːʃən] n resolución f

resolve [rɪ'zɔlv] n resolución f ▷ vt resolver ▷ vi: **to ~ to do** resolver hacer

resort [rɪ'zɔːt] n (town) centro turístico; (recourse) recurso ▷ vi: **to ~ to** recurrir a; **in the last ~** como último recurso

resource [rɪ'sɔːs] n recurso; **resourceful** adj despabilado, ingenioso

respect [rɪs'pekt] n respeto ▷ vt respetar; **respectable** adj respetable; (large: amount) apreciable; (passable) tolerable; **respectful** adj respetuoso; **respective** adj respectivo; **respectively** adv respectivamente

respite ['respaɪt] n respiro

respond [rɪs'pɔnd] vi responder; (react) reaccionar; **response** [-'pɔns] n respuesta; reacción f

responsibility [rɪspɔnsɪ'bɪlɪtɪ] n responsabilidad f

responsible [rɪs'pɔnsɪbl] adj (character) serio, formal; (job) de confianza; (liable): **~ (for)** responsable (de); **responsibly** adv con seriedad

responsive [rɪs'pɔnsɪv] adj sensible

rest [rest] n descanso, reposo; (Mus, pause) pausa, silencio; (support) apoyo; (remainder) resto ▷ vi descansar; (be supported): **to ~ on** descansar sobre ▷ vt: **to ~ sth on/against** apoyar algo en or

r

restaurant | 504

sobre/contra; **the ~ of them** (people, objects) los demás; **it ~s with him to ...** depende de él el que ...

restaurant ['rɛstərən] n restaurante m; **restaurant car** (BRIT) n (Rail) coche-comedor m

restless ['rɛstlɪs] adj inquieto

restoration [rɛstə'reɪʃən] n restauración f; devolución f

restore [rɪ'stɔ:] vt (building) restaurar; (sth stolen) devolver; (health) restablecer; (to power) volver a poner a

restrain [rɪs'treɪn] vt (feeling) contener, refrenar; (person): **to ~ (from doing)** disuadir (de hacer); **restraint** n (restriction) restricción f; (moderation) moderación f; (of manner) reserva f

restrict [rɪs'trɪkt] vt restringir, limitar; **restriction** [-kʃən] n restricción f, limitación f

rest room (US) n aseos mpl

restructure [ri:'strʌktʃə*] vt reestructurar

result [rɪ'zʌlt] n resultado ▷ vi: **to ~ in** terminar en, tener por resultado; **as a ~ of** a consecuencia de

resume [rɪ'zju:m] vt reanudar ▷ vt comenzar de nuevo

  Be careful not to translate **resume** by the Spanish word *resumir*.

résumé ['reɪzju:meɪ] n resumen m; (us) currículum m

resuscitate [rɪ'sʌsɪteɪt] vt (Med) resucitar

retail ['ri:teɪl] adj, adv al por menor; **retailer** n detallista mf

retain [rɪ'teɪn] vt (keep) retener, conservar

retaliation [rɪtælɪ'eɪʃən] n represalias fpl

retarded [rɪ'tɑ:dɪd] adj retrasado

retire [rɪ'taɪə*] vi (give up work) jubilarse; (withdraw) retirarse; (go to bed) acostarse; **retired** adj (person) jubilado; **retirement** n (giving up work: state) retiro; (: act) jubilación f

retort [rɪ'tɔ:t] vi contestar

retreat [rɪ'tri:t] n (place) retiro; (Mil)

retirada ▷ vi retirarse

retrieve [rɪ'tri:v] vt recobrar; (situation, honour) salvar; (Comput) recuperar; (error) reparar

retrospect ['rɛtrəspɛkt] n: **in ~** retrospectivamente; **retrospective** [-'spektɪv] adj retrospectivo; (law) retroactivo

return [rɪ'tə:n] n (going or coming back) vuelta, regreso; (of sth stolen etc) devolución f; (Finance: from land, shares) ganancia, ingresos mpl ▷ cpd (journey) de regreso; (BRIT: ticket) de ida y vuelta; (match) de vuelta ▷ vi (person etc: come or go back) volver, regresar; (symptoms etc) reaparecer; (regain): **to ~ to** recuperar ▷ vt devolver; (favour, love etc) corresponder a; (verdict) pronunciar; (Pol: candidate) elegir; **returns** npl (Comm) ingresos mpl; **~ (for)** a cambio (de); **by ~ of post** a vuelta de correo; **many happy ~s (of the day)!** ¡feliz cumpleaños!; **return ticket** n (esp BRIT) billete m (SP) o boleto m (LAM) de ida y vuelta, billete m redondo (MEX)

reunion [ri:'ju:nɪən] n (of family) reunión f; (of two people, school) reencuentro

reunite [ri:ju:'naɪt] vt reunir; (reconcile) reconciliar

revamp [ri:'væmp] vt renovar

reveal [rɪ'vi:l] vt revelar; **revealing** adj revelador(a)

revel [rɛvl] vi: **to ~ in sth/in doing sth** gozar de algo/con hacer algo

revelation [rɛvə'leɪʃən] n revelación f

revenge [rɪ'vɛndʒ] n venganza; **to take ~ on** vengarse de

revenue ['rɛvənju:] n ingresos mpl, rentas fpl

Reverend ['rɛvərənd] adj (in titles): **the ~ John Smith** (Anglican) el Reverendo John Smith; (Catholic) el Padre John Smith; (Protestant) el Pastor John Smith

reversal [rɪ'və:sl] n (of order)

inversión f; (of direction, policy) cambio; (of decision) revocación f

revert [rɪ'vɜːt] vi: **to ~ to** volver a

review [rɪ'vjuː] n (magazine, Mil) revista; (of book, film) reseña; (us: examination) repaso, examen m ▷ vt repasar, examinar; (Mil) pasar revista a; (book, film) reseñar

revise [rɪ'vaɪz] vt (manuscript) corregir; (opinion) modificar; (price, procedure) revisar ▷ vi (study) repasar; **revision** [rɪ'vɪʒən] n corrección f; modificación f; (for exam) repaso

revival [rɪ'vaɪvəl] n (recovery) reanimación f; (of interest) renacimiento; (Theatre) reestreno; (of faith) despertar m

revive [rɪ'vaɪv] vt resucitar; (custom) restablecer; (hope) despertar; (play) reestrenar ▷ vi (person) volver en sí; (business) reactivarse

revolt [rɪ'vəult] n rebelión f ▷ vi rebelarse, sublevarse ▷ vt dar asco a, repugnar; **revolting** adj asqueroso, repugnante

revolution [rɛvə'luːʃən] n revolución f; **revolutionary** adj, n revolucionario/a m/f

revolve [rɪ'vɒlv] vi dar vueltas, girar; (life, discussion): **to ~ (a)round** girar en torno a

revolver [rɪ'vɒlvə*] n revólver m

reward [rɪ'wɔːd] n premio, recompensa ▷ vt: **to ~ (for)** recompensar o premiar (por); **rewarding** adj (fig) valioso

rewind [riː'waɪnd] vt rebobinar

rewritable [riː'raɪtəbl] adj (CD, DVD) reescribible

rewrite [riː'raɪt] (pt rewrote, pp rewritten) vt reescribir

rheumatism ['ruːmətɪzəm] n reumatismo, reúma m

rhinoceros [raɪ'nɒsərəs] n rinoceronte m

rhubarb ['ruːbɑːb] n ruibarbo

rhyme [raɪm] n rima; (verse) poesía

rhythm ['rɪðm] n ritmo

rib [rɪb] n (Anat) costilla ▷ vt (mock) tomar el pelo a

ribbon ['rɪbən] n cinta; **in ~s** (torn) hecho trizas

rice [raɪs] n arroz m; **rice pudding** n arroz m con leche

rich [rɪtʃ] adj rico; (soil) fértil; (food) pesado; (: sweet) empalagoso; (abundant): **~ in** (minerals etc) rico en

rid [rɪd] (pt, pp ~) vt: **to ~ sb of sth** librar a algn de algo; **to get ~ of** deshacerse o desembarazarse de

riddle ['rɪdl] n (puzzle) acertijo; (mystery) enigma m, misterio ▷ vt: **to be ~d with** ser lleno o plagado de

ride [raɪd] (pt rode, pp ridden) n paseo; (distance covered) viaje m, recorrido ▷ vi (as sport) montar; (go somewhere: on horse, bicycle) dar un paseo, pasearse; (travel: on bicycle, motorcycle, bus) viajar ▷ vt (a horse) montar a; (a bicycle, motorcycle) andar en; (distance) recorrer; **to take sb for a ~** (fig) engañar a algn; **rider** n (on horse) jinete mf; (on bicycle) ciclista mf; (on motorcycle) motociclista mf

ridge [rɪdʒ] n (of hill) cresta; (of roof) caballete m; (wrinkle) arruga

ridicule ['rɪdɪkjuːl] n irrisión f, burla ▷ vt poner en ridículo, burlarse de; **ridiculous** [rɪ'dɪkjuləs] adj ridículo

riding ['raɪdɪŋ] n equitación f; **I like ~** me gusta montar a caballo; **riding school** n escuela de equitación

rife [raɪf] adj: **to be ~** ser muy común; **to be ~ with** abundar en

rifle [ˈraɪfl] n rifle m, fusil m ▷ vt saquear

rift [rɪft] n (in clouds) claro; (fig: disagreement) desavenencia

rig [rɪɡ] n (also: **oil ~** at sea) plataforma petrolera ▷ vt (election etc) amañar

right [raɪt] adj (correct) correcto, exacto; (suitable) indicado, debido; (proper) apropiado; (just) justo; (morally good) bueno; (not left) derecho ▷ n bueno; (title, claim) derecho; (not left) derecha ▷ adv bien, correctamente; (not left) a la derecha; (exactly): **~ now** ahora mismo ▷ vt enderezar; (correct) corregir ▷ excl ¡bueno!, ¡está bien!; **to be ~** (person) tener razón; (answer) ser correcto; **is that the ~ time?** (of clock) ¿es esa la hora buena?; **by ~s** en justicia; **on the ~** a la derecha; **to be in the ~** tener razón; **~ away** en seguida; **~ in the middle** exactamente en el centro; **right angle** n ángulo recto; **rightful** adj legítimo; **right-hand** adj: **right-hand drive** conducción f por la derecha; **the right-hand side** derecha; **right-handed** adj diestro; **rightly** adv correctamente, debidamente; (with reason) con razón; **right of way** n (on path etc) derecho de paso; (Aut) prioridad f de paso; **right-wing** adj (Pol) derechista

rigid [ˈrɪdʒɪd] adj rígido; (person, ideas) inflexible

rigorous [ˈrɪɡərəs] adj riguroso

rim [rɪm] n borde m; (of spectacles) aro; (of wheel) llanta

rind [raɪnd] n (of bacon) corteza; (of lemon etc) cáscara; (of cheese) costra

ring [rɪŋ] n (of metal) aro; (on finger) anillo; (of people) corro; (of objects) círculo; (gang) banda; (for boxing) cuadrilátero; (of circus) pista; (bull ring) ruedo, plaza; (sound of bell) toque m ▷ vi (on telephone) llamar por teléfono; (bell) repicar; (doorbell, phone) sonar; (also: **~ out**) sonar; (ears) zumbar ▷ vt (Brit Tel) llamar, telefonear; (bell etc) hacer sonar;

(doorbell) tocar; **to give sb a ~** (Brit Tel) llamar or telefonear a algn; **ring back** (Brit) vt, vi (Tel) devolver la llamada; **ring off** (Brit) vi (Tel) colgar, cortar la comunicación; **ring up** (Brit) vt (Tel) llamar, telefonear; **ringing tone** n (Tel) tono de llamada; **ringleader** n (of gang) cabecilla m; **ring road** (Brit) n carretera periférica or de circunvalación; **ringtone** n (on mobile) tono de llamada

rink [rɪŋk] n (also: **ice ~**) pista de hielo

rinse [rɪns] n aclarado; (dye) tinte m ▷ vt aclarar; (mouth) enjuagar

riot [ˈraɪət] n motín m, disturbio ▷ vi amotinarse; **to run ~** desmandarse

rip [rɪp] n rasgón m, rasgadura ▷ vt rasgar, desgarrar ▷ vi rasgarse, desgarrarse; **rip off** vt (inf: cheat) estafar; **rip up** vt hacer pedazos

ripe [raɪp] adj maduro

rip-off [ˈrɪpɔf] n (inf): **it's a ~!** ¡es una estafa!, ¡es un timo!

ripple [ˈrɪpl] n onda, rizo; (sound) murmullo ▷ vi rizarse

rise [raɪz] (pt **rose**, pp **risen**) n (slope) cuesta, pendiente f; (hill) altura; (Brit: in wages) aumento; (in prices, temperature) subida; (fig: to power etc) ascenso ▷ vi subir; (waters) crecer; (sun, moon) salir; (person: from bed etc) levantarse; (also: **~ up**: rebel) sublevarse; (in rank) ascender; **to give ~ to** dar lugar or origen a; **to ~ to the occasion** ponerse a la altura de las circunstancias; **risen** [ˈrɪzn] pp of **rise**; **rising** adj (increasing: number) creciente; (: prices) en aumento or alza; (tide) creciente; (sun, moon) naciente

risk [rɪsk] n riesgo, peligro ▷ vt arriesgar; (run the risk of) exponerse a; **to take or run the ~ of doing** correr el riesgo de hacer; **at ~** en peligro; **at one's own ~** bajo su propia responsabilidad; **risky** adj arriesgado, peligroso

rite [raɪt] n rito; **last ~s** exequias fpl

ritual [ˈrɪtjuəl] adj ritual ▷ n ritual

m, rito

rival ['raɪvl] n rival mf; (in business) competidor(a) m/f ▷ adj rival, opuesto ▷ vt competir con; **rivalry** n competencia

river ['rɪvə*] n río ▷ cpd de río; (traffic) fluvial; **up/down** ~ río arriba/ abajo; **riverbank** n orilla (del río)

rivet ['rɪvɪt] n roblón m, remache m ▷ vt (fig) captar

road [rəud] n camino; (motorway etc) carretera; (in town) calle f ▷ cpd (accident) de tráfico; **major/minor** ~ carretera principal/secundaria; **roadblock** n barricada; **road map** n mapa m de carreteras; **road rage** n agresividad en la carretera; **road safety** n seguridad f vial; **roadside** n borde m (del camino); **roadsign** n señal f de tráfico; **road tax** n (Aut) impuesto de rodaje; **roadworks** npl obras fpl

roam [rəum] vi vagar

roar [rɔ:*] n rugido; (of vehicle, storm) estruendo; (of laughter) carcajada ▷ vi rugir; hacer estruendo; **to ~ with laughter** reírse a carcajadas; **to do a ~ing trade** hacer buen negocio

roast [rəust] n carne f asada, asado ▷ vt asar; (coffee) tostar; **roast beef** n rosbif m

rob [rɔb] vt robar; **to ~ sb of sth** robar algo a algn; (fig: deprive) quitar algo a algn; **robber** n ladrón/ona m/f; **robbery** n robo

robe [rəub] n (for ceremony etc) toga; (also: **bath~**) albornoz m

robin ['rɔbɪn] n petirrojo

robot ['rəubɔt] n robot m

robust [rəu'bʌst] adj robusto, fuerte

rock [rɔk] n roca; (boulder) peña, peñasco; (us: small stone) piedrecita; (BRIT: sweet) = pirulí ▷ vt (swing gently: cradle) balancear, mecer; (: child) arrullar; (shake) sacudir ▷ vi mecerse, balancearse; sacudirse; **on the ~s** (drink) con hielo; (marriage etc) en ruinas; **rock and roll** n rocanrol m; **rock climbing** n (Sport) escalada

rocket ['rɔkɪt] n cohete m; **rocking chair** n mecedora

rocky ['rɔkɪ] adj rocoso

rod [rɔd] n vara, varilla; (also: **fishing ~**) caña

rode [rəud] pt of **ride**

rodent ['rəudnt] n roedor m

rogue [rəug] n pícaro, pillo

role [rəul] n papel m; **role-model** n modelo a imitar

roll [rəul] n rollo; (of bank notes) fajo; (also: **bread ~**) panecillo; (register, list) lista, nómina; (sound of drums etc) redoble m ▷ vt hacer rodar; (also: ~ **up**: string) enrollar; (cigarette) liar; (also: ~ **out**: pastry) aplanar; (flatten: road, lawn) apisonar ▷ vi rodar; (drum) redoblar; (ship) balancearse; **roll over** vi dar una vuelta; **roll up** vi (inf: arrive) aparecer ▷ vt (carpet) arrollar; (: sleeves) arremangar; **roller** n rodillo; (wheel) rueda; (for road) apisonadora; (for hair) rulo; **Rollerblades®** npl patines mpl en línea; **roller-skating** n montaña rusa; **roller skates** npl patines mpl de ruedas; **roller-skating** n patinaje sobre ruedas; **to go roller-skating** ir a patinar (sobre ruedas); **rolling pin** n rodillo (de cocina)

ROM [rɔm] n abbr (Comput: = read only memory) ROM f

Roman ['rəumən] adj romano/a; **Roman Catholic** (irreg) adj, n católico/a m/f (romano/a)

romance [rə'mæns] n (love affair) amor m; (charm) lo romántico; (novel) novela de amor

Romania etc [ru:'meɪnɪə] n = **Rumania** etc

Roman numeral n número romano

romantic [rə'mæntɪk] adj romántico

Rome [rəum] n Roma

roof [ru:f] (pl ~**s**) n techo; (of house) techo, tejado ▷ vt techar, poner techo a; **the ~ of the mouth** el paladar; **roof rack** n (Aut) baca, portaequipajes m inv

rook [ruk] n (bird) graja; (Chess) torre f

room [ru:m] n cuarto, habitación f; (also: **~ bed-**) dormitorio, recámara (MEX), pieza (SC); (in school etc) sala; (space, scope) sitio, cabida; **roommate** n compañero/a de cuarto; **room service** n servicio de habitaciones; **roomy** adj espacioso; (garment) amplio

rooster ['ru:stə*] n gallo

root [ru:t] n raíz f ▷ vi arraigarse

rope [rəup] n cuerda; (Naut) cable m ▷ vt (tie) atar o amarrar con (una) cuerda; (climbers: also: **~ together**) encordarse; (an area: also: **~ off**) acordonar; **to know the ~s** (fig) conocer los trucos (del oficio)

rose [rəuz] pt of **rise** ▷ n rosa; (shrub) rosal m; (on watering can) roseta

rosé ['rəuzeɪ] n vino rosado

rosemary ['rəuzməri] n romero

rosy ['rəuzɪ] adj rosado, sonrosado; **a ~ future** un futuro prometedor

rot [rɒt] n podredumbre f; (fig: pej) tonterías fpl ▷ vt pudrir ▷ vi pudrirse

rota ['rəutə] n (sistema m de) turnos m

rotate [rəu'teɪt] vt (revolve) hacer girar, dar vueltas a; (jobs) alternar ▷ vi girar, dar vueltas

rotten ['rɒtn] adj podrido; (dishonest) corrompido; (inf: bad) pocho; **to feel ~** (ill) sentirse fatal

rough [rʌf] adj (skin, surface) áspero; (terrain) quebrado; (road) desigual; (voice) bronco; (person, manner) tosco, grosero; (weather) borrascoso; (treatment) brutal; (sea) picado; (town, area) peligroso; (cloth) basto; (plan) preliminar; (guess) aproximado ▷ n (Golf): **in the ~** en las hierbas altas; **to ~ it** vivir sin comodidades; **to sleep ~** (BRIT) pasar la noche al raso; **roughly** adv (handle) torpemente; (make) toscamente; (speak) groseramente; (approximately) aproximadamente

roulette [ru:'let] n ruleta

round [raund] adj redondo ▷ n círculo; (BRIT: of toast) rebanada;

(of policeman) ronda; (of milkman) recorrido; (of doctor) visitas fpl; (game: of cards, in competition) partida; (of ammunition) cartucho; (Boxing) asalto; (of talks) ronda ▷ vt (corner) doblar ▷ prep alrededor de; (surrounding): **~ his neck/the table** en su cuello/alrededor de la mesa; (in a circular movement): **to move ~ the room/sail ~ the world** dar una vuelta a la habitación/ circunnavigar el mundo; (in various directions): **to move ~ a room/house** moverse por toda la habitación/casa; (approximately) alrededor de ▷ adv: **all ~** por todos lados; **the long way ~** por el camino menos directo; **all (the) year ~** durante todo el año; **it's just ~ the corner** (fig) está a la vuelta de la esquina; **~ the clock** adv las 24 horas; **to go ~ to sb's (house)** ir a casa de algn; **to go ~ the back** pasar por atrás; **enough to go ~** bastante (para todos); **a ~ of applause** una salva de aplausos; **a ~ of drinks/sandwiches** una ronda de bebidas/bocadillos; **round off** vt (speech etc) acabar, poner término a; **round up** vt (cattle) acorralar; (people) reunir; (price) redondear; **roundabout** (BRIT) n (Aut) isleta; (at fair) tiovivo ▷ adj (route, means) indirecto; **round trip** n viaje m de ida y vuelta; **roundup** n rodeo; (of criminals) redada; (of news) resumen m

rouse [rauz] vt (wake up) despertar; (stir up) suscitar

route [ru:t] n ruta, camino; (of bus) recorrido; (of shipping) derrota

routine [ru:'ti:n] adj rutinario ▷ n rutina; (Theatre) número

row¹ [rəu] n (Tin) fila, hilera; (Knitting) pasada ▷ vi (in boat) remar ▷ vt conducir remando; **4 days in a ~** 4 días seguidos

row² [rau] n (dispute) bronca, pelea; (scolding) regaño ▷ vi pelear(se)

rowboat ['rəubəut] (US) = **rowing boat**

rowing ['rəʊɪŋ] n remo; **rowing boat** (BRIT) n bote m de remos

royal ['rɔɪəl] adj real; **royalty** n (royal persons) familia real; (payment to author) derechos mpl de autor

rpm abbr (= revs per minute) r.p.m.

R.S.V.P. abbr (= répondez s'il vous plaôt) SRC

Rt. Hon. abbr (BRIT) (= Right Honourable) título honorífico de diputado

rub [rʌb] vt frotar; (scrub) restregar ▷ n: **to give sth a ~** frotar algo; **to ~ sb up** or **~ sb** (us) **the wrong way** entrarle algn por mal ojo; **rub in** vt (ointment) aplicar frotando; **rub off** vi borrarse; **rub out** vt borrar

rubber ['rʌbə*] n caucho, goma; (BRIT: eraser) goma de borrar; **rubber band** n goma, gomita; **rubber gloves** npl guantes mpl de goma

rubbish ['rʌbɪʃ] (BRIT) n basura; (waste) desperdicios mpl; (fig: pej) tonterías fpl; (junk) pacotilla; **rubbish bin** (BRIT) n cubo or bote m (MEX) or tacho (SC) de la basura; **rubbish dump** (BRIT) n vertedero, basurero

rubble ['rʌbl] n escombros mpl

ruby ['ruːbɪ] n rubí m

rucksack ['rʌksæk] n mochila

rudder ['rʌdə*] n timón m

rude [ruːd] adj (impolite: person) mal educado; (: word, manners) grosero; (crude) crudo; (indecent) indecente

ruffle ['rʌfl] vt (hair) despeinar; (clothes) arrugar; **to get ~d** (fig: person) alterarse

rug [rʌg] n alfombra; (BRIT: blanket) manta

rugby ['rʌgbɪ] n rugby m

rugged ['rʌgɪd] adj (landscape) accidentado; (features) robusto

ruin ['ruːɪn] n ruina ▷ vt arruinar; (spoil) estropear; **ruins** npl ruinas fpl, restos mpl

rule [ruːl] n (norm) norma, costumbre f; (regulation, ruler) regla; (government) dominio ▷ vt gobernar ▷ vi gobernar; (Law) fallar;

as a ~ por regla general; **rule out** vt excluir; **ruler** n (sovereign) soberano; (for measuring) regla; **ruling** adj (party) gobernante; (class) dirigente ▷ n (Law) fallo, decisión f

rum [rʌm] n ron m

Rumania [ruːˈmeɪnɪə] n Rumanía; **Rumanian** adj rumano/a ▷ n rumano/a m/f; (Ling) rumano

rumble ['rʌmbl] n (noise) ruido sordo ▷ vi retumbar, hacer un ruido sordo; (stomach, pipe) sonar

rumour ['ruːmə*] (US **rumor**) n rumor m ▷ vt: **it is ~ed that ...** se rumorea que ...

rump steak n filete m de lomo

run [rʌn] (pt **ran**, pp **run**) n (fast pace): **at a ~** corriendo; (Sport, in tights) carrera; (outing) paseo, excursión f; (distance travelled) trayecto; (series) serie f; (Theatre) temporada; (Ski) pista ▷ vt correr; (operate: business) dirigir; (: competition, course) organizar; (: hotel, house) administrar, llevar; (Comput) ejecutar; (pass: hand) pasar; (Press: feature) publicar ▷ vi correr; (work: machine) funcionar, marchar; (bus, train: operate) circular, ir; (: travel) ir; (continue: play) seguir; (contract) ser válido; (flow: river) fluir; (colours, washing) desteñirse; (in election) ser candidato; **there was a ~ on** (meat, tickets) hubo mucha demanda de; **in the long ~** a la larga; **on the ~** en fuga; **I'll ~ you to the station** te llevaré a la estación (en coche); **to ~ a risk** correr un riesgo; **run after** vt fus (to catch up) correr tras; (chase) perseguir; **run away** vi huir; **run down** vt (production) ir reduciendo; (factory) ir restringiendo la producción en; (car) atropellar; (criticize) criticar; **to be run down** (person: tired) estar debilitado; **run into** vt fus (meet: person, trouble) tropezar con; (collide with) chocar con; **run off** vt (water) dejar correr; (copies) sacar ▷ vi huir corriendo; **run out** vi (person) salir corriendo; (liquid) irse; (lease) caducar, vencer; (money etc) acabarse; **run out of** vt fus quedarse sin; **run over** vt (Aut) atropellar ▷vt fus (revise) repasar; **run through** vt fus (instructions) repasar; **run up** vt (debt) contraer; **to run up against** (difficulties) tropezar con; **runaway** adj (horse) desbocado; (truck) sin frenos; (child) escapado de casa

rung [rʌŋ] pp of **ring** ▷n (of ladder) escalón m, peldaño

runner ['rʌnə*] n (in race: person) corredor(a) m/f; (: horse) caballo; (on sledge) patín m; **runner bean** (BRIT) n = judía verde; **runner-up** n subcampeón/ona m/f

running ['rʌnɪŋ] n (sport) atletismo; (of business) administración f ▷ adj (water, costs) corriente; (commentary) continuo; **to be in/out of the ~ for sth** tener/no tener posibilidades de ganar algo; **6 days ~** 6 días seguidos

runny ['rʌnɪ] adj fluido; (nose, eyes) gastante

run-up ['rʌnʌp] n: **~ to** (election etc) período previo a

runway ['rʌnweɪ] n (Aviat) pista de aterrizaje

rupture ['rʌptʃə*] n (Med) hernia ▷vt: **to ~ o.s** causarse una hernia

rural ['ruərl] adj rural

rush [rʌʃ] n ímpetu m; (hurry) prisa; (Comm) demanda repentina; (current) corriente f fuerte; (of feeling) torrente m; (Bot) junco ▷vt apresurar; (work) hacer de prisa ▷vi correr, precipitarse; **rush hour** n horas fpl punta

Russia ['rʌʃə] n Rusia; **Russian** adj ruso ▷n ruso/a m/f; (Ling) ruso

rust [rʌst] n herrumbre f, moho ▷vi oxidarse

rusty ['rʌstɪ] adj oxidado

ruthless ['ruːθlɪs] adj despiadado

RV (US) n abbr = **recreational vehicle**

rye [raɪ] n centeno

S

Sabbath ['sæbəθ] n domingo; (Jewish) sábado

sabotage ['sæbətɑːʒ] n sabotaje m ▷vt sabotear

saccharin(e) ['sækərɪn] n sacarina

sachet ['sæʃeɪ] n sobrecito

sack [sæk] n (bag) saco, costal m ▷vt (dismiss) despedir; (plunder) saquear; **to get the ~** ser despedido

sacred ['seɪkrɪd] adj sagrado, santo

sacrifice ['sækrɪfaɪs] n sacrificio ▷vt sacrificar

sad [sæd] adj (unhappy) triste; (deplorable) lamentable

saddle ['sædl] n silla (de montar); (of cycle) sillín m ▷vt (horse) ensillar; **to be ~d with sth** (inf) quedar cargado con algo

sadistic [sə'dɪstɪk] adj sádico

sadly ['sædlɪ] adv lamentablemente; **to be ~ lacking in** estar por desgracia carente de

sadness ['sædnɪs] n tristeza

s.a.e. abbr (= stamped addressed envelope) sobre con las propias señas de uno y con sello

safari [sə'fɑːrɪ] n safari m

safe [seɪf] adj (out of danger) fuera de peligro; (not dangerous, sure) seguro; (unharmed) ileso ▷ n caja de caudales, caja fuerte; **~ and sound** sano y salvo; **(just) to be on the ~ side** para mayor seguridad; **safely** adv seguramente, con seguridad; **to arrive safely** llegar bien; **safe sex** n sexo seguro or sin riesgo

safety ['seɪftɪ] n seguridad f; **safety belt** n cinturón m (de seguridad); **safety pin** n imperdible m, seguro (MEX), alfiler m de gancho (SC)

saffron ['sæfrən] n azafrán m

sag [sæɡ] vi aflojarse

sage [seɪdʒ] n (herb) salvia; (man) sabio

Sagittarius [sædʒɪ'tɛərɪəs] n Sagitario

Sahara [sə'hɑːrə] n: **the ~ (Desert)** n (desierto del) Sáhara

said [sɛd] pt, pp of **say**

sail [seɪl] n (on boat) vela; (trip): **to go for a ~** dar un paseo en barco ▷ vt (boat) gobernar ▷ vi (travel: ship) navegar; (Sport) hacer vela; (begin voyage) salir; **they ~ed into Copenhagen** arribaron a Copenhague; **sailboat** (US) n = **sailing boat**; **sailing** ['seɪlɪŋ] n (Sport) vela; **to go sailing** hacer vela; **sailing boat** n barco de vela; **sailor** n marinero, marino

saint [seɪnt] n santo

sake [seɪk] n: **for the ~ of** por

salad ['sæləd] n ensalada; **salad cream** (BRIT) n (especie f de) mayonesa; **salad dressing** n aliño

salami [sə'lɑːmɪ] n salami m, salchichón m

salary ['sælərɪ] n sueldo

sale [seɪl] n venta; (at reduced prices) liquidación f, saldo; (auction) subasta; **sales** npl (total amount sold) ventas fpl, facturación f; **"for ~"** "se vende"; **on ~** en venta; **on ~ or return** (goods) venta por reposición; **sales assistant** (US),

sales clerk n dependiente/a m/f;

salesman/woman (irreg) n (in shop) dependiente/a m/f; (representative) n vendedor(a) m/f; **salesperson** (irreg) n vendedor(a) m/f, dependiente/a m/f; **sales rep** n representante mf, agente mf comercial

saline ['seɪlaɪn] adj salino

saliva [sə'laɪvə] n saliva

salmon ['sæmən] n inv salmón m

salon ['sælɔn] n (hairdressing salon) peluquería; (beauty salon) salón m de belleza

saloon [sə'luːn] n (US) bar m, taberna; (BRIT Aut) coche m (de) turismo; (ship's lounge) cámara, salón m

salt [sɔlt] n sal f ▷ vt salar; (put salt on) poner sal en; **saltwater** adj de agua salada; **salty** adj salado

salute [sə'luːt] n saludo; (of guns) salva ▷ vt saludar

salvage ['sælvɪdʒ] n (saving) salvamento, recuperación f; (things saved) objetos mpl salvados ▷ vt salvar

Salvation Army [sæl'veɪʃən-] n Ejército de Salvación

same [seɪm] adj mismo ▷ pron: **the ~** el(la) mismo/a, los(las) mismos/as; **the ~ book as** el mismo libro que; **at the ~ time** (at the same moment) al mismo tiempo; (yet) sin embargo; **all** or **just the ~** sin embargo, aun así; **to do the ~ (as sb)** hacer lo mismo (que algn); **the ~ to you!** ¡igualmente!

sample ['sɑːmpl] n muestra ▷ vt (food) probar; (wine) catar

sanction ['sæŋkʃən] n aprobación f ▷ vt sancionar; aprobar; **sanctions** npl (Pol) sanciones fpl

sanctuary ['sæŋktjuərɪ] n santuario; (refuge) asilo, refugio; (for wildlife) reserva

sand [sænd] n arena; (beach) playa ▷ vt (also: **~ down**) lijar

sandal ['sændl] n sandalia

sand: sandbox (US) n = **sandpit; sandcastle** n castillo de arena; **sand dune** n duna; **sandpaper** n papel m de lija; **sandpit** n (for children) cajón m

de arena; **sands** npl playa sg de arena;
sandstone ['sændstəʊn] n piedra
arenisca
sandwich ['sændwɪtʃ] n sandwich
m ▷vt intercalar; **~ed between**
apretujado entre; **cheese/ham ~**
sandwich de queso/jamón
sandy ['sændɪ] adj arenoso; (colour)
rojizo
sane [seɪn] adj cuerdo; (sensible)
sensato

Be careful not to translate **sane** by
the Spanish word sano.

sang [sæŋ] pt of **sing**
sanitary towel (us **sanitary napkin**)
n paño higiénico, compresa
sanity ['sænɪtɪ] n cordura; (of
judgment) sensatez f
sank [sæŋk] pt of **sink**
Santa Claus [sæntə'klɔːz] n San
Nicolás, Papá Noel
sap [sæp] n (of plants) savia ▷vt
(strength) minar, agotar
sapphire ['sæfaɪə*] n zafiro
sarcasm ['sɑːkæzm] n sarcasmo
sarcastic [sɑːˈkæstɪk] adj sarcástico
sardine [sɑːˈdiːn] n sardina
SASE (us) n abbr (= self-addressed
stamped envelope) sobre con las propias
señas de uno y con sello
Sat. abbr (= Saturday) sáb
sat [sæt] pt, pp of **sit**
satchel ['sætʃl] n (child's) mochila,
cartera (SP)
satellite ['sætəlaɪt] n satélite m;
satellite dish n antena de televisión
por satélite; **satellite television** n
televisión f vía satélite
satin ['sætɪn] n raso ▷adj de raso
satire ['sætaɪə*] n sátira
satisfaction [sætɪsˈfækʃən] n
satisfacción f
satisfactory [sætɪsˈfæktərɪ] adj
satisfactorio
satisfied ['sætɪsfaɪd] adj satisfecho;
to be ~ (with sth) estar satisfecho
(de algo)
satisfy ['sætɪsfaɪ] vt satisfacer;

(convince) convencer
Saturday ['sætədɪ] n sábado
sauce [sɔːs] n salsa; (sweet) crema;
jarabe m; **saucepan** n cacerola, olla
saucer ['sɔːsə*] n platillo; **Saudi
Arabia** n Arabia Saudí or Saudita
sauna ['sɔːnə] n sauna
sausage ['sɒsɪdʒ] n salchicha;
sausage roll n empanadita de
salchicha
sautéed ['səʊteɪd] adj salteado
savage ['sævɪdʒ] adj (cruel, fierce)
feroz, furioso; (primitive) salvaje ▷n
salvaje mf ▷vt (attack) embestir
save [seɪv] vt (rescue) salvar, rescatar;
(money, time) ahorrar; (put by, keep: seat)
guardar; (Comput) salvar (y guardar);
(avoid: trouble) evitar; (Sport) parar ▷vi
(also: **~ up**) ahorrar ▷n (Sport) parada
▷prep salvo, excepto
savings ['seɪvɪŋz] npl ahorros mpl;
savings account n cuenta de ahorros;
savings and loan association (us) n
sociedad f de ahorro y préstamo
savoury ['seɪvərɪ] (us **savory**) adj
sabroso; (dish: not sweet) salado
saw [sɔː] (pt **~ed**, pp **~ed** or **~n**) pt
of **see** ▷n (tool) sierra ▷vt serrar;
sawdust n (a) serrín m
sawn [sɔːn] pp of **saw**
saxophone ['sæksəfəʊn] n saxófono
say [seɪ] (pt, pp **said**) n: **to have one's
~** expresar su opinión ▷vt decir; **to
have a** or **some ~ in sth** tener voz or
tener que ver en algo; **to ~ yes/no** decir
que sí/no; **could you ~ that again?**
¿podría repetir eso?; **that is to ~** es
decir; **that goes without ~ing** ni que
decir tiene; **saying** n dicho, refrán m
scab [skæb] n costra; (pej) esquirol m
scaffolding ['skæfəldɪŋ] n andamio,
andamiaje m
scald [skɔːld] n escaldadura ▷vt
escaldar
scale [skeɪl] n (gen, Mus) escala;
(of fish) escama; (of salaries, fees
etc) escalafón m ▷vt (mountain)
escalar; (tree) trepar; **scales** npl (for

weighing: *small*) balanza; (: *large*)
báscula; **on a large ~** en gran escala; **~
of charges** tarifa, lista de precios

scallion ['skæljən] (*us*) *n* cebolleta

scallop ['skɔləp] *n* (*Zool*) venera;
(*Sewing*) festón *m*

scalp [skælp] *n* cabellera ▷ *vt*
escalpar

scalpel ['skælpl] *n* bisturí *m*

scam [skæm] *n* (*inf*) estafa, timo

scampi ['skæmpi] *npl* gambas *fpl*

scan [skæn] *vt* (*examine*) escudriñar;
(*glance at quickly*) dar un vistazo a; (*TV,
Radar*) explorar, registrar ▷ *n* (*Med*): **to
have a ~** pasar por el escáner

scandal ['skændl] *n* escándalo *m*;
(*gossip*) chismes *mpl*

Scandinavia [skændɪ'neɪvɪə] *n*
Escandinavia; **Scandinavian** *adj, n*
escandinavo/a *m/f*

scanner ['skænə*] *n* (*Radar, Med*)
escáner *m*

scapegoat ['skeɪpgəʊt] *n* cabeza de
turco, chivo expiatorio

scar [skɑː] *n* cicatriz *f*; (*fig*) señal *f* ▷ *vt*
dejar señales en

scarce [skɛəs] *adj* escaso; **to make
o.s. ~** (*inf*) esfumarse; **scarcely** *adv*
apenas

scare [skɛə*] *n* susto, sobresalto;
(*panic*) pánico ▷ *vt* asustar, espantar;
to ~ sb stiff dar a algn un susto de
muerte; **bomb ~** amenaza de bomba;
scarecrow *n* espantapájaros *m
inv*; **scared** *adj*: **to be scared** estar
asustado

scarf [skɑːf] (*pl* **~s** *or* **scarves**) *n* (*long*)
bufanda; (*square*) pañuelo

scarlet ['skɑːlɪt] *adj* escarlata

scarves [skɑːvz] *npl of* **scarf**

scary ['skɛərɪ] (*inf*) *adj* espeluznante

scatter ['skætə*] *vt* (*spread*) esparcir,
desparramar; (*put to flight*) dispersar
▷ *vi* desparramarse; dispersarse

scenario [sɪ'nɑːrɪəʊ] *n* (*Theatre*)
argumento; (*Cinema*) guión *m*; (*fig*)
escenario

scene [siːn] *n* (*Theatre, fig etc*)

escena; (*of crime etc*) escenario; (*view*)
panorama *m*; (*fuss*) escándalo; **scenery**
n (*Theatre*) decorado; (*landscape*)
paisaje *m*

Be careful not to translate **scenery**
by the Spanish word *escenario*.

scenic *adj* pintoresco

scent [sɛnt] *n* perfume *m*, olor *m*;
(*fig: track*) rastro, pista

sceptical ['skɛptɪkl] *adj* escéptico

schedule ['ʃɛdjuːl] (*us*) ['skɛdjuːl] *n*
(*timetable*) horario; (*of events*) programa
m; (*list*) lista ▷ *vt* (*visit*) fijar la hora
de; **to arrive on ~** llegar a la hora
debida; **to be ahead of/behind ~** estar
adelantado/en retraso; **scheduled
flight** *n* vuelo regular

scheme [skiːm] *n* (*plan*) plan *m*,
proyecto; (*plot*) intriga; (*arrangement*)
disposición *f*; (*pension scheme etc*)
sistema *m* ▷ *vi* (*intrigue*) intrigar

schizophrenic [skɪtzə'frɛnɪk] *adj*
esquizofrénico

scholar ['skɔlə*] *n* (*pupil*) alumno/a;
(*learned person*) sabio/a, erudito/a;
scholarship *n* erudición *f*; (*grant*) beca

school [skuːl] *n* escuela, colegio;
(*in university*) facultad *f* ▷ *cpd* escolar;
schoolbook *n* libro de texto;
schoolboy *n* alumno; **school
children** *npl* alumnos *mpl*; **schoolgirl**
n alumna; **schooling** *n* enseñanza;
schoolteacher *n* (*primary*) maestro/a;
(*secondary*) profesor/a *m/f*

science ['saɪəns] *n* ciencia; **science
fiction** *n* ciencia-ficción *f*; **scientific**
['-'tɪfɪk] *adj* científico; **scientist** *n*
científico/a

sci-fi ['saɪfaɪ] *n abbr* (*inf*) = **science
fiction**

scissors ['sɪzəz] *npl* tijeras *fpl*; **a pair
of ~** unas tijeras

scold [skəʊld] *vt* regañar

scone [skɔn] *n* pastel de pan

scoop [skuːp] *n* (*for flour etc*) pala;
(*Press*) exclusiva

scooter ['skuːtə*] *n* moto *f*; (*toy*)
patinete *m*

scope [skəup] n (of plan) ámbito; (of person) competencia; (opportunity) libertad f (de acción)

scorching ['skɔːtʃɪŋ] adj (heat, sun) abrasador(a)

score [skɔː*] n (points etc) puntuación f; (Mus) partitura; (twenty) veintena ▷ vt (goal, point) ganar; (mark) rayar; (achieve: success) conseguir ▷ vi marcar un tanto; (Football) marcar (un) gol; (keep score) llevar el tanteo; **~ s of** (lots of) decenas de; **on that ~** en lo que se refiere a eso; **to ~ 6 out of 10** obtener una puntuación de 6 sobre 10; **score out** vt tachar; **scoreboard** n marcador m; **scorer** n marcador m; (keeping score) encargado/a del marcador

scorn [skɔːn] n desprecio

Scorpio ['skɔːpɪəu] n Escorpión m

scorpion ['skɔːpɪən] n alacrán m

Scot [skɔt] n escocés/esa m/f

Scotch tape® (us) n cinta adhesiva, celo, scotch® m

Scotland ['skɔtlənd] n Escocia

Scots [skɔts] adj escocés/esa;
Scotsman (irreg) n escocés;
Scotswoman (irreg) n escocesa;
Scottish ['skɔtɪʃ] adj escocés/esa;
Scottish Parliament n Parlamento escocés

scout [skaut] n (Mil: also: **boy ~**) explorador m; **girl ~** (us) niña exploradora

scowl [skaul] vi fruncir el ceño; **~ at sb** mirar con ceño a algn

scramble ['skræmbl] n (climb) subida (difícil); (struggle) pelea ▷ vi **to ~ through/out** abrirse paso/salir con dificultad; **to ~ for** pelear por; **scrambled eggs** npl huevos mpl revueltos

scrap [skræp] n (bit) pedacito; (fig) pizca; (fight) riña, bronca; (also: **~ iron**) chatarra, hierro viejo ▷ vt (discard) desechar, descartar ▷ vi reñir, armar una bronca; **scraps** npl (waste) sobras fpl, desperdicios mpl; **scrapbook**

álbum m de recortes

scrape [skreɪp] n: **to get into a ~** meterse en un lío ▷ vt raspar; (skin etc) rasguñar; (scrape against) rozar ▷ vi: **to ~ through** (exam) aprobar por los pelos; **scrap paper** n pedazos mpl de papel

scratch [skrætʃ] n rasguño; (from claw) arañazo ▷ vt (paint, car) rayar; (with claw, nail) rasguñar, arañar; (rub: nose etc) rascarse ▷ vi rascarse; **to start from ~** partir de cero; **to be up to ~** cumplir con los requisitos; **scratch card** n (BRIT) tarjeta f de "rasque y gane"

scream [skriːm] n chillido ▷ vi chillar

screen [skriːn] n (Cinema, TV) pantalla; (movable barrier) biombo ▷ vt (conceal) tapar; (from the wind etc) proteger; (film) proyectar; (candidates etc) investigar a; **screening** n (Med) investigación f médica; **screenplay** n guión m; **screen saver** n (Comput) protector m de pantalla

screw [skruː] n tornillo ▷ vt (also: **~ in**) atornillar; **screw up** vt (paper etc) arrugar; **to screw up one's eyes** arrugar el entrecejo; **screwdriver** n destornillador m

scribble ['skrɪbl] n garabatos mpl ▷ vt, vi garabatear

script [skrɪpt] n (Cinema etc) guión m; (writing) escritura, letra

scroll [skrəul] n rollo

scrub [skrʌb] n (land) maleza ▷ vt fregar, restregar; (inf: reject) cancelar, anular

scruffy ['skrʌfɪ] adj desaliñado, piojoso

scrum(mage) ['skrʌm(mɪdʒ)] n (Rugby) melée f

scrutiny ['skruːtɪnɪ] n escrutinio, examen m

scuba diving ['skuːbə'daɪvɪŋ] n submarinismo

sculptor ['skʌlptə*] n escultor(a) m/f

sculpture ['skʌlptʃə*] n escultura

scum [skʌm] n (on liquid) espuma;

(pej: people) escoria

scurry ['skʌrɪ] vi correr; **to ~ off**
escabullirse

sea [si:] n mar ▷ cpd de mar,
marítimo; **by ~** (travel) en barco; **on the
~** (boat) en el mar; (town) junto al mar;
to be all at ~ (fig) estar despistado;
out to ~, **at ~** en alta mar; **seafood** n
mariscos mpl; **sea front** n paseo
marítimo; **seagull** n gaviota

seal [si:l] n (animal) foca; (stamp) sello
▷ vt (close) cerrar; **seal off** vt (area)
acordonar

sea level n nivel m del mar

seam [si:m] n costura; (of metal)
juntura; (of coal) veta, filón m

search [sə:tʃ] n (for person, thing)
busca, búsqueda; (Comput) búsqueda;
(inspection of sb's home) registro ▷ vt
(look in) buscar en; (examine) examinar;
(person, place) registrar ▷ vi: **to ~ for**
buscar; **in ~ of** en busca de; **search
engine** n (Comput) buscador m; **search
party** n pelotón m de salvamento

sea: seashore n playa, orilla del mar;
seasick adj mareado; **seaside** n
playa, orilla del mar; **seaside resort** n
centro turístico costero

season ['si:zn] n (of year) estación
f; (sporting etc) temporada; (of films
etc) ciclo ▷ vt (food) sazonar; **in/out
of ~** en sazón/fuera de temporada;
seasonal adj estacional; **seasoning**
n condimento, aderezo; **season ticket**
n abono

seat [si:t] n (in bus, train) asiento;
(chair) silla; (Parliament) escaño;
(buttocks) culo, trasero; (of trousers)
culera ▷ vt sentar; (have room for)
tener cabida para; **to be ~ed** sentarse;
seat belt n cinturón m de seguridad;
seating n asientos mpl

sea: sea water n agua del mar;
seaweed n alga marina

sec. abbr = **second(s)**

secluded [si'klu:dɪd] adj retirado

second ['sekənd] adj segundo ▷ adv
en segundo lugar ▷ n segundo;

(Aut: also: **~ gear**) segunda; (Comm)
artículo con algún desperfecto; (BRIT
Scol: degree) título de licenciado con
calificación de notable ▷ vt (motion)
apoyar; **secondary** adj secundario;
secondary school n escuela
secundaria; **second-class** adj de
segunda clase ▷ adv (Rail) en segunda;
secondhand adj de segunda mano,
usado; **secondly** adv en segundo
lugar; **second-rate** adj de segunda
categoría; **second thoughts: to have
second thoughts** cambiar de opinión;
on second thoughts or **thought** (us)
pensándolo bien

secrecy ['si:krəsɪ] n secreto

secret ['si:krɪt] adj, n secreto; **in ~**
en secreto

secretary ['sekrətərɪ] n secretario/a;
S~ of State (for) (BRIT Pol) Ministro
(de)

secretive ['si:krətɪv] adj reservado,
sigiloso

secret service n servicio secreto

sect [sekt] n secta

section ['sekʃən] n sección f; (part)
parte f; (of document) artículo; (of
opinion) sector m; (cross-section) corte
m transversal

sector ['sektə*] n sector m

secular ['sekjulə*] adj secular, seglar

secure [sɪ'kjuə*] adj seguro; (firmly
fixed) firme, fijo ▷ vt (fix) asegurar,
afianzar; (get) conseguir

security [sɪ'kjuərɪtɪ] n seguridad
f; (for loan) fianza; (: object) prenda;
securities npl (Comm) valores mpl,
títulos mpl; **security guard** n guardia
m/f de seguridad

sedan [sɪ'dæn] (us) n (Aut) sedán m

sedate [sɪ'deɪt] adj tranquilo ▷ vt
tratar con sedantes

sedative ['sedɪtɪv] n sedante m,
sedativo

seduce [sɪ'dju:s] vt seducir;
seductive [-'dʌktɪv] adj seductor(a)

see [si:] (pt **saw**, pp **seen**) vt ver;
(accompany): **to ~ sb to the door**

acompañar a algn a la puerta;
(understand) ver, comprender ▷ vi ver
▷ n (arz)obispado; **to ~ that** (ensure)
asegurar que; **~ you soon!** ¡hasta
pronto!; **see off** vt despedir; **see out**
vt (take to the door) acompañar hasta la
puerta; **see through** vt fus (fig) calar
▷ vt (plan) llevar a cabo; **see to** vt fus
atender, encargarse de

seed [si:d] n semilla; (in fruit) pepita;
(fig: gen pl) germen m; (Tennis etc)
preseleccionado/a; **to go to ~** (plant)
granar; (fig) descuidarse

seeing ['si:ɪŋ] conj: **~ (that)** visto que,
en vista de que

seek [si:k] (pt, pp sought) vt buscar;
(post) solicitar

seem [si:m] vi parecer; **there ~s to
be ...** parece que hay ...; **seemingly** adv
aparentemente, según parece

seen [si:n] pp of **see**

seesaw ['si:sɔ:] n subibaja

segment ['sɛgmənt] n (part) sección
f; (of orange) gajo

segregate ['sɛgrɪgeɪt] vt segregar

seize [si:z] vt (grasp) agarrar,
asir; (take possession of) secuestrar;
(: territory) apoderarse de; (opportunity)
aprovecharse de

seizure ['si:ʒə*] n (Med) ataque m;
(Law, of power) incautación f

seldom ['sɛldəm] adv rara vez

select [sɪ'lɛkt] adj selecto, escogido
▷ vt escoger, elegir; (Sport) seleccionar;
selection n selección f, elección
f; (Comm) surtido m; **selective** adj
selectivo

self [sɛlf] (pl selves) n uno mismo;
the ~ el yo ▷ prefix auto...; **self-
assured** adj seguro de sí mismo; **self-
catering** (BRIT) adj (flat etc)
con cocina; **self-centred** (us
self-centered) adj egocéntrico;
self-confidence n confianza en sí
mismo; **self-confident** adj seguro
de sí (mismo), lleno de confianza en sí
mismo; **self-conscious** adj cohibido;
self-contained (BRIT) adj (flat) con

entrada particular; **self-control** n
autodominio; **self-defence** (us **self-
defense**) n defensa propia; **self-drive**
adj (BRIT) sin chofer or (SP) chófer; **self-
employed** adj que trabaja por cuenta
propia; **self-esteem** n amor m propio;
self-indulgent adj autocomplaciente;
self-interest n egoísmo; **selfish**
adj egoísta; **self-pity** n lástima de
sí mismo; **self-raising** [sɛlf'reɪzɪŋ]
(us **self-rising**) adj: **self-raising flour**
harina con levadura; **self-respect** n
amor m propio; **self-service** adj de
autoservicio

sell [sɛl] (pt, pp sold) vt vender ▷ vi
venderse; **to ~ at** or **for £10** venderse a
10 libras; **sell off** vt liquidar; **sell out**
vi: **to sell out of tickets/milk** vender
todas las entradas/toda la leche; **sell-
by date** n fecha de caducidad; **seller**
n vendedor(a) m/f

selves [sɛlvz] npl of **self**

semester [sɪ'mɛstə*] (us) n
semestre m

semi... [sɛmɪ] prefix semi...,
medio...; **semicircle** n semicírculo;
semidetached (house) n (casa)
semiseparada; **semi-final** n semi-
final m

seminar ['sɛmɪnɑ:*] n seminario

semi-skimmed [sɛmɪ'skɪmd] adj
semidesnatado; **semi-skimmed
(milk)** n leche semidesnatada

senate ['sɛnɪt] n senado; **the ~** (us)
el Senado; **senator** n senador(a) m/f

send [sɛnd] (pt, pp sent) vt mandar,
enviar; (signal) transmitir; **send back**
vt devolver; **send for** vt fus mandar
traer; **send in** vt (report, application,
resignation) mandar; **send off** vt
(goods) despachar; (BRIT Sport: player)
expulsar; **send on** vt (letter, luggage)
remitir; (person) mandar; **send out**
vt (invitation) mandar; (signal) emitir;
send up vt (person, price) hacer subir;

(BRIT: parody) parodiar; **sender** n remitente mf; (of letter) n: **a good send-off** una buena despedida

senile ['si:naɪl] adj senil

senior ['si:nɪə*] adj (older) mayor, más viejo; (: on staff) de más antigüedad; (: of higher rank) superior; **senior citizen** n persona de la tercera edad; **senior high school** (US) n ≈ instituto de enseñanza media; see also **high school**

sensation [sɛn'seɪʃən] n sensación f; **sensational** adj sensacional

sense [sɛns] n (faculty, meaning) sentido; (feeling) sensación f; (good sense) sentido común, juicio ▷ vt sentir, percibir; **it makes ~** tiene sentido; **senseless** adj estúpido, insensato; (unconscious) sin conocimiento; **sense of humour** (BRIT) n sentido del humor

sensible ['sɛnsɪbl] adj sensato; (reasonable) razonable, lógico

  Be careful not to translate **sensible**
  by the Spanish word sensible.

sensitive ['sɛnsɪtɪv] adj sensible; (touchy) susceptible

sensual ['sɛnsjuəl] adj sensual

sensuous ['sɛnsjuəs] adj sensual

sent [sɛnt] pt, pp of **send**

sentence ['sɛntns] n (Ling) oración f; (Law) sentencia, fallo ▷ vt: **to ~ sb to death/to 5 years (in prison)** condenar a algn a muerte/a 5 años de cárcel

sentiment ['sɛntɪmənt] n sentimiento; (opinion) opinión f; **sentimental** [-'mɛntl] adj sentimental

Sep. abbr (= September) sep., set.

separate [adj 'sɛprɪt, vb 'sɛpəreɪt] adj separado; (distinct) distinto ▷ vt separar; (part) dividir ▷ vi separarse; **separately** adv por separado; **separates** npl (clothes) coordinados mpl; **separation** [-'reɪʃən] n separación f

September [sɛp'tɛmbə*] n se(p)tiembre m

septic ['sɛptɪk] adj séptico; **septic**

tank n fosa séptica

sequel ['si:kwl] n consecuencia, resultado; (of story) continuación f

sequence ['si:kwəns] n sucesión f, serie f; (Cinema) secuencia

sequin ['si:kwɪn] n lentejuela

Serb [sə:b] adj, n =**Serbian**

Serbian ['sə:bɪən] adj serbio ▷ n serbio/a; (Ling) serbio

sergeant ['sɑ:dʒənt] n sargento

serial ['sɪərɪəl] n (TV) telenovela, serie f televisiva; (Book) serie f; **serial killer** n asesino/a múltiple; **serial number** n número de serie

series ['sɪəri:z] n inv serie f

serious ['sɪərɪəs] adj serio; (grave) grave; **seriously** adv en serio; (ill, wounded etc) gravemente

sermon ['sə:mən] n sermón m

servant ['sə:vənt] n servidor/a m/f; (house servant) criado/a

serve [sə:v] vt atender; (customer) atender; (train) pasar por; (apprenticeship) hacer; (prison term) cumplir ▷ vi (at table) servir; (Tennis) sacar; **to ~ as/for/to do** servir de/para/para hacer ▷ n (Tennis) saque m; **it ~s him right** se lo tiene merecido; **server** n (Comput) servidor m

service ['sə:vɪs] n (gen) servicio; (Rel) misa; (Aut) mantenimiento; (dishes etc) juego ▷ vt (car etc) revisar; (: repair) reparar; **to be of ~ to sb** ser útil a algn; **~ included/not included** servicio incluido/no incluido (Econ: tertiary sector) sector m terciario or (de) servicios; (BRIT: on motorway) área de servicio; (Mil): **the S~s** las fuerzas armadas; **service area** n (on motorway) área de servicio; **service charge** (BRIT) n servicio; **serviceman** (irreg) n militar m; **service station** n estación f de servicio

serviette [sə:vɪ'ɛt] (BRIT) n servilleta

session ['sɛʃən] n sesión f; **to be in ~** estar en sesión

set [sɛt] (pt, pp ~) n juego; (Radio) aparato; (TV) televisor m; (of utensils)

settee | 518

batería; (of cutlery) cubierto; (of books)
colección f; (Tennis) set m; (group
of people) grupo; (Cinema) plató m;
(Theatre) decorado; (Hairdressing)
marcado ▷ adj (fixed) fijo; (ready) listo
▷ vt (place) poner, colocar; (fix) fijar;
(adjust) ajustar, arreglar; (decide: rules
etc) establecer, determinar ▷ vi (sun)
ponerse; (jam, jelly) cuajarse; (concrete)
fraguar; (bone) componerse; **to be ~ on
doing sth** estar empeñado en hacer
algo; **to ~ to music** poner música a;
to ~ on fire incendiar, poner fuego a;
to ~ free poner en libertad; **to ~ sth
going** poner algo en marcha; **to ~ sail**
zarpar, hacerse a la vela; **set aside** vt
poner aparte, dejar de lado; (money,
time) reservar; **set down** vt (bus, train)
dejar; **set in** vi (infection) declararse;
(complications) comenzar; **the rain
has set in for the day** parece que va a
llover todo el día; **set off** vi partir ▷ vt
(bomb) hacer estallar; (events) poner en
marcha; (show up well) hacer resaltar;
set out vi partir ▷ vt (arrange)
disponer ▷ vt (state) exponer; **to set out
to do sth** proponerse hacer algo; **set
up** vt establecer; **setback** n revés m,
contratiempo; **set menu** n menú m
settee [sɛˈtiː] n sofá m

setting [ˈsɛtɪŋ] n (scenery) marco;
(position) disposición f; (of sun) puesta;
(of jewel) engaste m, montadura f

settle [ˈsɛtl] vt (argument) resolver;
(accounts) ajustar, liquidar; (Med: calm)
calmar, sosegar ▷ vi (dust etc)
depositarse; (weather) serenarse; **to
~ for sth** convenir en aceptar algo;
to ~ on sth decidirse por algo; **settle
down** vi (get comfortable) ponerse
cómodo, acomodarse; (calm down)
calmarse, tranquilizarse; (live quietly)
echar raíces; **settle in** vi instalarse;
settle up vi: **to settle up with sb**
ajustar cuentas con algn; **settlement**
n (payment) liquidación f; (agreement)
acuerdo, convenio; (village place) pueblo

setup [ˈsɛtʌp] n sistema m; (situation)

situación f

seven [ˈsɛvn] num siete; **seventeen**
num diez y siete, diecisiete;
seventeenth [sɛvnˈtiːnθ] adj
decimoséptimo; **seventh** num
séptimo; **seventieth** [ˈsɛvntɪɪθ] adj
septuagésimo; **seventy** num setenta

sever [ˈsɛvə*] vt cortar; (relations)
romper

several [ˈsɛvrəl] adj, pron varios/as
m/pl, algunos/as m/f/pl; **~ of us** varios
de nosotros

severe [sɪˈvɪə*] adj severo; (serious)
grave; (hard) duro; (pain) intenso

sew [səʊ] (pt **~ed**, pp **~n**), vt, vi coser

sewage [ˈsuːɪdʒ] n aguas fpl
residuales

sewer [ˈsuːə*] n alcantarilla, cloaca

sewing [ˈsəʊɪŋ] n costura; **sewing
machine** n máquina de coser

sewn [səʊn] pp of **sew**

sex [sɛks] n sexo; (lovemaking): **to
have ~** hacer el amor; **sexism** [ˈsɛksɪzə
m] n sexismo; **sexist** adj, n sexista
mf; **sexual** [ˈsɛksjʊəl] adj sexual;
sexual intercourse n relaciones fpl
sexuales; **sexuality** [sɛksjʊˈælɪtɪ] n
sexualidad f; **sexy** adj sexy

shabby [ˈʃæbɪ] adj (person)
desharrapado; (clothes) raído, gastado;
(behaviour) ruin inv

shack [ʃæk] n choza, chabola

shade [ʃeɪd] n sombra; (for lamp)
pantalla; (for eyes) visera; (of colour)
matiz m, tonalidad f; (small quantity): **a
~ (too big/more)** un poquitín
(grande/más) ▷ vt dar sombra a; (eyes)
proteger del sol; **in the ~** en la sombra;
shades npl (sunglasses) gafas fpl de sol

shadow [ˈʃædəʊ] n sombra ▷ vt
(follow) seguir y vigilar; **shadow
cabinet** (BRIT) n (Pol) gabinete paralelo
formado por el partido de oposición

shady [ˈʃeɪdɪ] adj sombreado;
(fig: dishonest) sospechoso; (: deal)
turbio

shaft [ʃɑːft] n (of arrow, spear) astil m;
(Aut, Tech) eje m, árbol m; (of mine) pozo;

(of lift) hueco, caja; (of light) rayo

shake [ʃeɪk] (pt **shook**, pp **shaken**) vt sacudir; (building) hacer temblar; (bottle, cocktail) agitar ▷ vi (tremble) temblar; **to ~ one's head** (in refusal) negar con la cabeza; (in dismay) mover or menear la cabeza, incrédulo; **to ~ hands with sb** estrechar la mano a algn; **shake off** vt sacudirse; (fig) deshacerse de; **shake up** vt agitar; (fig) reorganizar; **shaky** adj (hand, voice) trémulo; (building) inestable

shall [ʃæl] aux vb: **~ I help you?** ¿quieres que te ayude?; **I'll buy three, ~ I?** compro tres, ¿no te parece?

shallow ['ʃæləʊ] adj poco profundo; (fig) superficial

sham [ʃæm] n fraude m, engaño

shambles ['ʃæmblz] n confusión f

shame [ʃeɪm] n vergüenza ▷ vt avergonzar; **it is a ~ that/to do** es una lástima que/hacer; **what a ~!** ¡qué lástima!; **shameful** adj vergonzoso; **shameless** adj desvergonzado

shampoo [ʃæm'puː] n champú m ▷ vt lavar con champú

shandy ['ʃændɪ] n mezcla de cerveza con gaseosa

shan't [ʃɑːnt] = **shall not**

shape [ʃeɪp] n forma ▷ vt formar, dar forma a; (sb's ideas) formar; (sb's life) determinar; **to take ~** tomar forma

share [ʃeə*] n (part) parte f, porción f; (contribution) cuota; (Comm) acción f ▷ vt dividir; (have in common) compartir; **to ~ out (among or between)** repartir (entre); **shareholder** (BRIT) n accionista mf

shark [ʃɑːk] n tiburón m

sharp [ʃɑːp] adj (blade, nose) afilado; (point) puntiagudo; (outline) definido; (pain) intenso; (Mus) desafinado; (contrast) marcado; (voice) agudo; (person: quick-witted) astuto; (: dishonest) poco escrupuloso ▷ n (Mus) sostenido ▷ adv: **at 2 o'clock ~** a las 2 en punto; **sharpen** vt afilar; (pencil) sacar punta a; (fig) agudizar;

sharpener n (also: **pencil sharpener**) sacapuntas m inv; **sharply** adv (turn, stop) bruscamente; (stand out, contrast) claramente; (criticize, retort) severamente

shatter ['ʃætə*] vt hacer añicos or pedazos; (fig: ruin) destruir, acabar con ▷ vi hacerse añicos; **shattered** adj (grief-stricken) destrozado, deshecho; (exhausted) agotado, hecho polvo

shave [ʃeɪv] vt afeitar, rasurar ▷ vi afeitarse, rasurarse ▷ n: **to have a ~** afeitarse; **shaver** n (also: **electric shaver**) máquina de afeitar (eléctrica)

shavings ['ʃeɪvɪŋz] npl (of wood etc) virutas fpl

shaving cream ['ʃeɪvɪŋ-] n crema de afeitar

shaving foam n espuma de afeitar

shawl [ʃɔːl] n chal m

she [ʃiː] pron ella

sheath [ʃiːθ] n vaina; (contraceptive) preservativo

shed [ʃed] (pt, pp **~**) n cobertizo ▷ vt (skin) mudar; (tears, blood) derramar; (load) desprender; (workers) despedir

she'd [ʃiːd] = **she had; she would**

sheep [ʃiːp] n inv oveja; **sheepdog** n perro pastor; **sheepskin** n piel f de carnero

sheer [ʃɪə*] adj (utter) puro, completo; (steep) escarpado; (material) diáfano ▷ adv verticalmente

sheet [ʃiːt] n (on bed) sábana; (of paper) hoja; (of glass, metal) lámina; (of ice) capa

sheik(h) [ʃeɪk] n jeque m

shelf [ʃelf] (pl **shelves**) n estante m

shell [ʃel] n (on beach) concha; (of egg, nut etc) cáscara; (explosive) proyectil m, obús m; (of building) armazón f ▷ vt (peas) desenvainar; (Mil) bombardear

she'll [ʃiːl] = **she will; she shall**

shellfish ['ʃelfɪʃ] n inv crustáceo; (as food) mariscos mpl

shelter ['ʃeltə*] n abrigo, refugio ▷ vt (aid) amparar, proteger; (give lodging to) abrigar ▷ vi abrigarse, refugiarse;

s

sheltered adj (life) protegido; (spot) abrigado

shelves [ʃelvz] npl of **shelf**

shelving [ˈʃelvɪŋ] n estantería

shepherd [ˈʃepəd] n pastor m ▷ vt (guide) guiar, conducir; **shepherd's pie** (BRIT) n pastel de carne y patatas

sheriff [ˈʃerɪf] (US) n sheriff m

sherry [ˈʃerɪ] n jerez m

she's [ʃiːz] = **she is**; **she has**

Shetland [ˈʃetlənd] n (also: **the ~s**, **the ~ Isles**) las Islas de Zetlandia

shield [ʃiːld] n escudo; (protection) blindaje m ▷ vt: **to ~ (from)** proteger (de)

shift [ʃɪft] n (change) cambio; (at work) turno ▷ vt trasladar; (remove) quitar ▷ vi moverse

shin [ʃɪn] n espinilla

shine [ʃaɪn] (pt, pp **shone**) n brillo, lustre m ▷ vi brillar, relucir ▷ vt (shoes) lustrar, sacar brillo a; **to ~ a torch on sth** dirigir una linterna hacia algo

shingles [ˈʃɪŋɡlz] n (Med) herpes mpl or fpl

shiny [ˈʃaɪnɪ] adj brillante, lustroso

ship [ʃɪp] n buque m, barco ▷ vt (goods) embarcar; (send) transportar o enviar por vía marítima; **shipment** n (goods) envío; **shipping** n (act) embarque m; (traffic) buques mpl; **shipwreck** n naufragio ▷ vt: **to be shipwrecked** naufragar; **shipyard** n astillero

shirt [ʃɜːt] n camisa; **in (one's) ~ sleeves** en mangas de camisa

shit [ʃɪt] (inf!) excl ¡mierda! (!)

shiver [ˈʃɪvə*] n escalofrío ▷ vi temblar, estremecerse; (with cold) tiritar

shock [ʃɔk] n (impact) choque m; (Elec) descarga (eléctrica); (emotional) conmoción f; (start) sobresalto, susto; (Med) postración f nerviosa ▷ vt dar un susto a; (offend) escandalizar; **shocking** adj (awful) espantoso; (outrageous) escandaloso

shoe [ʃuː] (pt, pp **shod**) n zapato; (for

horse) herradura ▷ vt (horse) herrar; **shoelace** n cordón m; **shoe polish** n betún m; **shoeshop** n zapatería

shone [ʃɔn] pt, pp of **shine**

shook [ʃuk] pt of **shake**

shoot [ʃuːt] (pt, pp **shot**) n (on branch, seedling) retoño, vástago ▷ vt disparar; (kill) matar a tiros; (wound) pegar un tiro; (execute) fusilar; (film) rodar, filmar ▷ vi (Football) chutar; **shoot down** vt (plane) derribar; **shoot up** vi (prices) dispararse; **shooting** n (shots) tiros mpl; (Hunting) caza con escopeta

shop [ʃɔp] n tienda; (workshop) taller m ▷ vi (also: **go ~ping**) ir de compras; **shop assistant** (BRIT) n dependiente/a m/f; **shopkeeper** n tendero/a; **shoplifting** n mechería; **shopping** n (goods) compras fpl; **shopping bag** n bolsa (de compras); **shopping centre** (US **shopping center**) n centro comercial; **shopping mall** n centro comercial; **shopping trolley** n (BRIT) carrito de la compra; **shop window** n escaparate m (SP), vidriera (LAM)

shore [ʃɔː*] n orilla ▷ vt: **to ~ (up)** reforzar; **on ~** en tierra

short [ʃɔːt] adj corto; (in time) breve, de corta duración; (person) bajo; (curt) brusco, seco; (insufficient) insuficiente; **(a pair of) ~s** (unos) pantalones mpl cortos; **to be ~ of sth** estar falto de algo; **in ~** en pocas palabras; **~ of doing ...** fuera de hacer ...; **it is ~ for** es la forma abreviada de; **to cut ~** (speech, visit) interrumpir, terminar inesperadamente; **everything ~ of ...** todo menos ...; **to fall ~ of** no alcanzar; **to run ~ of** quedarle a algn poco; **to stop ~** parar en seco; **to stop ~ of** detenerse antes de; **shortage** n: **a shortage of** una falta de; **shortbread** n especie de mantecada; **shortcoming** n defecto, deficiencia; **short(crust) pastry** (BRIT) n pasta quebradiza; **shortcut** n atajo; **shorten** vt acortar; (visit) interrumpir; **shortfall** n déficit m; **shorthand** (BRIT) taquigrafía; **short-lived** adj efímero; **shortly** adv en breve, dentro de poco; **shorts** npl pantalones mpl cortos; (us) calzoncillos mpl; **short-sighted** (BRIT) adj miope; (fig) imprudente; **short-sleeved** adj de manga corta; **short story** n cuento; **short-tempered** adj enojadizo; **short-term** adj (effect) a corto plazo

shot [ʃɔt] pt, pp of **shoot** ▷n (sound) tiro, disparo; (try) tentativa; (injection) inyección f; (Phot) toma, fotografía; **to be a good/poor ~** (person) tener buena/mala puntería; **like a ~** (without any delay) como un rayo; **shotgun** n escopeta

should [ʃud] aux vb: **I ~ go now** debo irme ahora; **he ~ be there now** debe de haber llegado (ya); **I ~ go if I were you** yo en tu lugar me iría; **I ~ like to** me gustaría

shoulder ['ʃəuldə*] n hombro ▷vt (fig) cargar con; **shoulder blade** n omóplato

shouldn't ['ʃudnt] = **should not**

shout [ʃaut] n grito ▷vt gritar ▷vi gritar, dar voces

shove [ʃʌv] n empujón m ▷vt empujar; (inf: put): **to ~ sth in** meter algo a empellones

shovel ['ʃʌvl] n pala; (mechanical) excavadora ▷vt mover con pala

show [ʃəu] (pt **~ed**, pp **~n**) n (of emotion) demostración f; (semblance) apariencia; (exhibition) exposición f; (Theatre) función f, espectáculo; (TV) show m ▷vt mostrar, enseñar; (courage etc) mostrar, manifestar; (exhibit) exponer; (film) proyectar ▷vi mostrarse; (appear) aparecer; **for ~** para impresionar; **on ~** (exhibits etc) expuesto; **show in** vt (person) hacer pasar; **show off** (pej) vi presumir ▷vt (display) lucir; **show out** vt: **to show sb out** acompañar a algn a la puerta; **show up** vi (stand out) destacar; (inf: turn up) aparecer ▷vt (unmask) desenmascarar; **show business** n

521 | **shut**

mundo del espectáculo

shower ['ʃauə*] n (rain) chaparrón m, chubasco; (of stones etc) lluvia; (for bathing) ducha, regadera (MEX) ▷vi llover ▷vt (fig): **to ~ sb with sth** colmar a algn de algo; **to have a ~** ducharse; **shower cap** n gorro de baño; **shower gel** n gel m de ducha

showing ['ʃəuɪŋ] n (of film) proyección f

show jumping n hípica

shown [ʃəun] pp of **show**

show: show-off (inf) n (person) presumido/a; **showroom** n sala de muestras

shrank [ʃræŋk] pt of **shrink**

shred [ʃred] n (gen pl) triza, jirón m ▷vt hacer trizas; (Culin) desmenuzar

shrewd [ʃruːd] adj astuto

shriek [ʃriːk] n chillido ▷vi chillar

shrimp [ʃrɪmp] n camarón m

shrine [ʃraɪn] n santuario, sepulcro

shrink [ʃrɪŋk] (pt **shrank**, pp **shrunk**) vi encogerse; (be reduced) reducirse; (also: **~ away**) retroceder ▷vt encoger ▷n (inf, pej) loquero/a; **to ~ from (doing) sth** no atreverse a hacer algo

shrivel ['ʃrɪvl] (also: **~ up**) vt (dry) secar ▷vi secarse

shroud [ʃraud] n sudario ▷vt: **~ed in mystery** envuelto en el misterio

Shrove Tuesday ['ʃrəuv-] n martes m de carnaval

shrub [ʃrʌb] n arbusto

shrug [ʃrʌg] n encogimiento de hombros ▷vt, vi: **to ~ (one's shoulders)** encogerse de hombros; **shrug off** vt negar importancia a

shrunk [ʃrʌŋk] pp of **shrink**

shudder ['ʃʌdə*] n estremecimiento, escalofrío ▷vi estremecerse

shuffle ['ʃʌfl] vt (cards) barajar ▷vi: **to ~ (one's feet)** arrastrar los pies

shun [ʃʌn] vt rehuir, esquivar

shut [ʃʌt] (pt, pp **~**) vt cerrar ▷vi cerrarse; **shut down** vt, vi cerrar; **shut up** vi (inf: keep quiet) callarse ▷vt (close) cerrar; (silence) hacer callar;

shuttle | 522

shutter n contraventana; (Phot) obturador m

shuttle ['ʃʌtl] n lanzadera; (also: **~ service**) servicio rápido y continuo entre dos puntos; (Aviat) puente m aéreo; **shuttlecock** n volante m

shy [ʃaɪ] adj tímido

sibling ['sɪblɪŋ] n (formal) hermano/a

sick [sɪk] adj (ill) enfermo; (nauseated) mareado; (humour) negro; (vomiting): **to be ~** (BRIT) vomitar; **to have ~** tener náuseas; **to be ~ of** (fig) estar harto de; **sickening** adj (fig) asqueroso; **sick leave** n baja por enfermedad; **sickly** adj enfermizo; (smell) nauseabundo; **sickness** n enfermedad f, mal m; (vomiting) náuseas fpl

side [saɪd] n (gen) lado; (of body) costado; (of lake) orilla; (of hill) ladera; (team) equipo ▷ adj (door, entrance) lateral ▷ vi: **to ~ with sb** tomar el partido de algn; **by the ~ of** al lado de; **~ by ~** juntos/as; **from ~ to ~** de un lado a otro; **to take ~s (with)** tomar partido (con); **sideboard** n aparador m; **sideboards** (BRIT) npl = **sideburns**; **sideburns** npl patillas fpl; **sidelight** n (Aut) luz f lateral; **sideline** n (Sport) línea de banda; (fig) empleo suplementario; **side order** n plato de acompañamiento; **side road** n (BRIT) calle f lateral; **side street** n calle f lateral; **sidetrack** vt (fig) desviar (de su propósito); **sidewalk** (US) n acera; **sideways** adv de lado

siege [siːdʒ] n cerco, sitio

sieve [sɪv] n colador m ▷ vt cribar

sift [sɪft] vt cribar; (fig: information) escudriñar

sigh [saɪ] n suspiro ▷ vi suspirar

sight [saɪt] n (faculty) vista; (spectacle) espectáculo; (on gun) mira, alza ▷ vt divisar; **in ~** a la vista; **out of ~** fuera de (la) vista; **on ~** (shoot) sin previo aviso; **sightseeing** n excursionismo, turismo; **to go sightseeing** hacer turismo

sign [saɪn] n (with hand) señal f, seña; (trace) huella, rastro; (notice) letrero; (written) signo ▷ vt firmar; (Sport) fichar; **to ~ sth over to sb** firmar el traspaso de algo a algn; **sign for** vt fus (item) firmar el recibo de; **sign in** vi firmar el registro (al entrar); **sign on** vi (BRIT: as unemployed) registrarse como desempleado; (Mil) alistar; (employee) contratar; **sign up** vi (Mil) alistarse; (for course) inscribirse ▷ vt (player) fichar

signal ['sɪgnl] n señal f ▷ vi señalizar ▷ vt (person) hacer señas a; (message) comunicar por señales

signature ['sɪgnətʃəʳ] n firma

significance [sɪg'nɪfɪkəns] n (importance) trascendencia

significant [sɪg'nɪfɪkənt] adj significativo; (important) trascendente

signify ['sɪgnɪfaɪ] vt significar

sign language n lenguaje m para sordomudos

signpost ['saɪnpəust] n indicador m

Sikh [siːk] adj, n sij mf

silence ['saɪləns] n silencio ▷ vt acallar; (guns) reducir al silencio

silent ['saɪlnt] adj silencioso; (not speaking) callado; (film) mudo; **to remain ~** guardar silencio

silhouette [sɪluː'et] n silueta

silicon chip ['sɪlɪkən-] n plaqueta de silicio

silk [sɪlk] n seda ▷ adj de seda

silly ['sɪlɪ] adj (person) tonto; (idea) absurdo

silver ['sɪlvəʳ] n plata; (money) moneda suelta ▷ adj (colour) plateado; **silver-plated** adj plateado

SIM card ['sɪm-] n (Tel) SIM card mf; tarjeta f SIM

similar ['sɪmɪləʳ] adj: **~ (to)** parecido or semejante (a); **similarity** [-'lærɪtɪ] n semejanza; **similarly** adv del mismo modo

simmer ['sɪməʳ] vi hervir a fuego lento

simple ['sɪmpl] adj (easy) sencillo; (foolish, Comm: interest) simple;

simplicity [-'plɪsɪtɪ] n sencillez f;
simplify ['sɪmplɪfaɪ] vt simplificar;
simply adv (live, talk) sencillamente;
(just, merely) sólo

simulate ['sɪmjuːleɪt] vt fingir,
simular

simultaneous [sɪməl'teɪnɪəs] adj
simultáneo; **simultaneously** adv
simultáneamente

sin [sɪn] n pecado ▷ vi pecar

since [sɪns] adv desde entonces,
después ▷ prep desde ▷ conj (time)
desde que; (because) ya que, puesto
que; **~ then**, **ever ~** desde entonces

sincere [sɪn'sɪə*] adj sincero;
sincerely adv: **yours sincerely** (in
letters) le saluda atentamente

sing [sɪŋ] (pt **sang**, pp **sung**) vt, vi
cantar

Singapore [sɪŋə'pɔː*] n Singapur m

singer ['sɪŋə*] n cantante mf

singing ['sɪŋɪŋ] n canto

single ['sɪŋɡl] adj único, solo;
(unmarried) soltero; (not double) simple,
sencillo ▷ n (BRIT: also: **~ ticket**) billete
m sencillo; (record) sencillo, single
m; **singles** npl (Tennis) individual
m; **single out** vt (choose) escoger;
single bed n cama individual; **single
file** n: **in single file** en fila de uno;
single-handed adv sin ayuda; **single-
minded** adj resuelto, firme; **single
parent** n padre m soltero, madre f
soltera (o divorciado etc); **single parent
family** familia monoparental; **single
room** n cuarto individual

singular ['sɪŋɡjulə*] adj (odd) raro,
extraño; (outstanding) excepcional ▷ n
(Ling) singular m

sinister ['sɪnɪstə*] adj siniestro

sink [sɪŋk] (pt **sank**, pp **sunk**) n
fregadero ▷ vt (ship) hundir, echar
a pique; (foundations) excavar ▷ vi
hundirse; **to ~ sth into** hundir algo en;
sink in vi (fig) penetrar, calar

sinus ['saɪnəs] n (Anat) seno

sip [sɪp] n sorbo ▷ vt sorber, beber
a sorbitos

sir [sə*] n señor m; **S~ John Smith** Sir
John Smith; **yes ~** sí, señor

siren ['saɪərn] n sirena

sirloin ['sɜːlɔɪn] n (also: **~ steak**)
solomillo

sister ['sɪstə*] n hermana;
(BRIT: nurse) enfermera jefe; **sister-in-
law** n cuñada

sit [sɪt] (pt, pp **sat**) vi sentarse; (be
sitting) estar sentado; (assembly)
reunirse; (for painter) posar ▷ vt (exam)
presentarse a; **sit back** vi (in seat)
recostarse; **sit down** vi sentarse;
sit on vt fus (jury, committee) ser
miembro de, formar parte de; **sit up** vi
incorporarse; (not go to bed) velar

sitcom ['sɪtkɔm] n abbr (= situation
comedy) comedia de situación

site [saɪt] n sitio; (also: **building ~**)
solar m ▷ vt situar

sitting ['sɪtɪŋ] n (of assembly etc)
sesión f; (in canteen) turno; **sitting
room** n sala de estar

situated ['sɪtjueɪtɪd] adj situado

situation [sɪtju'eɪʃən] n situación f;
"~s vacant" (BRIT) "ofrecen trabajo"

six [sɪks] num seis; **sixteen** num diez
y seis, dieciséis; **sixteenth** [sɪks'tiːnθ]
adj decimosexto; **sixth** [sɪksθ] num
sexto; **sixth form** n (BRIT) clase f de
alumnos del sexto año (de 16 a 18 años de
edad); **sixth-form college** n instituto
m para alumnos de 16 a 18 años;
sixtieth ['sɪkstɪɪθ] adj sexagésimo;
sixty num sesenta

size [saɪz] n tamaño; (extent)
extensión f; (of clothing) talla; (of shoes)
número; **sizeable** adj importante,
considerable

sizzle ['sɪzl] vi crepitar

skate [skeɪt] n patín m; (fish: pl
inv) raya f ▷ vi patinar; **skateboard**
n monopatín m; **skateboarding** n
monopatín m; **skater** n patinador(a)
m/f; **skating** n patinaje m; **skating
rink** n pista de patinaje

skeleton ['skɛlɪtn] n esqueleto;
(Tech) armazón f; (outline) esquema m

skeptical ['skeptɪkl] (US) = **sceptical**

sketch [sketʃ] n (drawing) dibujo; (outline) esbozo, bosquejo; (Theatre) sketch m ▷ vt: dibujar; (plan etc: also: ~ **out**) esbozar

skewer ['skjuːə*] n broqueta

ski [skiː] n esquí m ▷ vi esquiar; **ski boot** n bota de esquí

skid [skɪd] n patinazo ▷ vi patinar

ski: skier n esquiador(a) m/f; **skiing** n esquí m

skilful ['skɪlful] (US **skillful**) adj diestro, experto

ski lift n telesilla m, telesquí m

skill [skɪl] n destreza, pericia; técnica; **skilled** adj hábil, diestro; (worker) cualificado

skim [skɪm] vt (milk) desnatar; (glide over) rozar, rasar ▷ vi: **to ~ through** (book) hojear; **skimmed milk** (US **skim milk**) n leche f desnatada

skin [skɪn] n piel f; (complexion) cutis m ▷ vt (fruit etc) pelar; (animal) despellejar; **skinhead** n cabeza m/f rapada, (head) m/f; **skinny** adj flaco

skip [skɪp] n brinco, salto; (BRIT: container) contenedor m ▷ vi brincar; (with rope) saltar a la comba ▷ vt saltarse

ski: ski pass n forfait m (de esquí); **ski pole** n bastón m de esquiar

skipper ['skɪpə*] n (Naut, Sport) capitán m

skipping rope ['skɪpɪŋ-] (US **skip rope**) n comba

skirt [skɜːt] n falda, pollera (SC) ▷ vt (go round) ladear

skirting board ['skɜːtɪŋ-] (BRIT) n rodapié m

ski slope n pista de esquí

ski suit n traje m de esquiar

skull [skʌl] n calavera; (Anat) cráneo

skunk [skʌŋk] n mofeta

sky [skaɪ] n cielo; **skyscraper** n rascacielos m inv

slab [slæb] n (stone) bloque m; (flat) losa; (of cake) trozo

slack [slæk] adj (loose) flojo; (slow) de poca actividad; (careless) descuidado; **slacks** npl pantalones mpl

slain [sleɪn] pp of **slay**

slam [slæm] vt (throw) arrojar (violentamente); (criticize) criticar duramente ▷ vi (door) cerrarse de golpe; **to ~ the door** dar un portazo

slander ['slɑːndə*] n calumnia, difamación f

slang [slæŋ] n argot m; (jargon) jerga

slant [slɑːnt] n sesgo, inclinación f; (fig) interpretación f

slap [slæp] n palmada; (in face) bofetada ▷ vt dar una palmada or bofetada a; (paint etc) **to ~ sth on sth** embadurnar algo con algo ▷ adv (directly) exactamente, directamente

slash [slæʃ] vt acuchillar; (fig: prices) fulminar

slate [sleɪt] n pizarra ▷ vt (fig: criticize) criticar duramente

slaughter ['slɔːtə*] n (of animals) matanza; (of people) carnicería ▷ vt matar; **slaughterhouse** n matadero

Slav [slɑːv] adj eslavo

slave [sleɪv] n esclavo/a ▷ vi (also: ~ **away**) sudar tinta; **slavery** n esclavitud f

slay [sleɪ] (pt **slew**, pp **slain**) vt matar

sleazy ['sliːzɪ] adj de mala fama

sled [sled] (US) = **sledge**

sledge [sledʒ] n trineo

sleek [sliːk] adj (shiny) lustroso; (car etc) elegante

sleep [sliːp] (pt, pp **slept**) n sueño ▷ vi dormir; **to go to ~** quedarse dormido; **sleep in** vi (oversleep) quedarse dormido; **sleep together** vi (have sex) acostarse juntos; **sleeper** n (person) durmiente m/f; (BRIT Rail: on track) traviesa; (: train) coche-cama m; **sleeping bag** n saco de dormir; **sleeping car** n coche-cama m; **sleeping pill** n somnífero; **sleepover** n: **we're having a sleepover at Jo's** nos vamos a dormir a casa de Jo; **sleepwalk** vi caminar dormido;

(habitually) ser sonámbulo; **sleepy** adj soñoliento; (place) soporífero
sleet [sliːt] n aguanieve f
sleeve [sliːv] n manga; (Tech) manguito; (of record) portada; **sleeveless** adj sin mangas
sleigh [sleɪ] n trineo
slender ['slendə*] adj delgado; (means) escaso
slept [slept] pt, pp of **sleep**
slew [sluː] pt of **slay** ▷ vi (BRIT: veer) torcerse
slice [slaɪs] n (of meat) tajada; (of bread) rebanada; (of lemon) rodaja; (utensil) pala ▷ vt cortar (en lonjas), rebanar
slick [slɪk] adj (skilful) hábil, diestro; (clever) astuto ▷ n (also: **oil ~**) marea negra
slide [slaɪd] (pt, pp **slid**) n (movement) descenso, desprendimiento; (in playground) tobogán m; (Phot) diapositiva; (BRIT: also: **hair ~**) pasador m ▷ vt correr, deslizar ▷ vi (slip) resbalarse; (glide) deslizarse; **sliding** adj (door) corredizo
slight [slaɪt] adj (slim) delgado; (frail) delicado; (pain etc) leve; (trivial) insignificante; (small) pequeño ▷ n desaire m ▷ vt (offend) ofender, desairar; **not in the ~est** en absoluto; **slightly** adv ligeramente, un poco
slim [slɪm] adj delgado, esbelto; (fig: chance) remoto ▷ vi adelgazar; **slimming** n adelgazamiento
slimy ['slaɪmɪ] adj cenagoso
sling [slɪŋ] (pt, pp **slung**) n (Med) cabestrillo; (weapon) honda ▷ vt tirar, arrojar
slip [slɪp] n (slide) resbalón m; (mistake) descuido; (underskirt) combinación f; (of paper) papelito m ▷ vt (slide) deslizar ▷ vi deslizarse; (stumble) resbalar(se); (decline) decaer; (move smoothly): **to ~ into/out of** (room etc) introducirse en/salirse de ▷ **to give sb the ~** eludir a algn; **a ~ of the tongue** un lapsus; **to ~ sth on/off** ponerse/quitarse algo;

slip up vi (make mistake) equivocarse; meter la pata
slipper ['slɪpə*] n zapatilla, pantufla
slippery ['slɪpərɪ] adj resbaladizo
slip road (BRIT) n carretera de acceso
slit [slɪt] (pt, pp ~) n raja; (cut) corte m ▷ vt rajar; cortar
slog [slɒg] (BRIT) vi sudar tinta; **it was a ~** costó trabajo (hacerlo)
slogan ['sləugən] n eslogan m, lema m
slope [sləup] n (up) cuesta, pendiente f; (down) declive m; (side of mountain) falda, vertiente m ▷ vi: **to ~ down** estar en declive; **to ~ up** inclinarse; **sloping** adj en pendiente; en declive; (writing) inclinado
sloppy ['slɒpɪ] adj (work) descuidado; (appearance) desaliñado
slot [slɒt] n ranura ▷ vt: **to ~ into** encajar en; **slot machine** n (BRIT: vending machine) distribuidor m automático; (for gambling) tragaperras m inv
Slovakia [sləu'vækɪə] n Eslovaquia
Slovene [sləu'viːn] adj esloveno ▷ n esloveno/a; (Ling) esloveno; **Slovenia** [sləu'viːnɪə] n Eslovenia; **Slovenian** adj, n = **Slovene**
slow [sləu] adj lento; (not clever) lerdo; (watch): **to be ~** atrasar ▷ adv lentamente, despacio ▷ vt, vi retardar; **"~"** (road sign) "disminuir velocidad"; **slow down** vi reducir la marcha; **slowly** adv lentamente, despacio; **slow motion** n: **in slow motion** a cámara lenta
slug [slʌg] n babosa; (bullet) posta; **sluggish** adj lento; (person) perezoso
slum [slʌm] n casucha
slump [slʌmp] n (economic) depresión f ▷ vi hundirse; (prices) caer en picado
slung [slʌŋ] pt, pp of **sling**
slur [slɜː*] n: **to cast a ~ on** insultar ▷ vt (speech) pronunciar mal
sly [slaɪ] adj astuto; (smile) taimado
smack [smæk] n bofetada ▷ vt dar con la mano a; (child, on face) abofetear

▷ vi: **to ~ of** saber a, oler a

small [smɔːl] adj pequeño; **small ads** (BRIT) npl anuncios mpl por palabras; **small change** n suelto, cambio

smart [smɑːt] adj elegante; (clever) listo, inteligente; (quick) rápido, vivo ▷ vi escocer, picar; **smartcard** n tarjeta inteligente; **smart phone** n smartphone m

smash [smæʃ] n (also: **~-up**) choque m; (Mus) exitazo ▷ vt (break) hacer pedazos; (car etc) estrellar; (Sport: record) batir ▷ vi hacerse pedazos; (against wall etc) estrellarse; **smashing** (inf) adj estupendo

smear [smɪə*] n mancha; (Med) frotis m inv ▷ vt untar; **smear test** n (Med) citología, frotis m inv (cervical)

smell [smel] (pt, pp **smelt** or **~ed**) n olor m; (sense) olfato ▷ vt, vi oler; **smelly** adj maloliente

smelt [smelt] pt, pp of **smell**

smile [smaɪl] n sonrisa ▷ vi sonreír

smirk [smɜːk] n sonrisa falsa o afectada

smog [smɒɡ] n esmog m

smoke [sməuk] n humo ▷ vi fumar; (chimney) echar humo ▷ vt (cigarettes) fumar; **smoke alarm** n detector m de humo, alarma contra incendios; **smoked** adj (bacon, glass) ahumado; **smoker** n fumador(a) m/f; (Rail) coche m fumador; **smoking** n: **"no smoking"** "prohibido fumar"

▌ Be careful not to translate **smoking** by the Spanish word smoking.

smoky adj (room) lleno de humo; (taste) ahumado

smooth [smuːð] adj liso; (sea) tranquilo; (flavour, movement) suave; (sauce) fino; (person: pej) meloso ▷ vt (also: **~ out**) alisar; (creases, difficulties) allanar

smother ['smʌðə*] vt sofocar; (repress) contener

SMS n abbr (= short message service) (servicio) SMS; **SMS message** n (mensaje m) SMS

smudge [smʌdʒ] n mancha ▷ vt manchar

smug [smʌɡ] adj presumido; orondo

smuggle ['smʌɡl] vt pasar de contrabando; **smuggling** n contrabando

snack [snæk] n bocado; **snack bar** n cafetería

snag [snæɡ] n problema m

snail [sneɪl] n caracol m

snake [sneɪk] n serpiente f

snap [snæp] n (sound) chasquido; (photograph) foto f ▷ adj (decision) instantáneo ▷ vt (break) quebrar; (fingers) castañetear ▷ vi quebrarse; (fig: speak sharply) contestar bruscamente; **to ~ shut** cerrarse de golpe; **snap at** vt fus (dog) intentar morder; **snap up** vt agarrar; **snapshot** n foto f (instantánea)

snarl [snɑːl] vi gruñir

snatch [snætʃ] n (small piece) fragmento ▷ vt (snatch away) arrebatar; (fig) agarrar; **to ~ some sleep** encontrar tiempo para dormir

sneak [sniːk] (pt (us) **snuck**) vi: **to ~ in/out** entrar/salir a hurtadillas ▷ n (inf) soplón/ona m/f; **to ~ up on sb** aparecérsele de improviso a algn; **sneakers** npl zapatos mpl de lona

sneer [snɪə*] vi reír con sarcasmo; (mock): **to ~ at** burlarse de

sneeze [sniːz] vi estornudar

sniff [snɪf] vi sollozar ▷ vt husmear, oler; (drugs) esnifar

snigger ['snɪɡə*] vi reírse con disimulo

snip [snɪp] n tijeretazo; (BRIT: inf: bargain) ganga ▷ vt tijeretear

sniper ['snaɪpə*] n francotirador(a) m/f

snob [snɒb] n (e)snob mf

snooker ['snuːkə*] n especie de billar

snoop [snuːp] vi: **to ~ about** fisgonear

snooze [snuːz] n siesta ▷ vi echar una siesta

snore [snɔː*] n ronquido ▷ vi roncar

snorkel ['snɔːkl] n (tubo) respirador m

snort [snɔ:t] n bufido ▷ vi bufar

snow [snəʊ] n nieve f ▷ vi nevar;
snowball n bola de nieve ▷ vi (fig)
agrandirse, ampliarse; **snowstorm** n
nevada, nevasca

snub [snʌb] vt (person) desairar ▷ n
desaire m, repulsa

snug [snʌg] adj (cosy) cómodo; (fitted)
ajustado

○ **KEYWORD**

so [səʊ] adv 1 (thus, likewise) así, de este
modo; **if so** de ser así; **I like swimming
– so do I** a mí me gusta nadar – a mí
también; **I've got work to do – so has
Paul** tengo trabajo que hacer – Paul
también; **it's 5 o'clock – so it is!** son las
cinco – ¡pues es verdad!; **I hope/think
so** espero/creo que sí; **so far** hasta
ahora; (in past) hasta este momento
2 (in comparisons etc: to such a degree)
tan; **so quickly (that)** tan rápido (que);
she's not so clever as her brother
no es tan lista como su hermano;
we were so worried estábamos
preocupadísimos
3: **so much** adj, adv tanto; **so many**
tantos/as
4 (phrases): **10 or so** unos 10, 10 o así; **so
long!** (inf: goodbye) ¡hasta luego!
▷ conj 1 (expressing purpose): **so as to do**
hacer; **so (that)** para que +subjun
2 (expressing result) así que; **so you see,
I could have gone** así que ya ves, (yo)
podría haber ido

soak [səʊk] vt (drench) empapar;
(steep in water) remojar ▷ vi remojarse,
estar a remojo; **soak up** vt absorber;
soaking adj (also: **soaking wet**)
calado o empapado (hasta los huesos
o el tuétano)

so-and-so ['səʊənsəʊ] n (somebody)
fulano/a de tal

soap [səʊp] n jabón m; **soap opera**
n telenovela; **soap powder** n jabón
m en polvo

soar [sɔ:*] vi (on wings) remontarse;
(rocket: prices) dispararse; (building etc)
elevarse

sob [sɔb] n sollozo ▷ vi sollozar

sober ['səʊbə*] adj (serious) serio; (not
drunk) sobrio; (colour, style) discreto;
sober up vt quitar la borrachera

so-called ['səʊ'kɔ:ld] adj así llamado

soccer ['sɔkə*] n fútbol m

sociable ['səʊʃəbl] adj sociable

social ['səʊʃl] adj social ▷ n velada,
fiesta; **socialism** n socialismo;
socialist adj, n socialista mf; **socialize**
vi: **to socialize** alternar; **social life** n
vida social; **socially** adv socialmente;
social networking n interacción
social a través de la red; **social security**
n seguridad f social; **social services**
npl servicios mpl sociales; **social work**
n asistencia social; **social worker** n
asistente/a m/f social

society [sə'saɪətɪ] n sociedad f;
(club) asociación f; (also: **high ~**) alta
sociedad

sociology [səʊsɪ'ɔlədʒɪ] n sociología

sock [sɔk] n calcetín m

socket ['sɔkɪt] n cavidad f; (BRIT Elec)
enchufe m

soda ['səʊdə] n (Chem) sosa; (also: ~
water) soda; (us: also: ~ **pop**) gaseosa

sodium ['səʊdɪəm] n sodio

sofa ['səʊfə] n sofá m; **sofa bed** n
sofá-cama m

soft [sɔft] adj (lenient, not hard) blando;
(gentle, not bright) suave; **soft drink** n
bebida no alcohólica; **soft drugs** npl
drogas fpl blandas; **soften** ['sɔfn] vt
ablandar; suavizar; (effect) amortiguar
▷ vi ablandarse; suavizarse; **softly** adv
suavemente; (gently) delicadamente,
con delicadeza; **software** n (Comput)
software m

soggy ['sɔgɪ] adj empapado

soil [sɔɪl] n (earth) tierra, suelo ▷ vt
ensuciar

solar ['səʊlə*] adj solar; **solar power** n
energía solar; **solar system** n
sistema m solar

sold [səʊld] *pt, pp of* **sell**

soldier ['səʊldʒə*] *n* soldado; *(army man)* militar *m*

sold out *adj (Comm)* agotado

sole [səʊl] *n (of foot)* planta; *(of shoe)* suela; *(fish: pl inv)* lenguado ▷ *adj* único; **solely** *adv* únicamente, sólo, solamente; **I will hold you solely responsible** le consideraré el único responsable

solemn ['sɒləm] *adj* solemne

solicitor [sə'lɪsɪtə*] *(BRIT) n (for wills etc)* = notario/a; *(in court)* = abogado/a

solid ['sɒlɪd] *adj* sólido; *(gold etc)* macizo ▷ *n* sólido

solitary ['sɒlɪtərɪ] *adj* solitario, solo

solitude ['sɒlɪtjuːd] *n* soledad *f*

solo ['səʊləʊ] *n* solo ▷ *adv (fly)* en solitario; **soloist** *n* solista *m/f*

soluble ['sɒljʊbl] *adj* soluble

solution [sə'luːʃən] *n* solución *f*

solve [sɒlv] *vt* resolver, solucionar

solvent ['sɒlvənt] *adj (Comm)* solvente ▷ *n (Chem)* solvente *m*

sombre ['sɒmbə*] *(us* **somber)** *adj* sombrío

○ **KEYWORD**

some [sʌm] *adj* **1** *(a certain amount or number)*: **some tea/water/biscuits** té/agua/(unas) galletas; **there's some milk in the fridge** hay leche en el frigo; **there were some people outside** había algunas personas fuera; **I've got some money, but not much** tengo algo de dinero, pero no mucho

2 *(certain: in contrasts)* algunos/as; **some people say that ...** hay quien dice que ...; **some films were excellent, but most were mediocre** hubo películas excelentes, pero la mayoría fueron mediocres

3 *(unspecified)*: **some woman was asking for you** una mujer estuvo preguntando por ti; **he was asking for some book (or other)** pedía un libro;

some day algún día; **some day next week** un día de la semana que viene ▷ *pron* **1** *(a certain number)*: **I've got some** *(books etc)* tengo algunos; **as 2** *(a certain amount)* algo; **I've got some** *(money, milk)* tengo algo; **could I have some of that cheese?** ¿me puede dar un poco de ese queso?; **I've read some of the book** he leído parte del libro ▷ *adv*: **some 10 people** unas 10 personas, una decena de personas

some: **somebody** ['sʌmbədɪ] *pron* = **someone**; **somehow** *adv* de alguna manera; *(for some reason)* por una u otra razón; **someone** *pron* alguien; **someplace** *(us) adv* = **somewhere**; **something** *pron* algo; **would you like something to eat/drink?** ¿te gustaría cenar/tomar algo?; **sometime** *adv (in future)* algún día, en algún momento; *(in past)*: **sometime last month** durante el mes pasado; **sometimes** *adv* a veces; **somewhat** *adv* algo; **somewhere** *adv (be)* en alguna parte; *(go)* a alguna parte; **somewhere else** *(be)* en otra parte; *(go)* a otra parte

son [sʌn] *n* hijo

song [sɒŋ] *n* canción *f*

son-in-law ['sʌnɪnlɔː] *n* yerno

soon [suːn] *adv* pronto, dentro de poco; **~ afterwards** poco después; *see also* **as**; **sooner** *adv (time)* antes, más temprano; *(preference: rather)*: **I would sooner do that** preferiría hacer eso; **sooner or later** tarde o temprano

soothe [suːð] *vt* tranquilizar; *(pain)* aliviar

sophisticated [sə'fɪstɪkeɪtɪd] *adj* sofisticado

sophomore ['sɒfəmɔː*] *(us) n* estudiante *mf* de segundo año

soprano [sə'prɑːnəʊ] *n* soprano *f*

sorbet ['sɔːbeɪ] *n* sorbete *m*

sordid ['sɔːdɪd] *adj (place etc)* sórdido; *(motive etc)* mezquino

sore [sɔː*] *adj (painful)* doloroso, que duele ▷ *n* llaga

sorrow ['sɔrəʊ] n pena, dolor m
sorry ['sɔrɪ] adj (regretful) arrepentido;
(condition, excuse) lastimoso; ~!
¡perdón!, ¡perdone!; ~? ¿cómo?; **to feel**
~ for sb tener lástima a algn; **I feel ~ for**
him me da lástima
sort [sɔːt] n clase f, género, tipo; **sort**
out vt (papers) clasificar; (organize)
ordenar, organizar; (resolve: problem,
situation etc) arreglar, solucionar
SOS n SOS m
so-so ['səʊsəʊ] adv regular, así así
sought [sɔːt] pt, pp of **seek**
soul [səʊl] n alma
sound [saʊnd] n (noise) sonido,
ruido; (volume: on TV etc) volumen m;
(Geo) estrecho ▷ adj (healthy) sano;
(safe, not damaged) en buen estado;
(reliable: person) digno de confianza;
(sensible) sensato, razonable;
(secure: investment) seguro ▷ adv: ~
asleep profundamente dormido ▷ vt
(alarm) sonar ▷ vi sonar, resonar;
(fig: seem) parecer; **to ~ like** sonar a;
soundtrack n (of film) banda sonora
soup [suːp] n (thick) sopa; (thin) caldo
sour ['saʊə*] adj agrio; (milk) cortado;
it's ~ grapes (fig) están verdes
source [sɔːs] n fuente f
south [saʊθ] n sur m ▷ adj del sur,
sureño ▷ adv al sur, hacia el sur;
South Africa n África del Sur; **South**
African adj, n sudafricano/a m/f;
South America n América del Sur,
Sudamérica; **South American** adj, n
sudamericano/a m/f; **southbound**
adj (con) rumbo al sur; **southeastern**
[saʊθˈiːstən] adj sureste, del sureste;
southern ['sʌðən] adj del sur,
meridional; **South Korea** n Corea
del Sur; **South Pole** n Polo Sur;
southward(s) adv hacia el sur; **south-**
west n suroeste m; **southwestern**
[saʊθˈwestən] adj suroeste
souvenir [suːvəˈnɪə*] n recuerdo
sovereign ['sɔvrɪn] adj, n soberano/a
m/f
sow¹ [səʊ] (pt ~**ed**, pp **sown**) vt

sembrar
sow² [saʊ] n cerda, puerca
soya ['sɔɪə] (BRIT) n soja
spa [spaː] n balneario
space [speɪs] n espacio; (room)
sitio ▷ cpd espacial ▷ vt (also: ~ **out**)
espaciar; **spacecraft** n nave f espacial;
spaceship n = **spacecraft**
spacious ['speɪʃəs] adj amplio
spade [speɪd] n (tool) pala, laya;
spades npl (Cards: British) picas fpl;
(: Spanish) espadas fpl
spaghetti [spəˈɡetɪ] n espaguetis
mpl, fideos mpl
Spain [speɪn] n España
spam [spæm] n (junk email) spam m
span [spæn] n (of bird, plane)
envergadura; (of arch) luz f; (in time)
lapso ▷ vt extenderse sobre, cruzar;
(fig) abarcar
Spaniard ['spænjəd] n español(a)
m/f
Spanish ['spænɪʃ] adj español(a)
▷ n (Ling) español m, castellano; **the**
Spanish npl los españoles
spank [spæŋk] vt zurrar
spanner ['spænə*] (BRIT) n llave f
(inglesa)
spare [speə*] adj de reserva; (surplus)
sobrante, de más ▷ n = **spare part**
▷ vt (do without) pasarse sin; (refrain
from hurting) perdonar; **to ~** (surplus)
sobrante, de sobra; **spare part** n pieza
de repuesto; **spare room** n cuarto de
los invitados; **spare time** n tiempo
libre; **spare tyre** (US **spare tire**) n
(Aut) neumático (de LAM) de
recambio; **spare wheel** n (Aut) rueda
de recambio
spark [spaːk] n chispa; (fig) chispazo;
spark(ing) plug n bujía
sparkle ['spaːkl] n centelleo, destello
▷ vi (shine) relucir, brillar
sparrow ['spærəʊ] n gorrión m
sparse [spaːs] adj esparcido, escaso
spasm ['spæzəm] n (Med) espasmo
spat [spæt] pt, pp of **spit**
spate [speɪt] n (fig): **a ~ of** un

torrente de

spatula ['spætjulə] n espátula
speak [spi:k] (pt **spoke**, pp **spoken**)
vt (language) hablar; (truth) decir ▷ vi
hablar; (make a speech) intervenir; **to
~ to sb/of or about sth** hablar con
algn/de o sobre algo; **~ up!** ¡habla
fuerte!; **speaker** n (in public) orador(a)
m/f; (also: **loudspeaker**) altavoz m; (for
stereo etc) bafle m; (Pol): **the Speaker**
(BRIT) el Presidente de la Cámara de los
Comunes; (US) el Presidente del Congreso
spear [spɪə*] n lanza ▷ vt alancear
special ['spɛʃl] adj especial; (edition
etc) extraordinario; (delivery) urgente;
special delivery n (Post): **by special
delivery** por entrega urgente;
special effects npl (Cine) efectos mpl
especiales; **specialist** n especialista
mf; **speciality** [spɛʃɪ'ælɪtɪ] (BRIT)
n especialidad f; **specialize** vi: **to
specialize (in)** especializarse
(en); **specially** adv sobre todo,
en particular; **special needs** npl
(BRIT): **children with special needs**
niños que requieren una atención
diferenciada; **special offer** n (Comm)
oferta especial; **special school** n
(BRIT) colegio m de educación especial;
specialty (US) n =**speciality**
species ['spi:ʃi:z] n inv especie f
specific [spə'sɪfɪk] adj específico;
specifically adv específicamente
specify ['spɛsɪfaɪ] vt, vi especificar,
precisar
specimen ['spɛsɪmən] n ejemplar m;
(Med: of urine) espécimen m; (: of blood)
muestra
speck [spɛk] n grano, mota
spectacle ['spɛktəkl] n espectáculo;
spectacles npl (BRIT: glasses) gafas
fpl (SP), anteojos mpl; **spectacular**
[-'tækjulə*] adj espectacular; (success)
impresionante
spectator [spɛk'teɪtə*] n
espectador(a) m/f
spectrum ['spɛktrəm] (pl **spectra**)
n espectro

speculate ['spɛkjuleɪt] vi: **to ~ (on)**
especular (en)
sped [spɛd] pt, pp of **speed**
speech [spi:tʃ] n (faculty) habla;
(formal talk) discurso; (spoken language)
lenguaje m; **speechless** adj mudo,
estupefacto
speed [spi:d] n velocidad f; (promptness)
prisa; (promptness) rapidez f; **at full** or
top ~ a máxima velocidad; **speed up** vi
acelerarse ▷ vt acelerar; **speedboat**
n lancha motora; **speeding** n (Aut)
exceso de velocidad; **speed limit** n
límite m de velocidad, velocidad f
máxima; **speedometer** [spɪ'dɒmɪtə*]
n velocímetro; **speedy** adj (fast) veloz,
rápido; (prompt) pronto
spell [spɛl] (pt, pp **spelt** (BRIT) or **-ed**)
n (also: **magic ~**) encanto, hechizo;
(period of time) rato, período ▷ vt
deletrear; (fig) anunciar, presagiar;
to cast a ~ on sb hechizar a algn;
he can't ~ pone faltas de ortografía;
spell out vt (explain): **to spell sth out
for sb** explicar algo a algn en detalle;
spellchecker ['spɛltʃekə*] n corrector
m ortográfico; **spelling** n ortografía
spelt [spɛlt] pt, pp of **spell**
spend [spɛnd] (pt, pp **spent**) vt
(money) gastar; (time) pasar; (life)
dedicar; **spending** n: **government
spending** gastos mpl del gobierno
spent [spɛnt] pt, pp of **spend** ▷ adj
(cartridge, bullets, match) usado
sperm [spə:m] n esperma
sphere [sfɪə*] n esfera
spice [spaɪs] n especia ▷ vt
condimentar
spicy ['spaɪsɪ] adj picante
spider ['spaɪdə*] n araña
spike [spaɪk] n (point) punta; (Bot)
espiga
spill [spɪl] (pt, pp **spilt** or **-ed**) vt
derramar, verter ▷ vi derramarse; **to ~
over** desbordarse
spin [spɪn] (pt, pp **spun**) n (Aviat)
barrena; (trip in car) paseo (en coche);
(on ball) efecto ▷ vt (wool etc) hilar; (ball

etc) hacer girar ▷ vi girar, dar vueltas

spinach ['spɪnɪtʃ] n espinaca; (*as food*) espinacas fpl

spinal ['spaɪnl] adj espinal

spin doctor n informador(a) parcial al servicio de un partido político etc

spin-dryer (BRIT) n secador m centrífugo

spine [spaɪn] n espinazo, columna vertebral; (*thorn*) espina

spiral ['spaɪərl] n espiral f ▷ vi (*fig: prices*) subir desorbitadamente

spire ['spaɪə*] n aguja, chapitel m

spirit ['spɪrɪt] n (*soul*) alma; (*ghost*) fantasma m; (*attitude, sense*) espíritu m; (*courage*) valor m, ánimo; **spirits** npl (*drink*) licor(es) m(pl); **in good ~s** alegre, de buen ánimo

spiritual ['spɪrɪtjuəl] adj espiritual ▷ n espiritual m

spit [spɪt] (*pt, pp* **spat**) n (*for roasting*) asador m, espetón m; (*saliva*) saliva ▷ vi escupir; (*sound*) chisporrotear; (*rain*) lloviznar

spite [spaɪt] n rencor m, ojeriza ▷ vt causar pena a, mortificar; **in ~ of** a pesar de, pese a; **spiteful** adj rencoroso, malévolo

splash [splæʃ] n (*sound*) chapoteo; (*of colour*) mancha ▷ vt salpicar ▷ vi (*also: ~ about*) chapotear; **splash out** (*inf*) vi (BRIT) derrochar dinero

splendid ['splendɪd] adj espléndido

splinter ['splɪntə*] n (*of wood etc*) astilla; (*in finger*) espigón m ▷ vi astillarse, hacer astillas

split [splɪt] (*pt, pp* **split**) n hendedura, raja; (*fig*) división f ▷; (*Pol*) escisión f ▷ vt partir, rajar; (*party*) dividir; (*share*) repartir ▷ vi dividirse, escindirse; **split up** vi (*couple*) separarse; (*meeting*) acabarse

spoil [spɔɪl] (*pt, pp* **~t** or **~ed**) vt (*damage*) dañar; (*mar*) estropear; (*child*) mimar, consentir

spoilt [spɔɪlt] *pt, pp of* **spoil** ▷ adj (*child*) mimado, consentido; (*ballot paper*) invalidado

spoke [spəuk] *pt of* **speak** ▷ n rayo, radio

spoken ['spəukn] *pp of* **speak**

spokesman ['spəuksmən] (*irreg*) n portavoz m

spokesperson ['spəukspɜ:sn] (*irreg*) n portavoz m/f, vocero/a (LAM)

spokeswoman ['spəukswumən] (*irreg*) n portavoz f

sponge [spʌndʒ] n esponja; (*also: ~ cake*) bizcocho ▷ vi (*wash*) lavar con esponja ▷ vi: **to ~ off** or **on sb** vivir a costa de algn; **sponge bag** (BRIT) n esponjera

sponsor ['spɒnsə*] n patrocinador(a) m/f ▷ vt (*applicant, proposal etc*) proponer; **sponsorship** n patrocinio

spontaneous [spɒn'teɪnɪəs] adj espontáneo

spooky ['spu:kɪ] (*inf*) adj espeluznante, horripilante

spoon [spu:n] n cuchara; **spoonful** n cucharada

sport [spɔ:t] n deporte m; (*person*): **to be a good ~** ser muy majo ▷ vt (*wear*) lucir, ostentar; **sport jacket** (US) n = **sports jacket**; **sports car** n coche m deportivo; **sports centre** (BRIT) n polideportivo; **sports jacket** (BRIT) n chaqueta deportiva; **sportsman** (*irreg*) n deportista m; **sports utility vehicle** n todoterreno m inv; **sportswear** n trajes mpl de deporte or sport; **sportswoman** (*irreg*) n deportista; **sporty** adj deportista

spot [spɒt] n sitio, lugar m; (*dot: on pattern*) punto, mancha; (*pimple*) grano; (*Radio*) cuña publicitaria; (*TV*) espacio publicitario; (*small amount*): **a ~ of** un poquito de ▷ vt (*notice*) notar, observar; **on the ~** allí mismo; **spotless** adj perfectamente limpio; **spotlight** n foco, reflector m; (*Aut*) faro auxiliar

spouse [spauz] n cónyuge mf

sprain [spreɪn] n torcedura ▷ vt: **to ~ one's ankle/wrist** torcerse el tobillo/la muñeca

sprang [spræŋ] *pt of* **spring**

sprawl | 532

sprawl [sprɔːl] vi tumbarse

spray [spreɪ] n rociada; (of sea) espuma; (container) atomizador m; (for paint etc) pistola rociadora; (of flowers) ramita ▷ vt rociar; (crops) regar

spread [spred] (pt, pp ~) n extensión f; (for bread etc) pasta para untar; (inf: food) comilona f ▷ vt extender; (butter) untar; (wings, sails) desplegar; (work, wealth) repartir; (scatter) esparcir ▷ vi (also: ~ out: stain) extenderse; (news) diseminarse; **spread out** vi (move apart) separarse; **spreadsheet** n hoja electrónica or de cálculo

spree [spriː] n: **to go on a ~** ir de juerga

spring [sprɪŋ] (pt **sprang**, pp **sprung**) n (season) primavera; (leap) salto, brinco; (coiled metal) resorte m; (of water) fuente f, manantial m ▷ vi saltar, brincar; **spring up** vi (thing: appear) aparecer; (problem) surgir; **spring onion** n cebolleta

sprinkle [sprɪŋkl] vt (pour: liquid) rociar; (: salt, sugar) espolvorear; **to ~ water etc on, ~ with water etc** rociar or salpicar de agua etc

sprint [sprɪnt] n esprint m ▷ vi esprintar

sprung [sprʌŋ] pp of **spring**

spun [spʌn] pt, pp of **spin**

spur [spəː*] n espuela; (fig) estímulo, aguijón m ▷ vt (also: ~ **on**) estimular, incitar; **on the ~ of the moment** de improviso

spurt [spəːt] n chorro; (of energy) arrebato ▷ vi chorrear

spy [spaɪ] n espía m/f ▷ vi: **to ~ on** espiar a ▷ vt (see) divisar, lograr ver

sq. abbr = **square**

squabble [skwɔbl] vi reñir, pelear

squad [skwɔd] n (Mil) pelotón m; (Police) brigada; (Sport) equipo

squadron [skwɔdrən] n (Mil) escuadrón m; (Aviat, Naut) escuadra

squander [skwɔndə*] vt (money) derrochar, despilfarrar; (chances) desperdiciar

square [skweə*] n cuadro; (in town) plaza; (inf: person) carca m/f ▷ adj cuadrado; (inf: ideas, tastes) trasnochado ▷ vt (arrange) arreglar; (Math) cuadrar; (reconcile) compaginar; **al ~** igual(es); **to have a ~ meal** comer caliente; **2 metres ~** 2 metros en cuadro; **2 metres** 2 metros cuadrados; **square root** n raíz f cuadrada

squash [skwɔʃ] n (BRIT: drink): **lemon/orange ~** zumo (SP) or jugo (LAM) de limón/naranja; (US Bot) calabacín m; (Sport) squash m ▷ vt aplastar

squat [skwɔt] adj achaparrado ▷ vi (also: ~ **down**) agacharse, sentarse en cuclillas; **squatter** n okupa m/f (SP)

squeak [skwiːk] vi (hinge) chirriar, rechinar; (mouse) chillar

squeal [skwiːl] vi chillar, dar gritos agudos

squeeze [skwiːz] n presión f; (of hand) apretón m; (Comm) restricción f ▷ vt (hand, arm) apretar

squid [skwɪd] n inv calamar m; (Culin) calamares mpl

squint [skwɪnt] vi bizquear, ser bizco ▷ n (Med) estrabismo

squirm [skwəːm] vi retorcerse, revolverse

squirrel [skwɪrəl] n ardilla

squirt [skwəːt] vi salir a chorros ▷ vt chiscar

Sr abbr = **senior**

Sri Lanka [srɪˈlæŋkə] n Sri Lanka m

St abbr = **saint**; **street**

stab [stæb] n (with knife) puñalada; (of pain) pinchazo; (inf: try): **to have a ~ at (doing) sth** intentar (hacer) algo ▷ vt apuñalar

stability [stəˈbɪlɪtɪ] n estabilidad f

stable [steɪbl] adj estable ▷ n cuadra, caballeriza

stack [stæk] n montón m, pila ▷ vt amontonar, apilar

stadium [steɪdɪəm] n estadio

staff [staːf] n (work force) personal m,

plantilla; (BRIT Scol) cuerpo docente
stag [stæg] n cuerpo docente
stag [stæg] n ciervo, venado
stage [steɪdʒ] n escena; (point) etapa;
(platform) plataforma; (profession): **the
~** el teatro ▷ vt (play) poner en escena,
representar; (organize) montar,
organizar; **in ~s** por etapas
stagger ['stægə*] vi tambalearse
▷ vt (amaze) asombrar; (hours, holidays)
escalonar; **staggering** adj asombroso
stagnant ['stægnənt] adj estancado
stag night, stag party n
despedida de soltero
stain [steɪn] n mancha; (colouring)
tintura ▷ vt manchar; (wood) teñir;
stained glass n vidrio m de color;
stainless steel n acero inoxidable
staircase ['steəkeɪs] n = **stairway**
stairs [steəz] npl escaleras fpl
stairway ['steəweɪ] n escalera
stake [steɪk] n estaca, poste m;
(Comm) interés m; (Betting) apuesta
▷ vt (money) apostar; (life) arriesgar;
(reputation) poner en juego; (claim)
presentar una reclamación; **to be at ~**
estar en juego
stale [steɪl] adj (bread) duro; (food)
pasado; (smell) rancio; (beer) agrio
stalk [stɔːk] n tallo, caña ▷ vt
acechar, cazar al acecho
stall [stɔːl] n (in market) puesto; (in
stable) casilla de establo ▷ vt (Aut)
calar; (fig) dar largas a ▷ vi (Aut)
calarse; (fig) andarse con rodeos
stamina ['stæmɪnə] n resistencia
stammer ['stæmə*] n tartamudeo
▷ vi tartamudear
stamp [stæmp] n sello (SP),
estampilla (LAM), timbre m (MEX); (mark)
marca, huella; (on document) timbre
m ▷ vi (also: **~ one's foot**) patear ▷ vt
(mark) marcar; (letter) franquear; (with
rubber stamp) sellar; stamp out vt (fire)
apagar con el pie; (crime, opposition)
acabar con; **stamped addressed
envelope** n (BRIT) sobre m sellado con
las señas propias

stampede [stæm'piːd] n estampida
stance [stæns] n postura
stand [stænd] (pt, pp **stood**) n
(position) posición f, postura; (for
taxis) parada; (hall stand) perchero;
(music stand) atril m; (Sport) tribuna;
(at exhibition) stand m ▷ vi (be) estar,
encontrarse; (be on foot) estar de pie;
(rise) levantarse; (remain) quedar en
pie; (in election) presentar candidatura
▷ vt (place) poner, colocar; (withstand)
aguantar, soportar; (invite to) invitar;
to make a ~ (fig) mantener una
postura firme; **to ~ for parliament**
(BRIT) presentarse (como candidato) a
las elecciones; **stand back** vi retirarse;
stand by vi (be ready) estar listo
▷ vt fus (opinion) aferrarse a; (person)
apoyar; **stand down** vi (withdraw)
ceder el puesto; **stand for** vt fus
(signify) significar; (tolerate) aguantar,
permitir; **stand in for** vt fus suplir a;
stand out vi destacarse; **stand up** vi
levantarse, ponerse de pie; **stand up
for** vt fus defender; **stand up to** vt fus
hacer frente a
standard ['stændəd] n patrón m,
norma; (level) nivel m; (flag) estandarte
m ▷ adj (size etc) normal, corriente;
(text) básico; **standards** npl (morals)
valores mpl morales; **standard of
living** n nivel m de vida
standing ['stændɪŋ] adj (on foot) de
pie, en pie; (permanent) permanente
▷ n reputación f; **of many years' ~**
que lleva muchos años; **standing
order** (BRIT) n (at bank) orden f de pago
permanente
stand: **standpoint** n punto de vista;
standstill n: **at a standstill** (industry,
traffic) paralizado; (car) parado;
to come to a standstill quedar
paralizado; pararse
stank [stæŋk] pt of **stink**
staple ['steɪpl] n (for papers) grapa
▷ adj (food etc) básico ▷ vt grapar
star [stɑː*] n estrella; (celebrity)
estrella, astro ▷ vt (Theatre, Cinema)

ser el/la protagonista de; **the stars** npl
(Astrology) el horóscopo

starboard ['stɑːbəd] n estribor m

starch [stɑːtʃ] n almidón m

stardom ['stɑːdəm] n estrellato

stare [steə*] n mirada fija ▷ vi: **to ~
at** mirar fijo

stark [stɑːk] adj (bleak) severo,
escueto ▷ adv: **~ naked** en cueros

start [stɑːt] n principio, comienzo;
(departure) salida; (sudden movement)
salto, sobresalto; (advantage) ventaja
▷ vt empezar, comenzar; (cause)
causar; (found) fundar; (engine) poner
en marcha ▷ vi comenzar, empezar;
(with fright) asustarse, sobresaltarse;
(train etc) salir; **to ~ doing** or **to do
sth** empezar a hacer algo; **start off**
vi empezar, comenzar; (leave) salir,
ponerse en camino; **start out** vi
(begin) empezar; (set out) partir, salir;
start up vi comenzar; (car) ponerse
en marcha ▷ vt comenzar; poner en
marcha; **starter** n (Aut) botón m de
arranque; (Sport: official) juez mf de
salida; (BRIT Culin) entrante m; **starting
point** n punto de partida

startle ['stɑːtl] vt asustar,
sobrecoger; **startling** adj alarmante

starvation [stɑːˈveɪʃən] n hambre f

starve [stɑːv] vi tener mucha
hambre; (to death) morir de hambre
▷ vt hacer pasar hambre

state [steɪt] n estado ▷ vt (say,
declare) afirmar; **the S~s** los Estados
Unidos; **to be in a ~** estar agitado;
statement n afirmación f; **state
school** n escuela or colegio estatal;
statesman (irreg) n estadista m

static ['stætɪk] n (Radio) parásitos mpl
▷ adj estático

station ['steɪʃən] n estación f; (Radio)
emisora; (rank) posición f social ▷ vt
colocar, situar; (Mil) apostar

stationary ['steɪʃnərɪ] adj
estacionario, fijo

stationer's (shop) (BRIT) n
papelería

stationery [-nərɪ] n papel m de
escribir, artículos mpl de escritorio

station wagon (US) n ranchera

statistic [stəˈtɪstɪk] n estadística;
statistics n (science) estadística

statue ['stætjuː] n estatua

stature ['stætʃə*] n estatura; (fig)
talla

status ['steɪtəs] n estado; (reputation)
estatus m; **status quo** n (e)statu
quo m

statutory ['stætjutrɪ] adj
estatutorio

staunch [stɔːntʃ] adj leal,
incondicional

stay [steɪ] n estancia ▷ vi quedar(se);
(as guest) hospedarse; **to ~ put**
quedarse en el mismo sitio; **to ~ the
night/5 days** pasar la noche/estar 5 días;
stay away vi (from person, building)
no acercarse; (from event) no acudir;
stay behind vi quedarse atrás; **stay
in** vi quedarse en casa; **stay on** vi
quedarse; **stay out** vi (of house) no
volver a casa; (on strike) permanecer
en huelga; **stay up** vi (at night) velar,
no acostarse

steadily ['stedɪlɪ] adv
constantemente; (firmly) firmemente;
(work, walk) sin parar; (gaze) fijamente

steady ['stedɪ] adj (firm) firme;
(regular) regular; (person, character)
sensato, juicioso; (boyfriend) formal;
(look, voice) tranquilo ▷ vt (stabilize)
estabilizar; (nerves) calmar

steak [steɪk] n filete m; (beef) bistec m

steal [stiːl] (pt **stole**, pp **stolen**) vt
robar ▷ vi robar; (move secretly) andar
a hurtadillas

steam [stiːm] n vapor m; (mist) vaho,
humo ▷ vt (Culin) cocer al vapor ▷ vi
echar vapor; **steam up** vi (window)
empañarse; **to get steamed up
about sth** (fig) ponerse negro por algo;
steamy adj (room) lleno de vapor;
(window) empañado; (heat, atmosphere)
bochornoso

steel [stiːl] n acero ▷ adj de acero

steep [stiːp] adj escarpado, abrupto; (stair) empinado; (price) exorbitante, excesivo ▷vt empapar, remojar

steeple [stiːpl] n aguja

steer [stɪə*] vt (car) conducir (SP), manejar (LAM); (person) dirigir ▷vi conducir, manejar; **steering** n (Aut) dirección f; **steering wheel** n volante m

stem [stem] n (of plant) tallo; (of glass) pie m ▷vt detener; (blood) restañar

step [step] n paso; (on stair) peldaño, escalón m ▷vi: **to ~ forward/back** dar un paso adelante/hacia atrás; **steps** npl (BRIT) = **stepladder**; **in/out of ~ (with)** acorde/en disonancia (con); **step down** vi (fig) retirarse; **step in** vi entrar; (fig) intervenir; **step up** vt (increase) aumentar; **stepbrother** n hermanastro; **stepchild** (pl **stepchildren**) n hijastro a m/f; **stepdaughter** n hijastra; **stepfather** n padrastro; **stepladder** n escalera doble or de tijera; **stepmother** n madrastra; **stepsister** n hermanastra; **stepson** n hijastro

stereo [ˈstɪərɪəu] n estéreo ▷adj (also: **~phonic**) estéreo, estereofónico

stereotype [ˈstɪərɪətaɪp] n estereotipo ▷vt estereotipar

sterile [ˈsteraɪl] adj estéril; **sterilize** [ˈsterɪlaɪz] vt esterilizar

sterling [ˈstɜːlɪŋ] adj (silver) de ley ▷n (Econ) libras fpl esterlinas fpl; **one pound ~** una libra esterlina

stern [stɜːn] adj severo, austero ▷n (Aut) popa

steroid [ˈstɪərɔɪd] n esteroide m

stew [stjuː] n estofado, guiso ▷vt estofar, guisar; (fruit) cocer

steward [ˈstjuːəd] n camarero; **stewardess** n (esp on plane) azafata

stick [stɪk] (pt, pp **stuck**) n palo; (of dynamite) barreno; (as weapon) porra; (also: **walking ~**) bastón m ▷vt (glue) pegar; (inf: put) meter; (: tolerate) aguantar, soportar; (thrust): **to ~ sth into** clavar or hincar algo en ▷vi

pegarse; (be unmoveable) quedarse parado; (in mind) quedarse grabado; **stick out** vi sobresalir; **stick up** vi sobresalir; **stick up for** vt fus defender; **sticker** n (label) etiqueta engomada (with slogan) pegatina; **sticking plaster** n esparadrapo; **stick insect** n insecto palo; **stick shift** (US) n (Aut) palanca de cambios

sticky [ˈstɪkɪ] adj pegajoso; (label) engomado; (fig) difícil

stiff [stɪf] adj rígido, tieso; (hard) duro; (manner) estirado; (difficult) difícil; (person) inflexible; (price) exorbitante ▷adv: **scared/bored ~** muerto de miedo/aburrimiento

stifling [ˈstaɪflɪŋ] adj (heat) sofocante, bochornoso

stigma [ˈstɪgmə] n (fig) estigma m

stiletto [stɪˈletəu] (BRIT) n (also: **~ heel**) tacón m de aguja

still [stɪl] adj inmóvil, quieto ▷adv todavía; (even) aun; (nonetheless) sin embargo, aun así

stimulate [ˈstɪmjuleɪt] vt estimular

stimulus [ˈstɪmjuləs] (pl **stimuli**) n estímulo, incentivo

sting [stɪŋ] (pt, pp **stung**) n picadura; (pain) escozor m, picazón f; (organ) aguijón m ▷vt, vi picar

stink [stɪŋk] (pt **stank**, pp **stunk**) n hedor m, tufo ▷vi heder, apestar

stir [stɜː*] n (fig: agitation) conmoción f ▷vt (tea etc) remover; (fig: emotions) provocar ▷vi moverse; **stir up** vt (trouble) fomentar; **stir-fry** vt sofreír removiendo ▷n plato preparado sofriendo y removiendo los ingredientes

stitch [stɪtʃ] n (Sewing) puntada; (Knitting) punto; (Med) punto de sutura; (pain) punzada ▷vt coser; (Med) suturar

stock [stɔk] n (Comm: reserves) existencias fpl, stock m; (: selection) surtido; (Agr) ganado, ganadería; (Culin) caldo; (descent) raza, estirpe f; (Finance) capital m ▷adj (fig: reply etc) clásico ▷vt (have in stock) tener existencias de; **~s and shares** acciones y valores; **in ~** en existencia *or* almacén; **out of ~** agotado; **to take ~ of** (*fig*) asesorar, examinar; **stockbroker** ['stɔkbrəukə*] *n* agente *mf or* corredor *mf* de bolsa(s); **stock cube** (BRIT) *n* pastilla de caldo; **stock exchange** *n* bolsa; **stockholder** ['stɔkhəuldə*] (US) *n* accionista *m/f*

stocking ['stɔkɪŋ] *n* media

stock market *n* bolsa (de valores)

stole [stəul] *pt of* **steal** ▷ *n* estola

stolen ['stəuln] *pp of* **steal**

stomach ['stʌmək] *n* (*Anat*) estómago; (*belly*) vientre *m* ▷ *vt* tragar, aguantar; **stomachache** *n* dolor *m* de estómago

stone [stəun] *n* piedra; (*in fruit*) hueso (=6.348 kg; 14 libras) ▷ *adj* de piedra ▷ *vt* apedrear; (*fruit*) deshuesar

stood [stud] *pt, pp of* **stand**

stool [stu:l] *n* taburete *m*

stoop [stu:p] *vi* (*also: ~ **down**) doblarse, agacharse; (*also:* **have a ~**) ser cargado de espaldas

stop [stɔp] *n* parada; (*in punctuation*) punto ▷ *vt* parar, detener; (*break*) suspender; (*block: pay*) suspender; (*: cheque*) invalidar; (*also:* **put a ~ to**) poner término a ▷ *vi* pararse, detenerse; (*end*) acabarse; **to ~ doing sth** dejar de hacer algo; **stop by** *vi* pasar por; **stop off** *vi* interrumpir el viaje; **stopover** *n* parada; (*Aviat*) escala; **stoppage** *n* (*strike*) paro; (*blockage*) obstrucción *f*

storage ['stɔːrɪdʒ] *n* almacenaje *m*

store [stɔː*] *n* (*stock*) provisión *f*; (*depot; BRIT: large shop*) almacén *m*; (*reserve*) reserva, repuesto *m*; (US) tienda; **stores** *npl* víveres *mpl*; **to be in ~ for sb** (*fig*) esperarle a algn; **storekeeper** *n* (US) tendero/a

storey ['stɔːrɪ] (US **story**) *n* piso

storm [stɔːm] *n* tormenta; (*fig: of applause*) salva; (*: of criticism*) nube *f* ▷ *vi* (*fig*) rabiar ▷ *vt* tomar por asalto; **stormy** *adj* tempestuoso

story ['stɔːrɪ] *n* historia; (*lie*) mentira

(US) = **storey**

stout [staut] *adj* (*strong*) sólido; (*fat*) gordo, corpulento; (*resolute*) resuelto ▷ *n* cerveza negra

stove [stəuv] *n* (*for cooking*) cocina; (*for heating*) estufa

straight [streɪt] *adj* recto, derecho; (*frank*) franco, directo; (*simple*) sencillo ▷ *adv* derecho, directamente; (*drink*) sin mezcla; **to put** *or* **get sth ~** dejar algo en claro; **~ away, ~ off** en seguida; **straighten** *vt* (*also:* **straighten out**) enderezar, poner derecho ▷ *vi:* **straighten up** enderezarse, ponerse derecho; **straightforward** *adj* (*simple*) sencillo; (*honest*) honrado, franco

strain [streɪn] *n* tensión *f*; (*Tech*) presión *f*; (*Med*) torcedura; (*breed*) tipo, variedad *f* ▷ *vt* (*back etc*) torcerse; (*resources*) agotar; (*stretch*) estirar; (*food, tea*) colar; **strained** *adj* (*muscle*) torcido; (*laugh*) forzado; (*relations*) tenso; **strainer** *n* colador *m*

strait [streɪt] *n* (*Geo*) estrecho (*fig:*) **to be in dire ~s** estar en un gran apuro

strand [strænd] *n* (*of thread*) hebra; (*of hair*) trenza; (*of rope*) ramal *m*; **stranded** *adj* (*person: without money*) desamparado; (*: without transport*) colgado

strange [streɪndʒ] *adj* (*not known*) desconocido; (*odd*) extraño, raro; **strangely** *adv* de un modo raro; **stranger** *n* desconocido/a; (*from another area*) forastero/a

▌ Be careful not to translate **stranger** by the Spanish word *extranjero*.

strangle ['stræŋgl] *vt* estrangular

strap [stræp] *n* correa; (*of slip, dress*) tirante *m*

strategic [strə'tiːdʒɪk] *adj* estratégico

strategy ['strætɪdʒɪ] *n* estrategia

straw [strɔː] *n* paja; (*drinking straw*) caña, pajita; **that's the last ~!** ¡eso es el colmo!

strawberry ['strɔːbərɪ] *n* fresa,

frutilla (sc)
stray [streɪ] adj (animal) extraviado; (bullet) perdido; (scattered) disperso ▷ vi extraviarse, perderse

streak [striːk] n raya; (in hair) raya ▷ vt rayar ▷ vi: **to ~ past** pasar como un rayo

stream [striːm] n riachuelo, arroyo; (of people, vehicles) riada, caravana; (of smoke, insults etc) chorro ▷ vt dividir en grupos por habilidad ▷ vi correr, fluir; **to ~ in/out** (people) entrar/salir en tropel

street [striːt] n calle f; **streetcar** (us) n tranvía m; **street light** n (LAM), farola (SP); **street map** n plano (de la ciudad); **street plan** n plano

strength [strenθ] n fuerza; (of girder, knot etc) resistencia; (fig: power) poder m; **strengthen** vt fortalecer, reforzar

strenuous [ˈstrenjuəs] adj (energetic, determined) enérgico

stress [stres] n presión f; (mental strain) estrés m; (accent) acento ▷ vt subrayar, recalcar; (syllable) acentuar; **stressed** adj (tense estresado, agobiado; (syllable) acentuado; **stressful** adj (job) estresante

stretch [stretʃ] n (of sand etc) trecho ▷ vi estirarse; (extend): **to ~ to or as far as** extenderse hasta ▷ vt extender, estirar; (make demands) exigir el máximo esfuerzo a; **stretch out** vi tenderse ▷ vt (arm etc) extender; (spread) estirar

stretcher [ˈstretʃə*] n camilla

strict [strɪkt] adj severo; (exact) estricto; **strictly** adv severamente; estrictamente

stride [straɪd] (pt strode, pp stridden) n zancada, tranco ▷ vi dar zancadas, andar a trancos

strike [straɪk] (pt, pp struck) n huelga; (of oil etc) descubrimiento; (attack) ataque m ▷ vt golpear, pegar; (oil etc) descubrir; (bargain, deal) cerrar ▷ vi declarar la huelga; (attack) atacar; (clock) dar la hora; **on ~** (workers)

en huelga; **to ~ a match** encender un fósforo; **striker** n huelguista mf; (Sport) delantero; **striking** adj llamativo

string [strɪŋ] (pt, pp strung) n cuerda; (row) hilera ▷ vt: **to ~ together** ensartar; **to ~ out** extenderse; **the strings** npl (Mus) los instrumentos de cuerda; **to pull ~s** (fig) mover palancas

strip [strɪp] n tira; (of land) franja; (of metal) cinta, lámina ▷ vt desnudar; (paint) quitar; (also: ~ **down**: machine) desmontar ▷ vi desnudarse; **strip off** vt (paint etc) quitar ▷ vi (person) desnudarse

stripe [straɪp] n raya; (Mil) galón m; **striped** adj a rayas, rayado

stripper [ˈstrɪpə*] n artista mf de striptease

strip-search [ˈstrɪpsɑːtʃ] vt: **to ~ sb** desnudar y registrar a algn

strive [straɪv] (pt strove, pp striven) vi: **to ~ for sth/to do sth** luchar por conseguir/hacer algo

strode [strəʊd] pt of **stride**

stroke [strəʊk] n (blow) golpe m; (Swimming) brazada; (Med) apoplejía; (of paintbrush) toque m ▷ vt acariciar; **at a ~** de un solo golpe

stroll [strəʊl] n paseo, vuelta ▷ vi dar un paseo or una vuelta; **stroller** (us) n (for child) sillita de ruedas

strong [strɒŋ] adj fuerte; **they are 50 ~** son 50; **stronghold** n fortaleza; (fig) baluarte m; **strongly** adv fuertemente, con fuerza; (believe) firmemente

strove [strəʊv] pt of **strive**

struck [strʌk] pt, pp of **strike**

structure [ˈstrʌktʃə*] n estructura; (building) construcción f

struggle [ˈstrʌgl] n lucha ▷ vi luchar

strung [strʌŋ] pt, pp of **string**

stub [stʌb] n (of ticket etc) talón m; (of cigarette) colilla; **to ~ one's toe on sth** dar con el dedo (del pie) contra algo; **stub out** vt apagar

stubble [ˈstʌbl] n rastrojo; (on chin)

barba (incipiente)
stubborn ['stʌbən] adj terco,
testarudo
stuck [stʌk] pt, pp of **stick** ▷ adj
(jammed) atascado
stud [stʌd] n (shirt stud) corchete m;
(of boot) taco; (earring) pendiente m
(de bolita); (also: **~ farm**) caballeriza;
(BRIT) caballeriza; (also: **~ horse**) caballo semental ▷ vt
(fig): **~ded with** salpicado de
student ['stju:dənt] n estudiante
mf ▷ adj estudiantil; **student driver**
(us) n conductor(a) mf en prácticas;
students' union n (building) centro
de estudiantes; (BRIT: association)
federación f de estudiantes
studio ['stju:dɪəu] n estudio; (artist's)
taller m; **studio flat** n estudio
study ['stʌdɪ] n estudio ▷ vt
estudiar; (examine) examinar,
investigar ▷ vi estudiar
stuff [stʌf] n materia; (substance)
material m, sustancia; (things) cosas
fpl ▷ vt llenar; (Culin) rellenar; (animals)
disecar; (inf: push) meter; **stuffing**
n relleno; **stuffy** adj (room) mal
ventilado; (person) de miras estrechas
stumble ['stʌmbl] vi tropezar, dar
un traspié; **to ~ across, ~ on** (fig)
tropezar con
stump [stʌmp] n (of tree) tocón m; (of
limb) muñón m ▷ vt: **to be ~ed for an
answer** no saber qué contestar
stun [stʌn] vt dejar sin sentido
stung [stʌŋ] pt, pp of **sting**
stunk [stʌŋk] pp of **stink**
stunned [stʌnd] adj (dazed) aturdido,
atontado; (amazed) pasmado; (shocked)
anonadado
stunning ['stʌnɪŋ] adj (fig: news)
pasmoso; (: outfit etc) sensacional
stunt [stʌnt] n (in film) escena
peligrosa; (publicity stunt) truco
publicitario
stupid ['stju:pɪd] adj estúpido, tonto;
stupidity [-'pɪdɪtɪ] n estupidez f
sturdy ['stɜ:dɪ] adj robusto, fuerte
stutter ['stʌtə*] n tartamudeo ▷ vi

tartamudear
style [staɪl] n estilo; **stylish** adj
elegante, a la moda; **stylist** n (hair
stylist) peluquero/a
sub... [sʌb] prefix sub...;
subconscious adj subconsciente
subdued [səb'dju:d] adj (light) tenue;
(person) sumiso, manso
subject [n 'sʌbdʒɪkt, vb səb'dʒɛkt]
n súbdito; (Scol) asignatura; (matter)
tema m; (Grammar) sujeto ▷ vt: **to ~
sb to sth** someter a algo a algo; **to be
~ to** (law) estar sujeto a; (person) ser
propenso a; **subjective** [-'dʒɛktɪv] adj
subjetivo; **subject matter** n (content)
contenido
subjunctive [səb'dʒʌŋktɪv] adj, n
subjuntivo
submarine [sʌbmə'ri:n] n
submarino
submission [səb'mɪʃən] n sumisión f
submit [səb'mɪt] vt someter ▷ vi: **to
~ to sth** someterse a algo
subordinate [sə'bɔ:dɪnət] adj, n
subordinado/a m/f
subscribe [səb'skraɪb] vi suscribir;
to ~ to (opinion, fund) suscribir, aprobar;
(newspaper) suscribirse a
subscription [səb'skrɪpʃən] n
abono; (to magazine) suscripción f
subsequent ['sʌbsɪkwənt] adj
subsiguiente, posterior; **subsequently**
adv posteriormente, más tarde
subside [səb'saɪd] vi hundirse; (flood)
bajar; (wind) amainar
subsidiary [səb'sɪdɪərɪ] adj
secundario ▷ n sucursal f, filial f
subsidize ['sʌbsɪdaɪz] vt
subvencionar
subsidy ['sʌbsɪdɪ] n subvención f
substance ['sʌbstəns] n sustancia
substantial [səb'stænʃl] adj
sustancial, sustancioso; (fig)
importante
substitute ['sʌbstɪtju:t] n (person)
suplente m/f; (thing) sustituto ▷ vt: **to ~
A for B** sustituir A por B, reemplazar B
por A; **substitution** n sustitución f

subtle ['sʌtl] adj sutil

subtract [səb'trækt] vt restar, sustraer

suburb ['sʌbɜːb] n barrio residencial; **the ~s** las afueras (de la ciudad); **suburban** [sə'bɜːbən] adj suburbano; (train etc) de cercanías

subway ['sʌbweɪ] n (BRIT) paso subterráneo or inferior; (US) metro

succeed [sək'siːd] vi (person) tener éxito; (plan) salir bien ▷ vt suceder a; **to ~ in doing** lograr hacer

success [sək'ses] n éxito

> Be careful not to translate **success** by the Spanish word suceso.

successful adj exitoso; (business) próspero; **to be successful (in doing)** lograr (hacer); **successfully** adv con éxito

succession [sək'seʃən] n sucesión f, serie f

successive [sək'sesɪv] adj sucesivo

successor [sək'sesə*] n sucesor(a) m/f

succumb [sə'kʌm] vi sucumbir

such [sʌtʃ] adj tal, semejante; (of that kind): **~ a book** tal libro; (so much): **~ courage** tanto valor ▷ adv tan; **~ a long trip** un viaje tan largo; **~ a lot of** tanto(s)/a(s); **~ as** (like) tal como; **as ~** como tal; **such-and-such** adj tal o cual

suck [sʌk] vt chupar; (bottle) sorber; (breast) mamar

Sudan [su'dæn] n Sudán m

sudden ['sʌdn] adj (rapid) repentino, súbito; (unexpected) imprevisto; **all of a ~** de repente; **suddenly** adv de repente

sudoku [su'dəuku:] sudoku m

sue [su:] vt demandar

suede [sweɪd] n ante m, gamuza

suffer ['sʌfə*] vt sufrir, padecer; (tolerate) aguantar, soportar ▷ vi sufrir; **to ~ from** (illness etc) padecer; **suffering** n sufrimiento

suffice [sə'faɪs] vi bastar, ser suficiente

sufficient [sə'fɪʃənt] adj suficiente, bastante

suffocate ['sʌfəkeɪt] vi ahogarse, asfixiarse

sugar ['ʃugə*] n azúcar m ▷ vt echar azúcar a, azucarar

suggest [sə'dʒest] vt sugerir; **suggestion** [-'dʒestʃən] n sugerencia

suicide ['suɪsaɪd] n suicidio; (person) suicida mf; see also **commit**; **suicide attack** n atentado suicida; **suicide bomber** n terrorista mf suicida; **suicide bombing** n atentado suicida

suit [su:t] n (man's) traje m; (woman's) conjunto; (Law) pleito; (Cards) palo ▷ vt convenir; (clothes) sentar a, ir bien a; (adapt): **to ~ sth to** adaptar or ajustar algo a; **well ~ed** (well matched: couple) hecho el uno para el otro; **suitable** adj conveniente; (apt) indicado; **suitcase** n maleta, valija (RPL)

suite [swi:t] n (of rooms, Mus) suite f; (furniture): **bedroom/dining room ~** (juego de) dormitorio/comedor; see also **three-piece suite**

sulfur ['sʌlfə*] (US) n = **sulphur**

sulk [sʌlk] vi estar de mal humor

sulphur ['sʌlfə*] (US **sulfur**) n azufre m

sultana [sʌl'tɑːnə] n (fruit) pasa de Esmirna

sum [sʌm] n suma; (total) total m; **sum up** vt resumir ▷ vi hacer un resumen

summarize ['sʌmməraɪz] vt resumir

summary ['sʌmərɪ] n resumen m ▷ adj (justice) sumario

summer ['sʌmə*] n verano ▷ cpd de verano; **in ~** en verano; **summer holidays** npl vacaciones fpl de verano; **summertime** n (season) verano

summit ['sʌmɪt] n cima, cumbre f; (also: ~ **conference**, ~ **meeting**) (conferencia) cumbre f

summon ['sʌmən] vt (person) llamar; (meeting) convocar; (Law) citar

Sun. abbr (= Sunday) dom

sun [sʌn] n sol m; **sunbathe** vi tomar el sol; **sunbed** n cama solar;

sunblock n filtro solar; sunburn n (painful) quemadura; (tan) bronceado; sunburned, sunburnt adj (painfully) quemado por el sol; (tanned) bronceado
Sunday ['sʌndɪ] n domingo
sunflower ['sʌnflaʊə*] n girasol m
sung [sʌŋ] pp of sing
sunglasses ['sʌnɡlɑːsɪz] npl gafas fpl (sp) or anteojos fpl (LAM) de sol
sunk [sʌŋk] pp of sink
sun: sunlight n luz f del sol; sun lounger n tumbona, perezosa (LAM); sunny adj soleado; (day) de sol; (fig) alegre; sunrise n salida del sol; sun roof n (Aut) techo corredizo; sunscreen n protector m solar; sunset n puesta del sol; sunshade n (over table) sombrilla; sunshine n sol m; sunstroke n insolación f; suntan n bronceado; suntan lotion n bronceador m; suntan oil n aceite m bronceador
super ['suːpə*] (inf) adj genial
superb [suː'pɜːb] adj magnífico, espléndido
superficial [suːpə'fɪʃəl] adj superficial
superintendent [suːpərɪn'tendənt] n director(a) m/f; (Police) subjefe/a m/f
superior [suː'pɪərɪə*] adj superior; (smug) desdeñoso ▷ n superior m
superlative [suː'pɜːlətɪv] n superlativo
supermarket [suːpə'mɑːkɪt] n supermercado
supernatural [suːpə'nætʃərəl] adj sobrenatural ▷ n: the ~ lo sobrenatural
superpower ['suːpəpaʊə*] n (Pol) superpotencia
superstition [suːpə'stɪʃən] n superstición f
superstitious [suːpə'stɪʃəs] adj supersticioso
superstore ['suːpəstɔː*] n (BRIT) hipermercado
supervise ['suːpəvaɪz] vt supervisar; supervision [-'vɪʒən] n supervisión f; supervisor n supervisor(a) m/f

supper ['sʌpə*] n cena
supple ['sʌpl] adj flexible
supplement [n 'sʌplɪmənt, vb sʌplɪ'ment] n suplemento ▷ vt suplir
supplier [sə'plaɪə*] n (Comm) distribuidor(a) m/f
supply [sə'plaɪ] vt (provide) suministrar; (equip): to ~ (with) proveer (de) ▷ n provisión f; (of gas, water etc) suministro m; supplies npl (food) víveres mpl; (Mil) pertrechos mpl
support [sə'pɔːt] n apoyo; (Tech) soporte m ▷ vt apoyar; (financially) mantener; (uphold, Tech) sostener

▌ Be careful not to translate **support** by the Spanish word soportar.

supporter n (Pol etc) partidario/a; (Sport) aficionado/a
suppose [sə'pəʊz] vt suponer; (imagine) imaginarse; (duty): to be ~d to do sth deber hacer algo; supposedly [sə'pəʊzɪdlɪ] adv según cabe suponer; supposing conj en caso de que
suppress [sə'pres] vt suprimir; (yawn) ahogar
supreme [suː'priːm] adj supremo
surcharge ['sɜːtʃɑːdʒ] n sobretasa, recargo
sure [ʃʊə*] adj seguro; (definite, convinced) cierto; to make ~ of sth/that asegurarse de algo/asegurar que; ~! (of course) ¡claro!, ¡por supuesto!; ~ enough efectivamente; surely adv (certainly) seguramente
surf [sɜːf] n olas fpl ▷ vt: to ~ the Net navegar por Internet
surface ['sɜːfɪs] n superficie f ▷ vt (road) revestir ▷ vi salir a la superficie; by ~ mail por vía terrestre
surfboard ['sɜːfbɔːd] n tabla (de surf)
surfer ['sɜːfə*] n (in sea) surfista m/f; web or net ~ internauta m/f
surfing ['sɜːfɪŋ] n surf m
surge [sɜːdʒ] n oleada, oleaje m ▷ vi (wave) romper; (people) avanzar en tropel
surgeon ['sɜːdʒən] n cirujano/a

surgery ['sə:dʒərɪ] n cirugía; (BRIT: room) consultorio

surname ['sə:neɪm] n apellido

surpass [sə:'pɑ:s] vt superar, exceder

surplus ['sə:pləs] n excedente m; (Comm) superávit m ▷ adj excedente, sobrante

surprise [sə'praɪz] n sorpresa ▷ vt sorprender; **surprised** adj (look, smile) de sorpresa; **to be surprised** sorprenderse; **surprising** adj sorprendente; **surprisingly** adv: **it was surprisingly easy** me etc sorprendió lo fácil que fue

surrender [sə'rendə*] n rendición f, entrega ▷ vi rendirse, entregarse

surround [sə'raund] vt rodear, circundar; (Mil etc) cercar; **surrounding** adj circundante; **surroundings** npl alrededores mpl, cercanías fpl

surveillance [sə:'veɪləns] n vigilancia

survey [n 'sə:veɪ, vb sə:'veɪ] n inspección f, reconocimiento m; (inquiry) encuesta ▷ vt examinar, inspeccionar; (look at) mirar, contemplar; **surveyor** n agrimensor(a) m/f

survival [sə'vaɪvl] n supervivencia

survive [sə'vaɪv] vi sobrevivir; (custom etc) perdurar ▷ vt sobrevivir a; **survivor** n superviviente mf

suspect [adj, n 'sʌspekt, vb sə'spekt] adj, n sospechoso a m/f ▷ vt (person) sospechar de; (think) sospechar

suspend [sə'spend] vt suspender; **suspended sentence** n (Law) libertad f condicional; **suspenders** npl (BRIT) ligas fpl; (US) tirantes mpl

suspense [sə'spens] n incertidumbre f, duda; (in film etc) suspense m; **to keep sb in ~** mantener a algn en suspense

suspension [sə'spenʃən] n suspensión f; (of driving licence) privación f; **suspension bridge** n puente m colgante

suspicion [sə'spɪʃən] n sospecha; (distrust) recelo m; **suspicious** adj

receloso; (causing suspicion) sospechoso

sustain [sə'steɪn] vt sostener, apoyar; (suffer) sufrir, padecer

SUV (esp us) n abbr (= sports utility vehicle) todoterreno m inv, 4x4 m

swallow ['swɒləu] n (bird) golondrina ▷ vt tragar; (fig.: pride) tragarse

swam [swæm] pt of **swim**

swamp [swɒmp] n pantano, ciénaga ▷ vt (with water etc) inundar; (fig) abrumar, agobiar

swan [swɒn] n cisne m

swap [swɒp] n canje m, intercambio ▷ vt: **to ~ (for)** cambiar (por)

swarm [swɔ:m] n (of bees) enjambre m; (fig) multitud f ▷ vi (bees) formar un enjambre; (people) pulular; **to be ~ing with** ser un hervidero de

sway [sweɪ] vi mecerse, balancearse ▷ vt (influence) mover, influir en

swear [sweə*] (pt **swore**, pp **sworn**) vi (curse) maldecir; (promise) jurar ▷ vt jurar; **swear in** vt: **to be sworn in** prestar juramento; **swearword** n taco, palabrota

sweat [swet] n sudor m ▷ vi sudar

sweater ['swetə*] n suéter m

sweatshirt ['swetʃə:t] n suéter m

sweaty ['swetɪ] adj sudoroso

Swede [swi:d] n sueco/a

swede [swi:d] (BRIT) n nabo

Sweden ['swi:dn] n Suecia; **Swedish** ['swi:dɪʃ] adj sueco ▷ n (Ling) sueco

sweep [swi:p] (pt, pp **swept**) n (act) barrido; (also: **chimney ~**) deshollinador(a) m/f ▷ vt barrer; (with arm) empujar; (current) arrastrar ▷ vi barrer; (arm) moverse rápidamente; (wind) soplar con violencia

sweet [swi:t] n (candy) dulce m, caramelo; (BRIT: pudding) postre m ▷ adj dulce; (fig: kind) dulce, amable; (: attractive) mono; **sweetcorn** n maíz m; **sweetener** ['swi:tnə*] n (Culin) edulcorante m; **sweetheart** n novio/a; **sweetshop** n (BRIT) confitería, bombonería

swell [swel] (pt **-ed**, pp **swollen** or **-ed**)

n (of sea) marejada, oleaje m ▷ adj
(US: inf: excellent) estupendo, fenomenal
▷ vt hinchar, inflar ▷ vi (also: ~ **up**)
hincharse; (numbers) aumentar; (sound,
feeling) ir aumentando; **swelling** n
(Med) hinchazón f

swept [swept] pt, pp of **sweep**

swerve [swəːv] vi desviarse
bruscamente

swift [swɪft] n (bird) vencejo ▷ adj
rápido, veloz

swim [swɪm] (pt **swam**, pp **swum**)
n: **to go for a ~** ir a nadar or a bañarse
▷ vi nadar; (head, room) dar vueltas
▷ vt nadar; (the Channel etc) cruzar a
nado; **swimmer** n nadador(a) m/f;
swimming n natación f; **swimming
costume** (BRIT) n bañador m, traje m
de baño; **swimming pool** n piscina,
alberca (MEX), pileta (RPL); **swimming
trunks** npl bañador m (de hombre);
swimsuit n = **swimming costume**

swing [swɪŋ] (pt, pp **swung**) n (in
playground) columpio; (movement)
balanceo, vaivén m; (change of
direction) viraje m; (rhythm) ritmo ▷ vt
balancear; (also: ~ **round**) voltear, girar
▷ vi balancearse, columpiarse; (also: ~
round) dar media vuelta; **to be in full ~**
estar en plena marcha

swipe card [swaɪp-] n tarjeta
magnética deslizante, tarjeta swipe

swirl [swəːl] vi arremolinarse

Swiss [swɪs] adj, n inv suizo/a m/f

switch [swɪtʃ] n (for light etc)
interruptor m; (change) cambio ▷ vt
(change) cambiar de; **switch off** vt
apagar; (engine) parar; **switch on** vt
encender (SP), prender (LAM); (engine,
machine) arrancar; **switchboard** n (Tel)
centralita (SP), conmutador m (LAM)

Switzerland [ˈswɪtsələnd] n Suiza

swivel [ˈswɪvl] vi (also: ~ **round**) girar

swollen [ˈswəʊlən] pp of **swell**

swoop [swuːp] n (by police etc) redada
▷ vi (also: ~ **down**) calarse

swop [swɒp] = **swap**

sword [sɔːd] n espada; **swordfish** n

pez m espada

swore [swɔː*] pt of **swear**

sworn [swɔːn] pp of **swear** ▷ adj
(statement) bajo juramento; (enemy)
implacable

swum [swʌm] pp of **swim**

swung [swʌŋ] pt, pp of **swing**

syllable [ˈsɪləbl] n sílaba

syllabus [ˈsɪləbəs] n programa m
de estudios

symbol [ˈsɪmbl] n símbolo;
symbolic(al) [sɪmˈbɒlɪk(l)] adj
simbólico; **to be symbolic(al) of sth**
simbolizar algo

symmetrical [sɪˈmetrɪkl] adj
simétrico

symmetry [ˈsɪmɪtrɪ] n simetría

sympathetic [sɪmpəˈθetɪk] adj
(understanding) comprensivo; (showing
support): **~ to(wards)** bien dispuesto
hacia

> ▌ Be careful not to translate
> **sympathetic** by the Spanish word
> *simpático*.

sympathize [ˈsɪmpəθaɪz] vi: **to
~ with** (person) compadecerse de;
(feelings) comprender; (cause) apoyar

sympathy [ˈsɪmpəθɪ] n (pity)
compasión f

symphony [ˈsɪmfənɪ] n sinfonía

symptom [ˈsɪmptəm] n síntoma
m, indicio

synagogue [ˈsɪnəgɒg] n sinagoga

syndicate [ˈsɪndɪkɪt] n sindicato; (of
newspapers) agencia (de noticias)

syndrome [ˈsɪndrəʊm] n síndrome
m

synonym [ˈsɪnənɪm] n sinónimo

synthetic [sɪnˈθetɪk] adj sintético

Syria [ˈsɪrɪə] n Siria

syringe [sɪˈrɪndʒ] n jeringa

syrup [ˈsɪrəp] n jarabe m; (also:
golden ~) almíbar m

system [ˈsɪstəm] n sistema m; (Anat)
organismo; **systematic** [-ˈmætɪk]
adj sistemático, metódico; **systems
analyst** n analista m/f de sistemas

t

la prensa popular británica, por el tamaño más pequeño de los periódicos. A diferencia de los de la llamada **quality press**, estas publicaciones se caracterizan por un lenguaje sencillo, una presentación llamativa y un contenido sensacionalista, centrado a veces en los escándalos financieros y sexuales de los famosos, por lo que también reciben el nombre peyorativo de "gutter press".

ta [tɑ:] (BRIT: inf) excl ¡gracias!
tab [tæb] n lengüeta; (label) etiqueta; **to keep ~s on** (fig) vigilar
table ['teɪbl] n mesa; (of statistics etc) cuadro, tabla ▷ vt (BRIT: motion etc) presentar; **to lay** o **set the ~** poner la mesa; **tablecloth** n mantel m; **table d'hôte** [tɑ:bl'dəut] adj del menú; **table lamp** n lámpara de mesa; **tablemat** n (for plate) posaplatos m inv; (for hot dish) salvamantel m; **tablespoon** n cuchara de mesa; (also: **tablespoonful**: as measurement) cucharada
tablet ['tæblɪt] n (Med) pastilla, comprimido; (of stone) lápida
table tennis n ping-pong m, tenis m de mesa
tabloid ['tæblɔɪd] n periódico popular sensacionalista

  ⬤ **TABLOID PRESS**

  ⬤ El término **tabloid press** o
  ⬤ **tabloids** se usa para referirse a

taboo [tə'bu:] adj, n tabú m
tack [tæk] n (nail) tachuela; (fig) rumbo ▷ vt (nail) clavar con tachuelas; (stitch) hilvanar ▷ vi virar
tackle ['tækl] n (fishing tackle) aparejo (de pescar); (for lifting) aparejo ▷ vt (difficulty) enfrentarse con; (challenge: person) hacer frente a; (grapple with) agarrar; (Football) cargar; (Rugby) placar
tacky ['tækɪ] adj pegajoso; (pej) cutre
tact [tækt] n tacto, discreción f;
tactful adj discreto, diplomático
tactics ['tæktɪks] npl táctica
tactless ['tæktlɪs] adj indiscreto
tadpole ['tædpəul] n renacuajo
taffy ['tæfɪ] (us) n melcocha
tag [tæg] n (label) etiqueta
tail [teɪl] n cola; (of shirt, coat) faldón m ▷ vt (follow) vigilar a; **tails** npl (formal suit) levita
tailor ['teɪlə*] n sastre m
Taiwan [taɪ'wɑ:n] n Taiwán m;
Taiwanese [taɪwə'ni:z] adj, n taiwanés/esa m/f
take [teɪk] (pt **took**, pp **taken**) vt tomar; (grab) coger (SP), agarrar (LAM); (gain: prize) ganar; (require: effort, courage) exigir; (tolerate: pain etc) aguantar; (hold: passengers etc) tener cabida para; (accompany, bring, carry) llevar; (exam) presentarse a; **to ~ sth from** (drawer etc) sacar algo de; (person) quitar algo a; **I ~ it that ...** supongo

que ...; **take after** vt fus parecerse a; **take apart** vt desmontar; **take away** vt (remove) quitar; (carry) llevar; (Math) restar; **take back** vt (return) devolver; (one's words) retractarse de; **take down** vt (building) derribar; (letter etc) apuntar; **take in** vt (deceive) engañar; (understand) entender; (include) abarcar; (lodger) acoger, recibir; **take off** vi (Aviat) despegar ▷ vt (remove) quitar; **take on** vt (work) aceptar; (employee) contratar; (opponent) desafiar; **take out** vt sacar; (business) tomar posesión de; (country) tomar el poder ▷ vi: **to take over from sb** reemplazar a algn (about) desafiar; **take up** vt (a dress) acortar; (occupy: time, space) ocupar; (engage in: hobby etc) dedicarse a; (accept): **to take sb up on** aceptar algo de algn; **takeaway** (BRIT) adj (food) para llevar ▷ n tienda or restaurante m de comida para llevar; **taken** pp of **take; takeoff** n (Aviat) despegue m; **takeout** (US) n = **takeaway; takeover** n (Comm) absorción f; **takings** npl (Comm) ingresos mpl

talc [tælk] n (also: **~um powder**) (polvos de) talco

tale [teɪl] n (story) cuento; (account) relación f; **to tell ~s** (fig) chivarse

talent ['tælnt] n talento; **talented** adj de talento

talk [tɔːk] n charla; (conversation) conversación f; (gossip) habladurías fpl, chismes mpl ▷ vi hablar; **talks** fpl (Pol etc) conversaciones fpl; **to ~ about** hablar de; **to ~ sb into doing sth** convencer a algn para que haga algo; **to ~ sb out of doing sth** disuadir a algn de que haga algo; **to ~ shop** hablar del trabajo; **talk over** vt discutir; **talk show** n programa m de entrevistas

tall [tɔːl] adj alto; (object) grande; **to be 6 feet ~** (person) = medir 1 metro 80

tambourine [tæmbə'riːn] n pandereta

tame [teɪm] adj domesticado; (fig) mediocre

tamper ['tæmpə*] vi: **to ~ with** tocar, andar con

tampon ['tæmpɒn] n tampón m

tan [tæn] n (also: **sun~**) bronceado ▷ vi ponerse moreno ▷ adj (colour) marrón

tandem ['tændəm] n tándem m

tangerine [tændʒə'riːn] n mandarina

tangle ['tæŋgl] n enredo; **to get in(to) a ~** enredarse

tank [tæŋk] n (water tank) depósito, tanque m; (for fish) acuario; (Mil) tanque m

tanker ['tæŋkə*] n (ship) buque m, cisterna; (truck) camión m cisterna

tanned [tænd] adj (skin) moreno

tantrum ['tæntrəm] n rabieta

Tanzania [tænzə'nɪə] n Tanzania

tap [tæp] n (BRIT: on sink etc) grifo (SP), llave f, canilla (RPL); (gas tap) llave f; (gentle blow) golpecito ▷ vt (hit gently) dar golpecitos en; (resources) utilizar, explotar; (telephone) intervenir; **on ~** (fig: resources) a mano; **tap dancing** n claqué m

tape [teɪp] n (also: **magnetic ~**) cinta magnética; (cassette) cassette f, cinta; (sticky tape) cinta adhesiva; (for tying) cinta ▷ vt (record) grabar (en cinta); (stick with tape) pegar con cinta adhesiva; **tape measure** n cinta métrica, metro; **tape recorder** n grabadora

tapestry ['tæpɪstrɪ] n (object) tapiz m; (art) tapicería

tar [tɑː] n alquitrán m, brea

target ['tɑːgɪt] n blanco

tariff ['tærɪf] n (on goods) arancel m; (BRIT: in hotels etc) tarifa

tarmac ['tɑːmæk] n (BRIT: on road) asfaltado; (Aviat) pista (de aterrizaje)

tarpaulin [tɑː'pɔːlɪn] n lona impermeabilizada

tarragon ['tærəgən] n estragón m

tart [tɑːt] n (Culin) tarta; (BRIT: inf: prostitute) puta ▷ adj agrio, ácido

tartan ['tɑːtn] n tejido escocés m
tartar(e) sauce ['tɑːtə-] n salsa tártara
task [tɑːsk] n tarea; **to take to ~** reprender
taste [teɪst] n (sense) gusto; (flavour) sabor m; (sample): **have a ~!** iprueba un poquito!; (fig) muestra, idea ▷ vt probar ▷ vi: **to ~ of** or **like** (fish, garlic etc) saber a; **you can ~ the garlic (in it)** se nota el sabor a ajo; **in good/bad ~** de buen/mal gusto; **tasteful** adj de buen gusto; **tasteless** adj (food) soso; (remark etc) de mal gusto; **tasty** adj sabroso, rico
tatters ['tætəz] npl: **in ~** hecho jirones
tattoo [tə'tuː] n tatuaje m; (spectacle) espectáculo militar ▷ vt tatuar
taught [tɔːt] pt, pp of **teach**
taunt [tɔːnt] n burla ▷ vt burlarse de
Taurus ['tɔːrəs] n Tauro
taut [tɔːt] adj tirante, tenso
tax [tæks] n impuesto ▷ vt gravar (con un impuesto); (fig: memory) poner a prueba; (: patience) agotar; **tax-free** adj libre de impuestos
taxi ['tæksɪ] n taxi m ▷ vi (Aviat) rodar por la pista; **taxi driver** n taxista mf; **taxi rank** (BRIT) n = **taxi stand**; **taxi stand** n parada de taxis
tax payer n contribuyente mf
TB n abbr = **tuberculosis**
tea [tiː] n té m; (BRIT: meal) = merienda (SP); cena; **high ~** (BRIT) merienda-cena (SP); **tea bag** n bolsita de té; **tea break** (BRIT) n descanso para el té
teach [tiːtʃ] (pt, pp **taught**) vt: **to ~ sb sth**, **~ sth to sb** enseñar algo a algn ▷ vi (be a teacher) ser profesor(a), enseñar; **teacher** n (in secondary school) profesor(a) m/f; (in primary school) maestro/a, profesor(a) de EGB; **teaching** n enseñanza
tea: **tea cloth** n (BRIT) paño de cocina, trapo de cocina (LAM); **teacup** n taza para el té
tea leaves npl hojas de té
team [tiːm] n equipo; (of horses) tiro;

team up vi asociarse
teapot ['tiːpɒt] n tetera
tear¹ [tɪə*] n lágrima; **in ~s** llorando
tear² [tɛə*] (pt **tore**, pp **torn**) n rasgón m, desgarrón m ▷ vt romper, rasgar ▷ vi rasgarse; **tear apart** vt (also fig) hacer pedazos; **tear down** vt +adv (building, statue) derribar; (poster, flag) arrancar; **tear off** vt (sheet of paper etc) arrancar; (one's clothes) quitarse a tirones; **tear up** vt (sheet of paper etc) romper
tearful ['tɪəful] adj lloroso
tear gas ['tɪə-] n gas m lacrimógeno
tearoom ['tiːruːm] n salón m de té
tease [tiːz] vt tomar el pelo a
tea: **teaspoon** n cucharita; (also: **teaspoonful**: as measurement) cucharadita; **teatime** n hora del té; **tea towel** (BRIT) n paño de cocina
technical ['teknɪkl] adj técnico
technician [tek'nɪʃn] n técnico/a
technique [tek'niːk] n técnica
technology [tek'nɒlədʒɪ] n tecnología
teddy (bear) ['tedɪ-] n osito de felpa
tedious ['tiːdɪəs] adj pesado, aburrido
tee [tiː] n (Golf) tee m
teen [tiːn] adj = **teenage** ▷ n (US) = **teenager**
teenage ['tiːneɪdʒ] adj (fashions etc) juvenil; (children) quinceañero; **teenager** n adolescente mf
teens [tiːnz] npl: **to be in one's ~** ser adolescente
teeth [tiːθ] npl of **tooth**
teetotal ['tiː'təutl] adj abstemio
telecommunications [telɪkəmjuːnɪ'keɪʃənz] n telecomunicaciones fpl
telegram ['telɪgræm] n telegrama m
telegraph pole ['telɪgrɑːf-] n poste m telegráfico
telephone ['telɪfəun] n teléfono ▷ vt llamar por teléfono, telefonear; (message) dar por teléfono; **to be on the ~** (talking) hablar por teléfono; (possessing telephone) tener teléfono;

telephone book n guía f telefónica; **telephone booth**, **telephone box** (BRIT) n cabina telefónica; **telephone call** n llamada (telefónica); **telephone directory** n guía (telefónica); **telephone number** n número de teléfono

telesales ['teliseilz] npl televenta s (f(pl))

telescope ['teliskəup] n telescopio

televise ['telivaiz] vt televisar

television ['telivi3ən] n televisión f; **on ~** en la televisión; **television programme** n programa m de televisión

tell [tel] (pt, pp **told**) vt decir; (relate: story) contar; (distinguish): **to ~ sth from** distinguir algo de ▷ vi (talk): **to ~ (of)** contar; (have effect) tener efecto; **to ~ sb to do sth** mandar a algn hacer algo; **tell off** vt **to tell sb off** regañar a algn; **teller** n (in bank) cajero/a

telly ['teli] (BRIT: inf) n abbr (= television) tele f

temp [temp] n abbr (BRIT) (= temporary) temporero/a

temper ['tempə*] n (nature) carácter m; (mood) humor m; (bad temper) (mal) genio; (fit of anger) acceso de ira ▷ vt (moderate) moderar; **to be in a ~** estar furioso; **to lose one's ~** enfadarse, enojarse

temperament ['temprəmənt] n (nature) temperamento; **temperamental** [temprə'mentl] adj temperamental

temperature ['temprətʃə*] n temperatura; **to have** or **run a ~** tener fiebre

temple ['templ] n (building) templo; (Anat) sien f

temporary ['tempərəri] adj provisional; (passing) transitorio; (worker) temporero; (job) temporal

tempt [tempt] vt tentar; **to ~ sb into doing sth** tentar o inducir a algn a hacer algo; **temptation** n tentación

f; **tempting** adj tentador(a); (food) apetitoso/a

ten [ten] num diez

tenant ['tenənt] n inquilino/a

tend [tend] vt cuidar ▷ vi: **to ~ to do sth** tener tendencia a hacer algo; **tendency** ['tendənsı] n tendencia

tender ['tendə*] adj (person, care) tierno, cariñoso; (meat) tierno; (sore) sensible ▷ n (Comm: offer) oferta; (money): **legal ~** moneda de curso legal ▷ vt ofrecer

tendon ['tendən] n tendón m

tenner ['tenə*] n (inf) (billete m de) diez libras m

tennis ['tenis] n tenis m; **tennis ball** n pelota de tenis; **tennis court** n cancha de tenis; **tennis match** n partido de tenis; **tennis player** n tenista mf; **tennis racket** n raqueta de tenis

tenor ['tenə*] n (Mus) tenor m

tenpin bowling ['tenpin-] n (juego de los) bolos

tense [tens] adj (person) nervioso; (moment, atmosphere) tenso; (muscle) tenso, en tensión ▷ n (Ling) tiempo

tension ['tenʃən] n tensión f

tent [tent] n tienda (de campaña) (SP), carpa (LAM)

tentative ['tentətiv] adj (person, smile) indeciso; (conclusion, plans) provisional

tenth [tenθ] num décimo

tent: **tent peg** n clavija, estaca; **tent pole** n mástil m

tepid ['tepid] adj tibio

term [tə:m] n (word) término; (period) período; (Scol) trimestre m ▷ vt llamar; **terms** npl (conditions, Comm) condiciones fpl; **in the short/long ~** a corto/largo plazo; **to be on good ~s with sb** llevarse bien con algn; **to come to ~s with** (problem) aceptar

terminal ['tə:minl] adj (disease) mortal; (patient) terminal ▷ n (Elec) borne m; (Comput) terminal m; (also: **air ~**) terminal f; (BRIT: also: **coach ~**)

estación f terminal f

terminate ['tɜːmɪneɪt] vt terminar

termini ['tɜːmɪnaɪ] npl of **terminus**

terminology [tɜːmɪ'nɒlədʒɪ] n terminología

terminus ['tɜːmɪnəs] (pl **termini**) n término, (estación f) terminal f

terrace ['terəs] n terraza; (BRIT: row of houses) hilera de casas adosadas; **the ~s** (BRIT Sport) las gradas fpl; **terraced** adj (garden) en terrazas; (house) adosado

terrain [te'reɪn] n terreno

terrestrial [tɪ'restrɪəl] adj (life) terrestre; (BRIT: channel) de transmisión (por) vía terrestre

terrible ['terɪbl] adj terrible, horrible; (inf) atroz; **terribly** adv terriblemente; (very badly) malísimamente

terrier ['terɪə*] n terrier m

terrific [tə'rɪfɪk] adj (very great) tremendo; (wonderful) fantástico, fenomenal

terrified ['terɪfaɪd] adj aterrorizado

terrify ['terɪfaɪ] vt aterrorizar; **terrifying** adj aterrador(a)

territorial [terɪ'tɔːrɪəl] adj territorial

territory ['terɪtərɪ] n territorio

terror ['terə*] n terror m; **terrorism** n terrorismo; **terrorist** n terrorista mf; **terrorist attack** n atentado (terrorista)

test [test] n (gen, Chem) prueba; (Med) examen m; (Scol) examen m, test m; (also: **driving ~**) examen m de conducir ▷ vt probar, poner a prueba; (Med, Scol) examinar

testicle ['testɪkl] n testículo

testify ['testɪfaɪ] vi (Law) prestar declaración; **to ~ to sth** atestiguar algo

testimony ['testɪmənɪ] n (Law) testimonio

test: test match n (Cricket, Rugby) partido internacional; **test tube** n probeta

tetanus ['tetənəs] n tétano

text [tekst] n texto; (on mobile phone)

mensaje m (de texto) ▷ vt: **to ~ sb** (inf) enviar un mensaje (de texto) or un SMS a algn; **textbook** n libro de texto

textile ['tekstaɪl] n textil m, tejido

text message n mensaje m de texto

text messaging [-'mesɪdʒɪŋ] n (envío de) mensajes mpl de texto

texture ['tekstʃə*] n textura

Thai [taɪ] adj, n tailandés/esa m/f

Thailand ['taɪlænd] n Tailandia

than [ðæn] conj (in comparisons): **more ~ 10/once** más de 10/una vez; **I have more/less ~ you/Paul** tengo más/menos que tú/Paul; **she is older ~ you think** es mayor de lo que piensas

thank [θæŋk] vt dar las gracias a, agradecer; **~ you (very much)** muchas gracias; **~ God!** ¡gracias a Dios! ▷ excl (also: **many ~s, ~s a lot**) ¡gracias! ▷ **~s** to prep gracias a; **thanks** npl gracias fpl; **thankfully** adv (fortunately) afortunadamente; **Thanksgiving (Day)** n día m de Acción de Gracias

● **THANKSGIVING (DAY)**
●
●
● En Estados Unidos el cuarto jueves
● de noviembre es **Thanksgiving**
● **Day**, fiesta oficial en la que se
● recuerda la celebración que
● hicieron los primeros colonos
● norteamericanos ("Pilgrims"
● o "Pilgrim Fathers") tras la
● estupenda cosecha de 1621, por
● la que se dan gracias a Dios. En
● Canadá se celebra una fiesta
● semejante el segundo lunes
● de octubre, aunque no está
● relacionada con dicha fecha
● histórica.

○ **KEYWORD**

that [ðæt] (pl **those**) adj (demonstrative) ese/a; (pl) esos/as; (more remote) aquel(aquella); (pl) aquellos/as; **leave those books on the table** deja

thatched | 548

esos libros sobre la mesa; **that one**
ése(ésa); *(more remote)* aquél(aquélla);
that one over there ése(ésa) de ahí;
aquél(aquélla) de allí
▷ *pron* 1 *(demonstrative)* ése/a; *(pl)*
ésos/as; *(neuter)* eso; *(more remote)*
aquél(aquélla); *(pl)* aquéllos/as; *(neuter)*
aquello; **what's that?** ¿qué es eso (or
aquello)?; **who's that?** ¿quién es ése/a
(or aquél (aquélla))?; **is that you?** ¿eres
tú?; **will you eat all that?** ¿vas a comer
todo eso?; **that's my house** ésa es mi
casa; **that's what he said** eso es lo que
dijo; **that is (to say)** es decir
2 *(relative: subject, object)* que; *(with
preposition)* (el (la)) que etc, el(la) cual
etc; **the book (that) I read** el libro que
leí; **the books that are in the library**
los libros que están en la biblioteca; **all
(that) I have** todo lo que tengo; **the
box (that) I put in** la caja en la que
o donde lo puse; **the people (that) I
spoke to** la gente con la que hablé
3 *(relative: of time)* que; **the day (that)
he came** el día (en) que vino
▷ *conj* que; **he thought that I was ill**
creyó que yo estaba enfermo
▷ *adv (demonstrative)*: **I can't work that
much** no puedo trabajar tanto; **I didn't
realise it was that bad** no creí que
fuera tan malo; **that high** así de alto

thatched [θætʃt] *adj (roof)* de paja;
(cottage) con tejado de paja
thaw [θɔ:] *n* deshielo ▷ *vi (ice)*
derretirse; *(food)* descongelarse ▷ *vt
(food)* descongelar

Ⓞ **KEYWORD**

the [ði:, ðə] *def art* 1 *(gen)* el f, la pl,
los fpl, las (NB *el* immediately before f n
beginning with stressed (h)a; a+ el =al; de+
el = del); **the boy/girl** el chico/la chica;
the books/flowers los libros/las
flores; **to the postman/from
the drawer** el cartero/del cajón; **I
haven't the time/money** no tengo

tiempo/dinero
2 *(+adj to form n)* los; lo; **the rich and
the poor** los ricos y los pobres; **to
attempt the impossible** intentar lo
imposible
3 *(in titles)*: **Elizabeth the First** Isabel
primera; **Peter the Great** Pedro el
Grande
4 *(in comparisons)*: **the more he works
the more he earns** cuanto más
trabaja más gana

theatre ['θɪətə*] *(us* theater) *n*
teatro; *(also: lecture ~)* aula; *(Med: also:
operating ~)* quirófano
theft [θɛft] *n* robo
their [ðɛə*] *adj* su;**theirs** *pron (sing)*
suyo/(la) suya etc); *see also* **my; mine**¹
them [ðɛm, ðəm] *pron (direct)*
los/las; *(indirect)* les; *(stressed, after prep)*
ellos(ellas); *see also* **me**
theme [θi:m] *n* tema *m*;**theme park**
n parque de atracciones *(en torno a un
tema central)*
themselves [ðəm'sɛlvz] *pl pron
(subject)* ellos mismos(ellas mismas);
(complement) se; *(after prep)* sí
(mismos(as)); *see also* **oneself**
then [ðɛn] *adv (at that time)* entonces;
(next) después; *(later)* luego, después;
(and also) además ▷ *conj (therefore)*
en ese caso, entonces ▷ *adj*: **the ~
president** el entonces presidente;
by ~ para entonces; **from ~ on** desde
entonces
theology [θɪ'ɔlədʒɪ] *n* teología
theory ['θɪərɪ] *n* teoría
therapist ['θɛrəpɪst] *n* terapeuta *mf*
therapy ['θɛrəpɪ] *n* terapia

Ⓞ **KEYWORD**

there ['ðɛə*] *adv* 1 **there is, there are**
hay; **there is no-one here/no bread
left** no hay nadie aquí/no queda pan;
there has been an accident ha habido
un accidente
2 *(referring to place)* ahí; *(distant)* allí; **it's**

there está ahí; **put it in/on/up/down there** ponlo ahí dentro/encima/arriba/abajo; **I want that book there** quiero ese libro de ahí; **there he is!** ¡ahí está!
3 there, there (*esp* to child) ea, ea

there: **thereabouts** *adv* por ahí; **thereafter** *adv* después; **thereby** *adv* así, de ese modo; **therefore** *adv* por lo tanto; **there's = there is; there has**
thermal ['θə:ml] *adj* (in water) termal; (*paper*) térmico
thermometer [θə'mɔmɪtə*] *n* termómetro
thermostat ['θə:məustæt] *n* termostato
these [ðiːz] *pl adj* estos/as ▷ *pl pron* éstos/as
thesis ['θiːsɪs] (*pl* **theses**) *n* tesis *f inv*
they [ðeɪ] *pl pron* ellos(ellas); (*stressed*) ellos (mismos)(ellas (mismas)); **~ say that ...** (it is said that) se dice que ...; **they'd = they had; they would; they'll = they shall; they will; they're = they are; they've = they have**
thick [θɪk] *adj* (in consistency) espeso; (in size) grueso; (stupid) torpe ▷ *n*: **in the ~ of the battle** en lo más reñido de la batalla; **it's 20 cm ~** tiene 20 cm de espesor; **thicken** vi espesarse ▷ *vt* (sauce etc) espesar; **thickness** *n* espesor *m*; grueso
thief [θiːf] (*pl* **thieves**) *n* ladrón/ona *m/f*
thigh [θaɪ] *n* muslo
thin [θɪn] *adj* (person, animal) flaco; (in size) delgado; (in consistency) poco espeso; (hair, crowd) escaso ▷ *vt*: **to ~ (down)** diluir
thing [θɪŋ] *n* cosa; (object) objeto, artículo; (matter) asunto; (mania): **to have a ~ about sth/sb** estar obsesionado con algn/algo; **things** *npl* (belongings) efectos *mpl* (personales); **the best ~ would be to ...** lo mejor sería ...; **how are ~s?** ¿qué tal?
think [θɪŋk] (*pt, pp* **thought**) vi

pensar ▷ *vt* pensar, creer; **what did you ~ of them?** ¿qué te parecieron?; **to ~ about sth/sb** pensar en algo/algn; **I'll ~ about it** lo pensaré; **to ~ of doing sth** pensar en hacer algo; **I ~ so/not** creo que sí/no; **to ~ well of sb** tener buen concepto de algn; **think over** *vt* reflexionar sobre, meditar; **think up** *vt* (plan etc) idear
third [θə:d] *adj* (before n) tercer(a); (following) tercero/a ▷ *n* tercero/a; (fraction) tercio; (*BRIT Scol: degree*) título de licenciado con calificación de aprobado; **thirdly** *adv* en tercer lugar; **third party insurance** (*BRIT*) *n* seguro contra terceros; **Third World** *n* Tercer Mundo
thirst [θə:st] *n* sed *f*; **thirsty** *adj* (person, animal) sediento; (work) que da sed; **to be thirsty** tener sed
thirteen [θə:'tiːn] *num* trece; **thirteenth** [-'tiːnθ] *adj* decimotercero
thirtieth ['θə:tɪəθ] *adj* trigésimo
thirty ['θə:tɪ] *num* treinta

○ **KEYWORD**

this [ðɪs] (*pl* **these**) *adj* (demonstrative) este/a *pl*; estos/as; (neuter) esto; **this man/woman** este hombre(esta mujer); **these children/flowers** estos chicos/estas flores; **this one (here)** éste/a, esto de aquí ▷ *pron* (demonstrative) éste/a *pl*, éstos/as; (neuter) esto; **who is this?** ¿quién es éste/ésta?; **what is this?** ¿qué es esto?; **this is where I live** aquí vivo; **this is what he said** esto es lo que dijo; **this is Mr Brown** (in introductions) le presento al Sr. Brown; (photo) éste es el Sr. Brown; (on telephone) habla el Sr. Brown
▷ *adv* (demonstrative): **this high/long** etc así de alto/largo etc; **this far** hasta aquí

thistle ['θɪsl] *n* cardo

thorn [θɔːn] n espina

thorough [ˈθʌrə] adj (search) minucioso; (wash) a fondo; (knowledge, research) profundo; (person) meticuloso; **thoroughly** adv (search) minuciosamente; (study) profundamente; (wash) a fondo; (utterly: bad, wet etc) completamente, totalmente

those [ðəʊz] pl adj esos(esas); (more remote) aquellos/as

though [ðəʊ] conj aunque ▷ adv sin embargo

thought [θɔːt] pt, pp of **think** ▷ n pensamiento; (opinion) opinión f; **thoughtful** adj pensativo; (serious) serio; (considerate) atento; **thoughtless** adj desconsiderado

thousand [ˈθaʊzənd] num mil; **two ~** dos mil; **~s of** miles de; **thousandth** num milésimo

thrash [θræʃ] vt azotar; (defeat) derrotar

thread [θrɛd] n hilo; (of screw) rosca ▷ vt (needle) enhebrar

threat [θrɛt] n amenaza; **threaten** vi amenazar ▷ vt: **to threaten sb with/ to do** amenazar a algn con/con hacer; **threatening** adj amenazador(a), amenazante

three [θriː] num tres; **three-dimensional** adj tridimensional; **three-piece suite** n tresillo; **three-quarters** npl tres cuartas partes; **three-quarters full** tres cuartas partes lleno

threshold [ˈθrɛʃhəʊld] n umbral m

threw [θruː] pt of **throw**

thrill [θrɪl] n (excitement) emoción f; (shudder) estremecimiento ▷ vt emocionar; **to be ~ed** (with gift etc) estar encantado; **thrilled** adj: **I was thrilled** Estaba emocionada; **thriller** n novela (or película or film) de suspense; **thrilling** adj emocionante

thriving [ˈθraɪvɪŋ] adj próspero

throat [θrəʊt] n garganta; **to have a sore ~** tener dolor de garganta

throb [θrɔb] vi latir; dar punzadas; vibrar

throne [θrəʊn] n trono

through [θruː] prep por, a través de; (time) durante; (by means of) por medio de, mediante; (owing to) gracias a ▷ adj (ticket, train) directo ▷ adv completamente, de parte a parte; de principio a fin: **to put sb ~ to sb** (Tel) poner or pasar a algn con algn; **to be ~** (Tel) tener comunicación; (have finished) haber terminado; **"no ~ road"** (BRIT) "calle sin salida"; **throughout** prep (place) por todas partes de, por todo; (time) durante todo ▷ adv por or en todas partes

throw [θrəʊ] (pt **threw**, pp **thrown**) n tiro; (Sport) lanzamiento ▷ vt tirar, echar; (Sport) lanzar; (rider) derribar; (fig) desconcertar; **to ~ a party** dar una fiesta; **throw away** vt tirar; (money) derrochar; **throw in** vt (Sport) sacar; (include) incluir; **throw off** vt deshacerse de; **throw out** vt tirar; (person) echar; expulsar; **throw up** vi vomitar

thru [θruː] (us) = **through**

thrush [θrʌʃ] n zorzal m, tordo

thrust [θrʌst] (pt, pp **thrust**) vt empujar con fuerza

thud [θʌd] n golpe m sordo

thug [θʌɡ] n gamberro/a

thumb [θʌm] n (Anat) pulgar m; **to ~ a lift** hacer autostop; **thumbtack** (us) n chincheta (sp)

thump [θʌmp] n golpe m; (sound) ruido seco or sordo ▷ vt golpear ▷ vi (heart etc) palpitar

thunder [ˈθʌndə*] n trueno ▷ vi tronar; (train etc): **to ~ past** pasar como un trueno; **thunderstorm** n tormenta

Thur(s). abbr (= Thursday) juev

Thursday [ˈθɜːzdɪ] n jueves m inv

thus [ðʌs] adv así, de este modo

thwart [θwɔːt] vt frustrar

thyme [taɪm] n tomillo

Tibet [tɪˈbɛt] n el Tíbet

tick [tɪk] n (sound: of clock) tictac m;

(mark) palomita; (Zool) garrapata; (BRIT: inf): **in a ~** en un instante ▷vi hacer tictac ▷vt marcar; **tick off** vt marcar; (person) reñir

ticket ['tɪkɪt] n billete m (SP), boleto (LAM); (for cinema etc) entrada; (in shop: on goods) etiqueta; (for raffle) papeleta; (for library) tarjeta; (parking ticket) multa de aparcamiento (SP) or por estacionamiento (indebido) (LAM); **ticket barrier** n (BRIT: Rail) barrera más allá de la cual se necesita billete/boleto; **ticket collector** n revisor(a) m/f; **ticket inspector** n revisor(a) m/f, inspector(a) m/f de boletos (LAM); **ticket machine** n máquina de billetes (SP) or boletos (LAM); **ticket office** n (Theatre) taquilla (SP), boletería (LAM); (Rail) mostrador m de billetes (SP) or boletos (LAM)

tickle ['tɪkl] vt hacer cosquillas a ▷vi hacer cosquillas; **ticklish** adj (person) cosquilloso; (problem) delicado

tide [taɪd] n marea; (fig: of events etc) curso, marcha

tidy ['taɪdɪ] adj (room etc) ordenado; (dress, work) limpio; (person) (bien) arreglado ▷vt (also: **~ up**) poner en orden

tie [taɪ] n (string etc) atadura; (BRIT: also: **neck~**) corbata; (fig: link) vínculo, lazo; (Sport etc: draw) empate m ▷vt atar ▷vi (Sport etc) empatar; **to ~ in a bow** atar con un lazo; **to ~ a knot in sth** hacer un nudo en algo; **tie down** vt (fig: person: restrict) atar; (: to price, date etc) obligar a; **tie up** vt (dog, person) atar; (arrangements) concluir; **to be tied up** (busy) estar ocupado

tier [tɪə*] n grada; (of cake) piso

tiger ['taɪgə*] n tigre m

tight [taɪt] adj (rope) tirante; (money) escaso; (clothes) ajustado; (bend) cerrado; (shoes, schedule) apretado; (budget) ajustado; (security) estricto; (inf: drunk) borracho ▷adv (squeeze) muy fuerte; (shut) bien; **tighten** vt (rope) estirar; (screw, grip) apretar;

(security) reforzar ▷vi estirarse; apretarse; **tightly** adv (grasp) muy fuerte; **tights** (BRIT) npl panti mpl

tile [taɪl] n (on roof) teja; (on floor) baldosa; (on wall) azulejo

till [tɪl] n caja (registradora) ▷vt (land) cultivar ▷ prep, conj = **until**

tilt [tɪlt] vt inclinar ▷vi inclinarse

timber ['tɪmbə*] n (material) madera

time [taɪm] n tiempo; (epoch: often pl) época; (by clock) hora; (moment) momento; (occasion) vez f; (Mus) compás m ▷vt calcular or medir el tiempo de; (race) cronometrar; (remark, visit etc) elegir el momento para; **a long ~** mucho tiempo; **4 at a ~** de 4 en 4; **4 a la vez; for the ~ being** de momento, por ahora; **from ~ to ~** de vez en cuando; **at ~s** a veces; **in ~** (soon enough) a tiempo; (after some time) con el tiempo; (Mus) al compás; **in a week's ~** dentro de una semana; **in no ~** en un abrir y cerrar de ojos; **any ~** cuando sea; **on ~** a la hora; **5 ~s 5** 5 por 5; **what ~ is it?** ¿qué hora es?; **to have a good ~** pasarlo bien, divertirse; **time limit** n plazo; **timely** adj oportuno; **timer** n (in kitchen etc) programador m horario; **time-share** n apartamento (or casa) a tiempo compartido; **timetable** n horario; **time zone** n huso horario

timid ['tɪmɪd] adj tímido

timing ['taɪmɪŋ] n (Sport) cronometraje m; **the ~ of his resignation** el momento que eligió para dimitir

tin [tɪn] n estaño; (also: **~ plate**) hojalata; (BRIT: can) lata; **tinfoil** n papel m de estaño

tingle ['tɪŋgl] vi (person): **to ~ (with)** estremecerse (de); (hands etc) hormiguear

tinker ['tɪŋkə*]: **~ with** vt fus jugar con, tocar

tinned [tɪnd] (BRIT) adj (food) en lata, en conserva

tin opener [-əʊpnə*] (BRIT) n abrelatas m inv

tint [tɪnt] n matiz m; (for hair) tinte m; **tinted** adj (hair) teñido; (glass, spectacles) ahumado

tiny ['taɪnɪ] adj minúsculo, pequeñito

tip [tɪp] n (end) punta; (gratuity) propina, (inf) vertedero; (advice) consejo ▷ vt (waiter) dar una propina a; (tilt) inclinar; (empty: also: **~ out**) vaciar, echar; (overturn: also: **~ over**) volcar; **tip off** vt avisar, poner sobreavisar

tiptoe ['tɪptəʊ] n: **on ~** de puntillas

tire ['taɪə*] n (us) = **tyre** ▷ vt cansar ▷ vi cansarse; (become bored) aburrirse; **tired** adj cansado; **to be tired of sth** estar harto de algo; **tire pressure** (us) = **tyre pressure**; **tiring** adj cansado

tissue ['tɪʃuː] n tejido; (paper handkerchief) pañuelo de papel, kleenex® m; **tissue paper** n papel m de seda

tit [tɪt] n (bird) herrerillo común; **to give ~ for tat** dar ojo por ojo

title ['taɪtl] n título

T-junction ['tiː'dʒʌŋkʃən] n cruce m en T

TM abbr = **trademark**

○ **KEYWORD**

to [tuː, tə] prep 1 (direction) a; **to go to France/London/school/the station** ir a Francia/Londres/al colegio/a la estación; **to go to Claude's/the doctor's** ir a casa de Claude/al médico; **the road to Edinburgh** la carretera de Edimburgo

2 (as far as) hasta, a; **from here to London** de aquí a or hasta Londres; **to count to 10** contar hasta 10; **from 40 to 50 people** entre 40 y 50 personas

3 (with expressions of time): **a quarter/twenty to 5** las 5 menos cuarto/veinte

4 (for, of): **the key to the front door** la llave de la puerta principal; **she is secretary to the director** es la secretaría del director; **a letter to his wife** una carta o para su mujer

5 (expressing indirect object) a; **to give sth to sb** darle algo a algn; **to talk to sb** hablar con algn; **to be a danger to sb** ser un peligro para algn; **to carry out repairs to sth** hacer reparaciones en algo

6 (in relation to): **3 goals to 2** 3 goles a 2; **30 miles to the gallon** ≈ 94 litros a los cien (km)

7 (purpose, result): **to come to sb's aid** venir en auxilio or ayuda de algn; **to sentence sb to death** condenar a algn a muerte; **to my great surprise** con gran sorpresa mía

▷ with vb 1 (simple infin): **to go/eat** ir/comer

2 (following another vb): **to want/try/start to do** querer/intentar/empezar a hacer

3 (with vb omitted): **I don't want to** no quiero

4 (purpose, result): **I did it to help you** lo hice para ayudarte; **he came to see you** vino a verte

5 (equivalent to relative clause): **I have things to do** tengo cosas que hacer; **the main thing is to try** lo principal es intentarlo

6 (after adj etc): **ready to go** listo para irse; **too old to ...** demasiado viejo (como) para ...

▷ adv: **pull/push the door to** tirar de/empujar la puerta

---

toad [təʊd] n sapo; **toadstool** n hongo venenoso

toast [təʊst] n (Culin) tostada; (drink, speech) brindis m ▷ vt (Culin) tostar; (drink to) brindar por; **toaster** n tostador m

tobacco [tə'bækəʊ] n tabaco

toboggan [tə'bɔgən] n tobogán m

today [tə'deɪ] adv, n (also fig) hoy m

toddler ['tɔdlə*] n niño/a (que empieza a andar)

toe [təʊ] n dedo (del pie); (of shoe) punta; **to ~ the line** (fig) conformarse;

toenail n uña del pie

toffee ['tɒfɪ] n toffee m

together [tə'ɡeðə*] adv juntos; (at same time) al mismo tiempo, a la vez; ~ **with** junto con

toilet ['tɔɪlət] n inodoro; (BRIT: room) (cuarto de) baño, servicio ▷ cpd (soap etc) de aseo;**toilet bag** n neceser m, bolsa de aseo;**toilet paper** n papel m higiénico;**toiletries** npl artículos mpl de tocador;**toilet roll** n rollo de papel higiénico

token ['təukən] n (sign) señal f, muestra; (souvenir) recuerdo; (disc) ficha ▷ adj (strike, payment etc) simbólico; **book/record ~** (BRIT) vale m para comprar libros/discos; **gift ~** (BRIT) vale-regalo

Tokyo ['təukjəu] n Tokio, Tokío

told [təuld] pt, pp of **tell**

tolerant ['tɒlrnt] adj: **~ of** tolerante con

tolerate ['tɒləreɪt] vt tolerar

toll [təul] n (of casualties) número de víctimas; (tax, charge) peaje m ▷ vi (bell) doblar;**toll call** n (us Tel) conferencia, llamada interurbana;**toll-free** (us) adj, adv gratis

tomato [tə'mɑːtəu] (pl **-es**) n tomate m;**tomato sauce** n salsa de tomate

tomb [tuːm] n tumba;**tombstone** n lápida

tomorrow [tə'mɒrəu] adv, n (also: fig) mañana; **the day after ~** pasado mañana; **~ morning** mañana por la mañana

ton [tʌn] n tonelada (BRIT = 1016 kg; US = 907 kg); (metric ton) tonelada métrica; **~s of** (inf) montones de

tone [təun] n tono ▷ vi (also: **~ in**) armonizar;**tone down** vt (criticism) suavizar; (colour) atenuar

tongs [tɒŋz] npl (for coal) tenazas fpl; (curling tongs) tenacillas fpl

tongue [tʌŋ] n lengua; **~ in cheek** irónicamente

tonic ['tɒnɪk] n (Med) tónico; (also: **~ water**) (agua) tónica

tonight [tə'naɪt] adv, n esta noche; esta tarde

tonne [tʌn] n tonelada (métrica) (1.000kg)

tonsil ['tɒnsl] n amígdala;**tonsillitis** [-'laɪtɪs] n amigdalitis f

too [tuː] adv (excessively) demasiado; (also) también; **~ much** demasiado; **~ many** demasiados/as

took [tuk] pt of **take**

tool [tuːl] n herramienta;**tool box** n caja de herramientas;**tool kit** n juego de herramientas

tooth [tuːθ] (pl **teeth**) n (Anat, Tech) diente m; (molar) muela;**toothache** n dolor m de muelas;**toothbrush** n cepillo de dientes;**toothpaste** n pasta de dientes;**toothpick** n palillo

top [tɒp] n (of mountain) cumbre f, cima; (of tree) copa; (of head) coronilla; (of ladder, page) lo alto; (of table) superficie f; (of cupboard) parte f de arriba; (lid: of box) tapa; (: of bottle, jar) tapón m; (: of list etc) cabeza; (toy) peonza; (garment) blusa; camiseta ▷ adj de arriba; (in rank) principal, primero; (best) mejor ▷ vt (exceed) exceder; (be first in) encabezar; **on ~ of** (above) sobre, encima de; (in addition to) además de; **from ~ to bottom** de pies a cabeza;**top up** vt llenar; (mobile phone) recargar (el saldo de);**top floor** n último piso;**top hat** n sombrero de copa

topic ['tɒpɪk] n tema m;**topical** adj actual

topless ['tɒplɪs] adj (bather, bikini) topless inv

topping ['tɒpɪŋ] n (Culin): **with a ~ of cream** con nata por encima

topple ['tɒpl] vt derribar ▷ vi caerse

top-up card n (for mobile phone) tarjeta prepago

torch [tɔːtʃ] n antorcha; (BRIT: electric) linterna

tore [tɔː*] pt of **tear²**

torment [n 'tɔːment, vt tɔː'ment] n tormento ▷ vt atormentar; (fig: annoy) fastidiar

torn [tɔ:n] pp of **tear²**

tornado [tɔ:'neɪdəʊ] (pl ~**es**) n
tornado

torpedo [tɔ:'pi:dəʊ] (pl ~**es**) n
torpedo

torrent ['tɔrnt] n torrente m;
torrential [tə'rɛnʃl] adj torrencial

tortoise ['tɔ:təs] n tortuga

torture ['tɔ:tʃə*] n tortura ▷ vt
torturar; (fig) atormentar

Tory ['tɔ:rɪ] adj, n (Pol)
conservador/a m/f

toss [tɒs] vt tirar, echar; (one's head)
sacudir; **to ~ a coin** echar a cara o cruz;
to ~ up for sth jugar a cara o cruz algo;
to ~ and turn (in bed) dar vueltas

total ['təʊtl] adj total, entero;
(emphatic: failure etc) completo, total
▷ n total m, suma ▷ vt (add up) sumar;
(amount to) ascender a

totalitarian [təʊtælɪ'tɛərɪən] adj
totalitario

totally ['təʊtəlɪ] adv totalmente

touch [tʌtʃ] n (sense) tacto; (contact)
contacto ▷ vt tocar; (emotionally)
conmover; **a ~ of** (fig) un poquito
de; **to get in ~ with sb** ponerse en
contacto con algn; **to lose ~** (friends)
perder contacto; **touch down** vi
(on land) aterrizar; **touchdown** n
aterrizaje m; (on sea) amerizaje m; (us
Football) ensayo; **touched** adj (moved)
conmovido; **touching** adj (moving)
conmovedor(a); **touchline** n (Sport)
línea de banda; **touch-sensitive** adj
sensible al tacto

tough [tʌf] adj (material) resistente;
(meat) duro; (problem etc) difícil; (policy,
stance) inflexible; (person) fuerte

tour ['tʊə*] n viaje m, vuelta; (also:
package ~) viaje m todo comprendido;
(of town, museum) visita; (by band etc)
gira ▷ vt recorrer, visitar; **tour guide**
n guía mf turístico/a

tourism ['tʊərɪzm] n turismo

tourist ['tʊərɪst] n turista mf ▷ cpd
turístico; **tourist office** n oficina
de turismo

tournament ['tʊənəmənt] n torneo

tour operator n touroperador(a)
m/f, operador(a) m/f turístico/a

tow [təʊ] vt remolcar; **"on** or **in** (us)
~" (Aut) "a remolque"; **tow away** vt
llevarse a remolque

towel ['tauəl] n toalla; **towelling** n
(fabric) felpa

tower ['tauə*] n torre f; **tower block**
(BRIT) n torre f (de pisos)

town [taun] n ciudad f; **to go to
~** ir a la ciudad; (fig) echar la casa
por la ventana; **town centre** (BRIT)
n centro de la ciudad; **town hall** n
ayuntamiento

tow truck (us) n camión m grúa

toxic ['tɒksɪk] adj tóxico

toy [tɔɪ] n juguete m; **toy with** vt fus
jugar con; (idea) acariciar; **toyshop** n
juguetería

trace [treɪs] n rastro ▷ vt (draw)
trazar, delinear; (locate) encontrar;
(follow) seguir la pista de

track [træk] n (mark) huella, pista;
(path: gen) camino, senda; (: of bullet
etc) trayectoria; (: of suspect, animal)
pista, rastro; (Rail) vía; (Sport) pista;
(on tape, record) canción f ▷ vt seguir
la pista de; **to keep ~ of** mantenerse al
tanto de, seguir; **track down** vt (prey)
seguir el rastro de; (sth lost) encontrar;
tracksuit n chandal m

tractor ['træktə*] n tractor m

trade [treɪd] n comercio; (skill, job)
oficio ▷ vi comerciar, comerciar ▷ vt
(exchange): **to ~ sth (for sth)** cambiar
algo (por algo); **trade in** vt (old car
etc) ofrecer como parte del pago;
trademark n marca de fábrica; **trader**
n comerciante mf; **tradesman** (irreg)
n (shopkeeper) tendero; **trade union**
n sindicato

trading ['treɪdɪŋ] n comercio

tradition [trə'dɪʃən] n tradición f;
traditional adj tradicional

traffic ['træfɪk] n (gen, Aut) tráfico,

circulación f ▷ vi: **to ~ in** (pej: liquor, drugs) traficar en; **traffic circle** (us) n isleta; **traffic island** n refugio, isleta; **traffic jam** n embotellamiento; **traffic lights** npl semáforo; **traffic warden** n guardia mf de tráfico

tragedy ['trædʒədɪ] n tragedia

tragic ['trædʒɪk] adj trágico

trail [treɪl] n (tracks) rastro, pista; (path) camino, sendero; (dust, smoke) estela ▷ vt (drag) arrastrar; (follow) seguir la pista de ▷ vi arrastrar; (in contest etc) ir perdiendo; **trailer** n (Aut) remolque m; (caravan) caravana; (Cinema) trailer m, avance m

train [treɪn] n tren m; (of dress) cola; (series) serie f ▷ vt (educate, teach skills to) formar; (sportsman) entrenar; (dog) adiestrar; (point: gun etc): **to ~ on** apuntar a ▷ vi (Sport) entrenarse; (learn a skill): **to ~ as a teacher** etc estudiar para profesor etc; **one's ~ of thought** el razonamiento de algn; **trainee** [treɪ'niː] n aprendiz(a) m/f; **trainer** n (Sport: coach) entrenador(a) m/f; (of animals) domador(a) m/f; **trainers** npl (shoes) zapatillas fpl (de deporte); **training** n formación f; **to be in training** (Sport) estar entrenando; **training course** n curso de formación; **training shoes** npl zapatillas fpl (de deporte)

trait [treɪt] n rasgo

traitor ['treɪtə*] n traidor(a) m/f

tram [træm] (BRIT) n (also: **~car**) tranvía m

tramp [træmp] n (person) vagabundo/a; (inf: pej: woman) puta

trample ['træmpl] vt: **to ~ (underfoot)** pisotear

trampoline ['træmpəliːn] n trampolín m

tranquil ['træŋkwɪl] adj tranquilo; **tranquillizer** (us **tranquilizer**) n (Med) tranquilizante m

transaction [træn'zækʃən] n transacción f, operación f

transatlantic ['trænzət'læntɪk] adj transatlántico

transcript ['trænskrɪpt] n copia

transfer [n 'trænsfə:*, vb træns'fə:*] n (of employees) traslado; (of money, power) transferencia; (Sport) traspaso; (picture, design) calcomanía ▷ vt trasladar; transferir; **to ~ the charges** (BRIT Tel) llamar a cobro revertido

transform [træns'fɔ:m] vt transformar; **transformation** n transformación f

transfusion [træns'fju:ʒən] n transfusión f

transit ['trænzɪt] n: **in ~** en tránsito

transition [træn'zɪʃən] n transición f

transitive ['trænzɪtɪv] adj (Ling) transitivo

translate [trænz'leɪt] vt traducir; **translation** [-'leɪʃən] n traducción f; **translator** n traductor(a) m/f

transmission [trænz'mɪʃən] n transmisión f

transmit [trænz'mɪt] vt transmitir; **transmitter** n transmisor m

transparent [træns'pærnt] adj transparente

transplant ['trænspla:nt] n (Med) transplante m

transport [n 'trænspɔ:t, vt træns'pɔ:t] n transporte m; (car) coche m (SP), carro (LAM), automóvil m ▷ vt transportar; **transportation** [-'teɪʃən] n transporte m

transvestite [trænz'vestaɪt] n travestí mf

trap [træp] n (snare, trick) trampa; (carriage) cabriolé ▷ vt coger (SP) or agarrar (LAM) (en una trampa); (trick) engañar; (confine) atrapar

trash [træʃ] n (rubbish) basura; (nonsense) tonterías fpl; (pej): **the book/film is ~** el libro/la película no vale nada; **trash can** (us) n cubo or bote m (MEX) or tacho (SC) de la basura

trauma ['trɔ:mə] n trauma m; **traumatic** [trɔ:'mætɪk] adj traumático

travel ['trævl] *n* el viajar ▷*vi* viajar ▷*vt* (*distance*) recorrer; **travel agency** *n* agencia de viajes; **travel agent** *n* agente mf de viajes; **travel insurance** *n* seguro de viaje; **traveller** (*us* **traveler**) *n* viajero/a; **traveller's cheque** (*us* **traveler's check**) *n* cheque m de viajero; **travelling** (*us* **traveling**) *n* los viajes, el viajar; **travel-sick** *adj*: **to get travel-sick** marearse al viajar; **travel sickness** *n* mareo

tray [treɪ] *n* bandeja; (*on desk*) cajón m

treacherous ['tretʃərəs] *adj* traidor, traicionero; (*dangerous*) peligroso

treacle ['tri:kl] (BRIT) *n* melaza

tread [trɛd] (*pt* trod, *pp* trodden) *n* (*step*) paso, pisada; (*sound*) ruido de pasos; (*of stair*) escalón m; (*of tyre*) banda de rodadura ▷*vi* pisar; **tread on** *vt fus* pisar

treasure ['trɛʒə*] *n* tesoro ▷*vt* (*value: object, friendship*) apreciar; (*: memory*) guardar; **treasurer** *n* tesorero/a

treasury ['trɛʒərɪ] *n*: **the T~** el Ministerio de Hacienda

treat [tri:t] *n* (*present*) regalo ▷*vt* tratar; **to ~ sb to sth** invitar a algn a algo; **treatment** *n* tratamiento

treaty ['tri:tɪ] *n* tratado

treble ['trɛbl] *adj* triple ▷*vt* triplicar ▷*vi* triplicarse

tree [tri:] *n* árbol m; **~ trunk** tronco (de árbol)

trek [trɛk] *n* (*long journey*) viaje m largo y difícil; (*tiring walk*) caminata

tremble ['trɛmbl] *vi* temblar

tremendous [trɪ'mɛndəs] *adj* tremendo, enorme; (*excellent*) estupendo

trench [trɛntʃ] *n* zanja

trend [trɛnd] *n* (*tendency*) tendencia; (*of events*) curso; (*fashion*) moda; **trendy** *adj* de moda

trespass ['trɛspəs] *vi*: **to ~ on** entrar sin permiso en; **"no ~ing"** "prohibido el paso"

trial ['traɪəl] *n* (*Law*) juicio, proceso; (*test: of machine etc*) prueba; **trial period** *n* periodo de prueba

triangle ['traɪæŋgl] *n* (*Math, Mus*) triángulo

triangular [traɪ'æŋgjulə*] *adj* triangular

tribe [traɪb] *n* tribu f

tribunal [traɪ'bju:nl] *n* tribunal m

tribute ['trɪbju:t] *n* homenaje m, tributo; **to pay ~ to** rendir homenaje a

trick [trɪk] *n* (*skill, knack*) tino, truco; (*conjuring trick*) truco; (*joke*) broma; (*Cards*) baza ▷*vt* engañar; **to play a ~ on sb** gastar una broma a algn; **that should do the ~** a ver si funciona así

trickle ['trɪkl] *n* (*of water etc*) goteo ▷*vi* gotear

tricky ['trɪkɪ] *adj* difícil; delicado

tricycle ['traɪsɪkl] *n* triciclo

trifle ['traɪfl] *n* bagatela; (*Culin*) dulce de bizcocho borracho, gelatina, fruta y natillas ▷*adv*: **a ~ long** un poquito largo

trigger ['trɪgə*] *n* (*of gun*) gatillo

trim [trɪm] *adj* (*house, garden*) en buen estado; (*person, figure*) esbelto ▷*n* (*haircut etc*) recorte m; (*on car*) guarnición f; (*on ship*) arreglar; (*cut*) recortar; (*decorate*) adornar; (*Naut: a sail*) orientar

trio ['tri:əu] *n* trío

trip [trɪp] *n* viaje m; (*excursion*) excursión f; (*stumble*) traspié m ▷*vi* (*stumble*) tropezar; (*go lightly*) andar a paso ligero; **on a ~** de viaje; **trip up** *vi* tropezar, caerse ▷*vt* hacer tropezar or caer

triple ['trɪpl] *adj* triple

triplets ['trɪplɪts] *npl* trillizos/as mpl/fpl

tripod ['traɪpɔd] *n* trípode m

triumph ['traɪʌmf] *n* triunfo ▷*vi*: **to ~ (over)** vencer; **triumphant** [traɪ'ʌmfənt] *adj* (*team etc*) vencedor(a); (*wave, return*) triunfal

trivial ['trɪvɪəl] *adj* insignificante; (*commonplace*) banal

trod [trɔd] *pt of* **tread**

trodden ['trɒdn] pp of **tread**

trolley ['trɒlɪ] n carrito; (also: ~ **bus**) trolebús m

trombone [trɒm'bəʊn] n trombón m

troop [truːp] n grupo, banda; **troops** npl (Mil) tropas fpl

trophy ['trəʊfɪ] n trofeo

tropical ['trɒpɪkl] adj tropical

trot [trɒt] n trote m ⊳ vi trotar; **on the ~** (BRIT: fig) seguidos/as

trouble ['trʌbl] n problema m, dificultad f; (worry) preocupación f; (bother, effort) molestia, esfuerzo; (unrest) inquietud f; (Med): **stomach** etc ~ problemas mpl gástricos etc ⊳ vt (disturb) molestar; (worry) preocupar, inquietar ⊳ vi: **to do sth** molestarse en hacer algo; **troubles** npl (Pol etc) conflictos mpl; (personal) problemas mpl; **to be in ~** estar en un apuro; **it's no ~!** ¡no es molestia (ninguna)!; **what's the ~?** (with broken TV etc) ¿cuál es el problema?; (doctor to patient) ¿qué pasa?; **troubled** adj (person) preocupado; (country, epoch, life) agitado; **troublemaker** n agitador(a) m/f; (child) alborotador m; **troublesome** adj molesto

trough [trɒf] n (also: **drinking ~**) abrevadero; (also: **feeding ~**) comedero; (depression) depresión f

trousers ['traʊzəz] npl pantalones mpl; **short ~** pantalones mpl cortos

trout [traʊt] n inv trucha

trowel ['traʊəl] n (of gardener) palita; (of builder) paleta

truant ['truənt] n: **to play ~** (BRIT) hacer novillos

truce [truːs] n tregua

truck [trʌk] n (lorry) camión m; (Rail) vagón m tren; **truck driver** n camionero

true [truː] adj verdadero; (accurate) exacto; (genuine) auténtico; (faithful) fiel; **to come ~** realizarse

truly ['truːlɪ] adv (really) realmente; (truthfully) verdaderamente; (faithfully): **yours ~** (in letter) le saluda atentamente

trumpet ['trʌmpɪt] n trompeta

trunk [trʌŋk] n (of tree, person) tronco m; (of elephant) trompa; (case) baúl m; (US Aut) maletero; **trunks** npl (also: **swimming ~s**) bañador m (de hombre)

trust [trʌst] n confianza f; (responsibility) responsabilidad f; (Law) fideicomiso ⊳ vt (rely on) tener confianza en; (hope) esperar; (entrust): **to ~ sth to sb** confiar algo a algn; **to take sth on ~** fiarse de algo; **trusted** adj de confianza; **trustworthy** adj digno de confianza

truth [truːθ, pl truːðz] n verdad f; **truthful** adj veraz

try [traɪ] n tentativa, intento; (Rugby) ensayo ⊳ vt (attempt) intentar; (test: also: ~ **out**) probar, someter a prueba; (Law) juzgar, procesar; (strain: patience) hacer perder ⊳ vi probar; **to have a ~** probar suerte; **to do sth** intentar hacer algo; ~ **again!** ¡vuelve a probar!; ~ **harder!** ¡esfuérzate más!; **well, I tried** al menos lo intenté; **try on** vt (clothes) probarse; **trying** adj (experience) cansado; (person) pesado

T-shirt ['tiːʃɜːt] n camiseta

tub [tʌb] n cubo (SP), cubeta (SP, MEX), balde m (LAM); (bath) bañera (SP), tina (LAM), bañadera (RPL)

tube [tjuːb] n tubo; (BRIT: underground) metro; (for tyre) cámara de aire

tuberculosis [tjuˌbɜːkjʊˈləʊsɪs] n tuberculosis f inv

tube station (BRIT) n estación f de metro

tuck [tʌk] vt (put) poner; **tuck away** vt (money) guardar; (building): **to be tucked away** esconderse, ocultarse; **tuck in** vt meter dentro; (child) arropar ⊳ vi (eat) comer con apetito; **tuck shop** n (Scol) tienda ~ bar m (del colegio) (SP)

Tue(s). abbr (= Tuesday) mart

Tuesday ['tjuːzdɪ] n martes m inv

tug [tʌg] n (ship) remolcador m ⊳ vt tirar de

tuition [tjuːˈɪʃən] n (BRIT) enseñanza;

(: *private tuition*) clases *fpl* particulares; (*us: school fees*) matrícula

tulip ['tjuːlɪp] *n* tulipán *m*

tumble ['tʌmbl] *n* (*fall*) caída ▷ *vi* caer; **to ~ to sth** (*inf*) caer en la cuenta de algo; **tumble dryer** (BRIT) *n* secadora

tumbler ['tʌmblə*] *n* (*glass*) vaso

tummy ['tʌmɪ] (*inf*) *n* barriga, tripa

tumour ['tjuːmə*] (*us* **tumor**) *n* tumor *m*

tuna ['tjuːnə] *n inv* (*also: ~ fish*) atún *m*

tune [tjuːn] *n* melodía ▷ *vt* (*Mus*) afinar; (*Radio, TV, Aut*) sintonizar; **to be in/out of ~** (*instrument*) estar afinado/desafinado; (*singer*) cantar afinadamente/desafinar; **to be in/out of ~ with** (*fig*) estar de acuerdo/en desacuerdo con; **tune in** *vi*: **to tune in (to)** (*Radio, TV*) sintonizar (con); **tune up** *vi* (*musician*) afinar (su instrumento)

tunic ['tjuːnɪk] *n* túnica

Tunisia [tjuː'nɪzɪə] *n* Túnez *m*

tunnel ['tʌnl] *n* túnel *m*; (*in mine*) galería ▷ *vi* construir un túnel/una galería

turbulence ['tɜːbjuləns] *n* (*Aviat*) turbulencia

turf [tɜːf] *n* césped *m*; (*clod*) tepe *m* ▷ *vt* cubrir con césped

Turk [tɜːk] *n* turco/a

Turkey ['tɜːkɪ] *n* Turquía

turkey ['tɜːkɪ] *n* pavo

Turkish ['tɜːkɪʃ] *adj, n* turco; (*Ling*) turco

turmoil ['tɜːmɔɪl] *n*: **in ~** revuelto

turn [tɜːn] *n* turno; (*in road*) curva; (*of mind, events*) rumbo; (*Theatre*) número; (*Med*) ataque *m* ▷ *vt* girar, volver; (*collar, steak*) dar la vuelta a; (*page*) pasar; (*change*): **to ~ sth into** convertir algo en ▷ *vi* volver; (*person: look back*) volverse; (*reverse direction*) dar la vuelta; (*milk*) cortarse; (*become*): **to ~ nasty/forty** ponerse/cumplir los cuarenta; **a good ~** un favor; **it gave**

me quite a ~ me dio un susto; **"no left ~"** (*Aut*) "prohibido girar a la izquierda"; **it's your ~** te toca a ti; **in ~** por turnos; **to take ~s (at)** turnarse (en); **turn around** *vi* (*person*) volverse, darse la vuelta ▷ *vt* (*object*) dar la vuelta a, voltear (LAM); **turn away** *vi* apartar la vista ▷ *vi* rechazar; **turn back** *vi* volverse atrás ▷ *vt* hacer retroceder; (*clock*) retrasar; **turn down** *vt* (*refuse*) rechazar; (*reduce*) bajar; (*fold*) doblar; **turn in** *vi* (*inf: go to bed*) acostarse ▷ *vt* (*fold*) doblar hacia dentro; **turn off** *vi* (*from road*) desviarse ▷ *vt* (*light, radio etc*) apagar; (*tap*) cerrar; (*engine*) parar; **turn on** *vt* (*light, radio etc*) encender (SP), prender (LAM); (*tap*) abrir; (*engine*) poner en marcha; **turn out** *vt* (*light, gas*) apagar; (*produce*) producir ▷ *vi* (*voters*) concurrir; **to turn out to be ...** resultar ser ...; **turn over** *vi* (*person*) volverse ▷ *vt* (*object*) dar la vuelta a; (*page*) volver; **turn round** *vi* volverse; (*rotate*) girar; **turn to** *vt fus*: **to turn to sb** acudir a algn; **turn up** *vi* (*person*) llegar, presentarse; (*lost object*) aparecer ▷ *vt* (*gen*) subir; **turning** *n* (*in road*) vuelta; **turning point** *n* (*fig*) momento decisivo

turnip ['tɜːnɪp] *n* nabo

turn: **turnout** *n* concurrencia; **turnover** *n* (*Comm: amount of money*) volumen *m* de ventas; (*: of goods*) movimiento; **turnstile** *n* torniquete *m*; **turn-up** (BRIT) *n* (*on trousers*) vuelta

turquoise ['tɜːkwɔɪz] *n* (*stone*) turquesa ▷ *adj* color turquesa

turtle ['tɜːtl] *n* galápago; **turtleneck** (**sweater**) *n* jersey *m* de cuello vuelto

tusk [tʌsk] *n* colmillo

tutor ['tjuːtə*] *n* profesor(a) *m/f*; **tutorial** [-'tɔːrɪəl] *n* (*Scol*) seminario

tuxedo [tʌk'siːdəu] (*us*) *n* smóking *m*, esmoquin *m*

TV [tiː'viː] *n abbr* (= *television*) tele *f*

tweed [twiːd] *n* tweed *m*

tweezers ['twiːzəz] *npl* pinzas *fpl* (de depilar)

twelfth [twelfθ] num duodécimo

twelve [twelv] num doce; **at ~ o'clock** (midday) a mediodía; (midnight) a medianoche

twentieth ['twentɪɪθ] adj vigésimo

twenty ['twentɪ] num veinte

twice [twaɪs] adv dos veces; **~ as much** dos veces más

twig [twɪg] n ramita

twilight ['twaɪlaɪt] n crepúsculo

twin [twɪn] adj, n gemelo/a m/f ▷ vt hermanar; **twin(-bedded) room** n habitación f doble; **twin beds** npl camas fpl gemelas

twinkle ['twɪŋkl] vi centellear; (eyes) brillar

twist [twɪst] n (action) torsión f; (in road, coil) vuelta; (in wire, flex) doblez f; (in story) giro ▷ vt torcer; (weave) trenzar; (roll around) enrollar; (fig) deformar ▷ vi serpentear

twit [twɪt] (inf) n tonto

twitch [twɪtʃ] n (pull) tirón m; (nervous) tic m ▷ vi crisparse

two [tuː] num dos; **to put ~ and ~ together** (fig) atar cabos

type [taɪp] n (category) tipo, género; (model) tipo; (Typ) tipo, letra ▷ vt (letter etc) escribir a máquina; **typewriter** n máquina de escribir

typhoid ['taɪfɔɪd] n tifoidea

typhoon [taɪ'fuːn] n tifón m

typical ['tɪpɪkl] adj típico; **typically** adv típicamente

typing ['taɪpɪŋ] n mecanografía

typist ['taɪpɪst] n mecanógrafo/a

tyre [taɪə*] (us **tire**) n neumático, llanta (LAM); **tyre pressure** (BRIT) n presión f de los neumáticos

U

UFO ['juːfəu] n abbr (= unidentified flying object) OVNI m

Uganda [juː'gændə] n Uganda

ugly ['ʌglɪ] adj feo; (dangerous) peligroso

UHT abbr (= UHT milk) leche f UHT, leche f uperizada

UK n abbr = **United Kingdom**

ulcer ['ʌlsə*] n úlcera; (mouth ulcer) llaga

ultimate ['ʌltɪmət] adj último, final; (greatest) máximo; **ultimately** adv (in the end) por último, al final; (fundamentally) a or en fin de cuentas

ultimatum [ʌltɪ'meɪtəm] (pl **-s** or **ultimata**) n ultimátum m

ultrasound ['ʌltrəsaund] n (Med) ultrasonido

ultraviolet [ʌltrə'vaɪəlɪt] adj ultravioleta

umbrella [ʌm'brelə] n paraguas m inv; (for sun) sombrilla

umpire ['ʌmpaɪə*] n árbitro

UN n abbr (= United Nations) NN. UU.

unable [ʌn'eɪbl] adj: **to be ~ to do sth**

u

no poder hacer algo
unacceptable [ʌnəkˈsɛptəbl] adj
(proposal, behaviour, price) inaceptable;
it's ~ that no se puede aceptar que
unanimous [juːˈnænɪməs] adj
unánime
unarmed [ʌnˈɑːmd] adj (defenceless)
inerme; (without weapon) desarmado
unattended [ʌnəˈtɛndɪd] adj
desatendido
unattractive [ʌnəˈtræktɪv] adj poco
atractivo
unavailable [ʌnəˈveɪləbl] adj (article,
room, book) no disponible; (person)
ocupado
unavoidable [ʌnəˈvɔɪdəbl] adj
inevitable
unaware [ʌnəˈwɛə*] adj: **to be ~ of**
ignorar; **unawares** adv: **to catch sb
unawares** pillar a algn desprevenido
unbearable [ʌnˈbɛərəbl] adj
insoportable
unbeatable [ʌnˈbiːtəbl] adj (team)
invencible; (price) inmejorable; (quality)
insuperable
unbelievable [ʌnbɪˈliːvəbl] adj
increíble
unborn [ʌnˈbɔːn] adj que va a nacer
unbutton [ʌnˈbʌtn] vt desabrochar
uncalled-for [ʌnˈkɔːldfɔː*] adj
gratuito, inmerecido
uncanny [ʌnˈkænɪ] adj extraño
uncertain [ʌnˈsəːtn] adj incierto;
(indecisive) indeciso; **uncertainty** n
incertidumbre f
unchanged [ʌnˈtʃeɪndʒd] adj igual,
sin cambios
uncle [ˈʌŋkl] n tío
unclear [ʌnˈklɪə*] adj poco claro; **I'm
still ~ about what I'm supposed to
do** todavía no tengo muy claro lo que
tengo que hacer
uncomfortable [ʌnˈkʌmfətəbl] adj
incómodo; (uneasy) inquieto
uncommon [ʌnˈkɔmən] adj poco
común, raro
unconditional [ʌnkənˈdɪʃənl] adj
incondicional

unconscious [ʌnˈkɔnʃəs] adj sin
sentido; (unaware) **to be ~ of** no darse
cuenta de ▷ n: **the ~** el inconsciente
uncontrollable [ʌnkənˈtrəʊləbl]
adj (child etc) incontrolable; (temper)
indomable; (laughter) incontenible
unconventional [ʌnkənˈvɛnʃənl]
adj poco convencional
uncover [ʌnˈkʌvə*] vt descubrir;
(take lid off) destapar
undecided [ʌndɪˈsaɪdɪd] adj
(character) indeciso; (question) no
resuelto
undeniable [ʌndɪˈnaɪəbl] adj
innegable
under [ˈʌndə*] prep debajo de; (less
than) menos de; (according to) según,
de acuerdo con; (sb's leadership) bajo
▷ adv debajo, abajo; **~ there** allí abajo;
~ repair en reparación; **undercover**
adj clandestino; **underdone** adj
(Culin) poco hecho; **underestimate**
vt subestimar; **undergo** (irreg)
vt sufrir; (treatment) recibir;
undergraduate n estudiante mf;
underground n (Brit: railway) metro;
(Pol) movimiento clandestino ▷ adj
(car park) subterráneo ▷ adv (work)
en la clandestinidad; **undergrowth** n
maleza; **underline** vt subrayar;
undermine vt socavar, minar;
underneath [ʌndəˈniːθ] adv debajo
▷ prep debajo de, bajo; **underpants**
npl calzoncillos mpl; **underpass** (Brit)
n paso subterráneo; **underprivileged**
adj desposeído; **underscore** vt
subrayar; **undershirt** (US) n camiseta;
underskirt (Brit) n enaguas fpl
understand [ʌndəˈstænd] vt,
vi entender, comprender; (assume)
tener entendido; **understandable**
adj comprensible; **understanding**
adj comprensivo ▷ n comprensión f,
entendimiento; (agreement) acuerdo
understatement [ˈʌndəsteɪtmənt]
n modestia (excesiva); **that's an ~!**
¡eso es decir poco!
understood [ʌndəˈstʊd] pt, pp of

understand ▷ *adj* (*agreed*) acordado; (*implied*): **it is ~ that** se sobreentiende que

undertake [ʌndəˈteɪk] (*irreg*) *vt* emprender; **to ~ to do sth** comprometerse a hacer algo

undertaker [ˈʌndəteɪkə*] *n* director(a) *m/f* de pompas fúnebres

undertaking [ˈʌndəteɪkɪŋ] *n* empresa; (*promise*) promesa

under: underwater *adv* bajo el agua ▷ *adj* submarino; **underway** *adj*: **to be underway** (*meeting*) estar en marcha; (*investigation*) estar llevándose a cabo; **underwear** *n* ropa interior; **underwent** *vb* see **undergo**; **underworld** *n* (*of crime*) hampa, inframundo

undesirable [ʌndɪˈzaɪərəbl] *adj* (*person*) indeseable; (*thing*) poco aconsejable

undisputed [ʌndɪsˈpjuːtɪd] *adj* incontestable

undo [ʌnˈduː] (*irreg*) *vt* (*laces*) desatar; (*button etc*) desabrochar; (*spoil*) deshacer

undone [ʌnˈdʌn] *pp of* **undo** ▷ *adj*: **to come ~** (*clothes*) desabrocharse; (*parcel*) desatarse

undoubtedly [ʌnˈdautɪdlɪ] *adv* indudablemente, sin duda

undress [ʌnˈdres] *vi* desnudarse

unearth [ʌnˈɜːθ] *vt* desenterrar

uneasy [ʌnˈiːzɪ] *adj* intranquilo, preocupado; (*feeling*) desagradable; (*peace*) inseguro

unemployed [ʌnɪmˈplɔɪd] *adj* parado, sin trabajo ▷ *npl*: **the ~** los parados

unemployment [ʌnɪmˈplɔɪmənt] *n* paro, desempleo; **unemployment benefit** *n* (BRIT) subsidio de desempleo o paro

unequal [ʌnˈiːkwəl] *adj* (*unfair*) desigual; (*size, length*) distinto

uneven [ʌnˈiːvən] *adj* desigual; (*road etc*) lleno de baches

unexpected [ʌnɪkˈspektɪd] *adj*

inesperado; **unexpectedly** *adv* inesperadamente

unfair [ʌnˈfɛə*] *adj*: **~ (to sb)** injusto (con algn)

unfaithful [ʌnˈfeɪθful] *adj* infiel

unfamiliar [ʌnfəˈmɪlɪə*] *adj* extraño, desconocido; **to be ~ with** desconocer

unfashionable [ʌnˈfæʃnəbl] *adj* pasado o fuera de moda

unfasten [ʌnˈfɑːsn] *vt* (*knot*) desatar; (*dress*) desabrochar; (*open*) abrir

unfavourable [ʌnˈfeɪvərəbl] (*us* **unfavorable**) *adj* desfavorable

unfinished [ʌnˈfɪnɪʃt] *adj* inacabado, sin terminar

unfit [ʌnˈfɪt] *adj* bajo de forma; (*incompetent*): **~ (for)** incapaz (de); **~ for work** no apto para trabajar

unfold [ʌnˈfəuld] *vt* desdoblar ▷ *vi* abrirse

unforgettable [ʌnfəˈgetəbl] *adj* inolvidable

unfortunate [ʌnˈfɔːtʃnət] *adj* desgraciado; (*event, remark*) inoportuno; **unfortunately** *adv* desgraciadamente

unfriendly [ʌnˈfrendlɪ] *adj* antipático; (*behaviour, remark*) hostil, poco amigable

unfurnished [ʌnˈfɜːnɪʃt] *adj* sin amueblar

unhappiness [ʌnˈhæpɪnɪs] *n* tristeza, desdicha

unhappy [ʌnˈhæpɪ] *adj* (*sad*) triste; (*unfortunate*) desgraciado; (*childhood*) infeliz; **~ about/with** (*arrangements etc*) poco contento con, descontento de

unhealthy [ʌnˈhelθɪ] *adj* (*place*) malsano; (*person*) enfermizo; (*fig: interest*) morboso

unheard-of [ʌnˈhɜːdɔv] *adj* inaudito, sin precedente

unhelpful [ʌnˈhelpful] *adj* (*person*) poco servicial; (*advice*) inútil

unhurt [ʌnˈhɜːt] *adj* ileso

unidentified [ʌnaɪˈdentɪfaɪd] *adj* no identificado, sin identificar; see

also **UFO**
uniform [ˈjuːnɪfɔːm] *n* uniforme *m*
▷ *adj* uniforme
unify [ˈjuːnɪfaɪ] *vt* unificar, unir
unimportant [ʌnɪmˈpɔːtənt] *adj* sin importancia
uninhabited [ʌnɪnˈhæbɪtɪd] *adj* desierto
unintentional [ʌnɪnˈtenʃənəl] *adj* involuntario
union [ˈjuːnjən] *n* unión *f*; (*also*: **trade ~**) sindicato ▷ *cpd* sindical; **Union Jack** *n* bandera del Reino Unido
unique [juːˈniːk] *adj* único
unisex [ˈjuːnɪseks] *adj* unisex
unit [ˈjuːnɪt] *n* unidad *f*; (*section: of furniture etc*) elemento; (*team*) grupo; **kitchen ~** módulo de cocina
unite [juːˈnaɪt] *vt* unir ▷ *vi* unirse; **united** *adj* unido; (*effort*) conjunto; **United Kingdom** *n* Reino Unido; **United Nations (Organization)** *n* Naciones *fpl* Unidas; **United States (of America)** *n* Estados *mpl* Unidos
unity [ˈjuːnɪtɪ] *n* unidad *f*
universal [juːnɪˈvɜːsl] *adj* universal
universe [ˈjuːnɪvɜːs] *n* universo
university [juːnɪˈvɜːsɪtɪ] *n* universidad *f*
unjust [ʌnˈdʒʌst] *adj* injusto
unkind [ʌnˈkaɪnd] *adj* poco amable; (*behaviour, comment*) cruel
unknown [ʌnˈnəʊn] *adj* desconocido
unlawful [ʌnˈlɔːful] *adj* ilegal, ilícito
unleaded [ʌnˈledɪd] *adj* (*petrol, fuel*) sin plomo
unleash [ʌnˈliːʃ] *vt* desatar
unless [ʌnˈles] *conj* a menos que; **~ he comes** a menos que venga; **~ otherwise stated** salvo indicación contraria
unlike [ʌnˈlaɪk] *adj* (*not alike*) distinto de ora; (*not like*) poco propio de ▷ *prep* a diferencia de
unlikely [ʌnˈlaɪklɪ] *adj* improbable; (*unexpected*) inverosímil
unlimited [ʌnˈlɪmɪtɪd] *adj* ilimitado

unlisted [ʌnˈlɪstɪd] (*US*) *adj* (*Tel*) que no consta en la guía
unload [ʌnˈləʊd] *vt* descargar
unlock [ʌnˈlɒk] *vt* abrir (con llave)
unlucky [ʌnˈlʌkɪ] *adj* desgraciado; (*object, number*) que da mala suerte; **to be ~** tener mala suerte
unmarried [ʌnˈmærɪd] *adj* soltero
unmistak(e)able [ʌnmɪsˈteɪkəbl] *adj* inconfundible
unnatural [ʌnˈnætʃrəl] *adj* (*gen*) antinatural; (*manner*) afectado; (*habit*) perverso
unnecessary [ʌnˈnesəsərɪ] *adj* innecesario, inútil
UNO [ˈjuːnəʊ] *n abbr* (= United Nations Organization) ONU *f*
unofficial [ʌnəˈfɪʃl] *adj* no oficial; (*news*) sin confirmar
unpack [ʌnˈpæk] *vi* deshacer las maletas ▷ *vt* deshacer
unpaid [ʌnˈpeɪd] *adj* (*bill, debt*) sin pagar, impagado; (*Comm*) pendiente; (*holiday*) sin sueldo; (*work*) sin pago, voluntario
unpleasant [ʌnˈpleznt] *adj* (*disagreeable*) desagradable; (*person, manner*) antipático
unplug [ʌnˈplʌg] *vt* desenchufar, desconectar
unpopular [ʌnˈpɒpjulə*] *adj* impopular, poco popular
unprecedented [ʌnˈpresɪdəntɪd] *adj* sin precedentes
unpredictable [ʌnprɪˈdɪktəbl] *adj* imprevisible
unprotected [ˈʌnprəˈtektɪd] *adj* (*sex*) sin protección
unqualified [ʌnˈkwɒlɪfaɪd] *adj* sin título, no cualificado; (*success*) total
unravel [ʌnˈrævl] *vt* desenmarañar
unreal [ʌnˈrɪəl] *adj* irreal; (*extraordinary*) increíble
unrealistic [ʌnrɪəˈlɪstɪk] *adj* poco realista
unreasonable [ʌnˈriːznəbl] *adj* irrazonable; (*demand*) excesivo
unrelated [ʌnrɪˈleɪtɪd] *adj* sin

relación; (family) no emparentado

unreliable [ʌnrɪˈlaɪəbl] adj (person) informal; (machine) poco fiable

unrest [ʌnˈrɛst] n inquietud f, malestar m; (Pol) disturbios mpl

unroll [ʌnˈrəʊl] vt desenrollar

unruly [ʌnˈruːlɪ] adj indisciplinado

unsafe [ʌnˈseɪf] adj peligroso

unsatisfactory [ˈʌnsætɪsˈfæktərɪ] adj poco satisfactorio

unscrew [ʌnˈskruː] vt destornillar

unsettled [ʌnˈsɛtld] adj inquieto, intranquilo; (weather) variable

unsettling [ʌnˈsɛtlɪŋ] adj perturbador(a), inquietante

unsightly [ʌnˈsaɪtlɪ] adj feo

unskilled [ʌnˈskɪld] adj (work) no especializado; (worker) no cualificado

unspoiled [ˈʌnˈspɔɪld], **unspoilt** [ˈʌnˈspɔɪlt] adj (place) que no ha perdido su belleza natural

unstable [ʌnˈsteɪbl] adj inestable

unsteady [ʌnˈstɛdɪ] adj inestable

unsuccessful [ˈʌnsəkˈsɛsful] adj (attempt) infructuoso; (writer, proposal) sin éxito; **to be ~** (in attempting sth) no tener éxito, fracasar

unsuitable [ʌnˈsuːtəbl] adj inapropiado; (time) inoportuno

unsure [ʌnˈʃuə*] adj inseguro, poco seguro

untidy [ʌnˈtaɪdɪ] adj (room) desordenado; (appearance) desaliñado

untie [ʌnˈtaɪ] vt desatar

until [ənˈtɪl] prep hasta ▷ conj hasta que; **~ he comes** hasta que venga; **~ now** hasta ahora; **~ then** hasta entonces

untrue [ʌnˈtruː] adj (statement) falso

unused [ʌnˈjuːzd] adj sin usar

unusual [ʌnˈjuːʒuəl] adj insólito, poco común; (exceptional) inusitado; **unusually** adv (exceptionally) excepcionalmente; **he arrived unusually early** llegó más temprano que de costumbre

unveil [ʌnˈveɪl] vt (statue) descubrir

unwanted [ʌnˈwɒntɪd] adj (clothing)

viejo; (pregnancy) no deseado

unwell [ʌnˈwɛl] adj: **to be/feel ~** estar indispuesto/sentirse mal

unwilling [ʌnˈwɪlɪŋ] adj: **to be ~ to do sth** estar poco dispuesto a hacer algo

unwind [ʌnˈwaɪnd] (irreg) vt desenvolver ▷ vi (relax) relajarse

unwise [ʌnˈwaɪz] adj imprudente

unwittingly [ʌnˈwɪtɪŋlɪ] adv inconscientemente, sin darse cuenta

unwrap [ʌnˈræp] vt desenvolver

unzip [ʌnˈzɪp] vt abrir la cremallera de; (Comput) descomprimir

○ **KEYWORD**

up [ʌp] prep: **to go/be up sth** subir/ estar subido en algo; **he went up the stairs/the hill** subió las escaleras/la colina; **we walked/climbed up the hill** subimos la colina; **they live further up the street** viven más arriba en la calle; **go up that road and turn left** sigue por esa calle y gira a la izquierda

▷ adv 1 (upwards, higher) más arriba; **up in the mountains** en lo alto (de la montaña); **put it a bit higher up** ponlo un poco más arriba or alto; **up there** ahí or allí arriba; **up above** en lo alto, por encima, arriba

2: **to be up** (out of bed) estar levantado; (prices, level) haber subido

3: **up to** (as far as) hasta; **up to now** hasta ahora or la fecha

4: **to be up to: it's up to you** (depending on) depende de ti; **he's not up to it** (job, task etc) no es capaz de hacerlo; **his work is not up to the required standard** su trabajo no da la talla; (inf: be doing): **what is he up to?** ¿qué estará tramando?

▷ n: **ups and downs** altibajos mpl

up-and-coming [ʌpəndˈkʌmɪŋ] adj prometedor(a)

upbringing [ˈʌpbrɪŋɪŋ] n educación

f

update [ʌp'deɪt] vt poner al día

upfront [ʌp'frʌnt] adj claro, directo ▷ adv a las claras; (pay) por adelantado; **to be ~ about sth** admitir algo claramente

upgrade [ʌp'greɪd] vt (house) modernizar; (employee) ascender

upheaval [ʌp'hiːvl] n trastornos mpl; (Pol) agitación f

uphill [ʌp'hɪl] adj cuesta arriba; (fig: task) penoso, difícil ▷ adv: **to go ~** ir cuesta arriba

upholstery [ʌp'həʊlstərɪ] n tapicería f

upmarket [ʌp'mɑːkɪt] adj (product) de categoría

upon [ə'pɒn] prep sobre

upper [ʌpə*] adj superior, de arriba ▷ n (of shoe: also: **~s**) empeine m; **upper-class** adj de clase alta

upright [ʌpraɪt] adj derecho; (vertical) vertical; (fig) honrado

uprising [ʌpraɪzɪŋ] n sublevación f

uproar [ʌprɔː*] n escándalo

upset [n ʌpsɛt, vb, adj ʌp'sɛt] (irreg) n (to plan etc) revés n, contratiempo; (Med) trastorno ▷ vt (glass etc) volcar; (plan) alterar; (person) molestar, disgustar ▷ adj molesto, disgustado; (stomach) revuelto

upside-down [ʌpsaɪd'daʊn] adv al revés; **to turn a place ~** (fig) revolverlo todo

upstairs [ʌp'stɛəz] adv arriba ▷ adj (room) de arriba ▷ n el piso superior

up-to-date [ʌptə'deɪt] adj al día

uptown [ʌp'taʊn] (us) adv hacia las afueras ▷ adj exterior, de las afueras

upward [ʌpwəd] adj ascendente; **upward(s)** adv hacia arriba; **upward(s) of** más de

uranium [jʊə'reɪnɪəm] n uranio

Uranus [jʊə'reɪnəs] n Urano

urban [ɜːbən] adj urbano

urge [ɜːdʒ] n (desire) deseo ▷ vt: **to ~ sb to do sth** animar a algn a hacer algo

urgency [ɜːdʒənsɪ] n urgencia

urgent [ɜːdʒənt] adj urgente; (voice) perentorio

urinal [juərɪnl] n (building) urinario; (vessel) orinal m

urinate [juərɪneɪt] vi orinar

urine [juərɪn] n orina, orines mpl

US n abbr (= United States) EE. UU.

us [ʌs] pron nos; (after prep) nosotros; as; see also **me**

USA n abbr (= United States (of America)) EE.UU.

use [n juːs, vb juːz] n uso, empleo; (usefulness) utilidad f ▷ vt usar, emplear; **she ~d to do it** (ella) solía or acostumbraba hacerlo; **in ~** en uso; **out of ~** en desuso; **to be of ~** servir; **it's no ~** (pointless) es inútil; (not useful) no sirve; **to be ~d to** estar acostumbrado a, acostumbrar; **use up** vt (food) consumir; (money) gastar; **used** [juːzd] adj (car) usado; **useful** adj útil; **useless** (unusable) inservible; (pointless) inútil; (person) inepto; **user** n usuario/a; **user-friendly** adj (computer) amistoso

usual [juːʒuəl] adj normal, corriente; **as ~** como de costumbre; **usually** adv normalmente

utensil [juːtɛnsl] n utensilio; **kitchen ~s** batería de cocina

utility [juːtɪlɪtɪ] n utilidad f; (public utility) (empresa de) servicio público

utilize [juːtɪlaɪz] vt utilizar

utmost [ʌtməʊst] adj mayor ▷ n: **to do one's ~** hacer todo lo posible

utter [ʌtə*] adj total, completo ▷ vt pronunciar, proferir; **utterly** adv completamente, totalmente

U-turn [juːtɜːn] n viraje m en redondo

V

v. abbr = **verse; versus;** (= volt) v;
(= vide) véase

vacancy ['veɪkənsɪ] n (BRIT: job)
vacante f; (room) habitación f libre; **"no
vacancies"** "completo"

vacant ['veɪkənt] adj desocupado,
libre; (expression) distraído

vacate [və'keɪt] vt (house, room)
desocupar; (job) dejar (vacante)

vacation [və'keɪʃən] n vacaciones
fpl; **vacationer** (US **vacationist**) n
turista m/f

vaccination [væksɪ'neɪʃən] n
vacunación f

vaccine ['væksiːn] n vacuna

vacuum ['vækjʊm] n vacío; **vacuum
cleaner** n aspiradora

vagina [və'dʒaɪnə] n vagina

vague [veɪg] adj vago; (memory)
borroso; (ambiguous) impreciso;
(person: absent-minded) distraído;
(: evasive): **to be ~** no decir las cosas
claramente

vain [veɪn] adj (conceited) presumido;
(useless) vano, inútil; **in ~** en vano

Valentine's Day ['væləntaɪnzdeɪ] n
día de los enamorados

valid ['vælɪd] adj válido; (ticket)
valedero; (law) vigente

valley ['vælɪ] n valle m

valuable ['væljuəbl] adj (jewel) de
valor; (time) valioso; **valuables** npl
objetos mpl de valor

value ['væljuː] n valor m; (importance)
importancia ▷ vt (fix price of) tasar,
valorar; (esteem) apreciar; **values** npl
(principles) principios mpl

valve [vælv] n válvula

vampire ['væmpaɪə*] n vampiro

van [væn] n (Aut) furgoneta,
camioneta

vandal ['vændl] n vándalo/a;
vandalism n vandalismo; **vandalize**
vt dañar, destruir

vanilla [və'nɪlə] n vainilla

vanish ['vænɪʃ] vi desaparecer

vanity ['vænɪtɪ] n vanidad f

vapour ['veɪpə*] (US **vapor**) n vapor
m; (on breath, window) vaho

variable ['veərɪəbl] adj variable

variant ['veərɪənt] n variante f

variation [veərɪ'eɪʃən] n variación f

varied ['veərɪd] adj variado

variety [və'raɪətɪ] n (diversity)
diversidad f, variedad f; (type) variedad f

various ['veərɪəs] adj (several: people)
varios/as; (reasons) diversos/as

varnish ['vɑːnɪʃ] n barniz m; (nail
varnish) esmalte m ▷ vt barnizar; (nails)
pintar (con esmalte)

vary ['veərɪ] vt variar; (change)
cambiar ▷ vi variar

vase [vɑːz] n jarrón m

> ⚠ Be careful not to translate **vase** by
> the Spanish word *vaso*.

Vaseline® ['væsɪliːn] n vaselina®

vast [vɑːst] adj enorme

VAT [væt] (BRIT) n abbr (= value added
tax) IVA m

vault [vɔːlt] n (of roof) bóveda;
(tomb) panteón m; (in bank) cámara
acorazada ▷ vt (also: **~ over**) saltar
(por encima de)

VCR n abbr = **video cassette recorder**
VDU n (= visual display unit) UPV f
veal [viːl] n ternera
veer [vɪə*] vi (vehicle) virar; (wind) girar
vegan ['viːɡən] n vegetariano/a estricto/a, vegetaliano/a
vegetable ['vedʒtəbl] n (Bot) vegetal m; (edible plant) legumbre f, hortaliza ▷ adj vegetal
vegetarian [vedʒɪ'tɛərɪən] adj, n vegetariano/a m/f
vegetation [vedʒɪ'teɪʃən] n vegetación f
vehicle ['viːɪkl] n vehículo; (fig) medio
veil [veɪl] n velo ▷ vt velar
vein [veɪn] n vena; (of ore etc) veta
Velcro® ['vɛlkrəʊ] n velcro® m
velvet ['vɛlvɪt] n terciopelo
vending machine ['vɛndɪŋ-] n distribuidor m automático
vendor ['vɛndə*] n vendedor(a) m/f; **street ~** vendedor(a) m/f callejero/a
vengeance ['vɛndʒəns] n venganza; **with a ~** (fig) con creces
venison ['vɛnɪsn] n carne f de venado
venom ['vɛnəm] n veneno; (bitterness) odio
vent [vɛnt] n (in jacket) respiradero; (in wall) rejilla (de ventilación) ▷ vt (fig: feelings) desahogar
ventilation [vɛntɪ'leɪʃən] n ventilación f
venture ['vɛntʃə*] n empresa ▷ vt (opinion) ofrecer ▷ vi aventurarse, lanzarse; **business ~** empresa comercial
venue ['vɛnjuː] n lugar m
Venus ['viːnəs] n Venus m
verb [vəːb] n verbo; **verbal** adj verbal
verdict ['vəːdɪkt] n veredicto, fallo; (fig) opinión f, juicio
verge [vəːdʒ] (BRIT) n borde m; **"soft ~s"** (Aut) "arcén m no asfaltado"; **to be on the ~ of doing sth** estar a punto de hacer algo
verify ['vɛrɪfaɪ] vt comprobar, verificar

versatile ['vəːsətaɪl] adj (person) polifacético; (machine, tool etc) versátil
verse [vəːs] n poesía; (stanza) estrofa; (in bible) versículo
version ['vəːʃən] n versión f
versus ['vəːsəs] prep contra
vertical ['vəːtɪkl] adj vertical
very ['vɛrɪ] adv muy ▷ adj: **the ~ book which** el mismo libro que; **the ~ last** el último de todos; **at the ~ least** al menos; **~ much** muchísimo
vessel ['vɛsl] n (ship) barco; (container) vasija; see **blood**
vest [vɛst] n (BRIT) camiseta; (US: waistcoat) chaleco
vet [vɛt] vt (candidate) investigar ▷ n abbr (BRIT) = **veterinary surgeon**
veteran ['vɛtərn] n excombatiente mf, veterano/a
veterinary surgeon ['vɛtrɪnərɪ-] (US **veterinarian**) n veterinario/a m/f
veto ['viːtəʊ] (pl **-es**) n veto ▷ vt prohibir, poner el veto a
via ['vaɪə] prep por, por medio de
viable ['vaɪəbl] adj viable
vibrate [vaɪ'breɪt] vi vibrar
vibration [vaɪ'breɪʃən] n vibración f
vicar ['vɪkə*] n párroco (de la Iglesia Anglicana)
vice [vaɪs] n (evil) vicio; (Tech) torno de banco; **vice-chairman** (irreg) n vicepresidente m
vice versa ['vaɪsɪ'vəːsə] adv viceversa
vicinity [vɪ'sɪnɪtɪ] n: **in the ~ (of)** cercano/a
vicious ['vɪʃəs] adj (attack) violento; (words) cruel; (horse, dog) resabido
victim ['vɪktɪm] n víctima
victor ['vɪktə*] n vencedor(a) m/f
Victorian [vɪk'tɔːrɪən] adj victoriano
victorious [vɪk'tɔːrɪəs] adj vencedor(a)
victory ['vɪktərɪ] n victoria
video ['vɪdɪəʊ] n (film) vídeo (SP), video (LAM); **video call** n videollamada; **video camera** n videocámara, cámara de vídeo; **video (cassette) recorder** n vídeo (SP), video

(LAM); **video game** n videojuego;
videophone n videoteléfono; **video shop** n videoclub m; **video tape** n cinta de vídeo

vie [vaɪ] vi: **to ~ (with sb for sth)** competir (con algn por algo)

Vienna [vɪˈɛnə] n Viena

Vietnam [vjetˈnæm] n Vietnam m; **Vietnamese** [-nəˈmiːz] n inv, adj vietnamita mf

view [vjuː] n vista; (outlook) perspectiva; (opinion) opinión f, criterio ▷ vt (look at) mirar; (fig) considerar; **on ~** (in museum etc) expuesto; **in full ~ (of)** en plena vista; **in ~ of the weather/the fact that** en vista del tiempo/del hecho de que; **in my ~** en mi opinión; **viewer** n espectador(a) m/f; (TV) telespectador(a) m/f; **viewpoint** n (attitude) punto de vista; (place) mirador m

vigilant [ˈvɪdʒɪlənt] adj vigilante

vigorous [ˈvɪɡərəs] adj enérgico, vigoroso

vile [vaɪl] adj vil, infame; (smell) asqueroso; (temper) endemoniado

villa [ˈvɪlə] n (country house) casa de campo; (suburban house) chalet m

village [ˈvɪlɪdʒ] n aldea; **villager** n aldeano/a

villain [ˈvɪlən] n (scoundrel) malvado/a; (in novel) malo; (BRIT: criminal) maleante m

vinaigrette [vɪneɪˈɡret] n vinagreta

vine [vaɪn] n vid f

vinegar [ˈvɪnɪɡə*] n vinagre m

vineyard [ˈvɪnjɑːd] n viña, viñedo

vintage [ˈvɪntɪdʒ] n (year) vendimia, cosecha f ▷ cpd de época

vinyl [ˈvaɪnl] n vinilo

viola [vɪˈəʊlə] n (Mus) viola

violate [ˈvaɪəleɪt] vt violar

violation [vaɪəˈleɪʃən] n violación f; **in ~ of sth** en violación de algo

violence [ˈvaɪələns] n violencia

violent [ˈvaɪələnt] adj violento; (intense) intenso

violet [ˈvaɪələt] adj violado, violeta

▷ n (plant) violeta

violin [vaɪəˈlɪn] n violín m

VIP n abbr (= very important person) VIP m

virgin [ˈvɜːdʒɪn] n, adj virgen f

Virgo [ˈvɜːɡəʊ] n Virgo

virtual [ˈvɜːtjuəl] adj virtual; **virtually** adv prácticamente; **virtual reality** n (Comput) mundo or realidad f virtual

virtue [ˈvɜːtjuː] n virtud f; (advantage) ventaja; **by ~ of** en virtud de

virus [ˈvaɪərəs] n (also Comput) virus m inv

visa [ˈviːzə] n visado (SP), visa (LAM)

vise [vaɪs] (US) n (Tech) = **vice**

visibility [vɪzɪˈbɪlɪtɪ] n visibilidad f

visible [ˈvɪzəbl] adj visible

vision [ˈvɪʒən] n (sight) vista; (foresight, in dream) visión f

visit [ˈvɪzɪt] n visita ▷ vt (person (US: also: ~ **with**)) visitar, hacer una visita a; (place) ir a, (ir a) conocer; **visiting hours** npl (in hospital etc) horas fpl de visita; **visitor** n (in museum) visitante mf; (invited to house) visita; (tourist) turista mf; **visitor centre** (US **visitor center**) n centro m de información

visual [ˈvɪzjuəl] adj visual; **visualize** vt imaginarse

vital [ˈvaɪtl] adj (essential) esencial, imprescindible; (dynamic) dinámico; (organ) vital

vitality [vaɪˈtælɪtɪ] n energía, vitalidad f

vitamin [ˈvɪtəmɪn] n vitamina

vivid [ˈvɪvɪd] adj (account) gráfico; (light) intenso; (imagination, memory) vivo

V-neck [ˈviːnek] n cuello de pico

vocabulary [vəʊˈkæbjʊlərɪ] n vocabulario

vocal [ˈvəʊkl] adj vocal; (articulate) elocuente

vocational [vəʊˈkeɪʃənl] adj profesional

vodka [ˈvɔdkə] n vodka m

vogue [vəʊɡ] n: **in ~** en boga

voice [vɔɪs] n voz f ▷ vt expresar;
voice mail n buzón de voz
void [vɔɪd] n vacío; (hole) hueco ▷ adj
(invalid) nulo, inválido; (empty): ~ **of**
carente or desprovisto de
volatile ['vɔlətaɪl] adj (situation)
inestable; (person) voluble; (liquid)
volátil
volcano [vɔl'keɪnəu] (pl **~es**) n
volcán m
volleyball ['vɔlibɔ:l] n vol(e)ibol m
volt [vəult] n voltio; **voltage** n
voltaje m
volume ['vɔlju:m] n (gen) volumen
m; (book) tomo
voluntarily ['vɔləntrɪli] adv
libremente, voluntariamente
voluntary ['vɔləntəri] adj voluntario
volunteer [vɔlən'tɪə*] n voluntario/
a ▷ vt (information) ofrecer ▷ vi
ofrecerse (de voluntario); **to ~ to do**
ofrecerse a hacer
vomit ['vɔmɪt] n vómito ▷ vt, vi
vomitar
vote [vəut] n voto; (votes cast)
votación f; (right to vote) derecho
de votar; (franchise) sufragio ▷ vt
(chairman) elegir; (propose): **to ~ that**
proponer que ▷ vi votar, ir a votar; **~
of thanks** voto de gracias; **voter** n
votante mf; **voting** n votación f
voucher ['vautʃə*] n (for meal, petrol)
vale m
vow [vau] n voto ▷ vt: **to ~ to do/
that** jurar hacer/que
vowel ['vauəl] n vocal f
voyage ['vɔɪdʒ] n viaje m
vulgar ['vʌlgə*] adj (rude) ordinario,
grosero; (in bad taste) de mal gusto
vulnerable ['vʌlnərəbl] adj
vulnerable
vulture ['vʌltʃə*] n buitre m

waddle ['wɔdl] vi anadear
wade [weɪd] vi: **to ~ through** (water)
vadear; (fig: book) leer con dificultad
wafer ['weɪfə*] n galleta, barquillo
waffle ['wɔfl] n (Culin) gofre m ▷ vi
dar el rollo
wag [wæg] vt menear, agitar ▷ vi
moverse, menearse
wage [weɪdʒ] n (also: **~s**) sueldo,
salario ▷ vt: **to ~ war** hacer la guerra
wag(g)on ['wægən] n (horse-drawn)
carro; (Brit Rail) vagón m
wail [weɪl] n gemido ▷ vi gemir
waist [weɪst] n cintura, talle m;
waistcoat (Brit) n chaleco
wait [weɪt] n (interval) pausa ▷ vi
esperar; **to lie in ~ for** acechar a; **I
can't ~ to** (fig) estoy deseando; **~
for** esperar (a); **wait on** vt fus servir
a; **waiter** n camarero; **waiting list**
n lista de espera; **waiting room** n
sala de espera; **waitress** ['weɪtrɪs] n
camarera
waive [weɪv] vt suspender
wake [weɪk] (pt **woke** or **~d**, pp **woken**

or **~d**) vt (also: **~ up**) despertar ▷ vi (also: **~ up**) despertarse ▷ n (for dead person) vela, velatorio; (Naut) estela

Wales [weɪlz] n País m de Gales; **the Prince of ~** el príncipe de Gales

walk [wɔːk] n (stroll) paseo; (hike) excursión f a pie, caminata; (gait) paso, andar m; (in park etc) paseo, alameda ▷ vi andar, caminar; (for pleasure, exercise) pasear ▷ vt (distance) recorrer a pie, andar; (dog) pasear; **10 minutes' ~ from here** a 10 minutos de aquí andando; **people from all ~s of life** gente de todas las esferas; **walk out** vi (audience) salir; (workers) declararse en huelga; **walker** n (person) paseante m, caminante m f; **walkie-talkie** ['wɔːkɪ'tɔːkɪ] n walkie-talkie m; **walking** n el andar; **walking shoes** npl zapatos mpl para andar; **walking stick** n bastón m; **Walkman®** n Walkman® m; **walkway** n paseo

wall [wɔːl] n pared f; (exterior) muro; (city wall etc) muralla

wallet ['wɒlɪt] n cartera, billetera

wallpaper ['wɔːlpeɪpə*] n papel m pintado ▷ vt empapelar

walnut ['wɔːlnʌt] n nuez f; (tree) nogal m

walrus ['wɔːlrəs] (pl **~** or **~es**) n morsa

waltz [wɔːlts] n vals m ▷ vi bailar el vals

wand [wɒnd] n (also: **magic ~**) varita (mágica)

wander ['wɒndə*] vi (person) vagar; deambular; (thoughts) divagar ▷ vt recorrer, vagar por

want [wɒnt] vt querer, desear; (need) necesitar ▷ n: **for ~ of** por falta de; **wanted** adj (criminal) buscado; **"wanted"** (in advertisements) "se busca"

war [wɔː*] n guerra; **to make ~ (on)** declarar la guerra (a)

ward [wɔːd] n (in hospital) sala; (Pol) distrito electoral; (Law: child: also: **~ of court**) pupilo/a

warden ['wɔːdn] n (BRIT: of institution) director(a) m f; (of park, game reserve)

guardián/ana m f; (BRIT: also: **traffic ~**) guardia m f

wardrobe ['wɔːdrəub] n armario, ropero; (clothes) vestuario

warehouse ['weəhaus] n almacén m, depósito

warfare ['wɔːfeə*] n guerra

warhead ['wɔːhɛd] n cabeza armada

warm [wɔːm] adj caliente; (thanks) efusivo; (clothes etc) abrigado; (welcome, day) caluroso; **it's ~** hace calor; **I'm ~** tengo calor; **warm up** vi (room) calentarse; (person) entrar en calor; (athlete) hacer ejercicios de calentamiento ▷ vt calentar; **warmly** adv afectuosamente; **warmth** n calor m

warn [wɔːn] vt avisar, advertir; **warning** n aviso, advertencia; **warning light** n luz f de advertencia

warrant ['wɔrnt] n autorización f; (Law: to arrest) orden f de detención; (: to search) mandamiento de registro

warranty ['wɒrəntɪ] n garantía

warrior ['wɒrɪə*] n guerrero/a

Warsaw ['wɔːsɔː] n Varsovia

warship ['wɔːʃɪp] n buque m or barco de guerra

wart [wɔːt] n verruga

wartime ['wɔːtaɪm] n: **in ~** en tiempos de guerra, en la guerra

wary ['weərɪ] adj cauteloso

was [wɒz] pt of **be**

wash [wɒʃ] vt lavar ▷ vi lavarse; (sea etc): **to ~ against/over sth** llegar hasta/cubrir algo ▷ n (clothes etc) lavado; (of ship) estela; **to have a ~** lavarse; **wash up** vi (BRIT) fregar los platos; (us) lavarse; **washbasin** (us) n lavabo; **wash cloth** (us) n manopla; **washer** n (Tech) arandela; **washing** n (dirty) ropa sucia; (clean) colada; **washing line** n cuerda de (colgar) la ropa; **washing machine** n lavadora; **washing powder** (BRIT) n detergente m (en polvo)

Washington ['wɒʃɪŋtən] n Washington m

wash: washing-up (BRIT) n fregado, platos mpl (para fregar); **washing-up liquid** (BRIT) n líquido lavavajillas; **washroom** (US) n servicios mpl

wasn't ['wɒznt] = **was not**

wasp [wɒsp] n avispa

waste [weɪst] n derroche m, despilfarro; (of time) pérdida; (food) sobras fpl; (rubbish) basura, desperdicios mpl ▷ adj (material) de desecho; (left over) sobrante; (land) baldío, descampado ▷ vt malgastar, derrochar; (time) perder; (opportunity) desperdiciar; **waste ground** (BRIT) n terreno baldío; **wastepaper basket** n papelera

watch [wɒtʃ] n (also: **wrist ~**) reloj m; (Mil: group of guards) centinela m; (act) vigilancia; (Naut: spell of duty) guardia ▷ vt (look at) mirar, observar; (: match, programme) ver; (spy on, guard) vigilar; (be careful of) cuidarse de, tener cuidado ▷ vi ver, mirar; (keep guard) montar guardia; **watch out** vi cuidarse, tener cuidado; **watchdog** n perro guardián; (fig) persona u organismo encargado de asegurarse de que las empresasactúan dentro de la legalidad; **watch strap** n pulsera (de reloj)

water ['wɔ:təʳ] n agua ▷ vt (plant) regar ▷ vi (eyes) llorar; (mouth) hacerse la boca agua; **water down** vt (milk etc) aguar; (fig: story) dulcificar, diluir; **watercolour** (US **watercolor**) n acuarela; **watercress** n berro; **waterfall** n cascada, salto de agua; **watering can** n regadera; **watermelon** n sandía; **waterproof** adj impermeable; **water-skiing** n esquí m acuático

watt [wɒt] n vatio

wave [weɪv] n (of hand) señal f con la mano; (on water) ola; (Radio, in hair) onda; (fig) oleada ▷ vi ondear; (flag etc) ondear ▷ vt (handkerchief, gun) agitar; **wavelength** n longitud f de onda

waver ['weɪvəʳ] vi (voice, love etc)

flaquear; (person) vacilar

wavy ['weɪvɪ] adj ondulado

wax [wæks] n cera ▷ vt encerar ▷ vi (moon) crecer

way [weɪ] n camino; (distance) trayecto, recorrido; (direction) dirección f, sentido; (manner) modo, manera; (habit) costumbre f; **which ~? - this ~** ¿por dónde? or ¿en qué dirección? - por aquí; **on the ~** (en route) en (el) camino; **to be on one's ~** estar en camino; **to be in the ~** bloquear el camino; (fig) estorbar; **to go out of one's ~ to do sth** desvivirse por hacer algo; **under ~** en marcha; **to lose one's ~** extraviarse; **in a ~** en cierto modo or sentido; **no ~!** (inf) ¡de eso nada!; **by the ~ ...** a propósito ...; **"~ in"** (BRIT) "entrada"; **"~ out"** (BRIT) "salida"; **the ~ back** el camino de vuelta; **"give ~"** (BRIT Aut) "ceda el paso"

W.C. n (BRIT) wáter m

we [wi:] pl pron nosotros/as

weak [wi:k] adj débil, flojo; (tea etc) claro; **weaken** vi debilitarse; (give way) ceder ▷ vt debilitar; **weakness** n debilidad f; (fault) punto débil; **to have a weakness for** tener debilidad por

wealth [welθ] n riqueza; (of details) abundancia; **wealthy** adj rico

weapon ['wepən] n arma; **~s of mass destruction** armas de destrucción masiva

wear [weəʳ] (pt **wore**, pp **worn**) n (use) uso; (deterioration through use) desgaste m; (clothes) llevar; (shoes) calzar; (damage: through use) gastar, usar ▷ vi (last) durar; (rub through etc) desgastarse; **evening ~** ropa de etiqueta; **sports-~/baby-~** ropa de deportes/de niños; **wear off** vi desaparecer; **wear out** vt desgastar; (person, strength) agotar

weary ['wɪərɪ] adj cansado; (dispirited) abatido ▷ vi: **to ~ of** cansarse de

weasel ['wi:zl] n (Zool) comadreja

weather ['weðəʳ] n tiempo ▷ vt (storm, crisis) hacer frente a; **under**

the ~ (fig: ill) indispuesto, pachucho;
weather forecast n parte m
meteorológico

weave [wi:v] (pt **wove**, pp **woven**) vt
(cloth) tejer; (fig) entretejer

web [wɛb] n (of spider) telaraña; (on
duck's foot) membrana; (network) red
f; **the (World Wide) W~** la Red; **web
address** n dirección f de Internet;
webcam n webcam f; **web page**
n (página) web m or f; **website** n
sitio web

Wed. abbr (= Wednesday) miérc

wed [wɛd] (pt, pp ~**ded**) vt casar ⊳ vi
casarse

we'd [wi:d] = **we had**; **we would**

wedding ['wɛdɪŋ] n boda,
casamiento; **silver/golden ~
(anniversary)** bodas fpl de plata/de
oro; **wedding anniversary** n
aniversario m de boda; **wedding day**
n día m de la boda; **wedding dress** n
traje m de novia; **wedding ring** n
alianza

wedge [wɛdʒ] n (of wood etc) cuña; (of
cake) trozo ⊳ vt acuñar; (push) apretar

Wednesday ['wɛdnzdɪ] n miércoles
m inv

wee [wi:] (SCOTTISH) adj pequeñito

weed [wi:d] n mala hierba, maleza
⊳ vt escardar, desherbar; **weedkiller**
n herbicida m

week [wi:k] n semana; **a ~ today/on
Friday** de hoy/del viernes en ocho
días; **weekday** n día m laborable;
weekend n fin m de semana; **weekly**
adv semanalmente, cada semana ⊳ adj
semanal ⊳ n semanario

weep [wi:p] (pt, pp **wept**) vi, vt llorar

weigh [weɪ] vt, vi pesar; **to ~ anchor**
levar anclas; **weigh up** vt sopesar

weight [weɪt] n peso; (metal
weight) pesa; **to lose/put on ~**
adelgazar/engordar; **weightlifting** n
levantamiento de pesas

weir [wɪə*] n presa

weird [wɪəd] adj raro, extraño

welcome ['wɛlkəm] adj bienvenido

⊳ n bienvenida ⊳ vt dar la bienvenida
a; (be glad of) alegrarse de; **thank you
- you're ~** gracias – de nada

weld [wɛld] n soldadura ⊳ vt soldar

welfare ['wɛlfɛə*] n bienestar m;
(social aid) asistencia social; **welfare
state** n estado del bienestar

well [wɛl] n fuente f, pozo ⊳ adv bien
⊳ adj: **to be ~** estar bien (de salud) ⊳ excl
¡vaya!, ¡bueno!; **as ~** también; **as ~ as**
además de; **~ done!** ¡bien hecho!; **get ~
soon!** ¡que te mejores pronto!; **to do ~**
(business) ir bien; (person) tener éxito

we'll [wi:l] = **we will**; **we shall**

well-: well-behaved adj bueno;
well-built adj (person) fornido; **well-
dressed** adj bien vestido

wellies ['wɛlɪz] (inf) npl (BRIT) botas
de goma

well-: well-known adj (person)
conocido; **well-off** adj acomodado;
well-paid [wɛl'peɪd] adj bien pagado,
bien retribuido

Welsh [wɛlʃ] adj galés/esa ⊳ n (Ling)
galés m; **Welshman** (irreg) n galés m;
Welshwoman (irreg) n galesa

went [wɛnt] pt of **go**

wept [wɛpt] pt, pp of **weep**

were [wə:*] pt of **be**

we're [wɪə*] = **we are**

weren't [wə:nt] = **were not**

west [wɛst] n oeste m ⊳ adj
occidental, del oeste ⊳ adv al or hacia
el oeste; **the W~** el Oeste, el Occidente;
westbound ['wɛstbaund] adj (traffic,
carriageway) con rumbo al oeste;
western adj occidental, del oeste ⊳ n
(Cinema) película del oeste; **West Indian** adj, n
antillano/a m/f

wet [wɛt] adj (damp) húmedo;
(soaked): **~ through** mojado; (rainy)
lluvioso (BRIT: Pol) conservador/a
m/f moderado/a; **to get ~** mojarse;
"~ paint" "recién pintado"; **wetsuit** n
traje m térmico

we've [wi:v] = **we have**

whack [wæk] vt dar un buen golpe a

whale [weɪl] n (Zool) ballena

wharf [wɔːf] (pl **wharves**) n muelle m

○ KEYWORD

what [wɔt] adj 1 (in direct/indirect questions) qué; **what size is he?** ¿qué talla usa?; **what colour/shape is it?** ¿de qué color/forma es?
2 (in exclamations): **what a mess!** ¡qué desastre!; **what a fool I am!** ¡qué tonto soy!
▷ pron 1 (interrogative) qué; **what are you doing?** ¿qué haces or estás haciendo?; **what is happening?** ¿qué pasa or está pasando?; **what is it called?** ¿cómo se llama?; **what about me?** ¿y yo qué?; **what about doing ...?** ¿qué tal si hacemos ...?
2 (relative) lo que; **I saw what you did/was on the table** vi lo que hiciste/había en la mesa
▷ excl (disbelieving) ¡cómo!; **what, no coffee!** ¡que no hay café!

whatever [wɔt'ɛvə*] adj: **~ book you choose** cualquier libro que elijas
▷ pron: **do ~ is necessary** haga lo que sea necesario; **~ happens** pase lo que pase; **no reason ~** or whatsoever ninguna razón a la que sea; **nothing ~** nada en absoluto

whatsoever [wɔtsəu'ɛvə*] adj see whatever

wheat [wiːt] n trigo

wheel [wiːl] n rueda; (Aut: also: **steering ~**) volante m; (Naut) timón m ▷ vt (pram etc) empujar ▷ vi (also: **~ round**) dar la vuelta, girar; **wheelbarrow** n carretilla; **wheelchair** n silla de ruedas; **wheel clamp** n (Aut) cepo

wheeze [wiːz] vi resollar

○ KEYWORD

when [wɛn] adv cuando; **when did it happen?** ¿cuándo ocurrió?; **I know**

when it happened sé cuándo ocurrió
▷ conj 1 (at, during, after the time that) cuando; **be careful when you cross the road** ten cuidado al cruzar la calle; **that was when I needed you** fue entonces que te necesité
2 (on, at which): **on the day when I met him** el día en que le conocí
3 (whereas) cuando

whenever [wɛn'ɛvə*] conj cuando; (every time that) cada vez que ▷ adv cuando sea

where [wɛə*] adv dónde ▷ conj donde; **this is ~** aquí es donde; **whereabouts** adv dónde ▷ n: **nobody knows his whereabouts** nadie conoce su paradero; **whereas** conj visto que, mientras; **whereby** conj por lo cual; **wherever** conj dondequiera que; (interrogative) dónde

whether ['wɛðə*] conj si; **I don't know ~ to accept or not** no sé si aceptar o no; **~ you go or not** os vayas o no vayas

---

○ KEYWORD

which [wɪtʃ] adj 1 (interrogative: direct, indirect) qué; **which picture(s) do you want?** ¿qué cuadro(s) quieres?; **which one?** ¿cuál?
2 in which case en cuyo caso; **we got there at 8 pm, by which time the cinema was full** llegamos allí a las 8, cuando el cine estaba lleno
▷ pron 1 (interrogative) cual; **I don't mind which** el/la que sea
2 (relative: replacing noun) que; (: replacing clause) lo que; (: after preposition) (el)(la) que etc el/la cual etc; **the apple which you ate/which is on the table** la manzana que comiste/que está en la mesa; **the chair on which you are sitting** la silla en la que estás sentado; **he said he knew, which is true/I feared** dijo que lo sabía, lo cual or lo

que es cierto/me temía

whichever [wɪtʃ'evə*] *adj:* **take~ book you prefer** coja (SP) el libro que prefiera; **~ book you take** cualquier libro que coja

while [waɪl] *n* rato, momento ▷ *conj* mientras; (*although*) aunque; **for a ~** durante algún tiempo

whilst [waɪlst] *conj* = **while**

whim [wɪm] *n* capricho

whine [waɪn] *n* (*of pain*) gemido; (*of engine*) zumbido; (*of siren*) aullido ▷ *vi* gemir; zumbar; (*fig: complain*) gimotear

whip [wɪp] *n* látigo; (*Pol: person*) encargado de la disciplina partidaria en el parlamento ▷ *vt* azotar; (*Culin*) batir; (*move quickly*): **to ~ sth off/out** sacar/quitar algo de un tirón; **whipped cream** *n* nata or crema montada

whirl [wə:l] *vt* hacer girar, dar vueltas a ▷ *vi* girar, dar vueltas; (*leaves etc*) arremolinarse

whisk [wɪsk] *n* (*Culin*) batidor *m* ▷ *vt* (*Culin*) batir; **to ~ sb away or off** llevar volando a algn

whiskers ['wɪskəz] *npl* (*of animal*) bigotes *mpl*; (*of man*) patillas *fpl*

whiskey ['wɪskɪ] (*US, IRELAND*) *n* = **whisky**

whisky ['wɪskɪ] *n* whisky *m*

whisper ['wɪspə*] *n* susurro ▷ *vi*, *vt* susurrar

whistle ['wɪsl] *n* (*sound*) silbido; (*object*) silbato ▷ *vi* silbar

white [waɪt] *adj* blanco; (*pale*) pálido ▷ *n* blanco; (*of egg*) clara; **whiteboard** *n* pizarra blanca; **interactive whiteboard** pizarra interactiva; **White House** (*US*) *n* Casa Blanca; **whitewash** *n* (*paint*) jalbegue *m*, cal *f* ▷ *vt* blanquear

whiting ['waɪtɪŋ] *n inv* (*fish*) pescadilla

Whitsun ['wɪtsn] *n* pentecostés *m*

whittle ['wɪtl] *vt:* **to ~ away, ~ down** ir reduciendo

whizz [wɪz] *vi:* **to ~ past** or **by** pasar a toda velocidad

○ **KEYWORD**

who [hu:] *pron* 1 (*interrogative*) quién; **who is it?, who's there?** ¿quién es?; **who are you looking for?** ¿a quién buscas?; **I told her who I was** le dije quién era yo

2 (*relative*) que; **the man/woman who spoke to me** el hombre/la mujer que habló conmigo; **those who can swim** los que saben or sepan nadar

whoever [hu:'evə*] *pron:* **~ finds it** cualquiera or quienquiera que lo encuentre; **ask ~ you like** pregunta a quien quieras; **~ he marries** no importa con quién se case

whole [həʊl] *adj* (*entire*) todo, entero; (*not broken*) intacto ▷ *n* todo; (*all*): **the ~ of the town** toda la ciudad, la ciudad entera ▷ *n* (*total*) total *m*; (*sum*) conjunto; **on the ~, as a ~** en general; **wholefood(s)** *n(pl)* alimento(s) *m(pl)* integral(es); **wholeheartedly** [həʊl'hɑ:tɪdlɪ] *adv* con entusiasmo; **wholemeal** *adj* integral; **wholesale** *n* venta al por mayor ▷ *adj* al por mayor; (*fig: destruction*) sistemático; **wholewheat** *adj* = **wholemeal**; **wholly** *adv* totalmente, enteramente

○ **KEYWORD**

whom [hu:m] *pron* 1 (*interrogative*): **whom did you see?** ¿a quién viste?; **to whom did you give it?** ¿a quién se lo diste?; **tell me from whom you received it** dígame de quién lo recibí
2 (*relative*) que; **to whom** a quien(es); **of whom** de quien(es), del/de la que *etc*; **the man whom I saw/to whom I wrote** el hombre que vi/a quien escribí; **the lady about/with whom I was talking** la señora de (la) que/con

quien or (la) que hablaba

whore [hɔː*] (inf, pej) n puta

O **KEYWORD**

whose [huːz] adj 1 (possessive: interrogative): **whose book is this?**, **whose is this book?** ¿de quién es este libro?; **whose pencil have you taken?** ¿de quién es el lápiz que has cogido?; **whose daughter are you?** ¿de quién eres hija?

2 (possessive: relative) cuyo/a, pl cuyos/as; **the man whose son you rescued** el hombre cuyo hijo rescataste; **those whose passports I have** aquellas personas cuyos pasaportes tengo; **the woman whose car was stolen** la mujer a quien le robaron el coche ▷ pron de quién; **whose is this?** ¿de quién es esto?; **I know whose it is** sé de quién es

O **KEYWORD**

why [waɪ] adv por qué; **why not?** ¿por qué no?; **why not do it now?** ¿por qué no lo haces (or hacemos etc) ahora?
▷ conj: **I wonder why he said that** me pregunto por qué dijo eso; **that's not why I'm here** no es por eso (por lo) que estoy aquí; **the reason why** la razón por la que
▷ excl (expressing surprise, shock, annoyance) ¡hombre!, ¡vaya!; (explaining): **why, it's you!** ¡hombre, eres tú!; **why, it's impossible!** ¡pero sí eso es imposible!

wicked ['wɪkɪd] adj malvado, cruel

wicket ['wɪkɪt] n (Cricket: stumps) palos mpl; (: grass area) terreno de juego

wide [waɪd] adj ancho; (area, knowledge) vasto, grande; (choice) amplio ▷ adv: **to open ~** abrir de par en par; **to shoot ~** errar el tiro; **widely** adv (travelled) mucho; (spaced) muy;

it is widely believed/known that ... mucha gente piensa/sabe que ...; **widen** vt ensanchar; (experience) ampliar ▷ vi ensancharse; **wide open** adj abierto de par en par; **widespread** adj extendido, general

widow ['wɪdəu] n viuda; **widower** n viudo

width [wɪdθ] n anchura; (of cloth) ancho

wield [wiːld] vt (sword) blandir; (power) ejercer

wife [waɪf] (pl **wives**) n mujer f, esposa

Wi-Fi ['waɪfaɪ] n wifi m

wig [wɪg] n peluca

wild [waɪld] adj (animal) salvaje; (plant) silvestre; (person) furioso, violento; (idea) descabellado; (rough: sea) bravo; (: land) agreste; (: weather) muy revuelto; **wilderness** ['wɪldənɪs] n desierto; **wildlife** n fauna; **wildly** adv (behave) locamente; (lash out) a diestro y siniestro; (guess) a lo loco; (happy) a más no poder

O **KEYWORD**

will [wɪl] aux vb 1 (forming future tense): **I will finish it tomorrow** lo terminaré or voy a terminar mañana; **I will have finished it by tomorrow** lo habré terminado para mañana; **will you do it? – yes I will/no I won't** ¿lo harás? – sí/no

2 (in conjectures, predictions): **he will** or **he'll be there by now** ya habrá or debe (de) haber llegado; **that will be the postman** será or debe ser el cartero

3 (in commands, requests, offers): **will you be quiet!** ¡quieres callarte?; **will you help me?** ¿quieres ayudarme?; **will you have a cup of tea?** ¿te apetece un té?; **I won't put up with it!** ¡no lo soporto!
▷ vt (pt, pp **willed**): **to will sb to do sth** desear que algn haga algo; **he willed himself to go on** con gran fuerza de voluntad, continuó

▷n voluntad f; (testament) testamento

willing ['wɪlɪŋ] adj (with goodwill) de buena voluntad; (enthusiastic) entusiasta; **he's ~ to do it** está dispuesto a hacerlo; **willingly** adv con mucho gusto

willow ['wɪləu] n sauce m

willpower ['wɪlpauə*] n fuerza de voluntad

wilt [wɪlt] vi marchitarse

win [wɪn] (pt, pp **won**) n victoria, triunfo ▷vt ganar; (obtain) conseguir, lograr ▷vi ganar; **win over** vt convence a

wince [wɪns] vi encogerse

wind¹ [wɪnd] n viento; (Med) gases mpl ▷vt (take breath away from) dejar sin aliento a

wind² [waɪnd] (pt, pp **wound**) vt enrollar; (wrap) envolver; (clock, toy) dar cuerda a ▷vi (road, river) serpentear; **wind down** vt (car window) bajar; (fig: production, business) disminuir; **wind up** vt (clock) dar cuerda a; (debate, meeting) concluir, terminar

windfall ['wɪndfɔ:l] n golpe m de suerte

wind farm n parque m eólico

winding ['waɪndɪŋ] adj (road) tortuoso; (staircase) de caracol

windmill ['wɪndmɪl] n molino de viento

window ['wɪndəu] n ventana; (in car, train) ventanilla; (in shop etc) escaparate m (SP), vidriera (LAM); **window box** n jardinera de ventana; **window cleaner** n (person) limpiacristales mf inv; **window pane** n cristal m; **window seat** n asiento junto a la ventana; **windowsill** n alféizar m, repisa

windscreen ['wɪndskri:n] (us **windshield**) n parabrisas m inv; **windscreen wiper** (us **windshield wiper**) n limpiaparabrisas m inv

windsurfing ['wɪndsə:fɪŋ] n windsurf m

windy ['wɪndɪ] adj de mucho viento;

it's ~ hace viento

wine [waɪn] n vino; **wine bar** n enoteca; **wine glass** n copa (para vino); **wine list** n lista de vinos; **wine tasting** n degustación f de vinos

wing [wɪŋ] n ala; (Aut) aleta; **wing mirror** n (espejo) retrovisor m

wink [wɪŋk] n guiño, pestañeo ▷vi guiñar, pestañear

winner ['wɪnə*] n ganador(a) m/f

winning ['wɪnɪŋ] adj (team) ganador(a); (goal) decisivo; (smile) encantador(a)

winter ['wɪntə*] n invierno ▷vi invernar; **winter sports** npl deportes mpl de invierno; **wintertime** n invierno

wipe [waɪp] n: **to give sth a ~** pasar un trapo sobre algo ▷vt limpiar; (tape) borrar; **wipe out** vt (debt) liquidar; (memory) borrar; (destroy) destruir; **wipe up** vt limpiar

wire [waɪə*] n alambre m; (Elec) cable m (eléctrico); (Tel) telegrama m ▷vt (house) poner la instalación eléctrica en; (also: **~ up**) conectar

wiring ['waɪərɪŋ] n instalación f eléctrica

wisdom ['wɪzdəm] n sabiduría, saber m; (good sense) cordura; **wisdom tooth** n muela del juicio

wise [waɪz] adj sabio; (sensible) juicioso

wish [wɪʃ] n deseo ▷vt querer; **best ~es** (on birthday etc) felicidades fpl; **with best ~es** (in letter) saludos mpl, recuerdos mpl; **to ~ sb goodbye** despedirse de algn; **he ~ed me well** me deseó mucha suerte; **to ~ to do/sb to do sth** querer hacer/que algn haga algo; **to ~ for** desear

wistful ['wɪstful] adj pensativo

wit [wɪt] n ingenio, gracia; (also: **~s**) inteligencia; (person) chistoso/a

witch [wɪtʃ] n bruja

○ **KEYWORD**

with [wɪð, wɪθ] prep 1 (accompanying, in the company of) con (con +mí, ti, sí =

conmigo, contigo, consigo); **I was with him** estaba con él; **we stayed with friends** nos quedamos en casa de unos amigos; **I'm (not) with you** (*don't understand*) (no) te entiendo (*inf: person: up-to-date*) estar al tanto; (: *alert*) ser despabilado **2** (*descriptive, indicating manner etc*) con; de; **a room with a view** una habitación con vistas; **the man with the grey hat/blue eyes** el hombre del sombrero gris/de los ojos azules; **red with anger** rojo de ira; **to shake with fear** temblar de miedo; **to fill sth with water** llenar algo de agua

withdraw [wɪθ'drɔː] *vt* retirar, sacar ▷ *vi* retirarse; **to ~ money (from the bank)** retirar fondos (del banco); **withdrawal** *n* retirada; (*of money*) reintegro; **withdrawn** *pp of* **withdraw** ▷ *adj* (*person*) reservado, introvertido

withdrew [wɪθ'druː] *pt of* **withdraw**

wither ['wɪðə*] *vi* marchitarse

withhold [wɪθ'həuld] *vt* (*money*) retener; (*decision*) aplazar; (*permission*) negar; (*information*) ocultar

within [wɪð'ɪn] *prep* dentro de ▷ *adv* dentro; **~ reach (of)** al alcance (de); **~ sight (of)** a la vista (de); **~ the week** antes de acabar la semana; **~ a mile (of)** a menos de una milla (de)

without [wɪð'aut] *prep* sin; **to go ~ sth** pasar sin algo

withstand [wɪθ'stænd] *vt* resistir a

witness ['wɪtnɪs] *n* testigo *mf* ▷ *vt* (*event*) presenciar; (*document*) atestiguar la veracidad de; **to bear ~ to** (*fig*) ser testimonio de

witty ['wɪtɪ] *adj* ingenioso

wives ['waɪvz] *npl of* **wife**

wizard ['wɪzəd] *n* hechicero

wk *abbr* = **week**

wobble ['wɔbl] *vi* temblar; (*chair*) cojear

woe [wəu] *n* desgracia

woke [wəuk] *pt of* **wake**

woken ['wəukən] *pp of* **wake**

wolf [wulf] *n* lobo

woman ['wumən] (*pl* **women**) *n* mujer *f*

womb [wuːm] *n* matriz *f*, útero

women ['wɪmɪn] *npl of* **woman**

won [wʌn] *pt*, *pp of* **win**

wonder ['wʌndə*] *n* maravilla, prodigio; (*feeling*) asombro ▷ *vi*: **to ~ whether/why** preguntarse si/por qué; **to ~ at** asombrarse de; **to ~ about** pensar sobre *or* en; **it's no ~ (that)** no es de extrañarse (que +*subjun*); **wonderful** *adj* maravilloso

won't [wəunt] = **will not**

wood [wud] *n* (*timber*) madera; (*forest*) bosque *m*; **wooden** *adj* de madera; (*fig*) inexpresivo; **woodwind** *n* (*Mus*) instrumentos *mpl* de viento de madera; **woodwork** *n* carpintería

wool [wul] *n* lana; **to pull the ~ over sb's eyes** (*fig*) engatusar a algn; **woollen** (*us* **woolen**) *adj* de lana; **woolly** (*us* **wooly**) *adj* lanudo, de lana; (*fig: ideas*) confuso

word [wəːd] *n* palabra; (*news*) noticia; (*promise*) palabra (de honor) ▷ *vt* redactar; **in other ~s** en otras palabras; **to break/keep one's ~** faltar a la palabra/cumplir la promesa; **to have ~s with sb** reñir con algn; **wording** *n* redacción *f*; **word processing** *n* proceso de textos; **word processor** *n* procesador *m* de textos

wore [wɔː*] *pt of* **wear**

work [wəːk] *n* trabajo; (*job*) empleo, trabajo; (*Art, Literature*) obra ▷ *vi* trabajar; (*mechanism*) funcionar, marchar; (*medicine*) ser eficaz, surtir efecto ▷ *vt* (*shape*) trabajar; (*stone etc*) tallar; (*mine*) explotar; (*machine*) manejar, hacer funcionar ▷ *npl* (*of clock, machine*) mecanismo *m*; **to be out of ~** estar parado, no tener trabajo; **to ~ loose** (*part*) desprenderse; (*knot*) aflojarse; **works** *n* (*BRIT: factory*) fábrica; **work out** *vi* (*plans etc*) salir bien, funcionar; **works** vt (problem) resolver; (plan) elaborar; **it works out at £100** suma 100 libras; **worker** n trabajador(a) m/f, obrero/a; **work experience** n: **I'm going to do my work experience in a factory** voy a hacer las prácticas en una fábrica; **workforce** n mano de obra; **working class** n clase f obrera ▷ adj: **working-class** obrero; **working week** n semana laboral; **workman** n (irreg) n obrero; **work of art** n obra de arte; **workout** n (Sport) sesión f de ejercicios; **work permit** n permiso de trabajo; **workplace** n lugar m de trabajo; **worksheet** n (Scol) hoja de ejercicios; **workshop** n taller m; **work station** n puesto or estación f de trabajo; **work surface** n encimera; **worktop** n encimera

world [wɜːld] n mundo ▷ cpd (champion) del mundo; (power, war) mundial; **to think the ~ of sb** (fig) tener un concepto muy alto de algn; **World Cup** n (Football): **the World Cup** el Mundial, los Mundiales; **world-wide** adj mundial, universal; **World-Wide Web** n: **the World-Wide Web** el World Wide Web

worm [wɜːm] n (also: **earth ~**) lombriz f

worn [wɔːn] pp of **wear** ▷ adj usado; **worn-out** adj (object) gastado; (person) rendido, agotado

worried [ˈwʌrɪd] adj preocupado

worry [ˈwʌrɪ] n preocupación f ▷ vt preocupar, inquietar ▷ vi preocuparse; **worrying** adj inquietante

worse [wɜːs] adj, adv peor ▷ n lo peor; **a change for the ~** un empeoramiento; **worsen** vt, vi empeorar; **worse off** adj (financially): **to be worse off** tener menos dinero; (fig): **you'll be worse off this way** de esta forma estarás peor que nunca

alcalde; (: to judge) señor juez

worst [wɜːst] adj, adv peor ▷ n lo peor; **at ~** en lo peor de los casos

worth [wɜːθ] n valor m ▷ adj: **to be ~** valer; **it's ~ it** vale or merece la pena; **to be ~ one's while (to do)** merecer la pena (hacer); **worthless** adj sin valor; (useless) inútil; **worthwhile** adj (activity) que merece la pena; (cause) loable

worthy [ˈwɜːðɪ] adj respetable; (motive) honesto; **~ of** digno de

○ KEYWORD

would [wʊd] aux vb 1 (conditional tense): **if you asked him he would do it** si se lo pidieras, lo haría; **if you had asked him he would have done it** si se lo hubieras pedido, lo habría or hubiera hecho

2 (in offers, invitations, requests): **would you like a biscuit?** ¿quieres una galleta?; (formal) ¿querría una galleta?; **would you ask him to come in?** ¿quiere hacerle pasar?; **would you open the window please?** ¿quiere or podría abrir la ventana, por favor?

3 (in indirect speech): **I said I would do it** dije que lo haría

4 (emphatic): **it WOULD have to snow today!** ¡tenía que nevar precisamente hoy!

5 (insistence): **she wouldn't behave** no quiso comportarse bien

6 (conjecture): **it would have been midnight** sería medianoche; **it would seem so** parece ser que sí

7 (indicating habit): **he would go there on Mondays** iba allí los lunes

wouldn't [ˈwʊdnt] = **would not**

wound¹ [wuːnd] n herida ▷ vt herir

wound² [waʊnd] pt, pp of **wind²**

wove [wəʊv] pt of **weave**

woven [ˈwəʊvn] pp of **weave**

wrap [ræp] vt (also: **~ up**) envolver; (gift) envolver, abrigar ▷ vi (dress

warmly) abrigarse; **wrapper** *n (on chocolate)* papel *m*; (BRIT: *of book)* sobrecubierta; **wrapping** *n* envoltura, envase *m*; **wrapping paper** *n* papel *m* de envolver; *(fancy)* papel *m* de regalo
wreath [riːθ, *pl* riːðz] *n (funeral wreath)* corona
wreck [rɛk] *n (ship: destruction)* naufragio; *(: remains)* restos *mpl* del barco; *(pej: person)* ruina ▷ *vt (car etc)* destrozar; *(chances)* arruinar; **wreckage** *n* restos *mpl*; *(of building)* escombros *mpl*
wren [rɛn] *n (Zool)* reyezuelo
wrench [rɛntʃ] *n (Tech)* llave *f* inglesa; *(tug)* tirón *m*; *(fig)* dolor *m* ▷ *vt* arrancar; **to ~ sth from sb** arrebatar algo violentamente a algn
wrestle [ˈrɛsl] *vi:* **to ~ (with sb)** luchar (con or contra algn); **wrestler** *n* luchador(a) *m/f* (de lucha libre); **wrestling** *n* lucha libre
wretched [ˈrɛtʃɪd] *adj* miserable
wriggle [ˈrɪgl] *vi (also: ~ about)** menearse, retorcerse
wring [rɪŋ] *(pt, pp* **wrung)** *vt* retorcer; *(wet clothes)* escurrir; *(fig):* **to ~ sth out of sb** sacar algo por la fuerza a algn
wrinkle [ˈrɪŋkl] *n* arruga ▷ *vt* arrugar ▷ *vi* arrugarse
wrist [rɪst] *n* muñeca
writable [ˈraɪtəbl] *adj (CD, DVD)* escribible
write [raɪt] *(pt* **wrote**, *pp* **written)** *vt* escribir; *(cheque)* extender ▷ *vi* escribir; **write down** *vt* escribir; *(note)* apuntar; **write off** *vt (debt)* borrar *(como incobrable); (fig)* desechar por inútil; **write out** *vt* escribir; **write-off** *n* siniestro total; **writer** *n* escritor(a) *m/f*
writing [ˈraɪtɪŋ] *n* escritura; *(hand-writing)* letra; *(of author)* obras *fpl*; **in ~** por escrito; **writing paper** *n* papel *m* de escribir
written [ˈrɪtn] *pp of* **write**
wrong [rɒŋ] *adj (wicked)* malo; *(unfair)* injusto; *(incorrect)* equivocado,

incorrecto; *(not suitable)* inoportuno, inconveniente; *(reverse)* del revés ▷ *adv* equivocadamente ▷ *n* injusticia ▷ *vt* ser injusto con; **you are ~ to do it** haces mal en hacerlo; **you are ~ about that, you've got it ~** en eso estás equivocado; **to be in the ~** no tener razón, tener la culpa; **what's ~?** ¿qué pasa?; **to go ~** *(person)* equivocarse; *(plan)* salir mal; *(machine)* estropearse; **wrongly** *adv* mal, incorrectamente; *(by mistake)* por error; **wrong number** *n (Tel)* **you've got the wrong number** se ha equivocado de número
wrote [rəut] *pt of* **write**
wrung [rʌŋ] *pt, pp of* **wring**
WWW *n abbr (=World Wide Web)* WWW *m*

XL *abbr* = **extra large**
Xmas ['ɛksməs] *n abbr* = **Christmas**
X-ray ['ɛksreɪ] *n* radiografía ▷*vt* radiografiar, sacar radiografías de
xylophone ['zaɪləfəʊn] *n* xilófono

yacht [jɔt] *n* yate *m*; **yachting** *n* (*sport*) balandrismo
yard [jɑːd] *n* patio; (*measure*) yarda; **yard sale** (*us*) *n* venta de objetos usados (*en el jardín de una casa particular*)
yarn [jɑːn] *n* hilo; (*tale*) cuento, historia
yawn [jɔːn] *n* bostezo ▷*vi* bostezar
yd. *abbr* (=*yard*) yda
yeah [jɛə] (*inf*) *adv* sí
year [jɪə*] *n* año; **to be 8 ~s old** tener 8 años; **an eight-~-old child** un niño de ocho años (de edad); **yearly** *adj* anual ▷*adv* anualmente, cada año
yearn [jəːn] *vi*: **to ~ for sth** añorar algo, suspirar por algo
yeast [jiːst] *n* levadura
yell [jɛl] *n* grito, alarido ▷*vi* gritar
yellow ['jɛləʊ] *adj* amarillo; **Yellow Pages**® *npl* páginas *fpl* amarillas
yes [jɛs] *adv* sí ▷*n* sí *m*; **to say/ answer** = decir/contestar que sí
yesterday ['jɛstədɪ] *adv* ayer ▷*n* ayer *m*; **~ morning/evening** ayer por la mañana/tarde; **all day ~** todo el

día de ayer

yet [jet] *adv* ya; (*negative*) todavía
▷ *conj* sin embargo, a pesar de todo;
it is not finished ~ todavía no está
acabado; **the best ~** el/la mejor hasta
ahora; **as ~** hasta ahora, todavía

yew [juː] *n* tejo

Yiddish ['jɪdɪʃ] *n* yiddish *m*

yield [jiːld] *n* (*Agr*) cosecha; (*Comm*)
rendimiento ▷ *vt* ceder; (*results*)
producir, dar; (*profit*) rendir ▷ *vi*
rendirse, ceder; (*US Aut*) ceder el paso

yob(bo) ['jɔb(bəʊ)] *n* (*BRIT inf*)
gamberro

yoga ['jəʊgə] *n* yoga *m*

yog(h)ourt ['jəʊgət] *n* yogur *m*

yog(h)urt ['jəʊgət] *n* = **yog(h)ourt**

yolk [jəʊk] *n* yema (de huevo)

○ KEYWORD

you [juː] *pron* 1 (*subject: familiar*) tú;
(*pl*) vosotros/as (*SP*), ustedes (*LAM*);
(*polite*) usted; (*pl*) ustedes; **you are
very kind** eres/es *etc* muy amable; **you
Spanish enjoy your food** a vosotros
(*or ustedes*) los españoles os os (*or les*)
gusta la comida; **you and I will go**
iremos tú y yo

2 (*object: direct: familiar*) te; (*pl*) os (*SP*),
les (*LAM*); (*polite*) le; (*pl*) les; (*f*) la; (*pl*) las;
I know you te/le *etc* conozco

3 (*object: indirect: familiar*) te; (*pl*) os (*SP*),
les (*LAM*); (*polite*) les; **I gave the
letter to you yesterday** te/os *etc* di
la carta ayer

4 (*stressed*) **I told you to do it** a ti te dije a
ti que lo hicieras, es a ti a quien dije que
lo hicieras; *see also* **3; 5**

5 (*after prep: NB*: con +ti =
contigo: familiar) ti; (*pl*) vosotros/as
(*SP*), ustedes (*LAM*); (*: polite*) usted;
(*pl*) ustedes; **it's for you** es para
ti/vosotros *etc*

6 (*comparisons: familiar*) tú; (*pl*)
vosotros/as (*SP*), ustedes (*LAM*);
(*: polite*) usted; (*pl*) ustedes; **she's
younger than you** es más joven que

tú/vosotros *etc*

7 (*impersonal one*): **fresh air does you
good** el aire puro (te) hace bien; **you
never know** nunca se sabe; **you can't
do that!** ¡eso no se hace!

you'd [juːd] = **you had; you would**

you'll [juːl] = **you will; you shall**

young [jʌŋ] *adj* joven ▷ *npl* (*of
animal*) cría; (*people*): **the ~** los jóvenes,
la juventud; **youngster** *n* joven *mf*

your [jɔː*] *adj* tu; (*pl*) vuestro; (*formal*)
su; *see also* **my**

you're [juə*] = **you are**

yours [jɔːz] *pron* tuyo (*pl*), vuestro;
(*formal*) suyo; *see also* **faithfully; mine¹**
see also **sincerely**

yourself [jɔːˈsɛlf] *pron* tú mismo;
(*complement*) te; (*after prep*) ti (mismo);
(*formal*) usted mismo; (*: complement*)
se; (*: after prep*) sí (mismo); **yourselves**
pl pron vosotros mismos; (*after prep*)
vosotros (mismos); (*formal*) ustedes
(mismos); (*: complement*) se; (*: after prep*)
sí mismos; *see also* **oneself**

youth [juːð *pl* juːðz *n* juventud *f*; (*young
man*) joven *m*; **youth club** *n* club *m*
juvenil; **youthful** *adj* juvenil; **youth
hostel** *n* albergue *m* de juventud

you've [juːv] = **you have**

Z

zeal [ziːl] n celo, entusiasmo
zebra ['ziːbrə] n cebra; **zebra crossing** (BRIT) n paso de peatones
zero ['zɪərəʊ] n cero
zest [zest] n ánimo, vivacidad f; (of orange) piel f
zigzag ['zɪɡzæɡ] n zigzag m ▷ vi zigzaguear, hacer eses
Zimbabwe [zɪm'bɑːbwɪ] n Zimbabwe m
zinc [zɪŋk] n cinc m, zinc m
zip [zɪp] n (also: ~ fastener, (US) ~per) cremallera (SP), cierre (AM) m, zíper m (MEX, CAM) ▷ vt (also: ~ up) cerrar la cremallera de; (file) comprimir; **zip code** (US) n código postal; **zip file** n (Comput) archivo comprimido; **zipper** (US) n cremallera
zit [zɪt] n grano
zodiac ['zəʊdɪæk] n zodíaco
zone [zəʊn] n zona
zoo [zuː] n (jardín m) zoo m
zoology [zuː'ɒlədʒɪ] n zoología
zoom [zuːm] vi: **to ~ past** pasar zumbando; **zoom lens** n zoom m
zucchini [zuː'kiːnɪ] (US) n(pl) calabacín(ines) m(pl)